Twentieth-Century Literary Criticism

Archive Volume

Guide to Gale Literary Criticism Series

When you need to review criticism of literary works, these are the Gale series to use:

If the author's death date is:

You should turn to:

After Dec. 31, 1959
(or author is still living)

CONTEMPORARY LITERARY CRITICISM

for example: Jorge Luis Borges, Anthony Burgess,
William Faulkner, Mary Gordon,
Ernest Hemingway, Iris Murdoch

1900 through 1959

TWENTIETH-CENTURY LITERARY CRITICISM

for example: Willa Cather, F. Scott Fitzgerald,
Henry James, Mark Twain, Virginia Woolf

1800 through 1899

NINETEENTH-CENTURY LITERATURE CRITICISM

for example: Fedor Dostoevski, Nathaniel Hawthorne,
George Sand, William Wordsworth

1400 through 1799

LITERATURE CRITICISM FROM 1400 TO 1800
(excluding Shakespeare)

for example: Anne Bradstreet, Daniel Defoe,
Alexander Pope, François Rabelais,
Jonathan Swift, Phillis Wheatley

SHAKESPEAREAN CRITICISM

Shakespeare's plays and poetry

Antiquity through 1399

CLASSICAL AND MEDIEVAL LITERATURE CRITICISM

for example: Dante, Homer, Plato, Sophocles, Vergil,
the Beowulf Poet

Gale also publishes related criticism series:

CHILDREN'S LITERATURE REVIEW

This ongoing series covers authors of all eras. Presents criticism on authors and author/illustrators who write for the preschool through high school audience.

SHORT STORY CRITICISM

This series covers the major short fiction writers of all nationalities and periods of literary history.

ISSN 0276-8178

Volume 26

Twentieth-Century Literary Criticism

Archive Volume

**Excerpts from Criticism of Various Topics
in Twentieth-Century Literature, including Literary
and Critical Movements, Prominent Themes and
Genres, Anniversary Celebrations, and Surveys
of National Literatures**

**Dennis Poupard
Editor**

**Paula Kepos
Associate Editor**

**Gale Research Company
Book Tower
Detroit, Michigan 48226**

Contents

Preface

The study of literature embraces many disciplines, including history, sociology, psychology, and philosophy. To fully comprehend a literary work, it is often necessary to understand the history and culture of the author's nation, the literary movements the author belonged to or disdained, the political passions and social concerns of the author's era, or themes common to the literature of the author's nation. Thus, to gain a fuller perspective on an author, a student often needs to examine a great many social, historical, and literary factors.

Many schools reflect the necessity for such a broad view of literature by including historical and thematic surveys in their curricula. In these courses, themes that recur throughout many works of literature are examined, the literary tempers of various historical eras are assessed, and literary and critical movements are defined. Increasingly, comparative literature courses and thematic surveys of foreign literature are being offered by colleges and universities, introducing students to the most significant literature of many nations. In order to provide important information on the variety of topics encountered by the general reader or student of literature, *Twentieth-Century Literary Criticism (TCLC)* is extending its scope by creating the *TCLC* Archive volumes. Once a year, *TCLC* will devote an entire volume to criticism of literary topics that cannot be addressed by our regular format.

Scope of the Series

TCLC is designed to serve as an introduction to the authors of the period 1900 through 1959 and to the most significant commentators on these authors. Since a vast amount of relevant critical material confronts the student, *TCLC* presents significant passages from the most important published criticism to aid students in the location and selection of critical commentary. *TCLC* is a companion series to *Contemporary Literary Criticism (CLC),* which excerpts criticism on current writing. Because of the difference in time span under consideration *(CLC* considers authors who were still living after 1959), there is no duplication of material between *CLC* and *TCLC.*

Standard volumes of *TCLC* comprise surveys of the careers of fifteen to twenty authors representing a variety of nationalities. The authors selected include the most important writers of the era 1900 to 1959, as well as lesser-known figures whose significant contributions to literary history are important to the study of twentieth-century literature. Each author entry represents a historical survey of the critical response to that author's work: some early criticism is presented to indicate initial reactions, later criticism is selected to represent any rise or decline in the author's reputation, and current retrospective analyses provide students with the latest views. Every attempt is made to identify and include excerpts from seminal essays on each author's work.

Scope of the Archive Volumes

The *TCLC* Archive volumes will enhance the usefulness of the series by examining literary topics that cannot be covered under the author approach used in the rest of the series. Such topics will include literary movements, prominent themes or subjects in twentieth-century literature, literary reaction to political and historical events, studies of significant eras in literary history, prominent literary anniversaries, and examinations of the literatures of cultures that are often overlooked by English-speaking readers. For example, the first Archive volume will examine the history, themes, and major authors of the Harlem Renaissance, a movement that redefined the culture of black Americans; the portrayal in American literature of the businessman, a character type that has stimulated and provoked American authors and readers throughout the twentieth century; the literary reaction to the events of the Spanish Civil War, a conflict that profoundly shaped the political attitudes and subsequent works of many twentieth-century writers; the literary flowering in the Soviet Union during the period 1953 to 1963 known as the Thaw, when Premier Nikita Khrushchev relaxed state control of the arts; the centennial of the first appearance of Sherlock Holmes, one of the most beloved characters in literature; and a survey of Hungarian literature of the twentieth century, a period of great ferment in a nation isolated from Western readers by both language and politics.

The subjects of Archive entries are chosen for their usefulness and timeliness; the length of each entry is determined by the importance of the subject and the amount of criticism available in English. Subjects considered in Archive volumes are restricted as much as possible to the period 1900 to 1959. For this reason, we discuss only literary movements and subjects which saw their greatest influence in this period. In some cases this means that we will include discussion of authors who are covered in *CLC* or in *Nineteenth Century Literature Criticism (NCLC)*. For example, many of the writers of the Harlem Renaissance lived into the era covered by the *CLC* series (post-1959), yet the movement was born, had its greatest influence, and came to a close in the period covered by *TCLC* (1900-1959). To ensure a complete discussion of the Harlem Renaissance, the editors have included criticism of all important authors associated with the movement, regardless of death dates. However, we have duplicated no criticism from *CLC*.

Organization of the Book

This Archive volume includes excerpted criticism on seven topics. Each subject entry consists of the following elements:

- The *introduction* briefly defines the subject of the entry and provides social and historical background information important to an understanding of the criticism.

- The *criticism* is arranged thematically. Entries commonly begin with general surveys of the subject or essays providing historical or background information, followed by essays that develop particular aspects of the topic. For example, the entry devoted to the Harlem Renaissance begins with a section of survey essays defining the principal issues and figures of the movement. This is followed by sections devoted to the effect the audience had on the production of the literature, the principal themes and techniques of Harlem Renaissance literature, the movement as a reflection of cultural issues of concern to American society as a whole, and the achievement and continuing influence of Renaissance writers. Each section has a separate title heading and is identified with a page number in the table of contents for easy reader access.

  The critic's name is given at the beginning of each piece of criticism; when an unsigned essay is later attributed to a critic, the critic's name appears in brackets at the beginning of the excerpt and in the bibliographic citation. Anonymous essays are headed by the title of the journal in which they appeared. Many critical essays in *TCLC* contain translated material to aid users. Unless otherwise noted, translations within brackets are by the editors; translations within parentheses are by the author of the excerpt.

- Critical essays are prefaced by *explanatory notes* providing the reader with information about both the critic and the criticism that follows. Included are the critic's reputation, individual approach to literary criticism, and particular expertise in the subject under discussion. Also noted are the relative importance of a work of criticism, the scope of the excerpt, and the growth of critical controversy or changes in critical trends regarding the subject. In some cases, these notes cross-reference the work of critics who agree or disagree with each other. Dates in parentheses following a book title refer to the publication date of the book.

- A complete *bibliographical citation* designed to facilitate location of the original essay or book by the interested reader follows each piece of criticism.

- *Illustrations* throughout the entry include portraits of the authors under discussion, important manuscript pages, magazine covers, dust jackets, movie stills, reproductions of artwork, maps, and photographs of people, places, and events important to the topic.

- The *additional bibliography* appearing at the end of each subject entry suggests further reading on the subject, in some cases including essays for which the editors could not obtain reprint rights. The bibliography also includes the most important works discussed in the entry that are available in English, as well as anthologies of creative writing pertaining to the subject.

An appendix lists the sources from which material in each volume has been reprinted. It does not, however, list every book or periodical consulted in the preparation of a volume.

Cumulative Indexes

Each volume of *TCLC,* including the Archive volumes, contains a cumulative author index listing all authors who have appeared in the following Gale series: *Contemporary Literary Criticism, Twentieth-Century Literary Criticism, Nineteenth-Century Literature Criticism, Literature Criticism from 1400 to 1800,* and *Classical and Medieval Literature Criticism.* Archive entries devoted to a single author, such as the entry on James Joyce's *Ulysses* in this volume, will be listed in this index. Also included are cross-references to the Gale series *Short Story Criticism, Children's Literature*

Review, Authors in the News, Contemporary Authors, Contemporary Authors Autobiography Series, Dictionary of Literary Biography, Concise Dictionary of American Literary Biography, Something about the Author, Something about the Author Autobiography Series, and *Yesterday's Authors of Books for Children.* The index, which lists birth and death dates when available, will be particularly valuable for those authors who are identified with a certain period but whose death date causes them to be placed in another, or for those authors whose careers span two periods. For example, F. Scott Fitzgerald is found in *TCLC,* yet a writer often associated with him, Ernest Hemingway, is found in *CLC.*

Each *TCLC* Archive volume also includes a cumulative nationality index listing all authors who have appeared in regular *TCLC* volumes, arranged alphabetically under their respective nationalities.

Subsequent Archive volumes will cumulate a subject index derived from the table of contents to provide users with easy access to the topics covered in the Archive volumes. Titles discussed in the Archive entries will not be included in the *TCLC* cumulative title index.

Acknowledgments

No work of this scope can be accomplished without the cooperation of many people. The editors especially wish to thank the copyright holders of the criticism in this volume, the permissions managers of many book and magazine publishing companies for assisting us in securing reprint rights, and Anthony Bogucki for assistance with copyright research. We are also grateful to the staffs of the Detroit Public Library, the Library of Congress, the University of Michigan Library, the Wayne State University Library, and the University of Detroit Library for making their resources available to us. The editors also wish to acknowledge Ardis Publishers for the endpaper illustration of *Nyugat;* ARS NY/SPADEM for the endpaper illustration of Max Ernst; and ARS NY/ADAGP for the endpaper illustration of Tristan Tzara.

Suggestions Are Welcome

In response to various suggestions, several features have been added to *TCLC* since the series began, including explanatory notes to excerpted criticism, a cumulative index to authors in all Gale literary criticism series, entries devoted to criticism on a single work by a major author, and more extensive illustrations.

Readers who wish to suggest authors or topics to appear in future volumes, or who have other suggestions, are cordially invited to write the editors.

Authors to Be Featured in *TCLC*, Volumes 27 and 28

E. F. Benson (English novelist and short story writer)—An enormously popular author of the late nineteenth and early twentieth centuries, Benson is best remembered for his creation of the characters Dodo and Lucia, each of whom was featured in a series of novels that are considered masterpieces of Edwardian comedy.

Henri Bergson (French philosopher)—One of the most influential philosophers of the twentieth century, Bergson is renowned for his opposition to the dominant materialist thought of his time and for his creation of theories that emphasize the supremacy and independence of suprarational consciousness.

R. D. Blackmore (English novelist)—A minor historical novelist of the Victorian era, Blackmore is remembered as the author of *Lorna Doone.* This classic of historical fiction is often praised for its vivid evocation of the past and its entertaining melodrama.

Edgar Rice Burroughs (American novelist)—Burroughs was a science fiction writer who is best known as the creator of Tarzan. His *Tarzan of the Apes* and its numerous sequels have sold over thirty-five million copies in fifty-six languages, making Burroughs one of the most popular authors in the world.

Joyce Cary (Anglo-Irish novelist)—Regarded as an important contributor to the trilogy as a literary form, Cary wrote trilogies noted for their humor, vitality, sympathetic characterizations, and technical virtuosity.

Stephen Crane (American novelist and short story writer)—Crane was one of the foremost realistic writers in American literature. *TCLC* will devote an entry to his masterpiece, *The Red Badge of Courage,* in which he depicted the psychological complexities of fear and courage in battle.

Charles Doughty (English travel writer and poet)—Doughty is best remembered as the author of *Travels in Arabia Deserta,* one of the classics in the literature of travel and a celebrated model of epic prose.

F. Scott Fitzgerald (American novelist)—Fitzgerald is considered the principal chronicler of the ideals and disillusionments of the Jazz Age, and his *Tender Is the Night* is one of his most celebrated novels. In an entry devoted solely to this work, *TCLC* will present major critical essays examining its meaning and importance.

Fyodor Gladkov (Russian novelist)—A proletarian realist writer, Gladkov is best known for his novel *Cement,* which portrays the post-revolutionary collectivization of a cement factory.

Edmund Gosse (English novelist and critic)—A prolific man of letters in late nineteenth-century England, Gosse is of primary importance for his autobiographical novel *Father and Son,* which is considered a seminal work for gaining insight into the major issues of the Victorian age, especially the conflict between science and religion inspired by Darwin's *The Origin of Species.* Gosse is also important for his introduction of Henrik Ibsen's "new drama" to English audiences and for his numerous critical studies of English and foreign authors.

Muhammad Iqbal (Indian poet and philosopher)—Considered one of the leading Muslim intellectual figures of the twentieth century, Iqbal was a political activist and the author of poetry calling for social and religious reform.

Franz Kafka (Austrian novelist and short story writer)—Kafka's novel *The Trial* is often considered the definitive expression of his alienated vision as well as one of the seminal works of modern literature. *TCLC* will devote an entire entry to critical discussion of this novel, which has been described by Alvin J. Seltzer as "one of the most unrelenting works of chaos created in the first half of this century."

Henry Lawson (Australian short story writer and poet)—Lawson's stories in such collections as *While the Billy Boils* and *Joe Wilson and His Mates* chronicle the hard lives of working people in the backcountry of Australia and are considered characteristic of Australian writing of the late nineteenth and early twentieth centuries.

Dmitri Merezhkovsky (Russian novelist, philosopher, poet, and critic)—Although his poetry and criticism are credited with initiating the Symbolist movement in Russian literature, Merezhkovsky is best known as a religious philosopher who sought in numerous essays and historical novels to reconcile the values of pagan religions with the teachings of Christ.

John Muir (American naturalist, essayist, and autobiographer)—In such works as *A Thousand Mile Walk to the Gulf* and *The Mountains of California,* Muir celebrated the North American wilderness. He was also a prominent conservationist who was instrumental in establishing the system of national parks in the United States.

Eugene O'Neill (American dramatist)—Generally considered America's foremost dramatist, O'Neill is the author of works examining the implacability of an indifferent universe, the materialistic greed of humanity, and the problems of individual identity. *TCLC* will devote an entry to O'Neill's *Long Day's Journey into Night,* a portrait of a tormented, self-destructive family that has been called one of the most powerful dramas in American theater.

George Orwell (English novelist and essayist)—Designated the "conscience of his generation" by V. S. Pritchett, Orwell is the author of influential novels and essays embodying his commitment to personal freedom and social justice. *TCLC* will devote an entry to Orwell's first major popular and critical success, *Animal Farm,* a satirical fable in which Orwell attacked the consequences of the Russian Revolution while suggesting reasons for the failure of most revolutionary ideals.

Wilfred Owen (English poet)—Inspired by his experiences in World War I, Owen's poetry exposed the grim realities of war and its effect on the human spirit.

Benito Pérez Galdós (Spanish novelist and dramatist)— Considered the greatest Spanish novelist since Cervantes, Galdós is known for two vast cycles of novels: the *Episodios nacionales,* a forty-six volume portrayal of nineteenth-century Spanish history; and the *Novelas españolas contemporáneas,* explorations of social and ethical problems in twentieth-century Spain which have been favorably compared to the works of Charles Dickens and Honoré de Balzac.

Fernando Pessoa (Portuguese poet)—Pessoa is considered the greatest Portuguese poet since the sixteenth century, as well as a writer whose work epitomizes the experimental tendencies and alienated temper of the modern era. His most prominent theme—that an individual's identity is multifarious and indeterminate—is conspicuously reflected in the fact that much of his work was written under the names of various fictitious personas, for each of whom he created a distinct personality and literary style.

Luigi Pirandello (Italian dramatist)—Considered one of the most important innovators of twentieth-century drama, Pirandello developed experimental techniques including improvisation, the play-within-the-play, and the play-outside-the-play in order to explore such themes as the fluidity of reality, the relativity of truth, and the tenuous line between sanity and madness.

Alexey Remizov (Russian prose writer)—Best known for his ornate prose style, which influenced a generation of Soviet writers, Remizov was the author of an enormously diverse body of work, including realistic depictions of the Russian underclass, adaptations of Russian legends, mystery plays, religious parables, historical chronicles, memoirs, and recorded dreams.

Gertrude Stein (American novelist and critic)—Stein is recognized as one of the principal figures of literary Modernism, both as a brilliant experimentalist in such works as *The Autobiography of Alice B. Toklas* and *Tender Buttons* and as an influence upon a generation of authors that included Ernest Hemingway and F. Scott Fitzgerald.

Italo Svevo (Italian novelist)—Svevo's ironic portrayals of the moral life of the bourgeoisie, which characteristically demonstrate the influence of the psychoanalytic theories of Sigmund Freud, earned him a reputation as the father of the modern Italian novel.

Leo Tolstoy (Russian novelist)—Along with *Anna Karenina, War and Peace* is considered Tolstoy's most important work and one of the greatest works in world literature. *TCLC* will devote an entire entry to the critical history of this epic novel.

Thorstein Veblen (American economist and social critic)— Veblen's seminal analyses of the nature, development, and consequences of business and industry—as well as his attack on bourgeois materialism in *The Theory of the Leisure Class*—distinguished him as one of the foremost American economists and social scientists of the twentieth century.

Edith Wharton (American novelist and short story writer)— Wharton is best known as a novelist of manners whose fiction exposed the cruel excesses of aristocratic society at the turn of the century. Her subject matter, tone, and style have often been compared with those of her friend and mentor Henry James.

Thomas Wolfe (American novelist)—Wolfe is considered one of the foremost American novelists of the twentieth century. His most important works present intense and lyrical portraits of life in both rural and urban America while portraying the struggle of the lonely, sensitive, and artistic individual to find spiritual fulfillment.

Additional Authors to Appear
in Future Volumes

Abbey, Henry 1842-1911
Abercrombie, Lascelles 1881-1938
Adamic, Louis 1898-1951
Ade, George 1866-1944
Agustini, Delmira 1886-1914
Akers, Elizabeth Chase 1832-1911
Akiko, Yosano 1878-1942
Alas, Leopoldo 1852-1901
Aldrich, Thomas Bailey 1836-1907
Aliyu, Dan Sidi 1902-1920
Allen, Hervey 1889-1949
Archer, William 1856-1924
Arlen, Michael 1895-1956
Arlt, Roberto 1900-1942
Austin, Alfred 1835-1913
Bahr, Hermann 1863-1934
Bailey, Philip James 1816-1902
Barbour, Ralph Henry 1870-1944
Benét, William Rose 1886-1950
Benjamin, Walter 1892-1940
Bennett, James Gordon, Jr. 1841-1918
Berdyaev, Nikolai Aleksandrovich
    1874-1948
Beresford, J(ohn) D(avys) 1873-1947
Binyon, Laurence 1869-1943
Bishop, John Peale 1892-1944
Blake, Lillie Devereux 1835-1913
Blest Gana, Alberto 1830-1920
Blum, Léon 1872-1950
Bodenheim, Maxwell 1892-1954
Bowen, Marjorie 1886-1952
Byrne, Donn 1889-1928
Caine, Hall 1853-1931
Cannan, Gilbert 1884-1955
Carducci, Giosuè 1835-1907
Carswell, Catherine 1879-1946
Churchill, Winston 1871-1947
Corelli, Marie 1855-1924
Cotter, Joseph Seamon 1861-1949
Croce, Benedetto 1866-1952
Crofts, Freeman Wills 1879-1957
Cruze, James (Jens Cruz Bosen) 1884-
    1942
Curros, Enríquez Manuel 1851-1908
Dall, Caroline Wells (Healy) 1822-1912
Daudet, Léon 1867-1942
Delafield, E.M. (Edme Elizabeth Monica
    de la Pasture) 1890-1943
Deneson, Jacob 1836-1919
DeVoto, Bernard 1897-1955
Diego, José de 1866-1918
Douglas, (George) Norman 1868-1952
Douglas, Lloyd C(assel) 1877-1951
Dovzhenko, Alexander 1894-1956
Drinkwater, John 1882-1937
Dunne, Finley Peter 1867-1936

Durkheim, Émile 1858-1917
Duun, Olav 1876-1939
Eaton, Walter Prichard 1878-1957
Eggleston, Edward 1837-1902
Erskine, John 1879-1951
Fadeyev, Alexander 1901-1956
Ferland, Albert 1872-1943
Field, Rachel 1894-1924
Flecker, James Elroy 1884-1915
Fletcher, John Gould 1886-1950
Fogazzaro, Antonio 1842-1911
Francos, Karl Emil 1848-1904
Frank, Bruno 1886-1945
Frazer, (Sir) George 1854-1941
Freud, Sigmund 1853-1939
Fröding, Gustaf 1860-1911
Fuller, Henry Blake 1857-1929
Futabatei Shimei 1864-1909
Glaspell, Susan 1876-1948
Glyn, Elinor 1864-1943
Golding, Louis 1895-1958
Gould, Gerald 1885-1936
Guest, Edgar 1881-1959
Gumilyov, Nikolay 1886-1921
Gyulai, Pal 1826-1909
Hale, Edward Everett 1822-1909
Hansen, Martin 1909-1955
Hayashi Fumiko 1904-1951
Hernández, Miguel 1910-1942
Hewlett, Maurice 1861-1923
Heyward, DuBose 1885-1940
Hope, Anthony 1863-1933
Hudson, W(illiam) H(enry) 1841-1922
Huidobro, Vincente 1893-1948
Ilyas, Abu Shabaka 1903-1947
Imbs, Bravig 1904-1946
Ivanov, Vyacheslav Ivanovich 1866-
    1949
James, Will 1892-1942
Jammes, Francis 1868-1938
Johnson, Fenton 1888-1958
Johnston, Mary 1870-1936
Jorgensen, Johannes 1866-1956
King, Grace 1851-1932
Kirby, William 1817-1906
Kline, Otis Albert 1891-1946
Kohut, Adolph 1848-1916
Kreve, Vincas 1882-1954
Kuzmin, Mikhail Alexseyevich 1875-
    1936
Lamm, Martin 1880-1950
Leipoldt, C. Louis 1880-1947
Lima, Jorge De 1895-1953
Locke, Alain 1886-1954
Long, Frank Belknap 1903-1959
López Portillo y Rojas, José 1850-1903

Louys, Pierre 1870-1925
Lucas, E(dward) V(errall) 1868-1938
Lyall, Edna 1857-1903
Machar, Josef Svatopluk 1864-1945
Mander, Jane 1877-1949
Maragall, Joan 1860-1911
Marais, Eugene 1871-1936
Masaryk, Tomas 1850-1939
Mayor, Flora Macdonald 1872-1932
McClellan, George Marion 1860-1934
McCoy, Horace 1897-1955
Mirbeau, Octave 1850-1917
Mistral, Frédéric 1830-1914
Monro, Harold 1879-1932
Moore, Thomas Sturge 1870-1944
Móricz, Zsigmond 1879-1942
Morley, Christopher 1890-1957
Morley, S. Griswold 1883-1948
Murray, (George) Gilbert 1866-1957
Nansen, Peter 1861-1918
Nobre, Antonio 1867-1900
O'Dowd, Bernard 1866-1959
Ophuls, Max 1902-1957
Orczy, Baroness 1865-1947
Owen, Seaman 1861-1936
Page, Thomas Nelson 1853-1922
Palma, Ricardo 1833-1919
Papadiamantis, Alexandros 1851-1911
Parrington, Vernon L. 1871-1929
Peck, George W. 1840-1916
Phillips, Ulrich B. 1877-1934
Pinero, Arthur Wing 1855-1934
Pontoppidan, Henrik 1857-1943
Powys, T. F. 1875-1953
Prévost, Marcel 1862-1941
Quiller-Couch, Arthur 1863-1944
Radiguet, Raymond 1903-1923
Randall, James G. 1881-1953
Rappoport, Solomon 1863-1944
Read, Opie 1852-1939
Rebreanu, Liviu 1885-1944
Reisen (Reizen), Abraham 1875-1953
Remington, Frederic 1861-1909
Riley, James Whitcomb 1849-1916
Rinehart, Mary Roberts 1876-1958
Ring, Max 1817-1901
Rivera, José Eustasio 1889-1928
Rohmer, Sax 1883-1959
Rozanov, Vasily Vasilyevich 1856-1919
Saar, Ferdinand von 1833-1906
Sabatini, Rafael 1875-1950
Saintsbury, George 1845-1933
Sakutaro, Hagiwara 1886-1942
Sanborn, Franklin Benjamin 1831-1917
Santayana, George 1863-1952
Sardou, Victorien 1831-1908

Schickele, René 1885-1940
Seabrook, William 1886-1945
Seton, Ernest Thompson 1860-1946
Shestov, Lev 1866-1938
Shiels, George 1886-1949
Södergran, Edith Irene 1892-1923
Solovyov, Vladimir 1853-1900
Sorel, Georges 1847-1922
Spector, Mordechai 1859-1922
Squire, J(ohn) C(ollings) 1884-1958
Stavenhagen, Fritz 1876-1906
Stockton, Frank R. 1834-1902
Subrahmanya Bharati, C. 1882-1921

Sully-Prudhomme, René 1839-1907
Sylva, Carmen 1843-1916
Thoma, Ludwig 1867-1927
Tomlinson, Henry Major 1873-1958
Totovents, Vahan 1889-1937
Tuchmann, Jules 1830-1901
Turner, W(alter) J(ames) R(edfern) 1889-1946
Upward, Allen 1863-1926
Vachell, Horace Annesley 1861-1955
Van Dyke, Henry 1852-1933
Villaespesa, Francisco 1877-1936
Wallace, Edgar 1874-1932

Wallace, Lewis 1827-1905
Walsh, Ernest 1895-1926
Webster, Jean 1876-1916
Wen I-to 1899-1946
Whitlock, Brand 1869-1927
Wilson, Harry Leon 1867-1939
Wolf, Emma 1865-1932
Wood, Clement 1888-1950
Wren, P(ercival) C(hristopher) 1885-1941
Yonge, Charlotte Mary 1823-1901
Zecca, Ferdinand 1864-1947
Zeromski, Stefan 1864-1925

Readers are cordially invited to suggest additional authors to the editors.

The Businessman in American Literature

INTRODUCTION

"The business of America is business": this statement by Calvin Coolidge indicates a central preoccupation of American life. It is not surprising, then, that such a fascination should also be reflected in the American arts, though rarely in a manner that Coolidge would have found acceptable.

The ethics and activities of the businessman have figured prominently in American literature since Benjamin Franklin introduced "Poor Richard" to colonial readers in 1733, and authors have subsequently depicted the financial and moral dilemmas encountered in American business from a variety of perspectives. Recognized as one of the first and most influential business novels in American literature, William Dean Howells's *The Rise of Silas Lapham* (1885) presented a favorable portrait of its businessman-protagonist. However, in the decades that followed its publication, American novelists rendered increasingly negative, even contemptuous, characterizations of business leaders. In numerous novels of the early-twentieth century, including Theodore Drieser's *The Financier* (1912) and *The Titan* (1914), powerful industrialists are depicted as amoral tyrants ruled by their passion for wealth and power, while the title character of Sinclair Lewis's *Babbitt* (1922) became synonymous with vulgar materialism and spiritual bankruptcy. The late 1940s and 1950s saw a notable increase in the number of business novels, many of which were written by former executives. These novels, most prominently *Point of No Return* (1949) by John P. Marquand and *The Man in the Gray Flannel Suit* (1955) by Sloan Wilson, generally focus upon the "organization man" in the American corporate world, portraying the triumphs and tragedies met by individuals in pursuit of the American dream, with the major emphasis on the corruption inherent in business and businessmen.

Noting the hostility with which many authors have approached the subject of business, Van R. Halsey concluded in 1959: "The men who have played a dominant role in [American] economic development are presented either as immoral scoundrels of the worst sort, smashing everyone and everything that threatens their own self-interest, or, more recently, as frustrated, unhappy creatures condemned for life to a meaningless routine marked by moral compromises and petty goals, and completely devoid of any sense of fundamental values." Despite this predominantly unsympathetic characterization, or perhaps because of it, the businessman has been a subject of interest to generations of readers. In the following entry, critics examine the image of the businessman in twentieth-century American literature.

PORTRAYAL OF THE BUSINESSMAN

ROBERT P. FALK

[Falk is an American educator and critic whose numerous works reflect his interest in the literary history and business ethics of post-Civil War America. In the following excerpt, he analyzes the evolving portrait of the businessman in American literature from Benjamin Franklin's Poor Richard through novels of the mid-twentieth century.]

Turning the pages of a recent issue of *Harper's Magazine,* I stopped for a moment at a picture of Benjamin Franklin, one of those heroic portraits which seem to register all of the thirteen virtues in one determined expression. It rang a bell at once, as it was no doubt intended to do, signifying the confidence and financial security of the man who has "arrived." What secret did this man possess? the reader was asked. Write for a free copy of the booklet, "The Mastery of Life," to the Society of the Rosicrucians and learn to grasp the inner power of your mind. Follow Franklin's road to success and happiness. Here, still intact, was the earlier American dream of poor-boy-to-Senator, or rags-to-riches, apparently with enough vitality left to justify the considerable expense of a three-quarter page ad in *Harper's.* The legend has received no small amount of debunking in the century or so of its existence, but somehow it seems to have survived as a lure for those who will send for the pamphlet rather than buy a copy of Franklin's *Autobiography* and see for themselves.

Across the page in the same issue of *Harper's* was a column reviewing the new books of 1958 by Paul Pickrel. The author discusses the modern business novel, drawing a composite picture of the businessman as he emerges from the pages of a dozen or so books of 1958 about the men making money. Most of these "Martini operas" of the business scene today, he says, are written by "ad-men" in public relations or management-diplomacy. The main character is a youngish man who struggles alone and without an assured place in society against the bureaucracy of management, the pressures of competition, and "the stifling atmosphere that results from trying to do everything in groups."

This new businessman, says Pickrel, has not gone to the "right" schools and does not come from a background of social class or family connection. He is in his middle thirties, has a good income and bigger expense account, but no real security. He depends upon his talent to win him a place in society and a promotion in the Organization. His struggle to maintain himself and to keep someone from pulling the rug out from under him is the essence of the story. He is sometimes a family man and suburbanite with children to educate and a country club to join; but often he is quite alone and has time for nothing but the most elemental relations with women. He strives to hang on to his job not so much against others who would like to climb over him, but against the more elusive enemies—bigness, bureaucracy, and the indifference and ambiguity of the "front office." His prospects are usually left uncertain at the end of the book.

We shall see that certain resemblances do exist between Poor Richard and the "organized" man of today, but first we should try to account for the obvious changes. The great difference between the two figures is in the attitudes each took toward society and its attitude toward them. Here Franklin had much the better of his twentieth-century counterpart. For, since about 1830 or 1840, there has taken place a steady chipping away at the ideal of hard work and success to which his name has been irrevocably tied.

A counter-image has grown up to challenge the original and to tarnish somewhat the earlier American dream. There are many sources for this belittling tendency—the general "debunking" of great men, the revolt in the 'twenties of the younger generation, new tastes and changing values. More precisely, there have been two streams of anti-Franklin and anti-success philosophy—one from Europe and the other from Greenwich Village. The first originated with European critics of American materialism, Harold Laski, Max Weber, R. H. Tawney and their American followers who have identified Franklin with the "Protestant ethic" which in turn combined with the spirit of capitalism, thus endowing material success with the blessing of God. This concept is traced to the Puritans and ultimately to John Calvin, who have bravely borne the onus of everything that is considered wrong with American society today. And Franklin is placed in its mainstream as one who found religious sanction for what later developed into a competitive struggle for survival in the world of business.

The other support for the counter-image of the business ethic belongs to the history of Bohemianism in America, climaxed in the warfare between Greenwich Village and *The Saturday Evening Post*. Malcolm Cowley has described this "War in Bohemia" as a battle between the artistic ideals of self-expression and the middle-class doctrine of *production*. The *Post* had attacked the "Greenwich Village idea" about 1920 in a series of articles. The artists struck back from garret and cellar to defend the ideals of freedom, paganism, living for the moment. Marshalled against them were the full forces of the Protestant ethic—thrift, industry, self-denial, saving for the future and, above all, *production* of more and more goods without thought of their ultimate value. Cowley reads this story as one of final victory for Bohemia over Philistia, when ironically the revolt of morals and manners forced business to adopt the values of the Village in order to find new markets for its products. The new morality created a demand for cosmetics, cigarettes for women, movies, radios, automobiles. Gradually middle-class families began to yield to the looser standards of the Village until business found itself "going Bohemian."

But the victory, if such it was, was by no means final. Old ideas cling, and revolutions in folkways are seldom final. In the 'thirties, the old antagonism revived in political and economic terms. The welfare state of the New Deal won the national vote from the proponents of a more conservative business administration, and collectivism was in the saddle. World War II, however, brought regained prestige for business efficiency. It was generally agreed that production was a decisive factor in the victorious outcome over Fascism. Yet the basic controversy lay deeper than national issues, even wars; and the age-old struggle between poet and propriety, Bohemian versus bourgeois, and the ultimate conflict of goals between town and gown or academy and marketplace goes on beneath the changing social scene.

All this has had an indirect bearing upon the businessman of fiction and the gradual historical modification of the older portrait of Poor Richard. And if we take up the story during the 1830's, the bustling decade of Jacksonian Young America, we can see the beginnings of a new tradition of the businessman which was to develop somehow alongside the Benjamin Franklin myth, share some of its seriousness but at the same time

bring to it an element of humor and a critical edge which would lend support to the later and counter-image of Poor Richard. This change began with the Yankee peddler and confidence man.

In 1836 Thomas C. Haliburton, a Canadian writer, published the first of a series of books called *The Clockmaker; or the Sayings and Doings of Samuel Slick*. Building upon a tradition of the shrewd and rustic Yankee peddler, Haliburton struck a chord which first indicated that the businessman was to become identified with the national ethos. Sam Slick was a prototype of the ubiquitous Yankee salesman and clockmaker who could sell a $6.00 clock to a tight-fisted New England farmer's wife for $40.00 when she didn't even want one. Sam was a rustic Yankee doodle dandy, first cousin to Brother Jonathan who was the early Uncle Sam. As a businessman he was shrewd, succeeding by combining "soft sawder" with a knowledge of "human natur." Later, Sam became a storekeeper, interested in politics, a cracker-barrel philosopher like Jack Downing, speaking the democratic idiom—a combination of bad grammar and horse sense.

Sam Slick was a businessman not quite of the earnest and ambitious Poor Richard school, but admired nonetheless by readers of nearly twenty editions of Haliburton's series in Europe and America. As a real "slicker," however, he was outclassed by the frontier opportunist, Simon Suggs, invented by Johnson Hooper. Suggs was a genuine rascal of the flush times on the Mississippi whose motto was: "It's good to be shifty in a new country." But something of both Suggs and Sam Slick began to mingle with the Ben Franklin tradition in the years before the Civil War. Peddlers and confidence men combed the rural communities in the mid-west and mingled with the crowds on the steamboats plying the Ohio and Mississippi rivers. When Herman Melville in 1854 wrote his picaresque adventure of *Israel Potter*, he carried his folk-hero, a kind of early Huck Finn, through a series of frontier experiences which included the role of the long-legged, smooth-talking Yankee peddler. Potter goes to France and meets Ben Franklin, who is portrayed as a canny rustic in knee breeches doing Israel out of something at every turn and then reading him a moral lesson. "Every time he comes in he robs me," Israel complains, "with an air all the time, too, as if he were making me presents."

Melville wrote a tale of Wall Street called "Bartleby the Scrivener" and also another novel called *The Confidence Man* (1857) which combines in its main character the features of the Yankee peddler, Brother Jonathan, and Uncle Sam. "Confidence" is a word which can be taken in two quite opposite senses and Melville seems to show his character in the dual, contradictory roles of canny trickster and Christ-like preacher of faith in one's fellow man. Mark Twain's famous Colonel Sellers in *The Gilded Age* (1874) varied this pattern of the businessman, portraying him against the background of a rapidly expanding frontier society after the Civil War. Sellers is a likeable, impractical dreamer of getting rich through patent medicines and impossible gadgets which he never gets around to inventing.

But in the 1870's when fortunes were in the making and the fluid conditions of a swiftly-moving society allowed freedom and exploitation to prevail, the satirists were in the minority. The way to wealth became the American way of life and the successful businessman became the national hero. On the popular level this new attitude influenced several generations of American youth in the person of one "Ragged Dick," the first of a long series of boy-success stories by Horatio Alger. Dick was a bootblack, a bright boy who made the most of his chances, climbing the steps of the ladder, armed with prudential wisdom and Poor Richard aphorisms, to become in the end a rich and respected merchant. Tens of millions of Alger's books were sold between 1867 and 1910, and it would be hard to exaggerate their influence. As literature the stories were badly written, the characters typed, and the morality banal, but as doctrine for the values of individual enterprise and getting-ahead by pluck and luck (not by confidence-man tricks), their influence upon a generation of boys who became businessmen in the early years of the present century was tremendous. So great, indeed, was Alger's influence that when business conditions changed radically after 1920, many businessmen found themselves still clinging to the easy, ready-made philosophy of Ragged Dick long after it had lost its relevance to the existing situation.

On a higher literary level, however, the businessman was studied more seriously. To Henry James and William Dean Howells, he was the new man of America, a type that had to be reckoned with, and they devoted long novels to his literary portrait. In his novel *The American* (1878) James represented him as Christopher Newman, a typical American exploring the cultural values of Europe, the first tourist abroad. Newman was a millionaire from California involved in a romantic affair with Claire de Cintre, the daughter of an aristocratic French family down on its luck. James's portrait of Newman has certain satiric touches—he made money in leather and in washtubs, "which were lovely," he is an innocent abroad, naive about art and cultural things, and he is regarded by the French with a kind of legendary wonder as a Paul Bunyan of finance who owns an entire city in the West inhabited only by people who don't smoke cigars!

Newman is, however, no ancestor of George Babbitt. He belongs to the period in which the businessman was painted in heroic proportions, but without the taint that has come to be attached to his real contemporaries—Jim Fisk, Jay Gould,and Cornelius "the public be damned" Vanderbilt. Newman has their dash, daring, recklessness, and towering freedom of movement without their unscrupulousness.

> You stand up, so very straight, for accomplished facts [says his friend Valentin de Bellegarde]. You've made a fortune, you've raised an edifice, you're a financial, practical power.... What I envy you is your liberty, your wide range, your freedom to come and go....

In the end he proves morally the superior of his French counterparts, though frustrated in his hopes of marriage. Newman was constructed of romantic materials. Business was only a means to an end with him and he was indissolubly linked with James's concept of the idealized American type.

James saw his businessman through a European perspective. Howells, on the other hand, viewed Silas Lapham (*The Rise of Silas Lapham,* 1885) in terms of the workaday business life of a newly-rich, uncultured man involved in a moral problem and perplexed by his social-climbing family which seeks to crash Boston society. Lapham is Howells' answer to the charge that all businessmen of the Gilded Age were amoral tycoons and robber barons. His wealth came from a paint mine on the family farm in Vermont. He had forced his partner out of the business just before the value of the paint was to double, and the action, though not entirely one of greed, was done in a

spirit of selfishness. In the end, Silas makes amends for his action, goes into bankruptcy rather than make a deal which might have saved his business, but ruined many small investors. Lapham's ethics are sound, his intentions good, and his table manners atrocious. But Howells manages to make him believable and even sympathetic. Even now, his portrait of Silas Lapham rings truer than some of the pictures we have from historians who have described the real businessmen of the 1880's in terms of a social or economic "thesis."

James, in later books like *The Ambassadors* (1903), continued to hold to the favorable view of the businessman as representative American, but Howells became increasingly concerned over the class conflict, strikes, and labor disturbances of the late 1880's and early 1890's. In *A Hazard of New Fortunes* (1889) his portrait of Dryfoos, a later and degraded Silas Lapham, becomes increasingly critical, looking forward to the vogue of muckraking novelists of the turn of the century.

In the 'nineties the Social Darwinists began to create in American life a cult of muscle-worship which had important ramifications in politics, society, and business. Teddy Roosevelt charged up San Juan Hill in a symbolic gesture of might, right, moral athleticism, and virtues of the outdoor life. John L. Sullivan, "the Strong Boy of Boston," became a national hero, The Message to Garcia a national creed, the Gospel of Wealth a rationale of big business. William Randolph Hearst helped justify a questionable war with jingoistic journalism. In short, America was flexing its muscles in an effort, perhaps, to forget

THE

RISE OF SILAS LAPHAM

BY

WILLIAM D. HOWELLS

AUTHOR OF "A MODERN INSTANCE," "A WOMAN'S REASON," ETC.

BOSTON
TICKNOR AND COMPANY
1885

Title page of Howells's The Rise of Silas Lapham.

some of the disturbing forces which had threatened to erupt into class-conflict, Populist revolts, agrarian discontent, and labor troubles. In fiction there developed a cult of the strong.

Jack London wrote novels which glorified animals with human feelings and men who acted like wolves or Alaskan huskies. Frank Norris admired "the brutal bullying instinct" which prompted the struggles between freshmen and sophomores at Berkeley. He proceeded to write a series of novels about business which were a mixture of Darwinism and romance. Curtis Jadwin, the hero of *The Pit* (1902), is a capitalist and speculator formed on a grand scale who appeals to Laura Dearborn, the heroine, because of his masculine proportions, his broad strong hands, and his look of relentless, unswerving will and purpose. Uneducated and awkward among women, in art museums, and at the opera, Jadwin is nonetheless Laura's (and Norris') choice over the artist, Sheldon Corthell. She weighs the cult of the beautiful against the cult of the strong and casts her lot with Jadwin's because, daughter of the frontier as she is, she is fascinated by the drama of The Battle of the Street, the challenging struggle which went on in the wheat pits in the Chicago Board of Trade. "Only the strong and brave might dare it, and the figure that held her imagination and her sympathy was not the artist, soft of hand and of speech . . . ; but the fighter . . . hard, rigorous, panoplied in the harness of the warrior, who strove among the trumpets. . . ."

Here is the first clear portrait of the strong business-hero as a virile Roman, a larger-than-life representative of the American scene, a kind of Leatherstocking transferred to the Board of Trade. His motive is not money, but the excitement of the speculating game, the sense of power in cornering the market in wheat. He is impelled to gamble by a restless force within him and he is drawn further and further by a combination of luck and genius. In the end he is destroyed by a more powerful force than himself, the wheat, but Jadwin has become a tragic hero, a figure of romance, who gains stature even in defeat.

Jadwin stands alone, as all business heroes did in the strenuous age. There were others like him in the fiction of individual enterprise which preceded World War I. Van Harrington in Robert Herrick's *Memoirs of an American Citizen* (1905) rises from farm boy to senator by the application of Darwinian ethics to the meat-packing industry. He survives by the cult of the strong, by rejecting the tender conscience of women and the clergy, and by acknowledging that climbing the success-ladder is "no gospel game." His code is that of the jungle—"to live in any age," he meditates, "you have got to have the fingers and toes necessary for that age." Unlike Jadwin, Harrington's twin motives are money and power, to be like the other men of wealth he saw in Chicago. "What was the golden road? These men had found it—hundreds, thousands of them,—farming tools, railroads, groceries, gas, dry-goods. It made no matter what. . . . To take my place with these mighty ones—I thought a good deal about that in those days!"

Van Harrington is shrewd, strong, masculine, attractive, fundamentally honest, but willing to sacrifice principle rather than to fail or be crushed by others in his drive for power. He and Dreiser's Frank Cowperwood are full-blown Napoleons of muscular capitalism. Cowperwood, modelled on the career of the industrialist Charles Yerkes, accepts without question the doctrine that men are cannibals, living on weaker men. He is both an egotist and an intellectual. Business-success is for him a challenge. The world of money is a "game." Finance is an "art," like chess. His impulse is to exercise his talent, to test his strength, not greed or gain *per se*.

Dreiser follows the fortunes of his Nietzschean superman through two prolific novels, *The Financier* and *The Titan* (1912, 1914). After marrying the widow of a wealthy merchant, he gets a start in the brokerage business, edges craftily into politics, and manages to score a coup by cornering the field in street-railway securities. Sex rears its lovely head in the person of Aileen Butler, the daughter of a street-paving contractor with whom Cowperwood has done business. She becomes his mistress, but the girl's father has the relationship exposed by detectives and Cowperwood is arrested and sent to prison for embezzlement of municipal funds. He is soon pardoned and returns to Philadelphia where the failure of Jay Cooke in 1873 enables him to recoup his fortune and exploit the market for millions of dollars.

Cowperwood is a fairly simple combination of financier and lover, Machiavelli and Don Juan, merchant prince and "sexual freelance." Dreiser does not pull his punches in presenting without apology the jungle ethics of the strong man. A product of nature, he is not responsible for his superiority to the ordinary herd. It is he alone who moves forward despite the mass mediocrity. There is an epic quality about his portrayal of the rise of a powerful individual, succeeding because he is the fittest to survive among conditions of the struggle and competition for existence and for power. When he was interviewed and asked about the right and wrong of the financial titan's activities, Dreiser replied there was no such thing in nature as the right to do and the right not to do.

> The financial type is the coldest, the most selfish, and the most useful of all living phenomena. Plainly it is a highly specialized machine for the accomplishment of some end which Nature has in view. Often humorless, shark-like, avid, yet among the greatest constructive forces imaginable.

In his delineation of Cowperwood's love-life, Dreiser added a new dimension to the portrait of the businessman which was to become a pervading motif of the later, Freudian novel. Unlike Curtis Jadwin or Van Harrington, who find their married lives amusing but something of a hindrance in their drive for power, Cowperwood becomes deeply entangled in the "chemistry" of sex, almost to the point of making him a tragic figure and the victim of his own illicit passion. He escapes the penalty of this romantic flaw, however, and continues on toward his goal of power, wealth, intellectual superiority, and social nobility—or at least, as he says, the appearance of these things.

These and many other novels of the business superman, written in the first decade of the twentieth century, show characteristics almost unknown to earlier and later examples of the *genre*. For one thing they concentrate with gusto upon the details of such things as the complex workings of the grain exchange, the formation of combines and trusts, the fluctuations of prices, the hard bargaining behind closed doors, the maneuvering involved in cornering the market in railway securities. Such information is narrated with a view to communicating information and telling the "inside story," even where it adds little to the central plot. The main character is the man of individual enterprise, his decisions are vital, nor does he submit them to a committee. In the end, he is seldom regretful of his actions, even though he is not satisfied with the result, and if he is brought low, he retains the reader's sympathy as for a giant in chains.

The strong man of the 1890's and early 1900's in fiction carries over something of Ben Franklin's determination to get ahead, and something of the disregard for principle of the peddler and the confidence man. He is Algeresque, too, in his "rise" from poor boy to a position of respect and greatness. Unlike Franklin, however, he is not even slightly concerned with virtue or character for its own sake. He has no use for Christian morality or "gospel games." In fact, to judge from the three business-heroes we have described, the cult of the great entrepreneur does not bear out the theories of Max Weber, R. H. Tawney, and other historians that the Gospel of Wealth and the Protestant ethic tended to sanctify business by endowing it with the blessing of God. All of them reject Christian ethics in favor of the law of the jungle. They agree, in general, with Frank Cowperwood, who learned his lesson early as a boy passing a fish market and watching a lobster slowly devour a squid. The sight answered for him the riddle of life: "How is life organized?" he asked himself. "Things lived on each other—that was it."

The reaction against the cult of the strong began in the 'twenties when Sinclair Lewis in *Babbitt* dealt a death-blow to the business-hero of the Gilded Age. The strong, amoral tycoon became in his hands a timid follower of orthodoxy, a repeater of slogans, and a blundering pursuer of manicurists or neighbors' wives. Babbitt is a scarcely recognizable descendant of Frank Cowperwood or Van Harrington. The Alger-myth has disappeared. Babbitt does not rise, he simply wallows. He lives in a world of tasteless vulgarity, domestic boredom, and Rotarian boosterism. He is pathetic because his aims are so petty and he takes them so seriously. Lewis stacks the cards against him by depriving him of all largeness. His business is selling real estate (he prefers the term "realtor"), his ideals are defined by the Chamber of Commerce of Zenith and what Mencken called Warren Harding's "Eden of clowns." Babbitt is a *boobus Americanus* par excellence, though in the end he senses dimly that his life lacked something, a freedom to do what he wanted, and he clumsily but honestly encourages his son Ted to take the job he wants and work out his destiny in his own way.

A re-reading of *Babbitt* cannot but impress one with the brilliance of Lewis' satiric pen and his incomparable mimicking of the empty banalities, the "by-Gosh, by-Gee, by-George" imprecations of the middle-class cliche-expert. Babbitt is honest in business, but his honesty is somehow made to seem far less admirable than the unprincipled ambitions of Dreiser's Cowperwood—a fact which once again confirms the old literary truism that heroic irregularity can be made more attractive than timid respectability. As a portrait of the businessman, Babbitt is a figure of satire, a caricature.

But Lewis partially redressed the balance in Dodsworth, an automobile magnate who sells his business, like Christopher Newman, and sets out to find the larger life in Europe. He fails to adjust to a more complex and graceful civilization and returns to America, but his defeat has brought a certain depth to his character. He rises in the reader's esteem by courageously refusing to take back his pampered wife who has deserted him for an Austrian nobleman. Dodsworth is a partly tragic figure, instead of a ridiculous one, but like Babbitt, his soul has been damaged by the philistinism of his circumscribed existence. "He would certainly produce excellent motor cars; but he would never love passionately, lose tragically, nor sit in contented idleness upon tropic shores." The ideals of self-expression and Greenwich Village, which Lewis here exalts, would never be his.

The career of Sherwood Anderson, so nakedly revealed in his books (which are a melange of Freudian dreams, Bohemianism, the revolt against middle-class ideals, nudism, and other "wist-

ful idealizations of the male menopause"), epitomizes the conflict between art and business in the 1920's. In such novels as *Many Marriages* (1923) and *Dark Laughter* (1925), Anderson portrayed himself, a businessman in a small town at the age of forty, suddenly rebelling against the repressions of standardization, the acquisitive life, factories, families, Rotarianism, and the machine age. Like John Stockton in the latter novel, he undergoes a spiritual eruption and walks out of his old life into one of new freedoms, life on the Mississippi, bumming, loafing, and dreaming in an exhibitionist effort to recapture Mark Twain's mood. As a youth Anderson had thrown himself imaginatively into the excitements of the money-game and the thrills of business expansion. At forty he did a complete reversal, and his books were an expression of the traumatic division which overtook him at mid-life. His rebellion was as extreme as had been his earlier immersion in the American dream of success. Writing and sex became his new ideals. Like John Webster, one of his characters who had been a washing machine manufacturer living a middle-class family life, he felt that he had missed "Life." Webster takes to walking naked up and down before a picture of the Virgin Mary and finally leaves his home to run away with his stenographer.

But Bohemianism as a literary vogue spent itself somewhat by the end of the decade. *Dodsworth* was a sign that even the truculent author of *Babbitt* could see its limits. In 1927 Booth Tarkington wrote the most effective anti-Babbitt novel of the 'twenties in *The Plutocrat*, in which he neatly reversed the values which Mencken, Lewis, and Anderson had espoused. Earl Tinker, its hero, is a colorful, likeable businessman who finds himself in a Jamesian situation while on a vacation trip through Europe. He harks back in certain ways to the virile, Napoleonic businessman of an earlier time. Tinker is first seen through the eyes of Laurence Ogle, a young playwright who wears his Bohemianism on his sleeve as obviously as does Babbitt his Boosterism. Ogle falls in love with a mysteriously attractive woman of European origin, Mme. Momoro, who perversely seems to prefer the company of the poker-playing, cigar-smoking, rough-and-ready president of the Illinois and Union Paper Company. Tinker is conscious of his crudeness, but it never bothers him. In the end the turnabout is completed. Ogle and his ideals are discredited by contrast with the greater stature of Mr. Tinker who becomes, for all his superficial vulgarity, a formidable figure, generous-minded, responsible, and above all energetic. He is called a "New Roman," virile, triumphant, riding a white camel in barbaric pomp toward long-conquered Carthage. "He is a great barbarian," Mme. Momoro tells the disillusioned young playwright, "with great power. . . . He is as careless of his power as he is of everything else. Do you remember how he bought all the fruit at Gibraltar, and tossed it to those poor people in the steerage?"

Tarkington's effort to restore the businessman of the Howells and James era, however, ran counter to the trend, and the attack which had been Bohemian in the 'twenties, became doctrinaire and proletarian in the 'thirties. The muckraking novel of which Upton Sinclair's *The Jungle* (1905) had been a classic example—a socialistic account of the evils of the meat-packing industry in Chicago—returned with a new kind of Marxian bitterness during the New Deal and the depression decade. Ideology began to crowd out characterization, psychology, and humanity. In the hands of such writers as Dos Passos. Steinbeck. Robert Cantwell, Samuel Hopkins Adams, James Steele, Mary Heaton Vorse, and Christina Stead, the novel of business was used as a platform for various spokesmen of the social left.

In Dos Passos' *The 42nd Parallel* (1930) and *The Big Money* (1936) the focus is on the class war. He does not attempt an extended portrait of a businessman so much as a kaleidoscopic impression of a cross-section of American life in the 1920's in which a rootless, drifting population searches for freedom and personal liberty in the stifling atmosphere of a commercially-organized society. One of these people, Charley Anderson, is a kind of symbol of the evils of capitalism. He returns from the war as a hero, becomes a financier in Detroit, but gradually declines to become a waster, a drinker, and a failure. Dos Passos dreamed of some new organization of "the masses," or rather no organization at all, but a world in which property was abolished and man ceased the economic war against man. His was a voice crying in the wilderness: "Oh, if people would only trust their own, fundamental kindliness, the fraternity, the love that is the strongest thing in life."

Dos Passos could be more aggressive than this in attacks upon Henry Ford and the assembly line, and in these moods he more nearly expressed the virulence which characterized the depression novel. Frederick Wakeman in *The Hucksters* described Evan Llewellyn Evans, a soap tycoon, as a kind of Laskian monster, or a Marxian distortion of reality. Samuel Hopkins Adams's *Plunder* is a story of business corruption in Washington. All businessmen in the novel are "predatory," devoid of sensitivity, and look like "huge gorged saurians." All are five-percenters (before the term gained currency) out to deceive the government, manufacturing planes which "crashed in deathly heaps," shells which backfired and caused great slaughter on the ranges, ships which broke in two on the waves. *Plunder* is a narrative written without warmth or understanding, but in bitterness and spite.

After Dreiser the novels of business step up the pace of sex and sensationalism. Once seduction scenes begin to appear (and at first they were tentative, suggestive, requiring long chapters of preparation), the progress toward freedom is swift. Physical details enter more frequently, multiple scenes are employed, the description becomes increasingly frank and spirals to its climax in fewer pages and more gripping language. Sex becomes a release, an escape from the pressures of business life, but writers (and readers) love it for itself alone. Of Christina Stead's *A Little Tea, A Little Chat* (1948) John Chamberlain remarks that the businessmen "spend so much time getting in and out of bed that one wonders how they have time to make money." Mary McCarthy's *The Man in the Brooks Brothers Shirt* portrays the Bohemian-Philistine hassle in terms of a seduction on a transcontinental train of an *avant-garde* girl novelist by a traveling salesman for a steel company. The outcome is inevitable—the two worlds are incompatible.

It is no news at this point in history that the shadows of Marx and Freud have dominated the contemporary novel and affected markedly the portrayal of the businessman, as well as other characters of fiction. In the 'thirties it was 75 per cent Marx and 25 per cent Freud. Today, the percentages are reversed. In the 'thirties the anti-business novelist won easy victories. In his mind was an idealized form of state socialism, writes John Chamberlain in *Fortune* [see excerpt below]. He demanded a state-endowed social security, with drastic limits on freedom–for the businessmen. He tended "to contrast the world of free capitalism with a perfect socialized order that had no existence outside his own head." No mere human businessman, Chamberlain said, could stand up against a perfect figment of the idealist's mind.

After World War II there was a noticeable upturn in the number of novels devoted to the businessman, but the accent shifted away from depression and class-conflict themes to the problems of the youngish man who returns from military life to re-establish himself in the business world. Tom Rath, in *The Man in the Gray Flannel Suit* by Sloan Wilson, has become a symbol in the public mind of this new type. Unlike his counterpart of World War I, he is not a rebel, a wastrel, or a rich boy of the Fitzgerald era. Nor is he one of the brooding members of a lost generation. Instead, he is an "Organization Man." His wartime experiences have taken away his desire to struggle. There are plenty of jobs, and the problem is to get the best one possible. Tom Rath seeks security, a place in the exurbanite society of the big city, and he does not want challenge or responsibility. He is conservative, tired. He wants mostly to "get along." He is a bureaucrat.

Charley Gray in J. P. Marquand's *Point of No Return* is another of the post-war business executives who fits this pattern. The writer's interest is to show the business career from the point of view of Charley's home life, his wife, their prospects for joining the country club and achieving "status" in suburban society-life. The big question in the Grays' life turns on whether he will be promoted to a vice-presidency of the Stuyvesant Bank. Marquand is only incidentally concerned with the details of banking and investment, and the emphasis falls on delicate problems of diplomacy, Charley's relations with his boss, the whole touchy matter of "getting along" with his superiors, "togetherness," and his relations with his wife and children. Lunch at the Harvard Club is a ritual, learning to call the boss "Tony" instead of "Mr. Burton," exchanging gossip with the brass on his way to work in the commuter train—such are the details on which his future depends. Frustration and resignation are the keynotes of this novel. When the announcement comes that he has been promoted over his rival, Charley is not greatly moved. "It was like the time at Dartmouth when he had won the half-mile at freshman track. He felt dull and very tired."

Charley Gray and Tom Rath are in positions which are relatively secure, but from which there isn't much they can rise to, or struggle for. Their desire is to keep the status quo. They don't rebel because there isn't anything to rebel against. The "company" dictates their way of life, but it is a comfortable one and they don't protest. Such rebellion as they feel is a kind of puzzled questioning of the value of it all. The only escape from frustration is in dreams, remembered war experiences, or sex (like the "affair" in Italy which produced a child for Tom Rath and threatened to disturb his domestic security after the war).

Babbitt, too, had had moments of questioning whether it was all worth while. Novelists of more recent years find this tone of doubt, of wondering what it is all about, where it will all end, and what reason exists for pursuing the "old rat race" a prevailing motif in their treatment of the business executive in the Organization. In *Jefferson Selleck* (1951) Carl Jonas has portrayed a wiser, sadder, mellower Babbitt of the 1950's. Selleck is middle-aged, a partner in a small company manufacturing tune-playing automobile horns. After a heart attack he is advised by his doctor to occupy himself by writing his memoirs, thinking over his past. Like Babbitt, he is a small-town joiner, a Republican, a suburbanite, and a member of the country club. What values he finds in his past life show certain positive ideas about his middle-class experience. He believes in the principle of work because it is "not unlike religion" and it gives him a sense of continuity and a faith that the world will keep on turning. He is puzzled about his life, and not really articulate, but he comes to terms with it, with his family, marriage, and even the rather tentative religion he had practiced.

Revolt against conformity shows itself in some of the recent business fiction, but is more the exception than the rule. In *From the Dark Tower,* Earnst Pawel describes the kind of brainwashing which a large insurance company imposes upon its members, from the top executive on down. The president points out that no employee can live two lives, a private life and a company life. All must worship the Tower, which becomes a symbol of the extinction of the individual. In return it offers "security" and "togetherness," but these are not enough for Pawel's hero who finally has the courage to resign rather than accept a new position which is offered him.

Revolt of a different kind is the theme of Ayn Rand's *Atlas Shrugged,* an 1100-page tome about the search for a new world of science and industry, freed from the restraints, parasites, "looters," and all the vermin of governmental bureaucracy and labor unionism who try to force the still existent, old-style business tycoon to his knees. Miss Rand's book is a fantastic piece of rightist propaganda and science fiction, symptomatic, however, of the present tendency of multiple-bureaucracies and strangling organizations to throttle the drive of productive business to get things done. The revolt in *Atlas Shrugged* is that of a few dynamic producers against a society (rather vaguely described as "they") which would cripple production and send civilization back into a hand-craft barbarity. The producers symbolize "reason" and pit themselves against the enemy, the "mystics of the spirit" who would deny "reason" (i.e., material progress).

The recent "Martini operas" of business discussed by Paul Pickrel concern young men in TV and newspaper advertising, merchandizing in a department store, public relations, and the drug business. In *The Admen* Shepherd Mead is concerned with the efforts of a young adman to hold to certain standards of integrity and creativity against a corporation manufacturing Broil-Around Roasters. The president seeks safety and security, stifling the advertising game by old-fashioned ideas. In *A Really Sincere Guy* by Robert Van Riper, Bill McCrary is a typical hero of the latest business novel. He is a middle westerner, product of a small unfashionable college, with a big income, but no security except his job. His egotistic boss tries to force him, against his own principles, to undertake a campaign in favor of high tariffs. The conflict of ideals and company interests finally forces Bill to resign, though he holds to the belief that public relations is an honorable calling. *Pax* by Middleton Kiefer is the story of another adman, this one involved in selling a new tranquillizer named "Pax" before it has been unambiguously tested in the laboratory. Politics complicate the problem when a Senate committee begins to look into the practices of the drug industry. Joe Logan is a far-seeing hidden-persuader who succeeds in preparing the way for Pax by a subtle means of favorable propaganda for the Raven Pharmaceutical Company, but in the end his high-pressure public relations backfire on the company.

None of these Organization novels, with the exception of *Atlas Shrugged,* takes a black-and-white position either for or against business as such. Most of them lean in sympathy toward the individual businessman in his struggle against conformity and dishonesty and standardization, but the middle-man hero is by no means whitewashed. At least some of the taint of the Organization has rubbed off on him. In his relations with women,

he is usually faced with two alternatives—one of whom stands for values, the other for sex. Most of the novels turn on this theme: can a man maintain a certain integrity in the business world against the built-in timidity and conservatism of the Organization and its executives. (pp. 2-12)

Some of them recall the naturalistic fiction of Dreiser and Norris in setting out to tell the "inside story" of a certain business. The picture is usually a depressing one. *Pax,* for instance, shows the way in which the sales manager and the publicity man of a company which has produced vermifuges for the army attempt to launch an anti-histamine compound as a tranquillizer and to put it out without prescription in an advertising campaign to hit the big, national market. The drug has not been unambiguously tested in the laboratory, it circumvents the Pure Food and Drug laws, and is not even certainly a tranquillizing compound, but Joe Logan proceeds with the publicity, touching new heights of psychological hidden-persuading. One of his ideas is a radio commercial designed to create the need for the product by describing with sound-effects the strains and tensions of modern life. First, a soothing voice tells of the infinite peace of the embryonic soul in the womb. Then the announcer says: "Prepare for the trauma of birth!"

> (Another silence. Then suddenly, from a speaker in the back of the room, a woman's shriek cut through the silence, long and piercing.)

"From infancy onward," continues the voice, "you are subject to a thousand tensions . . . you try to relax. . . ."

> (A child's scream was cut off sharply by the squeal of brakes which merged with the sound of an automobile horn.)

Public relations has become the critical department of business in these novels. It controls sales, production, and overrides the will of the president himself. All depends upon its success, and it is not just the product, but the company itself which requires public sympathy, good relations, and a favorable press. There is a change here, even from the kind of organizational fiction which Marquand and Sloan Wilson wrote. The businesses themselves are marginal ones trying to become bigger. The businessman is in the middle position, hoping to pull off a "coup" and get a promotion through his own ingenuity and inventiveness. He lives hard, drinks for relaxation, and becomes cynical or has his natural cynicism confirmed by the business "game." Sex has now become a part of the game. He connives with a pretty secretary who is often a bosomy persuader on her own part. In the end he does not either rise or fall, in the older sense; instead his fate is left ambiguous or he rebels and throws up his work for a return to writing, art, or a more creative and less organizational activity.

Business itself, and social attitudes toward it, have changed vastly from the innocent days of Poor Richard to the present era of the Organization. "A penny saved is a penny earned" is nonsense in a day when a dollar spent for advertising means a quick return in dividends and sales. And it would be poor public relations for the owner of a printing shop to be seen trundling his supplies to work in a wheelbarrow or driving his own delivery truck. The struggle to succeed has shifted from the individual to the company—even to the business system itself—and even "Big Business" is in a vulnerable position, its security depending upon intangibles such as government bureaucracies, public opinion, big labor unions, or the foreign situation.

The businessman himself, however, is not so greatly altered as he might at first seem. He has passed through a series of evolving portraits in literature with a variety of disguises: a great American success, a shifty or cunning peddler, a confidence man, a representative American, a strong amoral titan of finance. He has been depicted as George Babbitt and as his opposite number. He has become a monster of the schools with a Marxian head, a Freudian body, Laskian arms and legs, and a Veblerian or Weberian appetite for lovely proletarian virgins in annual sacrificial rites.

Yet there are certain constants to the portrait, too. He has been steadily shown as the representative American type, shrewd and eager to get ahead, lacking in cultural and aesthetic appreciation, but equipped with wit, humor, and practical wisdom. From Franklin to Joe Logan he has consistently stood for the principle that business is not solely or even primarily concerned to make money, but rather that it is a "game" played for high stakes in which his satisfaction comes from measuring his own wit and skill against others, or against "society." And, throughout American literature, the novelist has been fairly consistent in standing for the individual in his struggle for recognition—at first against himself, then against society, and finally against the business organization itself. (pp. 13-14)

Robert P. Falk, "From Poor Richard to the Man in the Gray Flannel Suit: A Literary Portrait of the Businessman," in California Management Review, *Vol. I, No. 4, Summer, 1959, pp. 1-14.*

HENRY NASH SMITH

[*Smith is an American educator who has written extensively on American novelists, particularly the works of Mark Twain. In the following excerpt, he traces the changing portrayals of businessmen in American novels of the nineteenth and twentieth centuries.*]

The fictional businessman follows a reasonably clear line of development from the 1880's, when he first becomes conspicuous as a literary type, to the publication of Dreiser's *The Financier*. In the early novels the businessman is presented simply as a villain; in Dreiser's trilogy Frank Cowperwood is held up for the reader's admiration. What has changed in the interval is not the character and behavior attributed to the businessman but rather the criteria by which he is judged. Although writers since Dreiser show a greater variety of attitudes, the development of the value systems controlling the fictive world of the novel is the central theme to be noticed.

The early hostility of novelists to the businessman was due to the fact that they took the characteristic type to be a financier and stock-market operator on the model of Jim Fisk or Jay Gould, who were almost universally considered reprehensible. Examples are Zedekiah Hampton in H. H. Boyesen's *A Daughter of the Philistines* (1883), "Uncle" Jerry Hollowell in Charles Dudley Warner's *A Little Journey in the World* (1889), and Jacob Dryfoos in William Dean Howells's *A Hazard of New Fortunes* (1890). The very titles of these novels express the basic revulsion of their authors against the emergent financial and industrial system of the post-Civil War period. The new millionaires are Philistines (a term popularized in the late 1860's and 1870's by Matthew Arnold), and the social atmosphere that they have created is worldly in comparison with the quiet refinement of a vanishing older order. (p. 78)

All three fictional financiers have grown wealthy and powerful through speculation, first on a small scale in the Middle West,

then in the larger arena of New York. In accord with the sentimental convention that gave virtuous characters a monopoly of culture and sensibility, all three businessmen are depicted as coarse and vulgar. (p. 79)

Howells is more sensitive to moral nuances than Boyesen or Warner, but all three of these novels of the 1880's reveal an inchoate sense of guilt somehow related to the rapid economic expansion of the period. This feeling is almost certainly one cause of the general hostility that writers showed toward the businessman. He was a candidate for the role of scapegoat because he was an alien intruder into the fictive world. In contrast with the familiar protagonists of sentimental love stories, he seemed both crude and immoral. Yet he was acknowledged to be immensely powerful. He controlled the energies of economic, social, and political change; the future belonged to him; and no matter how many times the novelists might condemn the businessman to social rebuffs, rejection by the heroine, bankruptcy, public exposure for his crimes, or even suicide, they recognized at bottom that traditional manners and morals were doomed by the growing dominance of the business system.

This was disconcerting, because when New England could no longer serve as a moral base, the novelist analyzing the business system was left without a stable viewpoint from which to survey his subject. It was difficult to find the elements of an acceptable code of values within the system, yet he faced an even more difficult task if he attempted to construct a moral code not supported by some historical reality. Writers of fiction were thus, on the whole, committed to the belief that American life showed an increasing disparity between value and fact, between ideal and actual. Howell's hope that somehow, sometime, loving-kindness would yet prevail in the world has little support in the description of that world presented in *A Hazard of New Fortunes*.

But what if a writer should break with tradition and attempt to deal with the new capitalism on its own terms? In several respects Mark Twain's *A Connecticut Yankee in King Arthur's Court* (1889), published almost simultaneously with *A Hazard of New Fortunes*, is just such an effort. His undertaking was, to be sure, less deliberate than this statement implies. His rejection of literary tradition was not a conscious act but the result of his having developed within the quite different tradition of native American humor—the tall tale, the journalistic hoax, the comic burlesque. The impulse that eventually developed into *A Connecticut Yankee* was quite antiliterary—the notion of writing a burlesque of Malory's *Morte D'Arthur*, which is expressed in a dream recorded in Mark Twain's notebook in 1885. The economic and political implications of the story appeared only later, as it gestated over a period of years. Yet they were not irrelevant, for a cult of medievalism, and specifically of the aristocratic ideals of chivalry, had become one of the principal weapons used by genteel critics against the growing power of business in the nineteenth century.... For most readers in the 1880's the Knights of the Round Table had much the same status as the antitypes of the businessman conceived by the novelists. The very impulse to make fun of Malory was thus profoundly hostile to the Genteel Tradition; it implied taking the side of a modern world which everyone agreed was permeated with commercialism against the current conception of the aristocratic, noncommercial Middle Ages.

Quite early in the development of Mark Twain's burlesque, he began to give to his modern protagonist many of the traits that had been associated with the businessman in fiction. Hank

Morgan, the Yankee, is "practical," and devoid of poetry and sentiment. He is crude in his tastes, being for example very fond of chromos and repelled by medieval tapestries; he has no reverence for antiquity and tradition; and he takes a commercial view of everything, greedily seeking opportunities to make money and constantly using figures of speech derived from business transactions—contracts, discounts, bookkeeping, and operations on the market such as running a corner, selling short, and so on. Dropped suddenly and inexplicably into sixth-century Britain, he secures for himself the status and title of Boss, and sets about putting Arthur's kingdom on a business basis.

The important question is how Mark Twain justifies his generally favorable attitude toward such a protagonist. The reader familiar with earlier fictional portraits of the businessman will be struck by the fact that almost nothing is said about the financial system of Arthur's kingdom or the means by which the Yankee raises the capital necessary for his operations. It is true that eventually we discover the Round Table has been transformed into a stock board, but the protagonist himself does no trading on it, and until almost the end of the story it is no more than a bit of irreverence toward a prime symbol of chivalry. The only influence that speculation has on the plot is to foment a rivalry among the knights which sets off a civil war; and this event is a great misfortune for the Yankee because it leads to the collapse of his plans for reforming British society.

In other words, whether deliberately or not, Mark Twain shields his hero against the charge of gaining wealth through speculation. Thus despite Hank Morgan's indifference to culture and refinement, he is free of the graver taint of immorality that literary convention had associated with business enterprise. Furthermore, instead of causing poverty, the Yankee is determined to alleviate it. Mark Twain emphasizes the constructive functions of his nineteenth-century invader by making a distinction anticipating Thorstein Veblen's contrast between the engineer interested in production and the financier interested only in profits. The Yankee plans an industrial revolution in the backward feudal economy of sixth-century Britain by means of modern technology. He sets about building factories, workshops, mines, and systems of transportation and communication that will drastically raise the standard of living for the people as a whole. He believes that industrialization will also educate the workers. They will become enlightened through their contact with machines and will in this way become capable of participating as citizens in the republic that he hopes eventually to proclaim.

In making his protagonist a master technician and interpreting economic development as an increase in productive power rather than as a mysterious opportunity for speculators to enrich themselves, Mark Twain was taking over a rationale of capitalism familiar in economic and political discussion but previously unknown in fiction. His attitude toward industrialization throws into relief the primitive character of the economic ideas used by his literary predecessors. Even when writing in detail about financial transactions, earlier writers show no awareness that the speculative boom of the post-Civil War period was the result of an immense increase in production based on the mechanization of transportation and industry. (pp. 85-8)

The preoccupation of the novelists with the Napoleonic battles among captains of finance indicates that they gained their impressions of the new capitalism from newspaper reports of political scandals rather than from observing actual economic changes. They were almost totally ignorant of what was really going on in the American economy. Even Mark Twain, despite his intention to exhibit an industrial and managerial genius at work, is unable to give imaginative substance to the Yankee's activities because he simply does not know enough about the technology that he ascribes to his hero.

Yet the intention is there, and it represents a bold attempt to evaluate the industrial revolution from the standpoint of the business community itself rather than from the standpoint of genteel literary and moral tradition. As the agent of technological progress, Hank Morgan takes on a kind of Promethean stature, and through three-fourths of the story the reader can believe that Mark Twain has at last found a way to create an authentic capitalist hero—one who represents the operative values of his society and performs a significant action expressing these values. But the Yankee's civilizing mission ends in failure. The causes of his defeat are not clear because the plot loses itself in a maze of complications. Toward the end of the story Mark Twain seems to be moved by an emotional reaction against his own confident ideology in the earlier chapters rather than by any consistent line of reasoning. Yet from the tangle emerges one powerful conviction—the common people cannot be enlightened as the Yankee had hoped. He has not been able to educate the superstition out of them after all; they are but "human muck," chained forever by their own prejudices and fears of authority, unable in a crisis to resist the commands of their masters, the Church and the nobles. (pp. 88-9)

Although *A Connecticut Yankee* seems an anomaly in the series of realistic novels about the businessman, Mark Twain's use of a radically different fictional convention casts much light on the issues involved. The method of the fable brings out in bold relief the central myth of nineteenth-century American capitalism; it is indeed the myth of Prometheus, enemy of the reactionary and tyrannical gods of tradition, bringer of intellectual light and material well-being to the downtrodden masses. These achievements were what was usually meant by the term "progress," and the hold of the big businessman on the popular imagination depended on the belief that the achievements were *his* achievements. (pp. 89-90)

Dreiser's trilogy about Frank Cowperwood contains by far the most impressive portrait of a big businessman in American fiction. No later writer has brought to the subject anything like Dreiser's commitment, no one else has dealt with it at such length or with such intensity. Yet in characterizing Cowperwood, Dreiser has in the main simply taken over the familiar catalogue of the businessman's vices and presented them as virtues. For example, Cowperwood resembles many of his predecessors in being an unsatisfactory husband, but Dreiser makes the failure of his two marriages turn upon his sexual prowess; Cowperwood is irresistible as a lover, and he refuses to be content with one woman at a time. The moral indictment brought against the businessman by earlier novelists becomes a blueprint for Dreiser's demonstration that Cowperwood is superior to the moral and legal codes binding the average of mankind. The characterization involves ideas drawn at second hand from H. L. Mencken's *The Philosophy of Frederick Nietzsche* (1908). Cowperwood exerts the inexplicable charm of the superman because he is beyond good and evil; he has "no consciousness of what is currently known as sin."

Much of the vividness of Cowperwood as a character is due to Dreiser's evident sympathy with his protagonist's scorn for "the conventional mind." The novelist remarks in his own person that Addison, a powerful Chicago banker, was "ostensibly a church-member, a model citizen; he represented a point

Theodore Dreiser. The Bettmann Archive, Inc.

of view to which Cowperwood would never have stooped." In fact, the attitudes that had earlier been associated with New England and had provided the basis for literary condemnation of the businessman in the 1880's and 1890's are associated in Dreiser's fictive world with the "silk-stocking crew" represented by Addison—men and women of established social and financial position who dominate Chicago and against whom Cowperwood must fight his way upward. Virtually all Dreiser's allusions to morals carry the express or implied charge of hypocrisy. He contrasts "the cold political logic of a man like Cowperwood" with "the polite moralistic efforts" of the silk-stocking crowd, "who were content to preach morality and strive to win by the efforts of the unco good." And he calls the newspapers that criticize Cowperwood "those profit-appointed advocates and guardians of 'right' and 'justice'." (pp. 99-101)

Dreiser translates the older contrast between a virtuous, semi-rural New England and the wickedness of commercial-minded New York into a contrast between the families of established economic and social position in Chicago and aggressive new-comers like Cowperwood. He insists that traditional codes of conduct are rationalizations supporting the status of a ruling class; his admiration for Cowperwood expresses his own resentment of the silk-stocking crowd. Perceiving that the tradition supporting this class has lost its moral authority and become a mere ideology, the superman brushes it aside and makes his own rules. (p. 101)

Both the Promethean accomplishments and the ultimate failure of Cowperwood link him with that other subversive, Mark Twain's Connecticut Yankee, and back of him with Emerson's

conception of Napoleon as the representative figure of the commercial nineteenth century. Cowperwood's empire, like theirs, cannot survive him. It is dissipated amid the bickerings of heirs, creditors, administrators, and courts. Even though, as Dreiser says, a Titan may "for the hour illuminate the terrors and wonders of individuality," there awaits him "the eternal equation—the pathos of the discovery that even giants are but pygmies, and that an ultimate balance must be struck."

The dominant trend in fictional portraits of the businessman during the past thirty years has led in quite a different direction from the celebration of individualism. Within a decade of the publication of *The Financier* appeared an influential novel depicting the businessman as a helpless victim of social pressure. Cowperwood's "private law" is, "I satisfy myself." George F. Babbitt's valedictory cry is, "They've licked me!" and "I've never done a single thing I wanted to." The contrast almost seems contrived. Yet Cowperwood has had few literary descendants, whereas Babbitt, henpecked and coerced by his fellow members of the Boosters' Club, has been succeeded by a host of conformists from Dos Passos's fatuous public-relations counsel, J. Ward Moorehouse (in *U.S.A.*, 1930-36), to the organization men in the novels of Cameron Hawley and Howard Swiggett.

It is hard to believe that this sudden transformation in the fictional businessman accurately reflects a change in society itself. History, even in the twentieth century, does not move that fast. Perhaps Cowperwood should be considered an anachronistic figure representing a vanished era of moguls and robber barons, whereas Babbitt is an emergent type. By the 1920's the businessman had evidently ceased to be viewed by the literary community as a giant, whether admirable or menacing, and had become instead something of a buffoon. If we take Sinclair Lewis's novel *Babbitt* (1922) and Eugene O'Neill's play *Marco Millions* (1927) as characteristic of the decade, we can say that the businessman was viewed in literature from . . . [the perspective] of the artist, of the emancipated intellectual, a Bohemianism more vividly impressed by the businessman's philistinism and his ineptitude as a lover than by his power or wickedness. Given this comic stance, summed up in Mencken's jeering designation of the business community as the "boo-boisie," one could fill out the counts in Lewis's and O'Neill's indictment with relative ease from earlier novels. The only revision necessary in the established portrait would be a reduction in scale.

The relation between Dreiser's fictive world and Lewis's can be illustrated by the passage in which Babbitt encounters one Charles McKelvey at a dinner for alumni of the state university. McKelvey, says Lewis,

> . . . built state capitols, skyscrapers, railway terminals. He was a heavy-shouldered, big-chested man, but not sluggish. There was a quiet humor in his eyes, a syrup-smooth quickness in his speech, which intimidated politicians and warned reporters; and in his presence the most intelligent scientist or the most sensitive artist felt thin-blooded, unworldly, and a little shabby. He was, particularly when he was influencing legislatures or hiring labor-spies, very easy and lovable and gorgeous. He was baronial; he was a peer in the rapidly crystallizing American aristocracy, inferior only to the haughty Old Families. . . . His power was the greater because he was not hindered by scru-

ples, by either the vice or the virtue of the old Puritan tradition.

Babbitt, who is dazzled by this godlike figure, manages to entice the McKelveys to his house once for dinner, but the evening is painful as only Lewis can make such a scene painful, and the relation comes to nothing.

McKelvey is a diminished Cowperwood, yet even so he towers on the horizon of Babbitt's world with a remote grandeur. The reduction in scale of Lewis's protagonist corresponds to a change in literary modes; where Dreiser is serious and, in aspiration at least, epic, Lewis is comic and mock-heroic. (pp. 102-04)

The only significant effort to discover a source of value and hence a vantage point from which to pass judgment on the business system in the literature of the 1920's and 1930's was that of the radical left. . . . Conceivably, a novelist on the left might have shown a Cowperwood in conflict with the workers, but the hostility to the businessman in proletarian fiction precludes even this degree of respect for him. Dos Passos speaks for the decade of the depression when he ends his trilogy with the image of a young hitchhiker beside the highway trying to thumb a ride, while overhead in a Douglas airliner,

> The transcontinental passengers sit pretty, big men with bankaccounts, highlypaid jobs, who are saluted by doormen; telephonegirls say goodmorning to them. Last night after a fine dinner, drinks with friends, they left Newark. . . . The transcontinental passenger thinks contracts, profits, vacationtrips, mighty continent between Atlantic and Pacific, power, wires humming dollars, cities jammed, hills empty, the indiantrail leading into the wagonroad, the macadamed pike, the concrete skyway, trains, planes: history the billiondollar speedup, and in the bumpy air over the desert ranges towards Las Vegas sickens and vomits into the carton container the steak and mushrooms he ate in New York. No matter, silver in the pocket, greenbacks in the wallet, drafts, certified checks, plenty restaurants in L.A.

Recent novels of business—and there have been many of them—are in the main, as Albert Van Nostrand has pointed out in *The Denatured Novel* [see excerpt below], imitations and adaptations of John P. Marquand's *Point of No Return* (1949). The usual theme is the submergence of the individual businessman in the corporation, the System. But whereas Marquand treats this material satirically, his most popular successors, such as Howard Swiggett and Cameron Hawley, imply that the subordination of the individual to the system is inevitable and desirable. As William H. Whyte, Jr., remarks in *The Organization Man*, their slogan might be, "Love that system." Thus, to quote Mr. Whyte again, the search for a capitalist hero which reached its culmination in Frank Cowperwood has now been supplanted by the depiction of "Society as Hero." The dominant force is not an individual but an institution, the large corporation, which could be called a metaphor for society if these novelists were aware that the two ideas can be distinguished from one another.

Swiggett and Hawley habitually expose a businessman protagonist to the threat of failure, then reveal that the danger was only apparent. The protagonist is immersed in a corporation or a broader system of business relationships; he feels panic, but a mysterious power comes to his rescue. The fictive world

is shown to be controlled by forces beyond the knowledge or comprehension of the individual, yet in the end the determinism proves to be not malign but benevolent.

In Swiggett's *The Durable Fire* (1957) Stephen Lowry appears to be eccentric and refreshingly defiant of conventions when he is hired as vice president of Continental Industries Corporation, but when subjected to the stupid tyranny of a new president named Cramer, he proves himself according to the rules of the system. In an interview with the directors he steadfastly refuses to utter even an implied criticism of Cramer. The directors, who have already discovered that Cramer is incompetent, are ravished by this restraint; Lowry is a team man, he cannot conceive of insubordination. They tell him they are "deeply impressed, deeply, by the way you behaved in there and by what you would not be drawn into saying." It is a singularly passive way of proving one's capacity for executive responsibility. (pp. 105-06)

Twentieth-century American novels about business have identified a number of moral dilemmas inherent in a capitalist system, but they have not produced a character properly described as a capitalist hero. Frank Cowperwood is conceived on a heroic scale, but he cannot enact the role of a hero because he defies the moral standards of his society and is indifferent to its welfare. The protagonists of the Swiggetts and the Hawleys fail to perform a significant action; they are controlled by the implausible benevolence of the System. . . . Serious novelists of our day have not even attempted to consider the possibly heroic traits and accomplishments of the businessman. Virtually all of them create protagonists who are antiheroes—outcasts, pariahs, varying only in the manner and degree of their repudiation of a society portrayed as being coterminous with the business system. The search for a capitalist hero has thus led to no viable results, and there is little indication that it will be more successful in the future. For the stereotypes used by the popular novelists cannot sustain a character of real imaginative substance, and serious writers seem unable to take an interest in a system of values based on economic assumptions. (pp. 111-12)

> *Henry Nash Smith, "The Search for a Capitalist Hero: Businessmen in American Fiction," in* The Business Establishment, *edited by Earl F. Cheit, John Wiley & Sons, Inc., 1964, pp. 77-112.*

JOHN CHAMBERLAIN

[*Chamberlain is an American essayist and critic who has edited several popular American magazines, including* Harper's Magazine *and* Life, *and is noted for his writings on social and economic subjects. In the following excerpt, he surveys business fiction from the viewpoint of Mr. Tinker, a fictional businessman created by Booth Tarkington, in order to illustrate the anti-business viewpoint adopted by many American novelists. Chamberlain introduces his essay with the following note: "Readers of Booth Tarkington's* The Plutocrat, *one of the few sympathetic novels of the past thirty years about a businessman, will recognize [Mr. Tinker]. . . . He is twenty years older than he was in Mr. Tarkington's book, and the depression has tempered some of his natural ebullience. But for a man who is fast approaching the age of retirement he still has a lot of the old Adam in him."*]

Mr. Tinker, Chairman of the Board of the Illinois & Union Paper Co., Rock Island, Illinois, leafed through a thick volume by Harold Laski called *The American Democracy*. The book had been recommended to him by his son-in-law, the playwright Laurence Ogle, who still had hopes of making the old man something better than a "great barbarian." The "barbarian," who had organized several paper companies and virtually all of Rock Island's public utilities in his day, paused idly over some of the more fancy writing in Mr. Laski's outsize tome, then caught himself up short at a particularly offensive statement about the American businessman in a chapter on "American Business Enterprise." (p. 134)

"It is rare," so Mr. Tinker read to himself on page 170, "for businessmen to look upon their civic duties as important." Mr. Tinker, who had endowed two trade schools and run innumerable community-chest campaigns when he was younger, muttered something about stupid limey socialists who were little better than complete morons. Suddenly, however, the logician in Mr. Tinker smiled inwardly. For Laski, the pontifical and insufferable little know-it-all, had begun to involve himself in a series of wholly unconscious contradictions. On one page Mr. Tinker learned that he, Tinker, belonged to a species of indigenous American monster that specialized in subverting the press, bribing the government, shooting it out with labor, and packing the colleges with spineless professors who kowtowed to the monster's least responsible whims. But on quite another page he discovered that his business colleagues were leaders "in all charitable and religious activities." The U.S. businessman, so Laski said, was virtually an illiterate; he bought only the volumes that had been chosen for him by the Book-of-the-Month Club judges, and he dreamed himself to sleep in Pullman cars over the pemmicanized contents of *The Reader's Digest.* But more U.S. businessmen, so Laski recited on another page, had been to college than was the case with their "opposite numbers" in Europe. This business of being put through a chills-and-fever treatment by the omniscient but somewhat forgetful Englishman amused Mr. Tinker for a while. It was especially hilarious to note that the businessman monster who had complete control of the channels of communication in the U.S. had somehow forgotten to censor numberless leftist scholars, poets, novelists, sociologists, dramatists, law-school professors, and Supreme Court jurists whom Laski was forever quoting. (pp. 134-35)

Laurence Ogle, the son-in-law, was sitting on the porch when Mr. Tinker emerged from the house. "Hey, you," said Mr. Tinker somewhat unceremoniously, "were you really trying to give me the straight dope when you said this Laski knows America as few natives know it?"

"Why, yes," said Ogle, "*The American Democracy* has been likened to de Tocqueville . . ."

"Dee-who?" Mr. Tinker exploded. "Well, anyway, this Laski is about the stupidest ignoramus I've ever met. Why, the things he says . . ."

"On the contrary," said Ogle, "Laski is extremely well versed in American literature . . ."

"Oh, *literature,*" said Mr. Tinker, a great light dawning. "Well, I dare say you've got something there. He does seem to have read all the books written about America. Maybe that's what's the matter; maybe those novels he quotes are by stupid ignoramuses, too."

The encounter with Laski set Mr. Tinker to wondering about the profession of public relations. Mr. Tinker had paid out plenty to public-relations counselors in his time, and the money had sometimes been profitably spent. But every so often at his golf club he had heard a smart young man mutter "Babbitt," and the tag was still good for a snicker in 1948. Why couldn't the public-relations fellows make the U.S. forget that Sinclair Lewis fellow? Mr. Tinker had read *Babbitt* a long time ago, and had liked it. George F. Babbitt had seemed rather pathetic, but a good egg at bottom. As for Babbitt's being *the* U.S. businessman, however, Mr. Tinker had never been able to see it. George Babbitt just didn't get the fun out of life that he, Mr. Tinker, had managed to have. Babbitt may have been typical of a time and a place, provided that you remembered he was not in manufacturing or banking or any of the more solid businesses. The time and the place, however, had long since vanished. . . . Yet here, a quarter of a century after *Babbitt* had been written, Sinclair Lewis' title had a satirical magic that no Edward L. Bernays had ever been able to efface.

"Damn," said Mr. Tinker to himself, "these novelists may have something about public relations that I ought to get hep to. That old bird who said he'd rather write a nation's songs than its laws was way off the beam. He should have said he'd rather write a nation's novels. . . ."

But what, besides *Babbitt,* were the novels that had created the ugly picture of the U.S. businessman that Laski and his supercilious kind had picked up? Casting about him in the J. S. Opendyck Book Store, Main and Hobart streets, Mr. Tinker came across something called *The Hucksters.* It was, so the eager clerk assured him, the unvarnished truth about the advertising business. Mr. Tinker read a few pages in it and took it home. The portrait of Evan Llewelyn Evans, soap tycoon, was of just the type of monster that Laski had in mind when he was making some of his most offensive generalizations. Mr. Tinker mulled the matter over for a bit, trying to recall a single one of his acquaintances who could match old Evans for sheer nastiness. The effort was too great, and Mr. Tinker gave it up. This Frederic Wakeman who had written *The Hucksters,* so Mr. Tinker decided, must be something of a sorehead. Either that, or he knew where the money lay. Come to think of it, there was almost as much dirt in *The Hucksters* as there had been in his son-in-law Ogle's unfortunate first Broadway play. . . . Man, how Mrs. Tinker had hit the ceiling when she discovered that her daughter's suitor had written *The Pastoral Scene.*

"Ye gods and little fishes," said Mr. Tinker the next day as he flopped *The Hucksters* back on the bookstore counter, "is that the best you can do in a novel about business?"

The clerk assured him there were other portraits of businessmen. There was the father of the heroine in John Marquand's *B. F.'s Daughter,* for example. Mr. Tinker dutifully took Marquand home with him. He rather liked B. F., but there was a wistfulness clinging to him that seemed rather out of place. It was almost as if Marquand were trying to apologize for seeing anything good in a person who lived and breathed production. The B. F.'s that Mr. Tinker knew—and he knew dozens of them—were certainly not wistful. And if their day had passed they were most assuredly not aware of it. They seemed to be going ahead as if the market for refrigerators and paper bags and corn syrup and cars were insatiable. . . . Mr. Tinker reflected that Europeans, including Mr. Laski's countrymen, were perfectly willing to take any surplus American production they could get. But if the world was hungry for goods, why must the purveyors thereof be complete s.o.b.'s or wistful has-beens? Mr. Tinker frowned a little and went back to the bookstore.

What followed was one of the most revealing months of Mr. Tinker's life. He read every piece of fiction about the U.S. businessman that he could get his hands on, and the clerk was indefatigable in digging back through the book catalogues for more. Sometimes the clerk would come up with a novel that was fairly decent about business. There was Marcia Davenport's *The Valley of Decision,* for instance; it made the steel industry seem rather important. And there was a second business novel by Sinclair Lewis, one called *Dodsworth.* The hero of this novel, Sam Dodsworth, was no Babbitt; indeed, he got the same sort of pleasure in doing a good job of production that Mr. Tinker himself remembered getting when he was younger and more active in the affairs of the Illinois & Union Paper Co. But Dodsworth was a rarity among the fictional businessmen; strangely enough, he might almost have been blood brother to Mr. Tinker himself.

Mr. Tinker soon found that it was far from being a mere matter of Laski's having read *Babbitt* and *The Hucksters.* For a distilled malevolence, a cold and frightening spite, went into the painting of practically every fictional businessman whom Mr. Tinker encountered. As his month of reading passed, Mr. Tinker began to get something of a persecution complex. He snapped at his wife; he became morose at meals; and his daughter Libby, who was visiting for the summer in Rock Island along with her husband, Laurence Ogle, observed rather testily that there might be something to this new theory of the male climacteric. . . .

Mr. Tinker, who skipped with some sophistication each week through the Kiplinger Letter, rather prided himself that he knew something about Washington. Back in NRA days he had spent a good deal of time there on the paper manufacturers' code, and he had made a few visits to the capital during the war. He knew there was pressure brought to bear on politicians whenever contracts were to be awarded, but he also knew the pressure was furtive and ordinarily ineffective. Besides, as long as there was competition among the pressure groups, there was democratic safety of a sort; better a smattering of corruption than the bureaucratic deadness of even the most honest totalitarianism. It was with some anger, then, that Mr. Tinker read the latest novel about business corruption in Washington.

The book clerk, thinking to begin Mr. Tinker's literary education from the top down, had handed him Samuel Hopkins Adams' *Plunder.* This was a novel about a businessman's conspiracy to buy the government. The "hero" of *Plunder,* Martin Strabo, was a man utterly devoid of sensitivity who looked like "a huge, gorged saurian." His friends were "predatory, suggesting the greater carnivores. There was a lean vulture, an agile tarantula, and a lazily watchful snake among the types." There was Tom Frenchling, a manufacturer whose wartime airplanes "crashed in deathly heaps." There was Matty Matzenden, whose "shells backfired on the ranges with dreadful slaughter." There was Kellerby Smith, whose armor plate had certain peculiar pittings. There was Farson Crane, the shipbuilder whose ships broke in two on the ways. None of these could quite measure up to Marty Strabo, whose own grisly racket was a mixture called tozerite. Marty's bought doctors and chemists claimed that a suit impregnated with tozerite would protect one's virility against gamma rays from an atomic bomb, but the claims were as fraudulent as Tom Frenchling's airplanes or Farson Crane's gimp-backed ships. It bothered Marty Strabo not a whit when his son-in-law, a young army captain, got a near-cancerous condition of the arm during a military test of tozerite's insulating capacity. Strabo would have gone on selling the stuff if his own daughter or mistress had been killed by it.

Mr. Tinker couldn't quite put the plot of *Plunder* together with the fact that his friend Bill Newell of Bath, Maine, whom he had met on a fishing trip, had made ships that stood up magnificently throughout World War II. He couldn't quite square Matty Matzenden's defective shells and Kellerby Smith's porous armor plate with the Battle of the Coral Sea or the invasion at Omaha Beach. But when he filed his feeble demurrer, the clerk, in haste to break down what seemed his customer's invincible innocence, handed a bemused and querulous Mr. Tinker another lollapaloosa of a novel called *Coming Home,* by Lester Cohen. "This," said the clerk, "is not about Washington; it's about Pittsburgh. But you'll find Pittsburgh is part of a corruption that goes all the way up."

Obligingly, Mr. Tinker sat up until three in the morning reading *Coming Home.* He learned from Mr. Cohen that steel tycoons did indeed sell cracked steel to the government. He learned also about the nefarious tie-in that the steel business had with politicians such as the rascally boss, Stoney Pike, who could get workers fired by snapping his fingers. Somehow Pike's control of the workers didn't quite make sense to Mr. Tinker, who knew the C.I.O. had organized the steel industry before World War II, but he let this pass for the moment, and went back to the book clerk for more. The clerk handed him Norman Mailer's *The Naked and the Dead.* "You won't find much about businessmen in this," he said. "But there's some information in it that shows how our soldiers were corrupted in childhood by a business society."

Mr. Tinker took the book home to discover that an overwhelmingly masculine tycoon-father inevitably produces a son who combines military skill with homosexual urges. He also discovered that the role which an industrialist-father had played in making Mr. Mailer's Lieutenant Hearn an indecisive character was just as starkly inevitable as Nemesis in a Greek tragedy. Mr. Tinker, rather dashed by what was happening to his perspective, tried to laugh Mr. Mailer off. "After all," he said to himself, "this is a little too much even for the most credulous." But he noticed uncomfortably that *The Naked and the Dead* was at the top of the best-seller lists.

Back to the bookstore for more enlightenment, Mr. Tinker bought Christina Stead's *A Little Tea, A Little Chat,* a story about Wall Street and the cotton-brokerage business that the book clerk insisted was the real thing. Once, during a winter vacation at Biloxi, Mississippi, the Tinkers had met and played bridge with Will Clayton and his interesting family; and thus, somewhat illogically, Mr. Tinker was certain that any book about the cotton-trading business must have some of Mr. Clayton's own breadth and humanity in its pages. But *A Little Tea, A Little Chat* was even more fetid in its atmosphere than Mr. Adams' *Plunder.* The brokers who swarmed in and out of Miss Stead's story "loved the United States intensely, ferociously, with terror and greed." Some of them professed to be "socialists," and one or two of them even quoted Marx, but their verbal humanitarianism didn't keep them from bilking any widows and orphans who happened to be within reach. A good family man himself, in spite of one or two innocent dinners with the fascinating Madame Momoro whom he had met on that boat trip to North Africa, Mr. Tinker couldn't stand the pathologically intense sexuality that went with the brokerage business in *A Little Tea, A Little Chat.* "These fellows spend so much time getting in and out of bed," so Mr. Tinker told the bookstore clerk, "that I don't see how they ever have time to make money." "You'd be surprised," said the clerk, whose secret hero was a certain lawyer whose sexual prowess had been set forth in the Kinsey report. "Why, there are men in New York . . ." And the book clerk fell to dreaming while Mr. Tinker browsed through Hiram Haydn's *The Time Is Noon*, which he eventually took with him.

The Time Is Noon had a lot in it about the apparently interminable hypocrisies and frauds of advertising, and it seemed hipped on the theory that Cleveland, Ohio, is a barbarous jungle whose most wanton beasts are the big businessmen and manufacturers. In creating an athlete and a journalist Mr. Haydn restrained his pen, but with the scoundrelly Charles Hoyt, a savage son who is heir to his uncomprehending old man's steel business, Mr. Haydn really cut loose. Mr. Tinker said nothing the next week as he returned *The Time Is Noon* to the rental library, and when the clerk grew voluble on the wisdom and power of Robert Penn Warren's *At Heaven's Gate* he submitted meekly to the recommendation. The story in *At Heaven's Gate* did indeed bear out the clerk's words; Mr. Tinker read it with mounting appreciation of Mr. Warren's undeniable talent. But it was the same old tale of the corruption that business power works on ambitious men, the same old story of the rich father's children who make a cult of failure just to get even with the old man. Mr. Tinker began to wonder about the inability of even the best novelists to discover a new situation or a new plot; all the stories he had been reading lately were simply the old *Saturday Evening Post* convention of George Horace Lorimer turned upside down. He mentioned this to the bookstore clerk, but all he got by way of an answer was something about the "tragic sense of life." "I don't mind tragedy," said Mr. Tinker, "but don't tragic things ever happen to honorable people?"

The clerk's answer was enigmatic, but the books that he pressed upon Mr. Tinker continued to tell the same story. By reading Charles Yale Harrison's *Nobody's Fool*, Hugh MacLennan's *The Precipice*, and Herman Wouk's *Aurora Dawn*, Mr. Tinker learned all over again that advertising men are virtually incurable in their swinish hucksterism. Fascist-minded businessmen cackled so evilly in the background of Sinclair Lewis' *Kingsblood Royal* that Mr. Tinker looked one morning in the bathroom mirror to see whether a scarlet swastika had blossomed overnight on his chest. Mr. Tinker had been reading in *Fortune* about the wonderful business boom that was transforming the face of Texas and the Southwest, but Robert Rylee's *The Ring and the Cross* insisted that corruption is at the heart of Texas enterprise. The munitions business was thoroughly exposed in Taylor Caldwell's *Dynasty of Death* and in Upton Sinclair's nine volumes about Lanny Budd. The most despicable person in John Steinbeck's *The Wayward Bus* proved to be a businessman, and in MacKinlay Kantor's *Glory for Me* Sergeant Al Stephenson was tremendously unhappy as a banker because he had to associate with other bankers. Robert Wilder's *Written on the Wind* made a tobacco fortune seem loathsome. Even the circus business turned out to be dirty in Thomas Duncan's *Gus the Great*.

"Hm," said Mr. Tinker as he deposited on the book clerk's desk a load of rental-library stuff that he had taken away for the weekend, "it seems that every business is rotten. Maybe the newspaper and magazine business is an exception; at least these novels seem to get praised in the reviews, which would indicate a clear conscience on the part of the press tycoons." The clerk's answer to this was to hand Mr. Tinker Merle Miller's *That Winter* and Robert van Gelder's *Important People*. "Read these," he said, "and see what you think of those fascist reactionaries who twist and distort U.S. opinion. An honest writer hasn't got a chance in American journalism . . ."

"But just how do you explain the reviews that praise these books?" asked Mr. Tinker. The clerk looked a bit startled. By way of a reply he recommended Mary McCarthy's *The Man in the Brooks Brothers Shirt*, a story of how a traveling salesman for a steel company had seduced an *avant-garde* girl novelist on a transcontinental train. Mr. Tinker couldn't see just what this story had to do with his question, unless the clerk was trying obliquely to suggest that the *avant-gardistes* had managed to dominate the literary world in spite of their fascist employers. But the bitter tale conveyed a good deal more than Miss McCarthy may have realized, for it proved that contacts between novelists and businessmen were extremely unusual and haphazard. Bohemia and Philistia were apparently worlds apart, and neither country was fitted to understand the other.

After reading about twenty-five or thirty contemporary novels in which the U.S. businessman was cast in the role of heavy villain, it occurred to Mr. Tinker that such a stubborn convention must have roots as strong and heavy as those of the great oak of Guernica. "Tell me," he addressed the bookstore clerk as he handed back an anti-business play by Arthur Miller called *All My Sons*, "where did this idea that all businessmen have horns, hoofs, and a forked tail get its start?" "Oh, it's always been that way," said the clerk. "Have you ever read Theodore Dreiser's Cowperwood trilogy?"

Mr. Tinker had barely heard of Dreiser, but he had known about Charles Yerkes, the Chicago traction magnate of the nineties who had served Dreiser as the model for Frank Cowperwood. The agglutinative style of the three Cowperwood stories, *The Financier*, *The Titan*, and *The Stoic*, rather grated on Mr. Tinker, but he was vastly impressed with Cowperwood's satanic proportions and with Dreiser's knowledge of plain and fancy financial shenanigans. "Sure," he said to himself, "this is the way those streetcar franchises were sewed up in the nineties. It's always dirty when you have to get permission from a bunch of politicians to do business. But under socialism, where you have to get a politician's O.K. even to raise a few chickens, wouldn't it be a million times dirtier?"

Mr. Tinker would have forgotten his rhetorical question if he hadn't next encountered certain novels of the twenties and early thirties that stressed the war of class against class in a way that argued either socialist conviction or temporary delusion. The encounter set Mr. Tinker to wondering what the novelists wanted out of life. Did they really wish to be part of a society that was ordered from the top down by a governing caste charged with allotting each and every person to his station? Did they really wish to be told how much they could pay for goods, and in what proportion they could have them? Mr. Tinker couldn't really believe the novelists wanted socialism, or even the planned capitalism that results in majority dictation of what minorities are to do with their energies. No doubt some of the novelists thought they were merely anatomizing the abuses of capitalism. But as Mr. Tinker pushed his researches back into time at the Rock Island Public Library he was considerably shaken. He read some of Sherwood Anderson's novels in which businessmen suddenly flee their offices in middle age as though menaced by the plague. This Anderson fellow, who had deserted his own advertising business in middle life, seemed muzzy and hesitant about the future, but Mr. Tinker gathered that he had dallied with socialism for a period. Dreiser, he learned, had become a stalwart in Communist fellow-traveling circles before he died. In John Dos Passos' *The 42nd Parallel*, *Nineteen Nineteen*, and *The Big Money* there was a young fellow named Charley Anderson who had a lot of manufacturing know-how, but Charley threw his money around and got drunker and drunker as he grew older. Mr. Tinker couldn't quite judge what Dos Passos was up to, but he came away from the three Dos Passos books with the idea that Charley Anderson symbolized his creator's idea of what capitalism does to one's personality. It was a great relief to Mr. Tinker to learn that Dos Passos, when confronted with the miseries of life under Stalin's system, had had the honesty to change his mind about the U.S. way of doing business.

Dos Passos' many vociferous anti-business contemporaries seemed to have faded into silence in the 1940's; at least Mr. Tinker couldn't discover what they had been doing recently. But their novels of the early thirties—"proletarian literature," Mr. Tinker learned to call the type—still clogged the library stacks. The office staff of Edwin Seaver's *The Company*, the lumberjacks of Louis Colman's *Lumber*, the auto workers of James Steele's *Conveyor*, the southern milltown operatives of Mary Heaton Vorse's *Strike*, the workers in young Whittaker Chambers' fiction, the strikers in stories by Grace Lumpkin, William Rollins, Robert Cantwell, Jack Conroy, and John Steinbeck, all suggested the existence of a business system that was as virulently anti-people as Rasputin or Ivan the Terrible. "Well," said Mr. Tinker in an unwonted feeling of extenuation for a generation, "a bad business depression can do strange things to one's perspective." But Mr. Tinker could see that it wasn't just a matter of the 1932 depression as he read through the books of that wonderful period of his own youth that had come to an end with World War I.

Somehow Mr. Tinker had always regarded the first decade of the twentieth century as the peak period of human felicity. It shocked him, then, to learn from Jack London's *The Iron Heel* that U.S. capitalists were fascist-minded long before the world had ever heard of Hitler or Mussolini. The novels of Robert Herrick, in particular one called *The Memoirs of An American Citizen*, were so insistent about the lack of ethics among early twentieth-century businessmen that Mr. Tinker began to doubt his own father for a moment. When he came across Upton Sinclair's *The Jungle*, a story of the meat-packing industry, it made him marvel how he had survived the many cheap steaks he had eaten as a boy. And Frank Norris' *The Octopus* and *The Pit*, novels about wheat-growers and wheat traders in the nineties, suggested that farmers invariably get the dirty end of the stick. Since Mr. Tinker knew all about the "parity" principle that the New Deal had applied to U.S. agricultural prices— a principle based on the theory that farm prices were quite equitable in relation to industrial prices in 1912—he couldn't see that this view of the farmer's lot had any relevance to the decade that followed Norris' death. This made *The Octopus* less "universal" than its supporters would have had Mr. Tinker believe.

Going way back into the nineteenth century, Mr. Tinker discovered a rather heartening book about a business man called *The Rise of Silas Lapham*. Interested in its author, William Dean Howells, Mr. Tinker decided he would read up on Howells' biography. The experience was disillusioning, for Howells had ended his days as a socialist. It was then Mr. Tinker decided to stop reading fiction; the whole business was failing to make any connection with his own life. . . .

If Mr. Tinker had had time to continue his studies, they would have carried him deep into a type of speculation that Vernon Parrington, Edmund Wilson, and other good critics have given their lives to. What, indeed, conditions our attitudes toward the ways we make our living? The anthropologists return one

set of answers, the economists another, the Freudians a third, the religious seers a fourth. Truth in this field is a matter of complex variables, and no pat answer can be satisfactory to an inquisitive individual for very long. But the main reasons why the U.S. novelist looks upon the businessman with a jaundiced eye can be isolated.

In the first place U.S. business enterprise has not always been carried out within the scope of the ethics that must apply to it as a functional system. Free enterprise can work if it remains free enterprise, but when it becomes hypocritically entwined with tariffs and subsidies, and with sophisticated evasion of the old Anglo-Saxon common law relating to monopoly, it must breed contempt in those who insist that morality is a matter of practicing what you preach. Mr. Tinker, who came from a small town in the lush and folksy midlands, would naturally tend to overlook the breaches of business ethics that had occurred throughout nineteenth and early-twentieth-century history on the top levels of industrial and financial power. But as even he dimly realized, there *were* Cowperwoods—and Jay Goulds and Jim Fisks ("nothing is lost save honor")—in the business epoch of our grandfathers. They even have their less effective descendants today.

What Parrington calls the tradition of "critical realism" inevitably took note of U.S. business corruption where it existed. And if our latter-day novelists had continued the tradition of putting corruption within a perspective that also includes the comparative honesty of most business people there would be no cause for Mr. Tinker's complaints. But what gives Mr. Tinker's type of flareback its justification is that "critical realism" has ceased to exist. The modern novelist is emotional and subjective when he approaches the theme of U.S. industry; he does not look at it in the light of changes that he himself has helped to instigate. The case of Upton Sinclair is typical. His *Jungle*, a powerful piece of work up to the point where it ends on a pamphleteering note of abstract socialism, changed the ethics of the meat-packing industry; we have had no "embalmed beef" scandals since the Sinclair-inspired passage, in Theodore Roosevelt's time, of the Pure Food and Drug Act. Sinclair's subsequent attack on the labor practices of the Rockefellers' Colorado Fuel & Iron Co. led indirectly to an entirely new and thoroughly enlightened labor policy in the Rockefeller Standard Oil Co. of N.J. But Upton Sinclair, both as a novelist and as a tractarian, goes on writing about businessmen as though they were impervious to suggestion. Thus Mr. Sinclair writes off the solid accomplishments of his own long and busy life.

American critical realism developed as a part of westward expansion; it was a response to frontier conditions that demand a hearty and commonsensical way of looking at things. The frontiersman laughed and exaggerated; he made fun of rascality by creating the folk character of Simon Suggs, whose motto was "It's good to be shifty in a new country." Mark Twain pushed the tradition of frontier realism and laughter to a peak. But Mark Twain enjoyed business even though he satirized it. And the main object of his satire was the damned—but still beloved—human race.

Even when Mark Twain was writing, two alien traditions that are implacably hostile to "trade" and the "bourgeois" were establishing themselves in the U.S. The first tradition was bound up with the aristocrat's point of view, and it may be found in the novels of Edith Wharton, in Henry Adams' *Democracy*, and in the works of Henry James that have got away from James's own view of the American businessman as the great "innocent." The second tradition, which invaded the later novels of Howells and ultimately reached noisy fruition in the books of the "proletarian" 1930's, was that of literary socialism. Strangely, the second anti-bourgeois tradition has attracted many converts from the first.

It is with literary socialism and its various dependent "totalitarian" liberalisms that the note of belittling comes to be applied to the businessman. Balzac, who had a great influence on Karl Marx, may have caricatured the businessman, but his caricatures had great and sweeping vitality. The latter-day novelists who have picked up Marx would have done better if they had emulated their master and gone themselves to Balzac. As things stand, their own caricatures of the businessman do not derive from living examples but from a dry and doctrinaire attitude. Their businessmen characters are all clichés; their plots have no creative originality. Indeed, the latter-day novelists are not only anti-business; they are also anti-fecundity and anti-life. They break images without frenzy and without exhilaration. Instead of making fresh starts for themselves they seem bent on pursuing a Freudian quarrel with their fathers, most of whom happen to be businessmen. Thus maturity (which consists of making peace with your antecedents and going ahead with your own work) is denied the modern litterateur.

If Mr. Tinker had gone on from his novel reading to discover the real anthropologist's view, he might have reflected that the artistic camp followers of Karl Marx yearn secretly for a new type of feudalism. What they seemingly want is a new world of fixed status, with feudal protection (i.e., state-endowed social security) granted in return for feudal duties (drastic limits on what the individual may do with his own life energy). Well, the world has known many forms of social order since paleolithic times, and the more fixed or planned the order the less the freedom. In his anti-business animus, the modern novelist seems never to have reflected that a comparative audit of systems might show that free capitalism, if highly imperfect, is still not only the most productive but also the least bloody system the world has ever known. (pp. 135-48)

Since the modern anti-business novelist has never paused to make a comparative audit of systems, he tends to contrast the world of free capitalism with a perfect socialized order that has no existence outside of his own head. Naturally the anti-business novelist wins easy victories; no mere human businessman can stand up against a perfect figment of the idealist's mind. But if the novelist would ever stop to explore the actual operative mechanics of socialism, a mechanics that reduces the human being to living by permission of the political arm, he might lose his lust for easy victories.

Certainly no novelist who prides himself on being an original, a pathfinder, can go on repeating forever the same old clichés about the businessman; someday a novelist will go forth into the market place and use his eyes. (p. 148)

John Chamberlain, "The Businessman in Fiction,"
in Fortune, Vol. XXXVIII, No. 5, November, 1948,
pp. 134-48.

HENRY STEELE COMMAGER

[An American historian and educator, Commager is the author of several popular historical works which, according to Lawrence Wells Cobb, have allowed "scholars and lay readers both to 'get at' the sources of the American historical record and to understand their heritage more fully." Among his important works are The Growth of the American Republic (1930), which he coauthored with Samuel Eliot Morison and which long served as a college
history textbook, and Our Nation (1941), a popular and instructive textbook used in high school history classes throughout the United States. In addition, Commager's Documents of American History (1934) is regarded as one of the most valuable reference books of its kind. This work, which has had several editions, contains over six hundred documents illustrating the course of American history from the age of discovery to the present. In the following excerpt, Commager discusses anti-business novels by late-nineteenth- and twentieth-century American authors.]

American society of Veblen's generation may have been habituated to money standards, but it found few literary spokesmen to justify those standards or even to explain them. Who, in the half-century from Cleveland to Franklin Roosevelt, celebrated business enterprise or the acquisitive society—who aside from John Hay, Thomas Bailey Aldrich, Mary Halleck Foote, Booth Tarkington, and a miscellany of contributors to popular magazines whose efforts are now buried in oblivion? Almost all the major writers were critical of those standards, or contemptuous of them; they voted, as it were, for Bryan and the two Roosevelts and sometimes even for Eugene Debs and William Z. Foster rather than for McKinley, Taft, or Hoover. Those authors who repudiated the economic system outright were few; Mark Twain, Henry James, Willa Cather, Ellen Glasgow, and others accepted it tacitly, while such lesser writers as James Lane Allen, George W. Cable, and Sarah Orne Jewett took little thought of economic affairs. But the dominant trend in literature was critical: most authors portrayed an economic system disorderly and ruthless, wasteful and inhumane, unjust alike to workingmen, investors, and consumers, politically corrupt and morally corrupting.

This all but unanimous repudiation of the accepted economic order by its literary representatives is one of the curious phenomena of American culture. The tradition of protest and revolt had been dominant in American literature since Emerson and Thoreau, but the protestants had by no means monopolized the stage, and their protests had been, for the most part, political or social rather than economic. Never before in American literature and rarely in the literature of any country had the major writers been so sharply estranged from the society which nourished them and the economy which sustained them as during the half-century between the *Rise of Silas Lapham* and *Grapes of Wrath*. The explanation is elusive. It can scarcely be maintained that novelists from Howells to Steinbeck were unfamiliar with the scene they portrayed. Yet their findings did not correspond with those of more popular novelists and journalists, or, later, of Hollywood producers, radio script-writers, and advertisers—most of whom pictured a society that was prosperous, vigorous, harmonious, and contented. To suggest, however, that the novelists misrepresented their society presents difficulties equally perplexing; assuredly the society that cherished and rewarded them did not regard them as alien or false.

Whatever the explanation, the facts are incontrovertible. From the mid-eighties to the second World War the literary protest paralleled the political, and both were directed toward the economic malaise. (pp. 247-48)

The creator of Silas Lapham made not only the most authentic transcript of American society but the most penetrating analysis of American economy in the transition years from the Civil to the Spanish War. (p. 250)

[William Dean Howells'] criticism of the economic order of the eighties and nineties was fundamental yet expressed, for the most part, with such indirection that it lost its cutting edge.

William Dean Howells in his library at the time he was writing The Rise of Silas Lapham. *Culver Pictures, Inc.*

Only in his Utopian novels did he try a head-on attack, and they were perhaps his least successful. Yet the indictment is there, no less telling for the suavity with which it is presented. He did not fall into the error of idealizing the poor or scarifying the rich or of personifying the system which he abhorred in a series of villains: the amiable Silas Lapham is a millionaire, and Mr. Homo gets along very well with his hosts. There are, indeed, few villains in Howells and few heroes: life, as he saw it, was too complex for such simplifications, and he was too faithful a reporter to ignore the complexities. Even for those who are dubiously cast in the role of villain, Howells has more pity than contempt—Dryfoos with his millions, old, frustrated, and defeated; Northwick, dying in distant Quebec, gloating over the money he has embezzled but knowing, too, that he has missed what he wanted. All alike are defeated by the economic system they do not understand and cannot control— the wicked and the virtuous, the greedy and the generous, Silas Lapham who loses all save honor, Ansel Denton who ends in suicide, Julius Peck who abandons the ministry for work among the poor. They are defeated, as society itself is defeated, by the competitive spirit which brings out the worst in men, by commercialism which perverts values, by the World of Chance of modern business. (pp. 251-52)

Profound as was Howells' revulsion from the economic order, it was, in its literary form, curiously unreal and ineffective.

For Howells never understood the order which he hated as he understood the order which he had loved, never understood his economy as he understood his society. When he described society his art was as authentic as that of Jane Austen or Flaubert; when conscience drove him to economic issues he was vague and mystical. He did not know the world of the rich as Henry James knew it; he did not know the world of the poor as Dreiser knew it. He knew his middle-class, northern, feminine world better than any one else who has ever described it, and he knew what happened to the inhabitants of that world when they won unexpected riches or suffered unmerited poverty. He could explain what money did to old Dryfoos, what social ambitions did to Silas Lapham's daughters, how community opinion pressed on Adeline and Suzette Northwick, but he could not be similarly realistic when he tried to explain monopoly or the competitive system. (p. 253)

Howells was against the economic system without knowing much about business, as his friends, Lowell and Norton and Gilder, were against the spoils system without knowing much about practical politics. If, in the end, he accepted it, he was never reconciled to it, as these guardians of the genteel tradition were reconciled to a political system that at least shielded them from the dangers of populism and free silver. It is this unregenerate quality in Howells that is most illuminating, that fixes the pattern, as it were, for the literary interpretations of American economy during the next half-century.

The most distinguished of Howells' successors, Robert Herrick, was similarly unregenerate. His theme was essentially that which Howells elaborated in the novels of his middle period—the corrupting influence of material standards—but he presented it in a more modern style, the attack upon economic injustice more direct, the exposure of political implications more specific, the recognition of the effect upon the relations of the sexes more candid, the vocabulary more passionate. He began where Howells left off, and more than style and setting distinguish the portraits of Van Harrington from those of Silas Lapham and the elder Dryfoos. Although Herrick owed much to Henry George and Bellamy—witness *Clark's Field* and the Utopian *Sometime*—he belonged to the muckrake rather than to the earlier, and perhaps more innocent, protestant movement. (pp. 253-54)

It was a simple story which Herrick rehearsed in a dozen novels—the story of the crumbling of the old integrities, the integrity of professional skill, of business honesty, of political morality, of love itself, before the insidious demands of modern business. The moral, too, was simple and familiar: that the search for material rewards—money, power, social position—leads inevitably to disintegration and corruption. In *The Common Lot,* the architect who uses shoddy and permits jerry-building sees the luckless inmates of his ''fireproof'' tenement burn before his eyes; in *Clark's Field,* unearned increment on a Boston block infects all who profit or hope to profit from it; in *The Man Who Wins,* social rather than financial ambition thwarts the idealism of a physician; and in *Waste,* it is an engineer whose vaulting plans for a better society are similarly frustrated. Most thorough in its exploration of the pathology of modern business, most merciless in its findings, is *The Memoirs of an American Citizen,* the story of a self-made man who in his progress to power and wealth demoralized honest business associates, bribed judges, corrupted legislatures, and destroyed his family and his marriage. ''No business in this modern world,'' says Van Harrington, contrasting his methods, with those of his wife,

> could be done on her plan of life. That beautiful scheme of things which the fathers of our country drew up in the stage-coach days had proved itself inadequate in a short century. We had to get along with it as best we could. But we men who did the work of the world, who developed the country, who were the life and force of the times, could not be held back by the swaddling clothes of any political or moral theory. Results we must have: good results, and we worked with the tools we found at hand. (*The Memoirs of an American Citizen*)

It is this novel which illustrates most sharply the shift in animus from Howells to Herrick; not only in its portrait of the self-made man but in its philosophy of determinism, it anticipates the Dreiser of *The Financier* and *The Titan.*

If Herrick owed much to Henry George and Thorstein Veblen, his more popular contemporary, Winston Churchill, was inspired by the effervescent Theodore Roosevelt, and his books confess the character as well as the source of the inspiration. Like Roosevelt, Churchill found health in the pioneer virtues, blended romanticism with progressivism, came late to the realization of the corrupt alliance of business and politics, and

learned publicly the facts of political life. Like Roosevelt, too, he was a romantic turned reformer by circumstances—his own career in New Hampshire politics had something to do with it—a historian who celebrated the past and deplored the present but who viewed past and present alike through the glasses of sentiment. (pp. 255-56)

Like so many novelists of his generation Churchill was concerned with the pervasive immorality of modern business—the passing of professional integrity, the transfer of economic power from those who were builders and creators to those who dealt with paper, the growth of an interlocking directorate of industrialists, lawyers, bankers, and politicians, the perversion of older social and moral values to a search for prestige and power, the sacrifice to Mammon of love, honor, obedience, troops of friends. All this is most explicit in *A Far Country*—Churchill's major assault upon that alliance of business, politics, and law which was becoming so familiar a feature of the American landscape. It is a novelized version of *The Shame of the Cities* and a commentary on the blighting influence of the Darwinian and Nietzschean philosophies as applied to business practices. Hugh Paret who—like Van Harrington in *The Memoirs of an American Citizen*—tells his own story, is a product and a mouthpiece of these half-baked philosophies. Repudiating the professional standards that his father had maintained inviolate, he was early initiated into the new moral code:

> I learned that not the least of the functions of these representatives of the people was . . . to facilitate the handing over of the Republic's resources to those in a position to develop them. The emphasis was laid on development, or rather on the resulting prosperity for the country: that was the justification, and it was taken for granted as supreme. I listened with increased fascination to these gentlemen in evening clothes calmly treating the United States as a melon patch that existed largely for the purpose of being divided up amongst a limited and favoured number of persons. (*A Far Country*)

All this was hard to reconcile to traditional ethics, but ethics seemed increasingly irrelevant to modern life. ''It was impossible,'' Paret explained carefully to the friend he was about to rob,

> to apply to business an individual code of ethics—the two were incompatible, and the sooner one recognized that the better: the whole structure of business was built up on natural, as opposed to ethical law. We had arrived at an era of frankness—that was the truth—and the sooner we faced this truth the better for our peace of mind. (*A Far Country*)

The whole panel of lesser novelists of the Roosevelt-Wilson era, however they differed in background and training, united with Howells and Herrick and Churchill in pronouncing a verdict of guilty against American business and businessmen of this generation. It is the verdict to be read in *Coniston* and *Mr. Crewe's Career,* confused as they are with recommendations of mercy; it is the verdict that emerges from Phillips' numerous journalistic exposures—*The Master Rogue, The Plum Tree, Light-Fingered Gentry, The Second Generation*—the very titles suggest a mistrial; it is the verdict passed by William Allen White, who compromised less in *A Certain Rich Man* and *In the Heart of a Fool* than in practical politics; it is the verdict affirmed by the experienced Brand Whitlock in *The Thirteenth District* and *The Turn of the Balance;* it is the verdict delivered in Ernest Poole's *The Harbor* and in Abraham Cahan's *Rise of David Levinsky.* These judges were all, in their way, clement, all willing to accept sentimental confessions or romantic atonements or deathbed repentances. What they affirmed, with no little indirection, was argued with more brutal insistence by Theodore Dreiser and Upton Sinclair.

These two major critics of American society differed profoundly in philosophy but not in analysis or diagnosis. Where Sinclair was animated by love for his fellow-men, Dreiser regarded them with dispassionate objectivity; where Sinclair was a propagandist, Dreiser was a scientific observer; where Sinclair was a moralist, Dreiser pretended to amorality; where Sinclair was melioristic, Dreiser was desperate; where Sinclair regarded the titans of industry with loathing, Dreiser confessed a sneaking admiration for those who came to the top in the struggle for existence. But however deep these differences, the two novelists agreed in describing the economic order as inhumane and corrupt. Philosophically *The Jungle* and *Sister Carrie, The Metropolis* and *The Financier, Boston* and *An American Tragedy* belong in different categories, but as indictments of American economy in the first quarter of the twentieth century they are interchangeable. (pp. 257-58)

In the mid-twenties a distinguished historian described American civilization as "almost wholly a businessman's civilization." Perhaps the generalization had been valid since Appomattox, but its validity was more readily conceded in a decade when the president announced that the business of America was business and when a political campaign could substitute the promise of two cars in every garage for the more modest full dinner-pail of an earlier generation. The advertisers, the radio, the movies, popular journals and newspapers, even churchmen, hastened to welcome the "new era," and colleges and universities were zealous to confer their honorary degrees upon corporation lawyers and stockbrokers. A chorus of praise for what was now, in despite of Jefferson, called the American system ascended to the skies. No major novelist joined in the chorus: the novelists remained unreconciled and unregenerate.

Yet the direct assault of the Populist-Progressive era was abandoned. Muckraking had been played out, and there were no successors to *The Arena* or *McClure's* or *Hamptons,* or to Herrick and Churchill and Phillips and Whitlock. It was partly that, as William Allen White later recalled, "the whole liberal movement . . . which had risen so proudly under Bryan and Roosevelt and LaFollette, was tired. The spirits of the liberals . . . were bewildered." It was partly that the public, lulled into complacency by prosperity and disillusioned by the abortive crusade to make the world safe for democracy, was no longer interested in exposures. It was chiefly that the triumph of business was so spectacular and its battlements were so formidable, that it seemed invulnerable to direct assault. Protest persisted, but the attack, in so far as that term may be used, was oblique and insidious. It took the form of satire and of repudiation, and satire and repudiation are confessions of defeat.

The confession is written large in the literature of the twenties. For as the novelists contemplated the business civilization which reached its apogee in that decade they were uncomfortable rather than indignant, derisive rather than rebellious; their protest was personal and their estrangement private. They looked with disapproval, even scorn, upon the contemporary scene,

but they confessed no sense of shock, only a desire to shock. And what was perhaps most striking about the fiction which they wrote was not its overtones of satire and its undertones of antipathy and repudiation, but that the satire should be directed toward the middle classes rather than toward the rich, that the antipathy should be reserved for the social rather than the economic manifestations of the new era, and that the repudiation should be private rather than public. What these novelists lacked was what their predecessors so conspicuously had—sympathy, dignity, and purpose. They were not deeply moved by wrong because they had so little pity for the victims of wrong. They were not outraged by the violation of moral standards because they themselves were so unsure of their standards. They did not embark upon crusades because they had no program, only an attitude. They did not stand at Armageddon and battle for the Lord—how could they when they did not believe in the Lord?—but fled to Greenwich Village or to the Left Bank and thumbed their noses at the middle classes or at Puritanism or at the small town. Their greatest ambition was *épater la bourgeoisie,* their greatest triumph when the bourgeoisie acknowledged the shock.

Yet that triumph was brittle and evanescent. The economic hide was too thick for the barbs of the satirists, and the ultimate evidence of the futility of the attack was the enthusiasm with which it was welcomed by its victims. How completely mere satire failed of its purpose was made clear in the case of Sinclair Lewis, for when the public swarmed to buy his novels, when Main Street became a national shrine and Babbitt a folk hero, when the Pulitzer Committee found that *Arrowsmith* reflected the "wholesome atmosphere of American life," the joke was surely on Lewis himself rather than on Gopher Prairie or Zenith. Others who took refuge in satire or in malice suffered a comparable fate: the mordant Ring Lardner was regarded as a first-rate sports writer; the profoundly disillusioned Fitzgerald was acclaimed the spokesman for gilded youth; James Branch Cabell, whose repudiation of contemporary life was complete, achieved popularity because *Jurgen* contained passages esoterically erotic; Mencken, whose hatred of democracy was morbid, was embraced by all the young liberals; *The New Yorker* was welcomed as merely a humorous magazine, the fortunate successor to *Life* and *Judge.*

Of all the novelists of the twenties, it was Sinclair Lewis who gave the most elaborate report on his society and whose scenes and characters came most nearly to symbolize its meaning to the future. *Main Street* was published the year of Howells' death, and its author was, as much as any one could be, Howells' successor. Yet the contrasts between Howells and Lewis are more striking than the similarities. Both were observant and shrewd, both ranged widely over the national scene though rarely outside the middle classes they knew so well, both were realists and critics. Both were historians of the commonplace, but where Howells had rejoiced in the commonplace, Lewis found it intolerable. Both were interested primarily in character, but where Howells was concerned with its inner compulsions, Lewis was content with its outward manifestations. Both looked with skepticism upon the conventions of their day, but where Howells acquiesced in order to achieve intellectual freedom, Lewis battered so frantically against convention that he had no energy left to enjoy the freedom he won. Where Howells was urbane, Lewis was raucous; where he was judicious, Lewis was dogmatic; where he was affectionate—or at least compassionate—Lewis was scornful. Yet Howells' quarrel with his society was deeper than Lewis', his repudiation more fundamental. (pp. 260-62)

It is in *Babbitt* that we find the most extensive report on society in the twenties, and the contrast between Howells and Lewis can best be appreciated when we compare Silas Lapham with George Babbitt. Silas Lapham, for all his vanity, his weakness, his vacillation, his confusion, is a hero. He has dignity, integrity, and character. The battles he fights are real, like the Civil War battles in which he was wounded—the battle for his farm, for his factory, for his family, for his own integrity; the victories he wins, the defeats he suffers, are meaningful. Nor is the society in which he moves negligible, or the delicate issues of class relationships, business honesty, friendship and love. But what shall be said of Babbitt—that "walking corpse" as Parrington calls him—content with his dull life, his dull family, his dull house, his dull business, his dull town, his dull ideas, his dull virtues and duller vices, mouthing the platitudes of the Rotary Club and the Republican platform as if they were gospel? What but that he is not only a success, but the very symbol of Success, the symbol of the New Era. Babbitt is a caricature who came to life; here, as so often, nature conformed to art. (p. 263)

If it is illuminating to compare Silas Lapham with George Babbitt, it is no less than startling to contrast Van Harrington, Hugh Paret, and Frank Cowperwood with Dos Passos' representatives of Big Business, J. Ward Moorehouse and Charley Anderson. For those earlier titans of finance and of industry are amoral and ruthless, but they are never contemptible or obscene. They have certain standards of decency and some sense of honor, and they formulate what appears to them satisfactory philosophical rationalizations for their conduct; each, in his twisted way, thinks that he is serving some larger end

Dust jacket of Babbitt, *by Sinclair Lewis. Copyright 1922 by Harcourt Brace Jovanovich, Inc. Copyright renewed 1950 by Sinclair Lewis. Reproduced by permission of the publisher.*

of progress. Nor can their authors wholly abandon them or repudiate them: Van Harrington and Paret, we feel, may yet be saved, and as for the fabulous Cowperwood, Dreiser can scarcely conceal his admiration for the man who was, after all, merely obeying those laws of nature which Darwin and Nietzsche had deciphered. But Anderson and Moorehouse have no redeeming qualities, nor is their creator troubled for a moment by any twinges of sympathy for them. They inspire disgust and justify it. They are Ring Lardner characters who, according to their ruined standards, make good, and their success is the blighted success of Lardner's dopes.

Dos Passos shows us businessmen far more corrupt than any who crowd the pages of Howells or Norris or Churchill or Herrick—depraved as these authors, who came to maturity in the afterglow of the Victorian era, could scarcely imagine depravity. Yet the object of his antipathy is not, as with these earlier critics, the bad man. It is the system, and he is the first major novelist after Upton Sinclair to condemn capitalism itself. It is not a little curious that those novelists whose resentment was focused most sharply on malefactors of great wealth should have displayed them with certain redeeming qualities, while Dos Passos (as indeed Wolfe and Steinbeck and Farrell), who made clear that the malefactors are merely the creatures of their environment, should give us villains of unmitigated wickedness. The acquisitive society of the twenties was scarred and pitted with evil, but it was not wholly, not even mainly, bad, and we may well ask what it had done to deserve a portrait done entirely in black. (pp. 270-71)

Surveying the literature of the twenties, one of the most astute critics, Bernard De Voto, charged that the major novelists were victims of a literary fallacy—the fallacy that what they saw was the whole of America and that their report on it was faithful:

> The repudiation of American life by American literature during the 1920's signified that writers were isolated or insulated from the common culture. There is something intrinsically absurd in the image of a literary man informing a hundred and twenty million people that their ideals are base, their beliefs unworthy, their ideas vulgar, their institutions corrupt, and, in sum, their civilization too trivial to engage that literary man's respect. That absurdity is arrogant but also it is naive and most of all it is ignorant. For the repudiation was the end-product of systems of thinking, and the systems arose in an ignorance that extended to practically everything but imaginative literature and critical comment on it. (*The Literary Fallacy*)

Mr. De Voto, in short, was pained that the novelists did so badly by American civilization, that they emphasized its harrowing aspects and ignored its admirable. He wrote in 1944 when Americans, confronted with the greatest crisis of their history, had revealed qualities not wholly ignoble, and he asked how it happened that the walking shadows who strutted and fretted their hours through the pages of Lewis and Fitzgerald and Dos Passos were able to meet that crisis.

And it was, in fact, remarkable, a reflection on the accuracy of the literary interpretation. Yet Mr. De Voto's charge is a point of departure rather than a conclusion. No major critic denied that the novelists of the twenties and the thirties were alienated from their society: it is the theme of much of the writing of Edmund Wilson, of Lewis Mumford, of Maxwell Geismar and Alfred Kazin. What is important is to ask how this situation came about. How did it happen that novelists from Lewis to Steinbeck were uniformly critical of America's business civilization? How did it happen that, after Silas Lapham, almost the only respectable businessmen in American fiction are Booth Tarkington's Plutocrat—the dubious Earl Tinker—and Sinclair Lewis' equally dubious Sam Dodsworth? Mr. De Voto is inclined to blame the novelists, and his resentment against what appears to be calculated misrepresentation is not hard to understand. Yet it is difficult to believe that all the novelists were blind except those who wrote for the popular magazines, that two generations of writers could have been led astray. It is, after all, a serious reflection on the business civilization that it was unable to commend itself to artists who were, on the whole, men of good will. (pp. 273-74)

> *Henry Steele Commager, "The Literature of Revolt," in his* The American Mind: An Interpretation of American Thought and Character since the 1880's, *Yale University Press, 1950, pp. 247-76.*

HOWARD MUMFORD JONES

[*A distinguished twentieth-century American critic, Jones is noted for his illuminating commentary on American culture and literature. Awarded the Pulitzer Prize for his study of the formation of American culture in* O Strange New World *(1964), he is also acclaimed for his criticism in* The Theory of American Literature *(1948) and similar works in which he examines the relationship between America's literary and cultural development. In the following excerpt, Jones notes the changing portrayal of the fictional businessman from a respected member of the community to a shallow, despicable figure and evaluates reasons for the prevalence of the latter image in American fiction of the twentieth century.*]

According to the college of commerce, business in a stable society is a stabilizing influence. It offers talented persons a professional career which promises most of the solid satisfactions of life—domesticity, respect, recreation, culture, a responsible place in the community. Furthermore, if we are to believe the mottoes of the business clubs, it offers as well a remarkable opportunity to serve one's fellow man.

But if we close the catalogue of the college of commerce and shut our ears to the Rotary Clubs; and if, instead, we read the novels in which American authors have portrayed businessmen, we find the picture startlingly altered. Increasingly in the nineteenth century and overwhelmingly in the twentieth century, if novelists are to be believed, businessmen are by no means the admirable creatures theory requires them to be. Apparently, also, a business career does not offer the solid satisfactions of life. What the novelists say, the poets and the dramatists reenforce; consider, for example, *Death of a Salesman*.

What is even more remarkable, this devaluation of business as a way of life is, in terms of literary history at least, a relatively recent phenomenon. Formerly the tradesman was admired by writers; now writers scoff at the business leader. Of course there is a difference between the connotation of a word like tradesman and that of a term like businessman. The tradesman, until recently, was a middle-class merchant who perhaps lived above his shop, employed a clerk or two or a couple of apprentices, and kept his strongbox in his bedroom, which served the purposes of a bank. We have few such persons nowadays. Nevertheless, the difference between the tradesman and the businessman is not sufficiently radical to disturb the compar-

ison, since both seek an honest profit by the creation, transport, or sale of goods.

Now what is remarkable in the literary treatment of the tradesman, at least until the nineteenth century was well along, is that even when good-natured fun was poked at him, the tradesman was on the whole regarded by the literary world with considerable respect. (pp. 134, 136)

The middle-class tradesman respected by writers as different as Shakespeare and Richard Steele more and more disappeared from English fiction as the last century wore on. His place was taken by either or both of two figures: (1) an uncultured, lower middle-class tailor, grocer, or pharmacist, such as you find in the novels of H. G. Wells or Arnold Bennett; (2) a substantial, selfish, and altogether despicable man of property, subtly dissected by John Galsworthy in *The Forsyte Saga*.

In American fiction, except for the novels of Cooper (*Miles Wallingford, Afloat and Ashore,* and *The Sea Lion*), the businessman does not importantly appear until after the Civil War. But in the Gilded Age the speculator, the monopolist, the capitalist driven ruthlessly on by mere lust of power attracted the attention of writers. His figure begins to form in the half forgotten novels of the Grant administration. You can see him, in *The Gilded Age* by Charles Dudley Warner and Mark Twain, happily in cahoots with amoral politicians. By and by he attracts the attention of William Dean Howells, who in books like *A Hazard of New Fortunes* or *The Quality of Mercy* and, more important still, *The Rise of Silas Lapham*, is far kinder to him than are Howells' contemporaries.

Then, in the books of writers like Frank Norris and Theodore Dreiser the businessman emerges as the ruthless superman of the era of trusts, monopolies, political corruption, and the Darwinian struggle for survival. Curtis Jadwin in *The Pit* by Norris and Frank Cowperwood in Dreiser's trilogy of desire (*The Financier, The Titan, The Stoic*) are representative. What is remarkable in these figures is not merely their gigantic amorality but also the atrophy of their domestic affections and religious feelings—precisely those solid middle-class qualities that had seemed admirable to eighteenth-century writers. Cowperwood lures woman after woman to his bed, but he has no family life. Curtis Jadwin becomes so warped by the struggle on the board of trade that his wife is on the verge of eloping with another man when Jadwin's financial collapse throws him back into her arms, and the eyes of both husband and wife are opened to the ruin business has wrought.

With the passing of the assumption that business is mere tooth-and-claw competition, this type of business leader has tended to pass out of the financial world pictured in literature. Or, rather, he has passed over into illegal operations like bootlegging, shady politics, or racketeering. Novels like *To Have and Have Not, Little Caesar,* and *All the King's Men* show this change. With the loss of a sense of gigantic power, which, after all, has its fascination, the businessman in American fiction has dwindled; you can see the process in the novels of Booth Tarkington.

In novels today, I am tempted to remark, the power has gone but the unhappiness remains. The businessman in much twentieth-century fiction is almost invariably frustrated and unhappy. He is pictured as without religious belief, without a satisfactory home life, without a philosophy except in the shallowest sense, and without any real satisfaction in his mercantile career. The routine of his life, the mere making of money, does not satisfy—as witness *Babbitt* by Sinclair Lewis; *H. M.*

Pulham Esquire, Point of No Return, and other novels by J. P. Marquand (in which the advertising agency, the bank, or whatever it may be, invariably takes a beating); and *Jefferson Selleck* by Carl Jonas, the latest novel I have read with a business "hero."

If American novelists are accurate recorders of the age, it appears that a young man graduating from a college of commerce and entering upon a business career may look forward to a life of frustration:

Such a person is sure to find the office in which he works stultifying. His job will be meaningless; his companions are quietly to drown their sorrows in drink on weekends, or will vary this with furtive and unhappy love affairs in some of our resort towns. Promotion will be largely a matter of intrigue, the elements of which are to be sex, alcohol, flattery, and a shrewd eye for the weaknesses of the boss's wife.

His own wife, after the birth of their first child, will cease to understand him as she becomes more and more absorbed by the country club set; and, to the disgust of his plain but faithful office wife (his secretary, who wears glasses and secretly adores him), our young friend will take up with a blonde from an advertising office, the arty set, or the army crowd. This will get him nowhere and may of course cost him money.

By the time he becomes the vice president of the company, both business and life will have lost their savor. The memoirs he will secretly dictate, or the conversations he will have with an old college classmate who kept his integrity by joining some progressive political group, will show up the whole wretched sham for the benefit of posterity.

Such is the pattern of business life common in our novels. Does it not seem a little unrealistic? Inspection of life around us fails to reveal any such concentration of infelicity in what used to be called the counting-house. The papers are filled with their daily quantum of domestic unhappiness—desertion, divorce, suicide, murder—but it would be difficult to demonstrate that a higher proportion of these disasters is recorded of businessmen in proportion to their numbers than is recorded of any other occupation.

Novelists complain of the stultifying effect of routine in business offices, or declare that the relations of men in business are insincere; but I have yet to learn that the routine of a business life is any more galling than the routine of a life in education or the army or the printing of books. As for the charge of insincerity, the publishers' offices and the critical literary circles of the land are notoriously populated by what are called literary cliques; and if there is any calling in the world which is occupationally rife with frustration, gossip, innuendo, backbiting, back-scratching, and jealousy, it is the trade of being a writer.

This retort, however, is more ingenious than sound. To say that writers are traditionally a petulant crew does not prove that a career in business makes for happiness. Moreover, the persistence in fiction for over a century of the formula of the unhappy businessman is not thus lightly to be dismissed. As I think over the situation, it seems to me that one part of the literary indictment can be denied, but that the other part is not so quickly to be got rid of.

The part that can be dismissed is the assumption common among these novelists that businessmen are persons without culture. That there are and have been uncultivated persons in the business world is patent, just as there are persons in the

world of politics, in the army, in the church, and even in literature who are without personal refinement and without cultural responsibility. Uncultivated businessmen, however, are not uncultivated because they are in business; they are uncultivated for other reasons—family background, lack of opportunity, failure of education. (pp. 136, 138, 140)

But the other part of the indictment is more complicated. The dissatisfactions the novelists register with regard to business life are not merely that many men do not seem to rise above the level of money making or that the mere making of money seems to induce in some human beings a low and cynical attitude toward ethical principles. There is something deeper and more disturbing. They question the rationalization of modern business enterprise which, they say, increasingly depersonalizes and mechanizes human relationships. It is not merely that modern business seems to force square pegs into round holes, but also that modern business seems to force everybody into some sort of hole, whatever its shape.

The relationship of the eighteenth-century tradesman to his business was the relation of a painter to his canvas—he made it, he framed it, he owned it—whereas the relation of even a great business executive to that shadowy thing, a great corporation, is elusive, tenuous, and mechanical. The clerks the tradesman hired and the apprentices he trained were under a special and individual obligation to him, as he was to them.

Today, however, the new secretary is hired by the personnel department and has file X307S2; the new sales manager is mysteriously transferred from San Francisco to Atlanta by forces as impersonal as a hospital nurse; the new advertising man contributes a phrase to the proposed national campaign but does not shape that campaign, although he may lose his job if the campaign does not go well. (pp. 140, 142)

In such a world the quick-tempered Joe Zilch that we all know, the man who loves handpainted neckties, serves luke-warm martinis, plays a good game of canasta, and won't go to church except at Easter, dissolves into the male robot described by W. H. Auden when he wrote:

He was found by the Bureau of Statistics to be
One against whom there was no official complaint,
And all the reports on his conduct agree
That, in the modern sense of an old-fashioned word, he
    was a saint,
For in everything he did he served the Greater
    Community,
Except for the War till the day he retired
He worked in a factory and never got fired. . . .
Was he free? Was he happy? The question is absurd:
Had anything been wrong, we should certainly have
    heard.

The novelists claim that something is wrong and that they, at least, have heard. (p. 142)

> *Howard Mumford Jones, "Looking Around," in* Harvard Business Review, *Vol. 31, No. 1, January-February, 1953, pp. 133-42.*

[DANIEL SELIGMAN]

[*Seligman is an American magazine editor who has worked for several periodicals, including the* New Leader, American Mercury, *and* Fortune. *In the following excerpt, he disparages the negative stereotype of the businessman that has traditionally dom-*

inated American business fiction and examines characters in three business novels published in 1952.]

Three novels have been published this year in which American businessmen have been the protagonists: *Jefferson Selleck* by Carl Jonas; *Thudbury* by Clyde Brion Davis; and *Executive Suite* by Cameron Hawley. Conceivably, Edna Ferber's best-selling *Giant* might be added to the list, though the ranchers, cotton brokers, and oilmen who wander through her new novel, together with their be-minked wives, are Texans, or at least Ferberized Texans, before they are businessmen. (p. 111)

Three or four novels about business almost constitute a trend. It is, of course, a bit early to speculate whether we are now in for a prolonged vogue of business fiction. If we are, it is devoutly to be hoped that a few new stereotypes will emerge; or better yet, that novelists will stop thinking of businessmen as "types." Though novels about enterprise are still not very plentiful, attentive readers must already be heartily sick of the stock characters in this genre. The ruthless and rapacious tycoon, consumed by ambition and devoid of ethics, is becoming a little boring. And so is Babbitt.

As John Chamberlain once pointed out . . . [see excerpt above], one fixed ingredient of the American literary tradition has been hostility to business. The entrepreneur has characteristically been portrayed as shrewd but narrow-minded, friendly but self-serving, wanting love but ultimately undeserving of it. For some perverse reason, the home life of the fictional business-man has almost always been an unholy mess. Above all, he has been a cultural barbarian, whose appearance in novels has preceded by only a few pages his assertion that there is no higher form of art than a *Saturday Evening Post* cover, for which he would gladly trade a dozen Picassos.

To be sure, the misconceptions reported by Mr. Chamberlain appeared in novels that, by and large, had been written before the war. Of course, the businessman of the 1920's and 1930's was actually a more useful—and interesting—member of society than the novelists were willing to concede. But in any case there is now a mid-century businessman, even further removed from the old stereotypes. Have our contemporary novelists discovered him?

It is rather dismaying to have to report that two of the novels at hand deal with Babbitt. Indeed the dust jacket of *Jefferson Selleck* asserts proudly—and, on the whole, accurately—that its hero "is Sinclair Lewis' Babbitt thirty years later, a wiser and sadder and mellower Babbitt. . . ." The jacket of *Thudbury* also mentions Babbitt, but only to disclaim any imitation. It might appear to some readers, however, that Otis Thudbury is just a bigger, richer, and more aggressive Babbitt, who has all the least appealing qualities of Mr. Lewis' hero without the small-town sense of awe for the modern world that made the latter a somewhat sympathetic figure at times.

Before returning to these two efforts, it might be profitable to consider *Executive Suite,* in some respects the most interesting of the crop. Though the characters in this novel do not come fully to life in most cases, they are, at least, not caricatures. Their creator, Cameron Hawley, was until recently a busi-nessman himself—advertising director at Armstrong Cork—and his novel proceeds on the assumption, totally lacking in most of the novels examined several years ago by Mr. Cham-berlain, that the operations of a large business enterprise are exciting enough to be dealt with seriously and respectfully.

The story line itself is remarkably simple. *Executive Suite* opens with the sudden death of Avery Bullard, president of the Tred-way Corp., one of the largest furniture manufacturers in the country. Bullard, who had completely dominated the company, and his subordinates as well, died without having designated a successor. Virtually the whole of the book is concerned with the battle among the seven members of the board to name the next president. The shifting coalitions, the logrolling efforts of the chief contenders, the personality clashes, the conflicting ideologies of business, are all handled deftly by Mr. Hawley. His book is, in fact, a kind of sustained exercise in office politics, as well as a genuinely interesting novel.

There are, however, several aspects of *Executive Suite* that might puzzle business readers. Two ideas hang very heavily over the proceedings. The first is the author's notion that a successful business, even a large enterprise like the Tredway Corp., can be run only by a complete dictator, an overpowering personality. The second, which is somehow made to seem a corollary of the first, is that the boss must be a "production man" as opposed—not very subtly here—to a "moneyman."

The villain of Mr. Hawley's piece is the comptroller. His remarkable capacity for keeping a slew of figures at his fin-gertips is made to seem irritating rather than admirable. His cautious program for consolidating, rather than expanding, the company's successful operations comes out as a kind of be-trayal, though no evidence is presented to indicate that he is actually wrong. To make his point a bit more bald, Mr. Hawley has the comptroller playing the dirtiest game of office politics, wanting the presidency the most selfishly, and finally, at the crucial meeting, which ends with his defeat, expounding this static and un-American idea: "At the top level, the corporation must now be governed to be what its owners want it to be—a *financial institution. . . .*"

The comptroller, who is despised on all sides, is defeated after this speech by the young Vice President for Design and De-velopment, who melodramatically abandons his mild manner, takes the assemblage by the scruff of its neck, so to speak, and delivers a belligerent talk on production and leadership that carries the day. He is Cameron Hawley's business hero. If businessmen readers put down the book with no special enthusiasm for such a tartar as president of a modern corpo-ration, let them not be too exercised. It is a pleasure, at least, to pick up a novel treating of management problems that bear at least some resemblance to the real thing.

It might be noted, incidentally, that few corporations could exist for long if their office politics were played as fiendishly as at the Tredway Corp. (pp. 111, 126)

Fortune respectfully questions . . . whether any office politi-cian has ever got off such a brilliant ploy as the one credited in *Executive Suite* to the wily comptroller. The latter, since he was a relatively new member of the executive family, was seated at board meetings near the foot of the table, a discour-aging distance from the president. One day he suggested that the board meetings be held at a different hour—for reasons that seemed to be perfectly plausible. But when the board met at this new time, it was discovered that the sun shone fiercely into the president's eyes. He, therefore, got up and moved to the other end of the table. The comptroller now sat near the head, rather than the foot, of the table, directly to the presi-dent's right.

Jefferson Selleck and *Thudbury* are both essentially about busi-nessmen, rather than business enterprises. The reader is given heavy doses of their family lives, their personal finances, their politics (unenlightened conservative), their artistic and cultural preferences (unenlightened).

Selleck, though a bit on the oafish side, is a good enough fellow when you get to know him; Mr. Jonas' satire is patronizing and gentle, never shrill. Our hero runs a small midwestern company that manufactures musical auto horns. Though hardly a tycoon, he is at least a personage in Gateway City, which at one point almost had him for mayor. At the 1948 Republican convention, he was in charge of noisemaking for Taft, and though Taft, of course, did not win, Selleck was held to have discharged his responsibility very creditably. His great weakness, until a heart attack forces him to do some thinking about his life, is an irrational fear of change.

Before Selleck dies, however, he makes the discovery that change is not always to be resisted. The climax finds him going into business with his new son-in-law, a direct young type who is so enthusiastic about change that he has been making a mint in surplus government tankers. The moral at this point is somewhat blurred. Despite its obvious roots in *Babbitt,* and its rather murky philosophizing, *Jefferson Selleck* is an engaging little book, fortified throughout by an invincible good humor. As a portrait of a businessman, of course, it leaves us about where we were twenty-five years ago.

Thudbury goes back even further; it is a sort of fictionalized job of muckraking done in the spirit of Ida Tarbell. Though it is subtitled *An American Comedy,* the humor wears thin very quickly under the author's compulsion to make of Otis Thudbury the worst boor in business fiction. What we are left with, after 446 pages, is a memory of an industrial and banking big shot who had more money and influence than was good for him when he died in 1945. Just why the notion of flogging this particular dead horse kindled Mr. Davis' imagination is rather difficult for a bystander to say.

The paucity of good novels about business, especially about big business, remains something of a mystery. There is, of course, the difficulty that very few men of letters know much about the modern corporation. But this problem should not be insuperable. . . . (p. 126)

[Daniel Seligman], *"Author Meets Businessman,"* in Fortune, Vol. XLVI, No. 6, December, 1952, pp. 111, 126.

KENNETH S. LYNN

[*An American critic whose works evidence his conservative principles, Lynn is the author of numerous essays and books on American life and letters. In the following excerpt, he analyzes American business fiction since 1885 and discusses the increasingly sympathetic portrayal of businessmen in fiction and drama of the 1940s and 1950s, disputing the view of John Chamberlain (see excerpt above) and other critics that American literature of the twentieth century depicts businessmen in a uniformly negative light.*]

Indisputably it is true that some plays and novels of the postwar era present the businessman in fully as unflattering a light as was ever trained upon him in the past.

Frederic Wakeman's hucksters are as appalling as J. Ward Moorehouse, the public relations tycoon in Dos Passos' *The Big Money* (1936). Carl Jonas' Jefferson Selleck is as limited, culturally and politically, as Sinclair Lewis' George F. Babbitt. Clyde Brion Davis' *Thudbury,* Lester Cohen's *Going Home,*

and Samuel Hopkins Adams' *Plunder* conjure up ogres to rival the brutal fruit growers in John Steinbeck's *The Grapes of Wrath.*

Nevertheless, Chamberlain's lament [see excerpt above] that the businessman was still being treated with universal hostility was far from accurate even in 1948 when it was written—and it has become still less valid with the passage of time.

Like Arthur Miller, Chamberlain was haunted by the 1930's; he brought to his analysis of the succeeding decade a series of preconceptions which, if markedly different from Miller's, were no less vivid—so vivid that they prevented him from seeing that what was significant about the literary climate in the 1940's was not that it still resembled the climate of the 1930's, but how rapidly it was losing that resemblance.

Thus, neither of the heroes in the two most important business novels of the 1940's fits Chamberlain's description of the decade's anti-business bias. Monroe Stahr, the motion picture executive in F. Scott Fitzgerald's posthumous novel, *The Last Tycoon* (1941), was based on the producer Irving Thalberg, whom Fitzgerald regarded as a brilliant, humane, and imaginative man. Similarly Solon Barnes, the banker in Theodore Dreiser's posthumous novel, *The Bulwark* (1946), is portrayed as a tower of moral strength.

The 1940's were the years, too, when many writers, having discarded one set of opinions about the American businessman, were beginning to search for another. Dos Passos' career is typical in this regard; the image of the businessman in *Chosen Country* (1951) is much more flattering than the one presented 15 years before in *The Big Money.*

Finally, several of the novelists whom Chamberlain considered were not so easily labeled as he thought. If John P. Marquand has been even harder on the businessman in *Sincerely, Willis Wayde* than he was in *B. F.'s Daughter,* a novel which Chamberlain deplored, Marquand has also, in the person of Charley Gray in *Point of No Return,* presented an appealing young banker as his hero.

Most of the new generation of novelists who began to write in the 1940's and early 1950's have approached the businessman in a spirit which is quite different from that of the depression authors.

Many of the current crop of sympathetic business novels are in fact the work of men who have been, or who still are, businessmen. The author of *Father of the Bride* and *Mr. Hobb's Vacation,* Edward Streeter, is vice president of the Bank of New York. The author of *The Power and the Prize,* Howard Swiggett, was the managing partner of one firm and president of another before turning entirely to writing. Bissell's *7½ Cents,* Schisgall's *The Big Store,* Prosser's *Nine to Five,* Schoonover's *The Quick Brown Fox,* and Hawley's *Executive Suite* and *Cash McCall* are all business novels by men who have had business experience of one sort or another.

But whether by businessmen or not, the extraordinary spate of business fiction in recent years has been increasingly sympathetic with the aims and problems of the businessman. When the hero of Schisgall's *The Big Store* affirms that "any man who holds business in contempt today ought to have his head examined," he probably speaks for the majority of American business novelists who have been writing in the mid-1950's.

In view of all this evidence to the contrary, it is difficult to know what Sloan Wilson is thinking of when he asserts that "too many novelists are still writing as if we were back in the Depression years," for while it is clear that his celebration of *The Man in the Gray Flannel Suit* has enjoyed an extraordinary success, it is not at all clear (nor does Wilson enlighten us) as to just who these depression-fettered novelists are, or how many constitute "too many."

Life magazine is also alarmed that the most powerful nation in the world is not producing a more "affirmative" literature, but it should probably be remembered that only yesterday *Life* was calling for a tragic American art and that in any event the Luce publications are still too much under the spell of John Chamberlain's gloomy statistics to gauge with any accuracy just which way the tide of American business fiction is running. *The Man in the Gray Flannel Suit* is neither the exception that *Life* considers it nor as exceptional as Wilson believes it to be; it is the rule.

If the business novel is leaving behind it the atmosphere of gloom and the tone of accusation that was typical of depression times, the same thing may be said of the business drama. True, Arthur Miller's prize-winning *Death of a Salesman* (1949) continued in the same ideological vein as *All My Sons*. But in the mid-1950's the social realism of Broadway in the 1930's has largely given way to comedy (mostly of the musical variety); and if the businessman is still seen as an ogre, it is a cause not for alarm but for laughter.

The company directors in *The Solid Gold Cadillac,* for example, are shown to be a collection of stuffed shirts whose dullness is exceeded only by their avarice; but when the little stockholders—in the person of Josephine Hull—rise up and take over, the new popular regime acts as highhandedly as the unpopular old one, thus drawing the poison from the sting. For if the business world is here represented as a Milleresque zoo, the fact remains that a zoo which includes Josephine Hull is obviously a delightful place!

Similarly, in the highly successful musical, *The Pajama Game,* the satirization of depression views is elaborately worked out and in fact is the central humorous device of the play. The time-study man in the pajama factory announces at the very outset, "This is a very serious drama. It's a kind of problem play. It's about Capital and Labor." And in the course of the next two hours union leaders, the class war, the speed-up, and of course the businessman are all portrayed in the same spirit of mock-1930's hilarity. Once again, as in *The Solid Gold Cadillac,* the boss is exposed as a pompous crook, but it is his very crookedness that makes possible a painless settlement of the strike, and so in the end all is laughingly forgiven.

Noting the shift in attitude toward the businessman that has been going on in American writing since the early 1940's is not without interest, but the game of totting up the score for or against the businessman is finally a rather unrewarding occupation. The significant question is whether he has ever really been dealt with at all in our literature.

Half a century ago, Henry James looked back on the most distinguished literary career any American has ever enjoyed and concluded that his greatest lack as a novelist was that he had been "unprepared" and "uneducated" in the ways of the business world. Nineteen-twentieths of American life, in James's view, was taken up by "the huge organized mystery of the consummately, the supremely applied money-passion," and the doors of this life had been "inexorably closed" to him. (pp. 116-18)

As compared to the novelist informed enough and bold enough to deal with American business, James felt distinctly inferior. However, he drew comfort from the fact that he descried "no semblance of such a competitor slipping in at any door or perched, for raking the scene, on any coign of vantage."

In taking such comfort, James was of course well aware that his long-time friend and literary acquaintance, William Dean Howells, had dealt with commercial and financial life more than once and that in Howells' greatest novel, *The Rise of Silas Lapham* (1885), the hero was a paint manufacturer, a businessman. A colonel in the Civil War and a self-made business success, Silas Lapham was a mixture of shrewdness and generosity, of open-mindedness and prejudice; he was a man who had never quite got over his awe about Boston, and yet who could hardly be described as suffering from an inferiority complex. With his big hands and bluff, Vermont manner, Lapham was a marvelously realized character. How is it that James, knowing of Silas, could have descried no competitors raking the business scene?

James believed that the business civilization of America would yield its secrets only to "a really *grasping* imagination," and it was precisely this quality which he perceived that Howells did not have. Thus although many of the scenes across the whole length of *Silas Lapham* take place in the office, where Howells depicts Silas being interviewed by a newspaperman, dealing with his business rivals, and going about his daily business routine, they do not make the book a novel about business.

Howells' acquaintance with business was limited to his experience as a magazine editor; he was almost as much of an alien in State Street or Wall Street as James was, and his imagination was powerless to grasp what he did not know well. Despite Howells' superb characterization of Silas, the verisimilitude of the details of business life which he presents, and the fact that the central moral crisis involves a business decision, the imaginative center of the novel does not lie in the office but at home, in the private lives of the main characters. (pp. 118-19)

By starting Silas Lapham out in the office, then rapidly escorting him away from it, Howells set a precedent almost universally followed by other novelists who wrote about businessman in the 60-year period between the mid-1880's and the end of World War II. Henry Blake Fuller's *The Cliff-Dwellers* (1893), for example, focuses initially on the Clifton building in downtown Chicago, but midway in the story the scene shifts, and with it the nature of the novel.

Sinclair Lewis, in his influential novel, *Babbitt* (1922), states that for his hero, "the office was his pirate ship," and spends the first 32 meticulously detailed pages of the novel piping Babbitt aboard and the following 40 pages taking him through a typical workday. For the next 333 pages, Zenith's leading realtor is almost always out to lunch. Having established, by that typical workday (which, for all of Lewis' photographic and phonographic realism, is not nearly as convincing as Howells' business scenes), that Babbitt is a businessman, Lewis leads his hero out of the office and into a host of other activities, none of which has much to do with the money-passion.

In the process of moving away from the office, the American business novel in this period often becomes, as *Silas Lapham* did, a novel of manners, and the business hero ceases to be a businessman as such. What is important about the businessman in this kind of novel is not that he makes paint, or sells real estate, but that he is an American male of limited culture attempting to move in a more sophisticated world.

Following the example of Henry James, who may not have known business but did know what the American traveler in Europe was like, and who in his early novel, *The American* (1877), had dealt with the businessman as tourist, many novelists attempted to solve the problem of their business ignorance by sending their innocents abroad. If no American writer since James has ever achieved his mastery of the international theme, nonetheless the trip to Europe has served as a favorite escape route for novelists in search of a way out of the office. Both Lewis' *Dodsworth* (1929) and Tarkington's *The Plutocrat* (1927) are hardly concerned with business at all, but rather with the impact of Old World values on the New World consciousness. (Gazing at Gibraltar, Tarkington's hero exclaims, "What an ad!")

But whether or not the scene is Europe, the businessman in the novel of manners is operating in a woman's world. Sometimes—as in Frank Norris' *The Pit* (1903)—the woman is his wife. Sometimes—as in *Dodsworth* and James's *The Ambassadors* (1903)—she is his mistress. But whatever her status, it is almost always a woman who introduces the businessman to culture, who "shows him the sights," who gives him his education. In these novels, the world of serious male interest is far away.

Business novelists of the period who did not write the novel of manners wrote success stories. They began, not with Silas Lapham the successful businessman, but with Silas Lapham the poor farm boy, and traced his rise from rags to riches. While the authors of the success stories seemed ostensibly to be more concerned with the businessman in his role as businessman than did the novelist of manners, they avoided the office with almost equal zeal. Instead of writing about their heroes' occupations, they wrote about their personalities.

Thus Elam Harnish in Jack London's *Burning Daylight* (1910) maintains an office, but what he does for a living is almost irrelevant to what the novel is about. What counts, and counts supremely, is his Napoleonic force and energy, his rugged individualism; the office is simply the backdrop, the barely furnished stage, against which his titanic advancement from triumph to triumph is outlined.

In fact, the success story in this 60-year period was not a novel about business but a saga of self-realization. Whether the author, like Dreiser, glories in Frank Cowperwood's ascent to the financial heights in *The Titan* (1914), or, like Dos Passos, finds the transformation of young Johnny Moorehouse in *The 42nd Parallel* (1930) into J. Ward Moorehouse in *The Big Money* a shameful progress, the accent is on the hero's sensation of rising, not on the objective details of how the rise is accomplished.

Thus Dos Passos is exceedingly vague about the details of Moorehouse's public relations operation; what concerns him is the way in which power intoxicates Moorehouse and corrupts him, not how the power was acquired or is maintained. And when Frank Cowperwood swoops down on his office for a whirlwind round of financial and political manipulation that climaxes in the demolition of all opposition and ends with his departure for a rendezvous with his latest mistress. Dreiser is scarcely describing the business mystery; he is writing about the unconquerable Self. It is the defiant Cowperwood's attempt to be an American superman, not an American businessman, which is the subject of *The Titan*.

Caught between the novel of manners and the success story, the businessman in American literature has traditionally been the man nobody knows. For all of the increased interest in the businessman since the end of World War II, the enigma of the office continues to exist in contemporary writing.

Death of a Salesman, like almost all of Arthur Miller's plays, takes place at home and is primarily concerned with the struggle between a father and his children. Willy Loman is not a salesman; as his one trip to the office makes clear, his career is behind him, he is all washed up. Willy confronts not the customer but old age, the hollowness of his dreams, and the bitterness of his sons. Miller has strong opinions about business, but he deals with the businessman in a peripheral context because—seemingly—the only situation he can write about with sufficient dramatic energy to support the intensity of his feelings about business is family conflict.

The significance of *Death of a Salesman*, however, is not simply that it displays the traditional failure of the American writer to deal with business directly. What makes it a notable play is that Miller has made the tragedy of the Loman family emblematic, just as James did with his novels of manners, of the moral drama of life in a business civilization.

Miller is not concerned with the office life of his protagonist, but rather with the impact of office values on the personality of a father; yet the moral criticism of the businessman is no less profound for that. Willy the salesman was raised on what Zelda Fitzgerald once called "the infinite promise of American advertising." As a result, his capacity to face reality has been destroyed. Trying to become something he is not, Willy employs a false and inflated rhetoric to put himself across—an effort which ends in utter loss of self-awareness.

At the end of the play, when his son, Biff, goaded beyond endurance, yells at Willy, "Pop, I'm nothing! I'm nothing, Pop. Can't you understand that?" Willy flees in terror from the truth and kills himself. The attempt to sell yourself or your product involves the risk of selling out yourself; Miller sees this awful eventuality as peculiarly the businessman's tragedy.

A further distinction of Miller's play is that it has helped to broaden the definition of the business hero. Since the enormous success of *Death of a Salesman*, contemporary writers not only have dealt with the entrepreneur, the stock market king, or the captain of industry, but have increasingly portrayed their heroes as men who work for somebody else, as managers, junior executives, ad men, or salesmen.

A large proportion of recent business novels retain the success story form—the hero's rise to a higher position is the central plot. But, by muting the success hero's role in the enterprise in which he is engaged, many contemporary novelists have smashed through the old success story cliché that business is a one-man affair.

The best-known example of this trend occurs in the most popular business novel so far to appear in the 1950's, *The Man in the Gray Flannel Suit. . . .* (pp. 119-21)

Like Charley Gray in Marquand's *Point of No Return*, who came back from the war feeling that "it's all so superficial . . . the bank president and the big job, and what will happen to Junior, and whether a boiled shirt will help," Wilson's grayflanneled hero, Tom Rath, is troubled by the thought that his business suit is just another uniform and that he is marching in "a frantic parade to nowhere." The question whether Tom is willing to make the sacrifices of time and energy which are necessary in order to move out of the $10,000-a-year class to the head of the parade serves as the crucial issue of the novel.

This is a serious issue, and Wilson approached it with a certain imagination. His solution to the problem of dealing with the business life of his hero, in spite of his own business ignorance, was to give Tom Rath a most untypical job, a job altogether outside the official hierarchy, and unconcerned with the affairs of the broadcasting company where Tom is employed. Tom Rath is special assistant to the president, charged with writing a speech to help launch a mental health campaign in which the president is interested. The result is that Tom's day-to-day activities in the office have a concreteness, a dramatic credibility and interest, far superior to that found in most business novels.

Yet the solution is inadequate. Wilson makes the speech-writing task interesting, but he cannot imagine what else his hero does, and so Tom goes on, day after day, week after week, working and reworking that one speech. Between times, he gazes out of the office window and thinks about Maria, the girl he knew in Italy. But this stereotype of the war experience seems almost fresh by comparison with those scenes in which Tom's meetings with Ralph Hopkins, the president of the company, are described.

This top executive, it is clear, comes not out of Wilson's experience of things, but from his acquaintance with Freud and Riesman. Hopkins, we are informed in an appalling two-page summary of his psyche, has homosexual tendencies, which have caused him to have guilt feelings, which in turn have caused him to attempt to kill himself with overwork. As for Hopkins' social character, clearly he is what Riesman calls "other-directed"—he first-names everyone and is sensitively attuned to the thoughts and feelings of his subordinates.

But Freud and Riesman are no substitute for the art of fiction; psychology and sociology do not save Hopkins from being a totally unconvincing and lifeless character. If we have been provided with a Freudian explanation for Hopkins' hard work, we remain dramatically unconvinced that he has any broadcasting business on his mind whatsoever. If his character is just what Riesman's *The Lonely Crowd* says it should be, this scarcely makes credible the scene where Tom tells Hopkins he doesn't like Hopkins' version of the speech and is rewarded by an instant burst of presidential gratitude and an eventual offer of high executive office.

The scenes that take place at home have their share of clichés, too. Honesty is the best policy, not only in business but in marriage: Tom's confession to his wife that he has a bastard son in Italy magically serves to rekindle their burnt-out sex life. The evil servant, the old lady's will, and the mortgage on the house are among the other worn-out literary trappings that clutter up the Raths' life in Connecticut.

However, for all these clichés, it is in its picture of suburban living that the novel comes alive. The Raths' run-down house, with its crack in the plaster on the living room wall, its leaky faucets and scuffed-up doors, the suburban habit of giving cocktail parties which last until two in the morning because no one any longer has a maid to serve dinner, the problem of raising children amidst the hazards of chicken pox and television, the tension growing out of Tom's inertia and his wife's ambition (a tension with which *Point of No Return* is likewise concerned, as is also the TV play, *Patterns*), these are vividly presented details of the culture of Suburbia that lend the novel

a certain charm and, judging from the reaction of audiences to the movie, are the real source of its appeal.

Yet in the end Wilson cannot keep true even to what he knows. The serious problem on which the novel turns, whether Tom will devote all his time to the company in the hope of someday becoming president or work only a nine-to-five day so that he can be with his family, is completely undercut by a series of manipulated lucky breaks that make it possible for Tom to turn down the chance for the top in the knowledge that he and his wife are about to make a profit of $100,000 on a real estate deal.

What, in sum, starts out to be a genuine business novel undergoes the familiar transformation to sharply observed domestic comedy, then ends as pure soap opera.

At first glance it might appear that Marquand, in his 1955 novel, *Sincerely, Willis Wayde,* is merely working, however skillfully, in the familiar framework of the novel of manners. Like all of Marquand's best work, this novel is focused on the effort made by an outsider to force his way upward through the solidified social structure of an old New England town. Henry Harcourt, the head of the mill where Willis Wayde is first employed, is portrayed less as a businessman than as the representative of the old New England aristocracy, and Willis' own work in the mill is of secondary importance dramatically to his relationship with Harcourt's daughter, Bess.

Many of the scenes in the novel are typical Marquand studies of social unease and could just as easily have taken place in some of his other novels which do not deal with business: Willis arriving for tennis only to discover that he is humiliatingly overdressed, Willis arriving to take Bess to the theater only to find that she has made another date—clearly, the fact that in these scenes the outsider is a businessman is not important.

Yet Marquand is one of the more accomplished contemporary writers to deal with the business world. (Perhaps the most able is Louis Auchincloss, whose *A Law for the Lion* and *The Romantic Egoists* appeared in 1953 and 1954. Unfortunately, in neither of these books has Auchincloss turned his full attention to the great Wall Street law firms with which he is so obviously familiar; and while each contains glimpses of the business world that are extremely penetrating, they are only glimpses.)

In any event, aware of Howells' dilemma, Marquand has in some sense achieved a way out of it. Although, like so many other writers, he knows society well and the business world not at all, this has not prevented Marquand, in *Willis Wayde,* from writing about the businessman *as* businessman, because he has capitalized on his perception that business and society are no longer the mutually exclusive provinces they used to be.

When, for example, Sinclair Lewis wrote *Babbitt,* he showed that the attitudes and standards of the businessman had permeated every institution of American life—church, press, art museum, and so on. But business as such in Lewis' fiction was still conducted in the office; when Babbitt and his pals got together for a jolly booster's lunch, they were playing, not working. Willis Wayde, on the other hand, never stops working.

As Willis moves through the social world that Marquand knows so well, he is acting the businessman (or Marquand's idea of the businessman) quite as much as when he is at the office.

He does not withdraw his knee from touching Bess's under the table, since to do so might jeopardize a business deal. And although Sylvia, his bride, begs him not to, Willis insists that they spend their honeymoon in the company of P. L. Nagel and his wife because "it's important in a business way."

Two scenes take place in hotel bedrooms, but they are both business scenes, in the strictest sense. One shows Willis, who has already seen *Red, Hot and Blue* seven times, planning to attend the musical once again with some business acquaintances whose sex jokes, boozy good cheer, and fake palship constitute only the thinnest veneer for the most intense financial self-interest. In the second of these two scenes, the mocking bird sings in the Carolina sunset and Willis signifies his sell-out to Nagel with the announcement, "I want you to know in a very friendly way that you can't bribe me in that manner."

Willis' smooth, calculated sincerity—his business personality—is at work 24 hours a day, because all the world is his office. The final result of his unending deception is self-deception; like Willy the salesman, Willis the executive does not know who or what he is. Marquand is distressed by the human cost that the business invasion of the social world has entailed; but he has made a literary virtue out of that distress and has used his knowledge of the social world to penetrate part way the mystery of the money-passion.

Marquand's solution was a brilliant improvisation, but one would think that the new crop of businessmen-novelists would find it unnecessary; they, after all, know the office because they used to (or still do) work there. However, what is so striking about these novelists is that despite their knowledge they, too, have not found it possible to deal with the mysterious office, and have depended on traditional literary solutions for avoiding it.

For all of his 35 years of business experience, Howard Swiggett in *The Power and the Prize* focuses primarily on the relationship of his hero with a widowed Austrian refugee whom he meets on a business trip to London. After talking to the widow, the hero expresses the literary businessman's historic urge to be educated: "He felt ashamed that his appreciation was limited to a liking for beautiful sounds, particularly those made by the human voice, or a symphony orchestra playing 'Get Along, Little Dogies' in *The Plow that Broke the Plains.*"

The main difference between the story of the hero and the widow and James's *The American* or Lewis' *Dodsworth* is that Swiggett cannot write. Such business scenes as the novel contains are taken up with demonstrating the hero's superior character and why he deserves to be chairman of the board. In the end, he does get both the chairmanship and the widow, thus proving the author's contention that business is romantic, but raising the question as to why, then, he left it.

Schoonover's *The Quick Brown Fox* and Prosser's *Nine to Five* stick, as the title of the latter implies, pretty close to the office, but office gossip and office sex are the stuff of which these novels consist, and they are not so much business novels as novels of manners set in the office.

A vastly more comprehensive and detailed picture of what the office is like has been presented by Cameron Hawley than by any other American author. Both his *Executive Suite* and *Cash McCall* have been hailed as the business novel America has been waiting for. Dreiser and Lewis and Wilson have all known what the office furniture looks like, but Hawley knows not only that but also about tax losses and capital gains, about

Regulation W and the union check-off, about the production line and the designing room, and about machines and sales.

Yet if Hawley is knowledgeable about business, he is naive about literature and has only a rudimentary imagination, with the result that his image of the businessman is nothing but a hackneyed stereotype of the indispensable, lonely, all-knowing success hero, a pale, second-hand version of Frank Cowperwood.

Don Walling, in *Executive Suite*, knows that "there could be no partnership! That was ridiculous.... There was room for only one man at the top of the Tower . . . one man . . . one voice . . . one strong commanding hand!" And just as Walling sweeps everything before him in the directors' meeting and is elected president, so Cash McCall moves from one capital gains deal to the next with triumphant and scornful ease. Because his business heroes are such stereotypes, they are never able to make contact with the very real problems of the business world which Hawley presents so fully and convincingly.

There is nothing, finally, that Hawley's supermen cannot do, no one who can match Walling, no one who can stop Cash McCall as he storms down the runway in the converted B-26 which is his private plane and climbs high into the air, leaving the office behind.

The example of Hawley and the other businessmen-novelists demonstrates first of all that although most writers since Howells have seemingly been unable to write about business because it has not come within their experience of things, inside information is not necessarily the key to writing about the office; further, it recalls James's emphasis on "the grasping imagination" as the *sine qua non.*

Yet the history of the American imagination from James to the present testifies that no writer has ever succeeded in conveying in a literary work of art what goes on in the daily lives of millions of Americans. Whether this is the fault of the writers or of the subject is not clear. Books, conversational reminiscences, the briefest glimpse, the least hint, have proved sufficient for the imaginative recreation of other forms of human endeavor; Stephen Crane had never been under fire when he wrote *The Red Badge of Courage*, perhaps the finest of all American war novels. But, for whatever mysterious reason, no stimulus has similarly kindled the imagination of the writer about business.

It is always possible, of course, that the office will acquire its Stephen Crane at some time in the future. Yet, on the record, it would appear doubtful. (pp. 121-24)

> *Kenneth S. Lynn, "Authors in Search of the Businessman," in* Harvard Business Review, *Vol. 34, No. 5, September-October, 1956, pp. 116-24.*

WILLIAM G. SCOTT

[*An American educator and critic, Scott frequently writes on labor management and human relations. In the following excerpt, he analyzes the "hero-manager" in American fiction of the twentieth century.*]

Currently a battle is progressing among writers, revolving around the central issue of whether or not managers in this decade are regimented conformists, and whether or not a basic shift in values made them the way they are. Much of the commentary on this subject is quite stimulating. However, students of management in the rush to keep current on nonfiction literature in the field often overlook the contributions that the novelists have made which bear on the conformity problem and many other subjects of pertinence to management. (p. 1)

The young middle manager is the most frequently appearing hero in the novels, but in addition to him is a large assortment of other people. The middle managers, the top managers, the operators, and the wives of managers display a vast spectrum of emotions and motives.

Some of the characters in business novels are hedonists, some are human relationists, some are conformists, others are non-conformists. Despite this diversity of characterizations, one thing is fairly clear about the people who are portrayed in the business novels. It is that they move in a world of paradox. Some of the conflicts they bring on themselves, other conflicts they face are generated by the nature of the business system.

A few characters in the novels are steadfastly certain that their faith which guides them in the business world is right. More often, however, the fictional personality is not sure where his belief lies and is searching for conviction. (pp. 1-2)

With the notable exception of Babbitt, the hero-manager is a tough-minded individualist. He is a man who does things. He creates and loses fortunes; he influences the economy of the country; he exploits resources; he engages in shady operations; he makes and ruins thousands of lives. In short, the hero-manager performs in the best bravura tradition.

The early hero-manager was a believer in the individualistic ethic. He practiced a laissez-faire doctrine in his business career and his social life. He was not a conformist in the "organization man" sense. The organizations he created reflected his personality and required his existence for their survival. He was the top man in the organizational structure. For good or for bad, the early hero-manager was not run by the organization; he ran it.

However, the novelists of this period did not foresee a particularly prolonged future for the hero-manager they portrayed. Dreiser, for example, had Frank Cowperwood bloodied in two novels by the force of the mass. Dreiser and other important early business novelists seemed to be certain that individualism is quite futile.

If the managerial characters in Dos Passos' trilogy *USA* are overlooked, the hero-manager disappeared as a personality in [the 1930s]. The novels of this period were largely "system" oriented. Managers tended to be disembodied. They floated around in the background as tools of the capitalistic machine. Their job, willingly or unwillingly done, was to exploit the masses. Steinbeck in *The Grapes of Wrath* refers to managers impersonally as "They." "They" are the puppets of the capitalistic monster. The managers did not reappear as personalities until well into the 'forties.

Howard Upton grasps his literary cudgel and in the *Saturday Evening Post* defends the modern male in the business rat race. The critics of the businessman, relates Upton, feel he has succumbed to three peculiarly American evils—conformity, security, and the "buck hunt." The truth, Upton tells us, is that the Old Rat Race is not as bad as many writers would have us believe. Concluding his article, Upton says:

> But those who stay—those who elect to continue in the Old Rat Race—require neither apology nor explanation. They need not rationalize. When you look at the total picture, it is not the

militant nonconformist, cultivating a beard and painting seascapes in Sausalito, who is the hero of our age. The real hero is the fellow you see there with the brief case, waiting to catch the night plane to Houston to see what he can do about sacking up that big double-threaded pipe order.

This observation has much insight. However, while Upton thinks conformity to the Old Rat Race is praiseworthy, the novelists feel it is lamentable. The real significance of Upton's article is not what he says, but his compulsion to justify modern managerial work and life. Upton rails against the novelists' conception of the hero-manager. (pp. 2-3)

The new manager is a hero, not because he does great or daring deeds, but because he puts up with grinding mediocrity and conformity. [In John P. Marquand's novel *Point of No Return*] Malcolm Bryant, cultural anthropologist, says to Charley Gray, bank middle manager:

> "Charley," he says, "you've got a lot of guts."
> "How do you mean, guts?" Charley asked.
> "Saying what you do," Malcolm said, "doing what you do, takes guts. You're a very nice boy, Charley."

The temptation is strong to abstract a profile of the hero-manager from novels and show him as a conforming automaton. There would be some accuracy in such a profile, but it would not be a true representation. It would not be entirely accurate because there is also a spirit of rebellion in the hero's personality. To be sure, this spirit in some of the heroes is stifled, and in others it boils over. But in most cases, no matter what the hero does in the end, somewhere along the line he rebels.

The hero-manager is a dependent employee. He works for a company in which he occupies a management position somewhere at or above the middle. *He is not at the top or at the bottom of the managerial structure.* The hero-manager actively participates in or is directly affected by committee action. Hence, he is largely divorced from the necessity of making or carrying the responsibility of major decisions. In short, he is a member of a team.

As a team member, priority is given to "getting along with people." The manager should be a relationship expert. He has to "deal" with a large number of people at different levels and in different functions in the organization. Being a member of a team, the manager must constantly be aware that his actions contribute to the good of the group. If they do not, his managerial abilities are suspect, regardless of his success in performing the technical side of his job.

The amount of conformity, standardization, apple-polishing, and general banality to which the hero-manager often is subjected is appalling. The organization is a "velvet trap" that threatens to vaporize the hero-manager's individuality but offers security for this price.

And security is important because, like Charley Gray in *The Point of No Return,* many of the hero-managers have gotten themselves submerged by family and time-payment responsibilities. Continued attachment to the organizational umbilical cord is the easy way out for the hero-manager. As dependent employees, all they can sell are their brains, their individuality, and their lives.

They sell their lives because the influence of the job extends beyond the eight-hour day at the office. The organization lays down rules, formal and informal, governing the type of home in which they live, the kind of car they buy, the club to which they belong, and the acquaintances they make. It even determines the ideal mold into which a manager's wife should be pressed. (p. 3)

Conformity among the early hero-managers was pragmatic. When it paid to conform, they conformed. They discarded conformity when it was no longer useful. Only Babbitt made conformity a way of life. Today, for many hero-managers, security and conformity go hand in hand. Since security seems to be an important work motive, conformity results.

But this is too simple. Conformity arises from the nature of organizational systems. A growing government or business bureaucracy is an ideal medium for breeding standardization. Bureaucracy could not work without well-disciplined, conforming employees. This point is made by Ernst Pawel. In his book *From the Dark Tower* he presents a powerful indictment of a modern business bureaucracy. As he puts it, "the reign of the clerk in all its variations, from the Tower on the Square to the Superstate on the Volga, is dedicated to the extinction of man's awareness of himself.

The Tower, the center of a huge insurance company, is a symbol of the destruction of the person by the organization. The Tower, like "Big Brother," is mother and father to all, offering universal security. The fact that a manager sits at the top of the company or occupies a lowly rank is immaterial. He is a clerk who does the bidding of the organization.

Pawel looks sourly at another aspect of the modern corporation—the committee. The endless amount of committee activity to which managers are subjected is a product of business bureaucracy. Committee behavior is typified by compromise and thus places a premium on conformity. The committee conveniently relieves the individual from responsibility for major decisions. This fact, of course, increases personal security. (pp. 3-4)

As suggested before, conformity radiates beyond the company. The novelists see it extending into the manager's home life. The wife of the hero-manager in earlier novels was relatively detached from the business career of her husband. This situation is not always so in contemporary fiction. The wife frequently is intimately concerned with the progress of her husband in the company.

Nancy, Charley Gray's wife, is a good example of wifely preoccupation with her husband's business fortunes. She was not so much concerned that business success might be a source of satisfaction for Charley. Rather, a promotion means more money, and a surer route to the good life.

But what is the good life? Charley Gray is not sure. A better home, a better car, a nicer club, a good education for the children—all appear to be at stake. However, success seems to boil down to giving a man an opportunity to conform at a plusher level. So he gets a promotion! This means giving up one set of superficial acquaintances and assuming "friendships" with another set. The standards and values lived by do not change, despite changes in income.

The hero-manager and family live either in a suburb or what Spectorsky might call an exurb. For the hero-manager, home is like a dormitory; he spends his evenings and weekends there, but large portions of his hours awake are consumed by commuting and working in a urban center. The urban center in the novels often is New York City.

The wife, of course, remains at home in the community during the day. Her life is involved with children, "constructive" community activities, and other wives. These communities are matriarchies. Because of employment in distant locations, the hero-manager is physically removed from domestic problems. Rearing children and making important family decisions are left to the wife. The wife becomes quite pecuniary-minded since children and other matters associated with running a home and maintaining community status cost money. Naturally, when the husband and wife engage in a little introspection about the pleasure-pain calculus connected with making money, the wife usually is for a lot more "pain."

The wife also has to worry about company acceptance as well as being accepted in her community. Two recent novels by Howard Swiggett bring out some problems involving wife-organization relationships. Swiggett is engrossed in showing a foreign woman's reaction to American business patterns, and American response to foreign women. In both his novels, *The Power and the Prize* and *The Durable Fire*, the main female characters are European imports.

In these novels, the hero-manager is involved with a foreigner in some amorous capacity. Stephen Lowry (*The Durable Fire*) was married to an Estonian. Cleves Barwick (*The Power and the Prize*) got himself mixed up with a refugee pianist in England. The "carryings on" of these hero-managers with Europeans of "dubious" backgrounds was looked on with suspect by the top managers of their corporations. The bosses' worry was that the hero-managers' women might not "fit in" with the company family.

Being able to "fit in" naturally presumes some kind of mold to fit into. The novelists do not spell out the mold pattern. But the ideal and successful organizational wife is often depicted. She is intelligent but not too intelligent. She should be a white American of not too humble origins. The wife must dress well. Above all, she should never take a blatantly active part in pushing her husband. Rather, the ideal wife should operate in a "nice" way behind the scenes.

A system which demands identification and personality digestion is bound to cause even the least sensitive of souls to rebel. The novelists' treatment of the rebellious spirit makes an interesting analysis. The nature of rebellion is not the same among hero-managers, although the differences may be more a matter of degree than kind.

At one end of an extreme is Charley Gray. He feels his life is contrived, something out of a soap opera. Will Junior go to Prep school? Will the family get a new car? Everything depends on Charley's promotion. On the way to Tony Burton's house (Tony is Charley's boss) Charley begins to question the values of the whole thing, much to his wife's dismay. The dinner party, given by the Burtons for the Grays, is to be the setting for the "moment of truth" about Charley's promotion. Before the news is revealed Charley really does not give a damn about the new job. He actually feels free for the first time in a long time.

Of course, Charley does get promoted. Burton infers there was never any question of it. But Charley was dangled so long, so unmercifully, he was too numb to appreciate it. Naturally Charley accepts. What else can he do—he is at the point of no return.

Marquand's picture is one of helplessness and frustration for Charley and presumably for others like him. They have virtually no control over their destinies. Charley's rebellion was personal and ineffectual. Charley is caught.

Abe Rogoff, a character in Pawel's *From the Dark Tower,* is at the other end of the extreme. He lives in a suburb dedicated to security, conformity, and the "good life." Abe works for an insurance company which is dedicated to making money and converting employees to happy, satisfied nonentities. He is not about to let this happen to him. Abe is different from most hero-managers because he is an intellectual who never quite recovered from his Bohemian past. He is also a Jew, which is definitely against him as far as his company is concerned.

Abe sees his life much the same as Charley Gray—phoney and artificial. However, Abe had the courage to chuck it all when the boss offered him a new "challenge" in the company. Abe's rebellion is overt, but he was in a better position to pull out. At least he had certain literary talents which gave him some independence. Charley Gray had nothing to make him more than what he was, a dependent employee for the rest of his life.

There is a large assortment of other characters between the extremes of Gray and Rogoff. They are too numerous for a discussion of each. However, Tom Rath, the gray-flannel suit man, is important enough to receive some attention.

Rath is neither a Gray nor a Rogoff. If any parallels are to be drawn, Rath is kind of a post-World War II edition of Dos Passos' Charley Anderson to the extent that wartime experiences colored his civilian life. The reactions of the two are different though. Anderson is dead set on seeing how fast he can kill himself, whereas Rath wants to return to the quiet, secure life.

Tom Rath wants two things—money and security. He never really rebelled against the business system. Rath was a split-the-difference man. Rath acted quite consistently with this observation in his business career. He figured ten thousand dollars a year would be sufficient to entice him away from the Foundation for which he worked at the beginning of the story. The broadcasting company with which he was seeking a job offered him eight thousand; they settled on nine.

Tom Rath wanted a job which offered sufficient but not a lot of money. In turn, he was not willing to take on responsibilities which would separate him too much from his family. About the only rebellion on Tom's part was his refusal to accept more responsibility.

In this respect, there is an interesting contrast between Tom's and Hopkins's lives. (Hopkins is president of the company). Hopkins's marriage is a failure and his daughter a problem. Reason? Hopkins devoted too much time in the past to being a success. Tom does not want this to happen to him and his family. Justifiable? It depends on an individual's set of values. Yet someone has to sacrifice something for the sake of success and progress.

The moral of *The Man in the Gray Flannel Suit* is hard to determine. Probably it is "to each his own." But some writers see business breeding too many Tom Raths and not enough Hopkinses. The gray flannel suit has become a symbol and a specter of conformity.

Rebellion against organization has a curious counterpart. In several novels, the hero-manager has found a valley for himself. His valley is an idealized place. The peace, simplicity, and virgin beauty of "the valley" starkly contrasts with the world of business.

Cash McCall has his valley—Aurora. Jim Coutler, in Bernard Lester's *Weatherby Crisis,* has a retreat in a valley filled with happy rural folk. And Abe Rogoff, after he breaks with "The Tower," finds refuge, where else but in a valley out West. Ayn Rand has John Galt building a new world in a valley in *Atlas Shrugged.* Although the valley is quite real for these hero-managers, it also has certain allegorical qualities. The valley is *too* perfect; the life is *too* good; and the folk are *too* kind. The valley is roughly the equivalent of positive mental hygiene or tranquilizers. Some psychologists might say the valley represents a retreat to the womb.

A valley, as such, is not present in all the novels. But the fact that one exists in four lends a certain symbolic significance to it. It is a place to escape and to sublimate. The "valley" perhaps stands for sanity or a reality greater than business life. The hero-managers who have their valley seem to face life more confidently than those who do not.

As previously observed, the main character in contemporary fiction is usually a man who is located in the lower ranks of the organizational hierarchy. However, the novelists also treat the man at the top of the organization. Even though this man is not a central figure in novels, a few words about him would not be a waste.

These men at times exhibit considerable identification with the organization. Peabody is a case in point. He reveals to Abe Rogoff that a man cannot, absolutely cannot, no matter what his position is in a company lead two separate lives, meaning a private life and a company life. The private life of a manager must always be interpreted and conducted from the standpoint of what is good for the company. This is sound advice for avoiding a split personality, but at the same time it cuts off the private life of a manager as a source of expression. In part, Abe Rogoff rebelled against this philosophy.

In quite another vein is the "double standard" philosophy found among top managers. This philosophy assumes different forms. Salt, for example, objected strongly to Cleve Barwick's affair with a European pianist. On the other hand, Salt, himself, had kept a mistress for years. Apparently Salt interpreted his own actions as not having any effect on the prestige of the company. But Barwick's "indiscretion" might have serious foreign repercussions. The top managers' attitude seems to be that individualism is all right for them, but their subordinates should support a "team work" or "group first" philosophy.

More basic than the foregoing is the "double standard" philosophy applied to organization objectives. A knotty problem in Cameron Hawley's *Executive Suite* seems to turn on a "double standard" consideration. Don Walling, in his over-the-goal speech for the company presidency, emphasized two objectives. The first objective is structuring a company in which the men could take pride. The second objective is growth. These objectives are not incompatible. But together, in Walling's mind, they constitute ends which precede profits in a form that will be returned as dividends to the owners.

This attitude is curious but perhaps not unrepresentative of the real world. It could be that Don Walling is voicing the philosophy of an employee-management centered organization.

Growth, plus happy workers, indeed may be the monument to achievement for the professional top executive. The matter of the "double standard" comes in when a return to the absentee owners of the corporation is considered. Their place in the structure is apparently vague in Walling's scheme. Management's obligation to the stockholders, according to Walling, is to keep the company *alive*. The subtlety of Walling's argument is the shift in emphasis from the "pure" notion of management stewardship for the owners to a philosophy designed for management ego-satisfaction and worker welfare.

Sincerely, Willis Wayde, by John P. Marquand, is a "success" story about a man who possesses "classic" administrative qualities. Willis sees the "broad" picture. Much the same is true of Cameron Hawley's character, Cash McCall. The interesting feature about these two men is that they are able to move successfully in the ambivalent business environment which sways between the individualistic ethic and the human relations ethic. Indeed, they are sensitive enough to this environment to be able to exploit it for their own "unaltruistic" ends. Neither of the two fits the "organization man" prototype.

Willis Wayde is more reasonably a "Carnegie man" because he did not drink (to excess), speculate, or endorse notes. Cash McCall and Willis Wayde are smooth. But, more important, they grasp and intelligently apply administrative principles, and thus are led to success.

Cash McCall and Willis Wayde have administrative savvy. Both are professionals at the job of salvaging lost business causes. And although Willis is probably more identified with the firms which employ him, this does not prevent him from making changes advantageous to himself and, for that matter, to the company. (pp. 4-6)

A number of critics say that the dilemma of the modern manager arises from two conflicting systems of thought which are, as previously stated, the individualistic ethic and the human relations ethic. The current fad of the human relations point of view, so the argument goes, has as a by-product converted managers into conformists.

Without question, the presence of the human relations ethic in modern business has impressed itself on the novelists and the books they write. Many novelists react against the code of conformity which they see imposed by the human relations ethic. In a way, this adverse reaction parallels the criticism by earlier novelists of the individualistic ethic. Perhaps it is the function of the novelists to rebel against popular notions. (p. 7)

> William G. Scott, "The Novelists View Management," in The Atlantic Economic Review, *Vol. VIII, No. 10, October, 1958, pp. 1-7, 20.*

THEMES AND TECHNIQUES IN BUSINESS FICTION

VAN R. HALSEY

[*In the following excerpt, Halsey compares themes, characterization, and fidelity to the everyday realities of business in serious and popular American fiction from 1900 to 1959.*]

When the historian examines business fiction, he looks at a particular group of novelists and his guideposts are most often those novels written by such artists as Frank Norris, Theodore Dreiser, Sinclair Lewis or John Marquand. These novels and others like them written by outstanding American writers are well known. The authors are spoken of as social critics and, almost without exception since before the turn of the century, their novels have been attacks on business values and the businessman.

From the power-hungry Frank Cowperwood of the Dreiser trilogy to Marquand's other-directed Willis Wayde, the men who have played a dominant role in our economic development are presented either as immoral scoundrels of the worst sort, smashing everyone and everything that threatens their own self-interest, or, more recently, as frustrated, unhappy creatures condemned for life to a meaningless routine marked by moral compromises and petty goals, and completely devoid of any sense of fundamental values.

For every one of these books criticizing the businessman, there are published dozens of business novels which are generally much more favorable in their treatment. These are the marginal novels designed for the mass market in the hope that perhaps one out of a dozen may achieve a momentary success. Those who seek redress from the continuing literary assault look to these books. But because they are poor novels, poorly executed, they never achieve a permanent place in the annals of American literature, and five months after publication, copies of most of them can only be discovered in the Library of Congress or at remainder sales. From the books of H. K. Webster and Charles Lush of an earlier era to those of businessmen-authors Howard Swiggett and Cameron Hawley today this surprisingly large group of novels takes on the aura of the class B western. The "bad guy" always loses out or reforms, and the traditional values of individualism, honesty and hard work point to a rich and creative life for the hero. And it is this conformity to the current business ideology which gives them their brief success.

There is a third and larger body of fiction closely related to the second which is just now beginning to be adequately dealt with. This is the magazine fiction. The mass circulation magazines, *Munsey's, McClure's* at the turn of the century, and *The Saturday Evening Post, American Magazine* (until its recent demise) and *Cosmopolitan* today, have printed an interminable stream of sugar-coated, situational and stereotyped business stories. In character type and in plot resolution they are similar to the potboiler novel, and for purposes of this essay, the two bodies of fiction will be classified together as marginal literature.

Now, as William Van O'Connor and others have pointed out, the true artist is not necessarily concerned with adherence to actuality. His stories are not meant to be mere transcripts of social situations, and the "better he is as an artist the more likely it is that his imagination will have greatly transformed what he has taken from among commonplace data and events." It is the marginal literature, close to the realities of the street, which provides the social, historical documents. Does this dichotomy apply to American business fiction? And if it does, then in what respects has the critical novelist transformed reality? Where does his portrait of the businessman diverge? Is the marginal literature completely faithful to the facts as we know them, or are there significant transformations and blind spots here also?

An examination of all the business fiction in three periods at twenty-five year intervals beginning in 1900 points to the fact that the critical literature differs from the marginal in three areas: the biographical data, and status in the business institution of the major figures; the description of actual mechanical details of the business and the hero's values in conflict with the business ideology.

At the turn of the century, as the studies of William Miller and Mabel Newcomer have shown, the largest proportion of big business executives came from families of comfortable circumstances, as indicated by their fathers' occupations. They were the sons of independent business executives or professional men, and almost half of them had at least some college education. Miller found that in 1900 only 14 per cent of the executives studied had started their own firms, and 27 per cent inherited the business. "Almost half of the leaders of American business were men who had been salaried officeholders virtually their entire business lives." It is in the marginal literature that these statistics are given life. The critical novels ignore them completely. The works of Frank Norris, Dreiser and Herrick are almost entirely devoted to studies of self-made men who, with an eye on the main chance, have reached positions of tremendous power without benefit of formal education and without becoming enmeshed in a salaried bureaucracy.

Furthermore, in magazine stories such as those by Edwin LeFevre and in the novels of David G. Phillips and other hack writers of the same period, one finds the details of the day-to-day operations of business fully outlined. The technical procedures by which the stock market could be manipulated, a railroad made to yield a profit or a small mining company started and built up to produce a fortune are given careful and accurate attention. In the critical novels like *The Octopus, The Memoirs of an American Citizen* and *The Financier* the reader hardly gets a glimpse of the inside of the office or of the detailed planning and carrying out of Cowperwood's or Harrington's schemes. Often the businessman is as much concerned with the social amenities as with his business transactions.

The final point of difference, the author's treatment of conflict and its resolution, is precisely the area which in most cases determines the literary fate of the story or novel. The mundane handling of completely stereotyped characters and situations consigns the marginal literature to a quick oblivion. One can predict in almost every case how the story will end. The unscrupulous banker or stockholder either meets his match in the honest and courageous young businessman who exposes his chicanery, dies of a heart attack at the moment when ultimate power is within his grasp, is persuaded by some beautiful girl to reform his ways or finally sees that "money isn't everything." All situations are either black or white in these stories, whereas the critical writers achieve their strength and assure their novels a prominent place in the literary histories by their deft and perceptive handling of complicated personalities caught in conflicts which have no easy solutions. Brought up in a naturalistic world, Frank Cowperwood has no alternative to corrupting legislatures in order to gain the traction franchise he seeks. The rewards in business go to those like Herrick's Van Harrington in *The Memoirs of an American Citizen* who are strong enough not to let the dictates of moral conscience interfere with the practicalities of getting ahead.

Of the many changes in business organization that occurred by 1925, none was more significant than the revolution in leadership and control. As Walter Lippmann had pointed out [in *Drift and Mastery*] in 1914, "the administration of the great industries is passing into the hands of men who cannot halt before each transaction and ask themselves: what is my duty as the Economic Man looking for immediate gain? They have to live on salaries and hope for promotion, but their day's work

is not measured in profit." In the twenties for the first time, the dominant figure in business was the salaried executive, employed by a company in whose ownership he had usually only a minority interest. Newcomer's study shows that, as an occupational group, the salaried administrator increased most rapidly between 1900 and 1925. As at the turn of the century, the largest percentage of these businessmen were the sons of business or professional people, and Taussig and Joslyn found "an unmistakable positive correlation between degree of schooling and degree of business achievement." An examination of the critical novels for this period reveals that, as far as indicated by the author, all major figures are still the self-made men who own and almost single handedly run their businesses without benefit of any college education. Again, it is in the marginal literature that the significant changes in business are explicitly documented. Of the fifty-three magazine stories and eighteen potboiler novels in the period 1925 to 1927, exactly half have as their major characters men who have been to college and now find themselves employed in a bureaucratic "system" where raises and promotions are the rewards for steady plugging or aggressive salesmanship.

The best writers of the twenties were more divorced from the actualities of business than ever before or since. Babbitt, Dodsworth, Gatsby and the others are merely men who happen to have business as an occupation. What goes on at the office is a mystery. It is the writers of the marginal literature who know exactly how "The System" ensnares the individual, and who describe the debilitating effects of the bureaucracy, while Lewis only speculates about it and then has Sam Dodsworth retreat to Europe. And it is in the so-called popular literature of the day that one finds the beginnings of the switch from "inner-directedness" to "other-directedness" forcefully enunciated. This shift in emphasis from things to people can be seen in the magazine stories in which the young executive recognizes that his own personality is responsible for a large part of his sales, and in the marginal novels like Edwin Balmer's *Dangerous Business*. In the early days of the father's firm there had been no competitors, "so people had to come to John Rountree and he could succeed, dealing only in things." But conditions changed and if the business was to survive personal relations were required with many sorts of people. Unlike his father, who distrusted people, the son was peculiarly well suited to this new business world because he was endowed with the "ability to succeed by merely forming personal relations which set at nothing and ignored his father's training to things."

The discussion thus far indicates that the writers of this marginal literature demonstrated a rather broad, if at times superficial, knowledge of the everyday realities of business. But they have only a limited insight into the subtleties of human nature, and their concentration on the commonplace precludes any sensitivity to the broader ramifications of what they are reporting. The rebellion, and the repudiation of authority and conformity which characterized so many areas of life in the twenties also manifested itself in all the literature of that era. The crucial difference between the marginal and the critical literature is that in the former, rebellion paid off in terms of financial success, while in the latter, it only resulted in an acute perception of the man's own inner failures. The escapist literature always provided an easy out for the businessman. To regain his self-confidence and find a satisfying life he had only to go off and start his own business, find another job which suited him better or tell his dictatorial boss or nagging wife what he thought of them. It hardly needs to be said that these pat solutions are a far cry from the futility of a Gatsby who had realized all his ambitions, or the frustrations of a Babbitt involved in a mechanical routine from which there could be no escape.

There have really not been enough first-rate business novels since the war to allow any significant comparisons with the marginal literature. John Marquand's *Point of No Return* (1949) and perhaps his *Sincerely, Willis Wayde* (1955) are the only two critical novels which will have any lasting value. When *Time* proclaims that the ''new novels reflect new understanding'' of the businessman, it is speaking of the recent spate of marginal novels, stories and TV plays. This large body of second-rate fiction is being written either by former business executives like Cameron Hawley, Howard Swiggett, W. H. Prosser and J. G. Burnett or by people like Sloan Wilson and Ernst Pawell who have little knowledge of business, but who have read the work of David Riesman and William H. Whyte. In biographical detail and accuracy of business mechanics the first group of authors bears out the most recent sociological findings. The novels of the second group abound in other-directed types and organization men. As transcripts of the daily record they are good, but in their attitudes toward business and in the sticky righteousness of their heroes they are still conforming to the myths and ideals of the business community. When Cash McCall scorns the company man and refuses to believe that ''always the individual must submerge himself in the mass''; when the aspirants for Avery Bullard's desk in the tower in *Executive Suite* recognize that ''there always has to be one man at the top. It can't be any other way,'' they are expressing the idealistic conceptions of individualism which have been one of the distinguishing features of the marginal literature since 1900. *Point of No Return* is the only recent outstanding artistic work, and, in keeping with the tradition of the past fifty years, it is still another attack on business. Charley Gray, the banker hero, realizes that the inter-office rivalry for the vice-presidency and the conniving it entails is ''all so superficial. The values of it are childish. It hasn't any values at all.'' And when he finally gets the promotion, there is no sense of fulfillment, only the dull feeling that although it had its compensations, it was not what he had dreamed. (pp. 393-97)

The artist, literary or otherwise, places a high value on the aesthetic, symbolic, emotional and personal experiences of life. His outlook is quite a different one from that of the businessman who is concerned with the more practical, material aspects. This difference puts the artist in fundamental opposition to the business ideology. He dislikes and is essentially hostile to the things that business and businessmen stand for. The writers of artistic merit . . . have found an outlet for this hostility in continuing criticisms of the businessman, and, because of their talent for literary expression, their novels have received wide attention and acclaim. (pp. 397-98)

[The] novelists of the past half-century who have produced really serious works of art were not writing simply to photograph business scenes from life. What the true artist does, to paraphrase a comment of Arthur Miller's, is to project through his personal interpretation of common events what he sees as their concealed significance for society. (p. 399)

With the emphasis on the vulnerable spots, his attacks on business and the businessman have led the critical novelist to overemphasize the weaknesses and faults, to concentrate on one or two aspects of life, at the expense of a broader portrait. Perhaps, too, the inaccuracies that have been noted are due, in no little part to certain preconceptions that the artist has of the businessman, and to a lack of any real knowledge of business and

how it has changed. In his recent book, *The Attack on Big Business,* John D. Glover examines the pattern and essence of the mass of criticism against Big Business since it came into being. Using primarily non-fictional source material, he finds that throughout all the criticism there is a basically hostile and unrealistic concept of the business unit. He further suggests that ''Big Business as an outstanding stereotype, has served for many people the same purpose as 'the Jew' served the Nazis. It has been a useful bête noire or whipping boy on which to focus all kinds of hostility. One can not help feeling that his observation is applicable, in some degree, to the critical novelists.

For these reasons, then, and in spite of the value of their work, the great writers of this century have created a collective portrait of the businessman which is less accurate than that of the writers of popular fiction. (p. 400)

[Both] the marginal and the critical can provide valuable analytical tools for an examination of society. But the two bodies of literature must not be used indiscriminately, as is too often the case. The former portrays rather accurately the day-to-day realities of the market place, but in its banal solutions to the moral problems and anxieties it merely furthers the myths and creeds of the business community. Unlike the popular writer who seeks to satisfy a demand of the moment through a sentimental and naïve treatment of the more superficial aspects of life, the literary artist explores the psychological and moral ramifications of experience. The Lewises, Fitzgeralds and Marquands are, to use Ezra Pound's comment on the intellectuals, ''the antennae of the race.'' Their sensitive interpretation of life often results in the projection of meanings or the creation of symbols. The historian and the sociologist can learn what questions to ask of the era he studies from the great artist whose creative tasks often expose social predicaments before the society recognizes them. But because of the artist's hostility toward business and his concern with the individual, he consistently presents a distorted concept of the businessman. This concept has been and will continue to be widely disseminated for the very good reason that the novels embodying this critical view rank among the best artistic works of our literature. (pp. 401-02)

Van R. Halsey, ''Fiction and the Businessman: Society through All Its Literature,'' in American Quarterly, *Vol. XI, No. 3, Fall, 1959, pp. 391-402.*

DANIEL SELIGMAN

[*In the following excerpt Seligman laments the lack of artistry in American business fiction and examines recurrent themes in ten business novels of the mid-1950s:* The Durable Fire *by Howard Swiggett,* The Man Who Broke Things *by John Brooks,* The Merger *by Sterling Quinlan,* The Blue Chips *by Jay Deiss,* Expense Account *by Joe Morgan,* The Wall-to-Wall Trap *by Morton Freedgood,* The Empire *and* The Ruling Passions *by George de Mare,* The Wheeler Dealers *by George Goodman, and* The Big Company Look *by J. Harvey Howells.*]

Why has no one yet produced an important novel about American business? The U.S. has been called a ''business civilization,'' and it is certainly true that millions of its citizens are engaged, emotionally as well as economically, in the world of business. There is much that is humdrum in business life, but there is much, too, that can truly test the human spirit. There is certainly no reason why an important novel might not have a business background, or why its central figures could not be illuminated in the conflicts of business life. The trouble with the novels at hand is that the conflicts are set up strictly for their own sake; they are not intended to illuminate anyone or anything. Whatever their capabilities, which in some cases are manifestly low, the authors of these books have certainly not *aimed* to do much more than tell adventure stories.

They have, indeed, developed a literary genre in many ways akin to the Western. Like the characters who populate most Westerns, the executives in these books tend to be wooden as baseball bats; they are "types" from some literary Central Casting, rather than whole men whom we may care about. The background may be a walnut-paneled office, rather than purple sage, and the uniform may be flannel rather than rawhide, but the literary level is about that of an "adult Western." Even some of the story lines are similar: the familiar problems of the green young sheriff called upon to tame a tough, wide-open town is replaced in *The Ruling Passion,* by George de Mare, by the problems of an inexperienced young management consultant called upon to take over the presidency of a huge but run-down chemical company. Our heroes are armed now with expense accounts rather than six-shooters, and the objects of their pursuits are vice presidencies rather than cattle rustlers, but the literary difference is nominal. Indeed, one of the authors, George Goodman, invites the comparison with a Western by characterizing a Texan in his novel as "one of the fastest draws in the West with a tax table." Mr. Goodman's *The Wheeler Dealers* is an expert piece of slapstick that satirizes just about everything on Wall Street, especially brokerage-house market letters.

If the modern business novelist does not look deep into his characters, he also does not look far beyond the business itself, or have any coherent point of view of the business order as good or evil; the system is taken as "fixed." The "literary socialists" of forty or fifty years ago—e.g., Upton Sinclair, Frank Norris, Theodore Dreiser—were hostile to business, and tended to view it as corruptive of the individual and society; they were often unfair, but the passion behind their point of view—or perhaps simply the fact that they *had* a point of view—resulted in books of much greater stature than the recent business novels. Socialism, of course, seems much less relevant to intellectuals today than it did forty years ago; but the world is still full of social injustice, and of problems larger in significance than mere success-striving. The present batch of business novels have their setting in a curiously static world, devoid of social problems; at least, the executives who populate the novels never seem to talk about anything except their own companies, families, and girl friends. (p. 104)

The corporations we are privileged to spy upon in these books impose on their executives no end of moral dilemmas, physical strain, financial problems, sexual temptations, and competitive strivings. Conflicts arising out of these five kinds of problems provide the main themes of the modern business novel.

Moral dilemmas. These come in all sizes and shapes, but the most common theme is profits vs. principles. . . . In *The Blue Chips,* the central question is whether a drug company shall rush to market a new antibiotic that seems not to have been tested adequately. The book's cover asks: "Can a fiery young man dedicated to the austere morals of medicine resist the temptations of the big money in miracle drugs?" The final answer appears to be that he cannot, any more than he can resist the boss's daughter; but the dilemma is blurred somewhat because the author, Jay Deiss, never makes it completely clear whether the drug *was* tested adequately, or whether the com-

pany is really to blame for the debilitating side effects the drug turns out to possess. In most business novels, it seems safe to generalize, the horns of those moral dilemmas have not had expert sharpening. What the author presents as a supreme test of his protagonist's courage or integrity is often nothing more than a muddle—in which a sensible man's first move would be to demand more information.

Physical strain. It is no secret that many businessmen work long, hard hours under great stress, and that some are literally killed by their jobs. But it is hard to see how the U.S. could have a gross national product much larger than Paraguay's if real-life businessmen were felled by strokes, coronaries, emotional collapses, and alcoholic collapses as regularly as fictional businessmen are. In eight of the ten novels [discussed in this essay], one or more of these calamities befalls a central figure and alters the course of events dramatically—at least, drama is the author's intention. It may be significant that the two novels in which there are no collapses, *The Wheeler Dealers* and *The Man Who Broke Things,* are both about Wall Street "operators" rather than executives. In any case, the executive life is implicitly held responsible for the breakdowns that occur in the other novels. Oddly enough—or perhaps just because they are not very dramatic—ulcers do not figure importantly in any of the novels.

Just as amnesia is traditionally the most popular illness in radio soap operas, the heart attack is far and away the leading medical menace in business novels. In *The Ruling Passion,* the hero actually suffers *three* heart attacks, one on the day he fights with his boss in a management-consulting firm, a second when he is appointed president of Transcontinental Oil & Chemical, and the third just after he wins a bitter fight for control of the company. In *The Merger,* a novel about two young executives who manage television stations, one of them suffers a heart attack, and the other what is described, a bit vaguely, as "a general collapse," brought on by "this atmosphere, this terrible life." The heart attack serves some authors as a kind of large punctuation mark, to be placed after a turning point in the story; it has the effect, thereby, of reminding the reader how tough things are in the executive rat race. But the heart attack can also be useful in removing the hero's competitors from his path of advancement. The protagonist of one novel, who is a research scientist, rises to the top more or less literally over the dead bodies of two other scientists (one stroke, one coronary). The story line in another book hinges on a competitive struggle that breaks out after a heart attack lays low the company chairman.

The only medical problem comparable to heart attacks in business fiction is alcoholism. In one novel, a prominent executive actually ends up as a Bowery derelict. Another ends with the protagonist getting drunk after being fired as executive vice president, and setting out to sea alone in a small boat, still drinking.

Financial problems. "He lived like a king on the swindle sheet while his wife pinched pennies at home." This one-sentence summary appears on the cover of the Signet Book edition of Joe Morgan's *Expense Account,* probably the first novel in history to be built entirely around the problems and opportunities of expense-account living. The book chronicles the woes of Pete Cody, a $13,000-a-year executive whose company won't give him a raise but nevertheless forces him to live in a fairly elegant style. Pete runs wild on his expense account, which is not ordinarily questioned because everybody knows that Pete's job requires him to perform some expensive and sometimes unsavory operations, like procuring girls for clients. Even so, Pete has his problems. "I spent $607," he complains to an associate, referring to an evening on the town, "but the most I can get on the damn form is $522, and half of that is phony." His associate remarks sympathetically that "there ought to be a space for 'whoring' and another for 'gambling'" and advises Pete to put down some sizable sums for taxi and rail fare—even though he had not left the company's home city. Pete thereupon puts down $140 for taxi fare and $275 for train fare; and the company's auditor, after pondering the case carefully, approves the expense account.

Although *Expense Account* is unique in the attention it gives to the problem, several other books also have a lot to say about the financial squeeze on middle-rank executives. In *The Big Company Look,* the supervisor of brands for the United States Grocery Co. suffers an emotional crisis when a $4.63 check he has cashed at the office is returned for insufficient funds; with five days left until payday, he has to borrow money to cover the check. He too is somewhat imaginative with the expense account, but no one is as systematic about it as the hero of *The Wall-to-Wall Trap.* The latter describes his method as

> classic, pure, almost austere in its adherence to formula. First, referring to notes, I jotted down on a piece of scrap paper the precise amount of my own money I had spent, and the occasion of the expenditure. Then I invented three additional dates (people I *might* have bought lunch or dinner for), with appropriate sums for each. Next, I added four dollars to each legitimate item, and two dollars to each illegitimate item. I multiplied each entry by two, tacked on 68 cents to the topmost (a good-luck fetish), and added the whole. As a final step I transferred everything to the voucher, and signed my name with a sense of having been intensely scrupulous.

Sex in business. In all of these novels the heroes are repeatedly beset by sexual temptations. This can scarcely be considered surprising, since it is a plain fact that the business world is inhabited by men and women. At the same time, it may be questioned, again, how large the G.N.P. would be if real-life executives were implicated in as many affairs as fictional executives seem to be.

The sexual life of the fictional executive is, on the whole, sordid. Call girls are provided by the corporation in several of the books, and while our heroes generally decline this appurtenance of the executive life, it is clear that their associates are less fastidious. A sizable number of fictional executives appear not to have any sexual relations with their wives, either because they are concentrating their energies entirely on "getting ahead," or because there is an attractive and complaisant girl in the office. Some variant of the line, "What are you going to say tomorrow when you see me in the office?" (*The Big Company Look*), appears in several of these novels.

One recurrent theme, with overtones of both Freud and Horatio Alger, is the fatal appeal that the heroes of these novels often have for their bosses' wives, mistresses, and daughters. In *The Man Who Broke Things* the young newspaperman who has gone to work for promoter Hank Haislip makes a pass at Haislip's mistress but ends up marrying his daughter. In *The Blue Chips* the hero is seduced by the daughter of the chairman of

the board, and finally marries her (though his heart really belongs to a female laboratory technician).

But perhaps the most intriguing of all these executive-meets-girl situations is developed in *Expense Account.* In this novel the girl *is* the boss—i.e., the chairwoman of the board of the vast Cartwright Tool Co. She is a sensational brunette of thirty-odd, who dazzles any number of her employees by appearing in a bikini at an executive outing, and who at one point orders poor Pete Cody to help zip up her dress, insinuating meanwhile that he might have a try at zipping it down as well. However, the story ends happily with the chairwoman deciding to marry a European count and simultaneously offering Pete a big raise and promotion, though Pete decides to be a lawyer (presumably in partnership with men) instead.

Executive competition. Like *Executive Suite,* most recent business novels give us heavy doses of office politics. In the novels at hand, we may observe the manner in which the members of one company's publicity department strive to impose on each other the blame for bungled jobs; we see the making and unmaking of coalitions backing a candidate for the company presidency; we see the head of research slyly letting the president of a pharmaceutical company take credit for marketing a new drug, which, the research man knows, will soon prove to be a bust.... (pp. 105, 178-79)

[Most] of the novelists appear to believe that the "bad guys" are usually beaten in the end (as the double-dealing controller was in *Executive Suite*).

But there certainly are plenty of bad guys around, in these books, and plenty of frailties in the good guys. If these "business novels" had more genuine insight into badness and goodness, more insight into men and institutions, they might rise above the level of escape literature. Meanwhile they can be safely recommended to the businessman who wants something to take his mind off those real-life people and problems at the office. (p. 179)

> Daniel Seligman, "The 'Business Novel' Fad," in *Fortune*, Vol. LX, No. 2, August, 1959, pp. 104-05, 178-79.

A. D. VAN NOSTRAND

[*Van Nostrand is an American educator and critic. In the following excerpt, he demonstrates the influence of literary naturalism on American business fiction and examines varying treatments of the theme of success in John P. Marquand's 1949 novel* The Point of No Return *and five business novels of the 1950s that Van Nostrand considers inferior imitations of Marquand's work.*]

Popular fiction in America has always been in the peculiar position of having to justify success. The business novel is a persistent, local instance of this.

Success can be indiscriminately applauded, which is easy to do; it can be rationalized as inevitable and therefore right, which is a little more involved; or it can be explained, which is still more complex. Among contemporary business novels, the first which gained any popularity by trying to explain this inevitability was John Marquand's *Point of No Return* (1949). The present pathology of success in business novels really began with this book, which made a great many, and many different, audiences aware of a situation; and it made a singular impression on the book trade. In the flood of business novels which deluged the market after *Point of No Return* even the waves had waves. (p. 161)

Although not sensational, the book's sales were high, and they reflected the steady buying of distinctly different markets. The fact that eight different publishers have since anthologized parts of the novel indicates its appeal to a variety of tastes and judgments. Also, it had created this appeal at a time of a rising market for novels in paperbound editions. Mannerism was one obvious result. Clusters of business novels thematically similar to *Point of No Return* began to appear in the early fifties.

Point of No Return provided a point of departure for most of its successors. It dramatized a situation many novels have subsequently caricatured by exaggerating and simplifying it. But Marquand took a satirical—not a popular—view of his subject, and the mannerists, avoiding this view, have ended up with attitudes which do not fit the situation.

Marquand's novel dramatizes Charles Gray's career in the Stuyvesant Bank to that climactic point when he learns whether he or Roger Blakesley is to become the bank's newest vice-president. The job will ultimately lead to the presidency, and each man has committed himself and his family to a war of attrition for a prize which only one of them can have. It would seem so simple: Gray has an adversary competing with him for the favor of the bank's president, Tony Burton, yet this exhaustive personal conflict turns out to be irrelevant.

Gray realizes he cannot reduce the bank to any manageable or satisfying terms. "The Stuyvesant was the aggregate of the character of many individuals, who merged a part of their personal strivings and ambitions into a common effort." Gray conjures up metaphors to explain the bank to himself. "It was like a head of living coral rising above the surf, a small outcropping of a greater reef." And all of its individuals, from the doorman to the directors, "were . . . asses following their bundles of hay." "They were all on an assembly line, but you could not blame the line. It was too cumbersome, too inhumanely human for anyone to blame."

A few pages before the end of the novel, Gray is still trying to appraise it all. He and his wife have been invited to dine at Burton's home, obviously to be told the fate of his career. After a few more hours of attrition for the Grays, in social small talk with the boss and his wife, the gentlemen retire to the library, and Gray concentrates on the imminent disaster. In that short walk across the hall, "he was actually walking . . . over the road of his career, a feeble little human track like the progress of a sea creature in the sand."

Having seen his own tiny image, Gray begins to adjust to it. His career is as good as over, and he must retreat to a new position. He and his wife will sell their suburban house and move into a smaller place; they will give up their plans for the more exclusive country club and for private schools. He begins to realize how tired he has been. He will never have to try so hard again, or be so cautious or obsequious. Then a deep sense of relief overcomes him. " 'It's over,' he said to himself as he walked across the hall. 'Thank God, it's over.' It was the first time he had felt really free." But the shocking news of success explodes this peace.

Gray suddenly learns that he has won the job, in a manner that stuns him. Burton casually announces the fact, then shows surprise that there should even be any doubt. There has been no conflict between Gray and Blakesley as far as the Bank is concerned. "You never thought any of us were considering Blakesley seriously, did you?" Blakesley was just not the right material; and as for the vice-presidency, says Burton, "it never occurred to me that you'd have any doubts about it."

John P. Marquand. The Bettmann Archive, Inc.

It paralyzes Gray to learn that he has never had any control of the situation, that he has no more power to refuse the honor than he had in winning it. He feels dull and very tired. He foresees a new professional friendship with his employer, and transactions for a larger house, a new car, a more exclusive country club. Even before the end of the conversation he realizes he has never left the treadmill.

Gray has made no decision. His success, already decided for him, is analogous to his entire life. He cannot even discover where the point of no return occurred. There has been no point at all, but a line stretching back into his past, across which he could never step.

Growing up in a small New England village, Charles Gray has always known the primitive rituals of the caste system. But "system" means more in this book than merely social stratification. To Gray's father, for instance, it has meant the arrangement of one's whole economic existence. "The system is not fluid and it is very hard to beat," he says. "What system?" Charles asks. "Why, the system under which we live. . . . The order. There's always some sort of order."

The hero's father has cultivated an independence in social matters which has made him an eccentric to the rest of the community, as if he were trying to beat the system by scorning it; then, following the loss of an inherited fortune on the stock market, he proves his point by suicide. The son absorbs the lesson; as he later explains to his wife: "There's no use getting mad at the system. We're part of a system where there's always someone waiting to kick you in the teeth in a nice way." Gray solves the system by acceding to it, and the plot of the novel bears him out.

Charles Gray's debilitating success dramatizes the peculiar course of literary naturalism in America. You can see how small the businessman has shrunk when you measure Gray by another hero, Silas Lapham, about whom William Dean Howells wrote, sixty-four years earlier. The comparison is useful. *The Rise of Silas Lapham* (1885) presents a hero with a moral problem, involving financial success or failure, which he resolves by himself. Howells idealizes the individual's control of affairs, and thereby hangs another tale.

Silas Lapham manufactures a paint whose excellence has made him wealthy, and he determines to use this wealth to improve his family's social position. But Lapham has made a costly compromise with his conscience, having forced out of partnership the man whose money he once needed. When this partner returns and asks for help, Lapham's wife prevails on her husband to pay off his conscience. The ex-partner is dishonest, but Lapham pointedly ignores the bad risk and loans him large amounts just before his paint business begins to fail.

The hero must capitalize his business or go bankrupt, but he has loaned his capital and spent his credit. At this point the ex-partner reappears, having found some purchasers for the land Lapham holds as collateral on the loans, and which both men know to be worthless. The hero's dilemma is clear: to sell the land and recover his loss, or to refuse to sell and save the other party, and the author subjects him to all the tortures of righteousness.

Lapham spends the night pacing his room, and Howells likens his struggle to Jacob wrestling with the angel. Like Jacob, following the struggle, Lapham finds peace. He has victoriously decided to go bankrupt. Virtue triumphs. He loses the battle to win the great moral war.

The picture of this Victorian businessman wrestling with the angel apparently gratified the women who read the novel and dreamed of what a virtuous world it would be if their husbands would only listen to them. The fun of justifying success consisted in deciding the terms on which one would accept it. But what made the dream convincing was the assumption, which Howells shared with his readers, that man was a free agent in the first place.

Marquand and his readers share no such luxury. Within the literary history which contains both novels the fact of "scientific" determinism separates them. Toward the end of the nineteenth century, this doctrine became incorporated in a theory of composition known as literary naturalism, which aimed to document determinism in copious and authentic detail. With the illusion of complete objectivity, according to this theory, the novelist would prove that the individual man is a small and limited creature, determined by heredity or by the social or economic forces of his environment.

No one has yet written the novel which could perfectly conform to Emile Zola's definition of this theory—not even Zola. Because naturalism denies any special significance to human beings, it therefore denies the vitality of fiction. Nevertheless, the prestige of literary naturalism in Germany and France, the translation of Zola's literary criticism into English, and American fiction's affair with journalism have so influenced writers that virtually every economic novel in America after 1900 at least implies some reference to naturalism.

This theory reflects the change in the businessman from an active hero to a passive one, from a Silas Lapham to a Charles Gray. Business history records substantial cause for the ex-

tinction of a Silas Lapham from the business world. Lapham was an entrepreneur, owner and manager. During the twentieth century, however, business organization outgrew his kind. With the development of the great public corporations, even before World War I, ownership and control began to separate and to offer disparate images to the public mind.

During the thirties the concept of ownership changed as Big Business strenuously publicized the notion of a people's capitalism, dependent on many small stockholders. As for control, people gradually heard about a new kind of businessman, called the administrator. Here was a new image of the businessman. The image was anticipated by Adolphe A. Berle and Gardiner C. Means in their epochal study, *The Modern Corporation and Private Property* (1932). They discovered that some two hundred non-banking corporations dominated the national economy and that the control of these corporations lay not in their legal owners, the stockholders, but in their executive managers.

Manuals of business management sold briskly as early as the 1920's. By the time of World War II, James Burnham's *The Managerial Revolution* (1941) dramatized the new apotheosis of business administrators. The nation, said Burnham, must now acknowledge business managers as a new social group. This new professional manager actually controlled the instruments of production. But even the manager was only an employee. He had no function by himself. He was only a unit of the great business society.

No wonder Charles Gray sees himself as a small sea animal and the Stuyvesant Bank as the outcropping of a reef. *Point of No Return* uniquely represents its times, as Howells' novel once did. But in Marquand's view Charles Gray's promotion to the Bank's vice-presidency is distressing. This is where Marquand's successors part company with him. But they don't part very straight.

These mannerists exaggerate the plight of the businessman overcome by success, but they avoid any honest dilemma over it. Instead, they celebrate it. Their main problem, therefore, is to make it look as though there were a problem in the first place between the businessman and this benevolent business system. The best way to see this mannerism at work is to compare some of the caricatures of the passive businessman which followed *Point of No Return* to market.

Between 1952 and 1956, the five years during which the first paperbound edition of Marquand's novel remained in print, the most commercially successful business novels were Cameron Hawley's *Executive Suite* (1952) and *Cash McCall* (1954), Howard Swiggett's *The Power and the Prize* (1954,) and Sloan Wilson's *The Man in the Gray Flannel Suit* (1955). (pp. 162-67)

These books variously emphasize the most recognizable qualities of *Point of No Return*. A fifth novel, published during this period, is George DeMare's *The Empire—and Martin Brill* (1956). This novel amplifies the qualities of *Point of No Return* as well as those in its four other predecessors. But all of these latter novels are eclectic; they are all stylized.

The narratives differ. In all of them, however, a particular business enterprise becomes both the emblem and index of "the system." And most of them have inflated the net assets and size of the business and its control over the individual. The change from "company" to "corporation" and then to "empire" suggests their magnification of the system. Even Howard Swiggett's *The Power and the Prize,* the most apparently humanistic of them all, insinuates a benevolent determinism by a board of directors.

Swiggett's novel tells about Cleves Barwick, the executive officer of Allied Metals Corporation, and his endeavor to form an international company that will revolutionize the world production of nonferrous metals. But Barwick falls in love with a woman of whom the chairman of the board cannot approve. A refugee from Central Europe and a suspected Communist sympathizer, she would presumably become a liability to the Corporation. The chairman discredits Barwick's choice in such a way as to jeopardize the negotiations for the new company. Clearly, Barwick must choose between the woman and the company.

His defense of his fiancée rests solely on her denial of having been a Communist, and apparently he can reconcile the conflict only by lying. The Corporation's directors give him a chance to declare that he has already investigated her political past, thereby clearing the Corporation of any guilt which may befall her. Barwick refuses to lie, but an old movie "gimmick" saves him. The directors were merely testing his integrity. They know he has not investigated his fiancée, so instead of firing him for his testimony they promote him to the chairmanship of the board. With this endorsement he completes negotiations for the new company before embarking on his honeymoon.

Here is the old-fashioned conflict between love and duty, but Swiggett has updated it. The hero with a choice to make is not really a free agent. Although Barwick has maintained his right not to explain anything, the circumstances have been rigged. He is on trial before a jury which already possesses the facts and which conducts the prosecution. At the moment of his triumph Barwick is less the protagonist than he appeared. As with Charles Gray the system has acted benevolently, but in this novel nobody worries about it.

One might miss this subtle downgrading of the hero in an exalted system had not Howard Swiggett literally repeated himself in his next and final novel, *The Durable Fire* (1957). In this latter version of the same story the hero argues with his uninformed and hypocritical boss, and the case goes before the directors of the Corporation. It turns out, however, that these representatives of the benevolent system already know the facts and merely wish the hero to justify their decision in his behalf.

Business enterprise even more thoroughly pre-empts the individual in Cameron Hawley's *Cash McCall;* and by another round of inflation the presiding force of this business world appears even further removed from the company employees. This Olympian force is itself a business: the purchase and sale of corporations, sustained by the federal tax law's provision for capital gains. In this new world the oldtime religion of company loyalty loses favor, and the novel's apparent conflict proceeds from this fact.

Ownership has become a commodity. Brokers manipulate companies, often fraudulently for profit, denying the permanent value of a business and its service to the community. So it seems to Gil Clark, a young man dedicated to managing the Suffolk Moulding Company, which will apparently be sacrificed to this sort of manipulation. Gil finally meets his adversary, Cash McCall, the symbol of this system, the manipulator whose name has become legend.

But this Croesus confounds all expectations. He operates legally. "I don't make the rules, Gil. I only play the game. I never thought much of making the kick-for-point after touch-down, either, but as long as it's in the rule book, that's the way the game is played." What could be more American? Or more unassailably moral? "There's only one way I can get a wallop out of a deal like this, Gil. And that's by way of knowing that I haven't dug money out of another man's hide."

McCall is downright benign, as any magazine reader could tell in an instant: he is in his "late thirties, possibly forty . . . more like a professional athlete than a businessman." He also has impeccable manners, and although he owns unbelievable wealth (he smiles with a "purse-string puckering around the eyes") the name "Cash," rumors notwithstanding, he has legitimately inherited from his mother's family. Some more of his heritage conveniently explains his motives: through his father's futile wage-slavery Cash has learned to disdain company worship.

Having given him necessary credentials, the author enhances the hero with a kind of parental authority. He owns most of the corporations in sight, including the one which has currently employed Gil Clark. McCall has, in fact, secretly maneuvered that young man's career into his own orbit. As for Suffolk Moulding, the company whose disposition he presently controls, Cash McCall has only the most responsible intention. It turns out that young Gil Clark did not have any problem at all. He only thought he did.

McCall merges Suffolk Moulding with two other properties he has dramatically acquired, saving the stockholders—including a medical research foundation—from ruin, and so demonstrates his superiority to lesser-minded company men. His supra-business really nurtures what it seems to prey on. The benign force comfortably ruling the economic world, which depressed John Marquand's hero, has here become a happy inevitability.

This novel celebrates earned income—large amounts of it—for its own sake. Cash McCall even delivers a lay sermon, scolding Americans for their public discomfort over wealth. But faced with precisely this discomfort in the public mind and wishing to justify profit, the novelist traffics in attitudes. The sanctioning doctrine of Good Works has been at hand ever since Benjamin Franklin canonized the Arminian Heresy. So Cash McCall, like his patron saint, does well by doing good.

The happy doctrine of profit through Good Works also explains Cameron Hawley's earlier novel, *Executive Suite,* a splendid suspense story with a little something for everyone. This book deifies the materialist, but so covertly that the reader is never offended by his own appetite. The sudden death of Avery Bullard precipitates a crisis in the furniture business. Which of the five vice-presidents of the Corporation will succeed the late Mr. Bullard to the presidency? The leading contender is the controller, Loren Shaw, a relentless and aggressive man dedicated to company profits.

Shaw is a money grubber, a conniving materialist, and the book makes a heavy case against him, casting suspicion on all his motives. The movement in the company to stop Loren Shaw quickly settles on MacDonald Walling, the youngest of the vice-presidents. The erosive battle between these two recalls the earlier, mannered contest between Charles Gray and the man he thought he had to beat. In this one, however, Don Walling triumphs much more theatrically. He wins the directors' votes at a show-down with Shaw by an impassioned speech which states the theme of the novel—or seems to.

Walling's convictions are not at first entirely clear. He damns Mammon, specifically Loren Shaw's priority of stock dividends, he applauds high-quality products and recognizes the employees as human, and he promises new and greater growth for the Company. These comforting attitudes seem safe enough. But the rhetoric of Mr. Walling disguises some fortuitous illogic. Speaking in anger, he excoriates Avery Bullard, who had had an eye on the profits, who had "been so busy building a great production machine that he . . . lost sight of why he was building it." Yet Walling earns the vote, after some talk of making newer and better furniture, by promising to build an ever bigger company.

This young man surely offers the directors the image of his predecessor. But at the time the author throws the switch, after Walling's rhetoric, the directors scarcely realize that a vote for Walling is a vote for Shaw. This fact becomes magnificently clear when the visionary Walling appoints Shaw, the money-man, to the new executive vice-presidency, explaining: "I'll need somebody to help me keep my feet on the ground."

Further evidence of this union of purpose—presumably too complex—never reached the movies. In the film Loren Shaw bitterly concedes defeat, but not in the novel. Perceiving that Walling's presidency will be the best for Tredway and for its dividends, Shaw is among the first of the voters to throw his support to the young man. All's well with the company. The new president has sold a bill of goods. Unlike his adversary he has managed to present his materialism not merely as a matter of profit but as a mission to be celebrated. What counts with the directors is the moral hocus-pocus which disguises the materialism in the first place.

Slick fiction, John Marquand's included, contrives to make it easy for the hero to take what is coming to him. What comes is material well-being. But these later novels differ from their predecessor by renouncing the uncomfortable sense of compromise and by presenting instead some justification for the hero's happy retribution. The most striking example of such expedience is Sloan Wilson's *The Man in the Gray Flannel Suit.*

Like *Point of No Return* this tale begins in authenticity, telling the problems of a pleasant young man with his attractive wife and their average children, living in a normal, hectic world. Tom Rath has two problems, professional and private, which equally urge him on to self-discovery. Professionally, he must decide whether or not to be a businessman—to commit himself to executive endeavors in the communications industry—or to find a less demanding job which will offer dignity and spare time. Privately, he must decide whether or not to tell his wife about his paternity of an illegitimate child in Italy during the war. In the manner of a morality tale, each problem offers the hero neat and exclusive alternatives.

And he decides: professionally, to abandon the chance to be a gladiator and to accept the lesser job; privately, to tell his wife about his illegitimate son, and to secure her blessings in settling an annuity upon the lad. But as it turns out, the hero has had no problem at all, because he could afford, in each case, to make the morally preferable decision. In the novel's most revealing sentence, Tom Rath perceives that "money is the root of all order." Since he has inherited his grandmother's estate before having to decide his problems, his choices have none of the moral significance proclaimed for them. The hero has merely had to wait for circumstances to make it easy.

In this parody of Virtue Rewarded the reward comes first, and the author's contrivance makes a caricature of the benevolent society. When Tom Rath's legacy appears doubtful because of a counter-claim, for instance, a probate judge goes out of his

way to investigate the other claimant and to discover his dishonesty. The villagers, in effect, endorse a drastic exception to the zoning laws, allowing Tom the opportunity to turn his inherited land into a profitable development. Finally, when the hero denies the business opportunity offered him, even chastising his boss in the process, that unbelievably tolerant benefactor obtains for the hero a life-time sinecure.

It is all so appallingly easy. The novel scarcely honors its publisher's claim that it speaks for a whole generation. On the contrary, this hero's endowments are so special and his society's dispensations so tailored to his needs, that his gray flannel suit would not fit anyone else.

Stylization exaggerates gestures and attitudes. Each of these novels offers a comparative, and some a superlative, to what John Marquand has set down. Competition for the top job is more erosive, more obviously dramatic in *Executive Suite;* the hero is more willfully passive in Sloan Wilson's novel; and the company more specifically paternal in *The Power and the Prize,* yet dwarfed in *Cash McCall* by an economic force above and beyond even the corporation. In short, whatever the problem, it is more urgent in these eclectic novels.

These stylized attitudes are rendered by stylized conventions. The author's chore is to dispose satisfactorily of the hero's problem; or the other way around, to make it seem for awhile as though the hero has a problem. It is the same either way. Some evidence need only be planted early in the story, which the climax can then recall in reversing the situation. This is the "gimmick" in the magazines and the movies.

John Marquand plants his evidence for the climax of Charles Gray's struggle in a long, detailed flashback. This is Marquand's most prominent convention. The hero's past is the majority of the novel, and the whole of it is the evidence for the way things suddenly turn out. These latter novels by the other authors, however, stylize the effect of sudden reversal by leaving out the past which precedes it. The climax is more sensational that way, less mundane and more dream-like.

In *Point of No Return* the hero's success is decided for him because this is the way it has been all his life. The sequence of events accounts for this apparently incontestable logic. Marquand introduces the problem in the narrative present, then suspends it for a thorough and painstaking exploration of Charles Gray's past, during which the hero is seen time and again abiding by accepted conventions of behavior.

Growing up in a small town, Gray conducts a courtship across the tracks and then dutifully abandons it. He conforms to the accepted image of a young man in a brokerage house, even playing the stock market conservatively in an era of wild speculation. He repeatedly contemplates the joys of unconventional behavior, yet keeps his thoughts to himself. Tempering his private observations with public good sense, he earns the complaisance and benediction of friends and employers. This pattern repeats itself so often, throughout the middle half of the novel, that when Marquand resumes the problem of the vice-presidency, he has already and repeatedly signaled its resolution.

The narrative past has determined the narrative present. Charles Gray's conservative honesty in deference to the system is bound to win the system's approval. Once you know the past, granting a consistent character, there is no present problem. What at first appeared problematic turns out to be merely a foregone conclusion. So it is with H. M. Pulham and George Apley, in fact with most of Marquand's heroes.

Marquand manages a convincing surprise by making the evidence so obvious that the reader takes it for granted. The problem has apparently solved itself; it is a kind of optical illusion. This surprise by illusion is precisely the quality in Marquand's narrative method which succeeding novels have exaggerated. By a kind of fictional shorthand they have abridged the past tense, which in Marquand's novels solves the present problem.

None of these latter heroes has a past in the sense of a history already resolved. Except for fragmentary flashbacks identifying the characters, these novels remain continuously in the present. They have abridged that part of the narrative which accomplishes the solution, but they must still fulfill the fictional requirement of a conflict solved. They must come out even at the end. So instead of solving the problem they dissolve it.

This tour de force is like the solution to a puzzle, and just about as significant. Sloan Wilson's hero did not have to work at a distasteful job in order to support two families; he only thought he did, until his inheritance made everything dreadfully easy. Gil Clark, in Cameron Hawley's novel, merely thought the brokerage of corporations was malevolent, until Cash McCall revealed the truth. Don Walling never challenged the primacy of company dividends, in *Executive Suite;* it just took a little time for him to reveal himself as a more imaginative moneyman than his adversary. And was there ever any doubt that the directors would endorse Cleve Barwick's high-principled courtship? Only by assertion.

The difference between John Marquand's patently logical solution of a problem and the mere illusion of the problem in the first place also makes the difference between an attitude and the commercial exploitation of it. These latter books all say less than they seem to. By dismissing the problems they have posed they disqualify the attitudes these problems seem to have produced. The greater the exaggeration in the first place, therefore, the more obvious the fake. In the extreme this affliction reduces a novel to saying nothing of its own.

The fifth and most recent in this cluster of business novels, George DeMare's *The Empire—and Martin Brill,* reaches this point of oblivion. It tells of five employees in the public-relations department of a vast and anonymous organization. This nameless corporation, which sells an unknown product, is called merely "the Company," "the System," or "the Empire."

During World War II, the time of the story, the Empire's public-relations problem is to broadcast its vital importance to the national war effort. Its headquarters occupy a skyscraper in a large Eastern city, and the nerve center of these headquarters is on the top floor. The reader catches a glimpse of two vice-presidents, one floor below, mysteriously referring to the "Old Man," but that is as close as anyone gets to the soul of this system. According to the blurb on the paperbound edition (1957), "it might be called the story of the successful 'company man.' But it is also the story of hundreds of thousands of 'big company' employees whose dreams are never fulfilled, who find themselves imprisoned in a treadmill of frustration."

Of the novel's five case histories, one man commits suicide because his mistress denies him. The second becomes an alcoholic, loses his job, and tramps the streets. The careers of numbers three and four contradict each other. Number three stands firm on a moral matter (like Cleves Barwick in *The Power and the Prize*), gets promoted when events turn out to justify his position, and passes from view to the upper stories of the skyscraper.

Number four, who is morally dishonest, seeks preferment at the expense of his colleagues. When his connivance is discovered, the Empire awards him a horizontal promotion, and he passes from view among the lower stories of the skyscraper. The fifth man, Martin Brill, is the hero only by deference of the novel's title. He is kicked around the Empire and finally promoted to the chair of the man who first hired him. But on the way to this promotion he has suffered battle fatigue.

This schematization of the five characters accommodates the anonymity of the Empire. The only ruling force in the System is the irony of denial. The successful executive kills himself, the dedicated company-man gets fired. The employee who renounces preferment wins, and the one who puts it before all else loses. Martin Brill, the man alleged to have great expectations in the Empire, gets unaccountably shuffled off into a minor job and exiled from headquarters. Then, having given up, he unaccountably wins.

The anonymity, the irony, the lack of any cipherable plan, and the boss nobody ever sees are all symptoms of literary naturalism. Moreover, signs of earlier naturalists mark the final impression of this book.

> There in the misty afterglow of the fading light,
> it towered like a huge and shadowy fortress,
> heavy and sinister, rising out of the sea. It was
> the Building—the great, shadowy Building. It
> seemed to him, as he stood there gazing at it
> from the distance, as if it were a symbol of the
> whole vast Empire—the granite stronghold of
> the mysterious powers of the age—fabulous,
> immense, and strange. . . .
>
> . . . but the Company which would see thou-
> sands like them come and go, rise and fall,
> would endure, would remain there forever, sub-
> stantial, unchanging, powerful, enjoying a spe-
> cies of immortality, not as humans but as hu-
> manity itself, a monument to the creative force
> and endurance of collective men, no matter how
> mediocre—and to the power of human need.
>
> (pp. 167-76)

Perhaps there were more salable attitudes for this latter novel to absorb. The "system" in it is more pervasive than in *Point of No Return* and more impersonal than in *Cash McCall*. The retributions of the Empire recall the rewards and penalties of the board of directors in *The Power and The Prize*, although retribution no longer has any sense of necessity. *The Empire—and Martin Brill* attempts to show the *modus operandi* of the big company. But the anonymity defeats this, and the machinations degenerate instead into office politics, like those in *Executive Suite*.

The Empire—and Martin Brill is no copy. It is an original artifact. The author's personal experience in just such an actual business corporation, in fact, inspired his convictions. But he represented these convictions by literary conventions which served other needs in other novels. His compendium consequently attracts no central or compelling idea to his particular subject. Reading it is like wandering through a hall of mirrors, seeing only the distorted reflection of other books. (pp. 176-77)

A. D. Van Nostrand, "After Marquand, the Deluge," in his The Denatured Novel, The Bobbs-Merrill Company, Inc., 1960, pp. 156-77.

LEWIS A. LAWSON

[*Lawson is an American educator and critic. In the following excerpt, he analyzes picaresque elements in five novels set in the advertising and public relations industries.*]

The inception of the advertising/public relations novel is a comparatively recent development in the long history of that genre. In fact, this type of novel is scarcely fifteen years old, for *The Hucksters,* which John Kenneth Galbraith credits as the prototype, was published in 1946. Since that time, however, novels depicting the machinations of Madison Avenue have been published with ever increasing frequency. Three of the books to be discussed here, for example, were published in a single year, 1958. Even a cursory survey of the field reveals fifteen titles.

The reason for the growing frequency of publication for this type of novel is subject to speculation. One explanation could be that the frequency reflects the expanding public awareness of the role of advertising in contemporary culture. Or, a second, somewhat more cynical, reason could be that the public did not discover the type until it was exposed to the cinematic adaptation of *The Man in the Gray Flannel Suit.* (There was a movie made of *The Hucksters,* but it never quite got off the ground, as they say in the vernacular.) A third explanation could be that there is a psychological as well as an etymological relationship between *novel* as an adjective and *novel* as a noun. This type might be popular just because it is new.

It would be extremely ironic if the third explanation were to prove correct. The topical interest of the advertising/public relations novel is fresh; that much is granted. The public is very much fascinated by the cobra of Madison Avenue. The purpose of many of these novels, however, is stale. If nearly all novels may be classified according to one of three purposes, presentation of entertainment, presentation of a problem, or presentation of an historical background, as Thrall and Hibbard say [in their *Handbook to Literature*], then the advertising/public relations novel falls more clearly in class one than in classes two or three. Specifically, the novels are more closely associated with the *novela picaresca* than with any modern form of the novel. It could be, as it were, that the public is dallying with an aged harridan, who apears youthful only because she has applied another thick coat of cosmetic.

My observations are drawn from five novels, two of which describe advertising, and three public relations. The two advertising novels, *The Hucksters* and *The Insider,* present the same plot structure; the protagonist is caught between the Scylla of the agency and the Charybdis of the client. The three public relations novels, *The Man in the Gray Flannel Suit, A Really Sincere Guy,* and *Pax,* display similar plots also; the protagonist is caught between his employer and the public. If there is any difference in personality between the advertising man and the public relations man, it is that the public relations man is alleged to have a system of ethical values. He has qualms about lying to the public, while the advertising man considers lying as one of the better weapons of the contact man. The similarities between the two types of men far outweigh the

single difference, though. The hero-heel of each of these novels is handsome, virile, and oh so intelligent. Victor Norman, in *The Hucksters,* is explicit on this point: "Oh, everyone in the ad game is intelligent. They have to be. You see, admen are half-creative." Unfortunately for those who are interested, Norman does not elucidate upon the other half. One may suggest that they are half-procreative.

To return to the statement that these novels are contemporary manifestations of the picaresque, some similarities in form should be discussed. As in the case of the picaresque novel, the advertising/public relations novel lacks a convincing climax. There have been so many crises scattered throughout the books that when the conclusion comes, the reader feels that he has been left hanging. Perhaps these climactic episodes are an inherent part of the adman's life in reality, but if they are, they take the edge off the climax of the adman's story in fiction. Moreover, the climax does not reveal a character change in the protagonist. Frederic Wakeman has the original adman, Victor Norman, painfully give up his love rather than soil her with the life of an adman's wife. But by remembering that Norman goes to bed with a casual friend *after* meeting the woman he gives up so heroically and that he begins an affair with *her* only five days after meeting her, even though her husband is away at war and she is the mother of two children, the reader may conclude that Victor Norman has precious little character to develop. The working out of the plot of *The Insider* may also be cited as an example of a weak climax. Morton Noyes, the protagonist, is down to his last Upmann and about to be fired by his agency when his wife and father-in-law conveniently die, and he is bequeathed an estate of three million dollars. A quotation from Thrall and Hibbard has significance at this point in the discussion of a rogue:

> There is little character interest. Progress and development of character do not take place. The central figure starts as a *picaro* and ends as a *picaro,* manifesting the same aptitudes and qualities throughout. When change occurs, as it sometimes does, it is external change brought about by the man's falling heir to a fortune or by his marrying a rich widow. Internal character development is not a quality of the picaresque novel.

Still another instance is provided by Bill McCrary, in *A Really Sincere Guy,* who rebels against his agency and takes his best client with him to form a new agency. Is rebellion so simple on Madison Avenue? One wonders. The classic climax, however, is in *The Man in the Gray Flannel Suit,* where Betsy Rath, in a scene calculated to put tears in the unguarded sentimental eye, nobly forgives her public relations husband for his wartime private relations and agrees to support the product of that affair. Incidentally, Linda McCrary, in *A Really Sincere Guy,* forgives her husband's infidelity almost as easily. Is one to conclude that American husbands are finally beginning to be understood by their wives?

Concomitant with the charge that these novels lack credible climaxes is the accusation that they are highly episodic in nature. The hero progresses from one incident to another, but many of these incidents do not contribute to the development of the primary plot in any way. The affair between Joe Logan and Pat Crain is extraneous and adds nothing to the plot of *Pax,* albeit it does add that necessary ingredient for commercial success—sex—to the book. Being a sexual adventure, this incident serves as an illustration of others found in all of these novels. By depicting their heroes passing from one bedroom to another, the authors of these novels may have hoped to suggest that virility of flesh accompanies virility of mind. What one concludes, though, is that these affairs result from the frustration of their heroes and that the authors have chosen the only arena in which these characters can compete. Additionally, in being rogues, these characters must be engaged in questionable activities. Since the American public will not countenance overt illegal acts by its fictional heroes, why not choose the next best substitute—illicit acts—specifically sexual promiscuity, which the American public sees as a typically American trait? Victor Norman entertains four women in *The Hucksters.* Joe Logan has only one success in *Pax,* but she is a senator's daughter and would equal four ordinary women, so perhaps he should not be disparaged. Tom Rath, in *The Man in the Gray Flannel Suit,* and Bill McCrary, in *A Really Sincere Guy,* settle for one affair each, perhaps having the foreboding that they would be caught. Morton Noyes, in *The Insider,* has two affairs only, but then he is forty-eight years old and could quite possibly be slowing down his activities. The point is, the battle for frankness in modern fiction was hard fought. In the hands of a serious author, sexual activities certainly add depth to character development. Physical description of the type encountered in these books suggests prurient value only and thus encourage those who would censor literature.

While the hero of the contemporary advertising/public relations novel would at first seem to differ from his picaresque brother by being of a higher social level, one can only point out that little else is possible in the modern social structure. With the broadening of society in modern America, the rigid lines of social structure have been broken down, and in literature the economic conception of the pitifully poor has taken the place of the social conception of the rascally poor. One may refer to the proletarian novels for the new approach to the poor. By the other criterion, rascality, however, these men, Norman, Rath, and all, qualify as rogues. One adman in *The Insider* sums up the fictional credo of the advertising/public relations man when he says, "Give me my orders and I'll carry 'em out or die trying. If you tell me to sell crap, I'll sell crap—like a Harvard man should." Or Joe Logan, in *Pax,* is another case in point. He utilizes his genius for the building of an authentic American hero into a front man for an unethical ethical drug firm. He is very moral, though, and actually regrets having to use information gained by wire tapping, even to win his true love. Bill McCrary, in *A Really Sincere Guy,* steals a client, but he twists his standards to fit the American ideal of success at any cost. After all, the agency had been attempting to prostitute his belief about the sanctity of the low tariff.

On the content level none of the characters mentioned resolves to leave the advertising/public relations field. On the structural level none of the characters undergoes a convincing change in personality as a result of the climax through which he has been. There is a consistency here between the content level and the structural level, but this consistency only points further to the statement that the novels which these characters inhabit are novels of entertainment. Of course, this charge does not imply that diversion cannot be a legitimate purpose of the novel. Certainly, some very notable authors have chosen to call their work entertainment, and every novel should first of all be interesting. But to one who believes that the modern problem novel represents the flowering of the genre, the advertising/public relations novel, drawing its technical sustenance from a withered branch, appears to be a sterile bud. (pp. 249-51)

Lewis A. Lawson, "The Rogue in the Gray Flannel Suit," in College English, *Vol. 22, No. 4, January, 1961, pp. 249-52.*

EMILY STIPES WATTS

[*In the following excerpt from her study* The Businessman in American Literature, *Watts examines the depiction in American novels of individual businessmen in conflict with corporate capitalists and labor unions.*]

As early as 1901, Frank Norris had identified the corporation as an octopus, a monster in the form of a railroad that destroyed the farmers (even wealthy farmers), their homes, and their free lives. Norris's *The Octopus* was the first part of an unfinished trilogy that was ultimately intended to extol wheat as a life force. Within this framework, the corporation is seen as an evil.

> They [the Railroad] own us, these task-masters of ours; they own our home, they own our legislatures. We cannot escape from them. There is no redress. We are told we can defeat them by the ballot-box. They own the ballot-box. We are told that we must look to the courts for redress; they own the courts. We know them for what they are—ruffians in politics, ruffians in finance, ruffians in law, ruffians in trade, bribers, swindlers, and tricksters. No outrage too great to daunt them, no petty larceny too small to shame them; despoiling a government treasury of a million dollars, yet picking the pockets of a farm hand of the price of a loaf of bread.

> They swindle a nation of a hundred million and call it Financiering; they levy a blackmail and call it Commerce; they corrupt a legislature and call it Politics; they bribe a judge and call it Law; they hire blacklegs to carry out their plans and call it Organization; they prostitute the honour of a State and call it Competition.

If Norris considers wheat a life force, the monopolistic corporation is clearly a death force, something beyond the control even of its president, Selgrim. In fact, Selgrim himself is depicted in somewhat sympathetic terms as a man who has some compassion for his workers but who is himself caught up in the force of the corporation. Moreover, the group of farmers who form a league and who, in a communist-inspired novel, would have been depicted as proletarian heroes are here depicted as inept, dishonest, and disorganized, but also as a potentially violent mob—a potential "Red Terror." With such a dismal prospect for the future of humanity, it is probably no wonder that Norris turned to a mystical vision of wheat as a life force.

One remarkable quality of Norris's novel is its distinctions among different kinds of capitalists as businessmen. The farmers are both wealthy and poor and are generally depicted favorably, as are the small businessmen in the local community. The banker, however, is vicious and cutthroat—an agent of the railroad. The corporation and its officials are generally destructive and devious. What is perhaps more remarkable, given the 1901 publication date of *The Octopus,* is Norris's indictment of the unions as a cooperative and integral part of the corporate octopus. Striking brotherhood members are welcomed back to the company, but one nonmember of the brotherhood who worked during the strike is not only fired, but also blacklisted from work on other railroads. Norris was thus able to do what other American writers were generally unwilling (or unable) to do until much later in the century—to differentiate among capitalists, to distinguish between private capitalism and corporate capitalism, and finally to suggest that together the unions and the corporation might well be, despite their occasional conflicts, a powerful, destructive force against the individual's freedom.

In the 1920s, the middle-class businessman and the corporation president—Sinclair Lewis's Babbitt and Mr. Cady in Kaufman and Connelly's *Beggar on Horseback*—were depicted by the American artist as essentially identical, despite their different financial bases. In the 1930s, the entrepreneur—heroic because of his individuality and financial daring—appeared in Rand's *Night of January 16th*. Similar to Rand's Faulkner, but less a symbol and more a sympathetic character, is F. Scott Fitzgerald's Monroe Stahr, the protagonist of *The Last Tycoon,* a novel left unfinished at Fitzgerald's death in 1940, but published with outline and other material in 1941, with an introduction by Edmund Wilson. Far from being a negative and destructive character, the Hollywood producer Stahr is a strong-minded but compassionate tycoon surrounded by corrupt colleagues. As a kind of feudal lord of his studio, Stahr still has time to give personal help to a cameraman Pete Zavras and is willing to let the studio lose money on a quality picture, much to the disbelief and opposition of his colleagues. Reasons Stahr, "we have a certain duty to the public." The novelist Boxley, whom Stahr has hired to write scripts (and who undoubtedly is a reflection of Fitzgerald himself) recognizes that "Stahr like [Abraham] Lincoln was a leader carrying on a long war on many fronts; almost single-handed he had moved pictures sharply forward through a decade, to the point where the content of 'A productions' was wider and richer than that of the stage. Stahr was an artist only, as Mr. Lincoln was a general, perforce and as a layman." Cecilia Brady, the daughter of one of Stahr's corrupt partners, sees Stahr "as a sort of technological virtuoso."

This is not to say that Monroe Stahr does not embody several qualities already associated with businessmen by American authors. He is paternalistic in his approach to his corporation—a quality which indicates real weakness during his drunken discussion with the communist union organizer Brimmer. He is, moreover, relatively uneducated and, when he wants to learn about communism, he has "the script department get him up a two-page 'treatment' of the *Communist Manifesto.*" Although his paternalism makes it difficult for him to understand the union movement, he was perhaps correct in his suspicions for, as Edmund Wilson interpreted the outline of the unfinished portion of *The Last Tycoon,* Fitzgerald obviously "intended to exploit the element of racketeering and gangsterism revealed in the [union] organization."

Nevertheless, *The Last Tycoon* depicts Stahr as a kind of hero in Wilson's summary of the projected conclusion of the novel. "The split between the controllers of the movie industry, on the one hand, and the various groups of employees, on the other, is widening and leaving no place for real individualists of business like Stahr, whose successes are personal achievements and whose career has always been invested with a certain glamour. He has held himself directly responsible to everyone with whom he has worked; he has even wanted to beat up his enemies himself."

In the post-World War II period, other writers began to distinguish more carefully between the private capitalist, often a small businessman, and the corporate capitalist, in contrast to the pre-1945 writers, who generally grouped all businessmen together. The corporation, that octopus Norris had described nearly half a century before, became more clearly identified as a destructive force. The small, private businessman and the "businessman-employee" of a corporation become sympathetic characters at about the same time the National Association of Manufacturers substituted the phrase "American Free Enterprise System" for "American Capitalism" in their pronouncements.

One representative and well-known play which strikingly demonstrated the difference between a businessman and a destructive capitalist is Arthur Miller's *Death of a Salesman* (1949). Willy Loman is a white-collar worker, a middle-class man with middle-class ambitions for his sons, a salesman—a businessman. His employer, Howard Wagner, is a capitalist, a man for whom profit is more important than loyalty to a long-employed salesman. In a sense, Miller has simply substituted the businessman for the laborer or cabdriver of Odets's *Waiting for Lefty.* In either case, the capitalist and his system are seen as corrupting even for a salesman, a latter-day Yankee Peddler, like Willy.

The "system" run by men like Howard Wagner and, in *The Last Tycoon,* Pat Brady soon was more fully identified by our writers with corporate capitalism or big business. Correspondingly, the small businessman began to emerge as a kind of sympathetic antihero. The earliest, most explicit example is Morris Bober in Bernard Malamud's *The Assistant* (1957). Bober has owned his little neighborhood grocery store for twenty-one years but is slowly being put out of business by his rival, Heinrich Schmitz. A compassionate man, Bober extends credit to the poor of the neighborhood. "He had labored long hours, was the soul of honesty—he could not escape his honesty, it was bedrock; to cheat would cause an explosion in him, yet he trusted cheaters—coveted nobody's nothing and always got poorer. . . . He was Morris Bober and could be nobody more fortunate." Moreover, as Bober recognizes, big business is destroying the small businessman. "The chain store kills the small man."

Bober is the victim of a robbery, but because his cash register contains so little—$10, his entire day's take—he is hit and injured by the robbers. However, one of the robbers, Frank Alpine, feels so guilty that he returns to help Bober, and Bober, with great compassion, gives Frank a job. Frank takes over the store while Bober is recuperating and business improves, even though Frank pockets some of the money. In the end, Bober dies, and Frank rents the store and seems destined to repeat Bober's life as a marginal shopowner and a (converted) Jew. There are other small businessmen in *The Assistant,* such as the liquor store owner, Julius Karp, but Bober with his compassion and humanity represents "the persistence of [Jewish] values uncorrupted and the relevance of the Jewish tradition of idealism to life in present-day America," as observed by Josephine Zadovsky Knopp. It is significant that Bober, this symbolic figure, is a small businessman, a private capitalist, although an unsuccessful one to be sure; in the late 1950s, the American writer was not yet ready to grant both goodness and success to the small businessman.

Perhaps the most striking example of the post-World War II indictment of the corporation and the union is John Dos Passos's *Midcentury: A Contemporary Chronicle* (1961). Many of Dos Passos's themes had already been introduced in his 1930s trilogy *USA,* but in *Midcentury* the destructive nature of union-business cooperation is brought into sharper focus. Such entanglements, further compounded by Mafia and racketeering interests, not only make it nearly impossible for a private capitalist like Will Jenks to begin his own business, but they also take advantage of honest union men such as Terry Bryant. Although *Midcentury* is generally viewed as a pessimistic book that attacks all aspects of capitalism, critics seem to have overlooked the fact that Will becomes successful for a number of reasons, not the least of which is his aggressive advertising campaign to the people of the community—a campaign that asserts the value of free enterprise and the classical economist's argument against monopoly.

> In his releases Will took high ground. His fight for competition was a fight to preserve the free enterprise way, the American way.

> . . . Will had typed out a five page story explaining how the Halloran interests were strangling the growth of Duquesne by their monopoly of transportation through Redtop Cabs. . . .

> *Corrupt Labor joins corrupt Management to strangle Competition.*

Dos Passos depicts the early twentieth-century union movement favorably in the career of Blackie Bowman, an IWW and a self-proclaimed "atheist anarchist." At this early point of union development, Dos Passos implies, there was a need to fight the dominant business leaders, who employed violent tactics to break up the unions. However, the unions adopted these same tactics and allowed communists like Kate Levine to speak for them, as Dos Passos continues the story. In time, the union leader became only another kind of monopolistic, corporate capitalist investing union funds in private ventures and even, like the Worthingtons, assuming social pretensions which in earlier American novels were assigned to the newly rich industrialists. Lillian Worthington, wife of the president of the fictional International Rubber Workers Union, bought "a lot out near the Country Club. They built themselves a neat Cape Cod cottage on it, plain roomy and unassuming. They had to think of the girls growing up. Lillian was president of the PTA. She was in the League of Women Voters and was invited to join the Ladies' Garden Club. The girls were asked to the really nice dances."

Besides the union-business alliance, Dos Passos also condemns corporations for destroying free, entrepreneurial capitalism. As John P. Diggins has observed in *Up From Communism: Conservative Odysseys in American Intellectual History,* "Dos Passos was . . . convinced that those who controlled big business no longer represented capitalism." Jaspar Milliron meets opposition from high and distant corporate management when he attempts to implement a new production process for his company; an example of Veblen's industrial innovator, he is . . . "a technical virtuoso" defeated by unimaginative financiers. One of the financiers depicted by Dos Passos is Judge Lewin, who lives in the world of "pure finance."

> I do not consider myself an evil man, yet my business, my hobby, my science is that special little section of arithmetic known as finance . . . insignificant from the point of view of great minds like Einstein's or Spinoza's, but still a sort of poor relation of mathematics. When I assume control of a corporation through the use

of my own private skills, I have to consider it a problem in pure finance. I can't be bothered with what it takes or what it sells. I can't be distracted by worrying about administration, who gets fired from what job, all the grubby little lives involved.

Finally, Dos Passos also explores another danger for the entrepreneur—big government—a theme already introduced into American literature in Ayn Rand's *Atlas Shrugged* (1957). In one of the biographical sections of real people scattered among the sections of fiction, Dos Passos records the story of Robert R. Young, who gained control of the Allegheny Railroad with strong hopes of reforming and refinancing the failing line. He "talked public service and the interest of the small investor"; he "pleaded the cause of honest management, streamlining, modernization, service." But in the end he failed.

> He died many times a millionaire. Money meant power, but not power enough. He was a skillful financial manipulator but not skillful enough

> to bring a successful reorganization of the railroads out from under the dead weight of the bankers' interests and the insurance companies' interests and the brotherhoods' interests

> and the seventy year old senile strangling head of the bureaucracy of the Interstate Commerce Commission.

> Restrictions, procedures, prerogatives hampered his every move.

In the fictional sketches, Dos Passos criticizes the NLRB as ineffective in controlling the racketeering and violent elements in the unions. With this theme—big government as dangerous to both free enterprise and the individual—Dos Passos suggested a thematic trend for novels in the 1970s.

The dangers of corporate capitalism also continue to be a major theme. Most recently, the corporation office appeared like this in Joseph Heller's *Something Happened* (1974).

> In the office in which I work there are five people of whom I am afraid. Each of these five people is afraid of four people (excluding overlaps), for a total of twenty, and each of these twenty people is afraid of six people, making a total of one hundred and twenty people who are feared by at least one other person. Each of these one hundred and twenty people is afraid of the other one hundred and nineteen, and all of these one hundred and forty-five people are afraid of the twelve men at the top who helped found and build the company and now own and direct it.

In William Gaddis's *JR: A Novel* (1975), JR learns about the stock market in his sixth-grade class and, with a few telephone calls from a booth near the boys' room at his school, promptly builds a paper empire, a paper corporation. JR, the successful child capitalist, is a satiric portrait, a surrealistic spin-off of the corporate investor who, like Judge Lewin in *Midcentury,* is involved in the game of pure finance with no thought of responsibilities or consequences.

The only fictional character in American literature who has been able to confront heroically and successfully big unionism and big business appeared to be the small, self-employed businessman. Will Jenks managed with some success in *Midcentury,* but he played only a minor role in a large and complex novel. However, Ken Kesey centered an entire novel, *Sometimes a Great Notion* (1964), around a heroic small businessman, Hank Stamper. Stamper is a character whose origins can be described in terms of the heroism of Daniel Boone and Natty Bumppo. Owner of a small, family lumbering company in Oregon, Stamper was also an all-state football player and a veteran of the Korean war.

Kesey has consciously surrounded his fictional hero with a myriad of nearly mythological associations. Hank's intellectual brother Lee associates Hank with Daniel Boone: "Who played at Dan'l Boone in forest full of fallout?" Old Henry, Hank's father, is described as "a Norse hero . . . [an] old warrior." Although Hank realizes that "you can make the river stand for all *sorts* of other [sentimental, mystical] things," he himself is strong enough to confront the river and its force. "It was like me and that river had drawn ourselves a little contract, a little grudge match." Hank's personality becomes associated with tall tales. "Old Henry says Hank's so godawful stout because something odd happened to Hank's muscle tissue because of all the sulphur his first wife, Hank's real ma, ate while she was pregnant with him." The family motto is "NEVER GIVE AN INCH!" and at one point Hank announces, "I don't care much for cages."

Hank and his small lumbering firm are caught between the big lumber corporations, which seem to have captured the market and have been squeezing the small companies, and the union, whose members are striking Hank's small company. In order to fight the union, Hank hires only members of his family and even sends east for his half-brother Lee, who has failed his doctoral exams in literature and, at the time he receives Hank's letter, is popping pills and contemplating suicide. The union resorts to sabotage and violence, alternated with honeyed moralisms about teamwork and community spirit. On the other hand, Hank is able to deal with the large corporations at this time because they too are suffering from a strike and can meet their own contracts only by buying lumber from men like Hank.

Hank represents individualism—a self-sufficiency and strength traced to his nomadic, pioneering ancestors. Kesey quite properly does not put words like "free enterprise" and "capitalism" in Hank's mouth, but lets Hank speak out for an individuality that can be expressed through his business and through his ability to confront the unions, which to Hank represent only conformity and mediocrity. As Hank tells the union president, in response to his sweet sentiments about the common good and community spirit and the American way,

> "I'm just as concerned as the next guy, just as loyal. If we was to get into it with Russia I'd fight for us right down to the wire. And if Oregon was to get into it with California I'd fight for Oregon. But if somebody—Biggy Newton or the Woodsworker's Union or anybody—gets into it with *me,* then I'm for *me!* When the chips are down, I'm my own patriot. I don't give a goddam the other guy is my own *brother* wavin' the *American* flag and singing the friggin' 'Star Spangled Banner!'"

Hank's individual strength is ultimately and ironically a community strength, much as the king's strength was the community's strength in classical drama. When, at one point, Hank

appears to have given in to union demands, the town is sad and the high school football team loses a game.

In an innovative and startling fashion, Kesey has thus adapted an ancient myth. The interrelationship of leader and community in a modern democracy can never be that of the ancient leader, such as Oedipus, and his people. However, Kesey implies that the heroic and free individual such as Hank Stamper does indeed have a positive and healthy effect on his community. Hank's struggle to meet his business and moral responsibilities and his refusal to buckle to the unreasonable union demands and the union leader's sweet sentiments concerning community spirit make explicit the strength and integrity of the small businessman.

In contrast to Hank's strength is this description of the union members on their way to a meeting:

> And there is nothing like feeling special for hustling a citizen out to round up every other comrade he can locate with a corresponding feeling; there is nothing like a sense of *difference* for getting a man lined up, shoulder to shoulder, with everybody as different as he is, in a dedicated campaign for the Common Good; which means a campaign either for the ramming of that difference down the throat of an ignorant and underprivileged and *unholy* world—this is only true, of course, in the case of a bona fide *holy* difference—or, at the other extreme, a campaign for the stamping-out of the thing that caused the damned difference in the first place.

Thus, according to the narrator, the union members are joining to impose conformity to their own standards.

Hank's half-brother, Lee, is by contrast an academic, an intellectual, a socialist, who returns home not to help Hank but to destroy him. Lee hates Hank because Hank had slept with Lee's mother, Hank's step-mother, and because Lee hates Hank's self-sufficiency and strength. Lee reviles their father, Old Henry, because he is a capitalist. Lee attempts to win by losing, while Hank attempts to win by winning. When Lee seduces Hank's wife, Viv, he feels that he has defeated his brother. Although Hank falters and admits that he has learned something from Lee, it is finally Lee who stays with Hank and tells the reader what Hank's integrity means.

> For there is always a sanctuary more, a door that can never be forced, whatever the force, a last inviolable stronghold that can never be taken, whatever the attack; your vote can be taken, your name, your innards, even your life, but that last stronghold can only be surrendered. And to surrender it for any reason other than love is to surrender love. Hank had always known this without knowing it, and by making him doubt it briefly I made it possible for both of us to discover it. I knew it now.

The contrast of Hank and Lee is perhaps a variation of the old American theme of the westerner and the dude. The two men, however, more fully represent the independent individual of the free-enterprise system and the group-oriented, academic, intellectual socialist. During the 1960s, American authors had regularly been attacking academic intellectuals for one reason or another. Bernard Malamud's *A New Life* appeared in 1961; Saul Bellow's *Herzog,* 1964; and John Barth's *Giles Goat-*

Boy; or, The Revised New Syllabus, 1966. However, it is significant that the small businessman Hank has something to teach the academic Lee. Unlike Kesey's *One Flew Over the Cuckoo's Nest* (1962), in which McMurphy is simply an individualistic rebel against a system, the characters in *Sometimes a Great Notion* are more carefully specified and delineated. According to this novel, it is only the small businessman who is strong and self-sufficient enough to confront the union, big business, and academics and, at the same time, to bring strength to his community. (pp. 103-13)

> *Emily Stipes Watts, in her* The Businessman in American Literature, *The University of Georgia Press, 1982, 183 p.*

ADDITIONAL BIBLIOGRAPHY

Benedict, Stewart. "The Business Novel." *Papers of the Michigan Academy of Science, Arts, and Letters* XLV (1960): 447-53.
> Notes the disparity between fictional portraits of executives in post-World War II business novels and their real-life counterparts. According to Benedict: "The business novel . . . contains so many inherent limitations and circumscriptions that it can never become much more than eulogistic pamphleteering. Because, however, the type offers a wide variety of settings and is essentially romantic escapism in the trappings of verisimilitude, it can be expected to persist in our literature for a long time and eventually to take its place beside the historical novel as a major branch of second-rate fiction."

"Corporation Life Gets a Literature." *Business Week* No. 1292 (5 June 1954): 79.
> Discusses the trend in literature to present young, well-educated businessmen "pumping for the corporation, not for themselves."

"How Good an Operator Is Cash McCall?" *Business Week* No. 1372 (17 December 1955): 104, 106, 112, 114.
> Presents a discussion by members of the business community of Cameron Hawley's characterization of the businessman in *Cash McCall*.

"The Fiction-Eye View of Business." *Business Week* No. 1467 (12 October 1957): 187.
> Maintains that modern portrayals of businessmen in fiction present faceless executives who have conformed to the ideal of the "organization man."

Cawelti, John G. "Dream or Rat Race: Success in the Twentieth Century." In his *Apostles of the Self-Made Man,* pp. 201-38. Chicago: The University of Chicago Press, 1965.
> Socioeconomic study using characters from novels by Theodore Dreiser, F. Scott Fitzgerald, William Faulkner, and Robert Penn Warren to show the "failure of success" in the first half of the twentieth century.

Dreiser, Theodore. *The Financier.* Philadelphia: Century Bookbindery, 1986, 503 p.

Erskine, John. "American Business in the American Novel." *The Bookman* (New York) LXXIII, No. 5 (July 1931): 449-57.
> Notes the influence of foreign cultures on and the limited role of women in American business fiction, and considers the differences between American and European views of the American businessman.

Hawley, Cameron. *Executive Suite.* New York: Dell, 1986, 352 p.

Hicks, Granville. "The Fiction of Business." *Saturday Review* XLI, No. 38 (20 September 1958): 18.
> Review of *Venus in Sparta* by Louis Auchincloss, *The Big Company Look* by J. Harvey Howells, and *The Week of the Wives* by Sarah-Elizabeth Rodger. According to Hicks: "If these three novels have anything in common, it is their repudiation of the nineteenth-century concept of Economic Man. Not one of the many businessmen they portray is motivated by [enlightened self-interest] . . . ; their motives have to be tracked down in the deeper recesses of the psyche."

Howells, William D. *The Rise of Silas Lapham.* New York: Penguin Books, 1983, 352 p.

Kavesh, Robert A. *Businessmen in Fiction: The Capitalist and Executive in American Novels.* Hanover, N.H.: The Amos Tuck School of Business Administration, 1955, 12 p.
> Introductory survey concluding that "novelists have seized upon instances of business misbehavior and have constructed character sketches in keeping with the dynamic, ruthless stereotype or the plodding, unthinking one. But, as both the nature of business and its leaders shift . . . , can novelists claim that they are being realistic when they cling to memories of the past?"

Lerner, Max. "Capitalist Economy and Business Civilization: The Rise and Decline of the Titan." In his *America as a Civilization: Life and Thought in the United States Today,* pp. 274-84. New York: Simon and Schuster, 1957.
> Consideration of the business "titan" in American life and literature.

Lewis, Sinclair. *Babbitt.* San Diego, Calif.: Harcourt Brace Jovanovich, 1949, 408 p.

Malcolm, Donald. "Villains and Heroes in Business Novels." *The New Republic* 134, No. 2 (14 May 1956): 16-7.
> Unfavorable review of George de Mare's *The Empire,* which Malcolm calls "a fairly representative specimen of a new kind of novel about business. . . . It might be described as a 'sympathetic exposé' of big business, the purpose of which is not to stimulate correction of abuses but to indicate what a heroic little fellow the executive really is for managing to function under such circumstances."

Marquand, John P. *Point of No Return.* Chicago: Academy Chicago, 1985, 559 p.

Mattheissen, F. O. "The Business Novel." In his *Theodore Dreiser,* pp. 127-58. New York: William Sloane Associates, 1951.
> Examines Dreiser's characterization of Frank Cowperwood in *The Financier, The Titan,* and *The Stoic.*

McInnes, William. "Businessman as Hero." *America* XCIV, No. 2 (11 February 1956): 533-35.
> Offers a brief history of the businessman in literature and reviews Hawley's *Cash McCall* and Sloan Wilson's *The Man in the Gray Flannel Suit.*

Mctague, Michael J. *The Businessman in Literature: Dante to Melville.* New York: Philosophical Library, 1979, 86 p.
> Examines depictions of businessmen in works by selected authors from the Middle Ages through the eighteenth century, including Geoffrey Chaucer, William Shakespeare, John Milton, and Jonathan Swift, with a chapter focusing on Herman Melville's "Bartleby the Scrivener."

Rubenstein, Gilbert M. "The Businessman in Literature: Parts I and II." *American Book Collector* XVII, Nos. 8, 9 (April 1967; May 1967): 24-6, 30-1; 26-9.
> Survey of businessmen in Western literature from Genesis to the post-World War II business novel. According to Rubenstein: "The great modern American novel of business . . . is yet to be written, and there are very substantial difficulties in the path of the prospective author. If, as [John] Chamberlain suggests, the modern executive is less crude than Frank Cowperwood, less ridiculous than the ineffectual Babbitt, less of a sex-starved conformist than the man in the gray flannel suit . . . , the new novelist will have to convince the public that such a businessman exists."

Seager, Allan. "Executive Suite: The Power and the Prize." *Nation* 179, No. 24 (11 December 1954): 506-08.

Review of *The Power and the Prize* by Howard Swiggett and *Executive Suite* by Hawley. According to Seager: "Judged seriously as works of art, these books are sentimental, naive, and technically commonplace. But as documents they are fascinating."

Smith, Howard R. "The American Businessman in the American Novel." *Southern Economic Journal* XXV, No. 3 (January 1959): 265-302.

Detailed analysis of critical generalizations about the depiction of the businessman in American fiction, including the commonly held opinion that novelists consistently portray the businessman as a villain. Faulting the methodology of critics including Kenneth S. Lynn and John Chamberlain (see excerpts above), Smith concludes that most critical assessments of the literature have been inaccurate, and that "what is easily mistaken for an indictment of businessmen" is in fact a broader depiction of a general "process of civilizational deterioration."

Spectorsky, A. C. "*SR* Runs Six up the Flagpole." *Saturday Review* XLI, No. 45 (8 November 1958): 14-15, 30.

Review of six business novels—*The Admen* by Shepherd Mead, *The Merger* by Sterling Quinlan, *A Really Sincere Guy* by Robert Van Riper, *A Twist of Lemon* by Edward Stephens, *Pax* by Harry Middleton and Warren Kiefer, and *The Detroiters* by Harold Livingston.

Stedmond, J. M. "The Business Executive in Fiction." *Dalhousie Review* 42, No. 1 (Spring 1962): 18-27.

Maintains that "just beneath the pseudo-realistic surface of a good many modern business novels lurks the idea that the individual is powerless in the grip of society. Protest is not only futile it is in fact disloyal. What are required are 'positive' attitudes—meaning a refusal to criticize any aspect of present-day North American life. Great literature has never been 'positive' in this bland way."

Stessin, Lawrence. "The Businessman in Fiction." *Literary Review* 12, No. 3 (Spring 1969): 281-89.

Introductory essay discussing the changing view of business executives in twentieth-century literature.

Taylor, Walter Fuller. *The Economic Novel in America*. Chapel Hill: The University of North Carolina Press, 1942, 378 p.

Comprehensive study of the historical background and the major and minor practitioners of the economic novel. Taylor states that his "aim has been to describe and interpret the response given by American authorship to one of the major social forces of the latter nineteenth century—the rapid industrialization of our American society, the sudden maturation of the Machine Age."

"Businessmen in Fiction: New Novels Reflect New Understanding." *Time* LXVIII, No. 23 (13 December 1956): 86.

Notes a trend in literature toward appreciative portrayals of business executives. According to the critic: "One reason for the shifting attitude in fiction is that the new generation of business authors has often had first-hand business experience."

Van Nostrand, Albert D. "Fiction's Flagging Man of Commerce." *English Journal* XLVIII, No. 1 (January 1959): 1-11.

Companion piece to "After Marquand, the Deluge," excerpted above. In this essay, Van Nostrand introduces the subject of the businessman in American fiction by comparing William Dean Howells's *The Rise of Silas Lapham* and John Marquand's *Point of No Return*.

Walker, Charles R. "Business in the American Novel." *The Bookman* LXVII, No. 4 (December 1927): 401-05.

Discusses the novels of Dreiser, Sinclair Lewis, Frank Norris, and Upton Sinclair, noting that business and businessmen are rarely portrayed favorably in American fiction.

Westbrook, Wayne W. *Wall Street in the American Novel*. New York: New York University Press, 1980, 213 p.

Takes the viewpoint that "business and art have walked common ground, if not shared a common purpose in American history" and that American writers have used Wall Street in their works "not always to communicate matters on mere stock trading or money making, but often to portray deeper attitudes about American culture."

Whyte, William H. "The Organization Man in Fiction." In his *The Organization Man*, pp. 241-63. New York: Simon and Schuster, 1956.

Compares earlier and later business fiction and concludes that, whereas "in older fiction there was some element of conflict between the individual and his environment," in later works the American social and economic system is portrayed as "so benevolent that there is no conflict left in it for anyone to be rebellious about."

Wilson, Sloan. *The Man in the Gray Flannel Suit*. New York: Arbor House, 1983, 356 p.

Harlem Renaissance

INTRODUCTION

The Harlem Renaissance, which was also known as the Negro Renaissance and the New Negro Movement, is generally considered the first important movement of black artists and writers in the United States. Centered in Harlem, New York, and other urban areas during the 1920s, the movement constituted an unprecedented flourishing of cultural activity among black Americans. During this period, new and established black writers published more fiction and poetry than ever before, the first influential black literary journals were established, and black authors, artists, and musicians received their first widespread recognition and serious critical appraisal. Although widely diverse in content and style, works of the Harlem Renaissance were often characterized by heightened racial awareness, as many black authors and artists sought through their works to counteract white racial prejudices as well as to perpetuate African aspects of their cultural heritage.

Between 1890 and 1920, a series of crises in the agricultural economy of the southern United States, coupled with a shortage of labor in northern industrial centers, led to a migration of approximately two million black Americans from the rural South to the urban North. Their settlement in densely populated, segregated neighborhoods and participation in the urban industrial work force resulted in greater racial cohesiveness, and economic independence; as a result of these and other social factors, during this period black Americans became more militant in protesting their subservient social position. Their sudden prominence in urban life and increasing assertiveness met with resistance from conservative whites, provoking a revival of the Ku Klux Klan and an outbreak of lynchings and other incidences of violence motivated by racism. This period of social upheaval and conflict inspired black intellectuals to reexamine both their role in American society and their unique cultural heritage. This trend, which has been described as black Americans' "sociocultural awakening," came to be expressed in an outpouring of art, music, and literature. At the same time, growing interest among white Americans in jazz and blues music, the discovery of African sculpture by such modernist artists as Pablo Picasso, and subsequent interest in black culture in general gave rise to an increase in white patronage of black artists and recognition of black artistic achievement.

This phenomenon—which was formally recognized as a movement in 1925 with the publication of Alain Locke's anthology *The New Negro*—was widely considered a social as well as an artistic renaissance. In the introduction to his anthology, Locke assessed what he considered the developing social identity of the "New Negroes" of the 1920s: "In [their] group psychology we note the lapse of sentimental appeal, then the development of a more positive self-respect and self-reliance; the repudiation of social dependence, and then the gradual recovery from hypersensitiveness and 'touchy' nerves, the repudiation of the double standard of judgment with its special philanthropic allowances and then the sturdier desire for objective and scientific appraisal; and finally the rise from social disillusionment to race pride, from the sense of social debt to the responsibilities of social contribution, and offsetting the necessary working and

commonsense acceptance of restricted conditions, the belief in ultimate esteem and recognition." In an essay that has been described as the manifesto of the younger writers of the Harlem Renaissance, Langston Hughes utilized similar terms to present what he considered the movement's literary goals: "We younger Negro artists who create now intend to express our individual dark-skinned selves without fear or shame. If white people are pleased we are glad. If they are not, it doesn't matter. . . . If colored people are pleased we are glad. If they are not, their displeasure doesn't matter either. We build our temples for tomorrow, strong as we know how, and we stand on top of the mountain, free within ourselves."

While some prominent figures of the Harlem Renaissance supported this call for artistic independence, many differed with Hughes over the ultimate goals of the movement and the means by which these goals should be achieved. Some black critics, including W. E. B. Du Bois, Benjamin Brawley, and Allison Davis, stressed the usefulness of literature in fostering racial equality, arguing that social progress for black Americans could be promoted or impeded by their portrayal in literature and therefore black writers were obligated to depict black people in a favorable light. Others, including Locke, Charles S. Johnson, and Charles W. Chesnutt, decried such overt use of literature for the purposes of propaganda, advocating instead an artistic philosophy based on individualistic self-expression. While few black critics asserted the complete independence of art from social concerns, most believed that literature could best enhance the pursuit of racial equality by demonstrating that black writers could produce works rivaling or surpassing those of their white counterparts.

As most publishers and readers of works by black writers were white, the controversy was further complicated by the perceived expectations and demands of the white literary establishment. Many black writers felt that white readers and publishers were interested only in stereotypical depictions of the Negro as primitive, and that realistic treatments of black life were rejected by whites in favor of those which dealt with the more sensational aspects of Harlem nightlife and the supposed free sexuality of black people. While this "primitivistic" side of black culture was rejected by some black authors as a destructive stereotype, it was actively fostered by others who considered it a continuation of or return to African custom and a defiance of white puritanical morality. Such conflicts among artists and critics reflect the fragmented nature of the Harlem Renaissance, a movement with no formal structure or unifying ideology. The body of literature produced during the Renaissance period is similarly diverse, comprising works of every genre and a wide variety of styles and thematic concerns.

The Harlem Renaissance is considered to have ended with the depression of the 1930s, although some of its participants had already foreseen its dissipation. Langston Hughes, for example, noted that interest in Harlem nightlife and other aspects of black culture was a fad for many white people; he wrote, "I thought it wouldn't last long. . . . For how could a large and enthusiastic number of people be crazy about Negroes forever?" White patronage of black artists and publication of their works ceased with the onset of the Depression, which, as Hughes put it, "sent Negroes, white folks and all rolling down the hills toward the Works Progress Administration." As black intellectuals had few literary magazines and publishing houses of their own, the literary flourishing of the 1920s came to an abrupt end.

According to Margaret Perry, during the Harlem Renaissance "the black world came of age in an artistic sense," and most critics agree that between 1919 and 1930 black writers attained an unprecedented level of both literary achievement and public recognition. In providing black authors with their first widespread opportunity for publication by commercial publishing houses and promoting awareness of black cultural achievement among both black and white audiences, the Renaissance period fostered the development of black literature in every genre, producing an important body of work that continues to be read today and which has frequently been cited as an inspiration to later generations of black intellectuals.

PRINCIPAL ISSUES AND FIGURES

AMRITJIT SINGH

[*Singh is an Indian lecturer, educator, and critic. He has written extensively about black American literature, relating it to its sociological and folk origins. In the following excerpt from his study* The Novels of the Harlem Renaissance *(1976), Singh examines the social factors contributing to the Harlem Renaissance, traces the development of the movement, and presents the principal issues in the debate over the nature and function of literature by black Americans.*]

The 1920s in American history were marked by a sociocultural awakening among Afro-Americans. More blacks participated in the arts than ever before, and their number increased steadily throughout the decade. This florescence of creative activity extended to many areas—music, poetry, drama, fiction. In literature, the few Negro novels published between 1905 and 1923 were presented mainly by small firms unable to give their authors a national hearing. However, in the succeeding decade, over two dozen novels by blacks appeared, and most of them were issued by major American publishers.

The needs of this new black self-expression were served by magazines and journals, black as well as white. The twenties gave rise to all-black literary quarterlies and "little magazines," some of rather short duration, such as *Fire, Harlem, Stylus, Quill,* and *Black Opals.* The National Association for the Advancement of Colored People (NAACP) and the National Urban League both published powerful journals, *The Crisis* and *Opportunity* respectively, which encouraged young black writers. *The Messenger,* published by A. Philip Randolph and Chandler Owen, also made stimulating literary contributions from time to time. In addition, the leading journals in America published articles, short stories, poems, and reviews from black writers.

By the middle of the decade, many people had become conscious of this literary upsurge and tried to direct and influence its orientation. Alain Locke, describing himself later as a "midwife" to the younger generation of black writers of the twenties, propounded the concept of a Negro renaissance and tried to develop a movement of black American arts. In March 1925,

he edited a special Harlem issue of *Survey Graphic,* which he expanded later that year into an anthology entitled *The New Negro* [see Additional Bibliography]. This anthology contained the recent work of young black writers and called for continued attempts at racial self-expression within a culturally pluralistic American context. Many black writers answered Locke's call by offering accounts of all strata of black life, from Philadelphia's blue-vein "society" Negroes to Harlem's common folk, including streetwalkers and criminals.

Locke's anthology also initiated a debate on black writing that caused endless controversy in the twenties and continues vigorously today. The term "New Negro," though not original with Locke, caught on in black circles even more than his concept of cultural pluralism. New Negro societies sprang up in several large cities and it became fashionable to declare oneself a member of the New Negro coterie. (pp. 1-2)

The philosophical and spiritual relationship between the Renaissance of the twenties and black writing of the 1890s has been explored by Arna Bontemps. He lived during the Renaissance and has written persuasively on the chronology of events leading to it; he associates writers such as Paul Laurence Dunbar, Charles W. Chesnutt, W. E. B. DuBois, and James Weldon Johnson with the 1890s and regards Booker T. Washington as the most prominent leader of the period. Victor F. Calverton, who encouraged many black writers in his *Modern Quarterly* and edited the pioneering *Anthology of American Negro Literature* in 1929, seems to support Bontemps' view that the upsurge of black creativity in the twenties was an assertion and expansion, after a relatively long silence, of the mood that prevailed briefly toward the end of the nineteenth century. Calverton, however, sees the postwar New Negro movement not so much as a revival, but rather as "the hastening of an old birth which had formerly been retarded in its growth and evolution."

The most significant link between the two periods was W. E. B. DuBois. DuBois, sponsoring the Pan-African Congress in 1897, asserted that the black American could best further his cause by rejecting a servile imitation of Anglo-Saxon culture. And writing in the August 1897 issue of *Atlantic Monthly,* he expressed, in his now famous words, the paradox and ambivalence of the Negro's existence in America: "It is a peculiar sensation, this double-consciousness, this sense of always looking at one's self through the eyes of others, of measuring one's soul by the tape of a world that looks on in amused contempt and pity. One ever feels his two-ness—an American, a Negro—two souls, two thoughts, two unreconciled strivings; two warring ideals in one dark body, whose dogged strength alone keeps it from being torn asunder." In 1903, he crystallized his seminal concept of "double-consciousness" in *Souls of Black Folk* and averred that "the problem of the twentieth century is the problem of the color line." DuBois' book was read by many young writers of the Renaissance during their formative years. Claude McKay spoke for his contemporaries with his response to *Souls of Black Folk:* "The book shook me like an earthquake." DuBois' prophetic statements, however, were not fully appreciated until certain other social and political changes forced black Americans to find "a bond in their common grievances and a language through which to express them."

World War I became a major factor in the Afro-American's new awareness of himself and his relationship to American democratic ideals. War-born opportunities brought blacks to Northern cities in great numbers, accelerating the population shift generally known as the Great Urban Migration. During the war, black troops marched and fought alongside white Americans to make the world "safe for democracy." The Negro's experiences abroad revealed the discrepancies between the promise of freedom and his own status in American life; and he was led to hope that democracy would also be won at home. After the Armistice in 1918, the blacks became embittered and defiant to find the whites more than ever determined to keep the Negro in his place. As John Hope Franklin points out, it was not the timorous, docile Negro of the past who said, "The next time white folks pick on colored folks, something is going to drop—dead white folks." The threat posed to legalized white supremacy in the South by returning soldiers and the hostility aroused in the North by a rapidly expanding black population resulted in nationwide expressions of racial animosity. During the "bloody summer" of 1919, race riots erupted in more than twenty-five cities across the nation. Blacks fought back bitterly and audaciously. It was in reaction to these riots that Claude McKay wrote his now famous poem, "If We Must Die," published in *The Liberator.* And in an editorial entitled "Returning Soldiers" in *The Crisis,* DuBois declared:

> Under similar circumstances we would fight
> again. But, by the God of Heaven, we are cow-
> ards and jackasses if, now that the war is over,
> we do not marshal every ounce of our brain
> and brawn to fight a sterner, longer, more un-
> bending battle against the forces of hell in our
> own land.

Meanwhile, the urban migration continued. Stimulated by the promise of industrial jobs in the North in the wake of the cessation of European migration, hundreds of thousands of Southern blacks were pouring into Northern cities. By one estimate, over 500,000 lower-class blacks migrated north between 1910 and 1920, and during the twenties another 800,000 blacks abandoned the South, many of them Negro ministers and professionals who followed their clients. In addition, there were migrants from the Midwest, the West, and the West Indies.

The political and economic implications of this change can be understood best in the light of what went on in black America in the two decades preceding World War I. Booker T. Washington had been the acknowledged leader and spokesman of black Americans for many years. Since Washington did not agitate for social and political equality, he had the approval and confidence of the white industrialists and politicians both in the North and the South. His "Tuskegee Machine" exercised unprecedented control over federal appointments for blacks and funds for black colleges. Washington's accomodationist policy, however, had won very little for Negro citizens. In the last sixteen years of the nineteenth century, there had been more than 2,500 lynchings and they continued at a shocking rate into the twentieth century. Before the outbreak of World War I, the number for the century soared to more than 1,100, many of them taking place in the Midwest. Between 1916 and 1921, the Ku Klux Klan grew from an obscure society in Atlanta to a nationwide secret organization with a membership of over half a million. In 1924, the journalist Stanley Frost accurately described the Klan as "the most vigorous, active and effective force in American life, outside business." More than anything else, the urban migration shook the foundation of Washington's philosophy and confirmed the inadequacy of his program for industrial education that would have tied the black to an antiquated, preindustrial Southern economy. Washington failed to anticipate the predominantly urban role the Afro-American would soon acquire.

The black sharecroppers and farm laborers saw in their move to the cities "a new vision of opportunity, of social and economic freedom." In the Northern cities, they hoped to escape the poverty of Southern agriculture and the violence of racial bigotry. The urban migration also meant being crowded into segregated neighborhoods where the blacks could feel their powers as they never had before. They developed a new self-respect and racial consciousness. Segregation stimulated the growth of a black middle class whose main function was to provide services for the black community that did not interest the white businessman. Such services included barber shops, funeral parlors, restaurants, shoe repair shops, beauty shops, and grocery stores, but some Negroes also successfully ran employment and real estate agencies.

The shift to Northern urban centers had its unpalatable side too. First, white hostility threatened the very existence of black neighborhoods. The overcrowding in black communities led to disease and delinquency. Racketeers and profiteers exploited the new migrants, who were for the most part ignorant of the city's ways. Euphoria Blake in Wallace Thurman's *Infants of the Spring* tells how she moved from the South full of ideas about race uplift, but ended up exploiting her fellow migrants by being an intermediary between jobseekers and employers, between landlords and potential tenants. In addition, intraracial and interregional conflicts arose when blacks of different backgrounds were thrown together into areas only ten to twenty blocks long in most cities.

In many ways, Harlem was just another of the new black neighborhoods in Northern cities; it shared their advantages as well as problems. But Harlem differed in that it developed from a white, upper-middle-class suburb, and not from the continued decline of an already poor white area, as was usually the case. In 1925, in an article written for Locke's anthology, *The New Negro,* James Weldon Johnson comments:

> Harlem is not merely a Negro colony or com-
> munity, it is a city within a city, the greatest
> Negro city in the world. It is not a slum or a
> fringe, it is located in the heart of Manhattan
> and occupies one of the most beautiful and
> healthful sections of the city. It is not a "quar-
> ter" of dilapidated tenements, but is made up
> of new-law apartments and handsome dwell-
> ings, with well-paved and well-lighted streets.
> It has its own churches, social and civic centers,
> shops, theaters and other places of amusement.
> And it contains more Negroes to the square mile
> than any other spot on earth.

No wonder Harlem became "a symbol of elegance and distinction, not derogation." Since the promise of a better future seemed more tangible in Harlem, it attracted more migrants, intensifying the process of urbanization in a cosmopolitan setting. The community grew from 14,000 blacks in 1914 to 175,000 by 1925 and more than 200,000 by the beginning of the Depression. Negroes came from all parts of the United States, West Indies, and even Africa, and their interaction led to the growth of a highly race-conscious, sophisticated black community—something unprecedented in American history. Black writers, painters, and actors from all over the country experienced the magnetic pull of Harlem as the new cultural capital of black America. "In Harlem," wrote Alain Locke in the special Harlem issue of *Survey Graphic,* which he edited in March 1925, "Negro life is seizing upon its first chances for group expression and self-determination." The black's new

A family moving into Harlem around 1905.

self-help through emphasis on the great history and future of Africa, and a program of black capitalistic enterprise that took its cue, through Emmett Scott and others, from Booker T. Washington's philosophy and economic programs, and anticipated the work and ideas of Elijah Muhammad and his Nation of Ismal. Through his exaltation of blackness, Garvey gained followers among the demoralized blacks in urban ghettos all over the country.

However, the middle-class Negro leadership of organizations such as the NAACP, the Urban League, and the Brotherhood of Sleeping Car Porters was not prepared for the belligerent, separatist philosophy of Marcus Garvey. Almost all the black leaders of the period, including W. E. B. DuBois, James Weldon Johnson, Walter White, and A. Philip Randolph, were reformers rather than radicals; they saw Garvey as a threat to their influence on both blacks and whites and to the Negro's civil rights cause in the United States. They did not share Garvey's professed mystique of blackness, but found race pride a useful tool in the fight to obtain greater opportunities for black American citizens. Many Negro leaders, however, recognized that Garvey's sway over the masses represented something much deeper than a mere desire to migrate to Africa. In 1925, Charles S. Johnson admitted that Garvey had shown "the clairvoyance to place himself at the head of a docile sector of a whole population, which, in different degrees, has been expressing an indefinite restlessness and broadening of spirit." Randolph had helped Garvey in his early efforts to gain public attention and DuBois praised him for his sincerity and eloquence but felt that Garvey had "absolutely no business sense, no *flair* for organization." Writing in the August 1923 issue of *Opportunity*, Charles S. Johnson recognized Garveyism as an expression of the urge for racial self-determination, but characterized Garvey's method as "injudicious and bunglesome" and his program as "absurdly visionary and impossible."

Garvey continued to attack individual black American leaders and their ideas with a ferocious invective that finally brought angry responses from DuBois and others. Garvey refused to answer charges by DuBois and Randolph about the poor handling of business and management details relating to his many auxiliary organizations, such as Universal African Legion, Black Cross Nurses, the Universal African Motor Corps, and the Black Eagle Flying Corps. Since neither Garvey nor any of his followers knew anything about ships, they squandered hundreds of thousands of dollars when they purchased rundown ships at exorbitant prices for Garvey's Black Star Line. His efforts to colonize Africa were doomed to failure from the beginning because of a general lack of technical and business skills among his followers and Garvey's own ignorance of the geopolitical situation of the African continent. (pp. 10-11)

Garvey's significance, however, was far greater than his unsuccessful ventures indicate. Henry Lincoln Johnson, a black attorney who represented one of Garvey's codefendants at their trial for mail fraud in 1923, had said: "If every Negro could have put every dime, every penny into the sea, and if he got in exchange the knowledge that he was somebody, that he meant something in the world, he would gladly do it. . . . The Black Star Line was a loss in money but it was a gain in soul."

In many ways, the New Negro movement of the twenties was the educated, middle-class black's response to the same changes that magnetically drew the unlettered and lower-class Negroes to Garvey's ideas and programs. In keeping with the political thinking of organizations such as NAACP and the Urban League,

aspirations and continued frustrations instilled among the common folk a fiery brand of racial chauvinism; it also led to an assertion of black pride by a broad-based middle-class negro leadership. Because of the diversity of its population, Harlem also became an ideal testing ground for clashing racial and political points of view. What Roi Ottley said about Harlem in 1943 had perhaps even greater validity for the twenties: "It is the fountainhead of mass movements. From it flows the progressive vitality of Black life. . . . To grasp the inner meanings of life in Black America, one must put his finger on the pulse of Harlem." (pp. 5-9)

[The] most significant Harlem-related mass movement in the twenties was the "Back to Africa" movement of Marcus Garvey. A Jamaican by birth, Garvey came to Harlem in 1916, and, unlike any leader black America had seen before, he had the ability and charisma to "convince masses of ordinary black men and women of the notion of their collective potential." Garvey's ideas were not new, but he used his demagogic techniques effectively on his growing audiences. (p. 10)

The essence of Garvey's message was that black was superior to white and that the destiny of the Negro race lay in Africa, not America. Garvey won a large following estimated anywhere between half a million and six million. Although Garvey's followers did not all desire to exchange their present lot, however difficult, for an unknown future in Africa, they found in [his Universal Negro Improvement Association] a much-needed outlet for race pride and self-assertion. Garvey's movement constituted a promise to provide what most black folk had always cherished—an opportunity to work and achieve on a par with others. Garvey attempted to build black pride and the black culture enthusiasts advocated race pride and racial expression, without developing a mystique of blackness based on African roots. Instead, they emphasized race differences with the definite objective of achieving racial cooperation and harmony in a culturally pluralistic American society. That the Garvey movement and the New Negro phenomenon failed to interact in any meaningful way indicates the extent of class cleavage in the black society of the twenties. (p. 12)

The New Negro stressed and sometimes glorified certain characteristics of the race they believed to be uniquely Negro. Although their long-term goals were assimilationist, they recognized the value of racial institutions within the segregated community. To them, Harlem, with its churches, theaters, restaurants, and night clubs, typified the vitality and diversity of black life. Neither desiring an all-black nation in Northern America nor looking forward to an all-black republic in Africa, they extended the use of institutions such as the black press beyond their social and cultural roles in order to deal with political and economic issues of national importance.

The Harlem Renaissance was thus a logical extension in the areas of art, music, and literature of the New Negro's racial, cultural, and political thinking. Arna Bontemps traced the origins of the Renaissance to the year 1917, when Claude McKay published a poem entitled "Harlem Dancer" in an obscure magazine. "In that same year, James Weldon Johnson collected poems he had been writing in a small volume called *Fifty Years and Other Poems,* but none of these verses had the sock of Claude McKay's poetry or of Johnson's own later poems. A serious dramatic presentation with a black cast appeared for the first time on Broadway in that same year." Soon after, many black artists and musicians, including Roland Hayes, Duke Ellington, Louis Armstrong, Bessie Smith, Jelly Roll Morton, W. C. Handy, and Aaron Douglas, came to public attention.

By 1920 the "coon" shows of Tom Fletcher, Ernest Hogan, George Walker and Bert Williams had given way to the musical revues and plays at the Apollo, Lafayette, and Lincoln theaters in New York. Already, talented black actors and musicians—Josephine Baker, Charles Gilpin, Paul Robeson, Frank Wilson, Florence Mills, Irvin Miller, Noble Sissle and Eubie Blake—were giving spectacular performances in plays and musicals by both black and white dramatists. The great success in 1921 of *Shuffle Along,* produced by Flourney Miller and Aubrey Lyles, was followed by the moderate success of many black musicals. In Washington, D.C., Montgomery Gregory organized and directed the Howard Players between 1919 and 1924, and in Harlem, W. E. B. DuBois founded the Krigwa Little Theater Group in 1923. In 1925, Garland Anderson's *Appearances* became the first full-length play by an Afro-American produced on Broadway. It was followed in 1929 by *Harlem,* a collaboration between Wallace Thurman and William Jordan Rapp. In 1927, Alain Locke and Montgomery Gregory collected twenty one-act plays by white and black playwrights. The collection was entitled *Plays of Negro Life: A Source Book of Native American Drama,* and in the introduction Locke quoted Eugene O'Neill's forecast that "the possibilities are limitless and to a dramatist open up new and intriguing opportunities: the gifts the Negro can and will bring to our native drama are invaluable ones." In 1930, Willis Richardson edited *Plays and Pageants from the Life of the Negro,* twelve nondialect works by black authors.

Many young painters and sculptors traveled abroad and moved away from the academic realism and modified impressionism

associated with Henry Tanner. Locke's *The New Negro* was the first book to present a number of drawings and paintings indicating the new trends in Afro-American art. As Judith Wragg Chase points out, by the midtwenties, the first group-conscious school of Afro-American art was practicing a combination of realism, Americanism, and cultural racialism. Freed from the timid conformity of earlier generations, black American artists experimented in a variety of styles and attempted a more objective and effective self-portrayal. Among the younger artists who achieved striking pictures of black life and characters were Aaron Douglas, Richard Barthé, Hale Woodruff, James A. Porter, Lois Mailou Jones, Archibald Motley, Malvin Gray Johnson, and Palmer Hayden.

In literature, the first stage of the Harlem Renaissance culminated in the events that led to the publication of *The New Negro* in December 1925. The first of these events was a dinner at the Civic Club on 21 March 1924, for a group called the "Writers' Guild." Charles Johnson describes the dinner in a letter to Ethel Ray (later secretary to Johnson in his *Opportunity* office):

> You could have been of enormous assistance to me this past week when I was arranging for the "debut" of the younger Negro writers. It was a most unusual affair—a dinner meeting at the Civic Club at which all of the younger Negro writers—Cullen, Walter White, Walrond, Jessie Fauset, Gwendolyn Bennett, Alain Locke, M. Gregory, met and chatted with the passing generation—DuBois, Jas. Weldon Johnson, Georgia Douglas Johnson, etc. and with the literary personages of the city: Carl Van Doren, editor of the *Century,* Frederick Allen of *Harper's,* Walter Bartlett of *Scribner's,* Devere Allen of the *World Tomorrow,* Freda Kirchwey of the *Nation,* Paul Kellogg of the *Survey,* Horace Liveright of Boni, Liveright Publishers, etc.—about 100 guests and tremendously impressive speaking. I'll have an account of it in the magazine. It would have given you a first hand introduction to the "last worders" in literature. But principally it served to stimulate a market for the new stuff which these young writers are turning out. The first definite reaction came in the form of an offer of one magazine to devote an entire issue to the similar subjects as treated by representatives of the group. A big plug was bitten off. Now it's a question of living up to the reputation. Yes, I should have added, a stream of manuscripts has started into my office from other aspirants.

Most of the prominent writers of the Renaissance were present at this dinner. (However, Langston Hughes, Claude McKay, and Jean Toomer were out of the country at the time.) Paul Kellogg, the editor of *Survey Graphic,* was also present; he invited Alain Locke to be the guest editor of a special issue devoted to Harlem. Locke accepted the invitation and the March 1925 issue of the *Survey* was entitled "Harlem, the Mecca of the New Negro"; it became "the single most notable achievement of the journal in these years." Two printings totaling 42,000 copies were sold, a record unsurpassed by the *Survey* until World War II. Even before the issue came out, Albert and Charles Boni expressed interest in publishing it later in

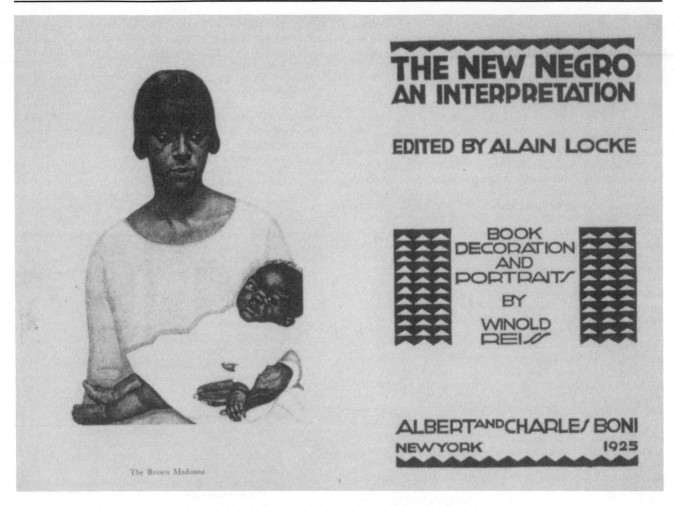

Frontispiece and title page of Alain Locke's anthology The New Negro.

book form and *The New Negro* was printed in a deluxe edition in December 1925.

In the words of Locke, *The New Negro* was put together "to document the New Negro culturally and socially,—to register the transformations of the inner and outer life of the Negro in America that have so significantly taken place in the last few years." He emphasized the need for and value of the Negro's self-portraiture, and he declared, "so far as he is culturally articulate, we shall let the Negro speak for himself." In a prophetic tone, Locke spoke of the New Negro in a national and international scope; he compared the New Negro movement with the "nascent movements of folk expression and self-determination" that were taking place "in India, in China, in Egypt, Ireland, Russia, Bohemia, Palestine and Mexico."

Locke, the first person to call the black arts movement of the twenties a renaissance, also became its major interpreter. He presented his views in four different essays included in his anthology, *The New Negro,* and continued to write review articles for *Opportunity* until 1945. With one or two exceptions, Locke chose pieces for *The New Negro* that illustrated his own philosophy. *The New Negro* contained a broad range of material—short stories, poems, one play, and many essays on aesthetic, historical, and sociological subjects. In addition, it contained illustrations by the young black artist Aaron Douglas and the Austrian artist Winold Reiss. To borrow the words of

Robert Hayden, "sophisticated and urbane, race conscious without being chauvinistic—there were several white contributors, for instance—it [*The New Negro*] presented facets of Negro life and thought that stimulated the imagination and challenged traditional prejudices."

Locke contended that a spirit of cultural nationalism, based on pride in the Negro's own traditions and folk arts, had led to a desire for self-determination and to "an unusual burst of creative expression." He compared the black's cultural reawakening to national movements in Ireland, Czechoslovakia, and Yugoslavia, but also saw the New Negro movement as parallel with and at the same time part of America's struggle to throw off European cultural hegemony and to develop its own literature, art, and music. Locke felt that the New Negro spirit embraced the masses as much as it did the Renaissance leaders and writers. "It is the rank and file who are leading, and the leaders who are following. A transformed and transforming psychology permeates the masses." He saw hope for the sharecroppers and plantation workers in their move to the urban setting; he placed great value on the cosmopolitan black communities in the North where blacks from diverse backgrounds could discover one another. He thought Harlem was a perfect example of this change, because Harlem was a point of contact for diverse groups with special motives, "so what began in terms of segregation becomes more and more, as its elements mix and react, the laboratory of a great race-welding."

Locke's philosophy of cultural pluralism is similar to the thinking of his white contemporaries Waldo Frank, V. F. Calverton, Randolph Bourne, and Van Wyck Brooks. Locke recognized that "the conditions that are molding a New Negro are [also] molding a new American attitude." To him, the racialism of the Negro was "no limitation or reservation with respect to American life, it is only a constructive effort to build the obstructions in the stream of his progress into an efficient dam of social energy and power." The choice for Locke, and for the white literary radicals, was "not between one way for the Negro and another way for the rest, but between American institutions frustrated on the one hand and American ideals progressively fulfilled and realized on the other."

Locke's optimism in *The New Negro* reflects the idealism of the American progressive reformers. Locke underplays the negative forces operating on the Negro and stresses the few hopeful signs on the horizon. He believed that the Old Negro had already become more of a myth than a man—the Negro who had for long been a formula rather than a human being—"a something to be argued about, condemned or defended . . . a social bogey or a social burden." At the same time, Locke saw the New Negro nourishing his racial roots and responding keenly to his responsibilities as a participant in the American experience. He defined as the creed of his own generation its

Alain Locke. Schomburg Center for Research in Black Culture, The New York Public Library, Astor, Lenox and Tilden Foundations.

belief in "the efficacy of collective effort, in race co-operation." He added:

> In this new group psychology we note the lapse of sentimental appeal, then the development of a more positive self-respect and self-reliance; the repudiation of social dependence, and then the gradual recovery from hypersensitiveness and "touchy" nerves, the repudiation of the double standard of judgment with its special philanthropic allowances and then the sturdier desire for objective and scientific appraisal; and finally the rise from social disillusionment of race pride, from the sense of social debt to the responsibilities of social contribution, and off-setting the necessary working and common-sense acceptance of restricted conditions, the belief in ultimate esteem and recognition.

The New Negro movement had no formal organization and its orientation "was more aesthetic and philosophical . . . than political." Of course, Locke never made high political claims for his philosophy of cultural pluralism. He made sure not to assign Harlem the political significance that places like Dublin and Prague had for cultural movements in New Ireland and New Czechoslovakia. And although he welcomed a scientific exposition of the Negro race by objective sociologists and anthropologists, he did not think more knowledge necessarily meant better treatment for blacks. He also observed that the New Negro was only a "forced radical"—a social protestant rather than a genuine radical, as he put it. Notwithstanding the basic soundness of his views on racial self-expression in a culturally pluralistic society, his contention that such self-expression "must lead to considerable further betterment of race relationships" is politically naive. Like the black political leaders of the period, Locke seems to have believed that the American system would ultimately work for the Negro, but he refused to take cognizance of the disagreeable political leverage the system recognized. Such an approach implied a relatively complete dependence of any black hopes for political change or reform upon white men of influence and their good intentions.

Strictly in terms of art and literature, however, Locke's views on racial self-expression by black Americans offered a valuable perspective for young black writers. In Locke's pluralistic view, there was no conflict between being "American" and being "Negro," but rather an opportunity to enrich both through cultural reciprocity. In a way, Locke was reinterpreting DuBois' "double consciousness" concept for aesthetic and cultural uses, and it seems there was enough room in Locke's view for many different kinds of talents to exist and thrive together. For *The New Negro*, he deliberately chose poems and short stories that illustrated his views about the use of folk culture and about "realism." Locke used the term "realism" rather loosely. He gives some indication of his meaning in an article written on French-African literature in 1924. In this article, Locke praised René Maran's novel *Batouala* for "its candor, its ruthlessness, and its humane but unemotional human portraiture." He also valued *Batouala* because it rejected "that decadent cult of the primitive which is the pastime of the sophisticated." Locke's realism has been defined negatively to include "works which were *not* in the genteel tradition, *not* melodramatic, sentimental, romantic or didactic; works in which the characters and situations were *not* idealized or sentimentalized, or viciously stereotyped. He also meant works which were *not* written in the Oscar Wilde manner of decadent sophistication."

Locke was, therefore, suggesting a well-balanced and flexible approach for the black writer to transform the richness and diversity, the intensity and anguish of the black American experience into the stuff of art and literature. He had little sympathy for the didactic and propagandistic literature that DuBois called for, nor did he want to inhibit the artistic depiction of the Negro by confining it to a particular class, group, or region. Alain Locke did not see any direct connection between the black American's "self-expression" and the African arts that had inspired and influenced the work of many European painters and sculptors. According to Locke, the most important lesson the black artist could derive from African art was "not cultural inspiration or technical innovations, but the lesson of a classic background, the lesson of discipline, of style, of technical control." At the same time, Locke emphasized the American identity of the young black writers by suggesting that "race for them is but an idiom of experience, a sort of added enriching adventure and discipline." He hoped in time to develop a Negro school of art and literature, with its own distinctive idiom and subject matter, that would parallel the growth of other "regional" and "local color" schools in American literature. To Locke, all such developments were a welcome indication of America's ethnic and regional diversity.

Locke's view of Afro-American artistic expression did not have a tremendous impact, even though Locke did more than write reviews and magazine articles to get his views across to the younger Renaissance poets and novelists. Most of the writers included in *The New Negro* were Locke's protégés, "men he knew personally, whose work he had encouraged, criticized, applauded, promoted and sometimes supported financially." Among the younger writers who received special encouragement from Alain Locke are Jean Toomer, Countee Cullen, Langston Hughes, and Rudolph Fisher.

Locke, however, was not alone in his encouragement of black writers. James Weldon Johnson was of great help to a number of young writers, especially Langston Hughes and Claude McKay. Johnson consistently praised and defended Hughes' blues-based poetry, and his sympathetic understanding of McKay's position on class issues sustained McKay through continual wrangles with black American leaders and critics. Although Walter White did not always succeed, he made genuine efforts to help in the publication of works by writers as diverse as Jean Toomer, Nella Larsen, Claude McKay, Countee Cullen, and Georgia Douglas Johnson. Carl Van Vechten was also instrumental in finding publishers for Renaissance writers. Victor F. Calverton, the literary radical, offered personal assistance to many black writers and encouraged them in his magazine *The Modern Quarterly.*

If anyone matched the enthusiasm and vigor of Alain Locke in promoting the concept of a renaissance in the twenties, it was the sociologist Charles S. Johnson, who was later to be the first black president of Fisk University. Johnson did not, however, share Locke's optimistic vision of cultural pluralism. Under the influence of Robert E. Park, Johnson saw the Afro-American as a marginal person, who, although rent by the conflict between two cultures, could stand apart and objectively view each. For him, the black's move from folk culture to industrial culture was an inevitable and painful process. Johnson was the first editor of *Opportunity,* and, for the five years he was editor, he stressed the need for the black American to advantageously understand and absorb this change from rural South to urban North. Although *Opportunity* placed more emphasis on creative writing than DuBois' *The Crisis,* it was

equally interested in examining migration, education, housing, health, and employment as they affected the daily lives of black Americans. As a pragmatist, Johnson offered incentives to youth authors through *Opportunity* literary contests, and encouraged contacts between the black writers and the white publishing world. His objective was, to use his own words, "to stimulate and encourage creative literary effort among Negroes . . . to encourage the reading of literature both by Negro authors and about Negro life . . . to bring these writers into contact with the general world of letters . . . to stimulate and foster a type of writing by Negroes which shakes itself free of deliberate propaganda and protest." In 1927, Johnson edited *Ebony and Topaz,* which in many ways was a companion volume to Locke's *The New Negro.* He intended *Ebony and Topaz* as an indication of the black writer's increasing maturity and independence in portraying black life. It is difficult today to account for all the factors that prevented the growth of a black American school of literature. Harlem Renaissance writing is marked by racialism, but the writers reflect the spirit of the times in their refusal to join causes or movements. "Individuality is what we should strive for. Let each seek his own salvation," says Raymond Taylor, the alter ego of Wallace Thurman in *Infants of the Spring.* As a creative writer, Zora Neale Hurston was interested not in social problems, but in the problems of individuals, black or white. Alain Locke's idea of a black literary movement had political implications, but he did not base it on a rigid social or political ideology. Locke's views were opposed by W. E. B. DuBois, Benjamin Brawley, and Allison Davis, who contended that black writers had a responsibility to defend and uplift the race by portraying educated, middle-class Negroes. Claude McKay, acutely conscious of his position as a black man in Western civilization, asserted his artistic independence while alternating between Marxist and nationalistic ideologies. Wallace Thurman, lost in the world of contemporary bohemia, would not compromise with the high artistic standards he set for himself and others. There were, however, many black writers of the period who—independently or under Locke's influence—resolved their dilemmas of conflicting racial and artistic loyalties in ways resembling Locke's approach. Among these writers are Langston Hughes, Jean Toomer, Rudolph Fisher, Eric Walrond, Sterling Brown, Arna Bontemps, and Zora Neale Hurston.

It is necessary to look outside Harlem and black America for the major explanation of the Harlem Renaissance writers' failure to develop into a cohesive group or movement. In discussing white interest in the Negro, Huggins argues that "the black-white relationship has been symbiotic, [and that] blacks have been essential to white identity (and whites to blacks)." In American history, this black-white symbiosis has resulted in the black being called on to uphold a new stereotype. In the twenties, both in Europe and America, interest in the Negro came to be focused around the cult of the primitive. It had become fashionable in the Jazz Age to defy prohibition and to find joy and abandon in exotic music and dance. In such an atmosphere "the Negro had obvious uses: he represented the unspoiled child of nature, the noble savage—carefree, spontaneous and sexually uninhibited." A popular misinterpretation of Freudian theory contributed to the promotion of primitivism. Freud was seen as exalting instinct over intellect in a revolt against the Puritan spirit. In his *Civilization and its Discontents,* Freud had contended that civilization is based upon renunciation of "powerful instinctual urgencies," and the privation of instinctual gratification demanded by the cultural ideal was a major source of neurosis. No wonder, then, that popularized Freudianism became "the rationalization of sex primitivism," and gave the ''cult of the primitive . . . an extraordinary foothold on this continent.''

The Negro fad of the twenties encompassed a new Euro-American interest in jazz, African art, and sculpture and a return to the values of a preindustrial society. But in the popular version of the fad the black was simply an uninhibited and unmechanized soul. Paul Morand, the French journalist, expressed gratitude for the Harlem black's contribution toward shattering ''the mechanical rhythm of America.'' With revealing imagery, he compares blacks on the subway, ''clinging with long hooking hands to the leather straps, and chewing their gum,'' with ''the great apes of Equitorial Africa.'' Young black girls playing on the streets with ''an animal swiftness, a warlike zest . . . savage and triumphant,'' suggested to him ''black virgins of some African revolution of the future.'' Morand was sure that if the policeman, the symbol of white civilization, were to vanish from the street corner in Harlem, this ''miniature Africa'' would immediately revert to a semi-savage state like Haiti, ''given to voodoo and rhetorical despotism.'' (pp. 13-21)

Carl Van Vechten's *Nigger Heaven* (1926) was the most influential novel, by a white writer, in establishing the image of the Negro as primitive. The book ran into several editions and sold over 100,000 copies; it initiated an unprecedented nationwide interest in the Negro and clearly demonstrated the commercial value of books written about the Negro. And although primitivism had different and wider uses for some black writers—especially Claude McKay—many of the Renaissance writers ignored the challenge of Locke's pluralistic vision under the bandwagon effect of Carl Van Vechten's *Nigger Heaven*. (p. 22)

Although a detailed analysis of *Nigger Heaven* may not be pertinent here, an evaluation of the influence of Van Vechten and his book on the milieu and literary careers of the Harlem Renaissance writers is. *Nigger Heaven* is the story of Mary Love, a prim and pretty Harlem librarian, who falls in love with Byron Karson, a struggling young writer. Byron, a recent graduate of the University of Pennsylvania, has been told that he has promise, which he interprets to mean: ''pretty good for a colored man.'' Like Ray in Claude McKay's *Home to Harlem*, Mary Love cannot take sex and love lightly. Randolph Pettijohn, the numbers king, desires her and offers her marriage. ''Ah ain't got no education lak you, but Ah got money, plenty of et, an' Ah got love,'' he tells her. Byron meanwhile fails to find a job compatible with his level of education and refuses to accept a menial job. The exotic and primitive aspects of Harlem life surround Byron's orgiastic affair with Lasca Sartoris, ''a gorgeous brown Messalina of Seventh Avenue.'' Lasca, however, deserts Byron for Pettijohn. Byron avenges himself by impulsively firing two bullets into the prostrate body of Pettijohn, who has already been killed by Scarlet Creeper. At the end, Byron surrenders helplessly to the police.

The unsettling effect of *Nigger Heaven* is best seen in the controversy its publication caused among early reviewers. Many white reviewers questioned its literary value. The *New Republic* thought the book was more successful as a traveler's guide to Harlem than as a novel, and the unimpressed *Independent* called it dull and disappointing in its attempt ''to prove that cultivated Negroes talk French and understand the scores of Opera.'' However, V. F. Calverton praised *Nigger Heaven* for its straightforward presentation of Negro life, and the *New York Times* critic, in a wholly favorable review, concluded that it was a study of the ''plight of Colored intellectuals.''

For the black reviewers Eric Walrond and Langston Hughes, the book was truthful and objective; Hughes described it as ''the first real passionately throbbing novel of contemporary Negro life.'' But the balance weighed heavily in favor of the book's black detractors. Offended by the title, many simply refused to read the book, and those who read it found the contents distasteful. Allison Davis accused Van Vechten of having ''warped Negro life into a fantastic barbarism,'' while J. A. Rogers suggested that ''Van Vechten Heaven'' would be a better title for the book, since Harlem seemed to provide ''release of soul'' for Van Vechten and others, who were satiated by the meager pleasures offered by the ''Nordic'' world. According to DuBois, the *Police Gazette* was likely to furnish material of a better quality than *Nigger Heaven*, which was ''neither truthful nor artistic. . . . It is a caricature. It is worse than untruth because it is a mass of half-truths''; it is ''ludicrously out of focus and undeniably misleading'' in trying to express all racial traits in the cabaret life of Harlem, when the overwhelming majority of blacks had never been to cabarets. ''The average colored man in Harlem,'' DuBois added, ''is an everyday laborer, attending church, lodge and movie and is as conservative and as conventional as ordinary working folk elsewhere.''

The specter of *Nigger Heaven* lurks behind almost all reviews written after 1926. Benjamin Brawley, Allison Davis, and W.

Advertisement for Carl Van Vechten's novel Nigger Heaven. *From* The Borzoi Broadside, *published by Alfred A. Knopf, Inc. Reprinted by permission of Alfred A. Knopf, Inc.*

E. B. DuBois asserted that some younger black writers and many white writers were misguided by *Nigger Heaven,* and they argued that the emphasis on the exotic and the primitive, the sensual and the bawdy in the depiction of the Negro was detrimental to the black's political future in the United States.

The fad of primitivism cannot be blamed entirely on Van Vechten or on the group of whites who wrote about the Negro in the twenties, but it is reasonable to conclude that the publication of *Nigger Heaven* made many black writers keenly aware of the commercial possibilities of the primitivistic formula, and made it more difficult for the Harlem Renaissance to develop into a black literary movement. The unusual success of *Nigger Heaven* and later of McKay's *Home to Harlem* clearly indicated an eagerness for works exalting the exotic, the sensual, and the primitive. This interest had "no minor effect on certain members of the Harlem *literati* whose work was just what the Jazz Age ordered." Thus, black writers who were willing to describe the exotic scene "had no trouble finding sponsors, publishers and immediate popularity." In his autobiography, *The Big Sea,* Langston Hughes recalled the pessimistic judgment of Wallace Thurman, who thought that the Negro vogue had made the Harlem Renaissance writers "too conscious of ourselves, had flattered and spoiled us and had provided too many easy opportunities for some of us to drink gin and more gin." (pp. 23-5)

W. E. B. DuBois set the stage for the controversy over the depiction of the Negro in literature around the issue of art versus propaganda. DuBois was steeped in the nineteenth-century genteel view of literature, and in his review of *The New Negro,* he attacked Locke's basic approach—that of fostering uninhibited self-expression and realism instead of promoting art for race uplift. He noted that *The New Negro* expressed "better than any book that has been published in the last ten years the present state of thought and culture among American Negroes," but charged that Locke's insistence on Beauty rather than Propaganda is likely "to turn the Negro Renaissance into decadence." In February 1926, DuBois followed his review of *The New Negro* by sending out a questionnaire for a symposium in *The Crisis* entitled "The Negro in Art—How shall he be Portrayed?" He objected to the concept of artistic freedom because, he said, "the net result of American literature to date [has been] to picture the twelve million black Americans as prostitutes, thieves and fools and . . . such 'freedom' in art is miserably unfair."

The results of the *Crisis* symposium on "The Negro in Art" are interesting as much for what they reveal about the aesthetic criteria of black (and white) critics of the Harlem Renaissance as for the light they throw indirectly on the continuing debate over Black Aesthetic today. DuBois anticipated the controversy over *Nigger Heaven* by raising, as the last and most important of his questions for the symposium, the issue of the young black writers succumbing to the temptation of following "the popular trend in portraying Negro character in the underworld rather than seeking to paint the truth about themselves and their own social class." Here are the six questions that preceded this:

> 1. When the artist, black or white, portrays Negro characters, is he under any obligations or limitations as to the sort of character he will portray?
>
> 2. Can any author be criticized for painting the worst or the best characters of a group?

> 3. Can publishers be criticized for refusing to handle novels that portray Negroes of education and accomplishment, on the ground that these characters are no different from white folk and therefore not interesting?
>
> 4. What are Negroes to do when they are continually painted at their worst and judged by the public as they are painted?
>
> 5. Does the situation of the educated Negro in America with its pathos, humiliation and tragedy call for artistic treatment at least as sincere and sympathetic as "Porgy" received?
>
> 6. Is not the continual portrayal of the sordid, foolish and criminal among Negroes convincing the world that this and this alone is really and essentially Negroid, and preventing white artists from knowing any other types and preventing black artists from daring to paint them?

The didactic tone of DuBois' questions is unmistakable; here as well as in the book reviews he wrote for *The Crisis,* DuBois demonstrates his limitations as a literary critic. DuBois' perceptive sociopolitical writings are impressive, but his literary criticism is outmoded and reveals his inability to break free of the limitations imposed by his New England Puritan background.

DuBois published excerpts from answers to his questions in various issues of *The Crisis* between March and November

March 1924 cover of The Crisis.

1926. The respondents to DuBois' symposium included the well-known white and black figures H. L. Mencken, Carl Van Vechten, DuBose Heyward, Mary White Ovington, Joel E. Spingarn, Sinclair Lewis, Sherwood Anderson, Vachel Lindsay, Julia Peterkin, Langston Hughes, Countee Cullen, Charles W. Chesnutt, Walter White, Jessie Redmon Fauset, Benjamin Brawley, and Georgia Douglas Johnson. However, Rudolph Fisher, Wallace Thurman, Claude McKay, Sterling Brown, Alain Locke, and Arna Bontemps were conspicuously absent from the list.

According to Clare B. Crane, DuBois must have been disappointed in the answers he received. Only Countee Cullen, Benjamin Brawley, and Jessie Fauset agreed with DuBois that writers were not completely free agents in choosing how to represent black life. Charles W. Chestnutt spoke for most when he declared: "The realm of art is almost the only territory in which the mind is free, and of all the arts that of creative fiction is the freest. . . . I see no possible reason why a colored writer should not have the same freedom. We want no color line in literature." In response to the second question, most answered that a writer could portray the best and/or the worst, so long as his portrait is reasonably accurate. Many respondents, including Countee Cullen, Vachel Lindsay, and DuBose Heyward, recognized that publishers are more concerned with the salability of a book than with its moral tenor or class orientation, but hoped that publishers would encourage writers who wanted to portray the potential drama in the lives of educated Negroes. Some suggested, in response to the fourth question, that the black novelist should get even by depicting the white man at his worst. (But this was easier said than done and easier done than published.) Mencken said that if he found the white man extremely ridiculous, "to a Negro, he must be a hilarious spectacle, indeed." Nobody denied the potential drama in the "pathos, humiliation and tragedy" of the educated black in the United States, but many respondents warned against giving in to propaganda in attempting a literary portrayal of the subject. Walter White found it necessary to recognize that every "honest craftsman . . . can only pour his knowledge and experience, real or imagined, through the alembic of his own mind and let the creations of his subjective or objective self stand or fall by whatever literary standards are current at a time." The sixth question apparently had wide-ranging racial implications in American society. DuBois felt, not unjustifiably perhaps, that the racist elements of American society would use the slightest scrap of evidence to support what they already believed—the inferiority of the Negro. In answering this question, Robert T. Kerlin anticipated Richard Wright's naturalistic fiction by suggesting that the black artist should depict the "sordid," the "foolish," and the "criminal" Negro in relation to "the environment and the conditions—of white creation, of course—which have made him what he is." And he added, "Let the black artist not hesitate to show what white civilization is doing to both races."

The last question on the list received its most provocative answer from Carl Van Vechten: "The squalor of Negro life, the vice of Negro life, offer a wealth of novel, exotic, picturesque material to the artist. On the other hand, there is very little difference if any between the life of a wealthy or cultured Negro and that of a white man of the same class. The question is: Are Negro writers going to write about this exotic material while it is still fresh or will they continue to make a free gift of it to white authors who will exploit it until not a drop of vitality remains?" Van Vechten's *Nigger Heaven,* published a few months later, signaled black writers to take up the challenge of exploiting the exotic material that lay close to their lives or face the threat of preemption. DuBose Heyward reflected on the broader implications of the question when he said: "I think the young colored writer in America need not be afraid to portray any aspect of his racial life. . . . I feel convinced that he alone will produce the ultimate and authentic record of his own people. . . . A real subjective literature must spring from the race itself." Charles W. Chesnutt, speaking from his long experience as a writer, attacked the propagandistic tenor of DuBois' question and asserted the primacy of aesthetic criteria in the writing and reading of literature:

> I think there is little danger of young colored writers writing too much about Negro characters in the underworld, so long as they do it well. Some successful authors have specialized in crook stories, and some crooks are mighty interesting people . . . there is no formula for these things, and the discerning writer will make his own rules. . . . The colored writer, generally speaking, has not yet passed the point of thinking of himself first as a Negro, burdened with the responsibility of defending and uplifting his race. Such a frame of mind, however praiseworthy from a moral standpoint, is bad for art. Tell your story, and if it is on a vital subject, well told, with an outcome that commends itself to right-thinking people, it will, if interesting, be an effective brief for whatever cause it incidentally may postulate. . . . But the really epical race novel, in which love and hatred, high endeavor, success and failure, sheer comedy and stark tragedy are mingled, is yet to be written, and let us hope that a man of Negro blood may write it.

(pp. 27-31)

Many Harlem Renaissance writers who led active lives past the twenties talked and wrote about the period, but Wallace Thurman provided the only detailed contemporary account of the movement. *Infants of the Spring* was published in 1932 toward the end of the Renaissance, a little before Thurman's untimely death; the book is a thinly veiled and largely undramatized fictional treatment of the black Renaissance writers. (p. 32)

Infants of the Spring presents mediocre artists lost in a web of frivolity and recalcitrance without purpose or privacy, unable to achieve anything worthwhile. (p. 33)

Although it is not necessary to fully agree with Thurman's cripplingly self-conscious judgment on individual writers, including himself, *Infants of the Spring* represents a coming-of-age of the Harlem Renaissance *literati.* It demonstrates the ability of the movement to evaluate and possibly modify its direction. Unfortunately, there was little opportunity for Thurman's criticisms to be absorbed. Two years earlier, the stock market had crashed, and white America's ability to sustain and enjoy the Negro fad had been severely hampered. Perhaps, as Ralph Ellison has pointed out, the black writer of the twenties "had wanted to be fashionable and this insured, even more effectively than the approaching Depression, the failure of the 'New Negro' movement." Black writers had "climbed aboard the bandwagon" of exoticism and decadence signaled by *Nigger Heaven* and enjoyed the era when the Negro was in vogue. By the midthirties, exotic and genteel novels were no longer popular with the publishers and were attacked by a new breed of black writers and critics. In early 1934, Eugene Saxton, who had handled McKay's work at Harper & Brothers, bluntly informed him that his popularity had been part of a passing fad. In 1940, Langston Hughes spoke for many when he said, "I had a swell time while it [the Negro Renaissance] lasted. But I thought it wouldn't last long. . . . For how could a large number of people be crazy about Negroes forever?"

It is unfair to evaluate the Harlem Renaissance by the hindsight judgments of Langston Hughes and Claude McKay, or the aesthetic criteria of the DuBois-Brawley school, or the theoretical constructs of Alain Locke, or even the detailed satire on its members and aims by Wallace Thurman. Intense intellectual and artistic activity created fruitful controversy over basic issues relating to art and its appreciation. The racial matrix of artistic expression received serious critical attention and some of the latter-day Afro-American concepts—such as Black Aesthetic—were prefigured in discussions of Harlem Renaissance artists. This is important, even though the attitudes of most Renaissance writers in these matters were characterized by ambivalence and tension, and they did not as a group develop common approaches, and many individual artists failed to resolve their conflicting impulses about race and art while others found only tentative solutions.

Two articles, along with the correspondence that followed from the two authors, contain the aesthetic and critical criteria that underlay black writing in the twenties. These are "The Negro-Art Hokum" and "The Negro Artist and the Racial Mountain," written by George S. Schuyler and Langston Hughes, respectively, for two consecutive issues of *Nation* in June 1926 [see Additional Bibliography]. The exchange between Schuyler and Hughes also confirms that a class bias was consciously or unconsciously at the root of most controversies among Renaissance writers and critics. Schuyler postulates that Negro art is simply an African phenomenon: "to suggest the possibility of any such development among the ten million colored people in this republic is self-evident foolishness." Spirituals, blues, jazz, and the Charleston are not racial expression, but "contributions of a caste in a certain section of the country." Otherwise, in literature, painting, sculpture, and drama, the American Negro has hardly produced anything racially distinctive, because "the Afro-American is merely a lampblacked Anglo-Saxon." He attributes the fad of racial differences to "a few writers with a paucity of themes [who] have seized upon imbecilities of the Negro rustics and clowns and palmed them off as authentic and characteristic Aframerican behavior."

With his uncompromising realism and keen observation, Schuyler notes the danger that any concept of racial difference will be used by Negrophobes and racists to prove the Negro's inferiority: "On this baseless premise, so flattering to the white mob, that the blackamoor is inferior and fundamentally different, is erected the postulate that he must needs be peculiar; and when he attempts to portray life through the medium of art, it must of necessity be a peculiar art." He responded to Hughes' defense of racial art by asserting that black masses in America were no different from the white masses and that both watched "the lazy world go round" and had "their nip of gin on Saturday nights."

Langston Hughes, in turn, noticed the taint of self-hatred in Schuyler's view of black art and culture. In his response to Schuyler's letter, Hughes wrote: "The very fact that Negroes do straighten their hair and try to forget their racial background makes them different from white people. If they were exactly like the dominant class they would not have to try so hard to imitate them." In his essay, he projected a culturally pluralistic view of black art that placed special emphasis on the integrity of the artist. He indicated that for most blacks and black artists, "the word white comes to be unconsciously a symbol of all the virtues. It holds for the children beauty, morality and money."

For Hughes, the whole issue of racial expression converged on the issue of class within the black group. The "low-down folks," Hughes said, "furnish a wealth of colorful, distinctive material for any artist because they still hold their own individuality in the face of American standardizations. And perhaps these common people will give to the world its truly great Negro artist, the one who is not afraid to be himself." Hughes refrained from using the black American's atavistic or African heritage as a point of departure from his white counterpart. He saw enough themes in the lives of black and white Americans to "furnish a black artist with a lifetime of creative work. To these the Negro artist can give his racial individuality, his heritage of rhythm and warmth, and his incongruous humor that, so often, as in the Blues, becomes ironic laughter mixed with tears." In direct response to Schuyler's charge that "Negro propaganda art, even when glorifying the 'primitiveness' of the American Negro masses is hardly more than a protest against a feeling of inferiority," Hughes contended that "until America has completely absorbed the Negro and until segregation and racial self-consciousness have entirely disappeared, the true work of art from the Negro artist is bound, if it have any color and distinctiveness at all, to reflect his racial background and his racial environment."

As a black artist, Hughes welcomed a growing middle-class black audience for his work, but regarded it as a potential threat to his artistic integrity. "The Negro artist works against the undertow of sharp criticism and misunderstanding from his own group and unintentional bribes from the whites." Using his own poems and Jean Toomer's *Cane* as examples of the kind of racial expression he approved and cherished, Hughes asserted his independence of both whites and blacks in what came to be known later as the literary manifesto of younger Renaissance writers:

> We younger Negro artists who create now intend to express our individual dark-skinned selves without fear or shame. If white people are pleased we are glad. If they are not, it doesn't matter. We know we are beautiful. And ugly too. The tom-tom cries and the tom-tom laughs. If colored people are pleased we are glad. If they are not, their displeasure doesn't matter either. We build our temples for tomorrow, strong as we know how, and we stand on top of the mountain, free within ourselves.

Langston Hughes' clear and resonant voice expresses the highest artistic ideals and achievements of the Harlem Renaissance. (pp. 36-9)

Amritjit Singh, "'When the Negro Was in Vogue': The Harlem Renaissance and Black America," in his The Novels of the Harlem Renaissance: Twelve Black Writers, 1923-1933, *The Pennsylvania State University Press, 1976, pp. 1-39.*

MARGARET PERRY

[*Perry is an American short story writer, poet, and critic. In the following excerpt, she introduces the most prominent authors of the Harlem Renaissance.*]

By the early 1920s there was something special emerging among the blacks, who—in the language of the day—were called colored or negro (small "n"), and the one thing that seemed to emerge was an interest in the black person's past. Perhaps the activity of this whole decade was no more than the following definition [by Joseph Jarab] suggests; but the main notion is all-important nevertheless: "The Harlem Renaissance was a renaissance in one sense only, namely in the renewed interest in the African part of the black American consciousness, which resulted in the programmatic use of the true values kept alive in black folklore." The past would be the touchstone, then—the black person's true ancestral past, which was rooted in Africa.

The definition of a period some claim did not exist represents a challenge that cannot be ignored: the Negro Renaissance, the Harlem Renaissance, the decade of the New Negro—whatever one pleases to call it—did exist in fact as well as in spirit. The term Harlem Renaissance is the most widely known and used, for it seems to help focus on the informing spirit that served to inspire black artists to produce poetry and novels, short stories and essays, music, and art. During this expanded decade—spanning approximately 1919-1934—the black world came of age in an artistic sense. It does not seem too strained to compare this volatile period to fifteenth-century Italy, as Walter Pater described the cultural setting: "Here artists and philosophers and those whom the action of the world has elevated and made keen, do not live in isolation, but breathe a common air, and catch light and heat from each other's thoughts. There is a spirit of general elevation and enlightenment in which all alike communicate. It is the unity of this spirit which gives unity to all the various products of the Renaissance. . . ." By the time World War I ended, black writers—just like the now more forceful, ordinary, non-artist blacks—felt freer and unshackled from the old images of the past. Emphasizing, in part, a commonality of the spirit that shaped their lives—that is, the African—the writers attempted to translate this newly found awareness into poems, plays, novels, short stories, and related literature.

The movement that gradually declared itself was self-consciously Afro-American: the African heritage was reclaimed and then proclaimed; slowly, and without a definite pattern, it was reshaped into an American idiom that supposedly stretched and spanned the years from capture, the "middle-passage," slavery, and the putative emancipation, up through freedom in a multitude of forms, to the variously defined period of the 1920s. If this decade, plus a few years, was ill-defined by its participants (and observers), it could be looked upon as a time of partial approaches towards self-realization, a time (in Harold Cruse's estimation) of "inspired aimlessness" [see Additional Bibliography]. (pp. xv-xvii)

The major writers of the Harlem Renaissance were few; the number of writers were many. Jean Toomer stands out as the most creative, because he experimented with style and form and the uses of symbols. Langston Hughes, who was much closer idiomatically to black life and to art that depicted ordinary black life, was the most inventive and unrestricted of the literary artists. In addition to these two most lasting examples of Renaissance writing talent are the following, in alphabetical order:

Countee Cullen
W. E. B. Du Bois
Jessie R. Fauset
Rudolph Fisher
Zora Neale Hurston
James Weldon Johnson
Nella Larsen
Claude McKay
Willis Richardson
Anne Spencer
Wallace Thurman
Walter White

The poets seemed to dominate the period, although some poets combined genres and produced fiction as well; Hughes, Cullen, and McKay, as well as Toomer, come to mind immediately. More short stories than are known were published; yet few Harlem Renaissance writers achieved mastery of this form. Rudolph Fisher was probably the best short story writer; McKay and Hurston also wrote some moving and well-told stories. Hughes represents the problem of attempting to define the Harlem Renaissance within the space of specific years: his best short stories appear in print from 1933 forward. (pp. xx-xxi)

One of the most consciously literary artists was Jean Toomer; he was deeply conscious of trying to shape his experiences and what he thought were the experiences of blacks into a form that became a work of art. His efforts to order experience into form, with meaning and emotion, were linked with his struggles to discover his personal spiritual and moral center. Toomer was also one of the few black writers who spent significant time with his white counterparts in Greenwich Village and in Europe. Thus, it is possible to connect him spiritually and thematically with some of the ideas that other writers of this period both in America and abroad were pondering—the lost generation writers, for instance: modern man's spiritual dearth, his lack of spiritual values; a rejection of bourgeois values; an obsession with death. Added to these areas of concern was Toomer's interest for a time in his genesis as an Afro-American—that strange anomaly that could make him black, although his own color was "white," as were his two wives. (Later, he was to repudiate his color, declaring he was of no race but solely of the human race.)

There are critics who may argue the aesthetics of Jean Toomer, writer—for he was enigmatic and contradictory. But he produced a complex, rich book about Negro life—*Cane*—which was published in 1923, demonstrating (particularly in the last section, "Kabnis") an artistic search for the black person's roots. As Robert Bone has stated, the figure of Father John in this section emphasizes Toomer's concern for this "link with the Negro's ancestral past" [see excerpt below]. Indeed, Toomer himself describes the following influence upon his life: "A visit to Georgia last fall [1921] was the starting point of almost everything of worth that I have done. I heard folk-songs come from the lips of Negro peasants. I saw the rich dusk beauty that I had heard many false accents about, and of which till then, I was somewhat skeptical. And a deep part of my nature, a part that I had repressed, sprang suddenly to life and responded to them."

Cane is divided into three sections; the first and the last are set in the rural South and the middle section takes place primarily in Washington, D.C. One has portraits of black life interspersed with impressionistic poetry. As an insistence, for example, upon the connection with the black race's past, Toomer writes: "the Dixie Pike has grown from a goat path in Africa." Toomer explores, often viscerally, the rural black life as it affects the poor men and women—especially the women. The circumscribed, restricted life of these individuals is the world

Arna Bontemps, Melvin B. Tolson, Jacob Reddix, Owen Dodson, Robert Hayden, Sterling Brown, Zora Neale Hurston, Margaret Walker, and Langston Hughes at a 1952 festival of black poets.

of Toomer's imagination and craft. We see this in such stories as "Fern," or "Esther," or in "Karintha"—the woman who is full of the seed for future generations, desired only for her body and not for her self. There is no escape for these women who demonstrate the waste resulting from incomplete lives—lives stunted and twisted by the fate of being black and poor in the white man's South of the 1920s.

The importance of *Cane* can be demonstrated by the last story, "Kabnis," which tells of a young man, Ralph Kabnis, moving from fear and ignorance to a greater awareness of himself and his roots. Within a brief space Toomer erects an illuminating edifice with characters inside who live forever in the reader's mind—Halsey, Lewis, Carrie K., Layman, for instance—because they each help Kabnis to define and find himself. And there is Father John, the archetypal father of blacks; a former slave, he is a symbol of the true past of the American Negro. With his enigmatic aid, along with that of others, Kabnis begins to come to grips with the past, not only by claiming his ties with the American South (i.e., Africa transplanted) but also by admitting to the past indignities of slavery and oppression.

Finally, in his efforts to find self, Toomer has explored the varieties of blacks living in the South and in the city in this small but impressive collection of tales that pulse with a vibrancy and intensity. *Cane* scholars battle with Toomer's mean-

ings, for it is a complex book—as complex, probably, as the man who wrote it and mused: "[*Cane* was] a swan song. It was a song of an end. . . . And why people have expected me to write a second and a third and fourth book like 'Cane' is one of the queer misunderstandings of my life."

While Toomer brought the African past into the rural South for that self-journey into one's true origins, Countee Cullen approached the meaning of his race and his place in American society with all of the contradictory emotional and psychological ambivalence that characterized the black bourgeoisie's probe into Afro-American cultural history. On the one hand Cullen stated, "I want to be known as a poet and not as a Negro poet," and on the other hand, "Most things I write I do for the sheer love of the music in them. Somehow I find my poetry of itself treating of the Negro, of his joys and his sorrows—mostly the latter—and of the heights and depths of emotion I feel as a Negro."

Countee Cullen was primarily a lyricist, influenced by romantic poets of the nineteenth and twentieth centuries; but he was also a man who was committed to pointing out the indignities heaped upon his people. Still, he was a true disciple of beauty, and he wanted his writing to reveal a sense of style and form and a consciousness of writing as art instead of polemic. Keats was perhaps the poet that Cullen most admired; also, his most characteristic lyrics show a penchant toward the style of A. E. Housman, Millay, and E. A. Robinson. Jay Saunders Redding called him the Ariel of Negro poets, one who "cannot beat the tom-tom above a faint whisper nor know the primitive delights of black rain and scarlet sun," a writer of "delightful love lyrics." Therefore, it is not surprising to note that, besides the race problem, Cullen's two most constant themes were love and death. Although considered by many critics as the least race-conscious poet, nevertheless, Cullen will be remembered, Charles Glicksberg has suggested, for his poems that deal with race or the race problem.

In defining the aspects of good poetry, Cullen stated: "Good poetry is a lofty thought beautifully expressed . . . poetry should not be too intellectual; it should deal more . . . with the emotion. The highest type of poem is that which warmly stirs the emotions, which awakens a responsive chord in the human heart. Poetry, like music, depends upon feeling rather than intellect, although there should of course be enough to satisfy the mind, too."

In trying to be raceless as well as to address the problems of the Afro-American in American civilization, Cullen represents the dichotomized black artist who would not repudiate his heritage but does not want to be judged solely in terms of it. Jessie Redmon Fauset, another Harlem Renaissance writer, was also of this persuasion, although her novels always dealt with the woes of the prejudice that the middle-class black faced. Langston Hughes, on the other hand, was of a vastly different cast of mind.

Hughes swaggered above the hurts and pressure of being black in America; he reveled in his blackness. A person—black or white—who did not know about or appreciate the ways of black folk was the deprived one in Hughes's canon of culture. And in his manifesto about art and culture Hughes declared: "We younger Negro artists who create now intend to express our individual dark-skinned selves without fear or shame. If white people are pleased we are glad. If they are not, it doesn't matter. We know we are beautiful. And ugly too. . . . If colored people are pleased we are glad. If they are not, their displeasure doesn't matter either." And Hughes was true to his declaration, frequently being castigated for his love of common blacks and his preoccupation with writing jazz and blues poetry. Nevertheless, it was at the beginning of his career—in 1925, when he won the *Opportunity* magazine's first prize for poetry with "The Weary Blues," a poem that was songful, idiomatic in vocabulary, full of jazz and blues sounds, with a tone that was unmistakably negroid—that Hughes demonstrated he was a poet to acknowledge.

The most distinct feature of Hughes's poetry, then, the metaphor of music—jazz and the blues—was a vital mode for expressing what the poet saw as the unique quality of black life in America. As he wrote in "Lenox Avenue; Midnight":

> The rhythm of life
> is a jazz rhythm—

Hughes can also be characterized as a poet of the city; in particular, Harlem is *his* city, and the people there are *his* people. His love for both place and people permeates his poetry, utilizing the themes of protest and pride, love for freedom, hatred and despair deriving from prejudice, and belief that the world will get better for blacks. Undergirding these themes is Hughes's strong belief in American democracy. As he once said in an interview, his primary aim was "to interpret and comment upon Negro life, and its relation to the problems of Democracy."

A writer who was much more critical of American life and American blacks was Claude McKay, who was born in Jamaica, West Indies, and who was a published author by the time he came to the United States in 1912. In his novel *Banjo* (a book berated by more conservative literary Negroes, such as W. E. B. Du Bois), McKay's character, Ray, who reflects his own thoughts, says: "We educated Negroes are talking a lot about a racial renaissance. And I wonder how we're going to get it. . . . If this renaissance we're talking about is going to be more than a sporadic and scabby thing, we'll have to get down to our racial roots to create it . . . [but] you're a lost crowd, you educated Negroes, and you will only find your self in the roots of your own people. You can't choose as your models the haughty-minded educated white youths of a society living on its imperial conquests." And, of course, many of the Harlem Renaissance writers thought they were going back to their roots when they portrayed "authentic" views of black life. McKay wasn't sure his fellow black writers were being that honest; yet it was McKay who repudiated his first poems, written in Jamaican dialect, and he avoided experimental forms and militant themes in most of his poetry. Even his inspiring poem "If We Must Die," written in 1919—supposedly in protest against the race riots (he later disclaimed this)—was in sonnet form.

Indeed, McKay employed the most traditional forms of poetic expression, the sonnet and other rhymed verse in iambic pentameter. There are vigor and passion in his poetry; there is also tenderness of the most romantic sort. His themes were remarkably consistent and they were reasserted later in his novels and short stories. There was the theme stemming from his being a black man—a bitter denunciation of racial prejudice. Then, McKay's nostalgia for Jamaica was exhibited in those poems celebrating the freer life, one that is close to earth and sky and water. This reverence for nature reveals the poet's longing for religion (nature, at first, is his religion). His subsequent conversion to Catholicism was not as uncharacteristic as some would have it. Even the symbols he used in his nature poetry point toward a preoccupation not only with anti-metropolis sentiments but also with humanity's religious dependency. The theme of alienation is iterated in McKay's poetry; but this concern is most vividly expressed through Ray, a character in two of his novels—a spokesman, obviously for McKay. This strong sense of alienation is expressed on two levels: black in the white world (black against white, and vice versa), and black against black. The latter level is almost exclusively portrayed in his novels, whereas the former emotion sustains the theme of many McKay poems, such as "Outcast," "Baptism," "Courage," and "America." McKay was also a talented short story writer who evoked the vital spirit of the ordinary Negro as well as the spiritual duality of the black intellectual.

Reminiscences, memories about World War I, do not haunt the writings of most Harlem Renaissance writers, but Claude McKay's work is a notable exception to this. Still, his productions can hardly be said to be overly concerned with the psychological inheritance of this war. Indeed, there may be a mockery of it as the "white man's war," inasmuch as Banjo—McKay's character who has had war experiences—is a deserter who proves the black man's invisibility in America: Banjo's status is neither validated nor invalidated as a defender or deserter of his country. He is simply ignored by America; he finds his place among the rejects of society.

Letter to Alain Locke by Claude McKay. Courtesy of the Alain Locke Papers, Moorland-Spingarn Research Center, Howard University.

Some people—Du Bois in particular—felt McKay exploited the theme of Negro primitivism. McKay, like Cullen, did not seem to live up to his expectations; thematic limitations may have been a major cause of this for both of these writers. Still, if McKay failed to live up to his potential he was also companion to others besides Cullen in this category of talented black writers of the 1920s and early 1930s. Wallace Thurman, aspiring to the greatness of masters such as Tolstoy, Melville, or Proust, turned bitter about the period that brought these writers accolades and attention.

Wallace Thurman wanted to be great and talented. He was the latter, but he squandered his talent and died young—as if to prove he was right to be disillusioned about his times. Langston Hughes describes him vividly:

> Thurman . . . was a strangely brilliant black boy, who had read everything, and whose critical mind could find something wrong with everything he read. . . . He wanted to be a *very* great writer, like Gorki or Thomas Mann, and he felt that he was merely a journalistic writer. His critical mind, comparing his pages to the thousands of other pages he had read, by Proust, Melville, Tolstoy . . . found his own pages vastly wanting. So he contented himself by writing a great deal for money, laughing bitterly at his fabulously concocted ''true, stories,'' creating two bad motion pictures for the ''Adults Only'' type for Hollywood, drinking more and more gin, and then threatening to jump out of windows at people's parties and kill himself.

Thurman was extremely skillful in writing about Harlem, indeed, he excelled at nonfiction, whereas he was weak as a novelist. Still, he must be mentioned for his acerbic novel about the Harlem Renaissance that cynically explores the people and the tenor of this time. In *Infants of the Spring* there is bitterness and tension; it is a book full of caricatures, a *roman à clef* that spares no one, not even himself.

Wallace Thurman was a confused intellectual who remained frustrated in both his personal and professional life; yet if he could have written as he lived, what an outstandingly interesting book he would have produced! Sadly, he died destitute at an early age—died after months of agony in the incurable ward on Welfare Island one cold December day. He was, perhaps, as Dorothy West reminisced, ''the most symbolic figure of the Literary Renaissance in Harlem.''

By contrast, Rudolph Fisher, B.A. and M.A. (Brown University, 1919 and 1920), M.D., Phi Beta Kappa, novelist and outstanding short story writer of the Harlem Renaissance, died in December 1934 as well—but in the Edgecombe Sanitorium in New York, in as much comfort as one can give a dying man. Fisher and Thurman, the first of the Harlem Renaissance writers to die, demonstrate the distinctions that existed among the black writers of this period.

Rudolph Fisher, who possessed a keen wit, a basically optimistic view of life, an observant mind, wrote short stories and novels (two) in a clear, direct, tidy style. He was a traditionalist in his manner of living and in his writing; yet he also had great humor and jollity. Once again, Langston Hughes captures a contemporary artist-friend:

The wittiest of these New Negroes of Harlem, whose tongue was flavored with the sharpest and saltiest humor, was Rudolph Fisher, whose stories appeared in the *Atlantic Monthly*. His novel *Walls of Jericho,* captures but slightly the raciness of his own conversation. He was a young medical doctor and X-ray specialist, who always frightened me a little, because he could think of the most incisively clever thing to say—and I could never think of anything to answer.

Certainly *The Walls of Jericho* was Fisher's major work, but he made his greatest contribution as a short story writer. (He was also the author of the first mystery novel by an American black: *The Conjure-man Dies.*) Fisher wrote the well-made novel and short story: everything is intact—theme, character, setting, dialogue—so that the reader is never at a loss about what the author is trying to accomplish. Fisher also possessed a witty style in both narration and dialogue: his language and style evoke experiences genuinely and appealingly. He captured black idiomatic language perfectly, and used it with grace and humor as well as with salty vigor.

In the short story, Fisher demonstrates a classic grasp of this most American of literary forms: from his stories there emerges a single effect, growing out of careful characterization and close attention to establishing and maintaining the features of a beginning, a middle, and an end. Yet Fisher never loses sight of his desire to go beyond the mere artistry of the form; he also stresses values that are important to Negroes within their unique culture, such as racial solidarity.

One important goal stressed by the well-educated, black bourgeois—such as Fisher or W. E. B. Du Bois or James Weldon Johnson—was that the depiction of Negroes in imaginative literature should show the wide range of Negro life and culture. The diversity of the Negro had suffered, it was felt, under the polarized, one-dimensional portraits painted by white post-bellum writers (and in some cases, by black writers, too, such as Charles Chesnutt). James Weldon Johnson, whose tastes were broad and varied, exemplified this diversity in both his life and in his writings. A poet, diplomat, novelist, musician, and lawyer, Johnson was a precursor of the Harlem Renaissance as well as a participant in the movement. In his autobiography, *Along This Way,* Johnson noted: "This was the era in which was achieved the Harlem of story and song; the era in which Harlem's fame for exotic flavor and colorful sensuousness was spread to all parts of the world; when Harlem was made known as the scene of laughter, singing, dancing, and primitive passions, and as the center of the new Negro literature and art. . . . But the sterner aspects of life in Harlem offer a unique and teeming field for the writer capable of working it. Under these aspects lie real comedy and real tragedy, real triumphs and real defeats. The field is waiting, probably for some Negro writer." Johnson was wise enough to see both sides of life, the real and the fictional. He contributed one novel—first published in 1912 and then reissued in 1927, during a vital year of the period. *The Autobiography of an Ex-Coloured Man* uses the standard theme of the "tragic mulatto," inherited from the late nineteenth- and early twentieth-century stories dealing with light-skinned blacks. But Johnson's skillful characterization, vivid descriptions of life in all strata, and his effective use of irony lift the novel above the ordinary ones that deal with this romantic idea (i.e., that the Negro who forsakes his own race suffers deep psychological and cultural loss that the "freedom" of whiteness can never replace).

Johnson was one of the older persons to achieve and maintain a large measure of fame during the Harlem Renaissance. Another was W. E. B. Du Bois, writer, editor of *The Crisis* (organ of the National Association for the Advancement of Colored People), pan-Africanist, and a person who was never without a strong opinion. For Du Bois, the Afro-American artist was inescapably enmeshed in the cultural and sociological atmosphere that had declared the black a second-class citizen. Therefore, to this vigorous intellectual giant of the twentieth century, "All art is propaganda." It was the dictum by which he wrote; it is not surprising that his fiction was weak and discursive, just as his essays and journalistic writings were insightful and challenging to the reader. His opinionated cast of mind made him difficult; but he was also a great encourager of the young writers of the Harlem Renaissance. Certainly his publication, *The Crisis,* provided an outlet for the publication of many pieces of literature that were produced during this period.

Du Bois and James Weldon Johnson, however, were not alone in providing encouragement and sustenance for the black writers who were emerging at this time. Charles S. Johnson, for instance, continues to be underrated as an important influence on the literary and personal lives of Harlem Renaissance writers; yet Langston Hughes has declared he "did more to encourage and develop Negro writers during the 1920's than anyone else in America." A specialist in race relations, and the first black president of the famous southern university Fisk (then for blacks only), Johnson's connection with the Harlem Renaissance was that of encourager, practical helper, and participant. He was the editor of *Opportunity,* and he found the money to support the prize contests of that magazine. He was also the editor of the collection of literature and the arts *Ebony and Topaz,* where he stated: "It is a venture in expression, shared, with the slightest editorial suggestion, by a number of persons who are here much less interested in their audience than in what they are trying to say, and the life they are trying to portray." And as the editor of this miscellanea, Johnson fits the description of an "entrepreneur of the Harlem Renaissance [with] . . . the third dimension as that of interpreter."

Alain Locke and Carl Van Vechten were likewise favorable and understanding interpreters of the period; and both were instrumental in helping the developing writers, even when these young people struck out on their own to produce a short-lived literary journal, *Fire!!* Carl Van Vechten's role has been inflated sometimes as well as being exaggerated in the other extreme to the point of minimizing the aid he provided. He introduced writers to publishers, invited blacks and whites interested in the arts to his parties, generally promoted black arts of all genre, and was the author of the infamous *Nigger Heaven* (a novel that outraged many blacks because of its title). Even after the Harlem Renaissance was long over, Van Vechten continued his interest in the writers, and he motivated his black friends to donate materials to Yale University to what has become a rich reservoir in black literature and culture: The James Weldon Johnson Memorial Collection of Negro Arts and Letters (dedicated on 7 January 1950).

As soon as the Harlem Renaissance was underway, a request was made to Alain Locke to edit a special edition of *Survey* magazine's "graphic" publication. The 1 March 1925 special issue was entitled "Harlem: Mecca of the New Negro"; the introductory essay was by Alain Locke. This same section was published, with some changes, during the same year [as *The New Negro;* see Additional Bibliography] and has become famous as the first anthology of writings by many of the Re-

Charles S. Johnson and Arna Bontemps. Shomburg Center for Research in Black Culture, The New York Public Library, Astor, Lenox and Tilden Foundations.

naissance writers. Locke's pronouncements captured part of the spirit and aims of the "New Negro," and expressed an assimilationist desire to contribute to American civilization the vestiges of Afro-American culture. In his introduction he states: "He [the new Negro] now becomes a conscious contributor and lays aside the status of a beneficiary and ward for that of a collaborator and participant in American civilization. The great social gain in this is the releasing of our talented group from the arid fields of controversy and debate to the productive fields of creative expression. The especially cultural recognition they win should in turn prove the key to that revaluation of the Negro which must precede or accompany any considerable further betterment of race relationships." The enthusiasm and optimism of the 1920s turned a bit sour in the heart of Alain Locke: he had not become bitter but he did question the quality of production, the sincerity of the praise and assessments, the depth of knowledge blacks really had of their past, and wondered if the overall failure to reach the heights he had expected had come from not shaping a new tradition out of the old. (pp. xxi-xxxi)

The writers of this period, in a self-conscious manner, had attempted to connect philosophy to art—the New Negro was one who had discovered his past, and therefore, was engaged in a cultural renaissance. There was also a relation to the nineteenth-century black "literature" of engagement—the slave

narrative, which depicted life as it was in the words of blacks rather than the sentimentalized yet basically racist (or at least unconsciously condescending) literature written by whites. The black writer had reclaimed his past and was to be interpreter of his own experiences. The buying audience, however, was mostly white.

> I was there. I had a swell time while it lasted. But I thought it wouldn't last long. . . . For how could a large and enthusiastic number of people be crazy about Negroes forever?

> The ordinary Negroes hadn't heard of the Negro Renaissance. And if they had, it hadn't raised their wages any.

And despite the desire to set the record straight, to correct the image, to explore or expunge the double consciousness, many of the writers failed to use their blackness to fullness and with total honesty in order to create that unique genre of American literature one calls black or Afro-American. When Langston Hughes declared in 1926: "We younger Negro artists who create now intend to express our individual dark-skinned selves without fear or shame," he was speaking for only a few of the writers. Most of the writers were not bold, nor were they blind to the implications of white patronage—whether direct (as in the case of Hughes's and Hurston's "godmother") or indirect through publishers and the reading public. The Afro-American soul was under close and curious scrutiny; it was a soul still awaiting a definition through imaginative art.

Still, the artistic world would never be quite the same: the exposure to black life, no matter how uneven, eager, frenetically presented, made an impact, if minor, upon the American cultural scene. The Harlem Renaissance movement basically existed outside mainstream America—including the literary scene. The work of the major black writers was reviewed, but the notion that this literature was an equal if colorful counterpart of literature produced by white writers did not exist in any strong sense. The black writer may have worked hard to correct the unfair and unrealistic images white writers had focused upon, but this didn't seem to matter in a national sense. There simply were no black parallels to Pound or Eliot, Fitzgerald or Hemingway or Faulkner. And the collective spirit vs. the individual's need for self-expression remained a frequently unspoken obstacle to creating a consistent, focused artistic movement. The complaint Cruse made in *The Crisis of the Negro Intellectual*—that the Harlem Renaissance was a period of ''inspired aimlessness''—is true in this sense of failing to emerge as a definite segment or stage in American literature and civilization during the time it existed. (One might safely question whether or not this is important.)

There was, of course, the precise economic factor that affected the movement—the Great Depression. Much white patronage simply disappeared. The movement petered out to an indefinite end. But in its heyday of glory and enthusiasm it was like nothing that had existed before or—some may argue—since that time. In any case, it may be possible to agree with the critic [George E. Kent; see excerpt below] who summed up the Harlem Renaissance, in part, this way: ''If today we can sometimes jog, rather than puff, down the road toward the self-definition, it would seem that the Harlem Renaissance was a father who should not go without thanks, or reverence.'' (pp. xxxv-xxxvi)

> *Margaret Perry, in her* The Harlem Renaissance: An Annotated Bibliography and Commentary, *Garland Publishing, Inc., 1982, 272 p.*

THE LITERATURE AND ITS AUDIENCE

ADEREMI BAMIKUNLE

[*In the following excerpt, Bamikunle discusses the influence of white readers' aesthetics and literary expectations on the literature produced by the Harlem Renaissance.*]

A lot has been said about the historical and sociological factors that led to the first major modern cultural and literary movement of black Americans, the Harlem Renaissance. Critics have pointed out the significance of events that arose from the First World War; the black participation in that war, the heroic return of the black brigade, the sense of pride engendered in the black race, the consequent rejection of the political status quo, the migration of Southern blacks to Northern cities; and the emergence of the Harlem Renaissance.

This gives the impression that the Harlem Renaissance was a sudden or impromptu development. But its roots go back to periods much earlier than the First World War and the sociological consequences of it. Rather, the First World War and

related social and historical events are catalysts that brought out the new feeling and attitudes that had been building up through the 1890s in powerful cultural and literary expressions that we call the Harlem Renaissance. Moreover the emphasis on historical and social factors has led to the neglect of the literary factors that contributed directly not only to the flowering of the Renaissance at the time it did but also to the general direction it took and its overall nature. (p. 33)

The first sizable reading public that the black writer has in the nineteenth century consisted of the abolitionists and their friends. The group wanted propaganda literature to further their cause. Naturally they turned to blacks who knew about black experience firsthand. Black writers began to have better access to publication. But as well as this may look to the development of black creative writing, it probably did more harm than good in forcing blacks to write according to a particular genre. It encouraged the genre or slave narratives, and since this was the only type of literature that served their purposes, it was primarily the main type of writing it published from black authors. Slave autobiographies and writings, which may be fictional but directed themselves towards black social problems, were what black authors could publish in abolitionist magazines. While I cannot argue that at that time in history blacks could have produced a Henry James or a Nathaniel Hawthorne, I can say that the restriction of the demand of publication led unfortunately to the impression that the slave narrative was the type of writing that blacks were capable of, not belletristic writing. As Julian Mason rightly observed, in the reviews of black authors between 1840 and 1865,

> some of the better books were completely overlooked or ignored and many of them were reviewed primarily because they wrote abolition literature.

When black authors were reviewed, the aesthetic qualities of their works received little or no attention from abolitionist reviewers, who were usually leaders of the critical reception of black works:

> Attempts at belles-lettres did not seem to interest reviewers much—works were not usually noted primarily for their literary aspects.

When nonabolitionist reviewers, who often came to hear of black authors from abolitionist magazines, did further reviews of black works, they took their cues from the abolitionists and emphasized only the social significance of the works. Nonabolitionists assessed the works primarily in terms of dangers that they posed to the social status quo. Such is this example of the review of *The Slave, or Memoirs of Archy Moore*, a fictional slave narrative, reviewed in the *Boston Daily Advocate* of January 14, 1837:

> Have you read Archy Moore? It is the most extraordinary book of the day, and will produce more sensation, if it is ever read south of the Potomac, than the massacre at Southampton. . . . Whether the sort of talent was got in this quarter, to produce a work of such intellectual power as a fiction, woven apparently out of terrible truths, we cannot guess; and how our good, comfortable, fat and easy friend Eastburn dare to put his name in the imprint as the publisher is a great marvel still. [It goes on to talk humorously of political consequences]. But the book is printed and can't be helped, and

everybody will finish it who reads five pages of it—. The book sellers won't dare to sell it, and a copy of it will never get into a southern latitude.

This reviewer completely ignored the aesthetics of the book to which he made a superficial praise before condemning the book as dangerous and advising that the book be withdrawn from sale. One has to agree with Mason that

> abolitionism and prejudice were the most important factors negatively and positively in the critical reception of American Negro authors between 1800-1865.

Thus, one of the most important things to note is that the abolitionist origins of black literature gave it inherent disadvantages. Because of the demands of the abolitionists, aesthetic qualities were not as prominent as they could have been. Yet nonabolitionist reviewers ignored this factor only to condemn the work as lacking in belletristic qualities. But above all, when reference was made to the aesthetic qualities of the works, it was usually by way of comparison or contrast with some notable American or English writer, the black writer's worth being measured in terms of how close to such a writer he was. Phyllis Wheatley, for example, was measured in terms of Alexander Pope: "The style of the poems is evidently formed, in a great degree, after that of Pope, a writer now in the golden age of his fame." Little or no attention was paid to the peculiar aesthetic qualities of the work itself, except as side comment.

This was the foundation of the pattern of critical reception of black literature by whites. As magazines were the major ways of disseminating literary opinions, the common reader had no alternative but to accept and help in perpetuating these same opinions about black literature. William Chawat, in his book *Literary Publishing in American 1790-1800*, noted that "the magazines, through criticism, had an opportunity for great influence on the reading public which was then reflected in the publishing world." But in the nineteenth century the situation was more serious for blacks because, again relying on the findings of Chawat, the "same publisher published magazines [that review books] and books [that are reviewed]." Many of the writers had to rely on magazines "as the primary method of publication." The short stories of Charles Chestnutt and the stories and poems of Paul Dunbar were first published in magazines. In this way it was more difficult not to write according to the taste of the publishers, the critics, and the reading public, all of whom were white.

Thus, before the notable period of Afro-American writing arrived (1885 from Chestnutt), a pattern had been established for its production and for its reception. Blacks were made aware that if they were to publish, they had to write about black life but in a manner that must appeal to white readers. This is why Charles Chestnutt, for example, had modelled some of his works on the doomed mulatto genre of prose writing which had been developed into a tradition by whites before he came on the scene. Perhaps more important is the manner in which they should write. They were made painfully aware that there are civilized standards of aesthetic forms. To produce a counterculture which does not conform to these standards was to write black literature, while to be a dignified writer was to conform to Western norms of literature. As Robert A. Bone has insightfully observed in the introduction to his book *The Negro Novel in America*, the black American has to be aware of belonging to two worlds at once:

The American Negro, however, has not one but two cultures to interpret. He bears a double burden, corresponding to the double environment in which he lives. He must be conversant with Western culture as a whole, and especially with the traditions of English literature of which he is a part and at the same time he prepared to affirm a Negro heritage as a legitimate contribution to the larger culture.

In these circumstances, black works of art are heavily compromised even before they are written. Between the publishers, the critics, the reading public, the language of expression, and the ideology they express, the material of black life and its natural form of expression are doomed to constant compromise. One wonders if an authentic black literature is even possible under these circumstances. In fact, what Ralph Ellison means when he says in his essay "Richard Wright's Blues" that

> . . . Negro life is a by-product of Western civilization, and in it, if only one possesses the humanity and humility to see, are to be discovered all those impulses, tendencies, life and cultural forms to be found elsewhere in Western society.

applies perfectly to black works of art, because as Houston Baker has rightly put it, black writers "were internally torn by the question of writing honestly and not being read or accepted by a white audience, or writing falsely and being read and accepted." (pp. 36-40)

The most important significance of this for us is the influence of all the above considerations on black writers. Stephen Bronz, in his book *Roots of Negro Racial Consciousness* [see Additional Bibliography], lays out in very neat interesting details the economy of Renaissance literature, giving us all the reasons why black writers could not ignore the larger white group in their bid to produce a counterculture:

> The very existence of the Harlem Renaissance depended upon white recognition and approval; since the negro [sic] book-buying public was limited, the interest of white publishers, critics, and readers was necessary for financial maintenance. White approval also was necessary because a main purpose of the Harlem Renaissance was to prove to whites that Negroes could be cultural peers.

For blacks who felt a strong obligation towards the black race there was bound to be conflict between that obligation and the constraints of writing within a white culture. The result is a split image which comes from trying to meet two obligations at once, represented by black and white demands or as is specific to the arts, black and white audiences. As James Weldon Johnson, himself a writer in the Renaissance movement, has affirmed, the desire to satisfy the white public was almost irresistible for black writers:

> I judge that there is not a single writer who is not, at least secondarily, impelled by the desire to make his work have some effect on the white world for the good of the race [see excerpt below].

The desired effect on whites may vary in emphasis from author to author, but it seems safe to say from the general notion of creating the New Negro which would counter the negative image of the Negro past, that many writers were concerned about proving that blacks could also create high culture. In itself, there would seem to be nothing bad in this, but this desire led to the adoption of artistic forms which focussed attention more on art than on subject matter and prevented men like William Stanley Braithwaite from addressing race issues.

Nearly all of the important artists of the pre-Renaissance, as well as Renaissance artists, were affected negatively by this desire for high culture. First, there was a rejection of other types of literature that were not considered high, even though they were more authentically black than some that were decked in borrowed conventional forms. Paul Laurence Dunbar, the first major black American poet, was quite disturbed that it was only his vernacular poems, and not his more romantic and cultured poems, that were accepted. His poem "The Poet" is a subdued indignation for this "belittling" of his works.

> He sang of life, serenely sweet
> With, now and then, a deeper nite
> From some high peak, nigh yet remote
> He voiced the world's absorbing beat
> He sang of love when earth was young
> And love, itself, was in his lays.
> But ah, the world, it turned to praise
> A jungle in a broken tongue.

The art which he condemns here as a "jungle in a broken tongue," vernacular poems, would appear to be more appropriate for a writer who wants to speak primarily to blacks, but Dunbar was more prepared to impress the "cultured" critics of his time.

This inclination to reject the folk qualities of literature which is associated with the past and "lowly" life of blacks can be said to be a general characteristic of the Renaissance. There are exceptions, of course, but the exceptions are rare and almost choked out by the general rule. Zora Neale Hurston collected oral black literature and transmitted some of it into literature of her own, but the controversy over the representation of low life, which was contrary to the aim of the Renaissance, prevented these from being among her popular works. (pp. 42-4)

This essay will not be able to examine the position of all the . . . Renaissance artists on this issue, but it will certainly not be complete if it does not treat Countee Cullen in relation to the issues under discussion. For one, he is probably the black writer of the Renaissance who best appealed to white readers, mainly because he was the one who best appropriated the literary convention of Europe and white America. Stephen Bronz sums up his indebtedness to these conventions when he says,

> Indeed his [Cullen's] poetry fitted the demands of most critics and readers. Though Cullen insisted that *he wished to write about universal subjects instead of about Negroes,* he found himself stressing racial themes. But he did so in a pleasing, impressive sounding nineteenth century poetic idiom marked by *imprecision and lack* of concreteness that considerably blurred the racial protests he was voicing.

Cullen is an example of Renaissance artists who got caught in a cultural tangle. He poured Afro-American materials into modes of art which emphasized forms and aesthetics at the expense of subject-matter. This at a time when Afro-American literature was the vanguard of the creation of a counterculture, is not only ironic but a disservice to the aims of the Renaissance.

Cullen's poetic philosophy aims, like the Romantic poetic philosophy of Wordsworth and Keats, at the creation of highly imaginative and lofty literature as opposed to realistic literature. Poetry, he says, is

> . . . a lofty thought beautifully expressed. Poetry should not be too intellectual. It should deal more . . . with the emotions.

It is not surprising that Cullen not only rejected dialect poetry, which is closely associated with black culture ("In a day when artificiality is so vigorously condemned the Negro poet would be foolish indeed to turn to dialect"), but again and again "reiterated his desire to be accepted as a poet, instead of a Negro poet." Cullen disagrees with the notion of a black school of poetry, denying that black poets have enough in common to justify this notion; instead, their works, he felt, should be regarded as part of English poetry: "Since theirs is also the heritage of the English language, their work will not present any serious aberration from the poetic tendencies of their times."

As Cullen sees it, black poetry is "a variety within a uniformity that is trying to maintain the higher traditions of English verse." It is obvious from his poetic practices and statements that Countee Cullen does not have the vaguest notion of creating a black counterculture. Instead, his movement is in the other direction, a running away from oneself in an attempt to make something new—no matter how unlike one's true self—that the world outside can respect as high culture. But the irony is that the literary convention that is being adopted to reach the "high pedestal of culture" is the same weapon that has been used to engender self-hatred in the black man, used to make him despise his culture that necessitated the Renaissance in the first place. This conclusion in the foreword of his anthology *Caroling Dusk* is nothing short of self-hatred in the poet:

> As heretical as it may sound, there is probability that Negro poets, dependent as they are on English language, may have more to gain from the rich background of English and American poetry than from any nebulous atavistic yearnings toward an African inheritance.

What has been said about Countee Cullen and James Weldon Johnson is to varying degrees true of the major writers of the Renaissance and of the cultural movement itself as a whole. The whole idea of the New Negro, as promulgated in *The New Negro* (1925) by Alain Locke [see Additional Bibliography], is an indication of the severance of links with the past. Perhaps this was necessary to give the black man a new image of himself. But then one cannot talk of a renaissance here, at least not in the sense of a revival of the past. There have been glib talks of the Renaissance writers turning to Africa for a glorious image for the black. A close look at Cullen's heritage will convince us that, on the contrary, the poet was laying to rest forever the last relics of a history and clutching the European and American civilization to himself with both hands.

However, turning back to the main points of this essay, we observe that European and white American literature and literary criticism—or rather the comprehensive language and linguistic practices, both as literature and as criticism—had combined to undermine the birth of a black counterculture long before such a culture was ever contemplated. This situation is not peculiar to the black experience in America, but is true of all situations in which a colored people brought up to admire the oppressing culture has made an attempt to fight back. In most instances, the oppressed uses the language which has been the weapon of his oppression to fight back. But the language is not an indifferent weapon. It is a medium for the expression of an ideology. Its literary and aesthetic practices embody the ideology or philosophic worldview of its users. To share a language is to partake, at least at basic levels, of these world or cultural views. Until the oppressed can find another language or means of expression which expresses a counter philosophy, it is virtually impossible to destroy an oppressing culture.

Afro-American writers, as well as other black writers fighting against colonizing cultures, found themselves caught in the ironies of fighting their oppressors using his own weapons. Literary criticism which determines what is good culture among what has been produced; white American notions of literature, with conventions of what is literary and what is not; the reading public, which has been nurtured on these conventions; the publishers who have made choices of what is publishable based on the taste of that public; and, the supreme irony of them all, the black intellectuals who set out to produce a new respectable culture but who turn out, despite their professions, to share the oppressors' philosophies—all combine to defeat the aims of the Renaissance. The best of Renaissance literature was written according to standards set to please the very forces that it should be fighting. (pp. 47-50)

Aderemi Bamikunle, "The Harlem Renaissance and White Critical Tradition," in CLA Journal, *Vol. XXIX, No. 1, September, 1985, pp. 33-51.*

JAMES WELDON JOHNSON

[*Johnson was a newspaper editor, lawyer, U.S. consul to Nicaragua and Venezuela, and Broadway songwriter, whose song "Lift Every Voice and Sing" has been adopted as the American black national anthem. Although he did not make his living as a writer, he was in fact a novelist, a writer of both conventional and experimental poetry, a literary and social critic, a historian, and an autobiographer. In addition to "Lift Every Voice and Sing," Johnson is known primarily for the novel* The Autobiography of an Ex-Colored Man *(1912), which was originally published anonymously and later reissued under his name in 1927. Providing psychological insights into the mind of a black man fleeing from self-understanding, the novel is considered the principal forerunner of the works of the Harlem Renaissance. Concerned in his literary works with the black individual's self-image and role in society, Johnson was labeled an Uncle Tom by later, more militant generations for his conservative approach to social change through education and legislation. Although he did not publish many works, Johnson contributed greatly to the development of a black voice in American literature. In the following excerpt from an essay written in 1928, Johnson discusses the problems faced by a black author writing for a biracial readership.*]

Now that the Negro author has come into the range of vision of the American public eye, it seems to me only fair to point out some of the difficulties he finds in his way. But I wish to state emphatically that I have no intention of making an apology or asking any special allowances for him; such a plea would at once disqualify him and void the very recognition he has gained. But the Negro writer does face peculiar difficulties that ought to be taken into account when passing judgment upon him.

It is unnecessary to say that he faces every one of the difficulties common to all that crowd of demon-driven individuals who feel that they must write. But the Aframerican author faces a special problem which the plain American author knows nothing about—the problem of the double audience. It is more than

a double audience; it is a divided audience, an audience made up of two elements with differing and often opposite and antagonistic points of view. His audience is always both white America and black America. The moment a Negro writer takes up his pen or sits down to his typewriter he is immediately called upon to solve, consciously or unconsciously, this problem of the double audience. To whom shall he address himself, to his own black group or to white America? Many a Negro writer has fallen down, as it were, between these two stools.

It may be asked why he doesn't just go ahead and write and not bother himself about audiences. That is easier said than done. It is doubtful if anything with meaning can be written unless the writer has some definite audience in mind. His audience may be as far as the angelic host or the rulers of darkness, but an audience he must have in mind. As soon as he selects his audience he immediately falls, whether he wills it or not, under the laws which govern the influence of the audience upon the artist, laws that operate in every branch of art.

Now, it is axiomatic that the artist achieves his best when working at his best with the materials he knows best. And it goes without saying that the material which the Negro as a creative or general writer knows best comes out of the life and experience of the colored people in America. The overwhelming bulk of the best work done by Aframerican writers has some bearing on the Negro and his relations to civilization and society in the United States. Leaving authors, white or black, writing for coteries on special and technical subjects out of the discussion, it is safe to say that the white American author, when he sits down to write, has in mind a white audience—and naturally. The influence of the Negro as a group on his work is infinitesimal if not zero. Even when he talks about the Negro he talks to white people. But with the Aframerican author the case is different. When he attempts to handle his best known material he is thrown upon two, indeed, if it is permissible to say so, upon three horns of a dilemma. He must intentionally or unintentionally choose a black audience or a white audience or a combination of the two; and each of them presents peculiar difficulties.

If the Negro author selects white America as his audience he is bound to run up against many long-standing artistic conceptions about the Negro; against numerous conventions and traditions which through age have become binding; in a word, against a whole row of hard-set stereotypes which are not easily broken up. White America has some firm opinions as to what the Negro is, and consequently some pretty well fixed ideas as to what should be written about him, and how.

What is the Negro in the artistic conception of white America? In the brighter light, he is a simple, indolent, docile, improvident peasant; a singing, dancing, laughing, weeping child; picturesque beside his log cabin and in the snowy fields of cotton; naïvely charming with his banjo and his songs in the moonlight and along the lazy Southern rivers; a faithful, ever-smiling and genuflecting old servitor to the white folks of quality; a pathetic and pitiable figure. In a darker light, he is an impulsive, irrational, passionate savage, reluctantly wearing a thin coat of culture, sullenly hating the white man, but holding an innate and unescapable belief in the white man's superiority; an everlastingly alien and irredeemable element in the nation; a menace to Southern civilization; a threat to Nordic race purity; a figure casting a sinister shadow across the future of the country.

Ninety-nine one-hundredths of all that has been written about the Negro in the United States in three centuries and read with any degree of interest or pleasure by white America has been written in conformity to one or more of these ideas. I am not saying that they do not provide good material for literature; in fact, they make material for poetry and romance and comedy and tragedy of a high order. But I do say they have become stencils, and that the Negro author finds these stencils inadequate for the portrayal and interpretation of Negro life today. Moreover, when he does attempt to make use of them he finds himself impaled upon the second horn of his dilemma.

It is known that art—literature in particular, unless it be sheer fantasy—must be based on more or less well established conventions, upon ideas that have some roots in the general consciousness, that are at least somewhat familiar to the public mind. It is this that gives it verisimilitude and finality. Even revolutionary literature, if it is to have any convincing power, must start from a basis of conventions, regardless of how unconventional its objective may be. These conventions are changed by slow and gradual processes—except they be changed in a flash. The conventions held by white America regarding the Negro will be changed. Actually they are being changed, but they have not yet sufficiently changed to lessen to any great extent the dilemma of the Negro author.

It would be straining the credulity of white America beyond the breaking point for a Negro writer to put out a novel dealing with the wealthy class of colored people. The idea of Negroes of wealth living in a luxurious manner is still too unfamiliar. Such a story would have to be written in a burlesque vein to make it at all plausible and acceptable. Before Florence Mills and Josephine Baker implanted a new general idea in the public mind it would have been worse than a waste of time for a Negro author to write for white America the story of a Negro girl who rose in spite of all obstacles, racial and others, to a place of world success and acclaim on the musical revue stage. It would be proof of little less than supreme genius in a Negro poet for him to take one of the tragic characters in American Negro history—say Crispus Attucks or Nat Turner or Denmark Vesey—, put heroic language in his mouth and have white America accept the work as authentic. American Negroes as heroes form no part of white America's concept of the race. Indeed, I question if three out of ten of the white Americans who will read these lines know anything of either Attucks, Turner or Vesey; although each of the three played a rôle in the history of the nation. The Aframerican poet might take an African chief or warrior, set him forth in heroic couplets or blank verse and present him to white America with infinitely greater chance of having his work accepted.

But these limiting conventions held by white America do not constitute the whole difficulty of the Negro author in dealing with a white audience. In addition to these conventions regarding the Negro as a race, white America has certain definite opinions regarding the Negro as an artist, regarding the scope of his efforts. White America has a strong feeling that Negro artists should refrain from making use of white subject matter. I mean by that, subject matter which it feels belongs to the white world. In plain words, white America does not welcome seeing the Negro competing with the white man on what it considers the white man's own ground.

In many white people this feeling is dormant, but brought to the test it flares up, if only faintly. During his first season in this country after his European success a most common criticism of Roland Hayes was provoked by the fact that his programme consisted of groups of English, French, German and Italian songs, closing always with a group of Negro Spirituals.

A remark frequently made was, "Why doesn't he confine himself to the Spirituals?" This in face of the fact that no tenor on the American concert stage could surpass Hayes in singing French and German songs. The truth is that white America was not quite prepared to relish the sight of a black man in a dress suit singing French and German love songs, and singing them exquisitely. The first reaction was that there was something incongruous about it. It gave a jar to the old conventions and something of a shock to the Nordic superiority complex. The years have not been many since Negro players have dared to interpolate a love duet in a musical show to be witnessed by white people. The representation of romantic love-making by Negroes struck the white audience as somewhat ridiculous; Negroes were supposed to mate in a more primeval manner.

White America has for a long time been annexing and appropriating Negro territory, and is prone to think of every part of the domain it now controls as originally—and aboriginally—its own. One sometimes hears the critics in reviewing a Negro musical show lament the fact that it is so much like white musical shows. But a great deal of this similarity it would be hard to avoid because of the plain fact that two out of the four chief ingredients in the present day white musical show, the music and the dancing, are directly derived from the Negro. These ideas and opinions regarding the scope of artistic effort affect the Negro author, the poet in particular. So whenever an Aframerican writer addresses himself to white America and attempts to break away from or break through these conventions and limitations he makes more than an ordinary demand upon his literary skill and power.

At this point it would appear that a most natural thing for the Negro author to do would be to say, "Damn the white audience!" and devote himself to addressing his own race exclusively. But when he turns from the conventions of white America he runs afoul of the taboos of black America. He has no more absolute freedom to speak as he pleases addressing black America than he has in addressing white America. There are certain phases of life that he dare not touch, certain subjects that he dare not critically discuss, certain manners of treatment that he dare not use—except at the risk of rousing bitter resentment. It is quite possible for a Negro author to do a piece of work, good from every literary point of view, and at the same time bring down on his head the wrath of the entire colored pulpit and press, and gain among the literate element of his own people the reputation of being a prostitutor of his talent and a betrayer of his race—not by any means a pleasant position to get into.

This state of mind on the part of the colored people may strike white America as stupid and intolerant, but it is not without some justification and not entirely without precedent; the white South on occasion discloses a similar sensitiveness. The colored people of the United States are anomalously situated. They are a segregated and antagonized minority in a very large nation, a minority unremittingly on the defensive. Their faults and failings are exploited to produce exaggerated effects. Consequently, they have a strong feeling against exhibiting to the world anything but their best points. They feel that other groups may afford to do otherwise but, as yet, the Negro cannot. This is not to say that they refuse to listen to criticism of themselves, for they often listen to Negro speakers excoriating the race for its faults and foibles and vices. But these criticisms are not for the printed page. They are not for the ears or eyes of white America.

A curious illustration of this defensive state of mind is found in the Negro theatres. In those wherein Negro players give Negro performances for Negro audiences all of the Negro weaknesses, real and reputed, are burlesqued and ridiculed in the most hilarious manner, and are laughed at and heartily enjoyed. But the presence of a couple of dozen white people would completely change the psychology of the audience, and the players. If some of the performances so much enjoyed by strictly Negro audiences in Negro theatres were put on, say, in a Broadway theatre, a wave of indignation would sweep Aframerica from the avenues of Harlem to the canebrakes of Louisiana. These taboos of black America are as real and binding as the conventions of white America. Conditions may excuse if not warrant them; nevertheless, it is unfortunate that they exist, for their effect is blighting. In past years they have discouraged in Negro authors the production of everything but *nice* literature; they have operated to hold their work down to literature of the defensive, exculpatory sort. They have a restraining effect at the present time which Negro writers are compelled to reckon with.

This division of audience takes the solid ground from under the feet of the Negro writer and leaves him suspended. Either choice carries hampering and discouraging conditions. The Negro author may please one audience and at the same time rouse the resentment of the other; or he may please the other and totally fail to rouse the interest of the one. The situation, moreover, constantly subjects him to the temptation of posing and posturing for the one audience or the other; and the sincerity and soundness of his work are vitiated whether he poses for white or black.

The dilemma is not made less puzzling by the fact that practically it is an extremely difficult thing for the Negro author in the United States to address himself solely to either of these two audiences. If he analyzes what he writes he will find that on one page black America is his whole or main audience, and on the very next page white America. In fact, a psychoanalysis of the Negro authors of the defensive and exulpatory literature, written in strict conformity to the taboos of black America, would reveal that they were unconsciously addressing themselves mainly to white America.

I have sometimes thought it would be a way out, that the Negro author would be on surer ground and truer to himself, if he could disregard white America; if he could say to white America, "What I have written, I have written. I hope you'll be interested and like it. If not, I can't help it." But it is impossible for a sane American Negro to write with total disregard for nine-tenths of the people of the United States. Situated as his own race is amidst and amongst them, their influence is irresistible.

I judge there is not a single Negro writer who is not, at least secondarily, impelled by the desire to make his work have some effect on the white world for the good of his race. It may be thought that the work of the Negro writer, on account of this last named condition, gains in pointedness what it loses in breadth. Be that as it may, the situation is for the time one in which he is inextricably placed. Of course, the Negro author can try the experiment of putting black America in the orchestra chairs, so to speak, and keeping white America in the gallery, but he is likely at any moment to find his audience shifting places on him, and sometimes without notice.

And now, instead of black America and white America as separate or alternating audiences, what about the combination

James Weldon Johnson. Courtesy of the Prints and Photographs Collection, Moorland-Spingarn Research Center, Howard University.

of the two into one? That, I believe, is the only way out. However, there needs to be more than a combination, there needs to be a fusion. In time, I cannot say how much time, there will come a gradual and natural rapprochement of these two sections of the Negro author's audience. There will come a breaking up and remodelling of most of white America's traditional stereotypes, forced by the advancement of the Negro in the various phases of our national life. Black America will abolish many of its taboos. A sufficiently large class of colored people will progress enough and become strong enough to render a constantly sensitive and defensive attitude on the part of the race unnecessary and distasteful. In the end, the Negro author will have something close to a common audience, and will be about as free from outside limitations as other writers.

Meanwhile, the making of a common audience out of white and black America presents the Negro author with enough difficulties to constitute a third horn of his dilemma. It is a task that is a very high test for all his skill and abilities, but it can be and has been accomplished. The equipped Negro author working at his best in his best known material can achieve this end; but, standing on his racial foundation, he must fashion something that rises above race, and reaches out to the universal in truth and beauty. And so, when a Negro author does write so as to fuse white and black America into one interested and approving audience he has performed no slight feat, and has most likely done a sound piece of literary work. (pp. 477-81)

> James Weldon Johnson, "The Dilemma of the Negro Author," in America Mercury, Vol. XV, No. 60, December, 1928, pp. 477-81.

JAMES WELDON JOHNSON

[*In the following essay, which was written in 1929, Johnson counters the claim that white publishers of the 1920s refused to publish works that portrayed blacks favorably.*]

Negro writers, like all writing folks, have many things to complain about. Writers have always felt and many of them have plainly said that the world did not fully appreciate their work. This attitude has seldom been justified. The great or good writers who have not been acknowledged as such by the generation in which they lived are rare. And where such acknowledgment has not been accorded by the generations which touched an author's life, posterity has hardly ever revoked the unfavorable judgment.

Nevertheless, writers have many good reasons for complaining; for their lot is a hard one. And it may be that Negro writers have some special good reasons for complaining; I am not sure that at the present time this is so. However that may be, there is one complaint that some younger Negro writers are uttering with greater and greater insistence which I do not think is based on the facts and which reacts to the injury of the writers uttering it. This complaint is: that the leading white publishers have set a standard which Negro writers must conform to or go unpublished; that this standard calls only for books depicting the Negro in a manner which tends to degrade him in the eyes of the world; that only books about the so-called lower types of Negroes and lower phases of Negro life find consideration and acceptance.

Now, in the first place, there is a certain snobbishness in terming the less literate and less sophisticated, the more simple and more primitive classes of Negroes as "lower." At least as literary material, they are higher. They have greater dramatic and artistic potentialities for the writer than the so-called higher classes, who so closely resemble the bourgeois white classes. The vicious and criminal elements—and we must admit that even in our own race there are such elements—are rightly termed "lower," but even they have more accessible dramatic values than the ordinary, respectable middleclass element. It takes nothing less than supreme genius to make middleclass society, black or white, interesting—to say nothing of making it dramatic.

But I am jotting down this brief essay with the prime purpose of pointing out the dangers, especially to young writers, in complaining that publishers refuse to consider their work because it portrays Negro life on too high a level. When a writer begins to say and then believe that the reason why he cannot get published is because his work is *too good* he is in a bad way. This is the way that leads to making a fetish of failure. It is a too easy explanation of the lack of accomplishment. It is this "superior work—sordid publishers—low brow public" complex that gives rise to the numerous small coteries of unsuccessful writers, white as well as colored; the chief function of the members of these coteries being the mutual admiration of each other's unpublished manuscripts. This attitude brings

its adherents to a position of pathetic futility or ludicrous superiority.

Within these seven or eight years of literary florescence I doubt that any first class publisher has turned down first rate work by any Negro writer on the ground that it was *not on a low enough level*. Now, suppose we look at the actual facts as shown by the books published in these recent years by leading publishers. Let us first take fiction and list the books depicting Negro Life on the "upper" levels or shedding a favorable light on the race that have been published:

There is Confusion	Jessie Fauset
Fire In the Flint	Walter White
Flight	Walter White
The Prince of Washington Square	Harry F. Liscomb
Quicksand	Nella Larsen
Dark Princess	W. E. B. Du Bois
Plum Bun	Jessie Fauset
Passing	Nella Larsen

Now, those depicting Negro life on the "lower" levels:

Cane	Jean Toomer
Tropic Death	Eric Walrond
Home to Harlem	Claude McKay
Walls of Jericho	Rudolph Fisher
The Blacker the Berry	Wallace Thurman
Banjo	Claude McKay

The score is eight to six—with *Tropic Death, Walls of Jericho* and *Cane* on the border line. In nonfiction the "upper level" literature scores still higher. In that class we have:

A Social History of the American Negro	Benjamin Brawley
Negro Folk Rhymes	Thomas W. Talley
The Book of American Negro Poetry	Ed. James Weldon Johnson
The New Negro	Ed. Alain Locke
The Book of American Negro Spirituals	Ed. James Weldon Johnson
The Second Book of American Negro Spirituals	Ed. James Weldon Johnson
Color	Countée Cullen
Caroling Dusk	Ed. Countée Cullen
Darkwater	W. E. B. Du Bois
Gift of Black Folk	W. E B. Du Bois
Plays of Negro Life	Ed. Locke and Gregory
God's Trombones	James Weldon Johnson
Copper Sun	Countée Cullen
Negro Labor in the United States	Charles H. Wesley
A Bibliography of the Negro in Africa and America	Monroe N. Work
What the Negro Thinks	R. R. Moton
Rope and Faggot	Walter White
An Autumn Love Cycle	Georgia Douglas Johnson

In the other column, in nonfiction, we have only:

The Weary Blues	Langston Hughes
Fine Clothes to the Jew	Langston Hughes

And it must be said that although Mr. Hughes shows a predilection for singing the "lower" and "humbler" classes of Negroes, these two volumes contain many poems that are highly inspirational.

In nonfiction the score is nineteen to two. I do not see how any one who looks at these figures can fail to see that the complaint against the publishers is not in consonance with the facts. I believe that Negro writers who have something worth while to say and the power and skill to say it have as fair a chance today of being published as any other writers. (pp. 228-29)

> *James Weldon Johnson, "Negro Authors and White Publishers," in* The Crisis, *Vol. 36, No. 7, July, 1929, pp. 228-29.*

THEME AND TECHNIQUE IN POETRY, FICTION, AND DRAMA

DARWIN T. TURNER

[*Turner is an American educator, poet, and critic specializing in black and Southern literature. In the following excerpt from an essay written in 1980, he examines prominent themes in Harlem Renaissance literature—contrasting the serious issues of black life treated in many works of the period with the qualities of exoticism and gaiety for which the Renaissance is often remembered—and assesses the lasting significance of the movement.*]

[There exists a tendency on the part] of many Americans to fix their attention on only a particular aspect of Black life in America—usually the most spectacular aspect. If they would twist the base of the kaleidoscope of Black life, the multicolored fragments would rearrange themselves into different patterns, some of them startlingly different. But few viewers choose to adjust the kaleidoscope.

As a result, out of the many patterns of Black life during the 1920's, the dominant image emblazoned on the vision of America is the Harlem Renaissance. By the same process, from the Harlem Renaissance itself, a Jazzed Abandon has become the most memorable spectacle. James Weldon Johnson's description of reactions to Harlem summarizes the legend of the Harlem Renaissance:

> It is known in Europe and the Orient, and it is talked about by natives in the interior of Africa. It is farthest known as being exotic, colourful [*sic*], and sensuous; a place of laughing, singing, and dancing; a place where life wakes up at night. This phase of Harlem's fame is most widely known because, in addition to being spread by ordinary agencies, it has been proclaimed in story and song. And certainly this is Harlem's most striking and fascinating aspect. New Yorkers and people visiting New York from the world over go to the night-clubs of Harlem and dance to such jazz music as can be heard nowhere else; and they get an exhilaration impossible to duplicate. Some of these seekers after new sensations go beyond the gay night-clubs; they peep in under the more seamy side of things; they nose down into lower strata of life. A visit to Harlem at night—the principal streets never deserted, gay crowds skipping from one place of amusement to another, lines of taxicabs and limousines standing under the sparkling lights of the entrances to the famous night-clubs, the subway kiosks swallowing and disgorging crowds all night long—gives the impression that Harlem never sleeps and that the inhabitants thereof jazz through existence.

Johnson continued, "But, of course, no one can seriously think that the two hundred thousand and more Negroes in Harlem spend their nights on any such pleasance." So we too can say, "Surely, no one seriously thinks that this picture or even the entire 'Renaissance' constitutes the totality of the patterns housed in the kaleidoscope of Black life during the 1920's, the decade of the 'New Negro'."

Even if one examines only the literary portraiture of the decade, one discerns more than a single image as the minute, tinted mirrors arrange and rearrange themselves into diverse patterns reflecting the actuality of Black life or reflecting the psyches of the Black and white artists who depicted that life. A knowledgeable individual twists the instrument to view the primitivism depicted by such white authors as Julia Peterkin, Eugene O'Neill, Sherwood Anderson, Dubose Heyward, Mary Wiborg, and William Faulkner, or the exotic abandon simulated by Carl Van Vechten. But a slight adjustment reshapes those images into the cultural elitism revealed by Van Vechten and cherished by W. E. B. DuBois. Another adjustment reveals the integrationist optimism of Langston Hughes, or the pan-Africanism of W. E. B. DuBois, or the Black nationalism of Marcus Garvey. Examine rural southern Blacks from the perspectives of Peterkin, Heyward, Faulkner, and Jean Toomer; or scrutinize the urban northerners of Toomer, Claude McKay, Rudolph Fisher, Langston Hughes, and Countée Cullen. Smile at the enthusiastic and naive Carl Van Vechtens, Mabel Dodges, and other white patrons as they prance about with their trophies collected on safaris into the Black jungles; then scowl at the lynchers painted by Claude McKay and photographed by Walter White. Admire the "patient endurance," with which William Faulkner colored his Dilsey; but do not overlook the militant impatience that inflames McKay's poetic voice. Consider the African nationalism vaguely sketched by Cullen, Hughes, and McKay; but compare it with Hughes' poetic demands for American integration and McKay's impressionistic sketches of the damnable siren, America, that fascinates, challenges, and captivates Blacks. Excite yourselves with sexual abandon garishly painted by Van Vechten, Anderson, McKay, and Toomer; but study also the conservative, often frustrated Blacks portrayed by Jessie Fauset and Toomer. Weep for the impotent failures depicted by O'Neill and Paul Green; but rejoice with the bold, determined aspirants of Fauset and Fisher. (pp. 195-96)

The image [of the nightclub Black] may have begun with *Shuffle Along* (1921), a brilliant and popular musical, written and directed by four Blacks—Flournoy Miller, Eubie Blake, Noble Sissel, and Aubrey Lyles. In the same year, *Shuffle Along* was succeeded by *Put and Take,* another musical by a Black—Irving C. Miller, who also produced *Liza* (1923), which was followed in the same year by *Runnin' Wild* by Miller and Lyles. The beauty of Afro-American chorus girls such as Florence Mills and Josephine Baker, the exotic foreign settings, the gaiety and the frenzy of these musicals and their successors may have cultivated in Broadway audiences a taste for particular depictions of Black life. Furthermore, these musicals may have created an image difficult to change.

Although it is located in the South, Sherwood Anderson's *Dark Laughter* (1925) conjures up the image of a joyful, untroubled people who, themselves freed from the need to read Freud, laugh gently at frustrated whites, who repress their own sexual desires. The image of joy continues in Carl Van Vechten's novel, *Nigger Heaven* (1926), set in Harlem. Although Van

Vechten later proclaimed his desire to familarize white readers with a cultural Black society which gives soirées and speaks French, he glamorized the Scarlet Creeper, a "sweetman" (gigolo), and he depicted Black night life with an excitement certain to allure readers.

The exoticism and gaiety appear in the works of Black writers themselves. Even Countée Cullen, known to subsequent generations as a somewhat prim purveyor of high art, contrasted the warmth of Blacks with the coldness of whites, wrote atavistically of the African rhythm inherent in the walk of a Black writer (in *Color,* 1925), and rhapsodized the wildness of the African heritage.

In his first collection, *The Weary Blues* (1926), Langston Hughes not only created jazz/blues poems but also wrote with an exuberance tending to promote the image of an uninhibited people:

>   Dream Variation
>
> To fling my arms wide
> In some place of the sun,
> To whirl and to dance
> Till the white day is done.
> Then rest at cool evening
> Beneath a tall tree
> While night comes on gently,
>   Dark like me,—
> That is my dream!
>
> To fling my arms wide
> In the face of the sun,
> Dance! whirl! whirl!
> Till the quick day is done.
> Rest at pale evening. . . .
> A tall, slim tree. . . .
> Night coming tenderly
>   Black like me.

Black novelists also contributed to the image of an uninhibited people whose lives are exotic whirls. In *Home to Harlem* (1928), Claude McKay, a Black West Indian, drowned social protest in a flood of night life—prostitutes, sweetmen, jazz, night club fights—as he told the story of a Black deserter from the armed services who searches through Harlem for the prostitute whom he loves. Succeeding novelists, such as Rudolph Fisher (*The Walls of Jericho,* 1928) and Wallace Thurman (*The Blacker the Berry,* 1929), seemed almost compelled to include irrelevant nightclub scenes as though they had become clichés of Black life.

It should not be wondered then that W. E. B. DuBois, editor of *The Crisis,* reserved sections of several issues to question whether writers and publishers shared his fear that Black writers were being encouraged to create derogatory pictures of Blacks. Seriously concerned about respectable images of Blacks, DuBois, more than two decades earlier, had rationalized their enthusiasm as a primitivism promoted by the experience of slavery, a primitivism which would be modified when Black Americans matured into the sophistication of Euro-American society. Now that his "Talented Tenth" seemed to promote spectacles of frenzy, however, DuBois suspected that their desire to publish persuaded them to ignore the truth of Black life and to pander to whites by creating images designed to titillate.

Beneath the surfaces of gay abandon during the 1920's, however, are more somber issues, more sober themes which should be examined more closely. The same writers who seem to rejoice in the enthusiasm of Black life also sounded what Langston

W.E.B. DuBois at work in the Crisis *office. Courtesy of NAACP.*

Hughes described as "the sob of the jazz band"—the melancholy undertone of Black life, ever present but sometimes unheard by those who fail to listen carefully.

Claude McKay pictured a Harlem dancer who guards her soul from the lascivious image suggested by her dance (*Harlem Shadows,* 1922), and Langston Hughes described the weariness of a jazz pianist (*The Weary Blues,* 1926). In *The Walls of Jericho* (1928) Fisher overshadowed the scenes of night life with a quieter depiction of the romance of two working people of Harlem. Thurman tempered his scenes of night life and dances in *The Blacker the Berry* by revealing that some Blacks visited dance halls not to gorge themselves with gaiety but to discover companionship to ease their loneliness. In the same novel a white Chicagoan confirms his impression that the exotic savagery of Harlemites is grossly exaggerated by their white press agents. While his actress-sister revels in what she considers the barbaric splendor of the Black club they visit, the Chicagoan sees a generally decorous behavior which assures him that Harlemites are no wilder than the Blacks he has known in Chicago (and perhaps not as wild as the whites in either city). Countée Cullen asserted that he wrote *One Way to Heaven* (1932) to counter Carl Van Vechten's *Nigger Heaven* by showing the humanity of Black life in Harlem. In scene after scene, Cullen balances superficial exuberance with sober explanation: The enthusiasm of a religious revival does not obscure the fact that in attendance also are some morally respectable Blacks who are not swept away by the emotion. The heroine, a morally circumspect, hard-working woman, has attended several revivals to which she has been indifferent. A male's illicit love affair is ascribed partly to the nature of the wandering male and partly to a desire to find companionship because his wife, who has become a religious fanatic, is engaged in an affair with Jesus.

These more serious vestiges of Black life in America should not be ignored when one considers the literature of the Renaissance; for, far from being mere entertainers, many Black writers regarded literature as a means of seriously examining problems of living. Moreover, they did not restrict their examinations to problems of Blacks in an adversary relationship with white society. Almost from the first they were concerned with issues which might be considered universal if American critics were more willing to discover universality in the lives of Black people.

The interest in human conditions appears in Jean Toomer's *Cane* (1923), the work of the Renaissance which is the best known and the most highly respected in academic circles. Toomer delineates many protagonists whose difficulties do not depend primarily upon their ancestry: Karintha has matured too soon sexually; Carma lives in a society which pretends that a woman should become sexless if her husband does not live with her; Esther cannot reconcile her sexual urges with the education by a society which has taught her that "good" girls do not feel such urges; John, in "Theater," cannot adapt his idealized romanticizing into a satisfactory relationship with an actual woman; Dorris, in "Theater," dreams of a companionship that will provide a real substitute for the artificiality of the theater; Muriel, in "Box Seat," fears to defy the little-minded, social regulators of the world; Avery finds it more pleasurable to be supported by men rather than to labor as a teacher in a normal school. The problems of these individuals may be complicated or intensified by their condition as Blacks in America, but the problems would exist regardless of their race.

Jessie Fauset, the too little-known author of *There is Confusion* (1924), *Plum Bun* (1929), *The Chinaberry Tree* (1933), and *Comedy: American Style* (1933), contrived her novels to focus on the problems of Blacks whose lives are not continuously affected by their interrelationships with whites. Most often their problems derive from their ambition or from a society excessively willing to evaluate individuals according to false criteria. In *There is Confusion,* for example, an ambitious young Black protagonist disrupts and nearly destroys the people around her because she tries to regulate their lives according to her delusions. Because she believes that people should not marry outside their class, she interferes with her brother's romance with a young woman whose family background is different. Doing "the right thing," by withdrawing from the relationship, the second young woman then rushes into an unfortunate marriage. Because the protagonist believes that suitors must be trained into suitably devoted servants, she refuses to apologize to the man she loves even though she is wrong. After he apologizes in order to effect a reconciliation, she delays a response with the deliberate intention of causing him to learn that he cannot win her too easily. She begins to realize her error only when he, jolted by her rebuff, proposes to a woman who offers him affection without reservation.

In stories which she published during the 1920's, Zora Neale Hurston of Florida explored such an "in-group" issue as the manner in which townspeople affect individuals by forcing them to act out of character in order to maintain the respect of the mob ("Spunk"). In addition, she vividly revealed the problems which disturb male-female relationships: the alienation which develops when a naive wife is seduced by a traveling salesman ("The Gilded Six-Bits"); the tragic consequences when a self-centered husband who has exploited his wife tries to replace her ("Sweat").

Black dramatists, such as Willis Richardson and Georgia D. Johnson, prepared domestic dramas for the Black community: the tensions between a man and his improvident brothers-in-law ("The Broken Banjo"); the pathos of a situation in which a child is permitted to die because the mother favors the healing power of faith above that of man's medicine.

In such ways as these, Black people of the Renaissance explored serious issues involving Black people but not deriving primarily from the racial ancestry or from their relationship with whites. This statement, however, should not encourage a fallacious assumption that the Black writers evaded their racial identity or ignored problems which do derive from interracial conflict. To the contrary, Black Renaissance writers frequently expressed concerns which strikingly anticipate major themes identified with the revolutionary Black Arts writers of the 1960's: a search for and affirmation of ancestral heritage, a feeling of alienation from the white Euro-American world; a presentation of and protest against oppression; and even militant defiance of oppression.

Just as Black Arts writers of today affirm their African heritage, so many Renaissance writers sought identity through identification with an ancestral past. Jean Toomer sought identity derived in part from the consciousness of the slave South and Africa (*Cane,* 1923, and "Natalie Mann"). As I have pointed out earlier, Countée Cullen proclaimed that the sober teachings of Christian civilization could not curb the memories and the urges which linked him with Africa ("Heritage"). Langston Hughes found pride in identification with a race so old in human history that it had lived when rivers were young ("The Negro Speaks of Rivers"). Although some of these ancestral searches may seem rhetorical rather than actual, although some of the thoughts of Africa are sufficiently atavistic to promote a concept of exotic primitivism, the quests respond partly at least to Alain Locke's urgings that Black artists search for subject and style in an African tradition.

For the Black American writer of the 1920's, however, the search for ancestry proved more difficult than for white Americans. Some Blacks, ashamed of their ancestry as slaves and as descendants of Africans whom they judged to have been savages, attempted to evolve more respectable ancestry from identification with former masters. In *There Is Confusion* (1924) Jessie Fauset suggested the problems sometimes posed by the quest for European ancestry. Moreover, Blacks who wished to affirm a Black heritage were forced to identify with a continent rather than with a particular tribe or nation. Hence, the identification sometimes became intellectual and abstract rather than personal. The problem is suggested by Hughes:

> Afro-American Fragment
>
> So long,
> So far away
> Is Africa.
> Not even memories alive
> Save those that history books create,
> Save those that songs
> Beat back into the blood—
> Beat out of blood with words sad-sung
> In strange un-Negro tongue—
> So long
> So far away.
>
> Subdued and time-lost
> Are the drums—and yet
> Through some vast mist of race
> There comes this song

I do not understand,
This song of atavistic land,
Of bitter yearning lost
Without a place—
So long,
So far away
Is Africa's
Dark face.

Failure to establish psychological identity with the Black heritage and corresponding awareness of exclusion from the European heritage sometimes produced a sense of alienation comparable to that expressed by Black Arts writers today. The feeling resounds vividly from McKay's "Outcast."

For the dim regions whence my fathers came
My spirit, bondaged by the body, longs.
Words felt, but never heard, my lips would frame:
My soul would sing forgotten jungle songs.
I would go back to darkness and to peace,
But the great western world holds me in fee,
And I may never hope for full release,
While to its alien gods I bend my knee.
Something in me is lost, forever lost,
Some vital thing has gone out of my heart,
And I must walk the way of life a ghost
Among the sons of earth, a thing apart;
For I was born, far from my native clime,
Under the white man's menace, out of time.

The serious themes that Renaissance writers explored most frequently, as might be expected, are protests against oppression. The presence of such themes has been obscured by three facts: (1) many readers remember the glamorous gaiety and forget the serious comments; (2) some protests appear as brief asides rather than fully developed explanations; (3) some protests seem mild because, rather than directly assaulting whites, they adumbrate the manner in which external oppression causes Blacks to oppress themselves. The way that serious protest can be ignored is evidenced by the customary reactions of casual readers to McKay's *Home to Harlem* (1928), which appears, even in this paper, as a prototype of a Black work that promotes exoticism. The vividly exotic spectacles blind many readers to McKay's presentation of such facts as the following: During World War I many Black soldiers who enlisted to fight for democracy were restricted to service as laborers; during the 1920's some Harlem clubs, whether owned by whites or Blacks, discriminated against Blacks by refusing them admission—except as entertainers or waiters; in many occupations Black workers surrendered their dignity to the caprice of white supervisors.

It is true that no *Native Son* burst from the Renaissance to denounce American oppression. But Walter White's novel *The Fire in the Flint* (1924) decries the brutality of lynchings, as does Claude McKay's "The Lynching." Toomer's "Blood-Burning Moon" and "Kabnis" (*Cane*) reveal the powerlessness of Blacks to protect themselves from white brutality: a successful self-defense summons the lynch mob as quickly as a murder would.

Much more prevalent is the Renaissance writers' tendency to attack oppression indirectly by showing how it causes Blacks to turn against themselves. Because color, as an evidence of African ancestry, was a shibboleth of whites against Blacks, many Blacks used color as a criterion of intra-group evaluation. In *The Blacker the Berry* the protagonist, because of her dark

skin, suffers within her family, in school and college, and in efforts to secure employment. Yet pathetically, as Thurman shows, the heroine cherishes the same criteria which have victimized her. She desires only men who are of lighter complexion and Caucasian appearance; and she undervalues herself, believing for a time at least that her Blackness is an ineradicable blot upon her record. In *Comedy: American Style* (1933) Fauset censured a Negro mother who values her children according to the degree of their approximation to Caucasian appearance. Walter White's *Flight* (1928) and Nella Larsen's *Passing* (1929) show the dilemmas of heroines who, repressed by the conditions of life as Blacks, attempt to improve their lot by passing for white.

In ironic repudiation of the images of Blacks as amoral beings, Jean Toomer repeatedly stressed the necessity for middle-class Negroes to liberate themselves from conscious imitation of the restrictive morality of Anglo-Saxons. "Esther," "Theater," and "Box-Seat" all reveal the frustrations of Black people who, desiring social approval, repress their emotions, their humanness. In "Kabnis" Carrie K., fearing censure by others, represses her instinctual attraction to Lewis. Paul ("Bona and Paul," *Cane*) loses a female companion because of his self-conscious desire to explain to a bystander that the relationship is not lustful. Toomer's most fully developed attack on middle-class morality appears in the unpublished drama "Natalie Mann." Mert, a school teacher, dies because she perceives too late that she must enjoy passion fully without concern for society's censure. Natalie, the protagonist, develops to this awareness only through the assistance of a Christ-like male who himself has experienced the rebukes of the middle class.

Toomer was not the only writer to question the excessive effort of Blacks to conform to the standards presumed to be those of whites. The protagonist in Walter White's *Flight* is forced to leave town and, temporarily, to deny her race because Blacks will not permit her to forget that she has had a child out of wedlock: her lover's proposal of abortion so diminished him in her esteem that she refused his subsequent efforts to marry her.

During the 1920's few writers reacted militantly to oppression with the kind of rhetoric for which Black revolutionary literature became notorious during the 1960's. There are several reasons. A generally optimistic faith that talented Blacks soon would merge with the mainstream muted rhetorical violence and violent rhetoric. Furthermore, publishers during the 1920's did not permit the kind of language and the explicit description of violent action which became almost commonplace in later decades. Third, the publishing houses were controlled by whites. It should be remembered that much of the Black revolutionary literature of the 1960's issued from Black publishers of poetry and in Black community drama.

Under the circumstances it is not surprising that the militant reaction often was expressed as self-defense, as in Claude McKay's well-known "If We Must Die" (*Harlem Shadows*). Less frequently came prayers for destruction, as in McKay's "Enslaved" (*Harlem Shadows*). Most often the militancy is a proud hostility toward whites. At the end of *Flight* the male protagonist learns why his father abhorred whites: they had deprived him of inheritance by refusing to recognize him as their offspring. In turn he refuses to permit an elderly white to ease his own conscience by making a monetary donation while continuing to ignore the blood relationship.

I cannot conclude without reassessing the significance of the literary Harlem Renaissance. If it is remembered for expression of gaiety rather than for the serious concerns of the Black authors; if it was a movement which involved only talented artists in one segment of the Black American population; if it reflects primarily the life of only one part of one city inhabited by Blacks; if it evidences little awareness of such a significant issue for Blacks as DuBois' dreams and promotions of Pan-Africanism and even less awareness of or respect for Marcus Garvey's Back-to-Africa movement—if the literary Renaissance is so limited, does it merit serious study? Was it, as Harold Cruse has suggested, an era to be examined only as a pathetic example of a time when Black artists might have established criteria for their art but failed to do so? Was it, as W. E. B. DuBois stated and as LeRoi Jones insisted more forcefully later, a movement that lost validity as it became a plaything of white culture? In fact, is the very attention given to it by historians of Black culture evidence of the willingness of Blacks and whites to glorify, or permit glorification of, inferior art by Blacks?

Each of these allegations has partial validity. But such objections based on idealistic absolutes fail to consider the actual significances of the literary Renaissance. First, in no other decade had Black novelists been afforded such opportunity for publication. If fewer than twenty original, non-vanity-press novels appeared between 1924 and 1933, that figure nevertheless exceeded the number published by American commercial houses in all the years since the publication of the first Black American novel, William Wells Brown's *Clotel* (1853). Even the Depression and the closing of some outlets could not dispel the new awareness that possibilities existed for Blacks who wished to write novels. The field was open to many writers, not merely to the individual geniuses—the Paul Dunbar or the Charles Chesnutt of an earlier decade. This productivity, as well as the later success of Richard Wright, undoubtedly encouraged such novelists as Chester Himes, Ann Petry, Frank Yerby, and William G. Smith, who developed during the late 1930's and early 1940's.

The literary examples and inspirations were not limited to the novel. Only a few serious Black dramas reached Broadway, but the enthusiastic establishment of Black community theaters during the 1920's furthered the creation of a Black audience for drama and promoted awareness of the need for writers to create material for that audience.

Perhaps the productivity in poetry had less significant influence because Blacks previously had found outlets for poetry—the national reputation of Paul Laurence Dunbar was known by Blacks. Moreover, poetry was still to be considered an avocation which one supported by revenue derived from a stable vocation. But there was hope that Black writers might be able to sustain themselves partly through grants, for Countée Cullen had established a precedent by winning a Guggenheim fellowship for his proposal of a poetry-writing project.

Of final benefit to future writers was the mere fact that entrées had been established. A Langston Hughes or Wallace Thurman or Countée Cullen or, later, an Arna Bontemps knew publishers and knew other people who might be able to assist prospective authors. In all these senses, the Renaissance was not a rebirth but, in very significant ways, a first birth for Black Americans in literature.

A second significance of the literary Renaissance is its inspiration for African and Caribbean poets such as Léopold Senghor, Aimé Césaire, and Léon Damas who, a generation later in the 1930's and 1940's, promoted Negritude, a literary-cul-

tural movement which emphasized consciousness of African identity and pride in the Black heritage. More than a decade after the Negritude writers, newer Black American writers of the 1960's looked to African Negritude for inspiration. Thus, both directly and circuitously, the Renaissance promoted Black American literature and Black consciousness of future decades.

Finally, the Renaissance has importance as a symbol. In many respects, the actuality of a culture is less important than the myth which envelops and extends from that culture. The memory that Black Americans had been recognized and respected for literary achievements, as well as other artistic achievements, established awareness that there could be a literary culture among Blacks. If the memory faded rapidly from the consciousness of white America, it did not fade from the minds of Blacks responsible for continuing the culture among their people. Marcus Garvey did not succeed in restoring Black Americans to Africa; consequently, he is remembered as a dream that faded. But the Renaissance, for Black Americans and others, has gained strength as the mythic memory of a time when Blacks first burst into national consciousness as a talented group that was young, rebellious, proud, and beautiful. (pp. 201-10)

> *Darwin T. Turner, "The Harlem Renaissance: One Facet of an Unturned Kaleidoscope," in* Toward a New American Literary History: Essays in Honor of Arlin Turner, *Louis J. Budd, Edwin H. Cady, and Carl L. Anderson, eds., Duke University Press, 1980, pp. 195-210.*

ROBERT A. BONE

[*Bone, an American critic and educator, is the author of the critical histories* The Negro Novel in America *(1958) and* Down Home: A History of Afro-American Short Fiction from Its Beginnings to the End of the Harlem Renaissance *(1975). A student of Afro-American, English, and American literature, with a special interest in Shakespeare, Bone has said of himself: "A white man and critic of black literature, I try to demonstrate by the quality of my work that scholarship is not the same thing as identity." In the following excerpt from* The Negro Novel in America, *Bone analyzes theme and technique in novels of the Harlem Renaissance.*]

Claude McKay has been called *l'enfant terrible* of the Negro Renaissance. Proud of his identification with the black masses and contemptuous of all things middle class, he led a successful revolt against the sanctimonious literary treatment of the Negro. "There was never any presentation more ludicrous," he maintained. McKay writes mockingly of "educated Negroes, ashamed of their race's intuitive love of color, wrapping themselves up in respectable gray." In his own work he exalts all that is colorful and distinctive in the Negro's cultural heritage. His insistence on legitimate differences is typical of the Renaissance generation. (p. 67)

With the appearance of *Harlem Shadows* (1922), a book of verse, McKay became a major figure in the Negro Renaissance. His publications include three volumes of poems, a collection of short stories, a book on Harlem, an autobiography (*A Long Way from Home*), and three novels.

McKay's first novel, *Home to Harlem* (1928), was an immediate popular success. Like many novels of the 1920's, it opens with a farewell to arms. Jake, the central character, goes AWOL from the white folks' war and comes "home to Harlem." He picks up a "tantalizing brown" for $50, but she returns his money as a gift, after leaving him during the night. The plot, which is little more than a device, concerns his attempt to find her again. The narrative structure is loose and vagrant, tracing Jake's movements from cabaret to "rent party," from poolroom to gin mill, from the docks to the dining car. McKay depends upon atmosphere to carry the book. The style is appropriately impressionistic, full of hyphenated adjectives aimed at vivid impressions of Harlem life.

The beginnings of a dramatic structure may be seen, however, in the characters of Jake and Ray. Jake represents pure instinct. Physical well-being—whether from good food, good liquor, or a good woman—is his prime value. Work when you feel like it. Loaf when the mood strikes you. Take life easy. Joy is the key word in understanding Jake; lust is a sign of repression: "Gambling did not have a strangle-hold upon him any more than dope or desire did. Jake took what he wanted of whatever he fancied and . . . kept on going." Through Jake, McKay strikes at the heart of the Protestant ethic. Jake's very existence is an act of affirmation, an injunction to enjoy life!

Ray is a young Haitian, consumed with a desire to write, whom Jake befriends on his railroad run. Ray embodies the dilemma of the inhibited, overcivilized intellectual. A misfit in the white man's civilization, he refuses to be penned in "like bank clerks in steel-wire cages." Yet he is unable, like Jake, to entrust himself wholly to instinct. For Ray, "Thought is suffering"— the opposite of joy. He is depressed by the state of contemporary society, which he describes as "the vast international cemetery of this century." His is that profound disgust which modern life sometimes evokes in men of artistic sensibilities.

Through a faulty denouement, the symbolic import of Jake and Ray is imperfectly conveyed. Ray, disgusted with all that is sordid and ugly in the lives of the dining-car waiters, ships out on a freighter bound for Europe. Jake, in the closing pages of the novel, finds his lost Felice, whose name signifies joy. By contrasting Jake's happiness with Ray's restless wandering, McKay attempts to convey the superiority of instinct over reason. But at bottom, Jake and Ray represent different ways of rebelling against Western civilization. Jake rebels instinctively, while Ray's rebellion occurs on an intellectual plane. Both characters acquire a broader significance only through their negative relationship to contemporary society. McKay's failure to develop this relationship is the failure of the novel.

Jake is the typical McKay protagonist—the primitive Negro, untouched by the decay of Occidental civilization. The validity of this symbol, however, depends upon McKay's view of contemporary life. Since the author cannot take this view for granted, he introduces himself into the novel as Ray, in order to expound it. But Ray hardly helps matters; in *Home to Harlem* he does little more than state his prejudices. As a result, the novel is left without a suitable antagonist. Jake and Ray are vivid enough, but what they would deny is not always clear. The novel, unable to develop its primary conflict, bogs down in the secondary contrast between Jake and Ray.

In *Banjo* (1929), the sequel of *Home to Harlem*, McKay comes closer to realizing his central theme. He is moving slowly toward the finished form which he finally achieves in *Banana Bottom*. The setting of *Banjo* has shifted from Harlem to the waterfront at Marseilles, but the main symbols are the same. Jake's role is played by Banjo, an irrepressible, joy-loving vagabond, while Ray is present once more to act as interpreter.

Part I presents the milieu and introduces the main character. The Ditch, familiar name for Marseilles' waterfront section,

makes the setting of *Home to Harlem* seem like a Victorian drawing room. Hoboes, panhandlers, pimps, prostitutes, sailors on shore leave, syphilitics, and beachcombers are its chief inhabitants. In the midst of this international flophouse lives Banjo with his "beach boys," from whom he hopes to fashion a jazz band. Part II witnesses the fulfillment of this ambition, as Banjo and his boys play "Stay, Carolina, Stay!" in a local bistro: "It was perhaps the nearest that Banjo, quite unconscious of it, ever came to an aesthetic realization of his orchestra." After a description of the breakup of the band and the subsequent troubles of the beach boys, Part III moves rapidly toward a denouement when Ray decides to cast his lot with "the Jakes and Banjoes of this world."

Ray editorializes freely throughout the novel, and from his lengthy discourses we can reconstruct McKay's indictment of European civilization. To begin with, Western society harbors against the colored man a not-so-blind prejudice, which is "controlled by the exigencies of the white man's business." Commercialism is the canker which is destroying the soul of the West. Hypocrisy is its handmaiden—a pious pose of patriotism, Christianity, and sexual purity which cloaks colonialism, economic rapacity, and bawdiness. An unwholesome attitude toward sex is warping the personality of "civilized" man: "Terrible is their world that creates disasters and catastrophes from simple natural incidents." Finally, a sterile trend toward standardization and conformity threatens to destroy the rich cultural diversity exemplified by such minorities as the Jews, the Irish, and the American Negro.

In dramatizing his indictment of Western civilization, McKay relies too heavily on Ray's rhetoric, but he also gropes toward a fictional presentation. The American steamship company named the Dollar Line, the brutality of the French police toward the beach boys, and a pornographic film of the "Blue Cinema" variety, help him to make his point. The French chauffeur, who intends to buy a suburban lot from his proceeds as a pimp, is a symbol of bourgeois respectability founded on sordid commercialism. The setting of the novel is likewise symbolic. Marseilles is the chief port of Mediterranean commerce and the crossroads of Europe and Africa. Its waterfront district provides a worm's-eye view of European civilization. But these scattered symbols can never replace successful characterization. Even in *Banjo*, McKay's antagonist remains an abstraction.

The protagonist of the novel, however, succeeds as both character and symbol. Convincing as a person, Banjo takes on additional depth, until in the end he comes to stand for a way of life. McKay expects us to see beyond the the Ditch to the positive values which Banjo embodies. A careless attitude toward money is central to these values. "Them's all sous-crazy, these folkses," Banjo says of the French. He plays jazz for fun, not for the commercial motives of the white musicians. He knows how to laugh, how to love, how to enjoy life in the carefree manner of the vagabond. Above all, he is a folk artist— a symbol of the Negro's inventiveness and creativity. His nickname and his instrument link him to the world of jazz, with all its connotations of impudence, freedom from restraint, spontaneous improvisation, and defiance of everything drab and respectable.

In seeking values to oppose to those of bourgeois society, McKay falls back upon a separate Negro culture. Banjo's devotion to "nigger music," the beach boys' gift of language, which Ray calls "their rich reservoir of niggerisms," and Ray's more sophisticated interest in African folk tales and primitive

Claude McKay. Courtesy of Joseph Solomon, Executor of the Literary Estate of Carl Van Vechten.

African sculpture are obvious manifestations of McKay's Negro nationalism. It follows from McKay's position that he must resist assimilation into the dominant culture. In all of his novels he bitterly attacks the mulatto middle class for its "imitativeness." The lower-class Negro's stubborn resistance to assimilation is the true theme of *Banjo*:

> That this primitive child, this kinky-headed, big-laughing black boy of the world, did not go down and disappear under the serried crush of trampling white feet; that he managed to remain on the scene, not worldly wise, not "getting there," yet not machine-made nor poor-in-spirit like the regimented creatures of civilization was baffling to civilized understanding. . . . He was a challenge to civilization itself.

McKay poses the central conflict in these terms: black vagabond vs. white civilization. At this point, however, the novel breaks down. Although the author intends a decisive rejection of "civilization" in favor of "Banjo," he cannot dramatize it successfully through the character of Ray. At the end of the novel Ray joins Banjo in the vagabond life. But Ray, who is more the child of modern civilization than he would care to admit, can never be a Banjo. His intellect is too great a barrier. For Ray no decisive choice is possible, but only a more or less unsatisfactory compromise: "Ray wanted to hold on to his intellectual acquirements without losing his instinctive gifts. The black gifts of laughter and melody and simple sensuous

feelings and responses." The novel thus slips out of a clear-cut dualism into a fuzzy dialectical structure—*thesis*, white civilization; *antithesis*, Banjo; *synthesis*, Ray.

Banana Bottom (1933) represents the culmination of McKay's search for a form. Cultural dualism is his central theme, and for its most successful expression he turns to his native Jamaica. Here the folk culture is more developed, and the clash between "native" and European values sharper. McKay has dispensed with Ray and achieved a proper distance between himself and his novel. The Craigs, a white missionary couple, are his first successful personification of Anglo-Saxon civilization. In Bita, their protégé, McKay has at last found his protagonist. Jake and Banjo, while they embodied McKay's values, were static characters. Ray, being an intellectual, was limited in his powers of renunciation. But Bita is a peasant girl, educated by white missionaries. Caught between two cultures, she is yet free to return to the folk.

The novel opens with the story of Bita's seduction by an idiot boy, at age twelve. Two different responses to this "tragedy" immediately set the stage for the deep cultural cleavage with which the novel deals. The Craigs adopt Bita and help her to overcome her "shame"; but Sister Phibby expresses an opposing view: "Although she thought it was a sad thing as a good Christian should, her wide brown face betrayed a kind of primitive satisfaction in a good thing done early."

After being educated in England by her benefactors, Bita returns to assist them with their missionary work. She soon becomes restless under the regimen of the Mission, and a struggle ensues between the gentle domination of the Craigs and Bita's desire to be herself. On the one side is the Christ-God, the Calvinist austerity, and the naive ethnocentrism of the Mission. On the other is the Obeah God, the primitive sexuality, and the simple values of the folk culture. Bita's choice is in the best Renaissance spirit: "I thank God that although I was brought up and educated among white people, I have never wanted to be anything but myself. I take pride in being coloured and different. . . . I can't imagine anything more tragic than people torturing themselves to be different from their natural unchangeable selves."

McKay uses sex as the chief means of dramatizing his theme. He understands that the major conflicts in a woman's life will be sexual, and that Bita's struggle with the Craig's will naturally assume this form. Bita rebels against her guardians by forming an attachment to a fun-loving, irresponsible scamp named Hopping Dick. In order to prevent her from backsliding, the Craigs try to arrange a marriage with a respectable young divinity student. Much to their consternation, the prospective bridegroom puts himself out of the running by defiling himself with a goat. Encouraged by her moral victory, Bita goes her own way, and the novel reaches a climax when she participates in an atavistic dance ritual. Since Hopping Dick is not a marrying man, Bita eventually settles down with Jubban, a sturdy black peasant, whose child she conceives during their engagement.

Sterling Brown has described *Banana Bottom* as a quiet story, quietly told. The novel moves at the leisurely pace of the life which it portrays. Its tone is tranquil, in contrast to the tumultuous quality of McKay's earlier novels. Ray's tirades are gone, along with the hyphenated adjectives which McKay formerly employed to present a panorama of urban life. He strives instead for a simplicity of style suited to his pastoral setting. Much of the novel is devoted to exotic descriptions of Jamaican peasant life. Partly ornamental, these scenes are also functional in revealing the beauty of the life which Bita embraces.

Although much of the tension in McKay's work derives from his Negro nationalism, it would be a mistake to conclude that his rejection of bourgeois society is based solely, or even primarily, on his experience as a Negro. McKay drew freely on his broader cultural heritage, and participated widely in the intellectual currents of his day. His social realism comes from the Dickens-Tolstoy-Zola tradition, his sense of satire from Shaw, Ibsen, and Anatole France. His emphasis on sex reflects his reading of Sherwood Anderson and D. H. Lawrence. Strongly influenced by Marxism, for a time he was associated editor of the *Liberator* under Max Eastman. In Paris he mingled freely with the cosmopolitan expatriates, from whom he discovered his basic affinity for Expressionism. Expressionism exerted a strong influence on most of the Parisian art colony of the early 20th century. At the core of the movement was a deep sense of alienation from modern society: to renew its waning vitality, art must turn from a decadent sophistication to the unspoiled outpourings of primitive man. Influenced by Freud and the new psychology, the movement exalted emotion over intellect, and in its extreme form (Dada) advocated the uninhibited expression of personal emotion, even at the sacrifice of intelligibility. As a result of this sudden enthusiasm for primitivism, the Negro—or rather an imaginary facsimile thereof—became an object of the white man's admiration and envy. Picasso discovered primitive African sculpture; Hugues Panassié introduced Europe to jazz; and authors like Gertrude Stein and E. E. Cummings made literary history with their characterizations of primitive Negroes.

None of this glorification of things Negro was lost upon a young writer of Claude McKay's temperament. It is a short step from Gertrude Stein's *Melanctha* with its central conflict between instinct and reason, to the characters of Jake and Ray. It is an even shorter step from Cummings' Jean le Nègre to McKay's Banjo. *The Enormous Room* (1922) and *Banjo* (1929) contain striking parallels, in both theme and situation. There is the same sordid environment with its "delectable (human) mountains"; the same senseless bureaucratic oppression by the French government; and the same uncorrupted primitives who resist integration into a degenerate society. Nor is it a matter of proving "influence"—these authors simply shared the same myth.

In the last analysis Expressionism is a form of escape. McKay anticipates his own spiritual flight when he writes of Ray: "Some day he would escape from the clutches of that magnificent monster of civilization and retire behind the natural defenses of his island, where the steam-roller of progress could not reach him." *Banana Bottom* is McKay's romantic escape from the machine age, and his symbolic link with the Expressionists. Like Gauguin, the founder of French Expressionism who sought inspiration in the South Seas, McKay found artistic fulfillment in his novel of West Indian peasant life. If McKay's spiritual journey carried him "a long way from home," in the end he returned to his native island.

In the summer of 1926, the *Nation* carried an article which was widely acclaimed as the literary manifesto of the New Negro. The main burden of the article was an attack on assimilationism. The writer urged the Negro artist to make full use of the colorful, distinctive material at his disposal, and to avoid the example of a Negro society woman who enthusiastically attended recitals of Andalusian folk songs but wouldn't be seen dead at a Bessie Smith recital of the blues. After calling upon the Negro artist to interpret the beauty of his own people, the article closed with a ringing declaration of independence: "We younger Negro artists who create now intend to express our individual dark-skinned selves without fear or shame. If white people are pleased, we are glad. If they are not, it doesn't matter. . . . If colored people are pleased, we are glad. If they are not, their displeasure doesn't matter either." The author of this manifesto was a young writer named Langston Hughes.

The importance of Hughes as a literary figure far transcends that of his only novel, *Not without Laughter* (1930). Primarily a poet, his verse was influenced thematically by the social realism of Lindsay, Masters, and Sandburg, and technically by the rhythms of jazz. His first two volumes of poems, *The Weary Blues* (1926) and *Fine Clothes to the Jew* (1927), provoked a fierce controversy because of their forthright and sympathetic treatment of lower-class Negro life. Hughes, perhaps more than any other author, knows and loves the Negro masses. His newspaper sketches of Jess B. Semple, an unlettered but philosophical Harlemite (just be simple), are among his finest literary creations. A prolific author, Hughes has published some seven volumes of verse, two collections of short stories, an autobiography, a book for children, and several plays, librettos, translations, radio skits, and magazine articles.

Not without Laughter deals with the childhood of a colored youth in a small midwestern town. The plot consists of Sandy's early experiences with school and work, with sex and race, and with his family, the major formative influence in his life. His grandmother, Aunt Hager, is a humble religious woman who has raised three daughters by taking in washing. Harriet, the youngest, is pleasure-seeking, rebellious, and bitterly resentful of racial injustice. Her secular values clash sharply with the religious zeal of her mother. Tempy, who has married well, is a social climber and a refugee from everything "niggerish." Anjee, Sandy's mother, lives from day to day between visits from her wandering husband, the guitar-plucking, blues-singing Jimboy.

Laughter is the central symbol of the novel—the complex, ironic laughter which is the Negro's saving response to racial oppression. The characters cluster around the poles of laughter and not-laughter. Jimboy and Harriet, with their low-down blues and comical dances, are the hub of laughter in Aunt Hager's household. Anjee, too, must be near laughter (Jimboy), at whatever cost. Hager and Tempy, for different reasons, represent the forces of sobriety. Hager's religion requires her to regard laughter as sinful, while for Tempy, laughter is an inexcusable digression from the serious business of accumulating property. Unfortunately, Sandy disrupts the symbolic unity of the novel. Presumably torn by the conflicting forces which divide the family, his inner struggle fails to materialize. There is no laughter in his life, but only an altogether commendable determination to be a credit to the race. At this point, the novel bogs down in hopeless ideological confusion.

The author sets out to make a defense of laughter. To those like Tempy who claim that Negroes remain poor because of their dancing and singing and easy laughter, Hughes replies: "The other way 'round would be better; dancers because of their poverty; singers because they suffered; laughing all the time because they must forget." Such a view of laughter rests on the assumption that "achievement," at least for the Negro masses, is largely illusory, and that some form of compensatory self-expression is therefore necessary. But it is precisely on this point that Hughes is most ambivalent. If he defends laughter, he also defends achievement: "I wants you to be a great man, son.'' ''I won't disappoint you, Aunt Hager.'' At the end of the novel, Sandy returns to school to fulfill his grandmother's dream.

In short, Hughes tried to reject the Protestant ethic (joy is wrong), while retaining the success drive on which it is based. It is an untenable halfway house, which Claude McKay and Jessie Fauset would equally scorn to occupy. In any event, Hughes' ideological ambivalence has disastrous aesthetic consequences. The novel and its main character simply part company. Instead of supporting the defense-of-laughter theme, Sandy emerges as a symbol of racial advancement, which is hardly a laughing matter. Given his main theme of suffering and self-expression, Hughes might better have written the novel around Harriet, who emerges from a life of prostitution to become ''Princess of the Blues.''

Not without Laughter has been compared in some quarters to the first book of the *Studs Lonigan* trilogy. No service is rendered either to American literature or to Hughes by this exaggerated claim. A mediocre novel, *Not without Laughter* was undertaken before its author was prepared to meet the rigorous requirements of the genre. Ideologically confused and structurally defective, the novel gives a final impression of sprawling formlessness. The author, to his credit, is fully aware of these shortcomings, if some of his friendly critics are not. In his autobiography, *The Big Sea* (1940), Hughes makes a courageous apology to the characters of his early novel: ''I went to Far Rockaway that summer and felt bad, because I had wanted their novel to be better than the published one I had given them; I hated to let them down.''

Among the poets of the Negro Renaissance there was none more talented than Countee Cullen (1903-46). While still an undergraduate at New York University, he had already placed poems in a dozen of the best literary magazines. Soundly educated at NYU and Harvard and thoroughly familiar with his literary past, Cullen was more sophisticated in technique and choice of subject than most Negro poets of the period. A Keatsian idiom, a biblical emphasis on moral paradox, and a somewhat self-conscious espousal of African primitivism are the distinguishing characteristics of his verse: His publications include seven books of poems, three plays, an anthology, and a novel, *One Way to Heaven* (1932).

Countee Cullen has often been described as one of the more ''respectable'' Renaissance novelists, with the implication that he avoided the ''sordid'' subject matter of the Harlem School. Nothing could be farther from the truth. Cullen neither exploited low-life material for its own sake nor avoided it when it served his artistic ends. Though distinctly not of a Bohemian temperament, neither did he value respectability above art. His mischievous sense of humor and his penchant for satire differentiated him from those Renaissance novelists who were forever defending the race before the bar of white opinion. Countee Cullen had a lighter and truer touch, which speaks for itself in *One Way to Heaven*.

Sam Lucas, the protagonist of the novel, is as typical a Harlem-School creation as Banjo or Jimboy. With the help of a missing arm, he makes his living as a professional convert. Traveling from one revival meeting to the next, he comes forward to the mourner's bench when the testimonials are nearly over and dramatically throws a deck of cards and a gleaming razor to the floor. Electrified by this eleventh-hour conversion, and moved to pity by his empty sleeve, the congregation can usually be relied upon to press a few dollars into Sam's good hand.

The narrative interest of *One Way to Heaven* centers upon Sam's relationship with Mattie Johnson, an attractive, hardworking dark girl. As the novel opens, Sam decides to try his luck in a large Harlem church, where a famous singing evangelist is preaching. Mattie, who is present in the audience, has stubbornly resisted the call of the evangelist, but where Heaven fails, Sam Lucas and the Devil succeed. Sam's cards and razor become the instruments of Mattie's conversion, and the glittering illusion on which she builds her faith. Subsequently Sam and Mattie marry, but Sam is a travelin' man, with none of the makings of a steady husband. Having left Mattie for another woman, he returns in the fullness of time with a fatal case of pneumonia, contracted during a drunken spree. The stage is thus set for the crowning irony of the novel. As Sam lies dying, he decides to simulate a death-bed conversion for Mattie's sake. Since his final act of deception is, so to speak, a benefit performance, Sam unwittingly accomplishes his own salvation.

The aesthetic design of the novel consists of variations on a theme. The moral ambiguity of Sam's life and death is echoed in the lives of the other characters. Both the evangelist and the Reverend Drummond are sincere men of God, but neither is above a little showmanship for the Lord's sake. The devout but worldly wise Aunt Mandy takes a practical view of Mattie's marital difficulties: ''Sometimes when the angels is too busy to help you, you have to fight the devil with his own tools.'' Even Mattie, ''the gentle servitor of the gentlest of all the gods,'' abandons her Jesus for a conjure-woman and nearly murders her husband's mistress. The author's point is clear: he that is without sin among you, let him cast the first stone at Sam Lucas.

Sam's cards and razor provide an appropriate symbol for Cullen's theme. Like people, the cards and razor contain potentialities for either good or evil. In Sam's hands, they are the tools of deceit, yet they are no less the instruments of Mattie's salvation. In Mattie's possession, they are the sacred tokens of her conversion, but in her extremity she uses them as a voodoo charm. When Sam asks Aunt Mandy, ''Don't you think that cards is evil?'' she replies, ''It all depends on the kind of cards you have and what you do with them.'' In Cullen's view the moral universe is infinitely complex. Form is unimportant; there is more than one way to heaven.

Attached to the main body of the novel by the thinnest of threads is a subplot which deals satirically with Harlem's intelligentsia. By the simple expedient of hiring Mattie out to Harlem's most popular hostess, Cullen creates a vantage point from which to launch his barbs. Constancia Brandon's *soirées* are attended by Harlem socialites, New Negro poets, inquisitive white intellectuals, Garveyites, and even a Southern Bourbon. Cullen deflates them all indiscriminately, exposing their foibles while respecting their essential humanity. Yet it is difficult to see how these satirical episodes are related to the rest of the novel. Clever but shallow sketches, they do not approach the depth of moral insight which Cullen achieves through Sam and Mattie.

In spite of its faults, *One Way to Heaven* overshadows the average Renaissance novel. Countee Cullen has a poet's way with words, for which much can be overlooked. He also has a sure instinct for drama, which at times invests the novel with surprising power. He manages symbols skillfully, and for the most part achieves convincing characterization. Yet in making a final appraisal, it is difficult to disagree with Blyden Jackson, one of the younger Negro critics, who speaks of Countee Cullen's *two* novels: the one "with the charm of a fairy tale," the other "too stilted and self-conscious for good satire."

The writers of the Lost Generation, as John Aldridge has observed, "were engaged in a revolution designed to purge language of the old restraints of the previous century and to fit it to the demands of a younger, more realistic time." Stein and Hemingway in prose, Pound and Eliot in poetry, were threshing and winnowing, testing and experimenting with words, stretching them and refocusing them, until they became the pliant instruments of a new idiom. The only Negro writer of the 1920's who participated on equal terms in the creation of the modern idiom was a young poet-novelist named Jean Toomer.

Jean Toomer's *Cane* (1923) is an important American novel. By far the most impressive product of the Negro Renaissance, it ranks with Richard Wright's *Native Son* and Ralph Ellison's *Invisible Man* as a measure of the Negro novelist's highest achievement. Jean Toomer belongs to that first rank of writers who use words almost as a plastic medium, shaping new meanings from an original and highly personal style. Since stylistic innovation requires great technical dexterity, Toomer displays a concern for technique which is fully two decades in advance of the period. While his contemporaries of the Harlem School were still experimenting with a crude literary realism, Toomer had progressed beyond the naturalistic novel to "the higher realism of the emotions," to symbol, and to myth.

Jean Toomer (1894—) was born in Washington, D.C., where his parents, who were cultivated Negroes of Creole stock, had moved in order to educate their children. Toomer's maternal grandfather, P. B. S. Pinchback, had been acting governor of Louisiana during Reconstruction days, so that tales of slavery and Reconstruction were a household tradition. Toomer was educated for the law at the University of Wisconsin and at the City College of New York, but literature soon became his first love. An avant-garde poet and short-story writer, he contributed regularly to such little magazines as *Broom, Secession, Double Dealer, Dial,* and *Little Review.* After a brief literary apprenticeship in cosmopolitan New York, he visited rural Georgia as a country schoolteacher—an experience which directly inspired the production of *Cane.*

During his formative period Toomer was a member of a semi-mystical literary group which included Hart Crane, Waldo Frank, Gorham Munson, and Kenneth Burke. Influenced philosophically by Ouspensky's *Tertium Organum,* they formed a bloc called Art as Vision—some of their catchwords being "the new slope of consciousness," "the superior logic of metaphor," and "noumenal knowledge." The group eventually split over the writings of Gurdjieff, the Russian mystic. So far did Toomer succumb to Gurdjieff's spell that he spent the summer of 1926 at the Gurdjieff Institute in Fontainebleau, France, returning to America to proselytize actively for his mystical philosophy.

In spite of his wide and perhaps primary association with white intellectuals, as an artist Toomer never underestimated the importance of his Negro identity. He attained a universal vision not by ignoring race as a local truth, but by coming face to face with his particular tradition. His pilgrimage to Georgia was a conscious attempt to make contact with his hereditary roots in the Southland. Of Georgia, Toomer wrote: "There one finds soil in the sense that the Russians know it—the soil every art and literature that is to live must be embedded in." This sense of soil is central to *Cane* and to Toomer's artistic

vision. "When one is on the soil of one's ancestors," his narrator remarks, "most anything can come to one."

What comes to Toomer, in the first section of *Cane,* is a vision of the parting soul of slavery:

> . . . for though the sun is setting on
> A song-lit race of slaves, it has not set;
> Though late, O soil, it is not too late yet
> To catch thy plaintive soul, leaving, soon gone.

The soul of slavery persists in the "supper-getting-ready songs" of the black women who live on the Dixie Pike—a road which "has grown from a goat path in Africa." It persists in "the soft, listless cadence of Georgia's South," in the hovering spirit of a comforting Jesus, and in the sudden violence of the Georgia moon. It persists above all in the people, white and black, who have become Andersonian "grotesques" by virtue of their slave inheritance. Part I of *Cane* is in fact a kind of Southern *Winesburg, Ohio.* It consists of the portraits of six women—all primitives—in which an Andersonian narrator mediates between the reader and the author's vision of life on the Dixie Pike.

There is Karintha, "she who carries beauty" like a pregnancy, until her perfect beauty and the impatience of young men beget a fatherless child. Burying her child in a sawdust pile, she takes her revenge by becoming a prostitute; "the soul of her was a growing thing ripened too soon."

In "Becky" Toomer dramatizes the South's conspiracy to ignore miscegenation. Becky is a white woman with two Negro sons. After the birth of the first, she symbolically disappears from sight into a cabin constructed by community guilt. After the birth of the second, she is simply regarded as dead, and no one is surprised when the chimney of her cabin falls in and buries her. Toward Becky there is no charity from white or black, but only furtive attempts to conceal her existence.

Carma's tale, "which is the crudest melodrama," hinges not so much on marital infidelity as on a childish deception. Accused by her husband of having other men ("No one blames her for that") she becomes hysterical, and running into a cane-brake, pretends to shoot herself. "Twice deceived, and the one deception proved the other." Her husband goes berserk, slashes a neighbor, and is sent to the chain gang. The tone of the episode is set by the ironic contrast between Carma's apparent strength ("strong as any man") and her childish behavior.

Fern, whose full name is Fernie May Rosen, combines the suffering of her Jewish father and her Negro mother: "at first sight of her I felt as if I heard a Jewish cantor sing. . . . As if his singing rose above the unheard chorus of a folksong." Unable to find fulfillment, left vacant by the bestowal of men's bodies, Fern sits listlessly on her porch near the Dixie Pike. Her eyes desire nothing that man can give her; the Georgia countryside flows into them, along with something that Toomer's narrator calls God.

"Esther" is a study in sexual repression. The protagonist is a near-white girl whose father is the richest colored man in town. Deprived of normal outlets by her social position, she develops a neurotic life of fantasy which centers upon a virile, black-skinned, itinerant preacher named King Barlo. At sixteen she imagines herself the mother of his immaculately conceived child. At twenty-seven she tries to translate fantasy into reality by offering herself to Barlo. Rebuffed and humiliated, she retreats into lassitude and frigidity.

Louisa, of "Blood-Burning Moon," has two lovers, one white and the other colored. Inflamed by a sexual rivalry deeper than race, they quarrel. One is slashed and the other is lynched. Unlike most Negro writers who have grappled with the subject of lynching, Toomer achieves both form and perspective. He is not primarily concerned with antilynching propaganda, but in capturing a certain atavistic quality in Southern life which defies the restraints of civilized society.

Part II of *Cane* is counterpoint. The scene shifts to Washington, where Seventh Street thrusts a wedge of vitality, brilliance, and movement into the stale, soggy, whitewashed wood of the city. This contrast is an aspect of Toomer's primitivism. The blacks, in his color scheme, represent a full life; the whites, a denial of it. Washington's Negroes have preserved their vitality because of their roots in the rural South, yet whiteness presses in on them from all sides. The "dickty" Negro, and especially the near-white, who are most nearly assimilated to white civilization, bear the brunt of repression and denial, vacillating constantly between two identities. Out of this general frame of reference grow the central symbols of the novel.

Toomer's symbols reflect the profound humanism which forms the base of his philosophical position. Man's essential goodness, he would contend, his sense of brotherhood, and his creative instincts have been crushed and buried by modern industrial society. Toomer's positive values, therefore, are associated with the soil, the cane, and the harvest; with Christian charity, and with giving oneself in love. On the other side of the equation is a series of burial or confinement symbols (houses, alleys, machines, theaters, nightclubs, newspapers) which limit man's growth and act as barriers to his soul. Words are useless in piercing this barrier; Toomer's intellectualizing males are tragic figures because they value talking above feeling. Songs, dreams, dancing, and love itself (being instinctive in nature) may afford access to "the simple beauty of another's soul." The eyes, in particular, are avenues through which we can discover "the truth that people bury in their hearts."

In the second section of *Cane,* Toomer weaves these symbols into a magnificent design, so that his meaning, elusive in any particular episode, emerges with great impact from the whole. "Rhobert" is an attack on the crucial bourgeois value of home ownership: "Rhobert wears a house, like a monstrous diver's helmet, on his head." Like Thoreau's farmer, who traveled through life pushing a barn and a hundred acres before him, Rhobert is a victim of his own property instinct. As he struggles with the weight of the house, he sinks deeper and deeper into the mud:

> Brother, Rhobert is sinking
> Let's open our throats, brother
> Let's sing Deep River when he goes down.

The basic metaphor in "Avey" compares a young girl to the trees planted in boxes along V Street, "the young trees that whinnied like colts impatient to be free." Avey's family wants her to become a school teacher, but her bovine nature causes her to prefer a somewhat older profession. Yet, ironically, it is not she but the narrator who is a failure, who is utterly inadequate in the face of Avey's womanhood.

In "Theatre" Toomer develops his "dickty" theme, through an incident involving a chorus girl and a theater-manager's brother. As John watches a rehearsal, he is impressed by Dorris' spontaneity, in contrast to the contrived movements of the other girls. He momentarily contemplates an affair, but reservations born of social distance prevent him from consum-

mating his desire, except in a dream. Dorris, who hopes fleetingly for home and children from such a man, is left at the end of the episode with only the sordid reality of the theater.

"Calling Jesus" plays a more important role than its length would indicate in unifying the symbolism of the novel. It concerns a woman, urbanized and spiritually intimidated, whose "soul is like a little thrust-tailed dog that follows her, whimpering." At night, when she goes to sleep in her big house, the little dog is left to shiver in the vestibule. "Some one . . . eoho Jesus . . . soft as the bare feet of Christ moving across bales of Southern cotton, will steal in and cover it that it need not shiver, and carry it to her where she sleeps, cradled in dream-fluted cane."

In "Box Seat" Toomer comes closest to realizing his central theme. The episode oopens with an invocation: "Houses are shy girls whose eyes shine reticently upon the dusk body of the street. Upon the gleaming limbs and asphalt torso of a dreaming nigger. Shake your curled wool-blossoms, nigger. Open your liver-lips to the lean white spring. Stir the root-life of a withered people. Call them from their houses and teach them to dream." (pp. 67-85)

The thought is that of a young man, whose symbolic role is developed at once: "I am Dan Moore. I was born in a canefield. The hands of Jesus touched me. I am come to a sick world to heal it." Dan, moreover, comes as a representative of "powerful underground races": "The next world-savior is coming up that way. Coming up. A continent sinks down. The new-

Jean Toomer. Courtesy of the Prints and Photographs Collection, Moorland-Spingarn Research Center, Howard University.

world Christ will need consummate skill to walk upon the waters where huge bubbles burst." The redemption motif is echoed in Dan's communion with the old slave: "I asked him if he knew what that rumbling is that comes up from the ground." It is picked up again through the portly Negro woman who sits beside Dan in the theater: "A soil-soaked fragrance comes from her. Through the cement floor her strong roots sink down . . . and disappear in blood-lines that waver south."

The feminine lead is played by Muriel, a school teacher inclined toward conventionality. Her landlady, Mrs. Pribby, is constantly with her, being in essence a projection of Muriel's social fears. The box seat which she occupies at the theater, where her every movement is under observation, renders her relationship to society perfectly. Her values are revealed in her query to Dan, "Why don't you get a good job and settle down?" On these terms only can she love him; meanwhile she avoids his company by going to a vaudeville performance with a girl friend.

Dan, a slave to "her still unconquered animalism," follows and watches her from the audience. The main attraction consists of a prize fight between two dwarfs for the "heavy-weight championship"; it symbolizes the ultimate degradation of which a false and shoddy culture is capable. Sparring grotesquely, pounding and bruising each other, the dwarfs suggest the traditional clown symbol of modern art. At the climax of the episode the winner presents a blood-spattered rose to Muriel, who recoils, hesitates, and finally submits. The dwarf's eyes are pleading: "Do not shrink. Do not be afraid of me." Overcome with disgust for Muriel's hypocrisy, Dan completes the dwarf's thought from the audience, rising to shout: "JESUS WAS ONCE A LEPER!" Rushing from the theater, he is free at last of his love for Muriel—free, but at the same time sterile: "He is as cool as a green stem that has just shed its flower."

Coming as an anticlimax after "Box Seat," "Bona and Paul" describes an abortive love affair between two Southern students at the University of Chicago—a white girl and a mulatto boy who is "passing." The main tension, reminiscent of Gertrude Stein's *Melanctha*, is between knowing and loving, set in the framework of Paul's double identity. It is not his race consciousness which terminates the relationship, as one critic has suggested, but precisely his "whiteness," his desire for knowledge, his philosophical bent. If he had been able to assert his Negro self—that which attracted Bona to him in the first place—he might have held her love.

In "Kabnis" rural Georgia once more provides a setting. This is the long episode which comprises the concluding section of *Cane*. By now the symbolic values of Toomer's main characters can be readily assessed. Ralph Kabnis, the protagonist, is a school teacher from the North who cringes in the face of his tradition. A spiritual coward, he cannot contain "the pain and beauty of the South"; cannot embrace the suffering of the past, symbolized by slavery; cannot come to terms with his own bastardy; cannot master his pathological fear of being lynched. Consumed with self-hatred and cut off from any organic connection with the past, he resembles nothing so much as a scarecrow: "Kabnis, a promise of soil-soaked beauty; uprooted, thinning out. Suspended a few feet above the soil whose touch would resurrect him."

Lewis, by way of contrast, is a Christ figure, an extension of Dan Moore. Almost a T. S. Eliot creation ("I'm on a sort of contract with myself"), his function is to shock others into moral awareness. It is Lewis who confronts Kabnis with his moral cowardice: "Can't hold them, can you? Master; slave. Soil; and the overarching heavens. Dusk; dawn. They fight and bastardize you. The sun tint of your cheeks, flame of the great season's multi-colored leaves, tarnished, burned. Split, shredded, easily burned."

Halsey, unlike Kabnis, has not been crushed by Southern life, but absorbed into it. Nevertheless, his spiritual degradation is equally thorough. An artisan and small shopkeeper like his father before him, he "belongs" in a sense that Kabnis does not. Yet in order to maintain his place in the community, he must submit to the indignities of Negro life in the South. Like Booker T. Washington, whose point of view he represents, Halsey has settled for something less than manhood. Restless, groping tentatively toward Lewis, he escapes from himself through his craft, and through an occasional debauch with the town prostitute, whom he loved as a youth.

Father John, the old man who lives beneath Halsey's shop, represents a link with the Negro's ancestral past. Concealed by the present generation as an unpleasant memory, the old man is thrust into a cellar which resembles the hold of a slave ship. There he sits, "A mute John the Baptist of a new religion, or a tongue-tied shadow of an old." When he finally speaks, it is to rebuke the white folks for the sin of slavery. The contrast between Lewis and Kabnis is sharpened by their respective reactions to Father John. Through the old slave, Lewis is able to "merge with his source," but Kabnis can only deny: "An' besides, he aint my past. My ancestors were Southern blue-bloods."

In terms of its dramatic movement "Kabnis" is a steep slope downward, approximating the progressive deterioration of the protagonist. Early in the episode Kabnis is reduced to a scarecrow replica of himself by his irrational fears. His failure to stand up to Hanby, an authoritarian school principal, marks a decisive loss in his power of self-direction. Gradually he slips into a childlike dependence, first on Halsey, then on the two prostitutes, and finally on Halsey's little sister, Carrie Kate. In the course of the drunken debauch with which the novel ends, Kabnis becomes a clown, without dignity or manhood, wallowing in the mire of his own self-hatred. The stark tragedy of "Kabnis" is relieved only by the figure of Carrie Kate, the unspoiled child of a new generation, who may yet be redeemed through her ties with Father John.

A critical analysis of *Cane* is a frustrating task, for Toomer's art, in which "outlines are reduced to essences," is largely destroyed in the process of restoration. No paraphrase can properly convey the aesthetic pleasure derived from a sensitive reading of *Cane*. Yet in spite of Toomer's successful experiment with the modern idiom—or perhaps because of it—*Cane* met with a cold reception from the public, hardly selling 500 copies during its first year. This poor showing must have been a great disappointment to Toomer, and undoubtedly it was a chief cause of his virtual retirement from literature. Perhaps in his heart of hearts Jean Toomer found it singularly appropriate that the modern world should bury *Cane*. Let us in any event delay the exhumation no longer.

During the 1920's when the advance guard of American letters fled overseas into exile, a strong detachment remained at home to fight a rear-guard action with the Philistines. Using satire as their weapon, such authors as H. L. Mencken, Sinclair Lewis, and James Branch Cabell maintained a running skirmish with those elements of the American population who were proud of their own ignorance. Echoes of this conflict could soon be heard in the Negro intellectual world, and the embattled novelists of the Harlem School quickly availed themselves of the striking power of satire. At the same time—and this is typical of the Negro's cultural history—specifically racial factors were at work behind this sudden penchant for satire.

Satire as a literary attitude was out of the question for the early Negro novelist. The social struggle in which he was engaged was too compelling, and humor too keen a blade for his blunt needs. Self-satire, moreover, could hardly be expected of those whose first impulse was to defend their race against the slanderous attacks of white authors. It was not until the freer atmosphere of the 1920's that satire came into its own. The novels of Countee Cullen and Rudolph Fisher contain nascent satirical elements, but Renaissance satire reaches its highest development in George Schuyler's *Black No More* (1931) and Wallace Thurman's *Infants of the Spring* (1932).

George Schuyler (1895-) was educated in the public schools of Syracuse, followed by eight years in the U.S. Army. Primarily a journalist, he began his career on an Army magazine called the *Service*. From 1922 to 1928 he was on the staff of the *Messenger*, a radical weekly founded by two Negro Socialists, A. Philip Randolph and Chandler Owen. From there he moved to a more lucrative position as a regular columnist for the *Pittsburgh Courier*.

Those who know George Schuyler only as the Westbrook Pegler of Negro journalism will be pleasantly surprised by *Black No More*. In his younger, more intellectual days, Schuyler possessed a ready wit and an authentic gift for satire. A disciple of H. L. Mencken, he regarded mirth as the proper antidote to folly. In *Black No More* he accords the same treatment to American racism which Mencken was currently administering to the American "booboisie."

The imaginary situation on which the novel turns is the discovery by a colored doctor of a glandular treatment which will transform Negroes into full-fledged Caucasians. As more and more Negroes vanish into the white population, panic seizes the nation. Race leaders tremble, for their profitable business and uplift organizations are faced with ruin. In the South the social structure completely disintegrates. Jim Crow facilities lie in idleness; ostensible white couples have colored babies; the Knights of Nordica (KKK) is taken over by former Negroes; and the party of white supremacy loses its *raison d'être*. The national balance of power is upset, and Black-No-More becomes the chief issue of a presidential campaign. In the end, life returns to "normal" when someone discovers that the ersatz Caucasians are a shade lighter than the garden variety. Segregation is promptly restored, based this time on the desideratum of a dark skin!

A satirist must have a consistent vantage point from which to rebuke his fellow mortals. It is not difficult to trace Schuyler's satire to its source. An occasional article in the *American Mercury*, founded by H. L. Mencken in 1924, emphasizes his debt to Mencken and to the tendency in American letters which he represents. During the 1920's Schuyler was active in the Socialist party, where he acquired an ideological basis for the satire of *Black No More*. Journalism also contributed to the development of his satirical powers. Schuyler's cutting edge was sharpened on his column in the *Messenger*, significantly titled "Shafts and Darts." Yet none of these explanations is sufficient in itself. It seems more likely, in view of the evident relish with which Schuyler lampoons the race, that assimilationism is the key to his satirical bent.

George Schuyler's writings provide, in fact, a classic study in assimilationism. In one of his early columns he vehemently attacks "the lie that Negroes wish to be white"; yet he based *Black No More* on this very conception. His attacks on Negro nationalism, whether of the Garvey or DuBois variety, run true to form. So, too, does his growing alienation from the realities of race. In his early days Schuyler was content to deny the existence of a distinctive Negro art; today he does not shrink from denying the existence of a Negro problem!

Perhaps more suggestive, from a theoretical point of view, is Schuyler's "red assimilationist" phase in the Socialist party. Beyond a doubt, one of the advantages which left-wing politics offers to the Negro is an opportunity to submerge his racial identity in a broader historical movement. His reference group is no longer ethnic but ideological; instead of striving exclusively for racial advancement, he participates in the struggle for social justice on a universal plane. It thus becomes possible for a Negro of Schuyler's temperament to move from a bourgeois to a socialist ideology—and back again—without relinquishing his basic assimilationist impulse. Schuyler's ideological vacillation assumes a certain consistency, if we look beneath the purely ideational level to the bedrock of social psychology.

Such an analysis of the roots of Schuyler's satire would be of limited interest if it merely cast light on the idiosyncrasies of a minor Renaissance novelist. As it happens, however, a similar pattern can be found in the work of Wallace Thurman. This literary parallel is not surprising in view of the close personal ties between Schuyler and Thurman. For a time they were colleagues on the staff of the *Messenger*, and Thurman apparently helped Schuyler to publish on more than one occasion. In turn, he was influenced by Schuyler's satirical bent, and in all likelihood by his assimilationist outlook.

Wallace Thurman (1902-34) came directly to Harlem from the University of Southern California. Employed as a reader at Macaulay's, he devoted his main energies to his first love, the Negro Renaissance. His home was a rendezvous for the New Negro coterie, and he himself became actively involved in the avant-garde Renaissance magazines, *Fire* and *Harlem*. Thurman first attracted attention as the co-author of a successful Broadway play entitled *Harlem* (1929). He wrote two novels, *The Blacker the Berry* (1929) and *Infants of the Spring* (1932).

"The blacker the berry, the sweeter the juice"—so runs the Negro folk saying. In a mood of bitter irony, Thurman borrows this phrase for the title of his novel about a dark girl who is the victim of intraracial prejudice. From the moment that Emma Lou enters the world—a black child rejected by her own parents—her pigmentation is a constant source of pain. It results in an unhappy adolescence, in social ostracism at a large California university, and in relentless discrimination when she seeks white-collar employment in Harlem. It leads to her sexual exploitation by a light-skinned lover and finally forces her to reconsider the whole pattern of her life.

Emma Lou's real tragedy is that she accepts the values of the system which torments her. Her use of bleaching agents, for example, betrays her unconscious belief in the magical power of a fair complexion. As the novel unfolds, she outgrows this crippling frame of reference and comes to recognize that her main enemy is within: "What she needed now was to accept her black skin as being real and unchangeable." This theme of self-acceptance is typically Renaissance: to be one's dark-skinned self and not a bleached-out imitation is the essence of emancipation. But Thurman's hard-won victory (the conflict he is acting out, through Emma Lou, is clear enough) does not prove to be decisive. His second novel shows him to be incapable of holding his feelings toward the race in stable equilibrium.

Infants of the Spring is a neurotic novel, in which Thurman broods introspectively on the "failure" of the Negro Renaissance. The novel opens with Laertes' advice to Ophelia, from which it derives both title and theme:

> The canker galls the infants of the spring
> Too oft before their buttons be disclosed,
> And in the morn and liquid dew of youth
> Contagious blastments are most imminent.

It was the canker of Bohemianism, in Thurman's eyes, which threatened to nip the New Negro Movement in the bud. The symbolic setting of his novel is Niggeratti Manor, where colored artists, writers, and musicians live in various stages of decadence and sterility. The central characters are Paul, a symbol of dissipated genius, and Ray, a young writer who struggles to free himself from an obsessive race-consciousness. Much of the "action" consists merely of dialogue, which serves to convey the author's impressions of the Negro Renaissance.

After a series of satirical sketches of leading Renaissance personalities, the novel draws to a depressing close. Paul commits suicide in such a manner that his masterpiece is destroyed. A drawing on the title page of the ruined manuscript pictures Niggeratti Manor with a foundation of crumbling stone: "At first glance it could be ascertained that the sky-scraper would soon crumble and fall, leaving the dominating white lights in full possession of the sky." The dream of the Negro Renaissance was, for Thurman, to end thus in disillusion and despair. The tone of the novel is too bitter, however, and Thurman's sense of personal failure too acute, to accept his critique of the Renaissance at face value.

It was appropriate enough that Thurman should seek to become the undertaker of the Negro Renaissance; at the time, he was busy digging his own grave with bad gin. His self-hatred, and the suicidal impulses which it engendered, were the central facts of his later years. No one who has read *The Blacker the Berry* will doubt that the source of this self-hatred was his dark complexion. The old struggle for self-acceptance, which Thurman had apparently won through Emma Lou, is reopened and finally abandoned through the character of Ray. "Eventually," Ray remarks, "I'm going to renounce Harlem and all it stands for." This mood of renunciation pervades *Infants of the Spring.* In his wholesale indictment of the Renaissance generation, Thurman was simply working out his self-destructive impulses on the level of a literary movement. The most self-conscious of the New Negroes, he ultimately turned his critical insight against himself and the wider movement with which he identified.

The satire of the Harlem School, though often directed against whites, is predominantly self-satire. As such it represents a gain in maturity, and a conscious rebellion against the "defensive" attitudes of the early Negro novelist. Nevertheless, the novels of George Schuyler and Wallace Thurman strongly suggest that Renaissance satire had its psychological roots in assimilationism. Since humor is often a form of veiled aggression, may not self-satire be a permissible form of self-aggression? Perhaps in a period which was predominantly nationalistic in tone, satire was the only available outlet for the assimilationist impulses of the more sophisticated Negro novelists. (pp. 67-94)

Robert A. Bone, "The Harlem School," in his The Negro Novel in America, *Yale University Press, 1958, pp. 65-94.*

MARGARET PERRY

[*In the following excerpt from her* Silence to the Drums: A Survey of the Literature of the Harlem Renaissance, *Perry provides a critical analysis of short stories of the Harlem Renaissance.*]

With few exceptions (e.g., Toomer, Fisher), the black writer of the 1920s gravitated to poetry or the novel, or both. Relatively few were attracted to the short story genre. Many of the short stories that did appear were limited in scope and form, numerous examples of which were published in Negro-owned periodicals. While the output of the individual short story writers was meagre, the total number of stories that appeared in magazines (primarily *The Crisis* and *Opportunity*) is surprisingly large. (p. 110)

In *The New Negro*, Alain Locke declared that "the artistic problem of the Young Negro has not been so much that of acquiring the outer mastery of form and technique as that of achieving an inner mastery of mood and spirit." Too many examples prove him wrong, however. The short story more than any other literary genre demonstrates the technical weaknesses of many of the young Harlem Renaissance writers. Another problem was the limited audience for fiction dealing chiefly with the Negro experience. As the compilers of *The Negro Caravan* pointed out:

> The short story as a literary form in America has always been intended primarily for popular magazine publication; . . . In this medium, more than in others, the Negro author faces the dilemma of the divided audience. With the exception of the journals [*The Crisis* and *Opportunity*] of two Negro organizations . . . and a few fugitive publications, there have been no magazines with a primarily Negro audience in which writers could place their short stories. . . . The necessity for magazine publication has affected the Negro short story profoundly.

And, yet, these young writers did produce some good short stories. The form was perfect for the purpose of brief illumination of selected segments of Negro life or for sharp portrayals of intense emotional moments. (pp. 111-12)

Rudolph Fisher, the master Harlem Renaissance craftsman of the short story, produced some of the more memorable literature in that period. (p. 112)

When Henry James enjoined other writers to "Dramatize! Dramatize!" Rudolph Fisher must have heard the master's voice. Fisher orders the experience of Negro life in sensitive dramatizations. Nowhere is this better accomplished than in two of his best stories, "The City of Refuge" and "Miss Cynthie." Both stories illustrate Fisher's ability to transform life into art through control of characterization, plot, and diction, and insistence on a single effect at the story's conclusion.

The dual theme in "The City of Refuge" is the death of innocence and the black man's ability to transcend disillusionment. The story centers on King Solomon Gillis, a large, innocent, ignorant black who "had shot a white man and, with the aid of prayer and an automobile, probably escaped a lynching.'' Fisher places the protagonist immediately into the setting, that home of homes for the Negro, Harlem, which Fisher ironically defines as a ''city of refuge.'' The author knows this is not always true, and his story is illustrative of the fact that Harlem, like the South, can be a place of confinement. (pp. 112-13)

The story is one of continual movement towards the entrapment and downfall of King Solomon Gillis. There is an added touch of irony in the name of the protagonist; the Biblical king has come down through literary history as the archetypal wise man, but King Solomon Gillis is far from wise. The story, indeed, relates with vivid economy just how unwise King Solomon Gillis is. Through flattery and guile and an eye for exploitation, Mouse Uggam, a resourceful drug pusher from Gillis's home town, uses him to pass along drugs without his understanding what he is doing. The set-up to trap King Solomon is planned in the second section where the subsidiary theme of confinement is stressed as well.

In the third section of the story, Mouse Uggam tightens his hold on King Solomon. Mouse has an uncanny talent for seeing through people, and thus he gets a job for Gillis which, in turn, works within the plan to have King Solomon to pass along drugs unsuspectingly. This section is rich in its evocation of Harlem language, atmosphere, and characterization. The American Negro's contempt for his black brothers from the West Indies is also deftly portrayed through attitude and dialect. Fisher's superior talent for realistic dialogue is in evidence in this section. In section four, Mouse Uggam sets up King Solomon's participation in drug pushing, and in the following section Tony Gabrielli, the owner of the store where Gillis works, sets Gillis up for entrapment by the police. The city of refuge is about to lose its character of sanctuary for one who symbolically and figuratively has fled another country. The last scene is laid, significantly, in a cavernous cabaret: it provides a contrast to King Solomon's first view of Harlem when, coming up from the subway, he was like ''Jonah emerging from the whale.'' Now he is in a place of entertainment that is in a low basement, reached by descending a ''narrow, twisted staircase.'' This is King Solomon Gillis's hell, although, as he is arrested (and deserted by Mouse Uggam who is, figuratively, a rat), he exudes an air that ''had something exultant about it.'' He is still a true believer in the black city with its ''cullud policemans,'' and despite his end he retains his humanity and a deep satisfaction in his racial identity.

Fisher was a traditionalist in his approach to literature. Hence, it is not surprising that ''The City of Refuge'' has the traditional short story form: a recognizable beginning, middle, and end. The story also exhibits Fisher's genuine ability to penetrate the black character with complete understanding.

His effortless, extraordinarily skillful delineation of character is revealed in one of his last stories, and perhaps his best, ''Miss Cynthie.''

Harmony between the ages is played out beautifully in this story. A stanza from Wordsworth fully expresses the theme and movement of ''Miss Cynthie'':

> Dust as we are, the immortal spirit grows
> Like harmony in music; there is a dark
> Inscrutable workmanship that reconciles
> Discordant elements, makes them cling together
> In one society.

As one critic [Oliver Louis Henry] has written, ''Reconciliation between the generations is the theme of this story.'' The theme is worked out almost melodiously, a talent that does not surprise those who knew ''Bud'' Fisher. He was a fine musician who had spent some time arranging Negro spirituals. (pp. 113-15)

Miss Cynthie, drawn with love and humor, represents the black grandmother archetype: shrewd, skeptical, religious, loving, giving, forgiving, and wise. As she says of New York during her first moments of arrival (and on her first trip of any kind), ''Reckon places is pretty much alike after people been in 'em awhile.'' It will take a lot to impress Miss Cynthie. She has come to visit her grandson, not knowing that he is a dancer and singer in Harlem. She had wanted him to be a doctor or preacher or at least an undertaker. For her, these professions fit in with her ideals and her admonition to Dave, ''Always mind the house o' the Lord—whatever you do, do like a church-steeple: aim high and go straight.'' Dave's plan is to introduce her to his profession by taking her to the club where he works, to let her see rather than to hear about what he does. He takes a chance on knowing her well enough to prove what he tells his wife, ''She's for church and all, but she believes in good times too, if they're right.'' As the reader and Miss Cynthie move from doubt to enlightenment and reconciliation, Fisher's use of song and rhythm reinforces the theme of union between the old and the young.

Fisher never loses sight of his desire to entertain as well as to reveal values held to be important to Negroes. Although Fisher was from the Negro bourgeoisie—his father was a minister— he was successful in depicting the black man from every strata of Negro society. This ability is reflected in the eight short stories which were published after ''The City of Refuge,'' culminating in his portrayal of the various sorts of Harlemites in his novel, *The Walls of Jericho* (1928).

John Matheus was generally an optimist and a believer in the ultimate conciliatory nature of man. We sense this in all of his work, with the exception of ''Clay,'' an impressionistic story pervaded by a mood of pessimism. In this story, as well as in ''Fog,'' there is a notion that death is the equalizer, that death brings together divergent men into oneness. This prevailing motif in Matheus's work, the reconciliation between men, is seen most clearly in his long narrative, ''Anthropoi.''

Although ''Anthropoi'' suffers from too much narration and too little action, the characterizations of Bush Winter, ''an oversized, swarthy, black-haired mulatto,'' and Demetrius Pappan, ''an undersized, swarthy, black-haired Greek,'' are successfully two-dimensional. Neither man is exceptional, but Pappan, despite his swarthiness, is able to take part in the Great American Dream of financial success because he is ''white.'' At one period in his American life he is a shoe polisher, polishing even the shoes of Bush Winter, and later he is the prosperous owner of a soda parlor where Bush and his family are not allowed to sit and drink. Later, their sons fight in the ''Great War''; each son's life is spared, and each son undergoes a change in self as a result of his war experiences. After the war, Bush Winter's son is no longer patient with second-class citizenship in a land made safe by his personal act of heroism (i.e., exposing himself to the constant possibility of being killed). Pappan's son, whose level of consciousness concerning people, right and wrong, and justice, has been raised, becomes indignant as he watches a Ku Klux Klan member rushing through town in a car with the American flag attached to it. This act of racist cowardice and ignorance arouses young Pappan to go see what will ensue. More Ku Klux Klan members enter town and there is a melee. The near-death of young Pappan during the ensuing riot brings his father to the realization that he and Bush Winter are "brothers under the skin": "They understood each other, these old, worn fathers, after all." The understanding blossoms, and in the end they are reconciled.

Matheus's social philosophy is dramatically displayed in his more important and famous story, "Fog." Although it is technically frail in style and transitional phrasing, its publication is nonetheless of great scholarly interest: it marks the modern beginning of the black writer's serious concern for writing a short tale that is both thematically and dramatically outside the folkloric tradition.

"Fog" is more complex than the bare plot reveals: a group of persons, multiethnic and multiracial, are on an interurban tramcar that must cross a bridge to arrive at its destination. The bridge gives out, but the people on the vehicle have enough time to escape the car. The fright from being so near death draws these people together and obliterates their ingrained animosities toward one another. The theme of death, or near-death, as the "great equalizer," combined with the symbols of fog (density) and the bridge (a nexus for divergent sides), leads into the story's strong redemptive motif. The story might even be considered propagandistic in its espousal of the idea of the equality of all men.

The fog is the focal point in the tale: it is not only a physical presence to be acknowledged, it is also a personification of the mental and emotional fog that clouds understanding from man to man. At the end of the story, the author (unfortunately, rather awkwardly) spells out the fog's symbolism: "The fog still crept from under the bed of the river . . . but from about the hearts and minds of some rough, unlettered men another fog had begun to lift." In "Fog," Matheus achieves a unity of action and tone. He is successful in creating a total effect that is carefully conceived from a central idea, or, more specifically, a dominant incident. The descriptive language establishes the physical surrounding. The use of dialect functions on two distinct but substantive levels: to signify actual ethnic differences and to indicate how little these differences mean in a moment of human crisis, in a moment when the common bond of humanity must serve individuals in a manner that enables them to overcome immoral or weak customs of a specific society.

The cast of characters is large and each is an obvious vehicle for the point that Matheus wishes to emphasize. Just as the fog operates on a level above a mere atmospheric element, each person is submerged as an individual in order to buttress the theme and resolution of the action. The two major weaknesses of the story are sometimes distracting, the use of clichés and the structural shakiness of shifting from one person to another within a short span of time. In the case of the latter weakness, it is inevitable that constant shifts in point of view in a short story will weaken the structure, for this is a technique better suited to the novel. As for clichés, there is no need, for instance, to use such phrases as "Madonna eyed Italian mother," "Court house, that citadel of Law and Order," or "The news spread like wildfire." The more serious flaws, however, are the constant shifting of action and the rotation of character presentations within a brief stretch of time. This accounts for Matheus's awkward transitional sentences, such as, "Now these series of conversations did not transpire in chronological order," and, later, the following superfluous statement: "What happened inside the heads of these men and women seemed to them to have consumed hours instead of seconds." Dorothy

Richardson, Joyce, and Woolf were demonstrating brilliantly how a writer could avoid such awkward phrasing and yet be dramatically and emotionally effective. In any case, this was not a new issue for the fiction writer, inasmuch as Flaubert discussed it when he wrote about what he wanted to accomplish in one of his famous moments in *Madame Bovary*. Time and spatial sequences are demanding problems for the writer, but "Fog" would have been enhanced if Matheus had been able to discover more subtle forms of expression. After all—and this must be remembered when assessing Harlem Renaissance literature—Matheus and writers like him were working for the most part within traditional stylistic forms.

The story's action is a lateral movement from the particular to the universal: a metaphoric use of the tramcar for the universe, and a grouping together of diverse persons to represent a cross-section of mankind becoming one in a cataclysmic moment. The physical salvation of these people parallels the theme of spiritual redemption. This dangerous moment represents a brief period when inner terror converges with outward commotion to form a bridge of understanding between divergent characters. Redemption through revelation? The author seems to point toward this idea. Thus we see that each person is tested in this moment of near-death. Our attention is focused on types of reaction rather than on individual ones because we do not know any character intimately enough to care for him personally. As readers, we can come away from this story in much the same manner as Crane's correspondent in "The Open Boat": "they felt that they could then be interpreters." Each character in "Fog," although seen fleetingly, becomes an interpreter of the event that touches everyone. (pp. 115-19)

Zora Neale Hurston did not exhibit any self-consciousness toward the provincial characters she created and, consequently, there is a sinewy, folkloric quality to her short stories. Hurston's characters live, for the most part, in an all-black world; when the white impinges on the black, each race maintains his societal role with abiding conviction. Thus, Hurston's black characters do not suffer from the sort of alternative black self-hatred/prideful self-love/hate-envy of white and black that characterize many other Harlem Renaissance fictional creations (e.g., McKay's Ray, Toomer's Kabnis, Thurman's Mary Lou, or some of the characters of Dorothy West). Zora Hurston's fictional style and characterizations were both deeply influenced by the colloquial, folk atmosphere of her native Florida where she collected folklore materials in connection with anthropological work she was doing with Franz Boas.

Several of Hurston's stories were published in *Opportunity* and serve as a good introduction to her artistic leanings toward folk literature. Her first story was "Drenched in Light," which at once displayed her ability to avoid one of the glaring weaknesses of her fellow black short-story writers, characterization. This is not to say that this is the strongest feature of her writing, but each person she created had a fullness of self while expressing a specific, unique culture. The naturalness of her narrative style may derive from her interest in folklore. The quality of her writing, unpretentious, somewhat colloquial, seems to grow out of her facility with dialect and her understanding of the psychology and motivation of country folk and the tales they told her. Her strongest, perhaps most interesting and intense story, "Sweat," certainly gives evidence of this facility. Even some of her lesser tales are noteworthy: they help to reveal, as Darwin Turner has said, that "she was one of the few Southern-born Afro-American writers who have consistently mined literary materials from Southern soil."

In "Drenched in Light," Isis ("Isie") Watts is a vital, energetic girl of eleven, full of liveliness, spunk, brimming joy, designated by her neighbors as being "different." Isis's intelligent vitality sets her apart from others in her farmland community in Florida. Clearly, Isis is Zora Neale Hurston as a young girl, or, at least, Isis is as Zora remembered her childhood self. The force of "Drenched in Light" lies in Hurston's portrayal of Isis in action before the reader: Isis poised with a razor as she prepares to shave her grandmother, Isis dancing ("she wheeled lightly about, hand on hips, flower between her teeth"), Isis wading in the water. The major weakness of the story derives from the author's acquiescence to a need to accept white appreciation even if it casts Isis into the role of the "happy darkie." The notion seems uncharacteristic of Hurston's writing, although numerous persons who have written about her personality suggest that she may have had a need for the paternalistic attitude of many of the whites she encountered. The approval that the happy little Isis derives from the white couple who pick her up is countered, in part, by the parallel need of the white woman to have "a little of her sunshine." The notion may have a distasteful, racial aspect, but the author has succeeded in presenting a strong character portrait and an interesting side-account of black life in rural Florida.

In the story, "Spunk," Hurston places the action within an all-black setting. The movement from beginning to end is ef-

Zora Neale Hurston. Courtesy of Joseph Solomon, Executor of the Literary Estate of Carl Van Vechten.

fectively rendered in sequences calculated to enrich the folkloric strains of this tale. There is also a mythic quality to this story of a dead man's revenge on his wife's lover. Certainly it is more than just a tale that "reveals the fickleness of the mob." The superstitiousness of the common black is portrayed, if somewhat superficially, and the unspoken philosophy of happy survival in a small, rural, all-black community underpins the simple plot of the tale. Spunk, whose character is developed from what others think and say of him (the reader encounters him only once), is a super-hero who meets his defeat through his first and only contact with fear. His true enemy is himself, not the bobcat which may be thought of as the reincarnation of the cuckold-husband. Although Spunk is acquitted of shooting Joe Kanty, Spunk's conscience does not free him of guilt. Thus, this he-man builds up a fear of the dead man that forces him to lose control of his actions. Spunk visualizes the dead Joe Kanty as the one who "pushes" him upon the electric tree-saw, and the other Negroes are not willing to disbelieve Spunk's fearful notion. Once laid low, the hero is no longer admired because there is no need to fear him. The one gesture of comfort given to him as he is dying (perhaps viewed as surety against Spunk's spirit) is to lay him "with his face to the East so's he could die easy." Now gone, Spunk becomes another part of the folklore of the past as the survivors continue with the business of living. (pp. 121-23)

Hurston successfully handled the important elements of the short story form—plot, diction, narration, and, especially, mood. Hence, we can overlook some of her more obvious faults, such as stilted conversation when she is not using dialect, her intrusion in narrative passages, and the relating of events as narration rather than as action. Hurston, however, does succeed, where other writers often failed, in presenting stories with a "preconceived effect" faithfully adhered to and achieved.

Arthur Huff Fauset wrote one remarkably good short story, "Symphonesque," which was awarded the first prize in the 1926 *Opportunity* contest and later was included in the O'Brien *Best Short Stories of the Year* collection. "Symphonesque" is a passionate, pulsing, tale of sexual desire, temptation, and resistance to both—a story of sin and salvation.

The author mingles black culture and myth in the orchestration of his tale. He makes effective use of musical terminology to indicate the emotional intensity of the story. Section I, *Allegro non troppo* and *Allegro vivace et capricioso*, introduces the reader to seventeen-year-old Cudjo, the principal character. Cudjo (note the strictly black name), awakening in his absolutely filthy cabin, proceeds to voice to himself a diatribe against the preoccupation of blacks with religion: "Al dis 'ligion ain't gittin' nobody nowheah. All it does, mek yo' feel good. Mek yo' feel lik yo' treadin' on soft cusions in Gawd's he'b'n." Just before these thoughts, Cudjo had felt a "curious shiver [course] slowly through his body." What we have, then, is the author establishing a pattern which serves as a leitmotif— the sacred and the profane at war in Cudjo's body and soul. The pervasiveness of religion is also a prime feature of the story. Cudjo attempts to mock and dismiss religion, and refuses, symbolically, the aid of Heaven: "He looked into the heavens.... His eyes could not stand the glare." Cudjo the elemental man, a "noble savage," the archetypal primitive, walks on. Yet, in another world, in another setting, he might have been a god or a hero. As he walks on, Cudjo continues to rail against God and His black followers, for to submit to the will of a being one cannot see seems incomprehensible, indeed, perhaps undesirable, to Cudjo. Yet, at the end of Section I he is among the church members who are colorfully preparing for the river-side baptism ceremony. Is it possible that Cudjo will be baptized and saved on this day? The reader wonders whether this is a possibility as the next section unfolds.

Part II, *Crescendo/Religioso Furioso,* opens with a vivid portrait of the preacher who is preparing to baptize the unsaved: "He was a tremendous black figure with a large round stomach that almost bulged out of his blue vest. . . . His corpulent body seemed like a huge inflated balloon made of thick rubber swaying upon two large resilient pillars." There is a certain mockery in the author's description; it is difficult, however, to ascertain if this is intentional or accidental. Since the story is primarily told from Cudjo's point of view, we also wonder how he would express it if he had the talent to use words like the author.

A commanding figure in this section is the exhorter who intones brief, repetitive verses to intensify the religious fervor of the already excited group. Fauset echoes the rhythmic stress of the exhorter who urges the crowd to respond in a typically black religious call-and-response pattern. Thus, Fauset is able to demonstrate the black man's African cultural heritage with dramatic artistry. The effect of this and other exhortations on Cudjo, along with the frenzied atmosphere, is electric and shamelessly emotional: laughing, screaming, and running amok briefly, Cudjo attempts to rescue a fainting young girl from baptismal immersion. Thrown out of the area of the baptism ceremony—symbolically excluded from the saved and those to be saved—Cudjo lies alone in a heap, isolated, confused (but not knowing why he is), while the baptism ceremony continues for people who have quickly forgotten that "black fool," that "outcast devil," Cudjo.

The third and final section is elaborately weighted down with the following musical notations: *Agitato/Agitato appassionato/ Smorzando et tranquillo.* The agitation from the religious ceremony is transformed in Cudjo into sexual terms, for his body is now aflame with the sensual desires of the flesh. His object is Amber Lee, singing sensuously in tall bushes nearby, Amber Lee who "feels only herself, her budding self." Although she is a pure young girl in the story, there is a touch of Toomer's Karintha in Amber Lee. Both serve as the archetypal Eve, or whatever African counterpart exists, the fecund temptress, the essential female.

Despite his passionate desire to seize Amber Lee and possess her, Cudjo hides and hesitates: here is the friend of his childhood, his playmate of old, an undefiled companion of his present everyday life. When he does manage to seize her, the fear and reluctance he sees in her eyes cool his ardor. He frees her, in shame, from his inflamed grasp and manages to apologize:

> Ah wouldn't hurt a hair on yo' head . . . Amber Amber Lee . . . un'stan' . . . ? Jes' want to scare mah lil' Amber Lee.
>
> He placed her gently on the warm grass and did not even kiss her.

His quelled passion is reminiscent of the wearied emotional and physical condition of the young girl who fainted at the baptism ceremony. She had been overwhelmed by the passion of religion, he by the passion of lust. Who, indeed, will be saved?

Fauset has shaped his story in a fashion that shows a direct outgrowth from the black oral tradition, both folk and religious. The story is enhanced further by his skillful use of symbols and symbolic language. The paralleling of Cudjo's sexual desires with the emotionalism of the baptismal service is an extremely effective narrative mode. Added to this is the masterful use of the church as in part symbol, in part metaphor: the church as the seat of the black man's emotional life, the church as the real world of black folk. Cudjo's rejection of this segment of his black self seems to boomerang and become a part of him despite his expressed sentiments of reproval. Thus, he is unable to carry out the inner urgings of his natural male inclinations when face to face with Amber Lee.

It doesn't seem unnatural that Fauset adopted the folk style for unfolding his tale; he was, after all, a collector of folk material from Nova Scotia and the Mississippi Delta. The tone of the story is established immediately: Cudjo, realizing that there is "somepin' mattah wid mah soul," is assailed by longings, fears, and personal revulsion. The intense heat of the day reinforces the notion of the soul's oppressiveness. In a way, the setting seems more African than Texan. The soul will be purified in one's native land, symbolically if not actually. Touches such as those describing the preacher's laugh as being "like the midnight cry of a panicky jungle cat," or personifying Cudjo's feet ("Did they not have ten eyes, as many noses, and mouths as well?") further illustrate Fauset's preoccupation with the spiritual and folk ties of the Afro-American with the land of his primary origins.

One critic characterized the Harlem stories in Claude McKay's short story collection, *Gingertown,* as being "on a very low level" whereas the Jamaican tales were described as "more exotic and more plausible." The Harlem stories, however, have a vigor deriving, perhaps, from the sordidness of their setting and their plots. In "High Ball," McKay displays excellent control of tone, characterization, and form. The story moves meaningfully from beginning to middle to dénouement.

The ingredients for drama are inherent in the situation in which the reader finds the black protagonist, Nation Roe, a successful singer-composer-pianist. Roe, recently married to a white woman, is becoming aware of her dissatisfaction with their mode of living. She complains that his friends, especially his white friends, do not care for her company and, therefore, exclude her from their gatherings. Nation—a simple man, a man of truth and inbred integrity—disbelieves her accusations because his closest friends, "colleagues to whom real merit was a thing considered above color," have never changed their attitudes toward him since his (to them) unpalatable marriage. McKay's description of Myra, the white wife, is swift and revealing: "She was rather a bloated coarse-fleshed woman, with freckled hands, beet colored elbows, dull-blue eyes and lumpy hair of the color of varnish." As Nation's best friend, George Lieberman, tells him after they have a heart-to-heart discussion about Myra: "If we were talking about a fish Myra would want to gut it right on the table; if it was about pigs she'd bring in the slops from the pen." Myra, quite simply, was a slut.

Myra is the crucial focal point of the story because it is she who effects the enlightenment and change in Nation. Myra is the one who spends a good part of her life guzzling gingerale highballs and running about low-type cabarets with her lesbian friend, Dinah. Nation's instincts, which lead him to dislike Dinah, are not alert to the same qualities in Myra. In the end, Nation must learn about his wife's rejection and betrayal of him after he has reached utter, yet unjustified, despair about the loyalty of his old friends. Insulting them, Nation flees to his home where he must bear the insult of insults, hearing his wife and her friends mocking him, calling him by a name Dinah had carelessly called him one day, "prune." Nation's final act of throwing out Myra and her friends leaves him alone with only the hurt of his knowledge. McKay has handled the story effectively enough to make this ending a natural and true conclusion.

Throughout the story the tone of gradual but impending devastating enlightenment about the character of Myra is maintained. Myra sets the pattern in motion by implanting the germs of doubt and distrust in Nation. The incidents that help to build towards the dénouement are significant in both tone and characterization. The tone, after all, influences both mood and character; if the tone is controlled, the purpose of a story is made clear and every movement and every character are governed by this control. McKay accomplishes this. For example, we see this when Nation is thrown into confusion in his effort to understand the mixed-up Myra:

> "I would like to go to some of those downtown parties."
>
> "They're mostly stags, though . . ."
>
> "Stags," she sneered, "*you* men! Don't mind about me, Nation. In fact, I really don't want to go to those affairs. Honest I don't. It's just some sort of jealousy. I don't care about anybody, as long as Dinah sticks to me."
>
> "And me?" asked Nation. "What about me?" He laughed.
>
> "Oh you know! I don't mean you. I mean Dinah compared to those downtown snobs."
>
> "You're a strange mixture, Myra. I kaint tell just what you want. I wish I could, for I want to please you always."
>
> She drank another highball.
>
> "Don't mind me, Nation. It's nothing really. I think I want things that I really don't want, but I have to want them because my friends think I should have them. I don't want anything and I want everything."
>
> "That's beyond me, Myra, like something outa big heavy books." And he went to his room to dress.

Moving closer to a despair he cannot fathom, Nation walks with his friend George down the streets after George has given his views about Myra (and after a subsequent unfortunate "racial" incident at George's home):

> A little later George and Nation left for the theatre. They strode along in silence. George desired to say something soothing to Nation, knowing that he was hurt, but he could not find a precisely appropriate phrase. Nation apprehended George's mood. He preferred that nothing further should be said about the incident, so he talked a great deal about nothing.
>
> At Broadway and Forty-third Street they parted a little awkwardly, each one going to his own theatre.

There is in this scene a sense of the closeness between these two men, and there is also a sense of impending massive un-

happiness awaiting both men. In the end, Nation's wrongheaded assessment of his friends and his diatribe against them wounds George in a manner that directly corresponds to Myra's damage to Nation's heart and ego.

The emotional effectiveness of the story derives from McKay's skillful handling of sequence and incident, characterization, and the full control he displays in narrative exposition and tone in the unfolding of this poignant tale.

In 1926 the second prize in the short story competition of the *Opportunity* contest was shared by Zora Neale Hurston for "Muttsy" and an unknown, first-published eighteen-year-old, Dorothy West, for her story entitled, "The Typewriter." . . . This prize story was her first, she claims; it is a strong beginning for an author who was to write a distinguished, engrossing novel, *The Living Is Easy* (1948).

The unnamed protagonist of "The Typewriter" is a hardworking, simple, honorable husband and father. He lives in Boston, having moved there from the South in his young manhood. He is a man now who admits to himself a disappointment with how his life has developed; his life is far below the economic and social levels he had envisioned for himself when he was a newcomer in Boston. "But, though he didn't know it," the author writes, "he was not the progressive type. And

Invitation to an awards dinner sponsored by the periodical Opportunity. *Courtesy of the Arthur B. Spingarn Collection, Moorland-Spingarn Research Center, Howard University.*

he became successively, in the years, bell boy, porter, waiter, cook, and finally janitor in a down town office building.'' We plunge immediately into the story that tells of this unachieving man's daughter practicing, upon a rented typewriter, the writing of business letters. To aid her, the father begins to dictate imaginary letters to and from important business people (e.g., Rockefeller, J. P. Morgan). To round out the verisimilitude, the father creates for himself the inflated persona whom he calls Mr. J. Lucius Jones. What originates as a favor to help his daughter achieve speed and accuracy with her stenography and typing becomes a fantasy-world into which the father hungrily escapes each evening, a fantasy-world where he transforms himself into a superior, achieving man. The daughter— the realist, an adultlike child in her materialist attitude—is unaffected by her father's emotional and psychological approach to their nightly exercise.

The daughter reaches a high level of proficiency, secures a job, and returns the typewriter to the rental agency. When her father discovers that the typewriter is gone his world is shattered: ''It burst upon him. Blinded him. . . . Why this—this was the end! The end of those great moments—the end of everything!'' What we have here is the portrait of a man of feeling who remains unfulfilled in his psychological and emotional relationship with his family. The influence of Dostoevsky here, and in a subsequent story, ''An Unimportant Man,'' is pervasive: the close identity of the father to his daughter evokes the Dostoevskian absorption with childhood and his belief in the incorruptible nature of children. It is only in the child's confrontation with the adult world that the process of ruination begins.

There is also the Dostoevskian tendency to emphasize confinement, in moral, psychological, emotional, and physical aspects: ''He would never be able to get away from himself and the routine of year'' (''The Typewriter''); and: ''And in that instant Zeb wanted frantically to break into that line. He didn't want to go home to Minnie, and a fretful baby, and a mother whose reproachful eyes spoke her unsatisfied hopes'' (''An Unimportant Man''). As it is, the men in both of these stories are confronted with incidents that thwart any escape from their confining world.

Dostoevsky's influence in these two stories (and in ''Prologue to a Life'') is implicit in the idea of salvation through suffering. (pp. 124-32)

In ''An Unimportant Man,'' the protagonist, Zeb, has finally passed his bar examination at the age of ''barely forty.'' At the end of the story, he is faced with the necessity of retaking the exam because of a technicality unrelated to himself. But Zeb, who has failed the examination on his first two tries, knows he cannot repeat the successful performance of his third try. He faces the realization that he will not escape the dreary destiny of other ''unimportant'' men. Zeb then turns his attention from himself to his daughter who is being repressed by her mother and grandmother. He decides to try persuading her to use her fine brain to succeed in some unnamed, professional career in place of seeking a dancer's way of life: ''He must save Essie from the terrible fate that had all but crushed his spirit.'' She must not become trapped as he had. This freedom and independence, gained through education, he thought, would prove more satisfactory to her in the end than a career based on her ''childish whim,'' dancing in clubs and cabarets.

In ''The Typewriter'' and ''An Unimportant Man,'' West gives examples of men caught up in the inescapable maze of an adulthood inferior to the one they had anticipated. Both men are childlike, and they satisfy themselves through the lives of their children, even though their communication with the children is partially defective. In ''The Typewriter,'' the other side of the father's nature, the submerged, uncharted area of his emotional life, is suddenly fulfilled by the fantasy-world he creates for his daughter's mechanical practice upon the typewriter. And Zeb, in his determination to help his daughter, enlarges his inner life as well. Through ''J. Lucius Jones,'' Zeb has performed an act that will save his daughter from the unfulfilled life he has.

The men in West's stories are unachieving, disappointed persons who still have retained a measure of innocence. This artlessness sets them apart spiritually from the women in her stories, who, discontented and frustrated by the confinement of their place in life, succumb to the realities of their second-rate lives. They retreat into an overtly bitter, unredemptive existence: Hanna Byde (in the story of the same name) laughs spitefully about botching up a suicide attempt and is contemptuous of the baby she is carrying; Net (the wife in ''The Typewriter'') constantly berates her husband; and Lily (''Prologue to a Life''), happy only as a mother, spurns a meaningful relationship with her adoring husband. The women are neurotics; the men are psychologically emasculated by women and society. Even the financially successful husband in ''Prologue to a Life'' is a victim of the emotional states of his wife and mother.

West's psychological soundness in her stories is not always supported by an adequate fictional style. She has many poorly constructed sentences, awkward descriptive clauses, overuse of the past tense, a tendency to intrude as author, clichés, and self-conscious dialogue that is often completely lifeless. (pp. 133-34)

West, in transcending her faults, managed to portray a special milieu of black life that other black short story writers rarely touched upon—the frustrated, urban middle class in its struggle to grasp the goods of American life. West attempted to explore the duality of human nature through these people, and in doing so she contributed some interesting, creditable stories that literary historians should not overlook. (p. 134)

Margaret Perry, in her Silence to the Drums: A Survey of the Literature of the Harlem Renaissance, *Greenwood Press, 1976, 193 p.*

STERLING BROWN

[*Brown, a noted authority on black literary history, is also a poet, folklorist, and educator. His anthologies and criticism, along with those of his older contemporaries Alain Locke and Benjamin Brawley, are considered among the most important contributions to the understanding of black literature. Brown investigated the folk culture of black people in semirural areas of Virginia, Missouri, and Tennessee, where he taught English courses. As the literary critic for the black periodical* Opportunity *during the Harlem Renaissance, he displayed a deeper understanding of the folk sources of literature than did critics whose lives and works were centered in Harlem and other northern cities. The poetry in his* Southern Roads *(1932), explores the complex psychology of black people in America while illustrating the irony of their lives. Noted for his pessimistic realism, Brown is credited with beginning a new era in black poetry by rejecting the artificial sentimentality of dialect poetry in favor of realistic examples of black folk life and language. In the following excerpt from his critical study* Negro Poetry and Drama, *which was originally published in 1937, Brown surveys poetry of the Harlem Renaissance.*]

The extensive migrations from the South, quickened by the devastations of the boll-weevil, the growing resentment at injustice, and the demand of northern industries; the advance of the Negro in labor, wealth, and education; the World War with its new experiences in camp and battle; the Garvey movement with its exploitation of "race," all of these contributed to the growth of the "New Negro." In 1935, Alain Locke, editor of *The New Negro* wrote:

> The intelligent Negro of today is resolved not to make discrimination an extenuation for his shortcomings in performance, individual or collective; he is trying to hold himself at par, neither inflated by sentimental allowances nor depreciated by current social discounts. For this he must know himself and be known for precisely what he is, and for that reason he welcomes the new scientific rather than the old sentimental interest.... Now we rejoice and pray to be delivered both from self pity and condescension.

The New Negro was marked by self-respect (which, admittedly at times, became self-preening) and by self reliance. He asked for less charity and more justice. Negro poetry reflected all of this. Coincidentally in the post-war years the "new poetry" appeared in American literature, and New Negro poets naturally shared in this movement's reaction against sentimentality, didacticism, optimism, and romantic escape. They learned to shun stilted "poetic diction," to use fresher, more original language and to humanize poetry. Race was no longer to be caricatured or neglected; they did not plead "for a race" but attempted to express it. At their best they belonged with the renascent American poets who "in the tones of ordinary speech rediscovered the strength, the dignity, the vital core of the commonplace."

The resulting poetry had five major concerns: (1) a discovery of Africa as a source for race pride (2) a use of Negro heroes and heroic episodes from American history (3) propaganda of protest (4) a treatment of the Negro masses (frequently of the folk, less often of the workers) with more understanding and less apology and (5) franker and deeper self revelation. Some of this subject matter called for a romantic approach, some for a realistic. (pp. 60-1)

Fenton Johnson's works show the two extremes of Negro poetry after 1914. Some of his poems are conventional in form and substance; others, patterned upon his fellow Chicagoan, Sandburg, are striking departures in Negro poetry. With Sandburg's technique and Edgar Lee Masters' outlook, Johnson included in *African Nights* snapshots of bitter experience such as "Aunt Hanna Jackson," "The Banjo-Player," "The Minister," "The Scarlet Woman" and "Tired." Unfortunately Johnson, like so many of his Negro contemporaries, fell silent shortly after these poems. Perhaps there was little audience for their pessimism, either within a race whose optimism is proverbial, or without, where the Negro's brooding over his lot is generally unwelcome. "The Scarlet Woman," educated for more than a white man's kitchen, is driven by poverty to street-walking, and gin is her only way of forgetfulness. "Tired" indicts civilization:

> I am tired of building up somebody else's civilization.... let the old shanty go to rot, the white people's clothes turn to dust, and the Calvary Baptist Church sink to the bottomless pit....

> Throw the children into the river; civilization has given us too many.

Negro "leaders" who direct the race into optimism, condemned this view of life, but it is tonic after such frequent insistence on "a good time coming bye and bye." Like so many modern poets, Fenton Johnson held to the words of Thomas Hardy that

> If way to the better there be, it exacts a full look at the worst.

Georgia Douglas Johnson continues in the main the [romantic tradition].... According to a sponsoring critic, Mrs. Johnson has "set herself the task of documenting the feminine heart ... and in a simple declarative style engages with ingenuous directness the moods and emotions of her themes." The poems in *The Heart of A Woman* (1918), *Bronze* (1922), and *An Autumn Love Cycle* (1928) are written to appeal to the heart, and are generally autumnal in tone. *Bronze* contains "Hegira," "The Octoroon" and "Aliens" upon race themes; one section "Motherhood" at times goes deeply into the tragic problems of Negro mothers aware of what faces their children. Though conventional in phrase and meter, her poems are skillful and fluent. Angelina Weld Grimké is the author of many musical lyrics, frequently in a carefully worded and cadenced free verse. Intellectual and sensitive to injustice, she has written poems of irony and quiet despair: a puppet player twitches "the strings with slow sardonic grin."

> Let us forget the past unrest
> We ask for peace.

She is influenced by imagism, but her images are of the twilight, or of winter.

Alice Dunbar Nelson, wife of Paul Laurence Dunbar, in addition to her better known sketches of Creole life, wrote many poems. These echo the romantic themes, some being concerned with descriptions of Nature "the perfect loveliness that God has made" in contrast with man-made imperfections. "I Sit and Sew" laments a woman's enforced inactivity in time of war.

More forthright, but done with less artistic care, are the poems of Walter Everette Hawkins. His book is called *Chords and Discords;* the "chords" are conventional lyrics about love or duty, but the "discords" foreshadow new Negro poetry. "The Iconoclast" and "To Prometheus" are self-consciously radical, but the theme was new for Negro poets. "A Festival in Christendom" describes a lynching, but since literary diction is used for lurid details, it does not succeed as poetry:

> Then from his side they tore his heart
> And watched its quivering fibres start.

In "Thus Speaks Africa" Hawkins combines race-pride and race-history in a manner favored by many contemporary Negro poets.

> I am Africa:
> Wild is the wail of my waters,
> Deep is the cry of my Congo.
> I laid down my life at Fort Pillow....
> I died on the flag at Fort Wagner
> My bones lie bleaching in Flanders.
> I was burned at the stake down in Georgia,
> I was fuel for the mob in Texas....

After such a catalogue, he states less convincingly:

> And then like the Phoenix of Egypt,
> I rose from the ashes immortal. . . .

Carrie W. Clifford in *The Widening Light* likewise looks forward anxiously to the bursting "full-flowered into life" of black folk choked into a death stupor. Many of her sonnets are race-conscious like "The Black Draftee From Dixie," which tells of one of the many soldiers who were lynched upon their return from overseas.

One of the many Negro poets who died young, Roscoe Jamison is best known for his poem "Negro Soldiers," beginning

> These truly are the Brave,
> These men who cast aside,
> Old memories, to walk the blood-stained pave
> Of Sacrifice, joining the solemn tide
> That moves away, to suffer and to die
> For Freedom—when their own is yet denied!

Similarly cut off at the outset of his career, Joseph Seamon Cotter, gifted son of a gifted father, left behind him a sheaf of poem *The Band of Gideon And Other Poems.* Cotter had a definite lyrical facility, seen in the title poem, "Supplication," and "Rain Music." Closer to the New Negro concern for social themes, done with quiet persuasiveness is

> Brothers, come!
> And let us go unto our God
> And when we stand before him
> I shall say—
> Lord, I do not hate,
> I am hated.
> I scourge no one,
> I am scourged.
> I covet no lands,
> My lands are coveted.
> I mock no peoples,
> My people are mocked.
> And brother, what shall you say?

Claude McKay's voice was the strongest in the immediate postwar years. Born in the West Indies, McKay soon after his arrival in America discovered the shams of "democracy." With Floyd Dell and Max Eastman he became one of the editors of *The Liberator,* a magazine dedicated to social justice. In the epidemic of race-riots occurring shortly after the war, a much quoted cry of defiance was McKay's

> If we must die, let it not be like hogs,
> Hunted and penned in an inglorious spot. . . .
> Like men we'll face the murderous, cowardly pack
> Pressed to the wall, dying, but fighting back.

"The Lynching" with its crowd where men were jostled by steely-eyed women and "little lads, lynchers that were to be," and "America," "which feeds me bread of bitterness" contain desperate truth. Africa is called, with point and power

> The harlot, now thy time is done
> Of all the mighty nations of the sun.

Street-walkers of Harlem, cabaret dancers, and urban workers are treated with understanding. McKay looks searchingly at reality and reveals its harshness. But there is a McKay other than the hater, the rebel, and the realist,—there is the dreamer, nostalgic for the sights and sounds of his native West Indies. "The Tropics in New York" is a poem of memory stirred by

the sight of West Indian fruits in a store window. "My Mother" is a simply, tenderly phrased reminiscence. "Flame-Heart," a listing of the delights of youth in Jamaica, is one of the best lyrics in Negro poetry. "Two an' Six" is a charming pastoral of Jamaican life, closer to Burns than to Dunbar. When McKay turned almost completely to prose fiction, Negro poetry suffered a real loss.

Anne Spencer is the most original of all Negro women poets. Her devotion to Browning, attested by one of her best poems "Life-Long, Poor Browning," results in a closely woven style that is at times cryptic, but even more often richly rewarding. She makes use of poetic tradition without being conventional, and of new styles with a regard for form; her vision and expression are those of a wise, ironic but gentle woman of her times. She is sensitive to natural beauty, praising her home-state Virginia:

> Here canopied reaches of dogwood and hazel
> Beech tree and redbud fine-laced in vines
> Fleet clapping rills by lush fern and basil
> Drain blue hills to lowlands scented with pines

"Neighbors," "I have a Friend," and "Innocence," convey a great deal, in the deceptively simple manner of Emily Dickinson. "Before The Feast of Shushan" is a poem of vivid sensuous beauty, telling an old story in modern terms. "At The Carnival" has a bitter wisdom; Mrs. Spencer sets before us graphically the drab cheapness: the blind crowd, the sausage and garlic booth, the dancing tent where "a quivering female-thing gestured assignations," the "Limousine Lady" and the "bull-necked man" in contrast to the gleaming beauty of the "Girl of The Tank." But

> Little Diver, Destiny for you
> Like as for me, is shod in silence;
> Years may seep into your soul
> The bacilli of the usual and the expedient;
> I implore Neptune to claim his child today!

Original, sensitive, and keenly observant, the poems of Anne Spencer should be collected for a wider audience.

Though better known as a novelist, Jessie Fauset is likewise a poet. Her interest in French literature is apparent in many titles of her poems, and in her translations of poets of the French West Indies, who should be better known. Most of Miss Fauset's personal poems are about love, written with a care for form, and an ironic disillusionment. "La Vie C'est La Vie," the best of these, sets forth a triangle of lovers, loving and unbeloved:

> But he will none of me. Nor I
> Of you. Nor you of her. 'Tis said
> The world is full of jests like these—
> I wish that I were dead.

"Oriflamme" celebrates Sojourner Truth, making her symbolic of the Negro mother, bereft of her children, "still visioning the stars."

Jean Toomer is best as a poet in the beautiful prose of *Cane* (1923). His few poems in the same volume, however, are original and striking. Jean Toomer has written that Georgia opened him up; "Reapers" and "Cotton Song," show this awaking to folk material. In "Georgia Dusk" there is a sense of the ominous mystery of the Southland:

> The sawmill blows its whistle, buzz-saws stop,
> And silence breaks the bud of knoll and hill . . . ,
> Smoke from the pyramidal sawdust pile

Curls up, blue ghosts of trees. . . .
. . . . the chorus of the cane
Is caroling a vesper to the stars. . . .

With a mastery of the best rhythmical devices of Negro folk-music, "Song of the Son" expresses the return of the younger Negro to a consciousness of identity with his own, a return to folk sources, to the "caroling softly souls of slavery"—

O land and soil, red soil and sweet-gum tree,
So scant of grass, so profligate of pines,
Now just before an epoch's sun declines,
Thy son, in time, I have returned to thee,
Thy son, I have in time returned to thee.
In time, for though the sun is setting on
A song-lit race of slaves, it has not set. . . .

In spite of the small number of his poems, Toomer remains one of the finest and most influential of Negro poets. His long silence has been broken with the publication of "Blue Meridian," a rather long poem calling for a "new America, to be spiritualized by each new American." In it there are only occasional references to Negro life:

The great African races sent a single wave
And singing riplets to sorrow in red fields
Sing a swan song, to break rocks
And immortalize a hiding water-boy. . . .

James Weldon Johnson has also felt the need of recording the lives and thoughts of those "leaving, soon gone." After collecting and editing two volumes of spirituals, he turned to the task, attempted in an earlier poem,—"The Creation," of fixing something of the rapidly-passing old-time Negro preacher. *God's Trombones, Seven Negro Sermons In Verse* (1927), was widely acclaimed. Material which is usually made ludicrous, is here invested with dignity, power and beauty. Convinced that dialect smacks too much of the minstrel stage, Johnson attempts to give truth to folk idiom rather than mere misspellings. The rhythms of these chants have true poetic quality. The advance from his earlier dialect "Jingles and Croons" is a great one; *God's Trombones* are truthful and sincere renditions of a belief and a way of life. There is the occasional grotesqueness of the folk preacher:

Wash him with hyssop inside and out
Hang him up and drain him dry of sin.

but there is the tenderness of the reference to Sister Caroline, down in Yamacraw, who had borne the burden of the heat of the day and to whom Death "looked like a welcome friend," and the intimacy of telling a novice in the mad, bad Babylon of scarlet women, dancing and drinking

Young man, young man,
Your arm's too short to box with God.

If the hell-border city of Babylon recalls Memphis, New Orleans, and Harlem, "The Crucifixion" and "Let My People Go" recall other Negro experiences:

Listen!—Listen!
All you sons of Pharaoh
Who do you think can hold God's people
When the Lord God himself has said,
Let my people go?

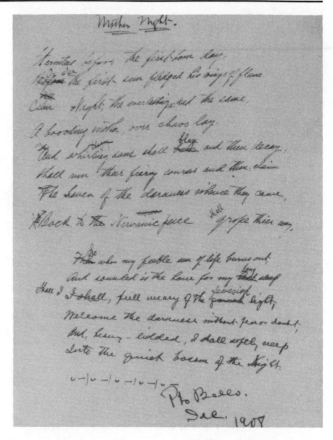

Manuscript of "Mother Night" by James Weldon Johnson.

The visionary qualities of the spirituals are seen throughout, especially in "The Judgment Day."

The sun will go out like a candle in the wind,
The moon will turn to dripping blood,
The stars will fall like cinders,
And the sea will burn like tar. . . .

The same visionary type of imagination is to be seen in *Saint Peter Relates an Incident of the Resurrection Day* (1930), a caustic satire of the treatment accorded Negro Gold Star Mothers. The Unknown Soldier, arriving in heaven, is discovered to be a Negro; the G.A.R., the D.A.R., the Legion, the Klan, the trustees of the patriotism of the nation are astounded and want him buried again. In these later poems, both the interpretation and the protest are less rhetorical and more dramatic than in *Fifty Years*, and consequently more persuasive.

Most precocious of contemporary Negro poets is Countee Cullen, who was winner of many nation-wide poetry contests in high school and college, and who published his first volume when he was only twenty-two. This volume, *Color* (1925), is by many critics considered Cullen's best. Like Dunbar's standard English poems, and Braithwaite's, Cullen's work is marked by technical skill; it is the most polished lyricism of modern Negro poetry. Cullen is a follower of tradition in English verse, of what he calls "the measured line and the skillful rhyme." His chief models are Keats and Edna St. Vincent Millay. But he has poured new wine into the old bottles. His gifts are fluency and brilliant imagery; he can convey deep emotion and concise irony. He writes of the gay abandon of lovely brown girls in Harlem "whose walk is like the replica of some barbaric dance'' but he is impressed with the transiency of happiness, ''the winter of sure defeat.'' He is capable of the tenderness of ''A Brown Girl Dead'':

> Her mother pawned her wedding ring
> To lay her out in white;
> She'd be so proud she'd dance and sing
> To see herself tonight. . . .

and of the epigrammatic:

> She even thinks that up in heaven
> Her class lies late and snores
> While poor black cherubs rise at seven
> To do celestial chores.

Cullen insists, as any poet should, that he wants ''no racial consideration to bolster up'' his reputation, and (a different thing, this) does not wish to be confined to ''racial'' themes:

> What shepherd heart would keep its fill
> For only the darker lamb?

It is nevertheless true, as James Weldon Johnson points out, that his best poems are those motivated by race. ''The Shroud of Color'' celebrates a mystical experience in which the poet turns from despair to identity with his people:

> Lord, I will live persuaded by mine own.
> I cannot play the recreant to these;
> My spirit has come home, that sailed the doubtful seas.

''Heritage'' is a statement of the atavism that was a cardinal creed of New Negro poetry, of ''old remembered ways'' from Africa persisting in civilization:

> I can never rest at all
> When the rain begins to fall
> Like a man gone mad with pain
> I must match its weird refrain. . . .

But the Africa is ''literary,'' and romanticized, and the theme is too close to Lindsay's ''Congo, creeping through the black.'' ''Heritage,'' for all of its color and facility, does not quite convince. Cullen has also written sonnets of protest. *The Black Christ* (1929) is a narrative poem about lynching, but like others of his late poems, relies more upon literature than life.

Langston Hughes is like Cullen in productivity and wide popularity. These two poets are about the same age; Hughes' *The Weary Blues* (1926) appeared the year after *Color*. Where Cullen is traditional in form, Hughes is experimental, substituting Sandburg for Keats, and going as far in metrical revolt as ''The Cat and the Saxaphone, 2 A.M.'' Cullen is subjective whereas Hughes is frequently objective and dramatic, concerned with the Negro masses. Cullen has most recently translated the *Medea* of Euripides; Hughes' most recent work is communist propaganda. Both poets have strains of pessimism, at times met stoically, but Hughes has now turned to a cause that he believes will usher in social justice.

In *The Weary Blues* Hughes helped to celebrate jazz-mad Harlem, but a note of sadness intrudes as in ''To Midnight Nan at Leroy's'' and ''Song For A Banjo Dance.'' He believes that

> We should have a land of sun. . . .
> And not this land where life is cold.

He, too, sings atavistically of Africa, of the boy in whose blood ''all the tom-toms of the jungle beat.'' But, aware that the dark peoples are caged in ''the circus of civilization,'' he turns realistically to description of his people. His folk portraits

are good in ''The Weary Blues,'' ''Aunt Sue's Stories,'' and the tender, stoical ''Mother to Son,'' one of the best Negro poems:

> Well, son, I'll tell you:
> Life for me ain't been no crystal stair. . . .

This interest is continued in *Fine Clothes To The Jew* (1927) in which he combines the melancholy and irony of the folk-blues. An abandoned woman sings

> Don't know's I'd mind his goin'
> But he left me when de coal was low. . . .

He gives dramatic sketches of city workers—elevator boys and porters ''climbing up a great big mountain of yes, sirs!'' ''Ruby Brown,'' like Fenton Johnson's acid sketches, and ''A Ruined Gal'' have shocked those who wish poetry to be confined to the pretty and sweet, but they ring true and sympathetic. Another side of Negro experience is made real in ''Feet o' Jesus,'' 'Prayer,'' and ''Angel's Wings.'' ''Cross'' is a quizzical, and ''Mulatto'' a direct commentary upon the bitter social fruit of race mixture.

Generalized interpretation of the race appears in ''I, Too Sing America'' and in ''A Negro Speaks of Rivers,'' one of his finest poems. He calls his people ''loud-mouthed laughers in the hands of fate,'' but is convinced that ''their soul has grown deep like the rivers.'' ''Minstrel Man'' takes an old concept and reveals a new truth:

> Because my mouth
> Is wide with laughter
> And my throat
> Is deep with song,
> You do not think
> I suffer after
> I have held my pain
> So long.

Hughes' awakened interest in communism has resulted in such poems as ''Good-Bye, Christ,'' ''Letter to the Academy,'' ''Elderly Race Leaders'' (which closes with twenty-four dollar signs), the ''Ballad of Lenin,'' ''Ballad of Ozzie Powell'' and the better ''To The Kids Who Die,'' ''America,'' and ''The Ballad of Roosevelt'':

> The pot was empty
> The cupboard was bare.
> I said, Papa
> What's the matter here?
> I'm waitin' on Roosevelt, son,
> Roosevelt, Roosevelt,
> Waitin' on Roosevelt, son.

Waring Cuney likewise absorbed something of the spirit of the blues and spirituals, and his poems, like those of Hughes, have a deceptive simplicity. ''I Think I See Him There,'' ''Troubled Jesus,'' ''Crucifixion'' and ''Wake Cry'' deal gently and truthfully with folk religion. ''Burial of The Young Love,'' ''The Death Bed,'' ''Threnody'' and ''Finis'' attain a true melancholy with economy of phrase. ''No Images'' tells of the girl who thinks ''her brown body has no glory.''

> If she could dance
> Naked,
> Under palm trees
> And see her image in the river
> She would know.

But there are no palm trees
On the street,
And dish water gives back no images.

Helene Johnson also writes with pride of race. Her "Sonnet to a Negro in Harlem" praises him for his magnificent disdain, his arrogant and bold laughter. Like Hughes, she believes his setting should be palm trees and mangoes. She writes in Harlemese a sketch of a jazz prince, with his shoulders "jerking the jig-wa." "Bottled" is a semi-humorous lament for a Negro "in trick clothes . . . yaller shoes and yaller gloves and swallow-tail coat," who would be beautiful back in pagan Africa. Gwendolyn Bennett's poems are generally race conscious; like most of the New Negro school, she writes in "To A Dark Girl":

> Something of old forgotten queens
> Lurks in the lithe abandon of your walk. . . .

Gladys May Casely Hayford, a native African, writes with a conscious desire to imbue her own people "with the idea of their own beauty, superiority and individuality, with a love and admiration for our own country which has been systematically suppressed." Her "Rainy Season Love Song" is colorful and warm, but the verse form is traditional in cadence and phrasing.

One of the best negro novelists, Arna Bontemps, is likewise a poet of distinction. His work is meditative, couched in fluent but subdued rhythms. It is poetry of the twilight, of reverie, as so much of Negro poetry, but the artistry is of high order. "Nocturne," "Nocturne at Bethesda," "Gethsemane," "Golgotha Is A Mountain" and "Return" are his best works, and their titles are indicative. Whether writing in the traditional forms or in free verse, Bontemps' concern seems to be music above all else. The symbolism is at times successful; "Nocturne at Bethesda" has racial import:

> . . . and why
> Do our black faces search the empty sky?
> Is there something we have forgotten? Some precious thing
> We have lost, wandering in strange lands?

One of the new Negro poets, Bontemps makes frequent reference to Africa, now grieving over the lost glory, now insisting upon his heritage, and now writing

> Those mountains should be ours.

Something of the attitude of the Garvey movement is to be seen in Lewis Alexander's poems to Africa: there is the allegiance to the "motherland," and a romantic faith in her resurgence.

> Rise from out thy charnel house to be
> Thine own immortal, brilliant self again.

This type of idealization of Africa was an attempted corrective to the typical undervaluation, but was more poetic dreaming than understanding. "The Dark Brother" pleads rhetorically for brotherhood. Lewis Alexander has also experimented with all types of poetry from the Japanese Tanka and Hokku to the Blues. Intellectual irony is in the free verse poetry of Frank Horne. "To A Persistent Phantom" and "More Letters Found Near A Suicide" are modern portraiture, vivid, racy and unhackneyed. "Nigger, A Chant For Children" is a recital of Negro heroism with the race-pride of the new Negro movement. One of the finest poetic re-creations of slavery days and characters was "Dead and Gone" by Allison Davis. This dramatic narrative (appearing in the only issue of the magazine *Harlem*) showed understanding and power.

Clarissa Scott Delaney wrote poems that bore witness to a spirit sensitive and in love with life. "The Mask" is a well done portrait. Sensitivity likewise marks the poems of Esther Popel Shaw. "Salute To The Flag" departs from her usual nature description; it attacks the shams of democracy by placing the patriotic teachings of the schools side by side with the newspaper report of a lynching. George Leonard Allen, a poet-musician of North Carolina, was awarded a prize for the best sonnet in a state-wide contest conducted by the United Daughters of the Confederacy. He wrote fluently of nature and music; before his untimely death he was attempting as well to deal with folk-experiences. Another southern poet, Jonathan Brooks, writes with quiet surety. His poems, generally religious in nature or in imagery, are thoughtful and moving. Simple in phrasing and rhythm, they are unobstrusively symbolic. A collection of them would reveal that Brooks has a talent of distinction. *Negrito* (1933) by J. Mason Brewer is commendable in its purpose of recording Negro experience in the southwest, but the shadow of Dunbar lies heavy and there is little reference to anything but the happier side of life.

Southern Road by Sterling A. Brown (1932) is chiefly an attempt at folk portraiture of southern characters. Brown sought to convey the tragedy of the southern Negro, in poems like the title poem, "Children of The Mississippi," "King Cotton" and "Sam Smiley," and the comedy in the Slim Greer series and "Sporting Beasley." The wandering roustabout is recorded in "Long Gone" and "Odyssey of Big Boy." The irony to be found in Negro folk-song appears in "Mr. Samuel and Sam." "Strong Man," making use of a refrain found in Sandburg—"The strong men keep coming on"—is an expression of the dogged stoicism Brown has found in Negro experience. He has made a fairly close study of folk-ways and folk-songs, and has used this in interpreting folk-experience and character which he considers one of the important tasks of Negro poetry. He is not afraid of using folk-speech, refusing to believe dialect to be "an instrument of only two stops—pathos and humor." He uses free verse and the traditional forms as well as folk-forms, and many of his poems are subjective. His second volume, to be called "No Hiding Place," re-explores the southern scene with more emphasis on social themes.

Trumpet in The New Moon by Welborn Victor Jenkins (1934), is a panoramic picture of the Negro in American life. It recalls Whitman in its patriotism (and its cataloguing) and Sandburg, but has an original place in Negro poetry:

> Remember the service:
>
> Come Susie, rock the baby— Go Hannah, get the
>   dinner—
> Uncle Jim, go plough the new ground—
> Here Sambo, grab my satchel and get to hell—
>
> Remember the sweat, the cotton fields, the lumber
> logs, the brick yards, the sawmills and turpentine
> plantation—all black labor.

Realistic and novel in detail, the poem repeats a pattern dear to Negro poets from Whitfield through Dunbar and James Weldon Johnson: the recording of Negro service will effect

> the joys of Rebirth and Regeneration
> At the solemn Love-Feast of Brotherhood and
>   Democracy.

Frank Marshall Davis is likewise panoramic in *Black Man's Verse* (1935). "What do You Want, America" like "Trumpets in the New Moon" lists the services of Negroes, but comments more sardonically on the abuses of democracy. Davis is at times a mystic escapist, but at his best he is bitterly realistic. "Chicago's Congo," "Jazz Band," "Mojo Mike's Beer Garden" "Cabaret" and "Georgia's Atlanta" are forthright transcripts of reality. "Lynched" is a powerful protest. Davis is satiric about Negro "society": Robert Whitmore, ruler of the local Elks,

> died of apoplexy
> when a stranger from Georgia
> mistook him
> for a former Macon waiter.

Davis at times leans heavily upon Masters and Sandburg, but his gift of realistic portraiture, his irony, and his knowledge of Negro life should stand him in very good stead. Richard Wright, likewise of Chicago, is not content with either listing Negro achievement or registering the abuses of American life. He believes in poetry as a weapon, and in his driving rhythms urges Negro workers to rise up like men, side by side with white workers, to estabish communism in America:

> I am black and I have seen black hands
> Raised in fists of revolt, side by side with the white
>   fists of white workers,
> And some day—and it is only this which sustains me—
> Someday, there will be millions and millions and
>   millions of them
> On some red day in a burst of fists on a new horizon!

Quite a few books of verse have been produced by Negro poets within recent years, which are romantic escapes for the sensitive authors from depressing actualities. *Make Way For Happiness* (1932) by Alpheus Butler promises "I will bring you pretty things measure for measure" and the resulting "prettiness" is trite. J. Harvey L. Baxter bewails the fallen estate of noble poetry which will still be sung

> As long as stars, or waves of sea.

That Which Concerneth Me (1934) is unconcerned with race experience or the revelation of a personality; what concerns the poet, according to Baxter, is "the song of rose and bee." "Eve Lynn's" *No Alabaster Box* is praised by her sponsor because "not once does she refer to the peculiar problem of her own group." Marion Cuthbert's *April Grasses* is generally escapist; the interesting subject matter Miss Cuthbert is acquainted with she seems to consider unfit for poetic expression. Mae Cowdery's *Lift Our Voices* contains too often vague yearning and the romantic worship of nature, but at times has poetic drive. These poets by denying racial, or even personal experience pretend to touch "universality," which according to one Negro critic, means a concern with the universe.

Contemporary Negro poets are too diverse to be grouped into schools. Certain chief tendencies, however, are apparent. More than Alberry Whitman, Dunbar, and Braithwaite, the contemporary poets, even when writing subjective lyrics, are more frankly personal, less restrained, and as a general rule, less conventional. They have been influenced by modern American poetry, of course, as their elders were by post-Victorian, but one of the cardinal lessons of modern poetry is that the poet should express his own view of life in his own way. It has been pointed out, however, that "bookishness" still prevails, that the so-called new poetry revival has left many versifiers

untouched. Secondly, more than the older poets who hesitantly advanced defenses of the Negro, the contemporary Negro poet is more assured, more self-reliant. He seems less taken in by American hypocrisy and expresses his protest now with irony, now with anger, seldom with humility. The poets who have taken folk-types and folk-life for their province no longer accept the stereotyped view of the traditional dialect writers, nor, lapsing into gentility, do they flinch from an honest portrayal of folk-life. Their laughter has more irony in it than buffoonery. They are ready to see the tragic as well as the pitiful. They are much closer to the true folk product than to the minstrel song.

It is not at all advanced that the contemporary poetry of the American Negro is to be ranked with the best of modern poetry. Too many talented writers have stopped suddenly after their first, sometimes successful gropings. The Negro audience is naturally small, and that part devoted to poetry, much smaller. Few Negro poets have the requisite time for maturing, for mastering technique, for observation of the world and themselves. Negro poets have left uncultivated many fields opened by modern poetry. Many still confine their models to the masters they learned about in school, to the Victorians, and the pre-Raphaelites. Almost as frequently they have been unaware of the finer uses of tradition. The reading world seems to be ready for a true interpretation of Negro life from within, and poets with a dramatic ability have before them an important task. And the world has always been ready for the poet who in his own manner reveals his deepest thoughts and feelings. What it means to be a Negro in the modern world is a revelation much needed in poetry. But the Negro poet must write so that whosoever touches his book touches a man. Too often, like other minor poets, he has written so that whosoever touches his book touches the books of other and greater poets. (pp. 61-81)

> Sterling Brown, "Contemporary Negro Poetry (1914-1936)," in his Negro Poetry and Drama and The Negro in American Fiction, *Atheneum*, 1969, pp. 60-81.

DAVID LITTLEJOHN

[*Littlejohn is a novelist, biographer, and critic whose works include* Black on White: A Critical Survey of Writing by American Negroes (1966). *In the following excerpt from that work, he criticizes the majority of fiction produced during the Harlem Renaissance for what he considers its superficial and trivial concerns and examines works by the best novelists and poets of the period.*]

In retrospect, the Harlem Renaissance of 1923 to 1933 seems far less important a literary event than it did to some observers at the time. There is no question of its importance as a progressive movement, both real and symbolic, in American Negro culture. The question is rather that of its substantial worth in any other context, or its relevance to subsequent generations.

It was, in part, one more fad of the faddish twenties—something modish and insubstantial, and perhaps even a little corrupt. The very title is journalistically pretentious. But however much fraud or fancy may have gone into it, the Harlem Renaissance had its lasting merits. First, the actual fact of literary maturity and independence coming to ten or twenty Negro writers in a very short space of time is notable both as accomplishment and as example: from then on other prospective Negro writers had at least a model and a chance for success. Secondly, the simple race-pride satisfactions in the spectacle were genuine and enduring, the spectacle of Negro poets and novelists being published, acclaimed, and accepted as writers in the first American rank, whether they belonged there or not. And thirdly, it gave us Langston Hughes. (p. 39)

The Harlem setting was an essential dynamic. America's major Negro metropolis scarcely existed in 1910, at the beginning of the great migrations of Southern Negroes. By 1925 it was, in James Weldon Johnson's proud words, "the greatest Negro city in the world." (p. 41)

Along with the new capital came, we are told, a "New Negro." The type was celebrated by Alain Locke in his introduction to *The New Negro,* a piece of militant, warfaring rhetoric. This New Negro was to assert himself proudly and independently, he insisted, to cast off the chains of servility and stereotype. Harlem was to be his glorious new spiritual home, the colorful symbol of his Coming of Age. He could now stand upright, and celebrate his race—his African heritage, his music, his "Negro blood." (pp. 41-2)

> Bliss was it in that dawn to be alive,
> But to be young was very Heaven.

Wordsworth's lines are doubly applicable to this particular "dawn," for the poet was writing of the promise of the French Revolution, out of the bleak perspective of his own later abject disillusionment; the lines bear a heavy charge of irony. And nothing freezes the Harlem Renaissance more into a past forever closed than a look back at the false, the pathetically high and unfulfilled hopes of its participants and observers. This is James Weldon Johnson, on the Harlem of 1925:

> It is not a slum or a fringe, it is located in the heart of Manhatttan and occupies one of the most beautiful and healthful sections of the city. It is not a "quarter" of dilapidated tenements, but is made up of new-law apartments and handsome dwellings, with well-paved and well-lighted streets.

He writes of "magnificent Seventh Avenue," of New Negro millionaires. "I know of no place in the country where the feeling between the races is so cordial and at the same time so matter of fact and taken for granted," he declares; "Nor is there any unusual record of crime. . . . Will Harlem become merely a famous ghetto?" he rhetorically asks. "Will it become a point of friction between the races in New York?" He thought not.

Since the pride and the vision have proved to be illusory, it is no wonder that much of the literature based on them now seems to us equally hollow. However well intended or well written the Harlem novels may have been, they depicted only a two-dimensional facade, with the third dimension built of hope. The hopes have crumbled, the facade has turned grimy, and now all the charm, the high color and high spirits, the joyful assertion of the instinctual-voluptuary new life-style of Harlem are the record of a pathetic delusion.

The celebrity, during the Renaissance, of such nonliterary figures as Paul Robeson, Ethel Waters, Louis Armstrong, Duke Ellington, Roland Hayes, Josephine Baker, and Bill Robinson may be accepted as genuine and earned; but the other side of the Harlem coin is represented by the cabaret-crawls of white Society up Lenox Avenue, the tremendous vogue for the Negro musical comedies of the decade—*Shuffle Along, Plantation Revue, Chocolate Dandies, Hot Chocolates:* an epochal cultural gap, as these titles make clear, divides the Harlem Renaissance from today.

But even in that dawn, there was much more to Harlem life than most of its recorders chose to show; they were painting not even its facade, but just the flaking top layer. Granted that Negro life in Harlem may have worsened perceptively in the interval, grown more tense and complex, even in 1925 it was not all brown jazz-babies and gin.

> Focusing upon carefree abandon, the Harlem school, like the plantation tradition, neglected the servitude. Except for brief glimpses, the drama of the workaday life, the struggles, the conflicts, are missing. And such definite features of Harlem life as the lines of the unemployed, the overcrowded schools, the delinquent children headed straight to petty crime, the surly resentment—all of these seeds that bore such bitter fruit in the Harlem riot—are conspicuously absent.
>
> [Sterling Brown, *The Negro in American Fiction*]

The comparison with the Plantation Tradition supports our own perspective. For all the novelty of the Harlem school, the two traditions share much of a common irrelevance today, and, as Brown points out, for much the same reason. A few writers tried to reach beyond the colorful superficiality (and of course there was good reason to assert and accentuate the merely colorful); to draw something more honest, more typical and complete. But too many were possessed by the artificial excitement, and by a view, ultimately, as outside and distant as Carl Van Vechten's. By their very literary stance—and this applies to the most famous, to Countee Cullen, Claude McKay, and Jean Toomer—they betrayed their own *difference* from the world they described. It is clear now that they did not, any of them, really undertand even the Harlem of 1925, let alone the Harlem to come. For a picture of Harlem we can accept as more convincingly complete, one must wait for a wiser, maturer art: Ann Petry's *The Street* (1946), Langston Hughes' later lyrics or *The Sweet Flypaper of Life* (1955), James Baldwin's *Go Tell It on the Mountain* (1953) or "Sonny's Blues" (1965). To complete a portrait-in-depth of the Negro capital (no one's romantic dream city any more), I would add two other recent works: Warren Miller's *The Cool World* (1959), the finest Harlem novel so far, though a white man's; and Claude Brown's artless and awful autobiography, *Manchild in the Promised Land* (1965).

The excessive concern for a colorful surface, for a skin that has long since scaled off, is one of the two elements of a built-in obsolescence in most popular Harlem Renaissance novels. The other is their fixation with the social mores of the Negro middle class.

As the Negro writer grew more self-conscious and professional, he was met by a growing Negro reading public: an urban (even suburban) Northern Negro bourgeoisis, with all the dull limitations of its class. These were his readers, more often than not, and it was their little anxieties he was to dramatize, their little lives he was to make exciting, their fantasies he was to enact. The results could hardly be good novels—they are as commercial as the hot Harlem nocturnes, though aimed at a different audience of mediocrities. (This is not to say that one novel may not be written to both, as several were.) Thousands of similar domestic novels, social-status tragedies, were written, are being written, by forgotten and prosperous whites.

What this fixation affords to the critical surveyor is a great repetitive wash of dull, in-group, Negro-for-Negro novels through the twenties and thirties, detailing not "The Ethics of Living Jim Crow" but the Anxieties of Living High-Brown. However extensive a white reader's sympathies may be, these accounts can have for him little more than an anthropological interest, distant and exotic, like Gulliver's reports on the Lilliputians.

What sort of details are included? Primarily the skin-shade mania of Negro society, which is reiterated to a point of mental paralysis: "White is right," goes the jingle; "yellow, mellow; black, stand back."

From this basic standard come the "blue vein" circles of light-skinned aristocrats; the desirability of "high yellow" girls (as employees, dates, wives, mistresses, whores), and the hapless sufferings of the unwanted blacks, like Wallace Thurman's Emma Lou; the social rule that one always marries a paler type, and "breeds to light"—and then the tragedy of occasional genetic throwbacks in one's offspring.

Beyond, there lies the vast melodramatic realm of the "passing" theme, of the uncertainties of those light enough to cross over the color line—a source of tasteless fantasy plots from Charles Chesnutt to Nella Larsen, related to the popular "octoroon" melodramas of the mid-nineteenth century. The Negro social novels of the twenties and thirties are filled with details of skin-lightening preparations, the tragicomic possibilities of racial confusion, and Whitmanesque lists of the rich varieties of Negro color:

> Ancient black life rooted upon its base with all
> its fascinating new layers of brown, low-brown,
> high-brown, nut-brown, lemon, maroon, olive,
> mauve, gold, yellow balancing between black
> and white. Black reaching out beyond yellow.
> Almost-white on the brink of a change.
> 　　　　　(Claude McKay, *Home to Harlem*)
> 　　　　　　　　　　　　(pp. 42-7)

At a further remove are the more commonplace details of a miniature society, which might seem hardly more bizarre than its white counterpart but for the fact that lightness of skin (and rightness of hair) is an important determinant of one's social rank. It *is* all a bit Lilliputian: all Society, let us grant, is artificial; but an imitation of an imitation comes closest to absurdity. Into this category of detail would fall the popular set pieces of Negro balls and socials; the details of fashions and costumes; and all the careful estimates of the social place of various churches, clubs, fraternal organizations, and neighborhoods. (Philadelphia, Washington, and Brooklyn all boasted a sort of old-guard Negro aristocracy, which sneered at the Harlem parvenus.) The phenomenon of the "dicty," or rising, class-conscious Negro, is viewed with scorn (or, more rarely, admiration) by almost *every* Negro writer of the period.

Add to this the endless intraracial wrangling over race pride and "assimilation," over the Negro press and the Negro pulpit, over "rising" and Heritage, over Africa and watermelons: it is all doubtless genuine, but it is also, to a white reader (and perhaps to some Negroes), very close and steamy, as would be the account of any subculture's taking itself too seriously, defining the world and its values exclusively in the terms of its own restrictive norms and concerns.

One can dislike all this inbred intensity, and yet grant the necessity of such concerns to the people involved. To the Negro writer and his world, such matters can quite conceivably assume a state of total and absolute consequence. They do in everyone's world.

One can dislike reading all these details, and yet further grant that the accounts may be useful. It is well, after all, for the white reader to know the inner details of the American Negro world. All such awareness of life "behind the wall" can have its value, if the white reader accepts the details not as exoticism or with condescension, but simply for what they are: the intramural behavior patterns of a small, semi-closed American society like his own.

Moreover, the frenzied little concerns of the Negro novelist's world, concerns over hair quality and skin shades and streets of residence, do at least take their ultimate source in the extramural anxiety, the race war: White is right. But such concerns can scarcely be regarded as a mark of adulthood, in any group. And reading of them, over and over, in these insular, middle-class novels, whether the concerns be viewed sympathetically or with scorn, is like reading a shelf-full of John O'Hara. It is all, finally, true to our own life or not, so inbred and childlike and petty, where one buys his clothes, by whom one is snubbed, to what club one can aspire.

One of the surest proofs of the maturity of Negro fiction since 1940 is the almost total absence of this area of argument, the supplanting of Jessie Fauset and Nella Larsen and Wallace Thurman by James Baldwin and Ralph Ellison and Ann Petry. (Dorothy West's *The Living Is Easy*, 1948, is the only notable hangover of this older and narrower breed.) The newer writers are obviously writing as men, for men, however much they may take their characters and issues from the worlds they know best; and not as middle-class Negroes for middle-class Negroes and the occasional white curiosity-seeking slummer. (pp. 47-9)

Three fictional works of the period, for three different reasons, should be exempted from this blanket dismissal: George Schuyler's *Black No More* (1931), Langston Hughes' *Not Without Laughter* (1930), and Jean Toomer's *Cane* (1923), which I shall discuss later on with his poetry.

I would exempt Schuyler's fantasy because, though broad, it is genuinely funny, the best satire to come out of the race war before *Purlie Victorious*. "Black-No-More," in the novel, is a gland treatment which turns Negroes into whites, changing all racial characteristics irrevocably. It sweeps the country, sends white America into a panic, upsets the social, political, and economic systems, and puts Negro leaders out of their jobs. In the end, a tantalizing new balance is restored with the discovery that *real* whites are slightly darker than chemical ones.

Schuyler writes flabbily, sad to say, without control—he was a muckraking journalist by profession—and dilutes the high potential of his provocative idea. His artillery is aimed every which way, and his plot line swoops from effective quasi-realism to outrageous burlesque. The mode, if not the intelligence, is comparable to that of Joseph Heller's *Catch-22*. In both cases the subjects—race war and "real" war—were well met by the wild, spleenful anarchy of attack. One such work per generation would be good for the national health. (p. 51)

Not Without Laughter deserves notice . . . as an antidote to the many shrill and artificial Harlem Renaissance novels.

It is not easy to define Hughes' achievement without making him sound corny or soft. Formulations of his work come out like Faulkner's stodgy explanations of his own novels, even to the motifs of "affirmation" and "endurance." *Not Without Laughter* belongs with the fiction of its simpler time. It is a gentle sequence of well-sketched social views, like so many

Negro novels of the period—the family gatherings, the colored ball, the pool hall. It even includes the standard caricature of the Episcopalian, anti-watermelon dicty.

Its special value, like that of DuBois' social essays, lies in its completeness and truth, its control and wide humanity. It is probably the most genuine inside view of Negro life available in the fiction of the period, comparable to later works like Ann Petry's. Like almost all of Hughes' work it is sad, to a degree, but never violent or bitter; it is touching, but never falsely sentimental. It is very small, really, in outline—a collection of the more or less connected stories of a family of very average, very attractive small-town Negroes in Kansas; but the stories flow with the warmth of genuine life.

The Harlem Renaissance novelists rode to fame, for the most part, on transient concerns, now as dated as their boxy orange bindings with art-nouveau lettering. The poets of the Renaissance, a quite different phenomenon, took themselves and their art far more seriously. (More seriously even than "themselves as novelists," since many were both.) They came closer to acting as independent, even aggressively independent, artists. Their range of style and experiment, their variety of subject and manner are more a dark reflection-in-little of the whole modernist foment of the decade, the decade of Picasso and Stravinsky (and, not irrelevantly, of the discovery of African Negro sculpture). If the novelists reproduce, in a sort of toy version, the period of Fitzgerald and Sinclair Lewis, of hip flasks and Babbitts, the poets reflect the concerns of the Sandburgs and Pounds and Amy Lowells. They were genuine Bohemians, hard-working artists doing their individual best, as poets are likely to be. Langston Hughes, properly, wrote their manifesto, their declaration of independence.

> We younger Negro artists who create now intend to express our individual dark-skinned selves without fear or shame. If the white people are pleased, we are glad. If they are not, it doesn't matter. We know we are beautiful, and ugly too. The tom-tom cries and the tom-tom laughs. If colored people are pleased, we are glad. If they are not, their displeasure doesn't matter either. We build our temples for tomorrow, strong as we know them, and we stand on the top of the mountain, free within ourselves.
> (Langston Hughes, "The Negro Artist and the Racial Mountain" [see Additional Bibliography])

The four most discussed Negro poets of the period, Jean Toomer, Countee Cullen, Claude McKay, and Langston Hughes, were all genuine poets of the new dispensation, not mere imitators or versemakers. Theirs is, really, the first American Negro writing one can judge absolutely, with no necessary reference to its context. They are better than the earlier Negro poets not because they are New Negroes, but because American poetry itself grew up in the 1920's, and they were there. Of the four, even the least worthy is of serious consequence, by comparison with earlier names in our survey. But only one has earned a place in the minor ranks of important *American* poets, regardless of race, creed, or color.

Langston Hughes belongs, fairly, at least as much in [a discussion of poets of the present generation]. . .—the generation since 1940—as in these back files of the Harlem Renaissance. At sixty-four, after thirty books and a "Langston Hughes Reader," he remains the most impressive, durable, and prolific Negro writer in America. His voice is as sure, his manner as original, his position as secure as, say, Edwin Arlington Robinson's or Robinson Jeffers'. He is the one sure Negro classic, more certain of permanence than even Baldwin or Ellison or Wright. By molding his verse always on the sounds of Negro talk, the rhythms of Negro music, by retaining his own keen honesty and directness, his poetic sense and ironic intelligence, he has maintained through four decades a readable newness distinctly his own. His finest book of poetry, *Montage of a Dream Deferred,* was written in the bop mode of the early fifties. In his latest work, designed for jazz readings in the sixties, he plays new games with typography, with inset prose dialogue, with dual columns of counter-pointed verse. Hughes is a true professional, like the hero of his fictions only deceptively "Simple." Younger artists and jazzmen, now that he is a Personality, a member of the National Institute, may suspect him of a degree of condescension, even conscious fraud. But the voice, at least, remains genuine. He has earned the tributes of translation and imitation, and has produced, for the white reader, a convincing, singing source book on the emotional life-style of the lower-class urban Negro in America, as valid as the blues.

Countee Cullen is a queer twentieth-century example of an English traditionalist, "loving the measured line and skillful rhyme," a good example of what becomes of a talent too rooted in the past. He could carve easily metered, run-on lines with a sophisticated and polished placing of words, an exact and unforced precision of accent, in the best manner of Tennyson or Keats. He could actually build sonnets, sonnets that worked, crisply and easily, on the stock sixteenth-century Renaissance love themes; little Herricky trifles on enrubied and palpitant hearts; or ballad-measure stanzas of a tired young aesthete's longing for death. He believed in Beauty, sang to Shelley and Keats ("And You and I, shall we be still, / John Keats, while Beauty summons us"), and altogether summons up the image of a flowing-tie, nineteenth-century poet. As the earlier Negro versemakers were bad nineteenth-century poets, Countee Cullen was a fairly good one.

But there are limitations to such precious, archaic skills. The diction (e.g., "sable breast") is bound to seem at times simply false. The style, so inadequately suited to his contemporary or even commonplace subjects, forces one to regard him not as an honest spokesman, but as a detached exquisite, a builder of poems, crafting elegant little reliquaries for his themes. The race-protest poems, in particular, come out sounding too frail and wood-windy, too mellow and suave. He had sipped of the New Harlem wine, and tried very hard to insist on his own "pagan blood"; but the false primitivism, the hopeful, distant assertion of his Congo heritage is unpleasantly clear:

> Why should he deem it pure mischance
> A son of his is fain
> To do a naked tribal dance
> Each time he hears the rain?

He should at least be given credit for "Heritage" (along with three or four other rereadable poems, "A Brown Girl Dead," "Incident," "Variations on a Theme"), the lead-off piece of the African heritage revival among New Negroes, which has never entirely died. Perhaps because I believe that no really intelligent American Negro could ever fall for the African heritage line (though many have)—there is so evidently no real contact between the cultures, the Ashanti warrior-kings are like ancestors bought from a genealogist or an art gallery, the whole jungle-blood affair reeks of adolescent daydreaming—I cannot take too seriously any of the great run of Negro poems or statements on the theme. But Cullen's effort is a decent, drum-beating, rollicking thing, with a few lines (''the unremittent beat / Made by cruel padded feet / Walking through my body's street'') that come near to convincing.

Claude McKay, as a poet, is most kindly served by reading a few of his strongest poems, or even selected lines. The more thoroughly one studies his work, the more disagreeably McKay is revealed as the small-souled declamatory propagandist we meet in his novels. The best poems from his angry series of race-war sonnets (''Baptism,'' ''If We Must Die,'' ''Outcast,'' ''Like a Strong Tree,'' ''The White House'') convey a bitter, masculine, very personal strength, a kind of enlightened crimson rant: the man loves to hate, and has objects worth hating.

There is nothing new or experimental about his efforts. At its best (or at the reader's most tolerant) his work seems to have a kind of harsh, proud seventeenth-century vigor, like Milton's sonnet ''On the Late Massacre in Piedmont'' (''Avenge, O Lord, thy slaughtered saints''). From another point of view, though, the diction may be seen as a kind of archaic British bluster (''O let us nobly die,'' ''Kinsmen,'' ''bend the knee,'' ''clime,'' ''making their mock at our accursed lot''); the best-known of his poems was once quoted by Churchill.

His strength *is* in his anger, in the fury of his rhythms and images and diction; his weakness lies in his small-mindedness and poetic inability. He writes in chunky, aggressively iambic, end-stopped pentameters, deep-chested rhetorical lines of accusation and defiance, full of mouth-filling vowels and chopped consonants. He will make a dozen bad mistakes per sonnet, and dip to all forms of archaism and syntactic ineptitude to crash his way out of a poem (''From dulcet thoughts of you my guts are twisted''). Looked at too closely, the ideas behind his angry rhetoric often show as incoherent black-racist propaganda. He is not a pleasant sort.

But often his verse can be carried along by the simple constant fire of his diction. And in his most successful angry sonnets, a small idea is sublimed into one compulsive image, a fine unity of image and structure pulls the whole together, and he is left with no room for the usual archaisms of diction or clumsiness of rhythm.

I would mention too his one most horrible, most captivating poem, ''The Desolate City,'' a potent nightmare allegory of the spirit as a city in plague, glutted with fine images of decay; and especially his ''Amoroso'' sequence of sex poems, more convincingly passionate than anything of Swinburne's. These are extraordinary things, celebrations of real copulations arguably better than his race-war sonnets. That none of the Negro anthologies includes them among his works is an interesting testimony to their effect.

Jean Toomer's career is still wrapped in foggy mystery: he wrote one esoteric work, difficult to grasp, define, and assess; he was associated with one of the more advanced white modernist cults, and adopted and taught Russian mysticism; and then he suddenly declared himself white, and disappeared.

His book, *Cane* (1923), is composed of fourteen prose pieces, ranging from two-and four-page sketches, to ''Kabnis,'' an eighty-three-page *nouvelle;* and fifteen detached poems set in between. About half the ''stories'' have tiny lyric refrains tucked inside them as well.

The prose pieces in the first section of the book are detached vignettes of high female sexuality among the Negro peasants of the Dixie Pike. They are drawn with the new honest art-fulness of the Stein-Anderson-Hemingway tradition, so crisp and icily succinct that the characters seem bloodless and ghostly, for all the fury of their indicated lives, all style and tone and suggestion. It is into this section that Toomer's finest poems are set—''Song of the Son,'' ''Georgia Dusk,'' ''Portrait in Georgia''—poems which reveal a great deal about his viewpoint and method. They are the most freely experimental Negro poems of the generation, far freer even than Langston Hughes' games with the rhythms of jazz and conversation. They view Southern Negro life with a chilling objectivity (''so objective he might not be a Negro,'' an early critic prophetically observed). Common things are seen as if through a strangely neurotic vision, transformed into his own kind of nightmare.

> Hair—braided chestnut, coiled like a lyncher's rope,
> Eyes—fagots,
> Lips—old scars, or the first red blisters,
> Breath—the last sweet scent of cane,
> And her slim body, white as the ash of black flesh after
>   flame.

In ''Song of the Son'' he tries to identify himself with the Georgia soil, but the very effort makes clear his distant view; the view of a sophisticated surrealist among an alien peasantry, a peasantry he transforms into something duskily primeval.

> O Negro slaves, dark purple ripened plums,
> Squeezed, and bursting in the pine-wood air,
> Passing, before they stripped the old tree bare
> One plum was saved for me, one seed becomes
>
> An everlasting song, a singing tree,
> Caroling softly souls of slavery,
> What they were, and what they are to me,
> Caroling softly souls of slavery.

The prose pieces of the second section support this view, though now his bony surrealist's objectivity is transferred to Northern urban Negroes. In the two key stories, ''Box Seat'' and ''Bona and Paul,'' he runs hot wires of anti-realism beneath a surface of realistic events, somewhat in the manner of Malcolm Lowry or John Hawkes, to imply a strange neurotic derangement in his characters. It is primarily a matter of imagery:

> Through the cement floor her strong roots sink
> down. They spread under the asphalt streets.
> Dreaming, the streets roll over on their bellies,
> and suck their glossy health from them. Her
> strong roots sink down and spread under the
> river and disappear in blood-lines that waver
> south. Her roots shoot down. Dan's hands fol-
> low them. Roots throb. . . .

The long story ''Kabnis'' that makes up the third part is crafted of nervous images and a strong sense of interior pain. The underground cellar symbolism is disturbing, as is, again, the utter objectivity of the narration. But the story drifts off into a hazy poetic incoherence, and—like most of the book, finally—is too insubstantial to be remembered. For all that, the book should really be allowed to come back into print. (pp. 52-60)

> *David Littlejohn, ''Before 'Native Son': The Renaissance and After,'' in his* Black on White: A Critical Survey of Writing by American Negroes, *Grossman Publishers, 1966, pp. 39-65.*

RICHARD LEDERER

[*In the following excerpt, Lederer discusses didacticism and aestheticism in protest sonnets by Claude McKay and Countee Cullen.*]

In literary criticism and the teaching of English, we often draw a useful distinction between didatic art and literary art. The first, we say, gives the impression that its purpose precedes its process, that an initial contention has been embodied in concrete terms. The weakness that threatens didactic art is that if the sole function of the process of the work is to embody its thesis, a fleshless, bloodless skeleton may well be the result.

Literary art attempts to reflect faithfully the complexities of life as it is actually experienced. What conclusions the literary artist may draw do not appear to be anterior; rather, they take their origins from the process in which they are latent. But the literary artist who lacks purpose or theme may create a corpse with all blood and tissue but no backbone, activity without direction. The four Harlem Renaissance sonnets ["If We Must Die" and "The White House" by Claude McKay and "Yet I Do Marvel" and "From the Dark Tower" by Countee Cullen]. . . exemplify the contrasts between the didactic and the literary, as well as the strengths and weaknesses inherent in each mode.

Coming on the outer beat of jazz and the inner beat of black pride and self-assertion, the Harlem Renaissance was an exhilarating literary movement that filled the 1920s with artistic outpourings, especially of poetry and the novel. Two of the poets at the very core of this Renaissance were Claude McKay and Countee Cullen.

Indeed, many scholars date the beginning of the Harlem Renaissance from the publication of McKay's "If We Must Die" in *Liberator* in 1919. McKay's protest sonnet gained additional fame when Winston Churchill quoted from it as a climax of his oration before the joint houses of Congress, as he sought to draw the United States into the common effort of World War II. McKay's "The White House" is a companion piece. . . . (p. 219)

In *Dark Symphony*, James Emanuel and Theodore Gross summarize McKay's fame as a poet:

> McKay's most enduring poems are his sonnets. . . . The subject of his finest poems varies, but the theme of protest is consistent and the moods of anger, frustration, or lament are pervasive; in all of these poems McKay insists that Negroes acknowledge and protest their common suffering, that they assert their dignity and "like men . . . face the murderous, cowardly pack, / Pressed to the wall, dying, but fighting back!"

"If We Must Die" and "The White House" possess clear strengths. To a remarkable degree McKay has been able to resolve the apparent paradoxes inherent in the term "protest sonnet." At times, McKay translates his aggressive emotions into forceful meters. Sound certainly echoes sense in the eleventh line of "If We Must Die":

> And fór their thóusand blóws deál óne deáth-blów!

And there is a quiet anger to the concluding couplet of "The White House":

> Oh, I must keep my heart inviolate
> Against the potent poison of your hate!

A second strength is simply that McKay grabs many . . . students with his furious "tell it like it is" (as they interpret it) style. Here is a poet who is a true revolutionary, who doesn't get hung up on aesthetic frills, who is "functional as a steel cable."

Then there are the weaknesses, first articulated by Harlem Renaissance critic William Stanley Braithwaite, who recognized McKay as "a genius meshed in a dilemma," at times writing with "wistful, sympathetic passion," at times the "strident propagandist." Indeed, the small souled declamation of the "strident propagandist" shrieks throughout the two sonnets. Churchill may well have felt a kinship with the blustering Britishisms of lines like "O kinsmen! we must meet the common foe! / Though far outnumbered let us show us brave, / . . . What though before us lies the open grave?" in "If We Must Die." And even if we grant some of this stiffness of syntax to McKay's Jamaican heritage and upbringing, what are we to make of the windy suspirations of "The White House": "And passion rends my vitals as I pass" and "Deep in my wrathful bosom sore and raw."

Most crucial, "If We Must Die" and "The White House" are remarkably devoid of concrete imagery and context. Only the hog similitude in the first and the image of the shut door in the second offer us any visual or tactile sense of setting or thesis. McKay tells all and shows little. As Cleanth Brooks and Robert Penn Warren, in *Understanding Poetry* point out in their analysis of Shelley's "Indian Serenade" ("I die! I faint! I fail!"), the characteristic danger of this kind of direct, intense poetry "is that the reader may feel that the statements are overstatements—merely absurd exaggerations." The historical context of "If We Must Die" is the vicious race riots of 1919, but that is hardly evident in the poem itself. The wounds that McKay exposes in his two sonnets speak to the reader like red mouths, but the hurt that suffuses Countee Cullen's "Yet Do I Marvel" and "From the Dark Tower" touch more deeply because that hurt emerges forcefully from a context of living images.

Countee Cullen felt that "good poetry is a lofty thought beautifully expressed." "Yet Do I Marvel" and "From the Dark Tower," also included in *Black Voices*, embody such a philosophy. The first, "Cullen's most famous and perhaps most representative poem," expresses the dilemma of the black artist in America. Cullen doubts not that God could, if He wished, explain the deepest paradoxes of our existence—the sightless, underground life of the mole; the fleshly mortality of man, fashioned in God's image; and the absurd rituals of Tantalus and Sisyphus. Yet the speaker still marvels that God could "make a poet black and bid him sing," that in a world of ugly prejudice God could ask a black man or woman to raise songs of beauty, that in a world of white deafness, God could impel a black artist to communicate.

The three quatrains lead nicely into the couplet. The images of the buried mole and Tantalus and Sisyphus subtly but unmistakably suggest the underground world in which the black reaches for the forbidden fruits of freedom, only to have them sway from his grasp, a world in which he is sentenced to absurd labor with no metaphysical meaning.

Cullen's Italian sonnet, "From the Dark Tower" published in 1927 with "Yet Do I Marvel" in *On These I Stand*, also illustrates his talent for marrying theme with process. The octave paints the Negro's plight with images of planting and music-making. Cullen states clearly that the enslavement of black people will not last forever. The sestet consists of three couplets, the first a striking metaphor of Negritude:

> The night whose sable breast relieves the stark,
> White stars is no less lovely being dark,

Countee Cullen. Schomburg Center for Research in Black Culture, The New York Public Library, Astor, Lenox and Tilden Foundations.

If one of the functions of poetry is to make rich what at first seems to be simple, then Cullen enhances the art of poetry in the last four lines. Here he returns to the imagery of planting, seeds, and fruits, and invests that imagery with a rich complexity and suggestiveness:

> And there are buds that cannot bloom at all
> In light, but crumple, piteous, and fall;
> So in the dark we hide the heart that bleeds,
> And wait, and tend our agonizing seeds.

Inevitably, Cullen's detractors find him too precious. In *Black on White,* critic David Littlejohn labels Cullen

> a detached exquisite, a builder of poems, crafting elegant little reliquaries for his themes. The race protest poems, in particular, come out sounding too frail and wood-windy, too mellow and suave [see excerpt above].

My personal response is to suspect that those who make such charges may be injecting political philosophy into their aesthetic criteria. In an age of sinuous militancy, it is easy to disparage Cullen because he does not call for action. In an age of unabashedly functional and revolutionary literature, it is easy to dismiss a "mere" lament as "detached" and "frail." But Cullen's poetry *is* action. While McKay stumbles over archaisms and syntactic potholes, Cullen marries medium with message and speaks articulately, as a whole artist and person, to the American consciousness.

Claude McKay has heated his poems at the fires of his convictions. But when he has finished, his works have cooled because they seem so removed from their source. Having examined the two didactic sonnets we have chosen, what do we know of the man Claude McKay? Very little: we sense him only as an abstract embodiment of the pride and anger of his race.

In contrast is the literary art of Countee Cullen. Here the artist has heated his convictions at the fires of his poetry. And so Cullen's works glow apart, generating their own heat from within. Despite the doubts that Cullen voices in the concluding couplet of "Yet Do I Marvel," he is indeed a poet, he is indeed black, and he does indeed sing. (pp. 221-23)

> Richard Lederer, *"The Didactic and the Literary in Four Harlem Renaissance Sonnets," in* English Journal, *Vol. 62, No. 2, February, 1973, pp. 219-23.*

CHERYL A. WALL

[In the following excerpt Wall examines works by several women writers of the Harlem Renaissance.]

[The] exciting atmosphere [of the Harlem Renaissance] stirred the interest of Black women as well as Black men. To a degree even greater than Black male writers, Black women had few models. Although Phillis Wheatley had been the heroine of the first chapter of Afro-American literary history, few nineteenth-century Black women had followed her lead. Of those who had, most printed their poems and novels privately. Only Frances Watkins Harper, an abolitionist and feminist as well as poet and novelist, achieved comparatively widespread recognition. Proportionately few slave narratives, the most important genre of nineteenth-century Afro-American literature, were written by women. By contrast, the most prolific novelist of the Harlem Renaissance was Jessie Fauset, whose four books were published over a ten-year period. Nella Larsen's novels were frequently reviewed and praised. For Zora Neale Hurston, the twenties were years of apprenticeship. Today her work is being rediscovered and acclaimed and she is being accorded her rightful place as a major writer of the period. The Harlem Renaissance was certainly not a male phenomenon.

As in other cultural awakenings, the renaissance produced more versifiers than poets, and a large number of these were women. No woman rivaled the achievement of Langston Hughes or Countee Cullen. Only in music did women and men share equal billing; Bessie Smith's reputation is as lustrous as that of any artist of the period. The twenties marked the heyday of classic blues singers, all of whom were female. Free of the burdens of an alien tradition, a Bessie Smith could establish the standard of her art; in the process she would compose a more honest poetry than any of her literary sisters'. They lacked the connection to those cultural traditions which shaped Smith's art; nonetheless, some produced work which "signified." The work of the greatest signifier, Zora Neale Hurston, was born, like Bessie's, from folk tradition and on occasion even from performance.

Nathan Huggins has described the debilitating effect on their art of Black writers' self-consciousness; this affected no group as severely as the female poets of the Harlem Renaissance. Their poems reflect far less of the race consciousness characteristic of their male counterparts. To understand their poems it is necessary to understand more about the context in which they were written. Black women were doubly oppressed, as Blacks and as women, and they were highly aware of the degrading stereotypes commonly applied to them. Some idea of the mood of the New Negro woman may be drawn from an essay by Elise Johnson McDougald who wrote;

> She [the Negro woman] is conscious that what is left of chivalry is not directed toward her. She realizes that the ideals of beauty, built up in the fine arts, have excluded her almost entirely. Instead, the grotesque Aunt Jemimas of the street-car advertisements, proclaim only an ability to serve without grace or loveliness. Nor does the drama catch her finest spirit. She is most often used to provoke the mirthless laugh of ridicule; or to portray feminine viciousness or vulgarity not peculiar to Negroes. This is the shadow over her.

This speaks to the negative images that defined Black women as mammies, mulattoes, and whores. The whore image was most vicious because it was the most difficult to defend oneself against; its victims conformed to no easily distinguishable physical type. It was fairly easy to know who was not a mulatto even if it was difficult to say for sure who was. In a society reluctant to recognize sexuality in most women: Black women were burdened with an almost exclusively sexual identity. Part of the conservatism found in the writings of the poets of the period reflects a determination not to conform in even the slightest manner to the hateful stereotypes. Certain subjects, particularly sex, were taboo, and the language was mostly genteel.

The best known poet of the period, Georgia Douglas Johnson, was born in 1886 in Atlanta, a self-described "little yellow girl." After graduating from Atlanta University, she continued her education at the Oberlin Conservatory. Johnson soon gave up her early ambition to become a composer. She had been working as a schoolteacher when President Taft appointed her husband recorder of deeds in Washington, D.C.; for years this post was the chief patronage plum offered the nation's Black politicians. The Johnson home was a favorite meeting place for young writers; Zora Neale Hurston was among those who participated in the literary discussions held there. Johnson's relatively high social status and educational accomplishment were typical of Black women writers of the day.

Johnson was the most conventional and popular of the women poets. Her supporters included the most respected literary men of her generation: William Stanley Braithwaite, W. E. B. DuBois, and Alain Locke wrote the introductions to her three volumes of poems. Perhaps, as the author of "I Want to Die While You Love Me," hers was considered the true voice of femininity. In any case, this became her most frequently anthologized poem:

> I want to die while you love me,
> While yet you hold me fair,
> While laughter lies upon my lips
> And lights are in my hair.
>
> I want to die while you love me,
> I could not bear to see,
> The glory of this perfect day,
> Grow dim—or cease to be.

> I want to die while you love me.
> Oh! who would care to live
> Till love has nothing more to ask,
> And nothing more to give?
>
> I want to die while you love me,
> And bear to that still bed
> Your kisses, turbulent, unspent,
> To warm me when I'm dead.

This regular meter and rhyme are characteristic of Johnson's work, as are the inverted syntax and poetic diction. Love is her favorite subject, rivaled somewhat by religion, and always treated sentimentally. While her poems are all derivative in the extreme, it is not difficult to see why they won her a popular following.

Some of the pressures operating in the lives of the women poets are illustrated by the fact that Johnson's first book of poems, *The Heart of a Woman,* published in 1918, contained no poems about Black life. Johnson's explanation for this, and evidently she felt compelled to proffer one, was that she wished to attract attention to her work using "universal" themes before she presented any poems with racial subject matter. Even in her second book, *Bronze,* racial references are oblique. Like Countee Cullen, Johnson feared the consequences of being labelled "a Negro poet." It is fully understandable that she would hesitate to experiment with language or theme, or in any way reject a tradition that had not yet admitted any Black woman— or man, for that matter. Her compromise necessarily yielded inferior verse.

A less popular but far more interesting poet was Anne Spencer (1882-1975), who began publishing during the renaissance years although she had long written poems for her private pleasure. Spencer was encouraged in her efforts by James Weldon Johnson, then field secretary of the NAACP and himself an important poet. At Johnson's suggestion, many Black writers began to make stopovers in Lynchburg, Virginia, Spencer's home, during their travels South; thus Spencer was kept abreast of ideas and trends in the New Negro movement. Johnson also arranged for the publication of Spencer's poems. Beginning with his seminal anthology, *The Book of American Negro Poetry,* which appeared in 1922, Spencer's poems became a staple of almost every major anthology of Black American poetry published through the 1950s. Still her poems were not collected into a volume until 1977.

Spencer used the traditions of English poetry, but she was not a conventional poet. Her best poems remain fresh and strikingly original. One of these, "At the Carnival," offers a finely hued, evocative description of a tawdry street fair. Onlookers like "the limousine lady" and "the bull-necked man," "the unholy incense" of the sausage and garlic booth, the dancing tent where "a quivering female-thing gestured assignations," and the crooked games of chance combine to produce an atmosphere of unrelieved ugliness and depravity. Yet the possibility of beauty exists even here, in the person of a young female diver, the "Naiad of the Carnival Tank." Her presence transforms the scene. Usually Spencer's references to reality are much more indirect; she rarely used racial themes in her poetry. An autobiographical statement she composed for Countee Cullen's anthology, *Caroling Dusk,* suggests the reason: "I write about the things I love. But have not civilized articulation for the things I hate. I proudly love being a Negro woman—it's so involved and interesting. *We* are the PROBLEM—the great national game of TABOO." Spencer's words reveal a tension that she never reconciled, aesthetically at least, and her poems contain few clues to their author's racial identity. But Spencer's poems evince a richness of imagery and verbal wit that render the epithet ''lady poet'' as wholly inappropriate for her as it is inevitable for Georgia Douglas Johnson.

Johnson and Spencer were considerably older than the best known New Negro poets, and neither lived in Harlem, which set the tone for so much of the literature. Perhaps as a result, their poetry is far from characteristic of the period as a whole. Younger women, like Gwendolyn Bennett and Helene Johnson, reveal a more typical race consciousness and a stronger empathy with the rhythms of Black urban life. In ''To a Dark Girl'' Gwendolyn Bennett projects positive images of Black womanhood:

> I love you for your brownness
> And rounded darkness of your breast.
> I love you for the breaking sadness in your voice
> And shadows where your wayward eye-lids rest.
>
> Something of old forgotten queens
> Lurks in the lithe abandon of your walk
> And something of the shackled slave
> Sobs in the rhythm of your talk.
>
> Oh, little brown girl, born for sorrows mate
> Keep all you have of queenliness,
> Forgetting that you once were slave,
> And let your full lips laugh at Fate!

Bennett's speaker echoes central themes of the period: the celebration of Blackness and the affirmation of an African heritage. But in choosing to make only vague references to the historical past, in relying on the simplistic contrast between queen and slave, she fails to make a memorable poetic statement even as she reinforces a necessary political one. Even when exploring racial themes Bennett chose not to employ characteristically Black language. Compare her poem to Nikki Giovanni's wildly inventive ''Ego Tripping'' which is also a tribute to Black women set in a historical context, but which is the work of a poet secure enough to experiment with language as boldly as she can.

The one female poet of the Harlem Renaissance who was inspired by the speech patterns of the newly urbanized migrants was Helene Johnson, whose ''Poem'' is immediately identifiable as belonging to the era:

> Little brown boy,
> Slim, dark, big-eyed,
> Crooning songs to your banjo
> Down at the Lafayette—
> Gee, boy, I love the way you hold your head,
> High sort of and a bit to one side,
> Like a prince, a jazz prince. And I love
> Your eyes flashing, and your hands,
> And your patent-leathered feet,
> And your shoulders jerking the jig-wa.
> And I love your teeth flashing,
> And the way your hair shines in the spotlight
> Like it was the real stuff.
> Gee, brown boy, I loves you all over.
> I'm glad I'm a jig. I'm glad I can
> Understand your dancin' and your
> Singin', and feel all the happiness
> And joy and don't care in you.
> Gee, boy, when you sing, I can close my ears
> And hear tom toms just as plain.

> Listen to me, will you, what do I know
> About tom toms? But I like the word, sort of,
> Don't you? It belongs to us.
> Gee, boy, I love the way you hold your head,
> And the way you sing, and dance,
> And everything.
> Say, I think you're wonderful. You're
> Allright with me,
> You are.

This is an exuberant celebration of Black culture during the 1920s. Johnson's use of free verse and Harlem slang liberate her poem. The Lafayette Theater was a Harlem landmark and it featured vaudeville entertainment by and for Blacks; its productions were both like and unlike the string of Broadway successes initiated by the legendary ''Shuffle Along.'' The audience here had a proprietary interest in the entertainment. In depicting a banjo-playing ''jazz prince,'' Johnson deftly suggests the legacy of slavery and its positive impact on a freer, more assertive period. She reclaims the banjo as a racial symbol, discarding its stereotypically servile associations. Likewise, she makes the singing, dancing Black man a positive figure, rather than the object of ridicule and condescension. Her speaker's self-consciousness about the word *tom toms* indicates Johnson's sensitivity to the dangers of exotic primitivism. This poet was not swept away by the atavistic currents of the time; her vision is securely rooted in urban reality.

Gwendolyn Bennett and Helene Johnson were rather late arrivals on the Harlem scene. Bennett's loyalties were divided between poetry and painting, and Helene Johnson was so young that she was scarcely taken seriously. Both published relatively few poems. Better known and more typical of the women of the period was the poetry of Jessie Fauset. (pp. 75-80)

Through her work on *The Crisis* and her personal acquaintance with writers of the Harlem Renaissance, Jessie Fauset emerged as an important figure in the Harlem literary community. Although it could pay very little, *The Crisis* was a major showcase for Black writers; among its other functions, it allowed them to become well known enough to attract the interest of White editors and publishers. As literary editor, Fauset decided what poetry and fiction would appear. Her literary tastes were far less conservative than those of DuBois, and she saw to it that *The Crisis* reflected a broad spectrum of the Black literature of the day. For example, it was Jessie Fauset who first received and read ''The Negro Speaks of Rivers'' in 1921. After showing the poem to DuBois, she wrote to Langston Hughes and thereby initiated a relationship that was to last throughout the decade. Years later, Hughes asserted that ''Jessie Fauset at the *Crisis,* Charles Johnson at *Opportunity,* and Alain Locke in Washington, were the three people who midwifed the so-called New Negro literature into being. Kind and critical—but not too critical for the young—they nursed us along until our books were born.'' Fauset took an active interest in the careers of young authors, lending advice and encouragement, and, like Georgia Douglas Johnson, opening her home as a salon where writers could share ideas and fellowship. Her solicitude was appreciated. In his memoir *A Long Way from Home,* McKay wrote of Fauset: ''All the radicals liked her, although in her social viewpoint she was away over on the other side of the fence.''

Unfortunately Fauset's own writing lacks the creative spark she admired and nurtured in others. The subject of most of her poems is love and the tone is usually ironic. It is not irony like that found in the blues however. The personae of Fauset's *vers de societé* sound more like the worldly wise lady of T. S. Eliot's "Portrait." Fauset's penchant for French titles strengthens this effect and places the poetry in what amounts to cultural limbo. Consider "La Vie C'est la Vie," her most often anthologized poem:

> On summer afternoons I sit
> Quiescent by you in the park,
> And idly watch the sunbeams gild
> And tint the ash-trees' bark.
>
> Or else I watch the squirrels frisk
> And chaffer in the grassy lane;
> And all the while I mark your voice
> Breaking with love and pain.
>
> I know a woman who would give
> Her chance of heaven to take my place;
> To see the love-light in your eyes,
> The love-glow on your face!
>
> And there's a man whose lightest word
> Can set my chilly blood afire;
> Fulfillment of his least behest
> Defines my life's desire.
>
> But he will none of me, nor I
> Of you. Nor you of her. 'Tis said
> The world is full of jests like these,—
> I wish that I were dead.

This poem moves carefully from the serenity of the first stanza to the agony and frustration of the last. On first reading, the concluding line is indeed shocking and affecting; the poem's sentiments have obvious popular appeal. But "La Vie C'est la Vie" has serious flaws. The first two stanzas need to move slowly if the contrast between external calm and inner turmoil is to be made clear, but each line should advance the poem's meaning. "Or else I watch the squirrels frisk / And chaffer in the grassy lane" adds little. The language shifts uneasily from the overly literary ("chaffer," "behest") to the mundanely popular ("love-light in your eyes," "love-glow on your face," and "set my chilly blood afire"). Although the poem may seem overly melodramatic in a setting of scholarly analysis, it is not so in the context of real-life experience. Consequently, it has retained a measure of appeal.

On the whole, Fauset's poetry is derivative in content and form; and although one recognizes that her love and command of the French language were genuine, her use of French phrases and titles in her poetry seems contrived. The poems seem intended to demonstrate their author's personal refinement rather than to gain appreciation for their own sake. Her self-proclaimed aim to tell "the truth about us" placed a similarly heavy burden on her fiction. Angered by the preponderance of degrading stereotypes about Black life generally and Black women in particular, she wanted to show that Black people were everything the stereotpyes said they could not be: intelligent and cultured, noble and respectable. The result was a strongly idealized portrait as distorted as the negative portrayals it attempted to displace. (pp. 81-3)

In many studies of the Harlem Renaissance, the names of Jessie Fauset and Nella Larsen (1893-1964) are closely linked. They are said to belong to the "rear guard" of the period, the keepers and defenders of the Black middle class. In some respects the style of their personal lives was similar. Like Fauset, Larsen was part of that elite group of Blacks, well educated and financially secure, whose posture was—in critic Hoyt Fuller's

sardonic phrase—"aggressively bourgeois." In dress, manner, and language, there was little to distinguish them from their White counterparts. Yet perhaps because she lacked Fauset's family connections, Larsen always remained somewhat estranged from the clannish Harlem bourgeoisie. Moreover, she scorned purpose novels, just as she scoffed at the often sententious rhetoric of racial uplift. She was attracted instead to psychological fiction and created characters who were far more complex and believable than Fauset's. Although it was little understood by her contemporaries, Larsen was as interested in exploring the effects of sexism as of racism; thematically, her writing remains remarkably fresh. (pp. 84-5)

Larsen's second novel, *Passing* (1929, has usually been described as the best fictional treatment of its very minor subject. Two characters, Irene Redfield and Clare Kendry, dominate the novel; both are attractive, affluent, and able to "pass." Irene identifies with Blacks, choosing to "pass" only for occasional social convenience, while Clare has moved completely into the White world. The trite plot unfolds; Clare, seeking thrills as much as identity, begins to make furtive trips to Harlem. Her White husband eventually follows and discovers her secret. Clare Kendry falls through a window to her death. However melodramatically, Larsen continues to survey the options open to supposedly privileged women and finds them wanting. So much energy devoted to keeping up appearances—as though their lives depended on it. Clare's life clearly did, and for others, relying on husbands for fine things, security, even identity, keeping up appearances was serious business indeed.

Genuine though it was, Larsen's talent bore relatively little fruit. Despite the critical success of her two novels and the Guggenheim Fellowship she was awarded in 1930, she subsequently published only one short story. Any number of nonliterary reasons have been proposed for Larsen's silence; intriguing though they are, they are so far unverified. That she had not solved several key literary problems is demonstrable. In both novels, Larsen's style is disturbingly flat, the dialogue often painfully stilted. On occasion the language is so studied in its sophistication that the characters sound like actors in a drawing room drama. When Larsen expanded the perimeters of her fiction beyond the insular middle-class world, her failure to accurately reproduce speech made her Alabama peasants unconvincing. A more fundamental problem is her inability to transcend the inhibiting convention of the "tragic mulatto." In *Quicksand*, where Helga's racial identity serves a thematic function as an emblem of "double consciousness," Larsen is able to work within the convention without being overwhelmed by it. In *Passing* though, where Clare Kendry's situation follows the pattern of the convention—the victim caught forever betwixt and between until she finds in death the only freedom she can know—the inevitable melodrama of the "tragic mulatto" weakens the credibility of the narrative. (pp. 88-9)

In a period when many Afro-American male intellectuals hoped to immerse themselves in the Black folk tradition, Zora Neale Hurston represented that tradition in the flesh. Born in the all-Black town of Eatonville, Florida, she was one of the few renaissance figures to know the rural folk experience firsthand. The stories, superstitions and songs of her childhood remained a vital part of her experience and informed everything she wrote: short stories, essays, folklore studies, plays, and novels. Hurston had studied anthropology at Barnard, and she liked to describe herself as "a literary anthropologist." Aesthetically through her fiction and scientifically through her ethnological studies, she sought to communicate the beauty and complexity of Black folk life. The stories she published in the 1920s, her first two novels, and the book of folklore *Mules and Men,* all recreated the world she had known in Eatonville. It was a world she wanted to explain and celebrate. Hurston described the rural customs and folkways with affection and respect. Drawing on Southern Black speech patterns, she shaped a literary language rich in wit and metaphor. Of particular interest in her fiction are the vividly realized female characters distinguished by their independence, inner strength, and common sense. Hurston believed she had discoverd a set of characters and situations unexplored in American literature. In her best work, she made them come alive in the reader's consciousness. Privately, Zora Hurston was an intense, dynamic woman who found it increasingly difficult to play the roles society imposed on her color and sex. Her behavior, especially during the Harlem Renaissance years, can most aptly be described by the Black English word *bodacious.* Needless to say, it sometimes evoked confused and bitter reactions from her fellows.

The 1920s were years of apprenticeship for Zora Neale Hurston. In courageous pursuit of the education she believed would free her, she was in 1920 a student at Howard University. Hurston had to work to support herself, and she could only attend classes intermittently. Nevertheless her talent and vibrant personality attracted the notice of Alain Locke, professor of philosophy, Rhodes Scholar, and a major catalyst of the nascent New Negro movement. Locke invited her to join The Stylus, a select campus writing club. The literary training at Howard inspired her to develop a voice but provided few useful models. Her first story, "John Redding Goes to Sea," was plainly amateurish; still Charles Johnson, editor of *Opportunity,* recognized Hurston's potential and asked for more material. She sent him "Drenched in Light," which became her first published piece. The story describes an encounter between an innocent and vivacious little Black girl and a somewhat jaded White couple. The woman is pleased, because "I want a little sunshine to soak into my soul. I need it." And the girl Isis is happy, because "for the first time in her life, she felt herself appreciated." While one can accept Isis's happiness at feeling "understood," it seems incumbent on Hurston to point out the limitations of this new understanding. Instead she seems oblivious to them. On another level, "Drenched in Light" echoes an attitude common in the twenties: Blacks in their childlike simplicity and gaiety could restore to Whites their seemingly lost capacity for joy and unencumbered emotion. Hurston, by drawing a child character, makes the myth somewhat less patronizing, but the artificiality of the story reflects the basic wrongheadedness of the idea.

Hurston's situation was inherently problematic. She had a sincere commitment to express the moral and aesthetic value of the folk culture that had nurtured her youth. Superficially, the *Zeitgeist* of the twenties welcomed a voice like hers; however, the prevailing myth of the exotic primitivism of Blacks distorted what she had to say. She persevered. Between 1925 and 1927 she wrote a series of short stories and occasional essays, all of which evince a consistent attempt to make her Eatonville experiences accessible to literature. The story "Sweat" is by far the best of Hurston's apprentice efforts. It prefigures several of the major elements in her mature work: the theme of marital conflict, a concern with the exploitation of Black women, a rural setting, and a liberal sprinkling of Negro dialect. Here no simplistic encounters between Blacks and Whites mar the credibility of the narrative, and Hurston invokes a reality that Bessie Smith's admirers would verify. (pp. 93-4)

Because of her style and subject, Hurston became associated with the so-called Young Turks of the renaissance. As one of their spokesmen, Wallace Thurman, explained: "They were interested in people who still retained some individual race qualities and who were not totally white American in every respect save color of skin." Oddly enough, even among those who shared a like literary sensibility, Zora Neale Hurston's reputation rested upon her gifts of bon vivant, raconteur, and wit—as performer rather than writer. She loved to regale audiences with the songs and stories of Eatonville; Arna Bontemps would later remark that her performances became part of the lore of Harlem. According to Langston Hughes, she was "certainly the most amusing" of the Harlem literati. In his memoir, *The Big Sea,* he recalls how Hurston once moved into an apartment and asked her friends to furnish it for her. At the housewarming, realizing that she had forgotten to request forks, she proclaimed it a *hand* chicken party. On another occasion, finding herself broke as usual and late for a downtown appointment, she walked to a Harlem subway station. She was stopped by a blind beggar holding out his cup: "'Please help the blind! A nickel for the blind!'' 'I need the money worse than you today,' said Hurston taking five cents out of his cup. 'Lend me this! Next time, I'll give it back.' And she went on downtown."

What is clear from the numerous "Zora stories" recounted by her contemporaries is that Hurston exemplified the Afro-American oral tradition. But while that tradition could mold the blues artistry of Bessie Smith, it was not in itself sufficient to sustain a literary voice. To become a creator as well as a performer, Hurston required an additional perspective. She found it in the study of anthropology. Upon enrolling at Barnard in 1925, Hurston had come under the influence of Franz Boas, the then preeminent American anthropologist. He and colleagues Gladys Reichard and Ruth Benedict gave Hurston a profoundly altered view of her Eatonville past. No longer were her Florida neighbors simply good storytellers, whose values were admirable, superstitions remarkable, and humor penetrating. As such, they had been well suited for local color fiction, but now they were part of cultural anthropology; scientific objects who could and should be studied for their academic value. The impact of this revelation was stunning. Hurston had seemingly found her singular mission. She was the one who would locate the folkways of Eatonville in what Benedict would later define as "patterns of culture." Anthropology was the tool with which the apparently immovable contradiction which stymied other Black intellectuals including Locke, James Weldon Johnson, and DuBois—that Blacks were the same as other Americans, yet different—could be resolved. In anthropology, the resolution was obvious. Particular cultural differences existed between Blacks and Whites, but all were bound in the same human condition. Blacks were neither exotic nor primitive. They had simply selected different customs from Benedict's "arcs of human behavior." By the time she graduated from Barnard in 1928, Hurston had done six months of field work, the preliminary research on which her pioneering *Mules and Men* would be based.

From 1927 to 1932, Hurston devoted all her energies to her work as a social scientist. She made long expeditions to Florida sawmill camps, Louisiana bayous, and Bahamian plantations, recording the folktales, songs, children's games, prayers and sermons, and hoodoo practices of the rural Black community. Hurston's writing conveys the extraordinary excitement she felt at being able to legitimize Black folk experiences from "shoutin' to signifyin'." Thrilled by her discoveries and im-

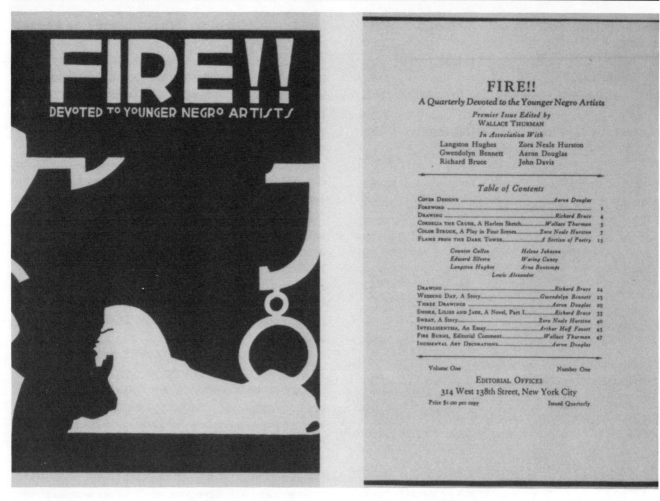

Cover and table of contents of the sole issue of Fire!!

patient with the prolonged process of readying material for scholarly publication, she first presented the folklore in a series of theatrical productions. These concerts, variously entitled "From Sun to Sun," "All de Livelong Day," and "Singin Steel," were given throughout the country, and Hurston performed parts in them herself. In an article, "Characteristics of Negro Expression," she had written that "every phase of Negro life is highly dramatised. . . . Everything is acted out." In these productions, Zora Hurston the artist demonstrated the truth of what Zora Hurston the social scientist had observed. Through her performances she was able to lay claim to her material in a far more intimate way than the academic setting could have allowed. And while Hurston was steadfast in acknowledging the benefits of her university education, she refused to let her voice be imprisoned behind ivied walls.

In the 1930s, Zora Neale Hurston bore the fruit of her labors. In the beautifully crafted novel *Their Eyes Were Watching God,* she broke the psychological chains for all time. No longer mammies, mulattoes, or whores, no longer afraid they would be mistaken for same, Black women in literature could begin to be themselves. (pp. 95-7)

> Cheryl A. Wall, *"Poets and Versifiers, Singers and Signifiers: Women of the Harlem Renaissance,"* in Women, the Arts, and the 1920s in Paris and New York, *edited by Kenneth W. Wheeler and Virginia Lee Lussier, Transaction Books, 1982, pp. 74-98.*

THEODORE KORNWEIBEL, JR.

[In the following excerpt, Kornweibel discusses theater of the Harlem Renaissance as reflected in the writings of drama critic Theophilus Lewis and examines Lewis's goal of creating a black national theater.]

The most thought-out and consistent commentary on black theater to be produced during the Harlem Renaissance was the drama criticism of Theophilus Lewis. From September 1923 to July 1927 he wrote monthly columns in the *Messenger* magazine, which dissected in honest yet sympathetic ways the foibles and shortcomings of black theater as well as the white stage that produced works on black themes. Mere criticism was not his end; rather, he intended to help provide an ideology for the development of a national black theater which would be both a source of a racial ethos and a repository of the race's genius. In so doing Lewis was articulating a primary goal of the New Negro spirit: racial self-assertion in the arts would provide the race with a cultural foundation derived from its own historical and cultural roots. Lewis's tools were alternately satire (of white stereotypes and of the lingering slave-psychology among blacks), compassion and sympathy (for the often amateurish efforts of little-theater groups), and exhortation (of playwrights to write serious drama, and of actors to demand serious and racially meaningful roles). Throughout, his columns were urbane and witty, at times biting, but never malicious. His fundamental theme, that the primary need of blacks in establishing their cultural independence was for a national black theater grounded, above all, in the works of black playwrights, was a justifiable criticism. Even as harsh a critic of the Harlem Renaissance as Harold Cruse, who seems not to have known of either Lewis or his criticism, would probably admit that Lewis was articulating the cultural nationalism that Cruse deems the key to the success or failure of independent black cultural development. (pp. 171-72)

Harlem was the black cultural capital of the country [during the 1920s], just as was New York for the nation as a whole. What passed for a national black stage (which played a circuit of New York, Philadelphia, Washington, and sometimes Chicago) had its inspiration and headquarters in Harlem. The most common and most popular type of theatrical entertainment was the musical revue; most revues played either at the Lafayette or Lincoln theaters, both white owned and operated. They usually consisted of a series of dance and musical numbers with an inevitable chorus-line of beautiful girls. The degree of excellence of acting, dance, and music, as well as taste, ran an expected full gamut. High theater it was not, but Lewis and others recognized that its best examples provided something invaluable to black audiences, if only productions composed, written, and acted by blacks.

Lewis was of two minds about the revues and low-humor comedies. Some were often cheap and tawdry, yet others could be elevating in their joy, mirth, and infectious music and dancing. They might provide absolutely no challenge to acting skills, yet still be perfect vehicles for such genuine stars as Florence Mills and Irvin Miller. The major problem with the revues was that the supply of fresh ideas and new dance combinations was easily exhausted. The programs at the Lafayette and at the Lincoln changed frequently, due to the almost insatiable demand for new revues, and the productions were not presented in repertory fashion, so that even the best-known and most-talented writers and producers borrowed shamelessly from previous successes.

A brief cataloguing of the revues noticed by Lewis from September 1923 to May 1926 (after which date he ceased, with one exception, reviewing them) gives a pictorial view of the black comedy stage in Harlem in these years. *The Sheik of Harlem,* starring Hattie King Reavis and Irvin Miller, allowed mid-1923 audiences to see "the frothy side of Harlem life" with all its foibles and vices prominently displayed, as well as a chorus of "as sweet a collection of baby vamps" as it had been the reviewer's pleasure to see in many a month. (Lewis's commentary, while not always employing flapper terminology, was usually spicy and interlarded with his admiration for the charms and beauties of the female form.) That the standard of quality was uneven at the Lafayette is evident from a later paragraph in the same review which briefly noticed a succeeding production, *Raisin' Cain,* which was "ancient and seedy stuff." Late in the same year Lewis caught *Follow Me* and thought it a poor piece, although the audiences liked it; this only proved to the reviewer how fastidious were the tastes of the Harlem show-going public. Succeeding shows reviewed were *Dinah,* with comic Irvin Miller, in late 1923, and *Come Along, Mandy,* early in 1924. Of a much higher standard of excellence was Lew Leslie's *Plantation Revue* (1924), starring Florence Mills. For this production Lewis did not reserve praise, although he attributed much of its success to Miss Mills, for whom he had unstinting admiration.

Success bred imitation, and *Club Alabam* at the Lafayette, following *Plantation Revue,* was merely a cheap replica of the former hit. Mid-1924 saw a new show by the noted comedy and music team Noble Sissle and Eubie Blake, *Chocolate Dandies,* which enjoyed considerable success and impressed Lewis as being sophisticated and urbane. The year ended with one of the most successful of all black shows of the twenties, *From Dixie to Broadway,* whose chief asset was Florence Mills. Lewis worshipped Miss Mills but was forced to admit that, on the whole, the show was an inferior production, most of which was "shoddy, garish and vulgar," with many of the ideas being "second-hand and cheap." Yet he predicted that it would make its producer, Lew Leslie, a wealthy man, and indeed the show was a great commercial success. Once again the pendulum swung to the mediocre and Lewis panned in succession *The Demi-Virgin, Pudden Jones,* and *Blackbirds of 1926.* The second reflected no credit at all on the race, in Lewis's opinion, as it continued the old association of comedy with a coal-black Negro, a jail record, and the trappings of the minstrel show. All that saved *Blackbirds* was Florence Mills; otherwise it was a rehash of older revues from which Lew Leslie had the gall to steal some songs and dance routines.

The best examples of the revue, however, served good purposes and could be justified as art. Lewis was honest enough to admit that he more often than not enjoyed the dancing, bawdy jokes, and shedding of clothes, as well as the humorous comment. He recognized the special liberties allowed by the Roaring Twenties and that its freedoms and joys might well not last:

> I look upon these musical shows and call them good. It is the business of the theater to satisfy spiritual craving. Whether the craving is refined or ethical is beside the point, so long as it's human. Since these shows satisfy a very definite and intense desire they are sound theater. So let us enjoy their verve, beauty and sin while we may, for the drear and inevitable day is coming when they will be against the law.

One revue that in early 1927 reached this higher plane was *Gay Harlem.* Unlike many of its type, this was not only entertaining but intelligent as well in its humor and poking satire. It did not display racial buffooneries and stereotypes of blacks, but portrayed in honest fashion the foibles and libertinage of black life. As such Lewis unreservedly defended its seminudity against the charge of encouraging a decline in modesty. Rather, a general societal decline in modesty had resulted in nudity on the stage. And that was precisely why the scantily clad performers were a valuable contribution to contemporary life and theater, for this was nothing less than art holding up a mirror to life. This was the musical revue at its best.

One of Theophilus Lewis's pet crusades was for an end to the belief that only light-skinned women were "beautiful." Nowhere was this color line more in evidence than in the choruses of the revues. The chorus line was often the highlight of an otherwise unspectacular production, and for many its scarcely clad, long-legged members were the main attraction of the evening's entertainment. But to see even a medium-brown girl was a rarity. The otherwise mediocre *Come Along, Mandy* had the "theatrical sensation of the decade—colored girls in the chorus!" The chorus of *Club Alabam,* however, was the usual "high yaller." And of the whole cast of *Blackbirds of 1926,* ironically, all the females but the two start actresses were "biological whites." It was thus with great pleasure and relief that Lewis caught a dance performance of the National Ethiopian Art Theater in which two of the dancers were genuinely black women. Lewis often attributed this discrimination to a psychology rooted in slavery, and it was certainly not confined to the musical stage; he was not successful in eradicating this judgment, however, and the white standard of beauty is still a burden on black performers to this day. Suffice it to say the ''New Negro'' perceived that along with a new definition of black culture would have to come new standards of aesthetics, of which color was a major problem.

The musical stage was not without importance, but Lewis, and probably any other serious student of the drama, would have insisted that it hardly served the functions of a race theater. It did provide employment for many actors and actresses and dancers, but only in the realm of comedy. The same held true for would-be playwrights: the musical stage was not the place for serious drama. And despite the protestations of James Weldon Johnson that the best musical revues broke completely with the minstrel tradition, there was certainly enough that was similar for younger critics to view it as a limited and stereotyped medium. It was clear to Lewis that a truly racial theater based on black values and rooted in the black consciousness would come about primarily through the medium of serious drama, for serious drama was the repository of a society's (or race's) collective spiritual life, culture, and character.

Some significant advances in the serious portrayal of blacks in drama were recorded by Lewis in the mid-1920s. First, there was promising activity coming from the (often short-lived) little-theater groups, of which more later. Equally as important was the occasional play, often written by a white, which presented blacks as believable and sympathetic characters and provided roles which were at the same time challenging to the competent actor, also sometimes white. Such a play was *Roseanne,* written by a white woman and starring in its original production in 1924 a white actress portraying a black character. Despite the lack of black personnel, Lewis praised it because it portrayed a believable Negro character ''without sentimentality or exaggeration.'' Of the white actress he admitted he had ''never believed a Caucasian could portray Negro feeling with such fidelity to the subject. It was simply astounding.'' Because of the truth of the whole production, Lewis felt that *Roseanne,* with the exception of Eugene O'Neill's plays on black themes, was the most significant dramatic work on black life up to that time.

Around the same period (early 1924) Lewis viewed a production by one of the little-theater groups, the Ethiopian Art Theater, entitled *The Gold Front Stores, Inc.* He credited this play with being the first full-length dramatic piece by a black playwright (Caesar G. Washington) who showed a knowledge of how to construct a believable play. The work was, surprisingly, a farce. Lewis feared that the play would not be acceptable to most other reviewers, however, because it was too genuine, it had ''too much niggerism'' in it. But this was precisely what made it an important production. The next important step he noted was taken by Eugene O'Neill in *All God's Chillun Got Wings* (mid-1924). Although Lewis thought it suffered by comparison with *The Emperor Jones,* he acknowledged that it was nonetheless a fairly authentic story in which Paul Robeson displayed some very sound acting. Lewis was of the opinion that this play was the most significant offering of the season because it showed that black people led lives, not in a vacuum, but in juxtaposition to others and to society. In addition the play gave black actors four major roles and in so doing greatly enriched black acting experience.

It was nearly two years before Lewis recorded another significant advance in black drama. This play was *Lulu Belle,* and while not perfect in either execution or conception, it presented some extremely well-drawn characters who expressed universal human emotions in a believable manner. In fact, the main character was so genuine that the white critics were confounded—he did not carry a razor, shoot craps, believe in superstition, or do anything that they believed the typical black should do. A year later, in 1927, another white-authored play was cited as an important contribution. *Earth* was ''an elaborately camouflaged Greenwich Village conception of an Uncle Tom's Cabin version of the Book of Job.'' In fact the play was nowhere near portraying black life accurately, but its conception of the classic dimensions of the Job story was faithful and spiritually moving. Lewis called it ''the best so-called Negro play since *The Emperor Jones,*'' and that was a compliment indeed. The acting was the finest he had seen from any black cast yet on Broadway, and he hoped that there would be more plays like it.

The fact that Lewis could praise several white plays for contributing significantly to black drama does not mean that he disregarded the New Negro goal of developing black playwrights in order to ensure that the race's life would be accurately portrayed. He saw this problem indeed. What the foregoing paragraphs tell us is that he was also concerned about the development of competent dramatic actors and a theater tradition at the same time. Lewis spent no little energy decrying the paucity of serious black dramatists and showed clearly how critical this was. More than once he said that the playwright was more important than the actor in the long run, and thus acting should not be developed at the expense of drama. Actors contributed little to civilization except the moment of their performance, although that might become tradition. But great drama, great plays, were enduring in tangible form. A playwright could create ''the idealization of race character which in the last analysis is the real meaning of Negro drama.'' All this meant that the first item of importance in the theater was the drama; then came acting, audience, and production. There were many sources to the problem of a lack of black dramatists—little public support, competing white drama, low public taste—all of which were valid complaints. But on occasion Lewis could not contain his disillusionment and disgust at the sorry state of black playwriting. In reviewing a play so bad he did not even name it, he noted that Charles S. Gilpin, probably the finest black actor then playing, had transformed his part into a thing of beauty. Yet why was he condemned to perform in such trash? Blacks simply would not write enough good theater to keep a fine artist like Gilpin well employed.

Another obstacle to the development of black theater was that of audience. At whom should the theater be aimed? The answer to this question depended on several variables, such as the affluence of patrons, the types of themes available, and the type of drama to be presented. In general, Lewis was distrustful of the willingness of the upper classes of black society to support meaningful theater. That group strenuously objected to the miscegenation theme of *All God's Chillun Got Wings:*

> There is a lot of talk about ''Art'' in this community nowadays. The best people are all hot for it. But when a craftsman [O'Neill] unveils his work and the best people immediately begin chattering about its propriety instead of discussing the competence of the execution one is moved to wonder whether their esthetic fervor is not bogus.

On the other hand, as Lewis admitted in a later analysis, much of the black audience was uncultured and coarse and thus many black entertainments naturally catered to this level. The result of this was that the more sensitive and imtelligent actors were driven out of the theaters. Things would be better if the higher classes attended more often and in so doing demanded a higher degree of fare. This might have the effect of raising the mean of race culture. Yet that might merely result in the type of Victorian censorship suggested in the quotation above. The fundamental problem with the upper-class or ''higher intellect'' black theater patron was that he went to the theater and often ignored his own tastes as well as the desires of the lower classes in the audience and demanded instead that the performance be geared to a set of standards alien to both—to white standards. This patron often insisted on the black theater copying the suave manners and conventions of the white theater, which at base reflected the racial experience and heritage of a different tradition. The result, Lewis noted, was sterility and artificiality.

To make a decision to cater to either portion of the potential theater clientele was difficult indeed, but Lewis recognized that the issue should not be straddled. Weighing the alternatives, he decided that to direct the appeal of the theater to a small group with relatively high but artificial standards of taste might have short-term benefits, but that in the long run it would be best to appeal to the group with lower but nonetheless genuine standards. After all, the lower group was the greater in number of a potential audience—and numbers pay. Such drama would be much more healthy than a snobbish, artificial ''high'' theater, and it would also keep more theaters in existence and provide a corps of competent performers. All this was not to say that the problems of a paucity of playwrights and of well-constructed plays and good roles would immediately cease to exist.

The weaknesses of the black theater were many, and most of them have already been touched upon. But two additional problems to which Lewis drew attention should be noted. One was the absence of actors with an understanding of the dignity of their calling. There were in fact plenty of black actors, but all too many were willing to play for low humor and obscenity. And it was plain that the black stage had more than enough low comedy already, even though Lewis could not resist taking some pride in this dubious achievement. The richness and variety of the black theater's lowest comedy, he claimed, far surpassed that found in the white theater, and in this respect the black stage enriched and helped to liberate the sexually repressed white world.

A second weakness was not unrelated to the first. It concerned the ownership and control of the theaters in Harlem. Lewis cited figures showing that white owners controlled 50 per cent of the theaters and 75 per cent of the patronage of blacks in New York. These whites were not cultured persons linked to the white stage—they were cheap vaudeville entrepreneurs and sideshow vendors. Most of the black owners were alleged to be of the same generally low character. Neither was qualified to make cultural contributions to the community. If they managed to uplift the theater it would only be because that would pay immediate profits, which was very doubtful; experimental and high-level theater was bound to lose money and would have to be underwritten by money-making popular theater. The influence of the white theater promoters was doubly pernicious; not only did they produce jaded theater, but they produced it for the tastes of voyeuristic whites who wanted black-and-tan entertainment. The wishes of the black audience were generally not considered. The lesson was clear to Lewis: ''. . . without economic autonomy the Negro stage can never become the flexible medium for the expression of the spirit of Negro people it ought to be.'' Needless to say, the domination of Harlem's theater (as well as cinema) entertainment by an alien ''cultural'' force was a major impediment to the ideology as well as the realization of independent black dramatic expression.

If Harlem's established theaters could not be depended upon to sponsor serious and probably unprofitable drama, the task then lay with little-theater groups. Lewis paid attention to such groups and was often solicitous of their efforts even in the face of very pedestrian and amateurish performances. He always managed to say something good about a particular evening's offering, for he regarded the little-theater movement as perhaps the only foundation on which a truly national black theater could be built. So even the most pathetic attempts offered some encouragement and hope.

Of the six theater groups which found mention in Lewis's columns, perhaps the most durable was the National Ethiopian Art Theater (NEAT). The first performance recorded by Lewis has already been mentioned: *The Gold Front Stores, Inc.*, which was noteworthy for being a dramatic work of competence authored by a black writer. The one-act play, however, was the more usual fare in the little theaters, and three such were reviewed from a performance in October 1924. Two of the three Lewis thought were mediocre, but one, entitled *Gooped Up*, written by a student at the NEAT school, was good in mirroring the real drama of black life. The NEAT also conducted dance classes, and it was at one of their recitals that Lewis had the pleasure of seeing a performance by genuinely black (as opposed to ''high yaller'') girls. The 1925 NEAT season closed with three one-acters, and the reviewer noted that the performances were encouraging and minus the gaucheries of previous productions. Two of the plays were of little value in themselves, but were good enough vehicles to be instructive to the actors.

The other theater groups mentioned by Lewis were the Tri-Arts Club, the Inter-Collegiate Association, the Sekondi Players, the Krigwa Players, and the Aldridge Players. The Krigwa Players Little Negro Theater was a project of W. E. B. Du Bois. In reviewing its first offering, Lewis was pleased to see that it had avoided spending all its energy on preparation and was instead getting out and actually performing. The acting could have been improved by being less reserved, but the evening was worth the time spent, since at least one of the plays (*Compromise*) proved to be a fairly serious discussion of real life, dealing with the theme of interracial, extramarital sexual relations. By the time of the opening of this group's second season Lewis was overlooking their stumbles with a ''tolerant eye.'' Around the same period the Aldridge Players put on three short plays by the black writer F. H. Wilson. Although ranging in dramatic content from fair to mediocre, they were nonetheless important because they had highly actable roles which were of great significance in building up the repertory experience so necessary for the little-theater movement. A plentiful supply of meaningful roles was more important at that early stage than fine plays.

Lewis's prescription for the health and vitality of the little-theater movement was a simple yet hard-to-achieve one: perform, perform, and perform some more. During its first year(s) of existence the most important thing was to keep putting on plays, mediocre though they may be. This would develop actors, and as they became more accomplished they would inspire dramatists to write good plays for them. And the frequent performances would create and begin to hold a public. All of this could be done without resident geniuses in either the acting or playwriting departments. Several famous white little-theater groups, Lewis noted, had succeeded without such exceptional talent. The crucial task was to develop competent acting quickly. But to do this any company would have to become at least semiprofessional. Good acting could be acquired in only two ways: hire already trained and competent professional actors; or pay resident amateurs who showed promise, so that they could afford dramatic training. In either case money was necessary. Who would provide funds? Lewis was confident that there was a segment of the population that could be induced to support such endeavors, but in order to secure its cooperation the productions of the group should be geared in their direction. That group Lewis defined as those who desired theater entertainment but were so dissatisfied with what was currently available that they would contribute toward subsidizing new theater more in accord with their tastes. But that returned the matter to the dilemma of the sophistication of the audience and its various ideas of artistic taste. There was no easy answer, and Lewis was perhaps more optimistic than was warranted; it was certainly not easy to keep a little theater alive during these years without some outside patronage or support which might or might not have strings attached.

Lewis saw the little-theater movement as a precursor and component of what he hoped would become a national black theater. To develop a race theater meant that a *national* theater must be constructed. It would have to be grounded on indigenous drama by its own playwrights or else it would become only the "sepia province of American Theater." Yet it must not isolate itself and address its appeal exclusively to black audiences. The problem lay in the nature of Harlem, where conditions were admittedly most propitious for the development of black theater. Even there only a fraction of the population, perhaps no more than five thousand, would initially support serious theater. Thus it must be on a low budget and repertory basis. It would have to educate and win its audience, and since much of that audience was conditioned by movies, the initial plays should be mostly melodrama, mysteries, and farce. But when the audience had been won over, more serious productions could be attempted. Finally, a nationwide network of several similiar repertory companies should be organized, so that productions could be exchanged. This was the stage at which a national race theater would come into being.

What was to be done about the matter of popular taste? First, the race theater would have to develop outside the houses controlled by whites. This would be relatively uncomplicated, although perhaps not too simple in execution. But the more serious problem lay in the concept of legitimacy. Lewis went to the heart of the matter when he noted that one of the fundamental causes of weakness in the black theater derived from its unwritten philosophy that the only "legitimate" theater was the white stage, particularly Broadway. The black theater had wrongly tried to excel at the things Broadway did. Negro theater had taken its instruction from the white stage, which too often portrayed blacks only in caricature. The Lafayette Players, the only permanent company of adult performers in Harlem, took their cues from Broadway and performed ten-year-old castoff plays from that stage. The Lafayette group had not only failed to encourage black playwrights but had not even kept pace with the white theaters it set out to emulate. Instead of crying for a "chance" on the white stage, Lewis asked, why not produce black drama on the black stage for black

audiences. With a contribution of a hundred dollars monthly from the five richest black churches in New York City, a resident company could employ Charles Gilpin and Paul Robeson on a regular basis and offer the finest of drama to black audiences. But did the public really want this? Aside from his own fulminations on the subject and an occasional column in *Opportunity,* Lewis claimed to have heard no complaint from the black public or cultural critics. It was not surprising, then, that the only serious attempts to create a black theater up to that time had been fostered by whites. Lewis described the result in September 1924: "What we call the Negro Theater is an anemic sort of thing that does not reflect Negro life, Negro fancies or Negro ideas. It reflects the 100 per cent American Theater at its middling and cheapest." (pp. 174-88)

The cultural ethos of the New Negro balanced two views on the subject of the race's contributions. On the one hand, blacks should strive to develop their own cultural institutions and ideals so that for the first time an accurate representation of black life would be available. In so doing the spiritual part of the racial heritage would be preserved and fostered. On the other hand, the contributions blacks made to culture would be to the whole of culture. The New Negro saw himself as contributing not only to his race, but also to American (and world) culture. It was not to be a separatist movement. Theophilus Lewis voiced these concerns, sometimes in very articulate fashion. In describing the process of enriching the racial heritage he advised that

> the Negro stage should be a vital force in the spiritual life of the race; it should constantly delight . . . and . . . exalt . . . and it should crystallize that delight and exaltation in a form worthy of being preserved as a part of our racial contribution to the general culture of mankind.

But he also saw the issue from a slightly more radical position, in which blacks would hold themselves somewhat aloof from American civilization, contributing to it, yet reserving judgment on whether or not to join it wholeheartedly. Lewis seemed to foresee the possibility of a Third World position from which dying civilizations could be viewed, but their contagion avoided. In other words, he was by no means sure that blacks should fuse themselves with white America and wholeheartedly embrace its destiny, cultural and otherwise:

> Now the Negro Problem is this: It is the question whether a youthful people living in the midst of an old and moribund civilization shall die with it or find themselves able to shake loose from its complexities and build their own culture on its ruins. . . . This condition of doubt will find its esthetic expression in dissonances of sound and color, and such explosive comedy and tragedy as results from the struggles of a passionate people to escape the restraints of the Calvinist version of the Ten Commandments.

The task for the Negro artist, then, is to observe the confusion of rusting flivvers, vanishing forests, migratory populations and expiring faiths which confronts him and reveals its meaning in a felicitous manner. He will show us, perhaps, the convulsions of a world breaking down in chaos. Perhaps the nuclei of a new world forming in incandescence. (pp. 188-89)

Theodore Kornweibel, Jr., "Theophilus Lewis and the Theater of the Harlem Renaissance," in The Harlem Renaissance Remembered: Essays, *edited by*

Arna Bontemps, Dodd, Mead & Company, 1972, pp. 171-89.

THE HARLEM RENAISSANCE AND AMERICAN SOCIETY

NATHAN IRVIN HUGGINS

[*Huggins is an American historian and critic specializing in black American history. In the following excerpt from his seminal study* Harlem Renaissance (1971), *he discusses the Harlem Renaissance artists' search for cultural identity as one facet of an attempt by American society as a whole to define its cultural character.*]

It is a rare and intriguing moment when a people decide that they are the instruments of history-making and race-building. It is common enough to think of oneself as part of some larger meaning in the sweep of history, a part of some grand design. But to presume to be an actor and creator in the special occurrence of a people's birth (or rebirth) requires a singular self-consciousness. In the opening decades of the twentieth century, down into the first years of the Great Depression, black intellectuals in Harlem had just such a self-concept. These Harlemites were so convinced that they were evoking their people's "Dusk of Dawn" that they believed that they marked a renaissance.

Historians have liked to use that word to characterize some moment when a "culture," once dormant, has been reawakened. But even the most conventional of them will confess the concept is a historical fiction, a contrivance of imaginations steeped in resurrections and similar rites of spring. Seldom, however, have the people—the subjects of such history—knowing their roles, inquired of themselves, "how goes the Renaissance?" While not so exaggerated, that was what Harlem men of culture were doing in the 1920s. (pp. 3-4)

Like others of that generation whose collective experience was World War I, Harlemites were caught up in its wake. Surely the ethnocentrism that generated self-determination as an Allied aim in that war informed a new racial awareness among blacks throughout the world. The war also forced a reevaluation of Western civilization and encouraged non-Europeans to esteem their own cultures as being as valid and civilized as Europe's. War-disillusioned white men (American and European), on the other hand, helped enhance a black self-concept through their own search for valid, authentic experience. Even before the war, Freud and the new psychology caused sophisticated people to deny the artifices of civility and manner and to seek the true self through spontaneity and the indulgence of impulse. In so far as Afro-Americans could see their own lives as being more natural and immediate than their countrymen's, they could be convinced that the mere accentuation of their characteristic spontaneity would work toward the creation of a new Negro, a new man. Indeed, if anyone doubted that the black man's time had come, he needed only look at the awakening of Mother Africa as evidenced in the recent European discoveries and appreciation of African culture and civilization. Such elements of the spirit of the age contributed to the Harlemites' view of themselves and their historic role.

While their world was different from ours—their attitudes and assumptions different—it is nevertheless familiar to us. I discovered that, when I looked through the eyes of those men who thought themselves the harbingers of the "New Negro," analogues to our own age of black self-consciousness were compelling. Their assertion of the militant self, their search for ethnic identity and heritage in folk and African culture, and their promotion of the arts as the agent which was to define and to fuse racial integrity resonate what we hear about us now, fifty years later. Black men of the 1920s, as easily as our own Afro-American contemporaries, talked of the end of Negro accommodation, of the importance of ethnic identity, of the new day a' dawning when black men would have and would wield power. Such similarities between now and then suggest fundamental characteristics of American racial life that have provoked the same questions and responses time and again. For, as all who have studied the story of the African in America will know (and as those Harlemites seemed not to know), the formulations of racial identity and culture in the 1920s were variations on earlier themes which have persisted into our own time. (pp. 6-8)

[To] speak of racial identity crisis is to distort, I have come to think. For, looking outside the confines of race, looking at the general American culture, one finds a no less persistent and recurrent demand to define American character and American culture. From Hector St. John Crevecoeur to Max Lerner, the effort to characterize "this American, this new man" has been an intense and serious national sport. Students of "American civilization" will also be familiar with the equally persistent (and compulsive) announcements of the "coming of age" of American culture. Such definitions of American character and trumpetings of cultural maturity seem necessarily repeated time after time, as if they had never occurred before. The simple matter is that Americans have been a provincial people, forever self-conscious of themselves and their society in the making, and pulled by the powerful gravity of the European civilization to which they are heir and, despite claims to independence, which they emulate. Negroes, no less than other Americans, have suffered this same condition. Even more so, in fact, for Afro-Americans have inhabited a special ethnic province within provincial America. They have been perplexed by the desire to emulate the European-entranced white American and by the equally appealing dream of self-definition through the claiming of their inheritance of African culture. But from the perspective of their ethnic province it has been impossible for black men to see how American their predicament is. White Americans and white American culture have had no more claim to self-confidence than black. The Negro has been unable to see the beam in the white man's eye for the mote in his own. For both black and white Americans art has been the more problematic because of these provincial uncertainties. (pp. 8-9)

Harlem intellectuals promoted Negro art, but one thing is very curious, except for Langston Hughes, none of them took jazz—the new music—seriously. Of course, they all mentioned it as background, as descriptive of Harlem life. All said it was important in the definition of the New Negro. But none thought enough about it to try and figure out what was happening. They tended to view it as a folk art—like the spirituals and the dance—the unrefined source for the new art. Men like James Weldon Johnson and Alain Locke expected some race genius to appear who would transform that source into *high* culture. That was, after all, the dream of Johnson's protagonist in *Autobiography of an Ex-Coloured Man* as he fancied symphonic scores based on ragtime. The same improbable will-o'-the-wisp entranced white musicians like Paul Whiteman and George Gershwin. It perplexed black musicians like James P. Johnson and Fats Waller. We now know better, but some would have

Sugar Hill, the most desirable of Harlem's neighborhoods.

said that Duke Ellington was mesmerised as well. Anyway, the promoters of the Harlem Renaissance were so fixed on a vision of *high* culture that they did not look very hard or well at jazz.

It is a real pity, because it would have been wonderful to have had contemporary accounts from curious and intelligent non-musicians of jazz in the making. We know that various versions of ragtime, New Orleans music, and the blues were being welded into a fresh musical idiom within earshot of all Harlemites. Louis Armstrong (occasionally in New York City), Jelly Roll Morton, James P. Johnson, etc., were at the prime of their creative lives. Duke Ellington, Fletcher Henderson, and Don Redman were already learning to give orchestral form to a music of improvisation and virtuosity. It is clear enough, now, that the blues were more than sad, bawdy, and entertaining songs. They were (not like spirituals) the ironic voice of free men, conscious of the unmitigating paradox of being free men and black men. Were it not for Langston Hughes, we would have almost no specific notice of that art from the Harlem writers. It is very ironic that a generation that was searching for a new Negro and his distinctive cultural expression would have passed up the only really creative thing that was going on. But then, it is not too surprising. People who are really engaged in creating a cultural renaissance are always too busy to think about the implications of what they are doing.

The black intellectuals were searching for their own identity, but they were bound up in a more general American experience

than a "Harlem Renaissance" would suggest. For black and white Americans have been so long and so intimately a part of one another's experience that, will it or not, they cannot be understood independently. Each has needed the other to help define himself. The creation of Harlem as a place of exotic culture was as much a service to white need as it was to black. So essential has been the Negro personality to the white American psyche that black theatrical masks had become, by the twentieth century, a standard way for whites to explore dimensions of themselves that seemed impossible through their own *personae*. The blackface minstrel show stylized a Negro character type that black men used to serve as a passport through white America. Yet, the mask demeaned them while it hid them. Thus the strands of identity for Afro-Americans in the 1920s were confounded in a tradition of white/black self-concept that could not be unraveled by simple proclamations of the birth of the New Negro. (pp. 10-11)

It was no mere coincidence that both Alain Locke and Van Wyck Brooks saw crisis in terms of cultural maturity. Americans have been consistently perplexed as to what culture is, what is distinctively American culture, and what of value America has contributed to Western civilization. Concern over the thinness of American culture forced many intellectuals to give continued backward glances to Europe. Sometimes the American's consciousness of Europe was ridiculed, as in the probing satire of Mark Twain, sometimes it was marked by a fascination with its richness, sophistication, and corruption, as with Henry

James. Always, it seemed culture was something alien to the fresh and rough American; always something learned, attained, achieved, never the natural gift of one's soil, one's land, one's blood.

Malcolm Cowley has made this point very well in *Exile's Return*. In its early pages Cowley explains why a group of young intellectuals around World War I felt no sense of value in their own experience and past. All of their education, as Cowley remembers, pointed them toward some other place than home. They were trained out of their regional dialects and into a colorless, school-learned Ameri-English which all of their teachers had dutifully acquired. The stuff of imagination, art, and literature was never pulled from the mysteries of their own country and the experiences of their own people. Rather, they were asked to dream of medieval European castles and English country life. It was as if the things that they could touch and see were unworthy of art and culture. Then, they were drawn to eastern colleges; fitting-rooms of culture, as Cowley remembers. Culture to the educated American had nothing to do with folk roots—one's past or one's life—rather, it was clothes that one could wear after a long process of divestment of the familial, the regional, the natural. Thus Cowley makes most understandable the feeling of uprootedness and alienation of the generation of young men who were in college, or had just finished college, around World War I. Set adrift from a past without meaning or value, or so their education had trained them to believe, they went searching for some roots in European civilization grafting themselves on to the only culture America had taught them to respect.

If anything, this alienation was more accentuated among Negro intellectuals. There had been little in the public schools or the colleges to give them a sense of their cultural past or the distinctiveness of their people. The black boy or girl who went to mixed northern schools and to white colleges could have expected little. But even the segregated southern schools provided little of their own past besides the names of heroines and heroes: Harriet Tubman, Sojourner Truth, Frederick Douglass, and of course Booker T. Washington. The fact that the line back to the past was snarled where enslavement and migration from Africa had begun made the racial past hazy, distant, and impossible to know. But even the more recent history of the Afro-American, that which could be touched and measured, seemed to provide little of the stuff for race-building. A society weaned on self-reliance and individual freedom could find little to honor in servitude, no matter how enforced. The shame that black men felt about their past was a measure of how much they had drunk up the values of the white American world around them. So they were left with the few names that had survived of the men and women who had defied oppression, achieved success in white men's terms, and who stood thus as proof that the past would not enslave blacks forever.

Shame of the past made the Negro reject much of the reality of his people's condition. In the mad rush from slavery, inferiority, and oppression into citizenship and manhood, much was garbled and confused. Those things reminiscent of the former condition—unskilled and field labor, enthusiastic religion—were to be denied. The professions (medicine, dentistry, law, the ministry, teaching, and undertaking) and business were to be embraced. One was to join the more sober Protestant denominations. It was not simply a matter of achievement or social mobility, these attainments were benchmarks measuring the distance a black man or woman had traveled from his past of chains. They were symbols which connoted to the Negro freedom and manhood. And they were not just in a few men's minds; they were built into those institutions, most of all the schools, charged with the impress of social values.

Of course, white schools transmitted "American culture," an ethnic cultural blandness—America was made up of many different peoples, but they were all the same. When the black child was well treated in such schools—not made to feel shame for his blackness—he was taught that he was like everyone else; a truth that his experience surely belied. And while Negro schools had many virtues in teaching the child that he had worth, they taught him also that he should be like white men, not like himself, and surely not like his father. It did not matter whether the teacher followed W.E.B. DuBois's philosophy of the "talented tenth" or Booker T. Washington's even more condescending notion that the Negro should prove himself acceptable as a citizen in white men's terms.

The point is not that teachers and schools were misguided or pernicious. White and black teachers gave many a young Negro his first feeling of genuine, personal worth. Rather, despite their best intended efforts they could not give to the black child a rich, dense, and mysterious sense of a past like that of traditional cultures. It was not merely that the ingredients were difficult to pull out of the American Negro's history, and that the sophistication and beauty of African cultures were not yet understood, but that the experience of American institutions worked against it. The object of American public schools was to make their charges American; which meant a rounding off of points of difference. Oriental and Jewish children were able to retain the gift of their past through special schools. But Negro children were swept into the cultural blender with other Americans, pulled into the vortex of Anglo-Saxon norms. Having no known culture to deny, the Negro was doubly damned. For when he discovered the emptiness and soullessness of the bland amalgam, or when he saw that the ultimate truth of the lie was that you had to be white, he had no place to return to. Adrift, his "shadow, so to speak, was more real to him than his personality."

Like white children, black children were taught that the speech of their fathers was not proper English speech. They were encouraged to leave behind their dialects and regional and ethnic idioms. The tales that they had heard the old folks tell were not the stuff of culture; they would read Jane Austen and Thackeray and dream of English romance. Nor were the special rhythms of their speech suitable for poetry when Keats and Shelley were the models. In time, they could learn to accept the spirituals, with their decorum and simple majesty, but never the more spirited gospel songs and surely not the profane blues. Culture was something distant and alien—generally English— to be studied, and, as Cowley remembers, fitted on like a suit of clothes. Negroes in provincial communities were introduced into Western culture by their churches. Vocal ensembles toured these towns, as well as soloists like Roland Hayes and Marian Anderson. Church members would sell tickets to a performance which would include the standard tour repertory with some spirituals. Local talent would be given a chance to perform, and there was always an elocutionist who would read from classical English literature. One would not have been surprised to find Browning Societies here and there in black communities. Of course, the experience of the people had been there all along. The folk wisdom that had sustained Afro-Americans through their most devastating trials persisted. The music in the language, the distinctive folk imagery, the drama of religion, the essential delight in music remained. In a very vital and real way, that folk culture and tradition was undergoing the genuine alchemy of art. Work songs, gospels, and hollers were being transformed into blues, ragtime, and jazz. But, strangely, although black intellectuals were quick to acknowledge the contribution of black music to American culture—the only distinctive American contribution as it was often put—they were rarely willing to claim it was *serious* music of high culture. And while many Harlem intellectuals enjoyed the music of the cabarets, none were prepared to give someone like Jelly Roll Morton the serious attention he deserved. Jazz was infectious entertainment and not an ingredient of high civilization. So, provincialism pulled the black intellectual—like his white American brother—away from the culture of his experience into the culture of his learning.

Since culture was not something that could be taken for granted, the announcement of its attainment by both white and black Americans seemed natural enough. The vogue of the New Negro, then, had all of the character of a public relations promotion. The Negro had to be "sold" to the public in terms they could understand. Not the least important target in the campaign was the Negro himself; he had to be convinced of his worth. It is important to understand this, because much of the art and letters that was the substance on which the New Negro was built and which made up the so-called Harlem Renaissance was serving this promotional end. Understanding this gives added meaning to the prose and poetry that were produced, and helps us appreciate their problems as art. Alain Locke and the others were correct in saying that there was a New Negro: an artistic self-consciousness of the Negro's human and cultural worth, the sense of an urgent need for self-assertion and militancy, and the belief in a culturally enriched past in America and Africa; these themes were real enough in the works of Negroes of talent. It was not merely Locke's imagination, although like an anxious parent he nurtured every suspicion of talent as if it were the bloom of genius. If the American context forced it to be artificial and contrived, it should not be thought Alain Locke's fault.

There is, however, a problem which promotions such as Van Wyck Brooks's New American and Alain Locke's New Negro share. It is in the metaphor itself. For whatever promise the new man has for the future, his name and the necessity for his creation imply some inadequacy in the past. Like the New Year's resolution or the "turning over a new leaf," the debut of the New Negro announced a dissatisfaction with the Old Negro. And since the New / Old dichotomy is a mere convenience of mind—Afro-Americans were really the same people all along—the so-called Old Negro was merely carried within the bosom of the New as a kind of self-doubt, perhaps self-hate. How can one take up the promotion of race (or nationality) through art without exposing this doubt? How can one say that Negroes are worthy and civilized and new men without at the same time acknowledging doubt and denial? Even the best of the poems of the Harlem Renaissance carried the burden of self-consciousness of oppression and black limitation.

Langston Hughes had just been graduated from high school in Cleveland and was on a strange journey to his father in Toluca, Mexico. His mother had made him feel guilty for wanting to go to college rather than to work, where he would be "of some use to her." While Hughes saw in his father a means of doing what he wanted—to go to college—he was perplexed because his father's bitterness had made him contemptuous of Negroes and a terrible man to live with. Hughes was on the train,

crossing the Mississippi River at sunset, when he wrote a poem on an envelope that has since been most often printed as characteristic of his work.

The Negro Speaks of Rivers

I've known rivers:
I've known rivers ancient as the world and older than the
    flow of human blood in human veins.

My soul has grown deep like the rivers

I bathed in the Euphrates when dawns were young.
I built my hut near the Congo and it lulled me to sleep
I looked upon the Nile and raised the pyramids above it.
I heard the singing of the Mississippi when Abe Lincoln
    went down to New Orleans, and I've seen its muddy
    bosom turn all golden in the sunset.

I've known rivers:
Ancient, dusky rivers.

My soul has grown deep like the rivers.

Hughes's use of the Mississippi here is traditional and symbolic. The river is an important symbol not only because it connotes the religious division between the temporal and eternal life, but because it is relentless, persistent, and timeless. It is eternity itself, with no beginning and no end. It pulls into itself the soil around it, and it sustains the life at its reaches. It is profound and enigmatic; its depths are somber and mysterious. And the rivers that Hughes mentions add to this point. The Euphrates, then thought the cradle of men, and the other three rivers are not only mother waters, sustaining life around them, but they have known the black man and the black slave. And Hughes says the black man has watched and known these rivers through the centuries, learned their inevitability, and, through them, sensed eternity. The black man, therefore, will persist because his soul has become one with the streams of life.

Hughes has managed in this poem to capture some of the force of the spiritual. Like many spirituals, it is so simple and clear a statement that it is difficult to argue the truth of the assertion. As in many spirituals, the Negro is the speaker and identifies himself with eternal forces, transcending the facts of life and the very conditions which make the statement necessary. And like many spirituals, there is great pathos in its promise of ultimate justice (the Negro's value is ultimate, indeed, eternal), because no other justice is possible (or likely).

Another poem of Langston Hughes's shows something more of his pathos.

Dream Variation

To fling my arms wide
In some place of the sun,
To whirl and to dance
Till the white day is done,
Then rest at cool evening
Beneath a tall tree
While night comes on gently,
      Dark like me—
That is my dream!

To fling my arms wide
In the face of the sun,
Dance! whirl! whirl!
Till the quick day is done

Langston Hughes. Schomburg Center for Research in Black Culture, The New York Public Library, Astor, Lenox and Tilden Foundations.

> Rest at pale evening. . . .
> A tall, slim tree. . . .
> Night coming tenderly
>   Black like me.

Each stanza, here, is a variation on the same dream; but what is most striking in this poem is Hughes's contrast of day and night—black and white. The poet, again the Negro, identifies himself with the night; doubtless white men and the white world are the day and the sun. The white day is frenetic, harsh, and hot, while the night is cool, gentle, and tender. But what is this dance that the poet wants to do? Is it one of joy, defiance, or abandon? One senses a kind of suicidal defiance, because the "place of the sun" (suggesting simple freedom) becomes "in the face of the sun" (suggesting defiance). Arms wide, body whirling and spinning, is this not in spite of the white-hot materialistic civilization? But the statement seems a death wish. The Negro is like the night, and the night is death. For the speaker, from the "quick" day, comes to rest here, with a coolness about him and a monumental "tall, slim tree" over him. The night that he welcomes is gentle, pale, and tender like the sleep of death.

Here, too, Hughes's poem touches one of the major themes of the spiritual. Whatever the anxiety and torment of life, death is always a guaranteed release. As in so many of the spirituals, death in Hughes's poem is a welcome friend. And here, too,

Hughes has joined the Negro to eternity and eternal forces through the simple association of the Negro with night and death, the untroubled, the tender and peaceful sleep. The white day passes, the sun sets, but the soft night, like the river, is eternal.

Like the spirituals, both of these poems gain power from the promise of a transcendent peace. Beyond the hardship and oppression of this life, there is an eternity and meaning which the poet claims to be his. The spirituals, unlike the poems, rest upon a metaphysic which insists that the "least of these" will be redeemed. It was not a racial matter; it was for all men. Negroes in religious expression found this message especially suited to their condition. When devout black men and women sang these songs, there was more than the self-pity of a lowly people claiming eternity for themselves. There was the sound of the triumph that Christianity promised, the glimpse of the eternity itself. So, while the spirituals were a racial expression, they were a universal message for all the dispossessed. Hughes's poems, on the other hand, are clearly racial. His poem is not merely speaking to the condition of everyman—that humbleness which Christianity promises to reward—but the condition of the Negro as a Negro. The pathos of his assertion is clear enough. But without the metaphysical or Christian justification, the claim to eternity and to ultimate worth lacks triumph and power. It is not that one denies the Negro's soul is deep or that justice to him is deserved and ultimate, but the secular expression lacks an important dimension. One need not ask a religious man why he feels it necessary to seek transcendent and eternal meaning for himself. But when a poet justifies his people in these terms, one suspects in him the initial doubt. There is doubt in the poet's mind, or he assumes doubt in his audience. Otherwise, he would not have to write about the matter in this way.

Ironically, the literature that was to be advanced as evidence of the Negro as a new man contained a strong odor of this pathos and self-doubt. It tainted all the pronouncements and exposed the vulnerability of the New Negro concept. Nowhere is this theme more clear than in one of Countee Cullen's poems:

> Yet Do I Marvel
>
> I doubt not God is good, well-meaning, kind,
> And did He stoop to quibble could tell why
> The little buried mole continues blind,
> Why flesh that mirrors Him must some day die,
> Make plain the reason tortured Tantalus
> Is baited by the fickle fruit, declare
> If merely brute caprice dooms Sisyphus
> To struggle up a never-ending stair.
> Inscrutable His ways are, and immune
> To catechism by a mind too strewn
> With petty cares to slightly understand
> What awful brain compels His awful hand.
> Yet do I marvel at this curious thing:
> To make a poet black, and bid him sing!

It may be argued that Cullen, influenced as he was by the English Romantics, was indulging in the self-pity that often captured those poets in their lesser expressions of inner anguish. There is something to this; Cullen turned to Tantalus and Sisyphus—mythological figures who fed the Romantic imagination—to give measure and equivalence to his torment. Yet, his torture is not personal, nor is it generic. It is racial, somehow the peculiar torment of black men who are sensitive and wish to sing. And Countee Cullen assumes that his audience, white and black, will know and immediately understand that there is a special godly and tragic condition here. But how can one know that? And why should everyone know that the black poet's trial is especially futile? Is it because he is wounded and limited? It could not be that he alone has more soul than voice to sing; that was the predicament of all poets, the Romantic would say. One cannot be sure what Cullen had in mind when he thought his reader would know the special curse of the black bard, but close to the surface is doubt which is not merely self-doubt but race doubt. Because it is a racial doubt and limitation rather than personal, the reader senses the pity of the futile effort, without the heroism of the tragic condition.

Such doubt and presumption of limitation were inextricably a part of the New Negro vogue. Just as Van Wyck Brooks's *America's Coming of Age* was condescending about American art and culture, assuming it limited and wanting, those promoting the New Negro, even as they proclaimed the Negro's worth, provided evidence that they had to assert and prove it.

Part of the assertion of the Negro's value was the assumption of militancy. The assertion that justice ultimately would be his was not enough for the New Negro. Indeed, that had been the problem with the Old Negro, the docile and patient retainer who knew that his reward would be in heaven. Hughes and the young Negro writers of the 1920s were not saying that. The Negro had ultimate, eternal human worth. It should not only be asserted, but the Negro should assume in the present the posture promised him in eternity. He should be a man like other men.

Thus, the other face of the New Negro's *persona* was militant and self-assured. Indeed, the only way he was to claim his true manhood was to demand redress of grievances, to fight back. Some of the poetry and prose of the 1920s by Negroes iterated this theme. The most notable was a poem by Claude McKay.

> If We Must Die
>
> If we must die, let it not be like hogs
> Hunted and penned in an inglorious spot,
> While round us bark the mad and hungry dogs,
> Making their mock at our accursed lot.
>
> If we must die, O let us nobly die,
> So that our precious blood may not be shed
> In vain; then even the monsters we defy
> Shall be constrained to honor us though dead!
>
> O kinsmen! we must meet the common foe!
> Though far outnumbered let us show us brave,
> And for their thousand blows deal one deathblow!
> What though before us lies the open grave?
> Like men we'll face the murderous, cowardly pack,
> Pressed to the wall, dying, but fighting back!

Here was none of the non-resistance that the Old Negro had preached, nor the tone of superiority and righteousness of pacifism. Black men must fight back. This was the message of East St. Louis, Illinois, and Houston, Texas. It was the same call to self-defense that the *Messenger* and W. A. Domingo had applauded. The poem, itself, as an expression of the new black spirit, alarmed conservative whites. Senator Henry Cabot Lodge had it read into the *Congressional Record* as evidence of the unsettling currents among black Americans. In later years, when Arna Bontemps collected on a phonograph record an anthology of Negro poets, McKay claimed that it was not just a Negro poem. He said, following World War II, that he

had never considered himself a Negro poet. He claimed that he had considered "If We Must Die" a universal poem, for all men who were "abused, outraged and murdered, whether they are minorities or nations, black or brown or yellow or white, Catholic or Protestant or Pagan, fighting against terror." Yet, in the *Messenger* in 1919 and in *Harlem Shadows* in 1922 no one could doubt that the author was a black man and the "we" of the poem black people too.

The search for a personality for the New Negro necessitated the rediscovery of a heritage. As much as the young Negro intellectuals wanted to proclaim a new day and to inter all vestiges of the old image, they felt a need to find justification in the past. The heritage was to serve the new image. So, much effort went into the explication of the Negro's folk traditions in America and into the interpretation of whatever was known of the civilizations of Africa.

The Negroes' importance to American culture, it was argued, was that he provided its only genuine folk tradition. From the Afro-Americans had come a rich and complex folklore and music which was the most distinctively American contribution to world culture. While the Negro had been denied by both whites and sophisticated blacks, he was unconsciously pouring out, in his own entertainment and for his own soul's needs, the raw folk materials upon which any American music or literature would have to rest. With this argument in mind, Negroes began to recover their folk traditions. Interestingly, sophisticated Negroes began to find value in the peasant character of the mass of American Negroes. After all, it was from the common man and the peasant stock that these ingenuous and fresh folk materials were being produced. (pp. 60-73)

The Negro intellectuals were attempting to build a race and define a culture. If there was validity in the notion of distinctive racial cultural contribution, it must be in the special experience of the race itself. So the whole people and the whole Afro-American experience had to be searched and exploited for clues to heritage. Folk materials and the expression of the common man had to be the essence of such a tradition. But heritage also demanded a continuity in the past, the transit of culture. When the promoters of the New Negro looked back to find his origins, or when they tried to discuss racial culture, they were always thrown back upon Africa.

Africa was an essential enigma in this culture-building enterprise. It was not only impossible for twentieth-century Afro-Americans to pick up any unsevered threads back to Africa, but it was difficult to find any correspondence between the cultures of Africa and that of the American Negro. Alain Locke, who was quite knowledgeable about African art, was quick to admit this. The African had a strong tradition of graphic and sculptural expression, but the American Negro, true to an ascetic Puritan tradition, had little visual art to show. The untutored Afro-American could sense no more in a piece of African sculpture than could a European. There were an ocean and an age of experience between the black men of the two continents. Yet, Alain Locke was convinced that African art held a key to Afro-American artistic expression.

African art was a legacy; its existence made evident the fact that black men were the craftsmen of a disciplined and classical art. So, the American Negro need not think himself "a cultural foundling without his own inheritance." He could be freed from imitativeness and indebtedness to the white Western culture. Thus, the knowledge of African arts should encourage American Negroes to pursue long-neglected lines: painting, sculpture, and decorative arts. Using his inheritance as a base, the American Negro, Locke dreamed, might then create new idioms from that tradition. With the African tradition to inspire him, the Afro-American could become the subject of art as well as the artist. He would be freed from the white dogma of beauty.

Locke observed that European artists had already been rejuvenated at the African fountain. Pablo Picasso and Georges Braque found in African sculpture the insight which led them into cubism. And sculptors like Constantin Brancusi and Wilhelm Lembruck were liberated through African sculpture to powerful restatements of human form. If they can, why can't we? Locke asked. Once known "and appreciated, this art can scarcely have less influence upon the blood descendants, bound to it by a sense of direct kinship, than upon those who inherit by tradition only, and through channels of an exotic curiosity and interest.''

Alain Locke did not need to wonder long. Negro painters and sculptors began experimenting with the African motifs. Richmond Barthé sculpted several figures which exhibited strong African influence. Aaron Douglas was more consistently devoted to the African legacy than Barthé. Douglas developed a style of drawing which employed stark black silhouette. The figures were always angular and stylized. Like African graphics, Douglas' drawings were more decorative than representational; they were stark blocks of design. In the 1930s Douglas developed this technique into a series of large murals, using flat colors. They were elaborations on his early work; Africa and the exotic dominated.

It was easier to use the African artistic tradition as a means of giving racial quality to art than it was to discuss the significance of Africa to the Negro. Alain Locke had found it difficult and was reduced to a simple assertion of faith in a valuable African legacy. Other Negro intellectuals were equally perplexed by the African heritage. All seemed to know, or sense, that Africa should mean something to the race; there should be some race memory that tied black men together; ambiguity and doubt always left the question unresolved, however.

Countee Cullen's poem "Heritage" did little more than show that poet's quandary. For he raised the question throughout the poem, what is Africa to me? It is a long poem, with unrelenting tetrameter and a regular aa, bb, cc, rhyme setting up a rhythmic beat that echoes Vachel Lindsay's "Congo." And although the question recurs, and the poet tells of Africa's enchantment, he never convinces the reader that the question is an honest one. Africa comes through as romantic and exotic, no more or no less real for him as a black poet than it would have been for a white one.

> All day long and all night through
> One thing only I must do
> Quench my pride and cool my blood,
> Lest I perish in their flood,
> Lest a hidden ember set
> Timber that I thought was wet
> Burning like the dryest flax,
> Melting like the merest wax,
> Lest the grave restore its dead.
> *Stubborn heart and rebel head.*
> *Have you not yet realized*
> *You and I are civilized?*
>
> So I lie and all day long
> Want no sound except the song
> Sung by wild barbaric birds
> Goading massive jungle herds,

> Juggernauts of flesh that pass
> Trampling tall defiant grass
> Where young forest lovers lie
> Plighting troth beneath the sky.

Doubtless, Africa was a large question for the black intellectual searching for identity and heritage. It was compelling because of the rootlessness and placelessness of the Afro-American and his search for the springs of a race's origins. It was not answered by the romantic ejaculations that Cullen used for passion. Langston Hughes came to the question more honestly in

Afro-American Fragment

> So long,
> So far away
> Is Africa
> Not even memories alive
> Save those that history books create,
> Save those that songs
> Beat back into the blood—
> Beat out of blood with words sad-sung
> In strange un-Negro tongue—
> So long,
> So far away
> Is Africa.
>
> Subdued and time-lost
> Are the drums—and yet
> Through some vast mist of race
> There comes this song
> I do not understand,
> This song of atavistic land,
> Of bitter yearnings lost
> Without a place—
> So long,
> So far away
> Is Africa's
> Dark face.

America and Americans were provincials. That was the problem. Black men as well as white men were forced through condition and education to look elsewhere for the springs of civilization and culture. Afro-Americans could not submit to the judgment that Europe was their cultural parent. Such an idea jarred reason, and relegated non-whites to aboriginal and primitive origins which denied them civilization. Whatever self-denial white Americans indulged in to tie themselves to Europe was intensified among blacks, whose road back to Africa was unclear; and when they looked they saw only a dark continent. It was dark because little was known about it; its civilizations and its people had not been high in the order of importance for European scholars. So, black men yearned, as American provincials, to find meaning and identity in Africa; their frustration was a measure of their Americanization. (pp. 78-83)

Nathan Irvin Huggins, in his Harlem Renaissance, *Oxford University Press, 1971, 343 p.*

ACHIEVEMENT AND INFLUENCE

GEORGE E. KENT

[*Kent is an American educator and critic. In the following excerpt from an essay written in 1972, he assesses the achievement of the Harlem Renaissance.*]

What finally does the Harlem Renaissance add up to in terms of achievement?

We must, in order to weigh its outcomes properly, acknowledge two facts: that today it bears the burden of heavy critical strictures, and that these strictures are, to some degree, an acknowledgment of its role as the father of many children whose features are likely to be looked upon suspiciously by the offspring.

But its negative criticism arose during its own time, and included participants in the movement. Alain Locke, its chief mentor, was eventually to see it as insufficiently socially conscious. Claude McKay was to repudiate his earlier fiction as he turned to Catholicism, and to describe the Renaissance as concerned more with racial uplift, superficial white acceptance, superficial values, than representing its own people or becoming something for them.

Langston Hughes, in *The Big Sea*, was to see the movement as a time when fun was to be had by all, but also as a rebirth whose good news the ordinary Black never heard of—and would not have had much time for anyway.

Then there was the bitter satire of its bohemianism, hustling and confusion by Wallace Thurman in *Infants of the Spring*.

Allison Davis, today a famous sociologist, and Sterling Brown saw as serious limitations of the movement its failure to dramatize the deeper qualities recognizable in ordinary Black people: fortitude, courage, and endurance.

Ralph Ellison has pointed out that it represented an ironic picture: a literature that was still a bawling infant choosing *decadence* as its model for expression. A judgment that is part of the charge that it swung open all doors to entry by whites questing for the exotic and the primitive. In this ritual, white Carl Van Vechten, through his novel *Nigger Heaven*, frequently is seen as a subverter of the fiction into the paths of blatant sexuality and sensationalism.

Harold Cruse, in *Crisis of the Negro Intellectual* [see Additional Bibliography], saw it as lacking a true forum for hammering out a common platform or a salon for promoting intellectual excitement. In place of the cultivated and devoted woman of the arts, such as Mabel Dodge could be for whites in Greenwich Village, the Renaissance had Aleila Walker, a vital Black woman who inherited a fortune from the hairstraightening enterprises of her mother. In her great parties, the good eating, good drinking, and good publishing contacts in an area too tightly packed with people to provide overall group communion seem to have been the main advantages.

And today's young writers, while conceding that the Renaissance left them a foundation, look askance at its failure to build lasting institutions and to truly address itself to a Black audience.

Certainly, a good deal of the movement is placed in perspective when we realize that, while the Marcus Garvey nationalist movement and the blues were allowed to make injections, they seemed to remain for most Renaissance writers superficial diversions, bastard brothers and sisters, lovable even in certain ways, but not eligible for Sunday company or a real dining room kind of intimacy.

It must be admitted that all charges are supportable, in varying degrees, but that some seem more applicable to a part of the Renaissance than to the whole. As a single example, Ellison's charge of decadence is more applicable to certain novels and stories than to poetry. What is needed is a very exhaustive study of all forces operating within the period, so that properly weighted judgment and completely accurate descriptions can be provided.

Meanwhile, we must acknowledge several accomplishments that were *fundamental*.

Certainly, no genre of literature went without substantial development. The short story in the hands of Toomer, Eric Walrond, and Langston Hughes became a much more flexible form for that moment of illumination of Black life. The novel, while not freed from the episodic structure or audible spasms in plot movement, provided memorable analyses that occasionally stopped just short of greatness. And the drama, while sneaking only occasionally through barricades to Broadway prominence as in the cases of Hall Johnson's *Run Little Children* and Wallace Thurman's *Harlem*, made progress in little theater and folk drama not known before, and the minstrel tradition was mortally wounded.

Although the loss of white patronage resulting from the stock market crash critically wounded the movement, it produced writers who were to persist and whose consciousness was to become an essential metaphor for Black realities of subsequent periods as they remained open to new tensions.

What we can see today, after all charges have been recorded, is that the Renaissance made paths through what had been stubborn thickets. It put muscles on nonliterary institutions, such as newspapers, the Urban League, the NAACP, labor leadership, which, however we may now categorize them ideologically, were to become powerful weightlifters. From a literary point of view, it made a strategic turn at the forks of the road. (pp. 78-80)

[The] Renaissance's dissociation of sensibility from constraining definitions enforced by white middle-class culture, though not radical, was essential, had a stronger grasp of the Black selfhood which W. E. B. Du Bois had described as under threat from the Blacks' double consciousness: the consciousness enforcing white definitions upon him; and the part that desired a full embrace of the universe.

If today we can sometimes jog, rather than puff, down the road toward self-definition, it would seem that the Harlem Renaissance was a father who should not go without thanks or reverence. (p. 80)

George E. Kent, "The Fork in the Road: Patterns of the Harlem Renaissance," in Black World, Vol. XXI, No. 8, June, 1972, pp. 13-24, 76-80.

ADDITIONAL BIBLIOGRAPHY

Arden, Eugene. "The Early Harlem Novel." *The Phylon Quarterly* XX, No. 1 (Spring 1959): 25-31.
   Discusses several early novels of the Harlem Renaissance and the black influx into Harlem.

Barret, Eseoghene. "The Harlem Renaissance." *Nigeria Magazine,* Nos. 122-23 (1977): 125-28.
   Short history of the Harlem Renaissance listing and briefly discussing several of its most prominent works.

Bell, Bernard. "Folk Art and the Harlem Renaissance." *Phylon* XXXVI, No. 2 (Summer 1975): 155-63.

Examines the relationship between black folk songs and the writings of the Harlem Renaissance.

Bone, Robert. *Down Home: A History of Afro-American Short Fiction from Its Beginnings to the End of the Harlem Renaissance.* New York: G. B. Putnam's Sons, 1975, 328 p.
Discusses the history of black American folk tales and short stories, examines the significance of a pastoral tradition in Harlem Renaissance literature, and provides individual analyses of several Harlem Renaissance writers, including Langston Hughes, Jean Toomer, Eric Walrond, and Arna Bontemps.

Bontemps, Arna. "The Negro Renaissance: Jean Toomer and the Harlem Writers of the 1920s." In *Anger, and Beyond: The Negro Writer in the United States,* edited by Herbert Hill, pp. 20-36. New York: Harper & Row, 1966.
Discusses *Cane* and its effect on Harlem Renaissance writers.

———, ed. *The Harlem Renaissance Remembered.* New York: Dodd, Mead & Co., 1972, 310 p.
Contains personal recollections of the Harlem Renaissance by Bontemps and essays by twelve critics, including Michael B. Stoff ("Claude McKay and the Cult of Primitivism"), Patrick J. Gilpin ("Charles S. Johnson: Entrepeneur of the Harlem Renaissance"), and Warrington Hudlin ("The Renaissance Re-examined").

Brawley, Benjamin. "The Negro Literary Renaissance." *Southern Workman* 56, No. 4 (April 1927): 177-84.
Berates black writers for what he perceives as a lack of aesthetic standards.

Bronz, Stephen H. *Roots of Negro Racial Consciousness: The 1920's, Three Harlem Renaissance Authors.* New York: Libra Publishers, 1964, 101 p.
Discusses the lives and works of James Weldon Johnson, Countee Cullen, and Claude McKay, which together Bronz considers to exemplify the various facets of the Harlem Renaissance.

Brown, Lloyd W. "The African Heritage and the Harlem Renaissance: A Re-evaluation." *African Literature Today* 9 (1978): 1-9.
Affirms the influence of African culture on Harlem Renaissance writing.

Brown, Sterling. *Negro Poetry and Drama. The Negro in American Fiction.* 1937. Reprint. New York: Atheneum, 1969, 209 p.
History of black poetry, drama, and fiction summarized to 1914 and examined in detail to 1936, containing numerous short sketches on individual writers and works.

Chamberlain, John. "The Negro as Writer." *The Bookman* LXX, No. 6 (February 1930): 603-11.
Discusses black writers from the 1880s through the 1920s.

Chapman, Abraham. "The Harlem Renaissance in Literary History." *CLA Journal* XI, No. 1 (September 1967): 38-58.
Compares the Harlem Renaissance to the Irish Renaissance of the early 1900s, discussing the importance of these movements to ethnic self-awareness.

Clark, Edward. "The Harlem Renaissance and Today." *Literatur in Wissenschaft und Unterricht* VIII, No. 2 (August 1975): 84-8.
Retrospective review of *The New Negro.*

Clarke, John Henrik. "The Neglected Dimensions of the Harlem Renaissance." *Black World* XX, No. 1 (November 1970): 118-130.
Examines the political and social background of the Harlem Renaissance and Marcus Garvey's "Back to Africa" movement.

Coleman, Floyd, and Richardson, John Adkins. "Black Continuities in the Art of the Harlem Renaissance." *Papers on Language and Literature* 12, No. 4 (Fall 1976): 402-21.
Demonstrates that aspects of African culture were preserved in the traditions and folk art of black Americans.

Cooley, John R. "*The Emperor Jones* and the Harlem Renaissance." *Studies in the Literary Imagination* VII, No. 2 (Fall 1974): 73-83.
Posits Eugene O'Neill's *The Emperor Jones* as an important precursor of black theater and the Harlem Renaissance.

Cooney, Charles F. "Walter White and the Harlem Renaissance." *Journal of Negro History* LVII, No. 3 (July 1972): 231-40.
Discusses the role of Walter White in assisting the publication of other black authors' works.

Cruse, Harold. "Harlem Background—The Rise of Economic Nationalism and Origins of Cultural Revolution." In his *The Crisis of the Negro Intellectual,* pp. 11-63. New York: William Morrow & Co., 1967.
Includes a discussion of both black and white literary activity in New York during the 1920s, examines the Harlem Renaissance as a historical event, and discusses several of its prominent writers.

Cullen, Countee. *Color.* 1925. Reprint. New York: Arno Press, 1969, 108 p.

Davis, Thadious. "Southern Standard-Bearers in the New Negro Renaissance." In *The History of Southern Literature,* edited by Louis D. Rubin, Jr., pp. 291-313. Baton Rouge and London: Louisiana State University Press, 1985.
Discusses Southerners involved in, and Southern influence on, the Harlem Renaissance.

Dean, Sharon, and Stetson, Erline. "Flower-Dust and Springtime: Harlem Renaissance Women." *The Radical Teacher* 18, n.d.: 1-8.
Examines the poetry of Georgia Douglas Johnson and Anne Spencer and the novels of Nella Larson and Zora Neale Hurston.

Diepeveen, Leonard. "Folktales in the Harlem Renaissance." *American Literature* 58, No. 1 (March 1986): 64-81.
Discusses black folktales and their incorporation into Harlem Renaissance poetry and fiction.

Du Bois, W. E. Burghardt. "Criteria of Negro Art." *The Crisis* 32, No. 6 (October 1926): 290-97.
Transcript of an address delivered at the Chicago Conference of the National Association for the Advancement of Colored People, in which Du Bois asserts that "all Art is propaganda and ever must be."

———. *Dusk of Dawn: An Essay toward an Autobiography of a Race Concept.* 1940. Reprint. New Brunswick, N.J. and London: Transaction Books, 1984, 334 p.
Autobiographical essay in which is developed much of Du Bois's thought concerning race relations and the advancement of blacks toward social equality.

Du Bois, W. E. B[urghardt] and Locke, Alain. "The Younger Literary Movement." *The Crisis* 27, No. 4 (February 1924): 161-63.
Review of Jean Toomer's *Cane* by Du Bois and of Jessie Fauset's *There Is Confusion* by Locke.

Fauset, Jessie. *There Is Confusion.* 1924. Reprint. New York: AMS Press, 1974, 297 p.

Ford, Nick Aaron. *The Contemporary Negro Novel: A Study in Race Relations.* 1936. Reprint. College Park, Md.: McGrath Publishing Co., 1968, 108 p.
Discussion of eleven black novelists.

Gallagher, Brian. "About Us, For Us, Near Us: The Irish and Harlem Renaissances." *Éire-Ireland* XVI, No. 4 (Winter 1981): 14-26.
Compares Irish literary activity in the early twentieth century to the Harlem Renaissance of the 1920s.

Gayle, Addison, Jr. *The Way of the New World: The Black Novel in America.* Garden City, N.Y.: Anchor Press, 1975, 339 p.
Examines novels by black authors from the nineteenth century to the 1970s. Gayle advocates a revolutionary role for the black writer.

Glicksberg, Charles I. "The Negro Cult of the Primitive." *Antioch Review* 4, No. 1 (Spring 1944): 47-55.
Disparages primitivistic aspects of black art, considering them artificial and a concession to white prejudice.

———. "Negro Poets and the American Tradition." *The Antioch Review* 6, No. 2 (Summer 1946): 243-53.

Discusses the role of the black writer in ending racial repression.

Gloster, Hugh M. "The Negro Renaissance" and "Fiction of the Negro Renaissance." In his *Negro Voices in American Fiction,* pp. 101-15, pp. 116-95. New York: Russell & Russell, 1948.
Examines forces that precipitated the Harlem Renaissance and discusses many of its important works.

Hart, Robert C. "Black-White Literary Relations in the Harlem Renaissance." *American Literature* 44, No. 4 (January 1973): 612-28.
Account of relationships between black writers and white writers and publishers during the 1920s. Hart concludes that most of the relationships took the form of white patron to black protégé.

Huggins, Nathan Irvin, ed. *Voices from the Harlem Renaissance.* New York: Oxford University Press, 1976, 438 p.
Anthology of writings from the Harlem Renaissance and the years immediately preceding and following it, arranged topically.

Hughes, Langston. "The Negro Artist and the Racial Mountain." *Nation* CXXII, No. 3181 (23 June 1926): 692-94.
Argues for a distinctively black voice in Afro-American literature.

——. *Not Without Laughter.* 1930. Reprint. New York: Macmillan, 1986, 320 p.

——. "Too Much of Race." *The Crisis* 44, No. 9 (September 1937): 272.
Speech concerning racism originally given to the Second International Writer's Conference in Paris in July, 1937.

——. "Harlem Literati in the Twenties." *Saturday Review of Literature* 22, No. 9 (22 June 1940): 13-14.
Reminiscences of Hughes's experiences in the Renaissance.

——. *Selected Poems of Langston Hughes.* 1959. Reprint. New York: Vintage Books, 1974, 297 p.

Johnson, Abby [Ann] Arthur. "Literary Midwife: Jessie Redmon Fauset and the Harlem Renaissance." *Phylon* XXXIX, No. 2 (June 1978): 143-53.
Discusses Fauset as one of the few black authors to write about the black middle class.

Johnson, Abby Ann Arthur, and Johnson, Ronald M. "Forgotten Pages: Black Literary Magazines in the 1920s." *Journal of American Studies* 8, No. 3 (December 1974): 363-82.
Examines several short-lived "little magazines" published by black writers during the 1920s.

Johnson, Abby [Ann] Arthur, and Johnson, Ronald M. "Reform and Reaction: Black Literary Magazines in the 1930s." *North Dakota Quarterly* 46, No. 1 (Winter 1978): 5-18.
Discusses various literary magazines during the period immediately following the Harlem Renaissance.

Johnson, Abby Arthur, and Johnson, Ronald Maberry. "Toward the Renaissance: *Crisis, Opportunity,* and *Messenger,* 1910-1928." In their *Propaganda and Aesthetics: The Literary Politics of Afro-American Magazines in the Twentieth Century,* pp. 31-63. Amherst: University of Massachusetts Press, 1979.
Discusses the three major black literary and political magazines of the 1920s and their impact on the development and popularization of black literature.

Johnson, James Weldon. *God's Trombones.* 1927. Reprint. New York: Penguin Books, 1976, 56 p.

Koprince, Susan J. "Femininity and the Harlem Experience: A Note on James Weldon Johnson." *CLA Journal* XXIX, No. 1 (September 1985): 52-6.
Examines Johnson's attitudes toward women as revealed in *God's Trombones* and *Black Manhattan.* Koprince finds that Johnson portrayed women as either sensual or maternal and notes the union of these qualities in Johnson's characterization of Harlem.

Larson, Nella. *Quicksand. Passing,* edited by Deborah E. McDowell. New Brunswick, N. J.: Rutgers University Press, 1986, 246 p.

Lewis, David Levering. *When Harlem Was in Vogue.* New York: Alfred A. Knopf, 1984, 381 p.
History of Harlem in the 1920s and 1930s, with emphasis on the Harlem Renaissance, popular culture and entertainment, and the influence of Harlem on the white culture of surrounding areas.

Locke, Alain, ed. *The New Negro.* 1925. Reprint. New York: Atheneum, 1975, 452 p.
Collection of poetry, fiction, and essays defining and promoting the aims of the Harlem Renaissance. Contributors include Jean Toomer, Countee Cullen, James Weldon Johnson, Langston Hughes, and Charles S. Johnson.

——. "Beauty Instead of Ashes." *The Nation* CXXVI, No. 3276 (18 April 1928): 432-34.
Asserts that black writers must and will continue to develop their talents and write mature work, rather than expending all their creative energy in undisciplined early works.

Makalani, Jabulani Kamau. "Toward a Sociological Analysis of the Renaissance: Why Harlem?" *Black World* XXV, No. 4 (February 1976): 4-13, 93-97.
Discusses why the Harlem Renaissance occurred when and where it did.

Margolies, Edward. *Native Sons: A Critical Study of Twentieth-Century Negro American Authors.* Philadelphia and New York: J. B. Lippincott Co., 1968.
Summarizes the history of black literature from 1900 to 1940 and provides individual studies of eight black authors writing between 1940 and 1968.

Martin, Tony. *Literary Garveyism: Garvey, Black Arts and the Harlem Renaissance.* Dover, Mass.: Majority Press, 1983, 204 p.
Examines Marcus Garvey and his relation to and influence on Harlem Renaissance literature.

McKay, Claude. *Selected Poems of Claude McKay.* 1953. Reprint. New York: Harcourt Brace Jovanovich, 1969, 110 p.

Mudimbe-Boyi, Mbulamwanza. "African and Black American Literature: The 'Negro Renaissance' and the Genesis of African Literature in French," translated by J. Coates. In *For Better or Worse: The American Influence in the World,* edited by Allen F. Davis, pp. 157-69. Westport, Conn. and London: Greenwood Press, 1981.
Discusses the effect of the Harlem Renaissance on black writers in France.

Osofsky, Gilbert. "Symbols of the Jazz Age: The New Negro and Harlem Discovered." *American Quarterly* 17, No. 2 (Summer 1965): 229-38.
Discusses the reaction of white Americans to the Harlem Renaissance.

Schuyler, George S. "The Negro-Art Hokum." *The Nation* CXXII, No. 3180 (16 June 1926): 662-63.
Denies that black American literature can or should be recognized as essentially different from white American literature.

Scruggs, Charles W. "Alain Locke and Walter White: Their Struggle for Control of the Harlem Renaissance." *Black American Literature* 14, No. 3 (Fall 1980): 91-9.
Examines the careers of and conflict between Alain Locke and Walter White. Scruggs views Locke as an idealist and White as a pragmatist, laments the fact that they could not work together, and interprets their struggle to indicate that the leaders of the Renaissance possessed more control over its direction than is generally recognized.

Singh, Amritjit. "Black-White Symbiosis: Another Look at the Literary History of 1920s." In *Studies in American Literature: Essays in Honour of William Mulder,* edited by Jagdish Chandler and Narindar S. Pradhan, pp. 154-68. Delhi: Oxford University Press, 1976.
Analyzes stereotypes of "black primitivism" which created popular interest in the Renaissance but limited the range of its authors.

Thurman, Wallace. *The Blacker the Berry.* 1929. Reprint. New York: AMS Press, 1972, 262 p.

Toomer, Jean. *Cane*. 1923. Reprint. New York: Liveright, 1975, 116 p.

Turpin, Waters E. "Four Short Fiction Writers of the Harlem Renaissance—Their Legacy of Achievement." *CLA Journal* XI, No. 1 (September 1967): 59-72.
    Examines short stories by Jean Toomer, Rudolph Fisher, Langston Hughes, and Claude McKay, and uses them to defend Harlem Renaissance writers from the charge that they merely perpetuated stereotyping of blacks.

Waldron, Edward E. "Walter White and the Harlem Renaissance: Letters from 1924-1927." *CLA Journal* 16, No. 4 (June 1973): 438-57.
    Utilizes White's correspondence to assess his role in the Harlem Renaissance.

Williams, John A. "The Harlem Renaissance: Its Artists, Its Impact, Its Meaning." *Black World* XX, No. 1 (November 1970): 17-18.
    Compares the Harlem Renaissance to the Black Power movement of the 1960s.

Williams, Sherley Anne. "Langston Hughes and the Negro Renaissance." *The Langston Hughes Review* IV, No. 1 (Spring 1985): 37-9.
    Examines two essays by Hughes on the Harlem Renaissance.

Hungarian Literature of the Twentieth Century

INTRODUCTION

Throughout Hungarian history the literature of the country has been shaped primarily by extraliterary factors, with accidents of language, history, and politics dominating the development of Hungarian letters. Principal among these factors is Hungary's linguistic uniqueness. With the exception of Finnish and Estonian, Hungarian is unrelated to any major European language, comprising radically different syntax and vocabulary and lending itself to a unique system of versification. The resulting obstacles to translation have severely restricted cultural exchange between Hungary and neighboring countries and have kept the development of Hungarian letters distinct from the intellectual development of Europe as a whole. This cultural isolation has contributed further to the strong sense of national identity that has traditionally informed Hungarian writing. Since the Middle Ages, Hungarian literature has been inextricably linked with national life, and the most prominent Hungarian authors have devoted their talents to such issues as political revolution and social reform. This tradition of social commitment has remained strong throughout the twentieth century, despite the influence of the iconoclastic modernist journal *Nyugat* and widespread acceptance of Western literary trends that eschewed social concerns in literature. During this era, the country has been repeatedly rent by social and political upheaval, with political forces intruding as frequently into literary affairs as writers have attempted to influence the course of politics. As a result, commentary on Hungarian literature is replete with references to its social and political milieu, making an understanding of the history of the period necessary to an understanding of the literary criticism.

At the turn of the century Hungary was ruled by the dual monarchy of the Austro-Hungarian Empire. With the collapse of the Empire at the end of World War I, the country was thrown into chaos. King Charles IV abdicated the throne in 1918, at which time Hungary was proclaimed a republic under a radical-socialist coalition government headed by Count Mihály Károlyi; however, Károlyi's government was short-lived, disbanding as the result of internal unrest and external pressure from the Allies. Leadership was assumed by the communist Béla Kun, who, in alliance with the Soviet Union, established a "dictatorship of the proletariat." Driven from power by the Rumanian army after a reign of 133 days, Kun's regime was succeeded in early 1920 by the conservative republican government of Miklós Horthy. Several months after Horthy's election, Hungary was devastated by the conclusion of the Treaty of Trianon, a settlement with the Allies resulting in the loss of over two-thirds of Hungary's territory and population to Rumania, Czechoslovakia, and Yugoslavia. The Horthy regime held power in what remained of Hungary throughout the interwar years, a period which saw the development of Populism, an influential literary and political movement dedicated to improving the lot of the peasantry. Declared a nonbelligerent upon the outbreak of World War II, Hungary entered into an alliance with Nazi Germany against the Soviet Union in 1941. In 1944 Hungary was occupied by the German army, and Horthy was forced to abdicate; the country was liberated and occupied the

following year by the Soviet army. With Soviet assistance, a coalition government was established under the domination of the Hungarian Communist Party. A succession of communist governments gradually suppressed dissent by means of an enormous state security force and by purging the army and civil service of individuals unsympathetic to the regime. Literary freedom was similarly restricted, with officials enforcing conformity to the doctrine of socialist realism by proscribing the publication of ideologically unacceptable writings and by sentencing dissident writers to prison and exile. Dissident writers contributed to an attempted revolution in 1956, but the rebellion was suppressed with the assistance of Soviet troops. Although the first five years following the uprising were characterized by severe repression, this reestablishment of communist authority was followed by a period of liberalization in human rights, religion, economics, and the arts. Since that time, the Hungarian cultural atmosphere has remained relatively liberal in comparison with the strict conformity enforced in some other Eastern-bloc nations, and although the tradition of social commitment in Hungarian letters remains strong, the past two decades have seen experimental literary forms gain greater acceptance from both the Communist government and the Hungarian reading public.

GENERAL SURVEYS

JOSEPH REMÉNYI

[Reményi was a Hungarian-born American man of letters who was widely regarded as the literary spokesman for America's Hungarian community during the first half of the twentieth century. His novels, short stories, and poetry often depict Hungarian-American life, and his numerous translations and critical essays have been instrumental in introducing modern Hungarian literature to American readers. In the following excerpt, he surveys twentieth-century Hungarian literature to 1955.]

Those who are more or less familiar with Hungarian history recognize its heroic aspects. Hungary's position as defender of Western civilization against Eastern attacks throughout the centuries is acknowledged even by historians who ignore the cultural qualities of the nation. Notwithstanding the inaccurate universal notion of Hungary's "inherent conservative or reactionary" disposition to which, of course, Hungarian liberals strenuously objected, there were those abroad who readily admitted the nation's contribution to intellectual and social progress. On the 11th of May in 1852 Ralph Waldo Emerson greeted Lajos Kossuth, the Hungarian democratic leader, on his visit to Concord and praised his political and humanitarian virtues. In *Ends and Means* Aldous Huxley writes with appreciation about Ferenc Deák, the nineteenth-century Hungarian statesman; he emphasizes his moral intelligence and sense of justice. The fact remains, nevertheless, that to have an over-all picture of any nation and to reach a plausible appraisal of the plus and minus characteristics of such a nation, it does not suffice to see her representatives solely as history's knights-errant, but one must find evidence by which to judge aright the total essence of her being. If, as Longinus in his dissertation *On the Sublime* remarked, "beautiful words are the mind's peculiar light," it is logical to assume that to account for Hungary's place in the realm of Western civilization (despite the ethically Eastern heritage of the Magyars) we must be interested in those forces that engaged the mind, the heart, the blood creatively, using words as a medium for the communication of aesthetically valid pursuits. Sometimes the internationally unheralded literary attainments of a nation may offer a more honest picture of her substance than the presumably factual authenticity of her picturesque features or political and social imperfections. At times unanalyzed statements contain the germ of misstatements.

Hungary's literary traditions are Western European. What Hungarian men of letters ardently desired was an acceptance of their "good Europeanism," enriched by the indigenous qualities of their national ethos. Consequently, when we discuss the Hungarian literary output of the past thirty years [1925-1955] it ought to be evident that the various literary trends of the West passed not unnoticed, but affected writers and poets and led to the production of works that convey the impression of clarity and confusion in the same sense as they are observable in the works of Western European creators. Dezső Szabó, one of the most able and forceful twentieth-century Hungarian writers, declared that "Hungary's destiny depends upon a unified Europe." It is not easy for non-Hungarians to comprehend this almost tragic accentuation of a "unified Europe" in relation-

Mihály Babits (left) and Endre Ady. From Endre Ady, *by Gyorgy Ronay. Editions Pierre Seghers, 1967. © 1967 Editions Seghers Paris.*

ship to the lot of the Hungarian nation. Too many fail to perceive the reason of this craving for a European order of a nation whose Finno-Ugrian language is definitely a liability in establishing relations with the outside world. At present Hungary is suffering terrible indignities as an Iron Curtain country: she certainly is not a Soviet satellite by volition or by a desire for uniformity based on the tenet of dialectical materialism, but in consequence of the unscrupulous schemer of Machiavellian politicians and of social upheavals whose threat hovered over the nation for many years past. Her geographical position, squeezed between the East and the West, made it easier for the Bolsheviks to bleed her unmercifully.

Oswald Spengler's Cassandra prophecies resound in the works of twentieth-century Hungarian creators. The voice of anxiety, despair, and *malgré tout* stubbornness implies a twofold consciousness: one regarding the universal spiritual-moral crisis of modern man, the other local, pertaining to the future of the Hungarian nation and the Hungarian language. (pp. 29-30)

Prior to World War I and between the two World Wars the Hungarian spirit went through a process of fermentation, manifested in the works of poets, short-story writers, novelists, playwrights, critics, sociologists, political scientists, historians, publicists, who ran counter to the accepted beliefs of the ruling classes and traditional literary taste or social standards. To capture the literary flavor of those times the best approach seems to be to scan the pages of *Nyugat* (West), a literary magazine, launched and edited by the critics Ernő Osvát and Ignotus, and after the end of World War I edited by Mihály Babits, the poet, translator, essayist, and critic, a seeker and often the master of classic perfection. In surveying the field of modern Hungarian literature one must stress the importance of the *Nyugat* writers who conceived literature either as a pure aesthetic experience or as a cathartic function in an Aristotelian sense. We must keep in mind that most of the creators grouped around this periodical not only were artistically sensitive but social-minded and spoke in behalf of the oppressed, exploited elements of Hungarian society, the landless peasants and industrial workers. Endre Ady, the greatest poet of this generation, is an interesting example of the intermingling of aesthetic finesse and social conscience. Writing about Endre Ady in his instructive essay on "Synaesthesia in Twentieth-Century Hungarian Poetry" [see Additional Bibliography], Arthur H. Whitney, the English critic, points to the Hungarian poet's use of synaesthesia "in a highly individual manner in which the normal value is entirely subordinate to a peculiar symbolism." Aladár Schöpflin, the Hungarian critic, states that "Ady dared to be different," but also refers to his "faith in the redemptive strength of the revolution." The term "revolution" had a Rousseauesque and not Marxist undertone. Zsigmond Móricz, the outstanding realistic novelist, frankly and brutally rejected the frustrating forces of the Hungarian mores. On a level of creative integrity and folk rhythm it is not difficult to establish bonds between the artistic psychology of Béla Bartók and Zoltán Kodály, the renowned composers, the "archetype" traits of "peasant" painters, and certain literary trends; the new creators showed courage and good sense when they tried to present a true picture of Hungarian life. It should be emphasized, however, that they did not conceive literature as a pretext for didacticism; they were essentially artists of the word, without being pontifical about their literary and national task. Milán Füst, Oszkár Gellért, Gyula Juhász, Anna Lesznai, Margit Kaffka, Frigyes Karinthy, Dezső Kosztolányi, Lajos Nagy, J. Jenő Tersánszky, Árpád Tóth, as poets, short-story writers, novelists, critics, were either nonpolitical in their ideological orientation or held the Hungarian historical and plutocratic classes responsible for the social and economic stagnation of the nation. Ferenc Molnár exhibited sophistication with his witty and technically efficient plays and narrative works; his plays, novels, and sketches are perhaps the best clue to an understanding of the Budapest-colored middle-class taste of twentieth-century Hungary. If it is aesthetic experience by which we get intrinsic value in its greatest purity, as Philip Blair Rice, the American critic, observed, one could say that Babits, Juhász, Kosztolányi, and Tóth are paramount examples of this doctrine; Molnár represents rather ingenuity than aesthetic sensibility. Novelists, playwrights, poets, critics, and literary historians, such as Kálmán Csathó, Kálmán Harsányi, Ferenc Herczeg, Jenő Pintér, Mihály Szabolcska (some of their works bear the stamp of creative authenticity), although contemporaries, were in subject matter or attitude closer to the nineteenth century, despite an awareness of the "disturbing issues" of twentieth-century chaos. Cecile Tormay, a novelist of some merit, paved the way to literary fascism. Zsolt Harsányi was popular as a writer of fictional biographies, Sándor Hunyadi as the author of short stories and plays, Irén Gulácsy as a historical novelist, and Gyula Krúdy for his atmospherical stories. It should be said here that besides Molnár's plays and stories other Hungarian works have been translated into English, French, German, Italian, and other languages.

While the *Nyugat* writers affected the following generation, especially in craftsmanship, and the Hungarian stage felt their impact in its improved histrionic art and stagecraft, there was one writer, Dezső Szabó, whose influence on the literary generation between the two World Wars was most impressive. At the outset of his literary life Szabó was associated with *Nyugat;* later he withdrew from this publication and developed an attitude which may be defined as a combination of populism, racial fanaticism, visionariness, an embodiment of ideas and ideals which were true and false. He considered himself a sort of *pontifex maximus* of the cultural life of his country. He was of reckless temperament, endowed with a Rabelaisian verbal imagination, and roamed through Hungarian history and the sphere of timely problems as if destiny had chosen him to keep the *corpus hungaricum* alive. Regardless of his inconsistencies, in which idyllism, romantic effusiveness, realistic bluntness, and violence, subtle and poor taste, bias and honesty and Coriolanus-spite mingled, his vitality, sometimes Balzacian, was undeniable. William Blake said that he was busy with the terror of thoughts; of Dezső Szabó it could be said that he was busy with the apocalyptic fears of his nation. In presenting the suffocating climate of Hungarian society and portraying the Hungarian past as a historical novelist would do, Zsigmond Móricz was a more balanced realist; he, too, lacked restraint, but he did not claim "infallibility of judgment," which characterized Szabó. Nonetheless, Szabó's exceptional ability must be admitted. His polemic writings, eloquence, and diatribes, his characterizations (albeit exaggerated), his unwillingness to be content with compromises, made of this novelist and pamphleteer a kind of apostle among the younger writers, and through his unconventional and controversial public activities he often made front-page news.

Under his influence writers and poets, chiefly of peasant background, many well-educated, felt released from their social inhibitions. The representatives of vested interests considered them poison ivy, but they were fearless and tried to curb the prejudices of the privileged classes. Most of them lived in very modest circumstances, yet their vulnerable economic state did not deter them from remaining faithful to their conviction.

Gyula Illyés, a "fellow traveler," one of the most gifted of those who transferred peasant vitality to letters, is today Hungary's unofficial poet laureate. László Németh is intellectually the keenest writer of this generation, a novelist, playwright, critic, and essayist, the exponent of "new humanism." He has an encyclopedic mind, though of some confusion. All he is allowed to do in totalitarian Hungary is to translate foreign books into his native tongue. Of the naturalistic novelists, short-story writers, and playwrights János Kodolányi is one of the most talented; his writings impress one like an electric current running through the gloomy existence of rich and poor peasants. József Erdélyi and a few more of the poets of the "populist" school adapted the meter and spirit of the intimate poetry of Sándor Petőfi, the greatest nineteenth-century Hungarian lyric poet, but, unfortunately, with fascist leanings. Several of these writers centered their activities in the *Falukutatók* (village investigators) movement: *Válasz* (Answer) was their periodical. Some of them were adamant in their insistence on the principle that only writers rooted in the Hungarian soil can wage a true war for a just social and political order. They remind one of the Russian *pochvenniki* in the nineteenth-century, a group to which Dostoevsky belonged for a time. It should be pointed out that every literary school of the West had its protagonists in Hungary: Expressionism, Surrealism, Futurism, New Objectivism, Activism, etc. Significantly Gyula Illyés, who is proud of his peasant ancestry and whose poetry crystallizes this pride, describes in one of his books a conversation with Tristan Tzara, the godfather of Dadaism. As Oszkár Jászi should be considered the sociological theoretician of the *Nyugat* generation, Gyula Szekfű, the historian, has a similar relationship to the peasant writers and their school. In his youth Szekfű supported the Habsburgs; later, he performed an ideological somersault and after the "liberation" of Hungary by the Soviets he became the first Hungarian diplomatic representative in Moscow. His friends maintain that it was not opportunism but pressure that impelled him to accept this mission.

Aside from the agrarian trend in Hungarian letters between the two World Wars, and during World War II, there were others who must be mentioned. Despite terrifying forebodings as to the future of the nation, in the shadow of Hitler and his Hungarian collaborators some poets and writers continued to concentrate on creative expression as an artistic responsibility. The periodical *Magyar Csillag* (Hungarian Star) became the successor of *Nyugat*. In manner and matter Hungarian poetry of this period is characterized by lyric poems in minor key akin to folk songs, dramatic and philosophical poems in major key, longer poems echoing folk ballads, loose versification or a firm control over the material, cosmic or personal symbolism and earthiness, an overwhelming sense of futility and yearning for hope, an aptitude for distinguished or delicate phrasing, original metaphors and mere technical dexterity, love and mysticism, intricate designs and attempts to free oneself from the complexities of modernity, participation in the life of the people and withdrawal from society. These contradictory elements reveal the restless impulses of the Hungarian poets and their many-faceted emotional, ethical, and intellectual interests. Poetry seemed like a cross-examination of man by destiny. Lőrinc Szabó is the most characteristic poet of this era. He remained intense even then, when he turned from his expressionistic manner to more traditional forms in search for philosophical security, thus indicating that his tendency toward solipsism and his desire to overcome it did not produce a peaceful spiritual solution of his problems.

For a time the historical and the war novel were regarded as the most successful fictional performance on the Hungarian literary scene; they were replaced by the pseudo psychology of "clever" novelists (misusing or abusing Freud), whose works were amorphous products serving the vogue of worldly superficialities. Other novelists or short-story writers—some excelling in composition, humor, irony, or unorthodox taste, or in assimilating foreign influences and harmonizing them with their own creative nature—stressed impersonality or distilled subjectivity. The works of several narrative writers confirmed Nikolai Berdyaev's observation about a certain type of the modern novel "as the most significant form of philosophical self-knowledge." Regrettably, the "philosophical" novels were rambling, diffuse, and cumbersome. The very best novelists, generally with a realistic attitude, combined popular success with artistic achievement. The novelists and playwrights, with few exceptions, were more flexible in their aesthetic views than the poets; this is demonstrated by the fact that it would be easier to select outstanding poems than prose works, although there were prose writers who achieved artistic flawlessness. The literary critics applied philosophical methods, historical, psychological, or sociological standards, or were impressionists. Some of the critics were concerned with ideas, reflecting the principles of Dilthey's *Geistesgeschichte* school; others were concerned with systematic criticism applied to form; some were moralists, others skeptics, some fanatical nationalists, others Thomists, humanists, psychoanalysts, or Marxists.

The psychological and imaginatively suggestive novels of Sándor Márai, the versatile and authentic poetry of Sándor Weöres and Zoltán Jékely (the former reminding one somewhat of Dylan Thomas), fully justify the claim that notwithstanding the censorship of the Horthy regime they were creators who would not permit political chicanery to destroy their aesthetic integrity. Foreign narrative, poetic, and critical works reached the Hungarian reader in translation. The repertory of the theaters in Budapest and in the provincial cities included many translated plays. Some of the poets, such as Géza Képes, Miklós Radnóti, István Vas, popular novelists, like Ferenc Móra and Lajos Zilahy, were harassed by the authorities. The most tragic case is that of Attila József (a poet in some respects similar to Federico García Lorca) who at the age of thirty-two committed suicide by throwing himself in front of a train. There was also a Catholic literary awakening, represented by Zsolt Aradi, Borisz Balla, Béla Horváth, Béla Just, Lászlo Mécs, Sándor Sik, who were identified with the periodical *Vigilia* (Vigil). Marxist writers and poets found outlet in the periodical *Munka* (Labor), edited by Lajos Kassák, the avant-garde poet and novelist, and on the pages of *Népszava* (Voice of the People), a daily newspaper. Often mediocre in artistic structure and concentrating on context, nonetheless some (for example, Andor Endre Gelléri, the short-story writer, who portrayed primarily social outcasts or "little people"—artisans, small shopkeepers of the city peripheries) conquered the handicaps of undesirable external circumstances and programmatic art with the sincerity of their convictions and ability.

Considering the stress and strain of life (the economic opportunities of the Hungarian man of letters were seldom favorable) and considering the "patriotic" restrictions of certain rigid codes to which "respectable" authors were expected to adhere, it is extraordinary indeed how well the scholarly type of literature, that is, research work, textual criticism, monographs, biographies, philological studies, developed in Hungary. The personal and the formal essay alike showed a heretofore unparalleled progress. The civilizing influence of the essayists reached many quarters. Their writings signified freshness of

expression and knowledge, scientific preciseness and discursive intelligence, a sense of the universal and a respect for details. Marcell Benedek, István Borsody, Gyula Farkas, István Gál, Albert Gyergyai, Gábor Halász, János Hankiss, János Horváth, Dezső Keresztúry, Károly Kerényi, Imre Kovács, Lajos Prohászka, László Cs. Szabó, Zoltán Szabó, István Sőtér, Antal Szerb, Tivadar Thienemann, József Túróczi-Trostler, Nándor Várkonyi, and others proved to be the intellectual conscience of their nation. They assigned themselves the task of inspecting the Hungarian creative and critical spirit in a manner which enabled them to show the wider horizons of the Hungarian literary genius; they also wrote a great deal on foreign subjects. Some were profound, some agile or dogmatic, others eclectic, but all—the older and younger alike—represented a truly cultivated mind. In opposition to the "manifesto" habit of "revolutionary" writers, they focused their attention with a singular perseverance on clear style, on the clarification of the turbulent spirit of modern times, on the intellectually integrated morality of information. They were not "above the battle"; in fact, some of them participated in it vehemently; but regardless of whether the past, the present, or the future was their main scholarly or literary interest, whether they moved on native or foreign grounds, their guiding principle was intellectual integrity. There was considerable good historical, philosophical, psychological, and sociological writing, too. (pp. 31-6)

> *Joseph Reményi, "Hungarian Literature during Three Decades, 1925-1955," in his* Hungarian Writers and Literature: Modern Novelists, Critics, and Poets, *edited by August J. Molnar, Rutgers University Press, 1964, pp. 29-39.*

ALBERT TEZLA

[*Tezla is an American critic, literary historian, bibliographer, and translator of Hungarian literature. In the following excerpt, he surveys the development of Hungarian literature from World War II to 1980.*]

More formidable impediments to the development of the literature of a small European nation can hardly be found than those present in Hungary during the postwar period. During these thirty years many historical events rent the intellectual and social fabric of the country. Hungarians had to bear the moral onus of the long alliance with Germany and of the savage acts of the native fascists, the Szálasi Arrow-Cross Party, in the closing months of the war. They had to restore the economic life of a land devastated by war and burdened by Soviet occupation. Their early attempts to revive national life occurred amid crucial struggles among political parties vying for popular support. When this discord ended with the sudden assumption of power by the Communist Party in 1948, Hungarians experienced radical upheavals in all parts of their lives. After eight years of the new social order, smoldering discontent with Party measures erupted in the Revolution of 1956, leaving Hungarians to face the consequences of the horrible bloodletting and the failure to reestablish a democratic government. The twenty years since that spontaneous uprising have witnessed the consolidation of a single-party socialist state, producing a profound impact not only on the economic and social life of the nation but also on the cultural policies that govern all the arts.

Even this brief summary of the chaotic and complex realities of postwar Hungary suggests that the circumstances in which creative writers had to work would pose grave barriers to the revival of literature and its evolution into a valuable interpreter of the human scene, as it had clearly shown signs of doing between the two world wars. In spite of the turmoil and uncertainty often attending these years, however, Hungarian authors developed a rich and varied imaginative literature, which, to a remarkable degree, eventually measured up to the enthusiasms and expectations that so many of them had expressed at the beginning of the post-war period.

At the end of the war, the atmosphere of freedom, unknown to Hungarian authors since the nation had been linked to Hitler's Germany in the mid-1930s, produced an outburst of literary activity. With censorship lifted and intellectual horizons unobstructed, all kinds of writing, including socialist, were published. There was much experimentation, and before long, many views of life and forms of expression existed side by side, particularly in poetry and fiction. This great surge of creativity was energized by many new journals that zealously advocated certain literary approaches, as well as partisan political viewpoints, and, for a time, found common ground in supporting humanistic principles. Although the struggle for power among the several political parties often interfered with literary activities, writers were vigorous enough to withstand the paralyzing effects of the worsening political atmosphere and to set in motion various trends so firmly that many outlasted

Tibor Déry. Reproduced by permission of Hans Christians Druckerei und Verlag.

the cultural policies put into effect in 1948, when the Communist Party took control of the nation.

Understandably, much of the imaginative literature appearing from 1945 to 1948 critically examined the events and social order of the previous twenty-five years that had culminated in the disaster of war. But, more significantly for the restoration of literature, authors probed issues ranging from current conditions in Hungary to the purpose of human existence and the nature of the universe. Certain poets among those who had established their reputations before the war stood out in this regard. There was Lőrinc Szabó, long an experimenter in verse forms, with his pessimistic view of humankind's struggle in an indifferent cosmos, and Milán Füst, a pioneer of free verse in Hungary, who rebelled against fate and felt deep compassion for humanity. Lajos Kassák, an early advocate of the avant-garde in both poetry and the visual arts, abandoned social themes to express his most intimate thoughts and feelings. Above the scene towered Gyula Illyés, the populist and poet of lyrical realism, who explored the issue of responsibility in the relationship between the individual and society, weighed thoughtfully the question of human efficacy, and viewed the problems of humankind from a historical perspective. István Vas, like Illyés a major inspiration for many young poets, was distressed by the anxieties pervading the times and offered the inherent strength of human reason and individual freedom as the best defense against calamity. Among the Communists, Zoltán Zelk pressed forward the need for revolutionary changes in the social and economic fabric, and László Benjámin, who published a volume of poems in 1939, urged radical reforms, based on his personal ideas, that would prepare the way for a socialist state. At the opposite pole, Sándor Weöres, divorcing himself from reality, searched for a private vision of a universal force that only a turning inward to the self could attain. These experienced poets were soon joined by those who would establish their place under conditions already looming on the political horizon. They fell into two groups. There were those who, as avowed Communists, dedicated themselves to the revolutionary transformation of their society: Ferenc Juhász, László Nagy, and István Simon, all of them from the poor social classes living in the villages. And there were those who, shocked by the moral implications of the war and Hungarian fascism, searched for new ethical and spiritual foundations on which to rebuild a relationship with life: Magda Szabó, who later wrote successful novels, János Pilinszky, Ágnes Nemes Nagy, László Kálnoky, and György Rába. The responses of these two groups and of prose writers who emerged at the same time to the stress and strain of impending historical events largely determined future trends in the post-war literature.

Prose fiction also manifested vitality at this time, although its themes and styles were not as various as those of poetry. For the most part, novelists and short-story writers preferred the values and attitudes of realism, and to arrive at a moral reckoning with their past, mainly re-examined Hungarian society since the end of World War I, analyzing sociologically and psychologically the semi-feudal social structure that lasted until 1945. This tradition, so firmly entrenched by the prolific and long career of Zsigmond Móricz, was best represented by several pre-war writers who were still active. Pál Szabó, another populist from the 1930s, portrayed peasant life and the conflicts between peasants and the intelligentsia. Péter Veres, then fifty years old, looked at peasant life in a satirical and humorous, though realistic manner. László Németh, more inventive than both, wrote his best novel, *Revulsion (Iszony)*, in 1947. It depicts the problems of a family and life in a village through the confessions of a wife whose marriage is falling apart. Also appearing at this time was fiction with a strong socialist theme, some of it written before the end of the war but not publishable until now. Probably the best example is Tibor Déry's *The Unfinished Sentence (A befejezetlen mondat,* 1947), which traces the gradual involvement of a middle-class intellectual in the cause of the working class between the two world wars, a narrative based on the author's past relationship with the proletariat. Another new current, one that soon caused serious problems for originality, was socialist realism. Béla Illés, an experienced writer just returned from Moscow with the Russian army, published a representative example, *Carpathian Rhapsody (Kárpáti rapszódia),* an affectionate portrait of Ukrainian life in the Carpathian Mountains, which appeared in thirteen editions between 1945 and 1960.

During these three years, other kinds of narrative representation did not develop significantly. They were present and had the potential to modify the realism that became such a fixture of the literary tradition. Unfortunately, the pressures of the times and social forces meant there was little opportunity to reconsider the purposes of prose fiction. To be sure, in the war years novelists were already experimenting with some elements of surrealism. Among the most accomplished were Emil Kolozsvári Grandpierre, György Rónay, István Sőtér, and Géza Ottlik, who were familiar with pre-war developments in the European novel and were associated with the progressive but short-lived literary periodical *Silver Age (Ezüstkor).* Some of the more promising authors among those making their debut immediately after the war vacillated between alternative styles and literary purposes. Imre Sarkadi turned to socialist realism for a time, believing that it served the needs of his country more productively than the realism of Zsigmond Móricz, which he had previously adopted; István Örkény, Ferenc Karinthy, and Lajos Mesterházi—who later became influential figures under changed historical conditions—first experimented with surrealism and then, for the same reason as Sarkadi, held up the mirror of socialist realism to their society—a mirror soon to be obligatory. Iván Mándy and Miklós Mészöly were also on the scene. Mándy was presenting an everyday world with an almost surrealistic mingling of the actual and the dream; Mészöly, who had quickly mastered the use of atmosphere in the short story to convey meaning, was experimenting with narrative techniques and style in search of new paths for Hungarian fiction. In 1948, amid these mixed trends and searchings, László Németh pointed the way that not only novelists but all writers must henceforth travel to foster a viable imaginative literature. In his view, the end of the war had brought a wider horizon to a literature that had just begun to mature between two world wars. "Now there is," he proclaimed, "no longer a national destiny; all humanity is now one nation, and the fate of everyone will be settled together: it is my right, indeed my duty to think about the whole human race." In the summer of that very year, the establishment of Communist control over national life abruptly arrested stylistic experimentation and the pursuit of Németh's concept of the writer's universal role.

The Communist Party's coming to power began the gravest period of literary creativity that Hungary had ever known. The Party's cultural policy seriously hobbled developments in imaginative literature for many years. Besides instituting radical economic and social changes and nationalizing all theaters and publishing houses, the government declared socialist realism, as promulgated in 1946 by Andrey Zhdanov in Russia, to be the sole course for the arts. In order to publish, writers were expected to adopt a schematic approach that interpreted reality

in accord with socialist principles as the Party hierarchy defined them. Essentially, schematism, or socialist realism carried to an extreme, demanded that the writer abandon the right to select themes, surrender a personal interpretation of issues, and forsake a distinctive style. Writers had to subordinate individual views and conform strictly to prevailing Party ideology. Accordingly, imaginative literature was to achieve victory in the class struggle against bourgeois elements, to glorify heroes of the socialist revolution and vilify its enemies at home and abroad, and to sing about five-year plans, agricultural cooperatives, common people enjoying the fruits of socialist policies, the imminence of the earthly paradise that socialism would inevitably create, and the battle against capitalists for world peace. Moreover, to attain its strictly didactic aim, the style of a work had to be democratized, made simple and clear, so that uneducated workers and peasants could grasp and pursue the objectives of socialism. Failure to comply with these dictates did not necessarily shut every door to publication, especially in periodicals. The slightest departure from them, however, brought published accusations that the author had abandoned the nation, betrayed the proletariat, become apolitical, or turned to romantic self-indulgence. The rigid enforcement of this cultural policy by severely party-minded critics in an atmosphere charged with political threat and insecurity left open only two paths to writers who did not espouse the values of socialist realism out of personal conviction but who chose to remain in Hungary. Neither boded well for the acceleration of the vital trends that had emerged between 1945 and 1948. Writers could carry out the official policy if they were willing to act against the grain of their individuality and work below the level of their true gifts—the path chosen by such important authors as György Somlyó, Gábor Devecseri, Imre Sarkadi, Ferenc Karinthy, and István Örkény. Or like Sándor Weöres, István Vas, János Pilinszky, Ágnes Nemes Nagy, Iván Mándy, Géza Ottlik, Miklós Mészöly, and others, they could leave the literary scene if they were not willing to compromise the integrity of their convictions and style.

This is not to say that all literature of high quality vanished from public view. However, the aggressive enforcement of schematism nearly brought the evolution of a diverse literature to a standstill, particularly during the early 1950s, an effect openly acknowledged today by Hungarian critics and literary historians. The drama, its revival hardly begun, was made ridiculous by the dogmatic presentation of social issues from everyday life. Lyric poetry, the most highly developed genre in Hungarian literature, became platitudinous, its imagery commonplace, its forms repetitious, and its thoughts impoverished. Given the circumstances, it is not surprising that even among those supporting socialism only the more accomplished poets were able to write lyrics worth reading. Illyés, his prestige as a revolutionary populist ensuring his authority, continued to treat a wide range of themes; and Benjámin, his convictions deeply rooted in revolutionary traditions, infused his endorsements of the social changes taking place with enthusiasm and intense feeling. Among the new poets, Ferenc Juhász, László Nagy, and István Simon also managed to convey genuine emotions because they envisioned a better future for the social classes who had only recently begun to enjoy economic and social benefits. Prose fiction, with Móricz and the recent socialist realists in the Soviet Union serving as its exemplars, suffered even more severely than poetry. Even such eminent older writers of realism as Déry, Pál Szabó, and Veres, who successfully adapted their works to socialist realism, could not always erase every trace of disharmony between the official style and their convictions. Many established novelists chose to write autobiographies, autobiographical novels, and novel cycles presenting broad pictures of recent times. And often the heaviest burden of schematism fell on such authors as Karinthy, Sarkadi, and Örkény, who were striving to discover their individuality under the self-censorship that their attempt to weld literary purpose with political ends inflicted on them.

But in the long run the regime was not able to force writers into a single mold. Resistance to schematism as administered chiefly by the doctrinaire József Révai surfaced early, often publicly. György Lukács, the renowned Marxist philosopher, aesthetician, and literary historian, took issue with Révai and gave legitimacy to the reality created by the imagination. In the spring of 1951 authors strongly protested its injurious effect on originality at the First Congress of Hungarian Writers, which was summoned to evaluate the literary developments of the previous three decades and to fix the role of literature in a socialist society. Its proceedings were reported in the periodical *The Star (Csillag)* and then were expanded into a book published in the same year. During the sessions Benjámin and Juhász objected to policies affecting literary creativity and pointed to their inevitable consequences. Benjámin criticized the poetry being published for flatness and lack of inspiration. The youthful Juhász complained about editors who accepted only works that slavishly adhered to the standards of schematism and attacked certain colleagues, including Benjámin, for their dull depictions of reality. And addressing the heart of the problem, he insisted that poets had the right to express their beliefs in a style natural to them. The next year Révai challenged the prestigious Déry for "misusing" socialist realism in *Answer (Felelet,* 1952), an attack that underlined the widening gap between official critics and the most important members of the writing community. Révai charged Déry with falling short of Party expectations because his youthful hero did not join the Communist Party. In reply Déry protested that he could not realistically make his bourgeois protagonist a member of a political group that in the 1920s, the time of the story, was merely an obscure "sect" in Hungary. During these years such clashes between official critics and writers were regularly reported in Budapest by two periodicals, *The Star* and *Literary News (Irodalmi Újság)* and in the provinces by literary and cultural journals like *Transdanubia (Dunántúl).*

The year 1953 saw a crucial stage in this conflict. This period known as the Thaw began when, as a result of massive economic disarray and Stalin's death, the liberal-minded Imre Nagy replaced Mátyás Rákosi. In this less oppressive atmosphere, writers increasingly ignored the demands of schematism. For example, Benjámin took a firm stand against Stalinism, and Illyés responded not only to domestic matters but to large philosophical questions and, at a more personal level, to the sad fact of aging and the inevitability of death. In the pages of *New Voice (Új Hang),* the vehicle of young writers, Juhász and Nagy freely divulged their gloom at what they found in the world around them. Juhász, whose "The Boy Changed into a Stag" W. H. Auden called one of the greatest poems of this century, shared with readers his agony at the sight of human suffering; Nagy, dismayed by the limited satisfactions that human toil brings, yearned for simple pleasures to enrich life, in "The Bliss of Sunday," one of his more compassionate poems. In a series of poems published in *The Star* and *Literary News* in August 1953, a new poet, soon widely read, Sándor Csoóri, cried out at the disastrous disruption of peasant life that collectivization had wrought. It was also significant that the poems of Weöres and Vas appeared again, first in journals and then as editions, and more slowly, also those of János

Pilinszky and Ágnes Nemes Nagy; and the fiction of Imre Sarkadi and Ferenc Karinthy, now critical of their society, was also published again. In an article appearing in *Literary News* in November 1953, István Örkény, who had suffered some of the severest treatment at the hands of official arbiters, captured the essence of the change that seemed to be taking place. He asserted that in the new climate a socialist writer no longer needed to embellish reality, that the truth as the writer saw it could be told without the guidance of official directives, and that, as always, the writer alone was responsible for what he or she wrote. This statement did not necessarily sound the death knell of schematism, but its wide acceptance by other Communist writers, even one as orthodox as the poet Lajos Kónya, augered well for fresh directions in literature.

At this time two developments in policy governing translations indicated that the literature of the West might again become more abundantly available than in recent years. Several publishing houses had, since 1950, been issuing translations of writings from all ages and literatures only as a secondary responsibility. Moreover, they published a narrow selection of twentieth-century works, preferring those of Russian writers and of western authors critical of their political and economic systems, such as John Steinbeck and Howard Fast. The unhappy consequence of this policy was that Hungarian writers, though not completely cut off from foreign literatures, were isolated from most of the more recent imaginative works in the West. This unfortunate situation was alleviated by the founding of two agencies that, unlike existing presses, were to publish translations only. The earliest of these is significant because of a change in its original scope. Created in 1954 to publish only translations of Russian literature, Új Magyar Kiadó (Európa since 1957) broadened its mission to include more recent examples of world literature. The importance of the second lies in its emphasis on immediacy. In 1956 a journal called *The World (Nagyvilág)* was founded to keep Hungarians informed of trends through translations of more recent works from all parts of the world. These two vehicles . . . opened ways to current writings that had a substantial impact on literary developments after the uprising in October of 1956.

The month of internecine bloodshed during the revolution and the Russian army's eventual crushing of all resistance left the Hungarian people with the tremendous task of restoring normalcy to their daily lives. During the period of consolidating the nation in compliance with socialist principles, writers, quickly recovering the momentum built up under the relaxed policies of the Thaw, advanced markedly toward a variety in imaginative literature not seen since the years immediately after the war. From 1957 to 1962 writers who supported the ideals of socialism abandoned schematism, and those who did not espouse socialism or strict didacticism in imaginative literature were again published in growing numbers.

Not unexpectedly, poetry resurged first. The many poets with various views and styles who were frequently published in the early 1950s soon appeared in anthologies. Those who were already familiar to readers before the revolution were included in a 1957 anthology entitled *105 Poems of 15 Young Poets (15 fiatal költő 105 verse),* which contained several selections by the promising Margit Szécsi and the brash Sándor Csoóri. This anthology is considered a milestone in the history of literary developments because not one poem evinced a trace of schematism. Quite different but equally important historically is another anthology, *Fire Dance (Tűztánc),* which was published the following year. The poets in this volume rose to the defense of the embattled socialist cause in distinctive ways. Among them were Mihály Váci and Mihály Ladányi, thirty-four and twenty-four respectively, the first furthering the interests of the proletariat and the liberation of all colonial peoples from imperialism, and the second lashing out against any middle-class weaknesses still present in Hungarian society. Also included was Gábor Garai, whose ethical view of revolutionary communism, and its extension to all humanity placed him in the forefront of post-1956 socialist poetry. To these two groups must be added two poets who, like Sándor Weöres, returned after a long absence: Ágnes Nemes Nagy and János Pilinszky. Nemes Nagy returned with *Heat Lightning (Szárazvillám)* in 1957, her first book since 1946, and Pilinszky with *On the Third Day (Harmadnapon)* in 1959, his first book of poems in thirteen years. Unlike the preceding poets, they were not concerned with political or purely domestic issues; their vision embraced all humankind as they explored the ethical implications of their inner conflicts. Both bore the wounds of their times. To offer consolation, Nemes Nagy, tormented by the susceptibility of human emotions to the deceptions practiced by the world, searched for those invisible points where the transient and permanent meet. Pilinszky was seared by the moral debacle of contemporary civilization, especially as symbolized by the inhumanity of the concentration camp, and he suffered the Stations of the Cross that marked humanity's way. The many strands of thought and expression represented by all these poets tied into a warp that ensured their personal growth and led to major developments in Hungarian poetry in the altered circumstances of the 1960s.

In this six-year period, prose fiction showed signs of developing beyond its traditional commitment to a realism characterized by sociological and psychological analysis, careful articulation of plot, strict adherence to time sequence, and detailed description. As in poetry, schematism vanished, and the way opened to fresh viewpoints and techniques. The elevation of fiction to new artistic levels required contributions from authors determined to express their interpretations of life in their own way. Casting off schematism entirely, both Imre Sarkadi and Ferenc Karinthy now assumed their true character. Sarkadi, unfortunately a suicide in 1961, freely criticized socialism for its deception of the people. Perceiving that even successful social reform would leave untouched many grave problems, he offered in his narratives the ethical insights of humanism rather than those of socialism. Like Sarkadi, Karinthy registered his criticism of the course that socialism had pursued in Hungary, and turning his fertile imagination to themes found in the life of a big city, he revealed a playfulness and narrative skill that later matured in a novel, *EPEPE (EPEPE,* 1970), a remarkable allegory of alienation and limitations in communication between human beings set in an imaginary metropolis.

Developments in fiction were also greatly influenced by a group of writers who emerged from 1953 on, many of them becoming major figures in the 1960s. In 1957 the short stories of the more important of these authors were collected in an anthology called *Initiation (Emberavatás),* its title taken from a story by Ferenc Sánta about a youth encountering the double-edged experience of becoming an adult. Unaffected by schematism and not strictly bound to traditional modes of realistic fiction, yet committed to socialism, these authors made clear early that they were seeking new paths in realism. Many succeeded, adding to those followed in the writing of Sarkadi and Karinthy. Among them, Sánta, Erzsébet Galgóczi, István Szabó, György Moldova, and István Csurka particularly introduced new themes and fresh techniques that helped to enliven fiction. Ready to

Lőrinc Szabó. Photograph by Lőrinc Szabó, Jr.

take issue with their society, they all focused on urgent matters. Sánta posed ethical issues, pondered the efficacy of revolution in producing constructive change, and extolled the role of the individual conscience, exalting the authority of the writer's conscience above everyone else's. Both Galgóczi and Szabó depicted the disruptions in peasant life resulting from collectivization, the former using nearly sociographical details lyrically and the latter applying psychological analysis. Moldova and Csurka, more oriented toward urban life, portrayed through penetrating satire and caricature the bizarre contradictions between socialist reality and its ethical ideal. Of course, many novelists and short-story writers then coming into their own, like the young poets included in the anthology *Fire Dance,* staunchly supported socialism. Noteworthy among them were Lajos Galambos, Károly Szakonyi, and István Gáll, who endorsed and defended the version of socialism that evolved after the Revolution of 1956.

These fundamental developments were importantly enhanced by the novels and short stories of two other groups of writers. Impetus was given to new trends by the long-delayed return of authors who had preferred silence to being stifled by schematism: Magda Szabó, Iván Mándy, Miklós Mészöly, and Géza Ottlik, who, like the poets János Pilinszky and Ágnes Nemes Nagy, were historically associated with the progressivism of the defunct periodical *New Moon (Újhold).* Magda Szabó published two novels, *Fresco (Freskó,* (1958) and *The Fawn (Az őz,* 1959), launching a new career; in her works, often concerned with the clash between old and new values, she used the stream-of-consciousness technique with special skill. Mándy, whose last book, excluding his stories for children, had been published in 1949, returned in 1957 to chronicle with almost poetic means the lives of unsuccessful characters living on the fringes of society in Budapest, such as those in "The Watermelon Eaters" or the mother in "A Summer Holiday," who is out of place in the new socialist order. Mészöly, who had not been heard from since 1948, published in 1957 a collection of stories, written during his silence, that reached sensitively for the innermost human emotions, often disclosing them, as in "Shade," in an atmosphere of elemental eeriness. Of this group, Ottlik achieved the most immediate and dramatic impact on readers. After publishing a book of short stories in 1957, he caused a sensation in 1959 with a novel, *School on the Border (Iskola a határon)*, in which he symbolized the innateness of human savagery with a shocking picture of young military cadets discovering within themselves many subtle ways to torture one another, somewhat as William Golding does in *Lord of the Flies*.

The second group consisted of three similarly minded writers who launched their careers in the middle of the decade. Like the authors who returned after several years' absence, László Kamondy, Endre Fejes, and Gyula Hernádi disclosed an independence in their choice of themes and styles. Kamondy, never touched by schematism and not attracted by socialist realism, published an edition of short stories in 1957 and in 1960 a sparsely phrased novel, *Descendant of the Apostles (Apostolok utóda)*, that demonstrated his penchant for careful psychological analysis and thoughtful exploration of intellectual and moral problems. After Fejes put out a collection of short stories called *The Liar (A hazudos*, 1958), which often portrayed characters living on the boundary between dream and reality, he next produced *Generation of Rust (Rozsdatemtő, 1962)*, a widely acclaimed novel that used cinematic techniques to draw a painfully detailed portrait of the life of a postwar middle-class family functioning with mistaken values. Of the three members, Hernádi, whose first stories appeared in 1954 when he was twenty-eight, revealed the most dynamic tendencies for experimentation, a feature of his creativity that links his spirit with that of the older Mészöly. In 1959 a collection of his short stories and his novel *On the Steps of Friday (A péntek lépcsői)* appeared. Both works were rooted in the suffering experienced by his generation as they searched for the meaning of life in the difficult times in which they grew up, and they already displayed the surrealistic touches that later became typical of his style as he continued to confront the agonizing moral choices contemporary humans must make. The large variety of themes and the many techniques present in the contributions of these two groups and of the authors previously discussed indicate that fiction was mustering new strength and many adherents during these six years, in spite of the near paralysis of originality and inspiration it had endured from schematism and the shambles in which the 1956 Revolution had left the nation.

The more temperate climate of the early 1960s brought the richest growth of Hungarian literature since the years immediately following World War II. By this time the consolidation of the nation's political and economic life in accord with Marxist-Leninist socialism, a process proclaimed complete at the Eighth Party Congress in 1962, had undoubtedly produced greater stability in the daily lives of the people. The reduction of tensions between the government and members of the writing community cultivated an atmosphere in which literary creativ-

ity could prosper more easily. Several changes in cultural policy made it possible for the activity stirring since 1956 to increase. Opportunities for publication were expanded, although state control of publishing houses and the burden of self-censorship remained in force. Authors were less and less isolated from the world community, especially the West, and the quickening flow of translations of the latest literature helped them to evaluate their writings in the context of world literature and to react to the newest currents of thought and style. Ampler opportunities to travel abroad also enlarged their perspectives, although such travel was subject to strictest government control. Hungarian authors actively participated in writers' conferences in the West, and many of them visited the United States through a long-term program instituted in 1964 by the Ford Foundation, which included the translation workshop and writers' conferences at the University of Iowa. Still another change was the publication of literary criticism that once again applied sophisticated individualistic methods of analysis. Authors of imaginative literature published treatises that freely explored the nature and function of literature, and their distinct speculations sparked readers' expectations of new literary experiences.

But the most liberating factor was the official acceptance of a role for the writer different from the prevailing one, a role that had already evolved to a significant degree but was only then being acknowledged, often tacitly. Writers felt freer to exercise the right that Juhász had so passionately claimed at the First Hungarian Writers' Conference in 1951: to use the creative imagination, even confessionally, to explore universal questions of human existence as the writer responded to their unfolding within the recesses of his or her inner world, stirring reflections in readers that led them to deeper perceptions of life. This new latitude and other signs of growing liberalization represented significant gains for writers determined to speak in their own voices, to discover what they are through self-realization. Of course, if they were to publish, they had to show moral purpose, and could not attack the regime, and always ran the risk that their works would be interpreted by established arbiters. But within these severe limits they secured the measure of freedom necessary to raise to new levels the literature that had been developing since the end of the war.

From this time on, literary activities became more vigorous and diverse. A new age seemed to dawn. Writers whose works were published before the war added to their achievements in climactic, often different ways. Among novelists Déry was, perhaps, the outstanding example of what the changed atmosphere made possible. Released in 1961 from prison and absolved in 1962 of all charges relating to his participation in the 1956 uprising, he disclosed new artistic tendencies. Exploring universal problems of life and the historical choices forced upon the human race, he wrote short stories and several novels that expressed a passionate concern about the destiny of twentieth-century civilization. Among them were *The Excommunicator (A kiközösitö*, 1966), a historical parable of the personality cult, and *Imaginary Report on an American Rock Festival (Képzelt riport egy amerikai popfesztiválról*, 1971), a terrifying account of human cruelty and barbarity drawing on the events of the 1969 Rolling Stones festival in California that culminated in a riot and the murder of a black youth by the Hell's Angels. Before his death at eighty-three in 1977, Déry added several other works to the body of his work: *Cher Beau-Père (Kedves bópeer*, 1973), an ironic and illusionless novel about an old man's infatuation with a young woman; *The One-Eared Man (A félfülü*, 1975), another ironic novel satirizing the absurdities of western life present in the kidnapping of Paul Getty, Jr.; *No Verdict (Ítélet nincs,* 1969), memoirs reflecting the adversities through which his generation had lived; and, in 1972 and 1975, editions of his meditations, which he called "flotsam," about daily life and the unique problems of the present century.

Poets well known before the war continued to contribute to developments, sometimes changing their views and feelings. Gyula Illyés, returning after a long absence, published seven books of poetry between 1961 and 1973, not to mention some plays, a philosophical novel on old age called *On Charon's Ferry (Kháron ladikája,* 1969), and several collections of essays. The lyrical realism of his poems remained, but their humanistic themes increased and focused on the transitoriness of life and the inevitability of death, becoming more philosophical and less engaged with domestic matters. István Vas, who still applied the rational faculty to human experience in precise verses that seldom used metaphorical language, now became a father figure to many of the younger poets. He faced life without illusion, and he viewed humanity somewhat skeptically. László Benjámin composed leaner lines, less adorned poetry than before, and although he remained a committed Socialist, he expressed some resignation and pessimism not present in his writings of the 1950s, and felt some doubt about the power of poetry to improve humans and society. And finally, Sándor Weöres particularly benefited from the more temperate climate, which gave a greater opportunity to share with readers the individuality of thought and style that he had always fostered. That course of development is made clear in a collection of his works published in 1970, augmented by a third volume in 1975. Magically versatile in devising form and selecting images, he widened and deepened his use of oriental and primitive myths, often in ways as arcane as those of William Blake, putting many of his best poems beyond the reach of translators. In such books of verse as *Fire Fountain (Tüzkút,* 1964), *Sinking Saturn (Merülő Saturnus,* 1968), and *Psyche (Psyché,* 1972), Weöres searched for humankind's place in the universe. These works created a cosmic and mythic world in which a passive inward-turning, made possible by oriental thought, mystically merged the self with a universal will of which all things in time are a manifestation, so that every aspect of conscious reality is transformed into ephemeral expressions of that universal will within the evermoving processes of time and nature.

Although these authors and others with long careers remained vital and influential, the literature of the 1960s and 1970s was chiefly in the hands of those new writers who had established their standing during the post-war years. Among the poets who had appeared in the historic anthology *Fire Dance,* Mihály Ladányi, Mihály Váci, and Gábor Garai were now well out in front. Convinced that poetry is an instrument of reform, Ladányi passionately opposed anything impeding socialism in Hungary. Váci defined the worth of his poetry solely by the extent to which it reached those who, in his view, had been trod upon by capitalism, seeking to embrace them with a love born of his sharing their suffering. Of the three, Garai grounded his revolutionary ideals most deeply on general philosophical and ethical principles. In time both Váci and Garai altered their attitudes to a degree. Before his death in 1970 at forty-six, Váci was troubled about the prospects of improving the human condition and unsure if the power of poetry could produce change; Garai did not modify his ideas, but his poems eventually evinced some dejection and feelings of isolation. With these poets must be included István Simon, whose career began

at the same time as that of Juhász and László Nagy, and also Imre Csanádi, whose first book was published in 1953. The tone of these two poets' commitment to the post-1956 socialist order is more subdued than that of any of the preceding. Simon, who died in 1975, offered to readers as much joy and escape from human cares as he possibly could, trusting ultimately in the strength to be discovered in the world of nature. Csanádi, whose meditative bent became more philosophical in the 1960s, expanded his themes beyond the peasantry, and humor gradually permeated his work. Attracted by the language of folk poetry and blending it with twentieth century speech, he speculated about human fate, attempting to reconcile individual destiny and the events of history, an effort effectively represented by a cycle of poems capturing in words the ancient Hungarian world of visual art.

But during these two decades, it was the poetry of Juhász and László Nagy that gained the largest following. Still avowed Communists, they suffered greatly from the painful paradoxes of events occurring since the revolution, and they experienced deep internal crises as they strove to bring their vision to their people. They wrestled with some of the most perplexing themes, Juhász reaching into the sciences for imagery and Nagy, though also using scientific images, always preferring natural and mythical imagery. The theme of death's inevitability is central to their thought, but each searched for consolation in different directions. Determinedly, sometimes desperately optimistic, Juhász sought the union of the self with the eternal universe. At first Nagy was confident that poetry had the power to create a valid relationship with reality for humankind, but he turned brooding and contemplative, seeking escape in poetry and finding solace in the supportive strength of love and, at times, relief in playful poetic moods. Experimenting freely with verse forms, as had the older Illyés and Vas, both poets contributed importantly to the variety of forms that became a prominent characteristic of the poetry of the 1960s and '70s, especially to the open and intricate long poem and the prose poem, which enabled the poets of the time to convey the layers of complexities they found in the turmoil of the present century.

Equally essential as Juhász and Nagy to poetic developments were János Pilinszky and Ágnes Nemes Nagy, who became increasingly influential. Neither of them as prolific as Juhász and Nagy and many other contemporaries and, like Emily Dickinson, favoring the short stanza and poem and the scrupulous crafting of images into almost aphoristic lines, they both sought an intellectually and emotionally acceptable reconciliation with the terrible moral violations of the self that pervade twentieth-century reality. Pilinszky, to whom the tragic collapse of morality during the war remained a permanent part of reality, struggled with his conviction that human beings can only passively register what is taking place in the world, that they do not shape it, that every experience simply happens to them. His sense of human tragedy is poignantly imparted throughout his career, in a poem as early as "Fish in the Net" ("Halak a hálóban," 1942) and as recently as "Self-Portrait 1974" ("Önarckép 1974"). Nemes Nagy, sharing this personally desolating view of the moral malaise of the world, nevertheless trusted that manifestations of a better existence for humanity could be experienced in the emotions stemming from the intellect under the disciplined expression of lyric poetry, a belief strikingly developed in the magnificent "Akhenaton" ("Ekhnáton").

Prose fiction prospered even more dramatically than poetry in the relaxed atmosphere. Freer to select and examine issues critically and to cultivate an individual style, novelists and short-story writers laid the foundations of a modern fiction that may achieve the stature of Hungarian poetry. In the fifteen or twenty years since the revolution, the post-war authors of fiction, like the poets who came to the forefront in the same period, searched persistently for life's meaning amid the turbulence of the contemporary world. Provokingly analyzing situations, they explored such overriding problems of twentieth-century civilization as the autonomy of the individual, the ethical nature of the human personality, and the clashes between the individual conscience and the demands of society. These key dilemmas were treated chiefly and most effectively by some of the authors who had appeared in *Initiation* back in 1957 and those present earlier who had refused to adopt the modes of schematism. On the whole these authors yielded less to the authority of the social system, and their narratives used their own motifs and problems to stimulate the readers' thought rather than to impose solutions on them. István Szabó, who died in 1976 at age forty-five, improved his narrative skills in short stories about peasant life, drawn, as before, from his personal experiences, and Erzsébet Galgóczi enlarged her perspective by creating peasant protagonists endowed with attributes that transcended the simple particularity of village life. It is Ferenc Sánta, however, who, not limiting his narrative sources to his early years in a village, cultivated a wide spectrum of human experience. The life of a village youth depicted in his early stories like "Little Bird" ("Kicsi madár") and "Fairyland" ("Tündérkert") was followed by portrayals of humans making ethical decisions in situations that historical circumstances visited upon them, as in "No More Dying Then" ("Halálnak halála"). Moral dilemmas dominated his explorations of the authority of the individual conscience, his seeking to account for the way Hungarians cruelly turned on one another during the revolution, and his raising the issue of the worth of revolutionary activity itself. It was also during this time that György Moldova and István Csurka, casting a critical eye at their society even more than before, satirized the contradictions they observed between principles and realities. Moldova, who also made major contributions to sociographic literature, wittily portrayed the foibles of Hungarians and the shortcomings of their society. After several novels about Hungarian life in the troubled 1950s, he published in 1972 a historical novel, narrated in the manner of old chronicles, about forty Hungarian Protestant preachers sentenced to the galleys in the seventeenth century for refusing to renounce their faith. In 1975 he completed the first part of a trilogy describing, through the life of a twelve-year-old Jewish boy, the tragic history of his people in Hungary from 1944 to 1945, when they fell victim to the vicious fascism of Szálasi and the notorious Arrow-Cross Party. Csurka also directed his biting satire at Hungarian society, at its political absurdities and the shortcomings of life under the new social order, as in works like in "The Two Rheumatics" ("Két reumás") and "The Passengers" ("Utasok"). His short stories, novels, and plays presented a bleak view of the human condition, an existence controlled by chance, despite humankind's confidence in the efficacy of planning and action. He often found in the life of gamblers and the race track the symbols for his interpretation of existence.

Perhaps the novelists who published again after a long silence evinced an even more distinctive choice of themes and techniques than did the preceding authors. Magda Szabó's frequent novels were soon translated into many languages. Using the unsettled history of twentieth-century Hungary and the responding flow of thoughts and emotions within her characters, she depicted the conflict between old and new concepts with warmth and psychological insight. From the mid-1960s on, Gyula Hernádi extended the scope of his themes to the problems of the Hungarian professional classes and, chiefly in the 1970s, to the intellectual and moral choices that history has imposed on contemporary humans. In 1971 his *The Fortress (Az erdöd)* appeared, a horrifying novel about successful businessmen paying for the opportunity to play at real war within a fortress in Greece staffed by mercenaries. He experimented with a mixture of real and surreal images, sometimes to intentional excess, as the title of the novel *The Dry Baroque* (*Száraz barokk*, 1967) implies. He often used nearly every style found in twentieth-century literature, including science fiction, the absurd, and the grotesque, as shown in a selection of short stories, *Gates of Logic (Logikai kapuk)*, published in 1975.

Three other writers had a most significant bearing on improvements in prose fiction: Iván Mándy, Miklós Mészöly, and István Örkény, who died in 1979. Mándy and Mészöly were building on careers that they had resumed shortly after the revolution, and Örkény, long silent after that upheaval, began publishing again in the mid-1960s. Mándy, whose novel *On the Touch-Lines* (*A pálya szélén*, 1963) was praised by Heinrich Böll, wrote with poetical concreteness about the world of the coffeehouse, the shabby side of the big city, and, later, the life of journalists, old-time movie stars like Greta Garbo, Harold Lloyd, the Danish comedians Zoro and Huru, and King Kong, and various activities connected with the cinema. His short stories and novels were influenced by surrealist modes and existential viewpoints, and they were unrelievedly pessimistic about the prospects of the human race. Mészöly, always in the vanguard of writers experimenting with narrative techniques and still arousing controversy, sought factual objectivity. Particularly effective was his portrayal of the inner states of characters, even their most irrational moments, through concrete details and facts, a mode typified by a novel, *Accurate Stories on a Journey* (*Pontos történetek, útközben*, 1970), in which he used the techniques of the *cinéma direct* to recount a woman's visit to the place of her youth. Earlier novels explored contemporary issues. *Death of an Athlete* (*Az atléta halála*, 1966), his first novel and first published book since 1957, related the tragic story of a man who, unable to find inner peace, drove himself to death seeking even greater achievements as a middle-distance runner; *Saul* (*Saulus*, 1968) chose the story of Saul from *Acts 8-9* to delve into the moral implications of power. Mészöly, who is inclined, as in "A Map with Lacerations" ("Térkép, repedésekkel"), to present characters, in transit without much regard for time sequence, was constantly concerned with the psychological conflicts of individuals who are incapable of making anything of themselves in the place they occupy, of establishing a constructive balance between themselves and that world. Örkény, the third of these major novelists, after a long and painful re-examination of his style and attitude toward civilization, decided that the grotesque was most compatible with his temperament. Returning with two books in 1967, he quickly took a commanding place in Hungarian literature with bold and absurd short novels—some adapted as plays—and many "one-minute stories" (*egypercesek*), a new grotesque-absurd genre pinpointing with amazing brevity, yet with deep meaning and often with affection, the problems plaguing human beings caught in the paradoxes of today's technological world.

The efforts of such writers as these produced radical changes in Hungarian fiction that continue today. Fiction, particularly the novel, has discarded, in the main, the episodic and descriptive techniques of realism and the panoramic mode in vogue for the more condensed and dramatic forms of the short novel. Rejecting the older modes that had developed as means of "reflecting" social reality, they chose the more startling and demanding forms of narration to impel the imagination to grasp the complexities of twentieth-century civilization: many-layered symbolic suggestion or exaggeration, the distortions of the grotesque and the absurd, the shaft of satire, and the shadings of irony. These experiments and the domestication of foreign literary influences promised the development of a prose fiction increasingly deserving of attention outside Hungary.

The appearance of many new authors primarily after the mid-1960s confirmed the creative vitality of poetry and fiction. The new poets generally fell into two categories: those who linked themselves with the works of Illyés, Juhász, and László Nagy, the last being especially influential, and those who were inspired by the poems of Weöres, Pilinszky, and Nemes Nagy. Among those in the first group were István Ágh, István Bella, Ferenc Buda, László Kalász, Sarolta Raffai, József Ratkó, and Simon Serfőző, who were called the Seven (*Hetek*) because they appeared together in an anthology. Often associated with them were Márton Kalász and Anna Kiss, who wrote differently and began their careers independently of them. These poets tended toward the autobiographical, often describing their struggles with poverty and declaring their devotion to those who had suffered economic hardship, and their support of the social order. Of the original Seven, three matured the most. Ágh began writing more intellectual and abstract verse than he had earlier, even though he was still commenting on the changes in his society, especially in the life of the peasant. Bella, influenced by László Nagy and Sándor Csoóri and partial to fixed poetic forms, called loneliness the major human experience, but frequently accepted the authority of ethical behavior in the relations between human beings. Ratkó, whose extensive use of detail gave his poems a sociographic character, made death the major theme of his poetry, devoting a large share of his more recent verse to struggles against senseless and premature death.

Belonging to the same poetic tradition were the Nine (*Kilencek*), who also appeared together in an anthology, *Unattainable Earth* (*Elérhetetlen föld*, 1969), a publication made possible by László Nagy, who also wrote the introduction and was their chief poetic inspiration. These young poets were László Győri, Benedek Kiss, József Konc, István Kovács, Katalin Mezey, Imre Molnár (later Péntek), János Oláh, Endre Rózsa, and József Utassy. In the beginning they wrote about their personal difficulties in life and voiced their protests. Their views reflected the sufferings endured by their parents' generation: the daily difficulty of making a living and the horrors of the war. Endre Rózsa and József Utassy became the most outspoken pleaders for justice, the former contemplative and philosophical, the latter energetic and dynamic. With the outstanding representatives of the Seven and the Nine must be mentioned Miklós Veress, who shared their desire to face life instead of retreating into a private world. By the mid-1970s Veress loomed large among the young poets holding this attitude. His successful blending of old and new themes, belief and skepticism, and seriousness and playfulness, combined with a mastery of a wide range of verse forms, revealed a poetic rigor that the bad health from which he had always suffered could not diminish.

Essential to the varied development of poetry were those young poets who chose Weöres, Pilinszky, and Nemes Nagy as their models. Like the older poets, they avoided the problems of national welfare in their works, preferring to unfold the innermost life of the human personality from highly distinctive viewpoints. They were greatly drawn to pessimistic philosophies, and their outlook on life was disillusioned and ironic. The earliest of these young poets were István Csukás, Tibor Gyurkovics, and Ottó Orbán. Csukás, whose first works drew on his boyhood years on the Great Plain, developed a style fusing folk and avant-garde poetry; Gyurkovics, whose style is highly condensed, composed love and confessional poetry and was deeply absorbed in his personal feelings and anxieties. Of the three, Orbán achieved the most dramatic evolution in theme and style, his technique and imagery substantially influenced by Weöres and by knowledge gained as a prolific translator of world poetry. Orbán mixed the ironic and the grotesque, and occasionally introduced obscenities. To this group of young poets must be added Imre Oravecz, György Petri, and Dezső Tandori. Both Oravecz and Petri cultivated the short lyric poem as their major art form, and Petri, whose disenchantment with existence often plunged him into deep pessimism, imbued his poems with the tones of self-mockery. Tandori, who also translated widely from world poetry, was the most versatile member of this group. Boldly, playfully experimental and inventive, he created unusual, even odd verse forms and altered the structure of long-established ones like the sonnet to express dramatically his pessimism about humanity's being able to escape finitude, to break out of the eternal limitation of time and space. In his view, human existence is completely determined; it is beyond the reach of assessment and improvement.

The future of prose fiction also remained auspicious. As is customary in Hungary, short stories and novels by new writers were published more slowly than works by new poets. But with the publication of their writings in growing numbers after 1965, the prosewriters gave clear evidence of following and modifying paths created by authors during the climactic stage of development in the first half of the 1960s. Three of the novelists who began publishing after 1965 were, like László Marsall among the new poets, in their later years. Two of them had been known as essayists, G. György Kardos and György Konrád. In 1968 Kardos published *The Seven Days of Avraham Bogatir* (*Avrahám Bogatir hét napja*), a story about terroristic activities in Palestine experienced by the author himself after World War II, which was followed in 1972 by *Where Have All the Soldiers Gone?* (*Hová tüntek a katonák?*), another story about Palestine, this time about Polish soldiers who are aliens in their present world and the one they left behind. Both novels demonstrate the author's sensitivity to dramatic situations and his power to create atmosphere and develop characters. In 1969 Konrád, whose works immediately influenced young writers, brought out *The Caseworker* (*A látogató*), a novel about the inefficacy of bureaucratic attempts to deal with social problems, which he followed with another novel, *The City Founder* (*A városalapító*), in 1977. Both works were translated into English. The third author was Anna Jókai, whose first book, *4447*, a novel, appeared in 1968, when she was thirty-six years old. Since then she has regularly published short stories and novels looking mainly at the difficulties of children and families and the life of women from a psychological viewpoint, though, as in "The Angel at Reims" ("A reimsi angyal"), she has treated other motifs effectively.

Unlike these three novelists, all the young prosewriters making their first appearance were born into the new socialistic society. This historical fact had a strong effect on their views of the times, perhaps even a surprising one. Unlike most of their predecessors and many young poets of their own generation, they did not, on the whole, look upon themselves as representing a particular social class or sociological background; thus they did not engage in the class struggle or use sociographic materials to the degree so common in earlier Hungarian fiction. Not burdened by programmatic commitments or by a sense of responsibility for the social system, they examined their world as independent minds relying on personal experiences, and they approached problems from a fundamentally humanistic stance. In general, they presented a picture of young people striving to gain control over their lives but, failing to achieve that autonomy, turning to a life of dislocation, of aimlessness. Among their most frequently used motifs were those of the generation gap—often symbolizing the protagonist's clash with society—of the search for employment, of trying to participate in a social order that seemed to push the young to its periphery. Amid dissatisfaction, disillusionment, and alienation, these new writers fixed their sights on the integrity of the individual personality and the means of achieving it. As they looked at the world and the internal distress of characters, they used mainly the representational modes of realism. Both Gyula Marosi and István Császár were concerned with the role of the individual in society. Marosi concluded that life does not provide opportunities for humans to accomplish great deeds, or nurture convictions able to move humanity to noble achievements. Császár often portrayed characters hopelessly trapped in tensions between themselves and the role society forced upon them, wearing masks to survive. Other writers using similar themes were Szilveszter Ördögh, Péter Módos, and István Csörsz. Ördögh delineated peasant life and the strain existing between peasants and their intellectually advanced children; Módos, whose first book, *The Run (A futás)*, came out in 1967, depicted the crises of adolescents and university students; and Csörsz successfully analyzed the mental states of members of the hippy generation.

Also among these young writers were those who, influenced by such authors as Mándy, Mészöly, and Örkény, took even greater care in choosing themes and stylistic techniques. Vilmos Csaplár, tending toward the grotesque, portrayed anxiety-ridden protagonists who were prevented by society from acting genuinely. Péter Lengyel turned to a different source of tension, the divided personality which is seeking to uncover some continuity between adulthood and childhood. Miklós Vámos was unhesitatingly critical of contemporary Hungarian life in his depictions of loneliness and isolation. Géza Bereményi also emphasized the tension between the individual and society, the frustration of personal dreams and desires, creating grotesque effects with blendings of reality and fantasy and frequently using historical materials. Gábor Czakó stood alone in his uncompromising ethical attitude toward human conduct. Exploring the inner stresses of characters whose personalities are being stifled by circumstances over which they have no control, Czakó nevertheless held them fully responsible for what happened, no matter how tragic the consequences to them. Most recently, Péter Esterházy, a descendant of the famous family, sparked a controversy among Hungarian critics and readers. Having published his first collection of short stories in 1976 and another in 1977, he revealed structural inventiveness in his latest and most successful major work, *Productional Novel (Ssshort [sic] Novel) (Temelésiregény [kisssregény] 1979)*. It mercilessly satirizes the learned institutes and work-places in Hungary dealing with problems of industrial and agricultural production and, in a set of notes longer than the novel to which

István Vas. Photograph by Gábor Komáromi.

it is appended, presented a picture of Esterházy's life and an exposition of the novel's genesis.

During the 1960s the Hungarian drama, still the least developed of the major literary genres, also responded to the relaxed atmosphere in ways that held promise for its future. After 1957, established authors like Tibor Déry, Gyula Illyés, and László Németh continued to write for the stage, often presenting domestic issues through past historical situations, with Déry occasionally examining contemporary problems satirically. And new post-war writers like Imre Sarkadi and Ferenc Karinthy pressed upon audiences, not so much political as moral issues, often in experimental theaters. The influence of Brecht was, of course, very strong, but as the cultural policy governing translations grew more liberal, other dramatists pointed to innovations for Hungarian playwrights to adapt. Their increasing familiarity with the works of O'Neill, Miller, Dürrenmatt, Tennessee Williams, Albee, who visited Budapest in fall 1963, and Pinter spurred them to consider new techniques and to widen the scope of ideas for dramatic representation. To these influences were added those of the Theater of the Absurd through the writings of Beckett, Ionesco, and Genet, not only their technique of imagistic patterns but also their concept of a bewildered humanity abiding in a universe without purpose and past comprehension. Under the impact of these influences and the greater opportunity to stage plays, drama began in the mid-1960s to lose the provincialism from which it had long suffered.

At this time the work of István Örkény was especially important. His plays, particularly *The Tóth Family (Tóték, 1967)* and

Catsplay (Macskajáték, 1970), which was adapted from his novel of the same name, were influenced by the absurdists and brought to the stage characters desperately trying to realize themselves in a world that always eluded their grasp. János Pilinszky's recent experiments with poetic drama also have injected new possibilities for the theater. Even more affected by the directorial techniques of Robert Wilson than by the dramatic modes of Beckett, he seemed to be abandoning the linear development of plot and character for unrelated scenes of states of mind in which past, present, and future frequently coalesce, as most recently in *Children and the Soldiers (A gyerekek és a katonák,* 1978), a three-part play that presents images of the horrors of war as if in a dream. The plays of István Csurka added liveliness to the drama. They are concerned with the absurdities of the Hungarian scene and the unhappy spectacle of humans completely controlled by chance, the latter concept being effectively portrayed in *Who Will Pay the Piper? (Ki lesz a bálanya?,* 1970), which consists entirely of a dialogue at a poker session between players completely out of step with life and unwittingly revealing themselves to one another. (pp. xix-xxxix)

Since the early 1960s Hungarian poetry and fiction have developed ever broader scope and refinement in the forms of expression. In the atmosphere of greater social stability and the acceptance of a more personal function for literature, growing numbers of Hungarian authors now offer their distinctive voices to world literature in its continuous effort at helping humankind deal with the conditions of life. Further enrichment of this literary experience is, as everywhere, largely dependent on leaving the creative spirit free to steer its own course and to share its vision with readers, a view openly endorsed by many critics in Hungary today. Clearly, the early challenges to schematism by many writers and their perseverance through the most trying historical circumstances have produced a diverse literature of high artistic quality, serving a centuries-old culture that has always given the literary imagination a paramount role in forming an understanding of the human condition. (pp. xxxix-xl)

> Albert Tezla, "Major Developments in the Imaginative Literature of Hungary since 1945," in Ocean at the Window: Hungarian Prose and Poetry since 1945, edited by Albert Tezla, University of Minnesota Press, 1980, pp. xix-xl.

MIHÁLY SÜKOSD

[*In the following excerpt, Sükosd discusses the essential qualities of twentieth-century Hungarian prose to 1968 and its relationship to world literature, stressing the purely national character of much of Hungarian fiction.*]

What is a writer to do who is born the son of a small people? So far as I know this problem has become relevant since the turn of the century in every country within the area that is often described as East-Central Europe. It is very much alive today [1968] in Polish, Czech, Serbo-Croat and Rumanian literatures, and due to . . . linguistic reasons it is most acute in Hungarian literature. This was true of the period between the wars, during the semi-fascist Horthy era; and it is equally true now, after the Liberation, in socialist Hungary.

Briefly, the problem is as follows. Owing to her unfortunate history, her long drawn out national dependence, and various other circumstances, Hungary was even in Eastern Europe one of the poorest and most backward countries. With the exception

of a few short moments, Hungarian history since the Turkish conquest has been one long series of tragedies. The ravages of war, revolutions conceived in unfortunate historical circumstances, revolutions which were suppressed, reaction following counterrevolutions, half a century's subordination within the Austro-Hungarian monarchy: I could go on at some length enumerating such historical events which mean little to the reader abroad, but which are nevertheless existential questions for the Hungarian educated classes. What was the result of this unfortunate historical background? For centuries, Hungarian economic development was retarded and one-sided; we never had a liberal-democratic era, and the country even today suffers from the fact that, unlike for example Czechoslovakia, we never had a twentieth century middle-class democracy. Hand in hand with this goes the backwardness of the modern social sciences, and the fact that the educated classes had no schooling in science. Compared with Western Europe, Hungary arrived in the twentieth century one whole century late. As a result, literature too has played a role different not only to the one it played in England and France, but also to the one it played in Scandinavia.

It was never the lot of the Hungarian writer to be merely a writer. Since a truly up-to-date philosophy, sociology and economics never existed here, a writer had to be politician, scientist and publicist also. Whether he wrote verse, novels, or plays, he had to put into them some sort of political or social programme or thesis. That is why for a long time the concept of the Hungarian writer was closely linked to that of prophet, leader of the people, social revolutionary. A particular theory and practice of "commitment" developed in Hungarian literature at a time when the notion was unknown in the West. That is why the best Hungarian writing always had something precisely definable to teach about the philosophy of history, political science and ethics. That is why for long periods at a time content was much more important here than form.

Present opinion is that this committed national literature had two faces. On the one hand, it spoke truly about the most important and decisive issues which affected Hungarians as a national and social unit. On the other hand, it was always in danger of being left out of or aside from the mainstream of world literature precisely because of its national content, so that it might be of only local or purely Hungarian significance— or, to put it bluntly, merely a provincial literature. Therefore it is understandable that the best Hungarian critics already in the thirties were repeatedly urging a synthesis of "Hungary and Europe" as an urgent task then facing Hungarian literature. But it was much easier to write a critical study about such a synthesis than to write a novel embodying it.

The lifework of Zsigmond Móricz, the greatest master of Hungarian prose in the first half of this century, expresses all the difficulties which any Hungarian author of talent has had to face. Móricz was a great writer. He knew men, and he knew life; he was productive; he had epic breadth; he knew how to construct a novel. In other words, he fulfilled all the conditions necessary to be a great master of prose. He accepted the role, and fulfilled the same task as Balzac and Thackeray and the great Russians about a hundred years before him. He was a late-comer among realists. He erected a monument to Hungarian society between the two wars in a series of broadly conceived novels. Even now, whoever wants to know how Hungarians lived between the turn of the century and the 1940s must consult Móricz. But how his novels stand up as works of art in the light of current taste is more difficult to assess.

Attempts have been made with the help of translations into various languages to secure a place in world literature for Móricz. None has succeeded so far and very likely will not succeed in the future either. This is probably not only because his novels were the children of a naturalist-cum-realist world which is no longer in tune with current practice in writing fiction. More likely it is because Móricz' novels are significantly Hungarian, and for the most part *merely* Hungarian, as regards the issues they raise. Zsigmond Móricz' principal tools were his own experience and his power of observation. Relying on them he created a world which, looked upon as a sociological and ethnological document, is of no interest to the non-Hungarian reader while at the same time its validity as fiction is not universal enough. For us Zsigmond Móricz is one of our great novelists; to others he seems uninteresting. There is a lot less interest in him than in the Scandinavian novelists of his time who in many ways resemble him.

The discussion still goes on with a degree of intensity after the ambiguous example of Móricz. What should the Hungarian novel be like? Is it for the writer to undertake a national and social mission through his work? Should he draft a moral code, a social proclamation, or a political confession in the guise of a novel? Or should he turn his back on national programmes in an attempt to adjust to the demands made by world literature?

Many have tried to produce a synthesis. A movement came into being in Móricz' lifetime partly under his influence, but it could not break through the limits of a merely local literature. It is usual to term those "populist writers" who took part in this movement. And a conspectus of some of their best work is available in English in *The Plough and the Pen,* an excellent anthology edited by Ilona Duczynska and Karl Polanyi, in which Canadian poets collaborated in producing English translations. The writers in this populist movement felt committed to the method of Móricz, and using his realist technique they examined various sections of Hungarian society and its problems. Today we regard them as having created lasting social documents, but not as having written novels that can be judged by world standards.—Or rather, those writers who were to outgrow the populist movement have shown, in those of their works which are part of world literature, what the potentialities of Hungarian writing are.

I would now like to mention two works which represent contradictory tendencies. *Puszták népe (People of the Puszta)* by Gyula Illyés appeared in 1936. An English-speaking or French reader will consider this book as written in a very modern genre. Illyés anticipated something of that mixed genre which is on the border line between fiction and sociology; these days it is one of the novelties of world literature, and is represented by works like Truman Capote's *In Cold Blood* and *mutatis mutandis* Oscar Lewis' *The Children of Sanchez.* Nevertheless, Illyés' work is significantly Hungarian. He wrote about the poorest section of Hungarian society between the wars, about the *zsellérs* (cottars) within the poor peasantry. He did not write a novel but instead the sort of work that stands outside any one genre with its rules. This we term *szociográfia* in Hungarian: one might perhaps call it a non-fiction novel in English, a genre where art can live side by side with legitimate documentary social observation.

The success of the erudite novelist, playwright and critic László Németh, who is only loosely connected with the populist movement, lay in yet another genre. His novel *Revulsion* has become world-famous in its German translation. It is worth examining precisely why this novel by such an extraordinarily productive writer succeeded in breaking through the barriers which normally enclose Hungarian literature. In this novel, whose technique resembles that of the great Russians, Tolstoy and Turgeniev, certainly to some extent László Németh succeeded in his attempt to create a closed self-regulating fictional world out of a hopeless marriage, out of the hell on earth which two people made for each other. Here there is psychological description paralleled only by Saul Bellow's *Herzog* in the literature of our day. However, this immanent fictional structure is so embedded in social reality, it offers such a detailed encyclopaedia of Hungarian provincial life, that the whole meaning of Hungary's history and recent past is made apparent without recourse to provincial or exotic colours.

Horthy Hungary had hardly collapsed in 1945 when the long years of Stalinism began. Zhdanovite "socialist realist" principles scarcely permitted any important works of literature to appear. After 1956, though, the literature of Eastern European countries showed great potentialities, and the first results can be observed in the development of the Hungarian novel.

In my opinion and in that of others, Jean Paul Sartre best expressed the situation confronting the literatures of socialist countries when in a recent interview he spoke of writing that deals with "the great adventure" of socialism. He mentioned the paradigm of a novel which embraces the historical period from 1917 to our day: what happened since the October Revolution, and in what way the Revolution itself changed. This kind of novel would convey the feeling of the victories of the revolutionary period, the sins of the Stalin era, and also the various tendencies in the years that have passed since Stalin's death. And the extent to which Sartre touches upon realities is demonstrated by nothing less than his old debating partner and philosophical opponent, György Lukács, who puts forward similar views in his recent critical study *Szolzsenyicin és a mai szocialista realizmus (Solzhenitsyn and Socialist Realism Today).*

Such a novel attempt to give expression to the totality of the revolutionary era has, we know, not yet really been made anywhere in Eastern Europe. Yet in Czech and Polish prose, as well as in the Hungarian novel, we find important initial steps from which have come certain results. In the first place I am thinking of the achievements of two "grand old men" of literature. Their genre and their methods differ. They are only at one in their intellectual approach, and in that they show the way to break through narrow national limits in order to communicate important artistic truths to the world at large.

One of them is Tibor Déry. I do not think there is any need to introduce him, at least by name, to the English-speaking reader. In the first period of his life as a writer he portrayed twentieth century Hungary in a powerful sequence of novels. As early as the thirties he wrote *Befejezetlen mondat (The Unfinished Sentence).* Within the circumstances and conditions then prevailing in Hungarian literature, Déry's novel reached the standards of Thomas Mann, Proust, and the Gorky who wrote *Klim Sangin.* With this novel and *Felelet (The Answer)* which followed in the 1950s, he established the genre of the modern Hungarian realist novel. His latest works approach the most modern type of Western novel without giving up anything of their independence. His novel which has the peculiar title of *G. A. ur X-ben (Mr. A. G. in X)* is surely one of the most ambitious in our entire literature. Déry depicts the world of an imaginary anti-society, through describing the imaginary adventures of an imaginary traveller who is lost in an imaginary town. It is a world which is one of the possible continuations of twentieth century reality—a horrifying one, but a possible one nevertheless. For the sake of greater artistic effect Déry does not even consider the other alternative, the possibility of harmonious development, so that he could then all the more convincingly depict the negative aspect in which man destroys himself knowingly and as part of a game. The reader does not know what he should marvel at more: the abstract suggestiveness of the fictional world which is worthy of Kafka, or the credibility of the realistic sections. And Déry, this artist who shows that he can renew himself even in old age, took a further step in his latest novel. *A kiközösítő (The Excommunicator)* deals with the activities of St. Ambrose, the great fourth century Bishop of Milan; but within this mock historical framework the ''great adventure'' of socialism becomes the subject of discussion. Ends and means, order and liberty, moral baseness and historical progress—all are discussed, and their dialectics are offered to us in this charmingly witty novel-parable.

József Lengyel's essentially modern life-work branches out in another direction. He has no wish to create a philosophical world-view through literature. He gives a picture of life as it is, authenticated by the admirable personal example of the author's own uncompromisingly moral position and by an artistic sense of the modern. József Lengyel is one of the few who have raised the twentieth century Hungarian avant-garde tradition to the level of great literature. He has never written a ''traditional'' novel. The genre to which his work belongs is difficult to establish. A substantial proportion of his short stories are not short stories at all in the strict sense. He prefers the tale, the short novel, the meditation, the autobiographical confession, or rather a personal mixture of all these. The works which achieve most impact are certain short and also longer stories. These carry not only the authenticity of personal experience but also achieve the objective distancing effect of the great epic writers in depicting the institutionalised aberrations of the Stalin era and the truth about the concentration camps. In this sphere he probably surpasses even Solzhenitsyn. The genre offers opportunities for a journalistic approach, for noble or ignoble flights of passion, for that angry pamphleteering which Arthur Koestler made world-famous. But in József Lengyel the immanent inner laws of great literature become true. His tales do not voice a single false ''foreign'' note. They present the institutionalised realisation of a dreadful practice with such truthfulness that nowhere in his work does the writer ever speak tongue in cheek or as if making it up; nowhere do we feel that the lucky survivor speaks from the point of view of knowing better now thanks to hindsight. This would ruin his work. József Lengyel writes out of the knowledge that is within him. He does not pass sentence, he does not judge, he only shows. In this way he establishes the lasting features of a negative era.

In Utrecht, in 1967, during a literary Round Table, I was asked whether I could name Hungarian novelists who associated themselves with any of the modern movements, for instance with the French *nouveau roman*. Then, as now, it was difficult for me to explain that putting the question in this way is inadequate when considering the situation of Hungarian prose.

At the beginning of my study I mentioned that the Hungarian— unlike the Western European or North American—novel has to this day to bear burdens which elsewhere belong to philosophy or sociology. This ideological content makes it impossible for it to associate itself wholeheartedly with modernistic movements which consciously brush aside the task of communicating content. There is no doubt that, as far as the twentieth century

Hungarian novel is concerned, authors (as well as works) who played no part in accepting tasks which were national were always in a minority. One ought to know in this connection that in pre-1945 Hungary a ferocious, and unfortunate, discussion raged for a long time· between the populists and the urbanists.—Or rather, between those who occupied themselves purely with the crucial issues of the nation and its peasant majority, and those others who felt attracted by Western examples and currents, the followers of cosmopolitan literature. This superfluous and inconclusive debate does not continue in our day, but even today one finds the opinion among wide sections of the Hungarian educated classes that a novel which is not linked to Hungarian traditions, methods, and experience must somehow be a relatively unimportant, second-rate work.

There is no doubt that certain non-national works which have appeared have done most to dissolve the traditional structure of Hungarian prose during the past fifteen years. I shall only mention a few titles and names: Géza Ottlik's novel *Iskola a határon (School at the Frontier)*, Miklós Mészöly's *Az atléta halála (The Death of an Athlete)*, Iván Mándy's short stories, and Gyula Hernádi's novels. These Hungarian writers actually appear to be more popular abroad, mainly where French and German are spoken, than in Hungary. They all break with traditional realism and attempt to attach themselves to the latest trends in the modern novel. Their subjects are Hungarian only in a remote, abstracted sense. Their world-view is derived from the natural sciences and cybernetics; they lean on neo-positivist, that is non-ideological, philosophy; the important thing they have to communicate is the isolation of man, man's ego, and his anxiety as a trembling individual held fast by impersonal powers. At present these writers are left in suspension, as it were, and in an ambiguous situation. They are published in widely-spoken Western languages, but they nevertheless not surprisingly fail to create a sensation in countries where they are lost amidst the huge annual crop of books. At the same time they are considered by a section of critical opinion in Hungary to be a peripheral current of little importance. The courses open to the Hungarian novel in the future may depend on whether these very talented and largely still fairly young writers can find their true selves, and from this standpoint be able to give greater permanence to the continuation of their present work.

Parallel with the modern current of writing mentioned above, there is a group of middle-aged as well as young writers who have chosen a more propitious path: the integration of national and supra-national material as an objective for the novel. What is significant as far as this current is concerned? In particular, there is the very interesting subject matter which they have selected for their fiction. It is as if the time had finally arrived for Hungarian writers to take up questions from Hungarian history which, although referring to the past, are also valid for the present. It cannot be regarded as mere coincidence that now, a quarter of a century after the end of the Second World War, the first important novels which deal with Hungary's role in that war are being written. As the whole world knows, Hungary was Nazi Germany's last ally. The exposure of this excusable and explicable, yet shameful and irretrievable fact was lost sight of in the Stalinist years. A simplistic diagrammatic way of looking at things had established itself; one spoke about a ruling class which alone was guilty, and about the common people who stayed pure, though impotent and incapable of action. This vulgarized proposition has only received more critical literary treatment in the course of the last few years. Tibor Cseres' *Hideg napok (Cold Days)* which deals with the Novi Sad massacre perpetrated by the Hungarian army, and the works of István Örkény and Ferenc Sánta, show how deeply fascism affected the world of the little man in a way which ever since then has led to distortions that are still very much alive today.

These novels which reach back to the war years are a long way from the usual type of war novel. To a large extent, the war and the states of mind associated with it are only a pretext. Their true subjects are the individual and society, power and morals, and the conflicts between them. What can a man do who is a subordinate, who is given a job, when faced with the abstract mechanism of carrying out a command? Does the way of life of insignificant people, of the eternal poor, change with the succession of historical periods? *Can* it change? Ferenc Sánta's novel *Húsz óra* (*Twenty Hours*), which examines the life of the Hungarian peasantry throughout the years which have passed since 1945, deals with such questions. The outstanding example of this genre is Endre Fejes' *Rozsdatemető* (*The Scrap-yard*) which has been translated into half a dozen languages. Since this novel looks like being the biggest international success that contemporary Hungarian fiction has enjoyed, it is worth taking a closer look at it.

Rozsdatemető runs altogether to two hundred pages. The material which it takes in is that of the traditional multi-volume family novel. The writer describes the fate of a half-peasant, half-workingclass family and of its various branches in twentieth-century Hungary, from the years before the First World War up to our day. He examines the social and psychological processes which an ordinary man, who thinks only of self-preservation, goes through in his desire to stay out of history, and the way he succeeds in doing so at the price of his own fall and inhumanity. Endre Fejes presents this huge mass of experience and information in an extraordinarily hard, pure, and economical novel. He breaks with traditional realism, but he also steers clear of abstract, non-figurative prose. With skilful use of flash-back, and thanks to his gift of synthesizing details which carry documentary conviction, Endre Fejes manages to say something of specific and indeed of general importance beyond the immediate subject of the novel, not only about twentieth century Hungary but also about that special Central and East European way of life of which Hungary is one example.

I have already mentioned that the representative novel about socialist East Europe, which Sartre and Lukács together have awaited so impatiently, has not yet appeared in Hungary. I believe that this is due not in the first place to the question of writing talent, but to the absence of the proper historical distance as well as to external and internal conditions which as yet are not altogether favourable. True, some important works of Hungarian prose and some trends seem to foreshadow the appearance of that paradigm of a novel described above; and we may hope that with its realisation, Hungary will shake off every objective handicap and impediment of its "small people's" literature and will then be able to speak with an equal voice in the chorus of world literature. This pattern of the novel of the future surprisingly resembles works from various other small Eastern European countries. I am thinking principally of the writings of the Poles Andrzejewski and K. Brandys, of Hrabal and Paral from Czechoslovakia, and of the Yugoslav Bulatinovic.

Though we cannot tell exactly what the Hungarian novel of the immediate future will be like, we have a pretty good idea what it will not be like. It is certain that it will break with that classic-realist structure which, as we saw, played a leading role in Hungary. It is also certain that the mainstream of the Hungarian novel will contain nothing like the French *nouveau roman* or Lawrence Durrell's tetralogy. The Hungarian novel will be able to say something truly important to the world when it finally integrates its own national, social, political and moral content, and applies to these a descriptive method of universalising power which transcends naturalistic petty details as well as ideologies. It seems that the most interesting Hungarian novelists, from József Lengyel and Tibor Déry, to Ferenc Sánta and Endre Fejes, are already working out such a genre. And this kind of novel will, if it resembles anything at all, remind us most of the modern American novel. It is no coincidence that the heritage of Hemingway and Faulkner can be discerned in contemporary Hungarian prose, not to mention living writers such as Salinger, Truman Capote and Updike. It is an instinctive, remote influence; it is no more than the similar expression in similar genres of similar experiences, or rather an attempt at it. It is a wide and modern genre within which the intellectual essay-novel has a place, as well as the philosophic parable or unembellished documentary novel.

In the last few years the Hungarian cinema—with a number of outstanding films, especially Miklós Jancsó's *Szegénylegények* (*The Round-Up*)—has become world-famous quite unexpectedly and without precedent. It is worth noticing that the Hungarian cinema's success has thus continued an East European artistic trend. First Polish, then Czech films have conquered the world, and in a number of works which deal with issues particularly relevant in small countries. Perhaps we may hope that in the years to come, when we enjoy more propitious external and internal circumstances, the Hungarian novel too will find, and retain, a place in the front rank of world literature. (pp. 111-19)

Mihály Sükosd, "Hungarian Prose Literature Today," in MOSAIC: A Journal for the Comparative Study of Literature and Ideas, *Special Issue: The Literature of Small Countries, Vol. 1, No. 3, April, 1968, pp. 110-19.*

GYÖRGY SOMLYÓ

[*In the following excerpt Somlyó offers an introduction to modern Hungarian poetry through 1966, examining the effect of Hungary's unique language and national experience on its literature and noting technical and thematic departures by Hungarian poetry from the broader European poetic tradition.*]

The postscript to the volume of T. S. Eliot's selected poems in the Hungarian language . . . draws an attractive and convincing parallel between the most influential modern English poet and Mihály Babits, one of the most significant Hungarian poets of the century, who occupied the same central position in Hungarian poetry before the Second World War as that occupied by T. S. Eliot in England up to his death. It would not be difficult to find parallels of this kind in other examples. The nervous intellectualism of Lőrinc Szabó, who died in 1954, his metallic staccato rhythms, the impetuous revolt of his early work, and the embittered classicism of his late period are not very different from the line followed by the poetic career of his contemporary, W. H. Auden. The representatives of the most distinctive trend among the younger poets refer themselves back, not without good reason, and in various forms, to Dylan Thomas. Ferenc Juhász, as he tells us in one of his essays, which reveals the tense, ecstatic manner of writing characteristic of his prose no less than of his verse, was interested during his short trip to England in almost nothing but following up through the streets of London the trail of his fellow-poet, whose meteoric career was cut short by his tragic end; and László Nagy not only employed all the magic of his language in his translations of Dylan Thomas, but also called on his skill as an artist to make an etching of Dylan Thomas and illustrate his poems.

The jigsaw game of comparative criticism could be continued further, and it would not be without value. It would demonstrate immediately and tangibly, that is to say, in the most readily comprehensible way, that this Central European poetry, in a language unrelatable to any of the great European tongues, can be drawn like water into the same channels and riverbeds that govern the poetry of the other and older European languages, into those that govern English just as easily as, in other cases, those of Russian or French poetry—and this would not be deceptive. Yet it could hardly avoid creating the impression that the poetry of these relative latecomers in Europe, who settled here in the tenth century, and who made unrivalled efforts to preserve their isolated language and develop it into a means of expression equal to the others in Europe, which are, in the final analysis, all related to one another, has no more to offer than a mere reflection of original European poetry—and such an impression would be doubly wrong. For the truth is that though Hungarian poetry, in all that we know of it today, is a thoroughly European phenomenon, born in and of Europe, it has carried within it, at all times and in all its highest moments, something extra-European—or as László Németh, a Hungarian writer of comprehensive vision, likes to call it, something "sub-European," something underlying Europe, something of the origins that have everywhere been lost, or at best preserved only in oral tradition and in the most secret layers of the language. And if it is true that it was always the challenge of the European spirit which brought forth its response sooner or later, it is equally true that it has always sought the answer to its own Hungarian questions.

It is therefore the more difficult approach that we have to choose instead of the easier and more attractive, even in a sketchy introduction such as this, which is simply designed to familiarize the reader with the problems, and not at all to provide all the answers to them. Attention must be called to the dissimilarities as well as the affinities. Anyone who undertakes to provide even a cursory insight into the Hungarian poetry of the last twenty or thirty years cannot avoid nor spare his readers the difficulties of the task. Not even if in the end it is scarcely more than a mere outline of them he is able to describe.

The first and most important is this: Not only is the particular aspect of Hungarian poetry which the present writer proposes to discuss unknown to the Western, and particularly the English reader, but equally almost the whole of its preceding seven hundred years of development. Not only, say, Sándor Weöres, that all-round athlete in the handling of modern Hungarian verse, but also János Arany (1817-1882), whose verbal mastery Weöres recreates with such felicity in a curious sequence of poems dedicated to his predecessor; not only Gyula Illyés, probably the last incarnation in Europe today of that nearly extinct species—the national poet—even though the International Poetry Biennale at Knokke-le-Zoute in 1965 awarded him the Grand Prix de Poésie, following Giuseppe Ungaretti, Saint-John Perse, Jorge Guillén and Octavio Paz; but also, for the most part, his direct poetic ancestor, Sándor Petőfi (1823-1849), whose legend, if not his real achievement, made a fleeting appearance in Europe in the second half of the last century.

Stephen Spender, in his essay *Poetry since 1939* (1946) wrote in the first few sentences: "During the war every country in the world has been barred off more or less completely from every other country. . . . This book is written simply to answer the question: What poems were written between 1939 and 1945 in Britain?

This is an important question which needs answering, because many people have not had the opportunity to find out the answer for themselves." And our position is that those who do not read Hungarian cannot find out the answer for themselves not only as to what poems were written between any given dates—since the Second World War, for instance, and in particular during the last ten years—but equally between 1190 (the date of the first known poem in Hungarian, *Mary's Lament*) and 1966. Poetry's kingdom is language. And the kingdom of the Hungarian language has been blockaded not only in times of war, but continuously cut off from most European languages. Yet every national poetry invariably carries within itself its whole history; all the geological and archaeological layers that go to make up a tongue are present in its poetry. "People bend language to serve them," writes Octavio Paz in his excellent essay on modern poetry, "but the poet serves language." Every poet has a co-author, even though unsolicited, in everything written up to that time in his language. The most beautiful poems of Illyés's late, that is, present period, without any direct reference or borrowing, echo overtones from the finest lines of Vörösmarty—the mid-nineteenth-century romantic poet—for all within ear reach of Hungarian. The magic wand of Sándor Weöres cuts the air to summon up shades of the deeply buried verse forms of Hungarian poetry. And there is hardly a writer of the present generation whose poems do not carry phrases in which one of Attila József's metaphors is concealed. Is it necessary to say anything more of this intrinsic law of poetry to the compatriots of T. S. Eliot?

Hungarian poetry lives and works in the heart of Europe with a certain understandable sense of resentment that so little of it has been allowed to pass into the bloodstream of European poetry. This is one of its undeniable peculiarities. This faint sense of wounded pride has not, however, on the whole led to any attitude of offended withdrawal or self-damaging rejection, which would have meant a tragic deprivation. True, such tendencies have indeed appeared from time to time in our cultural life, and on occasion, in conjunction with reactionary and retrograde political attitudes, have been a dominating influence for shorter or longer periods; sometimes with curious effects. One of them, which it is next to impossible to try to explain to the English or the West-European reader in general, was the intellectual erosion which cut such a gulf between the best of our writers in the inter-war years. This rift, which divided the "populists" from the "urbanists"—or, in simpler terms, between those drawing their chief inspiration from a country or peasant background, and those whose environment and experience was essentially urban—has not been so closed by contemporary democratic developments that we are not still aware of treacherous fissures quaking under our feet in an otherwise healthy intellectual atmosphere. There are—even today—men of considerable mental stature amidst us who feel it an irreparable loss for any poet not to have shared the intimate experience of nature of the Hungarian peasant. This desire to cling to the experience of the earth, increasingly outdated as it is becoming, might have something to do with the fact that Hungary is one of the few countries of Europe—or even the world—which have no sea. From primeval times onward the sea has given rise to the growth of urban cultures on the edge

Gyula Illyés. Photograph by Layle Silbert.

of unbounded nature—and from this absence of the sea men seem to believe that the only culture that matters is that of the indigenous tillers of the soil; they seem to have replaced the ancient assertion of European culture "water is best" by the illusion that "earth is best," while still sensible of the loss, still yearning for the sea, which has been the theme of not a few celebrated Hungarian poems.

For in fact only the merest fragments of even the greatest works of Hungarian poetry are to this day accessible in foreign languages at all; still fewer can be read in a worthy translation, and fewer still have been received with a proper appreciation of their value. At the same time almost the whole of European poetry can be read in Hungarian, for the most part in translations which can claim to compete with the originals, and have thus become integral components of our own national culture and poetry. It was no joking evasion when Mihály Babits, asked which was the most beautiful Hungarian poem, replied, "Shelley's *Ode to the West Wind,* as translated by Árpád Tóth."

The poet of the Renaissance set about assimilating the poetry of other lands in an uninhibited, confident, and—in the Schillerian sense—"naive" way of his own, by happily incorporating in his own work, even unconsciously, anything that pleased him in the way of form or feeling in the foreign verse he read. In the beginning Petrarch was not "translated" into French, English or Spanish; the European poets took him as their own, recreated or rewrote him, and thus fashioned out of him the French, English and Spanish poetry of modern times. With the development of humanist education, the appearance of philology and literary history, with the growing sense of the

inalienable individuality of poetic creation, poets could no longer wander in Eden plucking apples from each other's trees, that is, from the one and indivisible tree of universal poetry. Translation slowly turned into the scholarly occupation of supplying solid information, of research and the dissemination of knowledge, and imperceptibly it became the preserve of scholars, and got back into the poet's hands only on rare occasions. Pope's Homer, Baudelaire's Poe, Stefan George's complete Dante, or in recent English poetry Eliot's translations of Saint-John Perse and Day Lewis's Vergil are exceptional examples of poet's encounters with poets.

The Hungarian literature of translation, on the other hand, is an uninterrupted procession of such life-giving encounters. In theory and practice it is a unique amalgamation of the method of the Renaissance poet with the methods of the later philologists, our greatest poets have used their unique gifts, combining them with rigid scholarship, to produce the authentic taste of great European poetry for the Hungarian palate. As a result it has become an unbroken tradition of our literature that our greatest poets consider translation an integral part of their life-work, raising it, as it were, to the level of a special form of art. An indication of this is the type of Hungarian book rarely met in other literatures, in which a collection of translated poems by various foreign poets appears not under the name of the original foreign poets themselves but under the name of the Hungarian poet-translator, making it clear that they are considered as much part of his works as of their original authors. (pp. 108-11)

The only help Hungarian poetry has had in developing this special form of art has been precisely its curious, non-European language, which only began to be suspected of an affiliation to the Finno-Ugrian family of languages, with a few distant cousins in Europe, the Finns, the Esthonians, the Lapps, at the end of the eighteenth century. Paradoxically enough this isolated language, whose basic system of versification bears no resemblance to any other in Europe, lends itself quite easily to the adaptation of all European verse forms, including those which most modern European languages are no longer capable of recapturing. When in the sixteenth century the scholar poet of the French Renaissance, Antoine de Baïf, was making ineffective attempts to naturalize the hexameter, the first Hungarian distichs accommodated the classical measure as if nothing was more natural to it. Strangely enough, after German and later Russian, Hungarian, the most removed from the classic tongues, was to become the language in which the hexameters of the *Odyssey,* the peculiar strophic structures of Sappho, the iambic trimeters or even the most intricately patterned choruses of Sophocles, the dancing distichs of Ovid, could all be acclimatized with completely natural authenticity, while preserving their original character.

Parallel with this development the classical hexameter took its place among the standard forms of Hungarian verse; towards the end of the eighteenth and the beginning of the nineteenth century it dominated the poetry of the two main epochs in the revival of Hungarian letters, that is, the period of language reform and the subsequent age of political reform in the early nineteenth century. So deeply had it penetrated the blood-vessels of the Hungarian poetic language that it was to be heard as some extra-systolic arrhythmia beating through the irregular lines of the initiators and first masters of Hungarian free verse, Milán Füst, Oszkár Gellért, Illyés, and others. One of Babits's most fascinating and justly celebrated poems derives all its remarkable inner excitement and stimulus precisely from the ever-present rhythmic tension with which he deliberately strains against and periodically jolts us out of the chosen hexametric pattern, not unlike the Cubist technique of purposely playing colour against line.

In the years of fascism the hexameter verse of antiquity was revived, acting as a special form of protest. Many poetic careers began under its influence and even in later days were held in its enchantment, as for instance that of Gábor Devecseri. And Miklós Radnóti, murdered by the Nazis, turned to the hexameter in his last poems from the modern hell of our century, the forced labour camp, the last poems found on his body after death. On the edge of the mass grave this hallowed, pristine European measure became in itself the content of poetry: an appeal to the spirit of the true Europé. "Darling, speak truthfully: is anywhere left, where hexameters matter?"—the question, framed in a faultlessly Vergilian metre in the original Hungarian, could have been asked by no poet of any other European tongue in the tempest raging around him in June 1944, in any of those places where, as "Above Zagubica,"

> Hill-high here, vermin and rumour sharing,
> we Poles and we Frenchmen,
> Centuries-suffering Jews, magpie Italians,
> never-submitting Serbs.

This little pearl of modern Hungarian poetry unintentionally reflects the position of Hungarian poetry in Europe: it frequently differs from the others just where it has most successfully assimilated their traditions.

The fate and the sentiment expressed in Radnóti's poem is identical, more then than perhaps at any time, with the fate of so many of the poets—and peoples—of subjugated Europe—but the attitude, the metamorphosis by which fate is transformed into poetry, is very different. When recently Keith Botsford was kind enough to undertake the translation of this poem for the multi-language poetry almanac called *Arion*, which I edited, he had to make a special study of the rules and conventions of the English hexameter, only nominally in existence and very rarely used. The reader can judge from the two lines quoted above the extent to which his brave efforts have succeeded.

For Aragon, I think, is profoundly right when he says that "the history of all poetry is essentially identical with the history of its techniques." In the sixteenth century there was a Hungarian lyric poet, Bálint Balassi, an older contemporary of Shakespeare and Ronsard, who was one of the foremost minds of the age. Bálint Balassi pleaded the claims of earthly love with renaissance freshness and candour in cycles dedicated to his mistresses, just as Ronsard did, and with the same revealing passion as Shakespeare. But the prosody of these poems, the lines and the stanza forms, either of his own invention or adapted to many Hungarian and foreign melodies, are founded fairly and squarely upon the ancient inherited principles of Hungarian accented versification, which had no point of contact with the metric forms emerging at that time and soon to become predominant in Western, or for that matter, Eastern Europe. Of these forms, however, the most characteristic of the age, the sonnet, only appeared in Hungary at the end of the eighteenth century, to disappear again in the course of nineteenth-century romanticism—as indeed it did in most of Romantic Europe—re-entering the scene at the beginning of the present century as a specifically *modern* form, as a means of broadening and modernizing Hungarian poetry. Consequently there is an air of twentieth-century modernity about the sonnet in

Hungarian poetry, and the first significant example of the sonnet sequence in Hungarian, probably the most favoured form during the sixteenth century in Europe, is Lőrinc Szabó's *Twenty-sixth year,* published in 1957!

This also accounts for the stubborn persistence of set forms in present-day Hungarian verse. Some of these fixed forms have come into Hungarian poetry later than elsewhere and are therefore less worn and less fully exploited. What is more, since these forms have taken root by gradually ousting the ancient Hungarian system of versification, based on accent and not on length, their modern use tends to represent innovation, a modern breaking with national traditions, similar to the spread of free verse in French, English or Italian poetry. But it is precisely this aspect of them which translations cannot translate, which is one reason why translations of our most modern, adventurous poets strike a stiffly traditional and "classicist" note on the foreign ear.

The type of poetry written is dependent on what is needed and what is possible. In all societies and ages those literary forms of art come into being and reach maturity which are inspired by an inner need and favoured by the opportunities of the time. Hungarian literature of translation—as we have seen—sprang from the vital needs of Hungarian poetry and Hungarian culture, and the specific aptitudes of the language made it possible. At the same time Hungarian drama and prose, and particularly philosophy and criticism, have been consistently stunted in their growth by historical circumstances too complicated to discuss here. Accordingly the dominating form of literary art in Hungary has been, down to the most recent times, lyric poetry. This curious monopoly enjoyed by the lyric is a further peculiarity of our poetry which is apt to estrange or fascinate the foreign reader. As a result most of our poets, including those of today, have found themselves enriched, if burdened too, by the national and literary tasks, out of proportion with the tasks of a lyric poet as such, which they have had to assume. *Tout finit par la chanson*—says the French tag. With us it is really true. Everything, including drama and even political thought, pours into and pours out of lyric poetry. The repressed vitalities of all the other literary disciplines explode in the lyric. It has happened in other literatures too, but nowhere else does it seem to have been so persistent as in Hungary. All the lyric sap of the unlyrical French *siècle d'or* was absorbed into the reigning form of the age, the drama. Racine is looked upon to this day as one of the greatest French poets—certainly not on account of his psalms, insignificant both in number and in aesthetic value—but on account of his plays. Hungarian lyric poetry in the same way absorbed all the various elements crystallized in the novel, the drama, the essay or, for that matter, philosophy and political science in the literature of England or France. It is a platitude that only what cannot be said can be sung; but within the actual development of a particular literature that too may be suitable for poetry which remains unspoken in prose.

All this has given Hungarian lyric poetry a special significance and place in national life, and has at the same time imposed on it a burden often stretching the justified scope of lyric poetry beyond reason. Perhaps nowhere else in the world have so many poems—and good poems—been written which read as political leaders; and certainly not in countries where outstanding newspaper leaders, sometimes with a touch of poetry about them, are written in prose. Nowhere else are so many thoughts on public matters expressed in verse—not always of first-rate quality, be it said. The whole body of Hungarian poetry, it is fair to say, not excluding its best examples, contains more topical, more "foreign" matter than is good for it. It is in closer contact with journalism, and certain critics think this is a virtue. And if, on the one hand, it is just this quality which is liable to alienate the foreign reader at a time when *poésie pure* is in the ascendant, and the tendency is towards greater and greater abstraction, divesting poetry of everything but its ultimate inner core. On the other, it may also serve as a healthy impulse to restore the continually short-circuited current of poet and public in western lyrical poetry to normal functioning.

Innumerable contradictions are inherent in the position in which our lyrical poetry finds itself, at once exceptional, favoured and isolated. Owing to the comparative absence of philosophical literature in Hungary, practically all intellectual endeavour has thus been channelled into lyric poetry. The lack of a philosophical discipline, however, has proved a constant obstacle to the application of the rich concentration of ideas abounding in our poetry to a sensitive critical judgement and to a power of conceptualization. László Németh, writing to an Italian reader, diagnosed the problem correctly when he said: "When you have familiarized yourself with our literature you will be astonished how many great poets and writers have appeared and flourished in the past half century. But if you inquire how many of them have received satisfactory critical evaluation you will hardly find more than a couple; this creative profusion contrasts oddly with the indolence and lethargy shown in assimilating these riches and making them known." This state of affairs inevitably ends in a vicious circle, from which even the strenuous efforts recently made have found no way out. Throughout its history our poetry has never been weighed in the balance without our own national sensitiveness tipping the pointer one way or another. This fact is apt to blunt our own critical judgment, and the uncertainty which thus reveals itself in assessing our principal treasures acts as a further obstacle in preventing these values from appearing what they really are outside their language and country.

It is possible, therefore, that the whole of our classical poetry will remain for world literature nothing but a range of extinct volcanoes, and it is now too late for it to send its flames sweeping across the horizon, as it might have done in more favourable circumstances at the time of their activity or shortly afterwards. It is possible that Balassi, Csokonai, Vörösmarty, Arany, even Petőfi and Ady will continue to remain our exclusive treasures: genuine assets, pearls hidden in the pocket of a beggar's clothes; though there are signs that surprises might still occur. The poetry written in this century, however, might justly hope to render some retroactive satisfaction, as it were, to its predecessors, dispossessed from their place in international literature, and through its admission achieve, indirectly, a presence for them in the world.

This hope is held out for us by the ever livelier interest shown from all sides and the first not insignificant results of that interest; and the explanation for this promising change is to be found in the features of Hungarian poetry adumbrated in the foregoing sketch as well as in the general development of the poetry of our age.

Literary history in recent times has introduced a new concept, a typically world literary concept: coming too late. Two great prose literatures—Russian and American—have broken on to the world scene with such vehemence as can only be explained on the analogy of the energy produced by a time-lag. Defects or anomalies in development sometimes drive living beings into exertions at just that point of deficiency which enable them

not only to compensate but to outstrip the organic dysfunction. A drive of some kind, if of smaller proportions, seems to be developing at the present time within Hungarian poetry: it has drawn level with some of the major modern stages of European poetry a little late, but likewise in different circumstances, which has enabled it to give them a new content. And this arduous effort, spurring Hungarian art to catch up with European developments, is intertwined with an endeavour, very much of our time, which complements it to good effect.

One of the key problems facing art in our century is how to go beyond itself. It will assimilate anything alien to it, from primitive African sculpture to American jazz, from pre-Columbian folklore to Zen Buddhism. Hungarian art returned to primitive sources in a more direct way; all it had to do to tap them was to delve beneath itself; to carry out a few deep drillings, to put its shoulders to a couple of rocks and roll them away.

The convergence of these two lines of development has, through two exponents of genius, produced what is most peculiar in twentieth-century Hungarian art, and what might—and does—claim the attention of the world.

Béla Bartók and Attila József seem to have arrived in the seven-league boots of folk tales, covering century-long lags and, to extend the metaphor, leaping beyond the seven seas.

Their many differences apart—the musician representing the anti-fascist humanism of Thomas Mann, the poet a proletariat imbued with and bound by revolutionary ideology—they have three characteristics in common: their determination to make up for the time-lag, their search for the submerged world of the ancient Hungarian melodies, rhythms and symbols and their firm stand with all the most progressive contemporary European trends in society and the arts. In contemporary intellectual life they both represent more than the sum total of their achievements and their undoubted greatness as human beings; there is for us something more vital than all these in their intellectual aspirations: they both indicate the greater possibilities existing in Hungarian art. The real poetic creeds of contemporary Hungarian poets are revealed in the poems written to the memory of these two great predecessors. . . . It seems as if in some way every Hungarian poet can best define his true position and vocation by his attitude to these two masters.

The stimulating tension of the best of contemporary Hungarian poetry derives from the feverish tempo with which it tries to compensate for the time-lag and from the discovery of its own inner "otherness." And also from the fact that the process is taking place now, in the time of the building of socialism, entailing as it did so many tragic errors, but ultimately advancing our people and embarking it on the great stream of international history. Which, beyond everything else, means for poetry the electric atmosphere of a new public, such a close though contradictory contact, an uninterrupted dialogue, which in the contemporary world crisis of poetry and its public is a really remarkable and particular aspect of the Hungarian poet's inspiration.

Hungarian poets and their works, individually so different, are all in their several ways affected by these conditions.

Although in the period under discussion, the greater part of his work was in narrative and prose form, seventy-eight-year-old Milán Füst was the pioneer of modern Hungarian poetry, the creator of free verse in Hungarian. He has written no new poems for some time, but the influence of his earlier verse is strongly felt in the work of the best of our modern poets. He began as a master poet in his youth, and he has remained a master to this day.

His contemporary, Lajos Kassák, now in his eightieth year, the Nestor of Hungarian poets, has on the other hand reached new heights in his poetry after a long period of stagnation in later life. In his eighties—a rare occurrence!—he has shown his capacity to revive the initial note he struck with the *avant garde* in the first decades of this century, calling his peculiar brand of it "constructivism," which he has never for a moment abandoned. He has managed to maintain a freshness in the forms of simultaneist free verse which he favours, once shockingly novel, now long abandoned by almost all its European representatives, and which has really had its day, but which he has used in his latest verse to achieve a classic serenity paradoxically engendered within its own terms.

Gyula Illyés, next in age, commands the greatest authority among our living poets and exerts the widest influence. In the great variety of his work he sums up, as it were, all the contradictory possibilities of Hungarian poetry. A supporter of the Hungarian Council Republic, he began his career in Paris as an emigré in his early twenties, closely allied to the surrealists, and came very near to becoming a French poet, as his first poems, written in French, appeared in short-lived *avant garde* publications. His return home in the mid-twenties illustrates the duties which have always burdened Hungarian, as distinct from European, poetry; the young surrealist poet fresh from Paris became the spokesman of the lowest Hungarian peasant, the leading figure in the "populist" movement, one of the most seminal movements of Hungarian intellectual life during the inter-war years. Today, in the great synthesis of his maturity, his poems fuse things as far apart as automatic writing and primitive incantation.

László Benjámin and Zoltán Zelk coupled the extrovert, journalistic tradition of Hungarian lyric poetry, mentioned above, with a deeply introvert, self-tormenting moralizing tendency which—especially in Zelk's poetry—sometimes overwhelms one with the striking obviousness of the folksong. His long poem, entitled *Sirály* ("Sea-gull"), a powerful lament on his wife's death is one of the finest Hungarian poems in recent years.

István Vas has assimilated the conceptual incisiveness of English metaphysical poetry and the soul-searching openness of Villon, to blend them with a sense of history which turns the loss of illusions into a new hope, in which intellectual generalization is merged with specific autobiographical detail.

After a long and enforced silence János Pilinszky appeared again in the late fifties with his spare and compact verse struggling with the existentialist dilemma of "being and nothingness," and though living in a Catholic ambiance, still recognizably belonging to the age of socialism.

Producing thousands of lines luxuriating in metaphors, echoing the ecstatic tones of laments inherited from our Asiatic origins, a surrealist in the fifties and sixties whose apocalyptic visions affirm a socialist ideal of freedom—would this description fit a single European poet working today? The man it describes is Ferenc Juhász, and it could equally be applied to a few similarly inspired fellow poets such as, for instance, László Nagy.

And finally there is the generation of the last ten years, the poets grouped around the anthology *Fire Dance*, who appeared at a critical moment of our history, thus ensuring the continuity of Hungarian literature. Gábor Garai, Mihály Váci and a few others of the group are creating a related yet differing version of those new trends linked in Russian with the name of Yevtushenko or Voznesensky, in English with the *beat generation* or the *angry young men*.

There is no need to exaggerate the first signs of the awakening of a world interest in the work of these poets, which means so much to us. It is certain, however, that this incipient interest is wider and deeper than Hungarian poetry has experienced before. The growing number of translations of Attila József into French, Russian, German, Italian, Spanish, Serbian, Czech and lately into English, versions occasionally produced by excellent foreign poets, Miklós Radnóti's impact in Italy and Germany, comprehensive anthologies of Hungarian verse in Russian, English and French (of which by far the most significant has been the one edited by László Gara and published by Editions du Seuil in 1962 under the title *Anthologie de la poésie hongroise*), have been followed by volumes of selections from the work of Lajos Kassák and Gyula Illyés, translated into French, the introduction of István Simon to the Russian and Gábor Garai to the Slovak reading public, and finally the joint volume of Weöres and Juhász under preparation in the Penguin Poetry series have all helped to make Hungarian poetry better known than at any time before. And this wider hearing should act as a spur to our critics at home to reappraise various aspects of our lyric poetry and literature in this new situation. "At the gates of world literature"—this phrase would sum up some of the questions discussed at the Round Table conference held by the Hungarian Writers' Federation under the title "Hungarian poetry—European poetry," in the *Four Essays* on "the future of Hungarian literature" by László Németh, or in Tamás Ungvári's *World Literature—Hungarian Literature*.

How far has this sketch succeeded in its object? Early in the article I asked to be excused so that I need not end on a note of apology. Stephen Spender's essay had only to add one slender storey to the firmly-based edifice of the knowledge of English poetry. We are doing no more than putting up the scaffolding here—for a building which it will be up to the future to construct. (pp. 111-17)

György Somlyó, "A Short Introduction to Contemporary Hungarian Poetry," in The New Hungarian Quarterly, *Vol. VII, No. 23, Autumn, 1966, pp. 108-17.*

NYUGAT AND EARLY TWENTIETH-CENTURY LITERATURE

MIKSA FENYŐ

[Nyugat *(translated as "West" or "Occident") is considered the most important Hungarian literary journal of the twentieth century. Published between 1908 and 1941,* Nyugat *is credited with introducing contemporary Western European literary trends to Hungary. The journal served as a forum for many of the country's most talented and rebellious young writers, who sought to free both literature and politics from the predominant conservatism of the late nineteenth century. Miksa Fenyő was one of the founders of* Nyugat. *In the following excerpt, he discusses the magazine's creation, editorial orientation, and greatest writers, as well as the strong opposition of the Hungarian literary establishment to the journal's spirit of innovation and reform.]*

Whoever said the word *nyugat* or "occident" between 1910 and 1940 frequently used it to refer to a literary magazine and not necessarily to a direction or even to the Western Powers. This magazine was founded by several young Hungarian writers and poets in 1908 and was banned when the Hungarian government felt it opportune to do so under nazi-German pressure. This is quite understandable as the word "Occident" sounded like a provocation for the nazis and their Hungarian satellites who professed that the friendship with the axis was the only redemption for the country. The *Nyugat* magazine had to cease to exist but they could not banish its influence on the development of the Hungarian spirit.

I would not dare to step before the American reader if I did not know that the *Nyugat* and the spiritual collective of the writers who were discovered by this magazine had not grown in their influence beyond the framework which characterizes a well-edited literary magazine or review: high-level literary publications, essays on culture and politics, criticism, reviews. The *Nyugat* meant, however, much more, especially from literary or cultural points of view although it started in this vein. It meant much more in social respect, fighting for the freedom of the spirit and this was directly and indirectly felt in the entire field of public life. It was so because it expressed the ideas, the ideology that were generally considered to be present in the public life of the great western countries, and the magazine, together with its contributors, was always concerned that these be synchronized with the spiritual constitution of the Hungarian people.

I have no recollection of any other case in the Twentieth Century that a magazine had such a tremendous effect on the revitalization of its era's spiritual life as the *Nyugat* had in Hungary. (pp. 7-8)

Those who founded this review—and the author was one of them, followed its entire career with anxious interest—did not start their work with the intention to unhinge the Hungarian globe off its poles. They intended to tell the truth with courage like all the new papers profess to do especially if the founders are in their twenties. They were thinking of independent criticism which is not being tinted by adherence to any political party, which is not bound by academical dogmas and sanctified canons of literary societies. They planned and hoped to accomplish that without conceit but with spirit—*ridendo dicere severum*, as Nietzsche urged. That was what they were thinking about when they established the *Nyugat*. Several outstanding writers of the earlier generation sided with them who felt the same creative strength of literary freedom and they were followed by always new ones—and within less than five years the *Nyugat* became synonymous with a high sense of responsibility in the standard of the works published and in the ideas professed as well as in the mode of their expression and their style.

It seems, however, more opportune to describe more precisely the literary situation prior to the publication of the *Nyugat*, at the end of the last century and at the beginning of the present century which prevailed in Hungary instead of a rather rhetoric appraisal. (p. 8)

[It] is very close to a miracle that Providence gave the Hungarian people three such outstanding geniuses in the nineteenth century as Mihály Vörösmarty, Sándor Petőfi and János Arany whose oeuvres equal the works of the most outstanding literary figures in the Western literature. . . . This forceful development was shocked by the 1848 War of Independence and the crushing of the Hungarian nation's resistance by the Habsburg-Czarist Russian coalition. Petőfi lost his life on the battlefield. Whenever Vörösmarty sounded his lyre it was full of bitterness. "Mankind is a seed of dragon-teeth, and there is no hope, no hope" wrote Vörösmarty in one of his late poems.

Only János Arany survived the era of depradation. He turned to the Hungarian history and created the Hungarian epos, and the Hungarian ballad following the examples of the Hungarian populist and English examples. Until his death in 1882 János Arany was the most respected Hungarian poet and in fact the country's poeta laureatus. (p. 10)

In 1867 the nation and the King reached a reconciliation which was brought about by Ferenc Deák, the great Hungarian statesman. This period of reconciliation lasted from 1867 to the end of the first World War. It is worthwhile to describe this period's literature in a few lines. The era was a well-balanced period in the country's history, and the nation, in general, accepted the reconciliation. The feverish phenomena disappeared from the Hungarian literature and reflected the spirit of the reconciliation period which was as reassuring and as quiet as Ferenc Deák himself. Not because of a lack of excellent talent: János Arany enriched the Hungarian literature with many of his most outstanding works, Mór Jókai published his most beautiful novels towards the end of the century and Kálmán Mikszáth's enchanting talent developed in this era. . . . Quite a few great names could be mentioned from this period. Nevertheless, the era was stubbornly conservative which is often an asset in politics but results in a weakening of literary interest and aspirations. Goethe once said: "Der nicht vorwaerts geht der kommt zurueck" ["He who does not move forward moves backward"].

Thus, it is understandable that those who met around the table of Ernö Osvát in one of the literary cafés in Budapest raised the question: is it possible that Hungarian poetry ended with János Arany as professed by the critical literature at that time by stating almost as a dogma those aesthetic rules which were derived from the work of János Arany. Is it possible that the Hungarian novel has no other voice than the one with which Mór Jókai or Kálmán Mikszáth enchanted us? Is it possible that literature keeps its door closed before the political problems of vital importance and that social problems be taboos? Is is permissible that literary values be wasted because there is no one who would care about them? Aren't a few thousand people in Hungary—then having a population of well over 20,000,000 of which more than half were Hungarians—who could appreciate that talented writers and poets rallied to give something else than what was produced by the literature so far? That they could give "The new songs of the new times" as the great poet of the *Nyugat*-era Endre Ady put it?

Mihály Babits, another great poet of this era, wrote about the *Nyugat* a quarter of a century later: "until the publication of the *Nyugat* we had had no home; the *Nyugat* was created because the generation before did not want to know us." On the twenty-fifth anniversary of the *Nyugat*, Zsigmond Móricz, the greatest Hungarian narrator, stated in his solemn address: "When the *Nyugat* was established by Ignotus, Ernő Osvát and Miksa Fenyő, they have created a much needed and timely organ: they have given air and literary means of existence to what was then the young generation, to the writers and readers. It is not intended to be an accusation or an attack to state that the more mature writer generation which we found on the scene was painted by this movement. And today it is only a historical memory that the Academy, all the literary societies lined up

László Benjámin. Photograph by János Reismann.

against us at open and mass meetings at that time and formed a permanent front of the elderly people against the young.''

Those who launched the *Nyugat* on its literary career did not think about constitutional changes but had strong faith in the need of a radical reform in the literary field and were also convinced that this is the prerequisite of any other reform. They did not have a reform program which could have been put into solid form. They did not have any conception how a real urban middle class may be created, how the country might be freed from the chains of the rule of the counties and how to create a real parliamentary constitution. They had no such charter before them although many of them paid continuous attention to these problems. They knew, however, that as long as the voice of those who represent the elite of the intellectual life and especially the voice of the writers did not gain recognition as the expression of national sentiment in their aspiration within the national public there will be no chance for such a reform anywhere in the country. This review, therefore, deemed the creation of such a spiritual atmosphere its primary duty. Whether this attempt had had any result if the First World War had not interrupted it with such a devastating force is not worthwhile to meditate on.

Although the task undertaken by the young contributors of the *Nyugat* was very clearly seen in its outlines they were not prepared for the reaction created by their movement. Looking back from a distance of a half century it must be admitted that this reaction was a most inevitable one. The task of the Hun-

garian governments at any time after the Reconciliation was to preserve Ferenc Deák's work intact and the Hungarian middle class which found its place in this Francis Deákian frame identified its own interest with the interests of the Reconciliatory policy and regarded any reform attempt dangerous and almost rebellious. Not because there were no thinking and educated people who would feel the shortcomings of the system but they held the same opinion as Cardinal Retz who stated about any problem which might have created dissension between the ruler and the nation that the rights of the King and of the people ''can be best harmonized if they are not being discussed.'' They themselves felt good in this newly developed world because they received appreciation. While they sincerely admitted the shortcomings they did not attempt to introduce reforms. Mundus se expediet—everything will get well. It may be that they felt about this world like Homer who praised the wisdom of the gods for starting bloody wars in order to enable the late descendants to sing about them.

The debates about the *Nyugat* are still interesting especially from historical, and psychological points of view. These debates were continued with those who were not willing to tolerate the appearance of new poet personalities on the Hungarian Parnassus after the triumvirate of Vörösmarty-Petőfi-Arany. During the First World War the debate went on with those who did not consider the attitude of the writers of the *Nyugat* very enthusiastic. They expected war songs from them, the expression of sighs over the ruins of the Hungarian nation or they branded treason anything which had anything in common with a desire for peace. Later, the more courageous voice was criticized which dealt with the relationship of the two sexes and in general the tone in which sexual problems were discussed in the review. Objection was expressed to those writings which did not respect very much the rules of the positive religions, and to their tolerant and even understanding attitude toward the nationalities. They were accused of disrespect towards the traditions.

Those who attacked the *Nyugat* were led by two talented writers: Jenő Rákosi, the excellent publicist, editor of a nationalist daily of great reputation, and Ferenc Herczeg, an outstanding narrator, dramatist of German origin who, in the nazi times, excelled with his honest anti-nazi attitude. It is interesting to note that Endre Ady was in the center of fire of the attacks in any principal problem. He was the one who denied his Hungarian origin, who flouted his faith, who put Eros on the throne, in one word, he was the poete maudit, the damned poet. He answered the attacks in beautiful lyrical poems—it may be said that literature owes gratitude to the attackers. (pp. 10-12)

While it is impossible to condense an encyclopaedic appreciation of the forty immortals of the *Nyugat,* a few words must be said about the triumvirate of this review or about the triumvirate of the Hungarian literature in the twentieth century: Endre Ady, Mihály Babits and Zsigmond Móricz whose oeuvres were so generously granted by fate to the Hungarian people and which equalled the oeuvres of the nineteenth century triumvirate of Hungarian literature: Vörösmarty-Petőfi-Arany. (p. 13)

Endre Ady (1877-1919) was in my opinion, the greatest of Hungarian lyricists. His appearance on the Hungarian literary sky was a meteoric one. After a few small collections of poems in which as a provincial newspaperman he made his first attempts following the old traditions he published his volume *New Poems* in which he showed himself already as a fully developed genius. He was a sovereign master of the language and ''erased the notion of inexpressibility from the Hungarian language'' as it was said about him by an excellent expert of his literary art. He could express the most delicate, most refined sentiments, passions and suffering on his lyre with the magic of rhymes and rhythms, with such unparalleled suggestive force that the reader felt it his own. He complained in one of his poems:

> God, doubt, wine, women, sickness
> all inflicted wounds on my body and soul. . . .

And so is this expressed in his poetry. His is a pessimistic doubt, although, at the same time, he admits that ''life is not a great merry-making anywhere but can be amazing.'' A belief and doubt in God—a belief in gold and blood, in the power of Eros and in the mission of the Hungarian nation—to continue is of no avail because these words cannot give any concept of his own words. There is a striking similarity between his life and his outstanding predecessor, Sándor Petőfi. Petőfi's life was consumed—and his life was synonymous with his poetry— in the eternal struggle for his Hungarian people and for freedom. Petőfi died in action during the war of independence in 1849, fighting against the Czarist Russian invaders. Ady was a revolutionary, the deadly enemy of any reaction: The richness of instrumentation and the suggestive force expressing his struggles in his poetry almost defy the imagination. And as Petőfi died young on the battlefield, Ady, too, died at a young age, on a symbolical battlefield at a time when the end of the First World War, so tragic for the Hungarian people, tore his country apart. He sent a greeting to the victors and speaking about the sorrowful fate of the ''worn out poor Hungarian people'' he appeals to them by saying:

> Do not trample upon it too much,
> Do not stampede upon it too much,
> On our blood-weak, poor but beautiful heart
> Which wanted but to speed. . . .

Ady's influence on Hungarian literature was extremely great. It had a liberating effect: following his example the writers became more daring and spoke their own words and dared to speak about problems which were prohibited by the prevailing aesthetic literary rules. They also provoked the reaction and the debates cleared both the literary and political atmosphere. Each of his new volumes of poems was a new revelation; after each of his volumes his friends believed that there is nothing left and from this moment on he can but repeat himself. Nevertheless, each of his new volumes—and he published ten volumes of poems—was a great sensation. (pp. 14-15)

Mihály Babits (1883-1941). He is completely different in his spirit, language and style than his older contemporary, Endre Ady. The two great poets respected each other very much. There are many ways in the world of art and none of them is one-way. Babits was a poet of essayistic background and after Ernő Osvát's death he became the editor of the *Nyugat*. He was considered ''Poeta doctus'' by many because he was at home in the literature of every nation. Saint Augustine, Spinoza and Bergson were his friends. Babits translated Dante's *La Divina Comedia* into Hungarian. . . . He wrote a history of literature independently of the commonly made observations and statements on the basis of his own wide knowledge of the material. He was, however, above all a poet with the deepest thoughts and most artistic in style, in whose art the noble form was necessarily created by the noble content. His most beautiful poems are probably those which he wrote on his death bed sufferings from the lethal disease. Among them *The Book of Jonas* is the most moving.

Zsigmond Móricz (1879-1942), the greatest of Hungarian narrators. He wrote novels, short stories, reports which described the fate of individuals, their dramatic experiences, but in the background a decisive problem of the Hungarian people or a social question could be discerned. The tendency of the work, however, did not fog the masterful sketching of the narrative. His great historical novel, Transylvania, with Gábor Bethlen, Prince of Transylvania, as the hero, who was a great personality of the reformation, is a most exciting reading. He built up his story after careful and detailed study of the subject with such clearsight that the time he described grew into an entire era in world history and his people and crises threw some light on the people of today and on the problem of our time. His three volumes of short stories—*Seven pennies, Hungarians, Poor People*—must be especially mentioned. In an article written by the author about the *Poor People* during the First World War it was stated with the innermost conviction that Zsigmond Móricz would have deserved not only the Nobel Prize of Literature but also the Peace Prize. Mention must be made of his novel, *The Torch*, which was also published in the United States with the same title, although this translation gave a strongly distorted and shortened version paying attention only to the quick denouement of the plot. Móricz's biographic novel is also an excellent literary work. It is impossible to list all his very outstanding work and a separate article . . . would seem the most appropriate to make the reader acquainted with the literary work of this Hungarian genius. (pp. 15-16)

Finally, it must be mentioned here that the *Nyugat* followed and discussed with great interest the literature of the outside world, and especially American literature. Among them with the American classics such as Walt Whitman, Edgar Allan Poe, Herman Melville, Mark Twain, Washington Irving, and with those outstanding people who followed in their footsteps, Steinbeck, Faulkner, Hemingway, Pearl S. Buck, Willa Cather, Thornton Wilder, Dos Passos, Dreiser, Hergesheimer, Margaret Mitchell, Eugene O'Neill, Sinclair Lewis, Jack London, Vachel Lindsay, and others—and it should not be disregarded that all this was . . . when their names were less known than today. (pp. 18-19)

> *Miksa Fenyő, ''The Nyugat Literary Magazine and the Modern Hungarian Literature,'' in* The Hungarian Quarterly, *Vol. 3, Nos. 3-4, October-December, 1962, pp. 7-19.*

JOSEPH HELD

[*Held is a Hungarian-born American historian specializing in Eastern Europe. In the following excerpt, he discusses the origins and early years of* Nyugat *and the most important literary critics to contribute to the magazine.*]

[The Hungarian] authors emerging in the 1890s were impressionists; they believed that conformism was a great crime against literature. They rejected the belief in the objectivity of literary criticism, and they held that innovation was the most important task of a writer. They were the forerunners of the authors who were to set the tone of Hungarian literature in the new century. But there was a major difference between them and those who came to the scene in the 1900s. As Arthur Elek, a member of the younger generation later explained,

> What was only a shadowy promise, a surmise
> in the poetry [of the 1890s] became a con-
> sciously expressed thought in the works of the
> moderns. It was a consciousness of that rest-

lessness, of that dissatisfaction which was a sign of the age, expressed not only in their subject-matters, but also in their styles. . . .

The older writers, with few exceptions, continuously criticized the literary production of their younger colleagues, and these attacks were increasingly becoming political in content. The urban writers were forced by these attacks to seek out each other's company, and they soon established their own literary circles. Two of these circles, one in Transylvania in the city of Nagyvárad, the other at the University of Budapest, became the kernels of a literary movement that was destined to revitalize Hungarian literature.

The Nagyvárad-circle found its natural leader in the poet, Endre Ady. He was a most disturbing young man, openly and outspokenly contemptuous of conservative writers and of Hungary's social institutions, and deeply convinced of his own divine mission as *the* poet of the new generation. For him the art of poetry was only a means in the fight for a full life, against all that seemed to be standing in the way of the fulfillment of the destiny of the individual. His passion for the poor of the cities, his deep patriotism, his criticism of the Hungarian aristocracy's handling of the peasant question, made him into a genuine tribune of the people. He soon became a symbol of the impatient young men of the cities, determined to overthrow outdated institutions in literature as well as in politics. He was converted to Marxian socialism and welcomed the emergence of the radical and revolutionary movements in Hungary.

The young writers who lived in Budapest gathered in the literature classes of Professor László Négyessy at Budapest University; their leader was Ernő Osvát. This was a circle for self-education, one whose counterparts could be found in every *Gymnasium* and college in Hungary. A member of this circle described their early activities as having consisted of reading their poems and novels for each other, sometimes against the wishes of their professor, of criticizing and evaluating the works presented, and of discussing their plans. What made the Budapest-circle so important was that it was here where the first works of such authors as Gyula Juhász, Dezső Kosztolányi, Árpád Tóth, and others were presented. The young authors were determined to have their own journal in order to overcome the silence imposed on them by a conservative press which was not taking note of their activities. But their first efforts were unsuccessful.

> During the summer of 1900—or, perhaps, of 1901—. . . there appeared a call for subscriptions for a journal, signed by eight young men, in which they declared the publication of *Uj Figyelő* [*New Observer*]. But, except this declaration, nothing came of the projected journal, . . .

explained one of the participants of this venture. However, the eight young men were not easily discouraged. Next year they bought an already established family weekly, the *Magyar Géniusz*. As it turned out, however, this journal did not suit their purposes; it was supported by a conservative-oriented readership, and within half a year it had to be given up. Dezső Kosztolányi, one of the outstanding members of the group of young writers explained the reasons for this failure:

> In our country, unfortunately, the public is not yet mature enough to understand [modern literature]. . . . The fat-headed bourgeoisie still cannot get it into their heads that there is such

a thing as a modern poet in the world. They accepted one out of need as a court-jester; and that is Endre Ady. But of the rest they want to know nothing. . . .

Two years later Osvát allied himself with Miksa Fenyő, Artur Elek, Oszkár Gellért, and Lajos Hatvany [*Deutsch*], many of whom were to play an important role in the development of the new literature, all of them the rising young stars of the new writer-generation. Their journal, *Figyelő* [not to be confused with the *Figyelő* of the 1890s], published Ady's beautiful and controversial poem, *Harc a Nagyurral* [*Struggling with the Lord*], provoking immediate and furious attacks on the poet by the conservative critics. But subscribers were still hard to find and the journal ran out of funds in 1905.

A year later Ignotus, who was by then a friend of Osvát, started a new periodical. He was supported by the son of a well-known restaurant owner in Budapest, Antal Gundel. Seven issues of the journal appeared. But the father of the young Gundel disliked the adverse publicity that his son's activities generated, cut off his allowance and the paper folded. After all these activities, a new journal was begun by Osvát and Ignotus, the *Nyugat* [*West*], and it proved successful. Among its earlier financial supporters there were two firewood-dealers as well as Ferenc Chorin, one of the richest new manufacturers of Budapest.

Editor-in-chief was Ignotus; editors were Osvát and Miksa Fenyő, later also Hatvany and Ady. The first contributions published were written by Margit Kaffka, the first truly great woman-writer of urban Hungary; the poet Anna Lesznay, later to become the wife of Oszkár Jászi; György Lukács, already showing signs of his later fame as a Marxist thinker, and many others. They faced several serious challenges—mostly political in nature—before they were able to establish their credentials as great writers and thinkers. The secretary of the Kisfaludy Society, Gyula Vargha, fired a salvo against them at the annual meeting of the Society in which the character of future attacks was clearly outlined:

> . . . In our literature a new and dangerous ferment is now beginning. They [the young writers] are beginning to reject our national past using the Hungarian tongue for that purpose, to drag the great creations of the Hungarian past into the dust, and to inject the poison of alien thought into our literature. It is the sacred duty of the Kisfaludy Society to stop this destructive work and to defend the reading public from this poison of alien infection. . . .

As the partial list above shows, the contributors of *Nyugat* were a heterogeneous lot of authors. Not only were they coming from various parts of the country, professing often contradictory and opposing religious, political, and ideological convictions, but they also disagreed on their approach to literature. Some of them were avant-garde, while others retained a good dose of traditionalism in their works. There were among them Marxists, Jews, Christians, elementary school teachers, journalists, university students, and even medical doctors. Despite their heterogeneity as a group, they did succeed in creating a new literary movement. The very title of their journal provided them with a program: they considered it to be their task to "catch up" with Western ideas of freedom for the individual, of social equality and international brotherhood. They all regarded the "official" Hungarian literature sponsored by the

Academy and the Kusfaludy Society as being out of touch with new social realities. Some of them called for revolution in Hungarian intellectual life by transforming it to serve the needs of the urban middle class; others went further by advocating social revolution. The editors declared that they fully supported the idea of the freedom of literature from political interference. But they did not oppose the "right" of the authors to intervene in politics through their works. Rather, they advocated the right of the authors to set new standards for moral, ethical, and political values. The largest role in selecting works for publication fell to Osvát; in all this turmoil and clash of ideals he preserved high literary qualities for the journal, even in its political columns.

Osvát was an exceptionally able editor. His judgments of the literary merits of contributions to *Nyugat* was usually sound. He never hesitated to reject articles even by the best known authors if these did not measure up to his standards. He was generous in his defense of the young writers whose works he accepted for publication. He followed the labors of these authors with close attention; this was the way in which he discovered Zsigmond Móricz, Margit Kaffka, Dániel Jób, and Artur Elek. The *Nyugat* became, under his guidance, an observation point from which the best pieces of the new literature were introduced to the Hungarian reading public.

The first issue of *Nyugat* listed Ignotus as editor-in-chief. He was undoubtedly one of the most colorful and forceful characters in literary circles in Hungary at that time. He first aroused interest as a literary critic of *A Hét* in 1892 with his witty and sophisticated articles. From the very beginning of his activities as editor of *Nyugat*, he rejected the populist view which identified the Hungarian nation with the "sober peasant and the gentry of the countryside," and was deeply convinced that an artist was entitled to do everything for which he had a talent to do. His declared aim at the *Nyugat* was to defend the new literature from political interference. He was a fighting liberal in the true sense of the word, first among the defenders of the poetry of Ady. He proved himself an indispensable leader of the new literary movement.

The third editor of the journal was Miksa Fenyő, although his role as an editor was limited. He was more important as a first-rate propagandist for the *Nyugat*, and was extremely successful in gaining public attention for the journal. Moreover, he was a vigorous defender of the young writers, especially of Endre Ady. Finally, and this was not the least important of his activities, in the early days of the journal he often covered the deficits from his own funds.

Baron Lajos Hatvany, the scion of a Hungarian Jewish family, also played an important role in the early history of the *Nyugat*. He received an excellent education as the student of the conservative literary critic, Pál Gyulai. For this reason he was the last person to be expected to side with the poverty-stricken young generation of writers around the journal. But after reading Ady's poetry, Hatvany was converted to support the new literature. His great wealth, however, proved a handicap; despite the fact that he readily subsidized the journal, many of the contributors suspected him of having ulterior motives and never accepted him into their inner circles. (His disagreements with Osvát which eventually led to his break with the *Nyugat* will be discussed later.)

The first serious and recognized literary critic who followed Ignotus in supporting the young writers was Aladár Schöpflin. He worked for *Vasarnapi Ujság* [*Sunday News*] as a critic in the early 1890s and represented a new approach to literary criticism. Schopflin recognized that the literature of his time was changing as a response to changes in society. In Hungary, urban culture assumed an ever growing role while the cultural importance of the countryside was diminishing. He advanced the view according to which literary criticism should have to take into consideration the social background and origin of authors as these, he thought, determined the character and quality of their works. Throughout his life he remained devoted to *Nyugat* and what it represented, long after the original protagonists had departed from the literary scene.

The editors and contributors of *Nyugat* were quite conscious of the fact that, with them, a new age in Hungarian literature was beginning, although they could not yet measure the significance of their individual contributions. But if the social reform program of their counterparts [that of the political liberals such as Jászi and Mihály Károlyi] floundered upon the rock of conservative-nationalistic public opinion, the renovation of Hungarian literature did succeed. In this success the *Nyugat* played a decisive role.

At the turn of the century only "classical" Hungarian authors—and journals such as *Uj Idők*—were able to attract the attention of a sizeable reading public. Among these Gárodnyi and Herczeg competed with the works of the already dead Jókai. In general, they all wrote about Hungary's past. Herczeg often directly catered to the nationalistic passions of the gentry and to the gentle, syrupy romanticism of their women. Gárdonyi published highly readable historical novels that sold very well indeed. Naturally, when the *Nyugat* first appeared, the reading public idolizing Gárdonyi, Jókai, and Herczeg was baffled by it. Few of the conservative critics were alert enough to notice the quality of the new voices from the journal. But the openness by which the contributors treated sensitive subjects of patriotism and public and private morals, soon aroused interest, and indignation among the official guardians of Hungarian literature. Béla Tóth of *Pesti Hirlap* had already had an argument with Ady as early as 1906, when the poet's first controversial volume entitled *Uj Versek*, [*New poems*] appeared. The critic was appalled by Ady's unconventional verses and labeled him a "decadent young man." This label stuck: the entire generation of the *Nyugat*-writers was to be called decadent by their opponents for decades, an ironic, pre-Orwellian twist of existing realities.

The attacks on Ady and the young poet-generation clustering around him were intensified when, in 1908, the Nagyvárad-circle brought out the first volume of a two-volume anthology, *A Holnap* [*Tomorrow*]. This book contained poems by Ady, Mihály Babits, Margit Kaffka, and others. Now a hunt of the young writers began; Ady was accused of attempting to subvert the morals, language, and values of Hungarian society. Above all, the contributors of *A Holnap* were accused of being unpatriotic because they dared to attack Hungarian social and political institutions in their works. Jenő Rákosi, who was to lead the attacks on the *Nyugat* later, declared that the new poetry was not understandable. He suggested that the young poets were either crazy or consciously destructive, the followers of mad foreigners, especially the French. He constantly hammered away at what he called the "pollution of Hungarian literature by the young writers." His attacks came at a time when he was at the height of his influence as editor of one of the most prestigious journals of the Hungarian capital, *Budapesti Szemle*. His personal friends included most members of the older generation of writers, as well as Istvan Tisza. Soon even Tisza himself stepped into the fight by writing several articles—one under a pseudonym—in which he denounced the young writers as enemies of the Hungarian nation.

Tisza and the conservative critics were, of course, right. The contributors to *Nyugat* did reject the former's definition of what constituted the Hungarian nation. While Rákosi and his friends "decided to push for a chauvinistic program, and hoped for the internal strengthening [of Hungary] . . . by the setting up of intellectual censorship," the *Nyugat*-generation spoke of the urban masses as the new backbone of the Hungarian nation, and demanded the dismantling of official controls of literature. Perhaps the most poignant summary of the differences between the two sides was written by Dezső Szabó [he was to die of starvation in Russian-besieged Budapest in 1945, by then an influential populist-radical writer] as he remarked:

> Anyone possessing five- ten- or I don't even know how many thousands of acres of land, and is going to those who are suffering of starvation, saying: "do not bother with the acquisition of material wealth but go on starving for the homeland," is truly anti-national. He is anti-national because he is compromising the idea of the homeland. . . .

The arguments about the value of the new literature, therefore, were becoming more and more politically oriented. But it was not the doing of the young writers but of their opponents that forced the arguments in this direction.

Even the conservative critics who were willing to examine the *Nyugat* on the basis of its literary merits, came under fire. The case of János Horváth was typical. In 1910, Horváth wrote a book in which he tried to evaluate Ady's poetry from a conservative viewpoint, but on its own literary merits. First, he was warned by Tisza himself to leave the subject alone. When Horvath refused to abide by this warning, his subsequent writings were rejected by the conservative journals.

Dávid Angyal, another supporter of Tisza and Rákosi, charged that the quality of the writings published in *Nyugat* was too shallow and superficial to be called true literature. Fenyő and Ignotus took up the challenge, and charges and countercharges flew back and forth right up to the war and beyond.

After the revolutions of 1918-1919 and the collapse of Hungary, the *Nyugat* was accused by the conservative politicians of having prepared the way for these events. Again, these conservatives were, to some extent, right. But they forgot that the writers of the *Nyugat* began their work as reformers, aiming to overhaul Hungarian society through their writings; that they were driven, by the conservatives, into a corner from which the only way out was to support the revolutions. These writers represented a paradox in Hungarian history; they were deeply conscious of the dangers inherent in social revolution, but they could not avoid becoming its intellectual forbears.

There were serious internal dissensions which periodically shook the *Nyugat*. One of the most infamous disputes involved Ady in late 1908. It seems that the poet was having serious financial difficulties—which poet did not?—and he permitted himself to be persuaded by friends at the Singer and Wolfner Publishers to attack the *Nyugat* in return for some publishing favors. Thus, he proceeded to write an article in *Uj Idők* in which he asserted:

> I am not a delegate, or president, or member of any secret society. I have nothing in common with the so-called Hungarian moderns, and my

alleged literary rebellion is not a rebellion at all. Smart little men may succeed in attaching themselves to me because I am a patient man and a little out of touch with this world, but this is not my fault. There is a society in Melanesia called the duk-duk, a sort of primitive form of Free Masonry, whose leader seldom learns that he is the chief. Perhaps this is the kind of leader I am. . . . I don't know anything about the revolution that is allegedly being fought in my name. I do not consider myself to be more modern than Balassa, Csokonay, or Petőfi. I would not have a common cause with those who had even forgotten to learn Hungarian. I have nothing to do with those who had perhaps read a few cheap German books and now want to go on to redeem Hungarian literature. . . . I have the right to declare that I have a deep revulsion for those who are now agitating in my name, perhaps a deeper revulsion than some people feel toward me. There are a number of nobodys huffing and puffing in my name and are fighting on my behalf, and with whom I have nothing whatsoever to do.

Some of Ady's fellow contributors to *Nyugat*, who had compromised themselves by defending him, were deeply shocked and at least one of them, Dezső Kosztolányi, repaid the poet, long after his death, with a stinging denunciation. Others severed connections with him, including even Ignotus. But Osvát was now ready to show his qualities as an editor. Ady himself soon realized the magnitude of his mistake and wrote another article, this time against Ferenc Herczeg of the *Uj Idők*. The balance was thus restored, and the *Nyugat* came out in June, 1909, with an issue exclusively dedicated to Ady's poetry. It may be argued that Osvát realized that, without Ady, there was no new literature in Hungary. Being a shrewd editor, he sensed that the mirth that the "duk-duk affair" aroused in the reading public benefited his journal by calling attention to it. In any case, it was the Ady-number of *Nyugat* which established the poet as the darling of the progressive intelligentsia of Budapest and the hated adversary of the conservative critics.

Another dispute centered around Lajos Hatvany. He considered himself well-qualified to contest some of the editorial policies of Osvát; he possessed a great deal of self-confidence not only on account of his great wealth, but also because of his earlier success as a literary critic in Germany. His arguments with Osvát stemmed from this fact.

During the autumn of 1911, the *Nyugat* was incorporated, and Hatvany financed a *Nyugat* book publishing company. Several young authors, Ady among them, committed all their future works to this firm in advance. Hatvany gained an important leverage, and he used his influence in attempting to move the journal in a direction which, as it was feared by Osvát, would turn it into an old-fashioned family paper. Hatvany wanted above all to reduce the "propaganda" on behalf of Ady, and to slow down the publication of the works of newly discovered talents. Finally, he wanted to invite Géza Gárdonyi to become a member-contributor to the *Nyugat*.

Osvát opposed these plans. He considered Hatvany a second-rate writer in any case; he repeatedly rejected his manuscripts that Hatvany submitted for publication in the *Nyugat*. Eventually the bad situation became unbearable. Hatvany and Osvát argued over every major and minor policy decision. They disagreed over the merits of the works of Sándor Bródy, over the methods of financing the journal. Hatvany was determined to make the *Nyugat* self-supporting (which meant a greater reliance on conservative readers), while Osvát feared the "commercialization" of the journal. Finally Hatvany parted with *Nyugat* in June, 1912.

The polemics between the two gifted opponents, however, did not cease with Hatvany's departure. He continued his attacks on Osvát in various journals and this harassment finally led to a duel between them in which Hatvany was wounded. Deeply offended, Hatvany left Hungary not to return until the First World War was already in progress.

The exit of Hatvany left the *Nyugat* in a temporarily difficult financial situation. The director of the *Nyugat* Publishing Company, Mór Magyar, committed suicide partly because of his fear of bankruptcy. Ignotus took over as owner and editor together with Ady; but the latter was editor only in name, and Osvát remained for the time being in the background. But Osvát continued to control the editorial policies of the journal and decided upon accepting or rejecting manuscripts. The greatest loser in all this was Ady. Since all his works were tied up in advance for the *Nyugat* Publishing Company, he could not

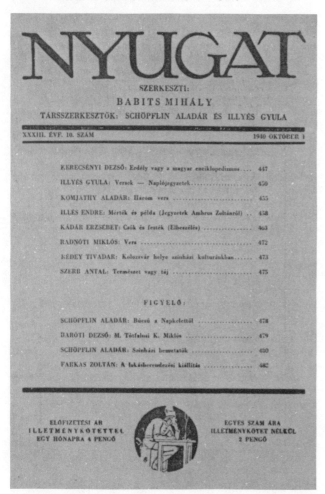

Cover of the October 1, 1940 issue of Nyugat. *From* Miklós Radnóti: The Complete Poetry, *edited and translated by Emery George. Ardis, 1980. Reprinted by permission of Ardis Publishers.*

publish them elsewhere. It took some years for the *Nyugat* to recover from the adverse financial consequences of this misfortune.

These disputes as well as the infighting ended the first and most exciting period of the *Nyugat*'s history. Although attacks against the journal—as well as against the new urban literature as a whole—were to continue unabated, these attacks were slowly losing their potency.

More and more middle class subscribers joined the *Nyugat* and acquired a taste for the strange symbolism and often beautiful writings of the new poets and novelists. The works of Mihály Babits, the thoughtful and beautiful poetry of Árpád Tóth, the sensitive and analytical novels and short stories of Margit Kaffka became classics of Hungarian literature.

However, all the excitement went out of the new literature with the end of the First World War; although the *Nyugat* was continuously published until 1941, it was no longer the experimental journal as it had been in the 1910s. Part of the reason for this was that the journal could not become a spokesman for public opinion; partly, because it had achieved a great intellectual success. Because, by the early 1920s, the new literature had become accepted as conventional; innovations were to come from other directions, not from the *Nyugat*.

The *Nyugat* was not a radical journal in the 1910s in the conventional sense of the word. Its editors were dedicated to a new respect for artistic freedom, regardless of the political convictions of the authors published by them. But the journal became radical in the context of Hungarian social, political, and cultural realities. It proclaimed artistic freedom when such a freedom was frowned upon by "respectable" society and, therefore, became embroiled in disputes over the politics of literature.

This article must, by necessity, be limited in scope; lack of space prevents a detailed inquiry into the individual achievements and lives of most members of the *Nyugat*-generation. One aspect of their activities, however, deserves a brief discussion, namely, the character and quality of the literary criticism produced by the *Nyugat*.

Among the critics who contributed to the *Nyugat*, Ignotus, Kosztolányi, and Schöpflin were the most important. Osvát and Fenyő also participated in the critical work of the editors, but they exerted their influence more by the acceptance or rejection of works for publication, than by writing. In general, all of the critics of the *Nyugat* were characterized by their reluctance to employ any rigid criteria in judging the merits of literary creations. They were content with permitting a poem or a short story to "penetrate their consciousness" while reading it in order to provide them with a "spiritual experience." By the intensity, or genuineness, of this experience they accepted or rejected a work of literature. At least, this was their loudly proclaimed aim. In practice, of course, they often deviated from such a strict observance of subjectivism.

Ignotus himself adhered closely to this ideal. According to him modern literature had but one task, namely, to be artistic. "There is no other rule in art except one; know how to express yourself." He further expressed this idea in an article which may be regarded as a guideline to his own critical activities:

> There are writers . . . whose aim it is to serve. Let these men be servers, and let their genius shine in the light of such a service. But there are others who are serving nothing—and this

is their service. Daumier is a genius of service, but Rembrandt *exists,* and he serves by simply being in existence. . . .

Ignotus rejected anything that went against this standpoint; this was the basis on which he turned against the chauvinistic nationalism in the literature of his time, because in the name of such chauvinism the conservative critics wanted to restrict artistic freedom. For the same reason, he fought against economic institutions that restricted the advancement of the individual; he wrote against the monopolistic control of Hungarian industry by big finance companies and banks, and against the large landholders of the aristocracy who controlled most of the arable land of Hungary. In this way he pronounced the "right" of the new literature to cast judgment over politics and politicians while, at the same time, fighting to limit the influence of the conservative politicians over the new literature.

At a first look, one could not find a greater contrast than that which existed between the cautious Schöpflin and the flamboyant Ignotus. The former believed in the necessity of analyzing the new literature by using the methods of sociology. He observed the growing compartmentalization of Hungarian society, and saw the development of the new literature as the expression of the emergence of the middle class as a cultural factor. He was, of course, right. Accordingly, he believed that the task of the literary critic was to trace the origin of literary creations to their social roots and understand them on their class merits. But, deep down, he did not live up to his rules. He was not really interested in "measuring exactly the faults and merits" of short stories, novels, and poetry, rather in understanding them, in experiencing them in his soul. He searched for the relationship between the individuality of the author and the uniqueness of his work, and by doing so he came close to the ideas professed by Ignotus. He had a flexible mind and his judgments were exceptionally sound. But he felt, as he later admitted, that this flexibility reduced his effectiveness as a literary critic.

Perhaps the purest of the Hungarian impressionistic critics was Dezső Kosztolányi. He regarded himself as being "homo Aestheticus," a man totally dedicated to the enjoyment of artistic beauty in life. He believed in the subjective merits of literature to such an extent that he considered all literary criticism as naive and futile. He confessed that he believed in the self-serving nature of literature:

> I confess that I do not despise rationalism to such an extent as those who marvel at the meaningless, as if it were the deepest of experiences. But I have to admit that I use [rationalism] little during my creative periods. I confess that I believe in the self-serving nature of poetry, namely, that a poem or a novel has no other purpose except that it has to be beautiful.

Such a preoccupation with the enjoyment of artistic beauty in literature had certain drawbacks for Kosztolányi as a literary critic. As one of his admirers later admitted, "Kosztolányi had shown little sensitivity to existing differences in values of the various literary creations. For him, any work of art, if it were well-done, if it expressed a certain measure of individuality, was equally worth while."

But such a weakness Kosztolányi shared with all the literary critics of the *Nyugat.* Perhaps their emphasis on subjectivity made these critics less valuable for the new literature than the writers whose original conributions they evaluated. But this

was only logical; the *Nyugat* was first and foremost a forum dedicated to the dissemination of first-rate urban literature, and literary criticism was secondary in importance for the editors and contributors of the journal. It was simply a weapon to be used against the detractors of the new literature.

As indicated before, the *Nyugat* was dedicated to the preservation of the autonomy of literature, against political interference. This the *Nyugat* did, indeed, achieve. Its editors refused to bend to conservative public opinion, to pressures coming from the Academy, and the various conservative literary societies, even when such an autonomy meant fewer readers—and less income. The *Nyugat,* therefore, became more than just another journal; it developed into an intellectual movement, eventually changing the character of Hungarian intellectual life. If such a change did not bring about, in time, important political and social innovations, it was not the fault of the young participants of this momentous movement. (pp. 275-86)

> *Joseph Held, "Young Hungary: The 'Nyugat' Periodical, 1908-14," in* Intellectual and Social Developments in the Habsburg Empire from Maria Theresa to World War I: Essays Dedicated to Robert A. Kann, *edited by Stanley B. Winters and Joseph Held, East European Quarterly, 1975, pp. 271-89.*

MARIO D. FENYO

[*In the following excerpt from an essay discussing the influence of* Nyugat *on social issues in Hungary, Fenyo characterizes the magazine's editorial policies on literature and politics.*]

Around [*Nyugat*] congregated most of the progressive writers (or modern as they preferred to call themselves) of talent, whether politically involved or not. As its title indicated, its writers and editors looked to the Occident, especially to France, as a source of inspiration and enlightenment. A substantial part of *Nyugat* was devoted to translations from or essays about French literature, although there was considerable delay in the acceptance of newer literary trends; for instance, *Nyugat* attempted to popularize symbolism at a time when it was already on the decline in France. While the writers and editors were primarily concerned with literary matters, they could not help but consider the milieu in which that literature emerged—the institutions of France, its political democracy—and the high level of culture of the public for whose benefit that literature was primarily created. Intellectual emulation, they assumed, would result in the emulation of social and political institutions as well—a fairly radical programme for pre-war Hungary. (p. 187)

What then was the political line of *Nyugat?* The three founders and editors of the review, Ignotus, Ernö Osvát and Miksa Fenyö, represented various nuances of the same political and literary creed. This creed, as already mentioned, was characteristically bourgeois: liberalism on the one hand, art for art's sake on the other. Yet the *art pour art* principle was not meant to be exclusive of other literary and aesthetic values. The slogan was, in part (but only in part), window-dressing to protect the review from the intervention of the authorities. If art was to stay out of politics, it was only fair that politics should stay out of art. When a socio-economic system is dominated by the interests of the aristocracy and of the gentry, as was the case in Hungary, art for art's sake must be viewed as a progressive ideal. Furthermore, in disregard of its own principles, *Nyugat* frequently published straightforward political articles, many of them penned by Ignotus himself. The editors did not seek to exclude literary works with a social or political content, quite the contrary: it might happen, for instance, that Osvát turned down a short story with the comment that "slapping society in the face does not necessarily make for good literature"; but it was permissible to slap society in the face. In other words, any work or theme was justified as long as it was engagingly written.

The editors of *Nyugat* were unquestionably liberal. Occasionally it even printed right-wing opinions and, during the first world war, a few war-mongering articles were published. Political and economic liberalism were gaining power in Hungary; true enough, as Dezső Szabó put it, but it stopped short of the Hungarian peasant, let alone the Hungarian worker. Nevertheless the process of liberalization in literature undermined not only the feudal establishment, but the liberal bourgeoisie itself. Inevitably the literature that appeared in *Nyugat* was subversive. Literature can become a guide to action; innovative literature may "free the spirit" and lead to innovation in political life. The novel, Marx and Engels claim, by conscientiously describing real social relations, by breaking down conventional illusions about those relations, can shatter the optimism of the bourgeois and instill doubt as to the eternal character of the existing order, even when the author does not offer any definite solutions and does not even line up openly on any particular side. For the most part, the writers of *Nyugat* were vaguely aware of these possibilities. The magnitude of the threat, however, was more obvious to the conservative writers and politicians. To appreciate fully the influence of *Nyugat*, one must read the attacks directed against it and trace these to their source. Its influence went far beyond its handful of subscribers. (pp. 188-89)

Mario D. Fenyo, "Writers in Politics: The Role of 'Nyugat' in Hungary, 1908-19," in The Journal of Contemporary History, Vol. 11, No. 1, January, 1976, pp. 185-98.

MIDCENTURY LITERATURE

LÓRÁNT CZIGÁNY

[*Czigány is the author of* The Oxford History of Hungarian Literature, *a comprehensive history from the Middle Ages to the present. In the following excerpt from that work, he discusses conservative trends in Hungarian historiography, philosophy, criticism, fiction, and poetry during the period between the world wars.*]

While the years preceding World War I had witnessed an imposing diversity of attempts to reform the social, economic, and intellectual conditions of [Hungary], the general climate of the inter-war years proved to be gloomy, and an anticlimax to the intellectual ferment of the *belle époque*. The primary cause of the narrowing intellectual horizon was undoubtedly the shock caused by the lost war, the ensuing convulsions—Red Terror, White Terror—and the complex problems, general misery, and intellectual bewilderment created thereby; society could not cope with them. The greatest damage to the national ego was that inflicted by the loss of two-thirds of historical Hungary's territories, which were ordered to be ceded to the successor states by the Treaty of Trianon in 1920.

Consequently the new regime, headed by Admiral Horthy, aimed at regaining these lost territories; the final and supreme aspiration in foreign policy during the next quarter of a century was the restoration of Hungary to the old, pre-1918 frontiers, an aspiration which successfully obscured all other issues, because, irredentist propaganda promised both social and economic salvation for the Hungarian masses after the regime's foreign policy objective had been achieved. In addition to the openly nationalistic character of the prevailing ideology, the "Christianness" of the regime's ideals was stressed. The adjective "Christian" was given racial overtones—the shining example of Christian values as opposed to "radical, subversive, Jewish machinations" which were largely blamed for the revolutionary upheavals in 1918-19. The "historic classes" could not forget their humiliation during the brief Communist interlude, and a universal scapegoat was needed for their wounded pride. They reasoned that as Hungarian Communists were predominantly Jews, Jewish participation in public life was to be restricted immediately lest the Bolshevik subversion should repeat itself.

This paranoid fear of Communism was the other main pivot around which "Christian-National" ideology turned. While Hungary was to be a bulwark against bolshevism and its assorted accomplices—socialism, radicalism, liberalism, cosmopolitanism, and freemasonry—which might attack from outside, within the country the "Christian-National" middle class, the backbone of society, had at all costs to be protected against these dangerous infections. Nevertheless the Horthy regime failed to accomplish its ideals; there was a considerable gap between theory and practice, not only because the regime did tolerate some genuinely liberal trends, particularly in literature and the arts, but mainly because it never became a right-wing dictatorship.

It also failed to produce significant literature which was unequivocally pro-establishment. A general survey of the existing trends shows this convincingly. The *Nyugat* movement survived and flourished. The prominent authors of its first generation . . . were at least uncommitted, if not outright critics of the establishment; writers of the second and third generations . . . were mostly apolitical, and the *neo-népies* ["neo-populist"] trend . . . was marked by an enterprising spirit which aimed at drawing public attention to social evils, thus perpetuating the traditional role of the writer in East European society as social conscience and spokesman of the opposition.

If "Christian-National" literature could not boast the kind of success that would withstand the test of time, there nevertheless emerged a generation of pro-establishment intellectuals whose significance reached far beyond the momentary support they lent to the regime; their ideas contributed salient features to the intellectual climate of the country in the first half of this century. (pp. 361-62)

Gyula Szekfű (1883-1955) [was] the leading historian and chief ideologist of the inter-war period. . . . As a young historian, he challenged nationalistic sentiment with a work which allegedly shed unfavourable light on a national hero (*Rákóczi in Exile*, 1913) and which involved him in a country-wide controversy, disproportionately greater than the significance of the new sources which made him reconsider the portrait of Prince Ferenc Rákóczi . . . as it was accepted by contemporary public opinion. Notoriety is not the best guarantee for scholarly work; Szekfű, however, was able to overcome his dubious fame.

His basic concept concerning Hungary's place in the family of European nations was put forward in *Der Staat Ungarn* (Berlin, 1917). Employing the method of the *Geistesgeschichte* School for the first time in Hungary, Szekfű expounded his conviction that Hungary had belonged to the so-called "Christian-Germanic cultural community" ever since its acceptance of Christianity ten centuries ago. [In a footnote, Czigány explains "Gestesgeschichte": "The German term is generally translated into English as "history of ideas" which is incorrect, or "intellectual history" which is even worse. Originally developed by W. Dilthey in Germany in the late 19th century, *Geistesgeschichte* regards history as being the product of the manifestations of "the creative spirit" which is irrational, hence no "laws" can be found in human evolution.] The underlying idea of this concept was, of course, the re-emergence in an acute form of the dilemma of "East" versus "West," since the original debate in the Age of Reform . . . had provided no reassuring answers. The implications of Szekfű's proposition were significant, because by narrowing the concept of "West" to the "Teutonic cultural community" it effectively supported loyalty to the House of Habsburgs; moreover, it paved the way ideologically for a German-Hungarian alliance during World War II.

New dimensions of Szekfű's ideas were displayed in his most influential work (*Three Generations*, 1920; with a substantial appendix: 1934), inspired largely by his pessimism, a pessimism generated by the recent national catastrophe, and particularly by his fear of revolutionary upheavals. Having reconsidered some of his earlier views, Szekfű came to the conclusion that recent history was a cautionary tale warning against violent changes such as those advocated by Kossuth and his radical followers. Szekfű's own ideal was gradual reform, as represented by the conservative Széchenyi. . . . He blamed the politicians of the Age of Dualism for their inept policy towards the nationalities, which, instead of assimilating them, aggravated the existing discord. In the *Appendix* (1934) he proved himself to be a relentless critic of what he termed *neo-Baroque* society.

Of Szekfű's numerous works, the *Hungarian History* (7 vols., 1929-33), written in collaboration with the medievalist B. Hóman, is undoubtedly the most significant. It fully displays his erudition by the superb handling of his material, his meticulous research and mature style, and last but not least, the refinement of his concepts. His position as a leading intellectual was acknowledged by his appointment to the editorship of the authoritative *Hungarian Review* (1927-44), a conservative forum of an indisputably high standard, whose series *Books of the Hungarian Review* published most of the best scholarship in the inter-war period.

By the late 1930s Szekfű found more and more points of disagreement with the regime, which resisted even moderate efforts at reform. In 1938 he resigned his office as editor, and in a series of articles he published a bitter critique of the policies which were leading Hungary to the brink of catastrophe for the second time in a quarter of a century ("Somewhere We Have Lost Our Way," *Hungarian Nation,* 1942-3). Disillusioned by the encroachment of racist theories on public life, Szekfű gave up his concept of the "Christian-Germanic cultural community," and after World War II he drew his conclusions from the fact that the Soviet Union had established a common frontier with Hungary; realizing that future Hungarian foreign policy could never disregard this new situation, moreover, the conservative thinker conceded the need for social revolution (*After Revolution,* 1947). Events vindicated his views and he accepted the appointment of ambassador to Moscow offered him by the post-1945 regime.

It was not by accident that the ideas of the *Geistesgeschichte* School acquired influence on Hungarian intellectual life after World War I. The prevailing general pessimism could find little relief in the study of "facts"; positivist scholarship therefore began to decline, and as an intellectual escapism *Geistesgeschichte* eminently served the meditative, subjective, and retrospective mood of the times, since its keywords were general comprehension, intuition, and "re-experiencing" (*nacherleben*). Soon *Geistesgeschichte* became dominant in all branches of the humanities; its forum was *Minerva* (1922-40), a periodical issued by the Minerva Society (1921-40) under the auspices of Pécs University. It was to Szekfű's credit that he often admonished some of its more fanciful excesses. For example, when Lajos Proházka (1897-1963) published a popular book (*The Wanderer and the Fugitive,* 1934) in which far-reaching parallels were drawn between the German and Hungarian "soul" based on "constant spiritual traits," Szekfű refuted most of its theses in *Hungarian Review.*

Independent-minded authors were unhappy about the way all intellectual phenomena were said to be derived from the universal manifestation of the *Zeitgeist,* which, in practice, stood for general and universal Western or rather German influence on Hungarian intellectual life. The populist writers . . . argued in favour of the sovereignty of the *népi* character of Hungarian culture. On the other hand, a small group of intellectuals, led by Károly Kerényi (1893-1973) set the classical tradition against the all-pervading *Geistesgeschichte* and the slowly penetrating "German cultural superiority" of the 1930s.

Kerényi's endeavour was significant not only because of its originality, but also because of its implications. His "discovery" was simple enough: although events preserved in myths may have never taken place, the gods of the myths have always existed as an "inner event," and consequently they cannot be erased from the deeper layers of human consciousness. Kerényi's aspiration was to free the gods of antiquity from the "fetters" of philology by establishing a "living link" with the classical Greek way of life. At the same time, his preoccupation with the gods of the Greeks aroused his interest in modern authors who created myths (e.g. James Joyce). When Thomas Mann became aware of the Hungarian scholar's interpretation of his *Magic Mountain* (e.g. Settembrini as a symbol of Hermes) they entered into a long and fruitful correspondence which contributed to the development of Mann's ideas about the function of myth in his tetralogy *Joseph,* based on Old Testament stories.

Kerényi was working on the same lines as Jung, the heretic disciple of Freud, whose convictions about the existence of religious instinct and the subconscious need for faith were the ultimate justification of his turning to mythology. Kerényi and Jung were bound to meet, and the meeting took place when the former left Hungary in 1943. They became lifelong friends and close collaborators (e.g. *Introduction to the Science of Mythology,* N.Y., 1949). Kerényi's own main contribution to the study of mythology is his concept of archetypal images in Greek religion, with the timeless faces of gods looking back on mankind to remind it of the primeval source of life and of the permanent aspects of existence. In tracing the origins of symbolism of gods and demigods, Kerényi, rebelling against the hyper-criticism of the positivists, accepted the proposition that all myths and traditions which contain elements of plausibility should be regarded as authentic unless proved otherwise. Kerényi's Greek ideals were remote from the main cultural aspirations of the Horthy regime, and after World War II his works were ignored until recently.

In the "Christian-National" public thinking of the inter-war period, however, the Churches were naturally prominent. Curiously enough the chief ideologist of the Catholic Church, Ottokár Prohászka (1858-1927), started his career with reformist ideals inspired by a sense of social responsibility and an aversion to the excesses of "intellectualism." His book on the latter (*Overgrowths of Intellectualism*, 1910) was banned by the Church. Yet he vehemently opposed all radical changes in society (*Culture and Terror*, 1918), was against modern literature as represented, for example, by the "decadence of Ady," and held "Jewish" capitalism responsible for all social diseases. Bishop Prohászka's main social ideal was a strong national middle class with pure Christian morals, and it was in order to promote this that he became the chief spokesman of the conservative backlash of the 1920s, serving its ideals with all his undoubted eloquence as a public orator. The leading figure in the Reformed Church, Bishop László Ravasz (1882-1975), was an equally talented orator; his homiletics, composed with rhetorical elegance, betrayed his literary ambition. A man of moderate views, Bishop Ravasz did much for the spiritual revival of Hungarian Protestantism, and for the fostering of the Protestant traditions of Hungarian literature.

The leading conservative literary forum of the period was *East* (1923-40). Its title suggested opposition to everything *Nyugat* stood for, and showed its preference for national traditions and values as opposed to innovation and fashionable foreign trends. *East* represented what was best in the "Christian-National" revival; the same cannot be said of the other leading organ, *New Times* (1896-1949), a consciously non-political weekly with literary ambitions, edited by Ferenc Herczeg . . . , the unofficial "Poet Laureate" of the regime. The popular and successful authors rallying round *New Times* were mainly entertainers, readily serving the illusions of their readers (who consisted predominantly of the "Christian-National" middle class).

The high standard of criticism in *East* was largely achieved through the efforts of one of its original co-editors, János Horváth (1878-1961), a scholar who was an outsider on the literary scene, and who after the first three years left *East* to devote his time entirely to teaching literature at Budapest University (1923-48). Both a student and later a professor at Eötvös College, Horváth was largely responsible for renewing literary scholarship, which had been in danger of losing its way in the maze of philological details at the turn of the century. The short period he spent in public affairs helped fulfil one of his lifelong aspirations, which was to create a valid approach to the study of literature. First he set out to establish his principles of investigation by claiming autonomy for literature. Former scholars, Horváth argued with convincing clarity, had usually regarded literature as a manifestation of the "national spirit," and treated it unhistorically by calling attention only to those of its aspects which had relevance for their own times, while ignoring the fact that literature is more than "what is written down"—it is an intellectual relationship between writer and reader through the written text. Horváth's conception of literature enabled him to employ a complex approach to his subject taking into account psychological, aesthetic, sociological, and historical considerations when describing literary phenomena ("Notions of Hungarian Literature," *Minerva*, 1922). By introducing novel concepts (e.g. *irodalmi tudat*) he effectively contributed to the understanding of literature. His theoretical approach was backed by a powerful memory, a lucid mind, and an ability to construct a coherent survey out of a multitude of philological data, the primary importance of which he un-

ceasingly stressed. His style is always clear and concise, and has a character of its own.

Horváth also criticized the stylistic excesses of the *Nyugat* writers; his critical remarks on neologisms, like his scholarly views, were never unfounded, and represented conservative taste at its best. In the 1920s, when he was participating in literary life, he clarified vexed questions in his essays ("Racial Issues in Literature," *Minerva*, 1922; or "The Rights and Limitations of Criticism," *East*, 1928) with disarming impartiality and imposing scholarship. After his withdrawal into the academic world, he made a direct impact on scholars only, yet his views were transmitted by the capillary system of literary scholarship to wider circles, and their influence can be felt even today. Of his pupils, probably Gyula Farkas (1894-1958) was the most controversial. In an attempt to explain literary movements more thoroughly, Farkas paid special attention to the background of writers, and in particular to the region they came from and their religion (e.g. in *The Hungarian Romantics*, 1930). Although there is no doubt about Farkas's intellectual honesty and integrity, his ideas, developed under the influence of the *Geistesgeschichte*, were later subjected to severe criticism; he was accused of racialist views after World War II, and he is largely ignored today.

While conservative ideas were represented by men of Szekfű's and Horváth's calibre, the artistic vision and the achievement of the conservative writers of fiction and poetry compare badly with the *Nyugat* generation, and with the populist writers. The editor of *East*, Cécile Tormay (1876-1937), for example, made her reputation as a public figure with *An Outlaw's Diary* (2 vols., 1921-2), in which she described with apparent disgust and aristocratic contempt the events of 1918-19. Her main thesis was that social radicalism was alien to the Hungarian character, which was basically contemplative and devoted to traditional values. As a novelist she was not without talent. She attracted critical notice with her first novel (*Stonecrop*, 1911); it was a work written with artistic care, although she sometimes yielded to mannerism (e.g. she seldom used sentences with subordinate clauses); her impressionistic descriptions were effective then, though they look somewhat dated now. The theme of *Stonecrop* is symbolic—it is the love-story of a Croatian married woman and a Hungarian railwayman from the Lowlands, showing the tragic incompatibility of people with different ethnic origins; there is little the individual can do against the basic law of nature, except to perish, as the Croatian woman does when she revolts against it.

The Old House (1914) is an ambitious undertaking—the story of three generations of a Budapest middle-class family of German extraction. Tormay's main concern is again with that "mystic" interrelationship between ethnic origin and regional characteristics which puzzled her in *Stonecrop*. Influenced by Thomas Mann's *Buddenbrooks*, *The Old House* delves into the decay and disintegration of the Ulwing family. It is the youngest member of the family, Anna, who understands the timeless unison between the native soil and the human soul: "Only those families survive which have their roots in the soil. In vain drops the seed on the city's pavement; no tree will grow out of it. Urban families are of houses which serve at best for three generations only." There is much nostalgia in the rolling sentences which evoke the atmosphere of a largely German Budapest of bygone days.

Tormay's last major work was to have been a historical trilogy, her death prevented its completion (*The Swan of Csallóköz*, 1934, and *On the Other Shore*, 1934). Set in the thirteenth century, the basic idea of the novel concerns the clash between Christian and pagan values, a subject which Herczeg also utilized successfully in his *Heathens*. . . . Inspired by the praiseworthy intention of lightening the general pessimism through evoking scenes of ''old glory,'' Tormay on the whole failed artistically in this lengthy novel, which was eventually completed by another writer using Tormay's original outline and published under the main title, *The Ancient Messenger* (1937). While Herczeg was careful not to give an unequivocal answer to the dilemma of ''East versus West,'' Tormay blamed Christian civilization for the decline of the originally martial spirit of the Hungarians. Her composition is careful, and abounds in stylistic embellishments, including refined metaphors, nevertheless the book produces a somewhat artificial effect.

Tormay's interest in historical novels was part of a general revival of the demand for historical fiction, with subjects invariably devoted to the national past. Conservative-Nationalist writers eagerly pampered the national ego: they were never at a loss when asked to gloss over selected topics and serve generous helpings of illusions up to their readers, whose spiritual hunger for feasting on past glories seemed insatiable. Seasoning was provided by Miklós Surányi (1882-1936), whose historical romances, padded with lengthy digressions on the social history of past centuries, contain larger-than-life figures, usually pursuing passionate love affairs. The glittering façades of the historical scenes always seem to cover deep human passions, and are never lacking in erotic detail (e.g. his novel about the romantic escapades of young Count István Széchenyi, *We Are Alone*, 1936).

Irén Gulácsy (1894-1945), on the other hand, looked to history to provide a lesson for the present. Her widely acclaimed novel (*Black Bridegrooms*, 1927) takes the reader to the early sixteenth century, the turbulent years of the Dózsa uprising and the battle of Mohács (1526) which resulted in the loss of national independence. Its timely message is that the lack of national unity leads to catastrophe; noble and heroic self-sacrifice is needed if it is to be averted. The novel is uneven; tragic scenes are often painted with overtly romantic colours—the writer lacked the strength to bridle her all too vivid imagination. Her language is highly original and metaphoric, abounding in little-known dialect words whose effect is lessened by their strangeness.

The novels of János Komáromi (1890-1937) still have an undeniable appeal and were very popular when they were published, mainly on account of the brooding atmosphere he was able to create in his descriptions of his native Upper-Tisza region. His poverty-stricken family background made him sensitive to the sufferings of others, which he always described with compassion and frequently with overflowing emotion. His main themes, besides his childhood experiences (*Students of Patak*, 1925, and *An Old House Beside the Road*, 1929), are derived from those terrible years which a generation spent in the trenches of the Russian Front and which irrevocably changed pre-war moral values. Komáromi was able to blend irony and nostalgia, and it is these qualities which make *Those Beautiful K. und K. Days* (1927) remarkable. The novel describes the hinterland activity of the Austro-Hungarian army, with its bureaucracy, inefficiency, and peculiar *esprit de corps*, although Komáromi is far less satiric than Hašek was in *The Good Soldier Schweik*. It was the local *kuruc* tradition in the county of Zemplén which Komáromi used as material for his historical novels, and popular heroes, like Jakab Buga or Tamás Esze, were the main characters in his stories, which were written

with Romantic exaggeration and much patriotic fire. All Komáromi's *kurucs* were penniless vagabonds or outlaws whose only asset was their fierce patriotism, which was still enough to defeat the better-equipped *labancs* who sided with foreign rule.

The general course historical fiction might take was perhaps epitomized by the rabid nationalism of Gyula Somogyvári (1895-1953), who became a best-selling author under the penname of *Gyula diák*. Somogyvári's ideals were the Hungarian military virtues shown during World War I (e.g. *The Almond Tree is In Bloom,* 1933), or the power of the Hungarian soil in assimilating foreigners. (*The Rhine is Obscured . . .* , 1935), both novels drawn in harsh colours and filled with profuse sentiments. One of his greatest successes was *And We Are Still Alive . . .* , (1936), the story of the revolt in Western Hungary after World War I which saved the city of Sopron and its environs from being ceded to Austria by forcing a plebiscite.

Those conservative writers who wrote less historical fiction devoted their energies to the ''back-to-the-soil'' theme. The heroine of Mária Szabó's (1888-1982) first novel, *Upward,* (1925) inherits a passion for the land, not the idle flame of possession, but an innate love of the earth and its fruits. When she comes into possession of the family estate she devotes herself entirely to its management, and becomes bound physically and spiritually to the earth. No doubt the novel, with its battles, triumphs, and defeats circling round Ágnes's struggle for the family seat and the resulting conflicts, is an epic representation of the lives of the Transylvanian landed gentry before World War I and the ensuing Romanian occupation. Yet some doubts linger whether the heroine's worship of Mother Earth in *Upward* is as genuine as Mária Szabó's imagination made it out to be—in her later novels, which are largely historical fiction, it was definitely her romantic imagination which gained the upper hand.

An entirely different aspect of conservative taste manifested itself in Kálmán Csathó's (1881-1964) novels and plays, which

Sándor Weöres. Photograph by Layle Silbert.

radiate a light-hearted, witty, and somewhat sardonic spirit. The world of Csathó is peopled with mischievous old gentlemen whose lives consist of endless anecdotes, related by the author with gusto and without excesses; his optimism is scarcely touched by the events of the immediate past. His heroines are interested only in making a good match, and then in preventing their husbands from unduly serious womanizing (*A Crow on the Church Clock*, 1916). This is a world which preserves all the fun of the *belle époque*, Hungarian style. The same can be said of Csathó's plays, which are permeated by a gay irresponsibility, and consistently lack social criticism. The best example of his craftsmanship is *You Only Smoke Your Pipe, Ladányi!* (1927), adapted from his novel of the same title (1916).

The demand for historical fiction created a special by-product: *vie romancée* ["fictionalized biography"], . . . addressed to a wide readership, which was impressed by the omniscience of authors who seemed to eavesdrop on the conversation of the famous. Reality and illusion mingled freely in this strange genre, which always displayed the facts with theatricality. Furthermore, for the sake of melodramatic climax authors often overstated their case or overplayed one single emotion. The most popular author of "fictionalized biography" was Zsolt Harsányi (1887-1943), who enjoyed success in many languages, including English in the late 1930s. His secret was a fast-moving and absorbing plot and an interest in psychological motives. He profited most by his keen eye for the consequences of early traumatic injuries to the ego. Having found the "key" to his chosen personality, he then wrapped the plot around the emotional strain thus discovered—lulling the reader into a comfortable feeling of having effortlessly acquired the secrets of his characters. The subject of his works were men who had left their mark on history, science, or the arts, and whose rejection of conformity usually landed them in clashes with society and/or authority. His best known works in English translations are about the love affairs of Liszt (*Hungarian Rhapsody*, 1935), *The Star Gazer* (1937) about Galileo, whose life suggests that man could think independently only at the risk of his own security, and *Lover of Life* (1940), about the flamboyant personality of Rubens.

Although Harsányi's works were not published in Hungary after 1945, the traditions of fictionalized biography were carried on and the genre is still popular. Perhaps the names of Sándor Dallos (1901-64) and László Passuth (1900-79) should be mentioned in this context. Of the latter's works, *Raingod Weeps Over Mexico* (1939) is a colourful epic of Cortez's Central American expedition, published in many languages, including English.

Although Catholic devotion continued to find an outlet in literature long after the Middle Ages, particularly in the works of Cardinal Pázmány or Count Zrínyi . . . , Hungarian literature became wholly secular from the Age of Enlightenment. In the late nineteenth century there appeared poets whose main themes were derived from religious piety and developed in the form of moral exhortation. They were all devoted servants of the Catholic Church; their poetry, however, did not attain the level of secular poetry. It was only at the beginning of this century that religious experience inspired works of merit, although Hungarian Catholic poetry never reached that intensity which characterizes, for example, the religious renewal in French literature after Baudelaire, because it often lacked the soul-searching and self-torment which make the French Catholic writers' search for refuge in religion a genuinely personal and poetic quest.

Catholic renewal fostered the new outlook of the *Catholic Review* (1887-1944); from the 1930s onwards, this journal contributed to the popularization of the modern Catholic spirit and ideals. On the literary scene, however, *Vigilia* (1935-)achieved prominence by offering scope to a new breed of Catholic writers who preached values until then very unfamiliar to the mainstream of Hungarian literature, which had always concerned itself with social reality, and on the whole lacked metaphysical inspiration. In addition *Vigilia* offered its pages to authors of the second and third generations of *Nyugat*, in a common protest against the new barbarism which was spreading on the Continent with awesome speed.

The Catholic revival was heralded by the poetry of Lajos Harsányi (1883-1955), whose early verses reveal Ady's influence in both imagery and language (*On New Waters*, 1908). His mature poetry developed from a sincere devotion to his calling as a priest, and an admiration for the solemn splendour of the Church and its traditions; in the background of this religious experience the reader always finds the tranquility of the Baroque churches and the scenery of Harsányi's native, rural Transdanubia. He also attempted to write longer meditative pieces about the philosophical relevance of religion (*Hagia Sophia*, 1913).

Ady's influence can also be detected in the early poetry of Sándor Sík (1889-1963), whose poetic meditations expressed the joy of the believers. Sík himself was aware that he was not acquainted with all aspects of human experience. Protected by his faith and by the power of the Church, he could sing only about religious devotion and nature, which linked him to eternity. His holy seclusion preserved the purity of his soul and of his poetry, which was devoid of any disquieting note; and it is precisely this lack of doubt, uncertainty, and mundane interest which make his poetic world limited in experience, if not in vision. Sík was also an accomplished translator and a versatile man of letters, whose literary studies displayed his conscious endeavour to maintain Catholic literary traditions (*Gárdonyi, Ady, Prohászka*, 1929; *Pázmány*, 1939; and *Zrínyi*, 1941) and to elucidate his aesthetic views (*Aesthetics*, 1943). As a professor of Hungarian literature at Szeged University before World War II, and as the editor of *Vigilia* afterwards, his contribution to the development of literary taste, particularly in the younger generation, is significant.

It was, however, László Mécs (1895-1978) who achieved real fame as a poet-priest. His poetry, in spite of its thin intellectual substance, has a commanding quality which stems from its vibrant exuberance, for Mécs possessed the secret of popular appeal. Armed with Ady's poetic innovations, and intoxicated by the sound of his own rich voice, this rhapsodic singer of joy, godliness, faith, and redemption is always filled with optimism. His rhetorical assertion that a universe created by God cannot be a place exclusively of injustice, squalor, and disaster found receptive ears in impoverished post-war Hungary.

A native of Upper Hungary, which was ceded to Czechoslovakia after World War I, Mécs represented the voice of the Hungarian minority living there (*Angelus at Dawn*, Ungvár, 1923), and soon became the object of a cult; his poetry recitals, given both at home and abroad, were stunning feats of performance. As a result of his success with large audiences in the 1930s Mécs made considerable concessions to popular taste. The authoritative poets of the *Nyugat* generations largely ignored him, and their verdict was followed by total and enforced silence after World War II; Mécs was denied all publicity, and was even imprisoned by the Rákosi regime. This conspiracy of silence makes it difficult to write about him; the uncritical adulation of the old fans of Mécs and the cold-shouldering of later literary public opinion make both criticism and praise difficult.

Paul Valéry, who wrote an introductory essay to one of Mécs's volumes in French translation praised his poetry unreservedly. It might well be that the great French poet was struck by the irresistible personality of Mécs, or admired those features of his poetry which he called Romantic and which were missing from his own lyrics. For Mécs, in spite of creating symbols and metaphors resembling those of Ady, did not conform to those poetic norms which were approved by Nyugat, and consequently by French poets, at the beginning of this century. His poems are built out of rhymes and rhythms (e.g. "The Ballad of the Universe," 1933), and the narrative element always prevails. The resulting poetry is therefore simple and easy to understand, sometimes it is even naïve or pedestrian; yet when recited its effect cannot be denied.

His themes are few—the world as seen through the unsophisticated eyes of a country priest. Mécs noticed social injustice and, although he was not interested in politics, he strongly protested against the totalitarian danger ("A Prayer for the Great Lunatic," 1942). He continued to write after World War II, without the slightest hope of ever being published. These later poems reveal his complete withdrawal into his immediate environment ("Canons Playing Cards," 1947), or give an ascetic inventory of his worldly possessions: "My country is in the moon. My house is on my back. / My larder is hidden in my knapsack. / This is how I confront winter." ("The Cranes Write a Capital V," 1951). When Mécs was allowed to reenter the outside world after his imprisonment, he was profoundly shaken at finding himself rejected and forgotten ("The Musings of Lazarus Resurrected," 1957). Yet he survived his trials and tribulations: his survival was due to the strength of his will—and perhaps to the fact that his faith remained unshaken—"Only the trade secrets of the saints are eerie: / How does the cage with the captive bird fly?" ("Nobert's Astral Moment," 1952).

It was not easy to be a Catholic poet in a country where the traditions of the Church demanded conformity from its members and the loyalty of its leaders to a foreign power, as if Catholicism were a Church of Austria. Béla Horváth (1908-75) was a layman; his early religious experiences were different from those of the priest-poets, for Horváth's God was essentially the "King of the Poor." Radical Catholicism, however, was not welcomed in Hungary in the 1930s, and Horváth had many clashes with the authorities, both secular and ecclesiastical. After World War II he lived abroad until 1962, when he returned completely disillusioned. He could not fit into the new Hungary he found, and eventually fell silent and died half-forgotten.

Horváth's basic poetic experience was derived from his humble origins; his radical Catholicism could not tolerate the social wrongs at which the Church seemed to connive. A brilliant craftsman when translating medieval Latin hymns, of which he was a connoisseur, Horváth's poetry reflected his everyday struggle to shed protective rhetoric and mannerism, and to face the problems of the self. His poetic development abroad displayed a gradual disappointment with Christian ideas and with the world at large. Rhetoric, however, was still with him: "I have nothing to do with the past and the future, / I have thrown away everything and move back to the heavens" ("Ultima

Verba," 1947); but occasionally he was able to look at himself with irony ("The Sorrow of the Patriot," 1953). The volume which he published abroad (Poems, Munich, 1955) contains some of his best verses (e.g. the inspired ode "A Flashing Light in Genoa," 1952). In the late 1950s Horváth turned to experimenting with avant-garde forms—genuine desperation, total pessimism about mankind's future, the fear of ecological disasters, and the rejection of Western values characterize these poems (The Age of Doom, 1962). Then he stopped altogether, he had no longer the faith to sustain himself as a poet.

Another layman, one of the founders of Vigilia, Béla Just (1906-54), was an exponent of French neo-Catholicism; his novels, written with intellectual honesty, document the conflicts between duty and conscience. His best known work was written after he had left Hungary. The narrator in The Gallows and the Cross (1954) is a prison chaplain, eventually imprisoned himself for assisting a condemned man to escape. The atmosphere of the death row in a Budapest prison during and shortly after World War II is presented in a simple and unembellished narrative; the portraits of the assorted prisoners (who include a mass-murderer and a prime minister) are drawn with valid psychological observation. The chaplain is linked to authority in the prisoners' minds, and his conscience is laden with controversial feelings. Just manages to describe the chaplain's moral struggle with convincing authenticity and uncomfortable honesty. This gifted writer is completely unknown in Hungary today. (pp. 363-74)

Lóránt Czigány, "Traditions, Traumas, and Quacks," in his The Oxford History of Hungarian Literature: From the Earliest Times to the Present, Clarendon Press, Oxford, 1984, pp. 361-80.

VALÉRIE KOREK

[In the following essay, Korek discusses Hungarian novels written between World War I and 1968.]

"Why should only that in which we differ from others be of value, why not also that in which we are one with them?" asked the poet and critic Ignotus, and Antal Szerb, the literary historian, stated that "Hungarian literature is an instrument in the orchestra of European civilization. . . . Acceptance is as vital for Hungarian literature as creation is." These are problems of authenticity versus influence, problems involving parallels and contrasts, that are legitimately matters of literary science. They will be kept in mind while passing in review some of the Hungarian novels written since the First World War. What looms in the background is, however, a less rewarding problem that transgresses the frontiers of art, the political intention behind writing or judging novels.

Good novels have seldom been written with preconceived intent, political or otherwise. But a system that denies individual liberty even to the most spiritual of personal acts—artistic creation—is apt to have a shotgun influence on works in the process of being written. Indeed, a whole apparatus of blurbs, jackets, prefaces, and a new literary history is busy evaluating and re-evaluating works of the present and the past.

Take, for example, the story of Tibor Déry (b. 1894) as divulged in The Revolt of the Mind: A Case History of Intellectual Resistance behind the Iron Curtain (1959) by two ex-Communist authors, Tamás Aczél and Tibor Méray, who fled to England after the Revolution of 1956. Are we reading a chapter of Koestler's Darkness at Noon, or merely a straight, eye-witness report on what the Minister of Education did to Déry, a card-carrying Communist since 1919, while "talking over" the problems of his forthcoming novel *Felelet (Answer)*? Déry's previous novel, the rambling, uneven *Befejezetlen Mondat (Unfinished Sentence,* 1948), was considered to be, by the omnipotent George Lukács, "one of the greatest works of our century" and given the highest literary award; but the manuscript of *Answer* apparently was not up to standards. Could it have been—as the authors, in a somewhat psychoanalytical manner, hint—that Comrade Révai, the Minister of Education, who was roughly Déry's age and a frustrated writer, gave vent to jealousy while tearing apart, indeed, practically, rewriting on the spot, Déry's *Answer* till it met the requirements of "socialist realism"? This spine-chilling meeting, which lasted into the small hours of the night, took place in 1952. In 1956, Déry wrote *Niki* (translated into many foreign languages), a story of a dog that keeps a woman company while her husband is a political prisoner. The day he is released, Niki dies. Because of the dog or because of the Revolution, Déry himseslf got a ten-year prison term, but was set free in 1960. In 1964, he gave a better answer to his Communist lords than his novel *Answer* had been, by writing the nebulous Kafkaesque *G. A. Ur X-ben (Mr. A. G. in X)*. Would the night-marish country "X," and the eerie Hotel Astoria, with its new electric bulbs but no switches, bathrooms without water, and never-halting elevators symbolize the old, "reactionary" Hungary, while "abroad," whence Mr. A. G. came, symbolized the new one? Or is it the other way around? "One cannot catch reality in *flagranti*. The only way to get to know it is to turn one's back on it," announces a judge while presiding over a murder trial (or over "socialist realism"?). If it was socialist realism, no one caught Déry this time. He added a double-somersaulting introduction to this curious travelogue, which, if nothing else, is an amazing exercise in intellectual vigor.

Is the answer, then, to outwit the cultural regime? Or do the regime's requirements grow more subtle as the years go by? (The year of Déry's ordeal, 1952, marked the high point of Stalinist terror.) It would seem, for example, that another talented novelist, Magda Szabó (b. 1917), enjoys popularity as well as approval because of a literary attitude that merely suggests her rejection of the "old system." Her stream-of-consciousness novels are about small-town petty intelligentsia mingling with the simple and the poor. Obviously, as in *Freskó (Fresco,* 1958), the minister drinks and beats his children, while the half-illiterate old servant is honesty in person. Her protagonists—invariably youngish females, father-oriented, hard, and without self-pity—could well be interpreted as good builders of socialism. Judged on the basis of her best novel *Az Oz (The Fawn,* 1962; translated into English), her writing is expressive as she spins a dramatic plot through the mental processes of remembering and associating. As for some of her other novels, one wonders whether her occasional disregard for grammar is part of the smoke screen to ward off critics. The fact that ten consecutive sentences have no subject makes reading difficult, and her practice of introducing dozens of nicknames that are more ridiculous than amusing, while reserving true Christian names for dogs and cats, is puzzling. Could pumping the oxygen of "people are not much good— why feel sorry for them?" into the poverty-infested air of Communism be subconscious misanthropy? Possibly the inborn pessimism of the author found a good sounding board in the politically determined gloom of her country.

Iskola a Határon (School on the Frontier, 1959); translated into English) by Géza Ottlik (b. 1912) appeared in a well-cut jacket that praises the author's "elegant style . . . which reminds one of the best writers in English prose. . . . [It is] about the education of future officers during the Horthy-period . . . the inhuman discipline the young were submitted to in order to teach them, through cruelty, how to torture others . . . that is, to make the victims of an immoral society into the defenders of it." True, *School on the Frontier* is a boarding school story, the prototype of which are the novels of L. P. Hartley or Graham Greene. But since a military academy is hardly a finishing school for genteel young ladies, there are rough goings-on and rough language in the school, which is located in western Hungary, near the Austrian border, independent of any specific political system. It is the world of turbulent adolescents sharing classrooms and bedrooms and suffering under discipline, a world in which "there was no plotting, lacking someone or something to plot against . . . except the inner structure of the world. . . . We lived in a tangible reality, not in the abstraction of laudable ideas or well-rounded stories. . . ." This tangible reality is mirrored in Ottlik's well-rounded story. As for the laudable ideas, the reader does not need prompting from the novel's pseudo-literary advertisers in order to find them.

On the premises of an industrial plant in Budapest, a man, having been hit during a violent argument by his brother-in-law, stumbled into the debris of a junkyard below and was killed instantly. "His judges will exercise clemency," says the author, Endre Fejes (b. 1923), of his hero in the introductory chapter of *Rozsdatemeto (Junkyard,* 1962), as he sets out to unfold a story of two generations, beginning in 1918, when János Sr. comes home from the wars. János Jr. was the killer. *Junkyard,* short and brilliantly constructed, portrays a changing world in which the fortunes of the working-class man were much the same whether he lived under a Habsburg king, Count Bethlen, or Comrade Rákosi. For forty years, whether they went to cafés-on-the-green to listen to Gypsy bands on Sunday afternoons or, decades later, formed their own jazz orchestra and packed sandwiches in nylon bags, they lived in the same room-and-kitchen apartment. Another impressive symbol in the novel is a lean, hard-working, loud-mouthed mother, whom the author never fails to call by her full maiden name. She sings the same self-made ditty at the cradle of her children and grandchildren, and invariably rises to occasions of christenings, engagements, or national events by "scouring the room, chalking the kitchen and frying fish." Is it possible that, fishing season or no, one can serve such meals in impoverished Budapest? Or did Fejes, at this specific point, ignore the requirements of socialist realism? In any case, with a truly epical, consistent characterization, he certainly made this proletarian *reine mère* unforgettable.

Few of the writers have been talented enough to avoid the issue of politics by letting it remain on the sidelines, like Ottlik and Fejes (no matter what their interpreters read into their novels). Some blatantly fell in line and, as people with little to offer, relied on their ancestry and became imitators, not always successfully. One of their father-images was Lajos Nagy (1883-1954), illegitimate son of a servant girl, and "a socialist," though (in his own words) "not a socialist writer, just: a writer." His two-hundred-page *Kiskunhalom* (name of a fictitious village on the Hungarian Plain; 1934) was described as a "sociographical novel." The opening page of this truly successful hybrid reads like a copybook: "Population 2687, territory . . . can be reached by rail . . . by water. . . ." As the pages turn, windows open from which figures emerge, a puppet show is set into motion, and behind the stage a voice relates not a story, but the everyday life of Kiskunhalom. The mailman goes on his daily round, the doctor calls, gossip spreads till the air thickens but then thins again in next morning's mist. Statistics get turned into individuals, while men are blurred back into data, through a good balance of detached words about people and facts that seem to carry emotions. Nagy has not overridden his device. In *Három Boltoskisasszony (Three Shopgirls, 1938)*, for example, he kept the village setting, but brought a dramatic plot into full bloom, as he did in his later novels as well.

A better social order had been much desired by the best of Hungarian storytellers, even if they did not adhere to any specific political movement and used no other means than artistic. This may be one of the reasons why politically well-connected art critics of the earlier period failed to appreciate them. In his autobiography, *Életem Regénye (The Novel of My Life, 1939)*, Zsigmond Móricz (1879-1942), son of a peasant and a village minister's daughter, hammers away at the problems of social justice. It becomes obvious, however, from his prolific novelistic output that, above anything else, he was interested in the human individual: the family, for example, the tragic entanglement of man and wife. Even his historical trilogy *Erdély (Transylvania, 1922-1935)* shows that his eyes were always on people—a perspective that made a novel about such an individualistic epoch as the sixteenth and seventeenth centuries into authentic history. His *Rokonok (Relatives, 1930)*, which tells about small-town nepotism and is hailed by today's critics as debunking the rotten administration of old Hungary, is really one man's story. Its hero, just risen to higher office, becomes innocently involved in illicit doings through a web of suddenly emerging uncles, brothers, and cousins, and is driven eventually to suicide.

"The freezing atmosphere of Hungary between the two World Wars was portrayed with the utmost authenticity in three masterpieces: Móricz's *Rokonok*, Milán Füst's *Advent*, and Dezso Kosztolányi's *Édes Anna*," states the opening lines of a preface written to a 1963 edition of the last mentioned novel: *Édes Anna*. Dezso Kosztolányi (1885-1936), one of the greatest lyric poets of the century, wrote *Édes Anna (Anna Édes)* in 1926. Like *Relatives, Anna Édes* also begins with the male protagonist being elevated to a high position, and, just as the first novel ends with suicide, *Anna Édes* ends with a double murder, committed by a nearly illiterate servant girl. But if Móricz's high-strung hero rides through tension-filled pages, Kosztolányi's translucent, simple style produces a realistic world "presented, with its many grotesque little features, entirely from the outside," as Antal Szerb remarked. Anna's own feelings are revealed but once, in the last chapter. She takes her low wages, long hours, and cot in the kitchen (on which she is seduced by the visiting nephew of the household) without complaint. Indeed, the reader is caught as unaware as the victims when Anna enters their bedroom with a kitchen knife. Not until the policeman tells her, "Thou knoweth, m'lass, this means the gallows," does she awaken, for the man has a broad, peasant's face, he might have been from her village, he called her "thou." Here the intimation of a message flashes through the reader's mind: the village as opposed to the city. But it is not easy to agree with the further elaborations of the 1963 preface and to read *Anna Édes* as "a social novel . . . hot with political emotion . . . in which Kosztolányi definitively turned his back on the inhuman system of gentry-Hungary." Instead of turning his back on anything, Kosztolányi faced the world with his poet's eye, and he had no comment, just a twinkle in that eye when Anna eventually escaped the gallows.

The third novel, Milán Füst's *Advent* (1920), could pass, perhaps, as one written with preconceived political motives, although not in the broad sense of "Communist versus old Hungary." Nineteen-twenty was the year of the "White Terror," an extended, cruel reaction to the "Red Terror" of 1919. In *Advent*, 1920-Hungary is cloaked as Catholic-persecuting England of the seventeenth century. Füst (1888-1967), according to his preface to a 1958 edition of his novel, "decided to awaken those who in the name of Jesus Christ practice inhumanity" by telling, in the first person, the story of a Catholic aristocrat in hiding: a timid young man, given to sobs as he trembles for his friends who have to face the unbending judges of the Church of England. Füst, as he states in the preface, "had shed bitter tears that year," which shows how well he situated his allegory: at a time when tears were not considered unmanly. Characteristic of Füst's writing is a firm hold on a single basic analogy to transpose the content of his story from that vantage point, stepping out of one reality in order to create another. His style carries full conviction with its mixture of stilted elegance and outspokenness, its *démodé* tone to suggest time-distance and, by the same token, detachment, and a mimicking of what seems like the translation from a foreign language. This is the technique of his five-hundred-page *A Feleségem Története (The Story of My Wife, 1942)*. The narrator is a Dutch ship captain, a big, uncouth man of little education and a fatal passion for a volatile, pseudo-intellectual *petite Parisienne*. The theme of his being cured and succumbing again runs in cycles of calmly-taken agonies and droll adventures, until the woman, loved through seven seas and seven hells, evaporates into an eerie mirage—death. By adhering to crisp, chronological storytelling and keeping his distance from first-hand reality, Füst has written an "arty" novel marked nowhere by deliberate effort.

Begetter of a peasant-hero who today is interpreted as having revolted against the "wrong" society, Józsi Jeno Tersánszky (b. 1888) has remained, like Füst, *persona grata* in Communist Hungary. His series of picaresque novels, *Kakuk Marci (could be translated as Marty Cuckoo, 1923-1937)*, are products of a boundless imagination that never trespasses on the grotesque and of a style that is unmatched in wealth and vigor yet never degenerates into folksiness. Marci is an ingenious village vagabond who fools everybody, including the *gendarmerie*, while fighting, cheating, and wenching his way on a grand tour across the country. This lovable rascal is a practical anarchist of the Romantic school, ready to outwit "right" or "wrong" society at any time. Tersánszky, author of countless good novels, was a native of Nagybánya, in Northern Transylvania, called "the Hungarian Barbizon"—an artists' colony where Hungarians and Rumanians, the well-to-do and the petite bourgeoisie, lived side by side in the picturesque foothills of the Carpathian Mountains. Such is the setting of *Rossz Szomszédok (Bad Neighbors, 1926)*. A son of the intelligentsia and a daughter of the lower classes live next door to each other. Fate appears in the guise of topography as the girl gets seduced at the fence which divides the two houses. She moves to Budapest and for a while is submerged in the *demimonde*, until eventually she wiggles her way up into a suitable marriage. But after some years, it is again the uncanny power of location, rather than love, that, on a visit home, lures the woman from her parents' dilapidated porch through the closed doors of the neighboring mansion. The denouement is literally around the corner as she gets caught in the act and thereby loses her hard-earned position—this time, for good. Although amusing details authentically reproduce the petty life of the small town and the soothing gaslights of irony shine over it, *Bad Neighbors* is nevertheless a dark story. Flaubert might well have helped to write it, but the prankish whistle of Kakuk Marci also lingers on its pages. According to *M. I.*, this novel has a message: Society forgives the well-to-do, while the poor remain guilty. If—and only if—there must be a message, is it not rather that men get away with more than women?

Another native of "the Hungarian Barbizon" was László Németh (b. 1901), playwright and novelist, now as before a major literary figure in Hungary. His most impressive novel, *Iszony* (*Revulsion,* 1947; translated into English), relates a woman's story in the first person, and conveys the conscious processes of a devilishly efficient, intelligent, loud, and tyrannical husband-hater. The story concerns two neurotics, a frigid woman who is essentially an inverted man, and a lazy, boisterous, oversexed weakling whom she kills, at the end, "accidentally" and without any regrets. *M. I.*'s thirty-page chapter on Németh hails *Revulsion* as one of the great novels of world literature. And this psychological double-portrait, achieved through minute descriptions of everyday life is, doubtless, a triumph in realism. But since Nellie has ecstasies (which she misses, rather deliberately, in bed) while preserving fruit, chalking the house, humiliating her husband in public, and indulging in soliloquies of scorn and self-pity, the style becomes overheated, as if her voice were declaiming lines from an outmoded tragedy.

Transylvania was the cradle of a specific civilization, with a spoken and written language richer, more original, and more pungent than the language elsewhere in Hungary. An independent principality for almost two hundred years, headed by great leaders, and also by clever men of political flexibility (some immortalized in Móricz's *Erdély*), Transylvania was able to save such values as were trampled on in the western parts of the country. Believers in individual freedom (predominantly Protestants), isolated in a far corner of Europe between high mountains and still cosmopolitan because of the region's foreign-language minorities, they went their own way in literature. The novels of József Nyiro (1889-1953) and Áron Tamási (1897-1966), for example, depict a beautiful, strange existence of shepherds and beasts, with the ever recurring drama of nature faced by the man who fights the elements and outwits everyone alive. Sometimes they almost create the one-dimensional world of the folktales, with its humorous peasant hero and a nature that yields to him, if need be, by miracle—a world that does not fail to impress readers who can sense, beyond a simple story, a very individualistic human consciousness.

The story of the clever mountaineer turned into tragedy in the late forties when Count Albert Wass (b. 1908) wrote *Adjátok vissza a Hegyeimet!* (*Giveth Back My Mountains!,* 1949). How the silent union of man and his native landscape becomes articulate during a long, historic manhunt is echoed by the linguistic crescendo of this Transylvanian writer, who shared the fate of his hero, and eventually fled the country.

Indeed, not only are the heroes' destinies noteworthy but also the authors' are as well, especially in times such as those decades in Hungary. Irén Gulácsy (1894-1945), in *A Fekete Volegények* (*The Black Bridegrooms,* 1926), told the story of the heroes who fought against the Turks in the Battle of Mohács. As Géza Ottlik in his *School on the Frontier* wrote concerning the four-hundredth anniversary of the disaster: "We got so used to celebrating lost battles that we survived. Perhaps because we consider defeat as made of denser fabric, as more important than victory—at any rate, it is more genuinely ours." After reading *The Black Bridegrooms,* however, one wonders whether Hungary could have ever recovered from 1526, such is the tragic impact of this book. Gulácsy was named, for her

accomplishment, "the adopted daughter of Transylvania," and was killed on the streets of Budapest by a bomb.

The year 1945—with its bombs, battles, and persecutions—marked the death of many intellectuals: poets, historians, writers. Antal Szerb, the literary historian, fell under the rifle butt of his labor camp warden. A prolific scholar of Hungarian as well as foreign literature, he was also the author of two novels. *A Pendragon Legenda* (*The Pendragon Legend,* 1934; translated into English), an entertaining parody of the English detective story, was followed by *Utas és Holdvilág* (*Traveler and Moonlight,* 1937). Although the title would suggest another take-off, perhaps this time on the Romantic novel, *Traveler and Moonlight* was conceived in a more solemn mood. True, the hero's road to Italy is paved with hilarity and paradox, but it eventually turns into a nostalgic path in the search for undefined ideals, half-felt and suppressed desires of the past. With his story of almost-forgotten memories that acquire life during a wildly adventurous journey, Szerb wrote a truly neo-Romantic novel in 1937. Two years later, World War II broke out and interrupted the era of an undecided dispute as to whether spirit or matter, individual liberty or compulsion, is predominant in human affairs. While *Traveler and Moonlight* is a farewell whispered to one of the many eclectic times of history, it is, being of the thirties, the closest to us. Like swinging in a hammock, far from heaven but still slightly above earth on a fall afternoon, reading this book gives the feeling of a minute rendering of every atmospheric friction that marks a sunset in autumn. Indeed, Szerb's story reminds one of Fitzgerald's *The Great Gatsby* and Erich Kestner's *Fabian:* What they had to

Lajos Kassák. Photograph by Károly Koffán.

tell about the twenties, Szerb says of the thirties. All three of these short novels have lively plots in the Romantic sense, rather than personal comments intended to revive a *Lebensgefühl*. Perhaps none of them will prove eternal classics, but they are the clearest-hued rainbows on the near-past's horizon.

Irén (1939) by András Hevesi (1902-1940) is a *roman à clef*, a day-by-day account of the author's short love affair with a girl who stepped out of his life with the same suddenness as that with which she entered it. The novel is written at the same ecstatic speed at which things happened to this sophisticated intellectual when he met a visitor from Transylvania—a plain girl, outlandishly dressed, but his equal in learning and appetite for adventure. The girl, however, was his superior in shrewdness, a true daughter of those hardy people who figure in the novels of Nyiro and Tamási, accustomed to outwitting nature and its creatures. Thus she went as she came, and the regrets were not hers. Anger and hurt male pride have seldom fathered a better story.

As a soldier in the French army, Hevesi died in 1940. Indeed, destiny took both Szerb and Hevesi at an early age. And destiny—of course, the fate of books is proverbial—somewhat earlier played a strange game with two Hungarian novels, when the first prize of two separate international contests were given to each respectively, before their authors were so much as known in Hungary. (Both emigrated later.)

Jolán Földes (1903-1960) wrote *A Halászó Macska Utcája* (*The Street of the Fishing Cat*, 1936, which was translated into twelve languages and sold one million copies in the first six months), a bittersweet story of post-1918 emigration. It was not the loss of country in any political sense, but poverty and unemployment that drove a Budapest working-class family to the picturesque slums of Paris. In telling her story, Földes lived up to the best nineteenth-century tradition by subduing sobs and laughter in the streets where simple people of barely articulated emotions lived. Thus absence of tragedy or comedy makes this short novel a paradigm of emigration's timeless tale.

A few years earlier, also in London, the first prize offered by another international contest was awarded to Ferenc Körmendi (b. 1900) for his *A Budapesti Kaland* (*The Budapest Adventure*, 1932). It is a long novel with a full cast and war-torn, bleeding Budapest as its stage. The story opens at a class reunion of disillusioned, unemployed young men, mostly veterans of World War I—a sordid evening, which brings the opening chapter of Werfel's *Abituriententag* to mind, as one of the men advances the idea of luring home an absent classmate who had emigrated and made good somewhere in Africa. The classmate might lend them money; he might also help them to leave the country. Subsequently, we learn the full story of the hero's hard-won success abroad up to the day when he accepts the invitation to spend a long, hot, and emotional summer in his home town: his tragic adventure in Budapest. Since a too readable plot frequently prejudices critics, only a few saw the psychological mastery in the follow-up of a love game, played by two with desperate consistency—for different aims—or, as the novel closes, the step-by-step account of a subconsciously planned suicide. True, the atmosphere of the book does not elevate the spirit. On the other hand, this meticulously executed picture shows a society whose despair stems from economic hardships that often override ideals.

A few months later, this time at home, Körmendi had a second novel published, *Ind. 7:15 via Bodenbach* (literally, "Lv. at 7:15 through Bodenbach," referring to the schedule of the Budapest-Berlin express, 1932; published in English translation as *Via Bodenbach*). While the clear, to-the-point style of everyday life, tinged with Budapest slang, is the same as that of the first novel, the elaborate, detailed realism of voluminous *Budapest Adventure* is limited in this short work to the supporting cast; otherwise *Via Bodenbach* is interior monologue in which free association, psychological flashbacks, and dilemmas of conscience thicken into a web, but without ever strangling the narrative, which reaches its climax through an utterly unexpected turn. It is not only the outer coincidence that recalls another story of a train ride, Michel Butor's *La Modification*, written thirty years later, but also the complex presentation of stream of consciousness. Moreover, Körmendi's protagonist remains just "he," with a minimum of features as compared to the other figures, who are clearly seen through a realist's eye, a device not far from Butor's innovation of the second-person narrative.

Eventual emigration was also in store for the two most read, most talked about, most compared, and, in short, most important novelists of the interwar period: Zilahy and Márai. Lajos Zilahy (b. 1891), a born storyteller and gifted with an inexhaustible imagination, continued in the tradition of the nineteenth-century novel of action, battle, and passion; a man who knew his ancestry, indeed wrote about it, and lived by the advice of his literary forebears. Also playwright and poet, Zilahy is a versatile observer of things and an avid reader of people's minds. His short *Halálos Tavasz* (*Deadly Spring*, 1922) is the story of a suicide the inevitability of which is so closely reasoned that it convinces more than a factual report ever could. The reader is first cajoled into believing in the perfect idyll between a lovely, highborn girl and an attractive, wealthy young man. Then clouds begin to form in this almost too-blue sky, and at first are only petty intrigues. But they subsequently gather momentum in an abyss of the human soul from which there is no exit. *Két Fogoly* (*Two Prisoners*, 1927) is a long novel about World War I, which separates a honeymoon couple forever. The wife becomes the prisoner of her own youth, her valiant but vain effort to remain faithful, while her husband is taken captive by the Russian Army. The privations of men thrown together in a Siberian camp, the hero's calvary from near-madness to frozen resignation and his eventually going native, are portions of the book that are worth rereading after forty years. The hero of *A Lélek Kialszik* (*The Soul Dies Out*, 1932) is a boy who comes to the United States. Since Zilahy's forte is the emotional, the ups and downs of homesickness lend psychological depth to an adventurous story of emigration.

Before leaving Hungary after World War II, Zilahy set about writing an epical work concerning a wealthy, absentee, unpatriotic family of aristocrats. *The Dukays* and *The Angry Angel* (both of which first appeared in English in 1949 and 1953 respectively) were on the best-seller list in New York. Later Zilahy reversed time and wrote *Century in Scarlet* (1965, directly in English) about an ancestor of the Dukays, a novel in the best style of the nineteenth century, with a hero far more lovable than the modern Dukays. Although in his journalistic work he was an alert critic of the regime that governed Hungary in the twenties and the thirties, Zilahy was not kindly treated by *M. I.* The pseudo-literary reasoning of such literary historians is not overly articulate, and their whimsical judgment of writers who emigrated—such as Körmendi, Zilahy, and Márai—should not be considered to be any more than sour grapes.

Sándor Márai's vast literary output, as it evolved, became the multiple target of Communist criticism. *M. I.* admits the impact

Márai (b. 1900) had on the intellectual reader as the thirties went through a veritable "Márai-fever," but he says further that the "famous-Márai-sentence" just "camouflaged reality and tricked the reader into an ecstatic acceptance of fiction." Is this sentence, which conveys a mood through clarity, with no poetic overtones but still satisfying the reader's emotional expectations, really a "trick"? Or is it rather Márai's own predicament, evoking a wish for feelings in which he cannot participate and perceiving only the outside of the complexity he has shown to others? What makes Márai's writing into novels is not boundless imagination or the rhythm of an inborn epic temperament but the mood of his sentences, his way of intoning feelings by a seemingly rational device—the atmosphere of some particular period conveyed by a single, archaic adjective, or that of comedy by a single, deliberate anachronism. *Béke Ithakában* (*Peace in Ithaca*, 1952) is typical of Márai's work. In this retelling of the closing parts of the *Odyssey*, Márai has Penelope begin her confession in the best style of a Budapest woman-of-the-world. "The consciousness of the human race never readily accepted the idyllic end of the epic," states Márai in the epilogue, after having added the twist of Ulysses' murder on his homecoming. The idyll in *Peace in Ithaca*, a sad-funny compromise, is contrived by Penelope, Telemachos, and Telegonos, another son and the killer of Ulysses. These three are first-person narrators of the novel, who chronicle, with admiring irony, the deeds of the ineffable traveler. Márai's travesty does not hit at them or the Homeric work; rather, it is against the social order, human and divine; against the law, which gets stricter as its purpose becomes more idiotic. "Was there ever a war that made sense? They rally to a rag, whether a banner or a petticoat . . . a delusion for which one has to die." Those grave words are Ulysses'; the storytellers themselves keep aloof from judgment and despair. "Behind the friendly surface of human and divine order there lurks a dark intent: madness . . . the best protection for us is to feign insanity as well . . . ," the hero advises his wife, though the narrators feign only detachment, which turns into the most pungent taste that ever spiced the Homeric story.

Another famous wanderer, Casanova, is the hero of Márai's *Vendégjáték Bolzanoban* (*Guest Performance in Bolzano*, 1940). Not unlike *Peace in Ithaca*, this novel is also merely an added incident to an often-told story. "You-alone-and-forever- . . . write these words with hyphens, will you?" dictates the hero to his manservant-scribe as he leaves the room for the yard to have his horses harnessed. The servant, alone in the room, bursts into a belly laugh. So ends the novel—a copybook sample of Romantic irony, an ending meant to lift the mask from the story, no matter how convincingly it had been told. *Guest Performance* is a torrid account of a passion that the "great lover" had nourished for long years and never consummated, reaching a dead end at a masked ball and in a long letter. The late baroque, a departing mood of life, is symbolized by the forty-year-old traveling salesman of love, who had just been chased out of another town. Márai's pithy, almost tongue-tied language triumphs in this novel and suggests the design of the baroque which was able to hold its overwrought ornaments—in other words, the impeccable proportions of its architecture—without the turbulent colors of its painting. The last passion of an adventurous time (the French Revolution was not far off), a farewell to a relentless and daring chase for personal happiness, was caught in one breath and exhaled in the last sentence of *Guest Performance*. The reasons for Márai's preoccupation with the lonely adventurer, the wandering exhibitionist admired by others but facing his own conscience uneasily, are obvious;

and his denouement technique suggests his well-adapted knowledge of Romanticism.

Márai's *Az Igazi* (*The True One*, 1942), like *Guest Performance*, also concludes on a note of Romantic irony. As in Németh's *Revulsion*, a woman's story is related in the first person. As if the author's feigned sex would allow him to be more talkative than usual, it is a deluge of words, conveying to a friend the fateful passion that the protagonist has for her husband, who, in turn, loves "the true one." A fascinating plot reveals "the true one" as a person without breeding or education, but while the narrator gives up her man, who is now united with the other woman, it is suggested that his attainment does not promise to be more than the mere outcome of a successful hunt.

A year later Márai wrote *Szindbád Hazamegy* (*Sindbad Returns Home*, 1943), which achieves a merger, indeed, a mystical union, of his own, crystalline style with that of the impressionist novelist Gyula Krudy, whose last days he evokes. However, he did not manage to unite his mood with his hero's in *San Gennaro Vére* (*The Blood of San Gennaro*, 1965, the somewhat briefer and smoothed out German translation of which appeared before the original: *Das Wunder des San Gennaro*, 1957). Was the death of an unnamed foreign transient in a southern Italian village an accident or suicide? Those who knew the man speak up, but their long monologues fail to paste the crumbling pieces of this narrative together, as question marks weigh heavily on the skeleton plot of a futile sacrifice. The Romantic irony of Márai's endings gives way to a skeptical double-split as one begins to suspect that the author does not believe his hero a savior any more than he believes in the recurring miracle of the Italian shrine. With the story, out went "the Márai-sentence," clipped to the bone, reversing every move of the story, and disappearing behind the wall of a self-conscious style. And still: "Unsteadfast, he went down the narrow gangplank, tottering, as people always do when they cross over water," relates the priest-witness of the accident, "but then again, he appeared, in the dark, as someone who walks *on* water." This could have been said about the author, as well.

The last word should be given to the first personage of this section, Lajos Zilahy, who greeted the poet-writer Gyula Illyés in 1962, on his sixtieth birthday, with *Vers Libre*, four lines of which are:

> Exile did not help Ovid or Turgenyev,
> Nor Zweig—to name just a few;
> Many a banished writer perished
> Of rantingly denied homesickness' cancer.

Zilahy's pessimism, of course, takes the long view. But if we consider 1956, which marked the last exodus, a remark of Kerényi's seems apt. Károly Kerényi, classicist and collaborator of C. G. Jung, said that exile might even add a new dimension to being a Hungarian. Indeed, newly-gained freedom of expression, fantastic experiences left behind, anger and indignation, all combined into a fictional explosive for some talented refugees. But just as explosives leave dregs, political manifestos and journalistic or autobiographical glossaries began to parade as novels, of tremendous interest to those engaged, but of ephemeral literary merit.

Unless it is thought cynical to judge works of art built on the horrible bloodshed and the destruction of an old city (for the second time in twenty years), two novels should pass as achievements of the Revolution. The first, *Tatárok a Széna*

Téren (*Tatars on Széna Square*, 1963) by Péter Halász (b. 1922) begins as a Communist judge condemns a young girl to death, a judge who, just a few days before, had hidden her after she had killed a notorious member of the political police. *Tatars* is the brief tale of an opportunist who, through the revelation of a god-sent, wondrous love, grows into a noble human being, but subsequently falls when he is terrorized into carrying on from where he had left off those few days ago. The judge's destiny was that of the Revolution, his road from redemption to renewed condemnation that of the country. Perhaps the ecstatic suddenness of all that happened made the horror of the situation bearable to man and the country as a whole, for no time was left them to grasp the triumph before tragedy hit again—a meager consolation, but part of the atmosphere in which this extraordinary novel was conceived.

The thread of *Tatars* comes to an end in November, 1956. *Nyugodt lehetsz Elvtárs* (*Rest Assured, Comrade*, 1959) by István Eszterhás takes place a few months later, in early 1957. Those were the days when a wave of terror had swept away the last vestiges of the Revolution and hit a crescent-shaped, dead-end street in a workers' district of Budapest, where about a dozen families lived, practically on top of one another, with adjoining backyards and windows that let glances slant in all directions. Suddenly one afternoon, a rumor began that the political police were about to raid the street. Most of Eszterhás' five hundred pages reproduce the ever-mounting electric shocks of hurried dialogue as men and women pass on warnings: flashbacks of their political pasts are given, while broken fragments of hatred or attraction are mended or torn apart in an effort to face the inevitable with precarious dignity. With the descending night, a murderous chase begins, and killed are the hunted and the hunters alike. "Rest assured, Comrade," says the villain-protagonist, a police captain to his superior, "it will never happen again." Richly spiced with the newest, Communist slang of Budapest, a powerful language complements this original narrative. As doorknobs change hands on the crescent, events move as if on a spiral staircase. Indeed, the technique recalls a revolving stage; the brevity of time and the staccato of the conversations add elements of drama to the novel. But the warmth with which its many characters smolder accounts for the best epic qualities of *Comrade*.

Leaving behind these novels, which were published on free soil, and picking up the thread of political intrusion in Hungarian literature, certain books bordering on the pure novel should be mentioned. The thread, lucky for their authors, gets thinner as novels such as the juvenile and the historical, as well as the autobiographical, are, by their very nature, less susceptible to political analysis. The juvenile novel in Hungary has a distinguished tradition, since works by the greatest novelists—Mór Jókai (1825-1904), Kálmán Mikszáth (1847-1910), and Géza Gárdonyi (1863-1922)—were "clean" stories and inspiring favorites with the young. As for current products, *Bogáncs* (*Thistle*, the name of a dog; 1963) by István Fekete (b. 1900) is a charmingly-written adventure story, and Magda Szabó has also a few successful juveniles to her credit.

Historical novels enjoy somewhat of a common ancestry with the juveniles, since almost all of Jókai and Gárdonyi's works deal with the past. Although Zsolt Harsányi (1887-1943) was practically slaughtered in the pages of *M. I.*, this branch of writing thrives mostly unmolested. Harsányi, who specialized in biography, recounted in *És Mégis Mozog a Föld* (1937) and *Magyar Rapszódia* (1936) the lives of Galileo and Liszt respectively, the English translations of which—*The Star Gazer*

and *Hungarian Rhapsody*—were at one time widely read in this country. He also wrote about the Hungarian King Matthias, the painters Rubens and Munkácsy, and several Hungarian poets of the past. Without too many personal speculations and comments, the habit of many biographers, the heroes' lives yield their psychological portraits. One learns from Harsányi's books the easy way, but one learns, nevertheless. Transylvania-educated László Passuth (b. 1900), with his rich style and astonishing knowledge, is concerned with chapters in history rather than individuals, and whether he takes his reader to Spain, Mexico, Italy, or Transylvania, his intrigues and romances of the past are presented in full panoply. Most of his work is translated into foreign languages.

Rózsa Ignácz (b. 1910) crossbred the historical novel and history in *Toroczkó Gyász* (*The Mourning of Toroczkó*, 1958). A legal battle fought by a mining village and its ruling family, which denied the community's exemption from serfdom granted to them by a medieval king, comes to a murderous conflagration in 1702, as the Unitarian church is surrounded by the landlord, aided by foreign militia, while the minister is performing a wedding ceremony. The *mémoires* of the minister's seventeen-year-old tubercular daughter is the fictional part of the book, and after death wrests the pen from her hands, Clio takes over and the story is brought up to the present day. *Toroczkó* is proof of the view that historical novels are best when their action reaches back only to the point at which the author can relate to his ancestral background. Ignácz, for example, was able to lean on the folklore and archives of her native Transylvanian environment, even on the oral tradition of her family. With versatile talent, she also wrote about the stream of consciousness of an old woman in *Titánia Ébredése* (*The Awakening of Titania*, 1964), and in *Róza Leányasszony* (*Damsel Rose*, 1942) immortalized Róza Laborfalvy, the great tragic actress of the nineteenth century who became the wife of Mór Jókai. Thus the author leads the way home to Mór Jókai, the foremost Hungarian storyteller of all times; and an essay on the modern Hungarian novel should perhaps end at this point, were it not for two autobiographies that are still worth mentioning.

Both were written, not by novelists, but one by a painter, Aurél Bernáth (b. 1895), and the other by a painter and poet, Anna Lesznai (1885-1966). They kept interesting company in historic times and were bent on revealing themselves only through others, while their artistic temperaments made them, although newcomers, masters of prose. *Igy éltünk Pannóniában* (*Such was Our Life in Pannonia*, 1958) and *Utak Pannóniából* (*Roads from Pannonia*, 1960; Pannonia was the ancient Roman name of Western Hungary) were the two volumes of Bernáth's reminiscences about the vineyard-bordered shores of Lake Balaton. This landscape, a favorite of artists and writers, is drawn by Bernáth as antiquity already knew it, a geographic reality which is likely to withstand more millenniums of political earthquakes.

Anna Lesznai was born in northern Hungary. Her *Kezdetben volt a Kert* (*At the Beginning Was the Garden*, 1966), a third-person narrative, is a three-generation story of two neighboring families which runs parallel to that of the villages that flank the two manor houses. The lives of poor Slovak peasants were—through their work, their subordination and its consequences, their loyalty or hatred—fused with those of the protagonists around the turn of the century. Doubtless the landowners set their hearts on improving the lot of the people, but they became involved in their own turbulent affairs and concentrated on

Budapest, where the heroine and her family remained for over a decade. After these years, during which Hungarian intellectual life was fermenting and was crossed at many points by the catastrophe of World War I, the family returned to the estate, which had been lost in the meantime, but was still overlooking the village, asleep in poverty and indifference, as before. The early twenties, *le temps retrouvé* in these thirteen hundred pages, brought a moment of atmospheric peace that only true artists are able to convey, although that time marks the dawn of the uneasy period during which the novels, reviewed here, were written. (pp. 122-39)

> Valérie Korek, "The Hungarian Novel in the Last Fifty Years," in Fiction in Several Languages, *edited by Henri Peyre, 1968. Reprint by Beacon Press, 1969, pp. 122-40.*

LITERATURE AND POLITICS

GEORGE GÖMÖRI

[*In the following excerpt from an essay written in 1966, Gömöri examines social and political consciousness in Hungarian letters, focusing on the debate between the Populist and Urbanist movements and on the adversary relationship between Hungarian intellectuals and their successive governments from 1920 to 1965.*]

Hungarian literature is *engagé* by nature. It is committed to the cause of national independence and social reform, freedom and justice. "It is *engagé* in the struggle for human rights . . ." [Gyula Illyés]. This does not mean that every Hungarian writer and poet of the last one hundred and fifty years has written about matters of national and social importance. But, the best of them have been compelled to act as spokesmen for the nation, and they have presented certain crucial problems with cogency and force. It is meaningless to talk about Hungarian literature without taking into consideration the social implications of every important novel or book of poetry, just as it is impossible to understand the recent history of Hungary without consulting at least some works of contemporary Hungarian authors.

The most conspicuous [social and literary] conflict of the [decades 1920-1960] may be defined broadly as the conflict between town and village. In non-industrial Hungary there were periodic conflicts between self-governing towns (often enjoying privileges granted to them by a royal charter) and the counties in which these towns were located. With the rapid industrialization of Hungary in the second half of the nineteenth century, however, the situation changed. The town-country conflict appeared on a new level, no longer as a quarrel between feudal lord and wealthy artisans but as a widening difference in living standards between peasants and town-dwellers. This was dramatized by the development of Budapest from a small provincial capital into a large metropolis. This development boosted the self-confidence of the bourgeoisie and caused frustrations for the provincial gentry, who despised trade and industry as "occupations unfit for gentlemen" and sought employment almost exclusively in the army and in the state administration. All the same, before 1918, anti-urban feelings were manifested only on rare occasions. Most Hungarians spoke with pride about Budapest and praised its natural beauty and its dynamism; to live in the capital was the dream of every ambitious young artist or intellectual in the provinces.

This glamorous image of Budapest underwent a great change after the collapse of the Monarchy, the Károlyi Revolution, and the unsuccessful experiment of the Hungarian Soviet Republic. Horthy's "national" counter-revolution and government came to power in an atmosphere of total defeat and in the shadow of the unjust and humiliating Peace Treaty of Versailles-Trianon. Hungary lost more than two-thirds of its territory, including such ancient cities as Nagyvárad (Oradea), Kolozsvár (Cluj), Kassa (Kosice), and Pozsony (Bratislava). Budapest, a sprawling capital and the center of Hungarian industry, became *the* city in Hungary, with an even higher concentration of industrial workers than before. The counter-revolution charged the atmosphere with an aggressive nationalism which was based on middle class reaction to radical social changes and which found a scapegoat for all Hungary's troubles in the conduct of the "unpatriotic" workers and "alien" intellectuals of Budapest. The governing elite—a mixture of the aristocracy and the gentry—declared itself innocent and put the blame on the German-Jewish bourgeois intelligentsia and the Socialist proletariat. The myth of the "sinful city" was born. A leading spokesman of the counter-revolution, Gyula Szekfü, pointed to the undeniable fact that capitalism in Hungary was "preponderantly Jewish" and that industrialization had been implemented with Austrian capital. He concluded that Budapest was not truly Hungarian in character and that "real" Hungarian culture could be found only in the "unspoiled" countryside. Szekfü claimed that the culture of the capital was a "Central European metropolitan Jewish culture" and maintained—even though his position was not in accord with the facts of cultural history—that "the cultural progress of modern Hungary . . . was basically nothing else but the saturation of the 'intellectual field' with Jews." The greatest poet of the pre-1918 period, Endre Ady, Szekfü regarded as talented but morally deplorable since, according to Szekfü, Ady "sold himself, body and soul to the new Budapest."

Szekfü's bitter and largely unjust condemnation of Budapest and all it had represented since 1867 was complemented by Dezsö Szabó, in his famous novel *The Lost Village* (*As elsodort falu*), in which he called for a national rebirth, defined in agrarian, collectivistic, and biological terms. Szabó's city could not have been more wicked, nor his village more lost and bewildered. In the novel, his gentry hero marries a peasant girl and helps to rebuild the war-devastated village. Szabó confessed that, like Ady, he believed great energies of the Hungarian peasantry remained untapped, but he preached a naive "peasant socialism" based upon a romantic and racially biased anti-capitalism and anti-Marxism. His message was well received in an era "when dissatisfaction spread over the country and impartial truth seemed an intruder" [Joseph Reményi]. It was to a large extent Szabó's myth of the "peasant saviour" that made the young generation which flocked to his lectures turn toward the village in the late twenties and early thirties.

Hungarian populist literature of the interwar period left an indelible mark on Hungarian thinking and influenced political movements both before and after the Second World War. Members of this social and literary movement "developed the new discipline of rural sociology; their novelists delved into the history of forgotten regions and social strata; their thinkers, breaking with feudalist tradition, posited the landless millions as the body of the nation" [Ilona Duczyńska and Karl Polanyi]. In other words, the populists explored the Hungarian village and described the living conditions of the most underprivileged stratum of the population, about which the average town-dweller knew very little.

At the same time, a political issue was raised: how could the deplorable poverty of the village be removed? On this question, the populist writers differed widely. In political terms, there developed a Center (democratic Left) which included Gyula Illyés, Zoltán Szabó and Imre Kovács. Some populists, such as Erdei and Darvas, became communists. Others, like Féja and Kodolányi, drifted to the Right, one populist poet, Erdélyi, actually becoming an extreme rightist, a writer of anti-Semitic doggerel. Dezsö Szabó's teachings—some of which the Master himself had repudiated by this time—proved to be a mixed blessing. Whatever his merits, his nation-concept was too narrow and had a divisive effect on the populists.

There is considerably less literature available on the urbanists, who were in theory antithetical to the populists. If the populist movement was not socially and politically homogeneous (not all of its members were of peasant origin), the urbanist camp was even less definable in these terms. Politically, it ranged from enlightened conservatives through liberals to Marxists. One cannot quite dispel the suspicion that the existence of the urbanists as a definable group was invented by some journalist who needed a counterpart to the populists. The differences between the two groups—both of which opposed the *status quo* perpetuated by the Horthy regime—were to be found in their respective social viewpoints, the political reforms they urged, and their cultural preoccupations. Among the "urbanists," both liberals and socialists regarded capitalism as a necessity; both gave priority to the problems of industrial production and distribution rather than to the revitalization of the peasantry, and both were convinced of the superiority of urban life. They generally sympathized with the activity of the populists, but they had misgivings about populist aims. With the notable exception of Attila József, they were more concerned with European cultural than with Hungarian national or social values, and they preferred *belles-lettres* to rural sociology. They rejected the myth of the peasantry, and viewed with mistrust and suspicion those *völkisch* ["racial"] tendencies that brought some populist writers very close to the formulation of a Hungarian National Socialist ideology.

In a sense, it was peculiar that the problem of populists versus urbanists could appear, and that political differences could alienate from each other two poets of such excellence as Attila József and Gyula Illyés. In other countries of Eastern Europe, the town-village controversy never reached such proportions, simply because industry was more evenly distributed and because there was more than one large town. About one-fifth of Hungary lived in Budapest in 1930, and this figure (much higher than in most other countries of Europe except Austria and Denmark) has not changed much in the last three decades. The controversy centered on the question of political priorities and was undoubtedly fanned by the ruling conservative clique which pursued a pseudo-liberal policy in the towns at the expense of the feudally ruled and terrorized countryside. This policy of *divide et impera* made the gap between populists and urbanists bridgeable only in books or poems where the two points of view could be blended in a higher, national *and* socially objective perspective. Only a few populists, such as Attila József, succeeded in achieving this synthesis. This poet of the proletariat *par excellence* understood the demands of the village and sought a solution for its misery. Although he did so from a Marxist standpoint, the populist leanings of his early youth must have influenced him. It was Attila József who, in a cycle of sonnets (*Hazám*) devoted to the analysis of social misery in Hungary, wrote these memorable lines about the mass emigration of the Hungarian peasantry before the First World War:

> Our many lords were not too lazy, or slow-witted
> to defend their estates against us,
> and one and a half million of our people
> staggered out to America.

The populist and urbanist attitudes could be reconciled only in a perspective that envisaged not merely reforms but radical and, if necessary, revolutionary changes in village and town alike. It would be unjust to say that urban poets, like Babits, were insensitive to the problems of the peasantry; but the older generation to which Babits belonged had never had, or had lost, the sociological interest and the radical fervor which were the mainsprings of the populist studies. The career of the poet Illyés is a fine example of how, in more fortunate cases, influences of village and town could meet and blend. He was born in a Trans-Danubian village, but in his early youth left Hungary for Paris where he lived for about six years. When he returned to Budapest, Illyés became the protegé of Babits, and later editor of the best literary periodical of the period, *Nyugat*. At that time he wrote much about the life of the village poor; his *People from the Puszta* was a most successful attempt at rural sociology in literary form. His populism did not prevent him from being thoroughly European and sophisticated. In fact, according to one critic, "as to his literary contacts and stylistic ideals, he stands . . . half-way between the *Nyugat* and the populists."

The radical transformation of the Hungarian social structure, hoped for by both Attila József and Gyula Illyés, took place in 1945. The Land Reform Bill of that year liberated millions of Hungarians from the feudal system under which they had lived for centuries. The village was, at last, given a chance to catch up with the town, and the economic revolution was followed by one in education. There were created state-supported but self-governing student hostels, called People's Colleges, which housed many bright young men who came from the countryside to the towns seeking higher education. These colleges were cradles of a new democratic intelligentsia. Although they were suppressed by the communist authorities in 1948 and 1949, it is interesting to note that at least three important Hungarian poets, and many writers, critics, scholars and scientists, grew out of this *milieu*.

The conflict between Budapest and the countryside could not be resolved in a year or two. Prejudice and economic conflicts of interest have survived the collapse of "Cloud-Cuckoo-Land," as a Hungarian poet once dubbed Horthy's Hungary. Although industrialization and the installation of electricity in most Hungarian villages paved the way for the disappearance of the worst discrepancies between town and country, many differences remained under the Communist facade of Socialist "national unity." With the forced introduction of Zhdanovist cultural policy about 1949, many pretended conversion to Marxism, or became fellow travellers. But it was clear, even to the casual observer, that under the veneer of Socialist unity old animosities remained. It was possible to detect in at least one of the major literary debates of the early fifties strong reminiscences of the old populist-urbanist controversy ("country lads" versus "young gentlemen"); and in some initial reservations of Communist writers to Imre Nagy's program in 1953, a fear of the "populist domination" of Hungarian literature was evident. In this period, some of the old anti-urban sentiments reappeared in stories by the ex-peasant writer Péter Veres, who censured the town for its frivolous bourgeois morality.

György Somlyó. Photograph by Demeter Ballas.

The one remarkable achievement of the Hungarian Zhdanovist *Kulturpolitik* was the creation of a united writers' front in opposition to it. This was real unity, not the earlier forced unity of slogans and pledges. Populists, Marxists and liberals were united in demanding a free press, a free literature and an independent national policy that would end Hungary's semi-colonial dependence on the Soviet Union. Their unity was demonstrated at the Annual Meeting of the Hungarian Writers' Association in September 1956, where the new Praesidium was elected from writers of all literary trends and political persuasions, with the exception of the Right-wing conservatives and the Stalinists. This consensus foreshadowed the great national consensus that made possible the revolution only a month later.

Since 1956 the whole conflict has lost its relevance. It is true that when some Revisionist writers were imprisoned after the revolution, the populists as a group were favored by the Kádár regime. But the regime did not succeed in playing off these elderly populist writers against their ex-communist colleagues. Before 1956, the most favored populist fellow-traveller was Gyula Illyés; now it is László Németh whose ''populism'' has always been less radical and more reformist-minded than that of Illyés. (pp. 152-57)

In the meantime significant changes have taken place in the social structure of Hungary. There has been a large change in the proportion of town-dwellers to rural inhabitants. There has been a movement into industry from the land. Particularly since the last collectivization drive of 1959-1961, which eliminated

most private land holdings in Hungary, the young people of the countryside have been moving in great numbers into towns. ''In the next decades . . . the last peasant generation will die out,'' forecasts one expert [István Márkus]. It is not only the traditional structure of the country which is affected by this change, but also the psychology of the individual going through the process of readjustment—a process which is a popular subject for writers of the younger generation.

The new intelligentsia, more than a third of which is of peasant origin, can play a positive role in the progressive elimination of the city-village conflict. But the centrifugal pull of Budapest on this intelligentsia can be a drawback for the country as a whole. The assimilation of the talented young men from the village into the metropolitan way of life will not necessarily benefit those who are still living in the rural areas. In this context, the career of the poet Imre Takács is very interesting. Takács came to Budapest with strong anti-urban inhibitions, and it took him a comparatively long time to get acclimatized to the city. His poetry has greatly benefited from his discovery and acceptance of those universal cultural values which are far more easily accessible in a large city than in a village. Nevertheless, having taken his degree at the University, Takács returned to his village. Later he moved on to a small town in the vicinity of Budapest where he continues to write good poetry—perhaps it is there that he can work best. It may well be that the elimination of the urban-rural conflict in Hungary can best be promoted by the demographic and cultural development of small and middle-sized towns, which can compete with Budapest and create new centers of cohesion in the country.

While the Hungarian village is slowly becoming more like the town, another antagonism, that of *different elites,* remains acute. Mutual respect and understanding between the political and the intellectual elite is desirable in any society. These two groups cannot achieve a complete identity of views since, as Mannheim points out in his *Ideology and Utopia,* the ''socially unattached intelligentsia'' judges events and situations from a ''total perspective'' which is not determined by the social origins or voluntary class-affiliations of its members. Nevertheless, the more open-minded, socially accessible and desirous of encouraging merit the governing elite, the less the chances that the intelligentsia will consistently oppose it. In countries where the elite in power is incapable of democratic and rational government, the intelligentsia will constantly question the right of this elite to rule. Although their lack of competence will not disqualify the rulers immediately—especially if part of the scientific and cultural elite is induced to cooperate by means of various concessions—as soon as the regime encounters a political or economic crisis, the intellectuals will be the first to raise their voice and demand changes at the top.

The Horthy regime that ruled Hungary for twenty-five years was the last thing the Hungarian intelligentsia, especially Hungarian writers, wanted. They were committed to liberal and democratic ideals; their patriotism was not reducible to chauvinism and irredentism. Leading Hungarian poets, like Ady and Babits, wrote bitter poems opposing the First World War, and many others, including Zsigmond Móricz, were persecuted by the counter-revolution for their Socialist sympathies. Scores of intellectuals emigrated in 1919, among them philosophers like Georg Lukács, writers like Kassák and Déry, and historians like Oszkár Jászi. After the turbulent period of anti-Socialist and anti-Semitic atrocities, known as the White Terror, the Horthy regime was consolidated and adopted a more liberal policy. Some of its intelligent spokesmen tried to establish a *modus vivendi* with the disenchanted intellectuals. But relations between the ruling elite and the intelligentsia were always strained, often to the point of open conflict. Even the friendly overture of the Fascist Gömbös, then Prime Minister of Hungary, toward the largely populist New Intellectual Front (Uj Szellemi Front) in the mid-thirties, failed in its attempt to domesticize the writers and ended in embarrassing failure.

From a social point of view, the Horthy regime was a retrogression. More social mobility existed in the days of Franz Joseph than at any time after 1920. Bibó stresses the "basic immobility of the counter-revolutionary construction," which no government could change as long as it respected the existing structure of property relationships. Although state scholarships existed for talented young people, there was little social or political outlet for the intelligentsia; it had to repent for the "sins" of the revolutions. Many Hungarians of Jewish origin were driven abroad by the *numerus clausus,* which barred them from higher education, but this did not mean that those who took their place at the University would have a better chance after graduation. The economic crisis of 1929-31 was a sobering shock for many young intellectuals in Hungary, creating large-scale intellectual unemployment and disrupting the tenuous security of the previous decade. The best of the national intelligentsia realized that racial preference would not solve the festering social problems. As a result, communist study groups were formed, and the real drive of the populists began. At the same time, a section of this intellectual proletariat became obsessed by the extreme "solutions" of the ultranationalists and found its way to Fascism.

The literature, especially the poetry, of the twenties and the thirties was full of social protest. In the twenties, emotion was dominant: the form was expressionistic and the revolt was anarchistic (Lörinc Szabó, the early József, Illyés). In the thirties, reason came into its own: the protest took a more scientific form, and there was a noticeable swing towards classicism (or realism). The latter trend was noticeable both in the works of the populists and in the poetry of Babits, the mature Attila József and Radnóti. Even the quality of negation was different. The wild and bitter confession of the young poet:

> I have neither father nor mother
> Neither God, nor country. . . .

became a well-defined statement:

> Out of the beerhall of our time
> I step, to clear thought and beyond.
> I'll never gobble my free mind
> to plod an idiot's servile round.

Attila József opposed the regime on three scores: as an individual, restricted in his freedom; as a member of the "superfluous" intelligentsia; and as a spokesman of the proletariat. Although his poems about workers and their life and aspirations are among the best Socialist poems of the century, what he expected from Socialism was *more, not less, freedom,* and less, not more, power for the state bureaucracy. Just as Ady played a role in the spiritual preparation of the democratic revolution of 1918, so it was Attila József's poems, imbued with the spirit of rebellion, that young Hungarian intellectuals used against the Stalinist regime in 1956.

After the war, the new political elite had a unique opportunity to reach an understanding with the non-Fascist part of the Hungarian intelligentsia. The latter was certainly prepared to make important adjustments in its way of thinking. The policy of the Hungarian communists in the first few years was one of great caution, as they initially did not want to alienate the intelligentsia. But as soon as they assumed complete control of the country in 1949, they changed their policy toward the old intelligentsia, which they decided to replace by a new, completely loyal intelligentsia. Education became the highest priority in communist Hungary after defense and industrialization. Yet the new generation of intellectuals turned out to be much less loyal and obedient than expected. The young writers and scholars developed an aversion to the Party's arbitrary interference in what they regarded as *their* field of competence; they also resented the stiff, sectarian and suspicious behavior of the Party elite. In 1956 a united front of old and new intellectuals emerged, and it was they who first challenged the Party leadership to a debate at the famous meetings of the Petöfi Circle. They fulfilled the traditional role of the Hungarian intelligentsia, representing not only themselves but also the nation which had no opportunity to speak for itself. The writers and scholars, who were often Marxists, criticized the Rákosi regime for its costly and wasteful industrialization drive, for the wretched state of agriculture which was a direct consequence of the overtaxation and collectivization of the peasantry, and for the systematic elimination of scholarly and artistic freedom. Between 1953 and 1956, Csoóri, Kuczka, Takács and others denounced the agricultural policy of the regime, and the leading Communist poet László Benjámin declared his revulsion at the police methods used by Rákosi against his political opponents. Tibor Déry's short stories cast light upon social conflicts unmentionable in "Socialist Realist" literature—the hostile attitude of the individual worker towards "his" state, manifested in stealing public property ("Behind the Brick Wall"), and the alienation of the ex-worker functionaries from their original background, dramatized in a chance encounter between a functionary and his old, morose, working-class father. The Party bureaucracy blocked the way of the reform-movement, but it was ill-equipped to cope with the open revolt of the writers which, in turn, succeeded in mobilizing the masses.

The revolution of October 1956 and the relief with which the greater part of the intelligentsia greeted the collapse of the regime shocked and infuriated the governing elite, which was mildly purged and hastily reorganized by the Kádár group in 1957. Kádár's initial liberal promises were soon shelved and the intelligentsia was brought into line with the alternating methods of police terror and tactical concessions. Yet, at the same time, a lasting concession was made to apolitical experts and specialists. Before 1956, no matter how brilliant, most specialists could not get leading posts without a Party membership card. In 1957, it was announced that specialists would be given a chance to reach such positions, but only if they did not involve themselves in politics. This concession improved the chances of the scientific, but only slightly that of the cultural elite. The Party elite is still in control of society, even if the former governing elite has been transformed into something of a new governing class which actually includes members of the scientific and the managerial elites.

If there is no identity of views, there is at least some sort of *identity of interest* within the new governing class. This is much less true for the most vocal part of the cultural elite. While their position has improved between 1961 and 1964, the scope of their activities and their influence is strictly circumscribed. Kádár's relative personal popularity as compared to Rákosi does not mean, for instance, that the writers are much happier with the present ideological inspector, Szirmai, than they were with Révai, or that they prefer the censorship of opportunistic and intimidated editors to the painful self-censorship exercised in the Rákosi Era. In the humanities, *political loyalty* still remains the supreme criterion for appointment to important posts at the University or in the administration. *Personal contacts* comes a close second. Scholarly merit and promising talent greatly suffer from the predominant influence of these two assets. It is no wonder that, in spite of the material incentives and awards offered by the State, the cultural elite feels frustrated: it has no political power—not even as a pressure group—and very little influence within its own field of competence.

The literary audience is much wider today than it was during the Horthy regime. Now even a mediocre young poet has a greater chance of selling his book than Attila József did in 1930. Nevertheless, the freedom of the written word has not become much greater. Rebellious books which were published by private firms during the Horthy regime and then confiscated by the authorities simply would not reach the printer today; the editors would withhold them from publication. The social influence of literature has somewhat declined when compared with the period 1953-1956, though it is greater than it used to be before the war, when the writers as such did not get a hearing from the governing elite. The communists have now ceased to regard writers as "pillars of fire" or "engineers of the soul"; they have been forced back to their traditional role as entertainers and educators.

Finally, let us single out two outstanding characteristics of contemporary Hungarian literature for analysis. The situation is now, in some ways, comparable to that of the late twenties. Now, as then, there is a strong sense of *disenchantment* in politics that leads to what may be called a "privatization" of literature. Drama and poetry are particularly affected. Writing about the contemporary Hungarian theatre, for example, a critic [István Hermann] called his essay: "The Disappearance of Public Matters." Poets also shun direct involvement in social and political issues; Benjámin, who between 1955 and 1956 published a cycle of outspoken anti-Stalinist poems, is now resigned to compromise:

> I do not want the world to cause pain
> to others! My nerves stock
> the horror of decimated generations.
> I gave up both attack and defense.

But it is not only the older generation that feels disillusioned and tired of political struggles. The character of the disillusioned communist turns up frequently in the writings of the young, whether it be the drama of Gyula Csák (*Peace to the Sinners*) or the poems of Mihály Ladányi. In Ladányi's case, the poet himself is disenchanted. He belonged to the group of those young poets who in 1957 supported the Kádár restoration in the belief that they were serving "the Revolution." Yet the more concessions the new regime made to the hostile majority of Hungarian society, the more it consolidated its non-oppressive power, and the more superfluous Ladányi and his friends became. His retreat into the world of anarchistic—somewhat beatnik—privacy is tinged with melancholy resignation:

> Everything that still has a magic
> sailed far away
> the day before yesterday.

At the same time, there are signs that indicate *the re-appearance of critical realism* in prose. This, of course, is also a logical outcome of the collapse of Stalinism, and a part of what Mannheim calls "the historical process of disillusionment." Yet unlike privatization, it also entails a certain faith in society, in the processes of social evolution. In the works of young writers, like Sántha and Csoóri, Galambos and Galgóczi, one meets complex characters and intricate conflicts: nothing is simple either in ethical or in social terms. Abuses of power, the arbitrariness of the governing bureaucracy, the inadequate methods in dealing with human beings—such are the problems raised and investigated by these writers. In some ways, they are continuing the tradition of Móricz and the populists—they are most competent when writing about the peasantry or the intelligentsia of peasant origin. There is one major difference between them and the populists: psychological factors play a far more important role in their stories. It is not so much the general trend of events that they are against, but the human consequences of mistaken or badly applied policies. Their critical realism is based on adjustment, not on rebellion; it aims to improve the regime, not to change it. (pp. 157-63)

> George Gömöri, "*Social Conflicts in Hungarian Literature, 1920-1965,*" in Journal of International Affairs, *Vol. XX, No. 1, 1966, pp. 151-64.*

WILLIAM JUHASZ

[*In the following excerpt Juhasz discusses Hungarian literature under communism, examining writers' treatment of ideological issues and the subjects of counterrevolution, religion, the Communist Party, and individual privacy. The essay from which this excerpt was taken was written in 1963, after Hungary came under the rule of János Kádár, whose government succeeded that of Mátyás Rákosi after the revolt of 1956.*]

Those who now seek to glorify the party's recent history are in many cases the same men and women who were persecuted during the years of the Stalin-Rakosi personality cult. The Kadar line goes to great lengths to extol the "good" party members who were imprisoned or executed by the Rakosi regime—not surprisingly, as Kadar himself, with many of his closest associates, was such a victim. Party literature endeavors to justify the politics of Kadar and his supporters by opposing them to both the stalinists and to the "counterrevolution" of 1956.

An example of this historical distortion is Gabor Csontos' short story "Felling the Idol" ("Balvanydontes," *Uj Iras* May, 1962). While it is a deplorable piece of fiction, it follows the current party line to the letter. It is the tale of a young man whose father—a "good" communist—has been tortured by the "bad" men in command. The son, in turn, suffers by association from the position his father has taken, and is turned down at the university; whereupon, in defiance of his father, he joins the "counterrevolutionaries" at the outbreak of the 1956 uprising. In the end, however, he does an about-face and kills a companion who has participated in the torture, robbery and murder of a communist, the implication being that the son of a "good" communist ultimately remains true to his father's convictions.

Nor is the regime above making a hero out of a sadist. Otto Javor's "The Sharpshooter" ("A Mesterlovesz," *Uj Iras*, July 1962) is about a trigger-happy soldier who, in the Horthy era, has dedicated himself with robotlike obedience to the extermination of the then-enemy Russians. In 1956, however, the automaton comes to life, decides he has been exploited, and, diverting his hatred to the "counterrevolutionaries," becomes an ardent defender of communism. (Javor tries to kill two ideological birds with one stone in making the local leader of the uprising a Hungarian-hating former Swabian Nazi, thus hinting at a sinister connection between Naziism and the revolution.) (pp. 6-7)

There are many indications that the regime believes its purposes are best served by the appearance of impartiality in literature dealing with the "counterrevolution." An example of the intended "soft sell" is Tibor Cseres' short story "Within Every Man His Own Enemy" ("Ember fia es farkasa," *Kortars*, November 1961), in which carefully measured doses of "sympathy" for the uprising prove even less persuasive and certainly less palatable than an open stand against the revolution.

Another version of the "soft sell" is the current "factual" school of revolutionary literature, in which "spiritual reconciliation" and "consolidation" are recommended. Denes Barsi, a populist, tells in his novel *Fever Curve* (*Lazgorbe*, 1962) of the disintegration of a rural collective at the time of the October Revolution, and of its later reconsolidation, made possible by the fact that "the rural souls have become reconciled." Barsi's hero is a young teacher from one of the urban centers of the Hungarian plain. As a member of the intelligentsia, he must be among the first to adjust to the defeat of the uprising, and moreover must see to it that the simpler folk become reconciled to the turn of events. Ultimately, the young man's gentlemanly and nationalistic instincts give way to sheer common sense, or, we suspect, the expedient of self-preservation.

The "counterrevolution," like Fascism during the Horthy era, thus remains a thorn in the side of the regime and a problem which requires constant attention. Although the revolution has been officially suppressed, it is still alive in people's minds. Party writers want to make it clear that such tendencies have no future.

In *Shackled* (*Guzsbakotve*), novelist Andras Tabak unmasks the enemy in a large Budapest machine factory. The workers in the plant have for some time planned a complete modernization of equipment, much of which is obsolete. The communist collective drafts a plan according to which operations can proceed as usual while reconstruction is going on. However, two hostile and egocentric engineers, with a following of "bourgeois riff-raff," insist on a work stoppage and succeed in getting their plan approved and accepted by the Ministry. A bit of sabotage by a "class alien" intensifies animosities, and some of the workers are laid off. October 1956 seems to herald a total victory for the "enemy," but the "good" and loyal workers are prepared for the showdown and, in spite of the dangerous climate generated by the uprising, carry the battle; the plant is rebuilt while a normal work program is maintained.

The ever-present enemy with which authorities are so preoccupied consists of the bourgeoisie, the gentry and any clandestine element which, while it purports to adopt modern ideological views, continues to uphold old world tradition and thought. The regime has recently had some misgivings as to the advisability of drawing attention to the problem, and party literature is constantly experimenting with various ways of dealing with it. Some of the more imaginative writers occasionally endow a bourgeois or a gentleman with such praiseworthy instincts as remorse and contrition, but this sort of treatment only thinly veils the author's obvious intention to discredit such people.

Imre Dobozi, a top party-scribe and regime-appointed secretary general of the Writers' Association, takes this approach in his short story "The Groom" ("Lovaszfiu"). Zsuzsa Thury, a communist author and the daughter of a talented realistic writer, enriches party literature with the same theme in "The Old Gentleman" ("Az oreg Urasag"), a short story from her 1961 collection *Patchwork* (*Cifra Szottes*). Their story line is standard: the "conversion" of the "gentleman" who grossly abused his power when he had it. In the "new" world, the people he had humiliated and otherwise victimized (i.e., the working class), now in a position to retaliate, prove to be above petty vengeance. The former master, grateful for their forbearance and impressed by their benevolence, is won over to their way of life and happily joins the community.

A major tenet of the Kadar regime is that the revolution was "reactionary." Because the superimposition of this view on literature severely limits freedom of thought and expression, serious writers are put in the agonizing position of having to reconcile obvious historical distortion with the apostolic aspect of their craft. Unquestionably, there are strenuous reservations which must be overcome or at least disguised. However, it is not important to search between the lines for what a writer may or may not really mean; what is significant to a study of literature is the artistic expression of the inner conflict involved. The agony of equivocation is not demonstrated by subject alone, but manifests itself in the peculiar attitude of the author as it emerges in his writing.

Lajos Galambos' . . . novel *Cold Since Yesterday* (*Hideg van tegnap ota*, 1961) is a love story with psychological overtones provoked by class consciousness. It tells of the attachment of a student of working-class background and the "class alien" daughter of a former fascist judge. The youth, sensing the gulf that separates them by virtue of class, origin, and character, decides the relationship must be broken off. According to the official literary formula, the story should end with this magnificent renunciation. Galambos, however, feels compelled to illuminate further the boy's inner conflict and introduces a sort of *deux ex machina* in the form of a psychological force. In a flashback, we learn about the boy's job, his parents whom he has abandoned, and his feelings about the cataclysm of 1956. It becomes apparent that the boy's dilemma stems from the defeat of the revolution and its ideology. He makes up his mind to renounce the girl because he wants to cut himself off from the old world she represents, but he is at the same time unable to adjust to the new one that has taken its place since October 1956. The process of his reconciliation with the new order of things is somehow identified with his relationship to the girl who, though a creature of the old world, becomes a sort of primordial symbol—the pure personification of woman, eternal virgin, wife, mother—above and beyond considerations of historical and political ideology. The road back is thus doubly hard, for the youth must come to terms with himself on two levels: private emotion and social consciousness.

Though critics complained that the "heroes in Galambos' novel react with strong aversion to world events," they commented favorably on the over-all literary merit of the work. "Compelled by its particular genre, the diverse components of his subjective but nonetheless valid theme are welded into a cohesive whole." (*Kortars*, October 1961.) (pp. 7-8)

[The poet Zoltan Zelk] played an important part in the revolt of the writers in 1956. Imprisoned following the defeat of the uprising, he was not published until April 1962, when *Kortars* carried three of his poems. The poems are thematically closely related, and yet they show interesting contrasts in attitude. The first, "Belated Verse on October" ("Kesei Sorok oktoberrol") is pure self-criticism of the sort demanded by the regime; Zelk confesses that he knew even at the time (1956) that the revolt was incited largely by reactionaries. The second, "Candlelight" ("Gyertyalang"), tells movingly of the kinship he has always felt with the poor folk. The third, and most personal, is a poignant expression of love and grief for his wife, who died during his incarceration. The woman never saw him after 1956, and her only thought was to wait for his return. Zelk feels she is waiting still. His great compassion, obscured in the less subjective contexts of the first two poems, is here amply demonstrated.

Young poet Andras Mezei, in an autobiographical poem entitled "Curriculum Vitae" (*Uj Iras,* August 1962), focuses his attention on two historical cataclysms—the Russian invasion and the October revolution—relating them to his own experience, and yet daring to suggest that their effects were not unqualifiedly beneficial.

> The day of reckoning amid the ruins has come twice in
>   my lifetime.
> The world that collapsed around me has been rebuilt
>   twice.
> Yet, how much of the great ideals have been left buried
>   under the smoldering ruins?

Mezei seems to be hinting that the success of the Russian invasion, like the failure of the revolution, caused "many great ideals" to remain lost in the rubble.

The case of Laszlo Benjamin is virtually unique in contemporary Hungarian literature, for he has managed to remain true to his humanitarian ideals without alienating the authorities and therefore without suffering their censure. Although a confirmed communist, he continues to voice the writer's agony of conscience over the defeat of the revolution. Benjamin has escaped the difficulties encountered by such men as Tibor Dery and Zoltan Zelk because, although at the time of Nagy's regime he spoke out for freedom of both the individual and the writer, he did not actually participate in the October Revolution.

Benjamin does not proclaim any "internal resistance." He demands only the restoration of those humanistic ideals which were crushed by the Soviet tanks. Personal liberty and freedom of the spirit should be, according to Benjamin, the primary characteristics of a real humanistic communism: "If humanity is crushed, as it was when the revolution was put down, what is there left of the communist ideal?" While this question *per se* is disturbing to the regime, because Benjamin asks it as a communist the authorities are reluctant to silence him. Rather, they hope that the younger generation of intellectuals will rally to his moderate views.

Evidently, in Benjamin's humanistic communism, no cause is so worthy that it justifies violence. Because of his restraint, Benjamin was able to make his voice—still the voice of conscience—heard again soon after the revolution. He was allowed to publish because the Kadar regime had no fear of his instigating another uprising, and because they realized that the total suppression of critical thought could create a potentially explosive climate. They wisely chose Benjamin as a sort of safety valve.

Ever since the days of Lenin, communists have been convinced that the West does not act on ideological principle, but rather professes a pseudo-ideology which it neither believes nor follows. Lenin, like all fanatics, was suspicious and mistrusting, and naturally feared the strength of the powerful organization which he saw in the Catholic church with her militant Jesuit forces. In point of fact, Lenin had far greater respect for the influence of Christianity than did Marx or Engels, who lived in an era when the enemy—the bourgeoisie and even the majority of the feudal class—were agnostics. From the point of view of moral and humanistic tenets, many communists consider themselves closer to "true christianity" than the hierarchy of church and priests, which in the communist view employs ideology only to ensure its power. In this sense, a reversion to "Leninist tradition" is in keeping with the militant anti-church attitude to be found in contemporary Hungarian literature. The tactics may have altered, with communism now attacking from a strangely defensive position, but the conflict continues.

The treatment of this antagonism in literature is an interesting phenomenon. In the first place, the writers must devote themselves to demonstrating the significance of an issue which writers and regime, as well as the public, know to have no contemporary validity. They go to great lengths to prove that there are and always have been dishonest priests, that the Word of God can be used for evil purposes, and that personal interest often plays a major part in the holiest of crusades. The sophisticated reader's immediate reaction is—so what? That's nothing new, and in any case has no bearing on the ultimate truth. As has been said, the writers are aware of the utter spuriousness of their arguments, but undertake nevertheless to dramatize them, perhaps as a result of a basic disapproval of the political role of the church in history, perhaps because of private animosities of long standing. These writers, though they may be neither artistically nor spiritually in sympathy with the party line, continue to act as prosecutors of religion, charging in most cases hypocrisy (moral and sexual) among priests and believers, as well as materialism, inhumanity, sadism, and finally, reaction.

Geza Feja, a leading sociologist of the populist movement and a man who was once persecuted for his support of the impoverished peasantry, takes out his religious antagonisms by the crudest of methods. These are to be found in numerous short stories and novels published since 1957. (Feja went through a brief period during which he strayed to the extreme right; as a result, he was unpublished for a decade after 1945.)

Another example of anti-church literature is Miklos Meszoly's short story "Papur," which is contained in a volume entitled *Dark Forebodings* (1958). Meszoly, one of the notable free spirits among the forty-year-old generation of writers, takes for his hero a sadistic village barber who makes an ostentatious display of feigned piety.

The principal characters of Magda Szabo's novel *Fresko* (*Murals,* 1958)—a work which brought her recognition in Western Europe—are also religious hypocrites, but the story is mainly notable for the fact that it attacks not only a man of the traditional church (in this case Protestant), but a pro-communist "peace priest" as well. Outwardly a family drama, *Freskos* focusses on the characters of the father, a former parish vicar, and his son-in-law, the pro-communist "peace priest" who has succeeded him. (Actually, the father has been ousted as a direct result of the communist take-over.) The innocent victim in the conflict is the vicar's daughter, who is disowned by her father for defying his authority and marrying communist Laszlo Kun (named for a paganistic Hungarian king of the Middle Ages).

László Nagy. Photograph by János Reismann.

The plot is developed largely through a series of monologues which characterize both father and son-in-law—professed Christians—as inhuman, tyrannical egotists. (pp. 8-10)

The two think alike: the old "gentleman" priest hopes for the return of the old order, so that his pride and ambition may be gratified by a restoration of power; the young man envisages the same sort of personal aggrandizement under communism. Each harbors a sinister vision of the world, a vision which entails the annihilation of the other.

Zoltan Galabardi's novel *Atkozottak* (*The Accused*, 1962) propounds in lurid detail the view that brutality and prejudice are inevitable components of the religious mentality. He tells the story of a wretched cripple who is born out of wedlock and left to die in the snowy streets of a poor Transdanubian village. The creature is taken in by childless peasants who bring it up with tender care and affection. As he grows up, the child comes to display great artistic gifts, making strikingly realistic statuettes from any material that comes to hand. However, he is ostracized by the rest of the village because he is illegitimate, for one thing, and because he is a cripple and therefore "different." The parish priest is the ringleader in his persecution, inciting hatred for the poor creature in order to divert attention from other more real problems. He persuades a simple parishioner that the boy has bewitched his wife, thus driving the man to an attempt on the lives of the cripple and his adoptive father. Other peasants, capable of slightly less primitive reasoning, prevent the murder, but the obsessed man finally suc-

ceeds in his crime by setting fire to the cottage at night. Both the cripple and his father die in the flames that, to all intents and purposes, the priest has ignited. To Galabardi, it is clear that the priest stands for all priests—a naturally malicious breed of men dedicated to the persecution of the poor, the simple and the unfortunate.

Laszlo Kamondy, on the other hand, tries to demonstrate in his novel *Apostolok utoda* (*Descendant of the Apostles,* 1960), that, even if a priest is basically honest and charitable, his unavoidable contacts with the evil, the unprincipled and the wicked will ultimately corrupt him and cause him to act wrongly. In Kamondy's story, a young priest falls in love with the pregnant, tubercular wife of his agnostic brother. True to his own ethics he resists his passion, and, true to his sacred duty, he persuades the woman not to have an abortion, though childbirth may endanger her life. Against the protests of her husband and her physician, the woman bears the child and dies. The young priest breaks down, unable to comprehend a God whose inexorable will it is to reward piety and righteousness with death. The priest's faith is later restored by the spiritual ministrations of an older churchman, who explains that the ways of God are unfathomable and not to be questioned.

The novel is marked by a running battle waged by its characters between personal will and the orders of the regime. The priests are judged guilty in the eyes of the regime because they have sacrificed a human life to a God the regime does not recognize. This, in the communist view, is tantamount to murder. And yet they are absolved because the party senses that it must respect the attitudes of its adversaries, to whom, like Abraham's offering up of Isaac, the sacrifice is "to the greater glory of God."

The cross-examination to which the author subjects his characters is to some extent dictated by regime policy, but Kamondy does not conduct it strictly along party lines. He does not commit himself with respect to the values denounced by the party. Rather, the characterizations and attitudes in this ostensibly anti-priest novel often reflect the views of such great writer-polemicists as Francois Mauriac and Georges Bernanos. Critical observations in anti-religious literature are often delivered with rather melancholy overtones: people are like that, but why? In most cases, authors are willing to concede that the reason—whatever it is—may lie outside the narrow bounds of clericalism.

The party is obviously a factor in contemporary Hungarian literature, making its influence felt in both treatment and subject matter. The question is, to what extent does it direct art? Does it operate as stage manager, or merely as a stage hand, shifting scenes while the plot develops of its own impetus? Is the party the hero, or simply a required prop like the make-believe swords in Shakespearean dramas? Whatever its function, "the party," as it applies to literature today, is written with a small "p" and should by no means be confused with The Party of the era of the personality cult. Although the "party" still bears some earmarks of stalinism, writers and critics have, by reducing it to the lower case, made a subtle distinction which enables them to expose and deplore the abuses of authority as perpetrated by The Party without risking an affront to "the party."

A communist writer who has gone farther than any other figure in Hungarian literature in unmasking stalinism and The Party is Joszef Lengyel. At the time of the first communist government in Hungary in 1919, he belonged to Lajos Kassak's avant-guard activist group, and fled to the Soviet Union after the Belakun regime collapsed. When Stalin came to power he was imprisoned and sent to punitive camps in Siberia. Released after Stalin's death, he returned to Hungary and in 1956 was published for the first time in 25 years. Lengyel's novels and short stories are a curious mixture of expressionist elements and the Soviet formalistic style. His short novel *Merges kis oregur (An Angry Old Man)*, which appeared in *Uj Iras* in June 1962, is an interesting dramatization of the question of police power. The importance of its publication was emphasized by a long critical commentary which accompanied the novel, condoning its approach to the problem but stressing the distinction that must be made between ''good'' and ''bad'' communists.

An Angry Old Man tells of the fate of Professor Andrian, a well-known university physicist. Old and somewhat eccentric, he lives quietly with his sister, taking no part or interest in politics or world affairs. One evening the police come and remove him to a prison, where he is thrown into a hideous cell crammed with hundreds of wretched men. Periodically, prisoners simply disappear; others are tortured and returned to the cell. In spite of incredible hardships, the inmates manage to maintain a certain solidarity and degree of morale among themselves, allocating the few beds to the sick and the tortured while the others try to sleep on the filthy floor. Nobody knows why he is there. The narrator suggests that their imprisonment ''will perhaps go down in history with the thousand and one nights of St. Bartholomew,'' but observes on second thought that this would be an inaccurate designation because ''what was being persecuted here was not a specific creed, not even a party, but everyman, sinner or not. The sinless were not brought here because of innocence, nor were sinners brought here because of their sins. At that time, there were a great many things you simply couldn't comprehend. . . .''

There is, for example, the story of the young engineer who describes the Queen Mary for his fellows—the largest ship in the world, on which, only two months ago, he sailed for the United States. ''This American trip is now being held against me,'' he says. ''I never asked to go on the mission. I was sent. Officially. They screened me carefully, and questioned me all about my loyalties, and I guess they cleared me because I was sent. . . . And now. . . .'' He can only shrug.

One day the professor's turn comes. He is taken from the cell and led to a small room, where a perfumed young inquisitor sits him down and orders him to write his confession. ''You will tell of your counterrevolutionary and spying activities, and of your terrorist deeds. You will tell us who made you join the organization, and the names of those you yourself have recruited. You will name three people.''

Professor Andrian naturally protests that he has nothing to confess, that he has never had the least interest in political affairs, much less joined any political organization. The repeated beatings and humiliations administered by the young official fail to force him to write a false confession. Returned to the cell, the professor asks one of the prisoners: ''Tell me, please. You say there are many party members in this cell. . . . What do they say to these 'confessions'?''

''Nothing. They understand it even less than we do. They just don't understand it. I'm a party member too, for that matter, and have been for five years. But even the old and seasoned warriors don't know what is going on.''

''You say they understand it even less. . . . What do you mean by that?''

''It's because they look for some legality in all this, and they don't find it. . . .''

The interrogations and beatings continue, until one day the professor is removed from the cell and does not return. The novel closes with the narrator's remark: ''Professor Andrian's story continued at the Twentieth Congress [of the CPSU]. Just after that, I heard that the physics faculty at the university was to be named after him.''

The point of the story is quite clear. It is a classic example of the sort of post-stalinist literature which attributes arbitrary abuses of power not to the party, but to individual communists who have allowed themselves to be corrupted into the service of the personality cult, or The Party.

The official critical view of such writing was expressed in the accompanying remarks of Mrs. J. Mathejka (probably a pseudonym) entitled ''What We Need and What We Don't.''

> In the field of literature and art, the issue is even more involved. In these areas, not only must we argue convincingly, but we must also strive to demonstrate that communist ideology and the communist party have nothing to do with the sinful and distorted methods of the personality cult. The serious and conscientious artistic representation of this tragedy must not be interpreted as a futile attempt to resurrect the past. On the contrary, it is in the interest of the future. Bourgeois ideology and revisionism will not profit by it.

> On the other hand, hypocrites will not be appalled by the mere fact that all these hideous things, which are so alien to us could have happened. They shed their tears over the politicians, writers and artists who, by telling what happened, put the issue of truth at the service of the party. . . .

> Arrest becomes the deepest layer of hell, and detention the starting point of the hideous journey. The human character of Professor Andrian, who was not a party member, his brutal flogging by the young inquisitor, the inhumanity of the entire inquisition, the wretched conditions of the cell—all these things serve to prove and document the simple fact *that all this is alien to the party, and was perpetrated against the will of the party.* [Author's emphasis throughout.] There are many seasoned old communists in the cell. What is their attitude toward all this, Professor Andrian asks. *They understand it even less,* is the reply, because they look for legality and do not find it. The truth of the matter is that at that time, all those who looked toward the socialist system for an answer looked in vain, *because a phenomenon alien to socialist legality had made its bloody and distorted way into socialist life.* This is what the Communist Party of the Soviet Union revealed at the Twentieth and Twenty-Second Congresses, and this is what the communist party has now put an end to, once and for all.

It may be asked, why must we return in our literature to this issue? Do we need this kind of literature? The answer to this is, we certainly don't need any sensationalist trash, but it would be a mistake to veto a real work of art just because it treats this topic. The personality cult is a thing of the past, and the party has made its revival impossible by forthright disclosure of the truth and by well-ordered enforcement of true leninist norms. However, certain facts may still be not quite clear in the minds of the people. For this reason we should not interfere with such literature, for in many cases light is best diffused by art, and art effects a kind of moral catharsis.

This commentary is possibly even more indicative of the state of Hungarian literature today than the novel itself, for by justifying the publication of Lengyel's story it takes a positive stand for a degree of free expression on the subject. The very fact that such a commentary accompanied the story is evidence that serious controversy preceded its publication, and it probably appeared over the protests of the more cautious. The critic in this case approves not only the subject but Lengyel's artistry as well, and in giving his story a clean bill of health asserts that such works serve a constructive purpose for the future of communism.

The pertinence of Lengyel's story is veiled by an intentional indefiniteness as to time and locale. It is not immediately clear, as the reader descends into the "deep hell" of imprisonment, that he is entering the past of the party, and not some grim period of Nazism. There is no specific suggestion that he is in the Soviet Union, though the possibility is always there. This uncertainty, we feel, is designed to provoke in us the nagging question, "Could it be that this sort of thing didn't happen only in Russia? Could this be Hungary, too, and we have never known about it?"

At the other end of the communist literary spectrum is Andras Berkesi, a devout party scribe who specializes in exposing the "counterrevolution." His novel, *Magany* (*Solitude*, 1961), is the confession of an inconstant heroine, and focuses on the bloody aftermath of the personality cult. Agnes is the daughter of a well-known physician and teacher, brought up in a liberal bourgeois atmosphere but predisposed to "prejudices, snobbery and lust." During the war she conducts a love affair with a member of the underground (we are not told whether or not he is actually in the party), who betrays his comrades for Agnes. After the takeover, Agnes transfers her affections to a real dyed-in-the wool communist—the exact opposite of her treacherous first lover. The true communist, however, is imprisoned during the Rakosi era, and the woman goes back to her turncoat. The emotional stresses and strains become too much for her, and she escapes them by suicide. Berkesi's point seems to be that the true communist must be on his guard for menaces from all sides: he suffers at the hands of those who adhere to the personality cult, of those who are not totally committed to the cause, and of course at the hands of class aliens like Agnes. However, by clinging to principles such a communist can endure, and he will in the end triumph.

To Istvan Katko too, it is not only the personality cult which threatens the well-intended. In his story "A nap adja az arnyekot" ("The Sun Makes the Shadow"), his hero, a prototype of the young peasant, is captured by the Russians at the front and sent to a Soviet prisoner-of-war camp where he is initiated into communism. Back in Hungary he joins the partisans, and after the takeover is elevated to the post of party secretary and political chairman of his district. Later, however, when the personality cult is discredited, he is unable to overcome his "petty king" attitudes and tactics, and, a misfit in the new order of things, he is driven to suicide.

Erzsebet Galgoczy, a talented journalist and authoress, is an example of the writer who has been profoundly influenced by the party. Her later novels, especially, reflect serious internal conflicts. [In 1953] Erzsebet Galgoczy worked in the turner's shop at the Gyor railroad car factory. She won the literary prize of the Student Youth Association for her short story "Szazszazalek" ("One Hundred Percent"), and was immediately hired by *Nepszabadsag* as a writer. She gained a great reputation for her work on the paper, but abandoned the security of her job to take a degree at the university. From that time on, her works began to "reflect the disappointment of a solitary and unbalanced soul." (pp. 10-13)

[In] *Feluton* (*Half Way*, 1961), she reveals that she "wanted to tell how a talented young man with a peasant background can get lost in the people's democracy." Her hero is an intelligent ambitious "middle" peasant with kulak relatives and some class-alien connections. In spite of these conditions of his birth, he becomes the chairman of a collective. When, during the revolution, the peasants try to break away from the compulsory collectives, he strives vainly to create in their place something new that will maintain the higher objectives of communism but which will also be more humane. Caught between the mill stones of party duty and his own humanitarian instincts, he sees no way out but suicide. His enemy, who has to a great extent manipulated the circumstances leading to his tragedy, is the party secretary—a rigid, jealous, and petty tyrant—the very personification of The Party.

Thus, in Galgoczy's novel, an individual acting on the best of intentions and at the same time believing wholeheartedly in lofty party ideals, is annihilated by The Party incarnate. Naturally, Golgoczy appeals to these higher ideals, but in vain. What remains is the naked expression of a truth—the fact that man is ultimately alone, and in many ways one cannot help feeling that the writer is speaking for herself as well as for her hero. One feels that both have become hopelessly entangled in their relationship with the party.

The role of both "The Party" and "the party" in literature—quite apart from any direct political function—is to observe and control the individual. Under this form of regulation, all that is personal or subjective is to all intents and purposes denied. Private life becomes communal life, and this transformation affects the writer both professionally and personally.

In a short story entitled "A stiglic" ("The Goldfinch"), Miklos Meszoly tells of a young Frenchwoman, Marianne, who comes to Budapest to start over after a life of conflicts and problems. The world she finds in Budapest is indeed new, and she becomes aware that she has given up her private life, for here even the most personal and intimate details of her life become public property. By sharing these things, she hopes that she can somehow impose some order on her experiences. "She is a kind of controller," says one of the other characters, hinting at the broader significance of the story. Marianne embarks on a love affair with a Hungarian painter who finds that only to her, a foreigner, can he express his innermost self. He confides in her the story of his youth, the painful memory of which is not yet public property. He was once a serious artist, but he has seen the fruits of his labor destroyed and can no longer sell his paintings. His liaison with Marianne is genuine and true, but it must be defended against the all-pervading Party, and therefore becomes public.

The Party is everywhere; it is not just an outside force. It is *inside* everything that lives, breathes and feels. But most of all The Party holds that everything is important to the public interest. Everyman's business is The Party's business. The Party is a presence which enforces a modus vivendi, and it is only the unquenchable determination of individuals to free themselves of its ubiquitous power that restores them to their rightful *human* condition.

The denial of privacy is a major theme in Hungarian literature. Even in Lengyel's *Angry Old Man* (see above), it is an issue. Andrian is emphatically and unquestionably a *private person*. Not only is he not in the party, his fundamental character—perhaps his only "crime," as he himself wryly observes—is his insistent "human being-ship." In this case, the *private* individual sacrifices his life by resisting totalitarian power, but the implication is that tyranny and terrorism are overcome not by the death of the tyrant, but by millions of such private resistances.

In Tamas Barany's novel *Uldozott vad* (*Persecuted*), the story of a scandal which threatens the social and professional life of a wronged woman, the question is less "what will the neighbors say" than "what will The Party say." What stand will The Party take on such-and-such an allegation, or to whatever new situation develops therefrom? Unlike Lengyel, Barany seems to suggest that the individual who strives to defend his or her private life is doomed.

The transformation of private life into a public affair is so commonplace a motif in Hungarian literature that it is frequently dramatized even by those who are known to make the greatest attempt to safeguard their artistic freedom. These do not, of course, make such an issue of the problem as do the strict party writers. Magda Szabo's characters, for instance, are *people*—flesh and blood human beings—and not socialist clichés. Though she is an avowed communist writer, in her hands and in the hands of authors of similar character and integrity, the question of "private versus public" becomes a spiritual rather than a political consideration, having to do with the larger issue of man and his common humanity. (pp. 13-14)

William Juhasz, "Writers and Politics," in East Europe, *Vol. 12, No. 7, July, 1963, pp. 6-14.*

LITERATURE SINCE THE 1956 REVOLT

IVAN SANDERS

[*Sanders is a Hungarian-born American critic and translator of Hungarian literature, most notably of works by dissident author George Konrad. In the following excerpt from an essay written in 1979, Sanders discusses works by the principal experimental novelists to emerge in Hungary during the 1960s and 1970s.*]

As recently as a decade and a half ago Hungarian fiction seemed as tradition-bound as ever. The celebrated novels of the late fifties and early sixties—Magda Szabó's *Az őz* (*The Fawn*), Tibor Cseres's *Hideg napok* (*Cold Days*), Ferenc Sánta's *Húsz óra* (*Twenty Hours*), Endre Fejes's *Rozsdatemető* (translated

into English as *Generation of Rust*)—stirred up excitement and cut to the quick by focusing on national traumas: the 1956 revolt, Hungary's participation in World War II, the anomalies of the post-war social transformation. These novels raised disturbing moral questions, challenged old certitudes and prompted a collective soul-searching; but for all their eager "form-breaking," their fashionably laconic language and abrupt shifts in point of view and time, they remained essentially realist narratives. By zeroing in on particular social environments, by flaunting local color and diction, they were in fact moving closer to naturalism than to realism. The commitment to the native anecdotal tradition was still so strong that truly experimental fiction didn't seem to have a chance.

It was in the 1960s that a number of modern Hungarian novels began to be translated into Western languages, and while they were generally well received, critics were struck by their quaintly old-fashioned qualities. "Backward-looking in both form and content," wrote Robert Stillwell of László Németh's *Revulsion*, a masterpiece of psychological realism, which was written in the forties but became widely known, even in Hungary, only after 1956. According to Stillwell, *Revulsion* was for people who "prize certain characteristics of 'older' European novels."

Of course there were innovative Hungarian prose writers before this time who had a discernible effect on the novelists emerging in the middle and late sixties, and perhaps an even stronger impact on a still younger generation of fiction writers who rose to prominence in the last six or seven years. In the 1930s Tibor Déry "modernized" the Hungarian novel not only by consciously utilizing the Proustian method of involuntary memory, with its juxtaposition of objective and subjective time and breakup of chronological narrative; he created a language that was as richly suggestive as it was minutely precise. The highlights of Déry's sprawling trilogy *A befejezetlen mondat* (*The Unfinished Sentence*) are elaborate introspections and lyrical descriptions, filled with microcopic and curiously impersonal details. Déry could remain painstakingly analytical even while orchestrating his monumental verbal set-pieces; he was a poet-turned-novelist who anticipated the *nouveau roman*, which may be one reason why he appeals to many contemporary prose writers.

Another conscious experimenter who began his work in the thirties, and one who is virtually unknown outside Hungary, is Miklós Szentkuthy. His first novel *Prae* is an undifferentiated hodgepodge of cultural history, psychological and literary analyses, personal recollections and reveries. Szentkuthy is, above all, a parodist who caricatures his own favorite periods and themes, including his despair about Western culture. He has often been compared to Joyce, though his meditations and associations are far more random and undisciplined than Joyce's. (In recent years Szentkuthy produced a brilliant, if idiosyncratic, translation of *Ulysses*.) Aside from a few sharp-eyed critics who recognized Szentkuthy's importance, few readers bothered with him in the thirties. Today his frantic parodies, his scintillating though aimless prose, his profound cultural pessimism are beginning to be more and more appreciated. The London-based Győző Határ is in many ways Szentkuthy's kindred spirit. Because he is an émigré writer, Határ cannot really be said to have a following in Hungary, though his extravagant pseudo-historical visions, iconoclastic meditations and baroque language are admired by many in his native country.

There are a number of influential Hungarian writers who began their careers in the forties but who—often because of the ups and downs of recent East European history—emerged as major literary figures only [since 1965]. Iván Mándy is a case in point. On the one hand he appears to be part of a tradition; his bittersweet nostalgia, his interest in marginal city types, in the lore and romance of the outskirts connect him to Gyula Krúdy, an early twentieth-century master, as well as to younger contemporary writers like Endre Fejes and György Moldova, who frequently write about these locales and types in their well-rounded stories. However, Mándy is unique in having abandoned traditional narration in favor of impressionistic suggestion. His "stories" are actually haunting daydreams, meandering dialogues about harried, déclassé intellectuals, forgotten silent screen stars, old-time soccer players, in which nostalgia turns to angst without warning. Mándy's motley cast of characters—small-time operators, losers, dreamers, vagabonds, youngsters, oldsters—are invariably revealed to be quietly suffering people. The author creates mood, builds character with minimal language, but the overall effect, dreamlike and often surreal, is highly evocative. There is a gossamerlike wistfulness in Mándy's sketches, though the sentiments and artifacts of a very prosaic world are never too far from his mind. This may explain why he too has much to offer to today's innovative writers.

István Örkény, another "late bloomer" who helped shape literary taste, is known as the exponent of the grotesque in Hungarian literature, even though much of his short prose and even some of his plays follow traditional patterns. It is in his remarkable "one-minute stories" (*egyperces novellák*) that Örkény really shifted gears. These radically abbreviated narratives, vignettes, verbal snapshots mock not only the neat structure of conventional fiction but its confident assumptions and pretensions as well. "Örkény experiments with anti-matter," writes Elemér Hankiss in a recent appraisal of the one-minute stories. "He takes a teaspoonful of this anti-matter . . . , dissolves it in our good old everyday reality, and then anxiously and slyly waits for the result. He wants to know what happens when the unusual suddenly disrupts the routine and the extraordinary mingles with the petty; when nonbeing overtakes being, or when History enters our everyday lives."

Both Mándy's elliptical, allusive language and Örkény's terse, deadpan prose work well in the medium of film; cinematic versions of their works have met with considerable success. Significantly enough, most of the innovative writers who achieved fame in the sixties have close ties with the world of film. Gyula Hernádi, who in his early short stories described the lives of urban loners with a verbal economy and psychological subtlety that remind one of Mándy's fiction, is director Miklós Jancsó's frequent scriptwriter and collaborator. Jancsó's stark, ritualized film parables (*The Roundup, Reds and Whites, Red Psalm,* et cetera) have become for many Western film buffs examples of characteristically East European treatment of historical-political reality. Hernádi's novels, though their starting point is either a carefully documented factual event or a skillfully understated piece of science fiction, are themselves parables. For example, *Sirokkó* (1969), one of his most puzzling and disturbing novels, is about the education of a would-be Croatian terrorist in a secret South Hungarian training camp. (There was indeed such a camp operating in the thirties, where members of the Croatian fascist organization, the notorious Ustaši, were groomed for acts of terrorism.) In a highly disjointed and oblique manner, *Sirokkó* relates how this man is brutalized and brainwashed by his "instructors." With his resistance worn down, his dignity destroyed and his secret anxieties kept cunningly alive, he becomes the perfect tool in the hands of his superiors.

Another Hernádi novel, *Az erőd* (*The Fort;* 1971), takes place on a Greek island. A group of international adventurers buy a superannuated military installation and turn it into a playground for jaded millionaires, who come here for the ultimate pastime: organized war games. Fighting against a crack army of professionals, they can be either attackers or defenders, can taste the thrill of victory or the anguish of defeat. The game is for real: within a two-day period the participants can kill or be killed. The high point of the novel is the confrontation between the authorities who want to put an end to the games and the trigger-happy mercenaries who stick to their stratagems to the very end.

As we can see, Hernádi is drawn to dramatically heightened situations that reveal the effects of physical and psychic manipulation—situations that test the limits of human endurance. He is careful, of course, to choose "safe" historical occurrences, and generalizes about the individual's helplessness in the face of various kinds of conditioning, though the careful reader can always detect allusions to the states of affairs closer to home. Gyula Hernádi relates his parabolic strategies, his predilections for stripped-down conflicts and head-on collisions to his involvement with film. He has said in an interview: "Our history is dominated by intense crises, extreme situations, and they also become the common experience of twentieth-century man. Because of its very nature, film has to be concise and intriguing; therefore it cannot dispense with situations in which human character, acts of courage and betrayal, rebellion and submission are revealed in all their nakedness."

Miklós Mészöly is another member of the "middle generation" of nonconformist prose writers who has been exploring the possibilities inherent in the medium of film. He is attracted to the objectivity and impersonality of cinematic expression, yet is well aware of the ambiguities behind its directness. Some of Mészöly's best essays are on film (on the work of Andy Warhol, Peter Fleischmann and others), and even in his literary criticism he uses concepts and criteria that are familiar to us from his analysis of film. He defines art in terms of process, articulation, "a school of spaciousness." Mészöly's best-known novel, *Az atléta halála* (*The Death of an Athlete;* 1966), examines the life and times of a popular long-distance runner. Some time after the athlete suffers a fatal heart attack, his girlfriend is asked to write his biography. She tries to piece together the story of his life from the available documentary evidence, but as she visits her companion's birthplace and talks to childhood friends, she becomes more and more uncertain of her subject. Her attempts to understand the runner, to put his life in perspective, to write a definitive biography, end in failure. "There are no neat explanations; there are only facts, it seems," she says at the end of the novel. "And strong, penetrating landscapes. There is Rogozsel Village and Burntstone Valley. And there is our own hesitation in the deserted village, on the moonlit heights."

The narrator-director of Mészöly's latest novel, entitled simply *Film* (1976), echoes those words when he says, after following an old couple on a Budapest street and making a number of insinuations about their past: "We wish to solve nothing; we simply want to cover a distance." *Film* reads like a tentative shooting script, a set of instructions and notes a director might be mulling over before (or while) shooting a segment. In introducing the eye of a camera and thereby achieving a degree of objectivity, Mészöly is clearly taking his cue from the *nouveau roman;* but he also seems to go beyond it, for by sizing up and arranging his *cinéma verité* subjects, by choosing appropriate camera angles and by looking for perfect visual effects, he estheticizes everyday reality and captures the process of elimination and selection inherent in the creative act.

Perhaps the most gifted Hungarian prose writer to have emerged in the sixties, George (György) Konrád, also has an interest in both the *nouveau roman* and film. Konrád, whose novels have been widely translated and acclaimed, began his writing career as a literary critic, and in his first essays, written on the French new novel, he discusses the relationship between film and novel. In his own first work of fiction, *A látogató* (*The Case Worker;* 1969), Konrád constructs a world of precisely observed objects. The visual impact of his vignettes about human misery and degradation is overwhelming. When the case worker, a tired, stoical and very humane bureaucrat, walks through a crumbling tenement, he sees

> discolored name plates, walled-up windows, shattered blinds, mutilated lions'-heads, eternally splotched and splattered doorways, urine-stained rosettes, sagging gutters and cables, eviscerated sirens, tumbledown fences with grotesque fleur-de-lys-headed spikes, ponderous padlocks guarding orphaned basements, abandoned brooms, mildewed piles of bicycle chains and cardboard trumpets, concrete boils marking the entrances of air-raid shelters, shot-up windows loosely-fixed with bricks, obsolete posters. . . .

Unlike Hernádi and Mészöly, Konrád is fond of lyrical, densely metaphoric expression. His novels are in fact formidable verbal edifices in whose nooks and crannies we find numerous capsule dramas, compressed landscapes, revealing snapshots. Konrád also favors succinct generalizations and aphorisms, though here too his point of departure is invariably a moment of lived reality. He worked as a superintendent in a child welfare agency when he wrote *The Case Worker;* later he had a position at the Institute of Urban Planning in Budapest, and his second novel, *A városalapító* (*The City Builder;* 1977), grew out of that association. In this recently published novel especially, personal experiences, memories, theories are subsumed into philosophical meditations, or transmogrified into frightening and fantastic visions. . . . Like other experimentalists of the sixties, Konrád tries to approximate the clarity and immediacy of film. But his language, because of its extraordinary power and plasticity, actually transcends film. "We have . . . been told that the old-fashioned printed word cannot match the film for vividness," writes Irving Howe in his review of Konrád's first novel. "But *The Case Worker* shows that language remains the greatest of human powers, with unrivaled capacities for evocation, parallel and echo."

George Konrád's language may be more exciting, more vibrant than that of many of his contemporaries, but he does share with Hernádi, Mészöly and others a penchant for unconventional, indeed unliterary imagery. Konrád and his generation are self-consciously intellectual writers, much more so than most of their predecessors, and this is reflected not just in their insistence on extraliterary points of reference, in their attraction to abstract metaphors and technical, scientific vocabulary, but also in the ease with which they broaden the conceptual framework of fiction. It goes without saying that awkward-sounding technical phraseology and the reliance on abstract sociological and historical models and geometric images seem very strange and jarring in a literature whose language for centuries has been a proving ground for lyric poets. There are many readers

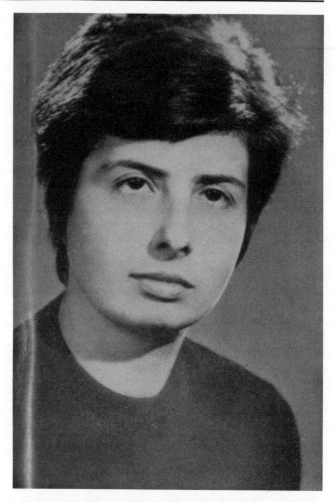

Judit Tóth. Photograph by László Kaszás.

who find the style of these novelists either too strained and artificial or stylistically impoverished. Just the same, we must realize that the use of technical imagery or metaphors in which the figurative terms are always abstractions is not all that new. In Hungarian literature we encounter them frequently in Tibor Déry's prose. Indeed, when we read, in George Konrád's *The City Builder,* that newborn infants are "declarative sentences that cannot be contradicted," or when a dead father's body is referred to as "this obscured attention, this wrinkle-free finality . . . this invulnerable nonpresence," we are reminded of passages in Déry's *A befejezetlen mondat* in which the main character is described as being as unobtrusive as a conjunction in a sentence, or where a bedraggled mass of workers streaming out of a factory is seen as "the solution to a shameless economic puzzle."

Another manifestation of the Hungarian new novelists' unconventional approach to fiction is their by now familiar practice of merging fact and fiction. Writers like István Örkény, Gyula Hernádi, Mihály Sükösd and others often incorporate in their novels and stories a wide variety of documentary material: letters, diaries, newspaper reports, historical narratives, manuscripts, archival material, et cetera. The result is frequently neither fiction nor nonfiction, but simply a *text,* a term very much in use in Hungarian literature today. The aim of these writers is not to give an all-encompassing, naturalistic sense of reality à la Dos Passos, but rather to exploit the ironic possibilities inherent in unusual editing and curious juxtaposition. For instance, István Örkény achieves stunning effects with his medley of classified ads, government regulations, names, inquiries, quotations. Underlying such collages is of course the notion that in a country with a turbulent history the most pedestrian written record may be more revealing than an elaborate work of fiction. At the same time, when a document is made part of a literary work, it becomes strangely tentative, equivocal—a fiction. Ultimately, the blending of fiction and nonfiction raises questions about both. The presence of documentary material in recent Hungarian novels about the Holocaust (in György Gera's *Terelőút* [*Detour*], for example, or in Mária Ember's *Hajtűkanyar* [*Hairpin Curve*]), or in a searching historical novel like Péter Dobai's *Csontmolnárok* (*Bone-Grinders*), not only reminds us of the inadequacy of fiction to deal with certain topics; it somehow also suggests the unreality of history.

The interest in literary nonfiction in Hungary is further evidenced by the popularity of memoirs, diaries, autobiographical novels. Much of contemporary Hungarian literature is retrospective; thus it is not surprising that writers examining their past respond eagerly to the modern novel's experiments with memory and time, or to its contemplation of the nature of fiction. Ten years ago, in his much-discussed autobiographical novel *Ítélet nincs* (*No Verdict*), Tibor Déry conjured up the spirit of his deceased fellow writers and poets, most of them modern classics by now, and while the spirits were realistically conceived, the subsequent portraits are full of little fictions. The author of another famous literary memoir, István Vas, impresses younger innovative writers with his sophisticated, sardonic prose style and lively interest in experimental literature. Vas sees his first autobiographical work, *Elveszett otthonok* (*Lost Homes*), in which he takes stock of middle-class values by carefully describing apartment interiors, ornaments, as a kind of proto-*nouveau roman*. In subsequent portions of his intellectual autobiography he continues to employ ingenious novelistic devices. In both *Nehéz szerelem* (*Difficult Love*) and the more recent "*Mért vijjog a saskeselyü*" (*Why Screeches the Vulture?*), he periodically leaps ahead in his narrative in an attempt to shed more light on the event under discussion. Yet another sign of the preoccupation with the past in Hungarian literature is the renewed interest in family histories. There are finely wrought, more or less traditional family chronicles (e.g., Magda Szabó's *Régimódi történet* [*An Old-Fashioned Story*]); but some of the latest ones—Péter Nádas's *Egy családregény vége* (*The End of a Family Novel*), which carries us back to a mythic past, or Géza Bereményi's fragmentary, multi-voiced *Legendárium*—reflect a newer literary sensibility.

Many critics have the tendency to relate nontraditional writing of any kind to the very latest avant-garde trend. The unconventional novelists of the sixties—their coldly precise, impersonal descriptions, technical vocabulary and fondness for abstractions notwithstanding—were not only following in the footsteps of the *nouveau romanciers;* many of their works reveal the influence of older trends and styles—the behaviorist school, for example, or existentialism—which ten to fifteen years ago were still considered daring and unorthodox in Hungary. In the background of many parabolic-allegorical novels we sense such models as Camus's *The Plague* and Golding's *Lord of the Flies*. The innovative writers of the seventies, most of them still under forty, seem to have different literary forebears. They have little use for stark allegories and moral fables. Having reached adulthood in the relatively tranquil and affluent sixties, they are a more self-centered, narcissistic generation;

their fiction is full of voluble self-appraisals. They can be charming or sullen or outrageous; they are also sensitive and inordinately curious. Most of them are obsessed with form and language and are far more interested in the process of creating fiction than with the end product itself. On the whole, they are closer in spirit to the more adventurous American "post-modernists" (Barthelme, Sukenick, Katz) than to the disciplined French innovators, and they owe a great deal to another American author, J. D. Salinger, whose works have been in vogue in Hungary ever since they were first translated in the early sixties.

It is surprising how many of these young prose writers seek to re-create the world of childhood and adolescence—most often their own—in their fiction. Reminiscences about youth, stories dealing with the wonder and pain of growing up have always been popular in Hungarian literature (they run the gamut, from Ferenc Molnár's sentimental *Paul Street Boys* to Géza Ottlik's chilling *School at the Frontier*), but writers like László Fábián, Miklós Vámos, Péter Esterházy and Peter Nádas explore the psyche of young people with an intensity and knowledgeability that is new. Of this youngest generation of innovative writers, Péter Esterházy (b. 1950) appears to be the most interesting. His first collection, *Fancsikó és Pinta* (1976), which he calls "stories strung on a piece of cord," is about two imaginary characters invented by a child hero to help him cope with the menacing goings-on in the adult world. Fancsikó and Pinta are meddlesome, impertinent and wise creatures; they have the wit and craftiness of the author and the innocence of their child creator. Some of Esterházy's stories are obviously autobiographical; his latest work, *Termelési regény* (*Production Novel;* 1979), ostensibly a takeoff on the socialist realist novels of the fifties, is in actuality a series of elaborate self-portraits. In these the author exhibits a sureness of touch, a mastery of language and a knack for controlled madness that is remarkable.

Esterházy's writing is full of comic asides, digressions, second thoughts and wordplay; he is exasperated by the arbitrariness of art and at times offers multiple versions of his narratives— he literally experiments on the printed page. He also parodies every conceivable literary convention, while at the same time cockily indulging in them. To a highly personal "situation report," parts of which are included in *Termelési regény,* Esterházy appends the following footnote: "Oh my gosh! After going over and correcting the text I note with embarrassment that it's the second time the word *slippers* came up. But then this must be a motif. And then what we have here is art. What do you know? Yet, I hadn't planned it that way. Just lucky, I guess. I simply write down this and that, and there it is: another pair of slippers. Of course, when I say art, I am not praising myself, but the world, in which slippers position themselves in such a way that sooner or later they become motifs." A passage such as this not only smacks of stylish metafiction; it also brings Salinger to mind, more specifically Buddy Glass, the self-reflective narrator of the later stories. Esterházy does in fact use a quote from "Seymour—An Introduction" as the motto of this particular narrative.

Another self-consciously literary artist who shares some of Esterházy's concerns is Dezső Tandori. A good bit older than Esterházy, Tandori is known mainly as an experimental poet, but in recent years he has branched out into prose as well. Esterházy's child hero relieves his anxieties and lives out his fantasies by inventing the puckish Fancsikó and Pinta; in his first volume of prose, "*Itt éjszaka koalák járnak*" (*Koalas*

Cross Here at Night; 1977), Tandori surrounds himself with charmingly guileless, Winnie-the-Pooh-like koala bears. Like Esterházy, Tandori creates self-contained worlds in which the author's real-life experiences, hobbies, eccentricities and private myths are transmuted into clever little fictions. In his two other volumes, *Miért élnél örökké? (Why Live Forever?;* 1977) and *A meghívás fennáll (The Invitation Stands;* 1979), Tandori's alter egos (D'Oré, D'Array) are busy relating incidents involving new pets—two tiny sparrows—and they lace these tales with reflections on seemingly insignificant childhood memories and mundane current happenings. Like Esterházy in his madcap "Spionnovella" ("Spy Story"), Tandori uses the familiar conventions of detective fiction, but only to emphasize the absurdity of these conventions. In general Dezső Tandori is preoccupied with esthetic problems. He has an insatiable curiosity about experimental artistic productions of all kinds, and a special interest in visual arts. (In some of his poems he offers verbal illustrations of works by his favorite painter, Paul Klee.) Yet the worlds created by Tandori and Esterházy are so private and allusive that much of the content remains obscure, despite the optimistic messages detected in the text by ideologically-oriented critics. It is the authors' playfulness and stylistic agility that prevent their obsessive self-exploration and involvement from becoming redundant and tiresome.

There is nothing lighthearted about the work of another gifted young writer, Péter Hajnóczy, although he too is preoccupied primarily with his own life, which, compared to that of his contemporaries, has itself been quite unconventional. Like Esterházy, Hajnóczy is blessed (or cursed) with a famous Hungarian family name; but unlike his fellow writer, he dropped out of school at the age of sixteen and . . . earned his living as a manual laborer. In most of his stories—he has published two slim collections since 1975—Hajnóczy writes about helpless Dostoevskian outcasts, misfits, down-and-outers, who nevertheless try, with pathetically poor results, to assert themselves, to rationalize their ills, to maintain their tattered dignity. In a few of his early stories Hajnóczy creates self-consciously grotesque, Kafkaesque situations—a man is grazed by a bullet and tries to convince himself that a bird-dropping hit his face; a butcher donates blood and for two months straight it keeps streaming from his arm—but in the majority of them nothing really happens. Characters register and contemplate external stimuli, mull over options, look for solutions but remain paralyzed. Their feverish mental activity is invariably contrasted with physical immobility. Yet even in their reduced state their compassion and yearning for freedom are undiminished. According to Péter Dobai, a friend and fellow writer, Hajnóczy is concerned mainly with "a workaday analysis of that non-romantic, non-Byronic, non-Schillerian . . . but cement-gray sense of freedom that emanates from our instincts, from the body, the mind; from words . . . dreams, memories."

In Hajnóczy's most recent work the single most powerful metaphor for human alienation and helplessness is alcoholism. His novel *A halál kilovagolt Perzsiából (Death Left Persia on Horseback;* 1979) is a devastating portrait of an alcoholic's personality. It is also more transparent, stylistically less challenging than the previous stories, though here again Hajnóczy resorts to interior monologues that convey the vulnerability and tenacity of a man with an addiction. As he reviews his relationship with women, especially his acquaintance with an ambitious, pragmatic Jewish girl, the novel's young protagonist seeks stability in a world made threatening and tentative by his drinking. At one point he contemplates an old shoehorn which bears the name of the owner of a forgotten shoe store.

A shoehorn may be somewhat unexciting, though it's certainly durable. Even in the event of war it enjoys relative safety. As a rule, guns are aimed at hospitals and apartment buildings, not shoehorns. And if someone had the bizarre idea of firing a cannon at Izidor Brasch's shoehorn, he'd surely miss; the thing is so light, the blast would just hurl it across the room. In all probability, only an atom or hydrogen bomb would be capable of destroying this shoehorn. But why would they drop a hydrogen bomb on Izidor Brasch's shoehorn? Come to think of it, there is no compelling reason to do it.

It would be incorrect to assume that contemporary Hungarian prose literature is dominated by experimental novelists. Not only are established writers in the mainstream committed to realism; many younger novelists are also returning to traditional forms. For example, the popular József Balázs has revived anecdotal realism in his absorbing stories about peasant anti-heroes caught in desperate historical situations. Moreover, such highly original Hungarian storytellers in neighboring countries as István Szilágyi (in Romania) and Nándor Gion (in Yugoslavia) likewise continue the realist tradition, although their exquisite craftsmanship and the psychological and mythic depths of their historical fictions also suggest a thorough assimilation of the post-realist tradition. According to someone like Gyula Hernádi, reductive "models" in literature present challenges to both author and reader. Ferenc Karinthy, a "hardcore" realist, believes, on the other hand, that "in practice an abstract parable about the relationship between state power and individual conscience, which can be variously interpreted and which many people can't figure out at all, is allowed to pass more easily than, say, a story about what really goes on in some of the cooperatives." Karinthy is no doubt right. But what he may not realize—and what many Hungarian new novelists do—is that there *is* an underlying continuity between various fictional modes. As George Konrád observed recently, "The novel always returns from its stylistic expeditions to the same point, and relates in new ways very basic, universal parables and fables." (pp. 589-94)

Ivan Sanders, "The Hungarian 'New Novel'," in World Literature Today, *Vol. 53, No. 4, Autumn, 1979, pp. 589-95.*

GEORGE GÖMÖRI

[In the following essay, written in 1973, Gömöri examines experimental trends in Hungarian theater of the 1960s and 1970s, focusing on the theater of the grotesque and the absurd and on historico-political dramas influenced by the theater of Bertolt Brecht.]

Until the mid-sixties there were few Hungarian plays to cause a stir outside Hungary. An obvious exception to this rule were the plays of Ferenc Molnár (1878-1952) and of some other Hungarian expatriates to the United States. None the less, Molnár's lyrical-symbolic, technically brilliant but socially anachronistic work belonged to a trend that, for a variety of reasons, could not be continued in Hungary after the Second World War. The work of other playwrights such as László Németh or Gyula Illyés proved to be less exportable—their plays were either technically too conservative or too centered upon national issues which sometimes gave them a touch of parochialism. In short, Hungarian drama has been for decades hampered by the conventions of Romantic and naturalistic tradition; even as late as 1965, in comparison with Poland or Czechoslovakia, the repertoire of Hungarian theatres looked somewhat antiquated. This situation, which was as much the consequence of political control and restraints as of the aesthetic standards long prevalent in Hungarian society, began to change gradually, and since 1969 we have witnessed the emergence of important new trends in the Hungarian drama. In life as well as in culture certain problems which had been either repressed or regarded as marginal now emerged with some force. Their expression in the theatre became possible largely because of external circumstances. With the inauguration of the New Economic Mechanism (an economic reform giving more autonomy to individual enterprises and genuine market forces) Hungarian society entered into a new phase of development; the political and managerial elite grew more tolerant toward experimentation in both literature and the arts. "Tolerance" in this context meant a relaxation of dogmatic control; such events as the Soviet-Chinese conflict, the repudiation of not only Stalin's but some of Khruschev's policies by the present Soviet leaders, the fragmentation of the world communist movement—these prepared the ground for a bolder questioning of earlier accepted "Communist" and human values. As a result, for example, the theatre of the grotesque and the absurd, which does not attack particular political tenets but questions the structure of everyday logic and puts in doubt the possibility of meaningful human communication, found in some important circles if not approval at least more understanding. The great international successes of Hungarian films, first of all Jancsó's in the sixties, also contributed to the revival of the drama in spurring playwrights to emulation. And, finally, imaginative productions of such authors as Dürrenmatt, Beckett, Brecht, Peter Weiss and Mrożek stimulated interest in the long-overdue "modernization" of Hungarian drama.

At present there are three trends which attract more than local interest. They may be representative of the Hungarian theatre of the future but they are not of the majority of theatrical productions at present. Because in Hungary—with the exception of amateur student groups—all productions are subsidized by the state, the repertory policy of theatres is strongly affected by two kinds of pressures: political-bureaucratic and commercial. A number of plays of the "correct" (i.e. Marxist) ideological content have to be put on regardless of the financial loss, and directors have a natural inclination to make up for the loss by staging light Western comedies or "proven" Hungarian and foreign classics. Thus the room for experimentation is definitely limited; only one or two theatres in Budapest are prepared to shock the audience with very unusual or openly controversial productions. In Hungary not only the tastes of the authorities but also those of the average theatre-goer are rather conservative.

As regards the new trends, the international theatre of the absurd gave inspiration to a number of plays, though the generally accepted Western definition of the absurd ("a caricatural mirror of man's metaphysical condition") cannot be applied even to these. Some authors, perhaps the most interesting ones now working for the Hungarian stage, cultivate a genre which I would describe as the "Hungarian grotesque"—a hybrid of the absurd and conventional realism, with a special emphasis on the absurdity of reality rather than on the reality of the absurd. Finally, the Germanic genre of the grand historico-moralistic parable (beginning with Brecht, practised by Hochhuth and Peter Weiss) has also gained ground in recent years, though in these Hungarian plays the sociological or quasi-documentary approach never really eradicates the author's insistence on his characters' deep psychological needs or peculiarities.

In the pragmatic but ideologically well-controlled political atmosphere of Hungary in the early sixties, the first experiments of the theatre of the "absurd" provoked surprisingly strong official strictures. Miklós Mészöly's play *Az ablakmosó (The Window-cleaner)* is a case in point. It is the story of a young couple's longing for privacy, whose attempts to love each other are constantly frustrated by the intrusions of the caretaker and a mysterious window-cleaner. The latter symbolizes the outside world or even the State which takes every opportunity to interfere in the lives of ordinary citizens. This, I think, is implied by the parallel we can draw between the window-cleaner whose job is to clean our window, that is "to improve our view," and the ideologist who claims that only his interpretation of reality makes us capable of seeing the outside world without delusion. The intruder, the ubiquitous State, manages to destroy personal happiness that is seeking refuge in the autonomy of love. Mészöly was castigated for his "existentialist" interpretation of human loneliness and human responsibility and attacked for the symbolic representation of power which, in his critic's opinion, blurred the difference between the power of "socialism" and that of "imperialism." *Az ablakmosó* was never published in book form, only in the provincial literary review *Jelenkor;* and to my knowledge it has not been produced in any Budapest theatre.

Mészöly's initiative was taken up some years later by Gábor Görgey, a young poet and translator. His *Komámasszony, hol a stukker?* (1969), translated into English as *The Pistol Shot,* was a clear product of the theatre of the absurd. In this short play we are confronted with an odd situation which can have a certain number of basic variants. Going through these variants constitutes the plot. Lock a number of people, each from a different social background, in an empty room; give to one of them a loaded pistol, and see what happens. Who will terrorize whom and what kind of "ideological" or pragmatic arguments will he use?—that is the question. The play, though quite effective, smacks of Mrożek; Görgey's scheme develops on lines recalling the "mad logic" of such plays as *Tango* or *At the Open Sea.* As in Mrożek's plays what matters is not what people say but what they do; power can be camouflaged by ideology to varying extents, but what matters is who holds the pistol. Görgey's scheme, by the way, is more static than that of Mrożek who in *Tango* shows not only the brittleness of ideologies but also the qualitative decline of those who wield power.

By 1968-69 the "theatre of the absurd" became a genre firmly entrenched all over Eastern Europe. In Poland, Mrożek and Różewicz found numerous followers; in Czechoslovakia, Václav Havel, Klíma and others were at the peak of their popularity; even in Romania, it became possible to write if not in an "absurd" then at least in an "absurdoid" vein. The distinction between these two labels was made by the gifted poet and playwright Géza Páskándi in the preface to his collected plays, partly to make it clear to all those concerned that he does not share the "pessimistic" philosophy of such Western colleagues as Ionesco or Beckett. Optimistic or not, the East European branch of the absurd has been more historicist in its outlook than its Western variety; few authors living in Prague or Budapest would be ready to accept absurdity as an unchangeable and eternal component of human life which deforms *every* social system.

Páskándi, incidentally, is a Hungarian author who lives in Romania. The question which ought to follow this qualification is: not how he came to write absurd plays, but why he did not start writing them earlier. For one belonging to a national minority of roughly two million people who live under the double pressure of a "fundamentalist" version of Marxism and an over-centralised and nationalistic Romanian-language administration, it is easy to develop a slightly schizophrenic disposition which is not unlike the world of the "absurd." Now the strange thing about Páskándi (who had been in jail for some years on the flimsiest charges of "conspiring against the state") is precisely his sanity. He writes "absurdoid" plays because he believes in much-maligned reason, and he regards himself as the defender of the rationalist tradition. His artistic aim is to exorcise the absurdity of social existence which is masked by conformist patterns of behaviour and institutionalized bureaucratic logic. If the theatre of Mrożek and of his spiritual ancestor S. I. Witkiewicz sometimes gives the impression of a brilliant puppet-show, more than one of Páskándi's short plays are like an elaborate chess-game played for life. Such is *A Bosszuálló, A Kapus, avagy: Kérjük a lábat letörölni* (*The Avenger, the Janitor, or else: Please Wipe Your Feet!*) the bizarre story of a crippled war veteran and his former commanding officer who is now Director of the Doormat Institute. The veteran kills the Director in revenge for the loss of his legs and is promptly appointed janitor by the New Director. The janitor's downfall happens when another crippled war veteran, also in a wheelchair, forces his way through the gate—the New Director used to be his commanding officer in the war. Another short play, *Külső zajok* (*Noises from Outside*) is a study in the psychology of intimidation through repeated assurances that there is absolutely no reason to fear anything or anybody. The scene is an office room, and a certain Mr. Kopa is left there, for no particular reason, just to keep watch. Though he does not utter a word, his mere presence creates nervousness among the clerks. From time to time an individual rushes in to assure and reassure everybody that "there is no reason whatever to fear Mr. Kopa." The clerks react to this with repeated statements of loyalty and utterances of official slogans; they cannot help fearing Mr. Kopa. The last word of the play—Mr. Kopa's menacing monosyllabic grunt: "What?"—shows that these fears were not unfounded. *Külső zajok,* written in 1964, gives a penetrating picture of bureaucratic paternalism in action. Though it has not been staged in Hungary proper, I would unhesitatingly call it one of the pioneering works of the *Hungarian* theatre of the absurd.

More recently some younger playwrights, whose experiences are quite different from those of Mészöly, Görgey and Páskándi, showed interest in an "absurdoid" interpretation of social reality. András Simonffy's radio-play *Szekrénylakók* (*Wardrobe-dwellers*) is among the most successful experiments of this kind. It tells the story of an amiable young couple who are reduced to living in a small room in the girl's parents' flat (there is an acute housing shortage in Budapest), but who get a majestic wardrobe for a wedding present. After a while, the wardrobe starts expanding; it would surely squeeze the young couple out of their room—unless they move into it. This step has its advantages; as not only the magic wardrobe but also the family expands, after a few years the tenants are quite content with their situation. Well, it's a bit dark in there, but warm and surprisingly comfortable. The symbolism of *Szekrénylakók* is not hard to decipher: the relationship between wardrobe and man reflects the power of things over people and also the "reification" of human individuals in situations beyond their control. Though Simonffy does not create a Kafka-

like nightmare, the play is steeped in irony and the last scene, when the husband loses his way in the wardrobe and shouts for help, shows the aimlessness of "petty-bourgeois" existence.

Simonffy's language, with its slangy and mock-historical references, could make translation of the play into English a difficult job indeed; the same problem arises in connection with István Örkény's plays. Örkény is a highly accomplished writer of fiction who gained popularity in recent years with his "minidramas" or "minimyths" in prose—grotesque snapshots which impress upon the reader the relevance of the extraordinary and atypical in life, giving an insight into "the cracks within reality." Örkény's first important play, *The Tót Family* (1967), was originally a short novel which he later adapted to the stage. It might well be the first genuine product of the Hungarian "theatre of the grotesque." This phrase is used here in contradistinction to the theatre of the absurd, which tends to create its own imaginary time and space. In Örkény's plays both time and place are concrete and historically defined; it is only the characters' behaviour that defies "common sense" and everyday logic.

The plot of *The Tót Family* can be told in a few words. During the Second World War, a major of the Hungarian army returns from the Russian front to rest and relax. He chooses for this purpose the quiet home of one of his subordinates whose parents, Mr. and Mrs. Tót (a very common name in Hungarian, like Smith or Miller), are only too eager to please him, for they believe that the major's good will is vitally important to the survival of their son. The major, however, turns out to be a psychopath who cannot sleep at night and needs company during his long vigils. Soon his presence completely disrupts the life of the Tót family. In the last scene the comedy turns macabre: Mr. Tót murders the Major and goes to sleep once again in his own bed. There is nothing absurd about this; in fact, I find the harassed Tót's final action understandable, very nearly rational. On the other hand, the relationship between the Major and the Tót family is specifically Hungarian, and its absurdity, though exacerbated by the war, is inherent in the pseudo-paternalistic attitude taken by the Hungarian upper classes (and the caste of Army officers) toward the "lower strata" of society. *The Tót Family* is a grotesque play with certain historical implications, a play that can be badly misinterpreted by stage directors who know about as much about Central European social relationships as they do of the geography of Tartary-Barbary.

Örkény's next theatrical piece, *Macskajáték* (*Catsplay*), can be dismissed here because, though it is amusing and well-constructed, it is traditional both in plot and technique. *Pisti a vérzivatarban* (*Steve in the Carnage,* 1969), however, is frankly experimental and in early 1973 it still awaits production in or outside Hungary. Though not exempt from Brechtian influences, to my mind this play is closer to S. I. Witkiewicz's theories about Pure Form and the kind of theatre he began to create in the nineteen-twenties. "What matters" wrote Witkiewicz "is the possibility of freely deforming life or an imaginary world in order to create a totality, the sense of which would be determined by a purely scenic construction and not by any exigencies of consequent psychology or action, corresponding to the rules of ordinary life." Örkény's title-character, Steve, is independent of the law of causality, and his actions are strange and often contradictory; none the less, the play has its roots in the absurdity of Hungarian (and in general East European) history and in the political predicament of these countries. As Steve informs the public:

> What you are going to see here is not much
> like other plays. It is not even a real play . . .
> just the frolics and capers of imagination. As
> it comes to your mind: just like in real life.

This statement will perhaps need some explanation. Örkény in *Steve in the Carnage* leads us through a series of irrational and absurd situations with which most citizens of his native country (or of the neighbouring countries) have had to cope during the past thirty-odd years. Steve's statement is deliberately ambiguous, for either you don't take seriously these situations—arguing that such things can happen only in a nightmare or in the mind of a madman—or else you admit that such things *could and did happen* in real life, thus marking life as a domain of "absurd" experience. In any case the border line between reality and imagination is blurred, and the reason for this is not "the absurdity of the human condition" but of a particular kind of human existence. For Ionesco the "conventional" is absurd; for Örkény and many of his fellow-writers the absurd seems at times almost conventional.

But back to Steve. He is both transmutable and expandable; depending on the situation, he is single or married, man or woman. During the war he is the commander of an execution squad, but, having given the order to shoot, he joins the crowd of civilians to be massacred. He is killed, and comes to life again; at one point he is (legally) two different persons. After the war when everyone is busy celebrating Steve, the New Heroic Man, in the whole country there is only one man who denies Steve's existence and that is Steve himself. Later "steve" becomes a unit of measurement. Still later, two men in leather jackets take away Steve, and, after a mock-trial where both prosecutor and defendant speak an emphatic nonsense-language, he is executed. People are forced to denounce him. After a while he is rehabilitated. In the sixties (?), he is arrested by the police for painting the hammer and sickle on the window of a first-class restaurant frequented by Western tourists. Still later, it looks as if Steve was the new Messiah. Finally, however, he decides to become completely and fully himself. Unfortunately the play has a strange and forced ending. The H-bomb having been dropped on Budapest, life starts again amongst the ruins. *Steve in the Carnage* is a modern morality play with a dialectically changing hero in whose life there are only two constants: his geopolitical situation and indestructible vitality. It is Örkény's most unconventional play to date, and even if it is not free of certain allusions, which require familiarity with Hungarian culture or history, its potential appeal to foreign audiences may be greater than that of *The Tót Family*.

Much younger than Örkény, but an established playwright with a genuine flair for the grotesque, is István Csurka. Of his plays, comedies verging on social satire, one could be singled out of special interest: *Ki lesz a bálanya? (Who Will Pay for the Ball?)*. Written in 1963 it could be staged only about five or six years later at the Thalia Studio Theatre, a small experimental theatre in Budapest. Although Csurka said in an interview that he "prefers humour to the grotesque," his play abounds in grotesque and tragicomic accents. One of the central characters (in the play "Czifra") is a dramaturge, modelled on Csurka's friend, who committed suicide and died in 1961. The whole play is set in Czifra's flat where three of his friends gather for their weekly poker party. During the game the players talk effusively; apart from habitual jokes, spontaneous curses and small talk, they also philosophize and assess their own way of life in clear-cut terms. One way or another all are depressed and dissatisfied: their complaints and angry confes-

sions reflect, and in my opinion faithfully so, the malaise of most young Hungarian intellectuals in the early sixties. In Act II we are treated to the following dialogue:

> ABONYI. Bullocky wants to discuss the responsibility of the intelligentsia, but lacks the power of self-expression. Whose deal is it? Do you have to fly off the handle just when my luck looks like changing?
>
> CSÜLLÖGH. None the less, we still represent the Hungarian intelligentsia, don't we? And none of us has ever done anything really beastly. But what did we do? Have we ever done anything at all?
>
> ABONYI. We tried.
>
> FÉNY. That's the most comfortable and most rotten lie in the world: we tried, but it was impossible. The truth is that we didn't even want to. If you really want to do something, you can't fail!

The seriousness of this collective self-criticism is temporarily reduced by the players' antics and the realization of their paradoxical dependence on each other: the chief loser has to borrow money from his partners to go on playing. And play they must, for such is the logic of their situation. The grotesque cardgame turns into tragedy in the last scene, when at dawn Czifra leaves his home for a Turkish bath, where—we already know—he is going to cut his veins in the bathtub. He is the symbolic sacrifice for all the omissions and could-have-beens of his friends, the once enthusiastic, now frustrated brotherhood of "useless intellectuals."

Ki lesz a bálanya? is a play not only for addicts of the poker game. Thanks to Csurka's insights into the mentality of his characters and his skill in highlighting their preoccupations, it becomes a penetrating study of intellectual behaviour patterns. Its production outside Hungary would nevertheless present difficulties. Csurka's play has a distinct Budapest air, the text being sprinkled with allusions, trying not only for foreigners but even for Hungarians of a different generation. For example, in the play Csüllögh is addressed by his partners as *Böhönye*. Rendering this as "Bullocky" is not bad, but it misses the implications; for Böhönye is a place-name, the name of a Hungarian village, close to which there used to be an Army camp for new recruits and University students in the early fifties, a training camp of a most unsavoury reputation. In other words, Csurka's translator should have intimate knowledge not only of Hungarian culture but also of recent history, even of "urban folklore." Admittedly, some of his other plays (for instance the excellent *Deficit*) lack this allusiveness, but *Ki lesz a bálanya?* is central to the understanding of Csurka's problems and complexes.

The third interesting new trend in the Hungarian theatre is grappling with problems of political power. Sándor Fekete's approach is documentary, or rather pseudo-documentary—his *Hőség hava (Thermidor)* is an ingenious effort to evaluate the downfall of the French Revolution in the light of contemporary evidence but from a modern point of view. How far can we sacrifice individual freedom in the service of revolutionary ideals? Was the Jacobin dictatorship in its last phase still a revolutionary form of government? Was Thermidor necessary, or was it unjustified, in view of what came afterward?

Miklós Radnóti. From Miklós Radnóti: The Complete Poetry, *edited and translated by Emery George. Ardis, 1980. Reprinted by permission of Ardis Publishers.*

Fekete contrasts the motives and later career of Fouché and Billaud-Varenne, both participants of the plot that smashed Robespierre. Fouché's career (he became Police Minister first under Napoleon and even for a while under Louis XVIII) proved that his motives in striking out against the Jacobin Terror were first of all personal, whereas Billaud-Varenne remained loyal to his revolutionary ideals even after he was deported to Guyana. The author's sympathies are clearly on Billaud-Varenne's side; and discussing Thermidor he makes him utter the axiom: revolutions can be destroyed only by the revolutionaries themselves. Once the spirit of the revolution "froze," its leaders were doomed. What makes Fekete's play interesting is its form which invites audience participation. He brings onto the stage five contemporary intellectuals (four men and one woman) who have a double function: they analyse Thermidor and its aftermath, giving their views on each historical character, but they also impersonate the characters they are talking about. This device is supposed to lead to a double identification process: the audience is not only to applaud or condemn Robespierre but also the moderate revolutionary Sándor who passes judgment on Robespierre. By evoking the last phase of the French Revolution, the five intellectuals in effect discuss the hopes, disappointments and weaknesses of contemporary revolutionary movements.

Páskándi's new play deals with the same problem from one particular angle. His three-act drama *A rejtekhely* (*The Hiding Place*) also takes place during the French Revolution, in the house of the cobbler Simon. According to some sources, the National Convention entrusted him with the "education" of Louis XVI's son. For Páskándi, Simon is a tragi-comic figure, a drunkard, torn between his political ambitions and fear of retaliation in the case that the Jacobins are defeated—"the customers will come back for their boots" which are of course still unmended—and he employs in his workshop three politically "unsafe" characters, just to cover himself in case things change. These people (who incidentally include Doctor Guillotin, inventor of the clever machine) regard the cobbler's house as the perfect hiding-place, while Simon's real alibi is the king's son whom he keeps in a permanent drunken stupor. One of Simon's powerful protectors is Danton—himself already under a cloud—who uses his house for the attempted seduction of a "Curious Countess," only to be interrupted by the visit of Saint-Just and Robespierre. The ensuing confrontation is perhaps the most dramatic scene in the play, though Páskándi's intentions remain unclear: is it Danton's "false loyalty" to the revolution that he deplores, or is it Robespierre's "false logic" which through the idolization of an abstract People leads to his isolation from real people? Perhaps both; but Danton's exuberant curses evoke more sympathy. The most pathetic figure in the play is clearly Simon himself: "he didn't learn politics but he forgot his craft," complains his wife. He is killed at the end of the play; but this cannot strike us as a climax after Thermidor, which happens almost unnoticed somewhere off stage in a third act which is somewhat disappointing. Even if we ignore the political dilemma implicit in Páskándi's play (is it better to be an onlooker rather than a player in the game of history?), *The Hiding Place* is still worthy of attention, for it gives an insight into human behaviour under extraordinary conditions, at the same time demonstrating the all-pervading nature of political terror.

Complex questions of political theory and revolutionary practice were raised by Gyula Hernádi in *Falanszter* (*Phalanstery*), a three-act play first staged at Pécs in 1972. Hernádi's name is widely known: he is Jancsó's idiosyncratic script writer, and also a pioneering, though often oddly elusive, author of experimental novels. In *Falanszter* he concentrates on the dramatic break up of a phalanstery, a Utopian community built on a Fourierist blueprint in the nineteenth century somewhere in Tennessee. Hernádi had probably read the story of Brook Farm (one of his characters is called Brisbane in the play) and other American Utopian communities. As in the film *Confrontations,* he synthesised diverse elements in his plot. His community breaks up after five years of existence and Hernádi traces the reasons for its failure back to a number of antagonisms, the most important of which is the implacable hostility of the local farmers. They strongly object to a community which is not merely preaching "lawlessness" and is living "in sin" but also gives shelter to runaway slaves. Their hostility is shared by the State administration, which investigates the circumstances of a murder case and singles out a runaway black as its main suspect. Another conflict, with even graver consequences, is shaping in front of our eyes between the "revolutionary idealists" and the "puritan empiricists" within the leadership of the community. The tragic disintegration of the phalanstery demonstrates the failure of the idealists to change human nature radically and achieve economic success *and* a maximum of individual freedom at the same time; though the motivation of Considerant—the idealist murderer in the play—is not entirely credible, Hernádi's play has a gripping plot; it is entirely relevant to the contemporary situation, to the world-wide search of young people for a meaningful and "organic" way of life. The author is certainly aware of this; while sympathetic towards the Utopian zeal of his more revolutionary heroes, he is rather pessimistic about the outcome of their social experiments which, if we understand him correctly, are destined to founder on a combination of human weakness and strong social inhibitions.

The three plays discussed above are all historical in one sense, but they also make unmistakeable references to the continuing relevance of certain problems in our own epoch. The same is true for Gyula Illyés' latest drama *Testvérek (Brothers)*. Illyés is a poet of international reputation and a prolific playwright; in his last but one historical play, he dramatized the siege of Montségur, the last fortress of the Cathar community in Southern France, the extermination of the "heretic" Cathars having been closest to medieval genocide. With *Testvérek* Illyés returned to Hungarian history, to an event which in 1514 foreshadowed the crucial defeat of Hungarian forces under the onslaught of the Ottoman Turks. The theme of his new play is the Dózsa revolt, the greatest *jacquerie* in Hungarian history, led by a Sekler nobleman. Illyés had already written one play on György Dózsa (in 1954) where he presented the leader of the crusaders-turned-peasant rebels as a man with a "national" mission impervious to the radical millenarianism of some of his followers. This first Dózsa was certainly idealized, not so much to fit Marxist as Hungarian national preconceptions and expectations. *Testvérek* is therefore Illyés' self-corrective variant of an old theme, with significant differences in the interpretation of György Dózsa's character. The "peasant king" is now seen as a strong Renaissance individual, whose pride and personal ambition played a not unimportant role in his accepting the leadership of the crusade which was turned against the lords once the Archbishop's order was revoked. This new Dózsa is an ambitious military leader, no prophet or ideologist but a man of action. Illyés creates a counterbalance to him in the figure of his brother Gergely, a former student of Cracow University who is an intellectual moralist by temperament. Gergely questions the necessity of rash engagement, points out the dangers of arbitrarily used power, and denounces political extremism as counterproductive to useful social action. If György stands for revolutionary action, Gergely represents the humanistic ideals of social liberation; the debate between the two brothers can be summed up as the verbal expression of "the schizophrenic condition of the revolution." Gergely's tragedy lies in his personal loyalty to his brother, though he has been constantly advising moderation. After the decisive battle at Temesvár he is captured and executed together with György.

Brothers is not the first dramatic parable by Illyés on the corrupting effects of power—his earlier *Kegyenc (The Minion)* had tackled a similar problem, in the context of imperial Rome. None the less, never before has he so clearly denounced violence committed in the name of whatever creed or ideology. His current influence and reputation in Hungary is very great, but it is hard to say whether his views are shared by all or his warning unheeded. Perhaps a message of this kind is already too vague, too general for the younger generation which seems to find absurd and grotesque plays more relevant to its own situation than even the most eloquent poetic voice of old-fashioned humanism. As for the kind of political theatre represented by Sándor Fekete or Hernádi, certainly it is closer to the heartbeat of our times than Illyés' historical drama. So far it has been drawing its themes from the remote past. Still, neither the French Revolution, nor the fate of a Utopian community

in the United States is near enough in time to involve the audience completely. At this point it is hard to say just where the limits of experimentation lie in this particular genre, but it is unlikely that the political theatre can develop much further without raising at least some problems of recent Hungarian history. If the present political climate does not change dramatically we may expect some bolder and more outspoken theatrical attempts at "national self-analysis" in coming years. (pp. 89-99)

> George Gömöri, "New Developments in the Hungarian Drama," in MOSAIC: A Journal for the Comparative Study of Literature and Ideas, Special Issue: The Eastern European Imagination in Literature, Vol. VI, No. 4, Summer, 1973, pp. 89-99.

ADDITIONAL BIBLIOGRAPHY

Cushing, G. F. Introduction to *Hungarian Prose and Verse*, edited by G. F. Cushing, pp. xi-xxxvi. London: Athlone Press, 1956.
  Concise survey of prominent literary figures from 1800 through the 1950s.

———. "Problems of Hungarian Literary Criticism." *The Slavonic and East European Review* 40 (1961-62): 341-55.
  Analyzes nationalism as the predominant characteristic of Hungarian literature.

Demaitre, Ann. "The Hungarian Shores of Realism." *Comparative Literature Studies* I, No. 4 (1964): 311-23.
  Recounts the debate that arose in Hungary after the death of Joseph Stalin between "the supporters of Marxist-Leninist literary orthodoxy and the advocates of an ideologically unobjectionable but more flexible interpretation of Marxist theories on literature and art."

Duczyńska, Ilona. Introduction to *The Plough and the Pen*, edited by Ilona Duczyńska and Karl Polanyi, pp. 17-29. London: Peter Owen, 1963.
  Details the history of the Populist movement in Hungarian literature.

"Kádár's Latest Offensive: Hungary's Populist Writers." *East Europe* 8, No. 2 (February 1959): 32-41, 57.
  Presents the history of Populism and the campaign by the Kádár government against Populist writers.

Fejtö, Francois. "The Crisis in Communism: The Revolt of the Hungarian Writers." *Partisan Review* XXIV, No. 1 (Winter 1957): 71-83.
  Relates the increasing conflict between Hungarian intellectuals and the Communist government in the years preceding the 1956 revolution.

Gömöri, George. *Polish and Hungarian Poetry, 1945 to 1956*. Oxford: Clarendon Press, 1966, 266 p.
  Examines the relationship of poetry to social and political developments in Hungary and Poland in the decade following World War II.

———. "Hungarian Literature." In *World Literature since 1945*, edited by Ivar Ivask and Gero von Wilpert, pp. 357-71. New York: Frederick Ungar Publishing, 1973.
  Surveys Hungarian literature from World War II to 1970.

Hegedüs, Adam. "Studies in Modern Hungarian Literature." *The Slavonic Review* X, No. 29 (December 1931): 293-300.
  Discusses the works of Endre Ady and other prominent twentieth-century authors.

Hungarian Short Stories. London: Oxford University Press, 1967, 432 p.

Short stories by twenty-two authors of the nineteenth and twentieth centuries.

"AB: Hungary's Independent Publisher." *Index on Censorship* 12, No. 2 (April 1983): 5-7.

Interview with the founders of Hungary's leading unofficial publishing house.

Juhasz, William. "The Writer and Society." *East Europe* 12, No. 1 (January 1963): 8-15.

Focuses upon the social convictions of the generation of writers of working-class and peasant background that emerged in Hungary after World War II, examining in particular these authors' attitudes toward the past and the old social order.

———. "Books and Readers in Hungary." *East Europe* 12, No. 3 (March 1963): 2-5.

Discusses publishing houses, the translation of foreign works, book sales, popular literature, and party-sponsored literature.

———. "The Literature of Solitude." *East Europe* 12, No. 12 (December 1963): 18-22.

Analyzes the themes of solitude and suffering in Hungarian literature, stressing the social and political ramifications of solitude in a communist society.

Klaniczay, Tibor, ed. *A History of Hungarian Literature*. Budapest: Corvina Kiadó, 1982, 572 p.

Introduces the principal literary movements and figures from the Middle Ages to the twentieth century.

Kovács, József. "Comparative Literature in Hungary: Prospects and Possibilities." *Neohelicon* X, No. 2: 147-62.

Traces the history of comparative literature in Hungary.

Mottram, Eric. "Access to a Nation's Culture." *The New Hungarian Quarterly* XXV, No. 95 (Autumn 1984): 87-9.

Tribute to the *New Hungarian Quarterly* on its twenty-fifth anniversary.

Ray, David, ed. *From the Hungarian Revolution*. Ithaca, N.Y.: Cornell University Press, 1966, 186 p.

Poems by the Hungarian authors most closely associated with the revolution of 1956; also includes several poems by Americans writing on the subject of the revolution.

Reményi, Joseph. "Recent Hungarian Literature." *The Hungarian Quarterly* II, No. 1 (Autumn 1936): 142-51.

Discusses the difficulty of translating Hungarian into other European languages and assesses the state of contemporary Hungarian literature, reviewing recent publications of poetry and fiction.

———. *Hungarian Writers and Literature*. New Brunswick, N.J.: Rutgers University Press, 1964, 512 p.

Reprints essays originally published in American, British, French, and Italian scholarly journals. Included are "Hungarian Writers and the Tragic Sense," "Modern Hungarian Literature in English Translation," "Hungarian Humor," and forty-two essays on individual authors of the nineteenth and twentieth centuries.

Sanders, Ivan. "Symbolist and Decadent Elements in Early Twentieth-Century Hungarian Drama." *Canadian-American Review of Hungarian Studies* 4, No. 1 (Spring 1977): 23-42.

Analyzes elements of Hungarian drama inspired by French Symbolism and Decadence, attempting in particular "to isolate certain thematic and stylistic traits . . . which reflect an awareness of the Mallarméan-Maeterlinckian notion of an internalized, 'detheatricalized,' evocative theater."

Tezla, Albert. *Hungarian Authors: A Bibliographical Handbook*. Cambridge, Mass.: Belknap Press, 1970, 792 p.

Attempts to present "a complete record of first editions, provides [an] extensive list of later editions, and notes the most important bibliographical, biographical, and critical materials for each of the 162 authors included."

Vajda, Miklós, ed. *Modern Hungarian Poetry*. New York: Columbia University Press, 1977, 286 p.

Contains poems by forty-one twentieth-century poets.

Whitney, Arthur H. "Synaesthesia in Twentieth-Century Hungarian Poetry." *The Slavonic and East European Review* 30 (1951-52): 444-64.

Detailed analysis of synesthesia in the works of Endre Ady, Mihály Babits, Gyula Illyés, Attila József, Lajos Kassák, Dezső Kosztolányi, and Arpád Tóth.

The Russian Thaw

INTRODUCTION

The Bolshevik Revolution of 1917 brought radical changes to Russian literature, as to all aspects of Russian life. Under the Marxist-Leninist theory by which the new Soviet state was governed, literature was regarded as a weapon in the class struggle between the proletariat and the bourgeoisie; as a result, freedom of expression in literature was considered subordinate to political concerns. In the years since the Revolution, successive Soviet leaders have consistently adhered to this basic principle; however, the actual degree to which literature has been forced to conform to governmental regulations, and the nature of those regulations, has fluctuated widely. The following entry concerns a period of liberalization in Russian intellectual life that occurred between 1953 and 1963, commonly known as the Russian Thaw.

Between 1917 and 1921 the Soviet Union was ravaged by civil war and famine, and few works of literature were published. The period of relative economic and political stability that followed, however, brought a resurgence of the modernist movement that had revolutionized the Russian literary world in the decade preceding World War I. Literary groups proliferated and vied for artistic hegemony, with authors engaging in heated public debates over the function of art and the artist in postrevolutionary society. Although works openly hostile to communism were censored, and proletarian literature was actively supported by the government, officials encouraged independence and diversity, resisting efforts of various radical and proletarian groups to secure governmental endorsement for their particular doctrines. As a result, works were published by writers of widely divergent political philosophies. These ranged from such groups as the Futurists, who pledged their unconditional support to the new regime, to the large number of writers grouped under the term "fellow travelers," who, although sympathetic to communism, insisted upon artistic and ideological independence, including the right to criticize the government.

This officially sanctioned diversity came to an end in 1928, when literature was placed under the supervision of the Central Committee for Literary Affairs, a government council that dictated to publishers which literary topics and styles were to be encouraged from Soviet authors. Four years later, independent writers' groups were disbanded and the Union of Soviet Writers was formed, with membership a prerequisite for publication. Thereafter it became increasingly difficult, and soon impossible, to publish anything that was not supportive of the Soviet system. Between 1932 and 1934, through a series of proclamations and resolutions, the government sanctioned an official literary doctrine called socialist realism, which has dominated the development of Soviet literature since that time. Socialist realism requires that literature function as an educational and propagandistic tool embodying three qualities: *partiinost,* or "party spirit," an enthusiastic and uncritical support of Communist Party policies; *narodnost,* or the use of literary forms meaningful to the masses; and *ideinost,* or the promulgation of the proletarian point of view. The doctrine prohibits all formalistic experimentation, calling upon writers to affirm the social order of Soviet communism in the realistic style of the great classics of nineteenth-century Russian literature. The application of this doctrine produced a body of works that typically utilize formulaic plots depicting heroic members of the communist proletariat engaged in struggle with the evil forces of capitalism—which are invariably defeated. Throughout the 1930s Soviet Premier Joseph Stalin continued to increase governmental control in all areas of Soviet life. He achieved this in part through massive purges, in which thousands of Soviet citizens, including many of the best writers of the era, were arrested for real or alleged ideological dissidence and executed or exiled to Siberia.

With the onset of World War II, the government sought to utilize literature as a weapon in the war effort, and state-imposed controls on literature were briefly relaxed. However, most Russian writers were caught up in the patriotic fervor of wartime and wrote little that did not conform to the nationalistic tenor of socialist realism. Following the war, the Soviet government took its most unequivocal steps toward total control of all aspects of Soviet intellectual and artistic life. Directed by Party spokesman Andrei Zhdanov (and therefore known as the *zhdanovshchina*), this campaign of repression was initiated by a resolution of August 1946, in which the journals *Zvezda* and *Leningrad* were condemned for publishing "ideologically harmful" literature. Singled out for criticism were authors Mikhail Zoshchenko and Anna Akhmatova, whose writings were denounced for embodying everything that should be abolished from a true Soviet literature: self-absorption, religious ideas, immorality, a regard for Western values, and Formalism—in Soviet jargon a blanket term of condemnation for any modern literary movements, such as Imagism, Symbolism, and Futurism, that originated in the decadent West and did not have specific Soviet application. This condemnation quickly grew into a torrent of abuse directed at authors in all areas of literature, and eventually spread to the theater, cinema, music, and science. The objects of Zhdanov's attacks were forced into public recantations of their works, and rigid restrictions were applied to the publication of new writing.

Stalin's death in 1953 brought an immediate relaxation of ideological control. Over the next decade, many of the excesses of Stalin's reign were openly acknowledged and repudiated by his successor, Nikita Khrushchev, and intellectual freedom in the Soviet Union reached its highest level since the 1920s. This period became known as the "Thaw," after a novel of that name by Ilya Ehrenburg that clearly reflected the liberal spirit of the era. Renewed excitement and vitality permeated the literary world, as formal experimentation gained limited acceptance and works treating previously forbidden themes were allowed publication; for the first time in twenty-five years, authors actively criticized hypocrisy and corruption in the Soviet government and provided realistic examinations of Soviet life. Literary theory again became a subject of public debate, with liberal writers and theorists openly opposing the Stalinists. The urgency and optimism of the period were best expressed in poetry, which became the most important vehicle of literary expression during the Thaw; poets became popular heroes, giving poetry readings to crowds numbering in the thousands.

In addition, works by previously proscribed authors from the West were translated into Russian, and many Russian writers whose works had been banned under Stalin were "rehabilitated," that is, their writings were republished or allowed publication for the first time.

Critics often refer to the "three Thaws," as the post-Stalin liberalization process followed a recurrent pattern of increasing artistic freedom cut short by a brief period of reaction. The end of the third and final Thaw coincided with Khrushchev's fall from power in the early 1960s. Many critics mark the end of the period with the 1963 trial of poet Joseph Brodsky, who was convicted of "parasitism" and exiled to Siberia, signaling a return to the repressive tactics of the Stalin era. The following entry presents commentary on the principal issues, figures, and works of the period of Soviet intellectual freedom between 1953 and 1963.

LITERARY HISTORY OF THE PERIOD

MARC SLONIM

[Slonim was a Russian-born American critic who wrote extensively on Russian literature. In the following essay he presents a history of the Thaw, tracing developments in Soviet literature and literary politics from the time of Stalin's death in 1953 through the early 1960s.]

Stalin's death on March 5, 1953, put an end to a regime of terror and opened a new era in the history of the Soviet Union. From that turning point the country developed under the banner of de-Stalinization—hidden in 1953, but more or less apparent in the next two years. Following the Twentieth Congress of the Party in 1956, de-Stalinization was intensified, especially after 1958 when Khrushchev consolidated his dominant position as the head of the government and the Party. Although the Russian Communists are reluctant to admit it, in these years, between 1953 and 1963, Soviet social, economic, political, and cultural life underwent a thorough revision. This process, of course, was far from smooth. The return to legality which helped to dispel the atmosphere of fear and suspicion resulted in the execution of Beria and other chiefs of the secret police. The rise and fall of Malenkov, Bulganin, Molotov, and many old-guard dignitaries were episodes in the furious fights and Byzantine intrigues among the rulers. The dismissal of 750,000 officials, mentioned by Khrushchev at the Twentieth Congress, and the reforms in the economy provoked strong opposition and discontent. And various dramatic events after Khrushchev's ascension to power indicated that the struggle between the revisionists and the Stalinists, or between the liberals and the conservatives, as the West called it, was actually a continuing contest between opposing factions. Each used technologists, professionals, intellectuals, and artists as allies or scapegoats in personal and political vendettas. An interminable series of moves and countermoves, of compromises, victories, and defeats accounts for the alternation of progress and reaction in all areas of Soviet life and particularly in literature and the arts. What happened in the community of writers in the decade following Stalin's demise corresponded to the changes within the Party and the government. Literature mirrored the general situation, offering a disturbing picture of thaw and freeze, as it was usually labeled in the Western press. The question was whether all these turns and oscillations pointed

toward a growth of artistic independence and a release of controls. In the following decade, particularly after the Soviet intervention of 1956-58 in Hungary, the fragility of great expectations and exaggerated hopes became rather clear: the basic structure of the regime did not change, and what prevailed were minor concessions and cautious reforms.

The effects of Stalin's passing were felt almost immediately: numerous writers, released from prisons and concentration camps, returned home; censors' attitudes became less rigorous; forbidden themes made a timid appearance in the press; discussions flared up in writers' gatherings; for the first time in many years well-known artists came out with bold statements. "Creative problems cannot be solved by bureaucratic methods," declared Aram Khachaturian, the composer. Ehrenburg reminded his readers in the October issue of *Znamia* (*The Banner*) that "in art statistics do not play the same role as in industry" and that Chekhov and Gorky wrote what and when they pleased without being prodded by functionaries and Writers' Unions. From all parts came evidence of the writers' dissatisfaction with the present state of affairs and with current literary production.

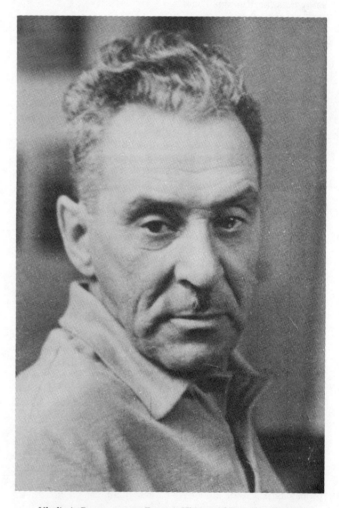

Vladimir Pomerantsev. From A History of Post-War Soviet Writing: The Literature of Moral Opposition, *by Grigori Svirski. Translated and edited by Robert Dessaix and Michael Ulman. Ardis, 1981. Reprinted by permission of Ardis Publishers.*

A great stir was caused by Vladimir Pomerantsev's article in the monthly *Novy Mir* of December 1953. It stated in plain words that Soviet literature lacked honesty and sincerity, that most contemporary works resembled gramophone records and repeated worn-out slogans *ad infinitum* without ever trying to represent truth and real life. "Even about love they talk as if they were making speeches in a public meeting," complained Pomerantsev. And he rebuked the foes of "subjectivity": "The history of literature shows that writers made confessions and not only sermons." In the summer of 1953 Olga Bergholz claimed in her *A Talk About Lyricism* that poetry is impossible without the author's self-expression as an individual. Excerpts from Tvardovsky's new poem "Afar Farther Yet" [also translated as "Distance beyond Distance"], although written in traditional style, had "liberal" overtones. *Volga Mother River* by Fyodor Panfyorov (1896-1960), serialized in August-September, contained a direct assault on bureaucracy and the "stultified" Party bosses who erected pompous public buildings instead of housing for the poor: "Forget about planning and think of people's needs," exclaims the hero of the novel. Panova's *The Seasons* pictured a member of the Communist upper crust as an egoist and profiteer driven to suicide by his own misdeeds; it also showed the moral confusion of Soviet youth and the rift between fathers and sons. And to climax all these signs of change, a new production of *The Bathhouse* by Mayakovsky was given on December 6 in the Moscow Theater of Satire, after an absence of a quarter of a century.

The new year 1954 came forth in an atmosphere of violent clashes between the "liberals" and the "conservatives." The latter, still occupying all the strategic administrative positions, opened fire against Pomerantsev, Panfyorov, and Ovechkin—the latter's *Weekdays of a District* being an unadorned report on the defects and miseries of provincial and village life. But all the efforts of the Stalinists to turn the clock back often proved to be ineffective.

The liberal campaign against "red tape," for example, continued with increasing zest, particularly in a number of new plays acclaimed by the public. *The Guests* by Leonid Zorin showed the moral decline of the bureaucrats: old Kirpitchev is an idealist and an upright revolutionary; his son Pyotr is a power-conscious "boss," remote from the people, a typical member of a reigning caste; and his grandchild is a "daddy's son," the idle and smug offspring of an upstart generation. After two performances the play was suspended. But then came another literary sensation: in May the magazine *Znamia* printed the first part of *The Thaw* by Ehrenburg (the second part came out in April 1956), and the title of this short novel served as the emblem of the whole period. Though far from being a masterpiece, it was avidly read by thousands and thousands because it mirrored their hopes for a milder climate after long years of tyranny. Readers got so enthusiastic about it that when it was released in book form on September 23, by the evening of that day all copies were sold out in Moscow.

Instead of focusing its attention on industrial and agricultural achievements, *The Thaw* deals with problems of love and personal happiness. The common trait of several couples of men and women in the novel is their inability to communicate and their reluctance to yield to their instinctual drives. Products of an era of constraint and repression, they all seem frozen, afraid of becoming frank and spontaneous. The disappearance of taboos and prohibitions, and the sentimental breakthrough of a warped and unhappy Soviet people represent figuratively the unfreezing of Russia. No less symbolic is the drama of Pukhov,

a conformist painter who has won money and recognition for his canvasses of smiling pioneers and joyful cow girls. When he encounters Saburov, a true creator who is starving in obscurity, he understands his own failure. The opposition of Pukhov's artificial potboilers to Saburov's deeply felt, semi-clandestine art was interpreted by the readers as a request for a complete revision of accepted aesthetic dogma. Other topical elements added to the popularity of *The Thaw:* the famous "doctor's plot" engineered by the secret police; the old men returning home after fifteen years in prison and exile; the creeping anti-Semitism, and various other indignities and wrongdoings. The topical and political impact of the novel apparently redeemed its obvious literary shortcomings: it lacked any depth and originality of characterization, its structure was loose, and its style journalistic, with the sharp black and white strokes so typical of Ehrenburg; but as a novel of ideological importance within a specific historical context, it remains a document of the period, and evidence of the turmoil Russia was passing through in the middle 'fifties.

The Stalinists, who were still strong in the Party hierarchy and in literary organizations, launched a counter-offensive the moment *The Thaw* (and Pasternak's poems) was published. In May Surkov, the poet and functionary, attacked Pomerantsev in *Pravda* for his "anti-Marxian revision of basic principles and Party decisions of 1946-1948." In other words, the diehards continued to defend Zhdanovism. Panfyorov was dismissed from the editorial board of *October* in June, and Tvardovsky from that of *Novy Mir* in August (for having published "harmful critical articles by Abramov, Shcheglov, and Lifshitz"). Four novelists and playwrights, including Nikolay Virta, were expelled from the Union of Soviet Writers; Ehrenburg. Pomerantsev, Panova, and Zoshchenko got "public reprimands," and Victor Mokrousov was thrown out of the Composers' Union "because of his careless attitude toward creative work." These restrictive measures were aimed at curbing the growing unrest of the intellectuals on the eve of the Second Congress of Soviet Writers, scheduled for December 1954, the first such reunion in twenty years. This fact alone was of tremendous importance, and the solemn reception offered by the government to the delegates, indicated the Kremlin's desire to establish a better relationship with the "engineers of human souls."

But of much greater significance was what the debates of the Congress revealed to participants and observers. Like all Soviet public gatherings it followed the inevitable ritual—invocation of Lenin, recitation of the Communist credo, sermons by the high priests of the state religion, and ecclesiastic jargon of the celebrants. But what went on behind this official facade showed confusion, discontent, and the rumbling of an approaching thunderstorm. Once given the opportunity to speak up, even within imposed limits, delegates poured out an amazing amount of complaints and "self-criticism." "Writers do not and cannot think all in the same manner," said Marin Franicevich, the guest from Yugoslavia. Several themes prevailed in the ten days' discussions. There was an almost unanimous condemnation of bureaucratic methods in literature. "Our Union of Soviet Writers," said Ketlinskaya, "resembles a ministry, with this difference that at the head of it are placed poets and novelists who have no administrative abilities and dream with nostalgia of their writing desks." And Ovechkin proposed fewer meetings on how to study life and how to write, more actual living and writing. No less unequivocal was the charge against the insincerity and the artistic poverty of current fiction. Caution prevented the speakers from criticizing the sacred theories of educational art and socialist realism, but they turned their guns on the discrepancy between the growth of the reading audiences and the inadequacy of the literary nourishment offered to them. In 1954 the USSR printed 231 million copies of fiction, declared one of the "revisionists," and had 380,000 libraries; the love of reading was universal, first printings of novels were sold out in a week—and what did readers find in all this avalanche of printed matter? "Communal apartments painted in gold, workshops in factories looking like laboratories, *kolkhoze* clubs resembling palatial mansions—a world of stage properties, of tinsel trinkets inhabited by primitives or model children made of wax"—this was Ehrenburg's description of contemporary literature. And the poet Lugovskoy stigmatized raw, uncouth works, hailed by the critics and honored by state awards, but essentially false or insignificant (Simonov called them "pastry-shop fabrications"). "Literature must return to great human problems," said Lugovskoy. "I am speaking of high and eternal things common to every man. The tragedy of jealousy and betrayal, disappointments in love and friendships, grief over the loss of dear ones—all this exists for us as for all human beings. . . . Where is it in our fiction? On our path we find the black shadows of stereotypes, coldness, incontestable thousandfold repeated ideas, all sorts of dull rot."

When it came to drafting final resolutions, such heretical voices were of course drowned in the usual babble of Communist phraseology, yet the writers did say that literature was lagging behind the impetuous development of Soviet society, that it did not satisfy the rapidly growing spiritual needs of the readers, that it did not create significant images of its contemporaries, and that many of its works ignored the contradictions and the difficulties of the times.

The writers pleaded for an expansion of the "permissible," for more latitude in the choice of themes and their treatment, and for less rigidity in official controls. In a way the Congress served as a catalyst. It is true that it did not weaken the Party's decision to maintain its hold over literature and to leave intact the organizational structure of the Union of Soviet Writers. But, on the other hand, the writers were assured that in the future they would be treated with more understanding, that their errors would not be considered crimes against the state, that the threat of arrests and repressions was definitively over, and that literature would henceforth be free to "present conflicts and contradictions that still exist in Soviet life." Certain facts seemed to confirm this attitude of the administration: Tvardovsky, Panova, Grossman, and other writers who had previously been reprimanded, were elected to the new Executive Board of the Union; Anna Akhmatova was re-instated as a member of the Union and ostensibly took part in the proceedings of the Congress. But the aftermath of the Congress was even more spectacular. The fall of Malenkov, the growth of the de-Stalinization movement, the humanization of the regime were felt throughout the country. In literature the speech by Mikhail Sholokhov at the Twentieth Congress of the Communist Party, published in *Pravda*, February 21, 1956, had a special impact. The honored dean of Soviet letters asked the delegates not to attach great importance to figures: the fact that the Union of Soviet Writers comprised "3773 members armed with pens should neither frighten nor rejoice the Congress," because the membership included a large number of "dead souls." And the high number of books printed in the last years should not be taken as proof of the great achievements of Soviet literature. "We must recognize," said Sholokhov, "that during the last twenty years we had but a handful of good, intelligent books, and huge piles of gray trash." He attributed this dearth to the alienation of the writers from life and the masses. But his main attack was against the Union of Soviet Writers. The latter, Sholokhov claimed, had been conceived as a creative collective but degenerated into an administrative organization, directed by Alexander Fadeyev, a power-hungry secretary general, who did everything except help writers to write. "Why nobody told him during the last fifteen years that a Writers' Union is not a military unit and certainly not a penal colony and that no writer wants to stand 'at attention' in front of Fadeyev, the general secretary?" "Prose writers did not go to Fadeyev to learn how to write because each of them had his own handwriting, his vision of the world, his style, and Fadeyev could not be and is not an infallible artistic authority." In the same way poets do not come to Surkov, the new secretary, to ask him how to write poetry because "he fails to understand that an orchestra is composed not only of drums and percussion instruments. . . . We do not need such literary leaders to whom none of their colleagues ever come to solve creative problems."

Among Sholokhov's many cutting remarks one must have hit Fadeyev most painfully: "Neither as secretary general nor as a writer has he done anything in the last fifteen years." Fadeyev the bureaucrat held dictatorial power over literature, but Fadeyev the writer must have realized that by obeying orders from the Kremlin and revising his *The Young Guard* he had mutilated the work and betrayed himself. After Stalin's death came his downfall as a Party functionary (he was demoted from a full fledged member of the Central Committee to that of a candidate). But loss of rank and addiction to the bottle were not the only causes of Fadeyev's disintegration. He was obsessed with a thousand doubts. Had he been right in following Stalin, in trying to regiment writers, in having participated in all the purges of the intellectuals? Now when the secret archives were dug up, the rumors went around Moscow that there were documents proving Fadeyev's role as a denunciator of Babel and Kirshon, probably of other writers. His whole life's work was challenged, and at the same time he, the man who wrote so many resolutions and instructions, was incapable now of writing a good story. In a moment of repentance and disgust, a bullet appeared to Fadeyev preferable to a life of deceit.

Fadeyev's suicide on May 13, 1956, rocked literary circles all over Russia but no explanation of his tragedy, except "illness," was ever given in the press, and standard text books (such as the third volume of the semi-official *History of Soviet Literature,* published in 1961) simply record that "he died" on such and such a date.

The Twentieth Congress of the All Union Communist Party and the "secret" speech by Khrushchev which gave a final consecration to de-Stalinization, and soon became known in the USSR and abroad, served to encourage Russian writers. A great many works published in the second half of the 'fifties were interesting and alive. Even though they were not masterpieces, they compared favorably with the mass production of the Zhdanovism era.

One of the best works was *In the Home Town,* a 1954 novel by Victor Nekrassov. Its hero, a young officer, returns from the front to find his wife with another man. His health is poor, he wanders amidst the ruins of a severely damaged city looking for a job, suffers from solitude and misery, is compelled to stay for a long while in the hospital, and then tries to re-adjust himself to civilian life. There is hardly any plot in this narrative, which tells of relations between ordinary people who all have their secret or manifest dramas, who lack food and fuel, but who crave above all human warmth, kindness, communication, and the modest niceties of existence. How different was this well written tale with its lyrical passages and muted tone, with its realistic portrayal of average Soviet men and women and their daily problems, from the "epics on heroes" made to measure a few years before. The Communist critics frowned at such a book, but readers refused to listen to them and brought the circulation of *In the Home Town* to one and a half million copies.

The main event of 1955 was the posthumous rehabilitation of writers who had been purged under Stalin and whose works and even names were proscribed for many years. The list included not only Babel, Bulgakov, Meyerhold, Vesyoly, Kirshon (executed in 1937 as a "Trotskyite"), but also members of The Pass, such as Ivan Katayev; Smithy poets, such as Kirilov, Gerasimov, Bakhmetiev; victims of the anti-Jewish campaign, such as Golodny and Bergelson (executed in 1952); and numerous Communist writers who were either killed or jailed during the trials and purges of the late 1930's, such as Koltsov, Yasensky, Serebriakova, and others. What was previously known only to a limited number of initiated through whispers and rumors was now revealed in the press. No details, however, were given about the fate of the martyrs: had they been shot, hanged, beaten to death, or had they died in prison and penal colonies? Of what had they been accused, had they been tried, what were the circumstances of their "elimination"? The reports on the writers who had perished offered only intimations, hints, euphemistic phrases which simply hid or veiled the horrifying truth.

In the meantime, rehabilitation served the purpose of the "posthumous homecoming." Special editorial boards were created

Victor Nekrasov.

for the publication of the "literary heritage of the deceased," and a series of their works appeared in new printings. (There were, however, significant exceptions, such as Pilnyak and Zamyatin, Mandelstam and Gumilev.) Bulgakov's plays were re-issued along with the poems of Pavel Vasiliev (1910-37) and novels by Artyom Vesyoly. Moreover, the stories by the expatriate Ivan Bunin, who always had strong admirers among Soviet authors (particularly Paustovsky, Lidin, Katayev), were offered to Soviet readers in large printings, with very mild expurgations. Other *émigré* writers who had died abroad (with the exception of Remizov and Zamyatin) were occasionally published in Soviet periodicals. Most spectacular was the official recognition of Dostoevsky as a great Russian classic, and the publication of his collected works for the 75th anniversary of his death. The living were also reinstated: Olesha returned to Moscow from Central Asia, Zabolotsky was published again, and Anna Akhmatova was hailed in the Literary Gazette as a "talented and noble creator of Russian poetry."

The rehabilitation of writers who had been banned since the 1920's and 1930's raised the problem of their place in Russian letters, and this, naturally, provoked a debate on the true evaluation of a period which the dogmatists rejected merely as an obnoxious survival of the Tsarist-capitalist tradition. In 1956, Simonov contended at the Moscow Congress of Teachers of Literature that the rehabilitation led logically to a revision of literary history; surveys of post-revolutionary prose and poetry could not ignore writers such as Babel, Olesha, Akhmatova, and others whose names had been hushed up for political reasons.

The "new look" in literature was also manifest in a changed attitude toward Western literature. Hemingway, whose works had been condemned for over fifteen years, made a comeback with *The Old Man and the Sea,* and translations of other American and European novelists were promised by *Foreign Literature,* a newly established monthly. Other new magazines (*Neva, Youth*), diverse publishing enterprises, literary panels, informal gatherings, and public discussions of best-sellers which attracted thousands of listeners, as well as a constantly increasing number of novels, tales, and poems by young authors, were among the signs of a cultural revival. An event of great resonance was the miscellany *Literary Moscow.* In its first volume it published poems by Akhmatova and Pasternak's essay on translating Shakespeare. The second volume contained poems by Marina Tsvetayeva, the great *émigré* poet who had returned to the USSR in 1939 and committed suicide in 1941. There were also stories conceived in the spirit of critical realism and several daring essays. In one of them the playwright Alexander Kron wrote: "a writer is an inventor, he works for the future, but a bent head cannot look forward." But the third volume of *Literary Moscow* never saw the light.

There is no doubt that by 1955 a large part of Soviet literature was breaking away from the official mold. The changes were wide-ranging and various. There was greater diversity of style, more inventiveness in plot, more freedom in the unfolding of a story. Such dangerous subjects as personal tragedies brought on by Stalinist terror were now treated. Since 1955-56 Soviet novels became populated by innocently condemned Communists, by non-Party convicts returning from exile, and by daughters and sons whose parents one night had been taken away for ever by the secret police. From *The Running Battle* by Galina Nikolayeva and *Not by Bread Alone* by Vladimir Dudintsev, to the novels of the 'sixties, such as *The Silence* by Yury Bondarev, *Kira Georghievna* by Victor Nekrassov,

The Living and the Dead by Konstantin Simonov, *The Wild Honey* by Leonid Pervomaysky—to mention only a few—the figure of the former inmate of a concentration camp or retrospective scenes of unjust, iniquitous arrests made their entry into Soviet fiction.

The general movement toward a critical representation of life was a reaction against the laudatory falsehoods and the "varnishings" of reality. Old and young writers competed with each other in exposing the concrete shortcomings of the system; only on rare occasions did their hints seem to touch the very foundations of the regime.

The main targets of this literature were the bureaucrats and the new ruling class, the Soviet aristocrats who had denatured the very ideals of the Revolution. Some short stories on this subject were so explicit that they obtained a huge success not commensurate perhaps with their artistic worth. In "Personal Opinion" Daniil Granin portrayed a Soviet engineer, the director of a research laboratory, who is afraid to form his own opinion; he is a coward and prefers to betray the truth rather than argue with his superiors and jeopardize his high position. "The Journey Home" by Nikolay Zhdanov depicted a high official of peasant extraction who, on a short and useless visit to his native village, is shocked by its poverty and deprivations, so leaves again in a hurry. The same theme is repeated in stories by Kazakov and other writers: the successful son or daughter returns home and feels the gulf between the city dwellers and the backward villagers who repeat Party slogans but live in primitive conditions. In "The Levers" by Alexander Yashin, *kolkhoze* administrators talk like human beings as soon as they are alone; they complain that Party bosses who come from the city keep on shouting "carry on" and are more interested in displaying high statistical indicators than in finding out how people live. The same men, however, themselves use the tired phraseology of the bosses as soon as they appear at a public meeting—because they are assigned the role of "levers" in the mechanism of the system. Yashin (1913-68) was also a master of lyrical prose, and his "Vologda Wedding," published in 1962, remains one of the most interesting descriptions of ancient rites and folklore in northern Russia.

The Twentieth Congress of the Party in February 1956 and the secret speech by Khrushchev, with his outright attack against Stalin, marked a watershed in the literature of social criticism. It reached its climax in the fall of that year when *Not by Bread Alone* by Vladimir Dudintsev (b. 1918) was serialized in *Novy Mir*. It did not rate very highly from a purely aesthetic standard; its structure was loose, its exposition was verbose, and its style was pedestrian, but it became a sensation and provoked riotous discussions and hundreds of articles. It was attacked and defended in special sessions of the Union of Soviet Writers, and it was talked about in Party councils and government meetings. Like *The Thaw* it articulated common moods and thoughts; it represented a whole movement within Soviet society. Khrushchev, in one of his speeches, dubbed Dudintsev "a calumniator who took a malicious joy in describing the negative side of Soviet life . . . in an unhealthy, tendentious, and obnoxious work." The leader failed, however, to explain why such a corrupt novel fascinated millions of readers and remained the focus of general attention for such a long time.

Not by Bread Alone has a complicated plot with twists and ramifications but its main theme is simple. It revolves around Lopatkin, a former physics teacher who became an inventor after the war and worked on a machine for the centrifugal casting of iron drainpipes. A single-minded lonely man, ob-

sessed by his project, he does not belong to the "gang," lacks the "right connections," and seems a dull nuisance to pedantic experts and ministry employees. His project is buried by red tape, while he is reduced to poverty and isolation. The only support he has comes from another defeated eccentric and from Nadia the wife of Drozdov, his chief enemy. At one point Lopatkin's invention interests the military, but this brings upon him the accusation of "divulging State secrets," he is arrested and sent to a concentration camp in the Arctic. His case is reviewed, however, thanks to an honest trial judge puzzled by some legal incongruities, and after Stalin's death Lopatkin returns to Moscow. He is rehabilitated, the army accepts his machine; yet all the functionaries who snubbed or crushed him are still around and Drozdov is about to become deputy minister. The evil is unpunished, the struggle goes on, and the "happy ending" is by no means a satisfactory and terminal solution.

Unlike other negative characters in Soviet fiction, Drozdov and the whole clique he represents are neither villains nor paid agents of American imperialism. They are Party members, solid citizens, and first-class business men. "I belong to the producers of material values," says Drozdov to Nadia who speaks about the importance of relationships among people: "matter comes first. Let us have things, we do not need to worry about relationships and then you will begin to hang little pictures and china plates on the walls." He dismisses all "ornaments," all superfluous "rubbish." He sees in Lopatkin one of those undisciplined idealists who are pitted against the collective, take fantasy for reality, and mumble "not by bread alone." Behind Drozdov stands a whole army of Party leaders, academicians, generals, experts, functionaries—all that "apparatus of the state" which has replaced the Old Guard of Communist intellectuals exterminated by Stalin. This officialdom consists of "monopolists," who have vested interests in the administration of the country, who form a sort of pale, a restricted area, and who curb mercilessly talented non-conformists such as Lopatkin.

By depicting Drozdov as the end result of the Communist regime, the novel goes beyond the "little defects of the mechanism." Within the limits of this kind of criticism permissible in the USSR, Dudintsev indirectly questions the whole system. At a discussion of the novel among Soviet writers Paustovsky declared that it signified the first round in the battle against the Drozdovs, "whom literature should fight until they are completely exterminated . . . the book expressed the anxiety we all feel about the moral aspect and purity of the Soviet man and our culture." The same critical spirit that made *Not by Bread Alone* so popular was in evidence in a steadily increasing number of stories and novels in the late 'fifties.

The rejection of the puritanism that was so typical of the previous period, formed another important trend in 1955-57. It colored most novels of social criticism. In *Not by Bread Alone* Lopatkin and Nadia, who leaves her husband, become lovers out of wedlock. In *The Running Battle* (1957), a very typical novel of the period, Galina Nikolayeva depicts the love affair between engineer Bakhirev, a married man and a Communist, and Tina, a young woman whose first husband has been "repressed." Their relations form a large part of the story which includes a great variety of material, from an impressive picture of Stalin's funeral, to the struggle between Bakhirev and Valgan, a factory director whose authoritarian ways have separated him from his comrades.

Family life, marriage and divorce, the deceptions and joys of love ceased to hover ashamedly in the background of Soviet fiction; they came boldly to the fore and were treated as extensively as the professional activities of heroes and heroines. Themes and figures completely ignored for twenty years suddenly erupted into novels and plays: there were illegitimate children, unfaithful wives and husbands, flirting young women, highly sexed men, and drinkers and gamblers. Personal problems, emotional conflicts, erotic troubles now took priority in numerous works. The success of such mediocre, rather dull novels as *Ivan Ivanovich* and its sequel, by Antonina Koptiayeva, or of *Elena* by Xenia Lvova, who alternated scenes of passion with quotations from Lenin, was due to the large role given to the private lives of their protagonists.

A heated debate was provoked by "A Long Conversation," a half-narrative poem by Paruayra Sevak, an Armenian poet, translated into Russian by Evgeny Evtushenko. It was a lyrical protest against Party interference in the intimate life of the hero, who has fallen in love with a married woman. The local Party organization tells the young man to stop, but he questions the right of the collective to make decisions in such matters. Finally his beloved comes to live with him—and he defends her action because her marriage was not based on real love. Many readers sided with the hero, others accused him of violating the very principles of Marxism, and an avalanche of enthusiastic or irate letters descended on the monthly that published the poem.

Nikolay Pogodin's drama *Petrarch's Sonnet* stirred up a similar controversy: it represented an aged Communist whose romantic love for a young girl is desecrated by the vulgar interventions of Party officials and the gossip and malice of "virtuous" citizens.

This more human and realistic approach to the problems of love and marriage was not by any means comparable to the freedom and bluntness with which they are treated in modern Western literature. It would be an exaggeration to say that Soviet fiction is the least erotic in the world, but the writers of the USSR prefer to ignore sex or just talk of it in a naïve and sentimental way: if they take it seriously they use allusions, symbols, and lines of dots. But the "unfreezing" of literature in the 1950's included not only love but all sorts of drives and emotions. In general, man's inner feelings were given more attention—hence the success of *The Turbulent Youth*, a romantic and psychological autobiography by Paustovsky, of *Serezha*, a delightful story of a child by Vera Panova, of *Probation* and *Cruelty* (in English, *Comrade Venka*) by Pavel Nilin, who raised problems of individual conscience in short novels that were alive with action. The tendency was to get away from dry rationalism, utilitarianism, and the whole negative attitude taken by "strong, dynamic, and scientifically oriented Communists" toward the "stuff and nonsense" of fantasy and intimate feelings. This explains why Semyon Kirsanov's long ballad "The Seven Days of the Week" was so widely read and discussed: in sharp satirical verse laced with mordant irony and thrusts that recalled Mayakovsky's manner, it told of an invention acclaimed by the Communist "organizational men"—the industrial production of hearts which could easily replace those in human breasts and eliminate the troublesome diversity and surprise of individual emotions.

Among the factors that seemed to indicate various changes in Russian letters of the 1960's, some hope was placed on encounters between Soviet and European writers in Venice, Zurich, and later in Rome, but all these meetings brought few satisfactory results and did not promote an end of Russia's cultural isolation. Translations of contemporary Western novelists and poets were avidly read, and though important authors were often submerged by inferior "representatives of progressive literature," in whom Communist critics tried to discover a counterpart to socialist realism, readers were quick to make the right choice. Of course, preference was given by Soviet publishing houses to American and European writers who were considered more or less safe ideologically—Theodore Dreiser for example—but large printings were also authorized of Sherwood Anderson, O. Henry, Steinbeck, Erskine Caldwell, G. B. Shaw, Richard Aldington, Galsworthy, Stefan Zweig, Thomas and Heinrich Mann, Saint-Exupery, Mauriac, Roger Martin du Gard, Sartre, Moravia, Levi, and many others. In some instances an author with no reputation at home would become a best-seller in the USSR for some special reasons (for example, the American Mitchell Wilson who writes about American physicists falling in love with Soviet women scientists). On the other hand, writers like Camus were not translated until the 1970's, and then mainly in periodicals, and Kafka's works appeared in a limited edition only in 1965.

In the theater, adaptations of stories by Stendhal, Balzac, Galsworthy, and Jack London alternated with plays by Shaw, Brecht, Lillian Hellman, and even Agatha Christie: *Dial M for Murder* and Christie's *The Witness for the Prosecution* were box-office hits in Moscow for two years. This is not surprising in a country where thrillers and detective stories are just tolerated, without being officially approved.

And, finally, the chief source of Western influence in Russia was the satellite countries, chiefly Poland and Hungary. The Russians may not have traveled extensively in Western Europe, but they did go very often to Poland, Hungary, Rumania, Czechoslovakia, Bulgaria, East Germany, and to a lesser extent to Yugoslavia. The impact of their contacts with poets, novelists, and artists of those countries was tremendous. Not only in private conversations, but in public conferences, congresses, and public discussions they were confronted with concepts that hailed creative freedom and unhampered search for new forms of expression. Even more shattering to the Russians was their hosts' low opinion of the theory and practice of socialist realism. The foreign visitors, who came to Russia from the "people's democracies," also brought with them forbidden books and ideas. All this sustained in the USSR a skeptical attitude toward the native brand of socialist realism.

In 1954, during the Second Congress of Soviet Writers, the definition of the official school was reduced to one sentence: "Socialist realism being the basic method of Soviet literature and literary criticism, requires from the artist a truthful, historically concrete representation of reality in its revolutionary development." The fact that the Congress dropped the embarrassing extension of this ambiguous formula, was of course, extremely significant but it did not help greatly. [In a footnote, the author explains: "This is what was judged superfluous by the Congress: 'Moreover, truthfulness and historical completeness of artistic representation must be combined with the task of ideological transformation and education of the working man in the spirit of socialism.' The ideas expressed in these requirements have never in fact been abandoned by the Communist Party in the USSR."] Simonov in a daring article (in the December issue of *Novy Mir*) recommended a revision of all the works published in the last decade, and criticized the very concept of the "Basic Method." An article by Netchenko in a specialist journal stated that 550 doctoral dissertations on

Soviet literature in the last decade were little more than padded newspaper articles and shed no light on the obscurities of socialist realism. Other rebels scorned the requirement of "truthful representation of reality." What criteria, they asked, were offered for judging the degree of this truthfulness—and who wanted a "false representation" anyway? What did all this rigmarole about historic concreteness and revolutionary development have to do with artistic accomplishment? And why is it that some words of Lenin in his "Party organization and Party literature," which belonged to a definite pre-revolutionary period and were written more than half a century ago, were not viewed now in their historical concreteness? Were they not applicable only to a given situation? Was it reasonable to proclaim them today as an unchangeable law? Some defenders of socialist realism emphasized its "particular content" and quoted again Lenin's words about "Party-mindedness." Others insisted that socialist realists possess a Communist outlook on reality and their creation was founded on a revolutionary, Marxist-Leninist approach to life. In this interpretation the stress was on the *Weltanschauung*, on the general philosophy of the writer, and not on his literary method. Since all Communist authors were supposed to have the same philosophy, not only did their works threaten to become terribly monotonous but the whole concept of socialist realism was rendered superfluous. This, by the way, was the argumentation of Soviet novelists such as Simonov and Ehrenburg (the latter wrote quite pertinently on the subject in his essay "Stendhal's Lessons"). Very close to them was the position of prominent European Communists. Georg Lucacz, the well-known Hungarian critic, expressed serious doubts about the Kremlin's cultural policy. He wanted socialism to become more humane and to favor free discussion. He disapproved of Soviet literature under Stalin and recognized that "the general public identified socialist realism with those mediocre mechanical works that Party critics praised to high heaven." Italian and French left-wing literati also attacked the intellectual ineptitudes and artistic failures of socialist realism. Never before was this "method" exposed in the West and in the USSR with such frankness, nor criticized with such energy. Whatever the Moscow press kept repeating in its declarations in the years 1955-58, and then again in the 1970's, the theory of socialist realism was dealt a mortal blow in Russia; and it never operated as a determining factor in the satellite countries of Europe or in Latin America (not even in Cuba). (pp. 320-37)

> *Marc Slonim, "The Thaw," in his* Soviet Russian Literature: Writers and Problems 1917-1977, *second revised edition, Oxford University Press, 1977, pp. 320-37.*

VICTOR ERLICH

[*Erlich is a Russian émigré educator and critic who has written extensively on Russian literature. In the following excerpt from an essay written in 1964, he examines works by the most prominent authors of the Thaw and discusses political reaction to their writings. In particular, he notes the decline in official tolerance of artistic experimentation and summarizes the moral effect of the period of the Thaw.*]

Writing about recent Soviet literature is a hazardous occupation. A Western chronicler of the post-Stalin literary ferment is as likely to overestimate an ephemeral trend as he is to miss a significant cue. He must be equally wary of premature euphoria and premature impatience. Last but not least, he has to do his best to maintain a viable balance between literary and political considerations.

The latter question was raised sharply by Mr. Andrew Field [see Additional Bibliography], a keen if somewhat petulant student of modern Russian literature. Mr. Field deplored the tendency prevalent in the West to discuss recent Soviet imaginative writing *sub specie* of its alleged ideological heterodoxy rather than of its literary texture. To do so, he argued with some cogency, is to fall prey to the Soviet fallacy we are so fond of decrying, notably to the habit of treating literature as a political weapon.

Mr. Field has a point, but it is one which can be easily misstated. To be sure, any body of literature worthy of the name—a rather important qualification, as we will see—deserves to be described and evaluated in literary terms. Granted, too, that some of the Western observers of the Soviet literary scene have precious little interest in literature. Yet the fact remains that while few literary manifestations of the post-Stalin "thaw" will repay close aesthetic analysis, many of them yield significant glimpses of the human reality hidden by the bland official façade—of unauthorized attitudes or hitherto unpublicized tracts of Soviet experience. And when, as in Solzhenitsyn's quietly harrowing tale, the taboo subject has the explosiveness of a long-denied nightmare, "no sane person," to quote Irving Howe, "can be expected to register a purely literary response."

Clearly what is needed here is not literary purism but respect for the autonomy of literary criteria. In many instances the literary judgment and the socio-political diagnosis are bound to be interrelated. Yet the former should not be confused with, or inferred from, the latter. We will do well to resist the temptation of proclaiming a nonconformist Soviet story or novel a literary masterpiece simply or largely because we have found it a major political event or a moving human testimony.

But then, one may interpose, what are the literary yardsticks that can be safely used in dealing with Soviet writing? Are we justified in applying Western criteria to a cultural situation so different from our own? I see no alternative to doing just that. To be sure, after two decades of stringently enforced sterility, it would be naïve and "ethnocentric" to expect a sudden literary resurgence, and ungracious not to take heart at whatever symptoms of a literary quickening come to the fore. But I submit that to measure the performance of Soviet writers by any other standards than the "Western" ones would be a sign of condescension rather than of understanding.

The post-Stalin literary discontent reached its first significant peak in 1956, a year described variously as the "interval of freedom" and the "year of protest." The faltering plea for a measure of creative integrity, heard during the first year after the tyrant's death, was vigorously re-echoed in the wake of Khrushchev's "secret" speech at the 20th Party Congress. The new leader's sensational attack on the "cult of personality" was seized upon by relatively independent-minded Soviet writers as a long-overdue occasion for some plain speaking, for an airing of accumulated grievances. The best-publicized and most characteristic symptom of this process was, of course, Vladimir Dudintsev's *Not by Bread Alone*. In some respects this drab but honest fictionalized tract hews quite closely to the conventions of the Soviet production novel. Suffice it to mention the puritan treatment of the "love interest": that strong-minded Russian woman Nadezhda Drozdov, who abandons her successful bureaucrat-husband to become the helpmate of the dedicated inventor Lopatkin, has to stand around for quite a while before she is taken note of by the scientist devoted single-mindedly to producing bigger and better iron drainpipes. Nor is the central theme of the book a novel one. The conflict between bureaucratic business-as-usual and individual initiative had served time and again in Soviet industrial fiction as a vehicle of "Bolshevik self-criticism," properly emasculated, to be sure, by the inevitable happy ending—a last-minute intervention of an aroused party secretary. On the face of it, *Not by Bread Alone* meets this requirement, too. After years of harassment and actual persecution, Dudintsev's lone-inventor hero is vindicated. His design for a pipe-casting machine is finally accepted.

What then, one may properly inquire, was all the shouting about? The fact of the matter is that at closer scrutiny the finale of Dudintsev's novel turns out to be less than reassuring. The villains of the piece, the self-serving bureaucrats who at the peak of their influence were powerful and unscrupulous enough to have the challenger sent to a forced labor camp—this was, incidentally, one of the first references to that uninstitution!—fail to receive their due. Though in effect they stand condemned of personal ruthlessness and of industrial sabotage, they are not fired but merely transferred to another branch of the system. The conclusion which suggests itself rather forcibly seems to be that the Drozdovs are too firmly entrenched in the apparatus to be easily dislodged. Dudintsev never says, nor does he appear to believe, that the system is rotten. Yet his narrative hints very broadly at the possibility that the rot had eaten deeply into the system.

Vladimir Dudintsev. Novosti Press Agency.

Who *are* the Drozdovs? The portrayal of the chief antagonist of Dudintsev's embattled hero is sociologically the most revealing aspect—and the only literary success—of *Not by Bread Alone*. A local boy who made good, a driven, hard-boiled, wily Soviet oganization man, Drozdov epitomizes the "new class," grasping, status-minded, and power-loving, glorying unabashedly in its material advantages and ever ready to invoke the "tough" Marxist-Leninist lingo as an alibi for its moral callousness. "This is not Turgenev for you," says Drozdov to his high-minded wife, "I am building the material base of Socialism."

I am reminded here of a passage from a little-known but remarkable novel by V. Kaverin, *Artist Unknown* (1930), built around the conflict between a single-track-minded Communist man of action, Shpektorov, and an engagingly quixotic painter, Arkhimedov. When the latter flamboyantly demands that the claims of Socialist morality be incorporated into the Five-Year Plan, Shpektorov retorts: "Morality! I have no use for the word. I am building Socialism. If I had to choose between morality and a pair of trousers, I would choose a pair of trousers." However, the similarity of phrasing should not blind us to the crucial difference between Kaverin's rough-and-ready pioneer of "Socialist construction" and Dudintsev's smug, latter-day *apparatchik*. As the process which Arthur Koestler had dubbed a breakdown of revolutionary incentives proceeds apace, what had been a rhetoric of crude yet genuine ideological commitment becomes a threadbare rationale for crass personal materialism. Perhaps Dudintsev said more than he knew.

Some of the implications of *Not by Bread Alone* were spelled out during a heated controversy which ensued. Predictably, the bureaucrats accused Dudintsev of slandering Soviet reality, while one of his most outspoken defenders, venerable and humane K. Paustovsky, delivered an impassioned attack on the insidious blight of "Drozdovism."

Dudintsev's profound distrust of the Soviet organization man was echoed in A. Yashin's story "The Levers," which shows how the party meeting ritual turns a group of humane and sensible men into unthinking robots. Another important theme of *Not by Bread Alone*—that of a chasm between bureaucracy and the "people"—found its way into many 1956 stories, most conspicuously "The Journey Home" by N. Zhdanov. While fiction was thus bringing to light some of the tensions and resentments smoldering within the allegedly harmonious Soviet society, the poets were rediscovering the need for emotional spontaneity, and the critics reaffirming the proposition ventured timidly in 1954 that in literature "sincerity" might be a more essential yardstick than political right-mindedness.

All this was more than the party was willing to countenance. Though no one had dared to question the validity of the system, to attack the fundamentals, the very volume and spontaneity of social criticism undertaken by honest Soviet writers posed a potential threat to the stability of the regime. The picture of Soviet reality which was emerging from 1956 Soviet fiction was too blatantly at variance with the official clichés. The cleavages and contradictions highlighted by the "thaw" writers were too profound and ubiquitous to be palmed off as mere bourgeois survivals or, for that matter, as residues of the Stalin era. In May, 1957, N. S. Khrushchev moved into the breach. In his first extended pronouncement on literature and the arts he took to task Dudintsev, *et al.*, for exaggerating the shortcomings of Soviet society and reminded the "ideologically confused" writers that their prime duty was to accentuate the positive. The defendants executed an orderly retreat, without, however, stooping to abject recantations, which had been part and parcel of the chastisement ritual in the Stalin days. The immediate effect of the unequivocal reassertion of the principle of party control over literature was a retrenchment rather than a rout, a muting of the attacks on the Establishment rather than a throwback to the bleak uniformity of Stalinism.

Though Khrushchev's harangue was boorish and occasionally grim, the official reaction was vastly outstripped in scurrilousness and unabashed nostalgia for the "good old days" of Stalinist regimentation by what might be called the vigilante counteroffensive. V. Kochetov, who has since become the recognized spokesman of literary zealots, struck back in a remarkably crude and venomous production novel, *The Brothers Ershov.* Kochetov's polemic with Dudintsev had the literary and moral finesse of a police report. The formula of *Not by Bread Alone* was stood on its head. In *The Brothers Ershov* the lone-wolf inventor who complains about being misunderstood and thwarted by the authorities turns out to be an embittered crackpot, while his chief ally is unmasked as a reactionary blackguard. Conversely, the plant manager is a paragon of integrity, and the party secretary a secular saint.

The rise of spontaneous literary bigotry underscored what has been since 1957 an essential facet of the Russian literary scene—notably the precarious coexistence of two camps which have been, somewhat misleadingly, labeled in the Western press as "liberals" and "conservatives." (The party has been shuttling uneasily between the two factions, trying to keep both in tow and to make alternate use of both without ever identifying itself with either position.) The die-hards, led by Kochetov, barricaded themselves in the literary journal *Oktiabr (October),* where they have been cultivating traditional Bolshevik pieties and pouring fire and brimstone on their "individualistic," "asocial," "aesthetizing" opponents. The "liberals" have found their chief outlet in *Novy mir (The New World),* which during the last years has featured, under the aegis of the resourceful poet-editor Tvardovsky, some of the most significant works of Soviet prose. In 1960 *Novy mir* published Dudintsev's engaging, if somewhat naïve, parable, *A New Year's Tale.* (In the West the story has been both overrated and overinterpreted. To my mind, it is neither the significant departure from the socialist-realist canon nor the subversive political allegory it was found to be by some overly excitable commentators, but simply an indication that Dudintsev has stuck to his guns: *A New Year's Tale* restates, this time in a safer, allegorical garb, Dudintsev's fundamental dichotomy of bureaucratic routine versus individual commitment.) A year later the journal opened its pages to an important story by Viktor Nekrasov, perhaps the most forthright present-day Soviet prose writer. "Kira Georgievna," an undistinguished but deeply humane and refreshing narrative, owes its appeal to a sympathetic portrayal of a rather unedifying heroine and a candid treatment of a delicate subject—the painful readjustment of a returnee from a forced labor camp.

The conspiracy of silence was broken, but the full story was yet to be told. In November, 1962, *Novy mir* presented to the Soviet public, with Khrushchev's personal blessing, A. Solzhenitsyn's *One Day in the Life of Ivan Denisovich.* The taboo was lifted. The dread institution, hitherto ignored or timidly hinted at, was now exposed to public view. The grim routine of what David Rousset has called "l'univers concentrationnaire," the unspeakable squalor and misery, the back-breaking labor, and the animal scrounging for scraps of food, is authenticated here by a wealth of detail and made more credible by the author's quiet, undramatic manner. *One Day* is not a horror story. Physical violence appears in the novel not as the central actuality but as an ever-present threat. When the shivering, hungry inmates start their forced march, the guards load their rifles: any false step will mean death.

The long, gruelling sequence from reveille to "lights-out," chronicled in Solzhenitsyn's unhurried narrative, represents an ordinary, in fact a relatively "lucky" day in the life of the tale's hard-working, good-natured protagonist. As the story draws to its close, Ivan Denisovich muses thus: "He'd had a lot of luck today.... They hadn't put him in the cooler; he'd finagled an extra bowl of mush at noon.... Nothing had spoiled the day and it had been almost happy."

The unwitting irony of this could not have been lost on Solzhenitsyn's readers. More broadly, one cannot help but wonder about the cumulative impact of this meticulously honest reportage in which thousands of Soviet citizens as innocent as Ivan Denisovich, as admirable as the brave naval officer Buynovsky, and as appealing as the gentle, devout Baptist Aleshka, are doomed to years of subhuman existence.

This is not to say, however, that *One Day* is an overt indictment of the system or that, as some overenthusiastic Western exegetes have argued, it implies the notion of the forced labor camp as a microcosm of Soviet society. For one thing, no work of fiction which could be legitimately interpreted thus would ever secure Khrushchev's personal authorization. For another, Solzhenitsyn's central narrative strategy obviates the need for, indeed eliminates the possibility of, an explicit verdict. Though technically *One Day* is a third-person narrative, the point of view is provided here by a "simple" peasant, whose potential for survival is considerably greater than his ratiocinative powers. This device, skillfully and consistently employed, is both a strength and a built-in limitation. The language of *One Day*—an effective blend of the earthy peasant vernacular with the harsh camp jargon which occasionally lapses into profanity—is a far cry from the colorless, timidly puritan prose of socialist-realist fiction. It is also testimony to Solzhenitsyn's sturdy sense of style—a quality which has not been very much in evidence in Soviet prose. Yet the sustained "folksy" stylization which lends solidity and color to the verbal texture of *One Day* limits the novel's scope and import. A reputable and well-wrought piece of writing as well as a major human and political event, *One Day,* as Irving Howe has acutely observed, is ultimately too "constricted" an affair to deserve some of the fulsome accolades that were heaped on it in this country.

Solzhenitsyn's keen ear for the leisurely rhythms of the Russian folk speech and his thoroughly un-Soviet affinity for Alesha Karamazov-like meekness are writ large in what is perhaps his most accomplished work to date, "Matryona's Home." The narrator of the story, who, not unlike its author, is a former political prisoner and a teacher, decides to "cut loose and get lost in the innermost heart of Russia, if there is any such thing." The phrase seems to suggest a hankering for some traditional Russian ambiance. In fact, both the language and the moral climate of "Matryona's Home" have a strikingly old-fashioned quality. The central figure in the story, a selfless, gentle, pure-of-heart peasant woman, makes one think of the quiet radiance of that chastened village belle Lukeria in Turgenev's "The Living Relics." When Matryona dies, a victim, symbolically, to her neighbor's brutal, unthinking acquisitiveness, the narrator is moved to comment: "We all lived beside her and never understood that she was the righteous one, without whom no village can stand nor any city. Not our homeland."

None of this was likely to please the official critics. Owing to Khrushchev's personal imprimatur, *One Day* enjoyed . . . a measure of immunity. But "Matryona's Home" was fair game. The story was promptly attacked for offering a distorted picture of the Soviet village. The implication that such "capitalistic" attitudes as competitiveness and greed were still rampant in the Soviet countryside was bound to be resented. Nor was Solzhenitsyn's positive message—his emphasis on personal "righteousness," on unaggressive goodness, so clearly at odds with the "struggle"—oriented and stridently public Soviet ethos—any less objectionable.

Both as revelation and as literature, Solzhenitsyn's best works represent the high point of present-day Russian fiction. Yet some of the younger Soviet prose writers have sounded notes that are both refreshing and symptomatic. Vasilii Aksenov's main significance thus far lies in his having tackled a phenomenon whose existence is strenuously denied by the regime's spokesmen—the cleavage between "fathers" and "sons." His lively, though occasionally banal, novel, *A Ticket to the Stars,* portrays with a degree of candor and sympathy the moral restlessness of Soviet teenagers. Characteristically, their adolescent rebellion is primarily a matter of an instinctive recoil from bureaucratic cant, from inspirational rhetoric. The novel's plot shuttles between two brothers, the dedicated and uncompromising young scientist Viktor and the "mixed-up" Dimka. Toward the end of the novel Viktor dies in a plane crash and Dimka vaguely reaches toward his older brother's "ticket to the stars." Curiously enough, the author allows him to do so, without protest, though at the moment the boy's only credentials are a distrust of "phonies," which makes one think of the hero of *Catcher in the Rye,* and a dogged insistence on personal honesty and authenticity.

In Iurii Kazakov, this undoctrinaire sense of individuality is coupled with a more finely modulated awareness of the emotional nuance than Aksenov seems capable of achieving. Kazakov's short stories have been compared to Chekhov's. The difference of stature between the two need not be insisted upon. Though possibly the most gifted and skillful among the young Soviet prose writers, Kazakov is a minor figure rather than a budding master. Yet there is something Chekhovian about the blend of sympathy and detachment in Kazakov's narratives and his steadfast refusal to moralize. To the considerable displeasure of the hacks, Kazakov shuns like the plague edifying themes and "positive heroes." The protagonists of his most characteristic tales (e.g., "Adam and Eve," "The Outsider") are loners, deviants, "offbeat" and unadjusted men. Their predicament is epitomized by the sullen and indolent buoy-keeper Egor in "The Outsider," who only in rare moments of shared bliss manages to rise above his usual torpor and break out of his isolation. Kazakov is a poet of brief but fateful personal confrontations, of fleeting yet significant moments. Apparently a faithful disciple of both Chekhov and Turgenev, Kazakov is finely attuned to subtle, barely perceptible shifts in interpersonal relations, to small cues which often make the difference between success and failure, between frustration or fulfillment in a long-awaited, hesitant encounter. This fundamentally un-Soviet sense of the fluidity and complexity of personal emotions goes hand in hand with a lyrical-descriptive evocativeness. Kazakov's protagonists typically have more rapport with nature than with society. The Russian countryside is a compelling presence in these stories, where a sudden radiance of Northern Lights breaks upon an encounter, now to illuminate a moment of shared joy, now to lend a wistful poignancy to the finale of a romance gone awry.

Yet when all is said and done, it is poetry rather than fiction that, in the last five or six years, has articulated most clearly the long-debased and ignored claims of the Self and projected most forcibly the sensitive young Russian's hankering for a life more varied, more open and venturesome than the one he had inherited. Inevitably the name of Evgenii Evtushenko comes to mind. Evtushenko has been described in the West alternately as Russia's angry young man and as Khrushchev's court poet. Both labels are misleading. A facile, derivative, often rhetorical versifier, Evtushenko is important and somewhat encouraging not because of the intrinsic value of his poems or his ideas, but because through his weaknesses as well as his strengths—his flamboyant vanity as well as his spontaneity—he has managed to dramatize the instinctive protest of his generation against the oppressiveness and bleakness of a world they never made. Though he has acted on occasions as the mouthpiece of the regime and will do so again, he has sincerity, élan, and the courage of his convictions, or, if one will, of his confusions. This courage was or seemed to be contagious. Evtushenko's much publicized attack on anti-Semitism, "Babi Yar," is a brave, deeply felt poem. But what made it an important public act was the vigorous response of Evtushenko's large and enthusiastic audiences. The roar of approval which, according to Patricia Blake's brilliant reportage [see excerpt below], would greet every reading of "Babi Yar" in the packed Moscow auditorium was not merely a dramatic indication of how sensitive young Russians felt about the Jewish tragedy. More broadly, it was a measure of their eagerness to take a vigorous stand on an issue evaded, indeed denied, by the regime, a gesture toward moral autonomy. The poetry readings, dominated by Evtushenko and the considerably more gifted Voznesensky, were generating a new sense of solidarity and dedication among the young, a harking back to some of the traditional ideals of the Russian intelligentsia.

Here, it seems to me, lay one of the major reasons why the Communist hierarchy chose to intervene once more. The threat of an independent public opinion did much to provoke Khrushchev's recent raid on the intellectuals. Another important factor was the resurgence of formal experimentation in poetry and the arts. It is noteworthy, and perhaps symbolic, that Khrushchev's spring campaign against the "liberals" was triggered by his visit to the exhibition of Soviet modernist artists. It seems that when confronted by abstractionist paintings, Khrushchev flew into a rage and declared war on the "filthy Formalist mess." The bureaucratic onslaught reached its peak in Khrushchev's March 8, 1963, tirade, in which he arraigned Evtushenko and Ehrenburg, Nekrasov and Aksenov, the poet Voznesensky and the sculptor Neizvestny.

Why was Khrushchev more exercised over a nonrepresentational painting than an explosive topical novel? Why is a lack of content deemed more objectionable in the Soviet Union than politically dangerous content? Perhaps what is involved here is a combination of a relentlessly instrumentalist approach to art with a totalitarian urge to control it. Though admittedly a gamble, an exposure of Stalin's concentration camps can be utilized by the party in furthering definable political objectives. Nonobjective art, as Khrushchev himself made clear in his March 8 harangue, cannot be used by "the people . . . as a tool of their ideology." For a Communist *apparatchik,* an art form which refuses to serve as a vehicle of propaganda is worse than useless. It is difficult to control what one does not understand. Hence, perhaps, the accents of genuine intellectual panic which crept into Khrushchev's nearly obscene outburst at the art exhibit of December, 1962. (pp. 405-14)

The two crack-downs have defined the limits of the party's tolerance of literary heterodoxy or, more broadly, of the concessions which present-day Soviet totalitarianism can make without changing its nature or losing its grip. Although the boundaries are more fluid than they used to be, and the hierarchy more vulnerable to societal pressures than it was under Stalin, the regime seems determined to block (a) explicit criticism of the bureaucratic Establishment, (b) a search for new, nonrealistic modes of expression, and (c) any literary movement or ferment which is likely to develop into an autonomous source of moral authority. For a full-scale repudiation of official ideology and aesthetics, one would have to turn to whatever samples of "underground" Soviet literature have come our way. It is only in a novel or story written, to use the Russian phrase, "for the drawer," or in the hope of being smuggled out abroad, that one can find a reference to the Stalin era as a "quarter of a century of tyranny unprecedented in the history of the world" [V. Tarsis]. By the same token, no narrative which has gotten past the Soviet censor could match the savage bitterness of N. Arzhak's "This is Moscow Speaking," where the narrator and his friends are apprised by the Soviet radio that "Sunday, August 10, 1960 is declared the Public Murder Day on which all citizens of the Soviet Union are given the right of extermination of any other citizen, with the exception of any persons metioned in the first paragraph of the annex to this decree. . . ." (Perhaps the most damning aspect of this parable lies in the fact that after the initial shock, the group managed to rationalize the gruesome announcement away and absorb it somehow into the fabric of everyday Soviet reality.) Finally, only "underground" could one stumble into the quasi-Orwellian vision of A. Tertz's *The Trial Begins* and the corrosive irony of his remarkable essay *On Socialist Realism,* an irony which testifies to a near-complete estrangement from the official ideology as well as a residual fear of abandoning it altogether.

It is in "Abram Tertz," whoever he may be, that one can see most clearly both the ideological and literary opportunities of underground Soviet writing and its apparent pitfalls. *The Trial Begins* is a remarkable, yet flawed story—an odd and perhaps not uncharacteristic mixture of nearly surrealistic suggestiveness with clumsiness and naïveté. Tertz achieves chillingly grotesque, Georg Grosz-like effects in the scene of an NKVD party. But the voyeurish eroticism of *The Trial Begins* strikes me as a rather adolescent and strained exercise in risqué sensuality, as a somewhat programmatic defiance of Soviet puritanism.

The dangers of writing by formula, or rather "counter-formula" (I. Howe), are still more apparent in Tertz's . . . *Fantastic Stories.* Aside from several brilliant passages, it is a disappointingly contrived book. Clearly, Tertz was trying to implement here his own much quoted plea for "a phantasmagoric art in which the grotesque will replace realistic description of ordinary life" (*On Socialist Realism*). Are we to conclude from this partial failure that there is something wrong with Tertz's program, or rather that he was not well equipped to carry it out? Or should we view the somewhat mechanical quality of Tertz's plots, shuttling as they do between science fiction and surrealism, between H. G. Wells and Kafka, as one more reminder that totalitarian thought control warps not only the conformist but the dissenter as well? Ironically, the very compulsion to protest, to say "no" in an underground rumble, which testifies to the writer's moral autonomy, can become a threat to his aesthetic freedom. Where thematic emphases are decided upon, in large measure, not as a matter of personal

vision or of structural necessity but as one of political intransigence, the system, so bravely and stridently defied, asserts its presence and retains its hold by effectively restricting the range of the artist's moral and aesthetic choice. (pp. 414-16)

With the partial exception of the best of Solzhenitsyn, Kazakov, and Voznesensky, the major literary products of the "thaw" have been heartening moral symptoms rather than significant literary achievements. Years of socialist-realist aridity must have taken a heavy toll. Moreover, aesthetic standards may well be more perishable, or may require a more systematic cultivation, than the basic human values. The bulk of Soviet prose fiction remains parochial, drab, and painfully dull. The writers whom I was discussing are a minority, though a vocal and, one hopes, a fairly influential one. And even here, more often than not, the level of performance and the degree of literary sophistication are far from impressive. It will take years, if not decades, until Soviet literature manages to repossess its own "modern" tradition, until it recaptures the vitality, the inventiveness, the free-wheeling experimentation of the twenties. (p. 417)

Victor Erlich, "Post-Stalin Trends in Russian Literature," in Slavic Review, *Vol. XXIII, No. 3, September, 1964, pp. 405-19.*

THOMAS P. WHITNEY

[*Whitney is an American critic and translator of Russian literature, most notably of works by Alexander Solzhenitsyn. In the following excerpt from an introduction to the anthology* The New Writing in Russia, *he recounts developments in Soviet literary politics during the period of reaction between December 1962 and June 1963.*]

On December 2, 1962, the paper *Pravda* published a front-page report on a tour by Nikita Khrushchev and other Soviet leaders of an exhibit of works of Moscow artists at the Moscow Central Exhibition Hall, sometimes known as "The Old Riding School" or more simply as the "Manezh." The press report of the tour constituted in fact a most important declaration of principles for Soviet art. And even though the specific target of the remarks by Khrushchev in the course of it was representational art—painting and sculpture—it obviously, from the very beginning, had a much broader significance than just these fields and was aimed with equal force at literature.

Soviet art, declared the *Pravda* report, citing Khrushchev, must faithfully depict the life of the people, inspire people to build communism, indoctrinate people in the best and most noble feelings, and arouse in them a deep understanding of the beautiful. The *Pravda* news "story" went on to deliver a bitter attack on abstract painting and sculpture: "It is impossible to observe without disturbance and outrage the smears on canvas (of the abstractionists) which are deprived of meaning, content, and form. These pathological eccentricities are a pitiful imitation of degenerate formalist art of the bourgeois West."

Pravda said that such creativity is alien to our people. Russians "reject it." Khrushchev went on to say, repeating that ancient banality of cartoonists and traditional critics when faced with modern art for the first time, that one could not tell whether the abstracts were upside down or rightside up, whether they were painted by human hands or by the tail of a jackass. Criticizing the organizers of the exhibition, Khrushchev condemned their "liberalism" and declared: "In the leadership of art there is required ideological consistency, adherence to principles, clarity, precision, and implacability toward any waverings or deviations from the main line of development of our art—the art of the people building communism.''

Actually, Khrushchev's remarks which were apparently made in the presence of a goodly number of people were evidently much more blunt than *Pravda* reported them—and even profane. The magazine *Encounter* for April 1963 quotes from an alleged stenographic report of the statements made at the Old Riding Hall—with Khrushchev declaring:

''People tell me that I am behind the times and don't realize it, that our contemporary artists will be appreciated in 100 years. Well, I don't know what will happen in 100 years, but now we have to adopt a definite policy in art, emphasizing it in the press and encouraging it materially. We won't spare a kopeck of government money for any artistic daubing. . . .

''As long as I am president of the Council of Ministers, we are going to support genuine art. We aren't going to give a kopeck for pictures painted by jackasses. History can be our judge. For the time being history has put us at the head of this state, and we have to answer for everything that goes on in it. Therefore, we are going to maintain a strict policy in art. I could mention that when I was in England I reached an understanding with Eden. He showed me a picture by a contemporary abstractionist and asked me how I liked it. I said I didn't understand it. He said he didn't understand it either, and asked me what I thought of Picasso. I said I didn't understand Picasso, and Eden said he couldn't understand Picasso either.''

Khrushchev was quoted as declaring to the artist Zheltovsky: ''We should take down your pants and set you down in a clump of nettles until you understand your mistakes. You should be ashamed. Are you a pederast or a normal man? Do you want to live abroad? Go on, then; we'll take you free as far as the border. . . . We have the right to send you to cut trees until you've paid back the money the state has spent on you. The people and the government have taken a lot of trouble with you, and you pay them back with this shit. They say you like to associate with foreigners. A lot of them are our enemies, don't forget.''

The next day after the report of the visit to the Old Riding School *Pravda* set off a press editorial campaign on the themes set by Khrushchev. The paper broadened the scope of the offensive to include literature and music. In music *Pravda* assailed Soviet musicians who devote themselves ''exclusively'' to imitations of ''rumbling jazz'' modeled after Western jazz leaders. (pp. 27-9)

Here, obviously, was the beginning of a major ideological campaign, guided and directed by the propaganda authorities of the Communist Party. Its slogans and its themes were clear. They added up to a vigorous reassertion of the same theses of socialist realism in art and literature which the Soviet Communist Party had so often repeated during and after Stalin.

How far would this go? What did it mean for writing?

A most ominous sign for the Russian writers and artists fully initiated into the intrigues of the Soviet artistic world—and who among them was not?—came on December 4, 1962, with the word that Academician V. A. Serov had been elected the new president of the Academy of Fine Arts. Serov's name was enough to frighten any liberal writer or artist in Moscow. He was an academic and socialist-realist painter *par excellence*. He had specialized in painting scenes from the revolution and other phases of the communist movement—and during the Stalin period the image of Joseph Stalin could sometimes be seen

in them, as for example in the painting which won him a Stalin prize, which showed the young Stalin standing behind Lenin at the time of the proclamation of Soviet seizure of power in 1917. He represented to the liberals pretty much the worst in the aesthetics of the personality-cult period, and from his new position he would certainly be able to hinder the work and attack the style of anyone who desired to paint or sculpt in a modern style on politically neutral or apolitical subjects.

Worst of all to show his new influence *Pravda* on December 9 published a major editorial by him on the theme of socialist-realism in graphic arts.

The storm warnings were up!

To a much greater extent than in the field of writing the dogmatists had managed to maintain in the field of the fine arts their positions of control over the major institutions and organizations of the system. As things had proceeded the liberal artists—and the liberal writers as well for they were nearly as concerned over the situation in the fine arts as in literature itself—had hoped that now there might be a change. But instead back went Serov into the saddle, and the prospect looked grim indeed.

The immediate result of all this was that two separate groups of prominent creative artists—principally writers—alarmed by the whole course of the new campaign, afraid for the loss of their newly won and insecure liberties, got together to compose letters to Khrushchev expressing the hope that there would not be any return to Stalinism in the arts and letters. (pp. 29-30)

Because of the great alarm obviously existing among the artistic intelligentsia, and in order to explain the new line, the Party leadership promptly called a meeting of Party political leaders, including Khrushchev and the Central Committee secretary in charge of ideological questions, L. F. Ilyichev, together with leading personalities from art and literature. Such meetings of political leaders with writers had occurred before—during the post-Hungary clampdown in 1957.

From this meeting, held at the Reception House on the Lenin Hills on December 17, there emerged two official documents. One was a short report that such a session had taken place, listing a few of the individuals who had spoken, including Khrushchev himself, giving nothing of the content of the discussion. The other was the text of the keynote report delivered there not by Khrushchev but by Ilyichev.

It apparently was a drama-packed gathering which lasted, it has been reported, for some ten hours! And it evidently saw some sharp exchanges. The usually well-informed correspondent of the Paris newspaper *Le Monde*, Michel Tatu, in a dispatch published in his paper on December 28, revealed that one work attacked was the new Thirteenth Symphony of Dmitri Shostakovich because it used, among a group of poems by Yevgeny Yevtushenko included with the music, the controversial verse about Babi Yar. Tatu's report on this was clearly accurate—since the Shostakovich symphony was later publicly attacked on exactly this ground after having been originally received by the Soviet press and radio in complete silence, except for one hostile innuendo aimed at it on December 25 in a lead editorial in the paper *Soviet Art*.

Tatu also reported an exchange between Yevtushenko and Khrushchev on the subject of the Soviet sculptor Ernst Neizvestny, who had been attacked by Khrushchev. Yevtushenko assertedly made a vigorous defense of his sculptor friend's patriotism and integrity. The article in *Le Monde* also reported some alleged strange charges said to have been made against Ilya Ehrenburg by the writer, Galina Serebryakova, which were supposedly too horrible to repeat and which were reportedly based on memoirs being written by the head of Stalin's former personal secretariat, Alexander Poskrebyshev. In reply to this it was said that the writer Mikhail Sholokhov, long hostile to Ehrenburg, had gone up to him and shaken him ostentatiously by the hand. This last incident, it must be said, seems a little unlikely.

The officially published text of the Ilyichev report at the meeting, at any rate, did not reflect any of the byplay and fireworks which clearly took place there. It was, in comparison with the original Khrushchev statements at the Old Riding School exhibit, rather less blunt and outspoken and had a slightly more tolerant tone. In art Ilyichev attacked, for the most part, only those same artists named in the original story of December 2. In literature the only personality whom he singled out for attack was a poet named Alexander Yesenin-Volpin, who had published some anti-regime verses in America. He had bitter words for this individual, but he did not extend his remarks to others. Basically, Ilyichev tried to build up a case to the effect that "formalists" in art were attempting to sneak into the graphic arts alien, bourgeois ideology, that not only were the "formalists" seeking a free way for their own works but that there was a plot to impose "formalism" on all the Soviet arts as the only tolerated trend.

Ilyichev had some strong words for Russian writers who hoped to be allowed to write as they please: "There are people who think thus and so: Since there is no longer arbitrary treatment in our country and since people are not arrested for political dissent, this then means that everything is permitted, and there are no limitations on what one wishes. One may not only paint ugly paintings, but one may praise them to the heavens as original searchings. One may slander the progressive traditions of our arts, but evidently one cannot defend them, because this, clearly, would be a 'limitation' of freedom, 'pressure' or the use of 'administrative' methods."

No, declared Ilyichev firmly, Soviet writers and artists must adhere to the principles of socialist-realism in their work. This, he said, did not exclude different approaches in form or searchings for new ways of expression. It did not mean that works could not be critical.

"The point is that while boldly exposing everything that stands in our way we must not deal blows at Soviet society itself."

The Party, Ilyichev indicated in no uncertain terms, would guide artistic processes in the Soviet Union.

Ilyichev was clearly the man who had been picked to carry the ball for the Party in this question of art. He made another important speech before a meeting of the Party's Central Committee's ideological commission, of which he was the chairman, with young writers, artists, etc., on December 26. This was a more detailed exposition of the Party position, naming a number of names among the writers. With a certain amount of moderation he criticized Yevgeny Yevtushenko and Andrei Voznesensky, for example. But he stated more strongly than before the basic line:

"The penetration of distortions and abnormalities into the world of art must come to an end, an atmosphere of intolerance toward manifestations of alien ideology, toward formalist gimmickry and tricks in art, must be established and a situation brought about which encourages the further consolidation of all the

Danil Granin. From A History of Post-War Soviet Writing: The Literature of Moral Opposition, *by Grigori Svirski. Translated and edited by Robert Dessaix and Michael Ulman. Ardis, 1981. Reprinted by permission of Ardis Publishers.*

forces of the intelligentsia in the arts on one basis, the foundation of Marxism-Leninism."

Once more he came down heavily on the concept of freedom of expression:

"Loud shouting about 'domestic freedom of self-expression' and haughty efforts to picture oneself as being 'in the vanguard of progress' and up above the people—who evidently are expected to strain their brains to comprehend the full 'depth' of artistic concepts and aesthetic 'subtleties' of certain persons who have wandered off the right path and are often nothing but fakers—these are simply anti-humanism of the purest type and the conceit that arises from lack of talent."

The year 1963 arrived with thundering utterances in *Pravda* by leaders of the "dogmatist" faction of writers and artists: on January 1 V. Kochetov, on January 2 G. Serebryakova and the sculptor S. Konenkov, on January 3 Alexander Chakovsky, and on January 4 the painter A. Laktionov. The series amounted to a whole barrage. The dogmatists were on the attack—and they were out for vengeance for the indignities they considered they had suffered from the liberals during the previous year or so.

That the "dogmatists" would have easier access to the important newspaper the *Literary Gazette* was assured by an "administrative" measure (obviously taken on the basis of an un-published Party decree) which reorganized the editorial board of that publication during the last week of December. The paper's editor-in-chief, V. A. Kosolapov, who had been running the publication was dismissed. Then there were fired—in January, a little later—six other editors of the paper out of fifteen. The editors dismissed were replaced.

This then was the situation as it stood in mid-January: There had been a dramatic reversal of the policy of liberalization in the field of art and literature. The "dogmatist" faction of the writers was engaged, with strong Party support, in an active offensive against liberal writers. The campaign was obviously only at its very beginning, and it was impossible to say how far it would go—but it looked to be in dead earnest. At the same time, up to the middle of January only a few particular targets for attack had been specifically named among the liberal writers—including the young poet Yevgeny Yevtushenko, and the senior writer, Ilya Ehrenburg.

How and why had this reversal of policy come about? It's worth examining this question closely since it illustrates so vividly the process of formulation of literary policy by the Party.

Two individual observers of the Soviet cultural scene have advanced some particular suggestions or theories on what happened. Professor R. Etiemble of the Sorbonne is one of these. He sees one particular villain in the piece—Academician Serov:

"Oddly enough there was hardly any reference in the press to the man who was most involved in the Old Riding School intrigues. He's no fool, this man, who is the pet aversion of all thinking people in Moscow. I mean by this Mr. Serov (he already knew whom I meant). Everyone knows, and everyone says that, having been beaten in the Moscow elections, and forced to take himself off to an obscure corner of the Urals, he swore he would have the blood of the insolent Muscovites. He is every bit as talented as Gerasimova and Laktionov and, as he did fairly well for himself in the happy days of the Personality, he is doing everything in his power to restore for his own ends the cult of that Personality.

"With this in view, he cunningly contrived the Old Riding School scandal, and induced the 'abstractionists' who were exhibiting their work privately to appear before the authorities. Taking advantage of the scandal, he had himself made president of the Academy of Fine Arts without any competition and there hopes to break the back of everyone who is any good as a painter or sculptor."

A different suggestion was made by the able commentator Alexander Werth, writing in *The Nation*. Werth considers that the "spark" that set off the fireworks of the Old Riding School exhibit and everything that followed was the "'Poets' Evening' of November 30" at the Luzhniki Stadium in Moscow, attended by some 14,000 people with an overflow of some thousands outside. At this gathering the biggest ovation of all went to poet Andrei Voznesensky—and Werth considers that this was too much for the authorities to take—because Voznesensky was the most "formalist" and "modern" of all the young poets. This event, he suggests, decided them to take decisive action to stem the "formalist," "modernist," "liberal" tide and impose a return to socialist-realism in all fields.

Now, both the demonstration for the most modern among the younger poets at the Luzhniki poetry declamation and the thoroughly effective political maneuvering of Academician Serov

presumably played their role. But, I would submit, they have to be looked at as parts of a far broader picture.

As has already been pointed out, the year 1962 was one of rapidly moving liberalization in the field of Russian literature. The liberals had taken a full measure of control over the Moscow Writers Organization—and excluded the dogmatists from any voice in the organization's affairs. The *Literary Gazette* was under relatively liberal editorship, and the literary journal *Novy Mir* was practically a party organ for the liberals, under the management of Alexander Tvardovsky, one of their leaders. In this situation writers had steadily become more and more outspoken—and this had culminated in the venturing into a new and very touchy field of writing—that selected by Alexander Solzhenitsyn in his novel on life in a Stalinist concentration camp. In painting too the liberal movement was well under way. In November the Moscow abstractionists held a private exhibit of their own—and it was well noted by Western journalists, as it was quite probably intended to be by its organizers, including a painter named E. Belyutin. Not only this but the abstractionist painters went so far as to defend their kind of art in a letter to the Central Committee of the Party.

Meanwhile, there cannot be the slightest doubt whatsoever that the great popularity of poetry recitations and readings on a large and small scale was causing alarm in official circles. These readings had several characteristics which were certain to raise the hackles of antagonism among people entrusted with indoctrination, propaganda, and security. In the first place there was an atmosphere of quasipublic demonstration about some of the gatherings. How could security people be certain things might not on some occasion get out of hand? In the second place, there was a kind of air of uncontrolled emotional tension quite contrary to the accepted official feelings of what public gatherings might be like. And third, the poetry readings provided the young poets with a means, evidently, of circumventing the censorship. This was an extremely significant loophole in the Soviet scheme of things. Poems printed in the press must have some kind of approval before they appear. Songs sung on stages must also have, under Soviet regulations, a "visa" from the artistic censorship—Glavrepertkom—by and large, at least that was the way it certainly always was. But the young poets' poems? The poets often recited—often at public demand—verses which had not been published or given a visa for public recital. Thus, Yevtushenko recited "Babi Yar" before it was shown to any editor, if one believes his account. Even more significantly, Yevtushenko, if one believes his own account and there is every reason to believe it, was reciting his quite political poem entitled "Stalin's Heirs" for a year before it was given a visa for publication—at the instance of Khrushchev himself, no less, to whom Yevtushenko had sent the poem. Not only were Party and other officials aroused by this sort of thing, but it also raised the keenest jealousy among the older established writers of the country, people like Mikhail Sholokhov, for example, who made an invidious reference to public poetry recitations at the Third Writers' Congress. After all, such people considered, naturally, that the young poets who had won themselves such enormous and quick popularity were upstarts and popularity-seekers. Such established writers, being themselves quite unlikely to inspire anything like a riot, naturally in some particular cases tended to take a dismal view.

All in all and adding everything up there certainly must have been by November 1962 a good number of rather alarmed people among those with most influence in the Soviet Establishment: officials in the propaganda and agitation apparatus, security people, Party secretaries, established writers and other artists whose personal positions were perhaps being affected adversely as they conceived it, and others, including even some of the topmost leaders of the body politic—all of whom had their sense of Soviet propriety wounded and their misgivings aroused by all the seemingly completely uninhibited and unrestricted "freedom" which was floating around Moscow.

But then there was another set of circumstances in the immediate picture—and this related to policy in the larger sense. The Cuban crisis burst upon the Soviet government at the end of September, and Khrushchev, to avoid war, surrendered to American demands to remove Soviet missiles from Cuban emplacements. Although in the long run this certainly meant no loss of a position essential to Soviet security—in the short run it was a blow to the prestige of Khrushchev at home and abroad. Furthermore, in the immediate sense it played into the hands of the Chinese communists who were already carrying on an intense political warfare against Khrushchev—hoping with the aid of "Stalinist" elements within the Soviet Communist Party to remove him from power. This continually more acute Chinese situation was a factor aggravating tensions within the Soviet Party. Khrushchev had other serious problems on his hands in 1962, for instance, problems of administration in agriculture and industry, which caused the leadership to convene a Central Committee meeting in late November to consider proposals for a radical reform of the Party organization and administration in the provinces.

The Soviet Premier was undoubtedly in a difficult position politically when the Central Committee met. It was in this particular situation that the question of Party policy in art and literature was raised in an urgent fashion before the Central Committee.

As Ilyichev later revealed in his own speech of December 17:

"A large group of artists sent a letter to the presidium of the recent Plenum of the Party Central Committee. They declared:

"'V. I. Lenin's theses and decisions of the Party on realist art are at present being contested by the formalists as obsolete. The formalists are aiming their declarations and actions at resurrecting formalist trends condemned in decisions of the Party.

"'We request the Party Central Committee to state just what in these decisions has become obsolete. If they have not become obsolete the declarations being made against these decisions in the press, on the radio, and over television have to be considered as revisionist and conducive to the infiltration of an ideology alien to us.'"

One can imagine that one of the leading spirits in the sending of this message was Academician Serov, of course. And one can also imagine that it was *not* sent without the knowledge of some elements in the topmost Party leadership—and perhaps even of the entire leadership.

It was rather reliably reported that Khrushchev in his final and concluding remarks at the November Plenum of the Central Committee touched among other things on the subject of literature.

Since at the time this report was published the spirit of the times seemed to be favorable to further liberalization it was presumed in the particular news report that Khrushchev's remarks were along these lines. In fact the text of Khrushchev's remarks was not published. And one can, in the light of the known fact that the question of the Party position on socialist-realism had been formally raised by "a large group of artists" before the Plenum—through its presidium—hypothesize that there was possibly an unpublished discussion of this problem at the Plenum—and a decision reflected in the events beginning December 2 at the Old Riding Stable. One is left wondering whether—if this hypothesis is correct—this was brought up at the Plenum with or without the knowledge and participation of Nikita Khrushchev himself—whether he was faced unwillingly and unwittingly with a situation in which others in the leadership forced him to reverse his policies or whether he himself perhaps had initiated this reversal, sensing the political need for a dramatic change in order to placate the more conservative elements in the Party. In a sense it is idle to speculate about this, though it is certainly an interesting and rather relevant question.

For the purposes of this [essay] it will be sufficient to chronicle in brief compass the further events from January to August 1963 in the Soviet literary-political arena.

During the month of January the campaign for socialist-realism in the arts and literature rolled on. It had various manifestations such as *Pravda*'s article on January 22 by Mikhail Sholokhov on the centenary of the birth of the Bolshevik writer, A. S. Serafimovich, author of one of the Soviet "classics" on the civil war. Sholokhov, putting himself on the side of the Party campaign, evidently declared in his tribute to Serafimovich that "only art which serves the interests of the people remains alive among the popular masses and has a right to live." He tried to draw a contrast—not very successfully, one feels—between Serafimovich who, he claimed, was popular and Ivan Bunin who died an emigré and who, Sholokhov claimed, was unpopular.

But this sort of thing was mere sniping. The big artillery was rolled out toward the end of the month and aimed at the main targets of the campaign. Thus, in *Izvestia* on January 30 V. Yermilov, a well-known Party representative in literary criticism, attacked Ilya Ehrenburg. His thesis was that Ehrenburg in suggesting or rather actually picturing himself during the years of Stalin's terror as constrained to silence for fear of doing harm to his country was being less than sincere and frank. According to Yermilov most Russians did not know that abuses of legality were taking place during the personality cult period. If, as Ehrenburg claimed he had, they had known about this then it was their duty to have spoken up. This in essence, as Ehrenburg pointed out in his reply published on February 6, was an attack on him as a person rather than as a writer. It impugned his courage and honesty. Ehrenburg replied rather pointedly that he knew of none who did speak out—none left alive anyway. Yermilov, who was granted the last word in the argument, returned to the attack on the same grounds as at first. What it all added up to was that *Izvestia*—and obviously the Party—was on the attack against the Ehrenburg memoirs. This was the kind of argument which it was difficult to win.

Izvestia on January 31 selected two more targets—first, the editorial board of the magazine *Yunost* for publishing some poetry by Andrei Voznesensky in the January number, and second, the editorial board of *Novy Mir* for publishing an essay by Alexander Yashin entitled "Wedding in Vologda" which allegedly slandered the author's native village, described in his essay.

On March 7 the leaders of the Party called a new meeting with writers and artists. There was a new Ilyichev speech on literature, a new and quite bitter attack on Ehrenburg, and, most importantly, a new Khrushchev speech. Since this was Khrushchev's first published personal major utterance of length and substance in this controversy it had great importance. It was not an encouraging speech—it seemed more Stalinist than anything the Soviet Party and government leader had uttered since the Hungarian aftermath in 1957. Khrushchev attacked the sculptor Ernst Neizvestny. He dwelt on the whole question of Ehrenburg and "silence" during the Stalin purges—offering a justification of Soviet leaders who had not intervened to stop Stalin. On the one hand, as it emerged from his speech, he and other Soviet leaders of the time had not known of Stalin's own personal involvement in the abuses of the terror and, on the other hand, in seeming contradiction, as it emerged from his account, he had saved some individuals and groups from the terror. He picked some other literary-artistic targets: the motion picture entitled *Zastava Ilicha,* Victor Nekrasov for his account in *Novy Mir* of his trip to the United States in which he found some things to admire in America and other things to criticize in Russia, and also Yevgeny Yevtushenko and his poem "Babi Yar." He delivered a justification of Soviet policy on the Jewish question in this connection. And then he went on to complain that since the publication of Solzhenitsyn's *One Day in the Life of Ivan Denisovich* Soviet magazines and publishing houses had been flooded with manuscripts about concentration camps. It was, he pointed out, a very dangerous and touchy subject.

All in all the Khrushchev speech of March 8, though a very interesting document, represented a clear step backward toward Stalinism in Khrushchev's attitudes on literature.

This meeting at the beginning of March set the stage for a much stepped-up campaign on the literary front: strong criticism of individual works in newspapers and magazines, various meetings at which some writers denounced other writers, and the criticized writers were required to "recant" their mistakes. The whole thing had a very bitter tone.

On March 15 *Pravda* carried a statement from sculptor Ernst Neizvestny which was a public "recantation." On March 29 in the press Andrei Voznesensky and Yevgeny Yevtushenko publicly admitted their errors and promised to do better in the future. On March 30 Alexander Solzhenitsyn's new story, "Matryena's Home," was gently criticized. On the same day Yevgeny Yevtushenko's *Precocious Autobiography,* published originally in Paris, was given the full treatment in *Komsomal Pravda* through the simple device of quoting its more provocatory remarks quite out of context—so as to give Soviet readers the impression, unfairly, that Yevtushenko had written an anti-Soviet booklet, which he had certainly not. Before that on March 22 the Young Communist League head, S. Pavlov, had attacked *Novy Mir* and *Yunost* for publication of allegedly offensive works—including "Oranges from Morocco" by Vasily Aksenov. On April 3 Aksenov, who had been rather constantly under attack, issued his declaration of recantation. Meanwhile, a meeting of the Moscow "artistic intelligentsia," called in late March, heard some quite violent attacks on the "formalists" in art and literature. This was mild, however, compared to the deep bitterness voiced in early April at a meeting of the Russian Union of Writers. It is worth quoting a paragraph from one of the speeches made at this meeting because it illustrates one aspect of the whole controversy.

Declared S. Baruzdin: "What did we fear? Being voted down by secret ballot? Having labels like 'dogmatist,' 'Stalinist,' etc., pinned on us? Or, last, were we perhaps afraid that our actions might have an impact on our own artistic fortunes, that we might not get into print, that we might be ignored, or that we might be beaten over the head with criticism from the noble standpoint of the 'struggle for quality'?"

The latter part of April saw some kind of a letup in the name-calling that was being so extensively and intensively indulged in by dogmatist writers who were out for revenge. But the general campaign continued without major new developments. As May proceeded preparations were going on intensively for the coming Plenum of the Central Committee called to discuss ideological issues. And it was in May that the first sign of a possible improvement in the literary climate appeared. This came in the form of the publication in the Soviet press of the full text of an interview given by Alexander Tvardovsky, editor still of the controversial *Novy Mir,* to the American correspondent Henry Shapiro.

Tvardovsky's interview, in gentle language but clear, defended his own original point of view and made clear that *Novy Mir* intended to go ahead with much the same program as in the past. In particular he went so far as to defend one or two of the works which had come under the most bitter attack during this campaign—including Alexander Yashin's essay on "A Wedding in Vologda" which he called "an excellent sketch" which is "full of poetry."

On June 18 the long-awaited Central Committee Plenum was called. The keynote address was given by Ilyichev again. He, however, added little so far as literature was concerned to things he had previously said—and the most important thing he came up with was a proposal that all the creative artists' unions be united in one big union combining graphic artists, composers, writers, etc. This was patently intended to submerge the highly liberal Moscow Writers' Organization and the Union of Soviet Writers in a mass of graphic artists and the like, and thereby establish a basis for a firmer control over writers.

Khrushchev also, of course, addressed the Plenum, but he had little to say about literature, nothing, at any rate, of much importance.

The Plenum ended after adopting a resolution which made the ringing declaration that: "To propagate peaceful coexistence of ideologies is treason to Marxism-Leninism, treachery to the workers' and peasants' cause."

Nothing was done immediately on the Ilyichev proposal for creation of one big union of creative artists.

So far as literature was concerned the Plenum turned out to be pretty much a big nothing. And for a pretty obvious reason.

What had happened was this: As the Plenum had convened the controversy—played up as an ideological controversy—between the Soviet Union and Communist China had broken completely and bitterly into the open. The Plenum, in this circumstance, turned principally into a platform for the delivery of statements mainly aimed at this issue and not at Soviet literature.

There was more to it than even this. From the West an olive branch had been offered—by President Kennedy. It was being looked at with the greatest of interest. The new test-ban treaty was already in the air—and much more. There was in Moscow a more relaxed atmosphere.

Not only this: Some of the Western European communists, in particular the Italians, had taken a rather negative attitude toward the whole campaign in literature. Much the same reaction had come from some of the more advanced East European communist countries—as, for instance, Poland.

Was there a new policy change in the air back toward liberalism in art? It seemed possible.

Ilya Ehrenburg came out of his seclusion a little later—to make a statement at an international writers' meeting to the effect that Soviet writers ought to be permitted to write experimentally for selected audiences. A few weeks earlier this might have sounded like some kind of treason to the Party line. But it didn't any longer. So rapidly could things shift in the Soviet Union.

Right after that two other similar developments followed. First, *Novy Mir* published a new story by Alexander Solzhenitsyn entitled "For the Good of the Cause," which was an attack on bureaucracy and disregard of human needs. This story was criticized by the assistant managing editor of the *Literary Gazette* just after it came out—the fact remained that it had appeared. Second, *Izvestia* on August 18 published on two pages the text of a new poem by Alexander Tvardovsky in which the poet, leader of the liberal camp of Soviet writers and editor-in-chief of the liberal literary journal *Novy Mir,* resurrected his famous wartime hero, Vasily Terkin, in order to put him in the unusual situation of being sent to "that world" only to find that it was run by an omnipotent bureaucracy and a leader who recalls Stalin. It is a satire—and an attack on Stalinism. And Tvardovsky read the poem, the paper announced over the signature of its editor-in-chief, Alexei Adzhubei, to Khrushchev in the presence of leading Russian and foreign writers. The poem is entitled "Terkin in That World."

In the light of these and other developments in the weeks preceding, an experienced American journalist present in Moscow at the time could predict with some assurance that new important novels, poems, and plays were in the offing and that a letup in the big clampdown of early 1963 was under way. (pp. 31-43)

Thomas P. Whitney, "Russian Literature and Soviet Politics," in The New Writing in Russia, *edited and translated by Thomas P. Whitney, The University of Michigan Press, 1964, pp. 3-51.*

SOCIALIST REALISM: THE THEORETICAL DEBATE

WALTER N. VICKERY

[In the following excerpt, Vickery discusses the critical debate over socialist realism that arose during the liberalization of 1955 and 1956.]

One indication of the vastly more liberal atmosphere that existed late in 1955 and in 1956 was the reopening of theoretical discussions of literature. Literature had, of course, been the subject of heated debate in the twenties and early thirties, but in 1934, at the meeting of the First Writers' Congress, the method of socialist realism was . . . officially defined, and the definition written into the Charter of the Writers' Union. For the next twenty years, the issue was, for all practical purposes, closed. Socialist realism, *partijnost'* ["party-mindedness"], and *tipichnost'* ["typicality"—used in the context of socialist realism to describe not that which is most common, but that which conforms to Communist ideology] became indispensable

parts of the paraphernalia of Soviet literary theory and were regularly used by the party to enforce its narrow, dogmatic, and rigid control. (pp. 99-100)

What took place in 1956 was not, strictly speaking, a debate. It lacked the conflicting schools of thought, the thrust and parry of true debate. It consisted rather of a number of liberally oriented articles which reached, if not a climax, at least a crescendo of outspokenness toward the end of the year. Before the Hungarian and Polish events these articles did not encounter really threatening opposition. Then, as the atmosphere changed, they began to come under attack. They were, along with various works of creative literature, condemned at several meetings that took place early in 1957. And there the debate ended. It is on these liberally oriented articles that attention will be focussed. (p. 101)

The two articles which created the biggest sensations are "On the Question of the Lag in Drama and the Theater," by B. A. Nazarov and O. V. Gridneva, and A. Kron's "A Writer's Notes."

Nazarov and Gridneva seek to define the contrast between what went on before and what came after 1936. And they bemoan the bureaucratic interference which has plagued the theater ever since. They point out bitterly that the regime had trusted the artists at a time when the ranks of the intelligentsia numbered many pre-revolutionaries. And this trust had been justified. Yet later, when the intelligentsia had become truly sovietized, the regime had transferred its trust to the bureaucrats! "Views were upheld which are diametrically opposed to those of Lenin. Nay more, the right is upheld to identify these views with the views of the entire people, to speak out on each isolated work in the name of the people." Various Stalinist intrusions into the world of art, including the 1946 decree on drama (which in tone closely paralleled the decree on *Zvezda* and *Leningrad*), are condemned. "It was precisely on the foundation of the cult of personality that from the mid-thirties there arose the conviction that success could be achieved by orders, directives, decrees or decisions."

The article does not suggest removing the theater from state control. On the contrary, the state must have control of all spheres of activity, but the forms of such control can differ. It is pointed out that literature, by virtue of the Writers' Union, does have a degree of autonomy, whereas the theater is still subject to direct administrative control. As a compromise, Nazarov and Gridneva suggest that the theater be removed from the domain of the Ministry of Culture and that an academy of arts or an academy of literature and art be set up. This would, they feel, provide a satisfactory fusion of control and local autonomy: "One thing is certain: the granting of autonomy [*samoupravlenie*] to the art of the theater will facilitate the realization of the views of V. I. Lenin, without which its renewed resurgence is impossible."

Kron's article leads off with a blistering and sarcastic attack not only on the cult of personality but on cults in any shape or form: "Cult is in its very essence antipopular [*antinaroden*]." Like Nazarov and Gridneva, Kron deplores administrative interference: "Art knows only one legitimate hierarchy: the hierarchy of talent. And this is established by time and by the people. When it is done swiftly and by secret order, the whole business is reduced to the habitual table of ranks, unjust in the eyes of contemporaries and ridiculous in the eyes of posterity." The system of awarding Stalin Prizes is condemned, as is also the established practice of publishing reviews by quite unknown critics claiming to speak "in the name of the people."

Kron also makes a sound point bearing on the then recent critical trend in Soviet literature, when he maintains that no orders or commands are required to right the situation. He sees the critical trend as a natural reaction to the past and feels that the balance will reassert itself without interference.

The time factor is of paramount importance here, for it has a direct connection with the question of literary theory. The year 1936 had seen the subjugation of the theater to the bureaucracy; 1932 had marked the founding of the Writers' Union; and a few years earlier Joseph Stalin, whose errors and tyrannies it was now permissible to decry, had started his rise to absolute power. This period also saw the rise of socialist realism. At the 1934 Writers' Congress the doctrine of socialist realism, for which Stalin had received no little credit, was given official blessing. Was not Soviet literary theory (and the whole doctrine and method of socialist realism itself) one more dictator's caprice?

The importance of the time factor was clearly recognized by those who, like Simonov, sought to stem the flood. In an article published in early 1957 Simonov charges, ominously enough, that efforts to overthrow the doctrine of socialist realism have a political character. He notes that attempts to date socialist realism have the aim of making it appear that socialist realism was imposed from above as a result of the cult of personality. He counters such charges by saying that socialist realism was practiced long before 1934 and that its formulation as a theory was thus no more than a response to pre-existing conditions. And he rejects all efforts to link socialist realism with the cult of personality: "An understanding of the people's role as the creator of history is one of the fundamental characteristics of the socialist-realist artist, and the cult of personality was in irreconcilable contradiction with this understanding."

This was really the only line that could be taken if the theory of socialist realism were to be salvaged from ruin. That the argument was not refuted was due less to any intrinsic merits it might possess than to the rapidly hardening political climate.

Can these extremely outspoken articles by Kron and by Nazarov and Gridneva be regarded as attempts to overthrow Soviet literary theory and Party control? I have already indicated why this is a difficult question to which no authoritative answer can be given. Nazarov and Gridneva, as we have seen, claim that they accept the idea of state control. Kron also makes a point of acknowledging the need for controls. But the sincerity of these authors was questioned in Soviet circles. Two separate *Kommunist* editorials went out of their way to doubt their avowed allegiance to the principle of Party guidance and to accuse them of attempting to be rid of Party control. Thus, for instance, we read: "Enumerating all the evils which allegedly lie in wait for the playwright on his 'thorny path,' Kron writes: 'It should not be concluded from this that in general art should not be under guidance.' But the whole emotional tenor of his article is such that in essence it calls in question the very bases of guidance in art." It is true that Soviet polemical techniques seldom attain a high ethical standard. False accusations would be no innovation. Were not the "cosmopolitan" critics found to be an "antipatriotic group"? Nevertheless I would tend to the view that more was known of the literary opinions of these three authors than they dared to put in print and that behind this smoke there was a genuine fire.

On the other hand, it is worth noting that the two articles in question deal with the theater and that they concentrate on administrative abuses rather than on literary theory. It is not surprising, as has already been pointed out, that some of the most violent statements, written and spoken, in recent years have come from people connected with the theater. Of all literary genres it is the theater which has most suffered from administrative interference. It would be perfectly logical to accept the broad premises of the theory of socialist realism and at the same time to resent government control most bitterly.

Whatever the underlying motives of Kron, Nazarov, and Gridneva—and I am inclined to think of them as "nihilistic"—it was certainly their articles which took the main brunt of hardline criticism in 1957. And in my view they did—under existing conditions—considerably less to advance the cause of liberalism than did other milder-mannered commentators. Their very sharpness of tone helped to precipitate a reaction which, it must be conceded, was in any case inevitable. Of greater interest and likely to prove of more lasting benefit to writers were other articles which sought mainly to show that the concepts of socialist realism, *tipichnost'*, and *partijnost'* had in recent years been "vulgarized" and misapplied; and that their abuse had stifled and impoverished Soviet literature. It is to these liberal articles that we now turn in an effort to determine what their prevailing line of thought was and in what way they could hope to improve the situation for the Soviet writer.

The first attempt to lighten the ideological load [was] the deletion from the Charter of the Writers' Union of the second half of the formula defining socialist realism. . . . [The Soviet Writers' Congress of 1934 defined socialist realism as follows: "Socialist realism, which is the basic method of Soviet artistic literature and literary criticism, demands of the artist a truthful, historically concrete portrayal of reality in its revolutionary development; whereby truthfulness and historical concreteness must be combined with the task of the ideological reforming and education of the toilers in the spirit of socialism." The 1954 Writers' Congress eliminated the second half of this definition. This] deletion found little sympathy with Party doctrinaires. The liberal tendencies which had manifested themselves at the Congress had produced their own reaction in the form of the rigid *Kommunist* article of January, 1955, which stressed the educational role of literature. But by the end of 1955 the political climate had so far improved as to make it possible for *Kommunist* to publish an editorial which had unprecedentedly liberal implications. *Tipichnost'* is the particular aspect of literary theory to which this editorial is devoted. The choice of subject was certainly not unconnected with Malenkov's fall from power.

The editorial sets out to correct past misinterpretations and abuses in the application of the concept of *tipichnost'*. . . . *Kommunist* now faces squarely up to the [danger that *tipichnost'* can be used to insist on the exaggeration of Soviet virtues and the embellishment of Soviet life] and condemns precisely this abuse.

> Theoretical confusion over the question of exaggeration has to a certain degree contributed to the appearance of works which incorrectly depict Soviet reality, in particular works which embellish Soviet reality. In fact, when writers take as their point of departure the idea that it is necessary consciously to exaggerate reality's positive manifestations, since only thus, they allege, is it possible to express in the fullest

possible manner the essence of a given social force, this leads to the ignoring of reality, to works which gloss over the difficulties of our work of building, even over its stages. Such a portrayal of life orients the readers incorrectly, educates them incorrectly.

The editorial seeks further to guard against the excessively narrow use of *tipichnost'* by insisting that *tipichnost'* cannot be identified with *partijnost'*.... *Kommunist* rightly argues that it is possible for a writer to possess *tipichnost'* without possessing *partijnost'* and, speaking of "contemporary progressive realist artists in capitalist countries," points out:

> For a number of reasons they do not yet accept *partijnost'* in literature, and some of them even reject it. The scholastic formula would have it that these artists cannot create typical images, since the typical is something in which *partijnost'* manifests itself. Yet these artists, striving to reflect life honestly and truthfully, do create vivid typical images and by their work do serve the cause of progress.... The question of the *Weltanschauung* of artists of different times and classes is an extremely complicated one. A concrete approach to the study of the phenomena of literature and art shows that the *Weltanschauung* of artists is very contradictory, and this cannot fail to manifest itself in their work.

This position certainly does not void the concept of *tipichnost'* of its sociological significance, for *Kommunist* speaks of "progressive" writers who "serve the cause of progress." But it does move it one step nearer to being an esthetic concept, or at least places greater emphasis on the esthetic.

Soviet theorists seek always to bolster their aruguments by reference to a Marxist authority. In this respect it is significant that Lenin's views on Tolstoy, which had long been neglected in favor of his pronouncements on *partijnost'* in literature, begin again at this time to claim widespread attention. Tolstoy's philosophical views were clearly opposed to Communism. This Lenin had noted. But he had also made the point that Tolstoy, consciously or not, had succeeded in "reflecting in his works at least some of the fundamental aspects of revolution." Further, he had "succeeded in conveying with great force the mood of the popular masses, oppressed by the social order of the day." This line of thought again places emphasis on the esthetic. And it tends to destroy or to weaken any direct correspondence between the artist's subjective intentions and the objective result. The *Kommunist* editorial, already referred to, is leaning in this direction when it states: "It is well known that an author's political views do not in artistic creation reveal themselves anything like as directly as in philosophy and other social sciences. There are even cases when the artist creates works whose objective significance is in contradiction with his political views and sympathies. Instructive in this respect, as Engels noted, is Balzac's work."

The support of Lenin's views on Tolstoy is also enlisted in a *Voprosy filosofi* article which makes essentially the same point. Speaking of Tolstoy, Balzac, and Shakespeare, the author, G. Z. Apresyan, contends: "They were realists, and therefore the objectively rational [*zakonomernoe*] often won the day over their personal sympathies and antipathies, over their subjective intentions."

Olga Berggoltz.

It is, of course, not so difficult to apply this view to writers of the past and to contemporary foreign writers not accepting Communism. A similar tolerance could scarcely be accorded Soviet writers. However, one implication was certainly not missed by the latter. A good artist, writing truthfully about life, will—through the esthetic qualities of his writing—almost inevitably tend to come up with worthwhile and progressive work. Balzac and Tolstoy may have been hopelessly mixed up, but, by the force of their art, they landed on the side of the angels. At the very least this approach makes for greater ideological tolerance and puts more emphasis on esthetic quality.

The desire was apparently widespread at this time to give the loyal writer his head, without quibbling about such details as his choice of theme, his subjectivism, or other weighty problems which had been wont to occupy the critics' attention. There seemed to be general recognition of the fact that different authors had different ways of getting through to the reader and that all these different ways were not necessarily incompatible with the requirements of socialist realism.

As has been already pointed out, the use of such concepts as *tipichnost'*, socialist realism, and *partijnost'* in the evaluation of literature depends on the political atmosphere that happens to prevail at any given time. Consequently, since the political atmosphere was relatively favorable by the end of 1955, it would be natural to expect the concept of socialist realism to be given a looser and less binding definition, in harmony with the liberalized definition of *tipichnost'* in the *Kommunist* editorial. This is indeed what happened. Outstanding among attempts to loosen the bonds is an article written by Simonov at the end of 1956. In this article . . . , Simonov reiterates the generally accepted view that socialist realism is a concept sufficiently broad to embrace many types of writing, including the romantic and other varieties. But he goes further than that and, in doing so, makes demands on the author that are too vague to have much meaning. "I have more than once heard writers who have made no small contribution to Soviet literature give approximately the following answer to the question as to what they understood by the method of socialist realism as applied to their own work: 'I believe in socialism, I write for the people on the basis of this belief, and I try to write as well as possible; if this is the method of socialist realism, then obviously I write according to this method.' "

The apathy of Simonov's imaginary writer toward theoretical questions would seem to be blatantly obvious, but Simonov goes on approvingly: "I personally think that it would be dogmatic pedantry to consider such an explanation unsatisfactory or inadequate when given by a writer who genuinely believes in socialism and who has in his work conveyed this belief to the reader." This requirement is so loose that it would scarcely have done violence to the fellow-travelers of the twenties.

Simonov is, of course, merely reporting the words of a hypothetical third party and asking for indulgence. But he himself goes out on a limb when he suggests, in the same article, that the concept of a "method" of socialist realism be replaced by the term "principle" of socialist realism. It is not my intention here to go into the niceties of language. "Method," as applied to socialist realism, is in itself a highly dubious and nebulous term which has acquired meaning in Soviet official jargon less through the intrinsic precision of the term than through force of habit. What Simonov strove to do in suggesting an alternative was to take the whole concept of socialist realism once and for all out of the hands of mistaken enthusiasts who might renew earlier attempts to impose on writers a socialist realist style. "Principle," which is, strictly speaking, equally meaningless in this connection, was for Simonov a broader term, and for this reason served his purpose.

During Stalin's life various works had been hailed as achievements of socialist realism not for their literary merit, but on political grounds, and for such extraneous features as the amount of zeal shown in paying homage to Stalin. Other works had been condemned as contrary to the spirit of socialist realism not because they lacked literary merit or were antisocialist, but because they had in some way sinned against the artificial canons erected from time to time. Part of the task of liberalizing the concept of socialist realism consisted in setting the record straight. Thus, A. Tolstoy's *Bread (Khleb)*, which had previously been hailed as a superb example of socialist realist art, was now seen to have been written under the influence of the cult of personality; whereas Sosyura's "Love the Ukraine" ("Lyubi Ukrainu"), previously condemned, was now seen to be a legitimate and patriotic work of socialist realism.

This adjusting of accounts and, even more important, the attempt to interpret socialist realism more loosely are part of one and the same general tendency, already noted in connection with *tipichnost'* : to free the writer from worry as to the minutiae of ideological conformity.

The same tendency is to be observed in the field of *partijnost'*. Outstanding on this problem was the much criticized article

by Ya. M. Strochkov, "On V. I. Lenin's Article 'Party Organization and Party Literature.' " Lenin's article had for a long time been used as a precedent by those who wanted to insist on the narrowest possible conception of *partijnost'* in literature. Actually it is doubtful whether Lenin, writing in 1905, ever intended his demand for *partijnost'* to apply to belles-lettres; it seems likely that Lenin was merely objecting to theorists who were then publishing in his Party journal, *Iskra,* political views which did not accord with those of the Party, or rather of the Leninist faction of the Party. But it had become customary in literary polemics to cite Lenin's 1905 pronouncements outside their historical context and to apply them mechanically to the current situation. Strochkov's article was an attempt to put Lenin's statements back into their historical context. Perhaps his most important contribution is his insistence that in 1905 the Bolsheviks were a minority party, whereas today they have with them the proletariat and the state. "After October 1917," Strochkov writes, "the working class and its Party became the recognized directing force of the state. The organized socialist working class used all means, including Soviet literature, for the re-education of the toilers and for the further development of their creative work. The working class began, as the leader of the country's entire life, to look at all spheres of social life from the standpoint of the state. Contemporary Soviet literature is developing as a part of the state and the people—in this lies its *partijnost'*." We have here two significant points. First, Strochkov emphasizes the difference between a minority party and a party in power. In the former case the only *raison d' être* is to gain power, and it is reasonable to demand that the party's publications pursue this aim. In the latter case the party becomes responsible for all the activities of the state and country which it controls. And these activities cannot be confined to politics alone. In fact, socialism in a socialist state is as broad as life itself, and it is therefore unreasonable to require that the writer convey in each work a narrowly political party message. Second, the last sentence quoted from Strochkov, which sees Soviet literature developing "as a part of the state and people," is of some importance, for it casts Soviet literature in a relatively passive role. Literature is seen as developing side by side with other aspects of Soviet life. And this is a position of relative comfort. Zhdanov, it will be remembered, called on writers to "help light up with a searchlight the road ahead." Strochkov seems willing to trade in the searchlight for the mirror. And, as the Russian proverb quoted by Gogol points out, the mirror is not responsible for all it reflects.

Thus in the three interrelated spheres of socialist realism, *tipichnost'*, and *partijnost'* the same general tendencies are seen to be at work. The attempt is being made: (1) to broaden theoretical requirements for the writer, to enlarge the scope and range of what is ideologically acceptable; (2) to relieve the writer of the invidious privilege of being the "educator" of his people; (3) to weaken the link or correspondence between the writer's subjective intention and the objective result; (4) to place greater emphasis on the esthetic.

One particular problem—that of portraying human character—is a constant headache for the Soviet writer and deserves special mention. . . . The problem is not here under discussion in its technical or purely literary aspects, but is studied, rather, as the end result of character portrayal: the way human beings are made to act in Soviet literature, their good and bad characteristics. In the final analysis this is the stumbling block over which the undisciplined Soviet writer invariably comes to grief. He may be told that his view of Soviet society is pessimistic, that he has nihilistic tendencies, that his characters are not typical, that his works lack *partijnost';* but these criticisms all boil down to the fact that the writer has produced negative characters of one sort or another and has portrayed them in a specific relationship to Soviet society. Are the vices of these negative characters mere capitalist survivals or are they produced by Soviet society?

The problem . . . is not merely one of glossing over Soviet vices or of presenting an overly optimistic picture of Soviet society, nor is it merely a question of misplaced chauvinism. It is also very much a theoretical question, closely related to Marxist ontology, to the Marxist credo, to the entire Soviet *Weltanschauung;* and it is significant that liberal theory in 1956 makes some attempt to ease the difficulties connected with this problem.

The main difficulty arises from the Marxist view of social consciousness—or human nature. "In the social production of their life," Engles writes, "men enter into definite relations that are indispensable and independent of their will; these relations of production correspond to a definite stage of development of their material forces of production. The sum total of these relations of production constitutes the economic structure of society—the real foundation, on which rises a legal and political super-structure and to which correspond definite forms of social consciousness. . . . It is not the consciousness of men that determines their being, but, on the contrary, their social being that determines their consciousness." Since the Marxist timetable sees human society as developing from one social stage to another, a higher one, it follows that human nature reflects this progress and itself improves.

This view is diametrically opposed to the view which Soviet writers like to identify with bourgeois thought, whereby man's nature is seen as immutable—as a sort of Schopenhauerian eternal battleground for the conflicting forces of vice and virtue. The Soviet view tolerates no immutability, looks forward to some sort of "withering away" of vice, and regards evil in Soviet man as a bourgeois survival, a remnant of capitalism. Marxism is, of course, very much the child of the optimistic and deterministic thought of the nineteenth century. The same glib optimism was expressed in Chernyshevsky's *What Is To Be Done? (Chto delat'?)*—and, incidentally, countered in Dostoevsky's *Letters From the Underground (Zapiski iz podpol'ya).*

Clearly the Marxist view of human nature imposes on the writer very definite restrictions. He is expected to castigate the old and affirm the new. And this he fails in some measure to do if he represents a negative character as being in any degree typical of Soviet man or as a product of Soviet society.

The demands made on writers by certain critics in the name of the Marxist doctrine had reached at times to the outer limits of absurdity. Even those works which were avowedly satirical in intention had been blamed for containing more negative than positive characters. They had been criticized because the negative characters emerged more vividly than the positive, or because a given character contained more negative than positive traits. Playwrights had been forced by this arithmetical logic to eliminate one negative character from a play and transfer some of his lines to a brother in vice. But subsequently (even before 1956) this mathematical computation of good and evil, of positive and negative, had been decried. Now a more liberal and common-sense viewpoint began to be expressed, even in the pages of *Kommunist.* "For a Profound Elaboration of the

History of Soviet Literature," which condemns many past errors and excesses, attempts to face up to this very issue of character portrayal: "It is obvious that it is not the character of the main hero which determines the essence of a work, but the idea which the work affirms, where the author's sympathies lie, with what force and depth the work expresses the social and esthetic ideal, in whose name the offensive is being waged against the old world, in whose name the new and conquering is glorified." So far so good. But a difficulty becomes immediately apparent when the article bolsters its arguments by reference to two examples: Aini's *Odina,* a Tadzhik work, and Sholokhov's *The Quiet Don.* Both deal with the early days of revolution. The heroes of both were formed in prerevolutionary times. Their failings can thus, from the Soviet viewpoint, be quite logically assigned to a presocialist stage of development. But the revolution is now more than forty years old. The situation becomes clearly much more complicated and more difficult when a character is represented as living today.

As Soviet society grows older and older, it becomes increasingly difficult to represent negative characters and characteristics as survivals of capitalism. It becomes increasingly difficult to avoid the impression—without doing violence to artistic truth—that many failings are either inherent in human nature or spring from the background on which the author depicts them.

My own view is that every society and nation, and sometimes even a locality, does tend to breed its own brand of vice and virtue but that no social order, however allegedly advanced, is likely to succeed totally in eradicating human frailty. The first proposition was made by Shcheglov when he expressed the view that Leonov's Gratsiansky was a product of Soviet society. The second proposition was implied by Pomerantsev in the following: "We will within two or three years make considerable improvements in material living conditions, but there is no direct line leading from them to the human soul. . . . It is clear that the eradication of these vices will require a great deal more effort and time than, for instance, the removal of our livestock shortage or of the lack of consumer goods."

Some theoretical efforts were made which come halfway to meet the problem. G. Glezerman states in *Kommunist:* "The moral-political unity of society means that society is free of class antagonisms, of conflicts and clashes between classes. But this by no means signifies the absence in society of non-antagonistic contradictions and conflicts. Yet over a long period in our literature and propaganda the idea—not always openly expressed, it is true—has been current that the existence of a moral-political unity in socialist society is incompatible with the admission that this society develops through contradictions. . . . All development, including the development of socialist society, is accomplished through the overcoming of contradictions, through the struggle of opposites." (pp. 103-21)

[This] article was written, at least in part, as an advance defense of Dudintsev's *Not by Bread Alone.* No mention is made of the novel, but the novel and the article appeared at the same time, and the latter directly parallels the main plot of the novel by singling out for criticism an [allegedly true situation on which the novel was based]. . . . Be that as it may, the significance of the statement cited above is clear. The writer, though still obligated to picture the old as yielding to the new, can represent human failing as a product of Soviet society, for even a socialist society develops "through the overcoming of contradictions."

The liberalism of Apresyan's *Voprosy filosofi* article has been noted in connection with his views on such writers as Shakespeare, Balzac, and Tolstoy; but he is no less liberal on the subject of contradictions: "Soviet reality does have its contradictions: some of them are overcome in the course of socialist construction; *but others arise.*" His reason for making this point, and its application to his view of literature, becomes apparent when he says: "As regards Soviet literature, it cannot of itself, as is well known, 'eliminate' any contradictions and must truthfully reflect what is in life; otherwise such 'elimination' will lead to the embellishment of reality." Apresyan clearly stands with those who would prefer to see literature as a mirror rather than as a searchlight.

Apresyan's article appeared in January, 1957. That the tide was turning at about the same time is clearly indicated by the publication soon after of an article by S. Kovalev which again raised the problem of contradictions. True, Kovalev recognized that socialist society was not fully equalitarian, thus admitting the possibility of contradictions. But basically he failed to endorse the views of Apresyan, for he made no mention of the fact that socialism might as it were generate its own non-antagonistic contradictions. Kovalev sees the shortcomings of Soviet society as "birth marks" inherited with the capitalist legacy. The material conditions under socialism had been such as to eliminate entirely some of these "birth marks"; thus, no one today wished to see factories owned by private capital; but some "birth marks," such as selfishness and careerism, still remained. It seems scarcely necessary to point out the extreme naïveté of the point he was trying to make. As to the "birth marks" and the whole conception of the article, the author was only rehashing the old and simple idea of capitalist survivals, and his conclusions fall far short of those reached by Apresyan. Kovalev's message, following an editorial which reaffirmed the validity and applicability under existing conditions of the "Zhdanov" decrees of 1946, must have been very clear to the Soviet literary world.

Kovalev's position was supported by the ever-adaptable Simonov. In December Simonov had come up with his revealing and liberal article, "Notes on Literature." Three months later, in March, 1957, he found it necessary to redefine his position. He did so in his later article, "On Socialist Realism," by pointing out the importance attached by those of liberal mind to the question of dates. Simonov is a skillful and farseeing debater with an eye for fundamentals. It is therefore not surprising that he saw this very question of human nature and character portrayal as one of cardinal importance. And he used it as an issue on which to throw down the gauntlet to the dissidents. "Do I believe," Simonov asked, "in the ability of man—man building socialism—to overthrow that which is old in the world and that which is old in himself? This is a fundamental question for the socialist-realist artist. Those who do not agree in their answers to this question are on different sides of the fence. For lack of faith in the ability of man to remake the world and himself is incompatible with the convictions of a writer who takes the socialist-realist position." (pp. 121-24)

Walter N. Vickery, "The Theoretical Debate," in his The Cult of Optimism: Political and Ideological Problems of Recent Soviet Literature, *Indiana University Press, 1963, pp. 99-124.*

NOVY MIR

HENRY GROSSHANS

[*During the 1950s and 1960s, the journal* Novy mir *("New World") served as the most important forum for radical fiction in the Soviet Union, publishing works by such authors as Vladimir Dudintsev, Vladimir Tendryakov, and Alexander Solzhenitsyn. In the following excerpt from an essay written in 1964, American critic Henry Grosshans discusses characteristic features of the fiction published in* Novy mir *and the controversy surrounding the journal's liberal editorial policies in the decade after Stalin's death.*]

Nine months after Stalin's death, in the December 1953 number of the Russian literary journal *New World,* appeared a twenty-seven page essay entitled "On Sincerity in Literature." Written by Vladimir Pomerantsev, this exercise in literary criticism bore all the outward marks of the usual Soviet text on esthetics. It had the common prosaic title, it was much longer than necessary, and at times it did not quite say what the author undoubtedly meant. But it did set forth the general outlines of a literary controversy that has lasted to the present time [1964], and it was an appropriate introduction to a sequence of events that was to make *New World* the most important literary publication in present-day Russia.

Pomerantsev's article was largely a repetitious restatement of the obvious. He attacked literary artificiality and didacticism, and he pointed out the discrepancies between the reality of modern Russian life and reality as portrayed in modern Russian literature. He argued that a writer's political reliability was of secondary importance and that the "degree of sincerity, that is, the directness of things, must be the first standard of evaluation" in any discussion of literature. He called for hard, cold honesty by Russian writers, and he claimed that insincerity was as great a sin as lying. According to Pomerantsev, Russian literature had been reduced to empty rhapsodies and stale clichés. Literary themes were conventional, while dialogue in most Soviet novels was "pure tirading in the style of a gramophone record."

But Pomerantsev went beyond a mere complaint about the "conditions of literary life." Indirectly, he questioned Soviet orthodox literary theory, the traditional Leninist subordination of literature (and all else in Russian life) to party direction and political manipulation. He ignored *partiinost* and *ideinost,* the two guidelines to proper literary conduct in the Soviet Union. And by contending that a writer's motives, especially when dealing with the human situation, may be ambiguous, Pomerantsev implicitly challenged the party leadership, which, in spite of its apparent dynamic appearance, is hostile toward anything creative or inexplicable, toward whatever does not fit accepted categories of thought, toward whatever is profoundly original.

Since 1953 over one hundred thick numbers of *New World,* whose editorial offices are located, perhaps symbolically, on the corner of Pushkin Square and Chekhov Street in Moscow, have been published. During the past ten years those responsible for the journal have done a great deal of coming and going and have taken a step in one direction and then a step in another. Editors have been replaced, apologies have been made for published material, and there have been spasms of self-criticism. At crucial times the publication has illustrated the method of survival in modern-day Russia, the "dialectical balance," a state of equilibrium achieved by distributing a common emphasis at all points of the compass and appearing on all occasions to be both suitably bold and suitably cautious. In 1956 the editors rejected the manuscript of Boris Pasternak's *Doctor Zhivago*, and *New World* played little part in the flowering of Russian poetry that occurred in the Soviet Union. Reviewers in *New World* have often allied themselves with conventional critics and have accused the young poets of being "loud-mouthed, quarrelsome, and impatient" and of preferring the "parabola" to the straight line. In fact, of all important Soviet literary reviews, *New World* appears to give the least space to poetry, and a reader must turn to other publications if he wishes to enter the lyrical and challenging world of Evgeny Evtushenko, Evgeny Vinokurov, and Andrei Voznesensky.

The very real contributions of *New World* should not be obscured, however, by the school-boy idiocy of canceling one good deed by a bad and thus coming up with a literary zero. The best of the literature published in *New World* has been a cultural commentary that has value and meaning. The journal has provided an alternative to the usual literary publication, with its wretched recital of the superficial and its vulgar collection of political, social, and esthetic footnotes. It has been a medium for literature rather than for literary jargon, and it has served as a haven for those cantankerous, talented men who possess the rare gift of intransigent integrity. Moreover, on the important issues, *New World* has been remarkably consistent, and the line leading from Pomerantsev's essay through the published works of Victor Nekrasov, Vladimir Dudintsev, Grigory Baklanov, and Vladimir Tendryakov to Alexander Solzhenitsyn's *One Day in the Life of Ivan Denisovich* is, as things go in this world, a straight one.

Since 1953 *New World* has been the target of almost continual attack by those who accused the journal of opposing the party attitude toward literature. The lack of optimism and the absence of typicality in much of the fiction published in *New World* offended the custodians of the official literary doctrine, who saw themselves and their ideas threatened by any questioning of traditional concepts and by any criticism of Soviet life. Some of these attacks were made by low-level party hacks; some were by Alexei Surkov, Vsevolod Kochetov, and Vladimir Yermilov, the leading party spokesmen on literary affairs. On several occasions Premier Khrushchev took part in the controversy. Such criticism was serious, for it involved literature in the problems of internal and external politics and raised questions of patriotism and political reliability. Thus in 1956, at the time of the Hungarian revolt, the journal *Communist* developed the following dubious historical interpretation in attacking the type of literature published in *New World:* "Events in Hungary have demonstrated the consequences of disregarding Leninist adherence to principle in questions of the guidance of literature and art." In a similar way, the tone of Khrushchev's comments on literary questions often appeared to be related to the interparty struggles that took place in the late nineteen-fifties and early nineteen-sixties.

Hardly an important literary or critical article in *New World* escaped criticism. One month after his essay was published, Pomerantsev was attacked for having ignored the question of *partiinost* and the task of literature in creating a new society. Vera Panova's *Seasons of the Year* was criticized for having failed to discriminate clearly between good and evil and for having "paid exaggerated attention" to the darker sides of Russian life. Victor Nekrasov's *In the Home Town* was accused of lacking a "sense of the spirit of the times; life flows on, but it is not transformed in the name of great purposes." A critic complained that Daniil Granin's *One's Own Opinion*

emphasized "hopelessness and futility," while Vladimir Dudintsev's *Not by Bread Alone*, which had been rejected by the Writers' Union publishing house and then accepted by *New World*, stirred up a storm in the Soviet Union. Attacks ranged from complaints about the lack of political clarity to suggestions that the work was a thinly disguised piece of treason. When Grigory Baklanov published his *An Inch of Ground*, a reviewer accused him of "Remarquism" and of cravenly imitating the style and form of Western writers. Vladimir Tendryakov's *Three, Seven, Ace* was scored for its lack of social motivation and for its presentation of characters without social consciousness: "They sleep and they work, they work and they sleep—that is how the author depicts them. They say 'we have launched another sputnik' and 'a bear has attacked an old woman near Kurenevo' in the same tone of voice. Clearly the former event excites them no more than the latter. Their minds are preoccupied above all with thoughts of the wages they will receive." Dudintsev's *New Year's Tale* offended a critic because of its lack of political content, which was certain to provoke "a host of perplexing questions" in the minds of readers. Ilya Ehrenburg's *People, Years, Life*, which began serial publication in August 1960, has been attacked for various reasons by various people ranging from Khrushchev and Kochetov to the lesser lights of the Soviet hierarchy.

At different times different official critics have taken the lead in pointing out the errors of *New World*. But the crux of such criticism, whether made in 1954 by Surkov or in 1961 by Kochetov, was the same, and the important issues at question have not changed. In 1954 Alexei Surkov, the First Secretary of the Soviet Writers' Union and a leader in the vicious "anticomparativist" and "anticosmopolitan" campaigns of the late nineteen-forties, attacked *New World* and set the pattern for those who were to complain about the type of literature being published in the journal. Surkov argued that he had originally regarded Pomerantsev's article as well as similar writings in *New World* as examples of carelessness on the part of the editors. This supposition had been wrong, however. Instead, Surkov discovered a premeditated policy, an echo of previous "cosmopolitan and nihilist" literary movements. The writing in *New World* was similar to that of the Pereval group of the nineteen-twenties and early nineteen-thirties, which had been linked with the "idealist" and "subjectivist" schools and with the Trotskyite opposition. This typical maneuver was, of course, intended to create the impression that those publishing in *New World* were influenced by antipatriotic and antiparty sources. In Surkov's opinion, Pomerantsev's article was an attack against "the foundations of our literature," against "Communist ideology," against the Leninist doctrine of *partiinost*, against socialist realism.

The same arguments against *New World* were still being used in the early nineteen-sixties. Vsevolod Kochetov, chief editor of *Literary Gazette* until the spring of 1959 and since early 1961 chief editor of *October*, attacked *New World* in a speech at the twenty-second party congress in the fall of 1961. Kochetov called for literature that would educate the people by positive example. He criticized Ehrenburg for his "crackpot memoirs" and for "grubbing about in human quarrels, in the trivia of everyday life," and he complained that journals such as *New World* had "consigned to oblivion the principal questions of our ideological and creative life." He also suggested that some of the leading writers of the *New World* group were indulging in "boudoir literature" and in the "bedroom lyric." According to Kochetov, "the world of such artists is not broad. It is really . . . about the size of the bed on which the action of a

The last editorial board of Novy mir *under the direction of Alexander Tvardovsky (center front), in 1970.*

great number of Western novels, stories, films, and plays is unfolded.'' This sinister (and false) description of writers who were concerned with the lives of private individuals and not with human beings as political mannequins was designed to darken their character by insinuating that they were immoral and were overly influenced by Western literary trends.

It has not been easy for the editors of *New World* to counter such criticism. Surkov and Kochetov are dedicated party servants, and they are adept at turning every literary controversy into a political polemic. Both are political activists, who lack real talent, and they are experts at hurling scurrilous abuse. Surkov called Pasternak a ''decadent esthete who enjoys a certain popularity in bourgeois circles in the West'' at a time when such denunciation could have resulted in exile, imprisonment, or worse, while Kochetov's best-known novel, *The Obkom Secretary,* was a turgid defense of the argument that party guidance is to be preferred to intellectual independence. Both are politically motivated human beings who are content with the political arrangement whereby they are manipulated from above and in turn manipulate those beneath them. Both are alert to discover any activity of the ''formalists'' and the ''abstractionists'' and to condemn such activity as the ''spawn of the capitalist world.'' For both men the production of literature is a relatively simple matter whereby clearly defined ''positive'' and ''negative'' characters engage in carefully staged combat which results in the destruction of evil, the triumph of good, and the glorification of Soviet society.

New World has also had to contend with Khrushchev, who speaks at random on literature as on all other topics. The premier, who apparently does not wish to interfere unduly in literary matters and who desires writers to follow the party line through their own volition and not through coercion, has occupied an ambiguous position in the Russian literary controversy of recent years. In 1957 he admonished writers to adhere strictly to the principles of socialist realism and to remember that they were the servants of the party. Two years later, however, he modified this stand and at the 1959 writers' congress refused to set down any specific literary program. He drew a distinction between ''party guidance'' and ''petty tutelage,'' implying that the first was good while the second was bad. He called upon writers to settle their own problems and pointed out that the party did not wish to concern itself in these matters. ''Therefore, comrades,'' he said, ''do not burden the government with such questions—decide them yourselves in a comradely manner.'' As long as writers did not engage in antiparty activity, some latitude was to be allowed, and he left the congress with the directive that might be interpreted as ''don't tease the goose.'' In late 1962 and early 1963, however, he again changed his mind. His general attack upon art in the Soviet Union included pointed comments about Ehrenburg and Nekrasov, who had published offensive material in *New World.*

His strictures on some of the writing appearing in the journal were in fact so severe that in the spring of 1963 there was a report that Alexander Tvardovsky had been replaced by Yermilov as chief editor of *New World*. The report was erroneous, and by the middle of the year Khrushchev had for the time being at least lost interest in literary problems.

Because these attacks were made in political terms, those in charge of *New World* were handicapped in defending themselves and were forced to give ground before any serious assault. In 1954, after Surkov's complaint about Pomerantsev's article, the editors confessed their sins, and in August chief editor Tvardovsky was relieved of his duties. The new editor, Constantine Simonov, also had his troubles, and in 1957 was involved in the controversy that developed over the publication of *Not by Bread Alone*. Simonov admitted that he had made a mistake in accepting Dudintsev's story and in early 1957 published a pedestrian defense of socialist realism and patriotic literature.

It was impossible, of course, to argue with Krushchev. But in 1959 and in 1961 Tvardovsky, who had been reappointed chief editor in 1958, made a public defense of the literary principles associated with *New World*. Tvardovsky was a speaker at the 1959 writers' congress. His remarks here were hardly revolutionary, and he balanced his words and avoided excessive liberality and offensive argumentation. But he did call for a new approach to literature in the Soviet Union and said: "We cannot go on living this way—this is what we must say to our literary yesterday and even to our today—and we shall not go on living this way." Following the congress, Tvardovsky became involved in a minor skirmish between the journals *Literary Gazette* and *Literature and Life*. An article in *Literature and Life* complained that some journals (obviously including *New World*) had attempted to establish certain "literary" standards that resulted in the rejection of many politically and ideologically correct works. The authors of this article argued that this procedure was in violation of the principles of socialist realism and that such a false "literary" attitude discriminated against any author who took the "correct ideological and political positions in his work." Tvardovsky answered the complaint in *Literary Gazette,* where he wrote that the *Literature and Life* writers were a disgrace to Soviet literature and that their defense of "mediocrity and dullness in art" was outdated and had no place in modern Russia. After the writers of the *Literature and Life* article had repeated their argument, an editorial in *Literary Gazette* put an end to the dispute by supporting Tvardovsky's contention that literary quality was the most important thing in any work of fiction.

In 1961 Tvardovsky addressed the twenty-second party congress assembled in Moscow. In the first real debate at a party congress since Stalin came to power, Tvardovsky opposed Kochetov and others who wished to hitch literature to the doctrine of socialist realism. He argued that too often political reliability in literature was merely an excuse for absurd tendentiousness and that the "positive hero" was, in spite of his virtues, unbearably dull. Such a person might be the best-hearted and most politically alert fellow in the world, but "just imagine being forced to travel with him from here to Vladivostok." Tvardovsky welcomed the "spiritual regeneration and liberation from certain restraints" that had taken place since the party congress in 1956. He did point out, however, that "we still encounter certain residual forms of previous habits of thought and literary practice." Soviet writing was too reticent. It lacked substance because of its "failure to speak out" and because of the "incomplete picture it gives of the vitality of life and the variety of its problems." Tvardovsky did not mention socialist realism or *partiinost,* but appeared to dismiss these concepts as extraneous to any debate on literature. To a great extent, his speech was a commentary upon Pomerantsev's essay of some eight years before, and he stressed his belief that nothing could compensate for "a lack of living depth and truth" and that one must write "without varnish, without sly glossing over of contradictions."

Tvardovsky's speech was neither profound nor original. But this was not unexpected. Literary arguments, especially when influenced by questions of politics, are usually poor, sterile things, and subtle and meaningful criticism is impossible in the Soviet Union. In 1955 the writer Valentin Ovechkin put it very well: "Confusion has appeared in our criticism. This is the result of addiction to official evaluations. There are no literary judgments, but there is literature. The shop is full of goods, but there is no inventory." In any consideration of *New World*, one must, in Ovechkin's words, look at the "goods" in the "shop" and after that he may, if he wishes, compile an "inventory."

About a dozen of the pieces of fiction published in *New World* in the past ten years are noteworthy literary efforts. This small collection includes Granin's *One's Own Opinion*, Nikolai Dubov's *A Difficult Test,* Baklanov's *An Inch of Ground,* Dudintsev's *New Year's Tale,* Lyubov Kabo's *On a Difficult March,* Nebrasov's *In the Home Town* and *The Second Night,* Solzhenitsyn's *One Day in the Life of Ivan Denisovich,* and Tendryakov's *Three, Seven, Ace* and *Justice.* Such a small group of titles may not constitute an excessively bountiful literary harvest to be gleaned from thousands of printed pages, but the collection probably compares favorably with that to be found in any other literary journal in or out of the Soviet Union.

These works all possess certain characteristics that identify them as products of the *New World* "school." Possibly the most important of these is a certain blunt contact with life that gives the fiction the smell of integrity. Both substance and style are direct. There are few literary twists, few literary tricks, and a minimum of literary finesse. The narratives are almost brutally developed, and there is a harsh dramatic quality in most of the stories that is similar to a slap across the face. There is little of the corrupt brightness and the moral evasion that robs so much literature, in Russia and elsewhere, of significance. The world of these writers, and in particular that of Nekrasov, Tendryakov, and Solzhenitsyn, is one of the moral paradox, of the spiritually mutilated individual, of the mysterious ambiguity of life. The characters portrayed are disfigured by their collisions with life, often flawed by their experiences, and usually broken by the hostile course of events. They are not revolutionary Men with the Capital *M* but Chekhovian men with the small *m,* overwhelmed by problems that reveal what has been called the "foul rag-and-bone shop" of the human heart. The most important fiction published in *New World* stresses the painful truth that underneath the tedious political and social world of everyday life there lies the nightmare world of the tortured individual and that the most common disease in society is the broken-heartedness of its individual members.

Thus Nekrasov's *In the Home Town* is a story of a returning soldier who finds himself alienated from his wife and his surroundings, while his *The Second Night* concerns the traumatic experience of an eighteen-year-old boy who kills a German soldier and then realizes that he has killed a fellow human being. Baklanov's *An Inch of Ground* presents a wartime episode where reason and justice have disappeared. A hero dies at the moment of his triumph, a competent but exhausted officer is reduced to the ranks, and a coward is promoted. In Granin's *One's Own Opinion* the central figure is a man who has fabricated his career through subterfuge and deception, by misrepresenting his own opinions and by suppressing the views of others. Once an enthusiast, he has learned the futility of struggling and has set out to achieve a position of strength so that he may then speak his own voice and redeem his transgressions. But he discovers that he has lost the talent for protest, that the road he is now on has no end, that no position is secure, and that he will always be as he is. Tendryakov's stories pose the questions of guilt and innocence. In his work evil is an integral part of human existence, while the devil alone knows what is just and he is a Don Quixote. Dudintsev's *New Year's Tale* is set in a strange world, one half of which is always in darkness, and is a parable, where the individual searches for self-realization and love.

The leading writers publishing in *New World* have refused to accept the argument that individuals are so much raw material to be used in realizing political and social schemes. They are uninterested in a literature of trivial virility, and they appear to agree with Boris Pasternak that the ultimate issues of life and death do not lie in the momentous upheavals of history but are revealed in the "life-within-a-life" which can be known only to each individual as he experiences it. The Soviet Union may be following a steady high road of historical purpose, but the individual Russian, is, again to use a Pasternak phrase, "a guest of existence," a more-or-less stumbling traveler between two way stations, a solitary soul who must find his own insights into his relationship with life. The ideal party member may be self-satisfied and content. But the typical Russian experiences great and recurring emotional crises in determining his role in the world and the meaning of that role. Political pronouncements and historical theories are of little assistance as each individual faces the terror of his own life, whether such a person is Dudintsev's scientist in his laboratory, one of Nekrasov's soldiers about his fire, Tendryakov's worker on the river, or Solzhenitsyn's prison inmate.

The writing in *New World* has also introduced the dominant quality of Soviet, and for that matter, of modern life. This is the complete loneliness of the individual. In the modern world every society requires a deep-seated habit of conformity, the "aggressive desire to do the right thing." This contributes to society's smooth functioning. But the more organized society becomes, the more isolated the individual. Conformism, careerism, slogans, flags, and political platforms do not provide effective links between him and the community. Moreover, the social and intellectual values forced upon the individual fail to answer any but the most superficial questions, and he is still faced with Tendryakov's presentation of the inevitability of evil and with Solzhenitsyn's query as to why men are inhuman.

There is much in this *New World* writing that is reminiscent of the classic Russian literature of the nineteenth century. The lessons of life in the Tolstoyan sense were modest ones and were usually defined in terms of love, friendship, useful work, and the realization that life, in spite of disappointment and suffering, is preferable to death. Such literature also expressed a fundamental anxiety about existence and continually called back into question the certainties and securities previously gained. In spite of its awesome straightforward quality, the writing of Tolstoy and Chekhov was highly contemplative and involved its characters in a constant intellectual and moral search for the meaning of their lives and of their relationships to the present and the future. In 1958, in a published interview, Dudintsev remarked on the connection between traditional Russian literature and modern Russian writing, and his comments would undoubtedly be endorsed by the other important contributors to *New World:* "When I was young I did not understand the characteristic feature of Russian literature. Now I am thirty-nine.... As I grew older, I began to understand it, to grasp its essential character.... The habit of pondering his fate is something you cannot take away from a Russian, and this most important trait has shaped all our artists."

To a large extent Pomerantsev's demands for sincerity in literature have been met by writers publishing in the journal in which he issued his call. Victor Nekrasov, for example, is accorded the highest possible compliment when he is called an honest writer (*chestny pisatel*) by his countrymen, and the same praise could be accorded Tendryakov, Solzhenitsyn, and others. These writers have cut through the platitudes of life and have established a meaningful moral relationship with their characters. They have attemped to make a valid and courageous analysis of the consequences of living. The "truly significant content, the fidelity to the great truths of life, the profound humanity in the approach to the portrayal of even the most difficult subjects," of which Tvardovsky wrote in the foreword to Solzhenitsyn's *One Day in the Life of Ivan Denisovich*, have become the recognizable characteristics of *New World* writing. (pp. 15-24)

> *Henry Grosshans, "Ten Years with Russia's 'New World'," in* Western Humanities Review, *Vol. XVIII, No. 1, Winter, 1964, pp. 15-24.*

ALEXANDER TVARDOVSKY/EDITH ROGOVIN FRANKEL

[*One of the most prominent figures of the Thaw, Tvardovsky is remembered as the editor-in-chief of* Novy mir *and the catalyst behind that journal's commitment to literary excellence and political outspokenness. Tvardovsky was also a highly-regarded poet of contemporary Russian life, whose best lyrics express his dedication to both the Communist Party and artistic truth. These equally powerful loyalties came into conflict during his editorship of* Novy mir, *as Tvardovsky was frequently the object of bureaucratic harassment for his journal's transgressions against prescribed artistic ideology. The following excerpt presents passages from Tvardovsky's* Za dalyu dal *(1961; Horizon beyond Horizon), an epic poem in which the author utilizes the device of a rail journey through the Soviet Union to prompt reflections on recent Soviet history and contemporary Soviet life. In this selection, Tvardovsky examines the state of literature and the situation of the literary artist in post-Stalinist Russia. Commentary is by Edith Rogovin Frankel, director of the Soviet and East European Research Centre at the Hebrew University of Jerusalem.*]

The single most outspoken work to appear in *Novy Mir* in the summer of 1953 was a poem, "Za dal'yu dal'" ("Distance beyond Distance"), by Tvardovsky.... The first instalment of the poem appeared in June and described the author's trip by train across the Soviet Union. Particularly striking were his stanzas on literature and literary criticism, which he incorporated as the subject of a night-time conversation among the passengers—two members of the reading public and the writer himself—of the railway compartment. One of them accuses the writer of not having an intimate tie with life:

> And how many of you are there in Russia alone?
> Probably five thousand or so.
> After all, it's not numbers that really matter,
> But life is passing you by
> While you probably lock yourselves up in your studies
> And guzzle vodka.

Another passenger complains of the standard socialist-realist novel:

> But their novels are all written
> Before they drop in, sniff the dust,
> Poke the concrete with a walking stick,
> Thus verifying volume one against life itself.
> Before you know it the novel and all that goes with it
>   are in top shape:
> A new method of bricklaying is properly depicted
> As is a backward deputy, a go-getter chairman,
> And a granddad marching on toward communism.
> She and he are both model workers,
> Then, the motor switched on for the first time,
> A party organizer, a snowstorm, a breakdown, an
>   emergency,
> A minister visiting the shops, and all
> Going off to a ball.
>
> And everything looks real enough, everything resembles
> That which is or which could be
> But as a whole it is so indigestible
> That you want to howl out in pain.

One reader becomes more outspoken as the conversation continues:

> No, say what you will, but voluntarily
> I will not agree, I will not give in.
> Life to me is pain and joy,
> I believe, I suffer, I love.
> I am happy to live, to serve my native land;
> I went and fought for it.
> I was born into this world for life—
> Not for editorials.
> I finish a book with irritation.
> My soul is sick: where is the ending?
> But there is no ending. There is a continuation.
> No, brother, that's too much. Have some decency.

And one nods:

> True, true.
> It's understandable, the criticism is well taken.

The writer finds that his own thoughts are ignited by this talk with his readers and feels that he himself would like to deserve their love, to reach "where the heat of living, truthful speech, and not the cold smoke of lies" is found. And so, for the sake of

> that priceless love,
> Having forgotten the bitterness of many years,
> Ready to work day
> And night—you are ready to burn up your soul.
> Ready to face
> All gossip and slander and to say
> Who gives a damn . . .

Alexander Tvardovsky. Novosti Press Agency.

But there is another passenger in the railway compartment besides the writer and his readers:

> Suddenly—a new voice from the upper berth:
> —It won't be published . . .
> —Meaning what?
> —I won't let it . . .
>
> This is not a stentorian outcry,
> No, but the particularly tough tone
> With which superiors usually
> Utter a refusal into the telephone.
> —It won't be published, he drawled a second time.
> —But who are you up there?
>
> —You know very well yourself . . .
> —But who?
> —I am your editor.

The irony in the situation is becoming apparent now. Tvardovsky the poet is portraying himself as a writer being hounded by readers because of the poor state of literature. But he suddenly finds himself being bullied by a demanding editor in the upper berth. As Tvardovsky was himself an editor as well as a poet we thus have Tvardovsky the writer fighting with his alter-ego, Tvardovsky the editor, and finding it difficult to work out a solution. The editor calls down mockingly from the upper berth:

> Well, it's incredible how ardent,
> How brave! And how you go back
> On your own words,
> How having amused yourself for a while,
> You sound your own retreat.
> What for? Because I am with you—
> Always, everywhere—I, your editor.

Tvardovsky attributes to his editor thoughts which he himself could only have regarded with dismay—is this criticism of some unnamed editors or an expression of self-criticism?

> You see, when bent over a blank sheet of paper,
> You're filled with creative thought,
> But you can't go a step without me, wise guy,
> Not a line and not a comma.

Although the writer tries to place the blame on the editor, accusing him of taking too much upon himself, the editor rejects the allegation, referring to the time-honored system of self-censorship:

> And lowering his voice ingratiatingly
> He answers:
> —I don't remove anything.
> Not at all. I delegate everything
> To you and your pen.
>
> It makes no sense for me
> To sweat over, to cross out, cursing fate.
> Understand? All my work
> You will do for me.
>
> . . .
>
> I prefer you above all,
> I set you up as an example: here's a poet
> Whom I simply do not read:
> There's no need to worry there.
>
> And he winked at me slyly
> As if to say, you and me, buddy, we're together all the
> way . . .

Tvardovsky has here identified himself as the "I" by having the editor refer to him not as a writer, but, suddenly, as a poet. He is becoming more entangled in his own literary figure and the dual nature of his own, Tvardovsky's, dilemma becomes increasingly poignant.

The conversation on the train remains unfinished and the problems unresolved. But the bitter quarrel between reader and poet, between poet and editor, has thus been introduced in the post-Stalin period, and well before the landmarks of the autumn Tvardovsky was thus outspokenly expressing the major conflicts of literary life. (pp. 21-4)

> *Alexander Tvardovsky/Edith Rogovin Frankel, "The 'Economic Thaw'," in her* Novy Mir: A Case Study in the Politics of Literature, 1952-1958, *Cambridge University Press, 1981, pp. 20-49.*

LITERARY MOSCOW

GRIGORI SVIRSKI

[*Svirski is a Russian-born novelist, short story writer, and screenwriter who worked as a successful author in the Soviet Union until 1964, when his writings were proscribed by the Soviet government in retaliation for his outspoken criticism of Soviet censorship. Thereafter Svirski supported himself by working on* Novy mir *as an editorial assistant, a position he secured through friends on the journal. In 1970 he was offered an opportunity to "reinstate himself" as an author by writing a novel acceptable to the Soviet authorities; however, he chose instead to emigrate to Israel. In the following excerpt, Svirski discusses the works in* Literary Moscow, *a liberal anthology of poetry and prose published in 1956.*]

1956 was the year of anti-Stalinism only in a manner of speaking. The "year" lasted from the end of the Twentieth Congress in the second half of February, when Khrushchev's speech in closed session opened the eyes of the whole world to the true nature of our "leader and teacher," until 30 June 1956, when the Central Committee started to beat a retreat. At a meeting in Moscow Anastas Mikoyan was soon to be heard berating members of the intelligentsia for "trying to stir up the elements."

All the same, Russian literature managed to have its say. As in 1953, for a very short space of time it achieved total mobilization. It was *Literary Moscow* which first attracted everyone's attention. Although it was an enormous volume, it did not contain even a third of the material prepared for it. Banned after the appearance of the second volume, *Literary Moscow* became not just a landmark in Russia's social and literary life, but a pinnacle heroically reached only after many losses. The greatest losses were the early death of Emmanuil Kazakevich who had nothing left to hope for after the routing of *Literary Moscow,* and the long isolation and illness of the writer and poet Aleksandr Yashin. When Yashin died, still unbroken, his funeral was held in the cemetery of his native village of Bludnovo in the Vologda district to the wailing and sermons of mourners from several northern villages. The funeral was conducted as if it were that of the last defender of the peasants.

However, all that was to come later. At the time, early in 1956, as I leafed through the first volume, which had just been passed for publication, I was delighted to see that among the editors were Konstantin Paustovsky, who in the past had always avoided open conflict with the authorities, and Emmanuil Kazakevich who had survived all the violent assaults directed at him and had again thrown himself into the fray, at least as an editor. Serving with Paustovsky and Kazakevich were Aleksandr Bek, Venyamin Kaverin, and Vladimir Tendryakov, each one of whom is a beacon in Russian post-war literature.

In the preparation of the first volume, there was a need to exercise some home-spun diplomacy, a touch of old-style politesse. When the editorial board was presented with something of an uncompromisingly explosive character, it would put it aside on the grounds that the first issue must present an almost "cloudless" picture, and be inoffensively round. "They mustn't take fright at what we're doing, otherwise they'll ban it. . . . They'll have to get used to us first and see that we're not rebels and not robbers who sound like nightingales. . . ." The first volume really was round and smooth . . . like a cannon-ball. That is why some shied away from it.

However, the important thing about this smooth first volume is that there were pearls to be found in the enormous pile of ''official dung'' made up of articles by people in authority such as Konstantin Fedin, Yevtushenko's empty verse and some sterile, although not always untalented, prose, including Kazakevich's novel *House on the Square,* which was hobbled by the constrictions of socialist realism.

The pearls attracted wide attention, as was only to be expected at a time when the scorched earth policy was being pursued with the greatest ferocity and the one or two break-throughs . . . in the publicistic area were the exceptions that proved the rule.

By 1956 the field of literature had indeed been reduced to burnt-out stubble. In the higher education establishments Professor L. I. Timofeyev's notorious literature textbook, . . . put out by *Uchpedgiz* as early as 1946, was still in use. Only two peasant poets—for some reason a rare phenomenon in a peasant country—appeared intact in it: Isakovsky and Tvardovsky. Esenin also reappeared in it, which was counted a historical victory of some kind. A third of Russian literature—the most probing, thoughtful and talented part—had disappeared from view. (pp. 97-8)

Literary Moscow made what was virtually a new start. It had a freshness and liveliness about it, especially in its poetry. It brought the reader the truth he had been thirsting for. The poems of Margarita Aliger and Nikolai Zabolotsky, who had returned from the concentration camps in poor health and in the last stages of exhaustion, attracted wide attention. In Margarita Aliger's verse the truth about the war seemed to come to life in all its vividness, a quality which seemed to have been lost after the first books by Kazakevich and Nekrasov.

> In Eastern Siberia is the village of Kukoy,
> A handful of huts above a river in the taiga.
> On the rise beyond the village are fields and meadows
> And beyond them, like a wall, the taiga.
>> In forty-one when the enemy was advancing
>> The village farewelled a platoon of fathers and
>> husbands,
>> A platoon of Siberian soldiers as they left their dear
>> taiga . . .
>> Not one came back.
>
> . . . No weddings are celebrated here, no children are
> born,
> Life is without adornment, without adventure.
> The villagers put out the lights very early,
> The accordion is never played in Kukoy,
> There are no parties, no fun,
> Just the sorrowing of widows which has lasted for
> years.
>> So what are my thoughts dwelling on?
> On the passing of the years of youth,
> Which can never have warmth blown into them or be
> brought back,
> And on our common lot, Kukoy,
> My strong, wise friend.

In it a Soviet poet, famous and seemingly without any worries, suddenly writes about sharing the fate of the village of Kukoy, which had in effect been wiped out by the enemy. It is well-known how the Siberians were slaughtered near Moscow—and not only near Moscow.

I remember the strong jolt this poem gave me when I first read it. It stayed with me mainly because it was the first breath of fresh air for a long time. Later I heard poems which were artistically stronger and more full of life than this one, but this was the first gulp of fresh air in the stifling atmosphere of censorship then prevailing.

Nikolai Zabolotsky's verse provided a similar breath of fresh air and similarly gave poetic expression to the truth—and his poetry was of a very high standard. Zabolotsky was a great Russian poet. After his return in a state of utter exhaustion from the camp, Zabolotsky published little of his own verse but more and more often published his translations from the Georgian. He lived outside Moscow, at first without the right to go into Moscow itself. Moscow was the territory of the man who had denounced him, Nikolai Lesyuchevsky, director of the *Sovetsky pisatel* publishing house. We were afraid that Zabolotsky, who had fallen silent in his corner in the forest, would never regain his strength and vigor. He turned out to be completing a new book of verse. On what subject?

> Starling, let me have a corner
> To live in your old starling-house
> I'll pledge you my soul
> For your sky-blue snowdrops.
>
>> Spring is whistling and muttering,
>> The poplars are in water up to their knees,
>> The maples are waking from their sleep
>> To flap their leaves like butterflies.
>
> There is such a mess in the fields
> And the streams are in such a muddle
> That if you leave your attic
> You can't rush at break-neck speed into the copse.
>
>> I am certainly one to try it,
>> But a wandering butterfly whispered to me
>> That whoever is noisy in spring
>> Has no voice left by summer.
>
> Turn to face the universe,
> Celebrating the sky-blue snowdrops
> And journey across the spring fields
> With the unconscious starling.

Another poem in the same vein is ''Morning'':

> Lovers break off their conversations,
> The last starling flies away,
> All day long the silhouettes of crimson hearts
> Fall from the maples.
>
>> Autumn, what have you done to us?
>> The earth is freezing in red gold.
>> The flame of sorrow is whistling underfoot,
>> Stirring the piles of leaves.

The mood of these poems is not a transient or a chance one. It makes itself felt again in ''The Cranes'':

> The cranes flew in a long triangle,
> Lost in the depths of the sky . . .
>
>> . . . Stretching out his silver wings
>> The leader led his small tribe
>> Across the whole wide vault of the sky
>> To the valley of abundance.
>
> But when a lake, transparent to the bottom,
> Flashed beneath their wings,
> A gaping black gun-muzzle
> Was lifted from the bushes towards them.

A beam of fire struck the bird's heart,
The quick flame flared and went out
And a piece of wondrous grandeur
Collapsed on us from the heights.

These lines may give some impression of the thoughts and feelings which seized the spent body of Russian poetry as epochs came apart at the seams. For some generations one age, the age of terror, had come to an end and a new one had begun which made it possible, over the graves of one's friends, to give meaning to the times they lived in and to one's place in the endlessly cruel and bloody stream. (pp. 98-101)

We were not surprised that there also appeared in *Literary Moscow* a new canto called "Childhood Friend" from Tvardovsky's epic poem "Vista beyond Vista" ("Za dalyu dal") in which one of Russia's most prominent poets, recognized as such by the country's leaders, joined those striding forward to greet those whom the leaders had thought were dead and buried long ago, and now tried not to notice. This canto is in the descriptive mode like much of Tvardovsky's poetry. Nevertheless I shall quote a few verses to remind the reader of Tvardovsky's attitude to those he walked with shoulder to shoulder until he died.

No sooner talk of wisdom—
When wood's chopped, chips fly, they say . . .
But no reward for such a fate
Is yet envisaged.

A pity . . . Anyway, here's a story
Which is very simple to tell.
Our train and one from the other direction
Were standing at Tayshet station in the taiga.

A man I usually held onto in my memory
Among my other losses
Like a border-line
Was there, alive—there he was.

I was not mistaken although
He'd worn that quilted jacket for years.
It was him! And he recognized me.
He shouldered his way toward me . . .

And a shameful feeling of fear
Of misfortune came for a moment . . .
But we were already shaking each other
By the shoulders and hands, saying "My old pal!"

"Old pal!" No suffering is stupid.
The whistle will blow either for him or me.
So after seventeen years apart—
Five minutes together.

The two streams of people could not be separated, even in literature. Admittedly, only Tvardovsky could be permitted this. (pp. 101-02)

In the same first volume of *Literary Moscow* there was a story by the talented writer Sergei Antonov called "The Questionnaire." As already mentioned, at one time Antonov's antipathy to politics led to his writing placid country tales while people in the countryside were dying from starvation. Many readers could not forgive Antonov this. Indeed, he did not forgive himself.

In "The Questionnaire" his main concern was to depict a callous manager for whom the answer to the question in the questionnaire "Were you at any time in occupied territory?",

a question which at that time could blacken the applicant's record irrevocably, was more important than the applicant himself. In choosing the theme of hard-heartedness, Antonov was punishing himself, but the reader no longer had any faith in the writer who had once forgotten people for the sake of a few lines of folkloric melodiousness. No mention was made of him at literary discussions, as if the subject were a shameful one.

All this—the village of Kukoy, the starling which lost consciousness, the starling which heard nothing of the woes of earth, and the meeting with the old friend on the station platform at Tayshet—all this was to be found in the first "overly cautious" volume, which was to be proof, as Bek imagined with his usual naïveté, of the editors' loyalty and law-abiding principles. (pp. 102-03)

It took just six months for the times to change, and to change decisively. At a reception at the Chinese Embassy, Nikita Khrushchev again declared himself a Stalinist. However, it was too late to ban the second volume of *Literary Moscow*. When it appeared, the whole country started talking about Alexander Yashin's story "Levers."

Yashin was a former peasant from the Vologda region whose ties with his native village remained strong all his life. He was a poet much in favor with the State, a Stalin Prize winner, a native son—in short, he "belonged." He was the last person the Stalinists expected this sort of thing from. This story cost Yashin his life, or at least shortened it, bringing a multitude of misfortunes on his family.

Yashin's "Levers" underpinned stories by Yuri Nagibin and Nikolai Zhdanov which I shall discuss later. His story rang an alarm-bell which made some people look up and listen and others act. Yet it is a simple story, which does not at first sight appear to be a call to action.

It is a story which no student of modern Russian literature should fail to acquaint himself with. It is a distillation of the wrongs not only of the past, but also of the present, and the future. It shows the sufferings of Russia crushed by arbitrary rule, with people deprived not only of the right to act, but also of the right to think—in other words, the right to a normal human existence which is inconceivable without the right to think about life.

It is not difficult to imagine how soldiers can be turned into "levers" and sent to fight the Czechs, for example. A soldier has sworn allegiance. He is ordered to shoot, and he shoots. The alternative is to be court-martialled or commit suicide— which also happened in Prague. Nor is it difficult to understand how Party functionaries become "levers." It is in the nature of their work. By way of compensation they enjoy a great number of privileges, not to mention a double salary. If they sell their independence, they do so consciously.

But how could the peasants, the mass of the people, become "levers"? This had not been discussed in Russia for a long, long time. "The people are silent"—as Pushkin tells us in *Boris Godunov*. And by its silence, Yashin seemed to be adding, it was furthering the ruin of the countryside and arbitrary rule—villainy, in a word. Yashin did not resort to Aesopian devices, but spelt it out in black and white.

This was perhaps the first post-war example of "folk" prose— earthy, solid, undiluted by the sometimes insipid, colorless language of the cities—entering the mainstream of Russian literature after a break of a quarter of a century. This "folk" prose became a continuing basis for a whole stream in post-war Soviet literature, later to be called "village prose" *(de-revenskaya proza).*

The story opens on a note which is almost symbolic in its everyday quality. Four men are sitting in the kolkhoz office smoking. There is so much smoke in the room it is almost impossible to breathe. Even the radio seems to be crackling because of all the smoke. The men can hardly even see each other through it. One of them says to the man next to him who is dropping live ash on himself: "If you burn your beard off, the cows won't be afraid of you any more." Unperturbed, his neighbor replies: "If they're not afraid any more, they might give more milk." They do not appear to be talking about anything important, just trifles. But in fact there is nothing trifling about this conversation. It introduces us to the main theme which the reader absorbs without realizing that it is the main theme.

Then comes another everyday scene from country life, again nothing out of the ordinary. It is an official aspect inasmuch as it is set in the kolkhoz office. The scene is in half-light. Here and there are posters and banners in honor of some special day—but they have been up all year. There is a list of kolkhoz members on the wall showing the number of work days to their credit, and an empty blackboard divided into two equal parts. At the top of one side is written "Black" (here are written the names of those with a bad work record.) The board itself is black like the kolkhoz members' life, but it is customary to consider one side "red" (which has connotations of "beautiful" in Russian)—there is an order from above to that effect.

An atmosphere of expectancy slowly builds up although nothing is directly said about it. Smoke, the blackboard, random snatches of conversation. There is no sugar in the village. Not that there is any complaint about it! One of the men sitting smoking says that the store manager "threw in a couple of kilos for me. Is he afraid of something, do you think?" The other says: "Of course he's afraid of something. I'm the new store manager now." The narrator explains that this man was made store manager because he joined the Party. When he joined a few months earlier he began expressing his opinion that all positions of authority in the kolkhoz should be occupied by Communists. How simple, how naively simple everything is. Once he has his Party card, he starts getting extra supplies. They now recall that the old store manager was caught stealing, which they had not known before. The new Communist store manager buys a fountain pen and starts wearing a tie. He joins the kolkhoz managers.

The atmosphere clears, despite the smoke. The main theme now starts to come through more and more strongly. "All right, so he took it [sugar]," said Shchukin after a moment's consideration. "But where's there any justice anyway? What happens to the sugar? Where's the soap and everything?" Another one of the men jokes: "What does justice matter to you? You're the store manager!"

Someone intones in a business-like way: "We must do the right thing. Everything depends on doing the right thing. Only I don't understand what's going on in this district. We're told to plan from below. Let the kolkhoz decide itself what it's best to sow and what not to sow—but they don't approve our plan. Three times they refused to pass it, then passed their own plan and insisted on it, too."

The conversation becomes deeper, passing from sugar and cows to the subject of how people's hands are tied.

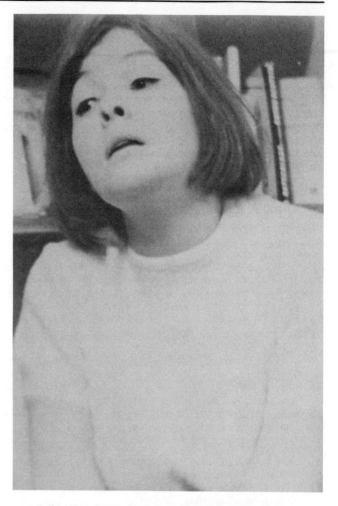

Bella Akhmadulina. From Ardis Anthology of Recent Russian Literature, *edited by Carl Proffer and Ellendea Proffer. Ardis, 1976. Reprinted by permission of Ardis Publishers.*

"There's justice for you. They don't trust us," says one of the characters. "Around here justice is made one of the directors so that it doesn't get upset or open its mouth," says another kolkhoznik and throws his cigarette butt into a pot. Shchukin the storeman gets his word in: "Do you mean to say that justice is only needed for meetings and public holidays, like criticism and self-criticism, and that it doesn't have any application to what we actually do."

And so the conversation goes on. It is a normal conversation among people who are sick of lies, although some people, like the store manager, are already managing to turn the situation to their own advantage. How easy it is to argue convincingly that since it is the Party which is in power and I am in the Party I am in power, so give me a post!

This utterly normal, confidential conversation between men from the same kolkhoz ends with one of the characters, who has visited the district boss, reporting what he said to him: "What are you doing to us, I said. The kolkhoz won't agree to changing the plan for the third time. You talk them into it," he said. "We talked you round when the kolkhozes were being set up, now you talk the others round. Implement the Party line. You're now our levers in the countryside."

This is the first mention of the word "levers." What is its meaning? How is it used? Why are people called "levers"?

Obviously so that official lies and unrealizable plans, ruinous plans, might triumph, so that the crops their grandfathers sowed and harvested for generations might not be sown, but instead what Moscow decided should be allotted to the different regions and districts.

How then could a district committee Secretary function? If he were honest, he would send off a protest and put his head on the block. If he were not honest, the system itself would pick him out like high-quality grain. Like attracts like. "He doesn't come out in the open with the people," the same kolkhoznik says of the district committee Secretary. "He knows full well that everyone in the kolkhoz gets a hundred grams per working day. Yet he keeps saying: 'Each year the value of a day's work grows and the people's well-being increases.' We haven't got any cows left on the kolkhoz, but he says: 'Each year the kolkhoz live-stock sector grows and strengthens.' He says to tell people that they're living badly for this reason or that at the moment, but they will live better—and then they'll work more willingly." But the district committee Secretary is lying.

If we consider that he lies not in his own words but in words taken from the speeches of the State's leaders such as Khrushchev and Bulganin, using official State-sanctioned stereotyped phrases, we can easily understand the enormous risk Alexander Yashin was running in his determination to make a break with the deeply rooted State system of lies. His break is a complete one. He sees right to the heart of his subject.

> Giving a small cough but remaining bent over, one of the men looked up and said somewhat hoarsely: "The top men in the district have forgotten how to talk to the people, they're ashamed. They understand what's going on but they're afraid to make a move. What do they mean—talk us round? . . . They expect us to be levers. . . . They see the houses boarded up in the village but don't want to say anything about it out loud. The only thing they're worried about is that they should have nice round figures in the reports."

The lamp starts to flicker and someone makes the casual remark: "Blast it, it'll go out without air. A lamp needs air too."

It is a friendly, frank conversation, all the more impressively true to life because of the casual details: the smoke, the blackboard one half of which it is obligatory to regard as "red," the lamp which *also* needs air.

Suddenly there is a noise in the cottage. An old woman's voice is heard crying out behind the big Russian stove: "Where do you think you're dropping your ash, you old carcass? You don't have to clean up!" The men are startled and look at each other. "Are you still here, Martha? What are you there for?" "You know what for! I'm watching you! You'll set fire to the office and I'll be dragged off to court. The broom's dry and you could easily drop a spark—God preserve us!" "Just go home!" "I'll go when I'm good and ready."

The men's conversation breaks off as if they feel guilty about something. For a long time they sit smoking in silence. When they start exchanging brief remarks again, the remarks are empty, not about anything or directed at anyone.

Finally, one of them, Shchukin, who has still not got used to his managerial position and is at heart still an ordinary kolkhoznik, suddenly cannot help bursting out into loud laughter: "What a fright she gave us, damn her!" They all exchange glances and also burst into laughter. "Gave us a fright all right, the old devil, roaring at us from behind the stove like that. I thought it was the boss himself come to catch us at it. . . . The way we got a fright, you'd think we were little boys stealing apples."

Laughter lightens the atmosphere and people begin to feel normal again. "What are we afraid of?" says Pyotr Kuzmich in a thoughtful and slightly sad way, "It is ourselves we're afraid of."

"It's ourselves we're afraid of." So that is the way things are. So this is what Russia has been brought to—not bureaucratic Russia, but grass-roots Russia, the mass of the people in whom everyone from Dostoevsky to the populists have put their trust, the true, peasant Russia untouched by lies. And it is a peasant poet with a Vologda way of speaking and thinking who tells us how frightened the peasant workers are, the Vologda peasants who stayed out of reach of the Tartar hordes and Genghis Khan. But not out of reach of Stalin and Khrushchev.

A woman teacher they have been waiting for arrives and the Party meeting they have gathered for begins. Sitting down, the teacher complains about the lack of wood at the school.

"We'll leave business till later," the chairman interrupts her. "First we must conduct the meeting. There's a long-standing requirement by the district committee that there should be two meetings a month, and we haven't managed to have a single meeting. How are we going to account for ourselves?"

Our despairing author's intent is now clearer. The proceedings at the Party meeting are wholly unnecessary. The meeting is not being held to attend to any business, but for the sake of making a report. This is an attack on the very foundations of the bureaucratic machine which without all this fuss would soon end up on the scrap heap.

Old Martha from behind the stove, who is not a Party member, the depths of Russia incarnate, and hope of the populists, has no difficulty in grasping what is going on. When they try to make her leave, she does not protest or kick up a fuss. Nor does she call the Party worker an old carcass this time, either, in her familiar, peasant way. "Carry on, carry on, I understand, I'm off." This is no longer an area of life where Martha has a right to say her piece, but a closed Party meeting.

The author is barely able to withhold his anger and irony. If it had been any stronger, it would have been virtually suicidal. "The earthy, natural element vanished entirely and the action shifted into another world, a complicated setting which was not wholly customary or comprehensible to these simple, warm-hearted people."

At this point a strange misprint made things worse. The author presumably meant to say that after Shchukin was appointed store manager, "there were no ordinary kolkhozniks left in the Party organization." (In Russian the difference lies in one letter: "ryadovykh kolkhoznikov i partorganizatsii ne bylo.") "That's not a chance misprint, but a deliberately malicious act—an act of sabotage!" claimed the frightened literary bureaucrats, playing safe.

The meeting, of course, drifts on in a flow of verbal garbage: ". . . this was not foreseen and allowed to take its own course. . . . Explanatory work was not taken up with the masses and consequently they were not convinced. . . ." Although the young Communist Shchukin sits in his corner making ironical remarks under his breath at the expense of the empty verbiage to which he is not accustomed, it is soon made plain to him who *is* experienced and in his element here. "All right, let him have his say. That's the way it's done! Piotr Kuzmich is carrying out his duties. That's the way it's done at the district level, and that's the way we do it. Like master, like man." They quieted down, ready to vote for whatever is necessary. "That's the way it's done!" Not long ago they were people, now they are people no longer, but levers.

The lifeless official part is over and some young people burst into the room impatient to begin a party—the room serves as both office and club for the kolkhoz, there being only one "official" building in the village. They fling open the windows. "It's so smoky in here," the girls cry.

It turns out that the smoke was no ordinary smoke, but Party smoke. Russia is smothered with smoke, stupefied with smoke, to the point of nausea and giddiness. When the poet's pen is guided by suffering and courage, his images have great strength. This poet had the determination to cry out for all Russia to hear: "We have been silent long enough! We're people, not levers!"

Alexander Yashin's "Levers," which aroused such lively interest among thinking people in Russia, could scarcely have appeared at all if it had been the only piece in the second volume of *Literary Moscow* attempting to throw some light on the "new class" of usurpers and destroyers. Apart from Yashin's story, which was as far-reaching as Russia's misfortune itself, there was also a story by Yuri Nagibin called "A Light in the Window."

Nastia, a maid in a rest house, keeps an empty room clean and tidy in readiness for "the big man," should he decide to turn up. There are rooms like this in every rest house and sanatorium, however unprepossessing, just in case "the big man" arrives—some government minister or factory manager, a Central Committee or district committee Secretary—every rest house has its own "big man." Sweeping out these uninhabited rooms and seeing the cramped conditions all around, Nastia is patient for a year and then she throws caution to the winds, ignores the ban on using the rooms, turns on the light, invites the janitor's children and a few friends in and settles down in front of the television as if she owned the place.

Seeing the light in the window of the room set aside for the "big man," the manager naturally hauls Nastia over the coals. As Nagibin describes it, there grows in the manager as he abuses Nastia "a sensation of intolerable self-disgust which penetrated right down to his fingertips."

Nagibin's story was almost as sharp-edged as Yashin's and possibly even more poetic. However, the impression it made on our generation in terms of its forcefulness and deep significance cannot be compared with the impression made by "Levers."

In the same issue of *Literary Moscow* there appeared a story by the Moscow writer Nikolai Zhdanov called "A Trip Home." The mother of an important Moscow big-wig, Varygin, dies at home in her village and her son goes home for the funeral. He returns to a world which he imagined no longer existed— a world of want. The furniture is rough, the old samovar is coming unsoldered. The junk in the room acquires a new significance in that it casts a different light on the visitor himself. The cracked and useless samovar lies on its side just like the visiting big-wig from Moscow. He, too, has come unstuck on his journey and is useless to anybody in his native village.

His mother waited for her son for many years, but he cut himself off not only from his village but also from his mother. He speaks a different language from the people in the village as if he came from another country. The following conversation takes place between a peasant woman who knew his mother and the former peasant lad:

> "Was she waiting for me to come?" he asked.
>
> "This year she didn't talk about it, but that summer when you promised to come she was very impatient for you to come. She kept saying: 'Any time now, any time now.' Then she quieted down. But she wasn't hurt about it, no. She understood how hard it is for a busy man to get away. I dare say you've gone farther than anyone else from our village."

After making some tea, she puts the cup in front of him and sits down at the table.

> "What I wanted to ask you is this," she went on. "Have they done the right thing by us or not? This year we sowed hemp, seventy-four hectares of it. The hemp had just flowered when the spring crops ripened. We wanted to harvest it and then stack it, but we were told to get on with the threshing and send it off. But if you don't bring hemp in at the right time, you won't get any seed."
>
> "She thinks there's something I can do about it," thought Varygin in dismay, trying to remember what was involved in harvesting hemp and where the bit about the seed came in. But he could not remember.
>
> Aloud he said: "It's a political question. The State must always come first for us. Everything depends on the level of consciousness of the masses." He fell silent, feeling that he had said the wrong thing.

If even Varygin was able to feel it, how much more able was the reader. The reader had been surrounded by Varygins for a long time. He had met them in Vera Panova's work after the war. Panova's Listopad was drawn more cautiously, but then times were different. There is nothing cautious about the way Varygin is drawn. He is not only callous, but does not even understand the language of the people, as if he were from another world. The only things he is left with are a feeling of guilt and the peasant woman's question: "Have they done the right thing by us?"

Nikolai Zabolotsky appeared again in the second volume. There was a whole collection of poems by this poet who had come to life again. One of his poems includes these three stanzas:

> As winter first advances,
> Wandering above the spacious Neva
> We compare summer's glow
> With leaves strewn along the shore
> But I'm a lover of old poplars
> Which try not to throw from their branches
> Their dry rusted shirt of mail
> Until winter's first blizzard.
> How shall I describe the similarity between us?
> Like a poplar, I'm not young either,
> And I too need a coat of mail
> To meet winter's approach and its deadly cold.

This poem clearly needs no commentary. This is the poetry of a master who did not believe in the warmth or even in the thaw which everyone believed had arrived. This great poet died like this, still frozen, in anguish that he had no protective armor to help him bear the cold. There were other poems like this in *Literary Moscow* and more came out later.

It was in the same issue of *Literary Moscow* that Ilya Ehrenburg introduced Marina Tsvetaeva to Soviet readers. It really was a case of introducing her as a new writer because by this time whole generations of readers had never even heard her name. After all, who would have dared tell them about a poet who had come back to her native land and then hanged herself?

This was a real break-through, a piercing of the ban which had sealed her off. Everyone hastened to make his contribution.

> My verses about youth and death
> —Unread verses!—
> Strewn about in the dust of shops
> (Where no one picked them up or does so now!)
> My verses, like precious wines,
> Will have their turn.

It was with these lines written by Tsvetaeva at the age of twenty that Ehrenburg opened his article on Tsvetaeva's poetry.

Ehrenburg, too, was in some haste. Tsvetaeva had perished as had her books and as had so many of Russia's best poets before her. Ehrenburg himself was not young and therefore he felt a sense of urgency. And Tsvetaeva had wanted to give voice to the same things he had wanted to express for many years:

> I refuse to be
> In the Bedlam of non-people,
> There I refuse to live.
> With the wolves on the squares
> I refuse to howl.

Of course, Ehrenburg explained, Tsvetaeva is talking about Fascism here—of the German variety. Up to this time Khrushchev alone was allowed to mention Stalinism, and only then in closed session at a Congress barred to the public.

It is to *Literary Moscow* that we are indebted for turning Russia's attention to this unknown poet. If *Literary Moscow* had achieved nothing else, apart from making Tsvetaeva's name known, it would have achieved much. But it did more—it went onto the offensive.

The editors seemed to have bided their time and then gone into the attack by publishing a number of critical essays and articles among which the most forceful was the playwright Alexander Kron's article about the destruction of the country's theatrical life. In it he accused the powers-that-be of "painting over existing contradictions" under the banner of "consolidation." It was indeed a despicable slogan, demanding as it did that writers unite with their hangmen. "There is no greater untruth than that the so-called no-conflict theory was the brain-child of creative artists," Kron wrote. "You might as well claim that it was the biologists' idea to ban the teachings of Darwin." In this way there was no direct accusation directed at the Party Central Committee. The artistic intelligentsia had successfully stormed new heights.

Kron wrote of an editor who regarded himself as a kind of watchdog: "It appears that as in the army a book has both a commander and a political commissar." "Art knows only one legitimate hierarchy," he wrote, "that of talent."

It is not hard to imagine the reaction to these words on the part of those at the top of the literary hierarchy—all the Surkovs, Fedins, Gribachevs and Korneichuks. There was a malicious joke circulating at Korneichuk's expense to the effect that if he wrote something good, he would sign it in full "Kornei Chukovsky" but if it was rubbish he would feel ashamed and shorten it to "Korneichuk."

"That is how the hierarchy is established among playwrights," Kron went on relentlessly. "There are general survey articles, signed by people no one has ever heard of—but this is of no importance since they are written in the people's name. "The people know and love such writers as. . . ." "Such writers are not carrying out their duty to the people. . . ." "Such plays have received some recognition among the people. . . ." "The people rejects such plays as. . . ." This magic formula, which obviates all necessity for arguing the case, is accompanied by a list of writers and plays.

The readers of Kron's article laughed, and of course nothing is as deadly as laughter. It was not something harmless that it was aimed at, however, but Stalinism, which knew how to crouch down on the ground like a mad dog and then suddenly spring up and bite. Kron was well aware of this, as were all the editors, and although he was well-known and the recipient of a number of honors, he still found the courage to say "I am attacking." "If drama is regarded as part of the greater body of Soviet literature, then there are no serious grounds for herding it into a cell," he concluded.

Kron's article caused the same panic as Yashin's article. Quite by chance I happened to be in the office of Nadezhda Chertova, Secretary of the Moscow Party organization, when Lesiuchevsky, director of the *Sovetsky pisatel* publishing house, rang her about the forthcoming discussion of *Literary Moscow*. It was a case of one hangman ringing another. On Chertova's desk lay the proofs of the third issue of *Literary Moscow* which was in fact fated not to appear. I shall never forget her shouting into the telephone: "We'll adopt an iron-fisted attitude to the discussion." Literature, of course, does not thrive on iron. The vocabulary of these mentors of literature and poetry is noteworthy. Over the years a special, lethal, violent vocabulary had been developed, the language of informers and those who carried out the sentences. The choice of language speaks volumes in itself, regardless of how it is dressed up.

Khrushchev was horrified by the Hungarian uprising and convinced, as only an ignoramus can be, that it was all the fault of writers—of the Petofi Circle in Hungary, and of the Moscow writers in Russia, and this led to an increase in the power and arrogance of the innumerable Chertovas and Lesiuchevskys. They regarded *Literary Moscow* as a rattlesnake which had slithered into their comfortable apartments. The most poisonous of all was, of course, Yashin's "Levers." They hammered away at it at all the meetings and set all the hacks onto it, all the modern Bulgarins and Greches. All the levers were pulled, all the stops were out.

How Russia's Party-appointed leaders took fright at Yashin's little tale! They started rushing off to the Central Committee, dredging up the old Stalinist terminology such as "ideological sabotage," the hot-lines to the Kremlin started buzzing, messengers ran back and forth as if a war had started and the enemy had to be repulsed immediately, today, for tomorrow would be too late.

With Russia's reading public Yashin's story had a stunning success. It helped many to stand up straight and acquire some realization of what was actually going on. It even allowed some to think things through to their conclusion. This was not an easy thing to do for people crushed by years of disinformation. It was this story which struck the heaviest blow, despite the insertions of the "co-author"—the pock-marks of the age—designed to soften the blow.

These pock-marks simply went unnoticed. After all, who could hold it against a writer if he did not want to be dragged straight off to the Lubianka away from his wife and six children, a writer who was also a talented poet, the support of a warm, close-knit family in the peasant tradition. The authorities soon made it their business to try to smash this family, something they did not take long to do. (pp. 105-15)

Alexander Yashin's fate was a tragic one. After "Levers" he was constantly under attack and being threatened. However Yashin would just spread his elbows on the rostrum and say with a knowing smile, as if he were just some country bumpkin: "I thought you'd thank me, but instead of that I'm really copping it from you." But it was pointless for him to pretend to be a country bumpkin. His smile was too frank, his eyes with their cunning peasant's squint too piercingly intelligent.

He kept on writing and did not retreat. A few things got into print, but most of his stories and poems stayed in his desk drawers. That is why in the later stories such as "My Rowan-berries" and "A Vologda Wedding" (*Novy mir*, no. 4, 1965 and no. 12, 1969) where he refuses to yield, he is so fresh and interesting.

Although his most valuable works have probably not been published, he still died a victor. (p. 115)

> Grigori Svirski, "The Year of Anti-Stalinism: 'Literary Moscow, I' " and "The Year of Anti-Stalinism: Fresh Insights, 'Literary Moscow, 2'," in his A History of Post-War Soviet Writing: The Literature of Moral Opposition, *edited and translated by Robert Dessaix and Michael Ulman, Ardis, 1981, pp. 97-103, 105-15.*

PASTERNAK, *ZHIVAGO*, AND THE NOBEL PRIZE

ABRAHAM ROTHBERG

[*One of the most heated controversies of the Thaw period concerned the foreign publication of Boris Pasternak's Doctor Zhivago and the subsequent award of the Nobel Prize in literature to Pasternak. In the following excerpt, the events precipitated by the novel's publication are recounted by American editor, novelist, and critic Abraham Rothberg.*]

Many liberal writers had been censured and criticized, some quite severely, during the years 1957 to 1959, but only one brought down the full wrath of the powers that be: Boris Pasternak, in 1958. Though Khrushchev was at that time striving to establish a more moderate, if not permissive, cultural policy, the Pasternak case showed how small the area of maneuver was for any writer in the Soviet Union.

Pasternak himself was a phenomenon in Soviet literary life, a major Russian poet who had managed to retain his integrity as a writer and as a man through all the vicissitudes of Communist rule. To have done so under Stalin was miraculous, and few, especially those of Pasternak's stature, had managed it. Yet

Pasternak, like Anna Akhmatova, who had also miraculously survived, had remained an influence and example for many of the younger generation of writers that the Party was most concerned to indoctrinate.

If Pasternak had survived, he had by no means flourished. Shortly after the end of World War II, when the Zhdanov decrees on the arts had shriveled the souls and the works of Soviet writers, Pasternak (with Akhmatova and Mikhail Zoshchenko) had come under severe attack from the regime and been expelled from the Writers' Union. At that time, Union secretary Fadeyev had criticized Pasternak for having contributed only a few second-rate verses to the Soviet war effort, though in the darker days of battle, the authorities had publicly commended his literary efforts and had, in fact, permitted two books of his poems to be published, in 1943 and 1945. But in the postwar political atmosphere of the restrictive and dogmatic Zhdanov decrees, Pasternak's mistress, Olga Ivinskaya, was arrested and tortured in an effort to make her confess that she and Pasternak were "Western agents." Ivinskaya's refusal to implicate Pasternak in any such trumped-up charges probably saved the poet from imprisonment, but resulted in Ivinskaya's serving a year in Lubyanka Prison and four years in a Siberian labor camp from which she was released (like Solzhenitsyn) only in the general amnesty after Stalin's death.

By and large, Pasternak had saved himself by devoting his gifts to the translation of foreign works into Russian—the major Shakespearean tragedies, Goethe's *Faust*, the works of the Hungarian national poet, Sandor Petöfi, and a group of Georgian poets; but mostly he had been "writing for the drawer." (Rumor had it that one reason Stalin kept Pasternak alive was because of his translation of the poets of Stalin's native Georgia, with which the dictator was pleased. Other rumors insisted that the Machiavellian Stalin deliberately permitted Pasternak to go on writing and living so that he could use him as an example of a true and gifted artist with which to goad more compliant but less talented hacks.)

The writer Valentin Katayev, who had himself survived the purges and was knowledgeable about the literary and political personalities involved, gave a quite different picture of how Pasternak survived. He told Harrison Salisbury:

> Pasternak was not a simple unworldly man as many of you in the West think. . . . He was a man of contradictions. He had his own character. But he wished to be part of the Establishment, to be recognized, to belong. He could have been a courtier of Stalin, if Stalin permitted this. He was not really a rebel at all.
>
> Mandelshtam was outspoken. . . . He was a real opponent of Stalin. I remember once he came to our house, it must have been 1936 or 1937. He was shouting against Stalin—what a terrible man Stalin was. We were terrified, my wife and I. We had two small children. Pasternak was never like that.

Some writers still blame Pasternak for not standing up more strongly to Stalin.

In April 1954, after not publishing in the Soviet Union since the end of the war, Pasternak took advantage of the first thaw to have ten of his poems published. These, later to be included in *Doctor Zhivago*, appeared in *Znamya* and soon came under official critical attack as pessimistic and decadent, and as examples of applying Pomerantsev's canons of "sincerity" to literature.

Shortly after the end of World War II, Pasternak had begun to write a novel which was eventually to become *Doctor Zhivago,* and by the end of 1955 he had finished his work on it. Taking advantage of the second thaw, in 1956, he circulated the manuscript to several publishing houses and magazines, among them the journal *Novy mir,* whose editorial board collectively sent him a personal letter of rejection which subsequently was to play a significant role in the government's condemnation of Pasternak and the novel. But at the time the authorities seemed to be considering a publication of a censored version of the novel—which Pasternak would have consented to—but no decision was forthcoming.

In the interim Pasternak had sent a copy of the manuscript of *Doctor Zhivago* to Giangiacomo Feltrinelli, a prominent Italian publisher and a member of the Italian Communist Party. Feltrinelli was empowered to arrange for publishing various foreign-language editions, and did so; at the same time, he prepared his own Italian translation of the novel. Then Moscow and Italian Communist leaders asked Feltrinelli to postpone the publication of the book for six months while the Kremlin decided what it was going to do. Subsequently, as the Italian publication date loomed closer, Anatoly Surkov, head of the Soviet Writers' Union, and a leading functionary of the Italian Communist Party combined to attempt to induce Feltrinelli to give up publishing the book altogether. They cajoled and threatened, warning Feltrinelli that if he issued the book he would be endangering Pasternak's life. Finally, a telegram bearing Pasternak's name came to Feltrinelli, and other foreign pub-

lishers who had contracted to publish the novel, requesting them to abandon publication. Feltrinelli refused, and *Doctor Zhivago* was published in Italy on November 15, 1957, to a chorus of praise, some notes of reservation and disappointment, and general agreement that the book presented serious criticisms of Soviet life.

But not until almost a year later, when on October 23, 1958, the Swedish Academy announced the award of the Nobel Prize in literature to Pasternak, did the storm break. On October 25, Pasternak cabled his acceptance (in French): "Immensely thankful, touched, proud, astonished, abashed."

On the same day, October 25, an anonymous article in *Literaturnaya gazeta* called down the rage of the Kremlin's rulers on Pasternak, accusing him of scorning the Russian people and the "Great October Revolution": "He says not one good word for our workers, peasants or soldiers," the paper pointed out, then went on to call Pasternak a slanderer, a base, small-minded, faint-hearted, and "malicious literary snob" whose novel had placed a "weapon in the hands of the enemy," for which this literary Judas had just been awarded his thirty pieces of silver, the Nobel Prize.

In the same issue, *Literaturnaya gazeta* printed the September 1956 rejection letter the editorial board of *Novy mir* had sent to Pasternak with a covering letter from the present editorial board saying that Pasternak had "flouted the elementary notions of the honor and conscience of a Soviet writer," and that the publication of the book abroad had raised an "anti-Soviet clamor . . . and is an act of pure politics hostile to our country and directed towards the fomenting of the cold war." (The covering letter of 1958 was signed by the entire editorial board, but only two of the members of that board—Konstantin Fedin and B. A. Lavrenov—were among the five signatories of the original rejection letter of September 1956. The other three were Konstantin Simonov, B. Agapov, and A. Krivitsky. In the obvious disparity between the two sets of signatures, Tvardovsky may deliberately but subtly have been making a point.) The rejection letter was a carefully thought-out and carefully written review of *Doctor Zhivago*. The editors refused to publish it for political reasons and directed their criticisms of the novel mainly to political issues in the manuscript because they believed that Pasternak had "written a political novel-sermon, par excellence." The rejection letter charged that the book depicted the Bolshevik Revolution and its aftermath as a disaster for the common people and the Russian intelligentsia alike and that because this hostility to the "socialist revolution" informed the entire work, it was something that "neither editors nor the author can alter by cuts or changes."

The letter also indicts Zhivago and, by implication, Pasternak for being intellectuals "bloated with a sense of [their] own self-importance," involved only with themselves and their own sufferings, turned against the revolution by physical discomfort and deprivation, feeling in no way a part of the nation or any responsibility to the people at large. "This is almost pathological individualism, a naive grandiloquence of people who cannot and do not want to see anything around them and who therefore attach a comically exaggerated importance to their persons"; "Zhivago sees the old life broken up and transformed around him in a brutal, costly, difficult process, the expediency of which can only be gauged from the standpoint of national interests, from the standpoint of a man who puts the nation above everything else. And this is precisely what Zhivago lacks."

Boris Pasternak. UPI/Bettmann Newsphotos.

Max Hayward gives an exceedingly subtle and intelligent interpretation of why the Soviet authorities hated *Doctor Zhivago* so much. He believes that Zhivago was one of the "great superfluous men of Russian literature," a man who despite his intelligence and good will could never sufficiently focus his gifts to act positively and effectively. What enraged the Party about the novel, Hayward believes, was that it treats Zhivago's ineffectuality with sympathy and in so doing appeals to "the non-activist people, mainly intellectuals, [and so] destroys the position of moral superiority that [the Communists] have created for the political activists." This is a shrewd insight, but it may be oversubtle and may overlook the main thrust of both the book and its threat to the Soviet regime. True, the Party has always been concerned with the "superfluous men" and "Oblomovist" inertia traditionally endemic among the Russian intelligentsia; but the *Novy mir* criticism is probably more to the point. What horrified the Party stalwarts was an evaluation of their achievement as an unmitigated disaster for everyone concerned. What appalled them was Pasternak's defense of the individual human personality as more important than any "collective": people, nation, state, Party. What defeated them was his refusal, in the novel as in life, to accept the transformation of society by brutal means: Pasternak (and Zhivago) could see such a transformation only as brutalizing. Pasternak has Zhivago say, "I was inclined towards revolution, but now I believe that nothing can be achieved by force." And when Zhivago says to Lara, "This construction of new worlds and transition periods is an end in itself to them [the guiding spirits of the Revolution and the Party]. This is all they know and all they can know. . . . A man is born to live, not to prepare for life," Pasternak is striking at the very taproot of the Party's perpetual (and megalomaniac) claim to direct and control the lives and sacrifices of more than two hundred million people now and for generations to come.

The type of campaign the regime directed against Pasternak would tend to confirm such an interpretation. Directly after the Nobel Prize award to Pasternak, Konstantin Fedin went to Pasternak and, as a friend of long standing as well as a writer and literary bureaucrat, warned, "Do you realize that this is not a question of literature, it is pure politics. You have become a pawn in the game that political intriguers are playing. You are now standing on the brink and if you overstep it you will sunder your connections with Russian literature and the Russian people." It was a warning and a threat that Fedin was to make again, some years later, to Solzhenitsyn, and in almost precisely the same terms.

On October 26, the very next day after Pasternak's cable accepting the award, one of Moscow's specialists in journalistic vituperation, David Zaslavsky, was let loose. In an article entitled "Reactionary Uproar over a Literary Weed," Zaslavsky attacked Pasternak as a writer of miniscule talents, isolated from Soviet life and the people, a man who had always been hostile to Marxist philosophy and to "socialist realism" in literature. He dubbed Zhivago an "infuriated moral freak," and said that the entire novel was "low-grade reactionary hackwork." Pasternak was merely a literary weed in the flowering garden of Soviet letters and if Pasternak had "a spark of Soviet dignity left . . . *he would reject the Nobel Prize*."

Though *Doctor Zhivago* was widely praised, even called a masterpiece, the acclaim was by no means unanimous, even among presumably objective critics. There were a wide gamut of reactions to the book and many dissenting opinions of its worth. Even the *Novy mir* letter of rejection contained some

telling literary, as distinct from political, criticism of the novel: remarks about hasty writing, disjointed impressions, and "lifeless and didactically dry sections especially in the second half of the novel." One of the more interesting evaluations was by the Yugoslav critic Mihajlo Mihajlov, who thought the novel artistically inadequate because the plot and general structure were rickety. Yet Mihajlov also thought the novel "unequaled in its time" in Russia. In judging Zhivago's career and character, Mihajlov singles out the same crucial scene that the *Novy mir* editors had, the scene in which the Bolsheviks shoot down the young boys from the White military academy. Both the critic and the editors saw in that scene the moral and political crux of the book. Mihajlov comments that Zhivago obstinately refused "to come to grips with the fact that there comes a time when not to resist is to be no longer a man."

October 27, 1958, the day following Zaslavsky's attack, the Writers' Union expelled Pasternak for "actions incompatible with the calling of a Soviet writer," and condemned him for aiming "against the traditions of Russian literature, against the people, against peace and socialism."

Two days later, on October 29, at Moscow's Luzhniki Sports Stadium, before an audience of fourteen thousand that included Khrushchev and many top Party leaders, Vladimir Semichastny, First Secretary of the Komsomol (a Stalinist and later head of the political police), descending to the nadir of abuse, compared Pasternak to a pig "who fouled the spot where he ate and cast filth on those by whose labor he lives and breathes." Semichastny then "suggested" that if Pasternak chose to become a real emigrant instead of an "internal emigrant," no obstacles would be put in his way; no one would stop his departure from the Soviet Union for a "capitalist paradise." (Such a threat had special meaning for Pasternak, because his parents, the painter Leonid Pasternak and the concert pianist Rosa Kaufman, and his two sisters had left the Soviet Union in 1921. Pasternak, however, had not considered emigration at that time, nor evidently at any time thereafter.)

The Party pressure had been swift, powerful, and overwhelming. Pasternak capitulated. On that same day, he took Zaslavsky's "advice" and sent a telegram to the Swedish Academy renouncing the Nobel Prize:

> Considering the meaning this award has been given in the society to which I belong, I must reject this undeserved prize which has been presented to me. Please do not receive my voluntary rejection with displeasure.

But Pasternak's abasement was not yet complete.

Two days later, on October 31, after showering a torrent of abuse on him as venomous as that of the professional Party hack journalists, the Moscow writers adopted a resolution asking the government to deprive the traitor "B. Pasternak" of his citizenship. Among those who attacked him were such well-known and reputedly liberal writers as Leonid Martynov, who had himself spent several years in one of the Arctic concentration camps and who would introduce himself with the words "Leonid Martynov, enemy of the people"; Boris Slutsky; Boris Polevoi, who called Pasternak a "literary Vlasov"; and K. L. Zelinsky who, in high dudgeon after reading *Doctor Zhivago*, reported: "I felt as though I had literally been spat upon. The whole of my life seemed to be defiled in the novel. Everything I had put my energy into for forty years, my creative energy and aspirations, my hopes, had all been defiled." The novel was execrated as written in mediocre prose and poorly constructed, with impoverished philosophy, but the focus of the attack was: "The novel portrays the whole of our people's struggle in the years of the Revolution and the Civil War, waged in the name of the enlightened ideas of the October Revolution, as a series of brutalities, executions and intrigues among leaders. A series of unjust acts—that is what the whole thing is made out to be." Because of that, *Doctor Zhivago* is simply an "apologia for treachery," and "a godsend for . . . our enemies."

On the next day, November 1, Pasternak wrote directly to Khrushchev, apologizing because he had not realized that he and his book would become the center of a Western political campaign; when he had realized it he had renounced the Nobel Prize. But, he continued—and here the note of pleading, though dignified, was plain: "I am linked with Russia by my birth, life and work. I cannot imagine my fate separate from and outside Russia. . . . A departure beyond the borders of my country would for me be equivalent to death, and for that reason I request you not to take that extreme."

Still Pasternak had not been made to drink the cup to its very dregs. On November 5, four days later, he made the required public self-criticism (and self-abasement) in *Pravda;* saying that he had never intended to harm either the state or the people, Pasternak confessed, "When I saw the scope of the political campaign around my novel and realized that this award was a political step which has now led to monstrous consequences, I conveyed my voluntary rejection on my own initiative and without any compulsion."

The assault on him now began to abate. In December, at the congress of the Writers' Union of the RSFSR, Surkov described Pasternak as a traitor, an apostate and a "putrid internal émigré." But what really concerned Pasternak were the threats to Olga Ivinskaya and her daughter. Once before, Ivinskaya had been his hostage to fortune, and his misgivings were not now misplaced, although the authorities did not take steps against Ivinskaya until after Pasternak was dead.

On February 11, 1959, the *London Daily Mail,* without the author's permission, published a brief Pasternak poem entitled "The Nobel Prize." Profoundly pessimistic, it lamented:

> But what wicked thing have I done,
> I, the murderer and villain?
> I made the whole world weep
> Over my beautiful land.
>
> Even so, as I near the grave,
> I believe the time will soon come
> When the spirit of good will prevail
> Over malice and evil.

Though appeals in behalf of Pasternak came from all over the world, from such eminent writers and intellectuals as Bertrand Russell, J. B. Priestley, Graham Greene, and even such Communist writers as Jorge Amado, the gifted Brazilian novelist, and Halldor Laxness, the Icelandic Nobel Prize winner in literature, who cabled his objections to Khrushchev directly, none seemed to have any effect.

Years later the conservative novelist Galina Serebryakova was to publish her reminiscences of Pasternak, in which she called *Doctor Zhivago* a boring novel and described Pasternak as a man "of great talent who sincerely loved his country in his own way and wished it to flourish, but was absolutely separated from its everyday labors and life. . . . The world was torn apart, steep icebergs rose and fell and new ones were born in pain,

but Pasternak covered his face with his hands and stood aside. Behind compassion he did not see the main thing. Mourning dead friends, he nevertheless did not venture out of his chocolate sphere."

Some critics believe that much of the clamor surrounding Pasternak and the novel was part of a power struggle in the Writers' Union. *Literaturnaya gazeta,* the organ of the Union, which led the attack on Pasternak, was then edited by Vsevolod Kochetov and his deputy editor, V. Druzhin, and both of them were die-hard dogmatists. When subsequently interviewed by Patricia Blake, Kochetov did say that he never wanted to see *Dr. Zhivago* published in the Soviet Union, because it was a badly written book. Even more, he opposed its publication, he said, because of its contents: "What would be your attitude towards a writer like Pasternak who described your countrymen as gangsters?" Therefore, I think the emphasis is misplaced. The Party leadership wanted Pasternak shamed and punished, and the dogmatists in the intra-Union power struggle may have taken advantage of that, but I doubt that it was the other way round. Harold Swayze points out that when *Literaturnaya gazeta* was "reorganized" in March 1959 to fit it into the "middle course" Khrushchev was trying to maintain, both Kochetov and Druzhin lost their jobs. Here, too, I believe that Swayze mistakes the way the regime, in punishing and rewarding people, uses its favors and those done for it. The desire to come to some accommodation with the writers in 1959 meant "appeasing" some of the liberal ones in a public way. Removing Kochetov, a liberal *bête noire,* and his deputy was a good "symbolic" political gesture. The excuse given to Kochetov and Druzhin may have been that they were being reprimanded for their role in the Pasternak affair, but it need not have been, and very likely was not, the essential reason.

In 1967, Werth was to report:

> Those who had taken part in the hounding of Pasternak, now a sick and deeply discouraged man, were feeling uneasy about it, too. They blamed not so much Pasternak as the Nobel Prize Committee, for having tried to stage an "anti-Soviet provocation" by awarding the prize to him. As for him, he was a "pigheaded old man" who had rejected even the slightest cuts and changes in the manuscript of *Dr. Zhivago.* "Of course, of course we would have published it"; and some even said, "It was a mistake we didn't print a small edition of even the full text; there would have been a few nasty notices in the press and that would have been the end of it." And it was said that Khrushchev, "who had never read a line of Pasternak in his life," thought it had all been rather a stupid mistake to make such a fuss.

But this was hindsight and a not unusual rewriting of Soviet history by the Party leadership and its stalwarts. (pp. 28-38)

> *Abraham Rothberg, "The Pasternak Case," in his* The Heirs of Stalin: Dissidence and the Soviet Regime, 1953-1970, *Cornell University Press, 1972, pp. 28-40.*

THE POETRY OF LIBERATION

YEVGENY YEVTUSHENKO

[Yevtushenko is the most popular contemporary Soviet poet, both in the USSR and throughout the rest of the world. He has toured the United States and Europe several times and is widely known for his dramatic public readings. His travels have been an acknowledged attempt to escape the chauvinistic isolationism of the USSR, and he often addresses in his work the need for world peace and understanding. In this regard, Yevtushenko perceives himself as a poet with a mission to take part in the political process of his age. His verse can be divided into two basic groups—lyrical autobiographical poems, which comprise his most accomplished work, and sociopolitical verses, which explore strengths and weaknesses of both Western and Soviet life. Although considered a propagandist early in his career, in his later work he has struggled for liberalization of Soviet life and a return to the humane ideals of the revolution, which stressed faith in the future of humanity. These works, including Baby Yar (1961) *and* The Heirs of Stalin (1962), *have had a strong political impact in the USSR. His frankness on some issues—particularly anti-Semitism and the tyrannies of Stalinism—have caused him trouble with the Soviet authorities. However, Yevtushenko generally stays within the limits of Soviet censorship and as readily attacks the moral and political problems of Western nations as he does of the Soviet Union. But even though he addresses the most important political issues of the age, critics generally find his civic verse blatantly didactic, prosaic, and often shallow. His personal lyrics are considered more interesting, both verbally and thematically; they portray a man who is unsure of himself and constantly concerned with his development, a portrait that many believe explained his strong appeal to Soviet youth in the 1960s and 1970s. In the following excerpt from his* Precocious Autobiography, *Yevtushenko comments on the role of poetry as the most popular medium of literary expression during the Thaw and on the nature of the liberalization movement of that period.]*

Poetry Day, which was later to become a national institution, was held for the first time in 1955. On that day poets stood behind the counter in all the Moscow bookstores, read their poems, and signed copies of their books. Several of us read our poems in a store in Mokhovaya Street, not far from the university.

I had no idea of what was coming.

About four hundred people squeezed into the bookstore which was bursting at the seams. Outside, a crowd of more than a thousand who could not get in were chanting in chorus: "Come outside! Come outside!"

We were literally carried out of the store and swept up the steps of the university. We began to read our poems. We all felt that something important was being expected of us. Love lyrics were applauded but the same expectation still shone in the eyes of our listeners. It came my turn. In front of me were fifteen hundred pairs of eyes. . . . I read the poem which the poet K had said was written for our enemies [one in a series of poems in which Yevtushenko criticized contemporary Russia's betrayal of the ideals of the Revolution]. But the young people who heard it took it not as an attack upon our country, but as a weapon in the struggle against those who were holding her back. . . . And fifteen hundred pairs of hands, raised in applause, voted for that struggle.

With the backing of the young, I wrote poem after poem calling for recruits to our side. Snobs reproached me with giving up "pure art." Dogmatists said menacingly that I was a "Nihilist." But I didn't give a damn about any of them. What

Yevgeny Yevtushenko. UPI/Bettman Newsphotos.

mattered to me were all those young eyes turned to me, waiting expectantly.

I saw that they needed my poetry, and that, by speaking of what was wrong with our society, I was strengthening, not destroying, their faith in our way of life.

The Soviet press, radio, and television were quite obviously failing to keep up with the rapid changes in the life of the country. The nation was demanding the truth about itself from its writers.

Literary criticism was lagging hopelessly behind events.

Fiction was on the move, but slowly.

But poetry had mobility.

To begin with, a poem takes much less time to write than a novel, and it can be read in public even before appearing in print. So I chose the public platform as the battlefield on which to defend my views.

I read poetry in factories, colleges, research institutes, in office buildings and in schools. The audiences numbered from twenty to a thousand. At that time poetry readings were hardly ever allowed in the big concert halls and I could not imagine that in 1963 they would draw fourteen thousand people to the Sports Palace.

The tradition of public poetry readings, started by Mayakovsky and later given up, was being gradually re-established. But it was not on anything like the scale it has reached now—unknown even in Mayakovsky's lifetime. (pp. 95-7)

I don't think the word "thaw," which Ilya Ehrenburg stuck so casually on this movement, is a very appropriate one. I have objected to it several times in the press and should like to object again. There is no doubt that it is spring. It is a rough spring, a difficult spring with late frosts and cold winds, a spring which takes a step to the left, then a step to the right, then a step back, but which is certain, nevertheless, to go on and take two or three steps forward. And the fact that winter should hold the earth so desperately in its grip and refuse to give it up is also quite in the order of things; but then, in the very counter-attacks of winter, one can sense its growing impotence—because times have changed. (pp. 99-100)

> *Yevgeny Yevtushenko, in his* A Precocious Autobiography, *translated by Andrew R. MacAndrew, E. P. Dutton & Co., Inc., 1963, 124 p.*

PATRICIA BLAKE

[*Blake is an American journalist, editor, and critic. In the following excerpt from her introduction to* Half-Way to the Moon, *an anthology of Thaw literature, she reports on a 1962 public poetry reading and discusses the poetry of performers Andrei Voznesensky, Bulat Okudzhava, and Yevgeny Yevtushenko.*]

It is the poets who communicate most directly to Soviet readers, possibly because of the traditional response to poetry in Russia, but more likely because the immediacy of the form meets the urgency of the need. "Poetry," wrote Mallarmé, "is the language of a state of crisis." Editions of 100,000 copies of Evtushenko's books have sold out within the first forty-eight hours of publication. Advance orders alone for Voznesensky's last book of verse, *The Triangular Pear* (1962), reached 100,000 two months before its publication. The poetry sections of Soviet book stores are fully stocked, however, with works by the old-guard poets which remain unsold from year to year. The quite inadequate size of printings of books by the new poets may have contributed to the rage for public readings which recently seized Russia—until both printings and readings were halted in the winter of 1963. The most spectacular of these readings took place in November 1962 in Moscow's Luzhniki Sports Stadium where 14,000 people gathered to hear Voznesensky, Akhmadulina, and Boris Slutsky. Poetry readings on a more modest scale had become the principal entertainment of intellectuals and students in Moscow, and in provincial towns as well, where poets went by the truckload. Even Mayakovsky, who spent his lifetime travelling across Russia declaiming his verse, never commanded anything like the following of these young people. (pp. 9-10)

I remember with particular vividness the scene I witnessed once at the entrance of an auditorium where several hundred students were clamouring to be admitted to a poetry reading. Seats were evidently still available—a number of official-looking men had just been let in without question. Among the young people in the crowd was a nineteen-year-old American student of Russian from the University of Indiana. Surely this very pretty and engaging girl could have charmed her way through police lines anywhere in the world, possibly even in Tirana or Peking; here, she was faced by a barricade of boys in their twenties, the *druzhiniki* (voluntary police) with red armbands and stony faces. The Russian students had taken up her cause and lifted her over the heads of the crowd. She cajoled the *druzhiniki*, she twiddled their Komsomol badges, then, having failed, burst into tears, crying, "But I've come all the way from Bloomington to hear Evtushenko!..." (p. 19)

[Of] all the well-known contradictions of Soviet society none has impressed me more than the contrast between the *druzhiniki* outside the auditorium and the people at the poetry reading inside.

This poetry reading was one of a series of six I attended in the public auditorium of Moscow's Polytechnic Museum in August 1962. These began at 5 pm and, with only brief intermissions, lasted until midnight. The auditorium was filled to capacity—about 700 people, largely students from the university and from various institutes where tickets had been distributed. A majority had brought books of poetry which they followed, like music scores, during the performance. On stage, before a blue velvet backdrop on which was lettered COMMUNISM IS THE YOUTH OF THE WORLD, THEREFORE YOUTH MUST CONSTRUCT IT, sat four poets, Evtushenko, Voznesensky, Bulat Okudzhava (the immensely popular half-Georgian, half-Armenian who accompanies his poems on the guitar), and a lesser-known poet, Sergei Polikarpov.

The first to read was the twenty-nine-year-old Voznesensky. An awkward figure, slight and singularly vulnerable, he stood before the microphone with his legs stiffly apart, his Adam's apple bobbing, bearing the applause and the shouts of acclaim from the audience as if they were blows. He announced the title of his poem "Fire in the Architectural Institute." "Fire! Fire!" he called out, "Oi! We're on fire!" This poem . . . is, of course, a joke on the Academy: "all those cowsheds decorated with cupids and those post-offices in rococo." It is also, I was told, a private joke shared by the audience (the Moscow Architectural Institute burned down when Voznesensky was a student there, consuming his designs together with his career as an architect).

He read poem after poem for perhaps an hour in a powerful, cultivated voice. His awkwardness had gone; now it was his listeners who appeared tense, straining forward to capture the flow of a language unheard-of in Russia in their lifetime. Here, clearly, was Russia's first modern poet. A prodigious technician, Voznesensky constructs his verse of assonances, rhymes, and puns which serve his intention rather as a brilliant orchestration serves a central musical idea. ("Form isn't what counts," he says. "Form must be clear, unfathomable, disquieting, like the sky in which only radar can sense the presence of a plane.") "I am Goya," begins one of his most extraordinary poems whose essential quality is not renderable in English. "I am Goya / eye sockets of shell craters have been picked out by an enemy / flying over a bare field / I am sorrow / I am the voice / of war / the embers of cities on the snows of the year '41 / I am hunger / I am the throat of a woman whose body like a bell / hangs over a naked square. . . ." In Russian the assonances are devastating: "Ya Góya . . . nagóye . . . ya górye . . . ya gólos . . . góda . . . ya gólod . . . ya górlo . . . góloi. . . ."

Most characteristic of Voznesensky's idiom are the abrupt shifts of tone and intention within the same poem, or even the same line; he is tender, jocular, mocking, and finally and most compellingly, ironic. He is a master of irony and to this end employs not only his technical resources (for example, juxtaposing, punning, or rhyming internally a pompous word with far-out slang) but also his alarming associations, fantasies and images, as in "The Skull Ballad" . . . where the decapitated head of Anna Mons, the mistress of Peter the Great, speaks to the Czar in these terms: "love is so small who cares for love / in times like these men build / and set a world on fire—you kiss / me State in blood in blood."

Andrei Voznesensky. From A History of Post-War Soviet Writing: The Literature of Moral Opposition, *by Grigori Svirski. Translated and edited by Robert Dessaix and Michael Ulman. Ardis, 1981. Reprinted by permission of Ardis Publishers.*

Even before the cultural purge released a torrent of abuse against Voznesensky, the conservative critics often accused him of "formalism" and ambiguity. To the first charge he answered, in "Evening on the Building Site," "They nag me about 'formalism.' / Experts, what a distance / You are from life! Formalin: / You stink of it, and incense." And again in "Anti-Worlds," which is a play on the concept of anti-matter, he wrote: "Ah, my critics; how I love them. / Upon the neck of the keenest of them, / Fragrant and bald as fresh-baked bread, / There shines a perfect anti-head. . . ." To the charge of ambiguity, he replied, in "Who are You?": "I am among avalanches / like the abominable snowman / absolutely elusive."

To his enemies Voznesensky is indeed elusive, but to his tremendous following he speaks more clearly than any writer in Russia. ("Here is a *real* poet," Evtushenko said to me when he introduced me to Voznesensky during an intermission. "He hasn't made his reputation through sensation—like some people one knows. . . .") Voznesensky often talks of his responsibility to the people who have given him their confidence: "When a man writes, he feels his prophetic mission in the world. The task of the Russian poet today is to look deep inside man. When I read my poetry to a great number of people, their emotional, almost sensual, expression of feeling seems to me to reveal the soul of man—now no longer hidden behind closed shutters, but wide open like a woman who has just been kissed." The response to Voznesensky that evening was like nothing I have ever observed in the West, either at the theatre or in a

concert hall, let alone at poetry recitals. As Voznesensky, smiling now, sweat streaming down his face like tears, was called back again and again to the footlights, I saw young men and women all around me rise and crying real tears call out their thanks.

I felt a little sorry for the poet to follow; it had to be an anticlimax. But no. Bulat Okudzhava, who appeared before the microphone cheerfully strumming a guitar, evidently inspires another sort of enthusiasm, and it broke the tension in the hall. A small dark man of thirty-seven with fuzzy, receding hair and a minute moustache, he is famous in Russia for his recordings of Odessa underworld songs (which circulate widely on tape), and for his own plaintively comic poems which he sings on public occasions in the manner of the French *chansonnier*. The audience seemed to know all his poems by heart and called for them by name: "Songs to Fools"; "So Long, Kid"; "Midnight Trolley-bus." "When I'm fed up / when despair comes over me / I jump into a blue trolley-bus," he sings pleasantly but tunelessly, "Midnight trolley-bus! Speed along the streets / roll around the boulevards / pick up those ship-wrecked in the night. . .!" However slight in substance, Okudzhava's little poems have charm, humour, and poignancy—qualities which appear all too rarely in Soviet literature.

Recently Okudzhava has begun to write fiction. His autobiographical novella, *Good Luck, Schoolboy!* . . . suggests that the strumming of the *chansonnier* conceals more serious intentions. For Okudzhava, who was wounded at the Front, the war remains the most meaningful experience of his life. And like so many of his generation, he is obviously weary of the hortatory tone of the majority of Soviet novels, plays and films about what is invariably called "the heroic feat of the People in the Great Patriotic War"; these serve only to de-humanize and diminish the feat of people (with a small "p"). Okudzhava's novella is one of the rare works of Soviet literature which deal sympathetically with the non-heroics of war—such hitherto unheard-of sentiments as the fear, bewilderment, and bravado of a teenage boy making his way across a German minefield. Inevitably the old guard critics were outraged. "Vindication of the fear of death!" protested A. Metchenko in *Kommunist* (March 1962), "Mawkish pacifism! Okudzhava is insulting the memory of those who died in order to save those who are living, including himself."

The next to recite was Evtushenko. His appearance brought forth cries of "Hi, Zhenya!" and "Give us *Babi Yar!*" and a barrage of paper pellets on which his admirers had written requests for their favourite poems. It was clear at once that this young man's popularity is extra-literary; although Evtushenko is gifted as a poet, it is the occasional boldness of his subjects which has made his national and international reputation—especially his protest against anti-Semitism. "Zhenya is a Columbus," one of his enraptured admirers told me. "He charts courses no one would dare dream of, and then everyone follows in his wake." Moreover, he is marvellously handsome and engaging. Dressed in a wildly-patterned American sportsshirt under a grey silk suit, he brushed back his blond forelock and waved familiarly at the audience. *"Horosho*—all right, you'll have your *Babi Yar."*

But first he read an unpublished poem: "How a Scoundrel Takes a Steambath." This is about a detestable bureaucrat. When he goes to the public steambath he pretends to be a real friend of the people; he is always ready to scrub the back of his neighbour, and he wears a *banny list* (a leaf from the birch twigs used to beat oneself in steambaths, which sometimes gets imbedded in the skin like a burr) as an "order of democracy." But while lying in the hot water he sighs and pines for Stalin. And at night, before going to sleep he always treats himself to a chapter or two of Kochetov (the Stalinist novelist who is the arch enemy of the liberal writers). The next morning he resumes his villainy. . . .

The audience roared with pleasure and then clamoured for *Babi Yar*. He reads it with unmistakable feeling, his arms open to the audience, his hands trembling a bit: "Today I am as old as the Jewish people / It seems to me now that I am a Jew. . . ." When he had finished, the crowd began pounding on the floor with their feet. "Again, at once!" He read it again, and later in the evening when the audience would not relent, read it once more. When this happened for the fourth time, Evtushenko shouted for silence and said, "Comrades, you and I have been in this hall for six hours and I have read that poem three times. I should think you would be as tired of hearing it as I am of reciting it." But again they pounded and once again he complied. It is a moving experience to hear this boy, so grave and so commanding, read *Babi Yar* to an audience of utterly mesmerized young Russians: "Let the Internationale ring out / When the last anti-Semite on earth is buried. / There is no Jewish blood in mine, / but I am hated by every anti-Semite as a Jew. And for this reason / I am a true Russian."

He also recited that evening a cycle of poems glorifying Castro's Cuba which seemed to justify the intransigent Soviet intellectuals' view that Evtushenko is deeply compromised by his concessions to the Establishment. One of these poems, "Three Minutes of Truth," suggested why popular enthusiasm for the Cuban revolution runs so high in Russia. The poem is about a *barbudo* who seizes a radio station during the Batista régime and, for three minutes speaks "the truth" to the people; he is then captured and shot. It ends with an exhortation by the poet who calls upon the youth of the world to remember this Cuban hero when they hear a lie: run the risk, even if it is death, but tell the truth. Evtushenko's intention may not be equivocal, but the poem, like the Cuban revolution itself, can be interpreted in more than one way. Whatever the reality of Cuba (and who in Russia can know?), for some it stands for what is most decent and pure in the revolutionary impetus; for others it means, simply, liberation from tyranny. (pp. 20-5)

> *Patricia Blake, in an introduction to* Half-Way to the Moon: New Writing from Russia, *edited by Patricia Blake and Max Hayward, Holt, Rinehart and Winston, 1964, pp. 7-39.*

THE END OF THE THAW: THE BRODSKY TRIAL

TRANSCRIPTION OF THE TRIAL OF JOSEPH BRODSKY

[Joseph Brodsky, a poet whose works were considered morally and politically subversive by the Soviet government, was tried for "parasitism" in early 1964, an event which many historians believe signaled the end of the post-Stalin liberalization process. Brodsky was convicted and sentenced to five years' labor on a collective farm, and in 1972 was forced to emigrate to the West. Since that time he has gained a reputation among Western critics as the greatest living Russian poet; in 1987 he was awarded the Nobel Prize in literature. The following excerpt is taken from a transcript of Brodsky's trial which was compiled by an anonymous reporter.]

Those arriving at the trial are greeted with the following sign:

THE HEARING OF THE PARASITE BRODSKY

The large hall of the Builders' Club is full of people.

ATTENDANT: Stand up! The court is coming! (p. 8)

JUDGE: . . . Citizen Brodsky, since 1956 you have changed jobs 13 times. You worked in a factory for a year, and then for half a year you did not work. During the summer you were with a geological expedition and then for four months you did not work. . . . *(She lists the places where he worked and the intervals which occurred between jobs).* Explain to the court why you did not work during the intervals and why you pursued a parasitic way of life.

BRODSKY: I did work during the intervals. I did just what I am doing now. I wrote poetry.

JUDGE: That is, you wrote your so-called poems? But what was the use of your changing jobs so often?

BRODSKY: I began to work at the age of 15. I found everything interesting. I changed jobs because I wanted to find out as much as possible about life and people.

JUDGE: And what good have you done for your country?

BRODSKY: I wrote poems. That's my work. I am convinced . . . I believe, that what I have written will be of advantage to people not only now but to future generations as well.

VOICE FROM THE CROWD: Listen to that! What an imagination!

ANOTHER VOICE: He's a poet. He should think that way.

JUDGE: So, you think that your so-called poems are of use to the people?

BRODSKY: Why do you refer to them as my "so-called" poems?

JUDGE: We refer to them as your "so-called" poems because we do not have any other conception of them.

PUBLIC PROSECUTOR SOROKIN: You speak about future generations. What are you? Do you feel that people don't understand you now?

BRODSKY: I didn't say that. It's simply that my poems have not been published yet and people don't know them.

SOROKIN: Do you feel that if they were known they would be given recognition?

BRODSKY: Yes.

SOROKIN: You say that you have a widely developed curiosity. Why did you not want to serve in the Soviet Army?

BRODSKY: I will not answer such questions.

JUDGE: Answer!

BRODSKY: I was deferred from military service. It was not a case of "not wanting" to serve; I was deferred. That's a different thing. I was deferred twice. The first time it was because my father was ill and the second time it was because of my own illness.

SOROKIN: Is it possible to live on the money you earn?

BRODSKY: Yes. Every day in jail I signed a paper to the effect that 40 kopecks [approximately 40 cents] had been spent on my welfare that day, and I used to earn more than 40 kopecks a day.

SOROKIN: But one has to buy shoes and clothes.

BRODSKY: I have one suit—an old one, but it is a suit, and I don't need another.

DEFENSE: Have your poems been evaluated by specialists?

BRODSKY: Yes. Chukovsky and Marshak spoke highly about my translations, better than I deserve.

DEFENSE: Did you have any connections with the translators' division of the Union of Writers?

BRODSKY: Yes. I appeared in an anthology entitled *For the First Time in Russian* and I read translations from Polish.

JUDGE: *(To the counsel for the defense)* You are supposed to ask him about his useful work, and instead you are asking him about his public appearances.

DEFENSE: His translations constitute his useful work.

JUDGE: It would be better, Brodsky, if you would explain to the court why you did not work during the intervals between jobs.

BRODSKY: I did work. I wrote poetry.

JUDGE: But this did not prevent you from actually working.

BRODSKY: But I was working. I was writing poetry.

JUDGE: But there are people who work in factories and write poetry, too. What prevented you from doing this?

BRODSKY: But all people are not the same. Even the color of their hair, the expression of their faces.

JUDGE: That is not your discovery. Everyone knows that. But explain to us, rather, how we are to evaluate your participation in our great progressive movement toward Communism.

BRODSKY: The building of Communism is not only just standing at a workbench or plowing a field. It's also intellectual labor which . . .

JUDGE: Leave off these high-flown phrases! Tell us, rather, how you plan to organize your labor activity for the future.

BRODSKY: I wanted to write poetry and to translate. But if this is contradictory to any generally accepted norms, then I will take on a permanent job and still write poetry.

ASSESSOR TYAGLY: In this country every person works. How is it that you have been doing nothing for such a long time?

BRODSKY: You don't consider what I do to be work. I wrote poetry and I consider this work.

JUDGE: Have you drawn any conclusions for yourself from what has been written in the press?

BRODSKY: Lerner's article was untrue. That's the only conclusion I have made.

JUDGE: So you have not drawn any other conclusions?

BRODSKY: No, I have not. I do not consider myself a person leading a parasitic way of life.

DEFENSE: You said that the article entitled "The Near-literary Drone" published in the *Evening Leningrad* newspaper is not true. In what way?

BRODSKY: The only thing that is correct in it is my name. Even my age is not right. Even the poems are not mine. In this article people whom I scarcely know or don't know at all are called my friends. How can I consider this article true and draw conclusions from it?

DEFENSE: You consider your work useful. Will the witnesses whom I have summoned be able to confirm this?

JUDGE: *(Ironically to Defense)* Is that the only reason you summoned witnesses?

PUBLIC PROSECUTOR SOROKIN: *(To Brodsky)* How could you make a translation from Serbian all by yourself without making any use of someone else's work?

BRODSKY: You are asking an ignorant question. Now and then an agreement with a publishing house comes with an interlinear translation. I know Polish and I know Serbian, but not as well. However, they are related languages, and with the help of an interlinear translation I was able to do my translation.

JUDGE: Witness Grudnina!

GRUDNINA: I have been supervising the work of young (beginning) poets for more than 11 years. For seven years I was a member of the committee on work with young authors. Right now I am guiding the poets in the upper classes in the Palace of the Pioneers, and I am also directing the circle of young literary enthusiasts from the Svetlana factory. At the request of the publishing houses I compiled and edited four collective anthologies of young poets in which more than 200 new names appeared. Therefore I have first-hand knowledge of the work of almost all the young poets in the city.

I know Brodsky's poems from 1959 and 1960 as the work of a budding poet. These poems were still in the rough, but they showed a brilliant originality of figures and images. I did not include them in the anthologies; however, I considered the author capable. I did not meet Brodsky personally until the

Joseph Brodsky. © Lûtfi Ôzkôk.

fall of 1963. After the publication of the article entitled "The Near-literary Drone" in the *Evening Leningrad* I sent for Brodsky to come for a talk with me, since the young people were besieging me with requests to intervene in the affair of the slandered man. To my question—What was he doing now?—Brodsky answered that he had been studying languages and working on literary translations for about a year and a half. I took some manuscripts of his translations so as to become familiar with them.

As a professional poet and a literary scholar I affirm that Brodsky's translations have been done on a high professional level. Brodsky has a specific talent for translating poetry that one does not find very often. He showed me work that he had done encompassing 368 lines of poetry, and in addition to this I read 120 lines of poetry which he had translated and published in Moscow editions.

From my personal experience in literary translation I know that such a volume of work would take an author not less than half a year of solid work not counting time spent in getting the poems published and consultations with specialists. The time necessary for such business is impossible to calculate. If we evaluate the translations which I have seen with my own eyes even at the lowest prices paid by the publishing houses, then Brodsky has already earned 350 new rubles [approximately $400] and the only question that remains is when will everything that he has done be published in full.

In addition to agreements for translations Brodsky showed me agreements for radio and television for which the work had already been completed, but likewise had not yet been paid for in full.

From conversations wih Brodsky and with people who know him I know that Brodsky lives very modestly, denies himself clothing and entertainment, and spends the major part of the day at his desk working. The money which he receives for his work he gives to his family.

DEFENSE: Is it necessary to have a general knowledge of the works of an author in order to be able to make literary translations of his poetry?

GRUDNINA: Yes, for good translations like those done by Brodsky one has to know the author's works and get a feeling of his style.

DEFENSE: Is the pay for translations less if one makes use of interlinear translations of the poems?

GRUDNINA: Yes, it is less. In rendering the poems of Hungarian poets into verse from interlinear translations I received one old-ruble less per line.

DEFENSE: Is it general practice among translators to work from interlinear translations?

GRUDNINA: Yes, everywhere. One of the most prominent Leningrad translators, A. Gitovich, translates from Old Chinese by using interlinear translations.

ASSESSOR LEBEDEVA: Can one learn a foreign language on one's own?

GRUDNINA: I learned by myself two languages in addition to those which I learned at the university.

DEFENSE: If Brodsky does not know Serbian, can he, despite this, make a first-rate literary translation?

GRUDNINA: Yes, of course.

DEFENSE: But do you not consider the use of an interlinear translation a reprehensible utilization of someone else's work?

GRUDNINA: God forbid!

ASSESSOR LEBEDEVA: Here is a book I have been looking at. There are only two short little poems of Brodsky's in it.

GRUDNINA: I would like to offer certain clarifications concerning particular aspects of literary work . . .

JUDGE: No, that won't be necessary. However, what is your opinion of Brodsky's poetry?

GRUDNINA: My opinion is that as a poet he is very talented and that he is head and shoulders above many who are considered professional translators.

JUDGE: But why does he work by himself and not frequent any literary organizations?

GRUDNINA: In 1958 he asked to belong to my literary group, but I heard that he was an hysterical young man and so I rejected him myself. This was a mistake and I regret it very much. Now I will gladly receive him into my group and will work with him if he wants to do it.

ASSESSOR TYAGLY: Have you yourself ever seen him actually at work on his poems, or has he been profiting by someone else's work?

GRUDNINA: I have not seen him sitting and writing, but I have not seen Sholokhov sitting and writing at his desk either. However, that doesn't mean that. . . .

JUDGE: It is awkward to compare Sholokhov and Brodsky. Is it possible that you have never explained to the young people that the State demands that they study? After all, Brodsky has gone through only seven grades of school.

GRUDNINA: His field of knowledge is very great. I became convinced of this from reading his translations.

SOROKIN: Have you read his bad pornographic poems?

GRUDNINA: No, never.

DEFENSE: Here is something I want to ask you, witness Grudnina. The following constitutes Brodsky's production for 1963: poems in the book entitled *Dawn over Cuba*, translations of poems by Galchinsky (to be sure, not yet published), poems in the book entitled *Yugoslav Poets, Songs of the Gaucho* and publications in *Kostёr* [The Bonfire]. Can this be considered serious work?

GRUDNINA: Yes, beyond a doubt. That is a full year's work. And payment for this work will not necessarily come immediately, but several years hence. It is incorrect to evaluate the efforts of a young author by the amount of money he has received in payment at the given moment. A young author may meet with failure which may necessitate a long reworking of what he wrote. There is a joke to the effect that the difference between a parasite and a young poet is that a parasite eats and does not work, whereas a young poet works and does not always eat.

JUDGE: We are not pleased with this statement of yours. In our country every person receives according to his effort, and therefore it cannot be that he has worked a great deal and received little for it. In our country, where such a great share of the wealth is allotted to the young poets, you say that they go hungry. Why did you say that young poets do not eat?

GRUDNINA: I did not say that. I said that it was a joke in which there is a grain of truth. Young poets have very uneven earnings.

JUDGE: Well, but this depends upon them. We do not have to explain that. Alright, you have explained that your words were a joke. We will accept this explanation.

A new witness is called: Efim Grigorevich Etkind, Member of the Union of Writers and teacher at the Herzen Institute.

JUDGE: Let me have your passport inasmuch as your last name is pronounced somewhat unclearly. *(She takes the passport.)* Etkind . . . Efim Gershevich [sic!] . . . You may speak now.

ETKIND: As part of my public literary work, which is connected with the education of beginning translators, I often have the opportunity of reading and listening to the translations of young writers. About a year ago I became familiar with the works of I. Brodsky. These were his translations of poems of the marvelous Polish poet Galchinsky whose poetry has not yet been widely translated here. The clarity of the poetical phrasing, the musicality, the passion and the energy of his verse produced a strong impression on me. I was also struck by the fact that Brodsky learned Polish by himself without any outside help whatsoever. He read Galchinsky's poetry in Polish with just as much enthusiasm as he read his own Russian translations. I understood that I had to do with a rarely gifted man and—not less important—a man with perseverance and a capacity for work. The translations which I had the opportunity of reading later served to reinforce my conviction. There were, for example, the translations he did of the Cuban poet Fernandes, which were published in the book entitled *Dawn over Cuba*, and those of the contemporary Yugoslav poets which are being printed in an anthology by the Goslitizdat [State Publishing House of Literary Fiction]. I talked a great deal with Brodsky and was amazed at how much he knew about American, English, and Polish literature.

The translation of poetry is the most difficult sort of work, demanding diligence, knowledge and talent. A translator can expect countless failures in this business and the material recompense is a thing of the distant future. A person can translate poetry for several years and not earn a single ruble for it. Such work demands unselfish love for poetry and for the labor involved in it. The study of languages, history, the culture of another people—all of this is, by far, not acquired immediately. Everything that I know about Brodsky's work convinces me of the fact that a great future awaits him as a poet-translator. This is not only my own opinion. The office of the division of translators, when it found out that the publishing house had broken the agreements made with Brodsky, came to a unanimous decision to intercede with the director of the publishing house to have Brodsky given some work and to have the agreements with him reinstated.

I know for a fact that the same opinion is shared by the great authorities in the field of translation—Marshak and Chukovsky, who . . .

JUDGE: Speak just for yourself!

ETKIND: Brodsky must be presented with the opportunity of working as a poet-translator. Far away from a large city where there are neither the necessary books nor a literary milieu, it is difficult, almost impossible. I repeat, I am deeply convinced that in this field a great future awaits him. I must say that I was greatly amazed to see the announcement: "The Hearing of the Parasite Brodsky." (pp. 8-11)

SMIRNOV *(Witness for the prosecution, head of the Department of Defense)*: I don't know Brodsky personally, but I want to say that if all the citizens of this country reacted toward the production of material wealth as Brodsky does, then it would take us a long time to build Communism. The mind is a dangerous weapon for its owner. Everyone has said that he is a smart fellow and practically a genius. But no one has said what sort of a person he is. He has grown up in an intelligent family, but he has only seven years of formal education. Let those present say whether they would like to have a son with only seven years of schooling. He did not join the army because he was the sole supporter of his family. But what sort of a breadwinner is he? Here they say that he is a talented translator, but why doesn't anyone say that he's all muddled up in his head? And what about anti-Soviet verses?

BRODSKY: That's not true!

SMIRNOV: He needs to change a lot of his thoughts. I am suspicious about the certificate that Brodsky was given in the "nerve" clinic concerning his nervous illness. This is nothing but his fancy friends ringing all the bells and demanding: "Save the young man!" But he should be treated with forced labor, and no one will help him, no fancy friends. I do not know him personally. I know about him from the newspapers. And I am acquainted with the certificates. I'm suspicious about the certificate which deferred him from service in the army. I'm not a doctor, but I'm suspicious about it.

BRODSKY: When I was deferred as the sole breadwinner of our family, my father was sick. He was in bed suffering from a form of necrosis, and I worked and earned our living. And after that I was sick. Where did you learn about me so as to speak that way about me?

SMIRNOV: I became acquainted with your personal diary.

BRODSKY: On what grounds?

JUDGE: I withdraw the question.

SMIRNOV: I read his poems.

DEFENSE: During the hearing it has turned out that certain poems do not belong to Brodsky. How do you know that the poems you read actually are his? After all, you are talking about unpublished poems.

SMIRNOV: I know and that's that.

JUDGE: Witness Logunov!

LOGUNOV *(Assistant to the executive director of the Hermitage Museum)*: I do not know Brodsky personally. I met him for the first time here in the courtroom. To live as Brodsky has been living is no longer permissible. I would not envy the parents of such a son. I have worked with writers and I have circulated among them. I compare Brodsky with Oleg Shestinsky. Oleg has traveled with a propaganda team; he finished the State University of Leningrad and the University of Sophia. And Oleg has also worked in a mine. I wanted to appear here to emphasize the fact that one must work hard and give up all one's cultural habits. Then the poems which Brodsky puts together would be real poems. Brodsky must begin his life anew.

DEFENSE: The witnesses should, however, be made to stick to facts. But they . . .

JUDGE: You may give an evaluation of the witnesses' testimony later. Witness Denisov!

DENISOV *(Pipe setter of the UNR-20)*: I do not know Brodsky personally. I am familiar with him from the press releases. I appear here as a citizen and a representative of our community. After the newspaper release I became indignant over Brodsky's work. I wanted to become familiar with his books. I went to the libraries. They didn't have his books. I asked acquaintances if they knew such a person. No, they didn't know him. I'm a worker. During my life I have changed jobs only twice. But Brodsky? I am not satisfied with Brodsky's testimony that he knew many specialties. You can't learn a single specialty in such a short time. They say that Brodsky passes himself off as some sort of poet. Why wasn't he a member of a single organization? Doesn't he agree with Dialectical Materialism? You know Engels considers that labor created man. But Brodsky is not satisfied with this idea. He figures it otherwise. Perhaps he is very talented, but why doesn't he make a name for himself in our literature? Why doesn't he work? I wish to suggest the opinion that I, as a worker, am not satisfied with his labor activity. (pp. 11-12)

JUDGE: Witness Romashova!

ROMASHOVA *(Teacher of Marxism and Leninism in the Muchina school)*: I do not know Brodsky personally. But I am familiar with his so-called activity. Pushkin said that talent is first of all work. But Brodsky? Does he work? Does he work on his poems so that the people will be able to understand them? I am amazed that my colleagues have created such a halo about him. It can only happen in the Soviet Union that a court of law would speak so benevolently to a poet and would advise him in such a comradely fashion to go and study. As secretary to the Party organization at the Mukhina school I can say that he is exerting a bad influence on the youth.

DEFENSE: Have you ever seen Brodsky?

ROMASHOVA: Never. But his so-called activity gives me the right to judge him.

JUDGE: But can you bring any facts to bear on the case?

ROMASHOVA: As a teacher of young people I know what they have to say about Brodsky's poetry.

DEFENSE: But do you yourself know his poetry?

ROMASHOVA: I do. It's horr-ible! I don't feel that it's possible to repeat them! They are hor-ri-ble!

JUDGE: Witness Admoni! Please give me your passport, since your last name is unusual.

ADMONI *(Professor at the Herzen Institute, linguist, literary scholar, translator)*: When I found out that Iosif Brodsky was being brought to trial for parasitism I considered it my duty to present my opinion also before the court. I feel that I have a right to do this on the strength that I have been working with young people for 30 years as a teacher in university courses and on the strength that I have been dealing with translations for a long time.

I know I. Brodsky hardly at all. We say "hello" to each other, but I believe we have never exchanged so much as two sentences with each other. However, during the course of, approximately, this past year or somewhat longer I have been following his translation work intently, both in his appearances at the translators' evenings (where the translators get up and read their translations) and also in his publications. Because these translations are talented and brilliant, and on the basis of these translations of Galchinsky, Fernandes and others, I

can with complete responsibility say that they demanded a tremendously great amount of work on the part of their author. They testify to the great mastery and cultural level of the translator. And wonders do not exist. Neither mastery nor culture comes by itself, but demands steady and persistent work for its attainment. Even if a translator works from an interlinear translation, he must, in order that the translation be worthwhile, form for himself an idea of the language he is translating from. He must acquire a feeling for the structure of the language, and he has to know the life and the culture of the people, and so forth. And Iosif Brodsky, in addition to this, even learned the languages themselves. Therefore it is clear to me that he is working, that he works intensively and persistently. And when today I learned—just today—that he had finished only seven grades of school, then it became clear to me that he must really have made a gigantic effort in order to acquire such mastery and such a cultural level as he possesses. What Mayakovsky said about the work of a poet is applicable to the work of a poet-translator: "You can go through thousands of tons of verbal ore for the sake of a single word."

The ukase by which Brodsky has been brought to account is directed toward those who do too little work and not against those who do not earn enough. Parasites are people who do not do enough work. Therefore the accusation against I. Brodsky as a parasite is nonsense. It is impossible to accuse of parasitism a person who works as I. Brodsky does, who persistently works a great deal, with no thought as to large earnings, who is prepared to limit himself to the bare essentials so as to be able to perfect himself in his art and to create worthwhile artistic works.

JUDGE: What was it you said about not judging those who do not earn enough?

ADMONI: I said that the essence of the ukase consists in the necessity of judging those who do not work enough and not those who do not earn enough.

JUDGE: What do you mean by this? Have you read The Ukase of May Fourth? Communism is built only by the effort of millions.

ADMONI: Every effort that is useful to society should be respected. (pp. 12-13)

JUDGE: Witness Voevodin! Do you know Brodsky personally?

VOEVODIN *(Member of the Union of Writers)*: No. I have been working in the Union for only half a year. I was not personally acquainted with him. He does not come very often to the Union, just to the translation evenings. He apparently understood how his poems would be received and therefore he didn't go to any of the other organizations. I read his epigrams. You would blush, comrade judges, if you read them. They have been here speaking about Brodsky's talent. Talent is measured only by public acclaim. And this acclaim does not exist and cannot exist.

A folder of Brodsky's poems was handed over to the Union of Writers. There are three themes in the poems. The first is the theme of estrangement from the world; the second is a pornographic theme; and the third is the theme of non-love for one's country and its people in which Brodsky speaks about another homeland. Wait, I think I can remember it . . . "Monotonous is the Russian crowd." May these disgraceful poems remain on his conscience! Brodsky as a poet does not exist. Translator—perhaps, but poet—no! I completely support the statement of our comrade who spoke about his son whom

Brodsky influenced perniciously. Brodsky tears the youth away from work, from the world and life. This is Brodsky's great antisocial role. (p. 14)

[After summary statements by the public prosecutor and defense counsel, the] court withdraws for consultation. A recess is announced. . . .

THE COURT RETURNS AND JUDGE READS SENTENCE:

Brodsky systematically does not fulfill the duties of a Soviet citizen with regard to his personal well-being and the production of material wealth, which is apparent from his frequent change of jobs. He was warned by the agencies of the MGB (Ministry of National Security) in 1961 and by the militia in 1962. He promised to take on a permanent job, but he made no decisions, he continued not to work, he wrote and read his decadent poems at evening gatherings. From the report of the committee on work with young writers it is apparent that Brodsky is not a poet. He was condemned by the readers of the *Evening Leningrad* newspaper. Therefore the court will apply the Ukase of February 4, 1961: to send Brodsky to a distant locality for a period of five years of enforced labor. (p. 17)

"The Trial of Iosif Brodsky," translated by Cullyer Bowen, in The New Leader, *Vol. XLVII, No. 18, August 31, 1964, pp. 6-17.*

ACHIEVEMENT AND INFLUENCE

ROBERT CONQUEST, RONALD HINGLEY AND G. R. URBAN

[Conquest is a poet, science fiction writer, and Kremlinologist who is best known for his poetry anthology New Lines *(1956) and his study* The Great Terror: Stalin's Purges of the Thirties *(1968). The latter work has been called the most complete, scholarly, and damning book written on the Stalinist terror. Hingley has written extensively on Russian literature and history and has translated the plays and stories of Anton Chekov. Urban is the director of Radio Free Europe's "Radio University" and the author of* The Nineteen Days, *an account of the Hungarian Revolution. The discussion that follows—an appraisal of intellectual freedom in the Soviet Union and Eastern Europe since Stalin's death—was broadcast to Eastern Europe as part of Urban's Radio University in 1964. In the following excerpt from that broadcast, the critics examine the political significance of art and literature under a totalitarian government, discuss the literary merits of works by several prominent writers of the Thaw, and attempt to assess the extent and nature of post-Stalinist liberalization.]*

URBAN: We are here to discuss Solzhenytsin's novel *One Day in the Life of Ivan Denisovich* and a number of similar books and plays on the Russian stage. The first quesion that I asked myself when I finished reading Solzhenytsin was: what are the limits of destalinization? Is this kind of novel a sign of destalinization only, or is it a sign that a more liberal atmosphere is now being ushered in in Soviet literature? Where does the one end and where does the second start?

HINGLEY: I don't think you can really compare Solzhenytsin's novel with any of the other so-called examples of destalinization, because it goes so very much further. I personally regard it as the only genuine piece of destalinization that we have ever had in the sense that it really does convey what it was like to be in a concentration camp. So far works of literature have referred to people who have returned from camps in a very cautious and vague sort of way. Here is a work which really

does describe what happens in a camp. This is a milestone, but I do not myself think that it heralds a new era of liberalism; as long as the party continues to keep overall control, it can stop it.

Also, it is rather significant that some of the people who wrote reviews in the Russian press praising Solzhenytsin's work, saying how wonderful this destalinization was, were in fact people who did very well out of it while it lasted. This puts me on my guard.

CONQUEST: I agree, but the question is: what is meant by destalinization and by liberalization? I am reminded of a remark made by a Russian writer to a Russo-American critic when he was in Moscow two years ago. The American said how much better things were in Russia, and the Russian writer replied: "Today, yes, but what about yesterday and tomorrow?" And I think your basic political point is that power to decide what will happen tomorrow to everybody and everything still remains entirely in the hands of the political apparat. They have relaxed, they are riding the horse with less nastiness—they are not lashing it or pulling at the bit—but they are still on it and they can do anything they wish. I do agree, on the other hand, that every time they do anything like allowing a Solzhenytsin book to be published, it makes it more difficult for them to tighten the reins again. But there has been no liberalization really. Liberalization involves allowing the people to have a voice, a real voice, not by permission but by right.

URBAN: You are both saying then that you can see no institutional guarantee that the changes will last. But what I am wondering is this: can you really stop the process? After 1956 there were periodic freeze-ups in the thaw, but taking the long view, the temperature curve has been rising all the time. Could the party really reverse this trend completely?

HINGLEY: As you know, more or less at the same time as this controversial novel appeared, the party brought out a whole series of pronouncements laying down the law on the subject of music, painting and so on. It is quite true that they cannot stop people thinking, but my impression at the moment is that the party is *prepared* to allow a little bit of fermentation. It is, from the party's point of view, a therapeutic fermentation and the party controls it.

CONQUEST: When you say '56, that is an interesting point: what exactly were they doing? What seems to have happened, to exaggerate it very slightly, was that Khrushchev and the people then allied with him allowed some liberalization of culture partly, not entirely, as a weapon against their opponents. When liberalization tended to boil over and produce more than they wanted, it did not worry them, but the next year, when Khrushchev had won, he mopped it up. All the extra, that we think of as liberalization, was wiped out. The power that he had tapped from the writers and the students was used against his opponents and when the job was done the writers were told to mind their business, which was socialist realism. Whenever there is a political fight in Russia, one side or the other is going to try to use all the forces it can muster against its opponents. Using Solzhenytsin's novel was—let us put it very crudely—a blow at Molotov. There was, I'm sure, much more to it than that, but I believe that this is one of the main motives of the Khrushchev faction: to use the novel against past, potential or future opponents.

URBAN: Developments in the satellite countries—and I am not sure if the two are comparable—don't quite bear out what you are saying: one's experience there has been simply that once you start a trend of liberalization, it carries its own momentum. We have seen this in Poland, we have seen it in Hungary and we are now witnessing it to some extent in Bulgaria and to a very significant extent in Czechoslovakia. You reach a point where you cannot turn the pages back again, you cannot say that we are not going to have this kind of writing because it is insidious and because it is seditious and so forth. Do you feel that there is, between the Russian mentality and satellite mentality, such a gap here that the two would be bound to run on different lines, that you can stop a fermentation in Russia, but you cannot stop it in the satellites?

HINGLEY: I think you cannot stop it in Russia in the sense that even under Stalin it went on, but I think you can effectively control it in so far as it is liable to have any practical impact. People will go on painting their private pictures or even writing for themselves and to some extent talking to each other. But the party at the moment is in a position to prevent any effective influence being exerted by these people on the broad public, and you may well be right that there is a difference here between the Russians and the satellites. After all the Russians have thirty more years of discipline behind them, and an even longer tradition of conformism.

CONQUEST: I agree entirely; the Russian apparat is a powerfully established force. Clearly, from 1956, the Hungarian is not; it is just a bunch of survivors now and the Hungarians have actually got rid of their old apparat leadership. The positions are not entirely comparable, but on the other hand I would agree that it would be very difficult even in Russia to go back in the sense of going back to saying Stalin was perfect—the party will not do that; the position the Russians are in now is something like 1928 or 1929 when there were the liberties we now speak of and yet there was a very tight dictatorship indeed. That dictatorship then developed into something worse. I think any political prediction, even in much less controlled societies, societies with many more variables, is extremely difficult. (pp. 3-4)

URBAN: Coming back to Solzhenytsin's novel: how would you describe the literary as distinct from the political merits of this book? Do we have here a book of major literary importance or just a text from which we can gauge the political temperature in the Soviet party?

HINGLEY: My own views are very strong on this. I think that we really do have a work of genuine literary value. After being starved under stalinism of anything, especially in the last years, of any literary merit, there was a tendency among Western critics to take something like Ehrenburg's or Dudintsev's wretched novels and to think that because these books said things that had not been said before, they must be good. My own tendency was to think the opposite; I was horrified by the dismal literary quality of Ehrenburg's and Dudintsev's writings. Solzhenitsyn's novel is quite different; it is almost, if not quite, a great work of literature. It is original, it breaks conventions which had formerly been obligatory.

URBAN: Conquest, would you agree with that?

CONQUEST: I am not really qualified to judge, but reading the English translation (the poorer of the two English translations) it does strike me that the thing you do notice is a total absence of the stalinist conventions. If I were told it was written by a German in Dachau or anywhere else I would be perfectly willing to believe it. It has the *feel* of world literature. I do not mean to say that it is not very Russian, of course it is; it has a terrific Russianness about it even in the translation; but it

Alexander Solzhenitsyn. UPI/Bettmann Newsphotos.

has this totally non-"communistified," non-"stalinified" air about it, a general human quality, and that is a remarkable phenomenon in a man who would doubtless have read the Russian classics but nevertheless would have been subjected to a great deal of orthodox theory of the novel.

URBAN: Do you mean to say that it speaks a language of its own, that it has its own distinctive style?

CONQUEST: I was thinking less of that really than of the structure, the things he thinks worth writing about, the points he thinks worth describing. There is an enormous lack of generalization to start with; the pieties are missing even when he describes a man who is thought to be a real spy. There is no talk about how awful it is to be a spy; and then when he talks about the Ukrainian nationalist rebels, there is not a word against them; they are just there.

HINGLEY: He goes even further than that because when he refers to the Soviet government, the Soviet power is *their* power—the *rulers'* power who are enthroned somewhere over and above the people. This is an extremely daring distinction.

CONQUEST: You don't get the feeling that Solzhenytsin is doing this for political reasons at all: this is just how a camp-man is feeling—it is *them*. But I feel that in a general way as well. His description of the guards is completely removed from stereotypes.

URBAN: Would you then agree that this is really a sign of going beyond a mere destalinization?

HINGLEY: There are two points here. The fact that the book was written is a sign that stalinization never worked at the level of a man like Solzhenitsyn who, after all, was an ordinary officer. It had never really got as deep as we always thought. The second point is: why was it allowed to be printed? I do not take a very high view of, let us say, Khrushchev's judgment in these matters. I do not suppose he saw all the implications.

My impression would be that he saw a good anti-stalinist thing and he said to himself: "We want anti-stalinism now, we want to say the past was foul when Stalin, Molotov, Malenkov and Co. were in charge, and this is as good as anything. Tvardovsky says it is good so let's print it." I do not think the political people were involved.

URBAN: My personal feeling is that a book such as Solzhenytsin's demolishes an important religious prop in communist thinking—it destroys the party's infallibility. We often underestimate the messianic features of communism. I don't think you can describe the horrors Solzhenytsin, or Lengyel in Hungary, described without driving the reader to the next logical question: if this could happen and is now admitted, the trouble must lie deeper than the whims of Stalin. I'm still not convinced that this kind of questioning can be controlled. I dare say Khrushchev did not foresee the repercussions of Solzhenytsin (although it would surprise me if a man such as Suslov did not), but the repercussions are there and I wonder how they might develop in future.

HINGLEY: I think you underestimate two things: the ordinary Russian's acute sense of the possible (I'm not saying this is a good thing but it is there) and the shortness of human memory, aided as it is in all totalitarian countries by the will to forget unpleasant things. Self-deception is a powerful force in political thinking and the Russian people had ample reason in their history to practice it. I'm not condemning self-deception (aren't we all deceiving ourselves at times?); in the history of some nations it was an important aid to survival. But a whole nation cannot for long live under the shadow of a disaster for which it was, in one way or another, itself partly responsible. The Germans cannot live (and cannot be expected to live) with Auschwitz and the Russians won't live with Stalin's camps. There is a psychological need in both these cases to get away from an oppressive past. The Russian people know from experience that the getting away has its limits and that is why I think that the repercussions of Solzhenytsin and of this whole genre of literature will not get out of hand. The satellites have different traditions and the problem there could be a very different one.

URBAN: I would agree with that. Already there are things happening in some of these countries for which I for one can find no parallel in Russia; of course, I stand to be corrected. In Hungary, for instance, a great deal of decadent, Western existentialist literature has been published in translation. The head of the state publishing house sponsors the publication of these books. Last year the same man came out with a tremendous attack in the official literary periodical saying very unkind things about these books which he himself had selected to be put on the market. His point was that these books were being made available in Hungarian to show the public what rotten, decadent Western existentialist literature was like and to discourage people. Now we know that the public is not at all discouraged and that these books are avidly read and often sold out the day they arrive in the shops.

My point is that, whatever the initial intention, once a thing is published it has its own momentum which you cannot stop, short of reinstating Stalin's terror at its worst. And that brings me back to our first point; I'm sorry to go on laboring this question but I think it is important.

CONQUEST: I don't think you can compare Russia with Hungary in this case. In Hungary there was nothing left in art except old stalinists and people who would have been Nagyists but for saving their skins, and now this trickling Nagyism is coming in again. The present Hungarian situation is certainly far more liberal than that in Russia; people can talk more or less freely, the political police do not drag them off to lunatic asylums—this sort of thing does not happen in Hungary, not now. Hungarians can come to the West, they can get Western books; Hungary is in a far better state that way than Russia. In Poland and Hungary they translate Kafka and Proust but they do not in Russia; the books are not available. I am sure your Hungarian has his tongue in his cheek to some extent in condemning the existentialists he publishes, or else he is a fool. But I am not sure whether all this makes an awful lot of difference because nobody in Russia among the intellectual classes, among the people who actually read seriously, ever thought anything different. If they have not got Kafka in Russian they read it in German.

I have not been in Moscow in many a long year, but in Moscow libraries, the libraries of the writers, in Ehrenburg's library, there is a mass of Proust and everything else, and the Russian intellectuals have never accepted the stalinist theory. They had to keep silent about it, but they never subscribed to the idea that these are not good writers. The fact that some of these writers are beginning to be printed again is an interesting *public* event, but it is not a *private* event in their minds; their opinion is settled already. This goes equally for students. The teachers in the Moscow Literary Institute never stop complaining that their students *will* read the wrong stuff, because the tradition trickles through in spite of all the efforts of the literary professors.

HINGLEY: All this is quite true but it remains the case that important books are not easily available, so that the general public simply have not read them because they have not been able to get hold of them. I know that forbidden fruit has a great lure for a lot of people, particularly the young generation. But—you will notice that I'm a born pessimist—for a book to make an impact on the public consciousness it has to be available in large numbers in the vernacular; and if it is not on the bookseller's shelves the non-specialized reader will just not make the effort to go after it. Of course, if you have a war or a revolutionary situation on your hands, a great many people will go out of their way to get forbidden literature. One did it during the last war, but I cannot see my white-collar Russian scurrying from library to library to find a German-language edition of Rilke's *Malte Laurids Brigge* or of Proust's *Time Regained* in French. We must not forget that most of us are too idle or stupid or both to do anything of the sort. I am therefore inclined to believe that non-publication in Russia is a pretty effective, although by no means foolproof, way of keeping the public ignorant.

Where I do see an important chink in this wall of ignorance is the infiltration of books from Poland. Many Russians read Polish, and the extent to which Polish books, pictures and periodicals reach the Soviet public is said to be considerable and highly influential. In any case I don't think that you can, in the long run, deny the Russian public something Poles, Czechs and Hungarians are allowed to read and see. There is too much official visiting and cross-fertilization going on for that to be possible. But in Russia the process may be slow. Perhaps if the Russians had staged a 1956 of some sort they too would be given a less carefully scrutinized intellectual diet.

URBAN: Evgenyi Yevtushenko has been given tremendous publicity in most Western countries. He has been travelling around and reciting his verse in America and Britain and Germany.

How would you describe the specific flavor of Yevtushenko's poems?

CONQUEST: A lot of Yevtushenko's reputation in the West is not, strictly speaking, literary at all. It is political in the sense that he is taken to be a great liberal—let us not define the term for the moment. About his verse: in the first place, even a foreigner who does speak Russian perfectly should be extremely chary of giving any personal judgment of verse, and I do not really want to do that. One curious thing about Yevtushenko's verse is that the Polish poets are terribly anti-Yevtushenko, they regard his poetry as square and ordinary and un*avant-garde*-ish. This seems to me very much a Polish reaction; Poles are very keen on being with Paris and I don't think this is fair. A Polish poet said to me "Yevtushenko is only Kipling." I said, "Yes, Kipling is a very good poet." This point had never occurred to him. Kipling is a good poet and this *avant-garde* business has rather died out in England. The feeling that the regular poets, indeed the rather rollicking poets, are not as good as the practitioners of the subtle doubletalk has gone. This urge for obscure symbolism and the shock-technique comes up every hundred years or so. We have always had it; we had it in the time of Charles I. It is now realized that Dryden is not a better poet than Donne, but a much plainer poet, and Yevtushenko is a plain poet. I admire much of his poetry, but subtlety is not one of its virtues; its qualities are vigor and liveliness. He has momentum, which is a good thing, particularly with long poems which are rare these days. Pasternak thought he was a good poet and I tend to agree with him.

If you talk about Voznesensky and his group, they are very much closer to the *avant-garde* ideals. But even Voznesensky is not really revolutionary. His poems owe their oddity, their appearance of not being good socialist realism, to his interest in words. He plays around with an immense amount of verbal repetitions and echoings and so on. That is all right, but it is not in itself a particularly obscure thing. It is irritating to somebody who feels the fact that two words rhyme or sound alike is irrational and in a sense uncommunist; but he has more subtlety and a more individual taste to him than Yevtushenko.

HINGLEY: I agree with what you say. I think Yevtushenko is nothing like as good a poet as Kipling. He has one great quality and that is his ability to declaim, particularly his rhythm. He could have been a first-class tympanist. Some of his poems are poor and even trite; but his rhythm as he speaks his verse is stirring.

We have to realize that Yevtushenko has changed— or so it seems to me. He has always had to compromise, as any Russian has to in order to be printed, but during the last year or so there has been more and more compromise and less and less liberalism. I can quote examples of this. You know his poem written in Helsinki, you have probably read his poems from Cuba. I was the first person to denounce Yevtushenko in the press; since then quite a lot of other people have done the same, but I described him as the poet laureate of Khrushchevism. This is perhaps a sneer. I do not want to suggest that I despise him, or that I think that he has completely sold out, but I think that he has half sold out. Of course, he is a living human being and is not anybody's slave and he may change, but at the moment his rôle is not one which I would particularly admire.

CONQUEST: In a way, Yevtushenko is writing public poetry and Voznesensky a more private poetry. I don't want to make a crass distinction between them; there are poems of Yevtu-

shenko which, although their clarity is great, are nevertheless private. Yevtushenko's great fault now is the bad public poem. His recent bad poems have been public poems. There was this absurd and dishonest poem about his behavior in Helsinki. Then there was his inordinate praise of Cuba. You may say that Cuba has a certain vitality and it can represent an idea of something livelier than Russia, but supporting it is not supporting anything resembling liberalism or democracy or freedom.

When you say that Yevtushenko is simply the poet laureate of Khrushchevism, I do not think that is quite right. He is the poet laureate of the extreme left edge of Khrushchevism which is not necessarily Khrushchev's real view at all; it is the left edge of Khruschev's present maneuver. "Babiy Yar," to do him justice, was not; it was beyond Khrushchev, it was pulling Khrushchev along. On the other hand, the poem on Stalin which people talk about as being such a great blow—well, it was published in *Pravda*, it might have been written by Agit-prop.

HINGLEY: "Babiy Yar" was written before Yevtushenko went sour.

CONQUEST: Yes, but the poem on Stalin could have been written in collaboration with the Secretariat. It represents the present line. (pp. 5-8)

URBAN: What do you think of the second version of "Babiy Yar," with the insert? It is a few lines where a Russian woman apparently comes in and saves a Jewish child, and then the Nazis come along and shoot the woman but the child is saved. What is even more peculiar is that Shostakovich's version of the setting of this poem in his new symphony has now also been changed to conform to the new words. I think this shows the most frightful lack of intellectual and artistic integrity.

HINGLEY: I would say that this confirms what I was saying. Yevtushenko has changed. Six months or a year ago he became more conformist, perhaps for some tactical reason; they have got on to him and got him to emasculate this poem from a political point of view.

CONQUEST: I do not think it is particularly emasculating it; it is putting in something that was not there already. But they have all done that for many a long year. Margarita Aliger did it with one of her poems. I had this poem translated in my collection and she wrote a long attack on me in one of the Russian magazines, *Inostrannaya Literatura,* saying that I had mistranslated it by leaving out two lines at the end. I thought "Good heavens, have I?" and I rushed back to the original and found I was exactly right, but the version I had taken came from 1956, and it was different from her collected poems which were published in 1958, and had two new lines added.

HINGLEY: I cannot agree that this addition is unimportant because we know that the Nazis killed Jews and also Russians, but the point of the poem, or one of the points of it, was to ventilate in public the fact that there is still some anti-Semitism in Russia. By adding these lines he makes a true comment, a fair comment, but in the context it alters the balance of the poem. Obviously it was induced and suggested to him.

CONQUEST: This poem is a political act rather than a poem. It is in verse, but it is a political gesture, and in adjusting a political act you are doing something slightly different from just rewriting a work of art. I agree with you that it does alter the tone, but it does not say that there is no anti-Semitism in Russia; it says there is some anti-Semitism.

HINGLEY: The real point here was not whether Yevtushenko condemned anti-Semitism or not, or so it seems to me, but that he made an unsolicited public political statement of any kind. The fact that it was anti-Semitism made it more important or more publicly interesting, but where he was a naughty boy was that without consultation he made a political statement, and he has now publicly shown that he can be controlled, and this is much more important than Jews or non-Jews.

CONQUEST: We should not judge, but I think we can register that it would be better if he had not added these new lines to his verses. It is difficult to say quite why, but one would somehow feel better if he had not, without wishing actually to enter into an adverse judgment.

HINGLEY: I do not think one should judge any of these people. We don't know the difficulties they labor under.

URBAN: What strikes me as even more important is that Yevtushenko, but the others as well, have these enormous public recitals in sports stadiums in Moscow. It is surely an extraordinary phenomenon that young poets get up on a podium and recite to the enthusiastic applause of ten thousand people.

CONQUEST: It reminds me of a remark of Paul Ignotus, the Hungarian writer, after the 1956 revolution when he fled to England. He said that during Rakosi's regime all the classics were read with immense gusto in Hungary and he asked if this indicated that they loved the classics. The answer was No. The only alternative was the party novel, and they would have preferred a good crime story or western, probably. When one says they go to poetry recitals, well, poetry is much the most difficult art for a totalitarian regime to control and it is always the first that escapes if there is the slightest liberalization. The guardians of orthodoxy can always complain about the plot of a novel: if the party secretary is made to look nasty the book is obviously out of line. But it is awfully difficult to know what is going on in a poem of Yevtushenko's. In these poems you get something which is not laid down for the poet by the government, and that is why you get these meetings at the statue of Mayakovsky, broken up however by the so-called voluntary detachments of young workers (or, to put it quite bluntly, auxiliary KGB squads). These recitals are a way of talking away from set texts and feelings, and people in Russia will queue up for anything that promises to give them a holiday from the stale pieties of official literature. (pp. 8-9)

Yevtushenko's recitals show the Russians to be anxious to satisfy a great many unsatisfied needs, but I don't think they spell danger for the government.

HINGLEY: I agree with what you say, but I think there is a little more to it than that. You are a poet and I speak as one who is not only not a poet but does not read very much poetry although at Oxford I teach it. I have always noticed how very unpoetically oriented the English are. Russians, I think, have a sort of appreciation of poetry which, on the whole, English people do not have, and even Yevtushenko's style of declaiming is much better than a BBC Third Program announcer or whoever they employ reading one of your poems. The Russians did have poetry recitals even under Stalin. A friend of mine was present at a reading given by Pasternak under Stalin and this was received with great enthusiasm. It is true that most East Europeans would rather be reading detective stories if they had a choice, but I think there is a sense in which the Russians are probably more receptive to poetry than we are.

At the same time I don't deny that the political element is extremely important. Can I draw a parallel here with funerals? We do not make much of poets here in England and we do not make very much of funerals. The funeral of a Russian writer—this is going back to tsarist times—has always been a great occasion; simply by attending the thing you were making a kind of political statement. Just as they make much more fuss of poetry, they make more fuss of funerals. This is perhaps sixty or seventy percent due to the fact that, when you cannot express political opinions, all sorts of apparently quite natural areas of behavior, which are taken for granted in a free country, become terribly sensitive. (p. 9)

URBAN: I think it is inconceivable that—given some social upheaval in England, which I think is highly unlikely—Mr. Eliot, or Mr. Auden would rush down to Westminster with petitions urging the government to do this or that, whereas it is quite conceivable, and it has actually happened, in Hungary, and I can see it happening again. I can quite see Yevtushenko and Voznesensky doing exactly that in some future upheaval.

CONQUEST: If England had been overrun by Germans in 1940 and a sort of petering-out puppet regime was here, you would get the same even in the older generation.

HINGLEY: I think that people are much the same everywhere. We talk about Eastern Europeans, we talk about Russians sometimes as if they were beasts in a zoo, and this is wrong as well as ridiculous. I think that very similar things, with certain differences in national outlook, would happen here. . . .

URBAN: But [what does leadership by the intelligentsia] really mean? Is it a good thing?

CONQUEST: In the country of the illiterate, the intellectual is king. Where students and intellectuals have influence, it is almost invariably a proof that the country is immature, I think any intelligent Russian would agree that Russia is immature politically, but this is not the same as to say that the Russian *intellectual* is immature. He is lacking in experience in certain respects, he is perhaps likely to be too theoretical, simply through detachment from real politics for so long, but the traditions involved are mature ones, right back to Pushkin. (p. 10)

URBAN: I am told that much of the new Russian poetry is extremely romantic and that these poems are all very brief, very sketchy and, in that sense, rather modern.

CONQUEST: I do get the impression from Voznesensky that he is very concerned to produce even a throwaway sentence in which every word has been considered. I do not quite get that from Yevtushenko, who sometimes dashes ahead like some good poets do. I do not mean that Voznesensky is pernickety; you know that awful feeling that every word has been thought out too much that you get with some poetry; he is not quite that, but I do feel he is taking care and he is not going to say a line more than he thinks is right. Some of his verse may sound diffuse, I agree on that, and I think it is true that, in a vague sense, his poems are romantic. But there were "romantics" under Stalin, too; then in 1956-1957, there were attacks on poets for dealing with the personal life at all, for mentioning bad moods, loneliness and so on. This does not fit in with the optimistic creed of communism. But I get the strong impression that this personal life is one of the integrities of the new poets and it will be very difficult to clear them out of it once they have established a right to it.

HINGLEY: This I think is the main gain since the death of Stalin; you can describe a mood, you can describe a personal predicament and you do not have to bring in politics. In prose, too, the writers are showing straightforward impatience with the official rubbish. There are, to be sure, references to politics; but there is the implication, which is quite clearly understood, that nobody with any sort of sense would pay any attention to the official line.

CONQUEST: This is a very important development. The official line is still being laid down, but the party is now a kind of adjudicator, someone standing in the middle saying ''that is right, that is wrong''; but people do not really have to take the party's guidance.

HINGLEY: The writers may, from time to time, have difficulty in being published, but the important thing is that the party's verdict is no longer accepted and nobody thinks it is.

CONQUEST: Also, there are competing factions who influence the party and one of the things you have now to take into account is that people can lobby to some extent.

URBAN: How would you describe these groups? I have a very rough division in mind and I can think of four different sections: you have your old stalinists, your Kochetovs and that kind of person who are on the way out, but still hold some position of power; then you have the official keepers of the scrolls: Khrushchev and Co., the people who utter pious platitudes on socialism and what is good for the party and the people; then the third group is your Yevtushenkos who wrote these letters of protest to Khrushchev and the party. They are free to publish, although they do not agree with the party line, but are nevertheless willing to compromise; and then the fourth group is the underground literature: Yesenin-Volpin, Tertz and all these people who send their manuscripts abroad or write for their desk drawers.

HINGLEY: I think that is a good division except one has to say that even within the groups there are people spread out on the spectrum. If you take the group of people who have published and yet protested—of which Yevtushenko is one, Ehrenburg is another, to some extent Paustovsky is another, and Viktor Nekrassov, who has written several rather interesting articles recently, is yet another—if you look at these individuals, they may fall in the same group, but they are not equal in terms of honorableness from my point of view. Some have a very clean record, some have a very dirty record, so there is quite a big difference within your groups, but I would accept your division.

CONQUEST: Mind you, I think you can be a very clean stalinist. Fadeyev was an honest stalinist, he committed suicide—of course—and the story is that he helped to get Pasternak out of trouble in 1948-1949, but Fadeyev was clearly an honest stalinist. The interesting point about that is that Stalin was not, and when you talk about Kochetov and others like him, to my mind they are fanatics in a sense in which Stalin was not. I can see Stalin easing up and getting rid of them if it suited his purpose (in fact, he did more or less at one time). But it is not quite true to call these hacks stalinists; they are sub-stalinists, they are people who have accepted Stalin's theoretical principles, but not what there was in Stalin's practical intelligence. Stalin was just concerned to keep himself in power and smash anybody who was against him; he was smart and he was prepared to maneuver if necessary. But the sub-stalinists never got down from the trees.

HINGLEY: I'm worried about the influence of your third group because I think the people in it are very mediocre. They are worse than mediocre, they are all the same: they cannot write, they cannot paint, they cannot write music, but there is a position of some honor for them in Soviet society, and certainly a great deal of perquisites, and they can boss around people who are much more capable than they are, which is a thing that mediocre people like to do in every country. In literature they are very much out on a limb at the moment and I feel sorry for them. I don't like some of the so-called new writers in prose who have been very much praised. I don't want to mention their names because I am for them politically. Some of them have made history simply by writing on new subjects. But what they have written has not been very good as literature.

CONQUEST: They caught the right moment and pushed the liberal front in literature as far as it would go.

HINGLEY: They have done their best and people have overpraised them both at home and in the West. Sometimes I have forced myself to read their writings because it is important; but then I have turned up a novel of Kochetov where you know exactly where you are, you are back in Stalin's day, and honestly I have read his latest novel, *The Secretary of the Obkom*, with enormous pleasure.

CONQUEST: It really is good?

HINGLEY: It is bad, it is terrible, it is like reading advertisements of a kind, you know Horlick's or something like that.

URBAN: It is like going to an old Chaplin film where you don't really laugh because the film is funny, but because you enjoy the tradition: you expect the chase, the fisticuffs and the demure miss—and you get them.

HINGLEY: Yes, it is a nostalgia. There is something oddly reassuring to see the tractor girl, the party secretary and all the other stereotypes back in their old places. For whatever reason, I can get more pleasure out of reading Kochetov than reading a mediocre liberal. Of course some of the liberals are more than mediocre, but there are plenty of mediocre ones and these include some well-known names. I would rather as a task read my Kochetov. He at least is unadulterated rubbish and you know where you are wih him.

URBAN: Don't forget that you are a decadent Western intellectual who judges these things by extraneous standards. Do you think the Russian reading public would take a similar view? I should hate to think it would. It might, I don't know.

HINGLEY: I shouldn't think so because they have had years when it was difficult to read anything contemporary that was not Kochetov. While I was reading the Stalin Prize novels I was also reading whatever Faulkner or Angus Wilson wrote and this made the Kochetovs bearable. Set side by side with a Wilson the official hacks were tremendously funny. If you were a Russian who did not read anything else, I can see that this would be a desperate matter.

URBAN: Going over to the visual arts. Hingley, why do you think that Khrushchev was so very harsh on abstract art at the exhibition he visited a few months ago? I don't quite see the difference between poetry and painting.

HINGLEY: It puzzles me, too. Khrushchev is well known to go off the deep end when he sees any sort of non-representational art.

CONQUEST: He may have been lured there by various cultural politicians, but I don't know why they bother so much about abstract art. They have a large apparatus of control which is fully occupied looking at the things that matter. Why they should bother with something that is purely a question of form, I don't know.

URBAN: *Is* it a question of form?

HINGLEY: It seems to be, does it not? They go crazy if they see a picture which is not like a photograph.

URBAN: It seems to me that poetry and prose lend themselves quite easily to the sort of message Khrushchev would like to have put across. It is simple enough to spell out your anti-stalinism in literature, but you cannot do it so easily with painting or sculpture, or can you?

HINGLEY: You can theoretically.

URBAN: How would you do that?

HINGLEY: You could have a picture of the same camp which Solzhenitsyn describes in his story, but, as far as I know, there has never been anything like it and I rather suspect it would not work. The verbal measure is the most effective one both in pleading for or against conventions and orthodoxy, at least on the popular levels.

CONQUEST: Apart from anything else there would be the purely practical problem here of creating a sort of traffic block in the art gallery, because if such a picture were put up in any of the Moscow galleries they would have to take it down because there would be people struggling and queueing up for weeks to see it. It may be just as simple as that.

HINGLEY: There are two different things here. One is that I am sure one could get a hack to do a picture of a concentration camp and it would not be of the slightest interest, except as a document. After all the new poets do not just write, even Yevtushenko at his worst does not simply hack out anti-stalinist poetry, he writes in a different genre and style, his method and feeling are different, and if you got a man to do a good concentration camp on canvas it would be an expressionist quasi-abstract—not a Picasso, but something like that. It would appeal to fewer people, a different lot of people. All I am saying is that the problem is a very complicated one and it would take books to analyze it properly.

The thing that strikes me about the evidence of Khrushchev's opposition to abstract arts is that it does show that basically the communist leaders feel that these pictures are subversive, that they distract attention from building socialism and that they tend to slip out of their control and competence. (pp. 10-12)

CONQUEST: This is simply the attitude of a primitive person feeling ill at ease politically, socially and intellectually.

HINGLEY: I think the real thing is that they fear the arts—when I say "they" I mean the most retrograde members in the party who are, on the whole, still making cultural policy. These people do not want great works of painting, sculpture or literature because they are too disturbing. This is a very old thing. It goes all the way back to Plato and we have seen it at work throughout history.

CONQUEST: Art symbolizes an alternative allegiance. If you are really enthusiastic about painting or music you are transferring enthusiasm which could be otherwise harnessed to the party's ends. You are depleting your stock of strong feelings for non-approved purposes. Abstract art could be a rival to

party ideology; it could siphon off the kind of emotion and intellectual vision which the party wants to keep for itself. (p. 13)

Robert Conquest, Ronald Hingley, and G. R. Urban, "Khrushchev and the Intellectuals," in East Europe, *Vol. 13, No. 2, February, 1964, pp. 2-14.*

THEODORE FRANKEL

[Frankel is a commentator on European and Soviet affairs. In the following excerpt, he evaluates the literary merits of dissident prose and poetry of the Thaw period.]

The thinness of the literary response to the thaw is suggested by the fact that only a handful of competent writers were engaged by it in their work. . . . Nor does one find any marked increase in diversity; the range of the Soviet literary imagination is still so restricted that the new directions which emerged during the thaw all seem to lead into the same three or four paths.

The first and most frequent tendency is found among orthodox followers of the party who are struggling to introduce some degree of artistic freedom and complexity into their celebrations of Soviet life. A good example is Vladimir Tendryakov's "Short Circuit," which, like many of his other stories, affirms the achievements of Communism while pointing up their moral costs. The hero of "Short Circuit" is a Khrushchev-like manager whose ability to make hard decisions under stress is shown to be bound up in a personality that is damaging to his family, his friends, and subordinates. Though a rather simple form of conflict for a writer to deal with, it still puts a heavy strain on Tendryakov's resources. Instead of moving toward a meaningful confrontation between political goals and moral scruples, he limits the issue by permitting all the key figures in the story to experience the same contradictory emotions in varying degrees. Thus the conflict between power and virtue remains unexplored, and Tendryakov's personal uneasiness toward his hero merely transmits itself to his equivocal and vacillating cast of characters. This is "constructive writing," to be sure, but at the expense of engaging the question it raises. There are a number of Central European writers who would know how to exploit the ambiguity of Tendryakov's situation, but lacking their gift of dual vision, he can only founder amid the disjunctions between political loyalties and personal consciousness.

There are many such holdovers from Stalin's world: heavy-handed social realists, inveterate moralizers who are redeemed, if at all, by their stubborn honesty in dealing with individual relationships. Even the best book in this genre, Vladimir Dudintsev's *Not by Bread Alone,* is undermined by its emphasis on the possibilities of making Communism more efficient and humane. A more extreme case of what Peter Benno calls "Stalinist literature *à rebours*" is the poetry of Yevgenyi Yevtushenko. When his anti-Stalinist poems "Stalin's Heirs," "Babi Yar," and "The Dead Hand" appeared in the West, Yevtushenko quickly acquired a reputation as a significant poet and a political rebel. On second look, he has turned out to be neither. Much as one hates to say so, the directness, simplicity, and sensitivity which made a poem like "Babi Yar" so effective in publicizing the plight of Soviet Jewry are not the qualities which of themselves make for major poetry. On the contrary, Yevtushenko's polemical verse, detached from its political content, seems unsophisticated and anachronistic, much as his lyrical poems are heavily romantic in their sentimentality and conventional in their non-conformity. Far from being a radical, moreover, Yevtushenko is a man so thoroughly conditioned by his Stalinist upbringing that his political vision goes no further than de-Stalinization combined with reform of the party. Indeed, Khrushchev's famous secret speech to the Twentieth Party Congress was more revolutionary than Yevtushenko's "Stalin's Heirs." Because of his youth and flamboyance, however, Yevtushenko became the political spokesman for the new generation, faithfully expressing in his "bohemian" way of life no less than in his poetry their repudiation of the past and their urgent, if vague, search for a better future.

Yevtushenko's importance derived from his role as the idol of the Russian students. And for a time he seemed to be the heir of those poet-leaders who might revive the distinctive tradition of a powerful civic literature. This possibility, however, was quickly nipped in the bud by the party, which took the sensible course of wooing the would-be rebel rather than attempting to silence him. Since Yevtushenko wished only to reform the Communist party, and since he needed to keep open the channels to the Kremlin if he was to remain the spokesman of his generation, he was easily seduced. (pp. 54-5)

In sharp contrast to this new civic literature is another category, which might be called the school of inner emigration, represented mostly by short-story writers who have turned their backs on politics and deal with the little incidents and poignancies of everyday life. A village carpenter drives his dying wife to the hospital and daydreams of having a meal in a fancy restaurant; an engineer on a brief vacation shows himself to be insensitive to the troubles of a young girl who happens to sit next to him on the bus; a truck driver picks up a woman hitch-hiker, fantasies a romance with her, and is brought down to earth by her insistence on paying him for the ride; a schoolgirl is punished by her friends for talking to a boy whom they have ostracized. From such sad, inconsequential stuff Kazakov, Nagibin, and [others] . . . spin their unadorned tales. The great popularity of these authors in the Soviet Union evidently derives from the ease with which readers can identify with the minor triumphs and sorrows of their characters, and with their predominant mood of fatalistic acceptance which reflects an enduring Russian trait—as well as the actual situation of the individual in Soviet society.

Lifelike, honest, tightly-structured, these modest stories are among the best-written literature produced in the Soviet Union. Nor are they quite as detached from the issues of Communist life as their authors and public like to believe. In a completely politicalized society, the very act of writing a deliberately non-political story is a protest, however weak, against the state. Moreover, being a species of socialist realism, this fiction cannot help but comment, indirectly but sometimes tellingly, on the conditions of Soviet life. One finds, for example, a devastating judgment of Soviet agricultural policy communicated by stories in which the emptiness of the peasants' existence is powerfully suggested by the pathetic modesty of their desires. Finally, the main characteristics of this literature—its understated style, its fatalistic philosophy, its focus on the individual—all serve by implication to debunk the bombast, the shallow optimism, and the inhuman stress on the importance of institutions which are the hallmark of the official literature.

This genre, though, is perhaps less subversive of the state than it is of the genuine talents of some of its practitioners. By hewing so closely to the surface of things, these writers inevitably scant the deeper layers of individual experience, just

as they tend to simplify and foreshorten social perspective through the brevity and narrowness of their tales. Thus is the Chekhovian sketch converted into a peculiar species of escape literature which evades the reality of social control in the Soviet Union by adopting the comforting fiction that only the individual counts. Yet what actually emerges from these stories is precisely the opposite point: it is the impotence of the individual we see, not his importance, in the endless procession of pathetic and nondescript Ivans and Natashas.

This central pretense concerning the individual accounts for much of the sentimentality that marks [these stories]. . . . It also explains the sense of incongruity that gradually takes hold of a reader who goes through a large number of such stories, for they register a consistently anemic response to the enormous realities of the Soviet state—the convulsions of Stalin's regime, the Second World War, and the domestic and foreign crises in which the Russian people have been and are involved. A constant preoccupation with the commonplace, however honorably motivated, cuts off consideration of larger and more decisive issues; and to humanize the Soviet character by reducing it to the purely personal is to narrow rather than broaden the horizons of consciousness.

While this self-limitation is the essence of the non-political Soviet writer's craft, it functions as a strategy for writers—like Aksenev, Okudzawa, and Solzhenitsyn—who attempt to offer serious comments on their society. Aksenev's "Half-way to the Moon" is the tale of a robust young lumberjack who falls in love with an airplane hostess—symbol of unattainable elegance and refinement—and, in the vain hope of meeting her again, flies back and forth on her route like a lost soul. Despite its whimsy, the story is coolly detached in its portrayal of Russia's confused and rebellious youth, and unlike the "inner-emigration" genre pieces, it aims at making a more than merely "personal" point. So, too, with Okudzawa's "Lots of Luck, Kid," a downbeat war novella whose non-hero, a likable peasant lad, tells in the first person singular "how I fought in the war, how they wanted to kill me, and how I made it through all right." And so, of course, with Solzhenitsyn's *One Day in the Life of Ivan Denisovich:* in this famous account of the daily struggle to stay alive in a Soviet labor camp, the very walls of the camp seem to come forward to bear unemotional witness to the sufferings of Ivan, the Russian Everyman.

Aksenev, Okudzawa, and Solzhenitsyn make up the small group of Soviet fiction writers who confront major social issues in a serious and solid way. They all feature the common man as a hero; and they all use his peasant heart and mind, his goodness and slyness, to serve as the recording center of consciousness. Generally, their style is naturalistic and highly idiomatic; indeed, all three writers are almost unintelligible in Russian unless the reader has an extensive knowledge of peasant dialect, adolescent slang, or the argot of labor-camp inmates.

In short, what we have here is a quasi-documentary form which permits the author to let "the facts" and "the people" speak for themselves. This is of obvious value in a society where the fear of repression and reprisal is still strong; the form also leans on a cherished populist tradition in Russian letters, and since it allows for easy identification on the part of the reader, it makes for a deep and lasting impact on a mass audience. Solzhenitsyn's spare tale of the Stalinist camps shook the Russians as Pasternak's complex novel never could have done.

Nevertheless, much of what has been said about the other types of contemporary Soviet fiction applies to the documentary protest novel as well. By depicting the social scene strictly as seen through the eyes of their simple protagonists—who are, moreover, deeply caught up in events—the authors deprive themselves of whatever larger awareness they have gained of the dynamics of the system; they also relinquish whatever distance they have been able to put between themselves and their social conditions, and they sacrifice any possibility of letting their art confront and transcend the conditions of life. More seriously, the narrow focus of the documentary form itself commits the author to a flat, oversimplified realism which cannot finally do justice to the surrealistic qualities of, say, Stalin's labor camps. The assumption of neutrality, the quiet style, and the very definite structure called for by the medium, produce an order and rationality which negate and betray the chaos and madness at the heart of whatever it portrays. Perhaps the best proof of this inherent tendency of the documentary form to diminish its subject is the fact that Khrushchev and his successors have been able to make use of books like *Ivan Denisovich* which, on the face of things, should have been a radical indictment of the entire system.

In the end, then, Solzhenitsyn and the others have failed to establish a significant political literature. One can point to the severe restraints on such writers in the Soviet Union, but it is also true that other writers of fiction like Sinyavsky-Tertz have chosen to remain unpublished in Russia rather than submit to the restrictive "objectivity" of socialist realism or its contemporary variants. If the "documentary" writers have lowered their sights to the "facts," one suspects that they have done so at least partly in order to write on the level of their imaginations.

This is particularly true, I think, of Solzhenitsyn. *One Day in the Life of Ivan Denisovich* and *Matryona's Home* are great documents, but their author is not a great artist. There is no resonance to his work, none of the richness one senses when a first-rate mind is in the background. His characters and situations, given to him by the times, are so powerful in themselves that they needed no more than an accurate observer, an honest craftsman—which Solzhenitsyn certainly is. When, however, he turns to more introspective material, as in his personal sketches, . . . one is immediately conscious of a commonplace, and rigid, sensibility. The cases of Aksenev, Okudzawa, and Dudintsev are not quite as clear-cut, but reading them, too, one becomes aware as much of their internal inhibitions as of the severe limits to acceptable Soviet writing during the thaw.

However, the full extent to which even the most liberated Soviet novelists operate under the dead hand of the Stalinist past—and the high price they must pay in terms of the limitations imposed upon their creative capabilities—is seen perhaps most clearly in the case of those novelists whose alienation from their society seems total. I am referring to the small group of writers whose sense of mission is so intense that, unable to publish at home, they smuggle their work abroad—including the recently-imprisoned Andrei Sinyavsky-Tertz and Yuli Daniel-Arzhak, and also Valery Tarsis, the author of "Ward 7."

What distinguishes these men is their determination to confront in their writings the major problems besetting Soviet society, paired with the recognition that they can do so only by resorting to unconventional literary idioms capable of reflecting the disjointed character of their time. (I shall limit myself in what follows to the work of Sinyavsky-Tertz, but my comments— particularly as they concern the "new style" and its implications—apply, with modifications, to Daniel as well. Tarsis

shares their political convictions completely, and their artistic orientation to a limited degree.)

In Sinyavsky's case, the close connection between political dissent and literary apartness was demonstrated, from the outset, by the joint Paris publication, in 1959, of the novella "The Trial Begins" and the critical essay, "On Socialist Realism"— both under the Tertz pseudonym. Then, it was the novella that caused most of the comment. For here, for the first time within the memory of our generation, could be heard the authentic, uncensored voice of the Russian intellectual—and that voice turned out to be surprisingly familiar; or so it seemed. Tertz, with his sophisticated, ironic, and self-deprecating view of personal relationships, and his high, grotesque style, was readily accepted in the West; there his intense political engagement was not only greatly admired for its courage, but also envied insofar as his targets—Stalin's camps, Russian anti-Semitism, Soviet bureaucracy—were the kind of visible, uncomplicated evils which Western society, with all its moral ambiguities, does not as a rule offer intellectual and artistic critics. Small wonder, then, that "The Trial Begins" received the lion's share of attention. In retrospect, however, the essay seems at least equally important, since it offers nothing less than a manifesto for a new Russian literature. It calls, in the most uncompromising terms, for emancipation from the "purposes" of Communism and the replacement of socialist realism by a "phantasmagoric" and "bizarre" style appropriate to the quality of life in the 20th century.

There can be little doubt that "The Trial Begins," and Tertz's subsequent stories and novels were meant to be the first specimens of this new Russian literature, or that Daniel's literary ambitions had also been defined in Tertz's essay. It is all the more ironic, then, that though "The Trial Begins" is a great work in many respects, it fails to measure up to Tertz's manifesto. For while the novella does indeed move away from Communist purposes and socialist realism, it does so not by progressing toward new artistic purposes and to a new idiom of its own, but by falling back, both in conception and style, on 19th-century Russian romanticism.

As it happens, there is an extended discussion of that movement in "On Socialist Realism," and the similarity between its governing themes, as seen by Tertz, and those which govern his own novels is striking indeed. According to Tertz, 19th-century Russian romanticism is dominated by the dilemma of the "superfluous" man, the intellectual who feels compelled by the absurdities and injustices of his age to search for a higher "Purpose" but is prevented from finding it by the stultifying effects of those very absurdities and injustices upon his own character. Writes Tertz:

> For all his generous purposes, he [the superfluous man] is unable to find a destiny and he presents a lamentable example of . . . purposelessness. He is as a rule a reflective character with tendencies to self-analysis and self-flagellation. His life is full of unrealized projects, and his fate is sad and slightly ridiculous. A woman usually plays a fatal part in it.

The part played by the heroine—one for which she is qualified by a "beautiful, magical, mysterious and not too concrete nature . . . is to serve as a substitute for the absent and desired Purpose." Tertz concludes that "Russian literature is full of stories in which an inadequate man and a beautiful woman meet and part without having achieved anything." Precisely.

And at bottom, Tertz's own novels are just such 19th-century stories, presenting in symbolic form the enduring plight of the Russian artist and intellectual who is unwilling to accept the purpose imposed upon him by the state and yet rendered incapable of realizing (and frequently of conceiving) his own purposes.

What, after all, is Karlinsky, the major figure in "The Trial Begins," but a man unable to find his destiny? Continually thwarted by an all-powerful, mean, and stupid authority, he finds that his intelligence, generosity, and wit only serve to bring home to him all the more poignantly his impotence—symbolized by his failure to satisfy either the beautiful Marina (a very obvious *ersatz* purpose) or himself; in the end he inadvertently contributes to sending a child to a labor camp.

And what is Lenny Makepeace, the hero of Tertz's latest book, but another superfluous man who, though magically endowed with power, fails to use it properly because he finds himself in an impasse where everything—Soviet society at large, the common people, his own nature—conspires against his discovering that new purpose which alone would permit him to enter into a saving communion with his people and his beautiful, mystical wife?

The style and the language of Tertz's novel belong no less to the 19th century than do his themes. Distinctive as is his "phantasmagoric" and "bizarre" style (and the similar style of Daniel) amid the flat conformity of socialist realism, it is hardly a literary departure on the scale of Joyce, say, or Rimbaud; it falls back, rather, on Gogol and the German E. T. A. Hoffman, whom Tertz invokes at the very conclusion of his essay.

In the end, what is most significant about this school—for all the brilliance of individual works—is precisely the discrepancy between intention and achievement, between the optimistic program of Tertz's manifesto and the unmistakable message of artistic impasse conveyed in his novels and stories. To be sure, the break with the oppressive present is accomplished, but only by way of regression—and that is a very high price to pay for independence.

Or perhaps it would be more accurate to say that Sinyavsky-Tertz and his friends paid the penalty for what turned out to be the impossible task of directly engaging the realities of Soviet politics in the old tradition of "civic literature"—i.e., in works that proclaimed, in however disguised a form, the indivisibility of politics and art and the political "mission" of the intellectual. Unfortunately, the Communist state has even stronger means at its disposal than Czarist Russia had to frustrate such autonomous purposes for a long, long time to come; as a result, writers like Sinyavsky and Daniel run not only the risk of prison and exile, but the more lasting danger of coming to see themselves, in their everlasting frustration, as "superfluous" men out of Gogol and Tertz.

Under the circumstances, it is not surprising that the writers who have best succeeded in freeing themselves are a few "pure" poets. Poetry generally depends to a greater degree than prose does on fresh language and new concepts: hence its irrepressible tendency—a tendency which Erich Auerbach has called the essence of literary progress—to slough off conventional responses and incorporate new realities. "In the Russian language," according to Wladimir Weidlé, "words seek to express not so much factual relations as the speaker's intention; they are oftener symbols than signals"; there is thus a natural correspondence between a poetic idiom and the Russian language itself which helps to explain why Russian verse in the post-revolutionary period has been more highly developed and innovative than Russian prose. There is also something of a Soviet tradition, going back to Mayakowsky, which, with notable exceptions, tends to give poets somewhat more latitude than writers of prose. But whatever the explanation, it is evident that a few Russian poets today enjoy greater freedom—above all, greater inner freedom—than other intellectuals.

Two of these poets are Andrei Voznesensky and Iosif Brodsky. . . . In his politics, Voznesensky has styled himself after Mayakowsky; though not a member of the Communist party, he wishes to purify and rejuvenate Communism, while (unlike his contemporary Yevtushenko) keeping his lyrical poems free of a political slant. In contrast to Voznesensky, Iosif Brodsky is a loner. His poetry is so apolitical as to be almost totally devoid of even topical allusions; however, he was exiled to Siberia . . . for having no profession other than writing poetry.

The idiom and vision of these poets are radically different from anything else to be found in Russian culture today. Their language is, above all, wilfully difficult, not to say hermetic. Voznesensky constantly changes rhythms and meters, and makes generous use of alliteration, sound associations, and assonances in heavily accented broken lines, while almost all of Brodsky's poems might be said to consist of the "broken strings of images" so cherished by Russian Imagists in the 1920's.

To be sure, a great many of the techniques employed—unexpected associations and contexts, concatenations of strange similes, omission of links between metaphors—date back to the 1920's. But if the poets of that generation defined their aim as "making it strange," those of today could more properly be said to be making their poetry "alienated." Here lies the difference between the two generations. The older one devised its innovations to keep abreast of what it took to be the current of history. For this reason the originality of its poetry is in the imagery rather than in substantive conception. The contemporary poets, on the other hand, must break with their times in order to express themselves; therefore the technical aspect of their innovations must be sustained by a genuinely distinctive vision.

In the case of Voznesensky, this quest for uniqueness originally involved an exploration of the self abstracted from society. Perhaps the most famous example of this early style is his "Parabolic Ballad":

> There was a girl who lived in my neighborhood.
> We went to one school, took exams together.
> But I took off with a bang,
>   I went sizzling
> Through the prosperous double-faced doors of Tiflis.
> Forgive me for this idiotic parabola
> Cold shoulders in a pitch-dark vestibule.

More recently Voznesensky has moved on to broader topics. In his long surrealistic poem, "Oza," he weaves together a number of 20th-century leitmotifs into a strange cacophonic symphony. His themes include the reversibility of time, the interchangeability of space, the meaning of technology for our age, the relevance of man to this world.

It is in Brodsky's poetry, however, that we encounter the most radical departure from Soviet norms: a poet in the grip of a metaphysical vision. In his great "Elegy for John Donne," Brodsky boldly describes the relationship between the 17th-century poet and his universe. He starts with an extremely long and almost hypnotic evocation of a primeval sleep descended on the English countryside:

> John Donne has sunk in sleep . . . All things
> beside are sleeping too: walls, bed, and floor—all
> sleep. The table, pictures, carpets, hooks and
> bolts,
>
> .   .   .
>
> This Island sleeps embraced by lonely dreams
> and every garden is now triple-barred.
>
> .   .   .
>
> The Hell-fires sleep, and glorious Paradise
> No one goeth forth from home at this dark hour.
> Even God has gone to sleep. Earth is estranged.

Then he addresses the soul of John Donne:

> And thou didst soar past God, and then drop back,
> for this harsh burden would not let thee rise
> to that high vantage point from which this world
> seems naught but ribboned rivers and tall towers—
> that point from which, to him who downward stares,
> this dread Last Judgment seems no longer dread.
> The radiance of that country does not fade.
> From thence our Lord is but a light that gleams
> through fog, in window of the farthest house.

And the poem ends:

> Sleep, John Donne, sleep. Sleep soundly, do not
> fret thy soul. As for thy coat, 'tis torn; all limp
> it hangs. But see, there from the clouds
> will shine the star that makes thy world endure till
> now.

Even from a reading of the English translation one is aware of being in the presence of a major statement which in its splendor and autonomy soars far above the flat rationalizations and "scientific" ideologies from which it has risen. It is a declaration of inner freedom so absolute that it has no need to assert revolt. Recognizing that Brodsky cannot be seduced, intimidated, hobbled, or driven into safe pastures, the courts have banished him into exile. Russia's greatness went with him. (pp. 55-9)

Theodore Frankel, "Art, Politics, & the Soviet Writer," in Commentary, *Vol. 41, No. 5, May, 1966, pp. 52-9.*

ADDITIONAL BIBLIOGRAPHY

Blake, Patricia, and Hayward, Max, eds. *Half-way to the Moon: New Writing from Russia.* Holt, Rinehart, and Winston, 1964, 276 p.
  Poetry and short fiction by authors including Andrei Voznesensky, Yuri Kazakov, Alexander Solzhenitsyn, and Yevgeny Yevtushenko.

Brown, Deming. "Literature Copes with the Present." In his *Soviet Russian Literature since Stalin,* pp. 285-309. Cambridge: Cambridge University Press, 1978.
  Examines the predominant themes in novels of the Thaw period and departures by these novels from the strictures of socialist realism.

Brown, Edward J. "After Stalin: The First Two Thaws." In his *Russian Literature since the Revolution,* pp. 190-221. Cambridge, Mass.: Harvard University Press, 1982.
  History of the Thaw and discussion of the period's most notable works.

Brumberg, Abraham, ed. *Russia under Khrushchev.* New York: Frederick A. Praeger, 1962, 660 p.
  Reprints thirty-eight essays originally published between 1954 and 1961 in the journal *Problems of Communism.* Authors include Victor Erlich ("Soviet Literary Criticism"), Max Hayward ("The Struggle Goes On"), and George Gibian ("Recent Soviet Literature").

———. *In Quest of Justice: Protest and Dissent in the Soviet Union Today.* New York: Praeger Publishers, 1970, 476 p.
  Reprints criticism, creative writing, speeches, letters, and other documents of contemporary Soviet dissent. Included are twelve documents detailing Alexander Solzhenitsyn's public protest against literary censorship during the late 1960s and the resulting campaign of governmental harrassment directed against him.

Ehrenburg, Ilya. *The Thaw.* Translated by Manya Harari. Chicago: H. Regnery, 1955, 230 p.

Field, Andrew. "The Not So Dissonant Voices in Soviet Literature." *The New Leader* XLV, No. 26 (24 December 1962): 15-16.
  Decries the tendency of American critics to overpraise politically dissident works of Soviet literature to the neglect of apolitical works possessing greater literary merit.

Friedberg, Maurice. *A Decade of Euphoria: Western Literature in Post-Stalin Russia, 1954-64.* Bloomington: Indiana University Press, 1977, 371 p.
  Details "the publication and official reception of the entire corpus of Western writing in post-Stalin Russia, particularly during the stormy decade 1954-64."

Gibian, George. *Interval of Freedom: Soviet Literature during the Thaw.* Minneapolis: University of Minnesota Press, 1960, 180 p.
  Examines Soviet literature of the mid-1950s, focusing on what Gibian considers the period's most important and frequently addressed themes: science, love, and villainy. Gibian also devotes a chapter to the literary and political significance of Boris Pasternak's *Doctor Zhivago.*

———. "Soviet Literature during the Thaw." In *Literature and Revolution in Soviet Russia, 1917-62,* edited by Max Hayward and Leopold Labedz, pp. 125-49. London: Oxford University Press, 1963.
  Categorizes works written during the Thaw on the basis of themes and ideological acceptability to the Soviet government. Gibian stresses the essential homogeneity of Thaw literature, noting that it "seems monotonous not merely when measured against the great Western achievement of the twentieth century—or the Russian authors of the nineteenth: it also fails in comparison with Isaac Babel, Yuri Olesha, and other authors of earlier Soviet decades."

Gladilin, Anatoly. *The Making and Unmaking of a Soviet Writer.* Translated by David Lapeza. Ann Arbor: Ardis, 1979, 166 p.
  Personal account of the Russian literary milieu of the 1950s and 1960s.

Hayward, Max. "Soviet Literature in the Doldrums." *Problems of Communism* VIII, No. 4 (July-August 1959): 11-16.
  Assesses the state of Soviet letters and reports on literary-political developments at the Third Congress of Soviet Writers. Maintaining that "freedom to express certain ideas is less important in art than freedom in the choice of form," Hayward argues that official restrictions on stylistic experimentation constitute the primary cause of stagnation in Soviet literature.

Hayward, Max, and Crowley, Edward L., eds. *Soviet Literature in the Sixties.* London: Methuen, 1964, 221 p.
  Contains essays by nine critics, including A. Gaev ("The Decade since Stalin"), Burton Rubin ("Highlights of the 1962-1963 Thaw"), and Rufus Mathewson ("The Novel in Russia and the West").

Hosking, Geoffrey. *Beyond Socialist Realism: Soviet Fiction since "Ivan Denisovich."* New York: Holmes & Meier, 1980, 260 p.
  Analyzes the works of eleven authors, including Vladimir Tendryakov, Alexander Solzhenitsyn, and Vladimir Voinovich. Not-

ing that "in the case of Soviet literature . . . a purely aesthetic approach is especially unfruitful," Hosking examines these works "for the light they throw on the author, his spiritual and intellectual world, and on the society in which he lives."

Johnson, Priscilla, and Labedz, Leopold, eds. *Khrushchev and the Arts: The Politics of Soviet Culture, 1962-1964*. Cambridge, Mass.: MIT Press, 1965, 300 p.

Essay by Johnson detailing Soviet literary politics between 1962 and 1964, supplemented by excerpts from documents of the period.

Lakshin, Vladimir. *Solzhenitsyn, Tvardovsky and "Novy Mir."* Translated and edited by Michael Glenny. Cambridge, Mass.: MIT Press, 1980, 183 p.

Refutes criticism of *Novy mir* and the portrayal of Alexander Tvardovsky in Alexander Solzhenitsyn's *The Oak and the Calf* (below), calling Solzhenitsyn's memoir a "display of naive, ridiculous self-aggrandizement." Also included in this volume are essays by Mary Chaffin ("Alexander Tvardovsky: A Biographical Study") and Linda Aldwinckle ("The Politics of *Novy Mir* under Tvardovsky").

Marsh, Rosalind. *Soviet Fiction since Stalin: Science, Politics, and Literature*. London: Croom Helm, 1986, 338 p.

Examines political and social aspects of scientific research as reflected in Soviet literature since Stalin's death.

Mathewson, Rufus W., Jr. *The Positive Hero in Russian Literature*. Stanford: Stanford University Press, 1975, 369 p.

Analyzes works by Boris Pasternak, Alexander Solzhenitsyn, and Andrei Sinyavsky in an attempt to demonstrate the essential continuity of Russian prose of the last two centuries.

McLean, Hugh, and Vickery, Walter N., eds. *The Year of Protest, 1956: An Anthology of Soviet Literary Materials*. Westport, Conn.: Greenwood Press, 1961, 269 p.

Selected drama, fiction, poetry, and criticism originally published in *Novy mir* and *Literary Moscow*, including works by Konstantin Paustovsky, Alexander Yashin, Nikolay Zhdanov, and Yuri Nagibin.

Medvedev, Zhores. *Ten Years after Ivan Denisovich*. Translated by Hilary Sternberg. New York: Alfred A. Knopf, 1973, 202 p.

Attempts to "give a picture of some of the social phenomena" of the decade between 1962 and 1972 by tracing the interrelated histories of Alexander Solzhenitsyn and *Novy mir*.

The New Writing in Russia. Translated by Thomas P. Whitney. Ann Arbor: The University of Michigan Press, 1964, 412 p.

Short fiction by Vasily Aksenov, Yuri Kazakov, Victor Rozov, Yuri Nagibin, and Vladimir Tendryakov.

Pasternak, Boris. *Doctor Zhivago*. Translated by Max Hayward and Manya Harari. New York: Pantheon, 1958, 558 p.

Rogers, Thomas F. *"Superfluous Men" and the Post-Stalin "Thaw": The Alienated Hero in Soviet Prose during the Decade 1953-1963*. The Hague: Mouton, 1972, 410 p.

Analyzes the theme of alienation in Soviet fiction and examines "the 'thaw' hero as both the outgrowth of a prior literary tradition and a distinctly new character creation."

Simmons, Ernest J. "Recent Trends in Soviet Literature." *Modern Age* 7, No. 4 (Fall 1963): 393-406.

Traces the recurrent pattern of liberalization and reaction in Soviet literary politics between 1953 and 1963 and examines works by the most prominent dissident authors of that period.

Solzhenitsyn, Alexander. *One Day in the Life of Ivan Denisovich*. Translated by Ralph Parker. New York: Dutton, 1963, 160 p.

————. *The Oak and the Calf*. New York: Harper & Row, 1975, 568 p.

Literary memoir. The chapter "Out of Hiding" recounts Solzhenitsyn's impressions of the editorial staff of *Novy mir* and the events leading to that journal's publication of *One Day in the Life of Ivan Denisovich*.

Spechler, Dina R. *Permitted Dissent in the USSR: "Novy mir" and the Soviet Regime*. New York: Praeger, 1982, 293 p.

Analyzes the literature of dissent published in *Novy mir* between 1953 and 1970 and attempts to assess the journal's influence on Soviet political, social, and literary policy.

Swayze, Harold. *Political Control of Literature in the USSR, 1946-1959*. Cambridge, Mass.: Harvard University Press, 1962, 301 p.

Detailed account of Soviet literary policy and politics.

Tertz, Abram. *The Trial Begins*. Translated by Max Hayward. New York: Pantheon, 1960, 128 p.

Sherlock Holmes Centenary

INTRODUCTION

One hundred years ago, in November 1887, Sherlock Holmes appeared before the public for the first time in the novel *A Study in Scarlet*. Published, after numerous rejections, in the somewhat sensational *Beeton's Christmas Annual, Scarlet,* Holmes, and the author, Arthur Conan Doyle, received little attention at the time. Such an inauspicious beginning is ironic considering the fact that in the ensuing century, Sherlock Holmes has become one of the most popular fictional characters in world literature. The Holmes adventures have so captured the imagination of readers that, over the years, thousands of letters have been written to Holmes by readers who believed that he truly existed. In fact, hundreds of critical articles and books have been based, with tongue firmly in cheek, on the premise that Holmes was a real individual. The authors of this type of commentary, called Sherlockian or Holmesian criticism, all have one thing in common: they approach their investigation of Holmes's life with absolute seriousness. According to Dorothy L. Sayers, "The rule of the game is that it must be played as solemnly as a county cricket match at Lord's. The slightest touch of extravagance or burlesque ruins the atmosphere."

But Holmes is of great interest to many besides the Sherlockians. Among the most popular stories ever written, the Holmes adventures have sold a tremendous number of copies and were the basis for one of the most popular series of movies ever made, starring Basil Rathbone as Holmes and Nigel Bruce as Watson. The stories are constantly reissued in various formats and new film versions appear almost as frequently. Some commentators have claimed that Holmes has become an intrinsic part of the Western cultural background, much like Don Quixote and Hamlet. Many critics have attempted to discern the reason for the depth of this popularity, and several of their conclusions are provided in the following entry. In addition, the Holmes stories are often examined for the light they shed on Victorian mores, since popular culture is often considered a useful indicator of the temper of an age. Several essays in the following entry discuss this aspect of Holmes scholarship. The entry also provides a brief biography of Arthur Conan Doyle, a history of the composition of the Holmes stories, a biography and character analyses of Holmes, and a discussion of Holmes's impact on the development of the detective story.

DOYLE'S LIFE AND THE COMPOSITION OF THE HOLMES STORIES

WILLIAM S. BARING-GOULD

[*An American critic and editor, Baring-Gould was a member of the Baker Street Irregulars and the Mystery Writers of America. He wrote* Sherlock Holmes of Baker Street: A Life of the World's First Consulting Detective (*see Additional Bibliography*)*, the first such full-length Sherlockian study, and a similiar "biography" of Nero Wolfe, the detective created by Rex Stout. Baring-Gould also edited* The Annotated Sherlock Holmes, *a profusely illus-*

London Regional Transport

trated and extensively annotated edition of the Holmes adventures. In the following excerpt from an introductory essay in that work, Baring-Gould discusses Doyle's early life to the time of writing the first Sherlock Holmes story.]

Arthur Conan Doyle, the author of the Sherlock Holmes stories (and of many other writings, fictional and nonfictional, which he held to be far more important works) was born at Picardy Place, Edinburgh, on May 22, 1859. He was the son of Charles Doyle, a civil servant and spare-time painter of Irish descent, and his wife Mary Foley Doyle, also of Irish parentage.

On both sides, the line was distinguished: Mrs. Doyle could trace her ancestry back to the ancient house of Percy-Louvain, three times allied by marriage with princesses of the Plantagenet line.

As for the Doyles, they came originally from Pont d'Oilly near Rouen, in Normandy. They took part in the conquest of Ireland, and in 1333, Alexander d'Oilly was granted lands in County Wexford by King Edward III. A Roman Catholic family, the Doyles of the 17th and 18th centuries were gradually evicted from their lands. At the beginning of the last century, John,

Sir Arthur's grandfather, left Ireland to settle in London. There, under the initials "HB," he soon became the leading political caricaturist of his day. He was the first but by no means the last of his family to enter the *Dictionary of National Biography*. Three of his sons won the same recognition: James, as a historian and genealogist; Henry, as an artist and Director of the National Gallery, Dublin; Richard, also an artist and a friend of men like Dickens and Thackeray. . . . (pp. 4-5)

Conan Doyle's schooling began at the age of seven and continued, when he was nine, at Hodder, the preparatory school of Stonyhurst College, which he attended until he was sixteen. A year of schooling at Feldkirch in Austria was followed by his return to Edinburgh in the summer of 1876. Edinburgh University had a well-deserved reputation for the fine medical training available there, and it was soon decided that young Arthur should become a doctor. He entered the University in October, 1876, and commenced what he later called a "long weary grind at botany, chemistry, anatomy, physiology, and a whole list of compulsory subjects, many of which have a very indirect bearing upon the art of curing."

Trying to help his family in vacation times (Charles Doyle fathered six other children), he worked as a medical assistant to doctors in Sheffield; Ruyton-of-the-eleven-towns, a tiny place in Shropshire; and Aston, Birmingham, where he was assistant to Dr. Reginald Ratcliffe Hoare at Clifton House, Aston Road North, a site now marked by a plaque (as is the birthplace of Sir Arthur Conan Doyle in Edinburgh).

It was here that Conan Doyle's first short story, "The Mystery of Sassassa Valley," was written and sold for £3 3s. ($15.75) to *Chamber's Journal,* where it was published in the issue of October, 1879.

In February of 1880, Conan Doyle accepted a job as surgeon on a whaling ship, the *Hope,* and spent seven months in the Arctic. In the latter part of 1880 he returned to Aston where he remained until early in 1881 as assistant to Dr. Hoare, after which he resumed his studies for the degree of Bachelor of Medicine, which he took in August, 1881, as he said, "with fair but not notable distinction."

A voyage to Africa as medical officer on the ship *Mayumba* followed; then he went into partnership, at Plymouth, with an explosive friend he had made at Edinburgh, Dr. George Budd. Through no fault of Conan Doyle's, there was friction between him and Budd, and he decided to leave. He arrived at Southsea, a suburb of Portsmouth, on an afternoon in July, 1882, picked up a house called Bush Villa (later renamed Doyle House by the owners; destroyed in the Blitz in 1941) at a rental of £40 ($200) a year plus another £10 ($50) in taxes, hung up his carefully burnished brass plate, and embarked on a practice that was neither very exacting nor very rewarding: he made £154 ($770) the first year, £250 ($1,250) the second, never more than £300 ($1,500).

It may be asked here why a man who was born a patrician should have been so poor and without influence at the very outset of his professional career; the scion of a family which, though far from wealthy, could yet afford to entertain the Prime Minister, Sir Walter Scott, Cardinal Newman, and other celebrated men at their dinner table. The answer lies in the fact that Conan Doyle, who had left the Catholic faith, considered it dishonorable to use his letters of introduction to the Duke of Norfolk, the Bishop of Southsea, and other Catholic notables.

Soon young Arthur Conan Doyle was engaged to Louise Hawkins, the daughter of one of his patients; she became his first wife on August 6, 1885, a month after Conan Doyle had taken his doctorate.

Meantime, between 1878 and 1883, Conan Doyle had written and sold a few short stories and had completed two novels, *The Narrative of John Smith,* lost in the post and never recovered, and *The Firm of Girdlestone,* which was then still making a dreary round of the publishers.

Now, in the March of 1886, with time on his hands and creditors at his door, young Dr. Conan Doyle—he was then only twenty-six—turned his mind to the writing of a detective story. (pp. 5-6)

Conan Doyle set out to create a private detective who would *not* fail in such an assignment because he would have developed "habits of observation and inference into a system," and he thought at once of one of his former teachers at the University, Joseph Bell, M.D., F.R.C.S., consulting surgeon to the Royal Infirmary and Royal Hospital for Sick Children, member of University Court, Edinburgh University; born in Edinburgh in 1837, he died in 1911.

A "thin, wiry, dark" man, "with a high-nosed acute face, penetrating gray eyes, angular shoulders" and a "high discordant" voice, Dr. Bell "would sit in his receiving room with a face like a Red Indian, and diagnose the people as they came in, before they even opened their mouths. He would tell them their symptoms, and even give them details of their past life; and hardly ever would he make a mistake."

Of the many anecdotes told of Dr. Joseph Bell, here is one of the lesser-known (from the *Lancet,* issue of August 1, 1956):

> A woman with a small child was shown in. Joe Bell said good morning to her and she said good morning in reply. "What sort of a crossing di' ye have fra' Burntisland?" "It was guid." "And had ye a guid walk up Inverleith Row?" "Yes." "And what did ye do with th' other wain?" "I left him with my sister in Leith." "And would ye still be working at the linoleum factory?" "Yes, I am." "You see, gentlemen, when she said good morning to me I noted her Fife accent, and, as you know, the nearest town in Fife is Burntisland. You noticed the red clay on the edges of the soles of her shoes, and the only such clay within twenty miles of Edinburgh is in the Botanical Gardens. Inverleigh Row borders the gardens and is her nearest way here from Leith. You observed that the coat she carried over her arm is too big for the child who is with her, and therefore she set out from home with two children. Finally she has a dermatitis on the fingers of the right hand which is peculiar to workers in the linoleum factory at Burntisland."

Here is how Conan Doyle himself wrote about this period in his life, in his autobiography, *Memories and Adventures:*

> I felt now that I was capable of something fresher and crisper and more workmanlike [than many of the detective stories that had been written up to that time]. Gaboriau had rather attracted me by the neat dovetailing of his plots, and Poe's masterful detective, M. Dupin, had from

boyhood been one of my heroes. But could I bring an addition of my own? I thought of my old teacher Joe Bell, of his eagle face, of his curious ways, of his eerie trick of spotting details. If he were a detective he would surely reduce this fascinating business to something nearer an exact science. I would try if I could get this effect. It was surely possible in real life, so why should I not make it plausible in fiction? It is all very well to say that a man is clever, but the reader wants to see examples of it—such examples as Bell gave us every day in the wards.

Again, in a letter to Dr. Bell dated May 4, 1892, Conan Doyle wrote:

> It is most certainly to you that I owe Sherlock Holmes, and though in the stories I have the advantage of being able to place [the detective] in all sorts of dramatic positions, I do not think that his analytical work is in the least an exaggeration of some effects which I have seen you produce in the out-patient ward. Round the centre of deduction and inference and observation which I have heard you inculcate I have tried to build up a man who pushed the thing as far as it would go—further occasionally—and I am so glad that the result has satisfied you, who are the critic with the most right to be severe.

Dr. Conan Doyle dedicated *The Adventures of Sherlock Holmes* to Dr. Joseph Bell. . . . (pp. 7-8)

This, then, was the *inception*.

But here let us try to be quite clear:

Bell himself states that Conan Doyle has made a great deal out of very little and proceeds to give the credit for Sherlock Holmes' genius to Conan Doyle's own gifts and training.

"You are yourself Sherlock Holmes and well you know it," he wrote to Conan Doyle.

Bell, undoubtedly, was the model for the consulting detective, Sherlock Holmes. But Bell was *not* Sherlock Holmes as we best know him. Save for his remarkable gift of deduction, Bell was never once able, in real-life crime cases, to show that he possessed any Holmesian powers; Conan Doyle, on the other hand, as we shall see, played a part in the investigation of many real-life crimes; certainly he was consulted by Sir Bernard Spilsbury, H. Ashton-Wolfe, and other criminologists and police officials.

Let us compare the character of Holmes with the character of his creator:

Holmes, like Conan Doyle, was partial toward old dressing gowns, clay pipes, keeping documents and lacking the time to arrange them, a habit of working with a magnifying glass on his desk and a pistol in the drawer. "Holmes' ancestors, like Conan Doyle's, were country squires," Professor Pierre Weil Nordon of the University of Paris has written . . . "the author's grandmother, Marianna Conan, was of French descent and Holmes' own grandmother was the sister of the French artist, Horace Vernet; Holmes' bank was the same as Conan Doyle's; he was offered a knighthood in the same year and in the same month as Conan Doyle was knighted; both evince a special

interest in Winwood Reade, or in the origin of the Cornish dialect; both loathe suffragettes; both wish with the same eagerness the establishment of a close alliance between all English-speaking countries. Finally . . . Conan Doyle, like Holmes, was treated by criminologists as one of their colleagues, and was honoured by them when they gave his name to police laboratories."

The story of Conan Doyle's ingenuity in transmitting news of the first World War to British prisoners in Germany is well known: this he did by sending books in which he had put needle-pricks under various printed letters so as to spell out the desired messages, but beginning always with the third chapter in the belief that the German censors would examine the earlier chapters more carefully.

We have said that Conan Doyle interested himself in many real-life crimes: he investigated the Mrs. Rome case (result unknown); he looked into the missing Dane case (solved); he went to the scene of the killing in the Thorne murder. A statement from a journalist, now in the Conan Doyle archives, attests that it was Conan Doyle who put the police on the trail of that infamous murderer Smith in the celebrated "Brides-in-the-Bath" case.

As examples of Conan Doyle's interest in fair play and justice, however, the best-known cases are those of George Edalji and Oscar Slater. [The critic explains in a footnote: George Edalji was sentenced in 1903 to seven years' penal servitude for horse-maiming. In 1906 Conan Doyle heard of this rather obscure case and, after exhaustive investigations lasting nearly a year, began a series of newspaper articles analyzing the incredibly weak evidence of the prosecution and making public "this blot upon the record of English justice." In consequence of Conan Doyle's endeavor, Edalji was released but denied compensation. In 1909, Oscar Slater was sentenced to death in Edinburgh for a brutal murder in Glasgow. This sentence was commuted to penal servitude for life. An unceasing battle was fought to prove Slater's innocence. Approached by Slater's lawyer, Conan Doyle took up this case of miscarriage of justice. It was not, however, until 1927 that Conan Doyle finally secured the release of Slater.]

That Conan Doyle had a gift of his own for making quick and accurate deductions has been demonstrated in "Some Recollections of Sir Arthur Conan Doyle." Here Dr. Harold Gordon tells how Conan Doyle once

> stopped at the crib of a young baby, about two and a half years old. The child's mother was watching at the lad's side. Almost without hesitation, Sir Arthur turned to the mother and said, kindly but with authority, "You must stop painting the child's crib." Sure enough, the child was in with lead poisoning. We were aware of the diagnosis, but asked how he had arrived at the right conclusion so quickly. He smiled as he answered, "The child looked pale but well-fed. He was listless and his wrist dropped as he tried to hold a toy. The mother was neatly dressed, but she had specks of white paint on the fingers of her right hand. Children like to sharpen their teeth on the rails of a crib—so lead poisoning seemed a likely diagnosis."

(pp. 8-9)

William S. Baring-Gould, "'I Hear of Sherlock Everywhere Since You Became His Chronicler'," in

The Annotated Sherlock Holmes, Vol. I *by Sir Arthur Conan Doyle, edited by William S. Baring-Gould, Clarkson N. Potter, Inc./Publisher, 1967, pp. 3-18.*

MICHAEL HARDWICK

[*Hardwick is an English critic, novelist, and dramatist. He and his wife, Mollie Hardwick, wrote* The Sherlock Holmes Companion *(1962) and* The Man Who Was Sherlock Holmes *(1964), considered major works of Sherlockian scholarship. Hardwick maintains that these earlier works have been superseded by his* Complete Guide to Sherlock Holmes. *In the following excerpt from that work, Hardwick provides a detailed chronological examination of Doyle's life during the years he was writing the Holmes stories.*]

In March, 1886, Dr. Arthur Conan Doyle began to write a detective story. He had no notion of becoming a professional writer, but he was full of ideas and replete with energy. All through his Edinburgh childhood his high-minded mother had told him tales of the romance and adventure of past ages. He wanted to write about those times, but he was conscious that he needed to learn the craft and gain the confidence which being published would bring.

He had plenty of leisure to work at it. After four years in medical practice at Southsea, a suburb of Portsmouth, he had few patients to attend. He was better known locally as a sportsman, debater, lecturer, campaigning public speaker, writer to editors, and convivial companion. (p. 13)

Plenty of stories, from the 18th century on, had included elements of crime and its investigation, and there had been books by former policemen and detectives about their real-life cases. The detective as an intelligent, idiosyncratic central character had emerged in the 1840s in Edgar Allan Poe's Dupin stories, followed in France by Émile Gaboriau, with his professional detective Lecoq and the amateur Père Tabaret. The first full-length English detective novel was Wilkie Collins's *The Moonstone,* 1868, with its sagacious Sergeant Cuff.

Doyle had read all these. Dupin had been one of his boyhood heroes, an investigator with analytical acumen and instinctive flair, though Poe's writing style was didactic and often heavy going. Lecoq was a dogged sleuth who owed many of his results to hunches, on which he acted with cunning and often in disguise. Gaboriau's stories were neatly plotted and briskly told, with plenty of dialogue. Doyle was confident that he could do something along these lines. He had ingenuity and natural zest, and ambition was urging him on: he was approaching his thirties, but, for all his varied talents, he had made no significant mark at anything.

A Study in Scarlet—he had thought of titling it *A Tangled Skein*—was written quickly in March and April, 1886. Too quickly, in fact; the "little novel," as his wife termed it, was only some 50,000 words. James Payn found some worthwhile things in it, but rejected it as neither long enough for a serial nor short enough for a single story.

The rebuff hurt, and there was more mortification to come. Several other publishers turned it down. After six months' toing and fro-ing with it, Doyle was relieved to get an offer at last, even though it was from a firm specializing in "cheap and often sensational literature." (p. 15)

He had asked for royalties, but had been refused. It was a case of going on hoping for a better sale elsewhere, or of accepting. Other "large thoughts" were pressing for his attention: an historical novel "seemed to me the one way of combining a certain amount of literary dignity with those scenes of action and adventure which were natural to my young and ardent mind." He accepted Ward, Lock, & Co.'s offer, forgot Sherlock Holmes for the time being, and concentrated on a story of the English Civil War, *Micah Clarke.*

Nevertheless, when *Beeton's Christmas Annual* for 1887 came out in late November that year, his hope for his detective story's success returned. *Beeton's,* founded in 1860 by Sam Beeton and his wife Isabella, of *Household Management* celebrity, was well enough respected for a shilling popular annual. The title *A Study in Scarlet* dominated its front cover; the few other contents were altogether subservient. Those were days when reviewers of fiction kept an eye on magazines, as well as books. "A. Conan Doyle," as he styled himself, believed that his "booklet" could catch on.

So far as the reading public was concerned, it didn't. A handful of reviewers commented, briefly but kindly, on the story's ingenuity. It was from behind the scenes that positive interest was to emerge.

Ward, Lock had been recommended to buy it by their chief editor, Prof W. J. Bettany, whose wife had read it for him and liked it. His report termed Doyle "a born novelist." He urged the editorial board to consider republishing it as a book on its own. Having to pay nothing further for that right, the firm's only risk was the production cost. They went ahead. *A Study in Scarlet* first came out as a book in the summer of 1888. (p. 16)

Micah Clarke, the novel about Puritan England which had resulted from Arthur Conan Doyle's "large thoughts" and a corresponding capacity for research, was finished by the end of February, 1888, between the appearance of *A Study in Scarlet* in *Beeton's* and as a book. It, too, went first to James Payn, of the *Cornhill.* He rejected it, reproving him, "How can you, can you, waste your time and your wits writing historical novels?" So began another depressing round of publisher after publisher. After nine months, when hope for it was almost gone, Andrew Lang accepted it for Longman's.

It appeared in February 1889 and got excellent reviews. Doyle believed increasingly that his future and fame would depend on historical novels. He pressed on fervently with the reading and note-making for a novel set even further back in time, which would glorify the bowmen, the knights and the chivalry of 14th century England.

It might have spelt the end of Sherlock Holmes and John H. Watson, MD. The legend, not yet established, might never have arisen, but for a recommendation by Payn to an American, Joseph Marshall Stoddart, recently appointed managing editor of *Lippincott's Monthly Magazine,* which was published simultaneously in Philadelphia and London. Visiting London in the summer of 1889 in search of fresh material, Stoddart gave a dinner party on 30 August. His guests were Oscar Wilde, at that time nearing the end of his term as editor of *Woman's World* magazine and still searching for his way to literary fame. T. P. Gill, MP, another witty Irishman, and Arthur Conan Doyle.

A jolly time was had by all. Oscar, as always, dominated the table-talk, impressing Doyle indelibly; but it was their host who did the most significant talking. He offered Wilde a commission to write the story which, as it turned out, would make him a cynosure of literary and society London, *The Picture of*

Dorian Gray. Stoddart's offer to Conan Doyle was not for anything in the historical line, but for another Sherlock Holmes story.

He couldn't afford to refuse. Medicine still brought little income. *Micah Clarke*'s sales were satisfactory, but not sensational. It would be months before the new historical novel would be finished, and an incalculable time before anyone might buy it. (pp. 36-7)

Wrenching his concentration forward five centuries, he sent Holmes and Watson into action again, in the case of *The Sign of the Four,* as it was titled before it was abbreviated to the less effective *The Sign of Four.*

Once more he wrote quickly and impatiently, not troubling to check certain details against ones in *A Study in Scarlet.* That had been set in 1881. *The Sign of the Four* belongs in 1888. In the seven years' interval, Watson's war wound has travelled from his shoulder to his leg—unless, that is, there had been a second wound, not mentioned in his earlier narrative.

The Sign of the Four was not meant to be a sequel. It was a one-off, written to oblige a well-wishing editor and to bring in some extra cash. If Doyle had had any higher hopes than that for it they would have been dashed, anyway. It appeared in *Lippincott's* in February, 1890, and attracted no special attention.

He managed to sell it to a few English provincial newspapers as a serial. Later in the year a London book publisher, Spencer Blackett, republished it. The book drew a few notices: "Dr Doyle's admirers will read the little volume through eagerly enough, but they will hardly care to pick it up again," one said.

A certain following does seem to be acknowledged, however, by the phrase "Dr. Doyle's admirers." He got one of the first literary agents, A. P. Watt, to represent him, and through him the story was serialized in George Newnes's weekly *Tit-Bits.* Holmes and Watson came to the notice of a new and different readership.

Doyle was not much interested. With the triumphant cry, "That's done it!" he had finished the historical novel which had become his obsession and which he was convinced was going to make him famous at last. This time there was no rejection by the *Cornhill.* Payn declared *The White Company* to be the best thing of its kind since Scott's *Ivanhoe,* and bought it for serialization. (p. 37)

The Sign of the Four opens by introducing another facet of Sherlock Holmes—as drug-taker. He explains to the disapproving Watson that he does it purely because he is bored from mental inactivity, an acceptable enough reason in the late Victorian context, before the regulation of narcotics and long before their misuse. Doyle gave Holmes the trait for no other reasons than to add to his idiosyncracies and point up his habit of slipping into introspection when he had no pressing work:

> My mind rebels at stagnation. Give me problems, give me work, give me the most abstruse cryptogram, or the most intricate analysis, and I am in my own proper atmosphere. I can dispense then with artificial stimulants. That is why I have chosen my own particular profession, or rather created it. . . .

We are told nothing of what has been happening to him or to Watson since *A Study in Scarlet.* It is a fair assumption, from

hints in later stories, that Watson had married and moved away, but had lost his wife within a year or little more and moved back to 221B. Holmes's professional life has clearly been in the doldrums of late, which makes all the more welcome to him and Watson the unexpected visit of a Miss Mary Morstan, sweet twenty-seven, blonde, dainty and refined, with an intriguing mystery to relate. (pp. 37-8)

[The elements of the mystery] include the Indian Mutiny, the Agra Treasure, a criminal alliance, blackmail and betrayal; and, credit where it is due, a testimonial to the capacity for staunch comradeship of a murderous cannibal named Tonga.

There is another outcome, concerning Watson and Miss Morstan. In what might so easily have been left as the last exchange between him and Holmes ever chronicled, Watson remarks, "The division seems rather unfair. You have done all the work in this business. I get a wife out of it, Jones gets the credit, pray what remains for you?"

"For me," says Sherlock Holmes, "there still remains the cocaine-bottle," and he stretches his long white hand up for it. (p. 39)

The White Company, [Doyle's] deeply studied and lovingly written story of the knights and bowmen of medieval England, was established in the *Cornhill Magazine* and attracting favourable comment. It remains the best known of Doyle's historical romances, although his favourite was *Sir Nigel,* its "sequel" set in earlier time. (p. 47)

A new monthly magazine had appeared on England's bookstalls. It cost sixpence, though it was claimed to be worth a

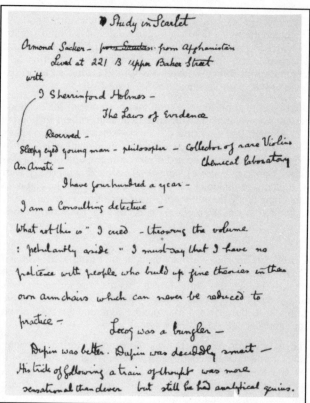

A page of Conan Doyle's notes for A Study in Scarlet. *Holmes is referred to by Conan Doyle's original name for the detective—Sherrinford.*

shilling. More than any other British magazine, it followed the style of such smart and lively American ones as *Harper's, Scribner's* and the *Century*. It was called the *Strand Magazine,* [owned by George Newnes]. (p. 48)

The first issue, of 112 pages with an illustration at every page opening and a free coloured print of a Royal Academy picture, duly appeared early in January, 1891. It sold 300,000 copies, a circulation figure without precedent on either side of the Atlantic.

There was no established pool of British writers of popular short stories. Most of the fiction carried in the first few numbers was in translation from French, Russian and other foreign originals. Just a few stories were by indigenous authors, who included Grant Allen, W. Clark Russell, Stanley Weyman, and E. W. Hornung. A story in the April issue, very short but with an ingenious plot involving the new phonograph machine, had the title "The Voice of Science." Its writer's name was not given. This was Conan Doyle's first contribution to the magazine which, more than any other, would be identified with his work for the rest of his life.

In recent years he had been thinking in terms of book-length themes. His passion for historical detail had meant much research, after which the story had to be written speculatively, then hawked around for sale. It was a long, slow process, which so far had failed to pay off in any big way. The *Strand,* whose policy was for each issue to be complete in itself, with no continuing serials, offered an excellent opening and ready payment to a fast writer whose notebooks were full of ideas for one-off tales. However, Doyle's mind had been tuned to broader conceptions, and he came up with an innovative compromise:

> It had struck me that a single character running through a series, if it only engaged the attention of the reader, would bind that reader to that particular magazine. On the other hand, it had long seemed to me that the ordinary serial might be an impediment rather than a help to a magazine, since, sooner or later, one missed one number and afterwards it had lost all interest. Clearly the ideal compromise was a character which carried through, and yet instalments which were each complete in themselves, so that the purchaser was always sure that he could read the whole contents of the magazine. I believe that I was the first to realize this and the *Strand Magazine* the first to put it into practice.

> Looking round for my central character I felt that Sherlock Holmes, whom I had already handled in two little books, would easily lend himself to a succession of short stories. These I began in the long hours of waiting in my consulting-room.

On Friday, 3 April, 1891, he wrote in his diary, "Sent A Scandal in Bohemia to A. P. Watt." A week later he recorded, "Finished A Case of Identity." The agent sent the two foolscap manuscripts together to [the *Strand's* literary editor] Greenhough Smith, who, forty years on, recalled his excitement on reading them: "I at once realized that here was the greatest short story writer since Edgar Allan Poe. I remember rushing into Mr. Newnes's room and thrusting the stories before his eyes."

Greenhough Smith asked for more, and A. P. Watt asked in return for £200 for a series of six. Each got what he wanted. Four more stories were delivered before May was out. The first of them, "A Scandal in Bohemia," appeared in the *Strand* in July, 1891, and the magazine's already increasing circulation figures began to rise perceptibly.

Doyle recognized that he had come to another of his life's crossroads. He did not arrive there in the best of shape. He had almost died that May from a severe attack of the influenza which was claiming many lives. Lying in bed in its aftermath, "as weak as a child, and as emotional," he nevertheless found his mind clear enough to assess his future:

> I saw how foolish I was to waste my literary earnings in keeping up an oculist's room in Wimpole Street, and I determined with a wild rush of joy to cut the painter and to trust for ever to my power of writing. I remember in my delight taking the handkerchief which lay upon the coverlet in my enfeebled hand and tossing it up to the ceiling in my exultation. I should at long last be my own master. No longer would I have to conform to professional dress to please anyone else. I would be free to live how I liked and where I liked. It was one of the great moments of exultation of my life.

He could not have been more mistaken in that notion of ceasing to have to do anyone else's bidding. Arthur Conan Doyle's career, more than almost any other writer's, was to be an example of a progenitor inescapably identified with his resented creation.

For the moment, though, Sherlock Holmes had his uses. The nonproductive medical practice was abandoned. . . . In [a] large, pleasant, rented house he settled immediately into a daily routine of work, punctuated with various sporting activities, during which his subconscious mind digested the rich diet of facts and thoughts that he had fed it.

His latest project—"some literary work worthy of the name"—was a novel about the Huguenots in 17th century Europe and America, *The Refugees*. He was not to be left in peace for long, though. The appearance of "The Boscombe Valley Mystery" in the October *Strand* meant that there were only two Sherlock Holmes stories left in stock. Greenhough Smith was asking for more. Conan Doyle replied that he would write a further six for £300. The acceptance came by return of post, with a request for speedy delivery. He had to put *The Refugees* aside and turn his imagination to Baker Street again. In the Christmas number, in which appeared the last of the first six adventures, "The Man with the Twisted Lip," A. Conan Doyle was the subject of one of the popular "Portraits of Celebrities at different times of their Lives." The piece incorporated timely tidings of comfort and joy: "It gives us great pleasure to announce that the extraordinary adventures of Sherlock Holmes, which have proved so popular with our readers during the past six months, will be continued in the new year."

The second six stories were written at high speed, all but one finished by mid-November. Reporting this in a letter to his mother, Doyle added, "I think of slaying Holmes in the last and winding him up for good and all. He takes my mind from better things." Her response spoke for hundreds of thousands of people in Britain and other parts of the world: "You won't! You can't. You *mustn't*." He picked up his pen once more to write the last of the dozen, ''The Copper Beeches.'' It was completed with Holmes alive and in excellent health. (pp. 49-51)

Newnes republished *The Adventures of Sherlock Holmes,* as they were titled generically, in volume form in 1892. Harper & Brothers, New York, also published them as a book that year. Both these editions used Paget illustrations. The stories had already gained popularity in America through newspaper syndication, and it was this series which implanted Sherlock Holmes firmly into the world's consciousness. (p. 51)

Sherlock Holmes's place was taken over in the July 1892 *Strand* by Dick Donovan, author and first-person narrator of a short-lived series with the generic title *A Romance from a Detective's Casebook.* Readers who found these exotic tales comparatively poor stuff could take comfort from an editorial note appended to the first one. It assured them that the interval was temporary only; Holmes would be back. . . .

Greenhough Smith, now the editor, had begun chasing him for more stories as early as February that year. He wrote to his mother, ''Under pressure I offered to do a dozen for a thousand pounds, but I sincerely hope that they won't accept it now.'' They did, of course. The best he could do to be free of Holmes for a time was to tell them they would have to wait. (p. 72)

The year 1892 saw Doyle expanding his range as a writer. He and J. M. Barrie had been at Edinburgh University at the same time, but hadn't become acquainted there (Doyle had also missed getting to know another great contemporary, R. L. Stevenson). Now they met at a literary dinner in London and became immediate friends. Barrie was in his period of transition from successful novelist—*A Window in Thrums,* 1889, *The Little Minister,* 1891—to dramatist. He was trying to write the libretto of a light opera for Richard D'Oyly Carte to produce at the Savoy Theatre. It was giving him problems, and he invited Doyle to collaborate on it.

Doyle had tried his hand at dramatic writing with a three-act play based on the American scenes in *A Study in Scarlet,* featuring a Watson character but no Holmes. By the time he had thought of submitting it somewhere, with the title *Angels of Darkness,* the Holmes-Watson partnership had become immutable and the play was abandoned for ever.

The exercise of working with Barrie stimulated him to try again on his own account. He adapted his own short story *A Straggler of '15* into a one-act play, about a dying veteran of the Guards reliving his finest hours. He sent it to Henry Irving, who bought it willingly, as an ideal vehicle for himself. *A Story of Waterloo* (later, simply *Waterloo*), with Irving as Corporal Gregory Brewster, was presented late in 1894 at the Prince's Theatre, Bristol, and then in London at the Garrick, in a double bill with the ever-popular *The Bells.* It proved an instant success. . . .

For Christmas 1892 the *Strand* was able to give its readers a present which many would treasure above most others. The December issue carried the first of what had been announced as ''a new series of The Adventures of Sherlock Holmes,'' ''Silver Blaze.''

The series of twelve stories ran in thirteen issues up to and including December, 1893, one of them, ''The Naval Treaty,'' spreading over two monthly numbers. (p. 76)

When Newnes reissued the series in volume form . . . in 1894, it had the title *The Memoirs of Sherlock Holmes.* One story, ''The Cardboard Box,'' had been omitted as not ''healthful''

enough for family reading: it involves sexual infidelity in marriage, leading to murder and mutilation. Its early scene in which Holmes deduces Watson's emotions from his friend's glances at his framed portrait of General Gordon, the hero of Khartoum, and his unframed one of the Rev. Henry Ward Beecher, the disgraced American evangelist, seemed too good to drop, however, so it had been transferred to the opening of another tale, ''The Resident Patient.'' (p. 77)

''It is with a heavy heart that I take up my pen to write these the last words. . . .''

It was with heavier hearts that *Strand Magazine* readers stared at the page which faced the opening of ''The Final Problem.'' It was occupied entirely by Sidney Paget's dramatic portrayal, stark and black as a Victorian funeral, of Holmes and another man, as yet unfamiliar, wrestling on the brink of a foaming mountain chasm. The deerstalker hat was already whirling away into the depths. The caption, ''The death of Sherlock Holmes,'' left no doubt that its owner was doomed to follow.

Nothing had prepared the readership for this. ''The Naval Treaty'' had just given them Holmes at his most perceptive and triumphant; the November *Strand* had carried no announcement that the next story would be the last ever. The better part of half a million subscribers in Britain and America opened the Christmas Number, anticipating the usual treat—and discovered this!

No wonder the letters of protest poured in. No wonder that jokers in the City of London put crape mourning bands round their top hats and coatsleeves. No wonder that women wept genuinely, and one was moved to begin her letter to Conan Doyle ''You Brute!''

He had struck, in both senses of the word. He had wanted to stop, but knew that he would be begged to go on and be offered financial incentives which would be hard to refuse. To place himself beyond temptation or compassion he introduced a hitherto unknown archenemy of Holmes, Professor James Moriarty. After a brief build-up of the background of this criminal genius and of the enmity between him and Holmes, he sent them to Switzerland, to struggle to a mutual death in the falls of Reichenbach. . . .

When Charles Dickens killed off Little Nell and Paul Dombey he did it with personal tears and real anguish. The innocents' deaths were artistic necessities and he could only join himself in grief with the many people who had written imploring him to spare them. Doyle's fatal deed was wholly premeditated, and unregretted. . . . George Newnes frankly admitted to his shareholders that the dispatch of Holmes had been ''a dreadful event.'' At one blow the mainstay of the *Strand*'s fiction had been knocked away. The roof did not cave in though. . . . The *Strand Magazine*'s circulation held up, even if monthly publication day no longer produced the bookstall queues, eager for each new Holmes adventure.

His had been the most extraordinary killing-off in all fiction: wilful, ruthless, and, to some readers' minds, callous, not only towards them, but to poor Watson who was left to grieve, though at least with a wife to console him. Doubly infuriating was the introduction in this last story, for no other purpose than to make Holmes's death plausible, of a character of such ripe potential as Moriarty. If a public which has given an author or dramatist its backing, and lifted him to fame, is justified in demanding more of what it wants in return, the people of all ages and both sexes who had made Arthur Conan Doyle the most eagerly read writer after Dickens had reasonable grievance against him.

When his blow hit his readers so devastatingly Doyle was out of the country and deaf to anguished howls. He was in Switzerland. . . . (pp. 103-05)

Doyle's most significant new creation in this period was Brigadier Etienne Gerard, of Napoleon's army, inspired by the recent publication of the memoirs of the real-life General Baron de Marbot, and further intensive reading in Napoleonic history. (p. 105)

While he was on tour [in the United States] he was given the news of the success at home of his play, *A Story of Waterloo.* Although he had to be patient, wherever he went, with the inevitable questions about Sherlock Holmes, he could contemplate a prosperous future without him.

The interchange of their names, which had always irked him, did not cease with time. "SHERLOCK HOLMES OFF TO THE WAR" headlined a newspaper report early in 1900 that Dr Conan Doyle had joined a privately-raised hospital going to tend fighting troops in South Africa. He had tried to enlist as a soldier, but went instead as an unpaid senior physician, paying for his butler to go with him.

It proved to be an extremely arduous experience. The hospital was established at Bloemfontein on 2 April, with the cricket ground for its site and the pavilion for its main ward. The Boers almost immediately captured the waterworks, cutting off the supply to the whole town. An epidemic of enteric fever struck down thousands of soldiers and civilians, all of whom had to be treated alike, with inadequate supplies of medical materials. The chief surgeon, a gynaecologist, left for England and the senior Army Medical Corps officer took to the bottle. Doyle was left to take over all the responsibility and a large part of the work, as many of his staff succumbed. A visiting journalist who asked him his favourite Sherlock Holmes story got short shrift. (pp. 105-06)

The Brigadier Gerard stories were established as a huge success. They and other serialized tales, *Rodney Stone* and *The Tragedy of the Korosko,* and the *Round the Fire* adventure series had kept his name in front of the *Strand*'s readers. All were republished in volume form and sold well, some hugely. The Sherlock Holmes editions kept on selling, too; and although he still refused to write new Holmes stories he had not hesitated to draw on existing ones in trying to write a full-length hit play. (p.106)

To his agent, A. P. Watt, any sign of his recountenancing Sherlock Holmes was too valuable to let pass. He persuaded Doyle to let him send the play to the American impresario Charles Frohman, a genius at promoting the right theatrical star in the ideally suited work. Frohman knew precisely whom to approach for a Holmes. The Connecticut-born William Gillette was not only his living image, but needed a new vehicle to follow his own *Secret Service,* which was nearing the end of its long run of success. . . .

Gillette was interested in the proposal, but didn't like the script. He asked if he might rewrite it. Doyle had no objection. After reading the published Sherlock Holmes stories for the first time in his life, Gillette began trying to reshape the play. He soon found that the only practical course would be to write a new one from scratch. Doyle, beyond caring by now, gave his permission. (p. 107)

He drew mainly on two stories: "A Scandal in Bohemia," for female interest and the plot of a blackmail case involving, among other things, some photographs; and "The Final Problem," so as to include Prof. Moriarty. Freed to go his own way, he wrote fluently, pausing only briefly to cable Doyle, "May I marry Holmes?" The uninterested answer was, "You may marry or murder or do what you like with him." Gillette did neither, but ended the piece with Holmes and the heroine, Alice Faulkner, in an embrace.

Gillette and Frohman were sure that the new four-act piece would be a success and Gillette took it to England for Doyle's approval. He had played in London, but Doyle had never seen him. Gillette wore a cape and a deerstalker to their first meeting, and Doyle was astonished to face a perfect embodiment of Holmes.

They were mutually charmed; Doyle liked the play immensely. After its New York opening, at the Garrick Theatre on 6 November, 1899, Frohman cabled him:

> SPLENDID SUCCESS WITH PRESS AND PUBLIC . . .
> "HERALD" ACCLAIMS IT AS DRAMATIC TRIUMPH.
> GILLETTE SCORED SUCCESS OF HIS CAREER.

Not all the critics agreed, but *Sherlock Holmes* ran for 236 performances, and for 216 at the Lyceum Theatre when Gillette brought his company to London, to open there on 9 September, 1901. His own restrained performance was considered intelligent, though rather grim. He remained identified with the role for the rest of his life, playing it for the last time in 1932, aged 78 (he died in 1937). Both he and Doyle, who was happy to give Gillette sole credit as author, but drew a percentage for the use of his material, prospered exceedingly from it. (pp. 107-08)

Dr. Conan Doyle came back from South Africa in July 1900. He had looked forward to the adventure as a tonic for his nerves, but he returned exhausted. He had not escaped the fever himself, and its after-effects persisted.

Nevertheless, he plunged into work. He was indignant about the British Army's outdated equipment and methods of fighting. He wanted to rebut ill-founded criticism of the personal conduct of the soldiery towards Boer prisoners and civilians. He wrote articles and letters to the press, and then a book, *The War in South Africa: Its Cause and Conduct.* It sold 300,000 copies in six weeks, with all the profits used to pay for foreign translations. He advocated teaching every man and youth in the country to shoot, in case of future emergencies, and set up the first civilian rifle-range in his own grounds. (p. 109)

By March 1901 the accumulation of pressures forced him to seek a short break. A golfing friend, Fletcher Robinson, accompanied him to Cromer, a Regency watering place on the North Norfolk coast, where they played the notable course. The Sunday afternoon of their stay was very cold. By the fireside in their sitting-room in the Royal Links Hotel was the place to be. They smoked and talked, and Robinson told him a story about a phantom hound on Dartmoor. . . .

The idea for a novel based on a legendary hound was roughed out between them that afternoon. Next month they were on Dartmoor together, tramping over the terrain and working further at the plot. Doyle had begun writing before he left the West Country; and, into a narrative whose first outline had been conceived without thought of them, Sherlock Holmes and John H. Watson insinuated themselves as central characters. (pp. 109-10)

The Hound of the Baskervilles is the best known and regarded of all the Sherlock Holmes stories. It is the longest by far, if the non-Holmesian flashback which takes up almost half of *The Valley of Fear* is discounted. It is replete with powerful elements: a legend of the supernatural, a sombre old house in a remote fastness of bleak moorland, a gigantic hound and a murderer at large, mysterious signallings, a woman's inexplicable sobbing in the still of night, and other suggestive sounds and sightings. For once, it has a personable, manly extrovert in Sir Henry Baskerville, and a sex-symbol in Beryl Stapleton, in place of the usual inadequate or eccentric male or perplexed girl.

It is not without significance, either, that Watson has his chance to remain centre-stage when Holmes is off. Doyle used Holmes for a change, instead of Holmes using him. The reader shares the feeling of vulnerability in Holmes's absence; and when he does show up, his impact is all the stronger for it. Meanwhile, Watson copes with events with resource and courage, and takes time and space in chronicling them, to describe the natural settings in evocative detail.

Doyle gave it his best. He wanted to write this story, his first dramatic novel for four years. Holmes or no, he wasn't impatient to get it over with. His writing did full justice to the elements of what has been widely recognized as the best of all mystery thrillers.

It ran in the *Strand* from August 1901 to April 1902, enabling Sir George Newnes (a baronet since 1895) to tell his shareholders at the annual meeting that circulation had leaped by 30,000 copies. He only regretted that he couldn't announce the return of Holmes; his creator was adamant that Holmes was dead, and *The Hound of the Baskervilles* merely a case previously unchronicled. (pp. 110-11)

Queen Victoria died in January 1901. Edward, Prince of Wales, had met Arthur Conan Doyle and was well aware of his work for his country, which he had capped with a thoroughly detailed work, *The Great Boer War*, widely praised for being as impartial as it was colourful.

It was not as Sherlock Holmes's creator that Doyle was offered a knighthood in the new monarch's first honours list, in 1902; it was for his service to the State. (p. 121)

Being Sir Arthur made no difference to his work. He was enjoying doing a further series for the *Strand*, entitled *Adventures of Gerard*. It started appearing in the month of his knighthood with "How Brigadier Gerard lost his Ear," and ran until May, 1903. By that time, sighs of relief were resounding in Newnes's offices. The September number ended with a triumphant announcement:

"THE RETURN OF SHERLOCK HOLMES"

The readers of the *Strand Magazine* have a vivid recollection of the time when Sherlock Holmes made his first appearance before the public, and of the Adventures which made his name a household word in every quarter of the world. The news of his death was received with regret as at the loss of a personal friend. Fortunately, that news, though based on circumstantial evidence which at the time seemed conclusive, turns out to be erroneous. How he escaped from his struggle with Moriarty at the Reichenbach Falls, why he remained in hiding even from his

friend Watson, how he made his re-appearance, and the manner he signalized his return by one of the most remarkable of his exploits will be found narrated in the first story of the New Series, beginning

In The OCTOBER NUMBER

He never said publicly precisely why he relented. All that is recorded is that an American publisher, no doubt near-frantic at the spectacle of the immense American success of *The Hound of the Baskervilles*, cabled an unprecedented offer. If the outcome of the struggle at the Reichenbach Falls could be explained away acceptably to readers, and Holmes could be believed to have survived, he would pay five thousand dollars a short story for a minimum of six and as many more as Doyle might care to write. A. P. Watt talked to Newnes, who readily added his own offer of a little over half the American rate. It meant, in all, some eight thousand dollars for each story in a series, plus what the subsequent book rights would earn.

Arthur Conan Doyle was a man of rigid principles. He was no dissembler, which is no doubt partly why he failed to get elected to Parliament in 1900 and 1906; he was too much his own man for party expediencies. Money, once he had it, mattered little to him. . . . But he was also a professional, and the package deal which Watt tactfully put to him was one which none but the most ivory-tower-bound author would have turned down. Besides, after years of freedom from the tyranny of Holmes he had quite enjoyed writing *The Hound*. Its huge success was the sort of thing that writers dream about. He sent Watt a laconic postcard: "Very well. A. C. D."; and became the highest paid writer in history so far. (pp. 121-22)

Holmes's version of what had happened to him was good enough to convince Watson. It has been much questioned in recent years, as scholars of the canon have picked over its inconsistencies and errors. It is argued that either Holmes told Watson what he wanted him to believe about his escape from death and his subsequent wanderings, or Watson made a hash of recording accurately what Holmes said to him. The simple truth is that Conan Doyle wrapped up his justification in a dramatic, zestful narrative, over whose fine detail no one but a Sherlockian scholar would bother to quibble. Contributing to a *Strand Magazine* symposium of how novelists of the day worked (December 1904) he confessed:

> In short stories it has always seemed to me that so long as you produce your dramatic effect, accuracy of detail matters little. I have never striven for it and have made some bad mistakes in consequence. What matter if I can hold my readers? I claim that I may make my own conditions, and I do so. I have taken liberties in some of the Sherlock Holmes stories. . . . That does not trouble me in the least when the story is admittedly a phantasy.

The manner of Holmes's supposed death made it possible to resurrect him without straining credence at all. If, instead of being presumed to have plunged into the cataract, without witnesses and without subsequent traces, Holmes had been shot to death, identified, buried, and memorialized, further narratives would have had to be like *The Hound*, set back in time before that fatal day in 1891. There are not the slightest grounds for suspecting that he realized this and changed the method of execution to leave himself a loophole. He wanted Holmes dead, and thought he had killed him.

Perhaps it is fanciful to suggest that he could not do it properly because, in a sense, he would have been killing something that was to a considerable extent a projection of himself. (p. 123)

Sherlock Holmes societies did not exist by the time his creator died in 1930. He was unacquainted with the recondite practices of reading hidden and wholly unintended meanings into Watson's prose and making play with his inconsistencies. If Holmes had been gunned down, slashed to ribbons, steamrollered, or even beheaded, someone would have come up with the theory that it had been a hoax to enable him to disappear for a while, or that Watson had made another of his mistakes. Doyle's explanation was enough for his readers, who only wanted Holmes back, never mind how. It worked, and the bookstall lines reformed in even greater numbers.

The series of thirteen stories known collectively as *The Return of Sherlock Holmes* began running in *Collier's* (New York) in September 1903. (pp. 123-24)

Doyle had written the thirteen stories comprising *The Return of Sherlock Holmes* in one batch, keen to be finished with them. The series had provoked a flow of correspondence from many parts of the world. The letters and cards were as often as not addressed to "Sir Sherlock Holmes" or "Sherlock Holmes, Esq., care of Sir Arthur Conan Doyle." "Sherlock Holmes, London" or "Conan Doyle, England" were enough address

Beeton's Christmas Annual, *containing the first appearance of Sherlock Holmes.*

to reach him. As well as requests for autographs and signed photographs there were gifts, including tobacco and smoking accessories, and even the occasional set of violin strings. Some people wanted advice and help with domestic problems, missing persons and other perplexities. Alfred Wood, Conan Doyle's Watsonian-looking secretary, some six years his junior and an associate since Southsea days, sorted out the saner ones for him to deal with.

Enthusiasm for Holmes was spreading. *Le avventure di Sherlock Holmes* had been published in Italy in 1895. *Das Zeichen der Vier* (*The Sign of the Four*) came out in Germany in 1903, followed next year by *Der Hund von Baskerville. Les Aventures de Sherlock Holmes* were introduced to French readers in 1902; but it was *La Resurrection de Sherlock Holmes* (*The Return*), and, that same year, 1905, *Nouveaux exploits de Sherlock Holmes* (a selection from *Memoirs* and *Return*) which really sparked off French enthusiasm: those and, in December 1907, the opening at the Théâtre Antoine, Paris, of Pierre Decourcelle's French version of Gillette's play. It became all the rage, running for 335 performances.

The new medium of film suited Holmes well. (p. 145)

Off the stage and screen, Sherlock Holmes had not been much in evidence since publication of *The Return*. There were people who said that he wasn't the man he had been before his "death." Certainly, some readers had taken to heart Watson's announcement, in "The Second Stain," of Holmes's retirement. Several respectable ladies wrote in, offering to be his housekeeper; one, more enterprising, added that she knew all about beekeeping and could "segregate the queen." There seemed a finality to his career this time which had never been acceptable through the Reichenbach Falls incident. He had been resurrected, had given a satisfactory number of encores, but had come to seem rather less than indispensable. Kipling, Wodehouse, Hornung, and others had become well accepted as writers of the *Strand's* contemporary short stories. Doyle was more familiar of late as the author of the long-running historical serial *Sir Nigel* (December 1905-December 1906), his "sequel," although set earlier, to *The White Company*. (p. 147)

Seven of the eight stories which comprise the collection entitled *His Last Bow* appeared at sporadic intervals during the years 1908-17. British publication was invariably in the *Strand Magazine*: Conan Doyle remained faithful to it for the rest of his life. His American magazine publishers, as well as his illustrators, had begun to vary. The story which made up the eight was "The Cardboard Box," considered unclean for book readers in 1894, but now cleared for the very different readership of *His Last Bow*, published in 1917. . . . (pp. 147-48)

It had been in 1902 that [Doyle] had found himself obliged to accept a knighthood. In one of the first Sherlock Holmes stories written at Windlesham, "The Bruce-Partington Plans," he let Holmes declare that he had no interest in seeing his name in the Honours List. It was many years later, in "The Three Garridebs," before Watson revealed that in that same year of 1902 Holmes had actually turned down a knighthood. It would not have done to let himself become Sir Sherlock Holmes: that would have been to surrender some part of himself to the Establishment.

Sir Arthur Conan Doyle did not let his title inhibit him. In issues of what he conceived to be public concern there was no greater patriot, but the rights of the voiceless underdog made him fight equally hard. He stood for Parliament twice, for the Unionist cause, because he was urged to, but his heart was not wholly in it. He stood up before audiences as what he was, and said what he thought and believed, which was not always what they wanted to hear from their candidate. He was not elected. He would have made an alert, noisy Parliamentarian, but not a successful one. He would not have been able to dissemble to suit party policy.

He fought his public campaigns chiefly through newspapers, pamphlets, and correspondence. Often, when his name was in the news, the ''Sherlock Holmes'' allusions were introduced—by others, never by himself. It is a measure of his integrity, rather than of any contempt for Holmes, that he never invoked him as a campaign ally. Without doubt, though, the creator of Sherlock Holmes, whose following never stopped growing, was noticed and listened to more readily for it. Holmes never ceased to have his uses, even if they went unthanked by his author. The public causes were many and varied. Some were urged on him, others were his own finding. He was more opinionated and impatient nowadays. Years of nerve-strain had changed his personality. He had always been able to write in any surroundings, oblivious to people or their noise. Now, he sometimes needed absolute peace and quiet. (pp. 149-50)

He had seen the First World War coming, and feared that the submarine and airship would give Germany victory by blockade. His solution was as simplistic and direct as all his notions: build a Channel tunnel. It would nullify the U-boat menace and give the army speedy access to France, which he was sure Germany would invade. A closely reasoned article in the *Fortnightly Review* stirred Parliament into setting up a commission to consider it. His estimate of the time it would take to build the tunnel was three years. A commission would be likely to waste most of that time simply grinding out its report. Some more dramatic means of alerting the nation was needed. He was its most widely read storyteller, so he would make his appeal with dramatic fiction.

''Danger!'', published in the *Strand* in July 1914, though written in 1913, showed a small power possessing a mere eight submarines frustrating the might of the Royal Navy by attacking all merchant shipping trading with Britain. Famine ensues, financial stability ends, and little ''Norland'' accepts a surrender.

To get his parable taken seriously, he asked Greenhough Smith to invite the reactions of a dozen naval experts. The consensus was politely dismissive of the submarine blockade as a weapon of attrition. One admiral likened the story to a Jules Verne improbability. Another declared, ''No nation would permit it, and the officer who did it would be shot.'' Two years later the German Naval Secretary was able to say in the Reichstag, ''The German people can thank the British Admiralty for disregarding the warning on U-boat warfare given by Sir Arthur Conan Doyle.'' (pp. 150-51)

In 1914 he offered the War Office his more active service:

> I have been told that there may be some difficulty in finding Officers for the New Army. I think I may say that my name is well known to the younger men of this country and that if I were to take a commission at my age it would set an example which might be of help. I can drill a company—I do so every evening. I have seen something of campaigning, having served as a surgeon in South Africa. I am fifty-five but I am very strong and hardy, and can make

my voice audible at great distances, which is useful at drill. . . .

(p. 151)

An official volunteer force was quickly established and the unit, recognized as the first of its kind, became the Crowborough Company of the Fifth Royal Sussex Volunteer Regiment. No. 184343 Private Sir Arthur Conan Doyle—''Ole Bill,'' as he termed himself—served in it all through the war. . . .

As in the matter of the knighthood, he turned to Holmes to grant him vicarious release. Sir Arthur Conan Doyle couldn't serve his country actively, but Mr Sherlock Holmes could, in the story *His Last Bow*. On 2 August, 1914, the date of this brief reunion between him and Watson to strike a blow for their country on the eve of war, Holmes was, in Watson's words, ''a tall, gaunt man of sixty,'' long since established in his solitary retirement. Sir Arthur Conan Doyle, on that date, was a gigantically-built man of fifty-five, a well-placed family man, prosperous, busy, though more with his crusades than with creative writing; the world's most widely-read storyteller, nevertheless: creator of the best known character in world fiction.

The stories collected in 1917 under the title *His Last Bow* add nothing much to the distinction of the canon of work which they had extended. It didn't matter. By then, the world, like the author, had graver preoccupations. (p. 152)

This brief Preface is from the volume.

HIS LAST BOW

> The friends of Mr Sherlock Holmes will be glad to learn that he is still alive and well, though somewhat crippled by occasional attacks of rheumatism. He has, for many years, lived in a small farm upon the downs five miles from Eastbourne, where his time is divided between philosophy and agriculture. During this period of rest he has refused the most princely offers to take up various cases, having determined that his retirement was a permanent one. The approach of the German war caused him, however, to lay his remarkable combination of intellectual and practical activity at the disposal of the government, with historical results which are recounted in *His Last Bow*. Several previous experiences which have lain long in my portfolio have been added to *His Last Bow* so as to complete the volume.
>
> JOHN H. WATSON, M.D.

(pp. 152-53)

In that fateful month of August 1914 . . . , the *Strand Magazine* ran another of its favourite kind of announcement: ''CONAN DOYLE'S GREAT NEW SHERLOCK HOLMES SERIAL 'THE VALLEY OF FEAR' THRILLING WITH INCIDENT AND EXCITEMENT WILL COMMENCE IN OUR NEXT NUMBER.'' (p. 172)

The fact that Britain and a large part of the rest of the world were at war by this time was no damper on the story's prospects. At that time of eagerness to get into the fight, with long lines of excited volunteers for ''Fred Karno's ragtime infantry,'' and stage revues with such titles as *On Duty* and *Business as Usual,* a brand new serial story about the omniscient man who never lost his battles against the agents of lawlessness and oppression could not have been more opportune: All this, and Sherlock Holmes, too!

Furthermore, the yarn turned out to be a cracker. Holmes scintillates from the start, swiftly sensing the evil shadow of Moriarty over the hurried communication from an informant within the Professor's oganization: demonstrating how, even without a key, Sherlock Holmes can crack any code, however abstruse; ribbing Watson for his development of an unexpected vein of pawky humour which is delightfully evident.

The Holmes-Watson relationship, so important to the spirit of the stories, and so missed when it is disregarded or fumbled, shows at its best in this one. More clearly than perhaps anywhere else, they revel in the extent and harmony of their friendship and rapport. The notion of the glacial know-all, contemptuously putting down his ingenuous, bumbling acolyte, could never be conceived by anyone beginning by reading this tale. They are pals, buddies, equals in their differing moulds. For a large portion of this longest of the Sherlock Holmes stories they are off-stage; but when they are on, they play to each other admirably. It is a story whose author clearly enjoyed writing it. (pp. 172-73)

A dramatic detective tale set in a rough-tough American mining community was an irresistible idea to Conan Doyle; but he had the notion of making it two tales, beginning with Sherlock Holmes investigating the murder of the American tenant of an ancient moated manor house in Sussex, whose wife and best male friend have some explanation to hide from the police which is not the obvious one.

Holmes's investigation is brilliant, carried out with all the flair and impudence, especially towards the police, which go with his best spirits. The story within the story, a flashback explanation of the American background to the case, takes up more than half of the novel's length. It is just another rough melodrama, with none of the panache of what has preceded it. It could have been expressed in one page, or even one paragraph; but it was the primary reason for the story's having been written at all, so we must be grateful, even if we skip it. The late Adrian Conan Doyle always insisted that its climactic line, "Birdy Edwards is here. I am Birdy Edwards!" was the most dramatic one his father ever wrote.

Conan Doyle must have known that the story would lose its impact with the shift from Sussex and Sherlock Holmes to America. . . . *The Valley of Fear* was "really two books with the Atlantic rolling between them." It is why it has been less regarded than most of the Sherlock Holmes stories; yet, in essentials and in exuberance of spirit, it is among the best. (p. 174)

Arthur Conan Doyle was a natural detective genius, who systematized his methods, partly on lines absorbed from [his medical school instructor Doctor] Joe Bell, and demonstrated them through Sherlock Holmes. It takes a genius to portray another so convincingly. It was something quite other than literary skill that made him able to invent crimes and their solutions, then reason backwards to recreate their details, and forward again to show Holmes's methods at work. If some of the plots seem old hat today, it is because they have been imitated and adapted so many times, and made over-familiar, in all sorts of guises. If some seem far-fetched, one has only to open any newspaper to read of people still falling for the same kind of confidence tricks (personally and nationally), still proving unable to temper passion with sanity, still being beastly to anyone and anything that it is in their power to oppress. The types of people and

crimes which repelled Sherlock Holmes are still with us, and the most sophisticated techniques available against them are in large part derived from the pioneering principles evolved for him by his creator. (p. 176)

The collection under the title *The Case Book of Sherlock Holmes* comprises the final twelve [Holmes stories]. (p. 184)

[Is it possible] that "The Veiled Lodger, Shoscombe Old Place" and "The Retired Colourman" were stories which Doyle had written before the war . . .? Did the editor of *Liberty* beg for a series for 1926-27, to which a preoccupied Doyle responded by letting his agent release these three rejects? To make a series of six, did he write up cursorily some of those stories which over the years hopeful imitators, American as well as British, had sent him and he had bought and put aside? These three, "The Blanched Soldier," "The Three Gables," and "The Lion's Mane," are sub-standard works, the first two of them displaying many Americanisms of language and style.

In this, as in detection, it is a capital mistake to theorize before one has all the evidence. Like others who have puzzled over the assemblage which is *The Case Book of Sherlock Holmes,* I can only echo, "The faculty of deduction is certainly contagious, Watson.". . . (pp. 184-85)

> *Michael Hardwick, in his* The Complete Guide to Sherlock Holmes, *Weidenfeld and Nicolson, 1986, 255 p.*

THE LIFE AND CHARACTER OF HOLMES

S. C. ROBERTS

[In the following excerpt, Roberts offers a "biographical sketch" of Holmes that does not venture into some of the more conjectural avenues frequented by Holmesians.]

"I am lost without my Boswell," said Holmes in a famous passage and while it must be admitted that Watson's narrative cannot wholly justify the claim:

> Quo fit ut omnis
> Votiva pateat veluti descripta tabella
> Vita senis

the life and character of Sherlock Holmes can nevertheless be reconstructed with a fair measure of probability.

In his family background the two most important elements were his descent from a long line of country squires and the fact that his grandmother was a sister of Horace Vernet (1789-1863), the third of a line of French painters. Holmes's tastes and habits were, indeed, so far removed from those of the squirearchy and Watson is so frequently at pains to emphasize the Bohemian character of life in Baker Street, that we are apt to forget how naturally and easily Holmes adapted himself to the country-house scene. With the Trevors at Donnithorpe or with the Musgraves at Hurlstone Manor or in Colonel Hayter's gun-room Holmes was completely at home; nor did he betray the slightest self-consciousness in dealing with such clients as the Duke of Holdernesse or the illustrious Lord Bellinger. But it was the Gallic side of Holmes's ancestry that more strongly influenced his way of life. "Art in the blood," as he remarked to Watson, "is liable to take the strangest of forms" and he attributed both his own and his brother Mycroft's achievements in the art of detection to their Vernet descent. (pp. 47-8)

While little or nothing is known of Holmes's relations with members of his family in France or elsewhere (except, of course, his occasional association with Mycroft), it is noteworthy that he seldom neglected the opportunity of investigating a French problem. As early as 1886 his practice had extended to the Continent. François le Villard, a rising French detective, translated several of Holmes's pamphlets, including that on the varieties of tobacco-ash, into French and was loud in his praise of Holmes's help in a difficult will case—*magnifique, coup de maître,* he wrote in his enthusiasm. In 1887 Holmes was engaged in foiling the "colossal schemes" of Baron Maupertuis and Watson hurried out to find him in a state of exhaustion in the Hôtel Dulong at Lyons; there followed an intricate problem at Marseilles and the case of the unfortunate Madame Montpensier, and in the winter of 1890-1 Holmes was retained by the French Government in a case of "supreme importance"; finally, in 1894, he was responsible for bringing the Boulevard assassin, Huret, to justice—a triumph which brought him a personal letter from the President of the Republic and the Order of the Legion of Honour. It is not without significance that Holmes accepted the Order; when he was offered a knighthood in 1902, he refused it.

But, to return to the background of Holmes's upbringing, very little can be inferred about his early education. If, like Watson, he had been at one of the well-known public schools, it is difficult to believe that Watson's narrative would not have included some chance allusion to it. It is, indeed, clear that Holmes had little interest in, or knowledge of, the manly sports and exercises which delight the heart of the normal Englishmen. His entire ignorance of famous rugby footballers astonished the simple soul of Cyril Overton ("sixteen stone of solid bone and muscle"), who found it hard to believe that anyone in England could be unfamiliar with the name of "Godfrey Staunton, the crack three-quarter, Cambridge, Blackheath and five Internationals." At the same time, Holmes admitted that amateur sport was the "best and soundest thing in England" and that he was himself a decent fencer, a good shot with a revolver, and definitely proud of his own proficiency in "the good old British sport of boxing."

That Holmes went to a university is, of course, quite definitely known. He told Watson that he was not a very sociable undergraduate, spending most of his time working out his own methods of thought, and that Victor Trevor was his only friend at college. The friendship was formed in a peculiar way, Trevor's bull-terrier "freezing on" to Holmes's ankle one morning as he went down to chapel. Much legitimate, and some extravagant, inference has been drawn from this incident. Bull-terriers are not allowed within the college precincts, so the attack must have occurred in the street. Therefore, it has been argued (and notably by Miss Dorothy Sayers), Holmes was living out of college in his first year; and therefore, as this was a distinctly Cambridge custom in those days, Holmes must have been at Cambridge. But the argument is not wholly conclusive; it is at least as reasonable to suppose that it was a Sunday morning service to which Holmes was on his way, and he may well have stepped into the street to buy a newspaper just before going to chapel. Or again, Trevor's dog may well have been tied up in the college porch, in accordance with Oxford custom. Apart from this, the tone of Holmes's commentary throughout the story of *The Missing Three-Quarter*

makes it impossible to believe that he was a Cambridge man. What Cambridge man talks of "running *down* to Cambridge?" Or, again: "Here we are, stranded and friendless, in this inhospitable town." This, surely, is the voice of a critical stranger, not of a loyal *alumnus.* (pp. 48-9)

It was the father of his friend Trevor who recommended Holmes to make a profession out of what had previously been "the merest hobby," and during the later part of his time at the university his fame spread amongst a small circle of undergraduates. Coming down from college, he took rooms in Montague Street near the British Museum and, as clients were few, he filled his time by a study of the various branches of science that were relevant to his prospective career. One of his earliest cases (*The Musgrave Ritual*), which may reasonably be dated about 1878, arose out of one of his rare undergraduate friendships, and early in 1881 came the famous meeting in the laboratory at Bart's, when young Stamford unconsciously acted as one of the great go-betweens of history and Holmes and Watson made their plans for the joint *ménage* in 221B Baker Street. In his account of the first adventure of the partnership (*A Study in Scarlet*) Watson introduces the character-sketch of his fellow lodger which must provide the basis for any biographical estimate—his late breakfasts, his alternating energy and torpor, his curious patches of ignorance (of Thomas Carlyle, for example, and of the Solar System), his violin-playing, his magazine article "The Book of Life." . . . Some of Watson's early impressions naturally need qualification. As has been more than once remarked, a man who quotes Hafiz and Horace, Flaubert and Goethe, cannot fairly be described as totally ignorant of literature, and one play of Shakespeare's (*Twelfth Night*) appears to have been his particular favourite since he twice quotes a line from it in very different contexts. Holmes, indeed, was very far from being a mere calculating machine. Watson was deeply, and properly, impressed by the compilation of "the great index volume" which served as Holmes's hand-made encyclopaedia, but it was a volume that showed some curious lapses. Under the letter V, for example, there appeared not only "Vigor, the Hammersmith Wonder" and "Vittoria, a circus belle" but "Voyage of the *Gloria Scott*" and "Victor Lynch, the forger"—exasperating entries for anyone wanting information about the *Gloria Scott* or Lynch. However, Holmes, no doubt, knew his own methods and by 1887, as has already been noted, he had become an international figure. The exceptional labours involved in the Maupertuis case had a serious effect upon his health, but he recovered in time to tackle the problem of the Reigate Squires and many others. Then came *The Sign of Four* and Watson's marriage (his first marriage) to Miss Mary Morstan. For a time the partnership was broken and it was only by hearsay that Watson knew of Holmes's summons to Odessa to investigate the Trepoff murder and of his mission on behalf of the Dutch Royal House. But the lure of 221B was strong and in 1888 the partnership was intermittently resumed, Mrs. Watson frequently encouraging her husband to respond to a tentative summons from his old friend. Thus Watson found himself engaged in the case of *The Five Orange Pips, The Naval Treaty, The Man with the Twisted Lip,* and many other famous adventures. What was described by Watson, in good faith, as *The Final Problem* belonged to the year 1891. But while Watson in the next few years was wistfully, and "with indifferent success," attempting to apply his friend's methods to the solution of the criminal problems of the time, Holmes was in fact travelling through Tibet and other distant countries. He spent some days in Lhasa with the head Lama, then went through Persia, paid

St. Bartholomew's hospital, scene of the momentous meeting of Holmes and Watson.

a brief visit to Mecca, and secured some useful information for the Foreign Office, probably at Mycroft's request, as a result of his interview with the Khalifa at Khartoum. Finally, he was engaged for some months in research in coal-tar derivatives in the laboratory at Montpelier. The dramatic "Return" to Baker Street occurred in 1894, and the years that followed were busy ones indeed. Watson more than once refers to the year 1895 as "memorable" and by the spring of 1897 the "constant hard work" was beginning to tell upon Holmes's iron constitution. One of his cases (*The Creeping Man*) occurred in 1903 and shortly afterwards he retired from active work and settled in Sussex. In a lonely house on the southern slope of the Downs "commanding a great view of the Channel" the great detective lived a placid life with his housekeeper and his beehives. A great change had come over him with the passing of the years. In his record of an early adventure (*The Cardboard Box*) Watson had noted that neither sea nor country held any attraction for Holmes and that among his many gifts appreciation of Nature found no place. But by 1907 Holmes had not only come to love the Sussex cliffs and downlands, but he had convinced himself that he had always aspired after a country life, solemnly referring to "that soothing life of Nature" as something for which he had yearned during the long years spent in London. Such is the power of Time to dull even a mind like that of Sherlock Holmes into forgetfulness— or was it just another Gallic touch, a *Recherche du temps perdu?*

But if Holmes fell into a mood of sentimental self-deception about his yearnings after Nature in his early days, there can be no doubt about the genuineness of his enjoyment of the Sussex downs and the Sussex coast, especially when, after a Channel gale, all Nature was "newly washed and fresh" and he would stroll along the cliff after breakfast and relish the "exquisite air." Nor was he idle. To the "little working gangs" of bees he devoted the same intense observation and analysis which he had before expended upon the criminal world of London, and it was with legitimate pride that he described his *Practical Handbook of Bee Culture, with some Observations upon the Segregation of the Queen* as the *magnum opus* of his latter years.

About 1912 this happy absorption in apiculture was dramatically interrupted. At that time the activities of Von Bork, *facile princeps* amongst the secret agents of the Kaiser, were causing grave anxiety at Cabinet level. Strong pressure was brought upon Holmes to return to active service, and the gravity of the situation was emphasized by his receiving a visit not from an under-secretary but from the Foreign Secretary and the Prime Minister himself. Holmes could no longer resist. He set off for Chicago, contrived to join an Irish secret society at Buffalo, and had some trouble with the police at Skibbareen. It was two years before the net was finally, and tightly, drawn and the full story of the capture of Von Bork in August 1914 is told in *His Last Bow.*

Of Holmes's way of life after 1914 no record survives. Whether he was ever again induced to emerge from his downland retreat seems doubtful. (pp. 50-2)

Such is the broad biographical pattern that can be woven with the threads drawn from the records of various adventures.

Why should it be deemed worthwhile to attempt such weaving? The answer is simple: the personalities of Holmes and Watson took such universal hold upon the hearts and imaginations of readers and have retained that hold so tenaciously over a period of sixty years, that their lives, their habits, and their characteristics have become an object of greater interest than the adventures which they shared.

"The truth is," wrote Johnson in a highly disputable passage in the Preface to his edition of Shakespeare, "that the spectators are always in their senses, and know, from the first act to the last, that the stage is only a stage, and that the players are only players."

Of the drama of Sherlock Holmes the very reverse is the truth. The spectators are not always in their senses and they refuse to treat Holmes and Watson as "only players." Conan Doyle, in spite of his own waning interest, created not puppets but characters whom his readers have insisted on regarding as flesh and blood rather than as dramatis personae. Never were two characters more desperately in search of an author than were Holmes and Watson in the years succeeding the tragedy of the Reichenbach Falls; and when *The Empty House,* the story that heralded "The Return," appeared in *The Strand* for October 1903, the scenes at railway bookstalls resembled the struggles in a bargain-basement. One critic remarked that, although Holmes was not killed when he fell over the cliff, he was never quite the same man afterwards. But for the common reader it was not the quality of the later stories that mattered; what mattered was Holmes's restoration to life, to detective activity, and to Baker Street. For Holmes returned to a familiar scene and a beloved companion: "It was indeed like old times when, at that hour, I found myself seated beside him in a hansom, my revolver in my pocket and the thrill of adventure in my heart." This was what Watson felt, and the renewal of the old-time thrill was communicated to a multitude of readers. The Baker Street *mise en scène* is indeed one of Conan Doyle's masterstrokes. In some way not easy to define, No. 221B has become the focal point of the metropolitan civilization of the nineties—the November fogs, the hansoms, the commissionaires, the gasogene, the frock-coats, the Wigmore Street post office. . . . Many of the adventures contain fantastic elements and conjure up scenes of distant devilry and romance; but Holmes and Watson always have their feet upon the ground. They travel on well-known railways, they frequent a well-known Turkish Bath establishment, they read the *Daily Telegraph,* they are in touch with all classes of society. If they are dealing with members of the middle class (doctors, solicitors, schoolmasters, engineers, tradesmen) they are treading on ground familiar to the great mass of readers; if, on the other hand, they are dealing either with Cabinet Ministers and political Dukes or with the crooks and loafers of London's underworld, they give the same readers the thrill that comes with an introduction either to the highest, or to the lowest, strata of society. But, in any event, the reader feels that he is encountering real people, people who do not demand of him any wide exercise of imagination. (pp. 52-3)

S. C. Roberts, "*A Biographical Sketch of Sherlock Holmes,*" *in* The Baker Street Reader: Cornerstone

Writings about Sherlock Holmes, edited by Philip A. Shreffler, Greenwood Press, 1984, pp. 47-54.

ALLEN EYLES

[*In the following excerpt, Eyles discusses what is revealed about Holmes's character in the first published adventure,* The Study in Scarlet.]

When the first Sherlock Holmes story, *A Study in Scarlet,* was written at Southsea, on the south coast of England, in 1886, Arthur Conan Doyle was 26 years old, having been born in Edinburgh on 22 May 1859. He had arrived at this mainly residential part of Portsmouth four years earlier, having chosen to set up in general practice on his own as a doctor here (he had previously assisted in a practice at Plymouth). . . . He had considerable spare time as patients were less than plentiful, and some of it he used to write short stories. (p. 10)

Arthur's stories were good enough to be published in magazines, although most appeared without name credit, and he did not earn enough to consider writing as more than a sideline. . . . On 6 August 1885, Conan Doyle married Louise Hawkins, the sister of one of these patients.

With the added responsibility of a wife, Conan Doyle decided to make a greater effort to develop a literary career, for his income as a doctor was barely sufficient to maintain a household. He knew that he had to make a name for himself by publishing a longer work. He was an admirer of the detectives created by Edgar Allan Poe (Auguste Dupin) and Emile Gaboriau (Monsieur Lecoq), as well as of the work of Wilkie Collins (*The Moonstone, The Woman in White*) and Israel Zangwill. But he wanted to do something different, and his inspiration for this was Doctor Joseph Bell, the surgeon and teacher of medicine during his student days at Edinburgh University. "Reading some detective stories, I was struck by the fact that in nearly every case their result was achieved by chance. I thought I would try my hand at writing a story where the hero would treat crime as Doctor Bell treated disease, and where science had taken the place of chance. The result was Sherlock Holmes." . . . (pp. 10-11)

The name Sherlock Holmes took time to evolve. Conan Doyle did not know what to call his detective at first. "One rebelled against the elementary art which gives some inkling of character in the name, and creates Mr. Sharps or Mr. Ferrets. First it was Sherringford Holmes; then it was Sherlock Holmes," he said in his reminiscences. The name Holmes was very likely suggested by the American jurist and medical pioneer, Oliver Wendell Holmes, whose impending visit to Europe was in the news—his authorship of monographs, his expert knowledge of tobacco and his analytical mind were all features that Sherlock Holmes shared.

As a cricket enthusiast and player, Conan Doyle would have known of the Nottinghamshire players Sherwin and Shacklock, who may have jointly suggested the detective's first name, and there was also a Devon cricketer actually called Sherlock. But it seems as likely that the name came from a prominent violinist, Alfred Sherlock, as Conan Doyle's sleuth also played the instrument.

Mindful of Lecoq's dim-witted associate, Father Absinthe, and also perhaps of Don Quixote's companion, Sancho Panza, Conan Doyle went on: "Holmes could not tell his own exploits, so he must have a commonplace comrade as foil—an educated man of action who could both join in the exploits and narrate them. A drab, quiet name for this unostentatious man. Watson would do. And so I had my puppets and wrote my *Study in Scarlet.*" . . . The name Watson did not register immediately; in early notes for the story, he was called Ormond Sacker.

It was on 8 March 1886 that Conan Doyle began outlining the story, which he initially called *A Tangled Skein.* He . . . did the real writing in three weeks, adopting what became his customary method of working backwards from the solution. He worked at all kinds of hours—between patients, early in the morning, late at night—but made few alterations to the handwritten sheets, finishing the story before the end of April. It was an awkward length—too long for a magazine, too short to encourage publication on its own—and there was difficulty in getting it accepted.

Finally, an offer came from Ward, Lock & Company, dated 30 October 1886: "We have read your story and are pleased with it. We could not publish it this year as the market is flooded at present with cheap fiction, but if you do not object to its being held over till next year, we will give you £25 for the copyright." Even more discouraging than the paltry amount and the absence of a royalty was the delay in publication. However, Conan Doyle reluctantly signed away all rights in *A Study in Scarlet* on 20 November 1886 for £25 and never received a further penny for it. A full year ensued before it was published as the principal attraction in *Beeton's Christmas Annual,* which sold out in a couple of weeks. (pp. 11-12)

A Study in Scarlet gives us a very thorough introduction to Sherlock Holmes and Doctor Watson. It is presented as "Being a reprint from the Reminiscences of John H. Watson, M.D., Late of the Army Medical Department," and it begins with Watson providing a short autobiographical sketch, describing how he is on leave to recover from the effects of injury and illness while serving during the second Afghan war. Lacking friends or relatives, Watson can no longer afford to stay in a London hotel, and a former acquaintance, whom he meets in the Criterion Bar at Piccadilly Circus, knows of someone wanting to share lodgings. Someone who is, however, "a little queer in his ideas" and full of "a lot of out-of-the-way knowledge," and who, moreover, conducts strange experiments, like beating corpses to discover how far bruises may be caused after death. We can hardly wait to meet such an intriguing figure, and it is in the chemical laboratory of a London hospital that one of the most significant and memorable introductions of all literary history take place.

> "Dr. Watson, Mr. Sherlock Holmes," said Stamford, introducing us.
>
> "How are you?" he said cordially, gripping my hand with a strength for which I should hardly have given him credit. "You have been in Afghanistan, I perceive."
>
> "How on earth did you know that?" I asked in astonishment.
>
> "Never mind," said he, chuckling to himself.

They agree to share the rooms that Holmes has found at 221B Baker Street, but it is some time before Watson discovers his companion's profession. After ridiculing a magazine article about the powers of observation and deduction, he learns that Holmes was its author. ". . . I have a trade of my own," says Holmes, "I suppose I am the only one in the world. I'm a consulting detective." And he explains how he knew that Watson came from Afghanistan:

> The train of reasoning ran, "Here is a gentleman of a medical type, but with the air of a military man. Clearly an army doctor, then. He has just come from the tropics, for his face is dark, and that is not the natural tint of his skin, for his wrists are fair. He has undergone hardship and sickness, as his haggard face says clearly. His left arm has been injured. He holds it in a stiff and unnatural manner. Where in the tropics could an English doctor have seen such hardship and got his arm wounded? Clearly in Afghanistan."

Holmes informs Watson that the police inspectors Lestrade and Gregson are apt to consult him over difficult cases: the two men are "the pick of a bad lot. They are both quick and energetic, but conventional—shockingly so." In fact, it is Tobias Gregson who invites Holmes to Brixton to see the body of an American, Enoch J. Drebber, which has been found in an empty house. From this first story we find Holmes venting his sarcasm on the police. Disgusted at the way the path to the house has been trodden over by the force, he remarks with acid humour to Gregson, "With two such men as yourself and Lestrade upon the ground, there will not be much for a third party to find out." Later he interviews the policeman who found the body and cruelly informs him, "I am afraid, Rance, that you will never rise in the force. That head of yours should be of use as well as ornament."

Holmes later brings off a dazzling *coup de théâtre* as, before the two police inspectors' unsuspecting eyes, he captures the cab-driver murderer after having lured him to 221B Baker Street on the pretence of picking up a customer. The text then turns into a third-person narrative relating events dating back to 1847 in the American wilderness that have culminated in the revenge murder of Enoch J. Drebber in London. This stodgy, dispensable, and controversial representation of Mormon history occupies a full third of the text before Watson is allowed to continue his reminiscences, in which the murderer confesses to his work in London and Holmes explains how he reasoned out the case. The police take all the credit in the press for apprehending the criminal, but Watson promises to publish the true account and display Holmes's achievements.

Here then, in this very first story, are the Holmes/Watson relationship and the pattern for later stories fully established. Watson displays himself as a simple man, prepared to make a fool of himself (and tell stories against himself), slow to understand Holmes's methods and ever ready to forgive his shortcomings as a human being. Watson's ordinariness contrasts with Holmes's cold, intellectual near-infallibility.

A Study in Scarlet is important for giving us the only full description of Holmes.

> His very person and appearance were such as to strike the attention of the most casual observer. In height he was rather over six feet, and so excessively lean that he seemed to be considerably taller. His eyes were sharp and piercing . . . and his thin, hawk-like nose gave his whole expression an air of alertness and decision. His chin, too, had the prominence and squareness which mark the man of determination . . . he was possessed of extraordinary delicacy of touch. . . .

This description forms one basis for judging the success of the artists and actors who have shown us Sherlock Holmes. Of Watson, we know from Stamford's description that he is "thin as a lath and as brown as a nut," but of course, this thinness may be a temporary state attributable to his poor health. The story also provides the only description of the Baker Street rooms: "They consisted of a couple of comfortable bedrooms and a single large airy sitting-room, cheerfully furnished, and illuminated by two broad windows." (No mention of a bathroom is ever made in any of the Sherlock Holmes stories.) There are references to "the landlady", but she is not as yet identified as Mrs. Hudson.

The story is far less interesting than the characterization of Sherlock Holmes. It has some very awkward developments; it is hard, for instance, to accept that Holmes could be fooled by a young man dressed up as an old lady, or that the murderer returned to the same Baker Street address that his mysterious accomplice had earlier visited. And the Mormon flashback commonly ranks as the least favourite episode among devotees of the Sherlock Holmes stories.

Conan Doyle makes an odd acknowledgement to the inspiration provided by previous fictional detectives. He has Watson tell Holmes, "You remind me of Edgar Allan Poe's Dupin." But he then has Holmes dismiss Dupin as "a very inferior fellow," prompting Watson to ask his opinion of Emile Gaboriau's Monsieur Lecoq. Holmes is even more dismissive:

> Lecoq was a miserable bungler; he had only one thing to recommend him and that was his energy. That book made me positively ill. The question was how to identify an unknown prisoner. I could have done it in twenty-four hours. Lecoq took six months or so. It might be made a text-book for detectives to teach them what to avoid.

Of course, Holmes rarely had any respect for other detectives, but it does make a reader wonder whether Conan Doyle shared the same view. When in 1912 Arthur Guiterman published a poem chiding Conan Doyle for being less than candid over his indebtedness to Poe and Gaboriau, the reply, titled *To An Undiscerning Critic,* was wittily composed:

> He, the created, would scoff and would sneer,
> Where I, the creator, would bow and revere.
> So please grip this fact with your cerebral tentacle:
> The doll and its maker are never identical.

(pp. 13-15)

Allen Eyles, in his Sherlock Holmes: A Centenary Celebration, *Harper & Row, Publishers, 1986, 144 p.*

PIERRE NORDON

[In the following excerpt from his biographical and critical study, Conan Doyle, *Nordon examines the development of the character of Holmes, noting such influences as Doyle's medical professor Joseph Bell and the atmosphere of fin de siècle decadence in literary London of the late 1800s. Nordon also discusses fundamental characteristics common to all the Holmes stories. In unexcerpted portions of the volume, Nordon discusses the popularity of the Holmes stories with the reading public, the importance of Watson's role in the stories, and parallels between the lives of Doyle and Holmes.]*

Sherlock Holmes figures in sixty narratives: fifty-six short stories and four full-length novels. Nearly all of these were published in the *Strand Magazine* before being collected into separate volumes between 1891 and 1927. The first novel, *A Study in Scarlet,* appeared in 1887, and it is in this work we first meet the detective. We are given a precise but undetailed description of his character, and the qualities which distinguish Holmes from common mortals are barely hinted at. According to Dr. Watson: "In height he was rather over six feet, and so excessively thin that he seemed to be considerably taller. His eyes were sharp and piercing . . . his thin hawk-like nose gave his whole expression an air of alertness and decision. His chin too, had the prominence and squareness which mark the man of determination."

The very stylisation of this portrait draws our attention to the essential qualities of the amateur detective: his energy and the acuteness of his senses. (p. 203)

[Sherlock Holmes] is generally accepted as the prototype of the detective, and if influence can be taken as the test of worth, Conan Doyle has certainly left an indelible mark on the detective-story. He also supplied Sherlock Holmes with a decor and orchestration that have helped make him as proverbial a character as Don Juan or Robinson Crusoe. His name has become almost a by-word. (p. 205)

The remarkable popularity of Sherlock Holmes's exploits in the United States is a literary fact which must be emphasised. Their being written in English is not enough to account for it and we must look for justifying circumstances both inside and outside the works themselves. As will be shown later, they make a strong appeal to American historical sense; two of the longer stories, *A Study in Scarlet* and *The Valley of Fear* are set partly in the United States, at the time of the conquest of the West, and belong to the American literary myth of the period. The sources for these books were largely American. Also Conan Doyle's works appeared at a time when the curiosity of the American public about Great Britain had taken a new lease of life, and when American literature often presented England and the English for the benefit of trans-Atlantic readers. The Adventures of Holmes give a condensed, accessible, coherent and intelligible picture of English life. Just as Conan Doyle's historical novels give the reader a sense of security with their coherent picture of English history, so the picture of English society in the Holmes stories is for the American reader a mirror of the "Old Country." To these reasons relating to the internal structure of Conan Doyle's books we must add others, probably less obvious, which depend upon the social conditions in America between 1900 and 1940. During this period crime became an acute problem, and figured widely in literature, the drama and the cinema. It is significant that the detective-story proper, and novels with a detective element, are even more popular in the United States than in England. Sherlock Holmes's Adventures have therefore as much ideological value in the United States as in England. But one of the short novels, *The Valley of Fear,* has a special interest for Americans. In it Conan Doyle describes a mining settlement, the miners themselves and, by implication, their managers. We know from various historical works (such as Henry Fern's biography of Mackenzie King) that the miner's conditions of life in some of these settlements were deplorable. Yet in *The Valley of Fear* Conan Doyle gives us to understand that the management was good. In fact Sherlock Holmes intervenes on this side. We see here how the Adventures of Holmes gave ideological security to Americans as well as to English. (pp. 209-10)

The fact that the publication of Conan Doyle's first books coincided with progress in the science of criminology raised the question as to whether these could be cause and effect and if so to what degree. Conan Doyle's first novel was not exclusively concerned with detection, but he prepared the way by insisting on the value of observation and scientific methods. When Dr. Watson first meets Holmes, he finds him in the middle of a chemical experiment. Afterwards he gives a proof of his skill by instantly recognising the origin of a mud-stain. Little by little the investigator becomes an expert criminologist. This is something that distinguishes Holmes from earlier fictional detectives and has aroused the interest of real criminologists, with Edmond Locard of Lyons among the foremost. It may be true ... that Sherlock Holmes knew nothing of the advances made in identification by finger-prints between 1880 and 1900. Sherlock Holmes makes only slight use of this science in the story called "The Norwood Builder." It is also possible that although he pays homage to Bertillon, Conan Doyle had never studied his findings in anthropometry. This does not alter the fact that *The Adventures of Sherlock Holmes* has been actually used as a text-book for the instruction of detectives. Locard tells us that a medico-legal study of the book was made by the Faculty of Medicine at Lyons at the request of Bertillon himself, and probably its influence still goes on. The criminologist Ashton-Wolfe wrote [in the *Illustrated London News* of February 27, 1932]:

> Many of the methods invented by Conan Doyle are today in use in the scientific laboratories. Sherlock Holmes made the study of tobacco-ashes his hobby. It was a new idea, but the police at once realised the importance of such specialised knowledge, and now every laboratory has a complete set of tables giving the appearance and composition of the various ashes, which every detective must be able to recognise. Mud and soil from various districts are also classified much after the manner that Holmes described.... Conan Doyle made Holmes a complex personality: not only a tracker, but a logician and an analyst, and thus evolved and disseminated successfully the constructive method in use to-day in all Criminal Investigation Departments. Poisons, hand-writing, stains, dust, footprints, traces of wheels, the shape and position of wounds, and therefore the probable shape of the weapon which caused them; the theory of cryptograms, all these and many other excellent methods which germinated in Conan Doyle's fertile imagination are now part and parcel of every detective's scientific equipment.

Nearer the present day, the German cipher expert Sittig gives Sherlock Holmes's creator the credit for describing the technique he himself used to decipher Cretan inscriptions.

Such indications as these go to show how wide an influence, even outside the literary context, Sherlock Holmes has had on the world of today. (pp. 210-11)

The character of Sherlock Holmes did not emerge fully-fledged from Conan Doyle's imagination. When questioned about the origins of his detective, Sir Arthur claimed for him one literary ancestor, Edgar Allan Poe's Chevalier Dupin, and another from real life, Dr. Joseph Bell, professor of medicine at the University of Edinburgh. Dupin and Holmes certainly have an

extremely striking family resemblance, and much has been written on the subject. They are both self-proclaimed rationalists. Both have a habit of beginning to tackle their problems with a period of often abstract preliminary reflection, and their subtle methods of analysis lead to results which astonish their listeners. Both enjoy giving displays of virtuosity disconnected with the affair on hand. And we find in them both, though in Holmes more than in Dupin, that casual dilettantism which coloured a whole current of sensibility at the end of the last century in England. Was the resemblance deliberate on Conan Doyle's part? Probably it was, because before he had even chosen his detective's final name (he was still "Sherrinford Holmes") he had already referred to him as Dupin's successor: "Lecoq was a bungler. Dupin was better. Dupin was decidedly smart. His trick of following a train of thought was more sensational than clever, but still."...

Conan Doyle explained Poe's influence on his imagination by his vivid memories of reading him in childhood. But if there is no need to say more about a writer so well-known as Poe, what do we know about Dr. Joseph Bell, Conan Doyle's Edinburgh acquaintance?

When Conan Doyle began to study medicine, Bell was already a well-known character in Edinburgh medical circles. He was born there in 1837 and his whole professional life had been spent in the town, starting as a mere hospital attendant and ending as head of the medical school and professor in surgery. He was also editor of the Edinburgh Medical Journal and had a considerable reputation among the students. He certainly made a deep impression on the young Conan Doyle. When the Sherlock Holmes myth took shape there were plenty of inquisitive people wanting to know if he had taken his model from life. He mentioned the name of the Scottish doctor, who was surprised and flattered to find himself the object of such unexpected publicity, but politely denied having had anything to do with the creation of Sherlock Holmes:

> Dr. Conan Doyle's education as a student of medicine taught him to observe, and his practise, both as a general practitioner and a specialist, has been a splendid training for a man such as he is, gifted with eyes, memory and imagination.... If in addition the doctor is also a born story-teller, then it is a mere matter of choice whether he writes detective stories or keeps his strength for a great historical romance as in *The White Company*.
>
> (pp. 212-13)

Since Bell and Conan Doyle had been on friendly terms for a great many years, it is a pity that Sir Arthur has not left us a detailed portrait of the Scottish surgeon. But we only find one well-known anecdote in his autobiography:

> In one of his best cases he said to a civilian patient: "Well, my man, you've served in the army." "Aye, Sir." "Not long discharged?" "No, Sir." "A Highland regiment?" "Aye, Sir." "A non-com officer?" "Aye, Sir." "Stationed at Barbados?" "Aye, Sir." "You see, gentlemen," he would explain, "the man was a respectful man but did not remove his hat. They do not in the army, but he would have learned civilian ways had he been long discharged. He has an air of authority and he is obviously Scottish. As to Barbados, his com-

plaint is Elephantiasis, which is West Indian, not British.'' To his audience of Watsons it all seemed very miraculous until it was explained, and then it became simple enough.

This sketch of Joseph Bell takes us straight back to Sherlock Holmes. It is too like Holmes to be true. Conan Doyle never describes Bell in a way that allows us to distinguish him from his fictitious character; it is as if Bell only existed for him as the function of a literary illusion. Nor is it possible to ignore the fact that there is only one passage in all the Holmes stories [''The Yellow Face''] in which the detective is described as behaving like a surgeon in front of an audience of students: ''Holmes was turning the pipe about in his hand and staring at it in his peculiar pensive way. He held it up and tapped on it with his long, thin forefinger as a professor might who was lecturing on a bone.''

Are we not then justified in suspecting that Conan Doyle's portrait of Bell was not entirely accurate? Or rather, can this portrait perhaps have been an artifice designed to strengthen the illusion that Holmes really existed, as a member of the Holmes-Watson partnership in the stories? How are we to discover whether Conan Doyle was aware of his own quasi-professional distortion of the old professor's portrait? It is certainly not impossible that Bell had some part in the birth of the Holmes cycle. Sir Arthur's anecdote about the surgeon bears the stamp of truth, and is a good example of what Sherlock liked to call his ''method.'' But it tells us less about Dr. Bell's particular mental gifts than about his ingenuity in showing them off to the best advantage, just as Sherlock Holmes liked to do. Even admitting that his memories of Bell were crystallized in the character of the detective, this idea of a formal dialogue controlled by the questioner was not original. It is found in early scientific writing, and Poe's Chevalier Dupin also amuses himself by reading the secret thoughts of the person he is talking to.

The inductive method, too, works on the same principle: observations lead to reconstructing the events connected with them. This method is used by such widely different writers as Defoe, Beaumarchais, Voltaire, Fenimore Cooper, to mention just a few. In his autobiography Conan Doyle tells us how he tried to imagine Bell as a detective: ''If he were a detective he would surely reduce this fascinating but unorganised business to something nearer to an exact science. I would try if I could get this effect.''

Baker Street, 1910.

Thus scientific prestige on the one hand and poetic realism on the other made it essential that a model for Sherlock Holmes should be found *a posteriori,* and that that model should be a man of science. We have very little idea what sort of man Joseph Bell really was, for Sherlock Holmes has blurred his outlines. While still a student, and before he had met Bell, the young Conan Doyle had probably begun inventing a rather vague imaginary character; then, when once he had fallen under the spell of his professor's personality, he found it intervening and filling out the details of his fictitious creation. To this extent perhaps it is true to say that Holmes reflects something of Dr. Bell's character. (pp. 213-15)

All the same, if he had not been linked with the collective consciousness and the sensibility of his readers, if he had not been in harmony with the ideological climate of the day, Sherlock Holmes would never have become an integral part of civilisation, as he is today. In so far as that climate impregnated Conan Doyle's ego, Sherlock represents that ego. And how could we identify ourselves with the hero if he did not emerge from the stories with sufficient consistency and a convincing enough individuality? Before making an inventory of the psychological contents of his character, we must first approach it from the periphery: contents is the appropriate word, because Sherlock Holmes was at first a mere outline, a type, a shape, an abstraction, before ever he developed a more complex interior and really began to exist. It seems as though Conan Doyle had always had two quite distinct images of Holmes in mind. Technically speaking, he is the ''detective''—that is part of the mechanism of the plot. Before being placed in ''a situation'' he has to ''function''; but no aesthetic value necessarily attaches to this functional aspect. Hamlet would not have been Hamlet if he were simply an avenger. It is probably because they have been unable to go further than Conan Doyle in giving their characters inner life, that subsequent detective-writers have so rarely succeeded in creating an original or convincing detective who is not a copy of Holmes. But Sherlock Holmes has another aspect, at first sight somewhat disconcerting and at odds with his essential function, but clearly important to his creator for it is already apparent in ''Sherrinford Holmes,'' the first sketch for Sherlock: ''a sleepy-eyed young man—philosopher—collector of rare violins. An Amati. . . .''

This psychological dualism is not found in Poe's Dupin; it harks back to a *fin de siècle* dandyism, first connected with a detective by Stevenson in ''The Dynamiter,'' a work written shortly before the appearance of Conan Doyle's hero:

> ''Do you then propose, dear boy, that we should turn detective?'' enquired Challoner.
>
> ''Do you propose it? No, Sir,'' cried Somerset. ''It is reason, destiny, the plain face of the world, that commands and imposes it. Here, all our merits tell; our manners, habits of the world, powers of conversation, vast stores of unconnected knowledge, all that we are and have builds up a character of a complete detective. It is, in short, the only profession for a gentleman.''

With perspicacious humour, Stevenson here clearly suggests a relationship between the detective as a social type and a middle-class ideology concerned with dignity, security and liberalism.

But in all the portraits of Holmes in the Adventures, this dualism is manifest—these two basic systems are always in opposition. Quite early on in the stories, we come across frequent comparisons of the detective to a fox-hound: "I was irresistibly reminded of a pure-blooded, well-trained foxhound as it dashes backwards and forwards through the covert, whining in its eagerness, until it comes across the lost scent."

Why a fox-hound? Because it calls up an image of exactly that controlled alertness which should be second nature to a detective in Holmes's own view, and also the most traditional of English sports—for we must not forget that Holmes is a gentleman. The metaphor emphasises the functional side of his character, and, by its allusion to hunting, that he belongs to the upper class. The fox-hound image seems so to have obsessed the narrator, that if he, or rather Watson, is to be believed, Holmes becomes almost literally metamorphosed, when is is in his own element, or his own field of action:

> Sherlock Holmes was transformed when he was hot upon such a scent as this. Men who had only known the quiet thinker and logician of Baker Street would have failed to recognize him. His face flushed and darkened. His brows were drawn into two hard, black lines, while his eyes shone out from beneath them with a steely glitter. His face was bent downwards, his shoulders bowed, his lips compressed, and the veins stood out like whip-cord in his long, sinewy neck. His nostrils seemed to dilate with a purely animal lust for the chase, and his mind was so absolutely concentrated upon the matter before him, that a question or remark fell unheeded upon his ears, or at the most only provoked a quick, impatient snarl in reply ["The Boscombe Valley Mystery"].

Here we see a man transformed with all speed into a fox-hound before our very eyes, until he seems almost to have lost the power of speech and be reduced to expressing himself by sounds. But the fox-hound motif recurs insistently: "Holmes hunted about among the grass and leaves like a retriever after a wounded bird." "See the fox-hound with hanging ears and drooping tail as it lolls about the kennels and compare it with the same hound as, with gleaming eyes and straining muscles, it runs upon a breast-high scent!—such was the change in Holmes since the morning." "In an instant he was tense and alert, his eyes shining, his face set, his limbs quivering with eager activity. He was out on the lawn, in through the window, round the room, and up into the bedroom, for all the world, like a dashing fox-hound drawing a cover. . . . Then he rushed down the stair, out through the open window, threw himself upon his face on the lawn, sprang up and ran into the room once more, all with the energy of the hunter who is at the very heels of his quarry."

In contrast to this imaginary and almost stereotyped vision of Holmes in action, or as a countryman, we have Holmes the Londoner. Here is a personality as entirely different as is Doctor Jekyll from Mr. Hyde—an absent-minded, taciturn, disturbing morphia-addict who is also a rather Bohemian, fastidious, sceptical music-lover. It is not so much a contrast between two aspects of the same person as one between two ways of life and modes of consciousness, the first sensitive and impressionable, the second intellectual. And this very coexistence of two antithetical sides to Sherlock Holmes's character is essential to his status as a hero:

> My friend was an enthusiastic musician, being himself not only a very capable performer, but a composer of no ordinary merit. All the af-

ternoon he sat in the stalls wrapped in the most perfect happiness, gently waving his long thin fingers in time to the music, while his gently smiling face and his languid, dreamy eyes were as unlike those of Holmes the sleuth-hound, Holmes the relentless, keen-witted, ready-handed criminal agent, as it was possible to conceive. In his singular character the dual nature alternately asserted itself, and his extreme exactness and astuteness represented, as I have often thought, the reaction against the poetic and contemplative mood which occasionally predominated in him ["The Red-Headed League"].

The picture of Holmes in his room in Baker Street, lying propped among a heap of cushions, with clouds of tobacco smoke rising through the dimness, evokes the characteristic pose of the "decadents." Cushions, tobacco—Holmes needs a special sort of environment and special stimulants in order to think; and he is a creative as well as an analytic thinker, as we shall have occasion to show. His addiction to morphine and cocaine (disapproved of by Watson) and to tobacco (which he tolerated) are the only links connecting him with the romantic idea of the artist, the decadent poet. It is easy for Watson, as a doctor, to trace the effects of narcotics in his friend's gaze—a gaze which clearly expresses Holmes's two modes of mental functioning, the extrovert and sensory, and the purely speculative. When he is under the influence of narcotics, Watson finds him even more mysterious than usual. As soon as he sees that dreamy look in Holmes's eyes, suspicions are aroused that were first hinted at in *A Study in Scarlet*:

> For days on end he would lie upon the sofa in the sitting-room, hardly uttering a word or moving a muscle from morning to night. On these occasions I have noticed such a dreamy, vacant expression in his eyes, that I might have suspected him of being addicted to the use of some narcotic, had not the temperance and cleanliness of his whole life forbidden such a notion.

Holmes's gaze, so faithfully rendered by Sidney Paget, soon becomes one of his most striking characteristics, indispensable to our image of his personality: "Holmes sat in his big armchair, with the weary, heavy-lidded expression which veiled his keen and eager nature."

As for the objects with which he surrounds himself in his Baker Street rooms, they tell us as much about him as clues do about a criminal, emphasising his interest in science and crime, and suggesting the intimate and endearing side of Watson's hero in terms that are sometimes not far from caricature:

> The rough-and-tumble work in Afghanistan, coming on top of a natural Bohemianism of disposition, has made me rather more lax than befits a medical man. But with me there is a limit, and when I find a man who keeps his cigars in the coal-scuttle, his tobacco in the toe-end of a Persian slipper, and his unanswered correspondence transfixed by a jack-knife into the very centre of his wooden mantelpiece, then I begin to give myself virtuous airs ["The Musgrave Ritual"].

Of all the objects associated with Holmes, the most familiar is of course his pipe. Is that because he prefers it to a cigar? No: it seems to mean more to him than a mere means of absorbing tobacco. It is, above all, the companion of his long, studious nights. (pp. 215-19)

The pipe is a necessary adjunct to his spells of thought, measuring their duration by the time taken to smoke a pipeful of tobacco.

> "What are you going to do then?" I asked.
>
> "To smoke," he answered. It is quite a three-pipe problem, and I beg that you won't speak to me for fifty minutes" ["The Red-Headed League"].

Thus Holmes's simple outline developed a certain number of clear and unforgettable features. . . . (p. 219)

However, neither of these two aspects of this outline are so much heroic, in the true sense of the word, as picturesque and remarkable. Homes's vocation as a fictional character, willed and designed by his creator, destines him to follow a certain career and play a certain part, even though the stages and episodes in it are only potential. He must therefore possess a certain number of attributes, and his figure must be set against an aesthetic or ethical background which brings out its essentially heroic quality, independent of the heroism of the adventures themselves.

One of these is his herculean strength, whether of muscle or endurance. We see Holmes being engaged as a stable-boy in order to get information about Irene Adler, and verifying a hypothesis with a harpoon. We see him twisting a poker in his powerful hands, and intimidating enormous men; and in *The Sign of Four* a professional boxer greets him as a colleague and regrets that he never became a pugilist. He is probably not addicted to any one sport (how could he possibly find time?) nor to any form of physical training; yet the drain upon his energies involved in the investigations in *The Hound of the Baskervilles* and "The Final Problem" is never too much for his strength. The opening of "The Reigate Squires" gives Watson the chance to talk of his friend's "iron constitution," which "however had broken down under the strain of an investigation which had extended over two months, during which period he had never worked less than fifteen hours a day, and had more than once, as he assured me, kept to his task for five days at a stretch."

Holmes's physical energy is backed up by his quite exceptional acuteness of the senses. His sensitive ear, which partly explains his love of music, enables him always to be the first to detect the approach of some criminal for whom he and Watson are lying in wait. In "A Scandal in Bohemia" he recognises the disguised voice of Irene Adler wishing him a rapid and ironical good-night, even though it is only slightly familiar to him. But his piercing sight is his most precious possession. From tobacco-ash to mud-stains, there is nothing he cannot identify, read and decipher with speed.

His deductions from objects in the Adventures are not always vital to the investigation. But their very superfluity only emphasises how superior Holmes is to the task he is carrying out and the society he has chosen to serve, and reveal his natural brilliance as a detective to every observer. They also contribute to the popularity of the Adventures, by turning them into a sort of parlour game. This aspect of the Holmes stories is not incompatible with their epic quality. Heroes start a fashion:

Holmes has as many eager imitators as Robinson Crusoe. Even in the text itself Sherlock is imitated by his brother Mycroft or by Dr. Watson, with varying degrees of success. Holmes invariably exercises his powers of deduction on commonplace objects. A hat in "The Blue Carbuncle" leads him to hazard a good many opinions about the health, age, habits and character of its owner, as well as his financial and family situation. In "The Yellow Face" he "reads" a pipe and in "The Golden Pince-nez" a pair of pince-nez, by means of which he is able to give an accurate description of an unknown man and woman— what modern detectives call an identikit. *The Hound of the Baskervilles* begins with his "reading" Dr. Mortimer's walking-stick, and this leads on to a playful dialogue of five pages in the course of which Holmes and Watson analyse the object according to the rules of the "method."

More often than not, it is the Doctor who gives his friend opportunities to display his deductive skill. In *The Sign of Four,* Watson's watch is the point of departure for a description of his deceased brother. In "The Stockbroker's Clerk" the detective takes a look at his friend's slippers. He notices that although they are new the soles have been slightly scorched. Did Watson perhaps get them wet and then put them in front of the fire? No, because in that case the label near the instep would have come unstuck from the damp. Watson must therefore have been sitting close to the fire, and since it is midsummer, it is obvious that he has had a cold. At the beginning of "The Crooked Man," Holmes deduces, from Watson's boots, that his patients are keeping him very busy and, also from his boots, in "The Disappearance of Lady Frances Carfax" that he has been to a Turkish bath. "Reading" objects and clothes is often merely a branch of "reading" their owners. The numerous instances to be found in *A Study in Scarlet* follow much the same plan as the anecdote about Joseph Bell quoted above. Holmes's first words to Watson after they are introduced come straight from the scene when Bell deduced that his patient was a veteran from Barbados: "You have been in Afghanistan, I perceive." An incident a little further on, where he identifies a commissionaire as an ex-sergeant of Marines, is a variation on the same theme. With "A Case of Identity" we gradually move on a little, and it is the profession of his client, Miss Mary Sutherland, that the detective spots at first sight. But Sherlock Holmes's most spectacular deduction makes the person concerned faint, because it brings back the memory of his troubled and threatening past.

Like the Chevalier Dupin, Holmes practises reading other people's thoughts, and here again Watson is very useful to him: " 'So, Watson,' said he suddenly, 'you do not propose to invest in South African securities?' " Afterwards he reveals his train of reasoning in six sentences. In another passage he guesses that Watson is speculating about the consequences of the American Civil War.

His deductions lead Holmes to make revelations which appear almost magical. And his fondness for doing chemical experiments adds to the air of mystery surrounding him. Watson tries to explain Holmes's two-sided nature in rational and intelligible terms: ". . . his extreme exactness and astuteness represented, as I have often thought, the reaction against the poetic and contemplative mood which occasionally predominated in him." But he soon gives up this theory and declares that his friend is superhuman, "a man whose knowledge was not that of other mortals."

It is clear that Watson is not thinking of the range of his knowledge so much as of his means of acquiring it. After all, the detective has confided his ambitions to him. Holmes's desire for power takes the form of a desire for knowledge. Like Le Sage's Asmodée he conjures up a view of the great city which is the field of operations assigned to him:

> If we could fly out of that window hand in hand, hover over this great city, gently remove the roofs, and peep in at the queer things which are going on, the strange coincidences, the plannings, the cross-purposes, the wonderful chains of events, working through generations, and leading to the most *outré* results, it would make all fiction with its conventionalities and foreseen conclusions most stale and unprofitable ["A Case of Identity"].

Although this dream is impossible to realise, Holmes has nevertheless travelled widely in the course of his career, not only in Europe but also in Asia, especially Tibet. This touch of the exotic in him, together with what might be called his Byronic side, helps convince us of his world-wide reputation and intimate knowledge of international criminal circles—an important point, because the first of the Holmes stories refers to similar cases with which Holmes was familiar when Watson got to know him: "There was the case of Von Bischoff at Frankfort last year. He would certainly have been hung had this test been in existence. There was Mason of Bradford, and the notorious Muller, and Lefevre of Montpellier, and Samson of New Orleans. I could name a score of cases in which it would have been decisive." (pp. 220-23)

His travels, his reading, his tastes have all helped him acquire those "vast stores of unconnected knowledge" described by Stevenson's character Somerset as being indispensable to "a complete detective." A brilliant talker when opportunity offers, he dazzles Dr. Watson just as much by his erudition as by his descriptions of travels in far countries:

> Our meal was a merry one. Holmes could talk exceedingly well when he chose, and that night he did choose. He appeared to be in a state of nervous exaltation. I have never known him so brilliant. He spoke on a quick succession of subjects—on miracle plays, on mediaeval pottery, on Stradivarius violins, on the Buddhism of Ceylon, and on the warships of the future—handling each as though he had made a special study of it [*The Sign of Four*].

Thus, while giving expression to the two chief trends of his creator's mind—his need for action and his need to dream—Sherlock Holmes developed a personality which roused a thrill of response in the latent romanticism of the reading public. (p. 223)

The adventures of Sherlock Holmes are separated sharply from the rest of Sir Arthur Conan Doyle's very varied output by the great social and literary success his detective achieved. The distinction has gradually been accepted both by public and publishers, and today no one would be likely to confuse an extract from one of the Holmes stories with a passage from any of the other books. Yet it is a distinction that has resulted from circumstances. Conan Doyle must have been unconscious of it when he was writing the first of the Sherlock Holmes stories, *A Study in Scarlet*, nor could he for a moment have imagined that fifty-nine other stories were to follow. So that what today seems to us a cycle or a saga, was not deliberately planned. When later on he spoke of the first of his Sherlock

Holmes stories, Conan Doyle made no attempt to attribute revolutionary significance to it *a posteriori*. *A Study in Scarlet* was just another new book: "I felt now that I was capable of something fresher and crisper and more workmanlike," he tells us in his autobiography. (p. 224)

How can one sum up the sources of the Sherlock Holmes Adventures? The formula he used to make them suitable for a magazine resulted in a success he had never dreamed of, nor even perhaps desired. As the cycle grew he came under more and more pressure from his own creation, and for a great many years the thread on which his days were strung was tightened by the fact that his imagination was caught in a trap. The intimacy this wove between the author and this series of stories during nearly forty years, gave them very visible organic unity. Technically speaking, the need for the plots to be as short and lucid as possible helped to build up the character of Holmes—the central point where all the threads met. (p. 237)

Every novel in which police and detectives play an important part is not necessarily a detective-story. One might mention works as different from each other as *Moll Flanders, Les Misérables, Crime and Punishment, Le Procès, Sanctuary* and a great many more. What is it about the Sherlock Holmes stories that makes them so typical of detective fiction? Firstly, it would seem, that everything to do with the investigation is given primary importance, to the detriment of the rest of the action and descriptions of persons and places. Also that in the detective story in general, and the Sherlock Holmes cycle in particular, time factors, characters and plot are controlled by aesthetic considerations belonging more to the domain of the theatre than the novel. We have to do with several hundred characters, almost all of whom appear in only one of the stories. What they are and what they do only interests us in so far as it concerns the hero. . . . [Whatever] their status in the action, whether the plot requires them to be princes or pariahs, they are technically speaking mere satellites. They fall into two groups or camps, according as to whether the hero is on their side or against them—a dualism that inevitably results in an almost Manichaean simplification of their psychological make-up. To know all is to forgive all: but criminals cannot be allowed to justify their crimes, the plot requires them to remain as they are. All that is necessary is to attribute their actions to one of the two motive forces to which all behaviour can be reduced—love or gain.

Let us consider the whole cycle of fifty-six short and four long stories, disregarding the distinction between innocent and guilty. In twenty of them either the central or subsidiary action depends on a love affair. Among eight murders motivated by jealousy, the rival is the victim in six and the unfaithful spouse in two. In these two last, one of the murderers is the husband "The Retired Colourman" and one the jilted fiancée "The Musgrave Ritual"; but the crime of passion plays only a secondary part in the plots. In only one story, "The Abbey Grange," do we find a drama of jealousy of the traditional type, and the victim is presented in such an unfavourable light that Sherlock Holmes allows the criminal to escape from justice.

If we examine these twenty plots we find that it is generally the victims who are involved in love affairs, whereas the criminals are invariably inspired by more sordid motives. We see from this that love is treated extremely unrealistically, never losing its pure and even sacred character, and in one case it is allowed to triumph over the law of the land. It must not therefore dominate the action. More often than not, whenever the plot seems to hinge upon a love affair, the final explanation

The Strand Magazine, *1891*.

accent, or are too episodic in character to create a macabre atmosphere. It is rare to find Holmes's investigations beginning with a bloody crime. Only seven stories start with a murder; the story called "Thor Bridge" seems to be an eighth but in reality is not.

Holmes's task is not therefore always to unmask or arrest a murderer. Very often the problems he is given to solve are nearer comedy than tragedy. Perhaps this is why Sherlock Holmes is so ready to describe them as "grotesque"—by which he means tragicomic. For instance the criminal may use a deliberate confusion of identity to achieve his ends: someone is forced to play the part of victim "The Copper Beeches, Shoscombe Old Place," or else the criminal passes himself off as the victim "A Case of Identity, The Man with the Twisted Lip, The Stockbroker's Clerk, The Norwood Builder" and deceives the reader, as well as Holmes and Watson. Or the detective may be asked to find a valuable piece of jewelry or a stolen document. But whether it is a question of finding insufficiently well guarded State secrets "The Naval Treaty, The Second Stain, The Bruce-Partington Plans" or of acting for private individuals, we find ourselves accompanying Holmes on a treasure-hunt that is exciting rather than really dangerous.

The unexpected appearance of someone after a long absence in a remote country is a specifically theatrical device, and Shakespeare, Molière, Racine and Beaumarchais among others have accustomed us to it. Whether he is the criminal, an inconvenient witness, or a redresser of wrongs, this individual is always a "skeleton in the cupboard" for the other characters, and the *deus ex machina* of the story. It will be noticed how frequently this theme occurs in the stories published between 1900 and 1910, when the author was having to make an effort to renew the series, and most of all in the *Return* stories, the first of which brings the detective once more on the scene. Perhaps it is too convenient a contrivance to satisfy aesthetic principles, but it at least allows Conan Doyle to conjure up an exotic and romantic background and give the Holmes cycle its epic quality.

The mysterious confines of the criminal world sometimes contain secret societies, whose activities do not escape Sherlock Holmes's vigilance, and introduce a disturbing note, as also do the cases of kidnapping he exposes in the course of his investigations. The criminal may perhaps want to get by force the services of someone with a particular skill ("The Engineer's Thumb, The Greek Interpreter"), or conceal the victim of some infirmity from inquisitive eyes ("The Yellow Face, The Blanched Soldier"). And there are five stories in which a guilty or innocent person tries to remain hidden or else pass for dead. Critics have amused themselves by pointing out the classical treatment of plots and situations; with this we find an atmosphere belonging more to the theatre than to the novel. It is hardly surprising that within the very narrow scope of these plots, Conan Doyle has only rarely introduced a sub-plot; but with the exception of "The Musgrave Ritual" (perhaps the most successful and characteristic of all the stories) when he does so this second plot spoils the balance. He nearly always preserves the unity of action, and this does not interfere with the intricacies of the plot, but facilitates them. Since these involve Holmes's adversaries as well as himself, an apparent equilibrium is maintained between the different forces in play. To destroy this equilibrium long before the *dénouement* would be to deprive it of all tension and therefore of interest.

The simplest stratagem used by Holmes is disguise. Dr. Watson, who is taken in every time, insists that his friend is a

brings more sordid motives to light. However there is one story, "The Missing Three-Quarter," in which exactly the opposite happens, and any reader familiar with the previous stories is as much surprised as the author evidently intended him to be.

The great majority of Holmes's adversaries are in complete control of their emotions, perfectly aware of what they are doing and therefore responsible; at least this is so in all the stories written before 1910. They represent the most formidable threat to the safe and well-organized class who profited from the established order in Great Britain before the First World War—the threat to property. Sometimes they are ordinary burglars, counterfeiters, or treasure-seekers; sometimes blackmailers, hired thieves or swindlers. It is not surprising that such characters as these should often have scores to settle among themselves, nor that three of the novels and nineteen of the Adventures should centre round the essentially dramatic theme of revenge.

The cycle is concerned with crimes of blood, but we never have to face unbearable scenes of slaughter, nor do we come across those "chain" murders so commonly found in detective-stories written after 1930. Some of the stories even make do without a corpse. Among the twelve stories of the first series of Adventures, nine contain no bloodthirsty crime at all. It is true that they become more common in the later stories, figuring in nine out of eleven stories in the *Memoirs* and ten out of thirteen in the *Return*. But the murders are used to give gifted actor with a talent for changing his walk or tone of voice. Holmes's love of disguise and stage-production even leads him to use a wax image of himself as a bait. But other characters in the stories share his taste for disguise. Some of his enemies use camouflage of a different sort, for instance in "Silver Blaze." Hiding-places also play an important part in their plans, and so sometimes do houses that have been faked, rather like boxes with double bottoms. Holmes never hesitates to fight his adversaries with their own weapons, force his way into a private house in disguise, or arrange a false alarm with or without the help of the official police ("Scandal in Bohemia, **The Norwood Builder**"). If the criminals set a trap to get him out of the way, Holmes and his devoted friend Watson divert their suspicions by pretending to follow the false trail. His sense of artistic perfection makes him aim at ingenious or spectacular *dénouements* ("The Dancing Men"), or indulge in the innocent pleasure of mystifying his own clients. The *dénouements* are particularly dramatic, and all with two exceptions ("The Yellow Face" and "The Missing Three-Quarter") turn out favourably for Holmes.

The aesthetics of the Holmesian cycle have the same advantages and disadvantages as those of the theatre. The psychological field is strictly limited, but situations and incidents can be exploited by good organisation and balance. A writer like Chesterton may have greater aesthetic subtlety, but whatever the merits of his detective-stories they have not the formal perfection we find in Conan Doyle. The danger of the theatrical treatment is that it may end in melodrama or *grand guignol*. It must be admitted that some of his *dénouements* are not free from melodrama—those of "The Yellow Face" or "The Beryl Coronet" for instance—but this is exceptional. As for *grand guignol*, it is hardly apparent in the stories written before 1910, which contain few scenes of horror, and those strictly subordinated to the needs of the action. However, after 1910 this element becomes much more common; the last fifteen stories are different from the rest both in their atmosphere and the part Sherlock Holmes plays in them.

In contrast to the problems in the earlier stories, we now find some actually morbid ingredient in the plots: for instance, a disease having all the appearance of leprosy ("The Blanched Soldier"), a case of mental abnormality in a child ("The Sussex Vampire"), a fantastic physical mutation of a Jekyll and Hyde description ("The Creeping Man"), a horrible mutilation ("The Veiled Lodger"). Some of the other Adventures are burdened with scenes of violence quite disconnected with the action. More or less imaginary poisons are used in some of the murder stories, and there are scenes involving gruesome discoveries. Conan Doyle only returns to his normal manner in the novel *The Valley of Fear* and the story of "Thor Bridge," the investigation develops in a similar way in both of these, and ends with the discovery of important evidence in a moat and a lake. Except for these two, the detection has lost some of its dramatic tension, the incidents are shorter and less numerous. The analysis is generally longer however, and in four of the stories Dr. Watson is no longer the narrator. We leave the glare of the footlights and move into a region of disturbing semi-obscurity, with something of the atmosphere of modern science-fiction about it. Holmes's personality suffers from these developments. He now gives us the impression of being a passive witness of events, rather than dominating and directing them. Henceforth we do not feel sure of his omnipotence. Of course he has sometimes been outwitted before ("Scandal in Bohemia, The Missing Three-Quarter"), but at least he did not then give the impression of having lost the initiative.

The plots of some of the final stories of the cycle are so paradoxical that he is obliged to be relatively inactive. In "Shoscombe Old Place" and "Thor Bridge," for instance, though there are apparently two murders to be solved, they in fact turn out to be natural death and suicide. The situation in "The Three Gables" corresponds with that of the first story of all, "Scandal in Bohemia," but Sherlock Holmes's role is reversed. Instead of being commissioned to find papers which would compromise his client, he is asked to forestall a burglary organised by an adventuress, far less attractive and alive than Irene Adler, in search of a document incriminating her. Moreover the story is bathed in an extremely changeable atmosphere, at times almost scabrous, at others frankly improbable. It is as if Sherlock Holmes's dwindling stature had thrown the story out of balance, with the result that these last stories do not have the eminently reassuring quality his resplendent presence conferred on the Adventures of the great period. (pp. 237-42)

> *Pierre Nordon, in his* Conan Doyle, *translated by Frances Partridge, John Murray, 1966, 370 p.*

GRAHAM NOWN

[*In the following excerpt, Nown analyzes the temperament, personality, and character of Sherlock Holmes, relying on evidence drawn directly, rather than inferred, from the stories.*]

Eighteen hundred and fifty four was a very good year for Holmes readers. So, too, were 1852, 1853 and 1855; while others prefer 1857, 1858 and 1867—all years in which students of the great investigator have pinpointed his birth. The precise location is another problem. Yorkshire's North Riding is the unanimous favourite, but some claim that he originates from Surrey (a theory prompted by his passing interest in newspaper county cricket scores), though Holmes seems far too outspoken for a Home Counties man. . . .

There have been many determined efforts to establish his genealogy and early life, most of them a heady mix of inspired juxtaposition, clever assumption and guesswork. Like all the better Holmesian research, it is artfully provocative stuff. . . .

Theories tumble with wit and erudition, arrogance and wild assumption, in attempts to clothe the world's most famous detective with greater reality than even Conan Doyle could muster. (p. 51)

Holmes as a young man was a reclusive individual. During two years at college, he tells Watson in "The Gloria Scott," he made only one friend, Victor Trevor.

> "I was never a very sociable fellow, always
> rather fond of moping in my rooms and working
> out my own little methods of thought, so that
> I never mixed much with the men of my year."

He was too preoccupied to be lonely, and took part in boxing and fencing, but was in need of understanding friends. Throughout his life Holmes rarely made time for small talk or cultivated acquaintances. He developed a long list of contacts for work, but his private circle remained small.

His sparse social life at college can be blamed partly on his course, which is never specifically mentioned in the stories: "My line of study was quite distinct from that of the other fellows, so that we had no points of contact at all." (pp. 51-2)

Inevitably, constant exposure to human weakness and the grimy side of life began to affect him, clouding his outlook but stopping short of obscuring his judgment. The burden of being the unsung arbiter of justice was to lose any enjoyment for the simplicities of life. Where others saw beauty, Holmes saw vulnerability. The spectre of crime hung everywhere, like the exorcist who sees evil where none yet exists.

"Do you know, Watson," he says rather bleakly in "The Copper Beeches," "it is one of the curses of a mind with a turn like mine that I must look at everything with reference to my own special subject. You look at these scattered houses, and you are impressed by their beauty. I look at them and the only thought which comes to me is a feeling of their isolation, and of the impunity with which crime may be committed there." Lesser men, unable to separate their line of work from relaxation, have suffered mental breakdowns, but Holmes was made of stronger stuff.

The pressure of constantly outwitting greed and criminal ingenuity might build up until he felt inclined to seize a ruffian by the lapels, but normally he disguised his emotions well. When his anger did boil to the surface there were undertones of violence. Holmes flushed with fury at the thought of James Windibank escaping justice in "A Case of Identity": "By Jove! It is not part of my duties to my client, but here's a hunting-crop handy, and I think I shall just treat myself to." . . . The unpleasant Mr. Windibank wisely took to his heels. In different circumstances he could turn his feelings to the cutting sleight. Even the King of Bohemia was not above the Holmes cold shoulder. "He bowed and turning away without observing the hand which the King had stretched out to him, he set off in my company to his chambers," Watson recorded.

Holmes's bizarre life left no room for romance. The Work was his mistress, dictating his moods and inspiration; without it he sank into boredom and the refuge of cocaine. Casework was his real drug, transporting him in bursts of energy to intellectual euphoria. When the great mind was at full stretch everything and everyone—including those who came to him for help—became secondary. "The status of my client is a matter of less moment to me than the interest of his case," he firmly declared in "The Noble Bachelor." (pp. 52-3)

Admittedly [Holmes's] behaviour veers towards the absurd at times, but Doyle always managed to keep a rein on his credibility.

Holmes's rural beginnings moulded him less than the tough realities of urban life. Like dozens of later fictional heroes he was the quintessential city detective, at home in dim dockland alleys or the palatial splendour of Belgravia. Despite being the first in a profession preoccupied with earning a living, money was of little consideration. Hunger for knowledge—whether bent over test tubes seeking new directions in forensic science, or scrutinizing people—drove him along. Yet, in his fascination with the small points of appearance, the details of gesture and speech, he missed the richness of relationships. The art of deduction reduced everyone he met to the level of a litmus held up to the light. Watson, in one of his rare flashes of perception, saw his friend, in "The Greek Interpreter," as "a brain without a heart, as deficient in human sympathy as he was pre-eminent in intelligence," which was also Doyle's view entirely.

Holmes was an emotional defective by choice, not circumstance. It would be tempting to feel sympathetic with a man whose pursuit of high ideals somehow left him sadly lacking, if it were not for the fact that he systematically suppressed and excluded all traces of emotion. "The emotional qualities are

antagonistic to clear reasoning," he stated with cold conviction in *The Sign of Four*. His reverence for reason and pursuit of logic made him a difficult companion—secretive, moody and with a humour which bordered on false heartiness. Perhaps only the well-adjusted and long-suffering Watson could have put up with him.

He was not without sensitivity, coaxing melancholy chords from his Stradivarius or relaxing with his rare books. This, perhaps, was a glimpse of the real Holmes, the human face which emerged only behind the closed doors of Baker Street. On one occasion the feelings he struggled hard to sublimate surfaced in public, to the amazement of onlookers. Lost in thought in "The Naval Treaty," he holds up a rose and tells those around him:

> "Our highest assurance of the goodness of Providence seems to me to rest in the flowers. All other things, our powers, our desires, our food are really necessary for our existence in the first instance. But this rose is an extra. . . . It is only goodness which gives extras." . . .

Whether Conan Doyle wrote this with a hint of a smile, we shall never know.

Women would certainly have found prolonged exposure to the great detective insufferable. As an investigator he had a healthy respect for their intuition, but he remained uncomfortable and reserved when dealing with them. Holmes was out of his element with the opposite sex. Intellectual achievement was clearly no help in such matters; spontaneity and emotional depth left him much to puzzle over. "Their most trivial action may mean volumes, or their most extraordinary conduct may depend upon a hair-pin or curling-tongs," he pondered in "The Second Stain."

He has all the appearance of a misogynist, but it is kinder to suppose that he was one of that rare and all-but-extinct breed, The Great British Bachelor. Holmes the consulting detective could turn on the professional charm to reassure a distressed client. Miss Stoner confesses her terror to him in "The Speckled Band," raising her veil to reveal "a state of pitiable agitation."

" 'You must not fear,' said he soothingly, bending forward and patting her forearm. 'We shall soon set matters right, I have no doubt.' "

As the accomplished actor and master of disguise he could slip into any part, even that of the seducer, with ease. In the case of "Charles Augustus Milverton," "the worst man in all London," Holmes dressed as a self-employed plumber in order to obtain information from Milverton's housemaid. Safely back in Baker Street he removed his disguise, sat by the fire and "laughed heartily in his silent, inward fashion," perhaps as much in surprise at his conquest as at the success of his ruse. Milverton was undoubtedly a bad egg and an unmitigated bounder, but Holmes carried his role beyond professional requirements and, astonishingly, proposed to her.

"Surely you have gone too far," cries Watson in alarm.

"It was a most necessary step," Holmes claims barely able to conceal his pleasure. "I have walked out with her each evening, and I have talked with her. Good heavens, those talks! However, I have got all I wanted." . . .

Holmes was, of course, referring solely to evidence gleaned in the course of duty, but the encounter certainly perked his sometimes jaded spirits.

He was aware of the strength of his passions. In "The Devil's Foot" he confesses that he has never been in love. But if he had, he says, and the woman he loved had been poisoned like the victim of the story, he would have gone to any length to seek revenge.

On rare occasions, in the presence of a striking woman, Holmes appears to have difficulty controlling his troublesome juices. In "The Solitary Cyclist" he found it impossible to refuse the "young and beautiful woman, tall and queenly," who rapped on the front door of Baker Street one night to beg his assistance. Despite the late hour his irritable nature melted. He seemed to struggle to resist her obvious charm.

Holmes asked her what was troubling her: " 'At least it cannot be your health,' said he, as his keen eyes darted over her; so ardent a cyclist must be full of energy.' "

He then "took the lady's ungloved hand and examined it with as close an attention and as little sentiment as a scientist would show to a specimen."

"You will excuse me, I am sure. It is my business," he murmurs.

A moment later he was touching her cheek: " 'There is a spirituality about the face'—he gently turned it towards the light. . . ." Given the formality of the times it was certainly curious professional behaviour for a gentleman with a lady client in the privacy of his rooms late at night, whatever her distress.

On other occasions, relaxing with the good Watson, his only confidante, he let slip his inhibitions about the opposite sex. Holmes felt that he could never trust a woman for fear that any close relationship would erode his powers of perception. They were his most precious possession, which not even love could be allowed to intrude upon. The prospect of losing his head over a woman was perhaps his greatest fear. When Watson tells him, at the end of *The Sign of Four*, that he is to marry Mary Morstan, Holmes's tactless reaction is to emit "a most dismal groan." His fixed views on the subject prevent him even from wishing his only friend well.

"I really cannot congratulate you," he says disapprovingly.

Watson, understandably, is a little hurt and to smooth things Holmes clumsily adds: "I think she is one of the most charming young ladies I ever met, and might have been most useful in such work as we have been doing."

He cannot resist using the occasion to express his own restricted opinion: "Love is an emotional thing," he tells the ever-patient Watson, "and whatever is emotional is opposed to that true, cold reason which I place above all things. I should never marry myself, lest I bias my judgment."

With the case successfully concluded, and Watson happily engaged, what is left for the great mind to occupy itself? " 'For me,' said Sherlock Holmes, 'there still remains the cocaine-bottle.' And he stretched his long, white hand up for it."

From this it would seem that Holmes's despair arises from his own innate selfishness, but, as always, there was perhaps more to the master than he cared to admit. Little more than a year previously he had been badly shaken by the unthinkable, seemingly impossible occasion of being outwitted by a woman.

More precisely, *the* woman, as Watson called her in "A Scandal in Bohemia." The dazzlingly beautiful contralto, Irene Adler—adored at La Scala and the Imperial Opera of Warsaw alike—shook his confidence so badly that he kept a photograph of her to remind himself that it could never be allowed to happen again. Irene outmanoeuvred him, forecast his moves and saw through his disguise. She even followed him herself, undetected, disguised as "a slim youth in an Ulster" and bade him goodnight. No mean feat considering Watson's recollection of her "superb figure."

Her cunning triumphed because of Holmes's blind spot, allowing his low regard for women to cloud his judgment. While he has been accused of overestimating the abilities of his male adversaries, he made the fundamental error of underestimating women. Had he Watson's appreciative eye for a pretty face, the embarrassing debacle might not have occurred.

"What a very attractive woman!" Watson exclaims, first setting eyes on Mary Morstan.

"Is she?" Holmes remarks languidly, "I did not observe."

"You really are an automation—a calculating machine," Watson says in exasperation. "There is something positively inhuman in you at times."

It was a trait the normally-meticulous Holmes should have come to grips with but, because of the nature of the subject, he considered it of little importance.

In "The Copper Beeches" his professional manner is at its patronizing best as he sits with his client, Miss Violet Hunter:

"I should feel so much stronger if I felt that you were at the back of me," she flutters.

"Oh, you may carry that feeling away with you," Holmes replies, stopping short of patting her. "I assure you that your little problem promises to be the most interesting which has come my way for some months."

The encounter raised Watson's romantic hopes for his friend. Alas, he was forced to record that Holmes, "rather to my disappointment, manifested no further interest in her when once she had ceased to be the centre of one of his problems, and she is now the head of a private school at Walsall, where I believe that she has met with considerable success." (pp. 54-9)

It was small wonder that Sherlock Holmes was prone to moods of deep emptiness. He had a few sporting activities and hobbies to balance his dedication to the Method, but they were always linked in some way to work. Without the demands of a case to solve, and his self-imposed abstinence from female companionship, there was only the dubious solace of drugs.

Holmes became attracted by the effects of cocaine three years after Josef Brettauer, a Trieste surgeon, demonstrated its use as an anaesthetic at the Heidelberg Congress of Ophthalmology in 1884. Its painkilling properties had been discovered by Karl Koller while working alongside Freud at Vienna's Allgemeines Krankenhaus on cures for morphine addiction.

Conan Doyle, as an eye specialist himself, would have been familiar with Brettauer's historic operation. Cocaine was hailed as a wonder drug, but, though it was not officially recognized as addictive until after World War I, Watson became suspicious of his friend's dependence on it. Holmes was injecting himself three times a day with a 7 per cent solution; an amount lower than the 10 per cent standard medical dosage of the period, but a sufficiently high daily intake to cause concern. His rooms, which had always had an untidy, Bohemian air, were becoming the dishevelled quarters of the *habitué*. In "The Dying Detective," Watson describes the mantelpiece as "a litter of pipes, tobacco pouches, syringes, pen-knives, revolver cartridges and other debris."

Holmes's depression and fluctuating moods may well have been intensified by cocaine, rather than alleviated by it. But the detective, laden with ennui, believed that its effect outweighed the risks to his health.

"I suppose that its influence is physically a bad one," he admits in *The Sign of Four*. "I find it, however, so transcendently stimulating and clarifying to the mind that its secondary action is a matter of small moment." Pessimism was probably an occupational hazard, but a man given to philosophizing on the futility of life is least suited to finding relief from drugs. "We reach. We grasp," he says in "The Retired Colourman." "And what is left at the end? A Shadow. Or worse than a shadow—misery."

The bachelor who distrusted women because they might interfere with his reasoning had little resistance to a substance which could destroy the same powers chemically. Watson's sound arguments did little to sway him:

> "But consider!" ... "Count the cost! Your brain may, as you say, be roused and excited, but it is a pathological and morbid process, which involves increased tissue change and may at last leave a permanent weakness. You know, too, what a blank reaction comes upon you. Surely the game is hardly worth a candle. Why should you, for a mere passing pleasure, risk the loss of those great powers with which you have been endowed? Remember that I speak not only as one comrade to another, but as a medical man to one for whose constitution he is to some extent answerable."

As a medical man in general practice Watson had a knowledge of the effects of cocaine which, in his day, would perhaps have exceeded that of a family doctor. As a friend to Holmes, he probably read up its properties in medical journals. Doyle himself, according to Prof. Michael Shepherd of the Institute of Psychiatry, took the drug gelsemium in experiments which he reported to the *British Medical Journal* in 1879. His studies may have given him the idea of adding the dimension of Holmes's addiction to the stories.

The detective knew that his own cure lay in work, but sufficiently taxing cases were not always available to occupy him. "Give me problems, give me work, give me the most abstruse cryptogram, or the most intricate analysis, and I am in my own proper atmosphere. I can dispense then with artificial stimulants." Despite Holmes's heavy use of cocaine, Watson was reluctant to broach the subject because his friend managed to effect such a "cool, nonchalant air." Yet the sight of his companion injecting himself in the privacy of 221B made him extremely irritable. For months Watson watched in despair as Holmes prepared his solution three times daily and, on one occasion, even offered him a "fix." (pp. 61-3)

Eventually Holmes, with the help of his good friend, appears to have reduced his cocaine habit to a containable level. The detective reciprocated with patient understanding about the doctor's gambling habits. (p. 63)

Holmes and Watson as depicted by Sidney Paget, the most famous illustrator of the Holmes stories.

Holmes received his clients in the sitting-room while Watson occasionally discreetly withdrew to his bedroom to ensure their privacy. It is not clear what they made of the great man, or indeed what they had been led to expect. Like any professional Holmes was not allowed to advertise his services. He attracted cases by recommendation, while his reputation was, of course, spread by Watson's published stories.

His roots in the squirearchy meant, to some extent, he was a gentleman of means, but he obviously had to earn a living. Holmes the self-employed businessman veered from the ruthless to the erratic, charging high fees to one client while refusing anything from another. Those who tramped wearily up the stairs to the sitting-room of 221B came from all levels of society, but Holmes—who displayed the qualities of Victorian liberalism—was unimpressed by rank or status. Indeed, he "loathed every form of Society with his whole Bohemian soul," Watson tells us in "A Scandal in Bohemia." It was one of his great redeeming features; an unexpectedly human quality beneath the calculating machine.

Holmes was an extremely complex and contradictory character, a tribute to Conan Doyle's skill at compressing both the scope and detail of a novel into short story form.

Professionally he had an easy courtesy which made even the most fraught client relax and talk in the homely disorder of his consulting-room. For a man who had poured so much into training and acquiring specialized knowledge, his career appeared to completely lack direction—a fact perhaps not unconnected with his fatalistic view of life. Watson could not help observing the absence of an overall scheme—his friend was happy to be successful with each case rather than expand his practice. Holmes, he tells us, could be found "alternating from week to week between cocaine and ambition, the drowsiness of the drug and the fierce energy of his own keen nature.'' Had he been taken in hand by an ambitious woman, who knows what different picture might have emerged—Holmes International plc? Perhaps we should be thankful for his bachelor Bohemianism.

He was, however, not as carefree about fees as his devil-may-care nature suggests. (''My professional charges are on a fixed scale—I do not vary them, save when I remit them altogether.'') Holmes wasted no time getting down to business with the King of Bohemia, for instance:

> ''Then as to money?''
>
> ''You have carte blanche.''
>
> ''Absolutely?'' he insists, to make his position doubly sure.
>
> ''And for present expenses?''

At this point the King takes a heavy chamois leather bag and counts out £300 in gold and £700 in notes. Holmes took the payment and ''scribbled a receipt.''

The King gave him a bonus of a ''snuff box of old gold with a great amethyst in the centre of the lid.'' Holmes also wore a valuable ring which sparkled on his finger. When Watson tackled him about it, he shrugged off the inquiries: ''It was from the reigning family of Holland, though the matter in which I served them was of such delicacy that I cannot confide.'' Queen Victoria, we are told, presented him with an emerald tie pin at Windsor in recognition of services rendered.

Holmes was extremely shrewd when it came to settling fees for his work. After recovering the precious stones in ''The Beryl Coronet,'' for instance, he secures his payment before he hands over the gems. He first ensures that he receives the money he had to pay out to get them back, then adds his fee on top:

> ''Three thousand will cover the matter. And there is a little reward, I fancy. Have you your chequebook? Here is a pen. Better make it out for four thousand pounds.''

We can safely assume that he lost no time putting it into his bank account. In the closing paragraph of *His Last Bow* he jumps into the car and orders:

> ''Start her up, Watson, for it's time that we were on our way. I have a cheque for five hundred pounds which should be cashed early, for the drawer is quite capable of stopping it, if he can.''

His earnings were considerable, enabling him to travel everywhere first class and support an expensive cocaine habit. Yet he preferred to share lodgings for the companionship and simple lifestyle. Money to Holmes was no more than a means of supporting himself; his real riches came from the higher things it could not buy.

The haphazard daily life of 221B was a sharp contrast to Holmes's precise and systematic investigating techniques. He equipped himself for every eventuality with a variety of eccentric tools—from his low-powered microscope to the dark lantern he used in ''The Red-Headed League,'' which could vary its output of light. At the heart of the paraphernalia was a filing system, intricately cross-indexed, to provide instant access to information.

''For many years he has adopted a system of docketing all paragraphs concerning men and things, so that it was difficult to name a subject or a person on which he could not at once furnish information,'' Watson tells us. (pp. 71-4)

Many of Holmes's cuttings were pasted in his Commonplace Book (''I read nothing except the criminal news and the agony column,'' he once said, though this was not quite true). In a private diary he kept a record of case histories. The filing method was so complex that it needed frequent attention, a task he tended to put off until the fancy took him. In ''The Five Orange Pips'' he ''sat moodily at one side of the fireplace cross-indexing his records of crime.''

At the scene of a crime he took in the stage and the leading characters at a glance, rarely telling Watson what was going through his mind. If something required closer examination he would take out the magnifying glass which generations of illustrators and cartoonists associated with him. In *A Study in Scarlet* we find Holmes brandishing his lens in full eccentric cry:

> He whipped a tape measure and a large round magnifying glass from his pocket. With these two implements he trotted noiselessly about the room, sometimes stopping, occasionally kneeling, and once lying flat upon his face. So engrossed was he with this occupation that he appeared to have forgotten our presence, for he chattered away to himself under his breath the whole time, keeping up a running fire of exclamations, groans, whistles and little cries. . . .

Whether this extravagant performance was to impress Inspectors Gregson and Lestrade of Scotland Yard is unclear. But they ''watched the manoeuvres of their amateur companion with considerable curiosity and contempt.''

Holmes had a long-running love-hate relationship with the Yard's detectives. He had as little regard for their methods as they had for his, and particularly disliked the way in which they took the glory for his inspired groundwork. In this same incident, when they ask his opinion, he replies with heavy sarcasm:

> ''It would rob you of the credit of the case if I was to presume to help you. You are doing so well now that it would be a pity for anyone to interfere.''

We can infer from this, and similar tart replies, that Holmes had more than a touch of the *prima donna* concerning his work. He did not suffer fools gladly, and he treated anyone of lesser intelligence rather brusquely. The police, portrayed by Conan Doyle as plodding and a trifle pompous, fall squarely into this category. Mr. Jones of Scotland Yard sums up the official view of Holmes when he patronizingly says in ''The Red-Headed League''; ''He has his own methods which are, if he won't mind my saying so, just a little too theoretical and fantastic, but he has the makings of a detective in him.''

Inspector Lestrade, ''the pick of a bad lot,'' is less restrained. ''I've wasted time enough,'' he remonstrates, rising to his feet, in ''The Noble Bachelor.'' ''I believe in hard work, and not in sitting by the fire spinning fine theories. Good day, Mr. Holmes and we shall see who gets to the bottom of the matter first.'' As he leaves he shoots a pitying glance at Holmes. Then, turning to Watson, taps his forehead with his finger and shakes his head solemnly.

Despite the friction, Holmes was on better terms with Lestrade than any of the other Yard officers. There was a hint of friendliness in their banter but, though their working relationship became quite close, the pair could never reconcile themselves to each other's methods. "That imbecile Lestrade!" Holmes calls him in "The Boscombe Valley Mystery."

Watson was not entirely taken with him either. "A lean, ferret-like man, furtive and sly-looking was waiting for us upon the platform. . . . I had no difficulty in recognising Lestrade of Scotland Yard." There was a keen, often caustic competitiveness between Holmes and his opposite numbers, and their exchanges were on many occasions loaded with mutual contempt. "Theories are all very well', Lestrade says, 'but *we* have to deal with a hard-headed British jury." For Holmes, who thrived on recognition (he was "as sensitive to flattery on the score of his art as any girl would be of her beauty"), denegration of his methods was not only an insult, but the mark of a buffoon. His responses varied from seething anger to self-deprecating good humour, depending how the mood took him. When the police refused to take his client's problem seriously in "The Five Orange Pips," Holmes shook his clenched hands in the air with rage. "Incredible imbecility!" he shouted.

Lestrade grew to respect the consulting detective's success rate, and, of course, the honours it brought him for appearing to have solved the crime. By the time they collaborated on *The Hound of the Baskervilles,* Watson noted a change; "I saw at once from the reverential way in which Lestrade gazed at my companion that he had learned a good deal since the days when they had first worked together." Indeed, Lestrade would even call on Holmes when a case was difficult, flop in the chair at 221B and confess; "I can neither make head nor tail of this business."

Patronizing as the Yard were, it was easy to see why they lost their patience with Holmes. Here was a well-paid private detective, picking only cases which interested him, tramping over clues and interfering with evidence, while they tried to carry out their duty. It was not so much Holmes's methods—they were seen as merely whimsical—but his secretiveness, which annoyed them. In addition, he had an irritating habit of pointing out clues without explaining how they were linked to the crime—often, it seemed, for his own amusement.

Lestrade summed up their feelings in "The Norwood Builder."

> "I don't know whether you are playing a game with us, Mr. Sherlock Holmes. If you know anything, you can surely say it without all this tomfoolery."

Watson also felt a victim of his stubborn insularity:

> "One of Sherlock Holmes's defects—if indeed one may call it a defect," he tells us in *The Hound of the Baskervilles,* "was that he was exceedingly loth to communicate his full plans to any other person until the instant of their fulfilment. Partly it came no doubt from his own masterful nature which loved to dominate and surprise those who were around him. Partly also from his professional caution, which urged him never to take any chances. The result, however, was very trying for those who were acting as his agents and assistants."

Holmes's attitude to justice and the law did little to cement his relationship with the Force. He was not above turning a blind eye to letting an offender escape if, in his view, justice had been done. He was also not averse to breaking the law himself in the course of his inquiries—cutting corners which the police could not. The reward lay in bringing cases to a swift and satisfactory conclusion; the penalty, in watching lumbering gentlemen of the Yard get the kudos. The fact that the Press were influenced by official statements must have made Holmes feel grateful for Watson's published accounts of his adventures.

The *Echo,* reporting the events of *A Study in Scarlet,* concluded:

> It is an open secret that the credit of this smart capture belongs entirely to the well-known Scotland Yard officers, Messrs. Lestrade and Gregson. The man was apprehended, it appears, in the rooms of a certain Mr. Sherlock Holmes, who has himself, as an amateur, shown some talent in the detective line, and who, with such instructors, may hope in time to attain to some degree of their skill. . . .

Holmes took it phlegmatically. He believed that he was not conceited about success, "If I claim full justice for my art," he explained in "The Copper Beeches," "it is because it is an impersonal thing—a thing beyond itself. Crime is common. Logic is rare."

When Holmes is first introduced to his new flatmate at the beginning of *A Study in Scarlet,* he good-humouredly warns Watson that he smokes shag tobacco and dabbles with chemicals. "Let me see—what are my other short-comings? I get in the dumps at times, and don't open my mouth for days on end. You must not think I am sulky when I do that. Just let me alone, and I'll soon be right." . . .

The doctor discovered that there were other shortcomings, but the odd couple became firm friends. Holmes, despite his rather frigid idiosyncracies, grew very fond of "good old Watson." He may not have possessed the detective's incisive mind, but he was loyal and reliable, a good man to have in a tight corner. When Watson arrived by train in "The Boscombe Valley Mystery," Holmes, pacing the platform was relieved to see him: "It is really very good of you to come, Watson. It makes a considerable difference to me, having someone with me on whom I can thoroughly rely."

So much so that, beneath his cool exterior, Holmes valued Watson's companionship more than he cared to admit. Peeling away the veneers of professional formality, secrecy and sarcasm, through which he distanced himself, we find a man of very human emotions. Conan Doyle buried them deep, but they are there, nonetheless. Holmes the self-sufficient adventurer would have found life very empty without his pedestrian friend. It was only when there was a real risk of losing him that his true feelings surfaced. Watson took a revolver bullet in the thigh in "The Three Garridebs." Holmes instantly dealt with the attacker,

> then my friends arms were round me and he was leading me to a chair.
>
> "You're not hurt, Watson? For god's sake say that you are not hurt!"
>
> It was worth a wound—it was worth many wounds—to know the depth of loyalty and love which lay behind that cold mask. The clear, hard eyes were dimmed for a moment, and the

firm lips were shaking. For the one and only time I caught a glimpse of a great heart as well as of a great brain. . . . His face set like flint as he glared at our prisoner who was sitting up with a dazed face.

"By the Lord, it is as well for you. If you had killed Watson, you would not have got out of this room alive."

It is, of course, the stuff of heroes—firm of jaw and true of heart. At least it would appear so. But Holmes under his normal composure left the good doctor in little doubt of his function in their relationship. In "The Creeping Man" Watson gives a rare account of how, beneath the simple, bluff exterior, he had Holmes quite firmly in perspective:

He was a man of habits, narrow and conceited habits, and I had become one of them. As an institution I was like the violin, the shag tobacco, the old black pipe, the index books, and others perhaps less excusable. When it was a case of active work and a comrade was needed upon whose nerve he could place some reliance, my role was obvious. But apart from this I had uses. I was a whetstone for his mind. I stimulated him. He liked to think aloud in my presence. His remarks could hardly be said to be made to me—many of them would have been as appropriately addressed to his bedstead—but none the less, having formed the habit, it had become in some way helpful that I should register and interject. If I irritated him by a certain methodical slowness in my mentality, that irritation served only to make his own flame-like intuitions and impressions flash up the more vividly and swiftly. Such was my humble role in our alliance.

Poor old Watson; but there were compensations. The action, danger and constant sense of living close to the madness made life at 221B appealing to an ex-military man obliged to seek his livelihood as a humdrum GP. When the time came Watson found no difficulty in departing for the fresh pastures of domesticity and marriage, but Holmes had no such comforts to console his restless spirit. He withdrew into his hard shell and devoted himself to the Method which held him more firmly than any religion.

Their friendship was founded on the attraction of opposites. Watson, on the whole, was made of more durable stuff. His resilience stemmed from a natural inclination to give and take. Holmes found reciprocation uncomfortable, even in the smallest things. "It was one of the peculiarities of his proud, self-contained nature that, though he docketed any fresh information very quickly and accurately in his brain, he seldom made any acknowledgement to the giver." Against the wise understanding of Watson, it indicated a weaker character. (pp. 74-81)

Physically he was immensely strong—capable of bending a steel poker with his bare hands—and extremely fit, despite his heavy smoking habits. He was an expert fencer, an enthusiastic amateur boxer who could handle himself well, and a formidable opponent with a singlestick—a heavy cane used in sabre practice, but more frequently for street fighting. Only his eyesight appears to have been slightly impaired, judging by the number of occasions he hands a paper to Watson and asks: "Would you read it to me aloud."

Holmes's robust constitution is something of a mystery, for he had little regard for diet—especially when working—and often looked haggard and drawn. In "The Five Orange Pips" he returned home "looking pale and worn. He walked up to the sideboard and, tearing a piece from the loaf, he devoured it voraciously, washing it down with a long draught of water."

"You are hungry?" Watson asks rather unnecessarily.

"Starving. It had escaped my memory. I have had nothing since breakfast."

Disregard for his health, and the tight rein he kept on his emotions, left him with a range of nervous mannerisms—the habit of rubbing his fingers together, throwing himself into chairs, and pacing restlessly up and down the sitting-room. We have no description of the carpet, but it was presumably quite threadbare in patches. When he was excited he tended to wriggle in his chair, like a schoolboy; when thoughtful he would draw his boney knees in a foetal position up to his hawk-like nose and close his eyes. He had a high-pitched voice, we learn in "The Stockbroker's Clerk," and a tooth missing from a fight in "The Empty House." At least one Holmesian expert adds to this a rather disturbing yellow smile from all that shag tobacco, which must have stained his teeth. But with Holmes's meticulous personal habits this was perhaps carrying realism too far.

"Sherlock Holmes was a man who seldom took exercise for exercise's sake," Watson tells us in "The Silver Blaze." "Few men were capable of greater muscle effort . . . but he looked upon aimless bodily exertion as a waste of energy. . . . That he should have kept himself in training under such circumstances is remarkable."

One saving grace was his humour, mischievous and a little forced at times, but giving nevertheless some spark of spontaneity to the impression of a walking calculator. Watson found his ideas of humour "strange and occasionally offensive." In "The Mazarin Stone" they were even considered "somewhat perverse." All were based, however, on an engaging philosophy that "life is full of whimsical happenings." And in the strange world of Sherlock Holmes it is a sentiment few would disagree with.

The Master, as Holmesians reverentially refer to the great detective, was the great Victorian hero—fearless, brilliant, ready to grasp life firmly by the lapels and, of course, British into the bargain. Not the blind patriot, but a reasoning man with a rounded view of the world. A man with a sense of common justice in a society besieged by lawlessness. A champion who turned every suburban reader's sense of indignation into action; who boldly went forth to show the well-intentioned but painfully slow police how it should be done.

On the surface Sherlock Holmes reads like Superman. But Conan Doyle, a master of his craft, sketched deep perspectives of arrogance and uncertainty which made him a flawed, but enduring, hero. There are those who strive to make him something different; those who play the game of pretending that Watson, not Doyle, wrote the stories. But Holmes is lovable because he *is* such a gawky, brilliant eccentric acting like a *Boy's Own* hero. In his more erratic moments he strayed dangerously down the path of Prof. Moriarty—an inspired mind blinded by its own brilliance.

Holmes himself admitted that the line between the crook and the detective was a thin one: "It is fortunate for this community that I am not a criminal.'' . . . Only his immense capacity for reasoning—and the stabilizing influence of Watson—prevented him from becoming the real Napoleon of Crime. (pp. 81-3)

Graham Nown, in his Elementary My Dear Watson: Sherlock Holmes Centenary, His Life & Times, *Ward Lock Limited, 1986, 143 p.*

THE METHOD

VINCENT STARRETT

[*Starrett was a Canadian-born American journalist, critic, and novelist. Considered an important Sherlockian scholar, he is also the author of numerous short stories, detective novels, and humorous sketches. In the following excerpt, Starrett discusses some of Holmes's methods of detection.*]

Holmes looked upon himself, it is to be remembered, as a machine. When he does not suggest it himself, the excellent Watson—like a Greek chorus—does it for him. Thus at the outset of the *Adventures,* and then not for the first time, we are reminded that ''all emotions . . . were abhorrent to his cold, precise, but admirably balanced mind. He was, I take it, the most perfect reasoning and observing machine that the world has seen.'' Deduction, of course, was his principal tool of office, and seldom was he at fault. Observation was a close and important second, but it was not always necessary for Holmes to *see* to understand. Pipe in mouth, with eyes half closed or shut, he could listen to a client's tale of mysterious horror and know the answer to the problem before the man had finished speaking. Whatever he might reveal to Watson, in advance of the ultimate revelation, reading the doctor's account of a recital in Baker Street one is always certain that Holmes, himself, is hot on the track. A particularly difficult case was sometimes a ''three-pipe problem,'' after the client had departed; but with Holmes of all people difficulty was only a word in the dictionary.

The importance of tobacco in Holmes's way of life, incidentally, has been pointed out by students of the detective's methods. ''He is,'' as Father Knox cheerfully admits, ''one of the world's great smokers'' [see excerpt below]. While occasionally he tossed a cigar case to Watson, he himself alternated between a pipe and cigarettes. The pipe was largely for his problems. In ordinary conversation, or when time was short, an occasional cigarette was sufficient. In nearly all the tales there is the pungent odor of tobacco smoke. The rooms in Baker Street must always have been full of it.

The drugs—cocaine and morphine—with which, during the early days of his association with Watson, he used to ''stimulate'' and ''clarify'' his mind, were seldom necessary during the *Adventures,* a reform for which Watson was, in large part, responsible.

The familiar Baker Street pose of lounging indifference, in a dressing gown, however, only masked the turnings of Holmes's restless mind. Bursts of almost demonic enterprise followed quickly, as a rule. In pursuit, he had amazing energy. Holmes at his utmost must have been a sight to strike the Scotland Yarders stiff with astonishment and dismay. Sometimes on hands and knees he traced a culprit's spoor across a sodden garden; and indoors, it is recorded, he often lay flat along the boards, with glass or measuring line to verify his suspicions

in the flagrant minutiae of a room's disorder. But there is nothing self-conscious about a machine dedicated to vengeance and retribution. Enviable indeed was the humble role of John H. Watson, whose privilege it was to watch; which Gregson and the others sneered. . . .

Granted the opportunity, gentlemen, . . . of recovering a single day out of the irrecoverable past, how would you choose to spend that sorcerous gift? With Master Shakespeare in his tiring room? With Villon and his companions of the cockleshell? Riding with Rupert or barging it with Cleopatra up the Nile? Or would you choose to squander it on a chase with Sherlock Holmes, after a visit to the rooms in Baker Street?

The notorious taste of Sherlock Holmes for theatrical arrangement and dramatic effects has been a subject of frequent comment; and so, too, has been his flair for sardonic epigram. His theatricality is evident in nearly all of the adventures. It is his most human failing—his appreciation of applause. It is the actor playing to his audience when he cries: ''Gentlemen, let me introduce you to the famous black pearl of the Borgias!'' It is the admirable manipulator of third-act surprises who serves up the missing naval papers, under cover, as a breakfast dish. In the matter of epigram, he is at his best where a flavor of paradox is involved, and two examples—celebrated by Father Knox as specimens of the *Sherlockismus*—are famous. As both

A letter from Doyle to his mother explaining his intention to kill Sherlock Holmes.

have been misquoted in that scholarly churchman's study, it may be well to restate them from the Watsonian text. The first is a snatch of dialogue from *Silver Blaze,* the speakers being Sherlock Holmes and Inspector Gregory:

> "Is there any other point to which you would wish to draw my attention?"
>
> "To the curious incident of the dog in the night-time."
>
> "The dog did nothing in the night-time."
>
> "That was the curious incident," remarked Sherlock Holmes.

The second, from *The Devil's Foot,* a later tale, is part of a conversation between the detective and a famous lion-hunter:

> "You came down here to ask me whom I suspected. . . . You then went to the vicarage, waited outside it for some time, and finally returned to your cottage."
>
> "How do you know that?"
>
> "I followed you."
>
> "I saw no one."
>
> "That is what you may expect to see when I follow you."

From this latter episode it is clear that Holmes was not above a bit of boasting on occasion; but it was never empty braggadocio. He knew his powers very well, and such boasting as he indulged in was usually ironic. There is a flavor of Dumas in his occasional rodomontade, a savor of d'Artagnan, who also made no brags that he was not able and willing to follow with performance. And the always tacit contempt of the detective for Scotland Yard was similarly well grounded; his tolerant scorn of the professional operatives is part of the very substance of the legend. Yet there is a certain apparent modesty that accompanies his transactions. "My trifling experience," he calls his greatest triumphs, when he speaks of them to Watson. False modesty, perhaps? Yet not quite false, nor yet quite modest. It is again the artist speaking, half depreciating the applause he has so well deserved. . . . "The stage," says Watson, "lost a fine actor, even as science lost an acute reasoner, when he became a specialist in crime."

It is obvious, also, that business lost a remarkable organizer. The number of assistants in the detective's employ—or ready to join his forces on a moment's notice—is not at any time explicitly set forth; but it must have been a large one. The ease and promptness with which a fine acting company was assembled to play their parts outside Miss Adler's window in *A Scandal in Bohemia,* points clearly to a highly perfected organization. And it is notorious that a veritable horde of gamins was at his call. Smart youngsters, too. "The Baker Street Division of the Detective Police Force," Holmes whimsically calls the gang at its first appearance, in *A Study in Scarlet*; in *The Sign of the Four* its members are the "Baker Street Irregulars." There are glimpses of them, here and there, throughout the *Adventures,* although their leader—a certain Wiggins—would seem to have been supplanted by one Simpson. It was Simpson, at any rate, who watched the rooms of Henry Wood in Hudson Street some months after Watson's marriage. (pp. 19-22)

Vincent Starrett, in his The Private Life of Sherlock Holmes, *revised edition, University of Chicago Press, 1960, 155 p.*

HOLMES AND THE VICTORIAN WORLD

IAN OUSBY

[*Ousby is an English educator and critic residing and teaching in the United States since 1968. He is the author of* Bloodhounds of Heaven: The Detective in English Fiction from Godwin to Doyle *(1976) and has contributed to the* Mystery Encyclopedia *and the* Mystery and Detection Annual. *In the following excerpt, Ousby examines the development of Holmes's character throughout the adventures, noting the various attributes that made Holmes a fit hero for the Victorian age.*]

It seems possible that Sherlock Holmes is the most famous character in English literature. At any rate, he is certainly a member of that small and oddly assorted group of literary figures—it includes characters as diverse as Hamlet and Robinson Crusoe—whose names and qualities are instantly recognized even by those who have never read the works in which they appear. To successive generations Holmes has been not merely the best-known of fictional detectives but the quintessence of the species: detection in the public mind is a deer-stalker, a meerschaum pipe, and an "Elementary, my dear Watson." For subsequent writers in the genre Doyle's work has been at once an inspirational example and an oppressive shadow in which to labor. Modern detective fiction abounds in direct and indirect tribute to Sherlock Holmes, in pale imitations of Doyle's formula and in desperate attempts to break from it.

The security of Holmes's niche in modern English folklore reveals the nature of Doyle's achievement. Earlier writers, like Waters and Gaspey, had made the detective the subject of casual and ephemeral hackwork, or like Godwin and Dickens, they had found in him the crystallization of serious interests. Doyle approached the subject as a workmanlike craftsman determined to write "light fiction" acceptable to an educated public in its moments of relaxation. He even resented the fact that the success of the Holmes stories distracted attention from his "higher work," those historical novels which read like ponderously fictionalized Macaulay. He produced some of the most satisfying middle-brow entertainment of modern times. The Holmes stories maintain a perilous balance: without ever attempting to engage the reader's sensibilities, they manage never to insult his intelligence.

In essence, the formula that underlies the portrayal of Sherlock Holmes is a simple one. The detective is a gentleman, polished and suave in his manners, but reclusive and eccentric in his habits. In his work he is unhampered by official rules, being in a very real sense a law unto himself, and is intensely individualistic. His methods combine the scientist's precision and attention to detail with the flamboyance of the showman and the *preux chevalier's* passion for justice and mercy. In general, the portrait is much like the popular conception of the academic or the intellectual, brilliant and wayward; and it is viewed through the eyes of the worshipful student, represented by the detective's satellite and biographer, Dr. Watson.

Seen in its historical perspective, the portrait of Holmes carries the mid-Victorian respect for the detective to new heights of hero-worship. In other ways, however, it represents a clean break with the stereotype evolved by Waters out of Gaspey and Vidocq, and continued by Dickens and Collins. Holmes is a private detective, not a policeman; a gentleman, not a modestly successful burgher; and is possessed by genius rather than endowed simply with native shrewdness. Doyle supplied the formula for which the writers of the 1870s and 1880s, in their disillusion with the police detective, had been fumbling. Moreover, as the success which was accorded his work in his day shows, he had created a figure uniquely attractive to the public for light reading. Sherlock Holmes, it may be said, was a cliché whose time had come; he was, contemporaries felt, the perfect hero for his age. (pp. 140-41)

As Doyle himself remarked in the Preface to *His Last Bow,* Holmes lived through three eras: the late Victorian, the Edwardian, and the Georgian. Doyle did not intend that Holmes's career should be so lengthy, and the chronicle inevitably has a haphazard and extemporaneous air: there are enough inconsistencies to have sustained a minor industry of mock scholarly exegesis and speculation.

The characterization of Sherlock Holmes also changes, reflecting the development of Doyle's own values as well as the different tastes of the various eras in which the stories first appeared. For the purposes of analysis the canon may be divided into three periods. The first of these is represented by *A Study in Scarlet* and *The Sign of Four* (1890), the earliest and weakest of the full-length novels. Here Holmes is not merely a less fully realized creation than he later becomes but is also more inhumanly dedicated to the principles of science and more tinged with Decadence. The second period begins with the series of short stories appearing in the *Strand* between July 1891 and June 1892, published in volume form as *The Adventures of Sherlock Holmes* (1892). In these tales and their immediate successors, *The Memoirs of Sherlock Holmes* (1894), Doyle found his true métier and his true audience: they are the best and most popular of his work. The Holmes of this period is more calculated to appeal to a middle-class readership than the earlier figure. He is moved as much by a passion for justice and a sense of *noblesse oblige* as by a love of scientific truth or artistic form. The final period, beginning in 1901 with Holmes's reappearance in *The Hound of the Baskervilles,* is one of progressive decline. By the time of the *Strand* stories, collected as *The Return of Sherlock Holmes* (1905), *His Last Bow,* and *The Case-Book of Sherlock Holmes,* the detective has become a more crudely drawn and less impressive figure than earlier.

From the beginning of *A Study in Scarlet* its hero is identified as a scientist, even before either the narrator or the reader is aware of the specific nature of his profession. By the time Holmes reveals to Watson, at the end of the second chapter, that he is a "consulting detective," the point has already been firmly established that detection is actually an extension of scientific principles into the practical affairs of men. (pp. 151-52)

Despite Doyle's determination to impress the picture of Holmes as a working scientist upon the reader, these laboratory scenes have a distinctly factitious air. Only in the passage from *A Study in Scarlet* is the object of the chemical test indicated with any exactitude. None of the scenes, moreover, is integral to the action of the story: Holmes's solution of his cases never depends on precise scientific details in the manner of, say, Austin Freeman's Dr. Thorndyke. Doyle is primarily interested in the superficially dramatic possibilities of the laboratory. The episodes are designed to impress the reader, as they do Watson,

with a sense of Holmes's powers; the effect is largely dependent on the vagueness of the reference.

The stories' relation to the details of contemporary science is tenuous. Holmes himself utters very unscientific judgments. In "The Blue Carbuncle" (1892) he bases a deduction on the idea that a man's intellectual capacities are reflected in his head size, while in "The Marzarin Stone" (1921) he defends his abstention from food during periods of intense work on the grounds that "the faculties become refined when you starve them." Dr. Watson, surprisingly, accepts this argument without demur. Nor are the references to criminological science more exact. In *The Hound of the Baskervilles,* the French scientist Alphonse Bertillon is referred to as the greatest contemporary criminological authority. Yet at the time the novel was published (1901-1902), Bertillon's work was largely obsolescent: his main contribution to criminology, an elaborate system of measurements designed to identify criminals, had proved cumbersome and was being superseded by the fingerprint system. Of fingerprinting there is only one mention in the Holmes stories, in "The Norwood Builder" (1903): here the detective treats the new system with disdain and shows that the police have been misled by their excessive faith in it.

In its general outline, however, Holmes's approach to detection participates intimately in that spirit of scientific rationalism which had come to dominate the intellectual climate of the late Victorian period. His use of disguise would have reminded contemporaries of Vidocq, as his interest in footprints would have recalled Gaboriau's hero, Lecoq. Above all, Holmes would have seemed to contemporary readers the successor to the methods of Cuvier, of Darwin, and of Huxley. The stories convert some of the most complex and disturbing issues of the period into the material for beguiling romance. (pp. 152-53)

Much of the work of nineteenth century science was directed toward the reconstruction of past events. By following the principles of inductive logic and noting the similar patterns of causation, scientists found in contemporary reality evidence of the prehistory of the world. Darwin could draw conclusions about the mechanisms by which species adapt from his observation of pigeons, as Cuvier could reconstruct the anatomy of prehistoric animals from a few surviving bones. The method received its most succinct exemplification in Huxley's lecture of 1868 to an audience of working men, "On a Piece of Chalk." Beginning with his lecturer's chalk, Huxley was able to work back to a complex geological map of the world's surface in prehuman times. The detail of contemporary life, the piece of chalk, spoke volumes of prehistory: "A small beginning has led us to a great ending."

Huxley's method is specifically echoed in Holmes's article "The Book of Life," quoted near the beginning of *A Study in Scarlet*: "From a drop of water . . . a logician could infer the possibility of an Atlantic or a Niagara without having seen or heard of one or the other. So all life is a great chain, the nature of which is known whenever we are shown a single link of it." In Holmes's work, as in that of contemporary scientists, the ability to get at the truth of things resides, in Walter Pater's phrase, in "a power of distinguishing and fixing delicate and fugitive detail." Whereas the scientists applied the method to the murky prehistory of the world, Holmes uses it to reconstruct mysterious criminal events. From the apparent trivia found at the scene of a crime he is able to draw dramatic and far-reaching conclusions. "Dear me, Watson," he chides his long-suffering colleague in *The Valley of Fear* (1914-1915), "is it possible that you have not penetrated the fact that the case hangs upon the missing dumb-bell?''

Taking their cue from Holmes's method, the stories themselves show a minute precision of description, a supreme attentiveness to the surface of life. The opening of *The Hound of the Baskervilles* gives a detailed account of the sort of walking stick a country doctor would be likely to own, while "The Bruce-Partington Plans'' describes what a clerk at the Navy Office might be expected to carry in his pockets on an ordinary day. Holmes's deductions allow the reader to find a meaning and an interest in such apparently mundane items. Just as Huxley had taught his audience to look at a piece of chalk with new interest, so Holmes teaches Watson and the reader to look upon the ordinary trivia of the physical world with renewed vision. Such trivia become the subjects of miniature romances, small human histories: the man's hat in "The Blue Carbuncle'' is made to tell a short sentimental tale of an unhappy marriage, while Watson's watch in *The Sign of Four* reveals a melodramatic chapter in the Watson family history.

To contemporaries, much of the attraction of Holmes would have resided in his ability to convey a sense of excitement about the ordinary physical world which they inhabited. His attentiveness to things does not merely refresh the spectator's vision; it imparts a sense of control. The scientific rationalists of the age insisted that their discoveries led to a new vision of human power. (pp. 154-55)

Holmes several times performs the archetypal role of the rationalist hero: he explodes superstitions and frees people from their influence. In "The Sussex Vampire'' (1924) he explains a case of supposed vampirism, and in "The Devil's Foot'' he tackles the notion of demonic possession. In *The Hound of the Baskervilles,* the most successful of the full-length novels, he shows that the apparently all-powerful hound of hell is merely a phosphorous-painted dog which can be killed with real bullets.

Holmes's scientism, stressed throughout the stories, helps to make him a fitting hero for his age. But in the earliest stories the intensity of his dedication to science can also make him a suspect and repellent figure. It is not that he approaches criminal and human problems with a methodology drawn from contemporary science. To him criminals and human problems are simply scientific puzzles, opportunities for a display of expertise. He is motivated solely by a passion for scientific truth; the fact that his work may serve the interests of justice, or that it may have painful human consequences, is of no concern to him. Standish, describing Holmes before his apearance in *A Study in Scarlet,* sounds an important note of warning: "Holmes is a little too scientific for my tastes—it approaches to cold-bloodedness. I could imagine his giving a friend a little pinch of the latest vegetable alkaloid, not out of malevolence, you understand, but simply out of a spirit of inquiry in order to have a more accurate idea of the effects. To do him justice, I think he would take it himself with the same readiness.''

This habit of mind is seen in action in *The Sign of Four,* when Holmes deduces from the watch which Watson has inherited from his brother a sad story of alcoholism and wasted talents. Intensely bound up in the problem in its purely scientific light, he suddenly pulls himself up and apologizes to Watson: "Viewing the matter as an abstract problem I had forgotten how personal and painful a thing it might be to you.''

This impression of a somewhat inhuman detachment from ordinary social values—from those values so solidly represented by Watson—is furthered by the overtones of Decadence which surround Holmes and his work in the two early novels. These books were written at a time when aestheticism was firmly established and Decadence was coming into fashion in literary circles; they draw upon this atmosphere in much the same way as they do upon the scientific and rationalist temper of the age. (pp. 155-56)

[Doyle's] detective is a recluse who holds himself aloof from ordinary men and ordinary existence; he alternates between bouts of nervous excitement and moods of dreamy languor in which he falls prey to melancholy brooding, consoles himself with extravagant extemporizations on the violin, or takes refuge (much to Watson's alarm) in a world of fantasy induced by cocaine. Doyle may have borrowed hints for the detective's eccentric habits from Poe; but he elaborated them in the light of what Poe's spiritual heirs, the Decadents of the late 1880s, had contributed to the myth of the sensitive genius.

With its reference to the terminology of Impressionist painting and its hint of the bizarre, the title of *A Study in Scarlet* would have appealed to Wilde and his contemporaries. The phrase is suggested by Holmes himself when he describes the book's main murder mystery as "the finest study I ever came across: a study in scarlet, eh? Why shouldn't we use a little art jargon? There's the scarlet thread of murder running through the colourless skein of life, and our duty is to unravel it, and isolate it, and expose every inch of it.'' The use of "a little art jargon'' is characteristic, for the Holmes of the early period regards detection as an art to be practiced for its own sake. Crime appeals not merely to the scientist's instinct for the puzzle but to the Decadent's love of "all that is bizarre and outside the conventions and humdrum routine of everyday life'' ("Red-Headed League''). Detection brings the artist that excitement in the exercise of his own powers which daily life commonly denies. "My life,'' Holmes tells Watson at the end of "The Red-Headed League,'' "is spent in one long effort to escape from the commonplace of existence. These little problems help me to do so.'' The effect of this rigidly aesthetic approach is much like that of the purely scientific attitude: seen as an activity to be pursued for its own sake, detection becomes divorced from any moral or social perspective.

Doyle's interest in Decadence, however, was of another caliber from his interest in scientific rationalism. His photograph shows him to have been the epitome of the military-looking, tweedy English gentleman; it bears a striking likeness to the reader's mental image of Dr. Watson. His life shows him to have been closer in temperament to the anti-Decadents than to the Decadents. He defended the conduct of the English troops in the Boer War, patronized amateur sport, and derided feminism. His favorite contemporary writer appears to have been Rudyard Kipling. Although he apparently liked Wilde as a person and wrote of his homosexuality with a surprising lack of cant, Doyle would no doubt have regarded the Decadent movement with much the same horror that modernism inspired in him. He belonged to a class of Englishmen who have traditionally had little time for dangerous, arty nonsense.

It therefore seems likely that he added the touches of Decadence to the characterization of the early Holmes in order to strike a topical note, and perhaps to gain a little of the publicity which Wilde and his colleagues were so adept at attracting. But by the mid-1890s and the trial of Wilde, Decadence would have been not merely less novel but dangerously associated with scandalous matters. Correspondingly, Holmes's Decadence is progressively muted after the two early novels. He continues to be attracted by bizarre details and to express a peevish anger at the commonplaceness of existence, as in ''The Norwood Builder,'' where he is even sufficiently antisocial to lament that the death of Moriarty has taken the fun out of detection. But the cocaine, surely Holmes's most blatant venture into Decadence, all but disappears after *The Sign of Four*; it is briefly alluded to in ''A Scandal in Bohemia'' (1891), the next story in the sequence, and in ''The Missing Three-Quarter'' (1904), where Watson expresses a passing fear that ''the fiend was not dead, but sleeping.'' Whereas the early Holmes was wont to retreat into narcotic fantasy at the end of a case, the later Holmes is more likely to propose that he and Watson dine at a fashionable restaurant or spend an evening together at the opera.

Although the detective continues to speak of his detection as an art to be practiced for its own sake, the phrase takes on more innocuous connotations: it usually means simply that he is not interested in financial reward or public praise. In ''The Bruce-Partington Plans'' the idea is translated into terms more comprehensible and acceptable to the ordinary rugger-playing Englishman: ''I play the game for the game's own sake.'' The main surviving evidence of Holmes's artistic temperament is his love of creating flamboyant and surprising effects, a habit more reminiscent of Poe's Dupin than of the Decadent artist, and one that has little to do with ''art'' except in the broadest sense of the term. Holmes surprises clients with on-the-spot deductions and arranges for artfully contrived denouements to his cases. (pp. 157-59)

As this severe modification of Holmes's Decadent tendencies would suggest, the detective becomes in general a more conventional figure than he had originally been. He becomes, it might be said, more like Watson. During the middle period, beginning with publication of the first short stories in the *Strand* in July 1891 and lasting until 1893, Doyle's characterization of Holmes was no doubt heavily influenced by the new readership to which the detective had been introduced. Reginald Pound, historian of the *Strand,* has noted [in his *Mirror of the Century: The Strand Magazine, 1891-1950*]: ''Certainly the middle-classes of England never cast a clearer image of themselves in print than they did in *The Strand Magazine.* Confirming their preference for mental as well as physical comfort, for more than half a century it faithfully mirrored their tastes, prejudices, and intellectual limitations. From them it drew a large and loyal readership that was the envy of the publishing world.''

The assimilation of Holmes into this format begins with a change in his physical appearance. In *A Study in Scarlet* Holmes had been described in the following manner:

> His very person and appearance were such as to strike the attention of the most casual observer. In height he was rather over six feet, and so excessively lean that he seemed to be considerably taller. His eyes were sharp and piercing, save during those intervals of torpor to which I have alluded; and his thin, hawk-like nose gave his whole expression an air of alertness and decision. His chin, too, had the prominence and squareness which mark the man of determination. His hands were invariably blotted with ink and stained with chemicals, yet he was possessed of extraordinary delicacy of touch, as I frequently had occasion to ob-

serve when I watched him manipulating his fragile philosophical instruments.

This is very different from the physical image of Holmes that emerges from the *Strand* stories. Doyle at that time usually avoided describing him in detail, but he did give tacit consent to the Sidney Paget engravings. These portray a figure very different from the powerful but ugly hero of *A Study in Scarlet*: handsome, intellectual, elegantly slim rather than ''excessively lean,'' and given to mildly dandified poses. When Doyle does refer to Holmes's appearance in the stories, it is in a way consonant with Paget's drawings: the reader glimpses his aquiline profile, his enigmatic smile, and his brooding eyes. He is not merely a striking but a suavely commanding figure.

A certain suavity also enters Holmes's social manners. In the early period, Holmes had been the living embodiment of Dr. Johnson's unclubbable man, a difficult and irritating person for Watson to live with. In the *Strand* stories the nervous excitability, the fits of melancholy, and the flashes of vanity remain; but Holmes has also become more charming and personable. In his dialogues with Watson before or after a case— and these occupy a surprisingly large part of each story—he develops a vein of pleasantly whimsical humor. In his treatment of strangers, visitors, and clients he is customarily the embodiment of the polished English gentleman. Of his treatment of social inferiors Dr. Watson records: ''Sherlock Holmes was a past master in the art of putting a humble witness at his ease, and very soon, in the privacy of Godfrey Staunton's abandoned room, he had extracted all that the porter had to tell.'' (''Missing Three-Quarter''). With the distressed women who form so large a part of his clientele, he is despite his misogyny, courteous and mildly avuncular. In the presence of a bullying villain like Dr. Roylott of ''The Speckled Band'' Holmes falls back on the English gentleman's traditional resort of impenetrable sang-froid and cutting irony. With an overbearing superior like Neil Gibson in ''Thor Bridge'' (1922) or the Duke of Holdernesse in ''The Priory School'' (1904), he is firm and dignified.

One consequence of Holmes's specialist mentality in the early novels was that, as Watson noted, ''His ignorance was as remarkable as his knowledge.'' In *A Study in Scarlet* he had never heard of Carlyle or of the Copernican theory of the solar system. By *A Sign of Four* his ignorance of Carlyle had been remedied, and at one point he showed himself the master of a formidably erudite vein of dinner-table conversation: ''He spoke on a quick succession of subjects—on miracle plays, on mediaeval pottery, on Stradivarius violins, on the Buddhism of Ceylon, and on the warships of the future—handling each as though he had made a special study of it.'' The *Strand* stories take Holmes's development as a man of culture further. In ''The Boscombe Valley Mystery'' he carries a ''pocket Petrarch'' to the scene of the crime and, to relax his mind from more serious matters, turns the conversation to George Meredith. In later stories he pursues ''laborious researches in Early English charters,'' . . . writes a monograph on the polyphonic motets of Orlandus Lassus ''said by experts to be the last word upon the subject,''. . . and develops theories about the origin of the ''ancient Cornish language.''. . . (pp. 159-61)

Holmes's emergence as a rounded man of culture is part of a progressive elaboration of his knowledge and talents which undercuts any sense that he is a specialist in the conventional meaning of the term. By the end of the saga he has shown himself to be expert in the following subjects, among others: tatoos, knots, ears, ciphers, bicycle tires, tobacco ash, newspaper types, perfumes, the development of English script, and names of American gunsmiths. His knowledge of each field has the profundity of the specialist, but its total range is that of the encyclopedist. In this respect Holmes's role is very like that which in "The Bruce-Partington Plans" he ascribes to his brother Mycroft:

> "Well, his position is unique. He has made it for himself. There has never been anything like it before, nor will be again. He has the tidiest and most orderly brain, with the greatest capacity for storing facts, of any man living. The same great powers which I have turned to the detection of crime he has used for this particular business. The conclusions of every department are passed to him, and he is the central exchange, the clearing-house, which makes out the balance. All other men are specialists, but his specialism is omniscience. We will suppose that a Minister needs information as to a point which involves the Navy, India, Canada and the bi-metallic question; he could get his separate advices from various departments upon each, but only Mycroft can focus them all, and say offhand how each factor would affect the other."

At a time when knowledge was becoming increasingly compartmentalized, this ability to master the various compartments and to range freely between them would have been peculiarly reassuring. Holmes, in fact, was designed to convince contemporaries that one of the traditional roles of gentility—that of the all-round man of knowledge, the liberally educated gentleman—could still survive.

The Holmes of the *Strand* stories becomes more and more the gentleman in his approach to his work. His fascination with the bizarre and his love of abstract scientific puzzles are assimilated into a larger concern for moral and social values. By the time of *The Hound of the Baskervilles* in 1901-1902 he can tell his client, Dr. Mortimer, with quiet pride: "In a modest way I have combated evil." To the Holmes of the middle period detection is a weapon in the struggle of right against wrong, or rather, since the stories are so deeply imbued with the spirit of gentility, the struggle of honor against scoundrelism.

This change becomes apparent shortly after the beginning of the first *Strand* series in 1891. At the end of his third case, "A Case of Identity" (1891), Holmes expresses his outraged sense of justice in the time-honored manner of the gentleman:

> "The law cannot, as you say, touch you," said Holmes, unlocking and throwing open the door, "yet there never was a man who deserved punishment more. If the young lady has a brother or a friend he ought to lay a whip across your shoulders. By Jove!" he continued, flushing up at the sight of the bitter sneer upon the man's face, "it is not part of my duties to my client, but here's a hunting-crop handy, and I think I shall just treat myself to—" He took two swift steps to the whip, but before he could grasp it there was a wild clatter of steps upon the stairs, the heavy hall door banged, and from the window we could see Mr. James Windibank running at the top of his speed down the road.

Such an outburst and such a threat would have been almost inconceivable on the lips of the cold-blooded scientist of *A Study in Scarlet* or the languorous Decadent of *The Sign of Four*. The early Holmes had little to do with riding whips or invocations to Jove.

This moral zeal and passion for justice complete Holmes's assimilation into the standards of gentility: he is the perfect gentleman hero, the embodiment of the values and aspirations of the contemporary middle-class public. He is also, in a sense, a fantasy version of Doyle himself, whose own life shows a continual aspiration toward perfect gentility. (pp. 162-63)

Where Doyle served his country both by active example and by polemical writing, Holmes becomes involved in counterespionage in a number of the stories—in "The Naval Treaty," "The Second Stain" (1904), "The Bruce-Partington Plans," and "His Last Bow." In "The Bruce-Partington Plans" he approaches the problem of stolen State secrets in a flippant manner, at one point telling Watson to occupy the time by beginning "your narrative of how we saved the State"; but his mission accomplished, he strikes the correctly genteel note of indifference to material reward for his services, though he does accept the gift of an emerald tie-pin from "a certain gracious lady in whose interests he had once been fortunate enough to carry out a small commission." In "His Last Bow"

Advertisement appearing in the Strand, *September 1903, heralding the return of Sherlock Holmes.*

(1917), which takes place on the eve of the First World War, Holmes speaks in tones of somber patriotism.

Apart from helping to protect his country from external danger, Holmes also defends the interests of the upper middle classes from internal threats. In "Charles Augustus Milverton" (1904) he combats the activities of a blackmailer who specializes in the private follies of the nobility. In general, Holmes presents himself as a suppressor of scandal and an enemy of unfortunate publicity. In "The Missing Three-Quarter" he angrily defends himself against the accusation that he is, by virtue of his profession, a public washer of dirty linen: "Incidentally I may tell you that we are doing the reverse of what you very justly blame, and that we are endeavouring to prevent anything like public exposure of private matters which must necessarily follow when once the case is fairly in the hands of the official police."

This aspect of the detective's role would have been especially important to contemporary readers, for during the late Victorian and Edwardian eras the reputation and self-respect of the upper middle classes were badly shaken by a succession of scandals, usually affairs of the gaming table or the divorce court.... To an age so frequently punctuated by public scandal Holmes, the enemy of the blackmailer and the scandalmonger, would have been a reassuring hero.

Holmes acts as the defender of upper middle-class values in other ways. On a number of occasions he protects clients who are deliberately presented as the epitome of characteristic English virtues. Hilton Cubitt of "The Dancing Men" (1903), whose wife is the victim of attacks by American gangsters, is a romanticized version of Dr. Watson: "He was a fine creature, this man of the old English soil, simple, straight, and gentle, with his great, earnest blue eyes and broad, comely face. His love for his wife and his trust in her shone in his features." The most extended handling of this theme occurs in *The Hound of the Baskervilles,* where Sir Henry Baskerville, the heir to the Baskerville estate, is a true chip off the old English block, despite his American upbringing: "He wore a ruddy-tinted tweed suit and had the weather-beaten appearance of one who has spent most of his time in the open air, and yet there was something in his steady eye and the quiet assurance of his bearing which indicated the gentleman." The story recounts the struggle to restore the English gentleman to his country estate, a fight in which Sir Henry himself is a passionate helper: "There is no devil in hell, Mr. Holmes, and there is no man upon earth who can prevent me from going to the home of my own people, and you may take that to be my final answer." By disposing of the myth of the spectral hound, Holmes is able to lift the family curse and to regenerate the manorial way of life.

Usually, however, the stories present Holmes as a solitary crusader on behalf of the weak and helpless individual. Like his creator, he plays the role of latter-day knight errant. As Pierre Nordon has suggested, he is "one of the last incarnations of chivalry in the literature of the English language." The weak may be the socially powerless, like Jabez Wilson in "The Red-Headed League" or Mary Sutherland in "A Case of Identity," or they may be unprotected foreigners, like the title character in "The Greek Interpreter" (1893) and the Italian couple in "The Red Circle" (1911). All of these characters Holmes helps with a splendid disregard for financial reward.

The chivalric knight is never more knightly nor more chivalric than in his protection of women. On a number of occasions Holmes rescues single women from dangerous situations, and

these tales fall into the familiar patterns of sentimental melodrama. "The Copper Beeches" tells the story of a governess working in an isolated country house who provokes the wrath of her employer by prying too deeply into the family secret that he keeps his disobedient daughter locked up in an unoccupied wing of the house. Both the setting and the situation are reminiscent of a stream of gothic governess fiction which had begun with *Jane Eyre*; Doyle appears to owe a particular debt to Florence Warden's *A House on the Marsh.* In "The Speckled Band" Holmes rescues the heroine from a murder attempt by her stepfather, a situation that had occurred in Miss Braddon's *Charlotte's Inheritance.*

The heroines of these stories are saved from physical harm. On several other occasions Holmes rescues women from sexual danger. In "The Solitary Cyclist" (1904) he manages to prevent a forced marriage. The most extended and lurid handling of the motif occurs in a late story, "The Illustrious Client." The heroine, Violet de Merville, is infatuated with Baron Gruner. As Colonel Sir James Damery explains to Holmes, "It is this daughter, this lovely innocent girl, whom we are endeavouring to save from the clutches of a fiend." Gruner, who collects rare china and keeps a record of his past love life in an album, is the epitome of corrupt sexuality, decadent but attractive: "cool as ice, silky voiced and soothing as one of your fashionable consultants, and poisonous as a cobra." Holmes approaches the task of rescuing Violet from Gruner with a rare passion, saying: "I was sorry for her, Watson. I thought of her for the moment as I would have thought of a daughter of my own. I am not often eloquent. I use my head, not my heart. But I really did plead with her with all the warmth of words that I could find in my nature." The hysterical note that the theme of sexual danger introduces into Doyle's writing reaches a crescendo in the denouement of this adventure: one of Gruner's ex-mistresses, now a fallen woman, throws vitriol in his face. (pp. 164-67)

To his role as protector of the weak, Holmes adds that of protector of the individual against the machine like bureaucracies which society has created. It is a role that Doyle himself played with some passion and intelligence; and as Doyle well knew, it is one which has a perennial attraction in popular literature.

"I am not the law, but I represent justice so far as my feeble powers go," Holmes explains in "The Three Gables" (1926). The distinction is an important one, and Holmes uses his status as private individual rather than public official for more than hushing up delicate scandals and correcting official wrongs. He is in a real sense a law unto himself: the representative of a private code of justice which transcends the technicalities or the inflexibilities of official law. On several occasions Holmes actually breaks the law. In "Charles Augustus Milverton" he and Watson break into the blackmailer's house to steal the contents of his safe. Holmes explains to Watson: "Since it is justifiable, I have only to consider the question of personal risk. Surely a gentleman should not lay much stress upon this when a lady is in most desperate need of his help?" Watson concurs: "The high object of our mission, the consciousness that it was unselfish and chivalrous, the villainous character of our opponent, all added to the sporting interest of the adventure." Holmes undertakes a similar burglary, this time of Gruner's house, in "The Illustrious Client." At the end of the story Watson records: "Sherlock Holmes was threatened with a prosecution for burglary, but when an object is good and a client is sufficiently illustrious, even the rigid British law becomes human and elastic. My friend has not yet stood in the dock.''

This private code of justice is to a large extent based on the genteel code of honor, and it can be both harsher and milder than the official law. Holmes feels justified in allowing the thief in ''The Blue Carbuncle'' to go entirely free, since it is the man's first offense and he seems sufficiently scared to be trusted not to err again. Holmes tells Watson sententiously, ''I suppose that I am commuting a felony, but it is just possible that I am saving a soul.'' Although the code allows for such moments of charity, it also sanctions a type of lynch justice against traditional social pariahs. Blackmailers and those who take advantage of helpless women are considered fair game. Holmes stands by without attempting to intervene while Milverton is murdered, and he threatens the villainous stepfather with a horsewhip in ''A Case of Identity.'' After another villainous stepfather, Dr. Roylott of ''The Speckled Band,'' has been poisoned by his own snake, Holmes remarks cheerfully: ''Some of the blows of my cane came home, and roused its snakish temper, so that it flew upon the first person it saw. In a way I am no doubt indirectly responsible for Dr. Grimesby Roylott's death, and I cannot say that it is likely to weigh very heavily upon my conscience.''

Believing that private revenge is sometimes justified, as he explains to Lestrade when declining to investigate Milverton's murder, Holmes also protects its perpetrators from the police whenever circumstances allow. He merely cautions the murderers in ''The Boscombe Valley Mystery'' and ''The Devil's Foot.'' The conventions of the genre in which Doyle was writing, however, do not allow such criminals to go entirely free: one suffers from a fatal illness, while the other vows to spend the rest of his life in Africa.

At such moments Holmes steps out of the role of detective and into the role of judge. Several scenes in the stories actually take the form of mock trials. At the end of ''The Abbey Grange,'' Holmes addresses the honest seaman who in a fit of passion has killed the bullying, drunken husband of the woman he loves:

> ''See here, Captain Croker, we'll do this in due form of law. You are the prisoner. Watson, you are a British jury, and I never met a man who was more eminently fitted to represent one. I am the judge. Now, gentlemen of the jury, do you find the prisoner guilty or not guilty?''
>
> ''Not guilty, my Lord,'' said I.

After a similar ''private court-martial,'' as Holmes calls it, of a cheating undergraduate in ''The Three Students,'' he subjects the culprit to a bracing moral lecture: ''As to you, sir, I trust that a bright future awaits you in Rhodesia. For once you have fallen low. Let us see in the future how high you can rise.''

Such speeches illustrate how much the Holmes of the *Strand* series has transcended the role of mere scientist able to clarify the facts. He occupies a position of almost Olympian superiority from which he can pass judgment on the affairs of men. This power, which seems like that of the presiding judge in a court, can also take on religious overtones, especially in some of the stories of the later period. In ''The Red Circle'' Holmes is consulted by a Mrs. Warren who explains that she had heard from a friend of ''the way in which you brought light into the darkness. I remembered his words when I was in doubt and darkness myself.'' The language suggests an appeal for spir-

itual help, and the detective displays appropriate powers of consolation: ''Homes leaned forward and laid his long thin fingers upon the woman's shoulder. He had an almost hypnotic power of soothing when he wished. The scared look faded from her eyes, and her agitated features smoothed into their usual commonplace.''

The same idea recurs in more pronounced form in ''The Veiled Lodger,''another of the late tales. The story involves no detection of Holmes's part; he merely goes to hear the confession of the title character to a murder in which she had been an accomplice. Taking down confessions is part of a detective's job, but Holmes's approach to the task is more sacerdotal than legal. He does not inform the police and treats the confession as if its purpose is solely to ease the guilty person's mind. At the end of the interview he divines that the woman is contemplating suicide and offers her philosophical consolation:

> ''Your life is not your own,'' he said. ''Keep your hands off it.''
>
> ''What use it it to anyone?''
>
> ''How can you tell? The example of patient suffering is in itself the most precious of all lessons to an impatient world.''

Like ''The Red Circle,'' ''The Veiled Lodger'' belongs to the final period of the Holmes saga, a period whose distinguishing feature is a decline in quality. This decline, though marked, is neither total nor entirely uniform. A story like ''Thor Bridge,'' for example, compares favorably with the best of Doyle's work. But on the whole the stories are either weakly plotted or heavily reliant on ideas that had already been better used. That delicate and playful sense of the bizarre which had distinguished Doyle's best work gives way to a cruder sense of the exotic and macabre: the late stories make use of leprosy, rare poisons, Oriental illnesses, rejuvenating drugs, and sea monsters. This desperate search for novel ideas is accompanied by a growing stress on the cruel, the gruesome, and the physically repulsive. In ''The Lion's Mane'' (1926) there is an almost gloating emphasis on the way the victim meets his death, while the title characters of ''The Blanched Soldier'' (1926) and ''The Veiled Lodger'' give lengthy accounts of their experiences in, respectively, a leper colony and a lion's cage.

In keeping with the grossly macabre tone of many of the later stories Holmes becomes a less suave and refined figure: his manners and his wit are at times considerably coarser and more brutal than before. Near the beginning of one of the worst stories, ''The Three Gables,'' he is threatened by a ''huge negro,'' the hired bully of a gang:

> He swung a huge knotted lump of a fist under my friend's nose. Holmes examined it with an air of great interest. ''Were you born so?'' he asked. ''Or did it come by degrees?''. . .
>
> ''I've wanted to meet you for some time,'' said Holmes. ''I won't ask you to sit down, for I don't like the smell of you, but aren't you Steve Dixie, the bruiser?''
>
> ''That's my name, Masser Holmes, and you'll get put through it for sure if you give me any lip.''
>
> ''It is certainly the last thing you need,'' said Holmes, staring at our visitor's hideous mouth.

Later in the story Holmes cross-examines a servant whom he has detected listening outside the door by the sound of her asthmatic breathing: "Now, Susan, wheezy people may not live long, you know. It's a wicked thing to tell fibs." He dismisses her with the valedictory: "Good-bye, Susan. Paregoric is the stuff."

The obvious xenophobia of the first passage and the snobbery of the second are both in character, for even at their best the Holmes stories hardly transcend the popular prejudices of their time. But what is new in the late stories is that such prejudices have become harnessed to so crude a conception of comedy. Earlier, Holmes had possessed a dry, effective wit reminiscent of Dr. Johnson. His new vein of repartee, however, aims at being debonair and succeeds merely in being vulgar; it reminds the reader of Sapper's hero, the brutish Bull-dog Drummond. The new humor is used to express not only snobbery and prejudice against blacks but also the anti-German hysteria bred by the first world war. Here is part of Holmes's conversation with Von Bork, a captured German spy, in "His Last Bow":

> "You are a private individual. You have no warrant for my arrest. The whole proceeding is absolutely illegal and outrageous."
>
> "Absolutely," said Holmes.
>
> "Kidnapping a German subject."
>
> "And stealing his private papers."
>
> "Well, you realize your position, you and your accomplice here. If I were to shout for help as we pass through the village—"
>
> "My dear sir, if you did anything so foolish you would probably enlarge the too limited titles of our village inns by giving us 'The Dangling Prussian' as a sign-post. The Englishman is a patient creature, but at present his temper is a little inflamed and it would be as well not to try him too far."

This story, originally entitled "The War Service of Sherlock Holmes," sheds light on the falling-off in the portrayal of Holmes. Much of the weakness of the later stories can be attributed to Doyle's growing boredom with both Sherlock Holmes and detective fiction and to his preoccupation with spiritualism—an interest that absorbed most of his time and energy during the last part of his life and which seems incompatible with the writing of tales or ratiocination. Yet it is also clear that, on a deeper level, Sherlock Holmes had by the time of these later tales outlived his proper era.

Holmes was a hero designed for the late Victorian and Edwardian period, and his triumphs reflect the age's belief in certain values: in the power of reason to control the environment and eliminate danger, and in the ability of the gentleman to enforce a sense of justice and fair play. On occasion the stories echo contemporary anxieties, as in their fear of scandal, but in general they express the self-confidence of the period. With their relaxed good humor they participate fully in the mood of what historians have come to call the "Edwardian Garden Party."

This mood and these values were shaken by the impact of the First World War on English culture. In his autobiography Doyle himself speaks of the prelude to the war in these terms: "I can never forget, and our descendants can never imagine, the strange effect upon the mind which was produced by seeing the whole European fabric drifting to the edge of the chasm with absolute uncertainty as to what would happen when it toppled over." This sense of large-scale events beyond the control of the individual, or even of human reason, is the exact opposite of the assumptions on which the Holmes stories were based. "His Last Bow" is thus, as its title implies, a swan song for Holmes and for the world he represents. It is not the final Holmes story—it comes only at the end of the penultimate volume—but it records, metaphorically, Holmes's death.

The mood of the story is bleak and elegiac. This atmosphere contrasts with the earlier stories, where spying and the security of the state had been treated with that light-heartedness which signifies underlying confidence. The threat to England's safety which Holmes had combatted in "The Naval Treaty" or "The Bruce-Partington Plans" belonged to the same level of fantasy as the threat to the honor of the king in "A Scandal in Bohemia." In "His Last Bow" the carefree extravagance which had distinguished the portrayal of Holmes survives only in flashes. He describes his exploits during the years when Watson had thought he was dead with the same panache that had characterized his earlier accounts: "When I say that I started my pilgrimage at Chicago, graduated in an Irish secret society at Buffalo, gave serious trouble to the constabulary at Skibbareen and so eventually caught the eye of a subordinate agent of Von Bork, who recommended me as a likely man, you will realize that the matter was complex." But more characteristic of the story is the concluding dialogue between Holmes and Watson, after the capture of Von Bork, the German agent:

> As they turned to the car, Holmes pointed back to the moonlit sea, and shook a thoughtful head.
>
> "There's an east wind coming, Watson."
>
> "I think not, Holmes. It is very warm."
>
> "Good old Watson! You are the one fixed point in a changing age. There's an east wind coming all the same, such a wind as never blew on England yet. It will be cold and bitter, Watson, and a good many of us may wither before its blast. But it's God's own wind none the less, and a cleaner, better, stronger land will lie in the sunshine when the storm has cleared."

The balance between grim foreboding and underlying optimism with which Holmes contemplates the prospect of war echoes the attitude Doyle himself later expressed in *Memories and Adventures*. The war, as Doyle describes it, brought personal loss and suffering, but it ended with a reassuring moral: 'We did not see the new troubles ahead of us, but at least the old ones were behind. And we had gained an immense reassurance. Britain had not weakened. She was still the Britain of old." In the story Watson, as always, represents the quintessential Englishman: honest, loyal, brave, but not especially intelligent. He remains the same, "the one fixed point in a changing age," and can look forward to the prospect of active service in the coming confict. Holmes, however, belongs to a more delicate breed: the individualistic and eccentric intellectual rather than the bluff soldier. As he tells Watson, he can only return to retirement after capturing Von Bork; and he implicitly identifies himself with those who may wither before the blast of war.

Doyle revived Holmes in several later stories, collected in *The Case-Book of Sherlock Holmes,* but the insight behind "His Last Bow" is essentially sound. The Holmes of the last volume is a figure adapted to the cruder, tougher mold of the postwar hero. Although later detective fiction abounded in copies of the earlier Holmes, in the fiction of the years immediately following the war he was succeeded by a hero of a very different type, exemplified by John Buchan's Richard Hannay and Sapper's Bull-dog Drummond. These men are like brutalized Dr. Watsons rather than like Sherlock Holmes. They are usually faced with immediate physical danger rather than with intriguing puzzles, and they rely more on physical courage and on fast reflexes that they do on refined speculation. As "His Last Bow" implies, the war had ushered in a world where figures like Holmes seemed less relevant than they did in the Edwardian era. (pp. 167-75)

> *Ian Ousby, "Arthur Conan Doyle," in his* Blood-hounds of Heaven: The Detective in English Fiction from Godwin to Doyle, *Cambridge, Mass.: Harvard University Press, 1976, pp. 139-75.*

CHRISTOPHER CLAUSEN

[*In the following excerpt, Clausen discusses Doyle's reflection of Victorian attitudes toward crime and civilization, examining in detail* The Hound of the Baskervilles, *which he considers Doyle's most artistically exemplary treatment of these themes.*]

Much Victorian literature makes it clear that for the comfortable classes in nineteenth-century England, crime and revolution were related concepts. Both were threats to the social order, and many people did not distinguish closely between them. For a variety of reasons—the growth of poverty and social unrest that followed the industrial revolution, the example of repeated revolutions on the Continent (Tennyson's "red fool-fury of the Seine"), the rise of socialism and of labor unions, the dependence of affluent households on servants whose loyalty might be questionable—those whose interests lay in the existing social order felt threatened and vulnerable throughout virtually the whole nineteenth century. Naturally they demanded protection.

Speaking of the mid-Victorian police force [in his *Mid-Victorian Britain, 1851-1875* (1972)], the social historian Geoffrey Best maintains: "I cannot rid myself of the impression that its main function was the protection of the property, the amenities and the institutions of the propertied: their homes and business premises, their parks and promenades, their religion and their politics. These good things badly needed protection." Although the middle and upper classes' sense of being a besieged minority eased somewhat in the second half of the century, it did not disappear either in country or in city. Furthermore, in the late 1870's Scotland Yard suffered a scandal that resulted in its reorganization and, for some time, a loss of public confidence. The country squire or West End gentleman who feels himself inadequately protected against foreign agitators, unionized laborers, reds, or simply vagrants is a figure of fun when he turns up in the plays of Shaw, but he had many real counterparts in the days when Sherlock Holmes began plying his trade. Any serious crime was a threat. An unsolved crime might be a mortal threat, for it left an unknown enemy at large, perhaps in one's own house. "The butler did it" was a revealing fear before it was a joke.

The crimes Holmes encounters include not only murder, the staple of later detective fiction, but blackmail of the rich and famous (e.g., "Charles Augustus Milverton"); theft on a grand scale, frequently from the aristocracy or from major institutions like banks ("The Red-Headed League"); attempts to inherit property and position illicitly (*The Hound of the Baskervilles*); revenge for crimes committed in the conquest of the Empire (*The Sign of Four*); a reign of terror by a corrupt labor union (*The Valley of Fear*); and crimes whose roots lie in radical political agitation ("The Red Circle"); and espionage that threatens the security of Britain itself ("The Naval Treaty," "The Second Stain," "The Bruce-Partington Plans," "His Last Bow"). Three of the four novels involve secret societies, a focus of much late-Victorian and Edwardian paranoia. The importance of these crimes is greater than that of the individuals who commit them or are their immediate victims. In solving them, Holmes does more than simply satisfy his clients or uphold the abstractions of the law. He single-handedly defends an entire social order whose relatively fortunate members feel it to be deeply threatened by forces that only he is capable of overcoming. "I am," he says in *The Sign of Four,* "the last and highest court of appeal in detection." When all else has failed—and the police almost always fail in the Holmes stories—the isolated, disclassed genius is the one who saves the day. No wonder that by the end of the cycle he has numbered among his clients Queen Victoria, King Edward VII, the pope, the king of Bohemia, the king of Scandinavia, the royal house of Holland, the sultan, and more than one British prime minister. (pp. 110-12)

Readers of the stories seldom ask themselves why the police should be such buffoons when confronted by an intelligent criminal. Such fumbling helplessness of course became one of the conventions of a rigidly conventional literary form, but a convention, at least while it is forming, generally reveals an attitude. I have already pointed out that the prestige of the police was low when Doyle began to write, and this historical fact has something to do with the popularity of an unofficial genius like Holmes. . . . The police are conventional not merely in the literary but also in the social sense of the word; they think and operate by coventions. As a result, they are often the victims of their own orthodoxy—of their social roles as respectable, practical, untheoretical men—whenever they encounter an especially bright or unorthodox criminal. They become blinded by their own unimaginative assumptions about how people act, which are those of the classes they are sworn to protect. No policeman is likely to deduce that a long-lost heir to a baronetcy will set himself up in the neighborhood under an assumed identity and train a gigantic hound to frighten the superstitious baronet to death; or that a butler will make use of a seemingly meaningless family ritual to steal the ancient crown of England; or that the supposed victim of a murder, a former detective himself, will in reality turn out to be the killer. All of these discoveries require a mind free from the assumptions of comfortable, law-abiding people. In extreme cases, society can be protected only by a man who does not share its orthodoxies, who sees through the disciplines of respectability, who despite his patriotism has little reverence for popular superstitions, who stands outside the normal system of rewards and punishments, who cares nothing for status and depends only on himself—a man, in short, who has more in common with many of the criminals he discovers than with many of his clients. The paradox of Holmes's eccentricity and isolation is one of the most important things that the stories seem to assert: in order to protect the social order effectively, one must separate oneself from it.

A figure who is at once so able and so detached could easily seem threatening to his readers instead of comforting. Holmes is rarely or never threatening, however, because his potentially corrosive intellect never questions the basic assumptions of his society. Crime or disorder results from a failure of individual responsibility, not of institutions. Generally speaking, Holmes finds aristocrats and industrialists unappealing, but he never says a word against either aristocracy or industrialism. Unattractive noblemen, even if they seem to form a remarkably large proportion of their caste, are not to be generalized into a condemnation of the nobility as an institution; they are merely individuals. The stories are consistently hostile to war, but the thought that England's preparations and policies (the subject of at least a half dozen stories) might contribute to the danger of war is never voiced. This is not to say that either Holmes or his author avoids contradicting all the prejudices of the time. Sometimes opinions are approvingly expressed that much of Doyle's original audience might have found excessively tolerant. Holmes is out-spokenly pro-American, for example, and in "The Yellow Face"—one of the many stories that have American backgrounds—a case of interracial marriage during Reconstruction is treated as a perfectly acceptable match. In matters of the first importance to his English audience, however, Doyle on the whole kept his character from stating unorthodox views. The interracial marriage is after all set in a remote time and place, not in England.

Holmes's social philosophy, if one may so describe such a random set of attitudes, is that while the existing order of things may be unattractive in many ways, his duty and vocation is nevertheless to protect it. One has the sense that both character and author feel any general remedy would be far worse than the disease. The total effect is somewhat similar to that in such Victorian novels of reform as *Hard Times,* where a vivid, detailed description of social and economic evils is followed by a vague, pious, and unconvincing conclusion. While Doyle's purpose, unlike Dickens', was not to encourage social change—quite the contrary—Doyle dealt with the potentially threatening implications of his stories in ways that are reminiscent of other Victorian writers who found themselves frightened by the undertones of their own realism. As Holmes's critical observations apply only to individuals, so his vocation, the solution of individual crimes, merely restores the social balance that each crime had upset. It never brings that balance into question, for the causes of disorder, where they involve more than individual motives, are not his concern. His few general reflections on justice, crime, and punishment are as indefinite as any Victorian conservative could wish. "What is the meaning of it, Watson?" he asks rhetorically at the end of "The Cardboard Box." "What object is served by this circle of misery and violence and fear? It must tend to some end, or else our universe is ruled by chance, which is unthinkable." No faith could be less threatening to the public on whom Holmes depended for his clients and Doyle for his readers.

Victorian writers from Disraeli to Dickens, from Tennyson to Arnold to Huxley, were almost obsessively aware of chaos lurking below the surface of civilized life, waiting for the opportunity to reassert itself. Not only the order of society but civilization itself was a precarious creation, maintained with immense effort against continuous threats. The theory of evolution gave to this pervasive fear a form that was at once scientific and iconographic, for the anarchic and bestial appetites that were so inimical to order could now be seen as survivals of primitive life, of the time when man was half an ape. Reason, morality, law, love, art—all the qualities that made civilization possible were late developments in the evolution of the species, and their hold on mankind was as yet so tenuous that the slightest emergency might reestablish the control of older, darker forces. "Move upward, working out

the beast, / And let the ape and tiger die," Tennyson had counseled in *In Memoriam*. Much Victorian opinion cried *amen* to the sentiment; only an optimistic few were at all confident that the ape and tiger had yet died out of human nature. "The highest type of man may revert to the animal if he leaves the straight path of destiny," as Sherlock Holmes puts it in "The Creeping Man."

Among the literary expressions of this set of attitudes, *The Hound of the Baskervilles* (1902) is one of the masterpieces. It is the most highly symbolic of all the Sherlock Holmes stories and the most carefully constructed of the novels. The phosphorescent hound itself, hurtling inexorably across the foggy wastes of Dartmoor after its victim, is the most powerful figure of horror in all the literature of crime, an apparition worthy to threaten not just the existing order of society but the order of the rational mind itself. It is fitting that the threat should manifest itself not in Holmes's own London, the capital of the civilized world, but in a remote rural area among the ruined dwellings of prehistoric man.

Holmes's predilection for London and antiromantic mistrust of the countryside are made clear from the start of his career and never change. London is the *locus* of all those aspects of civilization and intellectual progress that he values most highly. Rural England, on the other hand, has never altogether evolved out of barbarism. The ape and tiger retain a stronger hold there; law and reason are correspondingly frailer. Holmes makes his feelings clear in the early story "The Copper Beeches": "It is my belief, Watson, founded upon my experience, that the lowest and vilest alleys in London do not present a more dreadful record of sin than does the smiling and beautiful countryside." In *The Hound of the Baskervilles* we are never allowed to forget the contrasts between London and Dartmoor, and it is only by submitting to live for a time in a prehistoric stone hut on the moor that Holmes's London mind can defeat and partially exorcise the primitive forces arrayed against his client.

The early chapters of the book are heavy with references to nightmare, madness, the diabolical, and reversions to the primitive. Dr. Mortimer, who brings the case to Holmes's attention, is an archeologist and a specialist in atavistic diseases. His two published papers are significantly entitled "Some Freaks of Atavism" and "Do We Progress?" A man of scientific habits, London-trained, he finds himself wholly at a loss to understand the story he tells Holmes of the mysterious death of Sir Charles Baskerville. A "spectral hound," a "hound of hell" in the England of 1889? Yet he has seen the footprints in the yew alley beside the body of his friend. Having read Holmes the centuries-old legend of the nemesis hound, he does not know whether the tools of science will have any power to explain the horror on the moor. At the same time, he has won Holmes's respect by calculating the length of time Sir Charles had waited at the moor gate from the number of times that ash had dropped from his cigar. "It is evidently a case of extraordinary interest," Holmes declares, "and one which presented immense opportunities to the scientific expert." Dr. Mortimer is more doubtful:

> "There is a realm in which the most acute and most experienced of detectives is helpless."
>
> "You mean that the thing is supernatural?"
>
> "I did not positively say so."
>
> "No, but you evidently think it."

Holmes's reaction is comfortingly skeptical:

"I have hitherto confined my investigations to this world," said he. "In a modest way I have combated evil, but to take on the Father of Evil himself would, perhaps, be too ambitious a task. Yet you must admit that the footmark is material."

Soon Holmes prepares himself for the investigation of the case and the protection of the new baronet, Sir Henry Baskerville, by purchasing, characteristically, not a book of folklore or anthropology but an Ordnance Survey map of the area. A conversation with Watson foreshadows what is to come but hardly prepares us adequately for it. Watson comments:

"It must be a wild place."

"Yes, the setting is a worthy one. If the devil did desire to have a hand in the affairs of men—"

"Then you are yourself inclining to the supernatural explanation.'

"The devil's agents may be of flesh and blood, may they not?. . . Of course, if Dr. Mortimer's surmise should be correct, and we are dealing with forces outside the ordinary laws of Nature, there is an end of our investigation. But we are bound to exhaust all other hypotheses before falling back upon this one.". . .

The sense of foreboding, of menacing forces that transcend the ordinary powers of crime, increases markedly once the focus of the story shifts to Dartmoor. Holmes has already remarked, "I am not sure that of all the five hundred cases of capital importance which I have handled there is one which cuts so deep." When Watson approaches Baskerville Hall, we begin

Holmes and Moriarty, by Sidney Paget.

to wonder whether Holmes may this time be out of his depth. The very landscape conspires against rationality. "Over the green squares of the fields and the low curve of a wood," the normally unimaginative Watson describes gothically, "there rose in the distance a gray, melancholy hill, with a strange jagged summit, dim and vague in the distance, like some fantastic landscape in a dream." It is autumn. "The rattle of our wheels died away as we drove through drifts of rotting vegetation.". . . The nightmare landscape is not altogether uninhabited. Amid the bleakness stand the houses of Sir Henry's few neighbors and, farther away, the great prison of Princetown. There are soldiers on the road because a prisoner has escaped—a savage murderer, perhaps insane, with "beetling forehead . . . sunken animal eyes," later described as "half animal and half demon." A throwback to the primitive who might have stepped from one of Dr. Mortimer's papers, he is an appropriate inhabitant of this landscape, and it is fitting as well as chilling that after living for a time on the moor, he breaks his neck while trying to escape from the Hound.

At the center of this haunted wasteland, reducing even the Princetown prison to insignificance, is the great Grimpen Mire. "A false step yonder means death to man or beast," declares Stapleton, the naturalist, and Watson witnesses at a distance the death of a pony that has been caught in its grip. The pathways to the islands at the center of the bog are mysterious and dangerous; Stapleton warns Watson against trying to find his way there, adding: "That is where the rare plants and butterflies are, if you have the wit to reach them." As we learn eventually, the Hound of the Baskervilles is there too, awaiting the night when his master will have need of him. Meanwhile, the moor has become a place of horror to the local peasants, haunted by the sound of his baying, and even steadier observers find that the Mire has taken hold of their minds. "Life has become like that great Grimpen Mire," Watson says soon after his arrival, "with little green patches everywhere into which one may sink and with no guide to point the track."

By the end of the story, the rational mind is back on its throne, and the spectral hound is only a dead dog. But the outcome does not erase the impression of horror and unreason that has been so powerfully built up. Nor is it easily reached. Before it comes, Holmes must undergo an initiation by living on the moor, actually sleeping on the stone bed of vanished prehistoric inhabitants, and Sir Henry must confront the Hound alone, an experience that costs him a nervous breakdown. The forces of order and civilization are pitifully weak. The soldiers never come close to capturing the convict; indeed, they never appear again in the story. The police are never in evidence until Holmes summons them at the end. The local embodiment of the law is ridiculous: an eccentric landowner who indulges in petty lawsuits as a sport. No clergyman ever calls at Baskerville Hall. Dr. Mortimer is amiable but perennially baffled. And Stapleton, the man of science, proves to be the trainer of the Hound, the murderer of Sir Charles, the disguised next heir to the baronetcy, and a throwback to the most evil of all the Baskervilles.

The Hound of the Baskervilles is in fact a story of throwbacks from beginning to end. Civilization is not merely fragile; its representatives are paralyzed. Stapleton nearly wins, for he is masterful, imaginative, wholly unscrupulous, and more purposeful than any other character in the story except Holmes. Since Holmes is absent from nearly half the story—living out on the moor when Watson believes him to be in London—Watson and the reader alike have a frustrating sense of being at war with forces that are menacing, unerringly directed, and impossible to identify. Only when Holmes reappears, discovered by Watson in his stone hut on the moor, does the situation begin to clarify. When Watson notes that Holmes's chin was "as smooth and his linen as perfect as if he were in Baker Street," we know that civilization will win, though thanks only to a single champion.

Even at that, the moor almost defeats him. When Holmes orders Sir Henry to walk home at night as bait for the Hound and its master, a dense fog drifts inexorably across the path. Holmes, Watson, and Lestrade are forced to retreat to higher ground, and when they finally see the Hound come out of the fog, it is nearly upon its victim. Once again, everyone is paralyzed except the detective himself. . . . Holmes manages, just barely, to shoot the Hound and save his client's life. Stapleton escapes from Holmes and the law but apparently falls victim to the Mire. It is primitive nature, not the forces of order, that reclaims him in the end.

Holmes ultimately defeats Stapleton through what he calls "the scientific use of the imagination," and it is an impressive victory. Stapleton is the most powerful antagonist Holmes ever faces—"never yet have we helped to hunt down a more dangerous man than he who is lying yonder," he tells Watson near the end. Like Moriarty, who in the somewhat murky chronology of the stories is supposed not to have appeared on the scene yet, Stapleton is dangerous partly because he too represents the scientific intellect married to a Holmesian degree of determination. (He is, however, a much more realized and less abstract character than Moriarty.) He has become a dedicated student of the moor, and Holmes must do the same in order to defeat him. All the other characters appear puny and powerless in the setting of Dartmoor. One has the feeling that Holmes and Stapleton are equals who understand each other all along. On one occasion, Stapleton even impersonates Holmes. As Stapleton, his plans, and his hound are repeatedly described as diabolical, so Holmes is once half-consciously referred to by Watson as "our guardian angel." Their combat is inevitable and without quarter. Each is immensely resourceful but lonely, aided only by smaller figures who do not understand what they are doing. Each, in fact, deceives his closest associate.

The victory is won, the demons are exorcised; Holmes's solution to the mystery vindicates science and civilization. "We've laid the family ghost once and forever," he announces at the moment of triumph. But it is only a partial triumph, for the bleakness of Dartmoor and the Mire remains as impenetrable and unconquerable as any Wessex landscape in the novels of Thomas Hardy. Stapleton is apparently dead, but his legacy of malice survives him, for we have learned that he used to run a school. As he told it himself, soon after meeting Watson, "(T)he privilege of living with youth, of helping to mould those young minds, and of impressing them with one's own character and ideals was very dear to me." Seldom is Conan Doyle quite so ironic as this, but then seldom in the Holmes stories are the issues as large as they are here. Sir Henry, instead of entering into the enjoyment of his inheritance, has had to leave the country for a year's convalescent travel with Dr. Mortimer. Holmes, needless to say, is back in London, center of the world he represents. As the story ends, he is about to celebrate his commitment to civilization in an entirely appropriate and symbolic fashion—by taking Watson to the opera.

After *The Hound of the Baskervilles*, Conan Doyle published only one more Sherlock Holmes novel—*The Valley of Fear*

(1914), a second-rate thriller in which Holmes appears only at the beginning and end—and three collections of short stories. In two late stories, "The Devil's Foot" and "The Sussex Vampire," he tried to recapture the resonance and conviction of *The Hound of the Baskervilles*, but both stories are relative failures. The short-story form did not permit sufficient development to make the exorcism of the irrational fully persuasive. Furthermore, Doyle had by now grown tired of Holmes and Watson. Few of the stories in *His Last Bow* (1917) and almost none in *The Case Book of Sherlock Holmes* (1927), the last two collections, have anything like the depth or richness of even the less ambitious stories in the earlier volumes.

Perhaps Doyle's waning interest is sufficient to explain the decline, but there is another reason with effects that reached beyond Doyle. I have already pointed out that the seriousness and impact of the Holmes canon depended on the belief, shared by author and readers, that crime represented a potentially mortal threat to civilization and that the isolated but loyal detective was the only figure equipped to meet it. Early in the twentieth century, both halves of this belief became less plausible. The police (in England, at least) came to be more highly respected than before, and crime came to seem less pervasive and threatening. But I offer the speculation that the first World War was the crucial event that made the detective story a less serious form of entertainment than it had been at Holmes's peak. After 1918, it was no longer easy for a serious writer to believe that domestic crime was among the most important threats to the stability of civilization. War, revolution, or foreign enemies had permanently replaced it. Who could regard a solitary murderer, or even a Napoleon of crime, with the same gravity in an age of world wars and political upheavals?

One has the sense in reading the late Holmes stories of watching a play that has transferred to a smaller theatre near the end of its run. The wooden repetition of earlier plots in late stories like "The Mazarin Stone" and "Shoscombe Old Place" leads one to think that not only had Doyle tired of his characters, he no longer felt that crime was very important. As he became more and more devoted to spiritualism during and after the war, so Holmes in the late stories grows increasingly frustrated, as if conscious of the small scope in which his powers are effectual. "The ways of fate are indeed hard to understand," he exclaims in "The Veiled Lodger." "If there is not some compensation hereafter, then the world is a cruel jest." In "The Retired Colourman," the last story in the last collection, he is even more wistful: "but is not all life pathetic and futile? . . . We reach. We grasp. And what is left in our hands at the end? A shadow. Or worse than a shadow—misery." The Holmes who makes these statements is still a genius who solves crimes that baffle the police, but he has come a long way from the eager crusader who had just discovered a test for bloodstains. (pp 114-23)

Christopher Clausen, "Sherlock Holmes, Order, and the Late-Victorian Mind," in The Georgia Review, *Vol. XXXVIII, No. 1, Spring, 1984, pp. 104-23.*

JULIAN SYMONS

[*Symons has been highly praised for his contributions to the genres of biography and detective fiction. His popular biographies of Charles Dickens, Thomas Carlyle, and his brother A. J. A. Symons are considered excellent introductions to those writers. Symons is better known, however, for such crime novels as* The Immaterial Murder Case *(1945),* The Thirty-First of February *(1950), and* The Progress of a Crime *(1960). In the following excerpt, he discusses the relationship of the characters Holmes and Watson to Doyle and to his readers.*]

It is on the relationship of Holmes and Watson that the stories rest, for their first Victorian public and for us. Their fascination springs from the fact that they represent two parts of Doyle's own personality. In appearance Doyle resembled Watson, and many of his views were Watson's too. Watson-Doyle was a bluff Imperialist extrovert, whose opinions on art, politics and the proper ordering of society were conventional to the verge of philistinism. But Holmes-Doyle occupied the same skin as Watson-Doyle, and was a very different person. It was Holmes-Doyle who drew up the petition for Roger Casement's reprieve. Many liberals refused to sign it on moral grounds, but Holmes-Doyle did not flinch when shown the Black Diaries revealing Casement's homosexuality. It was Holmes-Doyle also who fought for years to prove the innocence of Oscar Slater, even though he detested the man he helped to free from prison.

Watson and Holmes together made up a double image of the conventional and the eccentric, the law-keeper and the law-breaker. The instant attraction held by the short stories for their Victorian audience from their appearance in 1891 was that they offered the chance of virtuous but outrageous excitement to readers whose lives were generally stodgy. The vast majority of Victorians and Edwardians were law-keepers. They respected the law because it was a powerful buttress for the support of bourgeois English society, which, at the end of the nineteenth century and the beginning of the twentieth, was thought to be threatened by the activities of the anarchists who assassinated McKinley in America and Carnot in France. Anarchism held a fascination for the respectable British, reflected in the way that the Siege of Sidney Street was instantly taken into the national folklore. Holmes was not an anarchist but he was a law-breaker, and such a figure could be admired if he was himself congenial. Hence the immense success of Raffles, the gentleman cracksman invented by Conan Doyle's brother-in-law E. W. Hornung. Raffles made his living by burglary, but his audience excused and loved him because he remained a gentleman.

Doyle did not approve of Raffles, saying severely to Hornung, "You must not make the criminal into a hero." Holmes of course is not a criminal, but he often engages in illegal activities, and he is a man outside ordinary society, a misanthrope, an emotionless reasoning and observing machine, and, when we first meet him, a drug-addict. The difference between the Victorian attitude to drug-taking and our own is shown by the casualness with which we are introduced to a Holmes who has been on three cocaine injections a day for months. Watson-Doyle regards this as regrettable rather than morally reprehensible. This early Holmes also showed a deep distaste, verging on contempt, for many human beings, and was immune to the charms of women. "He never spoke of the softer passions, save with a gibe and a sneer. . . . For the trained reasoner to admit such intrusions into his own delicate and finely adjusted temperament was to introduce a distracting factor which might throw a doubt upon all his mental results." Holmes was not exactly a Nietzschean Superman (Watson-Doyle thought that Nietzsche's philosophy was founded upon lunacy), but he was emphatically a Superior Man. It was comforting to have a man like that on the side of the right people, and he could be forgiven for breaking the law occasionally.

That quotation about the softer passions is from the very first short story, "A Scandal in Bohemia," and as time went on, the portrait of Holmes was made much less harsh. It proved

that he had turned to cocaine as a protest against the monotony of existence, and with Watson beside him and a case to work on, he was satisfied by pipe tobacco. The ignorance about the Solar System that he displayed early on does not seem to have lasted, and Watson was obviously wrong in putting "nil" against Holmes's knowledge of literature, philosophy and astronomy in the chart he drew up soon after their first meeting in *A Study in Scarlet*. The man then totally ignorant of literature was able later to quote Goethe, and to compare Richter and Carlyle. It would have been impossible for the Superior Man to have married, and Irene Adler of that first short story remained *the* woman, but the later Holmes often talks tenderly about the softer passions, particularly about a mother's love for her child. And in spite of occasional acerbities, Holmes's affection for Watson is so great that it embraces even his occasional stupidity and literalness. Watson is, as Holmes says on the last page of this book after a moment of Watsonic literalness, the one fixed point in a changing age. In one of the stories . . . , "The Devil's Foot," Holmes apologizes to his friend for having risked his life, and Watson answers with some emotion, because "I had never seen so much of Holmes's heart before." The affection is always apparent, even though Holmes was never able to bring himself to call his friend by anything but a surname. Watson reciprocated. It would hardly have done, after all, for a Superior Man to have been on Christian name terms with anybody.

In spite of Holmes's apology to Watson about leading him into danger, he was always prepared to ask his friend to engage in some joint illegal activity. "My dear fellow, you shall keep watch in the street. I'll do the criminal part," he says in "The Bruce-Partington Plans." He is not always so considerate, and indeed in this very story he has already given Watson the job of bringing round to him a jemmy, a dark lantern, a chisel and a revolver. A brisk little breaking and entering in "Wisteria Lodge" is justified by Holmes on the ground that a woman may be in danger of her life. "If the law can do nothing we must take the risk ourselves." Asked to produce his warrant in the affair of Lady Frances Carfax, Holmes responds by half drawing a revolver and cheerfully remarking, in the face of Holy Peters's description of him as a common burglar, that his companion also is a dangerous ruffian. It is plain that Watson thoroughly enjoys these excursions into illegal territory, strong in the knowledge that the law is being broken for the sake of virtue. He can never have felt this more fervently than when, in the title story, he helps to walk Von Bork down the garden walk of his long, low house by the sea, after Holmes has tricked the German spy. Useless for Von Bork to protest that "the whole proceeding is absolutely illegal and outrageous": Watson, like Holmes, knows that he is acting for a higher good. (pp. 8-11)

There are a dozen cases in which Holmes dispenses his personal idea of justice, most notably in "Charles Augustus Milverton," when the friends calmly decide not to reveal the identity of the woman who fires "barrel after barrel" of her revolver into the body of the blackmailer, and then grinds her heel into his face. Before Holmes, detectives in fiction had generally stayed within the law, but almost every Superior Man or Great Detective since then has bent the law a little or broken it outright. Few went so far as Philo Vance, who murdered a murderer by switching the poisoned drink meant for himself, but from Father Brown to Lord Peter Wimsey, Great Detectives acted as a final court of appeal, administering justice when the law faltered. Perhaps it is a good thing that there are fewer Great Detectives about nowadays.

Of course, the identification of readers with Holmes as Superior Man and law-giver is unconscious. . . . It is Doyle's skill as a story-teller, combined with the ability to bring those two strands of his own character so memorably to life in Holmes and Watson, that makes successive generations go on reading. (pp. 11-12)

Julian Symons, in an introduction to His Last Bow: Some Reminiscences of Sherlock Holmes *by Sir Arthur Conan Doyle, John Murray and Jonathan Cape, 1974, pp. 7-12.*

SHERLOCKIAN SCHOLARSHIP

CAIT MURPHY

[*In the following excerpt, Murphy provides a history of Sherlockian scholarship in the United States.*]

Sherlock Holmes stories have been translated into fifty-six languages, including Esperanto and shorthand. There have been at least 264 movies, 630 radio plays, thirty-two stage plays, twenty-five TV shows, and fifteen burlesques featuring the detective, as well as a ballet, a musical, and an oratorio. So familiar is Holmes that he is instantly recognized by his accoutrements alone—the deerstalker cap, inverness cape, and curved pipe—even by people who have never read a word of the stories. And like the woman who complained after seeing her first Shakespeare play that it used too many clichés, readers will find the Sherlock Holmes stories full of expressions that have entered our daily language. ("Elementary, my dear Watson" is not one of these, however; Holmes never uttered that phrase.)

As society moves further and further from the Victorian era, Sherlock Holmes only gains more fans, and more fanatical ones. Their passion for their hero has created a unique literary cult of personality. In the United States alone there are a hundred or so clubs devoted to "keeping green the memory" of Sherlock Holmes and Dr. John H. Watson, his trusty sidekick. People in at least ten other countries, including Denmark, India, Japan, Germany, Sweden, and, of course, Great Britain, share this peculiar obsession.

Holmes-worship can take some strange forms. For about twenty years one group, the Maiwand Jezails of Nebraska, has been trying to erect a statue in Afghanistan to commemorate the battle at which Watson was wounded. They finally worked out an agreement with the Afghans ten years ago, but then the government fell. Their mission was further complicated when the Soviets invaded the country. Still undaunted, they came up with the idea of traveling to Maiwand to inflate a portable monument there; however, no volunteers have come forward to make the trip.

Perhaps the most spectacular accomplishment of Sherlockians in recent times was the naming of Holmes Peak, outside Tulsa, Oklahoma. After a four-year struggle with the U.S. Board on Geographic Names and the Catholic Diocese of Tulsa, the Sherlockians prevailed. The Bishop of Tulsa, whose diocese owned part of the hill, at first refused to allow it to be named after Holmes, complaining that he wanted a name "more meaningful to His work." A timely letter to the Pope, reminding him of the numerous services Holmes had rendered to the Vatican, took care of that quibble.

Mostly, though, Sherlockians honor Sherlock Holmes and Dr. Watson by close scrutiny of the stories describing their adventures. As far as the untutored public knows, Dr. Arthur Conan Doyle created Sherlock Holmes and Dr. Watson while waiting for patients in his office in a London suburb. But true believers know that Doyle was merely the literary agent for his fellow medico, Watson. Holmes and Watson, these votaries maintain, actually lived; the chronicles of their adventures are factual case studies. The only mystery is why the four novels and fifty-six short stories of Sherlock Holmes—known as the Canon or the Sacred Writings—contain so many improbabilities, inconsistencies, and obvious fictions. If the stories are the Truth, then there must be logical explanations for any anomalies, and logical answers to any questions.

For example, why did Watson's wife call him James in "The Man With the Twisted Lip"? And how many times did Watson marry? The estimates range from one to five. Further, Watson clearly states in "A Study in Scarlet" that he was "struck on the shoulder by a Jezail bullet, which shattered the bone and grazed the subclavian artery," at the Battle of Maiwand, in Afghanistan, in 1880; yet in several later stories he complains of a wound in his leg, also caused by a Jezail bullet. Sherlock Holmes speaks of his time at university. But was it Oxford or Cambridge? (It is unthinkable that he could have gone anywhere else.) During the period that Holmes and Watson were said to room at 221B Baker Street, there was no 221. How could "The Adventure of Wisteria Lodge" have taken place in 1892, when Sherlock Holmes was presumed dead?

Sherlockians have addressed these issues with remarkable skill and wit. Mary Morstan Watson's curious lapse in calling her husband James has been explained by the suggestion that she was an agent of Professor James Moriarty. Holmes's archrival, and that "in a moment of carelessness, she addressed her husband while thinking of her mentor." From what we know of Mrs. Watson's character, this charge is an outrage. Likewise the idea that Mary was thinking of a former lover. A more plausible suggestion is that "James" was a code word between husband and wife to signal him to leave. Or perhaps Watson's real name was James and he simply used John as a pen name. Or maybe there were two Watsons—John died prematurely, and his brother James stepped into his place. Dorothy Sayers made the most convincing case. Noting that the good doctor's full name was John H. Watson, she theorized that the initial stood for Hamish, Scottish for James, and the Anglicization of his middle name was a private term of endearment.

Every aspect of the Sacred Writings has been subjected to the same close scrutiny. This tradition of the systematic study of the contradictions of the Canon, known as the game or the Higher Criticism, dates from January of 1902, when Frank Sidgwick wrote an open letter to Dr. Watson in the *Cambridge Review*, asking for the explanations of a number of chronological inconsistencies in "The Hound of the Baskervilles." Watson did not deign to reply.

Andrew Lang, a literary critic, followed Sidgwick's lead. In June of 1904 he published a devastating critique of "The Adventure of the Three Students," in which Sherlock Holmes discovers which candidate for the Fortescue Scholarship copied the examination papers. "Not one of the incidents could have occurred," Lang maintained, and he backed up this heresy with a convincing dissection of the case. No one listened to him, either.

Seven years later the world was better prepared for Ronald Knox's lighthearted essay "Studies in the Literature of Sherlock Holmes,'' delivered to the Gryphon Club of Trinity College, Oxford. Knox, a Catholic priest, parodied the ponderous critical approach of contemporary German biblical scholars by applying their heavy-handed methods to the Canon. He came up with a deutero-Holmes and a deutero-Watson, and propounded the eleven basic parts of a Sherlock Holmes story.

Even Doyle, the Literary Agent, who might have known better, was astonished by Monsignor Knox's insight. ''I cannot help writing to tell you of the amusement—and also the amazement—with which I read your article on Sherlock Holmes. That anyone should spend such pains on such material was what surprised me. Certainly you know a great deal more about it than I do.''

Doyle, of course, was far too modest. As long as he was alive, no one could know more about Sherlock Holmes. But after his death, in 1930, a lively scholarship emerged to answer the many questions he had left unanswered. The catalyst in this effort was the writer Christopher Morley, a co-founder of the *Saturday Review of Literature*.

Morley, an affable man, had the endearing hobby of founding clubs at the onset of a whim. Only a few survived the initial flush of enthusiasm. Among these were the Grillparzer Sittenpolizei Verein, or Grillparzer Morals-Police Association, and the all-male Three Hours for Lunch Club. The only rule was to keep Morley amused. Of the two, the GSPV was the slightly more formal organization—new members were required to register, by underlining a random passage from *The Collected Works of Franz Grillparzer*—and sometime in late 1932 or early 1933 a ritual of toasting and asking challenge questions from the Canon began. A round of drinks was the penalty for ignorance. Members of the GSPV took their drinking seriously, and so they began to study the Sacred Writings with a diligence worthy of Fortescue scholars.

Morley was delighted with the direction the GSPV was taking. Noticing that the last issue of the 1933 *Saturday Review* was due to come out on what he considered to be Holmes's birthday, January 6, he felt a natural impulse to have a party. The following week Morley described the gathering in his ''Bowling Green'' column as the inaugural meeting of the Baker Street Irregulars, named for the band of street urchins whom Holmes had deputized to ''go everywhere, see everything, overhear everyone.'' Until they read the column, none of the guests had had the slightest idea that a new club had been formed. Indeed, for at least one participant the most memorable part of the affair was a rousing game of Sardines, a kind of reverse hide-and-seek in which everyone has to squeeze together.

Morley later reprinted the facetious ''Buy-Laws'' of the BSI, devised by Elmer Davis—a set of largely disregarded rules concerning the disposition of the liquor bill. The Buy-Laws also called for an examination to determine membership in the BSI, but naturally no one dropped everything to devise one. Finally, Morley's brother Frank put together a Sherlock Holmes crossword puzzle during a tedious Atlantic crossing. The puzzle was published in the May 3, 1934, issue of the *Saturday Review*, and Morley promised full membership in the BSI to anyone who completed it satisfactorily. Of the fifteen acceptable responses, at least four were by women. Nevertheless, when Morley called the first formal meeting of the BSI, for June 5, 1934, he made it stag. The tradition has stuck ever since.

The 1930s and 1940s are recalled as the golden age of Sherlockian scholarship. The seminal works of the discipline were

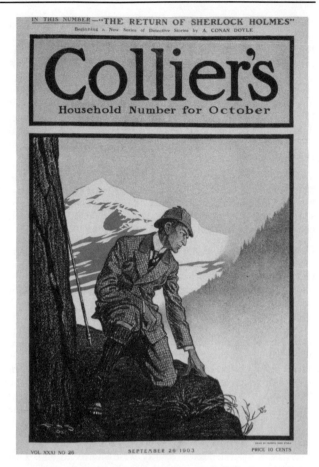

Cover of the American popular journal Collier's, *which serialized the Holmes stories in the States.*

published then, including *The Private Life of Sherlock Holmes* (1933), by Vincent Starrett; *Dr. Watson* (1931), by Sydney Roberts; *Sherlock Holmes: Fact or Fiction?* (1932), by T. S. Blakeney; and *Sherlock Holmes and Dr. Watson: The Chronology of Their Adventures* (1932), by H. W. Bell. Bell was the first to try to establish the exact order of the stories' settings, a task roughly comparable to translating the Rosetta Stone using a Berlitz phrase book.

With intellectual maturity came certain academic conventions. Jay Finley Christ devised a four-letter code to designate each of the stories, and the John Murray and Doubleday editions of the Canon came to serve as standard texts. Further, if one is going to examine subjects as different as Watson's love life (active) and medical training (competent), and Holmes's gunmanship (bad) annd fee schedule (non-existent), it helps to set some ground rules. Like the British Constitution, these rules are unwritten but widely respected.

There are three basic commandments. First, Sherlock Holmes, Dr. Watson, Professor Moriarty, and the whole cast of characters are assumed to have been people who actually existed. Second, the first commandment is never mentioned. Third, the questions of the Canon must be treated with seriousness. ''The rule of the game is that it must be played as solemnly as a county cricket match at Lord's,'' Dorothy Sayers wrote in 1946. ''The slightest touch of extravagance or burlesque ruins the atmosphere.''

Profile by Gaslight, published in 1944, pulled together the best of the early criticism. The contributors included Heywood Broun, Stephen Vincent Benét, Rex Stout, Christopher Morley, Dorothy Sayers, and Alexander Woolcott. The literary talents of such men and women could not long linger on a single subject without a magazine to express them. So in 1946 the *Baker Street Journal* was formed, with Edgar Smith, a vice-president of General Motors, as editor, publisher, and benign dictator, a position he held until his death, in 1960. Smith was the ideal man to run such a magazine: everyone loved him, and he had four secretaries.

The *Baker Street Journal* became the focal point for American Sherlockians, a sophisticated inside joke for the elect. As Christopher Morley once said when he compared the *BSJ*'s subscription list with its list of contributors, "Never has so much been written by so many for so few."

Occasionally, Sherlockians appeared in the public eye, perhaps to put up a plaque in St. Bartholomew's Hospital, where Sherlock Holmes and Dr. Watson first met, or to turn out in Victorian costume for the opening of the Sherlock Holmes train on the Baker Street line in London in 1953. In 1951 British Sherlockians had a field day when the London borough of Marylebone put on an exhibition devoted to Sherlock Holmes as its part of the Festival of Britain. The most popular feature was a full-size replica of the famous sitting room at 221B Baker Street. Even Queen Mary came for a peek. (Parts of the room may still be seen at the Sherlock Holmes pub in London.) The New York Irregulars even made the TV news, to their astonishment, when six women tried to force their way in to the 1968 BSI dinner. But mostly the Holmes fanatics were ignored. And that was fine with them.

These days of contented obscurity were shortly to end. One important sign that Holmes was becoming more than a literary cult figure was the publication of *The Annotated Sherlock Holmes,* by William S. Baring-Gould, in 1967. In two volumes and 1,512 pages Baring-Gould pulled together the best of the previous thirty-five years of Sherlock Holmes criticism. Each story was reprinted in full, with explanatory notes and illustrations filling the outer column. In addition, there were eighteen chapters to discuss separately such matters as the species of the snake in "The Speckled Band," the illustrators of Sherlock Holmes, the geography of the Baker Street rooms, and the biographies of Holmes, Watson, and Doyle.

Baring-Gould's thoroughness is astonishing. For example, when Sherlock Holmes tells Dr. Watson in "The Sign of the Four" that Watson's romanticized account of "A Study in Scarlet" produced "much the same effect as if you worked a love story or an elopement into the fifth proposition of Euclid," Baring-Gould approvingly cited an authority who notes that any other Euclidean proposition "would . . . have done as well."

Baring-Gould identified every town, every historical personage, mentioned. He explained the functions of forgotten Victorian objects like the gasogene and the tantalus. He translated the German and Latin that clogs the Canon, and he identified the numerous Shakespearean and biblical allusions. Most important to Sherlockians, he brought together in one place virtually all the best scholarship pertaining to the game. Like most Sherlockians, Baring-Gould didn't so much argue issues as pronounce dogma, but he was reasonably fair in giving those who differed with him a chance to air their views.

As soon as it was published, the *Annotated* was widely recognized as the apogee of the game. The unspoken question was, Was it the beginning of the end? For over thirty years hundreds of people had combed the Canon, hoping to catch Watson in an error. For a time this had been quite easy, but such coups were becoming as rare as hansom cabs and thrice-a-day mail. After all, one can discover only once that Watson mentions being wounded in two different limbs, or that the direction in which a bicycle has traveled cannot be determined by looking at the track made by its back tire, as Holmes says he determined it in "The Adventure of the Priory School." All kinds of ingenious ways to explain these errors may follow, but the thrill of discovery is gone. The early Sherlock Holmes criticism had thoroughly mined the nuggets from the Canon, and Baring-Gould put it all together. What was there left to do? Had the game been won?

As an informal community of eccentrics, Sherlockians did not hold conferences to discuss the question. They simply went on doing what they did best—quizzes, long dinners, longer cocktail parties—until a series of unrelated events changed the rules of their beloved game forever.

The first herald of a Sherlock Holmes revival was the Royal Shakespeare Company's 1974 production of William Gillette's classic melodrama *Sherlock Holmes.* Gillette wrote the play in 1899, having asked Doyle, "May I marry Holmes?" Doyle replied, "Marry him or murder him or do anything else you like with him." The play's first run lasted thirty years, and its author, who also played the starring role, became indelibly identified with the great detective, much as Yul Brynner would later become associated with the King of Siam. Indeed, when Frederick Dorr Steele began to illustrate the stories for *Collier's* magazine, in 1903, he simply drew Gillette. Any other portrait would have been unthinkable to his audience.

Gillette retired to his castle in Connecticut in 1932, and the play was pretty much forgotten. Initially no one wanted to step into Gillette's shoes, and later the play came to be regarded as a quaint chestnut from a bygone era, not nearly hip enough for the postwar theater. The RSC's decision to resurrect the play was surprising enough; the production's rousing success in both Britain and America was even more unexpected.

As *Sherlock Holmes* was enjoying its fifty-nine-week reign on Broadway, a thirty-year-old upstart named Nicholas Meyer published an inspired and iconoclastic pastiche, *The Seven-Per-Cent Solution.* Meyer claimed to have discovered a lost manuscript of Dr. Watson's; this described an incident in 1891, in which Watson supposedly lured a hopelessly cocaine-addicted Holmes to Vienna to be treated by Sigmund Freud. The book stayed on the *New York Times* best-seller list for almost a year. This was the first time a Sherlock Holmes book had been a best seller since *The Hound of the Baskervilles* was published, in 1902.

Although the public loved the book, many Sherlockians will never forgive its author for his presumption. Meyer's great sin was to make Holmes look ridiculous. That is simply not done. One form of the game, admittedly, is to reinterpret a story in order to devise a solution different from the one Holmes found, but this revisionism is tendered in a spirit of affection and honest intellectual inquiry. In depicting the Master as a pathetic drug addict and Watson as an underhanded schemer, Meyer committed sacrilege. And when he made a fortune off his blasphemy, this encouraged hacks to try to turn a quick buck off the resurgence of interest in Sherlock Holmes. A flood of bad, awful, and nearly criminal pastiches followed.

A long-term effect of *The Seven-Per-Cent Solution* was to awaken the reading public to the existence of the Sherlock Holmes cult. To be a Sherlockian became something of a fad. By the mid-1970s Sherlock Holmes societies loosely affiliated with the BSI could be found in forty-two states. Many of these new groups began their own publications: *Wheelwrightings,* published at a club called the Hansoms of John Clayton, based in Peoria, Illinois; the *Camden House Journal,* published by the Occupants of the Empty House, of DuQuoin, Illinois; *Columbine's New-Fangled Banner* of the Jefferson Hopes, of St. Louis; and *The Serpentine Muse,* published by the Adventuresses of Sherlock Holmes, of New York City, to name a few. As Holmes became more popular, the general level of scholarship began to sink. Far too many people with more spirit than judgment began to write inane articles about the similarities between Sherlock Holmes and Mr. Spock, or suggesting that Fu Manchu was actually Professor Moriarty.

To the utter dismay of many traditional players of the game, some of the new generation of Sherlockians seemed to delight in thinking the worst of Holmes and Watson. Yes, Holmes did occasionally take cocaine. No, he was not an addict and he did kick the habit. Yes, Sherlock Holmes and Dr. Watson lived together happily for years. No, they were not homosexuals. Yes, Holmes lived in London while Jack the Ripper was terrorizing Whitechapel. No, he was not Jack the Ripper. Until the 1970s it had not been necessary to say any of these things. Suddenly it was.

The *BSJ* is still pre-eminent in the realm of the Higher Criticism, where the literal truth of the Canon is unquestioned and the fact that Arthur Conan Doyle wrote the stories is conveniently ignored (Doyle's name has been booed at BSI dinners). Although it fell on hard times in the 1970s—at one point it failed to publish for an entire year—the *Journal* today is a slick magazine, published by the Fordham University Press and edited by a college professor: a far cry from the shoestring operation run by and for Christopher Morley's cronies. But in the realm of what might be called the new criticism, the best of the journals is the twelve-year-old *Baker Street Miscellanea,* which is independent of any club. The *Miscellanea,* and the new criticism in general (with some noteworthy exceptions), operate on the heretical assumption that Doyle created Sherlock Holmes and Dr. Watson out of his own creative genius. Jon Lellenberg, a founder and co-editor of the *BSM,* describes it as an "Arthur Conan Doyle journal masquerading as Sherlockiana." The *BSM* is far more interested in the life and times of Arthur Conan Doyle than in the minutiae of the stories. Sherlock Holmes and Dr. Watson are viewed in connection with Doyle's life and Victorian culture in general. "I figure the creator must be better than the creation—the more I admired Holmes the more I admired the man who created him," says Jack Tracy, the author of *The Encyclopedia Sherlockiana,* stating the (occasionally violated, as we shall see) creed of the new critics.

For the original Sherlockians, such a point of view was too prosaic. For Lellenberg, it only adds a fresh dimension to the game. "There's a fine line between fiction and reality, and we'd just as soon obscure it," he says. For example, he says, the rooms on Montague Street where Holmes lived upon first coming to London still survive; however, Doyle's house around the corner has been torn down. "That's were we hope to dupe the archaeologists of the future," Lellenberg says.

The new criticism has opened up the Canon to different kinds of questions. Instead of asking whether Holmes had an affair with Irene Adler, the heroine of "A Scandal in Bohemia," one asks whom Doyle was thinking of when he created her. Instead of arguing for the umpteenth time what university Holmes attended, the new critics wonder how Doyle came up with the unlikely name of Sherlock Holmes.

Michael Harrison, one of the icons of Sherlockiana, was the pioneer of this form of the game. In 1958 he wrote *In the Footsteps of Sherlock Holmes,* an informal tour of Holmes's Britain. Harrison assumed that every place mentioned in the Canon had an actual counterpart and then went all around Britain identifying them. *In the Footsteps* is still the guidebook of choice for Sherlockians on pilgrimage.

The emergence of popular-culture programs in colleges in the 1970s dovetailed neatly with the growth of interest in Sherlock Holmes. The stories began to be analyzed in terms of how they were created and how they reflected Victorian culture. A good example of this method is *In Bed With Sherlock Holmes,* a fine book despite its dreadful title. Its author, Christopher Redmond, examines the stories for their sexual undertones, to show how the Canon reflects Victorian mores. He also points out how Conan Doyle used the stories to reflect his own tangled private life. In "The Sign of the Four," written in 1889, when Doyle was a newlywed, the young heroine whom Watson marries bears a remarkable resemblance to the author's new wife. Tragically, Louise Doyle contracted tuberculosis in 1893, and four years later Doyle fell in love with another woman, Jean Leckie. There is no hint that Louise suspected the relationship, and Doyle remained faithful to her until her death, in 1906. Still, it is telling that at least nine of the sixty stories have a love triangle at their center—and almost all of these were written after Louise Doyle fell ill.

Conan Doyle and the Latter-Day Saints, by Jack Tracy, is another good example of the new criticism, but with a nostalgic twist of the old whimsy. Tracy identifies the literary sources from which Conan Doyle derived his mistaken notions of the Mormons in "A Study in Scarlet," and discusses the history and origins of anti-Mormonism. However, Tracy takes scholarly objectivity only to the edge of belief: he assumes that Doyle wrote the flashback passages of "A Study in Scarlet," but not the mystery itself, which was written by Watson. The rules of the game are not so easy to change.

In fact, for all its seeming intellectual rigor, the new criticism cannot wholly abandon the game; it differs from the Higher Criticism chiefly in that it tends to rely more on Victorian sources than on flights of fancy to make its points. In practice this means that startlingly different conclusions can be derived from the same data.

For example, in the manuscript of "The Adventure of the Second Stain" about 1,200 words are written in a strange hand. A contributor to the *Baker Street Journal* hypothesized that the writing was Watson's. Doyle's job, he argued, was to copy Watson's manuscripts, but when Watson had to add a section, he scribbled it in himself. The handwriting is a barely readable scrawl, as Sherlockians have long suspected that Watson's was. He was a doctor, after all, and such illegible handwriting would account for the errors of detail that riddle the stories. One can only pity the poor typesetter who had to deal with it.

When the editors of the *BSM* looked into the question of the second hand in "The Second Stain," they went about it very differently. By examining writing samples, they ruled out the possibility that the passage had been written by Doyle's secretary. They were also able to reject the idea that the scrawl was Doyle's "resting hand." Finally, they wrote to Dame Jean Conan Doyle, Arthur Conan Doyle's only surviving child, to ask if she could identify the writing. She wrote back promptly, and informed the breathless world that the writing was that of her mother, Doyle's second wife, Jean Leckie. Case closed. To the early practitioners of the game, this kind of intrusion of facts into the argument would have been considered rather rude. Now it is commonplace.

For the moment it appears that the new criticism is dominant. The traditional form of the game is simply too restrictive to engage the attention of the thousands of people who devote their energies to the Master. Michael Harrison bluntly dismisses the Higher Criticism as a "waste of time." This is going too far—Sherlockians still love the old game and play it to the hilt. But it is fair to say that while the Higher Criticism may not be played out, it is certainly played less.

The new criticism, too, has its limitations. Sometimes it has been far too successful in picking apart the stories. Take "The Adventure of the Speckled Band," which three polls of Sherlockians, and Sir Arthur Conan Doyle, have declared the best of the lot.

In the story an evil stepfather, the memorable Grimesby Roylott, has murdered one stepdaughter and is preparing to kill the other. Holmes deduces the plot from a leash, a dish of milk, a chair, a bed, a bellpull, and a ventilator. As he reconstructs the case, Roylott trained "a swamp adder . . . the deadliest snake in India," to climb down a bell rope and through a ventilator into his stepdaughter's room, to attack. Roylott calls the snake back by a low whistle, feeds it milk, and locks it back in his airtight safe. Holmes thwarts Roylott's attempt to kill the other stepdaughter by attacking the snake with his cane as it comes down the bell pull. Enraged, the snake returns through the ventilator and kills Roylott instead.

It is a thrilling tale, an entire Gothic novel in a short story. But wait. Snakes don't have ears, so they cannot hear a low whistle. Snakes can't climb ropes. Snakes can't survive in an airtight safe. There's no such thing as an Indian swamp adder. No snake poison could have killed a huge man like Grimesby Roylott instantly. Snake bites leave puncture marks, yet the coroner, who did a thorough examination of the first victim, saw nothing. And on and on. The story had been my favorite, but reading all this ruined it for me.

A good many other stories have been subjected to comparable treatment. In "A Critique of the Biologic Plots of Sherlock Holmes," which appears in *Beyond Baker Street*, a 1975 anthology of short criticism, a biologist named Edward Van Liere examines four stories whose plots turn on principles of science: "The Adventure of the Creeping Man," "Silver Blaze," "The Adventure of the Devil's Foot," and "The Adventure of the Lion's Mane." In a few spare paragraphs for each, Van Liere destroys the credibility of the plots, and then he claims, rather disingenuously, that he was only trying to "stir up interest in these fine tales."

I asked Otto Penzler, the proprietor of The Mysterious Bookshop, in New York, and the owner of the one of the largest collections of mysteries in the world—about 22,000 at last count—if he thought that this demolition of the plots of the stories could be a problem. Did it spoil the fun for Sherlockians to learn that the events in the tales could not possibly have happened? He smiled patiently and replied, "That's really only a problem for people too caught up in reality."

One might be excused for feeling, though, that the new criticism is itself sometimes too caught up in reality. Finding historical counterparts for the people, places, and events of the Canon is a great idea, but it can be taken too far. For example, Donald Redmond (Christopher's father), a librarian at Queen's College in Ontario, spent a year looking through Victorian telephone directories, street listings, and newspapers, novels, and magazines to try to match names that Doyle might have come across with names used in the Canon. The result is a 357-page volume, *Sherlock Holmes: A Study in Sources*. Occasionally Redmond discovers an interesting correspondence, but far too much of the book is composed of tidbits like this one, concerning Agatha, the housemaid in "The Adventure of Charles Augustus Milverton." Agatha is a minor character without a line of dialogue—she is never even given a last name. The obvious presumption is that Doyle simply scratched his head, thought Agatha a rather good name for a housemaid, and wrote it down. Not to Redmond.

> . . . there is no doubt about Agatha's original identity. She was Agatha, daughter of William the Conqueror and a character in Julia Pardoe's *Lady Morcar of Hereward,* a rather dull 1829 novel. Doyle had a copy of Pardoe's *Louis XIV* and undoubtedly knew her other works. . . . The conclusion of this identity for Agatha is, of course, that she never had a last name.

Elementary, perhaps, but dreary.

This sincere but stultifying stuff threatens to smother the inspired fancy that has been the hallmark of Sherlockian scholarship for more than two generations. There are already signs that Sherlock Holmes has gone establishment. The University of Toronto and the University of Minnesota have assembled Sherlock Holmes collections in their libraries. Minnesota even has the grandiose dream of a separate building or wing for its material. Stanford University has offered a course on the detective. John Bennett Shaw, the owner of the largest collection of Sherlock Holmes memorabilia in the world—20,000 items, including some 12,500 books—gives workshops at colleges around the country to introduce Sherlock Holmes criticism to the wider public. Christopher Morley and his drinking buddies would be astonished, and probably derisive, that what was their offbeat hobby has gained such respectable academic credentials.

They would also be stunned by the sheer volume of material that is being generated. The *World Bibliography of Sherlock Holmes and Dr. Watson,* prepared by Ronald De Waal and published in 1974, contains 6,221 entries. When he updated his magnum opus, six years later, De Waal had to add 6,135 more items. He is now working on a third volume which promises to be equally huge. Sherlock Holmes once told Neil Gibson, the Gold King in "The Problem of Thor Bridge," "I do not think that I am in need of booming." Nevertheless, the Sherlock Holmes boom shows no sign of losing force. (pp. 58-66)

Those who come to know the Master through the Sacred Writings can only regret that they will never chase the game afoot with him in person. They must be content with the sixty chronicles Watson left—a considerable consolation. And that seems to be enough. Another consolation was offered by Vincent Starrett, when he wrote that men who never lived can never die. "Shall they not always live in Baker Street?" Starrett wrote in *The Private Life of Sherlock Holmes*. "Are they not there this instant, as one writes? . . . Outside, the hansoms rattle through the rain, and Moriarty plans his latest devilry. Within, the sea-coal flames upon the hearth and Holmes and Watson take their well-won ease. . . . So they still live for all that love them well: in a romantic chamber of the heart: in a nostalgic country of the mind: where it is always 1895.'' (p. 66)

Cait Murphy, ''The Game's Still Afoot,'' in The Atlantic Monthly, Vol. 259, No. 3, March, 1987, pp. 58-66.

RONALD A. KNOX

[*Knox was an English essayist, critic, translator, and detective story writer who during his lifetime was renowned as one of the most influential Catholic apologists in England. His translations of the Latin New Testament in 1946 and the Old Testament in 1949 have been highly praised. The following excerpt, taken from the text of a lecture originally delivered to The Gryphon Club, Oxford, in 1911, is the first widely known example of Sherlockian scholarship. While most of Knox's cited ''sources'' are imaginary, by the 1930s and 1940s scholars playing the game of ''detecting the detective'' actually had a large body of exegesis in several languages from which to draw. For a complete discussion of the tongue-in-cheek nature of Sherlockian scholarship, see the excerpt above by Cait Murphy.*]

If there is anything pleasant in life, it is doing what we aren't meant to do. If there is anything pleasant in criticism, it is finding out what we aren't meant to find out. It is the method by which we treat as signficant what the author did not mean to be significant, by which we single out as essential what the author regarded as incidental. Thus, if one brings out a book on turnips, the modern scholar tries to discover from it whether the author was on good terms with his wife; if a poet writes on buttercups, every word he says may be used as evidence against him at an inquest of his views on a future existence. On this fascinating principle, we delight to extort economic evidence from Aristophanes, because Aristophanes knew nothing of economics: we try to extract cryptograms from Shakespeare, because we are inwardly certain that Shakespeare never put them there: we sift and winnow the Gospel of St. Luke, in order to produce a Synoptic problem, because St. Luke, poor man, never knew the Synoptic problem to exist.

There is, however, a special fascination in applying this method to Sherlock Holmes, because it is, in a sense, Holmes's own method. ''It has long been an axiom of mine,'' he says, ''that the little things are infinitely the most important.'' It might be the motto of his life's work. And it is, is it not, as we clergymen say, by the little things, the apparently unimportant things, that we judge of a man's character.

If anyone objects, that the study of Holmes literature is unworthy of scholarly attention, I might content myself with replying that to the scholarly mind anything is worthy of study, if that study be thorough and systematic. But I will go further, and say that at the present time we need a far closer familiarity with Sherlock's methods. The evil that he did lived after him, the good is interred with him in the Reichenbach. It is a known fact, that is, that several people contracted the dirty and deleterious habit of taking cocaine as a result of reading the books. It is equally obvious that Scotland Yard has benefited not a whit either by his satire or by his example. (pp. 145-47)

Any studies in Sherlock Holmes must be, first and foremost, studies in Dr. Watson. Let us treat at once of the literary and bibliographical aspect of the question. First, as to authenticity. There are several grave inconsistencies in the Holmes cycle.

For example the *Study in Scarlet* and the *Reminiscences* are from the hand of John H. Watson, M.D., but in the story of the ''Man with the Twisted Lip,'' Mrs. Watson addresses her husband as James. The present writer, together with three brothers, wrote to ask Sir Arthur Conan Doyle for an explanation, appending their names in the proper style with crosses after them, and an indication that this was the sign of the Four. The answer was that it was an error, an error, in fact, of editing. ''Nihil aliud hic latet,'' says the great Sauwosch, ''nisi redactor ignorantissimus.'' Yet this error gave the original impetus to Backnecke's theory of the Deutero-Watson, to whom he assigns the *Study in Scarlet*, the ''Gloria Scott,'' and the ''Return of Sherlock Holmes.'' He leaves to the proto-Watson the rest of the Memoirs, the *Adventures*, the *Sign of Four* and the *Hound of the Baskervilles*. He disputed the *Study in Scarlet* on other grounds, the statement in it, for example, that Holmes's knowledge of literature and philosophy was nil, whereas it is clear that the true Holmes was a man of wide reading and deep thought. We shall deal with this in its proper place.

The ''Gloria Scott'' is condemned by Backnecke partly on the ground of the statement that Holmes was only up for two years at College, while he speaks in the ''Musgrave Ritual'' of ''my last years'' at the University; which Backnecke supposes to prove that the two stories do not come from the same hand. The ''Gloria Scott'' further represents Percy Trevor's bull-dog as having bitten Holmes on his way down to Chapel, which is clearly untrue, since dogs are not allowed within the gates at either university. ''The bull-dog is more at home'' he adds ''on the Chapel steps, than this fraudulent imitation among the divine products of the Watsons-genius.'' A further objection to the ''Gloria Scott'' is that it exhibits only four divisions out of the eleven-fold division (to be mentioned later) of the complete Holmes-episode, a lower percentage than is found in any other genuine story. For myself, however, I am content to believe that this irregularity is due merely to the exceptional character of the investigation, while the two inaccuracies are too slight (*me judice*) to form the basis for so elaborate a theory. I would include both the ''Gloria Scott'' and the *Study in Scarlet* as genuine incidents of Holmes-biography.

When we come to the ''Final Problem,'' the alleged death of Holmes, and his subsequent return in an unimpaired and even vigorous condition, the problem grows darker. Some critics, accepting the Return stories as genuine, regard the ''Final Problem'' as an incident faked by Watson for his own purposes; thus M. Piff-Pouff represents it as an old dodge of the thaumaturgist, and quotes the example of Salmoxis or Gebeleizis among the Getae, who hid underground for two years, and then returned to preach the doctrine of immortality. In fact, M. Piff-Pouff's verdict is thus expressed: ''Sherlockholmes has not at all fallen from the Reichenbach, it is Watson who has fallen from the pinnacle of his mendacity.'' In a similar vein, Bilgemann asserts that the episode is a weak imitation of Empedocles on Etna, the alpenstock being left behind to represent the famous slipper which was revomited by the volcano. ''The episode of the 'Final Problem''' in his own immortal language, ''has the Watsons-applecart completely overturned.''

Others, Backnecke of course among them, regard the ''Final Problem'' as genuine, and the Return stories as a fabrication. The evidence against these stories may be divided into (a) those suggested by changes in the character and methods of Holmes, (b) those resting on impossibilities in the narrative itself, (c) inconsistencies found by comparison with the previous narrative.

(a) The true Holmes is never discourteous to a client: the Holmes of the ''Adventure of the Three Students'' ''shrugged his shoulders in ungracious acquiescence while our visitor . . . poured forth his story.'' On the other hand, the true Holmes has no morbid craving for serious crime; but when John Hector Macfarlane talks of the probability of being arrested, the detective is represented as saying ''Arrest you! this is most grati—most interesting.'' Twice in the Return he gibes at his prisoner, a habit from which the true Holmes, whether from professional etiquette or for other reasons, invariably abstains. Again, the false Holmes actually calls a client by her Christian name, an impossible thing to an author whose views had not been distorted by the erroneous presentation of him in the play. He deliberately abstains from food while at work: the real Holmes only does so through absent-mindedness, as in the ''Case of the Five Orange Pips.'' He quotes Shakespeare in these stories alone, and that three times, without acknowledgement. He gives way to ludicrously bad logic in the ''Dancing Men.'' He sends Watson as his emissary in the ''Solitary Cyclist,'' and this is elsewhere unparalleled, for in the *Hound of the Baskervilles* he himself goes down to Dartmoor as well, to watch the case incognito. The true Holmes never splits an infinitive; the Holmes of the Return-stories splits at least three.

(b) Is it likely that a University scholarship paper—nay, an Oxford scholarship paper, for the Quadrangle is mentioned in connexion with it—should be printed only one day before the examination? That it should consist of only half a chapter of Thucydides? That this half-chapter should take the examiner an hour and half to correct for the press? That the proofs of the half-chapter should be in three consecutive slips? Moreover, if a pencil was marked with the name JOHANN FABER, how could the two lettters NN, and these two only, be left on the stump? Prof. J. A. Smith has further pointed out that it would be impossible to find out from the superimposition of the tracks of front and back bicycle tyres, whether the cyclist was going or coming.

(c) As to actual inconsistencies. In the mystery of the ''Solitary Cyclist'' a marriage is performed with no one present except the happy couple and the officiating clergyman. In the ''Scandal in Bohemia'' Holmes, disguised as a loafer, is deliberately called in to give away an unknown bride on the ground that the marriage will not be valid without a witness. In the ''Final Problem,'' the police secure ''the whole gang with the exception of Moriarty.'' In the ''Story of the Empty House'' we hear that they failed to incriminate Colonel Moran. Professor Moriarty, in the Return, is called Professor James Moriarty, whereas we know from the ''Final Problem'' that James was really the name of his military brother, who survived him. And, worst of all, the dummy in the Baker Street window is draped in ''*the old mouse-coloured dressing-gown*''! As if we had forgotten that it was in a *blue* dressing-gown that Holmes smoked an ounce of shag tobacco at a sitting, while he unravelled the dark complication of the ''Man with the Twisted Lip!'' The detective, says M. Papier Maché, has become a chameleon. ''This is not the first time'' says the more ponderous Sauwosch, ''that a coat of many colours has been as a deception used! But in truth Sherlock, our modern Joseph, has altogether disappeared, and the evil beast Watson has him devoured.''

To this criticism I assent: I cannot assent, however, to the theory of the deutero-Watson. I believe that all the stories were written by Watson, but whereas the genuine cycle actually happened, the spurious adventures are the lucubrations of his own unaided invention. Surely we may reconstruct the facts

thus. Watson has been a bit of a gad-about. He is a spendthrift: so much we know from the beginning of the *Study in Scarlet*. His brother, as Holmes finds out by examining the scratches on the keyhole of his watch, was a confirmed drunkard. He himself, as a bachelor, haunts the Criterion Bar: in the *Sign of Four* he admits having had too much Beaune for lunch, behaves strangely at lunch, speaks of firing off a double-barrelled tiger-cub at a musket, and cautions his future wife against taking more than two drops of castor-oil, while recommending strychnine in large doses as a sedative. What happens? His Elijah is taken away from him: his wife, as we know, dies: he slips back into the grip of his old enemy; his practice, already diminished by continued neglect, vanishes away; he is forced to earn a livelihood by patching together clumsy travesties of the wonderful incidents of which he was once the faithful recorder.

Sauwosch has even worked out an elaborate table of his debts to other authors, and to the earlier stories. Holmes's stay in Thibet with the Grand Lama is due to Dr. Nikola: the cipher of the ''Dancing Men'' is read in the same manner as that in the ''Gold Bug,'' by Edgar Allan Poe: the ''Adventure of Charles Augustus Milverton'' shows the influence of Raffles. The ''Norwood Builder'' owes much to the ''Scandal in Bohemia'': the ''Solitary Cyclist'' has the plot of the ''Greek Interpreter'': the ''Six Napoleons'' of the ''Blue Carbuncle'': the ''Adventure of the Second Stain'' is a doublet of the ''Naval Treaty,'' and so on. (pp. 147-55)

[Taking] as the basis of our study, the three long stories, *Sign of Four*, *Study in Scarlet*, and *Hound of the Baskervilles*, together with the twenty-three short stories, twelve in the *Adventures*, and eleven in the *Memoirs*, we may proceed to examine the construction and the literary antecedents of this form of art. The actual scheme of each should consist, according to the German scholar, Ratzegger, followed by most of his successors, of eleven distinct parts; the order of them may in some cases be changed about, and more or less of them may appear as the story is closer to or further from the ideal type. Only the *Study in Scarlet* exhibits all the eleven; the *Sign of Four* and ''Silver Blaze'' have ten, the ''Boscombe Valley Mystery'' and the ''Beryl Coronet'' nine, the *Hound of the Baskervilles*, the ''Speckled Band,'' the ''Reigate Squires,'' and the ''Naval Treaty'' eight, and so on till we reach the ''Five Orange Pips,'' the 'Crooked Man,'' and the ''Final Problem'' with five, and the ''Gloria Scott'' with only four.

The first part is the Prooimion, a homely Baker Street scene, with invaluable personal touches, and sometimes a demonstration by the detective. Then follows the first explanation, or Exegesis kata ton diokonta, that is, the client's statement of the case, followed by the Ichneusis, or personal investigation, often including the famous floor-walk on hands and knees. No. 1 is invariable, Nos. 2 and 3 almost always present. Nos. 4, 5 and 6 are less necessary: they include the Anaskeue, or refutation on its own merits of the official theory of Scotland Yard, the first Promenusis (exoterike) which gives a few stray hints to the police, which they never adopt, and the second Promenusis (esoterike), which adumbrates the true course of the investigation to Watson alone. This is sometimes wrong, as in the ''Yellow Face.'' No. 7 is the Exetasis, or further following up of the trial, including the cross-questioning of relatives, dependants, etc., of the corpse (if there is one), visits to the Record Office, and various investigations in an assumed character. No. 8 is the Anagnorisis, in which the criminal is caught or exposed, No. 9 the second Exegesis (kata ton pheugonta), that is to say the criminal's confession, No. 10 the Metamenusis, in which Holmes describes what his clues were and how he followed them, and No. 11 the Epilogos, sometimes comprised in a single sentence. This conclusion is, like the Prooimion, invariable, and often contains a gnome or quotation from some standard author.

Although the *Study in Scarlet* is in a certain sense the type and ideal of a Holmes story, it is also to some extent a primitive type, of which elements were later discarded. The Exegesis kata ton pheugonta is told for the most part, not in the words of the criminal, but as a separate story in the mouth of the narrator: it also occupies a disproportionate amount of the total space. This shows directly the influence of Gaboriau: his *Detective's Dilemma* is one volume, containing an account of the tracing of the crime back to its author, who is of course a duke: the second volume, the *Detective's Triumph*, is almost entirely a retailing of the duke's family history, dating back to the Revolution, and we only rejoin Lecoq, the detective, in the last chapter. Of course, this method of telling the story was found long and cumbrous, but the French school has not yet seen through it, since the *Mystery of the Yellow Room* leaves a whole unexplained problem to provide copy for *The Perfume of the Lady in Black*.

But the literary affinities of Dr. Watson's masterly style are to be looked for further afield than Gaboriau, or Poe, or Wilkie Collins. M. Piff-Pouff especially, in his *Psychologie de Vatson,* has instituted some very remarkable parallels with the *Dialogues of Plato*, and with the Greek drama. He reminds us of the blustering manner of Thrasymachus when he first breaks into the argument of the Republic, and compares the entry of Athelney Jones: "Oh, come, now, come! Never be ashamed to own up! But what's all this? Bad business, bad business! Stern facts here, no room for theories," and so on. And when the detective comes back crestfallen after a few days, wiping his brow with a red handkerchief, we remember how Socrates describes the first time in his life when he ever saw Thrasymachus blushing. The rival theories of Gregson and Lestrade only serve to illustrate the multiformity of error.

But the most important point is the nature of the Scotland Yard criticism. Lecoq has his rival, but the rival is his own superior in the detective force, thwarts his schemes out of pique, and actually connives at the prisoner's receiving notes through the window of his cell. The jealousy of a Lestrade has none of this paltry spirit about it, it is a combination of intellectual pride and professional pique. It is the opposition of the regular force to the amateur. Socrates was hated by the sophists because they took money, and he did not. The cases in which Holmes takes money, explicitly at any rate, are few. In the "Scandal in Bohemia he is given £1,000, but this would seem to be only for current expenses, and may well have been refunded. At the end, he refuses the gift of an emerald ring. He will not allow the City and Suburban Bank to do more than pay his expenses in connection with the Red-headed League. He says the same elsewhere: "As for my reward, my profession is my reward." On the other hand, he takes £4,000 from Mr. Holder when he has recovered the missing beryls for £3,000. In the *Study in Scarlet,* when setting out in business, he says: "I listen to their story, they listen to my comments, and then I pocket my fee." In the "Greek Interpreter" he affirms that detection is a means of livelihood with him. And in the "Final Problem" we hear that he has been so well paid for his services in several instances to crowned heads that he is thinking of retiring from business and taking to chemistry. We must sup-

pose, therefore, that he did sometimes take payment, but perhaps only where his clients could well afford it. None the less, as compared with the officials, he is a free lance: he has no axe to grind, no promotion to seek. And further, there is an antithesis of method. Holmes is determined not to be led away by side issues and apparent pressure of facts: this it is that raises him above the level of the sophists.

If the sophists have been borrowed from the Platonic dialogue, one element at least has been borrowed from the Greek drama. Gaboriau has no Watson. The confidant of Lecoq is an old soldier, preternaturally stupid, inconceivably inefficient. Watson provides what the Holmes drama needs—a Chorus. He represents the solid, orthodox, respectable view of the world in general; his drabness is accentuated by contrast with the limelight which beats upon the central figure. He remains stable amid the eddy and flux of circumstance. (pp. 157-63)

Watson, like the Chorus, is ever in touch with the main action, and seems to share the full privileges of the audience; yet, like the Chorus, he is always about three stages behind the audience in the unravelling of the plot. (p. 164)

Watson is everything to Holmes—his medical adviser, his foil, his philosopher, his confidant, his sympathizer, his biographer, his domestic chaplain.... (p. 165)

And if the rival detectives are the sophists, and Watson is the Chorus, what of the clients, and what of the criminals? It is most important to remember that these are only secondary figures. "The murderers of the Holmes cycle," M. Papier Maché assures us, "are of no more importance than the murderers are not in *Macbeth.*" Holmes himself often deprecates Watson's habit of making the stories too sensational, but he does him an injustice. The authors of crime are not, in Watson, of personal interest, like the Duke in Gaboriau; they have no relation to the detective other than that which subsists between the sleuth-hound and its quarry—the author of the *Mystery of the Yellow Room* was a bungler when he made [his amateur detective] Jacques Rouletabille the criminal's natural son— they are not animated by lofty or religious motives like the high-flown villains in Mr. Chesterton's *Innocence of Father Brown*. All clients are model clients: they state their case in flawless journalese; all criminals are model criminals: they do the cleverest thing a criminal could possibly do in the given circumstances. By a sort of Socratic paradox, we might say that the best detective can only catch the best thief. A single blunder on the part of the guilty man would have thrown all Holmes's deductions out of joint. Love and money are their only incentives: brutality and cunning their indefeasible qualities.

And thus we arrive at the central figure himself, and must try to gather together a few threads in the complex and many-sided character. There is an irony in the process, for Holmes liked to look upon himself as a machine, an inhuman and undifferentiated sleuth-hound. "L'homme, c'est rien; l'oeuvre, c'est tout," was one of his favourite quotations.

Sherlock Holmes was descended from a long line of country squires: his grandmother was the sister of a French artist: his elder brother Mycroft was, as we all know, more gifted than himself, but found an occupation, if the Reminiscences are to be trusted, in a confidential audit of Government accounts. Of Sherlock's school career we know nothing.... (pp. 165-67)

Let us now take two pictures of Sherlock Holmes, the one at leisure, the other at work. Leisure was, of course, abhorrent to him—more so than to Watson. Watson says he was reckoned fleet of foot, but we have only his own word for it, and Holmes always beat him; beyond this alleged prowess we have no evidence of Watson's athleticism, except that he could throw a rocket through a first-floor window. But Holmes had been a boxer and a fencer; during periods of enforced inactivity he fired a revolver at the opposite wall till he had "marked it with the patriotic device V.R." Violin playing occupied leisure moments when Watson first knew him, but later it seems to be nothing more than a relaxation after hard work. And—this is very important—in this music was the exact antithesis of cocaine. We never hear of the drug being used in order to stimulate the mental faculties for hard work. All the stimulus needed he derived from tobacco. We all know, of course, that he smoked shag; few people could say off-hand what his pipe was made of. As a matter of fact, his tastes were various. The long vigil in Neville St. Clair's house was solaced by a briar—this is when he is hard at work; when he sees his way through a problem by inspection, as in the "Case of Identity," he takes down "the old and oily clay pipe, which was to him as a counsellor." In the "Copper Beeches" he takes down "the long cherrywood pipe with which he was wont to replace his clay when he was in a disputatious rather than a meditative mood." On one occasion he offers Watson snuff. Watson, by the way, smoked Ship's tobacco when he went into lodgings with Holmes, but must have replaced it soon after with a sterner stuff, thinly veiled under the *nom de plume* of Arcadia Mixture. This expensive product he did not abandon even under the exigencies of married life; though his circumstances were not those of affluence, since he had linoleum laid down in the front hall. But the pipe is not to Watson what it is to Holmes: to Holmes belongs the immortal phrase: "This will be a three-pipe problem." He is one of the world's great smokers.

Now let us see Holmes at work. We all know how brisk he becomes at the appearance of a client; how, according to the inimitable phrase in the Reminiscences: "Holmes sat up in his chair and took his pipe out of his mouth like a hound that has heard the View Halloo." We have seen him in the mind's eye prowling round the room with his nose an inch from the ground, on the look-out for cigarette-ends, orange-peel, false teeth, domes of silence, and what not, that may have been left behind by the criminal. "It is not a man," says M. Binsk, the great Polish critic, "it is either a beast or a god."

It is this charge of inhumanity brought against Holmes that I wish specially to rebut. True, he is reported to have been found beating the dead subjects in the laboratory, to see whether or no bruises could be produced after death. True, he was a scientist. True, we get passages like that in the *Sign of Four*:

> Miss Morstan: "From that day to this no word has been heard of my unfortunate father. He came home with his heart full of hope, to find some peace, some comfort, and instead—"
>
> She put her hand to her throat, and a choking sob cut short her utterance. "The date?" asked Holmes, opening his notebook.

But is it true to say that Holmes's anxiety to catch the criminal was not, like Watson's, due to a passion for justice, but to a purely scientific interest in deduction? Such truths are never more than half-truths: it would be hard to say that the footballer plays only for the goal, or that he plays only for the sake of exercise. Humanity and science in Holmes are strangely blended. At one moment we find him saying "Women are never to be

The Strand, *November 1926. The Stanley MacKenzie Collection.*

trusted, not even the best of them" (the coward!) or asserting that he cannot agree with those who rank modesty among the virtues, since the logician must see all things exactly as they are. Even his little sermon on the rose in the "Naval Treaty" is delivered in order to cover the fact that he is examining the window-frame for scratches. At another moment he is purchasing "something a little choice in white wines," and discoursing on miracle plays, on Stradivarius violins, on the Buddhism of Ceylon, and on the warships of the future.

But there are two specially human characteristics which come out at the very moment of action. One is a taste for theatrical arrangement, as when he sends back five orange pips to the murderers of John Openshaw, or takes a sponge into prison with which to unmask the man with the Twisted lip, or serves up the Naval Treaty under a cover as a breakfast dish. The other is a taste for epigram. When he gets a letter from a duke, he says: "It looks like one of those social summonses which call upon a man either to be bored or to lie." There is a special kind of epigram, known as the Sherlockismus, of which the indefatigable Ratzegger has collected no less than one hundred and seventy-three instances. The following may serve as examples:

> "Is there any other point to which you would wish to draw my attention?"
>
> "To the curious incident of the dog in the night-time."

"The dog did nothing in the night-time."

"That was the curious incident," remarked Sherlock Holmes.

and again:

"I followed you."

"I saw no one."

"That is what you may expect to see when I follow you."

To write fully on this subject would need two terms' lectures at least. Some time, when leisure and enterprise allow, I hope to deliver them. Meanwhile, I have thrown out these hints, drawn these outlines of a possible mode of treatment. You know my methods, Watson: apply them. (pp. 171-75)

> *Ronald A. Knox, "Studies in the Literature of Sherlock Holmes," in his* Essays in Satire, *1928. Reprint by Kennikat Press, Inc., 1968, pp. 145-75.*

DOYLE AND THE DEVELOPMENT OF THE DETECTIVE STORY

A. E. MURCH

[*In the following excerpt, Murch pronounces Doyle's Sherlock Holmes adventures a pivotal point in the development of detective fiction, finding that Doyle merged the best features of sensationalistic crime fiction with those of the intellectual detective story, and further contributed a valuable innovation by building a series of otherwise unrelated stories around a central recurring character.*]

There are in literature certain characters who have come to possess a separate and unmistakable identity, whose names and personal qualities are familiar to thousands who may not have read any of the works in which they appear. Among these characters must be included Sherlock Holmes, who has acquired in the minds of countless readers of all nationalities the status of an actual human being, accepted by many in the early years of the twentieth century as a living contemporary, and still surviving fifty years later with all the glamour of an established and unassailable tradition, the most convincing, the most brilliant, the most congenial and well-loved of all the detectives of fiction. (p. 67)

The reasons for the immense popularity of Sherlock Holmes are not hard to establish, and lie chiefly in Conan Doyle's inspired blending of two contrasting elements, the old and the new; mingling familiar, almost by that time traditional, features of the *genre* with startling, even sensational innovations. The time was exactly right in the 1890's for the appearance of a fresh detective hero of outstanding individuality, and to create him Doyle took the most notable characteristics of earlier fictional detectives and added to them the very qualities that the late Victorian general public admired most. Sherlock Holmes not only possessed far greater mental brilliance than his predecessors, but also a good social and cultural background, perfect respectability and integrity, the status of a "scientist," and an international reputation as a celebrity in his own field. Above all, he was an Englishman, while for the past fifty years, indeed ever since the time of Vidocq, all the celebrated de-

tectives of fiction—Dupin, Père Tabaret, Monsieur Lecoq, Rocambole—had been French.

Sherlock Holmes's skill in following a trail is a legacy from the Three Princes of Serendip, inherited through Voltaire's *Zadig,* a novel which Conan Doyle acknowledged as one of his sources of inspiration. The same faculty characterised the Indian trackers of Fenimore Cooper and of his successor in the same sphere, Captain Mayne Reid, who was Doyle's favourite author in his boyhood days. Sherlock Holmes could perform even more masterly feats of tracking, deriving remarkable information from footprints on a garden path or a snow-covered lane, the wheelmarks of a cab, or the traces left by a small bare foot on a windowsill. Holmes's kinship with the Redskin hunters is also apparent from his habit of silent laughter, his ability to go without food or rest when on the trail, and that "immobility of countenance" which made Dr. Watson more than once compare him to a Red Indian.

Like the almost legendary Vidocq, Holmes is a master of disguise, an accomplished actor and a man of great physical strength. They both have a sound grasp of criminal psychology and an encyclopaedic knowledge of criminal history which serves them well. Holmes once referred disparagingly to Dupin, calling him "a very inferior fellow, . . . showy and superficial," yet Dupin is the literary ancestor whom he most closely resembles. Like Poe's hero, Holmes is "unemotional," reasons with "ice-cold logic" and regards detection as "an exact science"; has a brilliant mind stored with all sorts of technical information; sometimes uses a newspaper advertisement to bring a suspect within his reach; can break in upon a friend's train of thought with an apropos remark after a quarter of an hour's silence. Both detectives express the opinion that when all impossibilities have been eliminated, what remains, however improbable, must be the truth; that an article is best hidden when left in full view; that an "abstract thinker" is the most formidable of all opponents, especially if he is a mathematician; that the more grotesque a mystery seems, the easier it will be to explain, while an apparently commonplace problem is the most difficult of all. They are both heavy smokers, take long walks through city streets at night, and hold a poor opinion of the police, whom they assist on occasion with brilliant deductions or inspired advice. Both are men of good family, bachelors with no interest in the opposite sex, and very little in their fellow-men, except as factors in a problem calling for the exercise of their analytical powers. They have their individual eccentricities, and while Poe comments on Dupin's "Bi-part soul," Dr. Watson mediates on Sherlock's "dual nature."

Both Dupin and Holmes are fortunate in having a faithful, long-suffering companion to chronicle with unfailing amazement and delight their various activities, their discourses on detective topics, but whereas Dupin's friend reveals little or nothing of his own individuality, Dr. Watson conveys his own character as clearly as he does the temperament and perspicacity of his famous colleague. He plays an active, if secondary, rôle in almost every story, serving not only as a foil to his brilliant friend but also as a figure with whom the reader feels a comforting comradeship when he, too, "sees but does not observe," and needs to have the implications of a clue explained. Dr. Watson, with his sturdy common sense and sincerity, his patient cheerfulness and instant readiness to face any danger beside his friend, stands almost as high as Holmes in the reader's affection. "The Lion's Mane," which lacks his presence, has lost an appreciable part of the characteristic savour, even though it is related by Holmes himself. The important part played by Watson, so different from the minor rôle of the narrator in Poe's tale of Dupin, is one of Conan Doyle's most pleasing innovations.

In spite of the similarities between Dupin and Holmes, the contrast between Poe and Conan Doyle, as writers of detective stories, could hardly be more striking than it is. Poe's tales are purely analytical discussions of the science of detection, argued out like a geometric theorem with no irrelevant detail. Though the subjects may be sensational, in their treatment we find little excitement and less romance. The characters, other than Dupin himself, are so lightly drawn that they have no personality, often not even a name, and the interest lies not in the people but in the things that have happened to them and the bonds of logic that link cause and effect. Of action or normal conversation there is practically none. Dupin moves in logical steps from the stated problem to its solution, and he is never wrong, never at a loss, never misled by a false clue. Doyle's stories are full of movement and animation. Men and women bring their personal troubles to Holmes (as they never did to Dupin) and the reader shares their dramatic moments, for much of the action takes place before his eyes. Sherlock Holmes is not merely an abstract logician, and is sometimes baffled, if only temporarily, or misled by conflicting evidence, even by unforeseen human reactions. On some occasions, as in "The Yellow Face," he is completely in error, but he loses no prestige thereby, his mistake making him seem still more convincingly human, and serving also to throw his almost invariable success into stronger relief. Poe was unfamiliar with Paris, and the French background he gave to his Dupin stories had no special significance in the plot. Victorian London, which Conan Doyle knew so well, gives its own characteristic atmosphere to the tales of Sherlock Holmes, so much so that the mere thought of that hero conjures up the great metropolis of the period, with its November fogs and August heat, its hansom cabs and gaslight, the docks and railway stations, the dignity of Westminster, the humdrum suburbs, the squalor of an East End opium den.

Conan Doyle admired Gaboriau for "the neat dove-tailing of his plot," and in his first novels of Sherlock Holmes (as distinct from the short stories) he followed Gaboriau's example of plot-construction, and found himself in the same technical difficulty, needing to break the thread of the detective interest to interpolate a long account of events that had taken place at some distant time or place. In *A Study in Scarlet* it is so abruptly done as to seem the opening of an entirely different story. In *The Sign of Four* it comes about more naturally, in the form of Jonathan Small's confession of his share in looting the Agra treasure during the Indian mutiny. Only once more, in *The Valley of Fear*, written a quarter of a century later, does Conan Doyle follow the same plan of construction, and this time he carefully reassures his readers, before transferring his story to America, that in due course they will "return to those rooms in Baker Street" for the conclusion of the tale. In this novel Doyle improved upon Gaboriau, and took an original step by making the interpolation another complete detective story with a different hero, "one of Pinkerton's best men, Birdy Edwards."

At the time when Conan Doyle began to write, detective fiction consisted mainly of two distinct groups, each designed to appeal to very different types of reader. The great majority of such stories were sensational, written for the uncritical general public, and seldom able to be read with interest a second time, once the secret was known. Side by side with these there was a growing popularity among more intellectual readers for the closely reasoned, more abstruse detective stories of Poe, which were repeatedly issued in new editions in this country and in France, as well as in his own country, especially from 1875 onwards. Conan Doyle contrived to combine the best features of both groups, and, by restraining the sensational within acceptable limits and explaining Holmes's deductions in such entertaining fashion, he evolved a new kind of detective story that pleased both types of reader. Sherlock Holmes's exploits are not simply tales of crime, nor mere puzzles that lose their interest as soon as they are solved. They can be read over and over again with renewed, even increased, appreciation for Holmes's detective acumen and the artistry with which the tale is unfolded.

When the reading public came to appreciate Holmes's powers in the *Adventures* they accorded him an affection that has scarcely diminished with the passing of more than a half a century. If, now and then, a plot contained some debatable statement, as, for example, Holmes's interpretation of the bicycle tracks in "The Priory School," or his inaccurate impressions of the rules of horse-racing in "Silver Blaze," Conan Doyle quickly learned about these discrepancies from readers' letters, or even from articles in the Press, but such comments did not ruffle his robust good humour. It is characteristic of well-written detective fiction that it stimulates the reader's mind almost equally to intelligent participation and analytical criticism. Mental effort on his part is essential to full enjoyment of the story, and he likes to increase his pleasure by exercising inductive reasoning upon the incidental details, provided always that the tale itself is sufficiently absorbing. The Sherlock Holmes stories quickly evoked this responsive interest, an interest which they still arouse in many critical minds seeking diversion.

Conan Doyle was singularly well equipped to produce fiction of this type. His prose was clear and factual, and he was mentally in tune with the spirit of sensational romance, for he loved action, adventure and tales of exciting quests. When little more than a youth, being troubled by religious doubts, he formulated for himself the rule: "Never will I accept anything which cannot be proved to me," and he made it his guiding principle through life, a principle that might well have served as a motto for Sherlock Holmes. . . . His long training in medicine enriched his mind in ways that had an important bearing on his work as a writer of detective fiction, giving him an intimate knowledge of all types of men and women and sharpening his inductive skill, his perception of the vital importance of *minutiae*. It also gave him, in the person of Dr. Joseph Bell, a prototype for the new "scientific" detective he was to create.

Holmes is introduced to the world as an expert in chemical research, a choice of profession very much in tune with the spirit of an age that was reaching out into scientific fields. On the historic occasion when Dr. Watson meets Sherlock Holmes for the first time, in the chemical laboratory at Bart's Hospital, Holmes has "just discovered a re-agent which is precipitated by haemoglobin and nothing else." "Practical?" cries Holmes in response to Watson's comment, "It is the most practical medico-legal discovery for years. Don't you see that it gives us an infallible test for bloodstains?" The same note is struck repeatedly. We hear of Holmes "spending seven weeks working out a few experiments in organic chemistry"; "settling down to one of those all-night researches which he frequently indulged in . . . stooping over a retort and test-tube"; "spending months on research into the coal-tar derivatives"; or discovering the decisive clue to a murder by testing a solution with litmus paper.

But it was not yet time for the appearance in fiction of a really scientific detective, such as Dr. Thorndyke and other specialists in this field who came later, for the average reader in the 1890's was scarcely able to appreciate chemical analysis as evidence. In spite of this flourish of test-tubes in the background, Holmes's experiments do little more than create the illusion of a scientific approach. He does not reason as a scientist in the cases related in detail, or make use of chemistry to solve the problems that form the framework of the plots. In *A Study in Scarlet* he believes that Enoch Drebber was murdered by poison, but he does not analyse the pills found later by the police. He tries them on his landlady's dog, and the little terrier's instant death satisfies the reader that the drug was lethal. The actual identification of the poison is a superfluous detail to him, as it is to Holmes. When, in "The Devil's Foot," Holmes at last comes to suspect that the burning of a mysterious brown powder has killed Brenda Tregennis and driven her brothers insane, he does not turn to his test-tubes, or, since he was on holiday in Cornwall at the time, send the powder to a local analyst. Instead, he arranges a rough and ready experiment to discover how the fumes would affect himself and Dr. Watson, with all but fatal results—a dramatic, rather than a scientific course of action.

In his early days of research at Bart's Hospital, Holmes was once seen "beating the subjects in the dissecting room with a stick, to verify how far bruises may be produced after death," but he is nowhere reported as using such knowledge, or, indeed, examining a body in a mortuary. The public was not yet ready for the detective with a scalpel, or for post mortem investigations such as were later performed so brilliantly by Sir Bernard Spilsbury in real life and Reginald Fortune in fiction. Holmes found his famous magnifying glass sufficiently informative for his purpose in most cases, though he sometimes used a microscope, as other detectives had done before him. He was, however, the first fictional detective to use a microscope for examining the dust extracted from his suspect's clothing, and this is perhaps his closest approach to "scientific detection."

In most cases, his successes depend far less upon science than upon his wide general knowledge, his quick perception of informative trifles, and in such matters the average reader can grasp his arguments with full appreciation. It needs no scientific training to perceive (or to agree) that a man writing on a wall usually does so at his own eye level, thus indicating his height; that only a strong man with special training could drive a harpoon through a human body; or that there is something sinister about a coffin which "took longer to make, being out of the ordinary." No one will deny that there are grounds for suspicion when a first-class workman accepts a job at half the usual wages, or when a governess is offered a situation at three times the normal salary. All through the series it is such clues as these, placed in passing before the reader, that enable Holmes to solve apparently inexplicable mysteries. Doctor Watson once exclaimed: "I had heard what he had heard, I had seen what he had seen, and yet from his words it was evident that he saw clearly not only what had happened, but what was about to happen, while to me the whole business was still confused and grotesque!" The reader feels the same mingling of frustration and curiosity, and not until he learns just where and when he has failed to notice the clues can he put the story down. (pp. 178-84)

It seems odd that Sherlock Holmes, who scrutinized footprints with such minute care on so many occasions, was so con-temptuous of fingerprints—an indication that the Red Indian out-weighed the scientist in him! In only one of his cases, "The Norwood Builder," is a fingerprint mentioned in any detail, and then it is a forgery, misleading to the police but not to Holmes, who "writhes with inward merriment" before explaining how simply such a print could be counterfeited. On a later occasion, in "The Three Gables," a pompous Inspector presumed to advise Holmes "never to pass anything, however trifling. There is always the chance of fingermarks or something." The remark was coldly ignored, and apart from these disparaging references there is scarcely a hint in all the Sherlock Holmes stories of this method of identification, and none of that familiarity with and respect for the work of fingerprint experts which became such a generally accepted feature in later detective fiction.

Conan Doyle, whose love for France was deep-rooted and sincere, repeatedly linked Sherlock Holmes with that country. His faculty of observation and deduction may have been inherited, he says, from his French grandmother, "the sister of Vernet, the French artist." Holmes was often engaged with French cases which are referred to in passing, that of the unfortunate Mme. Montpensier, for example, or of Huret, the boulevard assassin, "an exploit which won for Holmes a letter of thanks from the French president and the order of the Legion of Honour." Holmes frequently worked closely with the French police, and Dr. Watson records that one eminent detective, François le Villard, was so impressed with Sherlock Holmes's many monographs on technical aspects of detection that he translated them into French for the benefit of his colleagues.

The English police also valued Holmes's advise, and throughout his long career his services were available to help the professionals with any difficult case, from *A Study in Scarlet* (1887) to "The Retired Colourman" (1927). He had no great opinion of "the Scotland Yarders," in spite of their "quickness and energy," considering them "shockingly conventional," "lacking in imagination," sometimes even "obtuse to the point of imbecility," but he appreciated their persistence and their powerful organisation, and eventually found it a great convenience to be able to say: "Thanks to the telephone and the help of the Yard, I can usually get my essentials without leaving this room."

The numerous police officials who worked with him in turn, always began by distrusting his "far-fetched theories" and unconventional methods, but quickly came to value his co-operation, especially since he wanted no publicity, and never identified a criminal to them without at the same time giving them such clear proofs of his guilt that they ran no risk of losing their case in court. On occasion, however he deliberately refrained from revealing the entire truth to the police, reserving the right to with-hold information when he saw fit, though he never hampered or misled the official force. In "The Devil's Foot" he was scrupulous in leaving every clue for the police to find, if they could, but decided that in view of the special circumstances he was "not called upon to interfere." In "The Abbey Grange," also, he kept silence from similar motives, and never did Holmes let the police know that he and Watson had actually been present when a certain noble lady shot the blackmailing Charles Augustus Milverton.

In other murder cases when Holmes identifies the murderer, the guilty man may die of some long-standing disease, as in *A Study in Scarlet* and "The Boscombe Valley Mystery," or by some avenging stroke of Fate, as in "The Speckled Band" or *The Hound of the Baskervilles*. If he is to stand trial, the story closes with his arrest, and no more is heard of him. Apart from one brief newspaper report of an inquest in one of the early stories there are no court-room scenes, no dramatic trials such as had been popular in earlier detective fiction and would be so again; no attempt to follow a murderer along the sombre paths that lead from arrest to conviction and on to execution, that harrowing, inevitable sequence in the administration of justice which has disturbed the peace of mind of many sensitive investigators, from Walter Lester in *Eugene Aram* to Lord Peter Wimsey in *Busman's Honeymoon*. While recognising that some readers might wish to know what happened to the criminal, Watson dismissed the matter with the brief comment:—

> It has been difficult . . . to give those final details which the curious might expect. Each case has been the prelude to another, and, the crisis once over, the actors have passed for ever out of our busy lives.

Most of Sherlock Holmes's problems, in any case, are not concerned with murder but with less sensational crimes—burglary, fraud, blackmail, or the theft of important documents. Some of the most interesting do not treat of crime in the legal sense at all, but with human perplexities outside the scope of the law. Conan Doyle is unique among writers of detective fiction in the skill with which he so repeatedly weaves a fascinating mystery around some personal dilemma brought to Holmes by a distressed client—a missing fiancé, for instance, a husband's worry about his wife's health, or the disappearance of a rugby footballer on the eve of an important match. The reader finds additional pleasure in Holmes's frequent, intriguing little impromptu deductions about irrelevant matters, Dr. Watson's watch or Grant Munro's pipe, Dr. Mortimer's walking stick, or the profession of a casual passer-by; and a further savour is provided by the many tantalising hints of other mysteries which, for reasons of discretion, cannot yet be told, such as "The Case of the Two Coptic Patriarchs," "the truth about the Amateur Mendicant Society," or "the dreadful business of the Abernetty family."

In every story of Sherlock Holmes, the reader's interest is captivated not only by the detective's "unique methods," but perhaps to an even greater degree by "the singular personality of this remarkable man." Discussing his family link with Vernet, the French painter, Holmes commented that "Art in the blood is liable to take the strangest forms," and it may well have accounted for more than that hereditary aptitude for perception and deduction which he shared with his elder brother, Mycroft. There is artistry in his sense of the dramatic and in his skill as an actor. His impersonations deceive even his closest friend, and the reader is as amazed as Dr. Watson when Sherlock Holmes's voice is heard from a figure that till that moment has been fully accepted as a French workman, an elderly lady, a rough looking groom or a venerable Italian priest. (pp. 185-88)

Sherlock Holmes had many interests outside his professional activities, philology, for instance, and his study of ancient manuscripts or the music of the Middle Ages. He was an ardent lover of music, a composer as well as a capable performer, and the author of scores of treatises on abstruse subjects. Rather surprisingly, he was "one of the finest boxers of his weight," and it is a tribute to Conan Doyle's mastery of convincing detail that the reader can without hesitation accept Holmes in all these widely differing capacities. He had his eccentricities, his habit of countering boredom with cocaine, and now and then, like some of his French predecessors, he allowed his thoughts to stray to the other side of the fence. One of his

particular hobbies was the opening of safes, and in idle moments he would remark: "I have always had an idea that I could have made a highly efficient criminal," or "Burglary was always an alternative profession had I cared to adopt it." Yet his honour remained clear, and if, once or twice, he did break the letter of the law when all other means of achieving his purpose had failed, his motive was always to further the ends of justice, and he could say in all sincerity, "In over a thousand cases I am not aware that I have ever used my powers upon the wrong side."

The popularity of the Sherlock Holmes stories inevitably inspired many imitations and even burlesques, in none of which is the central character more than a puppet without life or personality, lacking everything except eccentricity. Such productions attested the vogue for detective fiction without affecting its development and they need not be examined here. . . . (p. 189)

Sherlock Holmes is a focal point in the evolution of the detective hero. He not only embodied the characteristics of his most notable predecessors, but also became the ancestor of almost all the outstanding twentieth-century detective heroes in English fiction, who reflect one or more of the varied facets of his personality, widely though they differ from him, and from each other, in other respects. Father Brown, with his intuition and his psychological flair; the scientist, Dr. Thorndyke, specializing in chemical analysis; Poirot, that neat little Belgian, and the burly French official, Hanaud, who so much enjoyed mystifying their friends, Captain Hastings and Mr. Ricardo, and arranging a dramatic denouement; Lord Peter Wimsey, who collected rare volumes and was a skilled musician; Reginald Fortune, enigmatic and sarcastic, who loved to work on his own and keep the regular police in suspense; all these and many others have a certain kinship with Sherlock Holmes.

With Conan Doyle, the detective story came at last to full fruition. His sincerity, his great skill as a writer, gave it a new distinction and won for it a wider, almost universal, acceptance as a literary form. It was by no means his only, or to him his most important, work, but the reading public of his generation recognised him as unquestionably a master of this type of fiction, which in his hands became a force potent enough to influence world trends in popular literature. For the first time, English detective fiction, which had received so much in earlier years from American and French sources, repaid that debt fully and created a new standard for developments in the twentieth century. (pp. 190-91)

> *A. E. Murch, "Sherlock Holmes," in her* The Development of the Detective Novel, *Philosophical Library, 1958, pp. 167-91.*

C. P. SNOW

[*Snow is an English man of letters who has also distinguished himself as a physicist and public servant. He has written science fiction and detective novels, but is best known for his popular* Strangers and Brothers *(1940-70), an eleven-novel series that examines questions of morality and power in contemporary England. In the following excerpt, Snow discusses the artistry of the Holmes stories, terming them the best of Doyle's literary work.*]

Conan Doyle had a singularly powerful romantic imagination. One can see it, not only in the Holmes stories, but in the books which, as with *Sir Nigel*, have not lasted so long (where Doyle, as modest as a successful writer can be, for once felt that he was being badly treated). One can see it in his life, the gallant crusades, the spiritualism, even his second marriage. In literature, to the depth and richness to which he possessed it, it is a rare quality, much rarer than most of those which we are inclined to venerate more. Balzac had it, so had Dickens, but other fine novelists, even some of the greatest, to nothing like the same extent.

It is probably impossible to capture a world audience without it. It is certainly impossible without it to produce a fictional person whose name becomes far better known than that of the author himself. How many people all over the planet could say something significant about Sherlock Holmes but would not have the faintest idea who created him! The number must be large. It is difficult to think of any similar case; perhaps the nearest equivalent would be the relation of Cervantes and Don Quixote.

The essence of an imagination such as Doyle's is that it simplifies and heightens. It can be benign, and give us a feeling of a desirable world—which most of the time he did. As I shall say in a moment, that is one of his delights. With some darker and more tormented souls (c.f. Dickens) it can be Gothic, or plain sinister. This quality was not entirely lacking in Doyle. No one could write "The Copper Beeches" or "The Speckled Band" without sadistic undercurrents disturbing him somewhere. But that does not leave a lasting effect as one reads. It is more like being taken back to childhood, hearing a storm thrashing about outside, and feeling comforted in a warm bed.

It is a mistake to think of his two great characters as caricatures. They are amiable archetypes—archetypes of what, in different moods, most of us would like to be, as brave and solid as Watson, as clever and superlatively effective as Holmes. These are, of course, desires which will never be fulfilled, but somehow we are safe. The whole environment gives us ultimate security. Adventure, risk, however timid we are, we have all had our flights of fancying them for ourselves—provided we come back intact, and bask in the comfort which is always residing deep down in the stories.

Remember, one feature of the author's imagination is that much of the grit of everyday life is washed away. Holmes and Watson aren't troubled about money. They have unqualified faith in each other's loyalty. They are not troubled about women, despite Watson's over-frequent marriages. Their attitude to women is chivalrous in the high Victorian manner (which incidentally, is a reason why Doyle's women are not satisfactory). Though their bachelor existence is happy-go-lucky and free from *Angst*, it is also respectably connected, again in the high Victorian manner. They have their place in the hierarchy, and it is a respected and influential place. Although Holmes sometimes produces admirable liberal sentiments about Board-schools as the lighthouses of the future, they take an entirely unaffected, unenvious pleasure in their connection with the eminent, especially with miscellaneous royalty. Note Watson's stupefied enthusiasm, in "The Adventure of the Illustrious Client,". . . when he catches sight of the brougham outside the door, and recognizes the armorial bearings. "It is a loyal friend and a chivalrous gentleman," says Holmes. "Let that now and for ever be enough for us."

Their pleasures are as unselfconscious and good-natured as that. Such pleasures have more charm than, with the top of our minds, we allow ourselves to think. Holmes and Watson are as unrancorous, as well-adjusted to turn-of-the-century England, as they are to their delectable cold suppers, presumably

Conan Doyle at his desk, allegedly writing A Study in Scarlet.

sent in from Fortnum's, after a successful case—though Holmes's choice of wine is sometimes distinctly eccentric. In spite of all the dramas and the occasional dangers, their lives are curiously soothing to read about. There is very little in any kind of literature which, in the last resort, bestows such reassurance and peace.

The truth is—this is often obscured—that the Holmes stories are a great artistic triumph, of a very strange kind, achieved without the writer's full engagement. That, of course, has happened to others. One of the most wonderful scenes in all literature, where Ivan Karamazov talks to his brother Alyosha in the garden, seems to have been written right against the grain, certainly against the conscious grain. Perhaps Doyle had one of those strokes of luck, which all writers know. After things which one has tried hardest to bring off have stayed half-dead, something else—maybe written without excitement or even interest—comes off with a dash, surprising the writer more than anyone else.

There is much more luck, sheer luck, in any kind of art than we care to recognize. A born professional like Doyle, slogging away, was likely to have it visit him once or twice. Before one or two suggestions why it visited him in the Holmes stories, it is perhaps as well to get rid of some illusions about them. They are not specially ingenious detective stories, and they didn't get much worse in that respect, simply because they were never very good. . . . "The Illustrious Client," "The Retired Colourman" and "The Sussex Vampire" are rather better than the average of the first two volumes. Doyle had nothing like the inventive skill of plenty of twentieth-century practitioners: compare Ellery Queen, John Dickson Carr, for psychological sleight-of-hand, Agatha Christie. There are dozens of others more cunning in these respects than Doyle. He was not a master of plot. His themes are nearly always more interesting than his plots, and his narrative, which rarely failed him, came more naturally than either.

Further, he was not a scientific innovator. He calms us with a faith in rationality: but, working in his period, anyone with a little curiosity about science could have done that. With enough self-hypnotism, it is possible to argue that he anticipated all scientific detective techniques. With enough self-hypnotism, it is possible to argue that he anticipated almost the whole of modern thought. You can make a plausible case, for instance, that he got in before Sir Karl Popper and Sir Peter Medawar on the hypothetico-deductive basis of the scientific process. All this belongs to the cheerful and agreeable Sherlockian fake scholarship, which is fine, so long as it doesn't detract from what Doyle could really do.

Some of that scholarship, though, does have a value in effectively revealing how often he was quite uncommitted to, or uninvolved in, the Holmes stories. One of my favourite pieces of this type is Mr. Michael Harrison's deadpan remark that Dr. Moriarty had three brothers, all rather surprisingly called James. (pp. 7-10)

Nevertheless, in these stories, uncommitted and careless as he often was, Doyle's temperament and gifts fused as they never did in anything else he wrote. His imagination needed tying down. He hadn't quite enough sense of the actual to make the fourteenth century concrete. His own London gave him just the sense of fact which he required. He had a beautiful gift for mood which, when Holmes and Watson were about, did not often run away with him. He shared their assumptions and their virtues, and, without effort, his own admirable personality showed through. Personalities as admirable as his are not common among writers, or, as far as that goes, anywhere else. Perhaps that is one reason why his work has inspired such affection. He was an extremely brave man, as Holmes and Watson are. He was as honourable as they are. He was generous and open-hearted. He was a specimen of Victorian England at its best. Incidentally, he was superlatively credulous, and even that leaves some endearing traces in the Holmes stories.

He was a good man, and somehow, with unusual percipience, first seduced by his restless imagination, his talent for atmosphere, the snugness of privileged London in the 'nineties, readers all over the world seem to have divined that goodness of his as a kind of sub-text.

It is a credit to public taste. (pp. 10-11)

Doyle understood a lot about evil, not so much about venality and corruption and shabbiness. That is another reason why the Holmes stories are nobler than this mortal life of ours. (p. 12)

> *C. P. Snow, in an introduction to* The Case-Book of Sherlock Holmes *by Sir Arthur Conan Doyle, John Murray and Jonathan Cape, 1974, pp. 7-12.*

HOWARD HAYCRAFT

[*Haycraft, an American critic and editor, has been termed a "connoisseur, historian, and bibliographer" of the detective story. In the following excerpt, Haycraft characterizes Doyle as a competent and vibrant storyteller, while discounting any particular originality or inventiveness on the part of the Holmes stories.*

Nevertheless, he notes several reasons why Holmes remains one of the best-loved characters in fiction.]

The rôle of Doyle and Holmes in resuscitating and rejuvenating the Poe-Gaboriau [detective story] formula was enormous and far-reaching. It is something of a paradox, therefore—but one which can not be ignored—that by modern standards the tales must often be pronounced better fiction than detection. They undeniably gave new life-blood to the form; they established a pattern which was to endure for a generation; yet it is certainly no disparagement to point out that they live to-day for the two immortal characters who move through their pages rather than for any particular excellence of plot or deduction. Subjected to purely technical analysis, in fact, they will be found all too frequently loose, obvious, imitative, trite, and repetitious in device and theme.

All the longer stories (with only the partial exception of *The Hound of the Baskervilles*) rely on painfully Gothic and antiquated treatment of the revenge motif. In two instances, *A Study in Scarlet* and *The Valley of Fear*, Doyle not only used without apology the creaking "flash-back" device, but did it so embarrassingly in the manner of Bertha M. Clay at her worst as to make the most ardent Sherlockian blush and hastily change the subject. The *Study in Scarlet*, in addition, violates two of the most sacred tenets of the detective story: the culprit is revealed to be one who has not, properly speaking, appeared previously in the story; and the solution is in large part based on information acquired secretly by the detective and not revealed to the reader until after the dénouement. The latter fault, in fact, tends to crop out in an embarrassing degree in many of the narratives.

Aside from his masterly creation of character, little real originality or inventiveness can be claimed for Doyle. Even *The Sign of the Four* bears a strong family resemblance in certain of its principal features to an older classic—Wilkie Collins' *Moonstone*. (Curiously enough, Doyle, who was ever ready to bow to Poe and Gaboriau as his masters in the craft, never properly acknowledged his indebtedness to his own compatriot.) The similarity of "A Scandal in Bohemia," among the shorter stories, to Poe's "Purloined Letter" has been mentioned in an earlier chapter; and certainly "The Dancing Men" could have been written only by an author who was familiar with "The Gold Bug."

On the whole, Doyle was happier in the short story than the longer form. Yet so faithful a disciple as Vincent Starrett pairs a sizable group of earlier and later tales, bearing plot resemblances that seem more than accidental: "A Scandal in Bohemia" and "The Norwood Builder"; "The Blue Carbuncle" and "The Six Napoleons"; "The Greek Interpreter" and "The Solitary Cyclist"; "The Naval Treaty" and "The Second Stain." Any discerning reader can easily expand the list. Repetitions of stock-characters, implements of crime and of detection, and similar minutiæ are even more numerous throughout the long saga. All these are integral weaknesses that can not be explained away, as certain others may be, by the obvious fact that Holmes came first in his particular field and has suffered from his imitators.

The detective himself has not escaped his share of just criticism. His frequent empiricism, his intolerance of others, his self-esteem got occasionally under even Watson's devoted hide. It was not without cause that E. W. Hornung, Doyle's brother-in-law and the creator of Raffles, once punned: "Though he might be more humble, there's no police like Holmes."

No offense is intended by these remarks; and none, one trusts, will be taken by even the most religious of Baker Street apostles. For Sherlock Holmes is a character who magnificently transcends the need for apology. What is it that has given him this opulent estate? For what excellent reasons do we forgive shortcomings we could condone in no one else? Why do we call his very absurdities beloved? The quality is at once simple and difficult to define—and one that many abler technical achievements sorely want. Lacking a single *mot juste* we may speak tentatively of "flavor." Or, to choose a hardier word, "gusto." One hesitates to use the overworked phrase "born story-teller"; yet Doyle's almost naïve zest was certainly a factor.

For it is not intricacy or bafflement that causes the tales to be read and re-read with a never diminishing thrill, when the slick product of to-day is forgotten in an hour. It is the "romantic reality" of their comfortable, nostalgic British heartiness. It is the small boy in all of us, sitting before an open fire, with the winter wind howling around the windows, a-wriggle with sheer pleasure. It is the "snug peril" of fin de siècle Baker Street, with hansom cabs rumbling distantly on wet cobblestones, and Moriarty and his minions lurking in the fog. It is the warmth behind drawn curtains, the reek of strong tobacco, the patriotic "V" done in bullet-pocks on the wall, the gasogene, the spirit lamp, the dressing-gown, the violin—and the "needle." It is the inevitable bell, the summons to duty and high adventure. It is "Sherlockismus," in the happy Carrollism of Father Knox:

> ". . . How do you know that?"
>
> "I followed you."
>
> "I saw no one."
>
> "That is what you may expect to see when I follow you."

It is the detective on all fours, nose to the ground, tracing a criminal's spoor with small animal sounds of happiness, like the human bloodhound he is. It is the triumphal return to 221-B, the "mission of humane vengeance" accomplished, the chase at end, the task well done. It is Holmes, beginning the explanation over one of Mrs. Hudsons's late suppers. It is Watson's wide-eyed and penultimate, "Marvelous!" It is Sherlock's final and superb, "Elementary!" (pp. 53-7)

Some one has accurately said that more has been written *about* Holmes (exclusive of the stories themselves) than any other character in fiction. A good half-dozen full-size published volumes are already given to his career and personality, and the number grows constantly, while the essays and magazine articles amount literally to hundreds; even Watson is achieving a respectable list of memorabilia in his own right. As Harry Hansen has pointed out, there is no other instance in literary annals where the *character* rather than the author is the subject of such fervid admiration.

But if, as these circumstances would seem to suggest, Holmes-worship has become something of a cult in late years, it is certainly defensible as the most innocent and least harmful of all its kind. Its unashamed insistence that what-never-was always-will-be stands in oddly human fashion for a Higher Sanity in a too-real world. (pp. 59-60)

> Howard Haycraft, *"Profile by Gaslight (Renaissance)," in his* Murder for Pleasure: The Life and Times of the Detective Story, *D. Appleton-Century Company, Incorporated, 1941, pp. 45-61.*

HOLMES'S CONTINUING POPULARITY

DON RICHARD COX

[In the following excerpt, Cox discusses reasons for the continued popularity of the Holmes stories.]

There have been many attempts made to explain the success of the Holmes stories. Doyle created in this series two of the most popular fictional characters of all time, characters who are instantly recognizable worldwide, even to those few who have not read the stories. Holmes and Watson repeatedly have been represented, alluded to, parodied, imitated, and caricatured in hundreds of movies, books, stories, articles, and advertisements. They can be seen on television, in the personages of Basil Rathbone and Nigel Bruce, stalking the moors looking for that infamous hound, and then, following the movie, appearing in a commercial selling Toyotas, being two of a small handful of literary figures such as Robinson Crusoe or Scrooge whom any reader can identify on sight. How did Doyle, whose other fiction is rather unmemorable, manage to score such a complete success in this series of tales that rival Shakespeare and Dickens in their popularity? There are several reasons.

First, there tends to be a somewhat cultlike following among readers of mystery fiction. Figures as diverse as Charlie Chan, Travis McGee, Hercule Poirot, Columbo, Miss Marple, Mike Hammer, Peter Wimsey, or Philip Marlowe reflect the phenomenon that began with Holmes and Watson. Fans of detective fiction like to see detectives develop and grow in a series of stories or novels. Because the central emphasis in the formula of detective fiction is usually on plot, characterization becomes secondary in the equation. Repeating a character, or allowing that character to develop gradually over a series of stories, allows both writer and reader to devote their attention to the central issue of the plot—the mystery. Furthermore, the repetition of the central figure or figures provides a constant viewpoint readers can rely upon as they attempt to unravel the puzzles for themselves.

As Doyle himself discovered when writing *The Hound of the Baskervilles,* it is simply much easier to use the personalities one has already created than to invent new ones, for the new ones must be accompanied by certain explanatory background information; they need a history or "life" to be believable. Detective fiction is of course not the only kind of fiction that utilizes the series format—children's books often come in series, for example, and there are the Brigadier Gerard and Professor Challenger series of Doyle—but fans of detective fiction tend to be somewhat avid readers, and most of them who find a character they like soon read the entire series and eagerly await more of the same. Since the sixty Holmes stories over a period of forty years represents one of the longest single detective series, one should not be surprised to find Holmes among the most popular of detectives. As one of the oldest detective series (the honor of creating *the* oldest must ultimately belong to Poe), it also stands to reason that Holmes is among the most popular simply because he has been around for so long.

A second factor contributing to the popularity of the Holmes cycle is the very successful pictorial treatment the stories have had nearly since their inception. Although Doyle's descriptions of the great detective and his friend are in themselves clear and memorable, if the series had continued with the type of illustrations we find in the early editions of the first novels it is safe to say that Holmes would not now be a figure visually identifiable to young and old. In what was an incredible stroke of luck, Doyle was able to secure Sidney Paget as the illustrator for most of the Holmes stories published in England. Paget clearly established the Holmesian profile that the American illustrator Frederic Dorr Steele perpetuated in the American publications of the stories, although Steele used as models both Paget's drawings and the American actor who brought Holmes to life on the stage—William Gillette.

The role of Gillette in contributing to the image of Holmes cannot be underestimated. He brought the deerstalker hat and the curved pipe to the characterization, two props that became permanent additions to later representations of the detective. Once this Paget-Gillette-Steele composite image was formed, Holmes became a rather firmly fixed and clearly identifiable figure that other illustrators did not alter, as though Holmes were a real person who "really looked" a certain way. For twentieth-century audiences, most of whom of course never saw Gillette, and many of whom have never seen the drawings of Paget or Steele, the tremendously popular series of fourteen movies starring Basil Rathbone and Nigel Bruce established the images clearly in the minds of millions. Although the Rathbone-Bruce series of films has been criticized for being unfaithful to Doyle's fiction (and it certainly is), the movies have always been popular and have contributed a great deal to the mythic dimensions of Holmes. Others since Rathbone have attempted the role, but Rathbone's physical resemblance to the Paget-Gillette-Steel representation has made his characterization the most popular and his face has blended with the others into the composite image of Holmes that is known the way the face of no other fictional character is known. Only Dickens and Shakespeare, besides Doyle, have had illustrators and actors contribute so successfully to bringing their characters to life.

Thirdly, the atmosphere of the stories is a powerful factor in their popularity. The dominant image that emerges from the cycle is one of Holmes and Watson prowling through the foggy streets of London in a world where, in the words of one writer, "it is always 1895." Even though Holmes and Watson attack a number of problems on sunny spring mornings and hot August afternoons, and work in the country almost as frequently as the city, those settings tend to be overlooked as readers remember only the "classic" atmosphere of some of the episodes. Reading is a solitary activity, a withdrawn activity, and the withdrawn atmosphere of Baker Street on a foggy London night is completely compatible with one's longing for retreat as he or she settles into a comfortable chair with a volume of Doyle in hand. There is a safeness one can sense in the picture of Holmes and Watson sitting snugly before their fire browsing through their papers or books in an idle fashion while outside the elements rage. It is a very comfortable world Doyle creates: inside are warmth, safety, light, and knowledge; outside are darkness, cold, and criminal forces.

The world of Baker Street is a world that is reassuringly far less complex than the real one. Messages are sent by telegrams, which usually can be traced. (Although there is a telephone in Baker Street in some of the later stories, Holmes does not seem to like to use this newfangled form of communication.) A railroad timetable (which apparently never needs updating) can provide definitive information about long-distance travel; for short distances, of course, there is a hansom cab on every corner (cabs which can also be traced if necessary). The news-

papers' "agony columns" (as Holmes refers to them) provide a kind of public bulletin board of information anyone can consult. Apparently everyone does consult these columns, for Holmes almost always gets instant responses to his advertisements and regularly discovers that the columns are being used to transmit secret and seldom encoded messages by people one might assume would choose a far less public and troublesome manner of communication. Personal security is also relatively simple in Holmes's world. A cane or stout stick is usually adequate protection; Watson's service revolver is an ultimate weapon of sorts, the absolute defense against any violence one might encounter. The very limited and contained nature of this environment makes it a safe retreat for readers because of its welcome predictability; the intricacies and uncertainties of life in the late twentieth century have no place in Doyle's simplified and well-ordered world.

Lastly, of course, the popularity of Doyle's two characters can be attributed to the personalities of the figures themselves. To say that Watson is beloved because he is loyal and devoted, or Holmes is popular because he is brilliant and fearless, however, is to miss the point. There are a number of admirable heroes in literature who have possessed any number of good qualities and not been nearly so well accepted by the public. Some of their secret lies in the interplay between the characters, the antithetical qualities they possess that cause them to complement each other. Watson is staid, for example, where Holmes is unconventional; Holmes is cerebral where Watson is physical; Watson is disciplined while Holmes indulges his many whims. We come to know these traits, these idiosyncrasies, how these characters will react to certain situations, and they themselves frequently display an awareness of their differences, giving added verisimilitude to their characterizations. Furthermore, by Watson's frequent allusions to cases that do not actually appear in the cycle (such as the infamous "Giant Rat of Sumatra"), Doyle suggests that his characters' lives extend much further than the series and thereby contributes a realistic fullness to their existence. There is the reliability of a solid friendship here, the predictability we come to expect from old companions when we have grown to know their habits nearly as well as we know our own.

The way readers relate to the personae of Holmes and Watson is also important. Watson, the narrative voice of almost all the stories, presents his case in a straightforward way. His method is the epitome of good common sense. Watson is frequently puzzled, sometimes reaches too quickly for the obvious, and often, when attempting to imitate the deductive thinking of his brilliant friend, arrives at an absolutely wrong conclusion even though he is reasoning from the same data as Holmes. Watson is human when Holmes is cold and indifferent, and readers no doubt sense in this rather practical physician the touch of humanity that makes him trustworthy. The reader can believe in these adventures because he knows that Watson reports them without exaggeration. In short, Watson reacts the way that a reader might in his shoes; one therefore identifies with his point of view.

Holmes is not perceived by Watson as an intellectual equal, and he is not seen that way by most readers either. Holmes is a kind of wizard with an endless array of tricks up his sleeve. His knowledge and skill make him virtually invulnerable, and his presence is as reassuring as Watson's revolver, but for very different reasons. Holmes continually demonstrates that the puzzles of life are always solvable, and that they are almost always far less complex than they first appear to be. Holmes brings with him his lantern of rational thought and repeatedly flashes it into the dark corners of human existence, showing us that the shadows lurking there are not to be feared. There is a paternal quality to his actions that reinforces our confidence and reassuringly convinces us that there exists in this man what he in turn found in his friend Watson, "one fixed point in a changing age." (pp. 178-83)

> *Don Richard Cox, in his* Arthur Conan Doyle, *Frederick Ungar Publishing Co., 1985, 251 p.*

ADDITIONAL BIBLIOGRAPHY

Atkinson, Michael. "Type and Text in *A Study in Scarlet*: Repression and the Textual Unconscious." *Clues: A Journal of Detection* 8, No. 1 (Spring-Summer 1987): 67-99.
Close study of the two separate narratives that combine to form the first Holmes story, *A Study in Scarlet*: the London-based mystery in which Holmes and Watson figure, and the long American flashback that explains the motivations of the characters.

Baring-Gould, William S. *Sherlock Holmes of Baker Street: A Life of the World's First Consulting Detective*. New York: Bramhall House, 1962, 336 p.
"Biography" of Holmes, using cleverly reasoned conjecture to flesh out a plausible life of the great detective. Baring-Gould includes a complete bibliography of the Holmes stories—with their authorship attributed to John H. Watson, M.D.— a separate bibliography of "The Higher Criticism," or works of Holmesian scholarship, and a bibliography of writings attributed to Sherlock Holmes.

———, ed. *The Annotated Sherlock Holmes*. 2 vols. New York: Clarkson N. Potter, Inc., 1967.
Profusely illustrated and extensively annotated edition of the Holmes stories and novels which Baring-Gould has arranged in the order he believes each case occurred. In an introductory section of essays, one of which is excerpted in the entry above, Baring-Gould discusses Doyle's life, the characters and possible inspirations for Holmes and Watson, notable illustrators of Holmes, stage and screen performances of the adventures, and other aspects of the stories and their settings. In various places throughout the text, Baring-Gould inserts Sherlockian essays on controversial, enigmatic, or entertaining matters from the narratives, such as the location of Watson's war wound.

Barolsky, Paul. "The Case of the Domesticated Aesthete." *The Virginia Quarterly Review* 60, No. 3 (Summer 1984): 438-52.
Explores aspects of Sherlock Holmes's character as a typical fin de siècle decadent aesthete, based perhaps upon Oscar Wilde, whom Doyle knew and admired.

Burgess, Anthony. "The Sainted Sleuth, Still on the Case." *The New York Times Book Review* (4 January 1987): 1, 26-7.
Discusses the Holmes centenary, suggesting that the stories' entertainment value and Holmes's vast popularity entitle Doyle to the claim of greatness as a writer.

Carr, John Dickson. *The Life of Sir Arthur Conan Doyle*. New York: Harper & Brothers, 1949, 304 p.
Anecdotal biography of Doyle.

Clark, Edward F., Jr. "Brag and Bounce." *The Baker Street Journal* n.s. 23, No. 2 (June 1983): 75-8.
Examines Holmes's tendency to contrive unnecessarily dramatic denouements to certain of his cases.

De Waal, Ronald Burt. *The World Bibliography of Sherlock Holmes and Dr. Watson: A Classified and Annotated List of Materials Relating to their Adventures*. Boston: New York Graphic Society, 1974, 526 p.
Inclusive bibliography of books and essays on Holmes and Watson.

Doyle, Arthur Conan. Preface to *The Case-Book of Sherlock Holmes*, pp. 13-14. London: Jonathan Murray, 1927.
Introduction to the final collection of Holmes stories, in which Doyle bids farewell to his most famous character, who "may perhaps have stood a little in the way of my more serious work."

Eco, Umberto, and Sebeok, Thomas A., eds. *The Sign of Three: Dupin, Holmes, Peirce*. Bloomington: Indiana University Press, 1983, 236 p.
Collection of essays discussing and sometimes comparing the methods of several fictional detectives.

Edwards, Owen Dudley. *The Quest for Sherlock Holmes: A Biographical Study of Arthur Conan Doyle*. Totowa, N. J.: Barnes & Noble, 1983, 380 p.
Biography which assumes an autobiographical link between Doyle's life and many incidents from his fiction.

Green, Richard Lancelyn, ed. *The Sherlock Holmes Letters*. London: Secker & Warburg, 1986, 266 p.
Reprints letters and periodical pieces pertaining to the Holmes stories and to the secondary body of Sherlockian scholarship.

Greene, Graham. Introduction (1973) to *The Sign of Four*, by Arthur Conan Doyle, pp. 7-10. Garden City, N.Y.: Doubleday & Co., 1974.
Maintains that the second Holmes adventure, *The Sign of Four*, is superior to *A Study in Scarlet* in character delineation, skillful scene-setting, and suspenseful incident.

Haining, Peter, ed. *A Sherlock Holmes Compendium*. London: W. H. Allen, 1980, 216 p.
Profusely illustrated collection of essays on things Holmesian.

Hall, Trevor H. *Sherlock Holmes: Ten Literary Studies*. New York: St. Martin's Press, 1969, 157 p.
Collection of Holmesian essays on such topics as Holmes's youth, his education, fondness for music, and relations with women.

———. *The Late Mr. Sherlock Holmes and Other Literary Studies*. London: Gerald Duckworth & Co., 1971, 142 p.
Collection of essays dealing with such aspects of Holmesian scholarship as Watson's marriages, the unpublished Holmes cases mentioned in the adventures, and Holmes's gourmandizing.

———. *Sherlock Holmes and His Creator*. New York: St. Martin's Press, 1977, 155 p.
Collection of essays, some purely Sherlockian, others concerned with Doyle's life, including his interest in a missing-person case that may have inspired the first Holmes adventure.

Hardwick, Michael, and Hardwick, Mollie. *The Sherlock Holmes Companion*. New York: Doubleday, 1962, 232 p.
"Scrapbook of Sherlockiana" including a list of characters, plot synopses, and profiles of Holmes, Watson, and Doyle.

———. *The Man Who Was Sherlock Holmes*. New York: Doubleday & Co., 1964, 92 p.
Biography of Doyle, concentrating on Holmes's popularity.

Harrison, Michael. *In the Footsteps of Sherlock Holmes*. Rev. ed. Newton Abbot, England: David & Charles, 1971, 292 p.
Retrospective survey of facts of everyday life in late nineteenth-century England related to the "life" of Holmes.

James, Clive. "Sherlockology." *The New York Review of Books* XXII, No. 2 (20 February 1975): 15-18.
Discusses sixteen essays and whole volumes devoted to the study of Sherlock Holmes, commenting somewhat sardonically on the cult of Holmesian scholarship.

Keating, H. R. F. *Sherlock Holmes: The Man and His World*. New York: Charles Scribner's Sons, 1979, 160 p.
Profusely illustrated volume relating the character of Holmes to his country and to his era.

Lawrence, Barbara. "Putting Women in Their Place: The Dichotomy of Irene Adler and Mrs. Hudson." *The Armchair Detective* 19, No. 2 (1986): 145-46.

Notes that only women ever outwitted Holmes, and claims that only women (and street urchins) ever assisted him in detection.

Liebow, Ely. *Dr. Joe Bell: Model for Sherlock Holmes*. Bowling Green: Bowling Green University Popular Press, 1982, 269 p.

Biography of the Edinburgh medical school professor who is widely believed to have partially inspired some of Sherlock Holmes's personality traits and methods. Liebow outlines the battle that Doyle's son Adrian has waged in his effort to disavow any connection between Bell and the character of Holmes.

Pearsall, Ronald. *Conan Doyle: A Biographical Solution*. London: Weidenfeld and Nicholson, 1977, 208 p.

Thorough biography discussing both Doyle's life and works. Pearsall places the Holmes stories in relation to the development of detective fiction.

Pearson, Hesketh. *Conan Doyle: His Life and Art*. London: Methuen & Co., 1943, 193 p.

Excellent critical biography.

Pointer, Michael. *The Public Life of Sherlock Holmes*. New York: Drake Publishers, 1975, 200 p.

Examines radio, stage, and film versions of the Sherlock Holmes adventures.

Rosenberg, Samuel. *Naked is the Best Disguise: The Death & Resurrection of Sherlock Holmes*. Indianapolis: Bobbs-Merrill Co., 1974, 198 p.

Examination of the Holmes stories as self-revelatory allegories on Doyle's part.

Sayers, Dorothy L. *Unpopular Opinions: Twenty-One Essays*. New York: Harcourt, Brace and Co., 1947, 236 p.

Contains four Sherlockian essays: "Holmes's College Career," "Dr. Watson's Christian Name," "Dr. Watson, Widower," and "The Dates in 'The Red-Headed League'." In her introduction to this volume, Sayers coined the term "Higher Criticism" for the elaborate game of scholarly exegesis of the Holmes stories, and established for its practitioners the incontrovertible rule "that it must be played as solemnly as a county cricket match at Lord's: the slightest touch of extravagance or burlesque ruins the atmosphere."

Seventeen Steps to 221B: A Collection of Sherlockian Pieces by English Writers. London: George Allen & Unwin, 1967, 181 p.

Compendium reprinting some major Holmesian essays, including contributions by A. A. Milne, S. C. Roberts, Desmond MacCarthy, Dorothy L. Sayers, Adrian Doyle, and John Dickson Carr.

Spruance, Sherril A. "Sherlock Holmes: His 100th Anniversary." *British Heritage* 8, No. 2 (February-March 1987): 39-44.

Notes the enduring popularity of the Holmes stories.

Stout, Rex. "Watson Was a Woman." in *The Art of the Mystery Story: A Collection of Critical Essays*, edited by Howard Haycraft, pp. 311-18. New York: Simon and Schuster, 1946.

One of the most widely known parodies of Sherlockian scholarship, in which Stout puts forth his theory that Doctor Watson was a woman—and Holmes's wife.

Symons, Julian. *Conan Doyle: Portrait of an Artist*. New York: Mysterious Press, 1987, 160 p.

Concise and informative introduction to Doyle's life and works.

Van Doren, Mark. "A. Conan Doyle: 'The Adventures of Sherlock Holmes'." In *The New Invitation to Learning*, edited by Mark Van Doren, pp. 236-51. New York: Random House, 1942.

Lively round-table discussion of various aspects of the Holmes stories, with Van Doren, Rex Stout, Jacques Barzun, and Elmer Davis.

Spanish Civil War Literature

INTRODUCTION

The Spanish Civil War profoundly stirred the imagination and emotions of writers throughout the Americas and Europe. This conflict between supporters of democracy, fascism, and communism encapsulated most of the ideological conflicts of world politics during the 1930s, and thus served as an ideal subject for writers who wished to treat these complex topics in a concentrated manner. To aid an understanding of the ideological and theoretical positions of the authors of this era, which is the intent of the following entry, it is necessary to first provide a brief overview of the events of the war.

The Spanish Civil War represented the culmination of many years of chaotic and bitter partisan politics and economic decline in Spain. Although the country enjoyed relative calm and stability under the military dictatorship of Miguel Primo de Rivera during the 1920s, his resignation in 1930 was followed by political and social unrest as successive governments futilely attempted to satisfy the demands of numerous parties and trade unions whose membership and influence grew rapidly in the 1930s. Among the most powerful of these groups were the C.N.T. (Anarcho-Syndicalist Trades Union), U.G.T. (Socialist Trade Union), and P.O.U.M. (Party of Marxist Unification) on the Left, and the Falange (Fascists) and C.E.D.A. (Catholic Party) on the Right. Following de Rivera's resignation, Spain was ruled briefly by a ministerial cabinet directed by a military general, but a rebellion of officers and civilians forced elections in April 1931, and a leftist government gained power. While the new government was engaged in constitutional reform, Anarchist revolts occurred in several parts of the country, and when elections were held again in April 1933, the Right emerged victorious. Many of the recently instituted reforms were repealed, while labor strikes and numerous local uprisings plagued the government. In October 1934, a violent revolt by miners took place in Asturias. Generals Francisco Franco and Manuel Goded were enlisted by the government to halt the rebellion, and Franco, without hesitating, sent in the Foreign Legion. The dispute was quickly settled, and Franco was celebrated as a hero for his decisive action.

Despite numerous changes of government (including seven in 1935 alone), the Right retained power until the elections of February 1936. For these elections, tentative alliances were formed by parties of the Left, which formed the Popular Front, and of the Right, which formed the National Front. The Popular Front won a majority, and optimistically set a new government in place, but bitter partisanship, street violence, and terrorism erupted almost immediately. A plot to overthrow the government—which would eventually ignite the war—was already being developed by General Emilio Mola, Franco, and others in May 1936. The military uprising was triggered in July by the assassination of the government opposition leader whom the conspiring generals supported.

The Nationalist (Insurgent) revolt began when a group of right-wing officers took control of an air base in Spanish Morocco on July 17, 1936, and similar uprisings soon occurred at military bases on the mainland. In Barcelona and Madrid, the

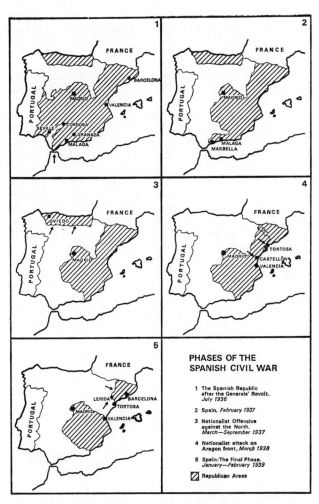

Phases of the Spanish Civil War. Reproduced with the kind permission of Wayland (Publishers) Limited, Hove, England.

Nationalists were defeated by the amateur militias of left-wing political parties and trade unions who had demanded arms from the indecisive Republican (Loyalist) government. After the initial skirmishes, during which the Republicans gained control of eastern and most of southern Spain, battle lines remained fairly stable for many months during a vicious war of attrition. The fascist governments of Adolf Hitler in Germany and Benito Mussolini in Italy provided military and financial assistance to the Nationalists, but few governments were willing to come to the aid of the Republicans. Most democratic nations, including the United States and Great Britain, adopted strict non-interventionist policies which outlawed even the shipment of arms to Spain. The Republicans did receive help from Joseph Stalin in Russia, but he extracted a high price for it—payment in gold upon delivery of military hardware and supplies and an ever-increasing communist influence in the Spanish government. They were also aided by over 40,000 foreigners who volunteered to serve in the hastily formed International Brigades. American volunteers served in the Abraham Lincoln Battalion, while battalions of Germans—often political exiles from Nazi Germany—joined British, French, Italian, and Mexican volunteers to fight for the Republic. The fall of Republican-held Catalonia in January-February 1939 signaled the demise of the Spanish Republic, which suffered an uprising within its own government in the final days of the war. General Franco assumed control of the government and continued to rule Spain until his death in 1975.

Occurring in an era of heightened international political awareness and activity, the war ignited the passions and imagination of intellectuals everywhere who traveled to Spain as correspondents, volunteers, or spectators. Many contemporary observers saw the Spanish Civil War as an opportunity to conclusively defeat the advance of fascism in Europe, while others, contemptuous of communism, worried that if the Republican forces won, Spain might become little more than a Russian satellite, controlled from Moscow by Stalin. Because of the intervention by Germany, Italy, and Russia, many historians now view the Civil War as a costly rehearsal for the Second World War, which began shortly after the conflict in Spain drew to a close. At the time, few in the international intellectual community could view the Spanish conflict dispassionately, and most fought—with a pen or with a gun—for the Republicans. From Britain came young, idealistic socialists and communists, such as W. H. Auden, Stephen Spender, John Cornford, George Orwell, and Julian Bell. From the United States came workers, journalists, and novelists, including Ernest Hemingway, John Dos Passos, and Alvah Bessie. Whether they had arrived in Spain as writers, or had never written before, many volunteers were inspired to record their experiences in poetry or prose. The following entry discusses the impact and concerns of the literature inspired by the Spanish Civil War.

TOPICS IN SPANISH CIVIL WAR LITERATURE

FREDERICK R. BENSON

[*Benson is the author of* Writers in Arms: The Literary Impact of the Spanish Civil War *(1967), a study in which he examines works by Ernest Hemingway, André Malraux, Gustav Regler, George Orwell, Arthur Koestler, and Georges Bernanos. In the following excerpt from that work, he discusses the historical importance of the war and introduces the principal ideological perspectives and literary forms of Spanish Civil War literature.*]

The total impact of the Spanish Civil War on Europe and America can never be measured with precision. In retrospect, the passions aroused by the conflict appear disproportionate to any military importance inherent in the struggle. For intensity of emotion, neither the First World War nor the Second World War exacerbated the feelings of people to the extent of those events in Spain from 1936 to 1939. More than any other crisis of the century, the Spanish struggle brought to the surface the incipient political philosophies and humanitarian hopes of an extremely social-conscious generation. For many intellectuals, their great interest in the Spanish conflict was not based on any exalted belief in the importance of the war for the future of mankind, but rather on the realization that something was

lacking in their own culture; that the backward, stagnant, and inefficient Spaniard could well compete, in the field of human values, with the efficient, practical, and progressive European. (p. xix)

Hugh Thomas has written that the Spanish Civil War "appeared a 'just war,' as civil wars do to intellectuals, since they lack the apparent vulgarity of [inter]national conflicts" [see Additional Bibliography]. To many antifascists, when all the parties of the left were ostensibly cooperating in the Popular Front, it seemed a moment of hope for a new generation rebellious at its inheritance of a cynical and hypocritical legacy. The democracies—England, France and the United States—had for years been absorbed in an effort to recover from economic disaster, and had shown neither vigor nor resolution in their attempt to contain Hitler and Mussolini. In describing the democratic perspective, Allen Guttman reflects that

> Spain seemed a last chance for a representative government and a pluralistic society in a Europe that had turned with frightening speed toward dictatorship and totalitarianism. At a time when militant Fascism deified the unreasonable, the Spanish Republic seemed to represent the Enlightenment's faith in reason as the faculty by which men govern themselves.

Thus, for many, the defense of the Spanish people was the embodiment of the forces of light struggling against the turbulent onrush of engulfing darkness.

With the perspective provided by the thirty-year interim since the outbreak of hostilities, the historical importance of the Spanish Civil War is clearly discerned. In the political and military history of the twentieth century, the Spanish conflict overshadows other national and international events which occurred between the two world wars. Although its concrete result was a fascist military triumph, it also offered to International Communism, with its discipline, its skillful propaganda machine, and the prestige derived from its defense of a humanitarian cause, the greatest political opportunity since the Soviet Revolution; it converted the concept of a unified front against fascism from a study in Marxist dialectics to a battlefield reality. For the Germans, Italians, and Russians, who undertook to advise, support, and exploit one side or the other, the war in Spain provided the opportunity to experiment with weapons and tactics. Politically, the war helped to delineate the European international situation, although at a tremendous sacrifice in men and ideals.

The Spanish Civil War was a conflict in which the military strategy was easily visualized and the ideological issues, at least on the surface, seemed clearly drawn. Since the area of struggle in Spain was confined, and the scope of the military action comparatively restrained, the voices of individuals were not submerged, as they were to be in 1939, by the vast machinery of modern warfare. It is not difficult to envision why so many intellectuals found in the outbreak of the conflict that thunderbolt from an increasingly clouding sky, something very like an act both of fulfillment and deliverance. As a result, when literature reflected social and economic problems, as well as the fears engendered by a series of political crises, the war not only served to bring these problems and fears into sharp focus, but became the counteraction that would conceivably contribute to their elimination. It provided writers with the opportunity to base their works on an actual event, an objective situation, which possessed tremendous power as a literary symbol. During the 1930s, an era of incessant social violence, depression, and revolution, climaxed by the Spanish Civil War, these authors felt themselves carried along by history. So traumatic was the impact of this period ending with the Second World War, that it can be said of a great many writers that nothing has happened to them since. If the nineteenth century did not end until 1914, the twentieth did not actually begin until the 1930s. In the democracies, the Spanish conflict ultimately proved to many writers that their political and social theories required closer scrutiny; that a cause which seemed just could nonetheless be corrupted; and that the violence of modern war could not be satisfactorily rationalized in ideological terms. Most intellectuals later conceded that abdication of responsibility by their democratic governments permitted the weak but representative Spanish Republic to be destroyed by fascist aggression; and they generally acknowledged that the defeat of the Loyalists was a major factor in encouraging the fascist dictators to extend their depredations in Europe, thus bringing about the Second World War. Only too late did they come to realize that what was occurring in that tormented country was neither a meaningless fratricidal strife nor a crusade in defense of Christian civilization, but a tragic prologue to the global struggle against international fascism.

Although the political and military history of the Spanish conflict has received considerable attention, less is known about the impact of the war on European and American literature, the importance of which is manifested in those writings dealing with the conflict. From a critical point of view, since 1945 there have been few works that can approach the distinction of the major literary efforts concerned with the Spanish Civil War. Authors of such international prominence as André Malraux, Georges Bernanos, François Mauriac, Jacques Maritain, Antoine de Saint-Exupéry, Louis Aragon, and Paul Eluard in France; George Orwell, W. H. Auden, Stephen Spender, C. Day Lewis, and Herbert Read in England; Ernest Hemingway, John Dos Passos, Theodore Dreiser, and Archibald MacLeish in the United States; and Ilya Ehrenburg and Michael Kol'tsov in Russia, all contributed to the literature of the Spanish Civil War. In South America the Chilean Pablo Neruda and the Peruvian César Vallejo committed their poetry to the Spanish cause. Most of the important writers were antifascist and their central themes were expressed in the context of their democratic traditions. This antifascist thesis was further strengthened by the writers who fled Hitler's Germany and Mussolini's Italy at this time: Gustav Regler, Arthur Koestler, Thomas Mann, Bertolt Brecht, and Ernst Toller from Germany; and Randolfo Pacciardi, Pietro Nenni, Palmero Togliatti, and Luigi Longo from Italy, each of whom later contributed to the literature of the war. In Spain as well, most literary figures, although deploring the extremism in both camps, were sympathetic to the cause of the Republic; few Spanish authors aligned themselves with the insurgents during the period of the conflict. Most Spanish writers and the literary world in general opposed the fascist cause, particularly following the senseless execution in the Nationalist zone of Spain's great poet, Federico García Lorca.

There was in Europe and the United States a small intellectual element on the right which hoped that the demise of the Spanish Republic would be followed by the rebirth of a nationalistic and aristocratic social order; George Santayana and Ezra Pound sympathized with this group. The only intense literary support for the Nationalist cause came from those Roman Catholic writers who saw in Franco's Nuevo Estado a promise of a Christian society in which the menace of communism would

be permanently eliminated. Paul Claudel was the leading figure of this group in France, but he was countered by such Catholic intellectuals as Mauriac and Maritain. With the possible exception of Stefan Andres' short religious novel, *Wir Sind Utopia,* an extremely moving portrayal of conversion and martyrdom, the literary efforts of the Catholic intellectuals were inadequate. The conservative and reactionary responses to the Spanish Civil War failed to produce a major work comparable to several written from a liberal perspective.

Supporters of the right, however, did not monopolize literary ineptitude. Of the considerable output by both sides recounting the war in Spain, much was amateurish and poor even by journalistic standards. The pamphlets, on-the-spot accounts and memoirs which were published shortly after the outbreak of hostilities, made no pretense beyond literary commercialism and are not worthy of serious critical consideration. A large portion of the literature written after the battlelines were drawn and the issues defined consisted of polemics intended to express political ideology. Such writings, often extremist in nature, either distorted or oversimplified the deeper meanings of the conflict. The vast literature on the subject available in books and periodicals was largely topical and evanescent. Much of it was marred by a surfeit of emotion; much was purely sensational; and a large portion of this writing, while passionately committed in sentiment, possessed little literary quality. Few works transcended the clichés of propaganda and found their inspiration in humanistic ideals rather than partisan politics.

The novelist possessed two distinct advantages over writers in other genres when discussing the disparate aspects of the Spanish Civil War. The extreme adaptability of his medium enabled him to cover a wider range than dramatists and writers in other fictional forms and to include within his work such widely diverse phases of the struggle as the siege of the Alcazar, the bombing of civilians in Guernica, the interparty strife in Barcelona, and the defense of Madrid. Thus, the novelist could establish a panoramic view of the war rather than be restricted to the presentation of an isolated theme or event.

Most significantly, the novelist was able to merge his ideas and ideals into the action he portrayed. During this period ideology had become very closely associated with politics in the minds of writers. The response to the conflict by European and American authors was affected by the same social and political forces which strongly influenced the literary movements of the decade. In the democracies there has probably never been a time when organized religion seemed as futile or lacking in reality as it did to many intellectuals when confronted with the human suffering of the depression years; at this same time, historical analyses seemed too remote to provide direction amidst the social protest and upheaval of the 1930s. No other philosophy appeared to fill the void. Political ideology alone seemed to provide a viable solution.

In view of the unique nature of the Spanish struggle, it is understandable that most of its literature is concerned with politics and hence may be termed "political"; in it political ideas play the dominant role and the political milieu is the dominant setting. Because of the close relationship between politics and the literary output of this war, it is difficult to judge the true merit of its product. The measure of effectiveness of a political novelist is his ability to explore ideology, which is necessarily abstract, through the experiences and feelings of his fictional characters. The important works of this genre concerning the Spanish conflict transcended the propaganda tracts of their contemporaries by generating such intense heat that the ideas expounded were endowed with a capacity for stirring the characters into action, while creating the illusion of an independent existence fused within the pattern of the novel. No other novels so well reflect the complexity of the issues involved and the various humanist interpretations of the conflict as those of André Malraux's *L'espoir,* Gustav Regler's *The Great Crusade,* and Ernest Hemingway's *For Whom the Bell Tolls.*

Three other novelists who chose the literary form of the personal narrative to present their experiences in Spain, George Orwell in *Homage to Catalonia,* Arthur Koestler in *Spanish Testament,* and George Bernanos in *Les grands cimetières sous la lune,* deserve consideration in a study of the literary impact of the Spanish struggle. The difference between these avowed personal narratives and the fiction of Malraux, Regler, and Hemingway is essentially one of degree rather than kind. The principal distinction between the personal narrative and the novel is the limitation of the former, which restricts its account to the single thread of personal experience, while the novelist may supplement or expand his narrative by an imaginative penetration into the experiences of others. The more autobiographical genre, however, if it is to be worthy of literary attention, must involve considerable selectivity and discrimination in ordering the writer's past experiences. The novelist follows a similar pattern but has greater freedom of selection and arrangement. The heavily autobiographical origins of the Malraux, Regler, and Hemingway war novels are unmistakable, and portions of the Koestler, Bernanos, and Orwell books may be considered in either category. The quality of these latter works provides a meaningful insight into the motivations of those authors who went to Spain, an insight which is not easily discernible in prose fiction. The responses of Orwell, Koestler, and Bernanos to the war, composed against a background of disillusioned hopes and irrevocable commitments, of political treachery, tortured hostages, air raids over placid villages, and mass executions, closely parallel the treatment of the issues by Malraux, Regler, and Hemingway, thus furnishing direct testimony to the importance of the conflict in its own time. These combined works form a history unsurpassed in knowledge of the issues and sensitivity to the sufferings of the Spanish people. Such evidence is extremely valuable in a study of the literary impact of the Spanish Civil War.

At the close of the fighting, the majority of Spanish writers who had aligned themselves with the Republican cause, such as Max Aub, Arturo Barea, Rafael Alberti, and Ramón Sender, were forced into exile and scattered throughout Europe and North and South America. The major theme of these writers was naturally concerned with the Spanish conflict. They had retained their loyalty, but having lost direct contact with their country, these exiles relied on vivid memories for their treatment of the tragedy which they had recently witnessed. Such memories were weighted with the hope and disillusionment accompanying a truly intense experience. So intensely bitter had the struggle been that these authors felt compelled to express a passionately partisan approach to the issues involved. They had participated in one of the most dramatic events of modern times, and it was inevitable that they should testify to their experiences. The martyrdom of their comrades, the poets Antonio Machado and Miguel Hernández, was perhaps the greatest contribution by creative writers in this decade to the spiritual life of Europe.

Inside Spain, since the end of the war, few works of merit have been published. The reasons for this are conjectural. Gov-

ernment censorship is perhaps a major factor, and possibly the Nationalist vantage point is less propitious for the exercise of the artist's imagination. In the years immediately following the conflict, no significant work concerned with the subject from a Nationalist point of view was produced. Recently, the Falangist author, José María Gironella, attempted to provide the Nationalists with a refutation of the interpretations of the conflict expounded by such Republican authors in exile as Barea, Aub, and Sender, as well as novelists of the stature of Hemingway, Koestler, Malraux, and Bernanos. Gironella's first novel, *Los Cipreses Creen en Dios* (1953), is worthy of consideration as an objective effort to explain the circumstances preceding the military uprising in July, 1936, while at the same time examining the conscience of the Spanish middle class during this period; his second novel, *Un Millión de Muertos* (1961), covering the events of the conflict, however, is little more than a caricature in its biased historical documentation of the three years of the war, accompanied by a tendentious interpretation of the facts involved.

The importance of the Spanish Civil War was diminished by the magnitude of the succeeding holocaust of World War II, but not in the eyes of Spanish authors. Although the immediacy of the Second World War discouraged potential foreign literature dealing with the Spanish struggle which might have been written between 1940 and 1945, this was not so with the native Spanish writers, particularly the Republican authors in exile. The impressive quantity and quality of the product of these authors, fiction as well as nonfiction, exceed all foreign treatment of the conflict and works on the subject published under the Franco regime. (pp. xix-xxvi)

The literature of the war in Spain is important because it reflects both the idealism and the subsequent disillusionment of many writers who had envisioned in the struggle of the Spanish people a great cause. No other circumstance is capable of altering the human condition as completely as war. The encounter with violence was to change drastically, not only the attitudes of these writers toward political ideology, but also their philosophy for establishing order in a chaotic world. The results of the encounter are manifest in the literature of World War II which is so obviously apolitical and in which writers seem to have extended beyond disillusionment to a desperate and consuming nihilism. If the writers of World War II cannot in any sense be called disillusioned, it is because they had been divested of their illusions before the great war had ever begun. The Spanish struggle had much to do with the destruction of the political drama of the 1930s, a destruction which left most writers without the direction provided by dogma and ideology when they were confronted by a far more widespread and devastating holocaust. Regarding the earlier conflict, Thomas eulogizes, "The struggle gave birth to a burst of creative energy in many countries . . . which can plausibly be argued as comparable in quality to anything produced in the Second World War. The few real masterpieces that were produced will survive as monuments to those who died." (p. xxix)

Frederick R. Benson, in an introduction to his Writers in Arms: The Literary Impact of the Spanish Civil War, *New York University Press, 1967, pp. xix-xxx.*

VALENTINE CUNNINGHAM

[*Cunningham is an English educator and critic. A contributor to the* Times Literary Supplement *and* New Statesman, *he is also the editor of the anthologies* The Penguin Book of Spanish Civil War Verse *(1980) and* Spanish Front: Writers on the Civil War

(1986). In the following excerpt from his introduction to the latter volume, Cunningham presents an overview of the role of writers and literature in the Spanish Civil War and the nature of the literature inspired by that conflict.]

[The] Spanish Civil War was . . . a war in which writing, text, image, and writers, artists, photographers, film-makers, poster-designers, print-workers played central and essential parts. In no war before this one had the means of propaganda been used on so massive a scale. This was the war in which the military importance of forces not visible on battlefields got open recognition. Mola invented the Fifth Columnist, in name if not in practice, when he boasted that his Four Columns advancing on Madrid were backed by a Fifth Column secretly waiting in the city to rise in Franco's favour. The propagandists became in this war a sort of open Fifth Column—a vital set of extra troops, an essential troupe of military extras. Never before had wartime printing presses worked so hard or printing-works turned out so many propaganda posters. Multi-colour printing techniques, still in their infancy, were exploited for the first time extensively in political warfare. The art of political photomontage had been developed in pre-Hitler Germany by people like John Heartfield just in time, you might say, for use in Spain. The documentary film, only recently brought to birth, mainly in England, found its apogee in propaganda movies, especially the Hemingway-Joris Ivens documentary film, *Spanish Earth*. In earlier times the occasional intellectual or writer had volunteered to travel abroad and fight in someone else's domestic cause. But this war had, as it were, numerous Byrons, even if some of them did only write for the newspapers. Many writers and artists fought and were wounded and killed in the First World War and some of them had been volunteers and not conscripts. But that was in an extremely large-scale conflict and most of the fighting writers had been coerced by their governments into taking part. What was startling and special about Spain was that this relatively small-scale war had so many voluntary writer-participants in it—whether they were doing medical work or actually fighting, were engaged in propaganda or political activities, or had gone to Spain simply to report events.

It is indeed extraordinary and quite distinctive that an Orwell or a Malraux, a Hemingway, an Auden, a Spender, a Claude Simon, a Simone Weil, should have wished to have done anything at all in this foreign conflict. It is characteristic of this extraordinary situation that at least one writer, the awful right-wing Roy Campbell, who in actuality got out of the country of his temporary residence as fast as he could when the war broke out, should have felt he must pretend he had been in the thick of the fighting and fake up quite untrue stories about how he had toted a rifle on behalf of his new-found Catholic faith and General Franco. It is indeed notable that in this war so many writer-volunteers should have got themselves killed for their decision to put aside their pens and books in order to bear arms or carry stretchers in Spain. Ralph Fox, John Cornford, Charley Donnelly, Christopher St. John Sprigg (or Caudwell), Julian Bell—to name only the British and Irish writers who were killed in Spain—all had much still to prove about their quality as poet or critic or novelist. Cornford, Bell and Donnelly in particular were only fledgeling writers. Each of them became, as Borges has put it of Byron, ''more important for his image than his work.'' But on any reckoning they make an arresting group. And merely making catalogues of the names of writers and artists who did something for the Republican side does bear out one of the major and distinctive claims of that side, that the forces of the legally elected Spanish government were struggling not just in the name of freedom and democracy against the forces of repression and Fascism, but were fighting for the survival of art and culture in free societies. (pp. xx-xxii)

In the Republican zones poetry became truly popular. Spanish poets like Rafael Alberti read to packed houses. Ordinary people on the Republican side were apparently much gladdened by the support they were getting from foreign writers. Poetry, as Spender argued in his Introduction to *Poems for Spain* [see Additional Bibliography] the anthology that he and John Lehmann brought out in 1939, achieved in Spain an extraordinary flowering, both among Republican Spaniards and in the ranks of the foreign militiamen. Writing was alive and well in the midst of the Spanish adversities (revolutions, especially in their early phases, have always been good for art). Some writers did, of course, support the Franco side, especially Roman Catholics such as Pierre Drieu La Rochelle, Evelyn Waugh, Roy Campbell, Hilaire Belloc and Arnold Lunn, people who feared communism more than anything, even than regimes that would savagely kill a Lorca, and who read Franco as the saviour of European Christianity against Stalin's Asiatic hordes. But even when you grant all the Rightists their due credit—and the anti-Republicans did include Ezra Pound and (more or less) W. B. Yeats and T. S. Eliot—the collective force of writers, artists and artistes supporting the Republic gives colour to the notion that on one side was Franco and his German and Italian allies and his Moorish mercenaries and on the other side was Sweetness and Light. (pp. xxii-xxiii)

But even had many more thirties writers and artists been in favour of Franco, the most important point hereabouts would have remained unchanged. And that is that Spain deeply engaged the world's writers and artists, their writing and their art, their words and images, in some way or another, on one side or another. For the writers of the thirties Spain was irresistible, magnetic, a very cynosure. Not surprisingly it became for them a test, indeed *the* test. There was intense pressure upon writers and writing to take sides, for or against the Republic. And sides were taken. The *Left Review* symposium published in 1937 with the title *Authors Take Sides on the Spanish War* not only managed to assemble an enormous band of Republican sympathisers and to winkle out only a very few Franco admirers, it also showed, and more crucially, just how few there were among British writers who were prepared to stand aside or back from the issue and profess themselves neutral. (p.xxiii)

''We are determined or compelled, to take sides,'' wrote the sponsors of the *Authors Take Sides* survey. And taking sides was not the only determination or compulsion around. Other compulsions vigorously converged in the matter of Spain. There was the compulsion to ''go over'' to Spain and the cause of democracy and the working-class not just in your head or your texts but also (as Marx and Engels had suggested bourgeois intellectuals would in Capitalism's late phases) actually, physically. There was the compulsion to bear arms, or to attend the Second Congress of the International Association of Writers that was held in Valencia, Madrid and Barcelona in July 1937, the compulsion to bear some kind of first-hand witness to events in Spain (a compulsion felt strongly on the Right as well as on the Left: but then being an I-witness in that era of fraught selfhood and compulsive testimony, that time when almost every other book had a title beginning *I*. . ., did come rather naturally to writers). And Spain's test, its set of tests, was experienced widely, especially on the Left, as a set of necessities. It is noticeable how greatly the very word *necessary* irked some readers when it appeared in Auden's poem "Spain." Auden, like lots of other writers, had taken on the personal Spanish burden of "The conscious acceptance of guilt in the necessary murder." The burden seemed at the time a necessary one. (When later Auden rejected the idea of that necessity he also dropped that word from his poem, and eventually he discarded the stanza that had once carried it.) "As an Englishman I am not in the predicament of choosing between two evils," Evelyn Waugh replied for *Authors Take Sides*. But he did choose, and choose, despite his resentment at being called a Fascist, for fascist Franco. His diary for 25 September 1936 shows him discussing the provision of "relief" for the Insurgent side at a meeting of the Catholic Archbishop of Westminster's "Spanish Association." You might in the event, of course, fail to satisfy Spain's various tests—as Auden feared he might ("I shall probably be a bloody bad soldier") and in effect did, and as poem after poem of Spender presents his cowardly poetic persona as doing ("Port Bou" is a good example). Turning yourself into André Malraux, the most satisfying western example on the Left, of the writer as Man of Action would be for most writers next to impossible. But the invitation to put yourself in for the examination was widely felt as ineluctable.

And if Spain's necessities tested thirties writers in their lives, it also provided tests for their writing. Bluntly put, thirties writing's preoccupation with questions of war, action, pacifism and the possibility of heroism in the light of the First World War, of Wilfred Owen's anti-war poetry and the absorbing failure of the "self-conscious" man of action T. E. Lawrence, its fascination with placing and displacing, with map-making and map-reading, with frontier-anxieties, with exile and abroad, its alertness to issues of class, revolution and the popularity of art, its talk of the revolutionary hour of the knife and the apocalyptic moment of decisive struggle: all these recurrent obsessions came suddenly very sharply and nastily to life in Spain. And not just on the Left. "Then Comrades come rally, And the last fight let us face," Leftists sang in The Internationale; John Cornford meditated on death "On the last mile to Huesca"; and the proletarian novels *We Live* and *The Land of the Leal* (both 1939) contrived to end their stories of working-class struggle with deaths in Spain; but Drieu La Rochelle's right-wing novel *Gilles* evinces an even stronger craving to have its hero come to an end masochistically in the Spanish fight.

Some writers' writing never recovered from the testing Spain gave it. Auden, for example, found it difficult to go on praising bombing planes and helmeted airmen after his Spanish experiences. Spender's poems abandoned any claim on revolutionary enthusiasm and started going in for stories of physical cowardice while he was still in Spain. And Spain had instant effects on people's texts, not least because a clear and central part of its nature was textual. This was a war that had been given a kind of proleptic existence in huge tracts of post-First World War writing. It was a war that provided the tragic enactment and instructive apotheosis of much main thirties writing in English. In Spain, as Auden's "Spain" has it, "the menacing shapes of our fever/Are precise and alive." There "our faces . . . are projecting their greed as the firing squad and the bomb." There "our moments of tenderness blossom/ As the ambulance and the sandbag;/Our hours of friendship into a people's army." MacNeice made the same sort of point in his *Autumn Journal:* "our spirit/would find its frontier on the Spanish front." These writers perceived Spain as being

dense with their own textualising. And when these textualised Spanish events got turned back into text by writers such as this it was scarcely surprising to find the shapes of the pre-Spanish fictions, the old metaphors, tones and themes still "precise and alive," or at least still powerfully in play and in debate. Critics would note, for example, how much John Sommerfield's style of battle reportage owed to Hemingway's fiction style (and, of course, Hemingway was himself also in Spain testing out his own textualised paper-courage in battle-front situations that generated not only more text in the shape of his newspaper stories but, eventually, the most famous example of the Hemingway fictional manner in his Spanish novel *For Whom the Bell Tolls*).

Sommerfield had his eye on the movies as well as on his copies of Hemingway's stories. He gave one section of his book *Volunteer in Spain* (1937) the title "War Picture." Spender called one of his poems "War Photograph." And these labels weren't just signalling how easy it was in Spain to feel that you were acting in a war movie or to read scenes of horror as if they'd already been snapped and developed and turned out as one of those atrocity photographs that so upset Virginia Woolf in *Three Guineas;* though such feelings were evidently widespread. Nor was this only because of Isherwood's famous granting of camera-status to the text of reportage, the discourse of the I-witness or reporter ("I am a camera"), though this too is not irrelevant. Even more importantly, it has to do with that instant conversion of events into images that writing, like photography, inevitably achieves.

And, naturally, once it has been written down or photographed, even the most painfully awful battle or scene of suffering finds itself clamped into the stilling embrace of the aesthetic, into the literary, imagic hold of text It is not, then—although it might at first appear so to the casual reader—the action of a dilettante or the pursuit of some obscene irrelevance that Cyril Connolly should in *Enemies of Promise* (1938) have chosen to reflect on the contributions to the *Authors Take Sides* survey in terms of their prose styles, or that so many responses to Picasso's Spanish drawings and his *Guernica* should have been built around the debates about social or socialist realism going on in the period. These reactions to textual matters, to manner, tone, style, this stress on cultural and critical relevance and on placings within the art-historical continuum were only acknowledging that Spain—so literary in any case to start with— existed for every reader of a book or an article about it, for everybody who saw the film *Spanish Earth,* for everyone who noticed a propaganda poster or cartoon or who heard a radio talk about the war, Spain existed *also* (and in most cases existed *only*) as text, as image. (pp. xxiv-xxvi)

It is because of its profound realisation of this inevitable process of textualisation and the difficulties thus sponsored for the observer stuck with the task of reading, that the meditation in Claude Simon's novel *Les Géorgiques* (1981) on a photograph of some Spanish volunteers is so important. It is a meditation that refuses to allow the experience and knowledge even of a Spanish veteran like Simon himself to inspire any special insight or intimacy. Even the general reader's feeling that the photograph is one (s)he has come across before is not allowed to help. The description acts with painstaking naïvety, scanning the image with minute care as if for the first time, pretending to come to it as from the pen of the merest uninitiated reader. And in refusing to accept anything as pre-read it mightily illuminates the serious drawbacks and difficulties, the postures and clenched fists of men that would indeed puzzle the uninstructed, the mystifyingly cut-off parts of bodies, the marred bits of the photograph, the dirt and the smoke that obscure and only half-reveal—all those features obstructing epistemological progress and hermeneutic satisfaction. And these are, in fact, the sort of barriers that always get in the way of making sense of and tracing out the meaning in any writing or photograph, even in writing and photography that have to do with an event as real and historical as Spain, but that custom and conventions of reading and interpretation encourage us to overlook. In treating Spain as mere text, and in offering a new piece of writing about Spain as an engagement not with the unmediated events of the past but as an intertextual dialogue with precedent images, writings, texts (*Les Géorgiques* includes a reinterpretation of one of Simon's own earlier Spanish fictions *Le Palace* and a rewriting of the French version of *Homage to Catalonia*) Simon isn't being quirky or fanciful, nor even wilfully French and post-structuralist; he's simply being wise and instructive. (p. xxvii)

[The] Spanish Front/Frontier is also that border at which fact overlaps fiction, and *vice versa*. What is more, because of the peculiar distortions of the ordinarily paradoxical dualities of the fact-fiction border that are brought about by the special Spanish circumstances, this particular frontier of the image and the real is an extraordinarily animated and difficult one. It is perhaps even the ultimate apotheosis of the terrible border tensions that so pack thirties writing.

Fiction, of course, always seeps into so-called factual writing. The two discourses are hardly ever completely separable. No effort at reportage can ever be a mere transcription of the real. And nobody in the 1930s, when documentary techniques and theories in photography, film and writing were being invented and developed, ever believed it might be. [The section-title "War Stories" in *Spanish Front: Writers on the Civil War*], which contains self-professed fictions, could just as easily be applied to much Spanish War writing, especially the reportage. After all, novelists write stories, and journalists "file" them. And this is a reflection whose implications might have saved some of Orwell's current detractors and defenders a deal of their trouble. The contributors to Christopher Norris's *Inside the Myth: Orwell; Views from the Left* (1984) make great, but unnecessary, play with mistakes of fact in *Homage to Catalonia*. Who does not make mistakes? Claude Simon, the apostle of Spain's textuality and narrativity, mounts a much more sophisticated attack. He accuses Orwell (and Orwell's readers) of the hypocritical pretence that *Homage to Catalonia* is telling the whole truth rather than composing a writing, arranging a narrative that, though it might contain some truth and even be essentially truthful, is by no means telling all the truth. Simon refers (in an interview in *The Review of Contemporary Fiction*, v, no. 1, 1984) to the suppressions and rearrangements implicit, if only to the alert critical intelligence, in *Homage*, a text that is, he declares, "faked from the very first sentence"—that arresting opening line, "In the Lenin Barracks, the day before I joined the militia, I saw an Italian militiaman standing in front of the officers' table." "If . . . critics," says Simon,

> find, after analysing it, that this sentence is innocent (what it says, and above all what it carefully omits to say) it is because they are singularly ignorant of the political circumstances in Barcelona at that time, and, in general, of the circumstances in revolutionary movements in Europe at that same period. I shall restrict myself to informing them that one

did not just wander casually into Republican Spain at that time, and that if there did exist in Barcelona something called the "Lenin Barracks" (or rather a "Cuartel Lenin"), there was also, not far away, a "Cuartel Karl Marx," and another invoking the name of Bakunin. The respective occupants of these various barracks considered each other to be "counter-revolutionaries" and thought only of the best way of eliminating them (as happened in May 1937 to the benefit of the Stalinists). To give an idea of the idyllic proletarian unanimity which then reigned in Barcelona, it should be recalled that the occupants of the Cuartel Karl Marx called the occupants of the Cuartel Lenin "hitlero-trotskyites." Finally, it was not "by chance" that a foreigner made for one of these cuartels rather than another: thus it was because I had a communist party membership card in my pocket at that period (September 1936) that I went straight to the Hotel Colon, which was then the headquarters of the PSUC [The United Catalan Socialist-Communist Party]. All these things (including the motives which led him to the Cuartel Lenin) are carefully suppressed by Orwell, until he gets to the account of the May insurrection, about which the uninformed reader will understand very little.

But Orwell himself, who carefully and with self-conscious craft reworked the material of his notes and diaries into texts like *The Road to Wigan Pier,* and was always quite consciously suppressing things (and not always just for reasons of narrative polish) would, I am sure have been surprised at Simon's fuss. Everyone in the thirties documentary movement would have assumed that Simon's suggestions about story-tellers' fakings went really without saying. What, though, gives the issue of narrativity special resonance in Spanish writing is that we know there was continual conscious and unconscious pressure upon writers to go in for suppressions and re-arrangements of their material to make the truths of the report conform not just to conventional narrative ambitions, pleasing form, and the like, but to the less reputable and continually shifting demands of some political party line. The results of serving those kinds of demands are undoubtedly sniffable in, say, the praise for Soviet equipment that gets into Sommerfield's *Volunteer in Spain*, or the way James Barke's Communists in *The Land of the Leal* preach up the current Communist International political line of the Popular Front, or in the technique developed in Republican propaganda posters of attacking the POUM [an independent Marxist party] and other non-Communist revolutionaries but in coded phrases about the dangers of pursuing social innovations and experiments while a war with Franco was still going on. But the textual results here are by no means the same thing as lying. Deliberate liars like Roy Campbell, floating untruths to increase his image as the most macho poet around, or a Black Propagandist like Claud Cockburn in his persona as *Daily Worker* Spain correspondent Frank Pitcairn inventing untruths to aid his own side, are relatively easy for readers to cope with. The case with a Capa photograph or an Orwell story is usually far less simple. It is the involvement of the would-be truthteller (such as Orwell clearly was) in the war of words, in the murky textual waters of propaganda and counter-propaganda inevitably tending to influence opinion and judgement, to colour narrative and handicap fact in its jockeying with fiction, which helps to make readers like Claude Simon so edgy.

And if Spanish propagandising exacerbated the normal fact-fiction problem, so also did the peculiarities of acquiring Spanish impressions. The rushed impressions of hasty visitors to any country are always unreliable and sketchy. And most writers about the Spanish War were essentially ignorant and short-term visitors, involved in an odd species of tourism. The acquaintance that a Hemingway or a V. S. Pritchett brought to his Spanish War writing was quite special and rare. And what the raw tourists were seeing was especially difficult to form impressions about. Spain in Civil War-time was no ordinary tourist spot. Civil War—Simone Weil makes the point as one of the writing-tourists, in a "Fragment" she jotted down probably around the time of her own aborted visit to Spain (it was published in 1960 in her *Écrits Historiques et Politiques*)—civil wars will turn any place into a shifty, kaleidoscopic object of focus:

> What is going on in Spain? Over there, everyone has his word to put in, his stories to tell, a judgement to pronounce. Right now, it's in fashion to go on a tour down there, to take in a spot of revolution, and to come back with articles bursting out of your pen. You can't open a newspaper or a magazine any more without coming across accounts of events in Spain. How can all this not be superficial? In the first place a social transformation can only be correctly appreciated as a function of what it means to the daily life of each of those who make up the population. It is not easy to get inside this daily life. Furthermore each day that passes brings new developments. Also, constraint and spontaneity, necessity and idealism are so mixed up that they generate inextricable confusion not only as to the facts, but also in the very consciousness of the actors and spectators in the drama. Right here lies the essential character and perhaps also the greatest evil of civil war. This is also the first conclusion to be drawn from a swift inspection of events in Spain, and what one knows about the Russian revolution confirms it only too amply. It is not true that revolution tallies automatically with an awareness of the social problem that is more elevated, more intense, clearer. It's the contrary that proves true, at least when revolution takes the form of civil war. In the howling gale of civil war, principles get completely out of phase with realities, every sort of criterion by which one might judge actions and institutions disappears, and social transformation is left completely to chance. So how can one report something coherently on the strength of a short stay and some fragmentary observations? The most one can hope for is to put together a few impressions, tug just a few lessons into the light of day.

Claude Simon accuses the "idyllic description" of Barcelona in the first part of *Homage to Catalonia* of being "little more than a comic tourist guide." But after all we have to afforce Simone Weil's observations with Auden's powerful suggestions about the malleability of Spain. The war, suggests the poem "Spain," is all things to all men (and women), it responds to whatever subjective needs the observer brings to bear on it. It's very like Hamlet's cloud formations, in fact, very like a whale if you want it to be:

> To you, I'm the

> Yes-man, the bar-companion, the easily-duped;
> I am whatever you do. I am your vow to be
> Good, your humorous story.
> I am your business voice. I am your marriage.

> What's your proposal? To build the just city? I will.
> I agree. Or is it the suicide pact, the romantic
> Death? Very well, I accept, for
> I am your choice, your decision. Yes, I am Spain.

The point rings truer and truer the more the touristic reader travels through the hundreds of pieces of Spanish War writing. Spain does indeed seem to have possessed the multivalence Auden ascribes to it. And in the writing . . . from various angles, male and female, democratic and liberal, insistently Communist, or Roman Catholic, or pro-POUM (like Orwell), or Trotskyite (like, well, Leon Trotsky), Spain remains—for such is the powerful persistence of writing—like that.

"I am your choice, your decision." And just as Spain came in the variety of readings that Auden suggested, so also those various readings have not remained an exclusive or static bunch of interpretations. Experience, the passage of time, the shifting realities of revolution and counter-revolution, the fluctuating political tides of the war, effected numerous changes in many individual readings. Powerful turns, dodges, shifts of perception and sympathy are the staple subject of many of the most impressive of the Spain texts: the loss of revolutionary faith manifested by Simone Weil's "Letter to Georges Bernanos" or by Auden and Isherwood's *On the Frontier;* the anger over the behaviour of the Spanish Catholic hierarchy that is evinced by the French Catholic Bernanos's *A Diary of My Times;* the marked turning away from the Communists and the British Left establishment in favour of the suppressed POUM in *Homage to Catalonia* and in numerous other texts of Orwell's; the sadness at a revolution's fade-out in Franz Borkenau's *The Spanish Cockpit;* the turn away from the Communist Party line about André Gide in the renegade Dutch Communist Jef Last's report on the International Writers' Congress. Lapsing and failing relationships with the gods people started off by worshipping are all over the place in these writings. Furthermore, Spain is still capable of sustaining new readings, it is a still reinterpretable, revisable set of texts. One aspect . . . to which previous generations did not pay particular attention is the role of women in this war. On the Republican side women fought, wore trousers in public, went about unchaperoned; they could practice birth-control and in some circumstances obtain legal abortions. One of the most prominent of Republican leader-figures was the woman Dolores Ibarruri known as "La Passionaria." On the other side, Franco's armies, egged on by the Catholic hierarchy, sought to restore traditional Spanish womanliness and Catholic motherhood. And we are now in a position to perceive women in Spain in the wider context of the twentieth-century struggle for women's liberation. The fairly well-known male story of concerned male artists and writers has now to be supplemented by the story of engaged women writers and artists. (pp. xxviii-xxxii)

But though the still resonant multivalence of Spain helps us notice the role of these New Women of the thirties, and allows us to afford a new place of honour to them and to their particular Spanish texts, what is also brought home by attending to the women's writings of this war is the degree to which female participation in Spain continued also in quite traditional modes. In Spain the men were still, by and large, going off to fight, leaving their women behind them to grieve their absence and their loss and/or to question the necessities that took their lives.

Virginia Woolf mourned the death of her beloved nephew Julian Bell and joined her interrogation of war's inevitabilities (in *Three Guineas*) with the pacifism Vera Brittain voiced in *Authors Take Sides* (a pacifism sponsored by the loss of a beloved in the First World War). Margot Heinemann was left behind, the recipient of John Cornford's letters from the Front with the ancient womanly task of composing the dead fighter's epitaph. Nan Green, whose husband the musician George Green was killed on the Ebro in the International Brigade's very last engagement, was left in like condition. She had also done what women have always done—she followed her man to the war, a modern version of the traditional female camp-follower, working with the medicals (who were organised by another wife, Winifred Bates, whose husband the novelist Ralph Bates edited the Brigade's paper *Volunteer for Liberty* and engaged in other male political activities). Rosamond Lehmann stayed behind to organise help for International Brigaders and was mighty gladdened when her wounded husband and ambulance-man Wogan Phillips decided not to return to Spain. These were traditional motifs and routines surviving alongside innovativeness of role and action. But then, a mélange of old and new is what keeps on marking the Spanish experience and the Spanish writings. In the end Spain failed to satisfy the deep political and artistic cravings of the thirties that it had focussed so sharply and had initially appeared able to resolve. There would be no utter renewal, no clean break with the past, no utopian resolution. Spain and its texts did not rewrite or iron out the paradoxes of the Great War and its texts. They did not fully answer the old questions about heroism and the life of action. They did not prove Wilfred Owen wrong about the bewildering but necessary alliance in war between feelings of disgust and outrage at the evil and futility of it all and feelings of love and admiration for the bravery of the soldiers and their pathetically and nobly borne sufferings. For Spain and its texts certainly do not sustain the earliest lyrical and romantic readings of the war as the zone where the necessary evils and terrors of revolution and war might after a temporary outing prove the gateway to happy conclusions. "Today the struggle": that was true. But tomorrow, after all, there still remained "the private nocturnal terror"; and the post-War "fun" that Auden hoped would eventuate from submission to purgatorial struggles "under Liberty's masterful shadow" was as elusive as ever—for the winners even more than for the losers. "There is," indeed, as Esmond Romilly said in his *Boadilla* (1937), thinking of his friends killed in the defence of Madrid, "something frightening, something shocking, about the way the world does not stop because these men are dead." History, in fact, could not manage much more than a grim Audenic "Alas" for anybody, on any side, whether actor or writer or reader. (pp. xxxii-xxxiii)

> *Valentine Cunningham, in an introduction to* Spanish Front: Writers on the Civil War, *edited by Valentine Cunningham, Oxford University Press, Oxford, 1986, pp. xix-xxxiii.*

STEPHEN SPENDER

[Spender is an English man of letters who rose to prominence during the 1930s as a Marxist lyric poet and as an associate of W. H. Auden, Christopher Isherwood, C. Day Lewis, and Louis MacNeice. During the war he visited Spain twice and wrote and lectured in England on behalf of the Republicans. Like many other artists and intellectuals, Spender later became disillusioned with communism, and although he may still occasionally make use of political and social issues in his work, he is more often concerned with aspects of self-knowledge and depth of personal feeling. In

the following excerpt, he introduces the reader to the major writers of the Spanish Civil War, their works, and their political ideals.]

[The] Spanish Civil War, in both its national and international aspects, had for thousands of people all over the world the appearance of being a direct confrontation between good and evil, right and wrong, freedom and tyranny. Something of this feeling of a crusade brushed off onto the very distinguished group of American reporters of the war who were situated in Madrid: Ernest Hemingway, his wife-to-be Martha Gellhorn, Lillian Hellman, and Josephine Herbst. "Spain" certainly brought out in Hemingway not only his courage but his great imagination and powerful intelligence. It must be admitted, too, that the Falangist supporters of Franco, basking in the blessings bestowed on them by the church, also saw it as a holy war and were supported in this by their few foreign sympathizers and volunteers. The philosopher George Santayana wrote, answering a correspondent:

> Spain has always been the most unfortunate of countries, and it is now having a hard struggle to throw the Bolshies off, that had got hold of her always execrable government. But my friends write that the young people are unrecognizable in their energy and discipline and that we shall soon see a new Spain as vigorous as in the Middle Ages. And of course Spain would not be alone in the transformation.
>
> —From a letter written from Mussolini's Rome, 1936; presumably not written as a joke.

Such medievalist black fervor can be set against Thomas Mann's introduction to an anthology called "Spain" published by the Socialist Alliance of Swiss Women:

> I shall be asked what I mean by "spirit" and what by "interest." Well, then: the spiritual, seen from the politico-social angle is the longing of the people for better, juster, happier conditions of life, more adequate to the developed human consciousness. It is this longing, affirmed by all those who are of good will. And "interest" is all that seeks to thwart this consummation, because it would thereby be cut off from certain advantages and privileges, seeks by every means at its command, not scorning the basest, even the criminal, or, well knowing that in the end it must fail, tries to put off as long as it can the evil day—for a little while, for a few decades. In Spain interest rages. Rages with a shamelessness such as the world has seldom seen. What has been happening there for many months is one of the most scandalous and mortifying pages which history has to show. Does the world see it, feel it? Only very partially.

Here, writing from Switzerland, Thomas Mann is seeing the Spanish Civil War as a microcosm of a Manichaean conflict between the forces of good and evil in the contemporary world—a view to which the character of Hitler surely lent force. Spain, that sunburned landscape cut off from the rest of Europe, historic home of saints, fanatics, and decadent monarchs, stimulated the imagination of the world. The idea of Apocalypse haunts the pages of André Malraux's novel about Spain, *L'Espoir* (translated under the title *Man's Hope*), as it does the pages of the Civil War in Gustav Regler's memorable auto-biography *The Owl of Minerva.*

For those non-Spaniards who went to Spain during the Civil War, the spectacle of the Spanish people was deeply moving. Most of these non-Spaniards were on the Republican side, though Roy Campbell's account of the liberation of Toledo from the Reds (and the horrors of the Red occupation before this) suggests that either side could strike the foreigner as heroic. Campbell's account of this episode strikes me as having an authenticity not present when he is evoking scenes of his own heroism.

W. H. Auden's description of Valencia (*The New Statesman,* January 30, 1937) could be multiplied by similar descriptions of Barcelona written by George Orwell, Cyril Connolly, and myself. We all discovered in ourselves feelings best expressed by Wordsworth in "The Prelude," describing his reaction to scenes he witnessed in France in the early days of the Revolution: "Bliss was it in that dawn to be alive." (pp. 5-7)

Looking back on Spanish events now, I feel that although there was something authentic about our Wordsworthian recognition of the joy of the people's freedom achieved, that we could not see any of the terrible murders happening behind this scene of revolution reinforces one of the great lessons of this century: that there is no trust to be placed in travellers' impressions of popular rejoicing soon after revolution.

Probably, too, if we had seen Valencia or Barcelona in the fall of 1936 and not in the spring of 1937, we would have had a less happy impression, for what we saw would have been chaos. Luis Buñuel, seeing the first days of the revolution, which, as he writes, "I personally had so ardently desired," relates that all he felt was shock:

> Elie Faure, the famous art historian and an ardent supporter of the Republican cause, came to Madrid for a few days. I went to visit him one morning at his hotel and can still see him standing at his window in his long underwear, watching the demonstrations in the street below and weeping at the sight of the people in arms. One day, we watched a hundred peasants marching by, four abreast, some armed with hunting rifles and revolvers, some with sickles and pitchforks. In an obvious effort at discipline, they were trying very hard to march in step. It seemed as if nothing could defeat such a deep-seated popular force, but the joy and enthusiasm that colored those early days soon gave way to arguments, disorganization and uncertainty—all of which lasted until November 1936, when an efficient and disciplined Republican organization began to emerge.

There may have been some efficiency after November 1936 in Madrid and some show of it in Valencia. But where else? Certainly not in Malaga before its fall to the Nationalists, as Arthur Koestler describes it in his terrifying account of the capture of that city by the Nationalists, still the most moving of all the documents bearing witness to the agony that was "Spain." Hemingway's *For Whom the Bell Tolls* does not approach it as felt truth, although Hemingway made a heroic effort to give a detached, complex, and objective picture of the war. It seems to me, however, that his novel, though magnificent, sinks under the weight of the effort. The point of view being Hemingway's own, he must need have an American hero,

Robert Jordan, who embodies Hemingway's own qualities—Robert Jordan is a strategist, a great lover, has shrewd political insight, is a writer, and while supporting the Republic, is also a Catholic. Moreover, much of the Spanish dialogue in the novel between Jordan and the Spanish characters is rendered into an English that reads like a literal translation of a Spanish grammar made by a Spaniard who does not know English.

Much of the literature of the Spanish Civil War written on the Republican side seems to show that the writers of it felt that there was a "truth" of "Spain" that remained independent of, and survived the mold of, Communism into which successive Republican governments were forced. Anti-Fascists who went to Spain and accepted Communism there as inevitable on the grounds of political exigence—and who later changed their minds about this, becoming anti-Communists—nevertheless retained their belief in the justice of the Republican cause. They did not renounce "Spain." This is true even of Arthur Koestler, who certainly experienced the worst that both sides had to offer. He became virulently anti-Communist, but he did not regret having supported the Spanish Republic.

The same was true of William Herrick, a veteran of the Lincoln battalion who was severely wounded outside Madrid, whose novel *Hermanos!* is both bitterly anti-Communist and profoundly sympathetic to the Spanish Republic. On the other hand, another veteran of the Lincoln battalion (and later one of the Hollywood Ten), the late Alvah Bessie, who wrote an affecting memoir of the war, *Men in Battle,* remained sympathetic to his old comrades.

Auden was one of those who, during the weeks that he was in Spain, seems to have accepted Communist policy as inevitable and necessary. This is what his poem "Spain" is surely about. In it he interprets the Civil War along strictly Marxist lines, seeing in it the classic "revolutionary situation." His reading of the war is in terms of historical materialism: Thesis (medieval Spain and the European past) = yesterday, that is, Franco. Antithesis (the struggle going on today against these obscurantist forces) = the Spanish Republic: "Today the struggle." Synthesis = tomorrow, when the Republic has won, through Communism, and after the Revolution (whose means have to be accepted as necessary), there is the withering away of the political state and entry into the post-political world of happy and virtuous Anarchy: "The walks by the lake, the weeks of perfect communion."

Auden combines in this poem the logic of Marxist theory with his own poetic logic of imagery evocative of past, present, future, concentrating on "Spain" in 1937—"Today the struggle." But in doing so, he arrives, quite logically, at conclusions that, politcally "correct," are alien to the poetic imagination, perhaps even alien to humanity, to what George Orwell called "decency." Accepting the Marxist view that Freedom is the recognition of Necessity, he grimly faces Necessity:

> Today the deliberate increase in the chances of death.
> The conscious acceptance of guilt in the necessary
>   murder.

Orwell seized on these lines to attack Auden for being an intellectual who approved of murder. By murder Orwell was here thinking of—or chose to pretend he was thinking of—the kind of murders then occurring in Spain as acts of private terrorism: someone being taken for a ride in a car into the country near Barcelona at night, then shot to death and his body thrown into a ditch. (pp. 8-11)

Auden could reasonably point out that when he wrote of "accepting" the "necessary murder," he did not mean terrorist acts of killing, merely that if you support revolution, you support murder. If you object to murder in war or revolution, you are a pacifist, and in "Spain" he has to recognize that he is not pacifist. Moreover, he might have argued, "Spain" is a poem about Historic Necessity, and the word "necessary" in such a context is almost inseparable from the word "murder." But surely he came to agree with Orwell to the extent of feeling that his conscientious attempt to politicize his poetry in support of "Spain" had led him into very alien territory. The fusion of political with poetic logic led out of poetry into the politics of exigence. He defended himself (rather unhappily) from Orwell's charges, but he brought against himself a (to him) still graver charge—of using poetry to tell lies. "Spain" ended with the lines:

> History to the defeated
> May say alas but cannot help or pardon.

Many years later, seeing a copy of the original pamphlet of his poem "Spain" (sold for Spanish relief) on a friend's bookshelf, he took it down and wrote, "This is a lie," against the last two lines. Poetry is, or can be, of course, history; but in poetry the defeated are not made non-persons, as they well may be in politics and as they are in Orwell's *1984*. In poetry, on the contrary, the defeated are often celebrated, given immortality.

After "Spain," Auden abandoned the attempt to fuse poetry with politics.

The English poets who joined the International Brigade considered that the necessity of fighting Fascism had become a more urgent task for them than writing poetry. If they continued to write it, they justified themselves for doing so by putting their poetry at the service of their politics. Many died too young for their views about politics and the war to develop beyond their initial sense of dedication to the cause, or even to see far beyond the international struggle against German, Italian, and Spanish Fascism to the particular Spanish tragedy (that which Hemingway made his tragic attempt to grasp in *For Whom the Bell Tolls*). John Cornford, however, wrote a kind of political poetry that, if he had lived, might have brought something new to modern poetry—the poetry of the intellectual will of the poet immersed in the class struggle. His poems were partly those of a soldier dedicated to the cause for which he was fighting and trying to steel his will by constantly reminding himself of the Fascist enemy. On the evening of battle, he prays (prays to what? To the party? To Karl Marx? All one can say is, he prays):

> Though Communism was my waking time,
> Always before the lights of home
> Shone clearly and steady and full in view
> Here, if you fall, there's help for you—
> Now, with my Party, I stand alone.

> Then let my private battle with my nerves
> The fear of pain whose pain survives,
> The love that tears me by the roots,
> The loneliness that claws my guts,
> Fuse in the welded front our sight preserves.

In other poems he tries to enter into the objective development of history, his own personality becoming, as it were, absorbed into it. This points to a kind of metaphysical secular poetry, materialist, yet in a humanist or Communist way, religious.

Of all the tragedies of the war perhaps the greatest was that of the destruction of what was surely a twentieth-century Renaissance of all the arts in Spain, particularly poetry. García Lorca, killed in the first few months of the war, is the outstanding figure in this Renaissance. (pp. 12-14)

Although, through his work in the theater—taking his plays to villages for performance to the workers— Lorca was a popular, almost a populist, writer; he was not a political figure. His great poem, "Death of a Bullfighter," written before the Civil War, can, in its somber evocation of a tragic Spain, be taken almost as a prelude to the drama of the war, taking death and violence, in the context of the bullfight, as its themes. It has a greatness similar to Picasso's painting *Guernica*. But having written this prelude so prophetic of the tragedy to come, Lorca, the poet who enchanted his fellow poets, not merely this side of idolatry but still more remarkably beyond literary jealousy, disappears from the scene, like Harlequin in the theater, through a trap door, or like Shakespeare's Ariel. (pp. 14-15)

A great deal of propagandist literature was written by Spanish poets during the Civil War. But it always seemed to me that the best Spanish poets (one being my friend Manual Altolaguirre) shrank from the extremes of anti-Fascist politicization of literature that the non-Spanish internationalist supporters of Spain imposed on it. The Spaniards did not write the kind of Communist anti-Fascist poetry fixing on Spain as its subject that was written then by French Communist poets—such as Aragon and Paul Eluard.

What the Spanish poets had to do was not be ideologists of propaganda but to burn in the flame of Spain's martyrdom, producing from it a cry beyond politics. There was one poet who did this—Miguel Hernández, a soldier fighting on the Madrid front. His is the authentic voice of "Spain" beyond ideology, where everything is reduced to the humanity acting and acted upon, pure witnessing of the most terrible events, the most outrageous injustices inflicted. In this poetry the war that was "Spain" becomes one with the international anti-Fascist war, because international anti-Fascism is seen as the response of the nations beyond Spain to the martyred Republic.

> Nations of the earth, fatherlands of the sea, brothers
> Of the world, and of nothing:
> inhabitants lost and more distant
> From the sight than from the heart.

> Here I have a voice impassioned
> Here I have a life, challenged and indignant,
> Here I have a message, here I have a life.

This is poetry hammered out of suffering, whose truth seems beyond dispute, outside politics, like certain poems of Whitman in *Drum Taps*. No wonder that Hernández died in prison where he was confined for years after the end of the war. "Spain" survives in his poetry.

Most of the writers of the Spanish twentieth-century Renaissance were scattered throughout the world after the war. They went into exile in France, in Latin and North America, in Russia. The line of this great intellectual flowering was broken. One consolation may perhaps be found, though, in the fact that the Spanish Civil War awoke among the writers of Latin America a consciousness of Spanish as a world literature which, during those years, became centered on the Spanish Republic in the writing of Pablo Neruda, Octavio Paz, and others. Perhaps "Spain" reborn into the world of the once worldwide

Spanish Empire will enjoy another Renaissance in the world literature of the twenty-first century. (pp. 15-16)

> *Stephen Spender, in an introduction to* Voices against Tyranny: Writing of the Spanish Civil War, *edited by John Miller, Charles Scribner's Sons, 1986, pp. 1-16.*

ARNOLD WHITTRIDGE

[*In the following excerpt from an essay originally published in 1940, Whittridge discusses the passion and belligerence that characterize much of the literature of the Spanish Civil War, comparing zealotry in the Nationalist-inspired poetry of Roy Campbell with that in the Republican-inspired poetry collected in the anthology* Poems for Spain *(1939).*]

[Two books] published in England, *Poems for Spain,* edited by Stephen Spender and John Lehmann, and *Flowering Rifle,* by Roy Campbell, prove that there are still plenty of young men in the world who agree with Emerson,

> 'Tis man's perdition to be safe
> When for truth he ought to die.

Poems for Spain is an anthology, ardently Communist in sympathy, of poems written by Englishmen most of whom served in the International Brigade. Several of the poets represented were killed in the war. *Flowering Rifle,* on the other hand, is a long poem by an exultant nationalist glorifying General Franco and all his works. No one can glance at these books and still complain that the poetry of to-day is too remote from the world in which we live. Excessive preciosity may be a fault of the modern school of poetry, but if so, it is a fault from which these particular volumes are entirely free. Roy Campbell and the poets of Spender's anthology are all in deadly earnest, and when men are in earnest, when they feel that everything they care about hangs on the success of their cause, their affectations melt away from them and they write with startling lucidity. No two men are more utterly different than Roy Campbell and Stephen Spender. They are different in temperament and inheritance, in intellect and in physique. It is impossible to conceive of a single axiom upon which they would both agree, except perhaps that the Spanish War was a clear-cut conflict between Right and Wrong. (pp. 457-58)

Spender is not a prolific poet. It is difficult for him to write poetry, because he is always tortured by the idea that poetry does not necessarily serve the cause of justice, and he is too much of an artist to deflect poetry into the channels of propaganda. His artistic conscience is always at war with his political and economic *credo.* To quote his own words, "I do not want to make poetry the instrument of my own will, so I have tried to divide prose from poetry, not as two separate branches of an art, but more as two separate ways of exercising one's consciousness." In other words, prose and poetry spring from different elements in his nature. This inner antinomy, this endless struggle within himself, was solved temporarily at least by the Spanish War. It affected him just as the outbreak of the World War affected Rupert Brooke. "Now, God be thanked Who has matched us with His hour. . . ." Spender's introduction to *Poems for Spain* is nothing more than Rupert Brooke's heartfelt cry translated into quiet unspectacular prose.

> Moreover, where the issues are so clear and
> direct in a world which has accustomed us to
> confusion and obscurity, action itself may seem
> to be a kind of poetry to those who take part

in it. Therefore these poems often seem like hasty transcriptions into words of an experience expressed not in words at all, but in deeds. "All a poet can do to-day is to warn," the greatest of the English war poets, Wilfrid Owen, wrote in 1918. That is true always of poetry written in the midst of a great social upheaval; but the poets of the International Brigade have a different warning to give from that of the best poets of the Great War. It is a warning that it is necessary for civilization to defend and renew itself.

Among the many tragic aspects of war, none is more ironic than the belief honestly held by both sides that civilization depends on their victory. Hegel's theory of tragedy applies to war just as truly as it does to drama. The essence of tragedy lies in the conflict between two conceptions of Right, rather than in the conflict between Right and Wrong. Roy Campbell is just as convinced as Stephen Spender and the poets of the International Brigade that if there is to be any freedom, education or leisure in the world, it will be only through the victory of the cause for which he fights:

> The Left possessed the all-compelling arms
> Which drove us from the factories and farms.
> Strike after strike was ordered and compelled
> And it was death if honesty rebelled.
> For they resented willingness and skill
> And that we could go fighting up the hill—
> As if a race of drones with guns and knives,
> Crazed with a creed that grudges and deprives,
> Can better men in whom the Faith survives
> Or clean the world before they clean their lives.
> The reformation of the whole world's sin
> Is not in other people, but within.
> They'll not tell you that the workers of the land
> Are not on Franco's side with heart and hand,
> And on "coercion" blame our eager toil
> To raise the ruined wall or till the soil.
> But of all bans the worst coercion still
> Is that which keeps the worker from his skill,
> All must that forced ineptitude refuse
> Which grudges prowess even to the thews,
> But in its hot intolerance more blind,
> Forbids the triumphs of the heart and mind.

That there is a splendid ideal latent in Campbell's satire is what Spender will never understand, and in the same way Roy Campbell is blind to the possibility of a more equitable world implied in Herbert Read's "Song for the Spanish Anarchists":

> The golden lemon is not made
>   but grows on a green tree:
> A strong man and his crystal eyes
>   is a man born free.
>
> The oxen pass under the yoke
>   and the blind are led at will:
> But a man born free has a path of his own
>   and a house on the hill.
>
> And men are men who till the land
>   and women are women who weave:
> Fifty men own the lemon grove
>   and no man is a slave.

Towards the end of the World War, men like Wilfrid Owen came to accept the Germans as in a sense partners in a common struggle of which the issue was in the hands of God. No such attitude can be discerned in the poets on either side in the Spanish War. Civil wars are notoriously bitter, but nothing is more eloquent of the efficiency of propaganda than the inability not only of the Spaniards but even of foreigners to discern any ray of justice in the other side of the case.

In one respect Roy Campbell is better qualified to speak of the issues involved than the various authors of *Poems for Spain,* because he lived in Spain for some time under the republican regime. Furthermore, he knew Spain not as a tourist or as a journalist, but as a breaker of horses. The poets of the Left Wing dismiss him as a talking bronco or a fake cowboy, but the fact that he earned his living in Spain lends a certain significance to his opinions. Once we accustom ourselves to his tendency to write at the top of his lungs, the sheer vitality of the man sweeps us off our feet. The first thing to remember about Roy Campbell is that he was born and brought up in South Africa, and that consequently the problems of an urban civilization have never come home to him as they have to Spender and other English poets brought up in cities. A boy who grows up on the veldt of South Africa develops a very different set of standards from the boy who grows up in the suburbs of London. (pp. 458-60)

As we would expect from a man who has lived all his life out-of-doors, who owns a fleet of fishing boats and wins prizes for steer throwing, he has small respect for *literati* and politicians. Up to the outbreak of the war in Spain he cared nothing for causes. He was hardly aware of the dislocation of the times, of class struggles and social injustice. The things that moved him to expression were long days in the sun, "an old unquenched, unsmotherable heat," the sierras "white with crimson crests, stained with sunset," "the snorting fillies of the sea," and what he calls "the red squadron of my dreams." It is easy enough to understand why he thinks that the engine of poetry can be driven only by the red fires of love and hate. He is a poet of extremes; that is his strength and weakness. He is in love with life, and also with death. Of a toreador, killed in the arena he can write:

> He was the bee, with danger for his rose!
> He died the sudden violence of Kings,
> And from the bullring to the Virgin goes
> Floating his cape. He has no need for wings.

His love of bull fighting is thoroughly characteristic. It is the supreme example of physical dexterity, danger, and cruelty which he accepts as an essential part in the pattern of life. A good deal of his poetry is insensitive and bombastic, but if we scratch the surface, we come upon an ecstasy, an intensity of emotion, and above all upon a sense that life is tremendously exciting, which has disappeared from the verse of his more sophisticated contemporaries.

War has a sobering effect upon most men, but it has not sobered Roy Campbell. It has not compelled him, as it does most men, to go back and examine afresh the standards by which he lives. He is like the juryman who refuses to listen to the other side of the case, because he has made up his mind. He hates the Marxian conception of life with a deadly hatred, and he has convinced himself that the International Brigade and its Left Wing sympathizers in England are the most contemptible of men. Religion was certainly one of the issues at stake in the Spanish war, but it was not the only issue, and Mr. Campbell

makes the mistake of writing as if the angels were all on one side and the devils on the other. From a polemical point of view, *Flowering Rifle* is a failure. Campbell is too much of a Hotspur to make a good advocate. Nor is he the kind of man to lure the wavering into his camp; he relies on crushing the reader into submission. In the long run, even those who agree with him will find the steady torrent of abuse monotonous. The defence of Alcazar, the miraculous march of General Franco to Toledo, these descriptions stand out like oases in a vast desert of invective. The satire is often telling, but a long satiric poem, however clever the satire may be, ends by wearying the reader. Only a real devotee of the eighteenth century can read the *Dunciad* with any pleasure, and Roy Campbell is not the artist in satire that Pope was.

According to his publisher, he succeeds in making live poetry out of economics and agriculture. That claim seems rather far-fetched, for there is nothing in the poem that the economist or the farmer would find particularly illuminating; but Campbell does succeed in presenting with great force a certain point of view that is to-day more than ever unpopular. Our sympathies are always ready to flow out to the individualists, to the rebels against society, whereas to Roy Campbell there is a more genuine romance in the achievements of organization. General Franco appeals to him as the leader of what must have seemed for a long time a losing battle against chaos. To those who have lived in a country given over to anarchy, the institution and defence of law and order must seem infinitely the most important, as well as the most romantic, thing in the world. The great heroes of antiquity, Theseus and Hercules, King Arthur and Charlemagne, spent their lives going up and down the land warring against devouring monsters, evil customs and every kind of lawlessness and injustice. Roy Campbell sees in General Franco another heroic champion of order. The poets of the Left see in him nothing but a ruthless enemy of individual freedom. These two conceptions are not as irreconcilable as they sound, but until they are reconciled, until the spirit of hatred and mutual contempt is purged, any poetry that comes out of Spain will be dangerously close to propaganda. What is perhaps of more importance to the average man, the peace itself will be dangerously insecure.

Poems for Spain, containing as it does the work of some thirty different poets, offers the reader a greater variety of interest than he will find in Roy Campbell's one long poem. Unfortunately the abuse of the other side, for no other reason than that it is the other side, is just as prevalent. Messrs. Spender and Campbell might have saved themselves, their printers and their public, no little trouble if they had read each others' manuscripts before going to press, and agreed to cancel all passages of hysterical denunciation. If the vituperation of Italy by the Left, and of Russia by the Right, could have been blue-pencilled by some dispassionate editor, the cause of poetry, and incidentally the cause of truth, would have been well served. Edgell Rickword's would-be satiric poem, "To the Wife of Any Non-Intervention Statesman," induces respect for the wife rather than contempt, once we have read Roy Campbell's diatribes upon those statesmen for their shameful failure to support Franco. The reader instinctively cries "A plague on both your houses." Rex Warner's "Arms in Spain" forms another companion piece to Campbell's innumerable outbursts against Jews and Reds:

> So that the drunken General and the Christian
>   millionaire
> might continue blindly to rule in complete darkness,
> that on rape and ruin order might be founded firm,
> these guns were sent to save civilization.

General Francisco Franco. The Granger Collection, New York.

Rubbish of this kind, of which Roy Campbell is equally guilty, might well be censored on the ground that it degrades poetry to the level of propaganda. To compare such writing with even one of the lesser known poems of the World War, Charles Sorley's sonnet ''To Germany,'' is to realize the difference between what is tragic and what is merely bad-tempered:

> When it is peace, then we may view again
> With new-won eyes each other's truer form
> And wonder. Grown more loving-kind and warm
> We'll grasp firm hands and laugh at the old pain
> When it is peace. But until peace, the storm,
> The darkness and the thunder and the rain.

In the World War men learned to fight without rancor, and their ability to rise above the passion of battle is a measure of the quality they had as poets. Behind the lines, in the fashionable clubs of London and Paris, feeling may have run very high, but not among the combatants themselves. Hatred is always sterile, and poetry produced in an atmosphere of hatred is bound to be ephemeral. Only occasionally have the poets in Mr. Spender's collection lifted the conflict on to the creative level attained by Charles Sorley.

W. H. Auden's ''Spain'' is one of the few poems in which the author grapples with the significance of the struggle to spectators outside Spain. Instead of merely recording his emotions, as countless other men have done, he has fashioned something new out of those emotions. In poetry there are architects as well as contractors, men who know how to design as well as men who know how to collect materials. In this poem Auden designs a brave new world, which he hopes will

rise like a phoenix out of the ashes of the war. Naturally he starts from a hypothesis which the other side would indignantly reject. The Spanish revolutionaries are taken to represent all the forces of progress, and they are depicted as struggling against picturesque customs and superstitions which have outlived whatever usefulness they may once have had:

> Yesterday the abolition of fairies and giants,
> The fortress like a motionless eagle eyeing the valley,
>   The chapel built in the forest;
> Yesterday the carving of angels and alarming
>   gargoyles. . . .

But the clue to the poem lies in his conception of progress:

> To-morrow, perhaps the future. The research on fatigue
> And the movements of packers; the gradual exploring of
>   all the octaves of radiation;
> To-morrow the enlarging of consciousness by diet and
>   breathing.

Mankind has fought for all sorts of things, for liberty, for land, for trade and for prestige, but to fight for the ''enlarging of consciousness by diet and breathing,'' to fight for a world which will ensure ''the research on fatigue and the movements of packers,'' whatever that may mean, seems to us utterly incomprehensible.

Auden has a way of jumping from the esoteric to the familiar, even to the trivial, so that we are not surprised when he suddenly discloses a very different aspect of the future:

> To-morrow the rediscovery of romantic love,
> The photographing of ravens; all the fun under
>   Liberty's masterful shadow;
> To-morrow the hour of the pageant-master and the
>   musician,
>
> The beautiful roar of the chorus under the dome;
> To-morrow the exchanging of tips on the breeding of
>   terriers,
>   The eager election of chairmen
> By the sudden forest of hands. But to-day the struggle.
>
> To-morrow for the young the poets exploding like
>   bombs,
> The walks by the lake, the weeks of perfect
>   communion;
>   To-morrow the bicycle races
> Through the suburbs on summer evenings. But to-day
>   the struggle.

Auden's choice of amusements is very English and very significant. When he discarded religion as a motive force in men's minds—God is airily disposed of as ''a dove or a furious papa or a mild engineer''—he was hard put to it to find a substitute. The best he can offer is a future of scientific progress, enlivened by the typical amusements of any English industrial community.

This conception of the future is echoed by all the poets in Mr. Spender's anthology. For them Spain is merely the arena where the fate of liberty and communism must finally be settled. John Cornford, one of the younger poets killed in the war, states the issue very clearly:

> Freedom is an easily spoken word,
> But facts are stubborn things. Here, too, in Spain
> Our fight's not won till the workers of all the world

Stand by our guard on Huesca's plain,
Swear that our dead fought not in vain,
Raise the red flag triumphantly
For Communism and for liberty.

Freedom is one of those chameleon words which is forever changing its meaning. To the romantic poets of the 19th century, to Browning and Swinburne as well as to Byron and Shelley, freedom was synonymous with nationalism. They dreamed of a free Italy, by which they meant a unified Italy. Roy Campbell belongs to the same tradition; Spain excites him just as the word "Italy" excited Browning. A Spaniard, even a Spanish radical, will feel at home in Roy Campbell's world, however much he may deplore it, but unless he has lived in Birmingham, Mr. Auden's Spain will seem strangely unfamiliar.

To one who clings tenaciously to the middle of the road, there is little to choose between the fanaticism of Spender's bellicose pacifists and the ferocity of Roy Campbell's nationalism. To say, as Philip Henderson does in his . . . book, *The Poet and Society,* that John Cornford was killed fighting for democratic government in Spain is absurd. He cared no more for democratic government than does Stalin. Now that Communists and Nazis have suddenly become blood brothers, the futile sacrifice of the men who died fighting in the International Brigade is more than ever evident. Spender was wrong when he said that the issues in Spain were clear and direct. On the contrary, they were peculiarly involved, but the quality of poetry written in the stress of war does not depend on the justice of the poet's cause, or upon the magnitude of the war itself.

To-day the world is involved in a much greater struggle, compared to which the Spanish war dwindles into insignificance, but the Spanish War did English poetry a good turn. It rescued it from a waste land, where it was dying of inanition. . . . War does not necessarily produce great poetry, but the poetry written by men fighting in a cause which they believe to be sacred is more likely to be genuine than the poetry that results from reading Karl Marx and Dr. Freud. One of the compensations of war, perhaps the only one, is that it increases the range, sensitiveness and depth of our emotions, and the safety valve for this increased emotion we usually call poetry. (pp. 461-66)

Arnold Whittridge, "English Poetry and the Spanish War," in The Dalhousie Review, *Vol. 19, No. 4, January, 1940, pp. 456-66.*

STANLEY G. ESKIN

[In the following excerpt, Eskin analyzes the political nature of Spanish Civil War literature.]

The Spanish Civil War literature, judged in terms of stature, reputation and mere survival, would seem to be a conclusive instance of the unviability of politics in literature. The success and excellence of documentary works like *Homage to Catalonia,* Hugh Thomas' brilliant history or the composite documentary film *To Die in Madrid* only accentuate what seems to be a dearth of imaginative literature, or a plethora of mediocrity. Only two books, I think, have survived at all in the general awareness of the reading public, Hemingway's *For Whom the Bell Tolls* and Malraux's *L'Espoir,* often regarded, even so, as inferior works in print only because of the fame of the authors. Yet to see this body of literature as exemplifying a kind of genre is to suggest the potential of the genre and occasionally to discover flashes of realization. (p. 76)

The encompassing topic of [Spanish Civil War] literature is partisanship: its function, possibilities, uses and perils in literature. . . . At one end of a scale, partisanship can be asserted loudly and directly; at the other end it can either be actively rejected or passively ignored; in between it can be variously qualified, fragmented, refracted, neutralized, etc. Even when the partisanship is straightforward and assertive it need not be exclusively considered as deliberate manipulation for utilitarian purposes, but may be seen as aesthetic principle dictating tone and structure. In other words, it is not always enlightening to think of the art as *used* for partisan ends: the partisanship *is* the art, whatever it may be worth.

The first rhetorical move that an author may make in the literary assertion of partisanship is in prefatory remarks, or, even before that, in dedications:

> This book is dedicated to the memory of eighteen hundred Americans who died in the ranks of the International Brigades during the second war of Spain's independence [*The Heart of Spain*].

> Dem Retter and Erneuer Spaniens, General Francisco Franco und seinem Soldaten ["To the deliverer and restorer of Spain, General Francisco Franco, and his soldiers," *Kriegsschule Toledo.*]

> This is a partisan anthology. It proceeds from the conviction that life, decency and progress were on the side of the Spanish Republic; obscenity, retrogression and death, the stigmata of its enemies [*The Heart of Spain*].

Establishing tone and expectations, such pronouncements have literary significance beyond their ideological content; what they signify, in a sense, is directness and assertiveness itself.

To carry the principle of direct partisanship into the body of a literary work various techniques are available. In dramatized or narrated fictions, one procedure is to set up a situation leading to a strong commitment through a series of obstacles, each surmounted interference solidifying the commitment in a rhythmic, crescendo movement. Ideological dialogue may provide opportunities for dramatized direct assertions, again with possibilities for a climactic rhetorical movement. And a definitive test of the commitment may be provided in the face of problems, action, danger and death. Young people may overcome the resistance of parents or teachers, girls the caution of their boyfriends, volunteers the disapproval of friends and the hostility of officials. At each step an assertion is made in word and in act, the one complementing the other. A likely climax of assertion is at the front lines (for the left, the battle of Madrid is perfect).

The congruence of word and deed is a central principle for the literature of direct affirmation, and the words may be not only those of public rhetoric but also of private reflection. Thus another pattern is the "realization-of-meaning" pattern: I look upon Spain and its struggle and I see what it means and I see that the meaning is both universal and intensely personal. Identities are found or recovered in situations simultaneously enacted and explicated. [Englishman Louis MacNiece] recalls a recent visit to Spain and reflects on how little he realized what Spain would soon come to mean: ". . . not realizing / that Spain would soon denote / Our grief, our aspirations." The war becomes a revelation of political truth and a clarification of one's own values and one's role. For German expatriates joining the Edgar André battalion [in the novel *Grüne Oliven und nackte Berge*] the sight of the Spanish coast signifies a recovery of their identity after years of exile, of assumed names, of concealment, of deceptions. Thus to the congruence of word and deed one should add the congruence of public and private, or political and personal, and these congruences subserve directness of partisan assertion.

Similarly, there is the pattern of political education—the political *Bildungsroman*—a useful technique that enables the author to express a great deal of political opinion or information in a dramatic context, to animate and personalize ideology by treating it, so to speak, embryologically, as a dynamic process in living personalities. Young men from upperclass families discover the falseness of their background from contacts with fellow-students; workers find their situation clarified by contacts with dedicated leaders at political meetings. In [*Kriegsschule Toledo*] a conflict develops between a visionary Falangist cadet and an apolitical, strictly military lieutenant, who, however, becomes "educated":

> How many Spanish officers acknowledged their adherence to the Falange Española and yet were no worse soldiers than he was! Did the Falange perhaps lay a bridge between the old order and the new, modern Spain forging ahead with its turbulent national power. Was it a bridge between the aristocracy, isolated in its class pride, and the simple Spanish worker, who loved his fatherland as ardently as they did, but who was in fact rejected by so-called "good society" and pushed into the arms of Bolshevism?

However, this pattern does not always directly subserve partisan affirmation, or may not subserve it at all: the education may be into the qualifying complexities of politics, or into, and thus out of, the nefariousness of politics.

Another literary method for affirming political commitment, familiar at least since the Romantic Movement, is the association of a political cause with positive energies like natural forces or sexual potency or a more general, unspecified sense of health and vitality. (pp. 77-80)

Another associational strategy to promote a political cause is enlisting art and culture. Both right and left can be quite explicit in asserting that their side represents art, culture and civilized values while their enemies are destroyers and perverters of these values. (p. 80)

In the literature [of the Spanish Civil War] the art-culture-politics nexus appears in various contexts. There is the straightforward enhancement of partisanship, as in a poem by Albert Brown, "From a Painting by Picasso," which sees the Loyalist cause as guaranteeing the future of artistic sensitivity, incarnate in a beautiful Picasso woman, but now threatened by "the magnified yap of a little dragon, / Dying with . . . disproportionate slaughter." At the beginning of *The Great Crusade*, Gustav Regler depicts his hero escaping Germany as the Nazis are destroying the great German cultural tradition, and finding himself at home once again in Madrid, in the company of Velázques and El Greco. A short story by Ruth Domino in *The Heart of Spain*, "The Wonderful White Paper," concerns a village schoolteacher who inspires both his pupils and the peasants to take up painting; they all become extremely enthusiastic about it, expressing in images their sense of social injustice and their dreams of a better life, until the whole project

is considered subversive by the authorities and brutally suspended. In other contexts the conjunction may be more ambiguous, with conflicts developing between artistic and political commitments: art and culture, once important to a character, now seem trivial and yield to more immediate imperatives; or, the commitment to art and culture, though far from trivial, must be heroically suppressed and the sensitive artistic soul cauterized for its rough and brutal political mission.

In lyric poetry, a simple mode of direct affirmation of partisanship is the clarion call (witness all the poems entitled "alerta," or "alarma"): the enemy is at the gate, the political issues are unequivocal, commitment is a categorical imperative. . . . The long-range political perspective of liberty, hope and a better future is concentrated on the immediacy of the defense of Madrid, and political lines are simplified to the confrontation between the heroic populace and the black Fascist beast of prey. Along these lines, a simple tactic to emphasize one's own side is to discredit the other by sheer invective and denunciation, and especially by pointing up the viciousness and brutality of the enemy and the suffering of his victims. The bombings by the right and the executions by the left acquire an almost emblematic status in the literature of the opposite side, arousing clear-cut *political* responses. Subtler effects are possible, as for example by presenting harrowing scenes of victimization from a seemingly detached, noncommittal, or at least non-commented, perspective, but suddenly injecting a few terse, well-placed and direct partisan barbs:

> Numerous peasants from the Tagus valley had taken refuge with relatives, each family with its donkey; amid the blankets, the alarm clocks, the bird cages, the cats carried in the arms, all of them, without knowing why, went toward the richer quarters—without panic, long accustomed to distress. The bombs fell in volleys. They would be taught to be poor as it is right they should be. [*L'Espoir*]

A less direct method to point up partisan commitment, yet direct in that it employs a simple reversal of perspective, is what we might call the pseudo-foreground or the false front: that is, telling a story ostensibly dealing with the "other side," while one's side appears in the background, but in such a way that what emerges most strongly is the commitment to one's own side. The main characters of a story, say, may be conservative or neutral persons in a Nationalist-occupied village and the plot may consist mostly of their activities against the Loyalists; but the perspective will be Loyalist and will in fact find its focus in figures outside the main plot but, like Fortinbras, prominent precisely because of their strategic position; and the main plot itself may turn either on a recognition of the "truth" by the main characters or on a particularly nefarious action by them that condemns the side they represent. The advantage of this method is a genuinely strategic one: the reader, in a manner of speaking, is hoodwinked into supposing that he is being shown a substantial image of the men and ideas of one side, but it all somewhat insidiously turns out to be a picture of the other side. (pp. 82-4)

Most of the complications that appear as one leaves direct assertions of partisanship take, in the end, one of . . . two directions: undermining partisanship, and indeed, the whole political dimension; or reasserting partisanship despite qualifications (or all the more deeply *because* of them). The literature of the left is of course far more significant in these matters than that of the right. The left is far more self-critical, partly because it is more wracked by intramural conflicts than the right. Minor conflicts of ideology occur in right-wing literature—as between a heavily religious orientation and a more secular Falangist activism or between pure militarism and political partisanship—but the definitive tone is of unquestioned and unified dedication. The historical factional disputes between Carlists, orthodox Monarchists, Falangists and right-wing Republicans have no effect on the Nationalist literature I have consulted. The literature of the left, however, reflecting deeper, more public and unresolved divisions, is a veritable anthology of factionalism. Commitment often is two-pronged, involving commitment to the Loyalist cause and commitment to a faction within it. The result, as regards the broader commitment, is often a strong qualification: you remain loyal to the Republic in terms of your own factional perspective while deploring and severely condemning the other factions. Thus one finds Anarchist condemnations of Communism and governmental Republicanism, Communist critiques of Anarchism, liberal critiques of Communism and Anarchism, etc. It is these party conflicts that are responsible for the juggling of initials—F.A.I., C.N.T., U.G.T., P.O.U.M.—that bewilders the novice and becomes so familiar to the student of the war. Complementing or counterpointing these conflicts are many others: front-line combatants vs. rear-guard militants (or shirkers), humanitarians vs. tough realists (or brutes), ideological (or non-ideological) flexibility vs. Party-line discipline (or dogmatic rigidity), loyalties of friendship or blood or human sympathy vs. political loyalties or necessities (or obsessions). The motifs one constantly encounters that qualify the Loyalist cause include the arbitrary arrests, imprisonments and executions by dubiously constituted revolutionary groups, the pathological obsession with spies, irresponsible and ignorant leadership, mob hysteria, etc.

A characteristic example of such cross-currents is a novel by Max Aub, *Campo abierto,* published a dozen years after the end of the war. In an early episode the student Vincente Dalmases, earnestly dedicated to Communism, runs into a conflict of Corneillan sharpness when his girl's father is arrested as a Fascist sympathizer and he is ordered to glean more information from him. He sticks with the Party but feels the conflict of loyalties acutely. Later we find him at the Madrid front, still troubled, but still committed, meditating at one point on a simple but moving vision of the new Spain that may arise if the Fascists are defeated:

> If we win. . . . What might we not make of Spain! A free and working Spain, a new Spain, where everyone has what he deserves to have. A Spain where the peasants own the land which they cultivate, a Spain where everyone knows how to read, a Spain with water. Yes, we will have water in Spain. And why shouldn't it have water if we determine that it will!

Vicente's story is only one of several almost independent plot lines, and nearly all involve conflicts with commitment. A Communist runs into trouble when he helps out an old acquaintance who turns out to be a member of the conservative Catalan league. An Anarchist fraternizes for a while with the Marxists, volunteers for the Aragon front, and is insidiously shot on the way by the Civil Guards along with the other Anarchist militiamen. An upper-class student who belongs to the Radical Socialists runs into a conflict between his humanitarian political ideals and the tyrannical rigor and uncertain justice of the popular tribunals trying political suspects; and

further conflict results from the arrest of his father, whom he barely manages to save by political pull—though here the lines of conflict are further complicated by the fact that his father *is* a dangerous rightist conspirator whose only response to his last-minute reprieve is a nasty, revengeful speech to his son. Another episode involves a volatile pseudo-Anarchist, basically a picaresque crook who heads a band of armed marauders, about whom leftist leaders argue as to whether he should be liquidated or whether he has some political value (the cross-currents here involve the doubts cast on a left that has included pure bandits among its militants, and further a certain conflict between the sympathy generated by the Anarchist's outrageous but engaging personality and the political necessity for getting rid of him).

The latter portion of the book is set in Madrid, and another gallery of characters appears, by no means all heroic. They include such types as the compulsive gossiper and rumormonger; the man who has gone to the mountains, fired a few shots and returns feeling he has saved the Republic; and the cynical, ambitious writer contemptuously aloof from the political turmoil. There are long-winded discussions among a group of intellectuals and professionals about the role of art in revolutionary politics, and conflicts between freedom and political discipline, the intractability of the Spanish character, etc. In the midst of all this Vincente Dalmases reappears, on leave from the front, listening bored and dejected to all this political babble. The tone of it all adds up to a strong irony against leftist commitment. Yet the categorical imperative and the glory of commitment are reasserted even more strongly. The Madrid defense may include a host of questionable types, but it plays its accustomed role in galvanizing political affirmation. (pp. 85-7)

The problems of partisan commitment complexly asserted, challenged and reasserted appear with a good deal of subtlety in what is probably the finest poem about the war, W. H. Auden's "Spain 1937," which has its own special way of dealing with political commitment. The poem has been the object of rather conflicting readings. Spender, in the preface to *Poems for Spain* [see Additional Bibliography], sees it as a political affirmation:

> It translates a political action into terms of the imagination and thus tests the implications of a particular, contemporary situation by the whole tradition of values which exist in poetry.

H. D. Ford, on the other hand, in *A Poet's War,* pointing out that Auden went to Spain briefly as a medical volunteer, returned to England, wrote the poem, then never uttered another word about Spain and shortly afterward turned away from his whole Marxist orientation, reads the poem as a kind of valedictory to political commitment, Auden's final gesture of commitment as he presents the ground for a rejection of politics:

> If "Spain," besides being a defense of the Spanish Republic, works out to its logical conclusion the Marxist hypothesis "which condoned the most reprehensible conduct so long as it advanced the socialist cause" . . . is it not possible to consider the poem Auden's renunciation of Marxism? . . .
>
> The severely impersonal quality of "Spain" might almost be taken as presaging Auden's withdrawal from politics. . . . We search for signs of his emotional involvement in the strug-

gle, but the search is futile. Auden the politically committed man eludes us.

Mr. Ford may be right in detecting an embryonic renunciation of Marxism; he argues from certain revisions which are less Marxist than the original, and from the concluding lines—"History to the defeated / May say Alas but cannot help or pardon"—which he feels would be unacceptable to a Marxist, for whom a Republican defeat would not mean the end of the struggle (though it does not seem to me that that is necessarily what Auden is saying; even if the Revolution wins out in the end the defeated in its momentary setbacks are still the defeated). In any case, the major theme of the poem is certainly not a turn from Marxism; it is the urgency of commitment in the Spanish struggle. Mr. Ford's remarks on the aloofness of the poet are quite acute. Auden does seem to be making an appeal for something for which he has no taste. But that is part of the point: the determination for commitment must be all the stronger in that it involves unpleasantness, danger and suffering:

> To-day the inevitable increase in the chances of death;
> The conscious acceptance of guilt in the fact of murder;
>   To-day the expending of powers
> On the flat ephemeral pamphlets and the boring meeting.

It is an unsentimentalized view of commitment, achieved precisely through the tone of detachment that Mr. Ford describes. What the poem loses in glamor it gains in the implied force behind the understatement, and the irregular refrain of "but to-day the struggle" becomes charged with an intensity all the more compelling for being withheld. Justifying the appeal for commitment is an Audenesque version of the long view of politics which, maintaining the tone of suppressed feeling, avoids the vatic, sweeping style that is the expected lyric voice for expressing the long view. It represents instead glimpses of past history and future possibilities in a series of concrete images:

> Yesterday the assessment of insurance by cards,
> The divination of water; yesterday the invention
>   Of cart-wheels and clocks, the taming of
> Horses; yesterday the bustling world of navigators . . .
>
> Yesterday the installation of dynamos and turbines;
> The construction of railways in the colonial desert . . .
>
> To-morrow, perhaps, the future: the research on fatigue
> And the movements of packers; the gradual exploring of
>   all the octaves of radiation

The specificity and sometimes homeliness of the catalogue mutes the grandiosity which would otherwise obtain in such a historical panorama. The long view of the panorama is effectively balanced by the close view of "the flat ephemeral pamphlet and the boring meeting"—the vision of progress by the prosaic mechanics that implement it—but both expressed in a gray, seemingly dispassionate tone that unifies them. The appeal itself, in the middle of the poem, maintains the tone. A personification of History or Evolution (he calls it "the life") is begged by the people and the nations to intervene:

>   O show us
> History the operator, the
> Organizer, Time the refreshing river . . .
>
>   Intervene. O descend as a dove or
> A furious pap or a mild engineer: but descend.

This is almost a parody of the kind of soaring personifications of historical processes that we find in Shelley and Swinburne, or even in Hardy's *Dynasts*. Even as a homely deity History does not descend but throws the issue squarely on human will, choice and commitment:

>   O no, I am not the Mover,
> Not to-day, not to you. To you I'm the
>
> Yes-man, the bar-companion, the easily duped:
> I am whatever you do; I am your vow to be
>   Good, your humorous story;
> I am your business voice; I am your marriage.
>
> What's your proposal? To build the Just City? I will.
> I agree. Or is it the suicide pact, the romantic
>   Death? Very well, I accept, for
> I am your choice, your decision: yes, I am Spain.

The ordinariness of some of the images ("the bar-companion," "your humorous story") and the irony of the more inflated ones ("the Just City," "the romantic Death") serve both to maintain the tone of understatement and to substantiate the principle of commitment by referring it to the real choices and actions of ordinary life rather than to transcendent visions. . . . "Spain 1937," it seems to me, is definitely a poem of commitment. If Auden's reservations about politics are responsible for the impersonal and subdued tone, that tone is nonetheless used effectively to urge "engagement." (pp. 88-91)

The political genre, more than most, invites consideration of its relationship to fact. Political works tend to involve a mixture of history and invention. The history, like any other historical writing, is more or less factual and has a variable relationship to the fiction. Authorial passages of general historical description (elections, changes of government, military campaigns, etc.) may be bodily interjected into the narrative. Or they may be filtered through the consciousness of a character, which can result either in a minimal fictionalization—the character merely as a gimmick for presenting the author's presumably factual observations—or a greater degree of fictionalization in which the character's personality and point of view must be taken into account. Or historical actions may be intertwined with invented ones, with a mixed cast of real and fictitious characters. Or fictitious actions may be closely based on historical ones but imaginatively heightened, condensed, concretized, or otherwise altered (a splendid instance is the opening of *L'Espoir,* as the railroad telephone central in Madrid contacts one provincial station after another on the night of the insurrection, learning in this way which towns are in Loyalist hands and which have yielded to the rebels). Similarly, imaginary characters may be close, but not quite factual, replicas of real models. Fiction may as easily be an instrument for historical documentation as history the occasion for fictional realization. It is sometimes difficult, in this literature, to distinguish between history and fiction. Going through the Lincoln Brigade anthology, *The Heart of Spain,* for example, which is full of unprefaced accounts of various aspects of the war, one is often uncertain whether one is reading reportage or fiction. Solano Palacio, the bitter Anarchist author of *Entre dos fascismos,* has also written straight reportage in *La Tragedía del norte* (1938) and *El Exodo* (1939). While it is formally evident which is fiction and which are reportage, the recollected impression of all three books is of identity of style, tone and perspective. It doesn't matter very much which genre he undertook to write. It is noteworthy that Hugh Thomas, that most scrupulous young historian, does not hesitate on occasion to use fictional works like *The Great Crusade* and *L'Espoir* as documentary evidence. (pp. 92-3)

Naiveté is an interesting subject in respect to political themes. First of all the author himself may be naive. Or he may assume a mask of naiveté for the purposes of the book: what Wayne Booth calls the implied author, as opposed to the actual author, is naive. Often one is unsure: is Upton Sinclair, in his melodramatic little novelette *No Pasarán!*, naive, or does he deliberately assume a naive stance as a rhetorical device, or does the heat of urgency impose a naivete he might not otherwise have? Some authors, perhaps, are born naive, some achieve naiveté, and some have naiveté thrust upon them. One could set up a scale of naiveté, with works like *No Pasarán!* at one end and, at the other, the highly sophisticated, unsentimental tone cultivated by Hemingway, Malraux, and Hermann Kesten. In addition, one should note the calculated use of that ancient literary formula, the naive observer: the tradition of Montaigne's cannibals, Gulliver, Candide, Rasselas, *Les Lettres persanes,* etc. This technique is either satirical or educational or both: that is, the naive character keeps encountering deplorable behavior and asking questions whose very simplicity pointedly exposes evils and follies; or the naive character, still asking simple questions, receives answers that contribute to his increasing awareness of the truth. (That kind of *Catch 22* of Spanish Civil War literature, Granell's *La Novella del Indio Tupinamba*, is a good example: the Indian who circulates through Spain trying to make sense of what he sees, though quickly enough abandoning his search and himself contributing to the hopeless nonsense of it all.)

More than any other major political event of recent history the Spanish Civil War raised the claims and the complexities of partisanship with a vivid concreteness providing ready-made images for literature. The war was an inexhaustible reservoir of objective correlatives. The symbols and emotions and drama, and even the ironies and paradoxes and tricks of perspective were all at hand in history and individual experience. Perhaps they were all too readily at hand, for one sometimes senses in some of these writers a compulsion to write imaginative literature which they might not have had without the political pressures and literary temptations afforded by the particular quality of this war. Furthermore, the Loyalist defeat produced a great number of exiles with time on their hands and a great weight in their hearts struggling to be expressed. If this means that too many dubious literary works were produced by men who should have stuck to journalism or school-teaching or political busy work, it also means that we have at hand an unusually broad range of literary efforts centered on an intensely political phenomenon. The inherent tendencies of literature both to universalize and to particularize provide a multiplicity of personality types, thematic patterns and characteristic incidents that could never be achieved in memoirs, reportage and straight historical reconstruction. On reflection, the literature of the Spanish Civil War is a paradoxical vindication both of literature and of the literary treatment of political themes. The paradox is the impression one has that a great deal about political experience has been revealed in a way that it could not otherwise have been revealed, but by a largely inferior literature. This seems true even about books that one may personally feel quite hostile toward on both literary and ideological grounds, yet from which one gains a sense of a political statement valuable precisely to the extent that it is imaged forth in literature, however incompetently, rather than plainly professed in polemical writing. (pp. 94-6)

Stanley G. Eskin, "The Literature of the Spanish Civil War: Observations on the Political Genre," in Genre, *Vol. IV, No. 1, March, 1971, pp. 76-99.*

ALLEN GUTTMANN

[*In the following excerpt, Guttmann examines the conflict between humanity and technology as a prominent theme in Spanish Civil War literature.*]

The Spanish Earth, a documentary film written in 1937 by Ernest Hemingway and directed by Joris Ivens, begins with the camera focused upon the soil itself. From the very beginning the film is an assertion of an intimate relationship between men and the land: "This Spanish earth is hard and dry and the faces of the men who work on [this] earth are hard and dry from the sun." The land must be defended, in the film as in reality, against an enemy armed with the most up-to-date mechanized equipment. The land is defended, and the film ends with the waters rushing through the newly constructed irrigation ditch and bringing life to the sun-baked soil. Floods of American aid never reached the Loyalists of Spain, but that is history's irony and not Hemingway's. *For Whom the Bell Tolls* begins and ends similarly—with the "pine-needled floor of the forest." The enemy possesses the weapons of a technological society and, in the eyes of the hero Robert Jordan, General Franco's Heinkels move like "mechanized doom." In both novel and film, there is a struggle between men and machines. (p. 541)

From his earliest stories, from Nick Adams episodes of *In Our Time* to the fable of *The Old Man and the Sea,* Ernest Hemingway has dealt, among other things, with man in the natural landscape. Even within the general lostness of *The Sun Also Rises,* the characters find themselves briefly while fishing in Spain, near Pamplona. For Hemingway, Spain is an elemental symbiosis of man and nature. . . . As if applying the old saw about Europe being cut off at the Pyrenees, Hemingway looks upon Africa and Spain as a unit. In *The Green Hills of Africa* the mechanized world enters to destroy the hitherto uncorrupted world of nature. The book opens with a hunt ruined by the passing of a truck. This is put into the simplest possible language: "The truck had spoiled it." Later, the theme is generalized:

> A continent ages quickly once we come. The natives live in harmony with it. But the foreigner destroys. . . . A country wears out quickly unless man puts back into it all his residue and that of all his beasts. When he quits using beasts and uses machines, the earth defeats him quickly. The machine can't reproduce, nor does it fertilize the soil.

What Hemingway seemed to discover in the Spanish war was that the machine is not merely passively destructive and biologically sterile: the war proved that the machine can also become an agent of destruction. Thus, writing in the *New Republic* in May 1937, he said:

> There is nothing so terrible and sinister as the track of a tank in action. The track of a tropical hurricane leaves a capricious swath of complete destruction, but the two parallel grooves the tank leaves in the red mud lead to scenes of planned death worse than any the hurricane leaves.

Before dramatizing in *For Whom the Bell Tolls* the conflict between the values associated with the natural landscape and the values associated with the machine, Hemingway wrote several short stories and also a play, all concerned with the Spanish Civil War.... The play, *The Fifth Column,* is set in Madrid's Hotel Florida. It is a wooden play about a Vassar girl (with long legs) and a counterspy for the International Brigades. If the play has any enduring meaning, it is that Ernest Hemingway could not dramatize the Spanish war with these stick figures; the play violates its author's own often-repeated rule—the writer must always tell the truth as he sees it, and the truth for Ernest Hemingway was not to be seen in the Hotel Florida. It was not even in Madrid; it was closer to the peasants and the gypsies, closer to the earth, closer to the pine-needled floor of the forest.

The first thing one notices about *For Whom the Bell Tolls* is, naturally, the epigraph taken from a meditation by John Donne. Ordinarily, we remember best the lines which give the book its title: "And therefore never send to know for whom the *bell* tolls; it tolls for *thee.*" Hemingway uses the epigraph as a statement of the theme of brotherhood, of human solidarity, of the involvement of all men in humanity itself. The statement, however, is not separable from the imagery of the passage:

> No man is an *Iland* intire of it selfe; every man
> is a peece of the *Continent,* a part of the *maine;*
> if a *Clod* bee washed away by the *Sea, Europe*
> is the lesse....

The images of the earth, of islands, continents, the main, a clod, are not accidental and not unimportant.... Hemingway's use of Donne's metaphor of the earth ... would be scant grounds on which to base a thesis if it were not for the accumulation of such seemingly trivial bits of evidence. Consider, for instance, two essays, both entitled "On the American Dead in Spain," in which Hemingway uses this same imagery:

> This spring the dead will feel the earth beginning to live again. For our dead are a part of the earth of Spain now and the earth of Spain can never die.

> The dead do not need to rise. They are a part of the earth now and the earth can never be conquered. For the earth endureth forever.

One need only finish the quotation, "And the sun also riseth," to feel the unity of Hemingway's best writing.

Robert Jordan, "a peece of the *Continent,* a part of the *maine,*" does *not* join the International Brigades. Two British volunteers described fighting in the wreckage of Madrid's University City, beneath the busts of "Plato, Spinoza, Aristotle and Voltaire," and behind bullet-proof "barricades ... of Indian metaphysics and early nineteenth-century German philosophy," but Robert Jordan joins a guerilla band in the mountains—a band which fights on horseback, a band whose previous accomplishments include the destruction of a troop-train. Robert Jordan fights side by side with Anselmo, a man of natural wisdom. The two trust each other by instinct, but Pablo, the leader of the band, is suspicious and grants the American an tentative approval only after witnessing his knowledge of horses, the same horses which subsequently bring out what little humanity is left in Pablo. Later still, horses play a vital role in the climax of Chapter XXVI, in the terrifying conflict between El Sordo's band, sprawled behind the dead bodies of their mounts, and the Fascist patrol. El Sordo's men hold out until the dive bomb-ers come. Then all is determined. On a hillside, where men are naturally accustomed to survey their dominions, the band is uncovered and helpless. They are all killed.

Those less grim sections of the novel, the episodes which concern the affair with Maria, have been condemned as extraneous, but, looking specifically at the theme of the earth and the machine, one notes that Maria, Roberto's beloved "rabbit," is somehow identified with the Spanish earth that was then being violated figuratively as Maria was violated literally. Maria's shaved head is so realistic a detail that one is surprised to see an obvious symbolism here as well. The *least* that one can say is that Maria's story parallels certain aspects of Spanish history. Paired with Maria is Pilar, a sort of Iberian Earth-Mother who is accustomed to having the world itself "move" during her love affairs, who had lived "nine years with three of the worst paid matadors in the world," and who reminds us again and again of the love-making and bull-fighting that, for Hemingway, represent Spain as it should have been.

In symbolic opposition to the cluster of values represented by the two bands, their mounts, and the earth itself, we have the steel bridge. Just as the lighthouse dominates Virginia Woolf's novel, so the bridge controls and unifies the action of *For Whom the Bell Tolls.* In one sense it is the center of a series of concentric circles; in another it is the point towards which the elements of the action converge. No matter what geometric metaphor is used to plot the book upon a plane surface, it is certain that the bridge is central. "That bridge," thinks Robert Jordan, "can be the point on which the future of the human race can turn." The character of each person is determined by his or her relation to the bridge. The steel bridge is the emblem of the technological society and at the same time the path over which the *Panzerdivision* of the enemy will come. Pablo is, of course, against the demolition of the bridge. Pilar is for it, because she understands its significance: "I am for the Republic.... And the Republic is the bridge." Robert Jordan defines himself by the bridge: "You're a bridge-blower now. Not a thinker." At the end, he once more identifies himself with the bridge: "As Jordan goes, so goes the bloody bridge...." The bridge *is* destroyed, but Robert Jordan, escaping on horseback, is hit by a shell fired from an enemy tank and mortally wounded.

One need not, moreover, rely exclusively upon the action of the novel or upon the symbolic oppositions, for the characters speak out. Anselmo asserts bitterly, "We must take away their planes, their automatic weapons, their tanks, their artillery, and teach them dignity." And Pilar is completely explicit: "The sight of those machines does things to me. We are nothing against such machines." Looking up at the Heinkels overhead, Robert Jordan thinks they are like "sharp-nosed sharks of the Gulf Stream," but only for a moment does he link the machine with the natural menace. As the tank was, in the dispatches which appeared in the *New Republic,* worse than the hurricane, so the bombers are worse than the very worst of nature.

> But these, wide-finned in silver, roaring, the
> light mist of their propellers in the sun, these
> do not move like sharks. They move like no
> thing there has ever been. They move like
> mechanized doom.

Clearly then, for Hemingway the Spanish Civil War was dramatized as, among other things, a struggle waged by men close to the earth and to the values of a primitive society against men who had turned away from the earth, men who had turned to the machine and to the values of an aggressive and destructive mechanical order. (pp. 543-47)

Early in the course of the Spanish war, the *New Republic*, which had printed Hemingway's dispatches from Spain, presented in an editorial the image of the machine-as-menace.

> Women and children torn to pieces by aerial bombs as they go to market, crowded building and boulevards . . . shattered by artillery, suburbs and outlying parks made into playgrounds for grinding tanks, men and women . . . sprayed to death . . . by machine guns in power-diving pursuit-planes—this is Madrid today.

There is no sense of human agency behind the weapons of the Fascists; there is only the sense of impotent humanity beneath omnipotent machines. This sense of impotence and this image of a conflict between men and machines runs through a variety of writings and is found in the visual arts as well. It is well, for the sake of clarity, to concentrate upon the most nearly ubiquitous symbol of technological warfare—the airplane.

Herbert Matthews, of the New York *Times,* described his own feelings of powerlessness before the then-experimental *Luftwaffe:* "It is a terrible moment when one can hear a bomber directly overhead, knowing its power of destruction and feeling so helpless." Irving Pflaum, of the United Press, admitted that his "one real fear" was "that methodical, systematic, terroristic bombing . . . may be one of the decisive factors in future wars. With me it was decisive. It licked me." Anna Louise Strong pictured Spain's "green civilian volunteers . . . raked by machine-gunning from the air. . . ." It was a form of attack "against which they were helpless." Similar observations were made by Edwin Rolfe in his history of the Abraham Lincoln Battalion, by Erskine Caldwell in his contribution to *Salud!* (a small anthology of writings on Spain), by Waldo Frank, who asked his readers to visualize "tens of thousands of bare breasts of simple men and women . . . there to confront the machine guns and bombing planes. . . ."

As this comment of Waldo Frank's suggests, the bombing planes were symbolically present in other novels than Hemingway's. The bomber quickly became part of the sound effects, part of the backdrop, for scenes of conflict. Of the best known writers, John Dos Passos uses this image of terror in *The Adventures of a Young Man* and Michael Blankfort uses it in *The Brave and the Blind.* Upton Sinclair brings his *No Pasaran!* to a dime-novel close in which two Americans, cousins who have volunteered for opposing sides, fight it out. The quality of the novel is reflected faithfully in the triumph of the foot-soldier (Loyalist) who "does in" his airborne relative (Fascist).

In addition to the numerous one-act plays which make symbolic use of the airplane, two verse plays for radio, by well-known writers, dramatize the air attack itself. Archibald MacLeish, who had joined Lillian Hellman in raising money for *The Spanish Earth*, wrote *Air Raid*, in which bombers are described by the narrator as a form of dehumanized menace.

> They swing like steel in a groove:
> They move like tools not men:
> You'd say there were no men:
> You'd say they had no will but the
> Will of motor on metal.

Implications of this vision become clearer as one recalls the visions of menaced primitivism that are found in MacLeish's earlier poem, "Conquistador." Lacking this element of overt primitivism but quite as bitterly written, Norman Corwin's play, *They Fly Through the Air With the Greatest of Ease,* was, like dozens of poems and hundreds of editorials, written as a response to the brutal bombing by the Germans of the Basque village of Guernica, a bombing which MacLeish denounced (in his speech to the 1937 meeting of the American Writers' Congress) as "the massacre of the civilian population of an undefended Basque village by German planes. . . . The Basques lie kicking in the fields where the machine guns caught up with them, and the Germans fly away."

When, as MacLeish in his speech emphasized, history consisted of horrors such as Guernica, it is not surprising that bombing planes appeared in the poetry of the Spanish war. Muriel Rukeyser has a long poem, "Correspondences," in which "crazies take to the planes" and the reader faces "machineries whose characters are wars." (Returning to America, she told New Yorkers that "The war there . . . is one of humans against guns.") Few poets wrote in her difficult experimental style; Norman Rosten's "Fragments for America" is completely exoteric. Nevertheless, his version of the unequal combat between men and machines is disquieting. He writes of a

> peasant who tried to stop an enemy plane:
> rising; ran cursing into the swift propeller
> to stop it with his hands; the plane rising
> . . . the sun shining on the stained steel. . . .

Langston Hughes wrote that "A bombing plane's / The song of Spain," and added further poems to show what he meant, poems like "Air Raid: Barcelona," and "Moonlight in Valencia," in which he links airplanes and death and destroys the traditional connotations of moonlight: "Moonlight in Valencia: the moon meant planes. / The planes meant death." Edwin Rolfe, in "A City of Anguish," describes Madrid under bombardment:

> All night, all night
> flared in my city the bright
> cruel explosions of bombs.
> All night, all night,
> there, where the soil and stone
> spilled like brains from the sandbag's head,
> the bodiless head lay staring;
> while the anti-aircraft barked,
> barked at the droning plane. . . .

Another poet, Boris Todrin, writes in a manner reminiscent of Hemingway's elegy to the American dead and the Spanish earth.

> Worn out fields where bomb and shell
> Scattered iron seeds of hell,
> Grow their scarecrow crops. The torn
> Bones will keep the roots of corn.

John Berryman's more complex poem, "1938," contains bitter comments on the Spanish war and on the war that was still in preparation.

> Across the frontiers of the helpless world
> The great planes swarm, the carriers of death,
> Germs in the healthy body of the air,
> And blast our cities where we stand in talk
> By doomed and comfortable fires.

In this helpless world beneath the iron bombers, poets found a metaphor grounded in reality. They found a still more specific metaphor when the "necessities" of modern warfare sanctioned the bombing of cities, for then it became "necessary" that children should die with their elders. Harold Rosenberg's eight-line "Spanish Epitaph" is representative of many poems:

> O tall men of Hades
> Have pity on this little one!
> His speech was not formed yet
> All he knew of life was laughing and growing
> Till the iron dropped on him out of the sky.
> O gaunt horses of Hades
> He has not even one weapon
> With which to defend himself.

Muriel Rukeyser's "M-Day's Child" contains this particular theme within the broader theme of mechanical horror.

> M-day's child is fair of face,
> Drill-day's child is full of grace,
> Gun-day's child is breastless and blind,
> Shell-day's child is out of its mind,
> Bomb-day's child will always be dumb,
> Cannon-day's child can never quite come,
> but the child born on the Battle-day
> is blithe and bonny and rotted away.

Aaron Kramer, Charles Norman, and Norman Rosten are three poets, of dozens, who wrote of the bombers and the children. (pp. 548-52)

These samples are a token of the pervasiveness, within American interpretations of the Spanish war, of the theme of conflict between men and machines, and of the image of the machine, especially the bombing plane, as the appropriate symbol for the terrible realities of the war. When we turn to the work of two European novelists, Ralph Bates and André Malraux, I believe that we can observe certain differences between the American and the European imagination. Ralph Bates' novel, *The Olive Field,* describes the tumult of the years preceding the actual outbreak of war. Agricultural laborers are pitted against effete landowners who collect ancient manuscripts and against ascetic priests who do not understand, as the workers do, that "the olive trees [are] the very spirit of the land." The action reaches a climax in the Left revolution of 1934, where, as Malcolm Cowley noted, the spontaneous action of the *dynamiteros* is overmatched by tanks and planes. (p. 553)

[Of] all writings on the Spanish war, Bates' short stories, collected in *Sirocco and Other Stories,* are closest to Hemingway's in tone and in theme. The protagonists are usually close to the land; their antagonists are associated with mechanized authoritarianism. In "The 43rd Division," published in *Harper's,* Bates' peasant-hero considers the Spanish war and condemns the new modes of warfare:

> The mechanical aid to the rebels was violating
> the nature of the Spaniard. Man to man, valor
> against valor; that was the Spanish way of fight-
> ing. Not factory against factory, bald-head en-
> gineer against peasant.

The crucial episode of this story embodies the same theme. An izard (a type of chamois) gives birth and a Fascist, equipped with a panoply of technical implements—Luger, Mannlicher-Cacano, Zeis range-finder, Leitz binoculars—kills the animal. Seeing this attack upon the natural order, the peasant-hero resolves his indecisions, vows to accept discipline, and is given command of a guerrilla unit. This story is more successful than Bates' accounts of men in the regular army because, in a sense,

the guerrilla unit is a compromise which permits the maintenance of a closeness to nature and, at the same time, the acceptance of a form of discipline. In literature both worlds were possible; outside of literature, Bates had to choose, and he chose the Popular Front of Juan Negrin and Julio Alvarez del Vayo, the discipline, the organization, the technological weapons, and the promise of a socialist Spain in which the machine and the olive tree are harmonized.

Excellent as many of these stories are, André Malraux's *L'Espoir* is the only piece of writing which compares with *For Whom the Bell Tolls* or George Orwell's magnificent *Homage to Catalonia.* No other European novel (of dozens) contains so much of the complexity of the Spanish Civil War. In *L'Espoir,* Hemingway's theme of primitivism—the affirmation of the natural man in the natural landscape—is sounded with a marvelous sense of the ambiguous overtones, and then subordinated to another theme. True to the European revolutionary tradition, Malraux debates and finally decides against the values of a primitive society. As Malcolm Cowley and Joseph Warren Beach separately noted, the struggle of the unarmed mobs against the troops of the Montana Barracks and the fight of the almost unarmed *milicianos* against tanks and armored trains, provide many of the most moving passages of the book, *but* this affirmation of the unorganized activity of the anarchists does *not* persist through the novel. The conflict between man and machine becomes less important as Russian equipment arrives. Scenes of heroic struggle against a mechanical enemy give way to descriptions of victory won by those who turn from the land in order to fight metal with metal. The somehow humanized "crates" of the circus-like volunteer air-force are replaced by modern flying machines; the pilots learn the necessity of obedience. As Malraux's spokesman argues, "Notre modeste fonction. . . . C'est d'organiser L'Apocalypse" ["Our modest function is to organize the Apocalypse"]. Realizing the hopeless situation of the unarmed human being, Malraux, like *most* writers, finds in this realization a call to action—the *milicianos* must be mechanized. Russian *chatos* climb into the air over Malraux's Madrid as they did over the Madrid of historical fact. It is true that the theme of discipline and the dramatic victory of the International Brigades at Guadalajara are interwoven with another strand, with the theme of primitivism and the uncoerced action of the peasants who, late in the novel, carry down from the mountains, in ritual procession, the survivors of a wrecked airplane; nevertheless, despite this extraordinarily moving episode, Malraux's *explicit* approval is with the organizers of the Apocalypse, with the Stalinists. (By "Stalinists" I mean those who followed the tactics of Georgi Dimitroff's "Popular Front" and whose ultimate strategy was the socialization and industrialization of a "progressive" Spain.) In taking this position, which F. W. Dupee lamented in the anti-Stalinist *Partisan Review,* Malraux was anticipating historical developments. As the war continued, discipline was imposed upon the militiamen and modern weapons were placed in the hands of the peasants; the *Volunteer for Liberty,* newspaper of the English-speaking battalions of the International Brigades, replaced pictures of "half-armed militiamen," firing from the earth at enemy planes, with pictures and charts of Soviet industrialization, with praise for the rigidly military *Ejército Popular;* James Hawthorne and Louis Fischer, correspondents for *New Masses* and the *Nation,* boasted of the "brand new beauty" of the Loyalists' airplanes, poets wrote elegies for Ben Leider, an American killed while flying in Spanish combat (Rosten wrote: "O Icarus, welcome him, / wingless now, and a wanderer"), and even Ralph Bates sounded the harsh call to discipline and argued that the "legendary time'' was over and had to be replaced by a more ''realistic'' attitude. In taking this position, however grudgingly, men like Malraux and Bates are, finally, representative of the main-stream of European radicalism, members of a tradition which has, for the most part, rejected the strong element of primitiv-istic anarchism found in American *and* in Spanish radicalism. (pp. 554-57)

Considering this theme of conflict between men and machines, it seems reasonable to suggest that at least part of the extraor-dinary fascination of the Spanish Civil War and part of the fanatical intensity of feeling among Americans here and in Spain, is related to a widespread if barely articulated (or even unarticulated) fear of the implications, and the actualities, of technological society. (pp. 557-58)

What Ernest Hemingway has done in *For Whom the Bell Tolls* has been to orchestrate and make central a theme which runs through scores of other writers and artists. He has, to change the figure, turned the various images of value into the characters of a drama, his version of the Spanish tragedy. Although the greatest caution must be exercised, we can surely study Hem-ingway's ordering of the historical events and speculate whether there is not within a vast complex of other and often contra-dictory values an association of freedom with the earth, of tyranny with machines; on the one hand, fertility and spon-taneity, and on the other, sterility and repression. The spectre of an urbanized, industrialized, mechanized and regimented world, a spectre that has haunted the romantic imagination since Blake's dark Satanic mills and Melville's Tartarus of Maids, seemed—to Ernest Hemingway, John Dos Passos, Waldo Frank, Archibald MacLeish, a few men like them—to have materialized, to have become the bombing planes over Madrid and Barcelona. Perhaps this is but, to use Ernest Cassirer's term, the symbol-maker's way of saying that capitalism was, in some countries, becoming Fascism. The problem is that the Marxists' vision of a Spain dotted with Magnitogorsks and Pittsburghs does not easily harmonize with the primitivists' vision of the Spain of Don Quixote and Sancho Panza, wherein, in John Dos Passos' phrase, we could find Rosinante on the road again. (pp. 558-59)

Joy Davidman, in her ''Letter to a Comrade,'' wrote bravely about the unarmed Loyalists,

> We have only the bodies of men to put together,
> the wincing flesh, the peeled white forking stick,
> easily broken, easily made sick,
> frightened of pain and spoiled by evil weather;
> we have only the most brittle of all things the man
> and the heart the most iron admirable thing of all,
> and putting these together we make a wall,

but Hemingway's interpretation seems closer to the historical truth when Robert Jordan is left, crippled and alone, waiting for the newest conquerors. Perhaps the novel is closer to his-torical fact only because *The Spanish Earth* failed to move us enough, because there were too many Stanley Baldwins and Cordell Hulls and too few Anselmos and Robert Jordans, be-cause the western democracies abandoned Spain to a choice between two forms of totalitarianism. Confronted by the mech-anized enemy, Hemingway's primitivism becomes an impos-sible vision, but that is *not* to say that the values associated with primitivism are not still valid ones; one need not be a primitivist to feel that technological society today is both re-pressive and frighteningly unstable. (p. 560)

Allen Guttmann, ''Mechanized Doom: Ernest Hem-ingway and the Spanish Civil War,'' *in* The Mas-sachusetts Review, *Vol. I, No. 3, May, 1960, pp. 541-61.*

BRITISH AND AMERICAN LITERATURE ABOUT THE WAR

JOHN M. MUSTE

[*An American educator and critic, Muste is the author of* Say That We Saw Spain Die: Literary Consequences of the Spanish Civil War *(1966). In the following excerpt from that work, he surveys the literary responses of British and American writers to the war.*]

In the first excitement of the Spanish Civil War, the literary mood of the writers who felt themselves involved, whether in physical fact or in spirit, was militant and combative. (p. 34)

The most blatantly propagandistic writing was turned out by such writers as Jack Lindsay, an English Communist who never went to Spain during the war, but whose poetry reflects no uncertainty about the merits of the struggle. Lindsay's poems try to make it perfectly clear that the Insurgents were no better than snakes, and that the Spanish Republic was defended by brave and heroic men. Other minor poets could work them-selves into transports of poetic wrath merely by reading news-paper reports and attending mass meetings, but few of them could match Lindsay for fervor and poetic blood lust.

Lindsay's technique consists largely of piling up ugly images to describe the heroes and villains of his poems. One opus, ''Looking at a Map of Spain on the Devon Coast,'' provides a sample:

> The brittle mask has broken, the money-mask
> that hid the jackal jaws, the mask of fear
> that twisted the tender face of love; and eyes
> now look on naked eyes. The map of Spain
> seethes with the truth of things, no longer closed
> in greed's geography, an abstract space
> of imports, exports, capitalist statistics,
> the jargon record of a tyrannous bargain.
> The scroll of injustice, the sheet of paper is torn,
> and behind the demolished surface of the lie
> the Spanish people are seen with resolute faces,
> They break the dark grilles
> on custom's stuccoed wall
> and come into the open. . . .

This poem, like so many other poems, articles, novels, plays, and manifestoes relies on images of violence combined with the jargon of left-wing propaganda to produce its emotional effect. The references to ''the truth of things,'' ''the scroll of injustice,'' and ''the Spanish people . . . with resolute faces'' are vague, and the images are overwrought. One has difficulty constructing a mental image of a map which is seething with truth.

Another of Lindsay's poems about Spain [''On Guard for Spain''] is one of the longest written about the war. It was called a ''mass declamation,'' intended for performance by a chanting chorus at rallies in support of the Loyalists. (pp. 35-6)

''On Guard for Spain'' . . . is a bombastic exercise of some three hundred and fifty lines, a riot of exhortation and images of blood and ravening wolves and evil crawling out of slimy holes. It is a kind of apotheosis of the militant propagandist poem, with its incredibly noble heroes and its absolutely evil villains, and it accepts and passes on myths of the Spanish War which had already gained currency. (pp. 36-7)

It is worth noting that Lindsay and those like him, including writers like John Malcolm Brinnin, Norman Rosten, Erskine Caldwell, Norman Corwin, Sylvia Townsend Warner, Ruth Deacon, or Theodore Kaghan . . . had their counterparts on the other side, most notably Roy Campbell, more recently the darling of American neoconservatives. Campbell, whose claimed experience in the war ought to have taught him to know better, wrote some of the most bloodthirsty poems to come out of this or any other war. *Flowering Rifle,* for example, in addition to asserting the power of prayer to bring down airplanes and capture tanks ("And with our Pater Nosters and Hail Marys / Were liming aeroplanes like tame canaries"), contains lip-smacking descriptions of the painful deaths of the "heathens":

> Blankets and petrol, then,
> And a great fire exploding, while the men
> Rush backward: and the brainyell of the crew
> Locked in and trapped, comes yodelling wildly through,
> While through the flaming reek of molten rubber
> Is heard the crack and hiss of human blubber,
> Which, when at last the whistling flames are dumb,
> For half an hour prolongs the dismal hum.

The same kind of ignorant callousness dominates other instances of propagandist literature. Upton Sinclair is only one of several writers who undertook novels which would show the absolute virtue of the Loyalist cause and the absolute depravity of the Insurgents. (pp. 38-9)

Sinclair's *No Pasarán!* is perhaps an extreme example, but it does serve as a demonstration of the tired devices that mark this kind of fiction. The hero is a poor young man of German descent who is taken up by rich relatives and exposed to a glittering social world. Unlike Dreiser's Clyde Griffith, however, he is eventually disgusted by the glitter and by his relatives, who turn out to be Nazis, and is drawn closer to a Jewish boy named Izzy, a Socialist, whom he has rescued from the brutality of the police. Sinclair takes us to a Bund meeting, where the storm troopers are warming up for a pogrom, and to a most inspirational and healthy social night at the local solidarity club, an affair which is unfortunately broken up by the Bundists. The hero, who has become disgusted with the casual promiscuity of his debutante inamorata, marries the virgin daughter of the lower classes, a paragon poor and ignorant, but sweet and loving. After a brief but ecstatic honeymoon, he is off with Izzy on a ship bound for the battlelines in Spain, a ship which also gives passage, coincidentally, to his Nazi cousin, who is off to join Franco. In a final apocalyptic scene in the trenches, our hero helps to save Madrid, and with his proletarian rifle kills his cousin, who happens to be strafing the trench in which he and Izzy are fighting. Sadly, Izzy is killed, but this gives Rudy the opportunity to rededicate himself to the struggle for liberty. Should the reader have any questions about the location of right and wrong in this short novel, Sinclair frequently takes time out from the action to explain the virtues of freedom, solidarity, and the proletariat, as well as the evils of anti-Semitism, oppression, and the idle rich.

The ludicrous melodramatics and the really startling coincidences are perhaps peculiar to the kind of author who could invent such a character as Lanny Budd. But Sinclair shared

with others a tendency to romanticize war beyond all recognition. . . . Sinclair and such other writers as William Rollins, Jr., Percy Westerman, Theodore Kaghan, or a dozen others, lacking the experience of war, lacked also the will or the ability to project themselves imaginatively into violent action, and were therefore unable or willing to deal with it realistically. What they produced might be temporarily exciting to the emotions, although even this is doubtful, but it could have little permanent effect. (pp. 40-1)

[Tales] of unrealistic heroism on your own side and evil deeds on the other are not the only means by which literature can be used to elicit sympathy and support for a cause, and not a few writers managed to be more realistic about war than either Lindsay or Sinclair without departing from stereotypes of good and evil. Men who had actually seen the war and participated in it could write books which were at once realistic in their descriptions of actual events and blatant appeals for the reader's sympathy for a particular point of view.

Ralph Bates, an English novelist who had been familiar with Spain during the early thirties, had before the war written a realistic and moving novel about life in a small Spanish village during the months immediately preceding the Asturian miners' revolt in 1934. In this novel, *The Olive Field*, it is perfectly clear that the author's sympathies are with the oppressed peasants; the revolt in Asturias has no genuine connection with the action of the novel, and is brought in to make a political point. Nevertheless, the characters have a life of their own, and seem to be more than the author's puppets. After the war had begun, however, Bates wrote a number of stories for journals as dissimilar as *Esquire* and *Left Review* while serving as a commissar in the International Brigades, and these stories are uniformly pointless and superficial. A typical story of this period deals with a small village near Madrid, recounting a series of incidents occurring in the town, incidents which share only location and the theme that peasants on the Loyalist side are uniformly brave, simple, and dedicated to their cause. The characters have no genuine existence, and Bates seems to have lost the feeling for Spanish peasant life which he manifested in *The Olive Field*.

John Sommerfield, another Englishman, demonstrates a different means of combining realistic description with slanted commentary. Sommerfield was a young Communist who was among the first to join the International Brigades. He fought in the defense of Madrid in the fall of 1936 and returned to England in time to write and publish his memoir, *Volunteer in Spain,* early in 1937. (pp. 41-2)

Sommerfield was among the men who were shipped, with very little training, to the defense of Madrid, and much of his description of warfare is realistic. He is most successful in *Volunteer* when he is simply reporting events or recalling what the men felt during the long waits between engagements or during the quiet nights along the front. At one point he provides a moving commentary on war's degradation:

> Here I lay, grovelling in a glorified ditch and
> gnawing at pieces of earthy tinned meat be-
> tween shell-bursts, listening tensely to the
> howling in the air that would tell me that one
> was coming our way, flattening myself against
> the ground with arms folded over head, waiting
> for the explosion and the hail of stones and
> shrapnel overhead, and then taking another bite
> of the meat. And the sun was down and the

cold night coming, and there was only an angry exhausted numbness in my mind, and a despairing craving for sleep and warmth. And every time I ducked and covered my head I felt degraded.

Such a passage helps to fulfill Sommerfield's promise to present a hard, realistic picture of the war. Other passages, however, reflect a tendency to slip from realistic detail into impressionistic pseudo-poetic descriptions of bombing planes, shellings, and rifle fire, which are strangely out of key with the realism. . . . Such flights intrude into the narrative pattern of *Volunteer,* tending to dim the harsh outlines of the battle scenes and consequently softening and glossing over the grimness of war.

The same effect is achieved by the frequent references in *Volunteer* to Sommerfield's political beliefs. Almost every event is given a dogmatic, ideological interpretation. The people on the Loyalist side are seen in a false light. When a poster evokes the memory of some militia girls he had seen in Spain, Sommerfield says of them:

> *They* were truly worth remembering, the living symbols of a whole generation of women who were freeing themselves from the bondage of centuries, from a triple burden of exploitation, religious, economic and sexual. A mute submissiveness still lingered in their large dark eyes, but the bullets in their cartridge-belts were to be directed against the defenders of their tradition.

Whenever the author comments on what he has seen in Spain, the result is passages like this, with the stock phrases (''bondage of centuries,'' ''burden of exploitation,'' ''living symbols of a whole generation,'') and its stock interpretation of Marxist-Stalinist doctrine: these girls are evidently unaware of the historical importance of their actions, but this hardly matters, since they have been selected by history to help usher in a new era. Seeing women as symbols relieves the observer of the need to see them as individuals, to see whether the ''mute submissiveness'' in their eyes is not really disgust at having to take part in men's bloody games, or to discover how they like being pawns of history. (pp. 43-5)

The jargon . . . seen in Sommerfields's description of the militia girls recurs throughout *Volunteer.* One of the most curious manifestations is a patent imitation of the famous discussion of heroic words in *A Farewell to Arms:*

> I don't know about heroism, I don't know about the history-book stuff; when you are in a war the orator's phrases and the newspaper words don't mean a thing; expressions like ''brave,'' ''victorious,'' ''gallant,'' become nauseous and shameful. Instead their meaning is transferred to certain places (so that when I spoke of young Simonie having been at Irun it meant everything) and to things that evoke the memory of certain scenes. And that song, the unforgettable voices and expressions of those men, the exhausted gestures of their limbs and bodies, the lines and composition of the shivering groups that they formed, conveyed in an instantaneous impression the whole of the ''heroism,'' the whole bones and guts of the Spanish people's struggle.

Sommerfield, after noisily renouncing the use of abstractions for describing war, immediately falls back on such more modern clichés as ''guts'' and such phrases as ''the Spanish people's struggle.'' Time and again Sommerfield deadens the narrative with similar injections of catch phrases and cant.

Sommerfield's problem is by no means unique. We find it also in such poets as John Cornford, Tom Wintringham, and Edwin Rolfe, and in some of the work of Ernest Hemingway. The writer is exposed to violence and sudden death, and he feels that he must report these experiences; at the same time he believes that the war is not only necessary but just, and that his book must show this. The result is clearly illustrated in the closing scenes of *Volunteer.* The narrative closes with a description of the men in Sommerfield's group; in a ravaged town behind the lines, they stand on a street where two dead Fascist soldiers lie. The brains of one of the dead men have spilled into the street, and a dog licks at the mess. A guard shoots the lean animal and then apologizes to the watching men: ''It has to be done. They get the taste for human flesh. It is bad. . . .'' His explanation is accepted and he returns to his post. Sommerfield concludes the narrative:

> And we stood there waiting, steel-helmeted, hung about with arms and ammunition, gas-masks dangling on our chests . . . ; and the rain came down, the broken water-main gushed continuously, the tall buildings gaped their wounds, and from the corpse in the street the blood and brains washed slowly away, mingling with those of the dead dog.
>
> It was as good a war picture as I could think of.

This is a memorable evocation of the futility and degradation of war, and a powerful metaphor of the bestiality and blood lust which accompany it.

To end on this note, however, would be bad politics, and so Sommerfield appends a chapter in which he repudiates his own metaphor. In his ''Final Note,'' he refers to the event just described as a ''sterile horror,'' and tries to show why that horror is not the important truth about Spain. Unfortunately for his purpose, he has nothing to set against his powerful image but a set of tired abstractions, justifying participation in this war (it is always *this* war) as an effective means of obtaining peace. Because this was an era of peace marches, the Oxford Pledge, and No-More-War, some kind of special pleading is necessary. The argument, however, is based upon such lame phrases as ''hatred of war,'' ''there are things worth fighting for and things that must be fought against,'' ''pure pacifism leads to sterility and in times of crisis to the abandonment of effective struggle against war,'' and references to ''peace-loving people.'' These phrases and their obvious aim show Sommerfield's awareness of the kind of debate that was going on among British intellectuals, but they lose their meaning when juxtaposed against the vivid image of the dead dog and the soldiers.

Civilians who had been caught in Spain by the outbreak of fighting, or who had gone there soon after, also managed to produce books about their experiences before the war was very old. Elliot Paul, who has since made a very good thing out of recapturing and sentimentalizing the past, tried his wings with *The Life and Death of a Spanish Town,* which is in many ways the most innocent of all Spanish Civil War memoirs. Out of an experience which in fact amounted to a defeat for the Loyalists, Paul constructs a hymn of praise to the Spanish people and to what he regards as their simplicity, their courage, and their belief in liberty and democracy. He mourns for a town captured by the Insurgents, but he shows no real awareness of the fate of such a town, nor of the reality of the struggle going on around him. Despite a fine assortment of ringing words and references to bloodshed, this is a most unwarlike book.

Paul's innocence seems to result from a combination of ignorance and sentimentality. His whole experience of the war was limited to a few months on the island of Ibiza, smallest of the Balearics, months when the only violence on the island consisted of a few scattered bombings and a nearly bloodless invasion. He speaks as an old hand at politics, but actually he knows next to nothing about Spanish political life. (pp. 45-8)

Spanish Town is a dull and foolish book when read today. In extenuation of its author, it should be pointed out that one reason for this has less to do with his own emotions or talents than with our own experience of destruction in the last twenty-five years. What seemed bloody and terrible in 1937 is to our jaded eyes only a minor incident. Paul regards the bombing of civilians towns as horrible and unthinkable, and so it is. But we live in a world in which a single bomb can obliterate an entire city, in which guided missiles can in a few hours or at most days destroy entire nations or the human race. (p. 51)

If our callousness helps to account for our lukewarm response to *Spanish Town,* however, the book itself is still the chief culprit. Paul was too concerned with himself, too simple-minded in his views of Spain and her problems, too ready with platitudes encased in hyperbole. His attitude toward the war is entirely emotional: his friends are good guys, they were for the Republic, they must therefore be "democrats," since in those loose jargon "good guys" and "democrats" are synonymous. The history of Spain before and during the Civil War belies Paul's implication that these primitives were political innocents. Such a view had a wide currency outside Spain in the early months of the Civil War, chiefly because it helped to counteract Nationalist charges that all Republicans were *ipso facto* Communists, but it had no basis in fact. (pp. 51-2)

Paul's book does not share with Sommerfield's an innocent and naïve belief in the automatic triumph of virtue which is ironic in view of the total defeat suffered in Spain by those whom they regarded as virtuous, but both books take too little notice of the true political nature of the Spanish Civil War. Paul writes from the point of view of an aging derelict made homeless by the war, while Sommerfield speaks with the voice of youth, typifying at least one group of the intellectual, idealistic, enthusiastic young men who made the difficult journey to Spain. (p. 52)

The line between the simple propagandist and the man who acknowledges the primacy of violence but tries to account for it in ideological terms is not an easy one to draw. The distinction may be clear, however, if we... [consider] Sommerfield's memoir, which is primarily devoted to celebrating the righteousness of the Republican cause and the heroism of its supporters. Whenever Sommerfield lets the mask drop far enough to reveal horrors . . . , he draws it up immediately; but, in such a poem as Edwin Rolfe's "City of Anguish," the mask slips too far and cannot successfully be replaced, so that the dogma is far less memorable than the experience of destruction. In the first four stanzas of this poem, Rolfe describes an air raid on Madrid from the vantage point of a roof

top, the destruction left by the bombs, and the appearance of the city in the light of the following day. The central concern of these stanzas is the senseless destruction of the city and its people:

> All night, all night,
> flared in my city the bright
> cruel explosion of bombs.
> All night, all night
> there, where the soil and stone
> spilled like brains from the sandbag's head,
> the bodiless head lay staring;
> while the anti-aircraft barked,
> barked at the droning plane,
> and the dogs of war, awakened,
> howled at the hidden moon.
> And a star fell, omen of ill,
> and a man fell, lifeless,
> and my wife fell, childless,
> and, friendless, my friend.
> And I stumbled away from them, crying
> from eyeless lids, blinded.
> Trees became torches
> lighting the avenues
> where lovers huddled in horror
> who would be lovers no longer.

Some of Rolfe's images are fairly conventional: "the dogs of war," and "the bright cruel explosion of bombs." Others are striking, including the image of the sandbag and the neat ironic shift from falling star to fallen man, wife, friend. Rolfe's skill in the poem is further shown in another passage whose rough alliteration is reminiscent of Ezra Pound's experiments with Anglo-Saxon versifications:

> Behind you the memory of bomb beats
> the blood in the brain's vessels—the dream broken,
> sleep pounded to bits by the unending roar of
> shell in the air, the silvery bombs descending,
> and spit of machine guns and the carnival flare
> of fire in the sky.

All of Rolfe's poetic skill goes into the rendering of violence. When he suddenly changes direction in midflight, and turns to a celebration of La Pasionaria, the Communist party's most popular symbol of the new Spain, his invention seems to desert him at once.

> After his food
> a soldier needs cigarettes, something to read,
> something to think about: words to pull
> the war-weary brain back to life from forgetfulness:
> spirited words, the gestures of Dolores,
> majestic Pasionaria, mother of revolutions,
> winner of battles, comforter of defenders;
> her figure magnificent as any monument
> constructed for heroes; her voice a symphony,
> consoling, urging, declaiming in prophecy,
> her forehead the wide plateaus of her country,
> her eyes constant witnesses of her words' truth.

Even if Pasionaria had been the heroine Rolfe makes her out to be, this passage does not fit in the poem. Images of destruction give way in these lines to the vague and honeyed abstractions which were a commonplace of militant left-wing polemic during the thirties, and to an image so imposing as to be inhuman and consequently false. The inappropriateness of this paean of praise is emphasized by Rolfe's return, at the end of the poem, to his earlier manner. In the fifth and final section we are plunged back into the realities of war, and we feel again the special shock that the brave young men of the Spanish Civil War endured when they discovered that, as Orwell put it, "the essential horror of army life . . . is barely affected by the nature of the war you happen to be fighting in." (pp. 75-7)

In "City of Anguish," Rolfe tries to use Pasionaria as a symbol of the ideals which make the war justifiable and therefore bearable. But he is not a good enough poet to accomplish this, and we may suspect that the reason for his failure was the fact that the destruction and chaos he witnessed made a far deeper impression on him than did the heroine. When he came to write the poem, in any case, he was able to render the horror far more vividly than its rationalization.

Time after time, in the work of men who had been made aware of the destructiveness and brutality of the war in Spain, we find a similar rendering of experience, accompanied by the attempts to use political belief as a talisman to keep reality at a distance. Time and again, in the work of many writers, we find that the reality overpowers the ideas. Arthur Koestler's publishers provided an example of this when they combined his harrowing "Dialogue with Death" with a disparate and unconvincing piece of hackwork purporting to give the facts about the war in Spain. As Koestler has since revealed, the more lurid sections of *The Spanish Testament* were the work of a Communist party propagandist in Paris.

Whatever the circumstances of its composition, the first part of this book leaves no lasting impression; rather the record of Koestler's capture and imprisonment, his mental processes while under sentence of death, remain with the reader. Implicit in *The Spanish Testament*, as in so much of the literature of this phase of the war, is the question: Can the war be justified if it causes such hardships? The affirmative answer is far less strong for Rolfe and Koestler than it was for Sommerfield or Lindsay.

More touching and on the whole more successful were the efforts of a young British poet, John Cornford, the golden young man of British Communism during the mid-thirties. (pp. 77-8)

Most of Cornford's verse is intended to urge the glories of the Communist party and to remind the individual of his duty to act as the party commands him to. His major theme is self-immolation, which is seen as a necessary concomitant to commitment. At the same time, his poems are not so much concerned with urging others to join him in the crusade as with the necessity for overcoming his own doubts and hesitations. In the poem "Full Moon at Tierz: Before the Storming of Huesca," he wills himself to act in the face of danger, since history no longer allows unlimited time for orderly progress:

> The past, a glacier, gripped the mountain wall,
> And time was inches, dark was all.
> But here it scales the end of the range,
> The dialectic's point of change,
> Crashes in light and minutes to its fall.

At such a time, the individual must act: "We are the future. The last fight let us face." The battle which impends is part of this final fight, and therefore of absolute importance in determining whether the ideals and ideology of communism will prevail. In the second section of the poem, Cornford seeks to draw strength from an invocation of party heroes like Maurice Thorez and Georgi Dimitrov, and from the party's own program: "Here what the Seventh Congress said, / If true, if false, is live or dead. . . ."

The pressures on the individual in such a situation are very strong, and Cornford admits his loneliness and his weakness; for the party or for history there are no hesitations or doubts, but the individual who serves them cannot be oblivious to his own problems:

> Though Communism was my waking time,
> Always before the lights of home
> Shone clear and steady and full in view—
> Here, if you fail, there's help for you—
> Now, with my Party, I stand quite alone.
>
> Then let my private battle with my nerves,
> The fear of pain whose pain survives,
> The love that tears me by the roots,
> The loneliness that claws my guts,
> Fuse in the welded front our fight preserves.
>
> Oh, be invincible as the strong sun,
> Hard as the metal of my gun,
> Oh, let the mounting tempo of the train
> Sweep where my footsteps slipped in vain,
> October in the rhythm of its run.

English poet John Cornford, 1936. Courtesy of Christopher Cornford.

Following a rather obvious structural pattern (the crisis; its importance; its meaning for the individual; resolution) Cornford in the final section evokes a vision of the world whose fate depends on events in Spain:

> Now the same night falls over Germany
> And the impartial beauty of the stars
> Lights from the unfeeling sky
> Oranienburg and freedom's crooked scars.
> We can do nothing to ease that pain
> But prove the agony was not in vain.
> England is silent under the same moon,
> From Clydeside to the gutted pits of Wales
> The innocent mask conceals that soon
> Here too our freedom's swaying in the scales.
> Oh, understand before too late
> Freedom was never held without a fight.
> Freedom is an easily spoken word
> But facts are stubborn things. Here, too, in Spain
> Our fight's not won till the workers of all the world
> Stand by our guard on Huesca's plain,
> Swear that our dead fought not in vain,
> Raise the red flag triumphantly
> For Communism and for liberty.

Cornford's poetry has serious failings. He is often awkward when struggling to work in the "correct" names of places and heroes. The regular rhyme pattern, varied occasionally by the approximate rhymes so characteristic of modern poetry (i.e., Aragon-begun-tone; roots-guts; nerves-survives-preserves) shows no special skill or real originality. To make too much of such difficulties, however, would be unfair. Surely it is asking a great deal to demand consummate technical mastery in verse written on battlefields. A more serious problem is Cornford's excessive reliance on the cant words and phrases drawn from Communist discourse: "history" and "freedom" used carelessly, "not in vain." As used here, such words do no more than arouse a sympathetic emotion in the reader, and repetition does not make them any more palatable ("freedom" is invoked four times in the final section, the phrase "not in vain" is used twice). It is impossible, twenty-five years after this poem was written, not to hear the false ring of this rhetoric, or to avoid the conviction that it was largely the unthinking acceptance and use of such terms that doomed most of the political poetry of the thirties to early obscurity.

But Cornford's poetry has important virtues as well as failings. "Full Moon at Tierz," whatever its weaknesses, displays a fine talent for metaphor. Cornford's use of words sometimes makes his verse flat, but the metaphors of the glacier as history, of time present as a "cataract" whose course men must try to direct, and of history as a train rushing into the future, have considerable power and originality. The first stanza of the final section, beginning "Now the same night falls over Germany . . ." is less melodramatic and more powerful than the similar final stanza of Auden's "Spain." These images help give the poem the "hard-muscled" quality which attracted John Lehmann's praise, and they redeem it from the banality of some of its diction. (pp. 79-82)

Many, like Cornford, Christopher Caudwell, Ralph Fox, and Charles Donnelly, to name a very few, died young, before the dimensions of their talent or its direction could become clear. Their deaths, and the work they left behind them, help to remind us that the Spanish Civil War was not merely a political struggle or an occasion for the composition of literary gems or dogmatic interpretations of history.

Cornford's poems, in particular, are interesting evidence that even under the stress of battle, an attempt could be made to apply the doctrines of a political ideology to the events in Spain. If Cornford is not so terrorstruck as Edwin Rolfe, he is far from being so glib and facile as John Sommerfield. (pp. 83-4)

"City of Anguish" and "Full Moon at Tierz," and the work of such soldier-poets as Tom Wintringham, Esmond Romilly, and John Lepper, show that men who had actually seen what war was like in Spain still struggled to find explanations in their beliefs. Day Lewis's poems show that civilians could also see both sides of the war, not only the "big picture" emphasized in the newspapers and magazines, but the destruction and its implications for the world. There is an interesting parallel between the poems of Wintringham, a hard-bitten veteran of World War I and of long service in the Communist party, and those of George Barker, one of the most powerful of the generation of British poets which came to prominence during the thirties.

Wintringham's poetry is dominated by the belief that ultimate victory in Spain will bring a new day bright enough to justify the sacrifices made in the war. Occasionally, in such a poem as "The Splint," Wintringham allows less ideological notions to intrude, but for the most part he saw the war as Armageddon, with himself and his comrades as the ushers of the future:

> Neither fools nor children we who are joining
> (Twenty years ago I knew war's face)
> We make what others wreck into our gaining,
> Into our choice.
>
> Our enemies can praise death and adore death;
> For us endurance, the sun; and now in this night
> The electric torch, feeble, waning, but close-set,
> Follows the surgeon's fingers; we are allied with
> This light.

Here, in contrast to Rolfe's shock at destruction, we are assured that the destruction will be given meaning. The cause is more important than the personal wound or the private fear; it is worth the sacrifice it exacts.

Wintringham makes this idea even clearer in the poem "Monuments," in which he suggests that all the relics of the war should be piled together: "Shell-splinters from University City," "a false coin stamped in Burgos by a traitor," "earth from the bullring / Where they shot the prisoners in Badajoz," and "earth from Durruti's grave," among other things. Such a collection will be a true memorial to the war and its victims:

> Take then these metals, under the deep sky
> Melt them together; take these pieces of earth
> And mix them; add your bullets,
> And memories of death;
> You have won victory,
> People of Spain,
> And the tower into which your earth is built, and
> Your blood and ours, shall state Spain's
> Unity, happiness, strength; it shall face the breath
> Of the east, of the dawn, of the future where there will
>   be no more strangers. . .

The difficulty with poems like "Monument" is not so much that the victory they forecast never came, but that they do not convince us that their victory would have been all they said, or that it would indeed have justified the sacrifices. Wintringham's images are more real than those of Jack Lindsay, and he does not shrug off the lessons of war as easily as did Sommerfield, but he is no more successful than they in giving life to his vision of the future. "Unity, happiness, strength" are far too vague when placed against the destruction seen in Rolfe's poems, or when compared to the work of writers like Alvah Bessie, Robert Payne, and Stephen Spender. There is a question here of poetic talent and of the opportunity for exercising it. George Barker, obviously enough, was a more gifted versifier than Tom Wintringham, a more practiced poet than John Cornford. Far from the actual fighting in Spain, Barker had time to develop his imaginative idea of the war and project his vision in words. These are enormous advantages, and it should not surprise us that when Barker gave voice to ideas similar to Wintringham's and Cornford's he should do so more skillfully.

The comparison is probably closest when we put Wintringham's notion of a monument from which the new Spain will arise next to Barker's poetic conception of the spirit of the Spanish people as a Phoenix which will arise out of the ashes of war. Barker's ability to conceive imaginatively a chaotic world undoubtedly stems from his vision of existence and his celebration of chaos as a necessary concomitant of a vigorous and pulsating life. In the special conditions of the Spanish Civil War, ideological considerations led many writers to gloss over the unpleasant facts of destruction; Barker turned those facts to the service of his vision.

In "Elegy for Spain," Barker provides a myriad of images of devastation, but speaks of the eventual triumph of the Loyalist cause as having been made inevitable by the blood shed in the war. The stanzas of dedication "to the photograph of a child killed in an air-raid on Barcelona" express horror at "the crime of the bloody time," but make it clear that the living must accept the challenge of the times: "And if I feel your gaze upon me ever, / I'll wear the robe of blood that love illumines." The recurrent theme of the poem itself is of death as a sacrifice to future greatness and future freedom. . . . (pp. 84-7)

Barker's poems of the Spanish Civil War raise problems that we have encountered before in different form. Like Sommerfield, Kaghan, Wintringham, and others, he does not accept destruction as a reason for surrender; on the other hand, he is less facile than Sommerfield, or such other rearguard writers as Norman Rosten and Norman Corwin, avoiding the easy assurance that victory *in this war* is made certain by "Irun's ruins." Barker envisions the world as an arena for continual struggle; if freedom is worth having, it demands sacrifices. (p. 89)

The most lengthy and laborious attempt to salvage some order out of chaos, and the best-known single work on the Spanish War, is Ernest Hemingway's *For Whom the Bell Tolls.* (p. 90)

This is the most impressive and memorable novel written about the Spanish Civil War, and while not Hemingway's best, it is his most ambitious, most difficult to evaluate, and most interesting. It is his most ambitious because he is working here with a broader canvas than in any of his other novels, attempting to give the book what has been called its epic scope by extending the action beyond the central character to the guerilla band which assists him, to the guerilla band of El Sordo, and beyond that to the headquarters of General Golz and the nerve center of Madrid. It is the most difficult to evaluate because Hemingway succeeds so brilliantly in solving some problems and fails so dismally in solving others. It is the most interesting because of its scope, because of its successes and failures, and because Hemingway attempts to do so many things he had

never done before, things which he never attempted again. (pp. 94-5)

Critics of the novel have called attention to its central problem, a problem deriving from Hemingway's special experience. Most of the writers who dealt with the Spanish Civil War came to Spain with what they thought of as firm political ideals, but with very little knowledge of violence or of how it might affect those ideals. For Hemingway, on the other hand, violence had always been a consuming interest; where others had to face the difficulties of fitting their new knowledge of violence into an ideological framework, with the alternative of abandoning their ideology, Hemingway had to try to change his interpretation of violence to fit his new view of the world. It is a critical cliché that in Hemingway's work before *To Have and Have Not,* violence is simply a condition of life, and a constant threat to the individual. Death or a wound may come from the uncontrolled violence of war or from the contained and circumscribed violence of the bull ring, but it is always a present possibility, no farther away than the next hour or the next day. The moral responsibility for violence is not laid at the door of any individuals or group; as one of the conditions of life, violence is not anyone's "fault."

In *To Have and Have Not,* Hemingway shifted away from this view of violence, although not very far away. Harry Morgan, like Jake Barnes or Frederic Henry, is a victim of forces beyond his control, forces which are given at least partial identification. In writing about the Spanish War, Hemingway went a good deal farther. Responsibility for the war and therefore for all of the violence is laid at the door of the Fascists. At the same time, the Loyalists must also engage in violence, and for the first time in Hemingway's writing, bloodshed is given a justification, since the Loyalists' violence is at the service of the people's desire to live in peace and with justice. The shedding of blood has come to involve moral responsibility. A further complication is the idea of duty. Other Hemingway heroes felt a need to act with courage and grace in the face of danger because of a sense of personal honor, imposed from within, or because they were committed to a code of behavior which their sense of personal honor would not permit them to betray.

With Robert Jordan, however, we have for the first time a Hemingway hero who believes that his actions can and will affect the destinies of other men, and who acts with the sense that he is therefore responsible to those others. Given his ideological reasons for joining the Loyalists, Robert Jordan submits to a discipline which is necessary to the successful prosecution of the war and which makes killing a duty. For the first time violence is at the service of Hemingway's vision of a world in which violence need no longer be a condition of life. This is a drastic change, and we have already seen Hemingway's attempts to adjust to it in *The Fifth Column* and the short stories.

Hemingway had to try, in *FWBT,* to show that an ideology he had only partly assimilated justified the violence of the war, and the major problems of the novel arise from this attempt. In the first place, Hemingway had to provide Robert Jordan with ideas and ideals which would justify his participation in the war and his submission to discipline. He had also to create a situation and characters which would account for Jordan's love for Spain and for the Spanish people. This was necessary both for the immediate purposes of plot and setting and for the thematic purpose of demonstrating the possibility of communication between men, the fraternity which is central to the novel's theme. The characters had to perform an ideological function in the novel, demonstrating the political awakening of the Spanish (and symbolically all) people, setting up ideological problems for Robert Jordan to solve, providing alternatives to his solutions of these problems, and showing the weaknesses as well as the strengths of the Loyalist side.

Beyond this, and of first importance, Hemingway had to provide the tensions and the conflicts which could test his ideas and his characters. This aspect of the political novelist's task has been described by Irving Howe [in his *Politics and the Novel*]: "He knows that his own momentum, his own intentions, can be set loose easily enough; but he senses, as well, that what matters most of all is to allow for those rocks against which his intentions may smash, but, if he is lucky, they may merely bruise." Hemingway provides these rocks in *FWBT* in the treachery of Pablo, the frivolousness of the gypsy, Anselmo's views on killing, the behavior of men like André Marty, the humanity of the Fascist soldiers, and even the necessity for submitting to Communist discipline. All of these suggest that Jordan's mission is futile or wrong, because the war may already be lost, or because nothing could justify the killing of enemies who share the common humanity. One of Hemingway's triumphs in the novel is his creation of realistic and believable "rocks," far more real and menacing than Philip Rawlings' "horrorous" or Dorothy Bridges' dubious charms. In so doing, Hemingway can draw upon the material and themes with which he is most familiar. He succeeds also in justifying the guerillas' participation in the war, because their commitment to the Loyalist cause comes directly from their experience and because Hemingway, in a remarkable feat of characterization, endows them with a strength and indomitability which enable them to maintain their commitment despite the depredations of war. But Hemingway does not succeed in justifying Robert Jordan.

Jordan is in many ways different from other Hemingway heroes. He is given the ability to make meaningful choices, he becomes involved in the violence of war because he makes such choices rather than by accident, and he believes in what he is doing, which implies a belief that violence can have a purpose and can result in some good. Nick Adams, Jake Barnes, Frederic Henry, and Harry Morgan all find themselves thrust into violent situations. . . . Robert Jordan, on the other hand, confronts the possibility of death because it is his duty to mankind. (pp. 95-8)

The reasons for Jordan's devotion to duty set him apart from the code heroes. This devotion is related to his sense of communion with other men, and forces him to act as he is ordered to, rather than as his emotions or his sense of honor might direct, because he accepts the assumption that following orders will contribute to some greater good. The Hemingway code implied a special knowledge of the conditions of life, a revelation of the imminence of violence, as well as the special necessity for acting well in the face of danger. (p. 99)

Jordan's distance from the code heroes is emphasized by the fact that there are opportunities in *FWBT* for the kind of fruitless but graceful act that would have appealed mightily to the narrator of [Hemingway's short story] "The Denunciation," notably when El Sordo's band is attacked on the mountaintop. But this kind of gesture is now referred to scornfully as the kind of thing that would appeal to Anarchists: "Whenever things get really bad they want to set fire to something and to die. It's a very odd kind of mind they have." Jordan does share some of the characteristics of the code heroes, notably the compulsion to exhibit physical courage, but this need cause no confusion. When he decides that he must go through with

his assignment despite all the portents of failure, his sense of duty, not the need to prove himself, decides him. At the end, when he is wounded too badly to escape with the others, his insistence on remaining behind is not motivated simply by a desire to die well; his act will give the others a better chance of escaping. (pp. 99-100)

Having given us this different kind of hero, Hemingway is faced with the necessity of justifying him, and he tries not only to validate Jordan's actions in the immediate setting of the Spanish Civil War but to extend this validation to a larger theme, the idea that there is a solidarity among men, that "no man is an island." The chief means of presenting these ideas is through Jordan's internal monologues and dialogues, similar in tone and style to the ruminations of Jake Barnes. Hemingway's failure to present these ideas convincingly is at the heart of the novel's difficulties, and to understand the reason for this we must look closely at the action which is a frame for the ideas, action which provides the rocks which Hemingway has set in the way of his purpose. (p. 100)

For convenience in discussion, the difficulties can be divided into two kinds, those which reveal weaknesses and failings on the Loyalist side and therefore cast doubt on the justice of the specific war Jordan is fighting in, and those which raise the question of whether any war can be justified. In a sense, these are the same thing. Given Hemingway's attitude toward the Spanish Civil War, it is clear that if any war can be justified on ideological grounds it must be this one; if this one is simply another example of senseless violence, then all wars must be so. In the context of the novel, however, we can make a distinction between those problems which relate to a particular cause and those which stand in the way of the novel's theme, the value of human life and the traditional democratic values.

A major difficulty of the war as Hemingway describes it is the character of the Spanish people. Robert Jordan, like Hemingway, has a deep affection for the Spanish people, but this does not prevent the author from including in the novel incidents which show what he regards as their natural cruelty and callousness toward human suffering, as well as their tendency toward treachery. (p. 101)

The cruelty of the Spanish people is present almost continually in *FWBT*, coming to the surface in such incidents as Pablo's killing of the other guerillas, in Agustín's lurid plans for punishing the Fascists after the war, in certain aspects of Pilar's treatment of Maria, and, most sharply, in Pilar's description of the killing of the Fascists in her town at the beginning of the movement. The method of execution she describes is so brutal that it disgusts everyone but the drunks, the Anarchists, and Pablo, but the violence generates its own momentum. (p. 102)

This scene, as described by Pilar, is one of the most memorable in the novel, and it helps to point out that atrocities are in the nature of war, not the exclusive property of one side or the other. At the end of Pilar's narrative, Hemingway tries to moderate what amounts to a criticism of the Loyalists by having Pilar say that the only worse day of her life was "Three days later when the fascists took the town." For once, however, Hemingway's favorite device of understatement is ineffective. The scenes described by Pilar remain in the reader's mind.

Hemingway also raises the problem of the political disputes among the Loyalists. At least in part, this is done to take the curse off Robert Jordan's acceptance of Communist discipline, and most of the criticism is directed against the Communists.

Other groups come in for critical comment, too, especially the Anarchists, and in the course of one of the abortive political discussions which checker the novel, Agustín puts a curse on all their houses, "And afterwards shoot the anarchists and the Communists and all this *canalla* except the good Republicans," but the Communists receive the lion's share. The most striking instances of this are the savage attacks on the idols of the Comintern, André Marty and La Pasionaria (Dolores Ibarruri). (pp. 102-03)

Hemingway's savagery in attacking Marty and Pasionaria seems to be both an expression of personal animosity and another gambit in that favorite indoor sport of the Spanish Civil War, dissociating oneself from undesirable elements. In the context of the novel, these attacks have a more immediate purpose as revelations of the weaknesses of even that party which provides the best discipline and the best program for winning the war. (p. 104)

In order to universalize his material, Hemingway also considers the larger problem of whether any war can be justified, whether any killing is right or even excusable. It is a problem he had never really investigated before his experience in the Spanish Civil War. Always before, in Hemingway's fiction, violent death had been almost a natural phenomenon, a condition of modern life. Now his hero must deal death, deliberately, in a new kind of situation. The morality of killing, even in a just cause, is mentioned so often in *FWBT* as to be almost an obsession.

The old man, Anselmo, states the question bluntly. He has been a hunter, and unlike Robert Jordan has gotten pleasure from killing animals, but he is deeply disturbed by the necessity for killing men. He has killed, he says: "Several times, but not with pleasure. To me it is a sin to kill a man. Even Fascists whom we must kill. To me there is a great difference between the bear and the man and I do not believe the wizardry of the gypsies about the brotherhood with animals. No. I am against all killing of men." (p. 106)

Anselmo is at one pole. At the other is Agustín, who also feels an emotion associated with killing: "And when I saw those four there and thought that we might kill them I was like a mare in the corral waiting for the stallion . . . the necessity was on me as it is on a mare in heat. You cannot know what it is if you have not felt it." (p. 107)

Jordan is neither Anselmo nor Agustín. He does not feel the sickness which Anselmo experiences when the necessity for killing confronts him; not only is he able to kill, he is able to order others to do so. On the other hand, he does share Anselmo's distaste for bloodshed, and while he knows the blood lust of Agustín, he also knows that it is dangerous. After he has shot the young enemy cavalryman from Tafalla who rides into the guerrillas' clearing, he warns himself that when killing becomes enjoyable, or an end in itself, it is disastrous:

> It is right, he told himself, not reassuringly but proudly. I believe in the people and their right to govern themselves as they wish. But you mustn't believe in killing, he told himself. You must do it as a necessity but you must not believe in it. If you believe in it the whole thing is wrong.

This is a far cry from the Philip Rawlings of *The Fifth Column,* who decidedly enjoyed killing. Hemingway, for whom hunting had always been the most enjoyable of sports, and upon whom

war and death had always exerted an unusual fascination, had in Spain been confronted with the moral problems of war in a way not suggested in his earlier work. Hemingway tries very hard in *FWBT* to show that killing cannot be justified in Agustín's terms, and that Anselmo's objections are of fundamental importance: "You have no right to do the things you do for all of them are crimes and no man has a right to take another man's life unless it is to prevent something worse happening to other people." (pp. 107-08)

If *FWBT* were a study in moral complexity, an investigation of the ironies and contradictions inherent in wars and in ideologies, the problem of justifying violence might well be one of the book's strong points. But Hemingway's purpose is to show the reader that Jordan's actions are morally right, because he is partaking in a just and necessary fight, and so, in Howe's metaphor, the moral dilemma of violence becomes one of the rocks past which the author must steer his craft. If the people of Spain are cruel and treacherous, if their leaders are corrupt and stupid, if the only group which offers a sensible program for winning the war is a haven for fools, madmen, and cynics, and if killing is always wrong, then the motives for Jordan's actions must be convincing indeed. That they are not is the measure of the novel's failure. (pp. 109-10)

When he tries to impart the rest of the message, the idea that a particular side in a particular war is right, Hemingway relies almost entirely on the thoughts he places in the mind of Robert Jordan. This in itself is a weakness, since it means, as Geismar pointed out long ago [in his *Writers in Crisis*] that the ideological point of the novel does not arise out of the action; it is rather imposed upon the action through Jordan's conversation and his thoughts. Still, the message might have been effective had Hemingway been able to make the expression of his ideas strong enough. But Robert Jordan seems not really sure of his reasons for fighting. He questions his own motives when he makes himself admit that he shares Agustín's blood lust at the prospect of killing, and throughout the book he cautions himself not to romanticize himself or the Spanish people. He does so in such a way as to convince the reader that, whatever his reasons, they are probably as shallowly sentimental as he himself fears they are. (pp. 110-11)

To put it in terms of this study, when it comes to giving his hero an ideological justification Hemingway is no more sophisticated or convincing than Upton Sinclair. (pp. 112-13)

FWBT deserves extended analysis because it demonstrates so clearly the dilemma of writers who continued to believe in the Loyalist cause, but who had seen and understood too much to be capable of the easy sophistries of the authors discussed earlier. They tried to avoid the simple black and white distinctions, and to look behind the political slogans to the realities they had themselves witnessed, an attempt in which they were not always successful. Their disillusion had not yet turned to bitterness, and when they despaired they often tried to cloak that despair with other themes; as *FWBT* shows, the result was often a failure. The symbols and the slogans which had seemed so pure to more innocent writers had become blurred in battle, and when they reverted to such symbols they often had a nostalgic quality. (p. 119)

The actual experience of battle, for all that young intellectuals might have learned of it vicariously from the realistic literature of World War I, was indubitably a shock. This is conveyed most clearly, perhaps, by a poem supposedly found on a leaf of notebook paper by a soldier in the International Brigades, and subsequently printed in the Spender-Lehmann anthology, *Poems for Spain:*

> Eyes of men running, falling, screaming
> Eyes of men shouting, sweating, bleeding
> The eyes of the fearful, those of the sad
> The eyes of exhaustion, and those of the mad
> Eyes of men thinking, hoping, waiting
> Eyes of men loving, cursing, hating
> The eyes of the wounded sodden in red
> The eyes of the dying and those of the dead.

The same spirit of revulsion is found in the same volume in the writings of such soldier poets as John Lepper and T.A.R. Hyndman. It finds its most vehement expression, however, in the poems of Stephen Spender. (pp. 120-21)

Of the ten poems about Spain which Spender . . . chose to include in *Collected Poems,* only one makes any overt statement of sympathy for the Loyalists. "Fall of a City" gives a picture of desolation and loss following an Insurgent victory. The words and deeds of the Loyalists, the deaths of men like Ralph Fox and Federico García Lorca, are "washed over with a smile/Which launches the victors where they win." The only consolation is that in defeat some memory of liberty may remain to inspire future generations:

> Somewhere some word presses
> In the high door of a skull, and in some corner
> Of an irrefrangible eye
> Some old man's memory jumps to a child
> —Spark from the days of liberty.
> And the child hoards it like a bitter toy.

This is hardly wild-eyed propaganda, but it is as far in that direction as Spender ever went in his poetry, however militant he may sometimes have been in his prose. In his other poems about Spain he is entirely concerned with the personal rather than the public aspects of the war.

Most of the other poems express a concern about the waste of war, the waste of effort, and of life itself. "The Room Above" is a lament for a lover who has departed for "sunbright peninsulas of the sword." "Thoughts During an Air Raid" considers the impersonality of statistics and casualty lists, and the fact that only a sense of personal loss can make clear the meaning of such statistics. . . . The irony of these poems stems from the bitterness which was Spender's most important legacy from his experiences in Spain, and which pervades all of these poems. Death for a cause might be attractive in the abstract, but as reality it was appalling. "A Stopwatch and an Ordinance Map," "In No Man's Land," and "Ultima Ratio Regum," all voice the question made explicit in the latter:

> Consider his life which was valueless
> In terms of employment, hotel ledgers, news files.
> Consider. One bullet in ten thousand kills a man,
> Ask. Was so much expenditure justified
> On the death of one so young and so silly
> Lying under the olive trees, O world, O death?

Spender seems to have been very nearly overwhelmed by the fact of death. Ideology fades out of these poems as violent death becomes an evil more immediate and therefore more terrible than political oppression or economic exploitation. In "Two Armies," Spender's subject is the eventual hatred of war itself felt by every soldier. . . . (pp. 123-25)

The nature of chaos is made explicit in the poem "To a Spanish Poet (Manuel Altolaguirre)." Here the poet's fear for the life of his friend leads him to an analysis of the state of the world which makes such fears inevitable:

> Perhaps it is we—the living—who are dead
> We of a world that revolves and dissolves
> While we set the steadfast corpse under the earth's lid.
> The eyes push irises above the grave
> Reaching to the stars, which draw down nearer,
> Staring through a rectangle of night like black glass,
> Beyond these daylight comedies of falling plaster.
>
> Your heart looks through the breaking ribs—
> Oiled axle through revolving spokes.
> Unbroken blood of the swift wheel,
> You stare through centrifugal bones
> Of the revolving and dissolving world.

This poem is the clearest manifestation of the effect that the horror of the war in Spain had upon Spender. He is still in control of his verse, on a technical level. The imagery, however, is unusually chaotic for Spender, as though only the images of madness could convey what he had felt and seen in Spain.

"Two Armies" and "To a Spanish Poet" are on a different level from Spender's other poetry of the Spanish War. These poems all share a preoccupation with death, but these two are evidence that in some extremity of horror or disgust the poet moved beyond pity and self-pity to a deeper perception of reality. (pp. 126-27)

As I have already noted, however, the same horror at events in Spain was shared by such fighting men as Hyndman, Lepper, and the anonymous author of "Eyes." It was also felt by an American, Alvah Bessie, who arrived in time to take part in the disastrous campaigns around the Ebro River in 1938, and who lived to write about his experiences in *Men in Battle.* Like John Sommerfield, Bessie was a dedicated Communist, who went to Spain to serve his party and advance the revolution, but the books of the two men are so different that they seem to record events that took place in different worlds. The two memoirs create a convenient measure of the distance between the world of the men who fought in Spain at the beginning of the war and those who were there at the end. Where Sommerfield records the exciting victories of 1936, Bessie ends his book with the evacuation of foreign volunteers, that last desperate move by the Loyalist government to win sympathy and help from France, Great Britain, and the United States. The men who were shipped out then knew a great deal more about war and defeat than Sommerfield could possibly have known.

Bessie's book is not distinguished in style or in structure. His prose is generally clear, with few blatant imitations of Hemingway and none of the flights of rhapsodic impressionism in which such writers as Sommerfield and Elliott Paul took delight, but there is so little tonal variation in *Men in Battle* that the final effect is to make everything Bessie reports seem dull and routine. The really impressive quality of the book is its accumulation of detail into what seems to be a truly objective record of the final months of the International Brigades. It is this factual quality which makes the book's heartbreaking bitterness so convincing.

One of the interesting elements in *Men in Battle* is that in its early chapters it bears considerable resemblance to *Volunteer in Spain*. Like Sommerfield, Bessie and the others in his group travel through France on their way to Spain, feeling the same exhilaration and the same nervousness that the early volunteers had felt two years before. . . . Only when Bessie tells of being assigned to duty does the real difference between the two experiences become clear to the reader.

After a brief period of training, Bessie is sent as a replacement to the Fifteenth International Brigade, being reconstituted after a disastrous retreat from Belchite. Bessie and the men he is with are nervous, fearful of battle but anxious to get into it, and still excited about the war. The veterans they join near the front are sick, angry, and disgusted. The encounter between the two groups is the classic confrontation of rookie and old soldier:

> Here was apparent total demoralization, utter fatigue, rampant individualism. The men criticized their command mercilessly; it sounded like treason to us. . . . They barked at each other and at us; they cursed continuously, making accusations that horrified the new replacements. . . . Irving N—was shocked, but not beyond speech.
>
> "Comrades," he said. "Do I understand you retreated and threw your guns away?"
>
> "Yeh," they said.
>
> "But comrades," he said, "that's cowardice. Don't you realize how difficult it is for the government to get arms? Don't you realize that unless we lick Fascism all over the world it won't be long before—"
>
> "Shit," some one said; they looked at him and spat. I expected them to tear him to pieces.

Not all the effusions of Sommerfield, the militant editorials in the *Daily Worker,* or the impassioned speeches of André Marty or Pasionaria would ever make war seem romantic again to men like these.

The war that Bessie knew had little of romance in it. (pp. 127-29)

The details of Bessie's experiences are presented with painstaking honesty, as if this war and its conditions had made rhetoric and heroic postures impossible. The one note in the book which might be called sentimental—the letters written by Bessie to his sons and his sons' answers—is unobtrusive, and it adds depth to our picture of the author. Otherwise, he is an objective recorder of action and his own emotions. He makes no attempt to hide the continual fear and discomfort he experienced as a front-line soldier, nor to explain away as "contributing to the greater good" his ultimately successful attempt to get a safer billet behind the lines. He writes also of the cowards and the deserters in the Brigades, and he describes the troubles between Spaniards and foreigners in the Fifteenth Brigade. All were part of the war he saw. (pp. 131-32)

Bessie's immediate response to his experiences in Spain was not unlike Stephen Spender's. Both men, in writing about Spain during the war or immediately after its close, were concerned with recording their horror at what they had seen or experienced. In *Men in Battle*, as in Spender's poems, political ideas fade into the background before the overwhelming fact of human suffering and the tragedy of defeat. Earlier, a comparison was made between Bessie's book and John Sommerfield's *Vol-*

unteer in Spain; a comparison of the conclusions of the two books is also instructive. Sommerfield ends his narrative with a picture of war's horror, and then appends a chapter in which he tries to use political emotionalism to explain away the horror. At the end of Bessie's book the Internationals are being withdrawn from the fighting, preparatory to being sent home:

> We were jittery, and the truck moved slowly down the long ramp toward the bridge, and slowly across the narrow, sounding planks. To your right was the collapsed skeleton of the old bridge that we had blown up to cover our retreat last April; it lay half in and half out of the water, like a wrecked dirigible. The farther shore was pitted with enormous craters left by the bombing that had been going on every day for two months now. We moved off the bridge and upgrade into the twin-town, Mora La Nueva, and I looked back at the yellow Ebro before we turned the corner. It was wide and placid in the brilliant sun; its surface shimmered with a million broken flecks of quiet light. I thought of Aaron.

The possibilities for an "up-beat" ending are here. There is the image of the placid river, amidst all the destruction, which could have been compared to the flow of history; the memory of the dead friend could have been turned into a sermon on the better world the dead had helped usher in, as Sommerfield did with John Cornford. But the book ends here. Aaron is dead and the war lost, and there is nothing more to say. . . . [*Men in Battle*] remains a book demonstrating vividly the way in which prolonged exposure to violence can turn idealism into ashes, and which shows that when no sacrifice will suffice, any slogan or dogma is irrelevant. For the duration of the time he took to write *Men in Battle*, at least, Bessie abandoned the tired abstractions and simply recorded an experience of desolation and defeat.

This desolation is also at the heart of three very different novels dealing with the Spanish War: Robert Payne's *The Song of the Peasant*, John Dos Passos' *Adventures of a Young Man*, and Humphrey Slater's *The Heretics*. Payne was one of the very few non-Spanish writers courageous enough to deal with the Spanish War in terms of Spanish characters, and the only one to give expression to the disillusion caused by the war among the Spanish peasants. His novel is set in a Catalan fishing village during the years 1935 to 1939. In the early part of the novel, Payne's primary purpose is to evoke the atmosphere of the village by showing us the lives of the fishermen and their close communion with nature. The early narrative is broken by extended and impassioned descriptions of the Catalan countryside and of the fishermen at work on the sea. The contrast between the natural lives of the villagers and the unnatural events of the war is made clear when the first mention of the war is followed almost immediately by a long rhapsodic passage in which a woman gives birth to a child in an ecstatic communion with nature. The outbreak of war is an unnatural birth, involving the violation of nature, in direct antithesis to the natural birth of the child, in which human and nonhuman become one.

Payne's peasants, unlike the noble savages of Elliott Paul's *The Life and Death of a Spanish Town*, are highly sophisticated in their politics, and in describing their existence before the war, Payne makes it clear that politics was an important part of their lives. The most important characters in *The Song of the Peasant* are Pere Campo, an Anarchist and the leader of the fishermen's cooperative, and Tomas Mora, a Communist stonemason. . . . Despite their differences, Campo and Mora are in fundamental opposition to the village priest, who defines his position in a defense of the right-wing government which held power before the elections of February, 1936: ". . . I beg you to discard impious thoughts and never allow yourselves to think evilly of the State which is also a representative pattern, not only of Christ but of Christianity. . . ." Such an attitude permits Campo and Mora to suppress their own differences and join in a common cause. (pp. 137-39)

The Song of the Peasant offers no consolation to its characters or to its readers. The destruction caused by the war is in the end pointless because the cause in whose name the war was waged has been lost. As in Bessie's memoir and Spender's poetry, *The Song of the Peasant* contains no direct condemnation of politics or political action, no attempt to put the blame for all this destruction on parties or dogmas. Instead, politics simply fade into insignificance beside the enormity of the degradations men are prepared to visit on one another and upon nature. Payne does not choose between the political ideologies of Mora and Campo; in fact, apart from his evident sympathy for the Loyalists, he is not much concerned with ideology. He makes clear, however, that both of his heroes are motivated by political concepts, and that neither anarchism nor communism is capable of sustaining its believers in a world whose only law is violence. To the men who hold them, such beliefs may seem worth fighting for, but in the end they are incapable of explaining or even ameliorating the disasters of the war.

There are a number of other writers in whose work the problems of politics are treated more directly, and in which politics is seen as one of the forces which cause disillusion. John Dos Passos, for example, had gone a long way down the road toward disaffection with left-wing politics before the Spanish Civil War broke out, and he was convinced that neither communism nor any other radical political or economic program could correct the weaknesses of our system. (p. 141)

The Adventures of a Young Man derives as much from his own disillusion with communism and its agents as from what he actually saw in Spain. Most of the action of the novel takes place in the United States, in the mill and mining towns whose strikes and riots attracted Dos Passos' sympathetic attention during the thirties, and in New York, where the traditional bohemianism of Greenwich Village became for a while almost indistinguishable from radical activism. But the story of Dos Passos' hero, Glen Spotswood, comes to its inevitable conclusion in Spain. (p. 144)

Adventures of a Young Man is Dos Passos' farewell to the radical movement and his explanation of his reasons for departing. He was to go on from this point to an interest in the early days of the United States, a period whose ideals he believed had been betrayed, and he has come to rest recently in the company of William Buckley and the group for which the *National Review* is home. In this trip through the political spectrum, so typical of our times, he does not seem to have lost his sympathy for the truly downtrodden. In this sense, he was still in 1939 the same writer who had grown so impassioned over the facts of Sacco and Vanzetti, and who had written after their execution, "All right; we are two countries." By 1939 he had, as he has written, "rejoined the United States," and he had long since dissociated himself from the Communist party, but he was still as angry at the treatment of the oppressed in *Adventures of a Young Man* as he had been at the plight of the miners in Harlan County or the industrial workers in Detroit in 1932.

What changed in the intervening years was the literary effect of his anger; in *USA* it was directed outward, with a cutting edge that revealed a sick society and showed at least some warmth for those who were trying to cure it. In *Adventures of a Young Man* the anger is gall; the society is no less sick, but social maladies have become less important than the author's bitterness at those who had been his allies, and who he feels have betrayed him. The betrayal was real enough, and in 1939 the revelation of this betrayal was still important, but after two decades the novel is as stale as the poems of Jack Lindsay or the heroics of *The Fifth Column*. All of its characters, including Glen Spotswood, are cardboard images, and the villains are no more human than Lindsay's "fascist monsters, slimed from the night." At the same time, *Adventures of a Young Man* demonstrates clearly the disillusionment with political ideas which became more common as the war in Spain continued. As the bitterness of the Loyalist defeat grew, so did the bitterness of those who felt that the defeat was caused, or at least contributed to, by those who fought on the Loyalist side but who insisted on having their own way in the prosecution of the war.

A more interesting and more rewarding book than Dos Passos', Humphrey Slater's *The Heretics*, develops the same idea, and Slater's target is once again the Communist party. One significant difference between the two novels resides in the fact that Dos Passos' antipathy toward the Communist party had its source outside Spain, so that his novel deals largely with events preceding the war. Slater, on the other hand, was a member of the Communist party who rose to the rank of Commissar of the Fifteenth Brigade, but who renounced the party because of his experience in Spain, and who denounced it bitterly in *The Heretics* and other books written after the end of World War II.

The Heretics is interesting not only for what it says about Spain but for its method. *The Heretics* is in fact two related short novels about two very different times; Slater attempts to draw parallels between widely separated historical events by putting into his narratives of these events two sets of characters with identical names. The first part of the novel deals with the Children's Crusade, that astounding blot on the record of militant Christianity, and does not directly concern us here; the second part deals with the Spanish Civil War. Wisely, the author has not attempted to make the two sections too closely parallel, nor does he make the characters in the second part similar to those in the first except in name. Both sections, however, illustrate a single theme: heresy and dissent, whether religious or political, are natural to the intelligent and sensitive, but they will always be sought out and punished by those in control of authoritarian societies. The political orthodoxies of our time are no more tolerant or flexible than was the religious orthodoxy of the Middle Ages. (pp. 145-47)

The Heretics is a generally successful fictional treatment of the war, and its attitude toward the Communist party as the dominant force in the Loyalist government gains credence because of the author's personal experience as a high-ranking agent of the party in Spain. The ending of the novel is bleak, but Slater avoids the unfocused bitterness of *The Song of the Peasant* as well as the note of personal pique which weakens *Adventures of a Young Man*. Slater makes perfectly clear his dislike of the Communist party's activities in Spain, but the first section and his treatment of individual characters throughout the book show that he regarded communism as only one of many monolithic ideologies. The enemy in *The Heretics* is not communism but orthodoxy. (pp. 150-51)

Spender, Bessie, Dos Passos, Payne, and Slater are by no means unique. Their response to the experience of the Spanish Civil War, in fact, helps to relate that conflict to every other war in which intelligent men have been forced to the understanding that belief is at the mercy of fact. Violence and betrayal cannot indefinitely, for most men of intelligence, be kept separate from the ideals for which they are used, and we do not need the literature of the Spanish Civil War to tell us this. It is nevertheless important that we see that for these men the shibboleths of twentieth-century politics, held as articles of faith for a time, simply disappear when the man becomes conscious that he can no longer accept them. Rolfe and Cornford might be dismayed by their experiences, but they responded by clinging the more fiercely to their beliefs. Spendor and the others abandoned those beliefs. (pp. 151-52)

Apart from a few brief works, only one book rises to the level of art, and that is the generally acknowledged classic of the Spanish Civil War, George Orwell's *Homage to Catalonia.* (pp. 167-68)

Homage was written and published in 1938, after Orwell had returned to England but before the war had ended. Unlike most of the other personal memoirs of the war in Spain (*Men in Battle* is another exception), *Homage* was not intended as propaganda for the Loyalist cause. Orwell knew that his book, or any other, was not likely to help that cause very much. The aim of the book was to clear up what Orwell thought were two major misconceptions: the myths about the life of the soldier in Spain, which had been created by books like *Volunteer in Spain,* and the myths about the nature of the struggle, which had been carefully nurtured by most of the left-wing press. If other books also claimed to tell the truth about Spain, Orwell's is unusual in being based upon what he had seen and experienced, and in the author's warning that the nature of truth is not always clear, nor his story the only story:

> I believe that on an issue such as this no one is or can be completely truthful. It is difficult to be certain about anything except what you have seen with your own eyes, and consciously or unconsciously everyone writes as a partisan. . . . Beware of my partisanship, my mistakes of fact and the distortion inevitably caused by my having seen only one corner of events.

Orwell's Spanish experience is largely the story of a series of accidents which placed him in particular places at critical times, and it is at first glance a simple story. He arrived in Barcelona in December of 1936, ostensibly as a correspondent, but he very soon joined the militia, because "at that time and in that atmosphere it seemed the only conceivable thing to do." At this juncture most of the armed men on the Loyalist side, especially in Catalonia, were in the militia units of labor unions and left-wing political parties. Because of the papers he carried, Orwell was enrolled in the militia of the small, independent left-wing party, POUM, and after the usual minimum of useless training was shipped to the front in Aragon, near Zaragoza. The front was inactive at the time, and he was quickly made aware of the vital concerns of trench warfare in Spain: "firewood, food, tobacco, candles and the enemy. In winter on the Zaragoza front they were important in that order, with the enemy a bad last."

Transferred to another sector of the same front, near Huesca, Orwell finally took part in a battle, an action typical in its indecisiveness of most battles in most wars. He was on leave from this front and in Barcelona when the fighting broke out there over the government's move to incorporate the militia units into the Popular Army and to appropriate the arms still held by the labor unions and political parties; the heart of *Homage* is the description of this fighting. When it had ended, Orwell returned to the front, was wounded by a bullet in the neck, and ultimately was invalided back to Barcelona. There, as a member of an outlawed militia, he found himself in danger of imminent arrest and possible execution, and with his wife he fled to France.

Orwell's attempt to provide an accurate account of the May fighting in Barcelona, and to examine the reasons behind that weird interlude, is the most important part of *Homage,* but since the book is arranged in a chronological pattern he deals first with his experiences as a soldier. His aim in the first part of the book is like that of Alvah Bessie in *Men in Battle.* Both show that even in Spain sleeping in the mud, struggling to keep warm, and firing and being fired at in anger were experiences less pleasurable and more dangerous than attending protest meetings or going on Young Communist League hikes. But the similiarity ends here, for Orwell describes events in the trenches to prepare the reader for more important later events, while Bessie's events seem almost to exist in a void. More important, Orwell is the better writer, with the ability to select from his experiences the critical incident or the typical gesture and to use it to illuminate his picture of war.

Orwell never permits his material to force him to the plodding, repetitious catalogues of events which make *Men in Battle,* for all its sincerity, ultimately a tiresome book. Orwell's sense of the ridiculous is most useful in his observations on the soldier's life:

> All of us were lousy by this time; though still cold it was warm enough for that. I have had a big experience of body vermin of various kinds, and for sheer beastliness the louse beats everything I have encountered. Other insects, mosquitos for instance, make you suffer more, but at least they aren't *resident* vermin. The human louse resembles a tiny lobster, and he lives chiefly in your trousers. Short of burning all your clothes there is no known way of getting rid of him. Down the seams of your trousers he lays his glittering white eggs, like tiny grains of rice, which hatch out and breed families of their own at horrible speed. I think the pacifists might find it helpful to illustrate their pamphlets with enlarged photographs of lice. Glory of war, indeed! In war *all* soldiers are lousy, at least when it is warm enough. The men who fought at Verdun, at Waterloo, at Flodden, at Senlac, at Thermopylae—every one of them had lice crawling over his testicles.

Passages like this show Orwell at his best—realistic as anyone could wish, but with his characteristic touch of outraged irony which debunks all grandiose notions of heroism, whether in this war or in any other. Only a very few writers, Orwell, Charles Donnelly, and perhaps Humphrey Slater, saw that the war in Spain was not altogether unique, was not the glorious crusade which the party-line organs (and liberal and left-wing journals in general) pretended it was. For the men who did the actual fighting, it was a war like any other, lice and all.

Orwell has other methods of deflating notions of exaggerated heroism. One of the most effective is employed in his description of his first departure for the front, which focuses on the personal discomfort and the reactions of the individual soldier, in sharp contrast to the description of a similar scene by John Sommerfield:

> I remember vividly the torchlit scene—the uproar and excitement, the red flags flapping in the torchlight, the massed ranks of militiamen with their knapsacks on their backs and their rolled blankets worn bandolier-like across the shoulder; and the shouting and the clatter of boots and tin pannikins, and then a tremendous and finally successful hissing for silence; and then some political commissar standing beneath a huge rolling red banner and making us a speech in Catalan. Finally they marched us to the station, taking the longest route, three or four miles, so as to show us to the whole town. In the Ramblas they halted us while a borrowed band played some revolutionary tune or other. Once again the conquering hero stuff—shouting and enthusiasm, red flags and red and black flags everywhere, friendly crowds thronging the pavement to have a look at us, women waving wildly from the windows. How natural it all seemed then; how remote and impossible now! The train was packed so tight with men that there was barely room even on the floor, let alone on the seats. At the last moment Williams' wife came running down the platform and gave us a bottle of wine and a foot of that bright red sausage which tastes of soap and gives you diarrhoea.

The method here might be called the double-delayed anticlimax; whenever Orwell shows us a side of war which might make us think that it is glamorous and exciting, he walks us three or four miles and produces the laxative sausage tasting of soap to remind us that modern war is never a boy's game. (pp. 168-72)

Orwell's portrayal of the soldier's experience is as crisp and as moving as anything to have come out of the Spanish Civil War, or for that matter any other war, but as I have said, in *Homage* this picture is primarily used as a means of preparing the reader to understand the context of the later events. Orwell's discussion of the war in *Homage* illustrates his later statement that "The outcome of the Spanish war was settled in London, Paris, Rome, Berlin—at any rate, not in Spain." It is a truism that nothing that happened in Spain during the war had as much effect on its outcome as the diplomatic actions of the great powers. It is also true, however, that among the events in Spain itself, those which took place behind the front lines were probably more important than any of the battles, and that one of the most crucial of these events was the May fighting in Barcelona in 1937. This fighting is the climax of Orwell's book. (p. 173)

There were, ... three main groups struggling for power in Catalonia: the PSUC, allied to the central government; the Catalonian *Generalitat,* established before the war and representative of the bourgeoisie; and the *ad hoc* Committee of

Fifteen, established in the early days of the fighting to direct left-wing opposition to the Insurgent revolt because it was feared that the Generalitat would be insufficiently militant—the Committee of Fifteen was dominated by the FAI (*Federación Anarchista Ibérica*). The Committee continued to direct military operations in the northeast, to the considerable annoyance of the central government in Madrid. Early in 1937, the Madrid regime undertook to establish a unified command which would incorporate the militia units formerly under party or union orders, a move which received scant support from the Committee of Fifteen. The PSUC, acting for the central government, was reluctant to move directly against the FAI or the Committee, which had too much popular support to be easy victims, but it could and did put pressure on the POUM. The POUM was a natural target, for although in practice it was allied with the FAI, it was a small and relatively powerless group. Suppressing it and appropriating the arms of its militia would show the power of the government. Because it was a Marxist group, but independent of Moscow, the POUM could be, and was, labeled "Trotskyist," a term roughly synonymous with Fascist and traitorous in the vocabulary of the time, but carrying the additional stigma of apostasy from the true faith. It was charged that this group had been negotiating with the Insurgents, and that its militiamen were therefore likely to turn their guns on their erstwhile allies whenever these negotiations proved fruitful. The charge was patently absurd, and has never been taken seriously by objective historians.

In Barcelona, however, the charges seemed extremely serious, and much of the bitterness of Orwell's story of the Barcelona fighting is accounted for by the attempt to label the POUM as a treasonous organization. But for these charges, Orwell says, he would have been willing to accept the official explanation of the causes of the incident. As it is, Orwell's analysis gains credibility from the fact that in the beginning he had been uninterested in the political differences on the Loyalist side, and had joined the POUM militia by accident. He had been generally unsympathetic to the POUM viewpoint, and as a soldier at the front "preferred the Communist viewpoint to that of the POUM." After his front-line hitch with the POUM, he decided to join the Communist-dominated International Column, and had taken steps toward that end at the beginning of his leave in Barcelona, but before definite arrangements could be made the fighting had begun. By the time it was over, four days later, the anti-POUM propaganda was accusing all the men in its militia of the gravest crimes:

> This, then, was what they were saying about us: we were Trotskyists, Fascists, traitors, murderers, cowards, spies and so forth. I admit it was not pleasant, especially when one thought of some of the people who were responsible for it. It is not a nice thing to see a Spanish boy of fifteen carried down the line on a stretcher, with a dazed white face looking out from among the blankets, and to think of the sleek persons in London and Paris who are writing pamphlets to prove that this boy is a Fascist in disguise.

This was bad enough, but in essence it was the usual interparty bickering on the left given added seriousness because men were killing each other. But the political quarrels were in this case little more than symptoms of what was to Orwell the real stake in the fighting: the revolution, and the attempt to betray it. For the early days of the war had been a time of genuine revolution in many parts of Spain, in which industries

George Orwell (far left) towering over his P.O.U.M. comrades in Barcelona. Centelles, Barcelona.

had been collectivized and large estates expropriated and divided among the peasants. In early 1937 the revolution had been halted and even pushed back, as the government undertook a policy whose aim was to show that Republican Spain was just another bourgeois democracy where foreign investments would be perfectly safe. Most of the other memoirs of Spain, and contemporary analyses of the Civil War, paid little attention to the revolution. Many of the foreign volunteers were unaware of it, and a good many volunteers as well as correspondents and observers accepted a party line which denied its reality. For Orwell, whose approach was nondoctrinaire and whose chief interest was in the fact that somewhere in the world the lower classes had briefly attained power, the revolution was of first importance.

It was the revolutionary atmosphere of Barcelona, late in 1936, that inspired Orwell to join the fighting in the first place, and that sustained him until he returned to the city at the end of April, 1937, to find the revolutionary atmosphere gone. (pp. 174-77)

The arrival in Barcelona was a distinct letdown for Orwell, but worse was to follow. The chapter dealing with the prelude to the actual fighting and with the outbreak is a story of mounting tension, suspicion, and hatred among people supposedly on the same side. The trouble lasted for only a few days (May 3-7) and even at its height there were occasions when the fighters on opposing sides talked with each other cordially, but the fighting was real enough. Within a day or two the entire city began to run short of food, and the pressures for a settlement soon became irresistible. The POUM, short of arms and ammunition and ignored by its Anarchist allies, capitulated. The whole episode was, for Orwell, profoundly disillusioning.

At this stage, Orwell inserts a chapter explaining the political situation, a device to which he has recourse several times in *Homage*. In beginning these chapters, he warns the reader to skip if he is interested in the narrative but not in the political involutions of his experience. Some readers have taken him seriously, and there have been occasional objections that these chapters do break up the continuity of the narrative. To so object is not only to reveal considerable naïveté, but also to underestimate Orwell's capacity for irony. For if the action of *Homage* has a theme, it is that the fighting and the other events can be understood only in terms of the politics which motivated the events, and that to anyone who does not understand the politics, the fighting must appear to be sheer madness.

These political chapters, although their insertion is perhaps slightly awkward, are therefore essential to the book, and on the whole probably the best method Orwell could have used for conveying the necessary information about the underlying motives for action. Certainly his method is preferable to the only real alternative: including political analysis as part of the description of the action, which would have been much more obtrusive and much more annoying. The political chapters perform another function for the reader, because they convey three fundamental elements of Orwell's character: his belief that the truth about events in war or politics is knowable, his belief that such knowledge is of first importance (in *1984* one of the abuses that he regards as most frightening is the ability of the regime to change the past by rewriting history), and his understanding that such truth is never simple. These are distinctive elements in all of Orwell's work, the novels and the essays as well as *Homage,* and they are worth bringing up again because Orwell's critics have tended to ignore the last of the three.

It is true enough that in one way Orwell was a simple man. He was not given to abstract thought, and one of his sympathetic critics has written that "Orwell was not prolific of ideas; he had a few basic ones, which he repeated over and over." But a number of writers have gone beyond this insight to the oversimplification that a kind of simple decency was the essential element of Orwell's character and of his writings. . . . (pp. 178-79)

There is, as Lionel Trilling has pointed out, something old-fashioned about the terms customarily used to describe Orwell—decency, virtue, simple honesty. They seem to place him in some earlier time, when politics was neither so complicated nor so desperate a matter as it has come to be in the twentieth century; and when "one's simple, direct, undeceived intelligence" was sufficient to an understanding of the problems of the day. But the use of such terms reveals more about the critics who use them than about Orwell.

Orwell may have shared with these critics a nostalgia for a simpler past—his yearning for a simple world in which men who shared goals could work together toward those goals is implicit in everything he wrote, and his idealization of an ordered past is manifest in *Coming Up for Air*—but he did not permit it to lead him to the conclusion that the present is also simple if one will only accept one of the dogmas that says it is simple. Orwell knew his experience to be a uniquely modern one, and his reaction to it was untypical only in that he was far less prone than most of his contemporaries to devote a good deal of time and energy to embracing dogmas and then reacting against them. Orwell knew as well as any of his contemporaries that all fighting faiths are less than perfect, that all utopias are illusions. But where others abandoned the faith and the fighting or denied the illusions, Orwell accepted what he saw and still maintained that it was not only possible but necessary to make choices in the light of continually changing realities, and to defend those choices. If the Loyalist cause was less than holy, if the revolution had been betrayed, if he himself had very nearly given his life for that cause only to be branded a traitor and forced to flee the country—that was too bad, and must be made known, but Orwell could not react to it by crying down a plague on all houses and retreating to the study of the classics, or of one's own navel.

History is conflict, and when history is being made it is important to see that neither side is perfect or near perfection, and equally important to make a choice: "I hope they win their war and drive all foreigners out of Spain, Germans, Russians, and Italians alike. This war, in which I played so ineffectual a part, has left me with memories that are mostly evil, and yet I do not wish that I had missed it."

Such a response may appear simple in its results, but it is not based upon a simplistic view of the world. As a modern man, Orwell was aware of the complexities of his world, and though he might deplore them he was fully involved in them. This is evident in the political chapters of *Homage,* as it is in most of his writings. His analysis of the political situation in Spain is lucid but not oversimplified: it was wrong of the government to suppress the revolution and to outlaw the POUM; at the same time there was a case to be made for a unified government and a centrally directed army, and neither of these was possible

if the revolution went forward and the POUM retained control of an independent militia. Still, the Barcelona fighting was part of an attempt at Communist control of Loyalist Spain, and this was bad; on the other hand, the Communists did offer discipline and a program for winning the war. The choices are not "simple." A "simple" man would probably never have seen the choices as Orwell saw them, certainly not with the same clarity combined with an awareness of complexity. It is perhaps one of his major virtues that Orwell tried never to evade an issue or a choice, even while he forbade himself the luxury of self-deception in describing the situations in which choices had to be made. (pp. 180-82)

> *John M. Muste, in his* Say That We Saw Spain Die: Literary Consequences of the Spanish Civil War, *University of Washington Press, 1966, 208 p.*

EBERHARD BRÜNING

[*In the following excerpt, Brüning employs a Marxist perspective to evaluate political ideology and literary artistry in American novels of the Spanish Civil War.*]

The Spanish Civil War from 1936 to 1939 was an international event with far-reaching consequences, not only of a political but also of a literary nature. The war in Spain attracted anti-fascist volunteers from numerous countries of the world and in so doing achieved [according to Eugen Varga in *20 Jahre Kapitalismus und Sozialismus*] "a new aspect of world historic importance: the practical international solidarity of the world proletariat in its struggle against fascism." (p. 42)

Among the writers of the United States who temporarily went to Spain at that time we find such well-known personalities as Ernest Hemingway, Theodore Dreiser, John Dos Passos, Dorothy Parker, Lillian Hellman, Josephine Herbst, Langston Hughes, Erskine Caldwell, Elliot Paul, Vincent Sheean, Malcolm Cowley, Waldo Frank, Edwin Rolfe, Joseph North, Herbert L. Matthews and Martha Gellhorn. Despite this great number of outstanding representatives of American literature, the literary output reflecting the events in Spain during the 30's, in high-quality prose genres, was comparatively small. On the other hand, reportage and war diary achieved great success. On the whole, the literary reflection of the Spanish War played almost the same role as the war itself: it was a prelude to the world-wide struggle which followed it, a struggle between the fascist states and those united in the anti-Hitler coalition, which later on became the subject for a real flood of war novels and stories. (p. 43)

The Spanish novel—that is, the only American novel whose complete story takes place in Spain at the time of the Civil War, from 1936 to 1939—is *For Whom The Bell Tolls* (1940), by Ernest Hemingway. If *any* modern American writer was predestined to write about the events in the Spain of the thirties, that writer was Ernest Hemingway whose personal relations with Spain reached far back into the twenties and were of profounder nature than those of a mere tourist. Who other than Hemingway himself is speaking through the mouth of Robert Jordan, who has written a book about Spain and about whom it is said: "He had put in it what he had discovered about Spain in ten years of travelling in it, on foot, in third-class carriages, by bus, on horse-and mule-back, and in trucks. He knew the Basque country, Navarre, Aragon, Galicia, the two Castiles and Estremadura well." (pp. 43-4)

In 1937, Cyril Connolly wrote in the English weekly *New Statesman and Nation*: "Hemingway . . . is obviously the person who can write the great book about the Spanish War." Hemingway's biographer, Carlos Baker, tries to prove in detail that *For Whom the Bell Tolls* is the "great book about the Spanish War." If, on the other hand, one takes a look at the representative and voluminous anthology, *The Heart of Spain*, one will search in vain for anything by Hemingway or any excerpt from his novel. The editor, Alvah Bessie, explained this "omission" with the following words:

> It was felt that Hemingway's talent and the personal support he rendered to many phases of the Loyalist cause were shockingly betrayed in his work *For Whom the Bell Tolls* in which the Spanish people were cruelly misrepresented and leaders of the International Brigade maliciously slandered. The novel in its total impact presented an unforgivable distortion of the meaning of the struggle in Spain. Under the name and prestige of Hemingway, important aid was thus given to humanity's worst enemies.

It is a fact that no other work by Hemingway has led to such controversial opinions in American and international literary criticism as has this novel on Spain. Ernest Hemingway describes in his book the lives and deaths of a group of antifascist partisans during four days of the year 1937. Robert Jordan, an American volunteer of the International Brigade, has moved far behind the enemy front line and deep into the mountainous countryside north-west of Madrid which is occupied by Franco's army. His aim, together with the Spanish partisans, is to dynamite a strategically important bridge at the same time that the Loyalist troups are launching an offensive. The bridge becomes a place of destiny for, and a tragic symbol of, all people involved in it. The preparations for its dynamiting, the necessary measures taken for their own personal security in order to guarantee the fulfillment of the order, and finally the considerations for a well-organized retreat after the explosion, involve the heterogeneous group of Spanish patriots in numerous problems and contradictions.

Jordan, the central figure of the book, is the well-known "Hemingway hero" whom we have encountered in many a previous work by Hemingway: the uprooted, lean, intellectual and ironic "he-man" with his liking for strong drinks and sexual debaucheries. It is said about him: "He fought now in this war because it had started in a country that he loved and he believed in the Republic and that if it were destroyed life would be unbearable for all those people who believed in it." Though he is able to find his way to the heart of a Spanish girl, who has suffered terribly under the fascists and who wins new courage to live, through her love of the American, basically he is living an isolated life—like all his literary predecessors—estranged from the world around him and without understanding of the real reasons why the Spanish people are fighting for the preservation of the republic—*their* republic—and are willing to lay down their lives for it. He cannot understand that the controversy between the fascists and the supporters of the People's Front bears the character of a class struggle and that the Spanish people are trying to get rid of hunger, exploitation, and bigotry once and for all. The Spanish peasants and workers fought with the courage of desperation and very often only with naked fists against those who were trying to re-establish the old conditions and who found ready help from foreign powers. They knew

what the putsch of the Franco-rebels meant for them and what dangers it implied—a rebellion which the great humanist writer, Thomas Mann, characterized in the following words:

> A general's rebellion undertaken in the service of the old powers of exploitation and suppression and, as it happened, schemed with speculating foreign powers, gets started and fails, is almost nearly annihilated, but is supported by foreign, liberty-hating governments, nourished and fostered with money, people and war material—all with the promise of economic and strategic advantages in the case of an insurgent victory!

But what is the opinion of Jordan-Hemingway about that? In one of the oft-quoted passages of the novel one can read:

> People should be left alone and you should interfere with no one. So he believed that, did he? Yes, he believed that. And how about a planned society and the rest of it? That was for the others to do. He had something else to do after this war. . . . What were his politics then? He had none now, he told himself. But do not tell anyone else that, he thought. Don't even admit that. And what are you going to do afterwards? I am going back and earn my living teaching Spanish as before and I am going to write a true book.

An American volunteer of the International Brigade without any political conviction? Hardly believable, but not at all typical of the three thousand-odd Americans who fought together with the Loyalists against the fascists and of whom Steve Nelson said in his book, *The Volunteers,* based on his own experiences and on facts: "All of us in this outfit are anti-fascists, and none of us is going to Spain for personal adventure. . . . Our boys know what they're fighting for. They're here because they want to be here. They came to Spain because they understood what this war is about. This is their war, and they know it, or they never would have come."

The above-quoted book by Steve Nelson, who as a political commissar took part in all important battles of the Spanish War, also contains the story "El Fantastico" which in its theme is similar to Hemingway's novel but, on the other hand, shows a basically different ideological conception. In "El Fantastico" too, the hero sacrifices himself after the fulfilment of his order—in Nelson's story it is the liberation of imprisoned Spanish labour leaders—to cover the retreat of his comrades. Whereas Robert Jordan does not really know what he is laying down his life for, El Fantastico is dying as a class-conscious worker and true revolutionary fully aware of his mission and strengthened by his glowing hatred of fascism.

The portrait of Jordan as an "unpolitical" soldier on the Loyalist side is quite obviously a distortion and mis-interpretation of the International Brigaders. Jordan's words, "I am going back and earn my living teaching Spanish as before," not only reveal a naïveté born of this so-called unpolitical attitude but also show the author's dangerous political blindness. The returning veterans of the Spanish War soon found out for themselves how it was about returning to their old jobs. Michael Gold writes in his vigorous and uncompromising analysis of Hemingway's book:

It is a sign of how ignorant of social reality Hemingway is that he can make this sound like some sort of cushy peace for a former Lincoln brigader. There were actually a number of university teachers in the Brigade. But when they came home, they found no such peace. They found boycott, persecution and blacklist.

Writers like Alvah Bessie and Irwin Shaw have clearly demonstrated the truth of this sober statement of Michael Gold in their novels some years later.

Additional to the problematic conception of the hero, *For Whom the Bell Tolls* contains a number of episodes—as for instance the notorious story about the brutal retaliation on the fascists by Pablo and his men—which make it clear that Hemingway's personal attitude as an anti-fascist, which is beyond any doubt, did not find a thorough and convincing literary interpretation. Hemingway did not want, as the critic Edwin Berry Burgum said, to write a "political" novel. He only wanted to use the political events as a background for his timeless story of an individual tragedy. Though we have no reason to doubt the author's subjective honesty or his sympathy for the Loyalists— the less if we take into consideration his personal attitude in Spain and his war reports for American newspapers and magazines—, it remains a fact, however, that in this novel Hemingway objectively served the enemies of the cause of the Spanish people. This was said by Marxist critics immediately after the publication of the book and remains true today. That in spite of its shortcomings the book could have a positive effect in the hands of progressive forces today, was recently confirmed by Fidel Castro, when he remarked that he and his guerilla fighters had taken *For Whom the Bell Tolls* with them into the mountains, "because it told us about modern civil war. Other books don't teach us this." The English Sunday paper, *The Observer*, published in its weekly "Profile," dedicated to Fidel Castro, in addition to the above-mentioned remarks the following interesting passage:

> Castro once asked a reporter why Hemingway, known to be a supporter of the revolution, hadn't made more public statements about it. The reporter said he assumed Hemingway didn't want to be involved in politics, and the whole Cabinet laughed. "We are not politicians," said Castro. "We made our revolution to get the politicians out. We are social people. This is a social revolution."

What was a tragic failure in the case of Hemingway and became unintentional support for the enemies of the Spanish People's Front, was out-and-out knavery and an intentionally barbed provocation in the case of John Dos Passos's literary contribution to the Spanish War. John Dos Passos, together with his friend Hemingway, went to Spain in the spring of 1937. Dos Passos published his personal experiences and impressions in his travel book, *Journeys Between Wars,* from which one can clearly perceive that the author was unable to make real contact with the country and the people, or with their complicated political and social problems, despite his many visits to Spain. He always remained the American tourist with whom the small discomforts of his travel caused by the war were more important than all essential phenomena of the world surrounding him. He was a "tourist" who visited the front line of Madrid. His so-called battle-report opens with the following sentences: "At the next barricade there's a small beadyeyed sentry who smilingly asks to see my pass. He's a Cuban. As Americans we

talk. Somehow there's a bond between us as from the western world."

This travel book also contains hints of an episode which Dos Passos seized as an opportunity to break finally with his convictions, so freely mouthed in former times. Dos Passos's Spanish translator was exposed as a fascist spy, condemned and executed. No one—not even Hemingway who had thoroughly looked into the case—was able to convince Dos Passos of the translator's guilt.

One certainly is right to assume that this event also lurks in the background of the novel *Adventures of a Young Man*. Moreover, one must interpret this book, published in 1939, as the final word of a long-drawn process of the author's retreat from the left movement of his country with which he had so much sympathized during the late twenties and the early thirties. If we have to mourn Hemingway's novel on Spain as an unlucky attempt at an "unpolitical" book, the novel in question now must be considered as a novel written with an intentionally political view in mind. It is the story of Glenn Spotswood, a young highly-strung idealist of the American middle class, who leads a miserable life for his faithfulness to principles but who hardly develops or matures as a character and is always suffering under the conditions surrounding him. Glenn is a man without any true convictions, mentally helpless, constantly wavering between pathetic heroism and lamentable defeatism. He becomes a member of the Communist Party and helps to organize miners on strike; then he turns his back on the Party since he is of the opinion that the Communist functionaries do not really represent the interests of the workers; after that he becomes the "spiritus rector" of a group of "disappointed revolutionaries" and goes to Spain where he is thrown into jail as a Trotskyite and "agent provocateur" and is finally forced to an unnecessary deed of courage by heartless and sadistic "Communist functionaries," on which occasion he loses his life to the bullets of the fascists. Glenn Spotswood's experiences in Spain, however, occupy only a small part of the book and are merely an instrument for the author to push his anti-Communist attitude to a certain climax, for he wants to have his main character understood as a victim of international Communism. It goes without saying that on the basis of this conception the author cannot spare a single word for the heroic struggle of the Spanish people or the solidarity of the anti-fascist volunteers from many countries of the world. His miserable "hero" is not only a caricature of a Communist but also of a member of the International Brigade, among whom, the writer says he feels "strange and lost, wishing he'd stayed home where he understood the language, where he had some way of doping out what things were about." Even the bourgeois critics leave no doubt that *Adventures of a Young Man* has to be seen as a turning point in Dos Passos's literary work—as a decisive step downward on the ladder of his artistic decline. Maxwell Geismar wrote in 1942: "*Adventures of a Young Man* is the final disestablishment of the spiritual values and intellectual themes which Dos Passos has built over the twenty years of social thinking and writing" [see Additional Bibliography]. Sixteen years later Geismar can only state flatly, in retrospect about the books published by Dos Passos in the meantime: "The decline of Dos Passos' work is another tragedy in contemporary letters."

"Every decent person wishes to help the democratic people's government of Spain. My help takes the form of a novel; also a job of publishing it so as to reach the masses." These are the first sentences of a one-page advertisement in the magazine

The New Republic, written and paid for himself by an American author. The author's name is Upton Sinclair and the pretentious and promising title of his novel is *No Pasaran!* (*They Shall Not Pass: A Story of the Battle of Madrid;* 1937). The title of this book so loudly introduced is misleading, for whoever expects a novel about the Spanish Civil War (one like the novels by the German writers Bodo Uhse or Eduard Claudius, perhaps) will find himself deeply disappointed. It is not only that the scene of hardly a fifth of the book is laid in Spain, but also that the author lacks the artistic accomplishment to live up to his material, that is, the literary remodelling of the certainly positive, though often very vague, political ideas which he has made the criterion for the plot. *No Pasaran!* is again one of Sinclair's many literary hybrids—partly a novel of the muckraking school, partly a moralizing political pamphlet—again a confirmation of what Lenin once said about this American writer, namely, "Sinclair is an emotional socialist, without theoretical education. . . . Sinclair is naive in his appeal, though this appeal is basically right. . . ."

Three volunteers (*Drei Freiwillige*—that is also the title of the German translation which was published by the Malik-Verlag in the same year) go, as convinced anti-fascists, to Spain and after a short training are rushed to the Madrid front where they defend the town against the attacks of the Moroccans. Their experiences, the inner as well as the outer ones, are hardly worked out, but remain somewhat shady. The reader cannot but avoid the feeling that the author is writing about something he only knows of by hearsay. Theorizing constantly suffocates the flow of action. The characters are reduced to mere objects for demonstration. Nevertheless, one should not overlook the author's honest intention, that is, his attempt to search for the essential facts behind the events in Spain and to uncover the fascist machinations.

We have already mentioned the fact that Spain and the Civil War are only dealt with in the smallest part of the novel. Becoming members of the International Brigade is the final stage of a process in the personal development of the three central figures whose thinking and actions were definitely influenced by the depression years.

The names Sinclair had chosen for his three heroes are symbolical: Rudy Messer, Izzy Bloch and Giuseppe Damile. Special attention is given to Rudy Messer, the "poor" relative of a wealthy and reactionary capitalist family of German-American origin. In addition to this Sinclair is interested—like Lewis in *It Can't Happen Here*—in exposing and attacking fascism and the followers of Hitler in the United States. It further is very instructive that Sinclair had chosen a Jewish worker as the ideological mentor of the son of a German-American capitalist. Above all, it is Izzy Bloch who finally wins Rudy Messer over to participate in the Spanish War.

Upton Sinclair took up the theme of the Spanish War once more in 1943, in the fourth volume of his Lanny Budd series. Extensive passages of this thrilling crime novel about the adventures of an extremely rich art dealer and amateur spy with Marxist inclinations deal with events of the Civil War—they describe, for instance, the enthusiastically greeted arrival of the International Brigade in Madrid—and show, despite a certain primitivism and irrationality of the plot, the author's endeavour to bring to light the legitimacy of the Spanish people's fight for freedom.

A middling position between novel and reportage is taken up by the interesting and moving work, *The Life and Death of a*

Spanish Town (1937), by Elliot Paul. Here the life of a small town (Santa Eulalia) on the Balearic Isle, Ibiza, immediately before and after the beginning of the Spanish Civil War is described. The book is in two parts. The first part gives a detailed description of the life and the activities of the inhabitants of Santa Eulalia, with whom the author deeply sympathizes and who consider him one of their own. The social order and the political attitude of the inhabitants, their opinion of the church, of the great landowners, of the Guardia Civil, of progress and reaction are thoroughly analyzed. This analysis is based on close and highly-differentiated observations which are used by the author's creative mind as minute, impressionistic components for his comprehensive study. The second part exclusively deals with the events on the island which took place between July 14 and September 15, 1936. Paul shows how these people described by him before became part of the revolutionary upsurge, were carried away by it and were finally crushed under the counter-revolutionary backwash. We become witnesses of the fascist putsch, and of the final victory of the rebel forces—events which are reflected in the mirror of the carefully depicted characters and their fate. The author never leaves any doubt that he is on the side of the Loyalists whom he actually helped to establish a democratic government in the town of Eulalia during that short period of their reign over the island of Ibizza.

Though the series of novels which directly reflect the Spanish Civil War is, on the whole, exhausted with the above-mentioned examples, one can nevertheless trace its literary effectiveness within the American novel right up to the present day. Indeed, it has in a peculiar, interesting and significant way taken over the function of a literary ferment which is used again and again by a great number of authors. One might even say that in certain respects the Spanish Civil War has become a literary cliché. American novelists, who intend to give one of their figures a "radical" tint, a progressive or even revolutionary background, very often make use of association with this important event of the thirties. Even the smallest allusion, however, to the Spanish War turns into a criterion of the author's political standing, because since the Cold War started, a pro-Loyalist attitude in the Spanish affair has been interpreted by so-called public opinion in the United States as an endorsement of Communism or as a subversive tendency. (pp. 44-51)

Ernest Hemingway said in his answer to the justified and necessary criticism of his anti-spy drama, *The Fifth Column* (1937), written in beleaguered Madrid, that it needs many plays and novels "to present the nobility and dignity of the cause of the Spanish people . . . and the best ones will be written after the war is over." And he was quite right, though he unfortunately failed himself "to present the nobility and dignity of the cause of the Spanish people" adequately or satisfactorily in his literary works.

Summarizing the impression of the material so far dealt with, we must come back to our introductory statement, namely, that such an important event as the Spanish Civil War has found comparatively little reflection in the American novel. There are probably two main reasons for this: firstly, the "little war" in Spain was actually only a prelude, a prologue to greater, world-wide events which very soon over-shadowed everything else and oriented the politically-minded writers towards new problems without providing them with the creative reprieve to tackle satisfactorily the Spanish tragedy; and secondly, a literary work on the Spanish Civil War always involved the author in a political and ideological confession in the sense of the old union song "Which side are you on?", and from which the bourgeois writer preferred to shy away even if he personally sympathized with the anti-fascist movement unequivocally. (pp. 54-5)

Eberhard Brüning, "The Spanish Civil War (1936-1939) and the American Novel," in Zeitschrift für Anglistik und Amerikanistik, Vol. 11, 1963, pp. 42-55.

ROWLAND SMITH

[*In the following excerpt, Smith discusses support for Franco among British literati, focusing on the political attitudes of Wyndham Lewis and Roy Campbell.*]

It is well known that British writers reacted passionately to the Spanish Civil War. The majority of those writing supported the Spanish Republic, and all those actually fighting in Spain were either anti-fascists or left-wingers. As a result there has been little attention paid to the British writers of the Right during the Spanish Civil War. There is general knowledge that Wyndham Lewis supported Franco as well as Hitler in the mid-thirties; that Evelyn Waugh, although not himself a fascist, had declared that he would choose to become a fascist rather than a communist if those were the only choices open to him. Edmund Blunden is known to have supported Franco. Roy Campbell's own tales of his exploits with Franco's armies are vaguely remembered, and it is widely known that his long and passionate poem, *Flowering Rifle,* is in praise of Franco's rebellion.

Beyond these vague impressions there is little common knowledge about the attitudes towards the war of the British literary Right. (p. 60)

The reasons for the lack of interest in the literary right-wing during the Spanish Civil War are clear enough. Not only was there no significant pro-Franco literature produced, but also several great pro-Republican works were written. The young left-wing writers who committed themselves to the Republican cause were vogue figures who attracted attention because they belonged to much-publicised coteries. The heroic romanticism connected with their commitment was an element in the situation which was bound to foster public interest. And when gifted young men like Christopher Caudwell, John Cornford, and Julian Bell were killed in Spain, the glamour of their cause was assured. There was no comparable glamour on the opposing side.

The left-wing writers whom we refer to rather loosely as the Auden group did not dominate the literary scene in the way their confident assertions would lead one to believe. Nevertheless, the established writers of the era remained uncommitted on the war, and therefore did not add their stature to the anti-Republican cause. . . . With big guns like Eliot remaining neutral, the field was inevitably dominated by the more numerous writers of the Left. (pp. 60-1)

It is, of course, not only the status or numbers of the writers supporting each side which affect the sympathy shown for their views. In retrospect the Spanish Civil War is usually seen as a preliminary to the Second World War; the dictators flexing their muscles and testing equipment in preparation for the real thing. Franco's terrorism, the cynicism of Hitler's and Mussolini's attitude towards non-intervention, their lies and manipulation of facts, are all seen as precursors to the European holocaust of 1939-45. As a result, pro-Franco writers are fre-

quently seen as part of the Axis propaganda machine. To be for Franco was to be for his allies too, for Hitler and Mussolini. Not to support the Republic was to accept the overthrow by military dictatorship of a democratically elected government.

There is a great deal of truth in this view. The two writers who supported Franco's cause most vigorously, Roy Campbell and Wyndham Lewis, were also, at the time, convinced that it was folly to oppose Hitler and Mussolini militarily. The degree of their admiration for Hitler's Germany varied constantly, but by and large it is true to say that until 1939 they were most sympathetic towards him. Both changed their opinions radically in 1939. In that year Lewis published an anti-Hitler book, *The Hitler Cult,* and, although living in Franco's Spain, Campbell began to think of enlisting in the British army once war had been declared. These writers' mistakes about Hitler were thus recognised by them before 1940, and can comfortably be placed as part of the general English-speaking gullibility of the 1930's. (pp. 61-2)

My aim in this [essay] is to discuss the attitudes of Wyndham Lewis in general and Roy Campbell in particular towards the Spanish situation, and to illustrate what led writers of such distinction to identify themselves with a cause which has become so distasteful. . . .

From the mid-twenties on Wyndham Lewis had set himself up as the prime "Enemy" of the new post-war mass society. As a casual member of London Bohemian circles in 1921-2, Roy Campbell had met Lewis and had become fascinated by his views. The poet's clashes with his native South African culture and with the British literary establishment had left him too an isolated "enemy" by 1931. In that year his satire, *The Georgiad,* had appeared. The satirised literary world turned a cold reviewer's shoulder to Campbell's work, and he himself began to lead an outsider's life, first in Martigues and later in Spain. Lewis's consistent attacks during the Twenties on the mediocrity and conformism of contemporary culture are more subtle and varied than Campbell's emotional reaction during the Thirties against a society he dislikes. But Lewis dislikes the same things that Campbell dislikes. (p. 62)

Lewis's distrust of coteries, and of mass-thinking, together with his firm belief in individualism, naturally made him an opponent of left-wing literary movements. His insight into the emptiness of their Utopian theory and abstract social values was balanced by a naivety in his attitude towards Hitler. After a brief visit to Germany, he published *Hitler* in 1931, which set out to illustrate Hitler's positive achievements and to discount his menacing statements and theories. From that point until 1939 there was warfare between him and the literary Left. In his attacks on English gullibility and Soviet hypocrisy he showed insight which history has confirmed. This insight was usually coupled, however, with absurdly naive attitudes towards the fascist dictators. . . . As part of his exposé of the one-sidedness of British public opinion, he tries to explain away Hitler's military aspirations, and to point to the real menace—Soviet manipulation of Western thinking. He sees Western blindness to the dangers of Soviet domination in Republican Spain as a significant illustration of the subservience of the democracies to Soviet propaganda. This is Lewis's most explicit commentary on the Spanish Civil War. His views on Spain are only part of a general attack on the English herd-mind, and, like his views on Hitler himself, were to be completely altered by 1939 in *The Hitler Cult.*

Roy Campbell's views on the Spanish Civil War were much more specific than his old mentor's, and held until his death.

They are derived from an essentially similar impulse, however: a passionate belief in heroic individualism, growing out of a real isolation, and a corresponding hatred of exclusive coteries or group-thinking of any kind. Like Lewis, Campbell associated group-thinking only with the group from whom he had suffered most—the literary Left. There was no equivalent in his own painfully isolated situation to the fascist automata whom he and Lewis mistakenly saw as a bulwark against leftist double-think. (pp. 63-4)

Campbell's long ''epic,'' *Flowering Rifle*, reflects every aspect of his political stand in Spain. . . . His total acceptance of Nationalist propaganda and his complete identification with the Nationalist cause are apparent throughout. The fact that he had been outside Spain for most of the war might be the reason for his absolute acceptance of the official Nationalist point of view. (p. 64)

Campbell's Spanish poems written before the outbreak of hostilities make clear his . . . delight in traditional, pastoral and religious values. At same time, he attacks bitterly any materialist outlook threatening those traditional values that were dear to him. In the poems written about the war itself, his conservative instinct and his wish to eliminate socialist activity are both naturally allied to Franco's cause. His religious convictions were also inseparable from his political convictions in the first few months of the war when a reign of terror was unleashed against the Church in Republican territory. Campbell's horror at the persecution of the Church is an inevitable reaction. But the political deductions he makes about that persecution ignore the fact that the Church itself played a political role in Spain and was seen by the Left as a consistent supporter of the military and landowning classes. (pp. 64-5)

Campbell's defence of the rising against a freely elected government is typical of Nationalist propaganda. At times he states that the elections were not democratic, and that the Popular Front was not representative:

> The votes, as if Democracy to slight,
> And show its rusted workings to the sight,
> Seated the left, yet counted for the right—
> And this in spite of violated urns,
> Shots at the booths, and falsified returns.

His criticism of the elections does not rely solely on allegations of the unfairness of the electoral procedure, however. A sense of the futility of democracy with its ''rusted workings'' underlies the complaint about the undemocratic nature of the 1936 elections. This attitude, of the falsity of the whole democratic system, is that which Campbell offers most frequently in *Flowering Rifle* as the reason for flouting its workings to establish ''order'' and control. ''Devout'' ''style'' is continually contrasted with the materialist values of democracy. The following lines are typical, both in their lack of poetic distinction and in their evocation of the mystique of the ordered and the uniform:

> Whether it's guns to fire, or bricks to pile,
> Matter is always sensitive to style
> (Which is the breathing rhythm of the soul)
> And shows itself Devout from pole to pole:
> In storms and shocks it always looks for order
> The waves in uniform, with silver border,
> Still fight to keep in equidistant ranks
> As we against artillery and tanks:
> Happier still to worship than to grovel
> It shows in the Cathedral than the hovel,
> And there of centuries will take the polish
> Requiring tons of Nitre to demolish:

> But when democracy begins to soar
> To whom the jail, the brothel, and the store,
> Stand for the Church, and tries for like proportions
> Matter complies with sorrowful distortions.

In contrast with these ''sordid,'' ''outworn'' conditions in the democratic state, Campbell describes the mystique of his ideal state. It is that of the ''clean rejuvenated nation,'' led by one leader to a purer form of national existence which spurns the degrading influences of both capitalism and communism. The influence of the fascist views of José Antonio Primo de Rivera and his Falange are clearly noticeable in these passages, which show the chivalric and Catholic overtones that distinguish Spanish fascism of the period. The leader principle can appear to be simply part of Campbell's fervid belief in the generalship of the war:

> It was not ''liberty'' that thus could level
> Mankind in common bondage to the Devil
> Nor yours, kind Labour, was this ghastly birth
> Of squalor—though to camouflage the stain,
> Our intellectuals take your name in vain;
> Only where Franco rules you seem to shine
> Whose influence reaches to our foremost line.

A sneer at false beliefs in ''liberty,'' the compliment to ''kind Labour,'' and the insistence on efficiency, when coupled with an assertion of the ''shining'' rule of the leader, are too close to the official fascist line to be accidental. The number of semimessianic leaders in *Flowering Rifle* is surprising. Calvo Sotelo and Salazar are celebrated in much the same way as Franco and José Antonio Primo de Rivera, the founder of the Falange. In each case, however, the mystical qualities associated with the leader cult combine in Campbell's political apologies with the suggestion of the health and new life which they bring:

> Creative rhythm shuns their blistered hands
> And is a thing no Fiscal understands
> While style and unity and emulation
> Inform each clean rejuvenated Nation,
> Wherever there's a Leader to rebel
> Against the outworn socialistic Hell,
> And muzzle up the soul-destroying Lie
> Which Lenin was the first to Magnify.

The idea of a clean rejuvenated nation in which all sectors of the population benefit from the central ordering principle of the leader, and which becomes an organic entity, is essentially the aim of José Antonio Primo de Rivera's fascism. In 1933 he wrote: ''The country is a historical totality . . . superior to each of us and to our groups. The state is founded on two principles—service to the united nation and the co-operation of classes.'' In the next year his views showed even more of the mystical quality of the fascist dream: ''Fascism is a European inquietude. It is a way of knowing everything—history, the State, the achievement of the proletarianisation of public life, a new way of knowing the phenomena of our epoch. Fascism has already triumphed in some countries and in some, as in Germany, by the most irreproachable democratic means.'' Before the Asturias rising he had written to Franco offering support for a military *coup d'état* to restore the ''lost historical destiny of the country.'' Even after his arrest in 1936 José Antonio continued in the same vein, and in May wrote an open letter from prison to Spanish soldiers in which he called for assistance to protect ''the sacred identity of Spain,'' continuing, ''in the last resort,'' as Spengler puts it, ''it has always been a platoon of soldiers who have saved civilisation.''

Campbell's old devotion to what is heroic and distinguished in life modulates easily into political views of this sort:

> The racket of the Invert and the Jew
> Which is through art and science to subdue,
> Humiliate, and to a pulp reduce
> The Human Spirit for industrial use
> Whether by Capital or Communism
> It's all the same, despite their seeming schism,
> In that for human serfs they both require
> Limpness, servility and lack of fire.

The heroic ethic in Spanish nationalism is intimately connected with the desire to resurrect the greatness of ancient Spain, and in that way is also connected with the belief in the Catholic character of the race and the part religion played in its past grandeur. Campbell's Catholicism is central to his thinking from this period until his death and is not in any way a convenient political concept for him. Nevertheless, his religious beliefs become part of his concept of the politics of the ideal state. In particular, his belief in the unyielding militarism of his cause and its need for realistic and often self-sacrificing surgery is closely linked to the concept of a redemptive sacrifice:

> The Christ of Salamanca teaches this,
> The devil-routing Lord of the Abyss
> Who, till this time of men resigned and bold,
> Ignatius was the last man to behold—
> Since then, till now, men fought for greed or lust
> To seize the booty or to bite the dust,
> But the old world is "braver" than the "new,"
> Can use it as its foot-stool or its shoe:
> Or when it rots as it's begun to do,
> As a sharp knife can cut that Stilton through
> Cough though the scientist or squirm the Jew,
> Or stink, abjectly dead, the poets too.
> That God was never brilliantined or curled
> Who out of Chaos saw his battles won,
> And gave, like Moscardo, his only Son,
> To save the charred Alcazar of the world.
> For of all gods, he only breathed our breath
> To live the solar myths, and conquer death.

Christ is the "Christ of Salamanca," explicitly associated with a Spanish religious leader in the devil-routing of the unfaithful, and quite clearly "Lord of the Abyss." So close is the identification of politics with religion that even the central sacrificial experience of the Christian faith is presented in terms of the siege of the Alcazar. Colonel Moscardo, besieged in the Alcazar, made a telephonic farewell to his son whom the besiegers finally executed after failing in their attempt to blackmail the colonel into surrender.

A sense of Christ's being a military ally of the Nationalists is repeated throughout *Flowering Rifle*, though when describing Christian persecution Campbell prefers to picture a loving and harmless Church. In the poem Christ can be the sword, and Mary the shield. God's vengeance is not often tempered with mercy:

> And well may they abominate the Sword,
> The bared and naked vengeance of the Lord—
> And curse the Soldier, him, the human brand,
> That came to lop the sacrilegious Hand,
> And root the godless vermin from the land.

The obviously biased tone of the passages I have quoted is one of the worst features of *Flowering Rifle*. An approval of the slaughter of one's enemies not only creates a sense of one-sidedness, however. Stephen Spender, in reviewing the poem, declared that there were many passages in it which made him physically sick. In spite of its excesses, though, there are successful moments in *Flowering Rifle*. At times Campbell can articulate his scorn for Utopian dreams of social progress. His insistence on the abstract and theoretic nature of communism at the expense of the real is his most consistent and sensible criticism of his opponents. Much more moving, however, are those passages in which he writes subjectively or imaginatively. At such moments he rises above political harangue. Typical is the passage describing his own fear in Toledo during the first days of the war:

> Cut off from the Alcazar as we lay
> With nothing save to listen and to pray,
> To listen and to start at fancied sounds
> While the Infernal searchers went their
>   rounds,
> And life, a fly upon a rum-glass rim
> Was subject to the vilest drunkard's whim.
>   .   .   .
> Abomination flawless and profound,
> Loathing turned joy, as if some fearful tumour
> Could find expression in the realm of sound:
> Or be translated by a rabid hound,
> With hoary mane erect and foetid breath,
> Into a cry whose echo in the gloom
> Would jog with fear the very bones of death
> And bristle up the grass upon the tomb.

The genuine quality in the lines gives them a conviction which totally eludes the denunciatory passages.

Lines in which Campbell describes an experience directly are similarly convincing:

> Cooped in a trench, it was my chance to study,
> My neighbour for a day or two, a bloody
> Unburied arm, left lying in the snow
> Which melted now its attitude to show,
> Quite independent of its late discarder,
> Clenching its fist on Nothing, clenching harder
> Than to a stolen penny clings a child:
> But to the desert scene unreconciled
> That seemed so well to sympathize with it,
> With knuckles so inextricably knit,
> It seemed against the Universe to hit,
> As it would storm and hammer at the sun
> Knocking for entry till the world be done.

His unconcerned acceptance of the severed arm creates an air of objectivity. The value judgments which he goes on to make grow so easily out of the experience as a whole and are founded on such a clearly personal and articulate reaction towards the communistic clenched fist that their effectiveness is independent of politics:

> But here his fury is external yet
> In frozen paroxysm fixed and set
> Constricted on the Nothing in its hold
> A clenched fist that Nothing can unfold
> Nothing can satisfy, Nothing appease,
> Though in its grasp that zeroid treasure freeze

And there is Nothing more for it to seize—
All that it wished to leave of the crushed world,
Compassed, and in its grip of lock-jaw curled—
And yet with its contorted boomerang
Of hate, it seemed my vigil to harangue
And on my mind, as on its table, bang.

Real experience informs passages like this. They embody an attitude towards the war which transcends political loyalty, although growing out of Campbell's own political convictions. He can be humane at times like this in the midst of what is a terrifyingly inhumane poem.

Campbell re-aligned his loyalties, and Lewis published *The Hitler Cult* in the last year of the decade. In later years Wyndham Lewis readily admitted how mistaken he had been in his attitude towards the fascist dictators. In his autobiography, *Rude Assignment* (1950), he dismisses his polemical works of the mid-thirties as ill-judged and harmful. (pp. 68-73)

Campbell never officially altered his position on the Spanish Civil War. He stood by his earlier views until his death in 1957, and a revised version of *Flowering Rifle* was published in the same year. However, once he had decided to support Britain in the war against Hitler, he developed a new *persona* which helped him overcome embarrassment caused by his Spanish crusade. From 1942-4 he was an N.C.O. in the British army. He adopted the manner of the cynical, worldly-wise Sergeant who has no illusions about the politics of the cause for which he is fighting. As an "old sweat" he must make a personal stand against tyranny even though he knows that all wars are really only fought for the benefit of a few politicians. All politics are now nasty and treacherous. In this way he can continue to attack the literary Left and also abandon his own support for the dictatorial Right without appearing to contradict himself. (p. 74)

Both Campbell and Lewis were badly mistaken in their attitude towards the Axis in Spain. Their insistence that the pro-Republicans were deluded, however, has in many cases been borne out by those pro-Republicans themselves. Although scorned at the time, their repeated attacks on the totalitarian politics of the communists within the Republic have been substantiated by many of the old Left. The sympathy which Lewis and Campbell had for Franco, Hitler, and in Campbell's case even fascist theory, severely limit their insights into the failings of the Republic, however. It is the old idealists of the Left who give the most moving statements of the cynical exploitation of ideals which supporters of both sides only partly sensed during the war itself. The ex-Comintern agent, Arthur Koestler, with a humanity which eludes Campbell and Lewis, had the last word on the tragedy:

> All this we know today, but we did not know then. We know now that our truth was a half-truth, our fight a battle in the mist, and that those who suffered and died in it were pawns in a complicated game between the two totalitarian pretenders for world domination. But when the International Brigades saved Madrid on November 8, 1936, we all felt that they would go down in history as the defenders of Thermopylae did; and when the first Russian fighters appeared in the skies of battered Madrid, all of us who had lived through the agony of the defenceless town felt that they were the saviours of civilisation.

(pp. 74-5)

Rowland Smith, "The Spanish Civil War and the British Literary Right," in The Dalhousie Review, *Vol. 51, No. 1, Spring, 1971, pp. 60-76.*

MURRAY A. SPERBER

[*A Canadian-born American educator and critic, Sperber is the editor of* And I Remember Spain: A Spanish Civil War Anthology *(1974) and* Arthur Koestler: A Collection of Critical Essays *(1977). Of his literary philosophy, he has written: "In my writing and teaching, I attempt to persuade people that politics informs all of life, including literature and film, and that the serious question for the artist is not how to escape from politics (those who try to flee merely serve the regime in power) but how best to become aware of politics and how best to integrate this awareness into one's life and work." Arthur Koestler was a Hungarian-born English novelist, nonfiction writer, and journalist who worked as a freelance reporter and Communist Party propagandist during the war. In part as the result of his experiences in Spain, where he viewed firsthand the increasingly brutal and totalitarian methods of Stalinist communism, Koestler came to reject a personal and political philosophy based on communism in favor of one based on individualism. In the following excerpt, Sperber examines the development of Koestler's political ideology, personal philosophy, and literary artistry as reflected in his writings about the Spanish Civil War.*]

Of the extraordinary amount of literature that came out of the Spanish Civil War, Arthur Koestler's work is considered among the best, usually ranked with the personal narratives of Orwell and Bernanos and the fiction of Hemingway. (p. 109)

Koestler's versions of his Spanish Civil War experience . . . form a unique microcosm of a period—the most important literary period—of his life. In *L'Espagne*, essentially a Comintern propaganda book, replete with atrocity stories and horrifying photographs, he reveals his ambivalent and doomed infatuation with the Communist Party as well as his dependence upon Willy Muenzenberg, the Comintern's "Red Eminence" (Koestler's phrase). In the first half of *Spanish Testament*, on his own in England, he falls into various didactic styles: sometimes he is the echo of Comintern propaganda, often he quiets to passages of liberal reason, and frequently he turns Marxist analysis into apocalyptic vision. But in the second or "Dialogue with Death" half of the book, he allows his individualism to emerge. Then, in the separate *Dialogue with Death* edition of 1942, he drops the chapters of historical and political analysis, over 180 pages, and concentrates on his private adventures in Spain, especially in the prisons of Malaga and Seville. The three different but complementary texts form a kind of modern *Bildungsroman:* the hero's character emerges from the trials and temptations of politics to discover spiritual meaning and to be born anew. (p. 110)

L'Espagne ensanglantée (1937) is written in a hectic, scattered, at times almost bloodthirsty style. Koestler worked under the direction of Willy Muenzenberg, head of the Comintern's Paris propaganda office, and his writing reflects Muenzenberg's literary injunction: "Hit them! Hit them hard! . . . Make the world gasp with horror. Hammer it into their heads. Make them *wake up* . . . !" (*Invisible Writing*). To establish Koestler's credibility, an editorial note describes him as an "*Envoye special du News Chronicle, journal liberal de Londres.*" (Muenzenberg arranged this cover and throughout his trips to Spain, Koestler did send a number of dispatches to the *News Chronicle*.) In the opening chapters of *L'Espagne*, he tells of his journey into

Rebel territory in August, 1936. He reports on Fascist atrocities in Seville (most of these accounts were dropped for *Spanish Testament* and therefore, were probably untrue), he visits the headquarters of the mad Rebel general, Queipo de Llano. . . . He then leaves Spain.

His personal adventures are muted, and he focuses the narrative on the Nationalist campaign. He retails, at length, atrocity stories and he participates fully in the propaganda war of the time. Years later, he portrayed himself as almost innocent in the writing of *L'Espagne,* as if he were mainly Muenzenberg's amanuensis, but considering Koestler's talent for vivid prose, he was probably more than a passive copyist when the atrocity stories were ladled into the book.

Koestler never states his personal feelings in *L'Espagne* but he suggests his confusion and pessimism. He fears lying—and according to his later memoirs, he felt that his life in the Communist Party was mainly a lie. . . . (p. 111)

After finishing *L'Espagne,* possibly to break out of his psychological and, at times, financial, political, and literary dependence upon and frequent rejection by Willy Muenzenberg (Koestler had been with him on and off for four years), he embarked upon other missions to Spain. That his psychic situation was becoming intolerable and that he felt compelled to cut through it by an extreme and dangerous act is one explanation of why on February 9, 1937, after rejecting numerous opportunities to leave the doomed city of Malaga, Koestler allowed himself to be captured by Rebel troops.

It was the London *News Chronicle,* ironically, after a vigorous campaign protesting the arrest and imprisonment of an "English liberal journalist," who helped most to secure his release from Nationalist Spain. He spent ninety days in prison, first in Malaga and then in Seville, under sentence of death and with no idea of what was occurring on the outside. Suddenly he was released, taken to Gibraltar and then to England, when he found himself front page news.

Immediately, for the *News Chronicle,* he wrote a factual, journalistic account of his adventure. In the five articles (May 23 to May 28, 1937), he described his arrest and imprisonment, including drawings of his cell, but he hardly mentioned his psychological experiences. The very last line of the final article indicates his feelings at this time: "It is still like a dream . . ." (his ellipsis).

Koestler's situation in England in late May, 1937, was complicated: if he revealed that he was a Communist, he would embarrass the people who had helped to secure his release and justify "Franco's propaganda which took the line that all democratic opponents of his regime were disguised Reds" (*Invisible Writing*). He felt that he had to maintain "the fiction of the *bona fide* Liberal journalist" and "A deception, once started, has a compelling momentum of its own" (*ibid.*). But possibly the role of liberal journalist was less troubling than continuing membership in the Communist Party. England, with its tradition of individualism, allowed Koestler's individualism to flower. During his political career on the Continent from 1931 to 1937, he had never squared his individualism with the demands of Party discipline—it was this struggle that shaped his off-again-on-again participation in the Party—but once in England, he could free himself of the major deception of his life—his self-deception concerning CP membership. In England, he could be rewarded financially, socially, and psychologically for working out in print what he termed his "voyage of discovery" (*Spanish Testament*), and although under the restraint

of having to pose as a liberal journalist, he found that less confining than Willy Muenzenberg's Comintern tutelage.

After completing his series for the *News Chronicle,* Koestler was asked by Gollancz to do a book on his Spanish adventures. When he wrote *Spanish Testament* in the summer and fall of 1937, his sense of self was very much in transition and the book reflects the transition. In the first half of *Spanish Testament,* he unsuccessfully combines elements of the propagandist's contempt for his audience with the liberal journalist's sympathy for a like-minded, individualist reader. Only when he defines the line between himself and "English journalists in particular, with their traditional feelings for level-headedness and decency. . . . But a civil war is in itself a somewhat indecent affair," does he move toward his own voice (and his eventual role as exile and prophet within English life and letters). So much for the public side of liberal journalism, Koestler is after the private element, subjective truth, and when he seeks it in the second half of *Spanish Testament,* "Dialogue with Death," the propagandist gives way to the psychological pilgrim and the author produces a coherent narrative.

Unlike *L'Espagne ensanglantée,* Koestler begins *Spanish Testament* with a first-person narrator and he tells the story of his initial visit to and escape from Rebel Spain (a Nazi journalist in Seville recognized him and he had to flee). He saturates the narrative with atrocity stories and luridly describes his adventures: during his interview with Queipo de Llano, "Spittle oozed from the corners of the General's mouth, and there was [a] flickering glow in his eyes. . . ." After the opening narrative, he launches a "Historic Retrospect" section, five chapters, one hundred and eighty pages in all, much of it cribbed from *L'Espagne.* But the changes are significant: the argument has been smoothed out, charts put into words, and English references added. The entire first half of *Spanish Testament* suggests that Koestler had not resolved his confusion and ambivalence about Willy and the Party—he did not resign for another six months—but at the same time, he sought a way out of the tension that his past created.

One of his solutions, mainly unconscious, was to fasten upon the apocalyptic element in Marxism. In passages that could have roared from the author of *The Eighteenth Brumaire,* Koestler shows how he had internalized Marx's apocalyptic style. Frequently he calls for the total break from the past—"once and for all sweeping away the economic foundations of feudalism in Spain"—and he sees no easy or reformist way to "the new era"—history requires revolution and apocalypse and "The receipt for [Republican] tolerance was handed . . . by General Franco on July 18th, on the point of a bayonet."

He goes beyond Marxism, however, in his fascination for and portrayal of the apocalyptic. For the political role of the Catholic Church, he invokes the rich Medieval apocalyptic tradition: "Infuriated crowds made attacks on churches and monasteries; they had not forgotten that . . . the machine-guns of antichrist had been trained on them from the fortress-like sacred building of Spain." The Nationalist Rebellion becomes "that curious blend of poison gas and incense which is characteristic of Francisco Franco's modern crusade." And the Moorish troops are the agents of apocalypse, demonic hordes embarked on "the barbarians' crusade."

That the Spanish Civil War prompted these apocalyptic descriptions was as much a result of the actual historical situation as Koestler's personal need and desire to focus on this aspect of it. He was hardly alone in seeing the war as apocalyptic, but because he saw his life at this time as a series of catastrophes, he was attracted to the most catastrophic element in the Spanish War.

The apocalyptic mode, however, allowed him a way out of his personal dilemma. Too often in the first half of *Spanish Testament*, he loses control because he cannot construct a framework within which to resolve his political, psychological, and literary tensions. Instead he erects a centrifugal machine, throwing its elements from the center. Only when he connects his private fears to world destruction fantasies, describing personal experiences in apocalyptic terms, does he locate his authentic voice.

This occurs in the second half of the book, "Dialogue with Death." A key passage, identical in the 1937 and 1942 texts, describes his thoughts on the eve of the fall of Malaga, with an Italian Army outside the defenseless city. He begins with a solemn incantation of the date, this important day in the life of Malaga (and of Arthur Koestler because of his arrest): "On this Sunday night, the seventh of February, nineteen hundred and thirty-seven, a new St. Bartholomew's Night is being openly prepared." His biblical cadence and imagery turns "An army of foreign invaders . . . encamped beyond the hills, recouping its strength" into a demonic horde, and he builds on this when he announces that "to-morrow," they "will invade these streets and drench them in the blood of the people." He plays on the phrase, "the blood of the lamb," because the people are childlike and innocent and the invaders, characterized by the repeated "they," senselessly cruel: "whose [the people's] language they do not understand, with whom they have no quarrel, and of whose very existence they were yesterday as unaware as tomorrow they will be indifferent to their deaths."

There is no indication of this passage in the *News Chronicle* series. Later in "Dialogue," Koestler describes the Nationalist take-over of Malaga—the town was almost deserted, it proceeded smoothly, with hardly a shot fired—and thus he acknowledges that his "St. Bartholomew's Night" did not occur. But six months after the fall of Malaga, he wrote this passage for "Dialogue" and four years later he kept it in *Dialogue*. The apocalyptic mode must have seemed absolutely true to him, representative of his feelings at the time, and as with most writers who invoke the apocalypse, he transmutes the political and psychological experience that sparked his feelings into annunciatory terrors. The final line of the passage—"There is still perhaps time to get away"—shows the connection between his demonic horde on the other side of the hills and his own person. Koestler, in fact, did not try to get away.

In "Dialogue"/*Dialogue*, Koestler tells the story of his imprisonment and his discovery of self. He later said that this was part of "the most important period in my life, its spiritual crisis and turning point" but "the transformation . . . took some time [to] seep through and alter my conscious outlook" (*Invisible Writing*). The before-and-after Koestler exists particularly in the textual differences between "Dialogue" (1937) and *Dialogue* (1942).

In the Foreword to "Dialogue," Koestler refers to himself as "a writer" and "a journalist," but for the 1942 Foreword, he mentions "the first person singular" and his string of "I's" leads into the first-person narrative of the text (throughout *Spanish Testament*, he had moved fitfully from third to first person and back again).

The successive Forewords point to Koestler's emerging individualism, and every change in the text underlines his new sense of self, as author, subject, political man, and psychological phenomenon. In the first half of *Spanish Testament*, the liberal journalist alternated with the leftist ideologue; in the "Dialogue with Death" half, when he concentrates on his personal experiences, he begins to work out the authorial synthesis that he completes in *Dialogue:* the lone individual within an apocalyptic world. In his life, especially after he left the CP in 1938, he moved to increasing isolation, in his writing, to prophecy. (pp. 111-16)

The major differences between "Dialogue" and *Dialogue* are personal and literary. Again and again, he reworks a passage or changes a word or two to emphasize his authorial character and/or to produce a greater literary effect. No doubt he rewrote partly because of his increasing familiarity with the English language and his dissatisfaction with the original text, but in so doing he also indicates his growing sense of himself as a writer, even a literary artist.

He takes turgid "Dialogue" passages of hundreds of words and by eliminating the verbiage, and often the sloppy sentiments, turns them into vivid, concise paragraphs. When he adds to the text, he gives it greater rhetorical force. His narrative character is more carefully drawn and he is more honest about his emotions. As part of his description of his breakdown in Malaga on the eve of surrender, he adds the paragraph: "Nothing doing without alcohol. The pressure of outward events has to be balanced by a certain inward pressure; the brain remains lucid but stark reality is agreeably blunted. And one no longer minds."

On the formal literary level, the deletion or addition of words, Koestler seems quite conscious; but on the political and psychological levels—the meanings and implications of these changes—he appears much less aware. He can present some of his private feelings, as in the passage on alcohol, but he is still unable and/or unwilling to tell the whole story of his Spanish War experiences. *Dialogue* has a more polished surface than the earlier version but Koestler's unconscious projections still break through, usually in odd, code-like ways. In a passage added for *Dialogue*, he describes a zealous political commissar:

> He is twenty-five and has been a member of the Socialist Youth from the age of eighteen. He knows all about the situation, and he knows that I know all about it, and that to-morrow the entire world will know all about it even if I don't cable a word. But his grey matter, soaked with propaganda, is proof against all realization of the truth.

The biographical detail that the fellow has been in leftist party politics for seven years (the years 1930-1937) appears gratuitous until connected to Koestler's own years in the Party: "I served the Communist Party for seven years (1931-1938)." He seems both to identify with the young Spanish politico and be repulsed by him. Since he added this to his text after he had ended his CP years, the "he," the politico, can be translated as the old, CP Koestler, and the "I" as the newly isolated and aware author writing about the "soaked with propaganda" politico.

Usually the *Dialogue* revisions are more in control than in this passage. Sometimes the changes are subtle and reflect an impulse to try to reenter and recreate feelings, especially those of his prison experience, and by implication, to reject the earlier version as incomplete or inaccurate. In 1937, in his conclusion to "Dialogue," he cannot articulate what has happened to him and as the "St. Bartholemew Night's" passage showed, he found it easier to project apocalyptic feelings upon Malaga, even Spain itself, than to focus on the momentous changes in his own life:

> Still more often I dream that I must return to No. 41 [his Seville prison cell] because I have left something behind there. Something or other, I don't know what.
>
> What was it, what have I forgotten? I must go back once again and take a last look round before the steel door falls to: this time not before, but behind, me.

When he comes to rewrite this passage for *Dialogue,* he has a better sense of what has occurred:

> Still more often I dream that I must return to No. 41 because I have left something behind there. I think I know what this something is, but it would be too complicated to explain.

"Dialogue"/*Dialogue* ends with Koestler flying out of Nationalist Spain in a small, open plane. The movement of the plane and the spectacular sensation of clouds, earth, and sky are reminiscent of the final flight in Malraux's *Temps de Mépris* (there, too, the political prisoner is flown to his freedom amidst much overt symbolism). For *Dialogue,* Koestler adds the Epilogue statement:

> Those who survived are now pursuing their dialogues with death in the midst of the European Apocalypse, to which Spain had been the prelude.

Koestler later chose to bury the first half of *Spanish Testament* and to deny the nature of the "Dialogue" half. Unfortunately for *Dialogue with Death,* the first half of *Spanish Testament* supplies a rhetorical element necessary for the whole *Dialogue* experience. Although the historical background is often inaccurate and overstated, in *Spanish Testament,* unlike *Dialogue,* the main participant, Arthur Koestler, is placed within history. Even when he tries to objectively present the background, he is subjectively involved. He is a partisan, and he convinces us, rightly, that there is no shame in being on the side of the Spanish Republic.

Spanish Testament is also crucial to *Dialogue* because within the first half of the book, Koestler captures the apocalyptic climate of the Spanish Civil War. He portrays and participates in the level of feeling that can lead men to kill "Reds" or "Fascists," "Workers" or "Priests," simply because they can pin those labels on their victims. By conveying this passion in the first half of *Spanish Testament,* he helps explain how and why the Seville prison and its executions can operate in *Dialogue.* Without the passion of the first half of *Spanish Testament,* reading *Dialogue* is somewhat like coming in for the last act of a drama: the level of emotion seems inappropriate to what is happening on stage.

An example of this discrepancy occurs when he is arrested in Malaga:

> While we are crossing the forecourt an officer of the Phalanx [Falange] prodded me on the chest. "*Ruso, Ruso*—a Russian, a Russian!" he exclaimed in the excited voice of a child which, when taken to the zoo for the first time,

shouts: "A crocodile, a crocodile!" I said that I was not a Russian, but he wouldn't listen to me.

> "Tonight you'll be flying off to your Moscow Hell," he said with a grin.

Within the context of *Spanish Testament,* after the long discussions of propaganda, especially the virulence and power of Franco's anti-Communist campaign, the Falangist's reaction makes sense. Without the context, as in *Dialogue,* his actions seem at once comic and gratuitously sadistic.

When, in the truncated version, Koestler begins his *Dialogue with Death,* he sees it personally, with few political implications. By leaving out the first half of *Spanish Testament* and rewriting the "Dialogue" half, his perceptions about death often become small, ironic jests. With a coherent *Spanish Testament,* all parts of *Dialogue* would assume a larger dimension: the relationship of politics to a man's life and death. *Dialogue* is merely that—a dialogue between a single man and the peculiar forces of his possible death (a sudden, almost unexplained potentiality). *Spanish Testament* might have been that— a testament to a wider experience.

Koestler has told the story of his Spanish War experiences one other time. In *Invisible Writing,* 1954, he attempted to analyse his motives and actions during his visits to Spain and describe his mystical experiences in cell No. 41. In five chapters, sixty-two pages in all, with great intensity, he tries to reenter and relive his Spanish War experience. The result is a form of therapeutic catharsis, one to complete as well as articulate what had occurred during the original experience. At one point in *Invisible Writing,* after connecting a troubling and recurring dream to a prison incident, he says, "the feeling of guilt on this particular count began to dissolve, and I began to take a more detached view of the incident." The psychic relief that comes from telling his most private version of the experience also allows Koestler to see his writings on the war in a new way—but to the end, he confuses the "Dialogue" half of *Spanish Testament* with the *Dialogue* revision:

> *Dialogue with Death* is an autobiographical sketch written at the age of thirty-two; the present chapter is an "explanation" of the same events, written at the age of forty-seven. I wonder what shape and colour they would take if I were to re-write them after another fifteen years have elapsed. Yet in intent each of these versions represents the truth, based on first-hand knowledge of the events and intimate acquaintance with the hero.
>
> (*Invisible Writing*)

He reveals his dialectical sense here; rather than try to arrest time as he so frequently did in the earlier versions, he acknowledges its flux and even seems content to flow with it.

Because of such moments, as well as the intensity that drives him through his self-examination, Koestler's Spanish War writings form a series of remarkable documents. When the 1954 memoir was published, some critics compared it to Rousseau's *Confessions.* Koestler's work is far too flawed to achieve Rousseau's rank but his Spanish War writings are important and when considered together, they form a unique record of a man's personal, political, and literary odyssey.

Writing was so integral to the experience that the works map the journey: from Communist Party propagandist and Willy

Muenzenberg's agent in *L'Espagne ensanglantée,* through the *News Chronicle* and *Spanish Testament* contradiction of liberal journalist and leftist ideologue, to Arthur Koestler, individual hero and prophetic figure in "Dialogue with Death" and especially its revision, *Dialogue with Death,* and finally, the self-analyst and mystic of *The Invisible Writing.* In their contradictions, unevenness and brilliance, Koestler's Spanish War writings reaffirm Isaac Rosenfeld's judgment that "it is precisely his limitations, by which he reflects his age, that give his utterances their authenticity for the age." (pp. 116-21)

> *Murray A. Sperber, "Looking Back on Koestler's Spanish War," in* Arthur Koestler: A Collection of Critical Essays, *edited by Murray A. Sperber, Prentice-Hall, Inc., 1977, pp. 109-21.*

FRENCH LITERATURE ABOUT THE WAR

CECIL JENKINS

[*The most renowned French work about the Spanish Civil War is André Malraux's novel* L'Espoir. *In the following excerpt, Jenkins analyzes prominent themes and techniques in the novel.*]

For Malraux himself, as for many of his admirers, *L'Espoir* remains his greatest achievement. However, certain of his critics have been embarrassed by what they have felt to be journalistic or propagandist elements in the novel, and have sometimes drawn rather purist distinctions between art and history, as between art and moral or political commitment. Yet the novel has never been a highly specific or "autonomous" form, it has frequently treated historical or political conflict, and it has certainly never excluded a moral viewpoint on the part of the author; some of the arguments advanced against *L'Espoir,* indeed, could be used against most of the great nineteenth-century novelists. (p. 87)

Malraux, in fact, was too ambitious a writer and had too high a view of himself as an artist to wish to write propaganda. He wished rather to pursue the attempt to establish his own myth of "quality" and "fraternity" and, since the acid test of a myth of this kind is its applicability to historical reality, the Spanish Civil War offered a peculiar challenge: a field of application at once promising and daunting. That he was focusing on one side in a historical conflict would not in itself have troubled him. Many great writers before him had done so, if only for reasons of manageability and clarity of viewpoint, and had still achieved universality to the extent that their work depended, not upon political particulars, but upon human values large enough to be inclusive of the other side. Malraux could not believe that his own universals of justice, brotherhood and human quality were inadequate, and he could in fact see beyond the battle to the tragedy of human strife itself.

However, there were special problems to the writing of *L'Espoir,* of course, and he was aware of them.

The first problem, which has some bearing on the charge that he was using "journalistic" material, was that he was writing about a violently contentious and highly symbolical historical conflict while it was actually going on. In practice, this meant that he could only impose his myth insofar as he was seen to respect the sheer size and diversity of a most complex situation—and insofar as he nevertheless imposed artistic unity upon his presentation of these first nine months of the war up to

March 1937. Now at the simple documentary level *L'Espoir* is still to be regarded as one of the most valuable accounts of the war. But the novel could only reasonably be called "journalistic" either if it were badly written, whereas it is generally brilliantly written, or if the historical detail were gratuitous in the sense that it was not subordinated to the overall artistic purpose. Yet Malraux surely maintains an almost astonishing thematic and artistic control over his material in *L'Espoir.* Nor is it reasonable, for example, to suggest that his account of the bombing of Madrid "dates" in that there was much more elaborate bombing of civilians in World War II. What then should we say of the historical content of the novels of Balzac or Tolstoy?

The second problem was of a moral and political kind. Those critics who see a propagandist intention in the work tend curiously to take Malraux's own distinction between "being" and "doing"—between the high aspirations informing a cause on the one hand, and the discipline, energy, and compromises needed to win a war on the other—in order to suggest that politically he falls clearly on the side of the latter. The irony of this is that it seems to get Malraux's own problem upside down. He himself, in almost obsessional fashion, sees the opposition between "being" and "doing" as a tragic one, and this tragedy is in the thematic sense the very subject of the novel. It is represented and debated, often in anguished terms, from beginning to end and Malraux, not being a propagandist, does not conclude. He was not after all dealing with some sort of private moral distinction, but with one of the great hard acts of historical life: that men fighting in the name of freedom may have to accept the hierarchized discipline of an army, may consider it necessary to bomb Dresden or obliterate Nagasaki—with the fact that, as one of his spokesmen says in the novel, there may be just causes but war itself can never be just. And by March 1937, that fact was already making itself felt in Spain. (pp. 87-9)

In seeking to turn immediate history into art without simplifying abusively or descending to propaganda, . . . Malraux was not only taking on a formidable descriptive and intellectual task. Given the passions which the war aroused, he was setting out to walk a tightrope. My own feeling is that, apart from minor uncertainties in the portrait of the character Manuel, he hardly ever, in the course of this very long novel tossed off in eight months, looks like putting a foot wrong. Richly human and glittering with talent as it is, this is surely one of the great political novels of the century. What is striking about the book, and what justifies its frequent lyricism, is the way in which it combines emotional involvement and analytical intelligence with an extraordinary detachment; almost every major character is not only troubled by the problem of ends and means but is stopped in his tracks, at one moment or another, by a sharp sense of the smallness and apparent gratuitousness of all human effort in the light of the indifference of the physical world and of eternity. "There is in this book," wrote Ramon Fernandez, "a desire to win and yet a subtle dislike of winning which for me constitutes its principal beauty." It is a measure of the literary distinction of the novel that it establishes the war in Spain not just as a battle or a political equation, but as a poignant human mystery. (pp. 89-90)

The first general impression one receives from *L'Espoir* is that Malraux has found a subject which has in some sense set him free: at once broadened his range of awareness and sympathy and unleashed the whole range of his literary skills. (p. 91)

This new freedom and this epic sweep are, of course, seen in the very structure of the novel. Part One, *L'Illusion lyrique,* which takes up about half of the work, ranges in a series of quickly alternating scenes from events surrounding the Franquist rebellion of July 18 in Madrid and in Barcelona, through the military action of the young Communist Manuel in the Sierra and the activities of Magnin's International Air Squadron outside Madrid and at Medellin, to the drama of the besieged Alcazar at Toledo and the loss of the city by the badly disorganized Republicans at the end of September—before settling on the personal tragedy of the Republican officer Hernandez. Part Two, also lengthy and named after the river Manzanares, covers the period from the start of November to early December, maintaining the interest in the Air Squadron and in the military situation of the International Brigades, but concentrating essentially on the defense of Madrid, before settling on the personal dilemma of Manuel. The much shorter Part Three, entitled *L'Espoir,* runs from February 8 to the latter part of March 1937, and includes the confused exodus from Málaga and scenes from the battles of the Jarama and Guadalajara, as well as the famous descent-from-the-mountain episode. However, this can convey only the broadest idea of the confident ease with which Malraux switches from one part of Spain to the other, and from one to another of a formidably large cast of characters.

The principle governing his technique is one of flexible juxtaposition: of locale with locale, and of action scene with meditative passage or conversation piece. He seems, one might almost say, to combine the advantages of the novel, the film and the play of ideas. Yet it is perhaps of the cinema that his art is most suggestive. His "scenes" tend to be stylized and finished units in themselves, within which he moves fluently from the panoramic to the closeup, often completing his fadeout interrogatively with a telling symbolical shot; the juxtaposition or "editing" of these scenes itself largely provides narrative perspective and continuity. His virtuosity is also seen in the skill with which he handles different levels of language, varied styles of conversation and gesture, and quite diverse types of action. Whether the immediate background is Toledo or a small village, whether he is describing a bombing raid, a tank attack, or an execution, he always seems to be able to provide the authentic detail—and the authentic oddity of incidental detail—which will establish the reality at once of the scene and of the character involved.

However, his narrative control is not simply a function of rhythm or of cinematic editing. For all the diversity of the scenes, we are concerned in the main with only two or three major centers of developing interest. And though he also contrives quite plausibly at certain moments to bring his major characters together, it is essentially in relation to their particular area of interest that he establishes each—providing each with foils and with such satellite or minor characters as need to be knitted successfully into the fabric of so ambitious and complex a work.

Thus the military aspect constantly involves the rising young Communist Manuel, with the Catholic Colonel Ximénès as foil, and such other significant figures as Heinrich. The Anarchist aspect introduces us to Puig, the Negus, and various spectacular minor figures. The aviation aspect centers upon the mustached French commander Magnin, but also involves the young Italian art historian Scali, and partly thereby the old sage Alvear. A special role is played by Garcia, anthropologist turned Intelligence chief, who is well placed to act as focus for discussion of the political and moral issues involved. Yet if Garcia is not unlike Malraux by dint of his turn of speech and formidable analytical power, Magnin—though Malraux has completely distanced him as to age and physique to obviate comparison with himself—perhaps remains closer to his creator by his deeper will to fraternity.

Beyond the structural control obtained through the exercise of this general relating principle, and quite apart from the intelligence and concern with which he isolates the central moral problem from a complex political situation, Malraux seems to possess his situation both in depth and in breadth. In depth, insofar as he can see the civil war in terms of Spanish history: the fresh ruins as a stage in a series going back to Christian, Roman, or Punic ruins. Not only has he the visual gift of rendering the Spanish light, the colors of a landscape or village rooftops, a detail of a building in Toledo or Madrid; he has the culture required to convey the agony of an Unamuno, or to set the present against the background of the country of El Greco, of Spanish Christendom, of the whole history of human effort in the peninsula. In breadth, he controls the situation by seeing it firmly in its international context. He points to the irony that Hitler's Junkers bombers were not quite the menace that the democracies had feared, or to the irony of Italian volunteers fighting Mussolini's Italians at Guadalajara. He already sees that the "Age of Fire" has begun with the bombing of Madrid, that all this is really the beginning of World War II, and that it will not be long before Japan itself "joins in the dance." He establishes the conflict as having worldwide symbolic importance.

It is by this multiple grid that Malraux orders his material and gives his novel relevance and resonance. Yet all this is governed by an ultimate control of a different and more fundamental kind, which everywhere informs the new richness of imagery and symbolic reference which has often been noted in *L'Espoir.*

Underlying the allusions to history or music or painting, the imagery of light and shade, or sun and snow, or sound and silence, there is again a constant principle of juxtaposition. The opposition may be ironic or absurd, comic or tragic: a barricade made up of confessionals, people undressed but otherwise unharmed by an explosion, a butterfly on a dead man's face, stuffed bears trembling in an air raid, a battle outside a sunlit cemetery, birds passing on their annual migration in the course of an air action. It comes out forcefully in the references to the carnival, the fairground, or the film set: militiamen, dressed in a style veering grotesquely between that of the Mexican revolutionaries and that of the Paris Communards of 1871, seen against the up-to-date Le Corbusier buildings of the airport; or homeless children seeking refuge beneath giant Disneyland figures during an air raid. It everywhere expresses the new kind of ultimate polarity which goes with the epic vision in *L'Espoir:* the constant opposition of illusion and reality, of the moment and the infinite, of the passionate "madness of men" and the idle indifference of sun-drenched cemetery, or shimmering plain, or evening red over snowy mountains.

The great paradox of *L'Espoir,* which takes it far above any vulgar propaganda, is seen in the new "cosmic" tone informing the meditative rhythms of the style itself. The typical ascending movement of the sentence is from the particular, through the collective, toward the eternal. "Everything seems to lead Malraux to turn his eyes towards the sky," as Girard puts it, "and night itself in *L'Espoir* seems to rise rather than fall." Strangely but logically, the very discovery of fraternity leads beyond fraternity. The Malraux hero escapes from his dark prison of solitude and anguish and, for the first time, sees the world beyond himself clearly. But now that the cosmos is no longer felt as the oppressive weight of night, it comes to be felt as something more mysterious still, and more daunting: as the ultimate indifference of daylight.

"The sun shone brightly upon the prostrate bodies and upon the blood": this short sentence, in the midst of a battle scene, is printed as a complete paragraph. The very reality of fraternity makes the human adventure seem stranger than ever, and raises the problem of "quality" to the highest metaphysical level. In the following very typical sentence we already see Malraux moving toward the later, reflective style of *Les Noyers de l'Altenburg* and *Les Voix du silence:* "Turning like some tiny planet lost amid the indifferent gravitation of astral bodies, the airplane waited for Toledo to pass beneath it, with its rebellious Alcazar and its besiegers alike swept along in the absurd rhythm of earthly things."

Malraux, on the ground, has discovered the reality of fraternity. Malraux, in his airplane, has risen far above the battle and discovered what he calls "geological indifference," or "geological serenity."

Malraux's opposition between "being" and "doing"—*Etre et faire* is the title of the first of the two sections in Part Two—has sometimes been taken as indicative that there are only two basic attitudes in the novel, and that he himself hovers uneasily between them. The truth is far from being so simple. There are, in fact, four basic attitudes in the novel and it is from the interplay between them, as well as from the formal or poetic persuasion of the work, that the final balance and meaning emerge.

At the immediate level, *être et faire* translates the broad opposition between Anarchists and Communists. As Garcia sees it, the Communists want to make something, whereas the Anarchists and such simply generous men as the officer Hernandez want to *be* something. The drama of their revolutionary situation is that they have to live according to conflicting myths: pacifism *versus* self-defense, the need to organize *versus* the Christian virtue of meekness, effectiveness in war *versus* justice. "We have to bring some order into these myths and transform our Apocalypse into an army, or die," he says. "There are no two ways about it."

The beginning of the war is the heyday of the Anarchists, the new dawn which Malraux, though he was temperamentally far closer to the Anarchists than to the Communists, calls the "lyrical illusion." Men who feel that they have been oppressed and humiliated for centuries, and with a romantic history of defeats behind them, come face to face with this sudden, miraculous "carnival of freedom" and want to see their individualist ethic realized at once: "to live," as the Negus declares, "as life ought to be lived, here and now, or die." The trouble, in Garcia's view, is that since this is not a peasant uprising but war against a mechanized modern army, their living may indeed turn out to be dying—and that these "semi-Christians," with their romantic taste for self-sacrifice, may settle for martyrdom all too easily. Like Puig, indeed, in an early scene, they tend to die heroically, but too soon. In their will to brotherhood and freedom and a certain personal nobility, they may incarnate for Garcia or for Malraux the deepest impulse underlying the cause, but it is not they who have the discipline necessary to forge the army that achieves the holding victory with which the novel ends. It is the Communists.

French novelist André Malraux.

To the Communists, the Apocalypse is necessarily provisional, an initial stage in the task of social construction. They tend realistically to be concerned not with the absolute but with the relative, less with nobility than with winning the war. "In the last analysis," says Pradas, "nobility is a luxury which a society can only afford at a late stage of development." For the Negus, who wants "to make neither a state nor a church nor an army, but men," the Communists have turned a cause into a party or yet another church. He sees them as corroded by discipline and the complicity of partisanship, while Magnin and Hernandez also discover that the Communists will put party before individuals or justice. For Garcia, who cannot accept what he sees as the denial of subjectivity and individuality implicit in the "objective" ethic of the Communists, they "have all the virtues of action, and those alone—but action is what is needed at this time."

The tragic nature, for Malraux, of this broad opposition in the initial stage of the conflict becomes clear. The Anarchists incarnate the profounder aspiration to fraternity and "quality," but are too romantically absolutist to adjust to the challenge of modern war. The Communists, with their rigorous relativism, their belief in the historical process and their equal courage, can certainly adjust to this challenge; but is there not the danger that their tough objectivism and exclusivism, together with the destructive nature of war itself, may drain the cause of its human meaning in the process?

Since the whole effort of the novel is to transcend the tragic dilemma implicit in *être et faire*, the center of gravity of *L'Espoir* is firmly placed outside this historical opposition between Anarchists and Communists. It is true that the logic of the developing military situation obliges Malraux to set up Manuel—who plays broadly the same role as the historical Lister, commander of the Communist Fifth Regiment—as being in a technical or formal sense the central figure of the novel. However, he possesses neither the importance nor the authority given to Garcia and he is presented, in opposition to such men as Enrique or Heinrich, as being a sensitive, intelligent young Communist who is tormented by the conflict between humanity and the cruel necessities of command. He feels that he is becoming "a little less human every day," and that "to be close to the Party is valueless if it means being separated from those for whom the Party is working." The military situation gives a certain tragic necessity to his loneliness, but his awareness of the fragility of his "terrible equilibrium" enables Malraux discreetly to "save" him from the party on the last page. Positively, therefore, as well as antithetically, he gravitates toward the group of characters who represent the third—and central—basic attitude in the novel.

Garcia, Magnin, Scali and such figures as Guernico and Ximénès, two Catholics who see themselves as fighting for Christ against both Franco and the Church of Spain, form a much more homogeneous group than might at first appear. Between them these men, non-Communist and intelligent as they are, constantly maintain Malraux's preoccupation with the quality of man, the idea of the role of the intellectual as custodian of human values, and the idea of the *difficulty* of being a man. Their political program proper is modestly stated: they want to improve the economic lot of the poor and to create a climate of justice and fellowship within which individuals may flourish freely. If the climate of fraternity is so important for them, it is because they see it as the condition of obtaining quality for the individual. They are fully aware of the opposition between "being" and "doing," or ethics and political action, but they also recognize the need to act in terms of this very reality. They are trying, in a word, to transcend the opposition and to act in such a way that *faire* expresses at least the direction of *être*.

In an important conversation with Scali, Garcia puts this view very forcefully. The war, he says, is a fact. The revolution through which they are living exists not as a solution to personal problems but as a historical reality. They are agreed as to the necessity of resisting fascism and are thus committed to winning the war. Even if there is the risk that a Communist victory may liberate the peasants economically only to enslave them politically, as Scali suggests, they are still forced at the immediate level to choose between the risks of action and . . . inaction. The choice is tragic, and action necessarily unjust, but they are placed in the midst of war and the good to which they aspire cannot be achieved through passivity. For an intellectual to say that he is leaving their cause because they are unjust is *immoral*, he says, for no party can be just. There can never be more than a *policy* of justice. That policy is theirs and it is up to them, by making their presence felt, to see to it that quality and freedom are maintained in Spain.

So central is this group that it is essentially among its members that the moral debate is conducted, and indeed a certain difference between Garcia and Magnin is important in the final balance of the novel. The three parts of the work are really three tiers of fictional persuasion in the service of an overall "argument." Part One presents "being" and "doing" as an *option* imposed by the Republican confusion which leads to the loss of Toledo. The tragedy of Hernandez, who morally commits suicide insofar as he does not seize the chance of escaping, does not lie simply in the world's denial of his generosity to the commander of the Alcazar—he tells his inter-

rogator that he might not be so generous the next time. It lies rather in his inability to live with the hard *fact* of the conflict between "being" and "doing." Part Two takes the problem a stage further, beyond the antinomic to the correlative—the title of the first section is *Etre et faire*, that is *"and"* rather than *"or."* Malraux indeed opens this section with several strong scenes showing a successful combination of "being" and "doing," emphasizing that "for the first time there was a fraternity which took the form of action." However, the graph of this part is similar to that of the first in that we end with the drama of Manuel, driven grievously to "choose between victory and pity" in dealing with deserters: a drama which is none the less real for being as it were the mirror image of that of Hernandez.

The "hope" which gives the title to Part Three does not lie simply in the military success after the defense of Madrid, but in Magnin's sense that it may be possible to cope with this contradiction more successfully than Hernandez or Manuel. To reinforce this "hope," Malraux holds back in time his "descent from the mountain" scene—which had historically taken place in December—and gives it climactic poetic force. It is because he has been so deeply moved by this experience that Magnin can come to feel that Garcia is not the ultimate oracle. Garcia declares in the last scene but one that "the age of Parties" is at hand—and, as Camus and others were to verify much later, this statement was prophetic enough. Yet Magnin has witnessed the simple, fundamental solidarity of the peasants on the mountainside, and can see obscurely in this a guarantee that fraternity is a reality which must finally prevail. Even so, the conclusion remains an open-ended and fragile one insofar as these men are uncertain about the outcome and constantly uneasy about the morally damaging effect of war itself.

This leads us finally toward the fourth basic attitude in the novel, represented by the very presence of the old sage Alvear and implicit in the "cosmic tone" in the writing itself. The authority of Alvear—as Malraux's friend André Gide at once recognized—lies in the fact that he states the idea of "quality" in terms of Malraux's long-standing obsession with the need for an "age of the fundamental" which will found Man and reason afresh. For him the Revolution is just another version of the old illusion of eternal life, a blind man's song of hope. His remarks linger on through the complex and delicate counterpoint through which Malraux builds up the final, mysterious meaning of his title. At the moral and political level of this moving and profoundly liberal novel he achieves a kind of positive equilibrium, but it is a difficult one, a fragile one, and a directly threatened one. And Alvear, with his reminder that there is "a deep and terrible hope in man" to which there can be no political answer, leaves it edged with black.

In the uneasy Europe of the eve of World War II, *L'Espoir* did not purvey a packaged political answer: far from it. It indicated hesitantly a difficult, if necessary moral direction, and asked some ultimate questions. (pp. 92-101)

Cecil Jenkins, "Brotherhood—and Beyond: 'L'Espoir'," in his André Malraux, *Twayne Publishers, Inc., 1972, pp. 87-102.*

SPANISH LITERATURE ABOUT THE WAR

JANET W. DIAZ

[*In the following excerpt, Diaz examines the treatment of the Civil War and postwar exile in the works of Spanish novelists Max Aub, Francisco Ayala, and Ramón J. Sender.*]

With the death of Francisco Franco, the long exile of the Spanish Republicans may be considered "officially" at an end, though no single termination date can be established. For Arturo Barea, Luis Cernuda, León Felipe (Camino Galicia), Juan Ramón Jiménez, Pedro Salinas and others, death in alien lands during the fifties and sixties ended hopes of return. Others, among them Ramón Pérez de Ayala, Alejandro Casona, Concha Castroviejo, Rosa Chacel, and Ramón Gómez de la Serna returned to Spain, some to die shortly and only Rosa Chacel to resume significant production upon reintegration to the mainland cultural panorama. Spain's outstanding novelists in exile, Max Aub, Francisco Ayala and Ramón J. Sender saw their return delayed still longer. None of these reestablished himself definitely in the peninsula, despite repeated visits by all three during the [1970s]. (p. 207)

Depending upon critical preferences, Aub, Ayala and Sender each have claims to consideration as Spain's leading post-war novelists. It is not the purpose of this essay to establish an order of relative importance either between them or with respect to counterparts in the peninsula. It may be affirmed with little fear of authoritative contradiction that Aub, Ayala and Sender compare favorably with writers who have emerged in Spain since 1939: Cela, Delibes, Matute, Goytisolo and many others. Relative merits aside, significant differences exist, some attributable to the fact of exile. The most obvious divergences are thematic; others are linguistic and stylistic.

On the thematic level, treatment of the Civil War from a Republican perspective is the province of exiles for many years, as is the theme of exile itself. Conversely, exile writings do not reflect Spain's post-war reality, given the lack of personal contact with conditions inside the national borders, but tend to nostalgic recreation of pre-war situations and events, or inquiry into the historical origins of the conflict. (pp. 207-08)

Aub, Ayala and Sender are unquestionably "exile" writers by any recognized definition, and despite differing socio-economic backgrounds and political ideologies, all were sufficiently identified with the Republic that remaining in Spain would have meant arrest, imprisonment and probable death. All were nationally recognized in Spain before exile; obliged to forge new careers elsewhere, they did so with commendable success. An overview of their lives and works before and during exile will clarify differences which may be attributable to the exile experience and provide a frame of reference for their writings relevant to the war and the theme of exile. (p. 210)

During the war, Aub was director of an important daily newspaper, Cultural Attaché of the Spanish Embassy in Paris, and Secretary General of the National Theatre Council. He collaborated (1938) with his friend André Malraux on the movie, *Sierra de Teruel*, based on *L'Espoir* (*Days of Hope*). With the Republican defeat in 1939, he joined the exodus to France where he was interned in a succession of concentration camps, witnessed the French defeat of 1940 and was moved from prisons in Marseilles and Nice to the nightmarish camp at Djelfa in the Algerian desert where he spent two years and wrote his poems, *Diario de Djelfa*. In September of 1942, he managed to escape, embarking in Casablanca for Veracruz. He arrived in Mexico a fugitive with little more than notebooks containing some manuscripts and outlines of projected writings. (p. 211)

The theme of civil war per se is pre-eminent in Aub's extensive production after 1936; even novels such as *La calle de Valverde* [*Valverde Street*] (dealing with the intellectual, artistic and moral climate of Madrid before the war) attempt to analyze

underlying causes of the conflict. The original plan for a cycle of five interrelated war novels under the common title of *El laberinto mágico* was amplified over some thirty years to include six long novels and a series of shorter narratives reflecting not only the war but years of exile. *Campo cerrado* [*Closed Field*] was described by Aub (in the third of his prefatory notes) as a "gallery" of characters historical and invented. An introduction both to the civil conflict and the novelistic cycle, *Campo cerrado* presents many characters who reappear in subsequent novels, and sketches the environment of Levantine villages, the socio-political climate of Barcelona's Anarchist proletariat neighborhoods, as well as a view of preparation for the Nationalist revolt in Barcelona.

Campo abierto (*Open Field*) was written some years after the third novel (*Campo de sangre* [*Bloody Field*]) but precedes it in the overall scheme. As the second of the novels in the cycle of *El laberinto mágico*, *Campo abierto* is divided, like its predecessor, in three parts: the beginnings of war and revolution in Valencia, a view of the Nationalist (Franco) zone in Burgos, and a summary of events of the first week of November in Madrid when the victorious advance of Franco's troops was temporarily halted. The prominence given theatrical activity in Valencia reflects Aub's own involvement. Another important theme (reiterated throughout the cycle) is the conflict between party discipline or political ideology and family ties or personal sentiment. There is no unity of plot, no protagonist in the traditional sense, in any of the three initial novels of the cycle; all three are collections of anecdotes, largely historical, portraying heroism and opportunism, personal tragedy and dissension within families, instant fortunes and economic ruin, political imprisonment and death, and the loves and betrayals engendered by war.

Campo de sangre reflects the tripartite division of the two preceding novels, with its first part presenting the situation in Barcelona on December 31, 1937. It focuses on executions in the Castle of Montjuich, with flashbacks to the past of three of those shot. The second part begins with the taking of Teruel by Republican forces and retrospectively recreates the life of Julián Templado (mouthpiece of the author). The third, in Barcelona some six weeks later, continues previously initiated episodes of amorous and political intrigue. Several pieces of short fiction—notably "El Cojo," "Una canción," "Cota," "La espera," "Santander y Gijón," "La ley," and "Un asturiano"—also belong chronologically to the early war years in their portrayal of events in the rear guard and on the battlefront.

By late 1938, the tide of war had clearly turned against the Loyalists, and Aub's account of 1938 and 1939 is correspondingly more somber. "Enero sin nombre" relates the evacuation of Cataluña following the Republican military collapse, and three novels of the *Laberinto* series also obsessively recreate this period. *Campo francés* (*French Field*) portrays the northward exodus of refugees, while *Campo del Moro* (*The Moor's Field*) recounts Coronel Casado's coup and the final days of the Republic in Madrid. *Campo de los almendros* (*Field of Almond Trees*) offers a nightmarish reconstruction of scenes in the port of Alicante as desperate hordes of troops and civilian refugees awaited ships which hopefully would carry them to freedom in exile, only to be trapped by the Nationalists and herded into concentration camps. A number of critics have commented upon Aub's seemingly excessive preoccupation with the final moments of the war (of little military significance) as compared with the lesser attention paid to more decisive episodes of the conflict. These observations overlook the fact that the narratives of the war's end also retell the exodus and the beginning of exile, probably of equal or greater import than military strategy for those who experienced them. Aub's drama, *Morir por cerrar los ojos* (*To Die in Order to Close the Eyes*) and several pieces of brief fiction are also related to the war's end and exile's beginning. Presentation of the exodus to France has a largely autobiographical basis, as do descriptions of concentration camps in the south of that country and in Algiers, and subsequent portrayals of the life of exiles in Mexico.

Campo francés . . . is something of a hybrid, with elements both of the novel and the cinema. Essentially a personal memoir of exile (the novelist states that only the three central characters are fictitious), it contains an impassioned indictment of French indifference to the plight of Spanish refugees, condemnation of what is seen as cynically brutal repression and a portrait of the government of Leon Blum as tacitly condoning this mistreatment. Several stories in *Cuentos ciertos* (*Stories That Did Happen*), and *Sala de espera* (*Waiting Room*) describe life in the North African prison camp of Djelfa, largely from Aub's own experience.

Works composed after 1944 reflect in increasing measure the life and influence of Aub's "homeland in exile," Mexico. With the fading hopes of return, an increasingly ironic tone invades his considerations of Spain. . . . Stories inspired by the life of Spanish exiles in Mexico include three in the collection, *La verdadera historia de la muerte de Francisco Franco y otros cuentos* (*The True Story of the Death of Francisco Franco and Other Tales*). The title tale and "La merced" (of which the former is a longer version) deal with the unreal quality of life of those exiles who continue to live in the past, clinging to hopes of the overthrow of Franco and refusing to see the changes wrought by time in themselves and in the Spain they nostalgically evoke. (pp. 212-15)

At the outbreak of the Civil War, Ayala was on a lecture tour in Argentina; with the fall of the Republican government (which he had served in several diplomatic posts), he chose exile in that country where he remained from 1939 to 1950, teaching sociology, translating and publishing a number of works of non-fiction. He then went to Puerto Rico and later to the United States, teaching in the universities of Chicago and New York.

Ayala's early vanguardist work differs markedly (as does Aub's) from his later publications. Beginning with *El hechizado* or "The Bewitched," which appeared after nearly a decade without fiction, there is a complete break with the pre-war style and a notable increment in the use of irony and satire. Two collections of brief fiction published in 1949, *Los usurpadores* (*The Usurpers*) and *La cabeza del cordero* (*The Lamb's Head*) have become contemporary classics. The unifying theme of the stories of *Los usurpadores* (set in many different moments of history) is man's desire for power and the "usurpation" or abuse thereof, with the resultant suffering. The four short novels of *La cabeza del cordero* treat a single central theme: alienation resulting from the crisis of the Spanish Civil War. The war is scarcely considered in its military aspects; Ayala's emphasis is upon the deterioration of interpersonal relationships and the effects of the conflict upon human emotion, war's tension which makes small differences insuperable, leading to intransigence and hostility. As elsewhere, Ayala is less interested in specific political ideology than in a search for the eternal causes of war and human conflict. His stated goal in writing of the Civil War is to present it in the guise of the human passions which nurtured it.

"La vida por la opinión," a story which Ayala has appended to later editions of *La cabeza del cordero,* presents two histories of "inner emigration" ending in exile, narrated by refugees (themselves the protagonists of their respective tales) to a third Spanish exile in Rio de Janeiro in 1945. Ayala spent that year in Rio, and it is not unreasonable to assume an identity between him and the Spanish exile who listens to and retells the stories in question, each the recounting of nine years of terror and fading hope that the Franco regime would topple, followed by identical decisions to leave the country. The first case is that of a man who assumed a false identity and moved frequently from one place to another, always living badly and believing himself pursued; the second literally buries himself alive in a hole beneath the floor of his mother's house, where he takes refuge from the onset of the war, as many similarly concealed themselves at the close of the conflict. The thematic nucleus of the tale is the fading hopes of all three for any possibility of return to democratic government in Spain. (pp. 216-17)

Ayala's focus upon both war and exile is more generic and universal, less personal and impassioned than Aub's, and his observations of the host countries contain less of the picturesque and folkloric, more of the urban, contemporary and collective (betraying the eye of the trained sociologist as opposed to that of the well-traveled layman). In his philosophical orientation, Ayala is closer to Sender, but more intellectual and abstract. A second factor approximating Sender and Ayala, not present in Aub, is the reflection in the works of each of long-time residence in the United States. (p. 219)

Misinformation and obscurity veil Sender's war-time activities, and while there is considerable autobiographical input in *Los cinco libros de Ariadna* (*The Five Books of Ariadne*), this is admittedly a fictionalized account where fact and fantasy are so interwoven as to make extrication of the factual well-nigh impossible. Interest in the Ariadna "books" centers upon Soviet trickery and treachery in dealing with the Republicans in the Spanish Civil War, despite a seemingly fantastic setting in time and space. The OMECC, a world organization resembling the League of Nations or the U.N. (and itself allegorical) convenes to investigate the causes and events of the Spanish Civil War, with Javier (Sender's double) and his lover, Ariadne, summoned to testify. The novelist is bitter in his satire of intervention by both Fascist and Stalinist factions, a chaotic recreation of the conflict and its confusion seen retrospectively nineteen years later.

The Civil War also figures in *El rey y la reina* (*The King and the Queen*), but largely as a background for the protagonist's inner struggle. Both allegorical and realistic, this narrative revolves upon a gardener's desperate efforts to protect the Duchess of Alcanadre from Republican militiamen during the war, while she remains in hiding in an unused tower of her Madrid palace. Poetic and symbolic, the story is also a study of sociopsychological conflict brought about by war's upsetting of conventional class relationships. A very different vision of the conflict is found in *Contraataque* (*Counter-Attack in Spain*), written under fire, wherein Sender combines journalism, propaganda and personal reactions.

Little is known of Sender's early exile after slipping across the border into France (December 1938) during the general retreat of Republican forces. His two motherless children, rescued from Nationalist Spain in 1937 by the International Red Cross, were taken from Pau to Paris, embarking with him for America in March, 1939. Two later novels, *La luna de los perros* (*The Moon of the Dogs*) and *En la vida de Ignacio Morel* (*In the*

Life of Ignacio Morel) reflect in some measure this period of Sender's life. (pp. 221-22)

The first two novels written following the war, [*Proverbio de la muerte* (*Proverb of Death*)] and [*El lugar del hombre* (*A Man's Place*)], explore the significance of individual and personal existence, reflecting Sender's desperate struggle following the Republican defeat. Faint echoes of Existentialism combine with a personal search for meaning. *El lugar, Crónica del alba* and *Réquiem por un campesino español* (*Mosén Millán: Requiem for a Spanish Peasant*), recreate nostalgically the Aragonese villages and countryside of the writer's youth. (p. 223)

Crónica del alba, first published separately and later as the beginning of the nine-part novelistic cycle, is the best known of Sender's works in the United States. It purports to be the deathbed autobiography of José Garcés, a thirty-six year old Republican army officer and friend of the author (another double, as shown by the names—José is Sender's middle name, Garcés his mother's—and the ages are identical). Recounting aspects of the novelist's life from age ten to after the beginning of the war, the novel contrasts youthful idealism and dreams with the dark realities of maturity in a free association sequence disregarding temporal order. One of Sender's crowning literary achievements, *Crónica del alba* with its lyrical, human, nostalgic and romantic combinations of humor and pathos tends to substantiate the affirmation that Sender's life provides a better novel than many creations of his imagination.

Réquiem por un campesino español, another masterpiece and a model of narrative economy, is both realistic and an allegorical exploration of the forces in conflict in the Spanish Civil War. There are two levels of narration present (wherein the village priest, Mosén Millán, prepares to celebrate a requiem commemorating the anniversary of the death of Paco el del Molino), and a retrospective reconstruction of the preceding thirty years comprising Paco's life as recalled by Mosén Millán. Paco has many attributes of Christ, while the priest, who christened him at birth and officiated at key events in his life is, Judas-like, his betrayer, witnessing his murder by Falangists. A *romance* (ballad) sung by the altar boy offers an ironic, objective counterpart to the self-serving recollections of Mosén Millán, an anonymous popular version of events. (pp. 224-25)

Following a divorce from his second wife in 1963, Sender moved to California living for a time in Hollywood and then in an artists' colony. He returned to the classroom from 1965 to 1971, teaching at the University of Southern California. The period is one of feverish literary fecundity but only a small minority of these publications are relevant to the war or the experience of exile.... *La antesala* (*Waiting Room*) takes place in Madrid during the closing days of the conflict, but the war is no longer the novelists's primary concern. Rather, he offers an often grotesque exploration of human limitations and failings, with only incidental reflections of Spain's recent history as the background. (pp. 225-26)

Sender, whose literary and intellectual contacts while in Spain were not with the vanguardist "Generation of 1927" influencing the early Aub and Ayala, but with the older "Generation of 1898," follows the autobiographical tendencies of these older writers, displaying little experimentation in his early publications. In contrast to Aub and Ayala who later draw away from stylistic complication and vanguardist fashions, Sender's post-war writings contain more Surrealistic touches than his realistic pre-war production. Nor is his work so clearly divisible on technical levels by reason of differing pre-war and post-war

devices and form. There is a continuity in Sender recently remarked by [Charles L. King]: "... most, if not all, of the major elements found in Sender's vast novelistic production are present in his first novel." ... Such continuity does not, of course, preclude changes in emphasis or the introduction of new thematic material reflecting changed locales and circumstances. While Aub and Ayala wrote relatively little of a political and combative nature in Spain, such polemics were Sender's daily bread. It may not be illogical, then, that his later writings composed at a distance from the revolutionary context are more contemplative and philosophical, proportionately less concerned with political issues and social criticism. Ayala, in turn, affirms the essential thematic and philosophical unity of his own work, technical and stylistic differences between the pre-war and exile production notwithstanding, and [Estell Irizarry's *Teoria y creación literaria en Francisco Ayala*] tends to support his contention.

The ideological differences between the parties of the Popular Front in Spain were notorious, and dissension within the ranks of its supporters weakened the Republican government from its inception. These differences continued to exist among the exiles, undoubtedly interfering with the formation of any significant *esprit de corps*. Sender in his youth was Anarchist, although not a party member; Aub's ideology approached the Socialist, and Ayala may be termed a Liberal. Only Aub seems to have associated closely and at length with other Spanish exiles; the other two not only moved away from the centers of exile concentration, but also from the predominantly Hispanic environment upon establishing themselves in the United States. It is in Aub's work that studies of the Civil War and exile predominate to the virtual exclusion of unrelated themes, while preoccupation with the military aspects of the war, with the exodus and personal experience of exile constitute a relatively small percentage of narratives of Ayala and Sender. The latter, the only combatant among the three writers, seems best able to leave the war behind and has cultivated many themes, classified by [Marcelino] Peñuelas in a rather lengthy listing wherein neither war nor exile figure as independent categories. (pp. 226-28)

Janet W. Diaz, "Spanish Civil War and Exile in the Novels of Aub, Ayala and Sender," in Latin America and the Literature of Exile: A Comparative View of the 20th-Century European Refugee Writers in the New World, edited by Hans-Bernhard Moeller, Carl Winter Universitätsverlag, 1983, pp. 207-31.

MARILYN ROSENTHAL

[*In the following excerpt, Rosenthal examines works by four Civil War poets who wrote in Spanish: León Felipe, Miguel Hernández, César Vallejo, and Pablo Neruda. Translations in brackets are by Rosenthal.*]

[César Vallejo, Pablo Neruda, Miguel Hernández, and León Felipe] are representative of Spain and South America, and have written some of the finest poems on the subject of the Spanish Civil War. Vallejo and Neruda are major figures of twentieth-century Latin American poetry. Despite their affinities, they also had different preparations and preoccupations.... [While] Neruda put his poetry at the service of his ideology, such ideology was not directly present in Vallejo's poems. Felipe was the most objective; he was also the oldest (fifty-two) at the time of the war. Hernández and Felipe were concerned with moral issues—in which politics seemed suddenly to deal with choices between life and death, civilization and barbarism. Felipe's background was the most academic. Any intellectual analysis of his poem "La insignia" ["The Insignia"] testifies to this. Hernández had done the least traveling, and had the weakest international perspective. His poetry was the least academic and most idealistic, and his audience was the simplest. Also, he was the only one of the four who had actually fought in the war, although they had all been in wartime Spain and had firsthand experience of the war.

At the outbreak of the war in 1936 Felipe was fifty-two; Hernández was twenty-six; Vallejo, forty-four; and Neruda, thirty-two. Felipe's life had been very much a part of everything that led up to the war. His exposure to the patterns of Spanish politics gave him a focus. Also, his presence in Mexico after its 1910 Revolution as well as during the political and cultural ferment of the 1920s molded his perspective. He had witnessed there the factions of the mid-1920s and the falling out among the groups that had overthrown the former dictatorship. The similar weakness of the Spanish Republican side was the main thrust of "La insignia." His background enabled him to be an objective commentator on the immediate circumstances and the entire period of the Spanish Civil War. (pp. 8-9)

From the tragic events of the Spanish Civil War, Felipe was able to write deeply motivated poetry. In 1937 he wrote "La insignia"; and in March of 1938, when the bombings of Barcelona worsened, he wrote "Oferta," which was combined in a book with "El payaso de las bofetadas y el pescador de caña." Both are tragic poems about the war. The latter work cynically considers the fate of Christ-like figures as this world goes: . . .

   —But . . . Don Quijote . . . is he crazy and defeated?
   Is he not a hero?
   Is he not a Promethean poet?
   Is he not a redeemer?
   —Silence! Who has said that he is a redeemer?
   He is crazy and conquered and now is only a clown . . .
   a payaso . . .
   Surely all the redeemers of the world have been crazy
     and defeated.
   . . . And clowns before turning into gods.
   Christ was also a clown.

                              (pp. 11-12)

Felipe has a declamatory, rhetorical style. When he claims he is not rhetorical, he means in the sense of not being complicated or artificial. Felipe frequently employs an enumerative technique. There are, also, many repetitions that emphasize through cumulative effects.

Even the beginning of ["La insignia"] is framed by the reiteration of the compound past form of *hablar*. The use of . . . ["Responsible ones / the great responsible one and the small responsible ones"] echoes from the first stanza. Obviously, Felipe has a strong point to make about those who are responsible, which reminds us of those dining on putrid food in Neruda's "Almería." The repetition emphasizes his scorn.

There is a highly dramatic effect produced as Felipe lists in repetitive form those among the dead whom he had counted. Blood was Hernández' metaphor for all the war dead, comparable in emotional impact with Felipe's counting of corpses. Vallejo's metaphor for the death of Spain in "Masa" ["Masses"] was one dead soldier, an equally powerful image. Felipe, by counting cadavers, is metaphorically holding up the bloody body of Spain.

Felipe subtitled ["La insignia"] "Alocución poemática" ["Poetic Speech (Address)"], which suggests a combination of poetry and prose. Spain and South America in the nineteenth century had a tradition of oratory, which they considered a distinct genre, and from which Felipe may well have inherited his oratorical style. An example of his style which combines poetic and prosaic elements begins ["One day you will die outside of your country. In bed perhaps. / In a bed of white sheets, with naked feet"]. . . . Felipe has illustrated here the poetic technique of concretizing experience in a graphic way. An individual on a white bed makes vivid Felipe's general disdain for cowards who run away to hygienic refuge. The sarcastic tone is unmistakable. Poetic qualities of the passage are the concrete imagery, repetition, condensation, informal grammar, emotional tone, and adjectival descriptions. Some of these qualities would also be true of rhetoric. The extension and logic of the narrative, the form in which the poet arranged it as if in a paragraph, and the lack of flowery speech are prosaic elements of Felipe's technique. His artistry derives not from the complexity of his metaphors but from the dramatic use he makes of his rhetorical technique. The poem is very stirring but its dramatic effect comes more from its structure than from its dramatic imagery. The structure could be considered architectural.

The poet often uses an irregular rhythm of short lines and short words. Some of the lines consist of only one word. He plays with length of line, gradation, and progressively lengthening (or shortening) repetition. Shrinking and expanding, his lines build up to a crescendo (or decrease) in which the last line is the culmination or diminution: . . .

   ["The historical curve of the aristocrat, since his
      popular and heroic origin, until his final present
      degeneration, covers in Spain more than three
      centuries.
   That of the bourgeoisie, seventy years.
   And yours, three weeks."] . . .

The length of the lines offers an imaginative parallel to the historical curve, a technique used by Walt Whitman also.

The vocabulary is both simple and serious, less difficult than that of Neruda or Vallejo. It is almost unpoetic in its everyday, straightforward syntax. . . . Felipe matches his bare words with what he hopes is a naked rhythm. The words, phrases, and framework are often repetitive. There is also a humble simplicity to the form and theme of "La insignia."

There is a development or progression of ideas in the poem as the poet introduces his role and explains what is wrong with the Republican side, which is precisely what he finds right about the Nationalist side. The bloody body of Spain is present throughout the poem. He distinguishes between the Spanish people and its divided leadership, and condemns the traitorous Nationalists, the fascists who side with them, and England, who remains neutral and thus tips the scales in favor of the Nationalists. The single insignia he recommends to the Republicans would represent Justice. He makes a clear distinction between the values of true Spain, the Spanish revolutionary, Man, Don Quijote, and Justice, and the values of their enemies—values of business and pragmatism.

"La insignia" is an intellectually critical poem as opposed to the emotionally empathetic poems of Hernández and Vallejo. While Neruda's poems are subjective, Felipe's vision is the most historically realistic. He predicted the outcome, he predicted the reasons for it, and he was right.

In sum, "La insignia" is a tremendous tour de force. It is not subtle and it is not especially metaphorical; the conception and technique of the poem are not so much poetic as rhetorical. It plays with repetition and cadence and has an architectural structure. The poem concretizes generalizations; for example, Felipe takes the fall of Málaga and the likely defeat of Valencia and makes them the metaphor for the larger death of Spain.

In his early works, Felipe was a human poet, a sad one, who saw human sorrows and society's evils. . . . He later adopted a more belligerent tone, almost declamatory, but filled with both epic and lyric force which can be seen in "La insignia." He viewed what he felt was a disintegrating world where positive, constructive efforts were futile. . . . (pp. 37-40)

The Spanish Civil War found [Miguel Hernández] in Madrid, where he immediately enlisted in the Republican army from a deep sense of social obligation and patriotism. He fought in the trenches, read his verses to fellow-soldiers, and escaped when he could to visit his fiancée, Josefina, in Orihuela. . . . In 1937, in the middle of the war, he married Josefina. In *Viento del pueblo,* published that same year, his style became graver and simpler. . . .

After the war, he was confined by the Franco Government in the Torrijos jail in Madrid and condemned to death for his political attitude during the war. Only at the intervention of some friends was his sentence commuted to thirty years' imprisonment.

In the long years of imprisonment, he wrote poems of great economy, simplicity, and feeling. (p. 41)

He died in prison—early in 1942, at the age of thirty-one—of typhoid fever and tuberculosis. His premature death cut short one of the most promising poetic careers of his day. . . .

From 1936 on, his main themes were his country, love, and death. The war in Spain elicited from him a passionate response and a loyal dedication. Recognizing the tragedy, he was still able to sustain inspired hope throughout the war. Even up to his own last miserable days, his unquenchable spirit conflicted with the despair of his real situation. . . . (p. 42)

Highly emotional in tone and full of vivid hyperboles, "Recoged esta voz" ["Hear This Voice"] may be classified as a wartime recruiting poem, its imagery derived from the passion of the battlefield. Discouraged by the course of the war (by 1937), Hernández asks for action by kindred spirits all over the world. He sees the war, then, not as a purely Spanish struggle. He feels the situation very intimately, as a Spaniard or Latin American would, and describes it from a firsthand point of view. Like Walt Whitman, he was there, but not just as a spectator—he had participated. His life was threatened and he, too, is being destroyed. It is a poem written out of the immediate circumstances of battle, revealing the poet's passionate, emotional involvement with no perspective of distance in time and space. . . . He is sunk in the midst of his people, as if in mire. Hernández notices bleeding wherever he goes—bleeding which is both physical and spiritual. There is an inundation of blood:

> ["Blood, blood through the trees and the soil,
>   blood in the waters, blood on the walls,
>   and a fear that Spain will collapse
>   from the weight of the blood which soaks through
>   her networks
>   right to the bread that is eaten."] . . .

The vision of blood is vivid: "sangrando por trincheras y hospitales" ["bleeding through trenches and hospitals"].

Hernández presents his people as violated and dying: the "¡ay! de tantas madres." These valiant people are being left "sin leche ni hermosura" ["without milk or beauty"]. Sweethearts find themselves alone, without hope or occupation. Cities are "de trabajo y de inocencia" ["of work and innocence"]. Those who fight are snatched daily from the hands of their mothers, to fight with farm tools against powerful weapons and die bravely.

On the other hand, the enemy is described as barbaric, criminal, and unconscionable, wanting Spain to be nothing but a vast graveyard. The image of the enemy is that of an animal predator living off weaker animals. They have hooves and fangs and destroy "como torbellinos" ["like whirlwinds"], while the poet's allies are like innocent children. Such a black-and-white vision shows the emotionality of the poet's commitment to the cause of the Republic. His poem shares with political cartoons an oversimplification and an intensity of the polarization between the two forces involved in the war, although political cartoons tend to be intellectualized while the poems of Hernández are not.

All around him Hernández sees chaos, mutilation, and death. Blood permeates everything, including the bread. There is a plethora of death images; Spain's life blood is being sapped, and Spain might collapse. The pervasive wind, like the ubiquitous blood, emanates from trenches and hospitals. It is the disturbed breath of a violated, desperate people losing a war. (pp. 53-4)

Spanish poet Miguel Hernández.

''Recoged esta voz'' is a passionate poem. . . . Pulling no punches, [Hernández] appeals to the strongest instincts and loyalties of his public. The audience he addresses is much simpler than that of Vallejo or Neruda (whose poems are less logical and more difficult to understand). The constant reminders of death . . . stress the urgent need for action. Hernández is addressing peasant soldiers so the imagery is rural and stated in terms understandable to the laborer: [''manufacturing tools,'' ''the mines,'' ''the plow,'' ''the pastures,'' etc.]. . . . Hernández, being of humble origin himself, felt very close to the proletariat.

The first-person presentation makes the poem personal and direct in its appeal. The poet's voice is the voice of Spain, its force derived from the clamor of Spain. . . . His feeling for collective humanity is like Vallejo's. (pp. 54-5)

Spain's hope, as in Vallejo's ''España, aparta de mí este cáliz'' [''Spain, Remove from Me This Chalice''], lies in the future and with a youth who will restore and beautify Spain. Not just chronological youth, but peasant and working youth; these peasants, because of their commitment, bravery, and passion, will overcome cannons and fighter planes:

> [''The youth that will save Spain, although it had to
> fight with a gun of nards
> and a sword of wax.'']. . . .

In his poetic vision, Hernández sees the disinherited masses pitted against force, but the strength of the people ''shall overcome.''

There are many images in the poem. In the first stanza of Part II, youth is symbolized as a sea with the characteristics of a horse: ''piafante'' [''pawing''] and ''pie calzado'' [''shoed foot'']. It is heroic, rebellious, and incorruptible. Hernández sees this vital force as composed of working men, and he eulogizes the common man with whom soldiers can easily identify.

In the second stanza, we have a variation of the title of the poem: ''recoged este viento'' [''gather up this wind'']. This wind contains blood and breath—vital, essential ingredients. The title of the poem is significant as the voice and wind fill the atmosphere with a tremendous energy and force.

In the ninth stanza, the poet addresses the same audience as in Part I: ''naciones, hombres, mundos'' [''nations, men, worlds'']. He looks on the war as offering some final hope—even if it brings temporary defeat and final death to some. He claims ultimate invincibility and victory for the brave youth of Spain, who are in perpetual and vigorous motion, communicating their dynamic qualities to everything they touch. . . . Hernández sees the young Spaniards as colts, bulls, and flowers, and he and they believe that to die is the highest achievement. They will be victors, even if dead; they will die proudly, saviors of Spain no matter what the odds, even if fighting with flower guns and wax swords—metaphorical terms of futility rather than effectiveness. The poem ends on a note of inspiration and idealism. The ending reaffirms the martyrdom the poet sees as the necessary and only possible answer, and is very similar to the message of ''Vientos del pueblo me llevan'' [''The Winds of My People Carry Me'']. (pp. 55-6)

Hernández speaks to soldiers as another soldier might. He has intentionally kept the poem simple in all ways and melodic in rhythm, because he has directed it to the common people. Since Hernández meant it to be a song, since it tells a sad tale of Spain with only romantic notions of victory, and since it is directed to the people, the poem might be considered a ballad. The structure is well defined, a rhyme scheme continues throughout. Hernández plays on the natural rhythm of the Spanish language, which tends toward the predominant accentuation on the penultimate syllable of words.

There is much repetition of words as well as sounds, which makes it easier to memorize. In the second stanza, ''aquí tengo'' [''here I have''] plus an indefinite article is repeated four times, the second and fourth being exact duplicates: ''aquí tengo una vida'' [''here I have a life'']. (p. 57)

The rhythm and repetition help to spell out the relentless message. There is some progression as Hernández makes his strongest plea at the end of Part I, and his most poetic claim for youth at the end of Part II. . . .

''Recoged esta voz'' is not polemical, nor is it especially narrative. Rather it is descriptive of a certain course of events through the presentation of a series of images. The poem is rhetorical and dramatic. Death is a major consideration. Hernández is emotionally committed to the Republican cause, and Hernández is highly subjective as he exaggerates his case in order to motivate and inspire his readers or listeners. The poet, coming from the working class, identifies with it, and directs his poem toward it. The poem was written by a soldier/poet very much involved in the war. (p. 58)

In 1930 [César Abraham Vallejo] and his wife traveled to Spain, where he met such writers as Salinas, Alberti, Unamuno, Gerardo Diego, and Lorca. By 1931 he was a communist and his writing became Marxist revolutionary propaganda. He became one of the founders of the Spanish communist cells. After another trip to Russia, he returned to Spain, going from there to Paris in a destitute state. He felt a deep nostalgia for Peru and his family and great indignation at the treatment of the Indian peasants.

The fascist uprising in Spain in July of 1936 disturbed him profoundly. He soon left Paris for Barcelona and Madrid. Returning to Paris at the end of December, he was completely absorbed in the Spanish cause. He left again for Spain in July of 1937. It was after this final visit to Spain, and after nearly fifteen years of poetic silence, that he turned his energy toward writing and revising the poems that comprise *Poemas humanos.* As the title suggests, he had a strong sense of human compassion and wished to extend his hand to anyone he felt needed it. . . . (p. 60)

Either during this time or shortly afterwards, he wrote fifteen poems inspired by the Republican cause, entitled *España, aparta de mí este cáliz.* It was printed by Republican soldiers, but the entire edition was lost in the disaster of Cataluña. These poems and the poems that comprise *Poemas humanos* are much more clearly expressed than the previous volume of poems, *Trilce* (1923), whose obscurity attached it to the surrealist movement in poetry. Perhaps, as in the case of Neruda, the brutal facts of the war jolted him into an interest in having his poems communicate a forthright message. On April 15, 1938, before the war came to an end, Vallejo died in Paris. (p. 61)

The themes of motherhood, death, and Man's isolation, suffering, and love are central to his poetry. It is clear that, although Vallejo cherished some inspired hope, he was skeptical and despairing over the outcome of the conflict. He had experienced at firsthand the horrors of Spain's Civil War, and was deeply concerned and involved. (p. 62)

The "responso" of ["Pequeño responso a un héroe de la República" ("A Brief Funeral Liturgy for a Hero of the Republic")] is a responsory, part of a church service sung in response to the reading of a text, but the poem itself hardly offers a formal religious context. There are, however, mystical circumstances, a religious occasion (a funeral), and a religious form to the poem. The poem concerns a small ritual (funeral) ceremony and offers a tribute to an unnamed, dead soldier of the Republic. The framework is localized and, basically, convincing. Vallejo's sentiments are clearly Republican; and the fateful battle at Toledo, where Republican forces failed to recapture the Alcázar, claimed many a hero.

The poem is not sequential. Rather, it is a succession of visual images that narrate an event. Many of the deaths emphasize physical and living aspects of the dead body and of those carrying it. Only remotely may it be considered a responsory: they go through the ritualistic motions of carrying the corpse during a funeral procession. Presumably, the body is buried. It may be supposed that some sort of anthem was sung on the same occasion—praising the enduring message of the "hero's" life and death, which is the main subject of the poem.

The hero is, in a sense, doubly dead: "cadáver muerto" ["dead corpse"]. His dead body is described in fragments: ["waist," "mouth," "navel," and "sleeve"].... Fragmentation seems appropriate to the shattering of a life. His navel may symbolize part of the heritage that his poetry offered. From his sleeve his writing hand is missing. His mouth would have offered his word. His body is dead, but his words (his poetry, his message, and perhaps the meaning of his whole life) which he gave birth to live on—in this way, too, the umbilical cord is related. What remains is his book, his testament: "Quedóse el libro y nada más" ["The book remained and nothing more"]. What this book symbolizes is debatable. It may represent more than one man's lifetime. Since the poetic sequence (*España, aparta de mí este cáliz*) centers on the murder of Spain, the book may represent, in a broad sense, whatever value Spain may have which would survive were she destroyed. (p. 63)

"Masa" informs us immediately that the battle is over and the combatant dead. We know that the poem was the twelfth of fifteen written by Vallejo in his Spanish Civil War collection. It is obvious that when he wrote it (1937) he was in despair over the outcome of Spain's war.

The first man to approach says to the dead man, "No mueras," because "te amo tanto!" ["Do not die," because "I love you so much!"]. Two others approach and make the same plea with the same result: "Pero el cadáver, ¡ay! siguió muriendo" ["But the cadaver, alas! went on dying"]. Then steadily increasing numbers surround the corpse, begging it not to leave them. Finally, when everyone in the world is there, with one common desire, the body resurrects, embraces the first man, and begins to walk.

The narrative is simple but its symbolism has large dimensions. A single dead soldier magnifies not just to the great body of all the war dead, but even to Spain itself. Spain's fall is Spain's death, but Spain, dead and dying (sic), resurrects (metaphorically, not literally). Spain in this poem symbolizes crucified humanity and, like the traditional figure of Christ, died for mankind and rose from the dead. The difference, however (and here lies the rub), is that Christ, being God-like, always had within him the power to be immortal. Spain had no such option. The cadaver views all of mankind sadly and, moved by their solidarity in love, faith, and hope, revives. It walks again as

if out of pity for suffering humanity. But could this miracle happen?

The title, "Masa," meaning "a mass of people," presents the poignantly romantic notion that Spain could be revivified by the love and hope of all the people in the world collectively. It is both idealized in its hoping and despairing in its impossibility. It is in its impossibility that it is so moving. It is the fantasy of a poet yearning to believe. Vallejo poeticizes the dream romantically, passionately, hopelessly.

But, from another viewpoint, an Hispanic poet could look at the total image of Spain, of its cities, of its people, dying and being destroyed, as the promise of a new Spain (this message underlay "España, aparta de mí este cáliz" also). Vallejo agreed with Hernández that death is inevitable, and Vallejo could further regard the war dead as not just dead and gone, but as part of a living army, sharing in the struggle and in the future with the people with whom and for whom they had fought.

The refrain, "Pero el cadáver, ¡ay! siguió muriendo," is a formal part of the structure of the poem and produces a cumulative effect of irony. It is like an undertow of fate and sadness. It is the last line of every stanza until the end, when the trend is reversed with "abrazó al primer hombre; echóse a andar..." ["he embraced the first man; he began to walk..."]. The reversal would lead us to believe that the love and religious faith (in the possibility of resurrection and in the individual Christ-figure) of all the people in the world (which is in itself impossible) could produce a miracle and save Spain. If this is what Spain's salvation depends upon, we are not much comforted.

The presentation of "Masa" is straightforward and relies on direct quotations. The structure of the brief poem is neat and simple. The vocabulary is limited to simple words and the dialogue is informal. There is a discrepancy between the mysterious, miraculous subject matter and the matter-of-fact tone.

It is curious that although Spain is "muerto" as of the second line, it continues dying in the refrain, as if it is in the process of becoming, and therefore retrievable, rather than an accomplished fact. The association of inanimate objects with animate qualities and vice versa is typical of Vallejo's (and Neruda's) poetry. In "Pequeño responso" the corpse sprouted and breathed.... (pp. 66-8)

It is a very human poem, resulting from the personal anguish of Vallejo, registering his ironic protest against injustice: Spain deserves to be transformed. Vallejo obviously had a strong impulse for human solidarity, and this poem reveals his interest in man individually and collectively; after all, there is no landscape in the poem, only people and feelings. It is a sad, lyrical poem, expressing high idealism. (p. 68)

The title [of "España, aparta de mí este cáliz"] (the same as that of the volume which contains the poem, along with fourteen others by Vallejo on the Spanish Civil War) is from the Bible. It is taken from Christ's words in the garden of Gethsemane: "O my Father, if it be possible, let this cup pass from me" (Matthew XXVI: 39; Mark XIV: 36; Luke XXII: 42). Vallejo changed it to "España, aparta de mí este cáliz," replacing Father with Mother Spain. The story behind the Biblical quotation is that Christ had had a premonition that he would be betrayed and that he would soon die. He had also prophesied that the next time he drank from the cup he would be beyond death, in the Kingdom of God. The chalice, then, symbolizes death. The night that Christ was apprehended, in a moment of weakness, as if he might change his fate, he asked that the cup be taken away. It was not and he went on to fulfill his divine destiny. A comparison is being made between his position—what he stood for, what he died for, carrying his own cross, being resurrected—and that of Spain, whose fate the poet is anguishing over, and would challenge if he could, Spain might be said to be dying for the sins of mankind, and Spain looks to its children as Christ might have looked to his disciples.

Vallejo addresses the poem to the future, to the "Niños del mundo" ["Children of the world"]. Spain's war has international implications. These children are "hijos de los guerreros" ["sons of fighters"] who represent multifarious nationalities.... Vallejo means children who are children not only by age, development, activities, but in a sense, too, children of the Spanish world. Latin American countries may be considered children of Mother Spain. As a Peruvian, Vallejo would have such a perspective.

The poem is a personification of Spain—in the first stanza as a huge image in the sky whose forearm is held in the grip of two earthly metal plates, which literally may refer to "armaments" or "engravings" that are opposing one another, and symbolically allude to the two distinct camps into which Spain, and the world, too, is divided. The poet then captures, by a series of images, some universal qualities of children: . . .

> ["how aged are her concave temples!
>   how early in the (history of the) sun what I was
>   telling you!
>   how soon in your chest (figuratively, heart) the
>   ancient sound!
>   how old the "2" in your copybook!"]
>
>   (pp. 70-1)

Spain represents to Vallejo not just the mother country, but the mother language, the source of civilization and religion as well. It is both a terrestrial image and a celestial one. (p. 72)

Despite its tragic circumstances, there is hope in the poem that Spain can be saved. Reviewing the image of Spain [in "España, aparta de mí este cáliz"], we may conclude that she extends up to the sky and down to the earth and that she is divided between two forces. Her fall is impending. She is in the clutch of the power of these opposing forces. She is both mother, familial and religious, and teacher of religion, language, culture. Mother connotes security, comfort, sustenance, nonabandonment. Teacher suggests learning, mental development, language, religion. In these two capacities, Spain would suggest to Spaniards and Latin Americans a long association of love, tradition, and civilization. Spain's energies are being drained, and in her hand is the skull of life. If she falls, life falls. The choice of children as part of the imagery in this poem is especially apt. Vallejo is able to play upon the powerful bond between children and their mother. Also, in their vulnerability and innocence, children and mothers evoke our emotions.

The poem is well unified in its imagery, the metaphors consistent with childhood. There is the pervasive, hovering image of Spain, and the reiteration of her possible fall. There is the focus of the poem toward the children, and the successions of images to represent the various aspects of Vallejo's vision. In the first stanza the children are presented. Spain, whose image has been suggested in stanza one, is further clarified in stanza two. In stanza three the fall of Spain is indicated by the effects it would have upon the children. Stanza four symbolizes the

dimensions of the war. Here, for the first time, the "I" (the narrator and the poet himself, I presume) directs the children. Stanza five expresses other fatal implications of Spain's fall: "está en su mano / la calavera . . . aquélla de la vida" ["in (Spain's) hand is / the skull . . . that of life"]. The final stanza offers the crux of his message to the children. The poet lists the contingencies upon which to base their (the children's) decision to take over. He exhorts that if the tragedy does occur, they should go forth and reclaim Spain, with all of its implications for the world. There is hope that the surviving children of the world will provide a better future. (pp. 72-3)

Neruda left Chile in 1927, proceeded to Europe, traveled in the Orient, where, between 1927 and 1932, he lived successively in Rangoon, Colombo, Singapore, and Batavia, visiting adjacent areas of Asia and Oceania, and was Chilean consul in Calcutta. On his return to Chile in 1933, Neruda was assigned first as consul to Buenos Aires (1932-1933) and then to Madrid (1933-1937), where he was received with admiration and acclaim by a generation of Spanish poets: Federico García Lorca, Rafael Alberti, Luis Cernuda, Miguel Hernández, and Manuel Altolaguirre. In Madrid, too, his first and second *Residencias* first appeared together, with enormous success, in 1935.

When the Civil War broke out in Spain in 1936, Neruda, heedless of diplomatic protocol, made no secret of his antifascist convictions. His active role in radical politics from 1936 on was to result in conflict with the Chilean government, expulsion, and, finally, exile. (p. 74)

The title [of Neruda's "Explico algunas cosas" ("I Explain Some Things")] is intimate in the first person. Although one might expect the poem to be defensive, Neruda explains his change in poetic aesthetics aggressively and even bitterly. In part the poem represents a coming to terms with himself and his readers about his new aesthetics, and in part it offers a particular perspective on the war. Neruda was in Spain both as a poet and as a man, and the war had a profound effect upon him in both capacities. Neruda sees himself in the role of a poet in the war (Felipe does, too) and translates the Spanish catastrophe into a personal one.... Neruda begins on an intimate key, conversationally, with "preguntaréis" ["you will ask"], which is addressed to a familiar, collective "you." It is a confession to fellow poets and students since it is they who would read his poetry. "Os voy a contar todo lo que me pasa" ["I am going to tell you all that happens to me"]—it is what is happening that is forcing him into a reappraisal of himself as a poet.

"Explico algunas cosas" is a poem transitional in his career from an earlier poetry . . . which he echoes in the first stanza, only to reject in favor of a new poetic style. It is a re-examination of where he stands and where his poetry stands.

In his early poetry, before the *Residencias*, Neruda had demonstrated a lyric inclination, while concerned as a human being with problems of coping with love, death, abandonment, and loneliness. Elements of nature, very personal emotions, and artistic consciousness affected this poetry. His later experience aroused his political conscience. His commitment (to communism) was ideological, not artistic, but caused priorities within his verse to shift. His vision became less introspective and more outward-directed toward experience which involved him as a person and as a poet. (p. 79)

["Explico Algunas Cosas"] is a critical point in the evolution of Neruda as a poet and as a social animal. And his decision is to put his poetry at the service of his commitment—which is clearly implied in his poem.

Typical of Neruda's poetry (as of Vallejo's) had been the juxtaposition of animate and inanimate objects, such as, from the first stanza: "la metafísica cubierta de amapolas" ["the metaphysics covered with poppies"]. The fragrance, color, and life force of poppies contrast strikingly with the philosophical abstraction of metaphysics. Both Vallejo and Neruda had the knack of making disparate things live with each other, their logic often deriving from emotion rather than intellect. (p. 80)

The life/death contrast of the imagery of the poem is striking. It is as if someone came along and knocked over and leveled everything, leaving nothing. This image of destruction leads up to the total holocaust of the final stanza, consisting of the repetition three times of "venid a ver la sangre por las calles" ["come see the blood in the streets"]. Blood is a frequent image of Neruda's poetry as we see also in "Almería" and "Llegada." The image is as terrifying as that of Hernández in "Recoged esta voz." . . . (p. 82)

In the final stanza, there is repeated play upon the same words, [as in Lorca's poetry]. . . . Like the imagery of Hernández, the poem offers a growing crescendo of destruction.

Neruda is considering his own poetry in relation to what is happening (1937), but it is not an intellectual exercise. In the heat of a traumatic experience, the poem offers a re-evaluation of how the poet stands in relation to the large, collective experience outside himself. In view of the overwhelming facts, everything else becomes essentially academic. His style has changed from being obscure, metaphysical, and inner-directed to being a poetry of emotional, as well as ideological, commitment. Putting his poetry at the service of his beliefs, he wishes to present his doctrine clearly and simply. He uses fewer images, and there is an emphasis upon direct communication. Between 1936 and 1939, when the Spanish Civil War exploded upon the world of his tradition, culture, and language as well as upon the routine of his life in Madrid, Neruda offered to the world a changed heart and a new source of perception firmly aligned with suffering and embattled mankind. His communist affiliation engaged his political conscience and artistic talent on the side of the Republic.

There is poetic intensity in the choice of strong words to dichotomize the opposing factions (Nationalist vs. Republican), in the careful repetitions, bitter accusations, and acid declaration of Spain's tragedy as well as his own. There is artistic tension in terms of language and imagery.

Neruda chose to cast this most personal poem in the form of a soliloquy. It is as if he were thinking aloud in reordering his values and life. The poem includes a re-evaluation of his poetry in view of the Spanish tragedy and a nihilistic picture of devastated Spain. It indicates an ideological background and offers a battle cry of revenge.

The twelve stanzas, of varying length and form, condense his emotional and intellectual response, but also allow him a flexible framework in which to build up the intensity of the poem. (pp. 84-5)

Neruda wrote "Llegada a Madrid de la Brigada Internacional" ["Arrival in Madrid of the International Brigade"] about a particular event. On October 20, 1936, Franco issued the general order for the capture of Madrid. On November 8 the first units of the International Brigades, formed at Albacete, arrived in Madrid. Some 3000 men, mostly Germans and Italians, many of them veterans of World War I and of fascist concentration camps, marching with absolute precision and singing revolutionary songs, paraded across the embattled capital. In total, there were to be twenty-odd nations represented in the International Brigades. The poem enshrines a moment, and without that moment the poem would not live. (pp. 87-8)

In the first stanza Neruda refers to the Brigade in the third person. Stanza two describes the destruction to the city and its inhabitants before their arrival. In stanzas three and four the poet calls them "camaradas" and "hermanos" ["comrades" and "brothers"], expressing increasing gratitude. He is expressing a comradeship based on the commitment of one human life to another. In the final lines the soft quality of "un inmenso río con palomas" ["an immense river with doves"] is juxtaposed with the hardness of "un valle de duras rocas" ["a valley of hard rocks"] and "acero" ["steel"]. This represents the very essence of hope: the illusion or ideal combined with the hard determination which gives it the ability to survive.

The poem expresses tremendous gratitude. It has an epic, larger-than-life quality and an ode-like tone. The whole vision of the Brigade filing into an embattled Madrid is panoramic and muralistic. Neruda describes the city prior to their arrival: the sense of apprehension and doom, the unhappy circumstances, the physical climate. Then he presents his proud feelings upon their arrival in glorified, idealistic terms. The Brigade's arrival is an inspiring experience, and one can almost hear martial music in the background.

The language is like that of a Spanish Civil War campaign song. The song/poem offers a hymn of gratitude to the volunteers who have come to help defend Spain. It is the intent which is of primary importance, and the language is the product of an intent both hyperbolic and glorifying. The combative elements of the language are like those of Hernández.

But the language is not especially original. The evocative details of Neruda's previous poetry are not present here. He is dealing in semantic generalities. The epithets are designed to evoke an emotional reaction not so much from their graphic suggestiveness as from the subjectivity of their connotations. Neruda has given us his highly emotional response to the ideological potential of the circumstances, and his canvas is huge. But the resulting poem is politically more stirring than poetically. (pp. 89-90)

On May 29, 1937, the German battleship *Deutschland* was attacked off Ibiza by two Republican aircraft. Thirty-one of the ship's company were killed and many others wounded. The Germans (especially Hitler) were furious, and at dawn on May 31 the Germans took their revenge. A cruiser and four destroyers appeared off Almería, on the southeastern coast of Spain, and fired 200 shots into the town, destroying thirty-five buildings and causing nineteen deaths. The Republic considered bombing the German fleet in the Mediterranean in retaliation, but there was too much pressure against it from fear of setting off world war. For reasons, then, mostly political, the incident of Almería was "forgotten."

Pablo Neruda did not forget. The destruction to an innocent Almería, chosen as a convenient victim by such powerful adversaries, enraged the poet. Neruda metes out his particular retribution in an extravagantly ironic manner. He carefully sidesteps the German involvement and names the types of people he held responsible for the inception and maintenance of the war: "el obispo," "el banquero," "el coronel y la esposa del coronel," "ricos de aquí y de allá," "embajadores, ministros, conmensales atroces, / señoras de confortable té y asiento'' (the religious leaders, financial controllers, army officials and their wives, the rich from all over who lend support to the Nationalist side, and the political leaders and idle aristocracy whose activity as well as neglect help to destroy the Republic). Neruda emphasizes the class struggle underlying the war, as Sender suggests it in ''Ultima Ratio Regum.'' It is the rich against the poor, the powerful minority with its material and social advantages against the masses. (pp. 91-2)

Neruda uses the metaphor of a variety of nauseating ''edibles,'' such as garbage and suffering-thickened blood, to express his own revulsion toward those he holds responsible for the tragedy. This particular punishment suggests Cronos of Greek mythology, who ate his own children, as well as Atreus, who killed Thyestes' young children and had them served up at a banquet. Ironically, Neruda is concentrating on those who might, ordinarily, take sensuous pleasure in what they were eating. The food he introduces is calculated to curdle in their stomachs and to send a shiver through their flesh. The blood he would offer them is hardly meant with sacred and mysterious reverence, buth with hate, contempt, and horror. Neruda is telling the beneficiaries of his contribution to their breakfast table (the first food of the day) that they will eat the results of what they have created for the rest of their lives. That particular philosophy is reminiscent of the Bible's ''what you sow, you shall reap'' and ''by their fruits shall ye know them,'' and also of the Mosaic law ''an eye for an eye, a tooth for a tooth.''

The imagery is visual and olfactory (''humeante y ardiente''). These potential gourmands will be made to smell, see, and swallow the carrion of their making. The poem is unflinching in its viewpoint and unsparingly graphic in its cannibalism. The recipients will sit there as mute victims of their own atrocities.

The ideological vision is of those with wealthy interests feeding on the innocent bodies of children and other victims to sustain themselves. This vision is Goyaesque (cf. his war sketches) in grotesqueness. Neruda transforms his ideological commitment into a plastic one which is overwhelming. It reminds me, also, of Jonathan Swift's ''A Modest Proposal,'' in which instead of abstracting the problem of starving people, Swift suggests that the children of the poor be served up to their parents in a cannibalistic orgy. (pp. 92-3)

It is obvious that Neruda meant the poem to be repetitious as well as inexorable. It is undoubtedly part of Neruda's irony that the poem should be stated with a variety of metaphors rich in adjectives, and frequent alliteration, assonance, and repetition. The sharp contradiction between the apparent generosity and the obvious bad faith of the giver is strengthened by the simplicity of the images. The poetic devices and lyrical qualities jarringly emphasize his bitterness. The poem's ironic vituperation is as strong as that of the Bible's Psalm 137.

''Almería'' is epic in its larger-than-life imagery and Neruda speaks not of individuals but of broad categories of types. The imagery is much more graphic than that of ''Llegada.'' There is a richness not only of emotional commitment, but also of language and imagery. The strength of its poetic language gives ''Almería'' a raison d'être that rises above its meaning, which is not true of ''Llegada.'' ''Llegada'' is a poem of a particular time and place. ''Almería'' is more powerful and durable.

All four poets (Felipe, Hernández, Vallejo, and Neruda) sympathized with the Republican side, sharing deep reactions to the war. All of their poems analyzed here in depth were written,

by coincidence, in 1937. Vallejo's presentation was in most personal terms. Neruda (''Llegada'' and ''Almería'') wrote about specific events, as did Felipe in ''La insignia'' (the fall of Málaga and the threat to Valencia). Hernández had a more generalized approach, with insinuations about political background. He saw the need to unite the nations of the world (''Recoged esta voz''). Vallejo included mention of Toledo in ''Pequeño responso'' but mostly generalized. Felipe had the most transcendental view, but Neruda, too, saw the war in international dimensions. Felipe was able to criticize the Republican side for a lack of unity, while admiring the cohesion of the Franco side. He bitterly condemned England for her motives in failing to intervene on the side of justice. He is the most historically realistic of the four. The Republican side was, indeed, hopelessly divided, which weakened its effectiveness and helped bring on its defeat. The prophetic ending of ''La insignia,'' however, intimates that Spain and Justice will somehow resurrect. By 1939 Felipe's poems became completely pessimistic. (pp. 93-4)

As to the durability of these war poems, we might ask whether they would survive outside their historical context. Although Felipe's poetic speech deals with particular circumstances, it is elevated to a transcendental plane. It derives its value from the fact that the poet does not speak through the mouths of certain men or names, but represents Man and is addressed to Man. Felipe is essentially concerned with Man. Felipe's poem goes beyond the Spanish Civil War to the hopelessness of all war. He is concerned with the ultimate brutality and horror of all war. . . . He points to the grotesque discrepancy between the horrible carnage and the political in-fighting. His poetry has ideological survival value, being based on political truth, and his understanding of human nature (though cynical) rings true. The poem has artistic survival value in the form of its dramatic elements, architectural form, skillful repetition, vivid images, emotionally-suggestive language, and emotional impact. His concern for the Republicans can be compared to his feeling for the loneliness and anguish of the exile in ''Español del éxodo y del llanto''; both have universal application.

Being completely caught up in the situation, Hernández wrote of the desperation and carnage of any war, with feelings of brotherhood, despair, and inspiration. His poems are exciting, full of energy and ideals, and have lyrical qualities which suggest they will last. The nature of Vallejo's poetic conception transcends the Spanish Civil War to include all of mankind. Besides, his poems are lyrical, intense, vivid, and beautiful in any context. His poems will survive because they are poetically conceived and because his message of compassion, feeling, and frustration-hope has universal meaning. His capacity for suffering reaches all humans. Of the three poems by Neruda considered here, ''Explico'' has the most artistic quality and ''Llegada'' the least. ''Llegada'' is the most limited of the three both in scope and artistry, but it does contain insights into human nature. Readers can identify with the bitterness and resentment of ''Almería'' with or without knowing the historical circumstances. (pp. 99-100)

Marilyn Rosenthal, ''Civil War Poets of Spain and Latin America,'' in her Poetry of the Spanish Civil War, *New York University Press, 1975, pp. 6-101.*

GERMAN LITERATURE ABOUT THE WAR

GERHARD MACK

[In the following excerpt, Mack surveys works written about the Spanish Civil War by writers in exile from Nazi Germany.]

Many of the most prominent names of German exile literature . . . made their mark on [the history of the Spanish Civil War] through their literary efforts. A major facet of this literature was the novel. Undoubtedly the most renowned work of this genre was Hermann Kesten's *Die Kinder von Gernika*. As Pablo Picasso was moved by the brutal bombardment of Guernica to paint his famous fresco, so Kesten wrote his novel to denounce the notorious air raid on that Basque city. In a masterful narrative which Thomas Mann termed "undoubtedly one of the peaks of (Kesten's) creative endeavors," he compared the Civil War to a family quarrel: "Seen close at hand, a revolution resembles a family squabble."

The author made his work even more meaningful, however, by going beyond a description of the war to the study of human nature itself. Kesten saw the coexistence of good and evil in this conflict, especially amidst the greatest adversities. In vividly executed scenes, Kesten depicted the horror of the bombardment, while simultaneously maintaining a stylistic mastery of undisputed beauty: "Guernica burned to ashes, and its people burned to ashes. . . . The altar burned, the church burned. The wool on the sheep burned, as did the hair of the sheepherder. . . . Far into the horizon, the anguished sky bled. Dead telephone wires trailed over demolished houses. Blackened trees thrust forth their stubs like beggars. No one gave alms. Some people were naked. No saint shared his cloak" (*Gernika*).

Arthur Koestler was another exile author who wrote eloquently of the Spanish Civil War. While his *Ein Spanisches Testament* is in actuality an autobiography, it nevertheless is one of the most important works associated with German exile writers and the Spanish Civil War. It was especially significant in that it was not merely a historical report on atrocities perpetrated by the rightists in taking the city of Malaga, but also an autobiographical introspection of his plight as a prisoner condemned to death for his earlier work in revealing the cruelties of the Franco forces.

Koestler's inherent objectivity was manifested in his criticism of the Republicans' lack of leadership and discipline, and the cowardice in their premature retreat from Malaga. In infinite detail he contrasted the monotony of life in prison with the agony of a man condemned to death. In moving passages he maintained that once this anguish is overcome, one can experience the most perfect sense of complete freedom. The essential theme of the book revealed itself in the fusing of a nation's suffering in one man. Additionally, *Ein Spanisches Testament* also revealed that Koestler's experiences in Spain (and also the Moscow Purge Trials) were directly responsible for his decision to leave the Communist Party—in spite of the fact that a world-wide free Koestler movement was mounted in his behalf and was instrumental in finally attaining his freedom.

Another well-known work dealing with the Spanish Civil War was *Torquemadas Schatten*, a novel written by the German émigré, Karl Otten. Set in Mallorca, it dealt with the criminality of fascism which befell the citizens of the island who theretofore had been living in harmony with nature. Otten com-pared the plight of the Mallorcans with the Jews, Moors, and Christian "heretics" persecuted by the infamous Grand Inquisitor. Otten's idealism ultimately revealed itself, however, in the conclusion that good is indestructible, and in the final analysis will triumph.

Another less-known but important historical novel was Ernst Sommer's *Botschaft aus Granada*. As in Otten's work, the atrocities of the Grand Inquisitor also served as a point of departure for commentary on the Republican struggle. Sommer drew the analogy of the Jews' expulsion from Spain in 1492 and the German refugees' plight in the 1930's. By interweaving the fate of the émigrés with Christopher Columbus' historic voyage, the author imparted even greater meaningfulness to the struggle. The New World, and also the future of the émigrés, represented uncertainty, but also great hope.

An additional, far more extensive, segment of exile literature evoked by the Spanish Civil War were the many lyrical and poetic works written by the German émigrés. This body of literature was, in fact, so extensive that it still cannot be adequately surveyed. Amongst these poems, the many *Kampflieder* ["combat songs"], written to inspire both renewed courage in the soldiers and international resistance, were the most significant. Undoubtedly one of the most prominent of the *Kampflieder* was Karl Ernst's verse, "Spaniens Himmel breitet seine Sterne über unsere Schützengräber aus." The inherent emotionalism of this work led to its adoption as the song of the International Brigades. It was immediately translated into several languages, and is still popular in East Germany today.

Another prominent writer associated with the *Kampflieder* was Erich Weinert. As a staunch Communist who was passionately anti-fascist, he projected all of his creative energies into the Republican struggle. Some of the recurrent themes found in Weinert's poems were the heroism of the combatants, the condemnation of "fascist atrocities," and the appeal for a common resistance in the fight by all those who cherish freedom. This poet-militant beseeched his audiences, "Do you not hear the fire bells ring in Europe?"

Other German exile writers were notable for the many ballads they wrote, both to inspire courage in the soldiers and to expose the alleged atrocities of the Rightists. Many, although unable to participate in the actual fighting in Spain, took what was for them the only available alternative—the writing of poetry—to protest the "inhumanity of the fascist aggressors." In one of these ballads the excruciating physical torment of a Republican soldier whom the Rightists substituted for a bull in the arena was depicted. The preoccupation with such brutal themes in fact seemed to border on what one critic [Frederick B. Benson] has called the "pornography of violence."

Other ballads propounded the same theme of the cruelty of the war. In one work the insignificance of a child's life is asserted in the public apathy concerning his death. In another Britain is castigated for her unwillingness to involve herself in the Republican struggle.

Still other well-known ballads included Bertolt Brecht's "Mein Bruder war ein Flieger," and Erich Arendt's collection of poems, *Bergwindballade*. Brecht's poem satirically recounted the exploits of a fighter pilot whose ultimate "conquest" was his grave. The simplicity and sardonic satire of this ballad manifested its inherent literary merit.

Erich Arendt's volume of poems, which dealt in part with his experiences in the Spanish Civil War, did not appear until 1952.

Anti-Nazi Germans of the International Brigade in Madrid. UPI/Bettmann Newsphotos.

The very title of the volume itself, in fact, was meant to symbolize the spirit of resistance of the Spanish people. Many of the poems in this collection, however, also compared the Republican struggle with the Russian revolution. Although this collection reflected Arendt's idealism and adherence to Communist doctrine, he enriched German literature through his frequent usage of the popular *flamenco* form.

While the works cited here constitute only a small segment of the large body of poetry occasioned by the Civil War, the inherently belligerent tendency of this genre is self-evident. The emotionalism of the *Kampflieder* in particular was made apparent by the poets' accusations, calls-to-arms, and propaganda. For these German exile writers, poetry became a weapon in the fight against fascism.

The foregoing examination of German exile literature occasioned by the Spanish Civil War should demonstrate that the influence of this conflict on these authors was, if varied, indeed profound, and generated a strong, uniform commitment. These writers, whether in active battle or with the weapon of the written word, identified with the cause of the Republic and supported it in their struggle for freedom against the common enemy, fascism. Although many of these authors were Leftist, and indeed, in some cases, convinced Communists, their support of the Republican cause should not be dismissed solely as Communist-influenced. Many so-called ''bourgeois'' writ-

ers such as Thomas Mann, Franz Werfel, and Hermann Kesten, who were not professed Communists, renounced their traditional poetic isolation to join socialist writers in a common front against what they viewed as the threat of fascism. After many years of political exile, they finally saw a ray of hope, an opportunity to end the blight which had settled over Germany. In their constant reference to the ''Other Germany,'' they were asserting that Hitler alone did not constitute the spirit of the German nation.

In addition, much of the literature which originated under these circumstances was propagandistic and therefore is mainly of interest from a historical perspective. Nevertheless, the large body of artistically redeeming literature of this period probably will continue to form a part of our literary repertoire. In fact, an important indicator of this significance of this phase in the history of German exile literature is its growing popularity with scholars, in contrast with the heretofore more historical examination of the Spanish Civil War. While East German literary historians initially attempted to exploit the role of German exile authors in Spain from a Communist perspective, earnest attempts are also being made now in the West to clarify the effect of this conflict on the German émigrés.

In sum, then, it is evident that most of these works reflected some definite literary quality in their evocation of the significance and panorama of the Spanish Civil War. It should be remarked parenthetically that even the propagandistic works demanded some degree of expression to appeal to the intellectual audience whom these writers were addressing. While the authors were uniformly dedicated to what they viewed as the anti-fascist struggle, the inherent idealism apparent in their works was all-pervasive. They sought the abolition of fascism, and looked toward the dawn of a world free from injustice. The lasting significance of the commitment of the German exile writers to the Republican cause, however, is to be found in their united defense of freedom and humanity at a dark time in world history. That the Republic was ultimately defeated cannot detract from the sense of purpose of their action. (pp. 65-7)

> Gerhard Mack, "German Exile Authors and the Spanish Civil War," in Proceedings: Pacific Northwest Council on Foreign Languages, *Vol. XXX, April 19-21, 1979, pp. 64-7.*

POLITICAL IDEALISM AND WAR LITERATURE

HUGH D. FORD

[*Ford is an American critic and educator whose works reflect his interest in the writings of American and British authors who remained in Europe after the close of the First World War. In the following excerpt from his* Poets' War: British Poets and the Spanish War, *he discusses British poets as Republican partisans and as literary artists, examining the nature of their loyalty to the cause and the expression of their social and political ideals in their poetry.*]

It is evident that most of the British poetry of the Spanish Civil War has far more historic value than intrinsic literary worth. Only a few Spanish war poems can compare favorably, either technically or thematically, with the best poems written about the two world wars. Yet their weaknesses must not dim their importance as a repository—at once exciting, hopeful, and sad—of the social and political attitudes of a generation of British poets. If we have enough charity to make allowances for all the verbal pyrotechnics and the technical pretentiousness, as well as for the overt oversimplifying and romanticizing of the struggle, which are the chief faults of their work, we can, perhaps, agree that collectively these poets implemented their belief in the Spanish Republic by creating a literature that is at least morally earnest if it is not technically distinguished. Besides intensifying their political beliefs, the Spanish struggle moved their consciences as men; it aroused in them a greater concern for humanity. Backing the Republic transcended just supporting the liberal-democratic tradition represented by the Azaña government; it meant being on the side of social justice and progress; it meant defending civilization itself. As poets, their duty to mankind was clear, and if it was manifested in ringing challenges to the conscience of Western humanity, it was not because they had abjured their responsibilities as poets but because they were aware of them.

There is considerable acumen in Spender's assertion that he and his colleagues "may . . . have written, during the Spanish Civil War, the English poetry of a just democratic war against Fascist tyranny." The description is applicable to the work of nearly all the [British poets writing on the Spanish Civil War]. . . . Most did not even visit Spain. They knew little or nothing about the internecine feuding among the political groups supporting the Republic, and they relied—probably too much—

on the announcements of the Popular Front for information about the struggle. Moreover, they probably acceded too readily to the vision that the Republic represented "democracy" (it did, of course, but they accepted it dogmatically, and not after proper reflection), that the choice was between fascism and "democracy," and that their duty was to support the Republic. When duty demanded attending or speaking at Popular Front rallies, or at the "boring meeting," or, as was more often the case, employing their talents to write the "flat ephemeral pamphlet," or verses acclaiming the Republican cause, they responded. Forsaking the traditional privacy of the artist, and perhaps even artistic ambitions for the "democratic" cause was a costly but necessary sacrifice. Among other things, it meant collaborating with political parties and individual politicians more closely than ever before. If acting for the public interest conflicted with the responsibility they felt toward their art, there was at least the consoling and encouraging factor that the right action might help restore democracy in Spain, and deter the Fascist dictators from further aggression.

Now that we can see the Spanish war from the other side in time, and have been forced to view it through the dark prisms of Arthur Koestler and George Orwell, and have heard that Stalin betrayed the Republic and turned Spain into a "convenient killers' lane" for political unreliables, and that after the war he even went so far as to liquidate many of the Russians and Spaniards who presumably knew too much about what had happened in Spain, it is tempting to conclude that these poets were merely docile pawns in a power struggle, that they were duped by cynical politicians, and that their ideals turned out to be ideological chimeras. Whatever truth this conventional literary picture of the Spanish war many possess—and its most recent supporter, Julian Symons, is a most knowledgeable critic of the thirties—it seems to me to fail to take into account two important matters: first, the knowledge that was not available to most people, including the poets, at the time of the war; second, the possibility of retaining a belief in the justice and purity of the Spanish war despite whatever pernicious schemes any political group might have tried to carry out in Spain. Who among these poets, even among the Communists, was perspicacious enough to foresee, in 1936-37, the outcome of the war, or to suspect how much falsehood and distortion existed beneath the surface? And even when a few, such as Auden and Spender, found instances of dishonesty or ruthlessness, their first reaction was to assume that the situation probably made a certain amount of persecution and chicanery unavoidable. Of course they were disturbed, and rebelled against the "deliberate lie," but they also went on supporting the Republic. At least for awhile, even in Spender's case, a few wrongs did not soil the just cause. Condoning what seemed impure was not simple self-deception either. Most of these poets were not completely ingenuous. If war contained the sordid, it also promised to win what was worthwhile, and if the latter had to be achieved partly by ignoble means, then this was only one of many paradoxes of war.

Contributing to the legend that these poets somehow failed to act responsibly during the Spanish war is the belief that in the long run they were ineffective. For all their foresight and concern and sacrifice, the Spanish Republic did lose and six months later the Second World War did begin. Had they, then, expended themselves for a lost, or as it is often called, an illusory cause? It would be going beyond the bounds of this study to go into the reasons for the defeat of the Spanish Republic, except to say that, at bottom, they were mostly political and that the burden of guilt must be shared partly by the democracies and not by Russia alone. But despite the loss of the Republic and the failure of these poets to effect social change, it seems to me completely unfair to dismiss them, ex post facto, as poets who betrayed their functions as poets, or who abjured their responsibilities as men. The lost battle does not lessen the really generous idealism and industry and hope and purpose that they put into it. To scorn their defense of the Republic is to mock their belief in humanity at a time when it was above all needed. To berate their sense of purpose, which was predicated on the belief that the individual could alter the course of events, is to belittle their determination to confront fascism when appeasement was winning applause. Certainly, it can be said that those who fought in Spain did so primarily for political reasons. But they were also conscious of their role as defenders of Europe's spiritual and cultural tradition. In the largest sense, Ralph Fox, Charles Donnelly, John Cornford, Christopher Caudwell, and Julian Bell died for this tradition. Those who never ventured to the battlefields made fewer and, of course, less important sacrifices, but they nonetheless responded to the challenge of their time by sacrificing, in some degree, their artistic hopes for the sake of mankind. The loss of the Republic reflects no discredit upon their participation in the struggle to preserve it.

The only illusions a few of these poets had concerned the morality of politicians and political parties, or their ability to combine the functions of poet and politician. The point often

Stephen Spender with a child, Calle Lista, Madrid, March 1937. Marx Memorial Library.

overlooked by commentators on the Spanish war is that the ideals these poets believed in and, in some instances, fought for, were and are noble ones. In the widest sense, it is of little importance whether the poet happened to be a Communist or not. If a Communist, he was most likely a dedicated Marxist, and consequently not apt to object to the operations of the NKVD [the forerunner of the KGB] in Spain or to the infiltration of Communists into military and governmental positions. And above all, he was under no illusions about respecting the rights of uncooperative groups like the POUM [a independent Marxist party]. If he was a non-Communist, he either cooperated with Communists, or dissociated himself from organizations in which Communists were influential and supported the Republic as an individual. As for the claim that the Soviets betrayed the Spanish Republic—and the claim has been vigorously supported—it is still a moot question whether the real betrayer was not the democracies, England, France, and even the United States, all of whom hid behind nonintervention policies while Russia became the only major nation to assist the Republic. Furthermore, the Loyalists were able to fight as long as they did only because Russia sent supplies, whether or not for Stalin's own benefit. It is not so simple to contend that the Spanish Civil War produced a crop of disillusioned idealists, for among the Communists there was only Koestler, and among the socialists and liberals there were only a few, such as Orwell, who continued to support the Republicans even while he somewhat unreasonably excoriated the Communists. The point is, there were few among these poets who really felt that they had been betrayed, that they had been duped or cheated by the Soviets or anyone else. Those mainly responsible for the belief that Stalin betrayed the intellectuals who supported the Republic are Koestler, who, as a dissident, was interested mostly in justifying his defection, and Orwell, who, by his own admission, was politically naïve when he joined the POUM and who, after all, saw the war only in Catalonia.

But, it might be asked, did not Auden, Spender, and Day Lewis experience something like betrayal when, during the Spanish war, they discovered that the cause they were espousing was being sullied by political chicanery despite their own good intentions? And did they not declare that a philosophy that pursued its ends by the most reprehensible means had become intolerable? And was not this nearly an open condemnation of Marxism, and hence an admission that they had been mistaken, if not actually betrayed? While the answer to each question is yes, there is some doubt about whether their encounter with Marxism really ended with a feeling that they had been betrayed, or whether, during the period of the Spanish war, they had learned not only that war was unpleasant, but that Marxism made unusually heavy demands in a time of crisis, demands that afforded more insight into the movement they had aligned themselves with than they had ever had before. In other words, having been forced into closer relations with Marxists at all levels, did they finally comprehend that there was a difference between professing to be a Marxist and actually being one? If so, was not their experience more like a revelation than a betrayal?

As much as their vociferous colleagues, Auden, Spender, and Day Lewis wanted to be useful, and their contributions to the cause were considerable. Auden went to Spain, at least with the intention of volunteering for ambulance duty, wrote "Spain" and donated the receipts to Spanish Medical Aid. Spender joined the Communist Party, made three trips to Spain, spoke at Popular Front rallies, attended Writers' Conferences, and in a spate of articles published between 1936 and 1939 defended the legitimacy and morality of the Madrid government. He celebrated the heroism of the international volunteers, praised the meticulous care with which the Republic had handled Spain's art masterpieces, and confirmed the agony of Spain which Picasso had epitomized in *Guernica*. In writing alone, Spender did more than either Lewis or Auden to advance the Loyalist cause. Lewis, already a Communist when the war started, performed, until the spring of 1938, innumerable tasks for the party and the Republic, the extent of which can be measured partly by the artistic sacrifices they incurred. Besides these specific duties, they all lent their names to pro-Loyalist groups, appeared at demonstrations sponsored by the Popular Front, signed petitions, and answered questionnaires.

But, ironically, it was this very willingness to sink their individualities in the collective forces of politics that led ultimately to a repudiation of the political life. An event as momentous as the Spanish war was needed to push them into the noisy hurly-burly world of mass demonstrations and expediency. But they nevertheless accepted it all hopefully, although apprehensively, and gave it their full support. How else could they hope to be really effective in the struggle to save civilization from fascism? The sacrifice in terms of time lost to their art was of minimal consequence if collective action worked to deter the enemy. The world of political exigency and intrigue, however, proved to be as disruptive and disconcerting to Lewis, Spender and Auden as the sudden embroilment in warfare had been to Cornford, Bell, and Donnelly. Somewhat at a loss as to how they could make themselves useful, they rather docilely obeyed the whims and crude directives of party leaders, who generally lacked the insight to use them and other intellectuals effectively. Gradually, they lost faith in their abilities as amateur politicians, partly because they objected to the ethics of expediency and the moral duplicity of the propagandists and parties with whom they worked. They became increasingly skeptical of the choice they had made and, finally, they withdrew completely from political life. Auden retired first, in 1937, and Lewis and Spender followed not long afterward. And in each case, the reason for withdrawing was the same: the belief that a worthy goal could be attained without having to resort to cynical and corrupting means, which in the long run could only damage the goal.

It seems evident now that the slogans and rigid ideology and opportunism of the extreme Left, which they had at one time treated with "considerable levity or scepticism," had finally become too powerful for their separate individualities as writers, and that unless they removed themselves from the political realm quickly they, like Orestes, would be pursued forever "by Furies of Ends and Means, Propaganda and Necessity." Withdrawal was in no sense a surrender, or an admission that fascism could not be contained. It was done partly in the interests of self-defense, to decide how their own beliefs, which had grown firmer as a result of their political experience, might be made more effective. That their retirement from politics in no way signified that they were abandoning the Republican cause both Spender and Lewis confirmed at the time.

All that really happened was that a close-up view of political life had led to shedding some political illusions. Left-wing politics proved to be too potent for them to accept, and they consequently made some revaluations about how social change could best be effected. To say, then, that they were betrayed one has to assume that they had been deliberately hoodwinked, tricked, or misled. That they were mistaken about Marxism there can be no doubt. But when they became aware of their

own errors, they readjusted their views, which they could not have done prior to the Spanish war, because it was only during that war that they discovered what political commitment really involved.

If we consider the war as a crucible which tested the charges that Cornford, Caudwell, and Bell made against Auden, Spender, and Day Lewis, we must concede that it verified most of their accusations. As a group, they resisted placing their talents as poets at the disposal of propagandists or political groups; they scrupulously put their art above politics, and it remained, as Caudwell had predicted, bourgeois rather than revolutionary, by which he meant that they would continue to write for a middle-class audience rather than for the "people." Neither did they declass themselves to achieve that amalgamation with the workers which, according to the Marxists, was the talismanic rite that permitted one to write as a true revolutionary. They remained what they had essentially always been: middle-class intellectuals, with a penchant for social change and all that promised improved conditions, whose poetry alternately showed a revolutionary zeal and respect for art, but who stood outside the class struggle and hence maintained that a division between life and art existed.

That Spender, Auden, and Lewis were primarily poets, not politicians, and that they were inspired first of all by the Loyalist cause and not Marxism, their Spanish war poems abundantly show. In verse free from political slogans and cant words, polemics and dialectics, they consciously strove to avoid the pitfalls of the political poem. Nonconformists in both form and content, they insisted, even under the pressure of war, on the artist's inviolate right of choice. And perhaps it is for this reason that their Spanish war poems, generally, lack a feeling of *élan*. Auden's "Spain," despite the poet's efforts to impregnate the struggle with meaning, is at bottom a denial of Marxism. The intellectual vigor, the cosmic sweep, and the vitality of metaphor all help to transform the struggle into something unprecedented and even magnificent. But Auden seemed so painfully aware that, although the balance of justice resided with the Republic, the struggle would demand tremendous sacrifice, and that ideals could not substantially lessen the pain of that sacrifice. At best, "Spain" commented on the historical and social significance of the war, but at the center of the poem exist a vacuity, an emotional void, an absence of commitment, which, paradoxically, helps to explain its partial failure as well as its reputation as a poem considerably above the caliber of most Spanish war verse. Auden shunned the excesses of propagandist verse, but he did not conceal, even under the grand metaphorical layers, an emotional and perhaps even an intellectual inadequacy to deal with the Spanish war. The studied, hypothetical content and elegant form arouse speculation, but the poem never suggests that Auden is doing more than stating an argument. We are intrigued by his brilliant insights, but they leave us unmoved.

Lewis' poems, though decidedly more partisan in feeling than Auden's, are almost politically neutral. They celebrate universal themes suggested by the war: man's irrepressible desire for freedom, the cruelty involved in war, and the idealism that prompts men to volunteer to fight in another country. Even in "The Volunteer," his tribute to the British members of International Brigades, Lewis avoided assigning to them any definite political motives that would explain their presence in Spain. The only certainty is that the volunteers presage a new social integration and greater freedom. *The Nabara* celebrates the same theme: freedom is more than a word, a belief decidedly nonpartisan and timeless.

The exclusion of political ideology from war verse is best illustrated in the case of Spender. For personal reasons, he was perhaps more deeply involved in the Spanish war than either Auden or Lewis, although for him politics counted too. But despite this Spender rigidly omitted from his war poetry all but what was "true to his own experience," which disallowed any overt acclamation of the Republican cause with which he was so closely associated in public life. Most of his poetry, therefore, is an examination of the human predicament, the hopeless confusion of men caught up in the chaos of war and their inability to adapt to it or escape from it. Thus, its negative quality is unmistakable, and its inchoate antiwar sentiment is redolent of Owen and Sassoon. Only the "smaller unheroic truths" of Spender's experience in Spain come through, and too often they are somewhat commonplace thoughts on suffering, fear, and death. In "Fall of a City," the one poem where the ideological meanings of the war emerge, Spender adumbrated the hope that flowered even as the tragedy of defeat overtook the Republicans. But since only this poem and "At Castellon" are ones in which Spender turned away from the "smaller unheroic truths," and since neither does more than suggest the idealistic side of the war, we must conclude that Spender was—quite rightly—asserting his belief in the inviolability of the artist and his art. That is, Spender must have assumed that an examination of ideals or aims, regardless if he happened to agree with them, lay outside his immediate experience and was therefore unsuitable for poetry. Such a view, while it no doubt kept Spender from writing the deliberately propagandistic poem, scarcely allowed him all the materials he needed to write circumspectly about this most idealistic of all wars.

The most conspicuous weakness of the war verse written by poets who remained in England during the conflict is its contemporaneousness. In their opinion, so many and so urgent were the immediate needs—the need to ridicule nonintervention out of existence, the need to warn the world of the spread of fascism—that there was no time left to ponder anything except the most pressing demands of the moment. Eager to function as Cassandras whose prophecies would be heeded, they mistakenly ignored two matters that reduced their influence both as prophets and poets. First, they knew almost nothing about warfare; and second, and more important, they had almost no idea of the complex origins of the Spanish war. As a result, they depended for the content of their verse upon the press, or more often upon experienced propagandists like Charles Duff, Willi Muenzenberg, and H. C. O'Neill. Instead of being the shapers of opinion, they became the ones whom opinion shaped. What the time needed, they felt, was not interpretations or personal reactions to war so much as concise directives about what had to be done to effect a Republican victory in order to prevent world catastrophe. Toward this end, they argued that their verse made a major contribution.

Obviously, they ignored C. Day Lewis' admonition that one must write only about what one experiences first as a man rather than as a poet. And the poems of Gawsworth, Mallalieu, Heinemann, Richardson, Warner, Lindsay, Rickword, and Howard illustrate the difficulty of attempting to fit one's poetic talent into a rigid political movement. Nearly always the result was either verse journalism or rhetoric, which sometimes unashamedly echoed the oratory of Popular Front speakers, or pilfered their slogans and clichés. Almost everything about it was synthetic. Grafting onto a poetic structure the inflexible dogmatism of their outlook on Spain proved disastrous. Seldom

were slogans successfully assimilated and transposed into the substance of poetry.

Unlike their colleagues in England, Cornford, Donnelly and, occasionally, even Wintringham expressed some antiwar feeling alongside the expected doctrinaire political pronouncements. When the experience of war became the raw material of their verse, the result was poetry that conveyed an intense and sincere emotion, often in language that was at once simple and lucid and yet capable of suggesting the emotional overtones of the situation. In this sense, at least, there was a unity of word and deed in their best poetry. Cornford and Donnelly, besides showing more technical promise than Wintringham and most of the others, alone seemed capable of transcending the particular and the demands of political orthodoxy and attaining something like universal significance in their verse. As seminal poets they demand attention.

But because the Spanish struggle was not just an ordinary war for the Marxist poets, they felt the need to reinforce its peculiar meanings. They believed they had to explain not only their part in the war. But, more importantly, they believed they had to justify its tremendous cost. to this end, they often turned their verse into a platform for a political ideology, and it was when they tried to vindicate or sanctify the Republican cause, which they regarded as embodying the goals of communism, that their poetry was in danger of becoming a treatise. For supporting a conflict by ideological reasons meant subsuming its meaner aspects in favor of its supposedly more positive ones. It meant distorting an ugly experience so that it became something wholesome and even heroic. While Wintringham's attempts to use ideology to justify the pain of war degenerated into misrepresentation and patent falsehood, the similar efforts of Cornford and Donnelly benefited from at least being rendered more poetically. Wintringham saw the war first as a political commissar; Cornford and Donnelly were more apt to view it as poets. The doctrinaire elements in their exhortative stanzas, although less bulky and pronounced, nonetheless seriously damage the over-all effect of their poems. The conclusions of Cornford's "As Our Might Lessens" and "Full Moon at Tierz," for example, illustrate the compulsion he felt to include certain ideological pronouncements. This is not to say that Marxism was incapable of generating poetry. Rather, it was too often a case of the ideology being unimaginatively rendered, as dogma rather than poetry, as theory rather than thought which was the result of an intensification process involving the poet and the ideas.

As for the remainder of the volunteer-poets, little needs to be said. Being participants, they were naturally closer to the heat of the struggle than most, which no doubt made any concentrated creative work exceedingly difficult. In attempting to reproduce the effect which the war made upon them, or more simply, to document as realistically as possible their own observations, they lapsed into a pretentiousness of style which, in turn, either created unnecessary confusion or blurred the overall effect of their poetry. As art their verses scarcely count. But taken as somewhat ingenuous yet serious attempts to record the impression of a powerful social event, these slight verses reveal the fugacity of political ideology. What Hyndman, Lepper, Birch, Branson, and Marshall recorded bespoke a lot less about their devotion to a political ideal than their disgust with the entire experience of war.

Proof that the war could appeal to poets for reasons besides its immediate political and social importance is found in the poems by three poets who had only tenuous connections with the Left. Barker, Read, and MacNeice sympathized with the Republic, but their main concern was not a Loyalistic victory. It was something more personal and, in a sense, more significant than victory. Barker's three poems, especially *Calamiterror,* form a study in self-integration, which culminated in "Elegy on Spain." The theme is the poet's development, his turning away from excessive self-interest toward greater compassion and oneness with humanity, and it was the Spanish war which embodied these qualities that helped to effect his integration. Barker's steady advance toward greater social responsibility unify these poems.

The engaging idealism of the Spanish anarchists appealed to Read's rather exalted concept of anarchism. Although it could be argued that his interests were basically social, it is apparent that his belief in anarchism necessitated seeing it as apolitical and as a philosophy of life based on organic change and freedom. His espousal of anarchism, therefore, differed from the emotional sort of homage most Leftists paid to the Republican cause. Where the verses of the latter bayed the slogans of the Popular Front, Read managed to convey the essence of anarchism in spare yet impressive images.

Roy Campbell and Louis MacNeice had at least one thing in common. Prior to the outbreak of the Spanish war, both remained well outside the realm of politics. The political currents stirred up by the war impressed both poets, particularly Campbell. However, his embroilment in the struggle came about primarily because of a wish to defend the Catholic faith and to castigate his literary enemies, rather than from any desire to propound the merits of fascism. Since the disposition of friends and foes on the Republican and Nationalist sides coincided so completely with his likes and dislikes, the urge to condemn or extol proved far stronger than the need to see and feel the misfortunes of war. Except in a few short verses, Campbell used his Spanish war poems as convenient and, at times, devastating sounding boards for his long pent-up grudges. And when he stopped venting his spleen, he marveled at his own prescience, or expounded on the wondrous nature of the Church. MacNeice's political involvement in the Spanish war was even less complete than Campbell's; in fact, it is a moot question whether MacNeice felt any political commitment at all. Like Campbell, who was inspired by the courageous Carmelite priests at Toledo, MacNeice felt that the resurgence of human values in war-weary Barcelona was a moving and awesome testament of man's goodness. His whole concern was with the sense of human dignity that had somehow managed to assert itself even in the midst of war.

Although the matter of writing "poetry for the people" has been mentioned in various places, the subject should be amplified a bit more here, for the reason that many believed the Spanish war might effect a closer relationship between poet and public. David Daiches, for example, writing shortly after the war had ended, noted that the Spanish war had given the "first real impetus to this [unification] movement," and prophesied that "the struggle for Spain against the fascist invader" would "one day be seen to have meant more for English poetry than the Greek struggle for independence meant for the Romantics of the early nineteenth century." Communists like Cornford, Caudwell, and Fox had expounded upon the need for a "people's literature" long before the outbreak of war in Spain. But the possibility of a truly formidable proletariat literature seemed immeasurably greater once the war had begun. Of course, not all who sympathized with the Spanish workers would consent to write for the masses. But many felt that the struggle in Spain was symptomatic of some sort of new integration of the classes, which would affect the nature of literature.

The strongest agitators for integration of poet and public turned out to be the amateur poets who published *Poetry and the People,* the repository for most of the verse written by members of the Poets' Groups formed by the Left Book Club. Their objectives were to "stimulate and encourage the poet to write out of his experience, to reflect the life and feelings of his fellowmen, to arouse an interest in such poetry among the people, and bring the poet and the people into as close a contact as possible for their mutual understanding and enjoyment." Appeals went out from *Poetry and the People* for verse that was "vivid, real, alive," that "appealed to people on the basis of their own real life experience." The response, though large, was hardly aesthetically satisfying. Beginners had no idea of how to go about writing a poem, and their first efforts were embarrassing imitations of school verse on which had been grafted some revolutionary material. No matter how bad the verse was, the editors, themselves poets, felt that a start had been made toward reaching a mass audience. What Jack Lindsay, Janet Watson, Miles Carpenter, Julius Lipton and other more or less professional poets on the staff of *Poetry and the People* learned, however, was that most workers could be made to listen to a poem, providing it was easily understood, but that they were unable to write a decent line.

To say, however, that this work presaged the fusion of the literary world with the world at large, or with the laboring classes, necessitates asking the related question of why the movement, once started, failed to continue. One answer, no doubt an obvious one, is that it became increasingly difficult for poets to find new "mass" themes once the focus and stimulus provided by the war had ceased to exist. As Julian Symons noted in his evaluation of the period, the end of the war meant the end of Spain as a "symbol of hope, pride, and reproach." Moreover, it terminated "a whole way of life." A few months after the fall of Madrid—and after the Nazi-Soviet pact—"the great tide of left-wing feeling had receded beyond the bounds of vision, and the land it had covered was as smooth, almost, as though the tide had never been." The retreat from large social themes to more subjective material was the inevitable result.

The poetry of the Spanish Civil War marks, then, not only the climax but also the end of a phase of British poetry. At no time during the decade had so many poets written so much about a single social event. Never before had they been so closely identified with a popular movement that embraced so many disparate elements. Never before had verse been forced to bear so many extraliterary functions. But despite all the sincerity and moral integrity that lay behind this poetry, it reinforces the lesson that good crusaders do not necessarily become good poets. The majority of them, with the noteworthy exceptions of Auden, Spender, Lewis, Barker, Read, and MacNeice, turned their verse into a tool with which to cajole, coerce, badger, and threaten their countrymen into supporting the Spanish Republic. Instead of interpreting their times, they sought to transform them. This is perhaps the worst result of the generally unhappy relationship between poetry and politics.

Perhaps the best that can be said for their work is that it is a fascinating and invaluable mirror of an era, reflecting what Elizabeth Bowen has called the Romantic Movement of our century. The comparison is not inappropriate. Just as the first and second generation Romantics of the last century imbibed the spirit of revolutionary ideals from France, Spain, and Greece and envisaged the dawn of a new world, so the British poets of the Spanish war thrilled to the prospect of turning ideals into realities. Their generous idealism and compassion and purpose were exhausted on behalf of a cause which, despite all the political distortions it has undergone, embodied as much truth and nobility as any which excited Byron, Shelley, or Wordsworth. And the majority of British poets have never lost faith in this cause. They have perhaps become suspicious of ideology. But they have not stopped believing that the Republican cause stood for tolerance, freedom, and human dignity. (pp. 252-71)

[As Hugh Thomas] has pointed out, the Spanish war was the last in a series of liberal European revolutions. But it was also the precursor of the social revolutions which have flared up on all continents since the end of the Second World War. Its position as perhaps a turning point in European history can be suggested for still another reason. And that is, that the issues about which the war was fought are the very issues which continue to divide the world today. It is unnecessary to say more than that these issues remain unresolved, and that, therefore, in an important sense the Spanish Civil War is not yet finished. Perhaps it is also unnecessary to remind the reader at this point that among those who first saw the need to resolve such issues were the socially conscious poets of the 1930's. (p. 271)

> *Hugh D. Ford, in a conclusion in his* A Poets' War: British Poets and the Spanish Civil War, *University of Pennsylvania Press, 1965, pp. 252-71.*

RONALD RADOSH

[*Radosh is an American historian and critic who contributes essays and reviews to various political journals. His works often reflect his view that "the study of history does not allow us to reach back to the past and find ready-made answers for today. Rather, it does allow us to learn how we got to where we are so that individually and collectively we can formulate relevant alternatives for the present and become actors in making our own history." In the following excerpt from an essay written in 1986, Radosh examines what he considers the deluded idealism and corruption of intellectual integrity of many authors who devoted themselves and their writings to the Republican cause.*]

Coming to terms with the truth about the Spanish Civil War seems more than ever to pose insurmountable difficulties for those intellectuals—perhaps the majority—who were brought up to believe that Spain in the Thirties was the one great cause in that "low dishonest decade," as Auden called it, which need never be either reconsidered or repented. Yet the publication of two new anthologies on the fiftieth anniversary of the war—Valentine Cunningham's *Spanish Front* and John Miller's *Voices Against Tyranny* [see Additional Bibliography]—together with the discussion they have generated come as a sober reminder that this is a subject that remains part of the unfinished business of recent intellectual history. "No episode in the 1930s," Paul Johnson has aptly observed [in his *Modern Times: The World from the Twenties to the Eighties*], "has been more lied about that this one, and only in recent years have historians begun to dig it out from the mountain of mendacity beneath which it was buried for a generation." Judging from some recent commentaries on Spain in the Thirties, there are still many intellectuals who would prefer—even today—to let the terrible truth remain buried rather than have their fantasies of a noble past destroyed. (p. 5)

Understanding some of [the history of the Spanish Civil War] is a prerequisite for evaluating the story of the Western intellectuals and their response to the Civil War. . . . Alfred Kazin [see Additional Bibliography] and others make much of Orwell's statement that though there was much he did not understand and did not even like about revolutionary Barcelona, "I recognized it immediately as a state of affairs worth fighting for." The quotation is accurate, but those who cite Orwell tend to omit the careful distinction he made between the original revolt and the very different reality after 1937. Orwell recognized this new reality full well, and he did not like what he saw. While he heralded Spain of August 1936 as a people's revolt, he had reached the sad conclusion that by January of 1937 "the Communists were using every possible method, fair and foul, to stamp out what was left of the revolution." He went on to cite, as one of his reviews reprinted in *Spanish Front* reminds us, "the ceaseless arrests, the censored newspapers and the prowling hordes of armed police," comparing the situation to a "nightmare." Does anyone really think that this was the Spain that Orwell saw as worth defending and fighting for?

Spain, as Mr. Kazin has so eloquently reminded us, became the central metaphor for artists, intellectuals, and writers of the 1930s. Hemingway immortalized the conflict in *For Whom the Bell Tolls,* although the veterans of the International Brigades were angered by his critical portrayal of the fanatic French commissar, André Marty. Nicknamed "the butcher of Albacete" because of his murder of at least five hundred of his own men for desertion or Trotskyism, Marty is believed to have killed, by a minimum count, one-tenth of all the volunteers who died in Spain.

"Madrid is the heart," of a world, a civilization and an ideal, Auden opined in his poem "Spain" (1937). He spoke for a generation when he said one had to put aside "the walks by the lake . . . the bicycle races." There was only one task: "But to-day the struggle." [The anthologies by Cunningham and Miller] remind us of just how much the attitude epitomized by Auden's poem (which he subsequently—to his honor—repudiated) was typical of the intellectual response at the time. They also serve to remind us, as Paul Johnson wrote, that "the intellectuals of the Left did not want to know the objective truth; they were unwilling for their illusions to be shattered. They were overwhelmed by the glamour and excitement of the cause and few had the gritty determination of Orwell to uphold absolute standards of morality."

In this respect, the role of Stephen Spender is particularly instructive. Spender has written the introduction to John Miller's anthology, *Voices Against Tyranny,* and he uses the opportunity to reflect on what Spain meant to the writers and artists of his generation [see excerpt above]. Spender now says that Auden, who had been criticized by Orwell for the poem on Spain, "came to agree with Orwell to the extent of feeling that his conscientious attempt to politicize his poetry in support of 'Spain' led him into very alien territory"; it opened him, Auden felt, to the grave charge of "using poetry to tell lies." Hence, because of the concluding lines of "Spain," Auden never allowed it to be reprinted during the remainder of his lifetime. The last lines of the poem had declared that

> History to the defeated
> May say Alas but cannot help nor pardon.

Auden commented that "[T]his is a lie." As for himself, Spender now admits that "there were atrocities on the Republican side perhaps equalling those committed by the rebels.'' On the subject of atrocities, however, he never refers to Arthur Koestler's account, in *The Invisible Writing,* of the way Comintern propagandist Otto Katz manufactured phony fascist atrocities out of his office in Paris. This is an important part of the story, for Stalinism was thus aided, as Paul Johnson writes, ''not only by superb public relations but by the naïveté, gullibility and, it must also be said, the mendacity and corruption of Western intellectuals, especially their willingness to overlook what W. H. Auden called 'the necessary murder.' ''

One might hope that, fifty years later, Western intellectuals would have more perspective on the events that once moved them into such tight corners. Yet, judging from Spender's introduction to *Voices Against Tyranny,* Spain still appears to be what Spender calls a simple ''direct confrontation between good and evil, right and wrong, freedom and tyranny.'' In this view, there was only one bad side—that of Franco. Spender does observe that Auden and he too curbed their true shock over things like the destruction of the churches. Looking back, he reflects, there was an authentic Wordsworthian recognition of the joys of rebellion, but he bemoans the fact ''that we could not see any of the terrible murders happening behind this scene of revolution.'' He now acknowledges ''that there is no trust to be placed in travellers' impressions of popular rejoicing soon after revolution.''

Spender, however, is still being disingenuous. His own career is a salutary reminder of how total identification with the ''right'' side corrupts intellectual integrity. One of the documents reprinted in Valentine Cunningham's *Spanish Front* is Spender's ''I Join the Communist Party''—printed in the London *Daily Worker* in 1937—in which Spender apologized for first doubting that the Moscow trials were anything but honest, and explained that he now understood the nature ''of the gigantic plot against the Soviet Government.'' This early heresy, Spender told his new comrades, occurred because he was then only ''a liberal approaching communism.'' Now that Spender understood that Stalin was right, he was ready to join the Party, evidently a necessity if one desired to go to Valencia to engage in anti-Fascist propaganda.

Having joined the Party, Spender became an ardent spokesman for it. In that capacity, he took part in the International Writers' Congress held in Madrid in 1937. . . . In Spain, Spender recorded, he and other delegates were ''treated like princes or ministers . . . riding in Rolls Royces, banqueted, fêted, sung and danced to,'' all while the battle raged around them. The same Writers' Congress was noted for its conclusion, which consisted of a massive attack on André Gide, who was excoriated as a ''fascist monster'' for the book he had recently published criticizing the USSR.

Spender's 1937 account tells how they were ''woken up at 4 a.m. by the air-raid alarms,'' as the reality of the war intruded upon the Congress. Evidently, it did not intrude too much for Spender to proclaim that the Spanish writer José Bergamín was the right man to rebuke Gide, because Bergamín had a ''mind which sees not merely the truth of isolated facts which Gide observed in the USSR, but the far more important truth of the effect which Gide's book is going to have.''

If Spender bought the classic rationale of the Stalinized intellectual, it was this affair that caused another participant in the Congress, the Dutch Communist Jef Last, to suffer a severe disillusionment. . . . Last could not accept the argument, presented to him by Egon Erwin Kisch, that when you hear of a Fascist bombing of a school you have ''to defend everything that has been done on our side, *even the trials!*'' Acting alone, Last protested against the Soviet delegates' demands that Gide be attacked by the Congress. Indeed, he pointed out, few in attendance had even read the book they were being asked to condemn. Gide had not been translated into Spanish and his book was not available anywhere in Spain.

Spender then stood with the regular Communists. Later, of course, he broke with them, and today he writes that there is a '' 'truth' of 'Spain' that remained independent of, and survived the mold of, Communism into which successive Republican governments were forced.'' (pp. 8-10)

But when Spender was in Spain—at the very time he was attending the 1937 Congress and spoke in Britain on behalf of aid for the International Brigades—he privately held to a different ''truth.'' It is to the credit of Valentine Cunningham that he includes the remarkable letter which Spender wrote to Virginia Woolf on April 2, 1937, in which the poet reflects that ''politicians are detestable anywhere,'' and that Spain has shown him ''the lies and unscrupulousness of some of the people who are recruiting at home'' for the International Brigades, including those ''of the *Daily Worker.*'' (p. 10)

Since Spender never said anything similar in public—and does not say anything like this in print even today—his letter is riveting. ''The sensitive, the weak, the romantic, the enthusiastic, the truthful live in Hell,'' he wrote to Woolf, ''and cannot get away.'' The Hell he spoke of was not that of Franco. ''The political commissars . . . bully so much that even people who were quite enthusiastic Party Members have been driven into hating the whole thing.'' Spender told the story of one veteran he spoke with, who ''complained to me bitterly about the inquisitional methods of the Party.'' Noting that it was a lie that the men were volunteers who could leave when they liked, Spender wrote Woolf that actually they were ''trapped there,'' and wounds or mental collapse were not considered grounds for leaving, ''unless one belongs to the Party élite and is sent home as a propagandist to show one's arm in a sling to audiences.'' Bitterly, Spender revealed that his closest friend fought in an offensive in which the men were sent to be slaughtered, with only olive groves for protection. After his friend's mental collapse, Spender tried to hire him as his personal secretary. The Party refused, and sent the man back to battle. He sought to escape, and was then put in a labor camp. Spender asked that nothing he had written be repeated, particularly ''the more unpleasant truths about the Brigade.''

Privately, Spender sought to help such men leave Spain, and he condemned the total fanaticism of the Party leaders who were really ''unconcerned with Spain'' and were intolerant of any dissent. But such truths had to be carefully guarded. Thus, Spender asked Woolf to quote his letter anonymously ''to any pacifist or democrat who wants to fight.'' Privately, he hoped they would refrain from enlistment with the International Brigades. Publicly, Spender towed the line, and his published poems supported the cause. Of the martyred John Cornford, he said, in a review written in September of 1938, that he exemplified ''the potentialities of a generation'' that was fighting ''for a form of society for which [it] was also willing to die.'' When Spender wrote the letter to Virginia Woolf, was he secretly hoping that she would show it to Cornford before he made the fatal decision to join the battle, as Cornford wrote, ''whether I like it or not''?

How are we to judge a writer who says one thing to a friend in private and quite the opposite to an innocent and credulous public on such a momentous issue? It is no wonder that Richard Gott was recently moved to observe that, the more we gain some historical perspective on Spain, "the more blurred becomes the morality." It is worth remembering, however, that there *were* some writers who grasped the morality of the situation at the time, and showed an exemplary bravery and candor in acknowledging the villainy of their chosen side. The Catholic writer Georges Bernanos, once a supporter of the rightist and anti-Semitic Action Française, saw firsthand the horror of the atrocities perpetrated by the Franco forces and sanctified by the Catholic priests. In his searing account from *A Diary of My Times* (1938), which appears in the Cunningham anthology, Bernanos tells of "the organizing of Terrorism" by the Italian Black Shirts brought to Majorca by Franco. Bernanos recoiled in horror at the figure of three thousand killed by right-wing death squads, as we would call them today, in a brief seven-month period. On that small island, he wrote, one could "witness the blowing-out of fifteen wrong-thinking brains per day." Hating "the sound and sight of it," Bernanos told the world the truth, despite the fact that it meant he was criticizing his own side. Bernanos saw that civil war meant "there is no longer any justice," and he pointed out that even moderate Republicans were shot "like dogs just the same," even though they had nothing to do with the Red Terror of Barcelona. To this Catholic intellectual, civil war meant terrorism had become "the order of the day."

On the Left, Simone Weil was Bernanos's counterpart. "[H]oping every day," she wrote in a letter to Bernanos, ". . . for the victory of one side and the defeat of the other," Weil went to Spain in August 1936. After two months there, Weil no longer saw the war as one "of starving peasants against landed proprietors and a clergy in league" with them, but instead she viewed it as "a war between Russia, Germany and Italy." . . . What Weil objected to was the relentless pleasure in murder that occurred on all sides. Killing "Fascists" and seeing them as beasts made the Republicans, in Weil's view, no better than the enemy; they too were excluding "a category of human beings from among those whose lives have worth." Such behavior, she wrote in her letter to Bernanos in 1938, soon obscured "the very purpose of the struggle." . . . "An abyss separated the men with the weapons," Weil wrote, "from the unarmed population," an abyss Weil saw as similar to that which separated "the rich from the poor." Hence Weil felt that Bernanos, a monarchist, was closer to her than the proletarian comrades of the Aragon militia she had come to Spain to support.

If the Spanish War was a "People's War," as Valentine Cunningham claims, "the most potent and emotionally engaging focus of thirties democratic struggles and progressive working-class ambitions," it was also a writers' war, in which almost all writers felt the need to take sides. It is true that most writers of merit were on the Republican side. But can one say with a clear conscience that the forces of the Republic were fighting, as Cunningham suggests, for the survival of art and culture in free societies, when, had the Red side won, such a free society would have been just as much at risk as it was after the Franco victory?

Orwell had warned, in the concluding pages of *Homage to Catalonia,* that one should beware of partisanship, and of the distortion caused by his having seen only one corner of events. And he warned that readers should "beware of exactly the same things when you read any other book on this period." What happened, of course, was that writers went to Spain and,

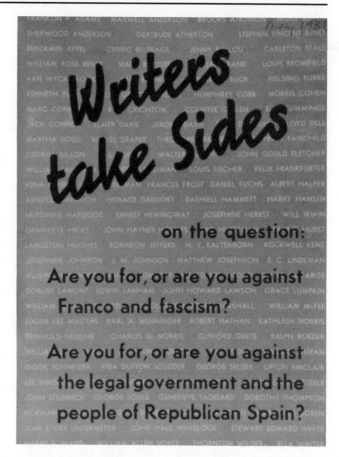

Cover of Writers Take Sides.

on the basis of brief tours, committed themselves and their art to the cause. Weil noted that it was "in fashion to go on a tour down there, to take in a spot of revolution, and to come back with articles bursting out of your pen." She noted such endeavors had to be superficial, especially since in the gale of civil war and revolution "principles get completely out of phase with realities," and the criterion for judging events disappears. How, she queried, could one "report something coherently on the strength of a short stay and some fragmentary observations?" (pp. 11-12)

We need to be especially alert to the accounts of the International Brigades in Spain, for on this subject particularly a great deal of emotion has been invested and a great many lies told. When, some years ago, Orwell condemned a memoir by the International Brigidista John Sommerfield as "sentimental tripe," he wrote that "we shall almost certainly get some good books from members of the International Brigade, but we shall have to wait for them until the war is over." Such a book was in fact written. . . . [In the novel *Hermanos!* William Herrick] has given us what is perhaps the first honest portrayal of the war from within the Brigades in Spain, a searing, tough indictment, filled with the bitter reality of youthful bravery and idealism crushed by the agenda of the Comintern and its decision to allow so many thousands to die for nothing. . . . And another, younger novelist, David Evanier, continues the tradition with his forthcoming novel of the Old Left; a recently published excerpt ["How Sammy Klarfield Became a Vacillating Element in Spain"] pertaining to the International Brigades traces one veteran's destruction as part of his experience with the Soviet tank corps.

Reading the committed partisans of the Left so many years later cannot but leave one with a bitter taste. How weak seem the partisans, and how prescient seem those who had doubts and expressed them. Indeed, one is struck by the intellectual courage it took to give anything but the expected answer, particularly when the question was framed, as it was in 1937 in a declaration "To the Writers and Poets of England, Scotland, Ireland and Wales" by Auden, Spender, Neruda, and Aragon: "Are you for or against . . . the People of Republican Spain? . . . it is impossible any longer to take no side." Those who answered by insisting that no side be taken must be given high marks for intellectual fortitude, and for refusing to ride with the herd.

Aldous Huxley spoke a simple truth when he replied, to those who demanded he side with the Reds, that dictatorial Communism would produce "results with which history has made us only too sickeningly familiar." T. S. Eliot replied that, while he was sympathetic to the Republicans, "it is best that at least a few men of letters should remain isolated." Condemned as a Fascist for these sentiments, Eliot at least was able to stay aloof from the foolish chorus of Stalinist hosannas in which the rest of the intellectuals joined. Was he not correct, then, to claim that, were the Left to win, it would "be the victory of the worst rather than of the best features . . . a travesty of the humanitarian ideals which have led so many people" to work for the Republic? Eliot was wrong, I think, to have opposed lifting the embargo on arms. Despite the tragedy of the conflict—and the evils of Communism—the main threat to the world in the Thirties was that of the menace of aggressive Hitlerism. But Eliot was right, after all, on the moral issue involved, that democracy had little to do with supporting either "Berlin or Moscow."

Those who argued that the Fascists killed Lorca—and therefore all writers must stand with the Republic—would be hard pressed to refute the argument of Salvador Dali that Lorca's "death was exploited for propaganda purposes," and that personally the poet was "the most a-political person on earth."

Undoubtedly, some did side with the Republic because of a valid opposition to Fascism, and because the Republic had the support of the populace. But who can question the accuracy of Vita Sackville-West, who addressed the hypocrisy of the call to support "the *legal* Government of Spain"? "Is this because it is the *legal* Government," she asked, "or because it is a Communist Government?" . . . Noting that, if legality were the issue, these writers would have to support the existing regimes in Italy and Germany if rebellion broke out against them, Sackville-West identified the real issue: ". . . you want to see Communism established in Spain as well as in Russia, and you do not care a snap of the fingers whether a Government is 'legal' or not." Demanding frankness, Sackville-West challenged what she called the "subterranean forms of propaganda." (pp. 13-14)

Jason Gurney [in *Crusade in Spain*] . . . speaks the clear truth when he writes that "nobody, from either side, came out of it with clean hands." A member of the British section of the International Brigades, Gurney noted that he and his comrades "had wilfully deluded ourselves into the belief that we were fighting a noble Crusade because we needed a crusade—the opportunity to fight against the manifest evils of Fascism . . . which seemed then as if it would overwhelm every value of Western civilization."

Gurney felt, writing in the mid-1970s, that "[W]e were wrong, we deceived ourselves and were deceived by others." But he

argues as well that their fight was not in vain, and he does not regret his own part in that fight. "The situation," he says, "is not to be judged by what we now know of it, but only as it appeared in the context of the period." But much *was* known then, and suppressed by those who knew. Gurney would have it both ways. History has taught him the truth about Communism. But he still insists that because "others took advantage of our idealism in order to destroy it does not in any way invalidate the decision which we made." And this man who claims to understand history gives his last word to the blabbering of "La Pasionaria," Dolores Ibarruri. This famous Communist deputy, who sang the praises of the departing brigidistas as they were suffering the consequences of her betrayal, went immediately thereafter to Moscow, where she remained in exile until Franco's death. Those brave men who gave their lives had allowed themselves to be part of an ideological and propaganda instrument forged by the Comintern for its own purposes. Had they looked closer, they could have discerned the truth at the time. In 1986, those who still respond to the Spanish Civil War as simply "our cause" have no excuse. (pp. 14-15)

Ronald Radosh, "'But Today the Struggle': Spain and the Intellectuals," in The New Criterion, *Vol. V, No. 2, October, 1986, pp. 5-15.*

ADDITIONAL BIBLIOGRAPHY

Blotner, Joseph L. *The Political Novel*. Garden City, N.Y.: Doubleday & Co., 1955, 100 p.
    Offers brief descriptions of political novels including many based on or influenced by the events of the Spanish Civil War.

Burgum, Edwin Berry. "Ernest Hemingway and the Psychology of the Lost Generation." In his *The Novel and the World's Dilemma*, pp. 184-204. New York: Oxford University Press, 1947.
    Discusses Hemingway's responses to the conflict in Spain as expressed in his fiction. According to Burgum: "No reader can escape a certain awareness, to be sure, of the mood of despondency in which *For Whom the Bell Tolls* leaves him. But the significance of this mood is obscured by the sustained breathlessness of the action and especially by the interest in the personality of the hero."

Compitello, Malcolm Alan. "The Novel, the Critics, and the Civil War: A Bibliographic Essay," *Anales de la Narrativa Española Contemporánea* 4 (1979): 117-38.
    Briefly surveys criticism of Civil War literature in post-Franco Spain.

Cowley, Malcolm. "A Congress in Madrid." *New Masses* XXIV, No. 7 (10 August 1937): 16.
    Report on the July 1937 conference of the Writers' International Association for the Defense of Culture held in Madrid and attended by Cowley, Rafael Alberti, André Malraux, Gustav Regler, Stephen Spender, Alexei Tolstoy, Sylvia Townsend Warner, and others.

Cunningham, Valentine, ed. *The Penguin Book of Spanish Civil War Verse*. New York: Penguin Books, 1980, 510 p.
    Compilation of works by prominent authors of the Civil War as well as poems by lesser known writers of the period. In his introduction Cunningham chronicles the involvement of British poets in the war, maintaining that "Spain was . . . in more ways than one a test. Above all, it was a test for truthfulness, and truthfulness in poetry. The propaganda case—that this was an heroic, righteous cause, a just war fought for democracy and freedom—was, at least at first, in fact the case, and so 'propaganda' poems, as many of them were, have a pointful role, for they bear pertinently on the truth of the matter."

―――, ed. *Spanish Front: Writers on the Civil War*. Oxford: Oxford University Press, 1986, 388 p.

Comprehensive collection of poetry and prose which includes excerpts from the survey *Authors Take Sides on the Spanish Civil War* (1937). Also reprinted are works by Hemingway, Malraux, Spender, W. H. Auden, Roy Campbell, John Cornford, T. S. Eliot, Graham Greene, Arthur Koestler, Thomas Mann, George Orwell, Leon Trotsky, Evelyn Waugh, and Virginia Woolf.

Geismar, Maxwell. "Ernest Hemingway: You Could Always Come Back" and "John Dos Passos: Conversion of a Hero." In his *Writers in Crisis: The American Novel, 1925-1940*, pp. 37-87, pp. 88-140. Boston: Houghton Mifflin, 1942.

Considers Hemingway's *For Whom the Bell Tolls* and Dos Passos's *Adventures of a Young Man* in the context of American fiction and in relation to other political novels of the period. According to Geismar: "When we compare *For Whom the Bell Tolls* with comparable works of its own genre, the revolutionary novels of André Malraux, for example, or the anti-Fascist work of Ignazio Silone, the difference in quality becomes apparent. *For Whom the Bell Tolls* hardly reaches into the depths and nuances of its theme."

Hart, Henry, ed. *The Writer in a Changing World*. Equinox Cooperative Press, 1937, 256 p.

Includes three essays on the Spanish Civil War: "Spain and American Writers" by Archibald MacLeish, "Writers Fighting in Spain" by Martha Gellhorn, and "The Writer and War" by Hemingway.

Hemingway, Ernest. *For Whom the Bell Tolls*. New York: Charles Scribner's Sons, 1983, 482 p.

Hoskins, Katharine Bail. *Today the Struggle: Literature and Politics in England during the Spanish Civil War*. Austin: University of Texas Press, 1969, 294 p.

Examination "concerned chiefly with artists of high abilities who, at least during the thirties, dedicated their talents to the propagation of certain social and political ideas," including Auden, Greene, C. Day Lewis, and Bernard Shaw.

Kazin, Alfred. "The Wound That Will Not Heal: Writers and the Spanish Civil War." *The New Republic* 195, No. 8 (25 August 1986): 39-41.

Personal and literary reminiscences.

Koestler, Arthur. *Spanish Testament*. London: Victor Gallancz, 1937, 384 p.

Malraux, André. *Man's Hope*. Translated by Stuart Gilbert and Alastair MacDonald. New York: Grove Press, 1979, 511 p.

English translation of Malraux's novel *L'Espoir*.

Marquis, Alice Goldfarb. "'*Es geht um Spaniens Freiheit*': German Writers and the Spanish Civil War." *The Durham University Journal* LXXI, No. 2 (June 1979): 151-67.

Details the careers of several writers exiled from Nazi Germany who participated in the Spanish Civil War, including Koestler, Regler, Alfred Kantorowicz, and Ludwig Renn.

Michalczyk, John J. *André Malraux's 'Espoir': The Propaganda/Art Film and the Spanish Civil War*. University, Miss.: Romance Monographs, 1977, 185 p.

Considers *Espoir* "one of the most important of the approximately 500 films made about the Spanish Civil War," noting that it is a film "out of which the political principles as well as the deepseated feelings of the characters flow humanly and artistically. The idealism and realism experienced during the Spanish crisis are present, but it is the humanism shared by the people and exhibited by Malraux which is the overriding, integrating factor."

Miller, John, ed. *Voices against Tyranny: Writing of the Spanish Civil War*. New York: Charles Scribner's Sons, 1986, 227 p.

Reprints works on the Spanish War by Auden, Hemingway, Koestler, Malraux, Mann, Orwell, Spender, Luis Buñuel, Salvador Dali, John Dos Passos, Theodore Dreiser, Federico García Lorca, Wyndham Lewis, Louis MacNiece, Edna St. Vincent Mil-

lay, Pablo Neruda, Dorothy Parker, Pablo Picasso, Kenneth Rexroth, Antoine de Saint-Exupéry, and William Carlos Williams.

Muggeridge, Malcolm. "Exploding Bombs and Poets." *T & T: Time and Tide* 42, No. 19 (11 May 1961): 785-86.

Offers commentary on prominent literary participants in the Spanish Civil War in a review of *The Spanish Civil War* by Hugh Thomas.

Orwell, George. *Homage to Catalonia*. San Diego, Calif.: Harcourt Brace Jovanovich, 1969, 232 p.

Pritchett, V. S. "The Spanish Tragedy." *The New Statesman and Nation* n.s. XV, No. 374 (23 April 1938): 734, 736.

Reviews Orwell's *Homage to Catalonia* and Geoffrey Brereton's *Inside Spain*.

Read, Herbert. "Poetry in My Time." *The Texas Quarterly* 1, No. 1 (February 1958): 87-100.

Includes a brief discussion of the major English poets of the 1930s—Auden, Day Lewis, MacNiece, and Spender.

Romeiser, John Beals. *Red Flags, Black Flags: Critical Essays on the Spanish Civil War*. Madrid: Studia Humanitatis, 1982, 261 p.

Contains essays examining the war writings of Alberti, Hemingway, Malraux, Orwell, Regler, Louis Delapree, and Langston Hughes.

St. Martin, Hardie. "Poetry in Spain since the Civil War." *Mosaic* 2, No. 4 (Summer 1969): 41-52.

Examines works by Gabriel Celaya, Miguel Hernández, José Hierro, and Blas de Otero, among others.

Samuels, Stuart. "The Left Book Club." *Journal of Contemporary History* 1, No. 2 (1966): 65-86.

Includes brief descriptions of works distributed through the book club which focused on the Spanish Civil War.

Sanders, David. "Ernest Hemingway's Spanish Civil War Experience." *American Quarterly* XII, No. 2, Pt. 1 (Summer 1960): 133-43.

Assesses Hemingway's works set in Spain in a discussion of *For Whom the Bell Tolls*.

Scarfe, Francis. *Auden and After: The Liberation of Poetry, 1930-1941*. London: George Routledge & Sons, 1942, 208 p.

Examines the works of several poets who figured prominently in the literature of the Spanish Civil War, including Auden, Day Lewis, MacNiece, and Spender.

Schwartz, Kessel. "The *Pueblo*, the Intellectuals and the Spanish Civil War." *Kentucky Romance Quarterly* XIV, No. 4 (1967): 299-310.

Maintains that "many [Spanish] intellectuals thought that a valuable literature might evolve from the war itself, feeling that the 'crisis of thought' was linked to the hunger and oppression of the workers with whose salvation would come that of thought."

Spender, Stephen. "Worshipers from Afar: Stephen Spender." In *The God That Failed*, edited by Richard Crossman, pp. 229-73. New York: Harper & Brothers, 1949.

Discusses his attempt to reconcile politics with art through subscribing briefly to communism. According to Spender: "Almost the whole literature of the Spanish War depicts the energy of a reviving liberalism rather than the Communist orthodoxy which produced an increasingly deadening effect on all discussion of ideas, all witnessing of the complexity of events. The best books of the War—those by Hemingway, Koestler, Malraux, and Orwell—describe the Spanish tragedy from the liberal point of view, and they bear witness against the communists."

Spender, Stephen and Lehmann, John, eds. *Poems for Spain*. London: Hogarth Press, 1939, 108 p.

Early anthology including important works in English as well as translations from the Spanish of Miguel Hernández, Pablo Neruda, and others. In his introduction Spender notes that "poets and poetry have played a considerable part in the Spanish War, because to many people the struggle of the Republicans has seemed a struggle for the conditions without which the writing and reading of poetry are almost impossible in modern society.''

Sperber, Murray A., ed. *And I Remember Spain: A Spanish Civil War Anthology*. London: Hart-Davis, MacGibbon, 1974, 337 p.
Collection of international writings on the Civil War, arranged by author under such headings as ''Volunteers,'' ''Reporters,'' ''Tourists,'' and ''Witnesses.''

Thomas, Hugh. *The Spanish Civil War*. New York: Harper & Brothers, 1961, 720 p.
Generally considered the standard history of the Spanish War.

Tierney, William. ''Irish Writers and the Spanish Civil War.'' *Eire-Ireland* VII, No. 3 (Fall 1972): 36-55.
Discusses the activities and writings of Irish authors, including General Eoin O'Duffy, Charles Donnelly, and Peadar O'Donnell.

Varela, Lorenzo. ''Ballads of the Spanish People.'' In . . . *And Spain Sings: Fifty Loyalist Ballads Adapted by American Poets,* pp. xiii-xv. New York: The Vanguard Press, 1937.
Examines the resurgence of the ballad form in popular poetry of the Civil War.

Waugh, Thomas. '''Men Cannot Act in Front of the Camera in the Presence of Death': Joris Ivens's *The Spanish Earth*—Parts I and II.'' *Cineaste* XII, Nos. 2, 3 (1982; 1983): 31-3, 21-9.
Presents production and critical history of *The Spanish Earth*, analyzes filmic techniques used by Ivens, and recounts Hemingway's contributions to the project as writer and narrator.

Weintraub, Stanley. *The Last Great Cause: The Intellectual and the Spanish Civil War*. New York: Weybright and Talley, 1968, 340 p.

Describes the involvement of intellectuals as participants in the conflict and offers critical appraisals of their works about Spain. Weintraub concludes that ''The impact [of the Civil War] on literature has often been to render suspect much of the writing inspired by the lost, and afterwards unfashionable, cause, although writers of real worth—whatever history's eventual verdict on the Republic—were no less mistaken or misled than the politicians or the journalists, nor did they take refuge in dogma or fall back less on slogans.''

Wood, Neal. ''To the Left.'' In his *Communism and British Intellectuals,* pp. 37-74. New York: Columbia University Press, 1959.
Discusses the political mood of Britain in the 1930s. Wood pays special attention to the generation coming of age in the thirties, including poets Auden, Day Lewis, and MacNiece.

Woodcock, George. *The Writer and Politics*. London: The Porcupine Press, 1948, 248 p.
Includes essays on Koestler, Orwell, and Ignazio Silone, in an examination adopting a ''social approach to literature.''

Writers Take Sides: Letters about the War in Spain from 418 American Authors. New York: The League of American Writers, 1938, 82 p.
Responses by American writers, including Hemingway, Sherwood Anderson, Pearl S. Buck, E. E. Cummings, Theodore Dreiser, William Faulkner, Dashiell Hammett, Katherine Anne Porter, Irwin Shaw, John Steinbeck, Thornton Wilder, and William Carlos Williams, to the questions ''Are you for, or are you against Franco and fascism?'' and ''Are you for, or are you against the legal government and the people of Republican Spain?''

Ulysses and the Process of Textual Reconstruction

INTRODUCTION

The first edition of James Joyce's *Ulysses,* published in 1922, was introduced with an unusual note from publisher Sylvia Beach: "The publisher asks the reader's indulgence for typographical errors unavoidable in the exceptional circumstances." The circumstances surrounding the composition and publication of the novel were indeed exceptional, involving amateur typists, typesetters who spoke little or no English, and an author with failing eyesight who made multiple revisions of each episode in proof stages and added nearly one-third of the text after the book had been typeset. As published, the resulting text contained nearly five thousand errors of typography and transcription. Correction proved impossible for editors of the next nine editions of *Ulysses,* which were published between 1926 and 1968. Since each episode of the novel had been separately composed, revised, and transcribed, and each of the various versions of each episode had been discarded, lost, or sold to collectors, there existed no complete text in the form Joyce had intended for publication. Thus, subsequent editions were of necessity based on the faulty text of 1922.

In 1977, researchers at the University of Munich under the direction of Hans Walter Gabler undertook the monumentally complex task of comparing all surviving documents of the novel's transmission, including fragments of manuscript, typescript, galleys, and page proofs, in an attempt to reconstruct the text that Joyce intended to publish. Collating the results of his research with the help of a computer, Gabler assembled his findings in a format suitable for both reading and scholarly investigation: the right-hand pages present the reading text, that is, the reconstructed text that Gabler considers to most closely reflect Joyce's intent, while the left-hand pages present every element of text appearing in the various documents of transmission, chronologically arranged with superscript notations indicating at which stage each element was introduced into the process. Issued by Garland Publishing in 1984 in three volumes totaling nearly two thousand pages, *Ulysses: A Critical and Synoptic Edition* was immediately acclaimed a landmark work of textual reconstruction. As Gabler's work diverges in significant ways from traditional principles of textual reconstruction, his edition also prompted renewed discussion of the theoretical foundations of textual editing. The following entry presents commentary on the "new *Ulysses*"—including the nature of Gabler's emendations, his editorial principles and procedures, and the accuracy and ultimate value of the new edition—as well as on the theoretical issues of textual editing raised by Gabler's work.

THE NEW *ULYSSES:* EVALUATIONS

JEFFERSON HUNTER

[In the following excerpt, Hunter reviews the Gabler edition of Ulysses *and discusses the nature of Gabler's emendations.]*

James Joyce. The Granger Collection, New York.

In "Lotus Eaters," the fifth episode of *Ulysses,* Joyce sends Bloom on his desultory way through the warm morning thinking about Guinness swirling in lazy pools and the cooling narcotic effect of a cigar. In equal measure Bloom likes the weakly stimulating effect of an epistolary flirtation with Martha Clifford. A letter from Bloom has apparently asked her to call him a dirty name; now, in a letter sent to "Henry Flower" at the post office, Martha types, mingling real prurience with feigned offense in a way that nicely matches Bloom's interest in the punishment she threatens, "I called you naughty boy because I do not like that other world. Please tell me what is the real meaning of that word?" That is, in most editions of *Ulysses* she types "I do not like that other world." The carefully proofread two-volume set issued by John Lane in 1936 emends "world" to "word," which of course is right in the abstract but wrong in the vicinity of Martha Clifford (she also types "if you do not wrote" and "my patience are exhausted"). The emendation makes nonsense of Bloom's later thought "I do not like that other world she wrote." To this, modestly heroic, he adds "No more do I," turning away from the death-world of "Hades" to "warm full-blooded life," making vitalist morality out of typographical accident. Meanwhile *all* current editions of *Ulysses* omit Martha's lazy question mark after "Please tell me what is the real meaning of that word."

How do we know Martha made mistakes if they are missing from the texts we read? The answer is that they and thousands of other niceties of Joyce's imagination have been restored in a new, three-volume text, *Ulysses: A Critical and Synoptic Edition,* the product of seven years' unremitting labor on the part of a computer and a rigorously scientific German bibliographical team headed by Hans Walter Gabler. Gabler and his associates have masterfully analyzed the relevant documents: the working drafts (some extant, some inferred from later witnesses), the copies made for the serializations in *The Little Review* and *The Egoist,* the typescripts produced by various machines and various typists (some accurate, some kin to Martha Clifford), the overlay upon overlay of changes, the proofs sent back from the bemused printers in Dijon, the corrected and hugely extended proofs by Joyce (a third of the novel was written in the margins of the printed sheets), the errata lists seldom error-free themselves and even more seldom incorporated into later printings. *Ulysses* was copied by amateur "improvers" of its inconsistencies and set into type by Frenchmen. Finally, it was checked by an author who had bad eyesight, an imperfect memory, and other things on his mind (chiefly, the writing of the last episodes of the novel). If Joyce was a Stephen Dedalus in revising his work, a perfectionist with a cursed jesuit strain that would allow no stopping short of the fullest meaning, the most artful phrasing, he was a Leopold Bloom—"Black conducts, reflects, (refracts is it?), the heat"—in transcribing it. He made mistakes in copying, failed to catch the mistakes of others, and based revisions on mistakes. Someone—not Joyce, in this instance—read Bloom's version of Molly's version of "metempsychosis" and refused to believe it; Gabler's edition gives us back the wonderful "metamspychosis." Someone took Buck Mulligan's repeated exclamation points out of "Telemachus"; they are now restored. A typist dropped four words from the old milkwoman's dialogue in the same episode, then dropped a few more from her reckoning of the bill; now her sums make sense. On and on the corrections go, averaging out at seven per page, striving mightily against that inherent propensity of print to err which Joyce acknowledged in the newspaper account of Dignam's funeral, where "L. Boom" is listed among the mourners.

A great many of the changes are minor, matters of format, capital letters, and italics. Hundreds if not thousands of commas are replaced or removed. With all these finicky details, significant only in their cumulative effect, to manage, it is little wonder that Gabler calls the change from "shrunken breasts" to "shrunken paps" a "weighty" revision. On the other hand, in a novel as obsessively contrived as this one, every change is in some sense weighty. It makes a difference that Bloom, as he moves along the street toward Dlugacz the porkbutcher, meditating on a more romantic journey through strange lands, thinks that he might "Dander along all day," not "Wander along all day" as we have previously read. It makes a greater difference that in "Scylla and Charybdis" Stephen enunciates, as he has done in no edition before this one, the mysterious "word known to all men." Overcoming for a moment his fear of the big words that make us so unhappy, he actually says, with extraordinary appropriateness, "Love, yes." The two words (as Richard Ellmann has noted [see excerpt below]) join him with the Bloom who tells the enraged Citizen what life is—"Love . . . the opposite of hatred"—and the Molly who ends the book with an affirmation.

The labors which produced this new *Ulysses* are recorded in a substantial apparatus of footnotes, textual notes, historical collation list, bibliography, and fifty-page Afterword explaining, among many other things, the rationale of the "copy-text." This is not the first printed edition, but a "continuous manuscript text" consisting of the holograph drafts in the Rosenbach Manuscript [a manuscript copy of the novel sold by Joyce to collector John Quinn and now owned by the Rosenbach Museum in Philadelphia], Joyce's autograph changes (where these survive), and other drafts, additions and changes which have not survived but which may reasonably be inferred from the testimony of later documents. The Afterword [see Additional Bibliography] is not easy going. Only students of textual criticism will be able to read it with pleasure (or be in a position to assess all the decisions it reveals), will be able to pick their way confidently through the thickets of compositional documents and transmissional documents and to join knowledgeably in the grave morrice, as Joyce put it in another context, of lemma and stemma. Gabler's prose, as read by a nonbibliographer at least, sometimes breaks down under the weight of the information it tries to impart. . . . Still, bibliographers are not obliged to be stylists. What counts is the rigor and consistency of Gabler's editorial judgment, the clarity of *sigla* and abbreviations in the apparatus, and above all the reliability of the critical text printed on the right-hand pages of Gabler's three volumes. It cannot be doubted that this text is comprehensive and accurate. Six decades after its first publication, *Ulysses* has become available. (pp. 315-17)

On the left-hand pages of the three volumes is a "synoptic" text; that is, a text identifying in chronological order all of Joyce's changes to a given *Urtext.* Compositional analysis, formerly dependent on the juggling of volume after volume of draft versions in *The James Joyce Archive,* is now a matter of mastering some symbols and scanning a page. An astonishing amount of information emerges from all the superscript numbers and letters, brackets within brackets, and carets rotated in various directions (to indicate various "overlay levels"). Take an apparently unremarkable lunch-time passage from "Lestrygonians." Disgusted by all the boltings and wolfings he sees in the Burton restaurant, Bloom has fled to Davy Byrne's quiet pub. There he wonders what to order. The original draft has Bloom moving briskly to a decision:

> Sardines on the shelves. Potted meats. What is home without Plumtree's potted meat? Incomplete. What a stupid ad. With it abode of bliss. Lord knows what concoction.
>
> —Have you a cheese sandwich?

Joyce revised the draft (which is now lost) after it had been fair-copied, the revisions being recoverable from the typescript version. He put an exclamation point after "ad" and allowed Bloom to go on a bit about the ad's stupidity ("Right under the obituary notices too"), altering this immediately to "Under the obituary notices they stuck it." "Dignam's potted meat" finds its way into the text: Bloom can't forget the funeral. "Cannibals would with lemon and rice. White men too salty. Like pickled pork" all comes in, the product of Bloom's travelogue-exotic imagination. "Pork" starts still another train of thought in this haphazard Jew: "Cauls mouldy tripes windpipes faked up. Kosher. Hygiene that was what they call now." Later, in 1921, Joyce added a four-line insert beginning with "Yom Kippur fast spring cleaning of inside" and ending with cheese, which "digests all but itself. Mity cheese." At this stage the revised passage was put in type.

From mid-August to mid-October of 1921 Joyce worked over the proofs of this part of "Lestrygonians" in at least four stages or levels, the first being the most important: he added brief extending phrases ("No meat and milk together" after "Kosher," for example), one splendid pun ("Ham and his descendants musterred and bred there"), and Bloom's recollection of a dirty limerick about cannibals. At last the passage had achieved its final form:

> Sardines on the shelves. Almost taste them by looking. Sandwich? Ham and his descendants musterred and bred there. Potted meats. What is home without Plumtree's potted meat? Incomplete. What a stupid ad! Under the obituary notices they stuck it. All up a plumtree. Dignam's potted meat. Cannibals would with lemon and rice. White missionary too salty. Like pickled pork. Expect the chief consumes the parts of honour. Ought to be tough from exercise. His wives in a row to watch the effect. *There was a right royal old nigger. Who ate or something the somethings of the reverend Mr MacTrigger.* With it an abode of bliss. Lord knows what concoction. Cauls mouldy tripes windpipes faked and minced up. Puzzle find the meat. Kosher. No meat and milk together. Hygiene that was what they call now. Yom Kippur fast spring cleaning of inside. Peace and war depend on some fellow's digestion. Religions. Christmas turkeys and geese. Slaughter of innocents. Eat drink and be merry. Then casual wards full after. Heads bandaged. Cheese digests all but itself. Mity cheese.

—Have you a cheese sandwich?

The textual story does not quite end here, however. The proofs returned from Dijon pedantically inserted a comma after the first word in "Eat drink and be merry" and changed "Mity" to "Mighty." Joyce failed to undo the changes, and all published editions before this one have reproduced them. We have grown used to "Mighty cheese," a Bloomian phrase if there ever was one. Should we keep it? Should we assume that Joyce, in failing to correct the meddlesome French compositors, tacitly approved their alteration? Gabler says no, in this case and in nearly all the other cases of "passive authorization." He reminds us that Joyce was not reading proof against copy and argues that the novelist was simply making too many revisions to catch every error. Perhaps. No one doubts that Joyce made mistakes, passive and active, nor that he insisted on having his own way about the details of *Ulysses* and wanted his manuscript reproduced exactly. But a Joyce unfixated on perfection and open to experience—open to someone else's accidental improvement of his text—is at least conceivable. That hero of openness to experience Bloom could pluck "musterred and bred" from the shelves of Davy Byrne's pub, and his creator could pluck "Mighty cheese" from a proof.

"ITHACANS VOW PEN IS CHAMP," as the headline in "Aeolus" runs. Gabler is a conservative editor, one reluctant to depart from James the penman's "continuous manuscript text." He will let what seems an obvious repetition stand—"His fingers drew forth the letter the letter and crumpled the envelope in his pocket"—because the Rosenbach Manuscript reads that way, interpreting (unconvincingly) the second "the letter" as a piece of interior monologue. He admits authorial revisions into the text even though they contradict information

given elsewhere. Many of these contradictions derive from the confusions and faulty memories of characters. But the characters are not always as confused as Gabler thinks. In "Nestor," Stephen sorrowfully reviews his debts, beginning with those to Mulligan: "nine pounds, three pairs of socks, ties." A typescript overlay of 1921 inserts "one pair brogues" into this list and the words are duly admitted, though as Gabler's textual note comments, "Episode 1 at 8.14-21 indicates that neither were the (black) brogues Mulligan's, nor had Mulligan procured them for Stephen." But the difficulties here are the editor's, not Stephen's or Joyce's. Page 8 of Episode 1 mentions the secondhand black *breeks,* not brogues, which were worn by some "poxy bowsy" and now fit Stephen "well enough." These breeks or trousers, moreover, do seem to come from Mulligan. Who more likely than he to get them off a patient in the Mater and Richmond? When Stephen taps his way across the shells of Sandymount Strand in "Proteus," thinking "My two feet in his boots are at the ends of his legs, *nebeneinander* ['side by side'],'' he accurately describes his borrowings.

In the old familiar text of *Ulysses* the Idiot at the Mabbot street entrance to nighttown lifts his palsied left arm and gurgles "Grhahute!" As revised, he gurgles "Ghahute!" It seems unlikely that ground-breaking interpretations of the novel will follow from this change, but no one can say what is likely to happen once Joyceans have pondered the separate and cumulative effect of the thousands of changes now recorded. It will take time to digest the corrected *Ulysses,* perhaps correct a few of its corrections, and apply its lessons to our longstanding debate about what the work is. In the old-fashioned view (to simplify), *Ulysses* is a novel, though a highly unconventional one and one growing more unconventional as it goes along, and like all novels reproduces in words the events and sensations of experience; it gives us Dublin and Dubliners on a June day. In the new-fashioned view, *Ulysses* is radically anti-novelistic, a sequence of styles following their own rules, perhaps even an autonomous verbal structure. One eye-catching change in the new edition would seem to support the new-fashioned view: following Joyce's consistent manuscript practice, Gabler has marked the opening of direct speech by *un-indented* dashes, and thus made it less distinct from narrative or interior monologue, less "privileged," less a reliable transcript of talk heard in Dublin. But the newly formatted quotations are only marginally less distinct. The dashes are still there; shifts in narrative authority are still signalled. And many of Gabler's new readings localize direct speech more finely than ever. As the Citizen excoriates the French ("never worth a roasted fart to Ireland") he claims they are making an "entente cordial" with perfidious Albion. You can hear him getting his Irish tongue around those two words as you could never quite hear him pronouncing, in the old version, a carefully italicized *"Entente cordiale."* In "Circe," the coyly playful Josie Breen orders Bloom to account for himself "this very sminute," while the excited Mary Driscoll defends herself with "As God is looking down on me this night if ever I laid a hand to them oylsters!" We owe both "sminute" and "oylsters" to Gabler, which is to say that we owe to him a sharper sense of the world, actual or imagined, in which Josie, Mary, Bloom, Stephen, Molly, and all the rest of them dwell, dream, love, hate, use words. "Word" and "world": what Martha meant and what she typed, what her letter consists of and what she herself is made by. Back and forth between the two great subjects of *Ulysses* the reader must go, freely letting language play, strictly holding language to its task of rendering Dublin.

The zigzag journey will be pleasanter now that we know the language is really Joyce's. (pp. 317-20)

Jefferson Hunter, ''I Do Not Like That Other Word,'' in The Hudson Review, *Vol. XXXVIII, No. 2, Summer, 1985, pp. 315-20.*

HUGH KENNER

[*Kenner is the foremost American critic and chronicler of literary Modernism. He is best known for* The Pound Era *(1971), a massive study of the Modernist movement, and for his influential works on T. S. Eliot, James Joyce, Samuel Beckett, and Wyndham Lewis. In addition to his reputation as an important scholar, Kenner is noted for his often eccentric judgements and a critical style that relies on surprising juxtapositions and wit. In the following excerpt, he discusses the corruption of the text of* Ulysses *and the results of Gabler's reconstruction.*]

''Trieste-Zurich-Paris,'' runs the familiar endline, ''1914-1921.'' It may now be extended: ''Charlottesville-Philadelphia-Buffalo-Cambridge-Austin-London-Munich, 1977-1984.'' This is a wholly new *Ulysses*, the implications of which we will be years absorbing. It alters the received text at some 5,000 places, say seven instances per page. The changes run from commas deleted to whole lost sentences recovered.

All versions of the received text descend from the Shakespeare & Co edition of 1922, which contained an apology for ''numerous typographical errors unavoidable under the exceptional circumstances.'' The circumstances were exceptional indeed, and included twenty-six French compositors who had no English, one composing-room foreman who had just enough to be a menace, numerous amateurs transcribing the author's holograph single-space on borrowed typewriters, and an author who hadn't actually finished the book when its typescripts went to the printers, and was simultaneously (a) composing two whole episodes while (b) trying to cope with proofs on the margins of which he (c) added some 30 per cent of the final text while (d) intermittently rolling on the floor with pain, having suffered an attack of iritis that entailed medical prohibition of any reading or writing at all.

Consider moreover that the whole huge work was set by hand. Machine-setting would have been straightforward. A man with his fingers on a keyboard and his eyes on the page can copy a language he doesn't know, letter after letter. But if instead he's setting type by hand he must memorize a gibberish string, find the characters in his typecase, return to where he left off, memorize a new string. One danger is that he'll not return to where he left off but to some later place that resembles it.

That happened when Leopold Bloom was wondering what it's like to be blind:

> How on earth did he know that van was there? Must have felt it. See things in their forehead perhaps: kind of sense of volume. Weight or size of it, something blacker than the dark. Wonder would he feel it if something was removed . . .

Joyce wrote that, a typist typed it; then a typesetter in Dijon scanned it. For a French eye English upper-case W is a handy checkpoint: an alien letter like the German umlaut or the Norwegian slashed o. So the Dijon compositor set a string that ended with ''Weight.'' He then re-entered at the wrong ''W'' and continued from ''would he feel it,'' producing the garble ''Weight would he feel it if something was removed'': ten

words skipped. In 1936 a Bodley Head proofreader, making ready the first legal British edition, sensed something amiss and patched it with punctuation. So the Penguin, set from the Bodley Head, reads ''Weight. Would he feel it if something was removed.'' Only now does the Gabler edition restore what Joyce wrote.

Those were pre-Xerox days, when typescript copies were scarce. The typists routinely made three, and when two had gone to the *Egoist* and the *Little Review*, that left one for Dijon and none for the author. When they sent back proofs from Dijon they held on to the typescript, with the result that Joyce was not reading his proofs against anything save his general memory of the sense. This is one reason so many things slipped by him. And the imagination (he himself said it, echoing Shelley) is ''a fading coal''; weeks, months, even years later, confronted with cold characters on a page, he patched manifest botches any old way, powerless to restore what he'd once hammered out at the forge of Daedalus.

Thus on one great page, where we're amidst perfection, he had conceived Bloom walking down Grafton Street, allured by the exhibits in shop windows: ''Cascades of ribbons. Flimsy China silks. A tilted urn poured from its mouth a flood of bloodhued poplin: lustrous blood. The huguenots brought that here. . . .'' And Bloom's mind jumps to a remembered performance of Meyerbeer's opera: ''*Lacaus esant tara tara*. Great chorus that. *Taree Tara*. Must be washed in rainwater. Meyerbeer. *Tara: bom bom bom*.'' ''*Lacaus esant*'' means that Bloom has Italian sounds in his head, but, not knowing the language, doesn't know where the words divide. But the typesetter thought it meant that the author was trying to spell French, and he supplied a pedantic *La cause sainte*. This Joyce corrected to equally pedantic Italian, *La causa è santa*, losing a ''taree'' or so in the process. And the fine phonetic rendition of what went through Bloom's head—a precision that had faded from Joyce's mind between 1918 and 1921—was lost for sixty-two years.

The typesetters' French fluency was a nuisance more than once. ''Entente cordial,'' wrote Joyce, faithful to how The Citizen pronounced it. The ''correction'' to ''cordiale'' again destroyed a precision. Before the text even reached Dijon transcribers had mangled it. Like the French printers, some of Joyce's typists seem to have thought him a feckless amateur. Such a one was the helpful soul who inserted ''hundreds'' of commas and some schoolmarm reparagraphings into ''Eumaeus,'' the rhythm of which is improved markedly by restoring the holograph readings. Others were simply careless, like the one whose primitive machine bollixed the book's opening episode, ''Telemachus.''

Joyce had carefully styled this episode to resemble a mechanically hearty Edwardian novel. No act lacked its adverb: things are said and done ''coarsely,'' ''solemnly,'' ''smartly,'' ''sternly.'' Buck Mulligan likewise spoke exclamatorily, with ''!'' affixed to fully fifty-five of his utterances: ''Come up, Kinch! Come up, you fearful jesuit!'' But when these pages were transcribed, the typewriter lacked an exclamation point and the typist didn't know a trick to synthesize one. Though perfunctory efforts to write them in were made, a surprising forty-seven of these Mulliganesque vulgarities got lost. Now that we have them back in we can feel their cumulative effect, especially striking since in later episodes Joyce hardly ever marks audible speech with that sign. A bouncy fellow, Mulligan. He has no inside. Blazes Boylan, even, gets three words of interior monologue. Mulligan gets none.

Such details can be restored, as they can't be for Shakespeare, thanks to the preservation of an extraordinary array of transmitting documents. Joyce wrote every word of *Ulysses* by hand. The so-called Rosenbach Manuscript in Philadelphia is essentially his fair copy of each successive episode, made either for the typist or for John Quinn at a point when he (prematurely) judged it finished. Sometimes the typists worked from the Rosenbach sheets. Sometimes they and Joyce copied from different stages of a lost final working draft, the progress of which can often be gauged by comparing transcriptions. (Gauging its progress is one way to tell auctorial improvements from scribal errors.) And stage after stage of proof-sheets, in the wide margins of which Joyce kept on composing, were bought from Sylvia Beach, in her time of financial distress, by American libraries that may have thought they were acquiring souvenirs but in fact were making precious evidence safe in fireproof vaults. (Left with Miss Beach, it would all have gone through the Occupation; during which who knows?)

We don't have all of anything: not all the holograph drafts, nor all the typescripts, nor all the proofs. Luckily, what we do have dovetails and overlaps sufficiently for Hans Walter Gabler to have reconstructed with considerable confidence what he calls "the continuous manuscript" of *Ulysses*. "Continuous" is the word to be aware of. There is no single document that enshrines the author's final intentions, and there never was. Given the complex history of transmission, it is pointless to think of starting from an extant text and "correcting" it. Efforts in that direction have been made, with the result that all available texts contain approximately the same number of errors, the cost of each correction being some novel botch. The technique of the new edition was instead to build up the complex text as it was built up originally, and so arrive at a final version the way it would have been arrived at in 1922 if no one had made any mistakes. This has entailed massive collation of documents scattered in half-a-dozen places. Two technologies made that possible: facsimile reproduction, and the computer.

A fine three-volume facsimile of the Rosenbach MS was issued by the library that owns it in 1975. Less fancy, but serviceable, facsimiles of nearly everything else were published by Garland in 1977-9 in sixteen volumes of their *James Joyce Archive*. Thus, copies of virtually everything needful could be gathered into one room in the *Rechenzentrum* ["computer center"] in Munich. What the computer did was to prepare lists of differences between parallel documents, locating the places where decisions had to be made, by a scrupulous editor. It also prepared the "reading" text from the "synoptic" text, stripping off the apparatus and inserting the footnote codes. The idea was to minimize the tax on human attention.

For you never know when human inattention will botch something, or attention uninformed make matters worse. The printers of this edition received computer-generated pages, with instructions to print them by offset and change nothing. They luckily sent a preliminary run of sheets to two or three handy experts for final checking. One of them, Michael Groden, turned to the end of "Ithaca" to admire the final period, now for the first time restored ("La réponse à la dernière demande est un point" ["The response to the last question is a dot"]. Joyce had written, and printers have responded both by nothing and by big black dots you could hide a flea beneath). And before Groden's eyes, the final period was—missing! Uninformed human attention had had its carnival. The embarrassed printer explained that he'd whited the little dot out, thinking it was a dust spot. So much for good intentions. Computers have the merit of entertaining no intentions.

So on the left-hand page we can watch Joyce and his amanuenses build up the text, layer by layer, levels of accretion and deletion set off by an intricate apparatus of sigla. And on the right-hand page we enjoy an unencumbered reading text, with numbered lines. Not that the left-hand page should be disregarded as mere testimony to editorial homework. As you grow used to its sigla, you can watch in fascination the working of Joyce's mind. Writing "Scylla and Charybdis," he had remembered how incandescent lamps first appeared in libraries, where the newest technology—today, the computer—is always invoked to ensure the safety of holdings. (The fumes from earlier lights were bad for paper.) So, recalling a filament's novelty, he had made John Eglinton look "in the tangled glowworm of his lamp." Years later, reading proofs of "Nestor," where the rare word "candescent" similarly hinted at electric lights in the Bibliothèque St Geneviève in Paris, 1902, he chose to amplify the hint, inserting a phrase about brains "under glowlamps impaled, with faintly beating feelers." Had he been browsing in the *OED*? It explains sense 1.d of "incandescent" by "the *glowlamp* as distinguished from the *arc light*." The whole incident can be pondered like a symbolist poem, Joyce having been early to realize that the editors of the *OED* were among their century's poets.

Elsewhere, deletions transmit what he later chose not to specify. Blazes Boylan, we learn from a phrase cut out of "Sirens," was "about thirty years" old, to Bloom's thirty-eight. The

---

ULYSSES

by

JAMES JOYCE

will be published in
the Autumn of 1921

by

"SHAKESPEARE AND COMPANY"

— *SYLVIA BEACH* —

8, RUE DUPUYTREN, PARIS — VI·

Front cover of the prospectus for the first edition of Ulysses. *Sylvia Beach Collection, Princeton University Library.*

"pony" Alf Bergan orders in Barney Kiernan's was a pony of stout. And we can watch Joyce have second thoughts about making Bloom address the cat "in mockery." That was too close to a Stephen-phrase about Mulligan. The second thought was "mockingly." But it is the novelties of the reading text that will arrest most students. Time and again Joyce wrote "wrong" words—phonetic transcriptions, intentional typos—which someone, a typist or the Dijon foreman, set "right." Stephen's "blue French telegram, curiosity to show" was a curiosity when it read "Nother dying come home father." But a typist who made the correction to "Mother" deprived "curiosity" of its point.

The phonetic renditions in which *Ulysses* abounds were especially apt to get normalized. Thus in "Proteus" Kevin Egan lifts up his voice:

> O, O, the boysof
> Kilkenny . . .

You can guess where a space got inserted. In "Lotus Eaters," Bloom's mind heard a sung phrase, "dearer thaaan them all," but two a's dropped out. One instance of "ray of hope" in the hope-bereft "Sirens" was meant to be "ray of hopk," synchronized with a cork coming out of a bottle. Bloom's panic at the end of "Lestrygonians" read "Ah soap there I yes" before the printers' foreman's pen changed "I" to "!" and someone else stuck in a comma after "Ah." And when Molly Bloom in "Calypso" pronounced her second most famous word she said "Metamspychosis," bringing it three-quarters of the way to what Leopold later remembers as "Met him pike hoses." His version was a puzzle during all the decades when the text contained not a thing remotely like it.

Everywhere, in this new version, the book is firmed up. In "Telemachus," Mulligan's harangue about diet and sanitation prompts the old milkwoman to ask if he's a medical student.

> —I am, ma'am, Buck Mulligan answered.

> —Look at that now, she said.

> Stephen listened in scornful silence. She bows her old head to a voice that speaks to her loudly, her bonesetter, her medicineman: me she slights . . .

Stephen's pique has point because she's said something obsequious ("Look at that now"); but in no text of *Ulysses* up to this one has she said anything at all, a typist having skipped a line. So we've been bullied, till this year, by a more paranoid Stephen, offended merely by atmospheres.

In "Nestor," Old Deasy's sententiousness—"All human history moves toward one great goal"—has its proper reek of cliché now that the restored word "human" restores its iambic pentameter. In "Proteus" Stephen's "Ought I go to a dentist, I wonder, with that money? That one. This. Toothless Kinch, the superman" gives the phrase "That one" a point it lacked when "This" was missing; he is testing teeth with his tongue. The fine paragraph that begins "The grainy sand . . ." now contains a bejewelled sentence: "Unwholesome sandflats waited to suck his treading soles, breathing upward sewage breath, a pocket of seaweed smouldered in seafire under a midden of man's ashes." The last thirteen words are only now restored. Joyce added them on the third level of proofs, but something happened; we've been reading a mutilated version. Heretofore, too, we've read how Bloom remembered a magical moment: "Hidden under wild ferns on Howth below us bay sleeping

sky." Insert the absent colon after "sleeping" and watch it clear up. And it isn't true that Mrs McGuinness, "stately, silverhaired, bowed to Father Conmee from the farther footpath along which she smiled"; in fact, "she sailed"—think of 1904 skirts.

Perhaps the most remarkable restoration is the five lines a typist's eye skipped over in "Scylla and Charybdis." "Will any man love the daughter," Stephen is asking apropos of Shakespeare's *Pericles*, "if he have not loved the mother?" And then (what has not been in print before):

> —Will he not see reborn in her, with the memory of his own youth added, another image?

> Do you know what you are talking about? Love, yes. Word known to all men. *Amplius veri alius alicui bonum vult unde et ea quae concupiscimus.*

So a circuit is completed when in "Circe" he (*eagerly*) asks his mother's ghost, "Tell me the word, mother, if you know now. The word known to all men." Before the lost phrases were given back to us, that appeal connected with nothing.

The last quotation also illustrates a general principle. In his holographs, Joyce deeply indented paragraphs of narration and interior monologue, but the dash that introduces reported speech he did not indent but wrote flush with the left margin. This was so contrary to continental usage there was no way to make a French printer reproduce it. Yet it is intrinsic to the conception of a book where narrator and reader are granted no privileged aloofness from the vocal antics. We and Dickens, for example, are secure in our superiority to Pecksniff; Pecksniff when he opens his mouth can but confirm by his every trick of idiom the moral limitations we and Dickens cozily perceive. So we and Dickens enjoy a mutuality Joyce will never permit. Joyce, it is well known, disliked the look of quotation marks. We may now join Colin MacCabe in suspecting that he disliked even more their air of fencing off and *exhibiting* speech. The novelists of class-ridden England thought of speech as the means by which people gave themselves away, and grew adept at phonetic renditions. But despite the multiplicity of Dublin dialects, Joyce employs phonetics only when an Irishman is imitating a foreigner, English or American, or when what is being recorded or remembered is not speech but song. And whatever the complexity of *Ulysses* he will not let his reader feel safely intimate with a benign intelligence at the book's centre. What he wanted is what we're shown in the new edition: the dash for a speech, less visible than the indent for a real paragraph. Only in "Circe," where you can seldom believe they were spoken, can your eye pick out speeches easily from the page. Speech and narrative cede flow to one another unobtrusively, the narrator's but another voice amid voices. That surly dog the dramatized narrator of "Cyclops" is less exceptional than he appears.

The decision to restore the flush-left dash *passim* runs counter to a cautious bibliographical maxim that what the author has passed in proof has authority. Joyce after all passed hundred of proofsheets with the dash indented. Another maxim states that the latest reading we have in the author's hand is the one we are bound by. On that principle we'd be stuck with *La causa è santa* for the Meyerbeer fragment. And what of the moment when, on the third set of "Ithaca" proofs, Joyce inserted a farrago of calendrical lore copied from inside the front cover of Thom's 1904 directory, then added on his own, in a holograph that survives, "MXMIV"? Professor Gabler correctly I think, has emended to "MCMIV," with a note that there were no further proofs on which it could have been corrected. Elsewhere, though, as with the unindented dash, he hasn't been intimidated by any number of proofs. For, despite responsible efforts to make the editing seem maximally scientific (the buzz-word is "critical"), there's no concealing the final court of appeal: scrupulous informed judgment. Editing is not a science and a computer couldn't have done it. Critical science, with computer assistance, can do no more than array the often intricate evidence.

In saying that I think the "MCMIV" emendation correct, I am dismissing arguments erected by people I respect, notably by Professor Patrick McCarthy, pertaining to the "unreliable narrator" of "Ithaca." (But if you prefer that version, the evidence is preserved in the textual notes.) Weighty issues, as Sherlock Holmes said, can hang upon a bootlace; likewise upon one letter of the alphabet. Written language can do but two things: make a list, tell a story. Blindly "scientific" editing gravitates toward listwork. There is security in lists. But behind Gabler's virtuoso performance lie reconstructed stories and his confidence in their details, a confidence he asks us to share.

For example: in the text we've always had, Bloom's budget for the day puts the price of a cake of Fry's Chocolate at a penny, 0-0-1; that had been typist number three's substitution for a shilling, 0-1-0. In making his list of errata for the second Paris impression, Joyce did not change the price of chocolate but instead altered the newly erroneous subtotal, to 0-17-5. Was Joyce conceding that Fry's chocolate sold for a penny? Should editor, like author, leave the price and change the sum? Gabler says not. "The sum of 0-17-5 which [Joyce] thereby leaves in Bloom's pockets would comprise pennies—and this cannot be, for Bloom has given his last coppers—literally 'the last of the Mohicans'—in payment at the cabman's shelter." So in the new text the price of chocolate reverts to a shilling, and Bloom's pocket-money to 0-16-6.

That overrides the author's latest inscription. I don't know how it agrees with 1904 chocolate prices. But it evidently corresponds not only with a Ulysses cross-reference but with a scenario whereby (1) the typist didn't correct an error of fact but simply made a mistake; (2) Joyce didn't see the error in the list but caught the resulting fault in the arithmetic, having (3), when he wrote of "the last of the Mohicans," and then made the original list, had all his wits about him, whereas when he saw to the errata the coal had faded. Confidence in such a story is what underlies the emendation.

That is the governing principle of the newly edited Ulysses, and some of the stories it implies are far too intricate to summarize here. We come back repeatedly to an arcane mixture of principle and judgment, and some of the judgments are sure to be disputed. However disputable, though, they are never capricious. Their basis is always an effort to reconstruct, on evidence not always as full as we'd wish, incidents in an intricate 1914-21 story.

The late John Hayward, many years ago, complained that whereas T. S. Eliot claimed to have given him "the first copy off the press" of Four Quartets, the copy in question contained an emendation inserted late in the press run. The formidable Fredson Bowers, Professor of Bibliography at the University of Virginia, received the complaint and addressed himself to it. What, he bade Mr Hayward imagine, had become of the first sheet off the press? Yes, it rested at the bottom of the pile of printed sheets. Which sheet, then, did the binder pick up first?

The one at the top of the pile, therefore the last one printed. Hence Mr Hayward's perplexity. The first copy from the bindery is the last from the press. What Professor Bowers did was to reconstruct a story, with agents manipulating physical things. Bowers was Professor Gabler's mentor, and his lessons have been taken to heart: however intricate the chain of reasoning, see that it hangs together as a story. So far, I've found only one editorial decision I deplore. "—I wouldn't do anything at all in that line, Davy Byrne said. It ruined many a man the same horses." Into that beautiful unpunctuated sequence a typescript, allegedly "copied from a lost final working draft," introduced a comma after "man." The edition accepts this comma as authorial. Now there is one story I simply don't believe. (pp. 771-72)

Hugh Kenner, "Leopold's Bloom Restored," in The Times Literary Supplement, No. 4241, July 13, 1984, pp. 771-72.

RICHARD ELLMANN

[An American biographer and critic, Ellmann is the author of the highly acclaimed critical biography James Joyce (1959; revised 1982) and the editor of The Critical Writings of James Joyce (1959) and Letters of James Joyce (volumes 2 and 3, 1967). In the following excerpt from an essay written in 1984, he discusses the importance of a passage restored by Gabler—in which Stephen pronounces the "word known to all men"—to the ultimate meaning of Ulysses.]

For the purposes of interpretation, perhaps the most significant of the thousands of small changes in Gabler's [Ulysses] has to do with the question that Stephen puts to his mother at the climax of the "Circe" episode, itself the climax of the novel. Stephen is appalled by his mother's ghost, but like Ulysses he seeks information from her. His mother says, "You sang that song to me. Love's bitter mystery." Stephen responds eagerly, "Tell me the word, mother, if you know now. The word known to all men." She fails to provide it. This passage has been much interpreted. I suggested a dozen years ago that the word known to all men must be love. Hugh Kenner has suggested that it is "perhaps" death—a revelation that would hardly require a mother's ghost to divulge. Another writer, Thomas Sawyer, in the James Joyce Quarterly, proposes that the word known to all men is "synteresis," which would seem rather to be the one word unknown to all men. Anyway, synteresis, meaning conscience as a guide for conduct, is too cold and moralistic a concept for the excited Stephen to claim such prominence for it.

Gabler has happily recovered a passage that was, it seems, inadvertently left out of the "Scylla and Charybdis" episode. When Stephen is talking about Shakespeare's affection for his granddaughter, he suddenly bethinks himself, in a passage that the typist probably skipped because two closely succeeding paragraphs ended in ellipsis. He says, "Do you know what you are talking about? Love, yes. Word known to all men. Amor vero aliquid alicui bonum vult unde et ea quae concupiscimus. . . ." The rather tortured Latin, which uses the vocabulary of Thomas Aquinas though I have not found in his works the exact passage, means, "Love truly wishes some good to another and therefore we all desire it." (In Exiles Richard explains love to the skeptical Robert as meaning "to wish someone well," as in the Italian, "Ti voglio bene.") In this view Stephen is following his master Dante, who has Virgil say, in Canto XVII of the Purgatorio—that canto in which the meaning of purgatory is set forth—"Neither Creator nor creature, my son, was ever without love . . . and this you know." . . . (p. 30)

Now that we can be certain that the word known to all men is love, we can verify the implications of Stephen's question. He is asking his mother to confirm, from the vantage point of the dead—for he thinks she may know *now*—what from the vantage point of the living he has already surmised. Presumably the dead can fathom the "bitter mystery." (It will be remembered that at the end of *A Portrait* his mother hopes that he will learn elsewhere what the heart is and what it feels, and Stephen says "Amen" to that.) Stephen is of one mind with Leopold Bloom, who at an equally tense moment in the "Cyclops" episode declares, "But it's no use. . . . Force, hatred, history, all that. That's not life for men and women, insult and hatred. And everybody knows that it's the very opposite of that that is really life." "What?" says Alf. "Love," says Bloom. "I mean the opposite of hatred."

Bloom's simple statement is immediately mocked. The citizen comments, "A new apostle to the gentiles. . . . Universal love." John Wyse Power offers a weak defense, "Well . . . Isn't that what we're told? Love your neighbour." "That chap? says the citizen. Beggar my neighbour is his motto. Love, moya! He's a nice pattern of a Romeo and Juliet." The citizen has quickly changed his tack from mocking love to mocking Bloom. At this point the inflationary narrator—Pangloss in contrast to Thersites—takes up the love theme.

> Love loves to love love. Nurse loves the new chemist. Constable 14A loves Mary Kelly. . . . Jumbo, the elephant, loves Alice, the elephant. Old Mr. Verschoyle with the ear trumpet loves old Mrs. Verschoyle with the turnedin eye. . . . His Majesty the King loves Her Majesty the Queen. . . . You love a certain person. And this person loves that other person because everybody loves somebody but God loves everybody.

Does this twaddle invalidate Bloom's remark? Some have said so, but we may find the mockery less telling if we remember that it parodies not only Bloom but Joyce's master, Dante, and Dante's master, Thomas Aquinas. (Aquinas says, in the *Summa Theologica* I, that God is love and loves all things.) It is the kind of parody that protects seriousness by immediately going away from intensity, as Bloom drops the subject and leaves. Love cannot be discussed without peril, but Bloom has nobly named it.

The larger implications of *Ulysses* follow from the accord of Bloom and Stephen about love. Both men are against the tyranny of Church and State, and the tyranny of jingoism—tyrannies that make history a nightmare. What they are for is also explicit. If we consider the book as a whole, the theme of love will be seen to pervade it. "Love's bitter mystery," quoted from the poem of Yeats which reverberates through the book, is something Stephen remembers having sung to his mother on her deathbed. It is something that Mulligan, though he quotes the song too, cannot understand, and that is alien to the experience of Boylan as of Thersites. But Bloom does understand it, and so does Molly, and both cherish moments of affection from their lives together as crucial points of reference.

The nature of love has to be more intimately anatomized, subjected to attacks of various kinds. In the "Nausicaa" episode Gerty McDowell claims soulful love, yet her physical urges make their sly presence felt. The body pretends to be soul but

isn't. In the following episode, the "Oxen of the Sun," the medical students scorn love and deal only with the intromission of male into female parts. The soul pretends to be body but isn't. In "Circe" Stephen opposes the forces of hatred, violence, and history in the form of the British soldiers, his mother's threats of hellfire, and Old Gummy Granny's insistence that he lose his life for Ireland. Bloom similarly opposes the soldiers, the sadistic nun, and the Gardai (the Irish police), as well as the sexual brutality of the brothel. He does so largely out of concern for Stephen—comradely and paternal love being among the forms that love takes. At the end of the "Circe" episode Bloom confirms Stephen's theory of artistic creation as like natural creation, when he imaginatively evokes the figure of his dead son, Rudy, not as he was when he died at eleven days, but as he might be at eleven years. Finally in the last episode of the book, Molly Bloom, after some equivocation between her physical longing for Boylan and her thoughts of Bloom, comes down firmly on the side of Bloom and of their old feelings for each other. She proves by her discrimination that love is a blend of physicality and mentality.

Joyce is of course wary of stating so distinctly as Virgil does to Dante his theme of love as the omnipresent force in the universe. But allowing for the obliquity necessary to preserve the novel from didacticism, the word known to the whole book is love in its various forms, sexual, brotherly, paternal, filial, and is so glossed by Stephen, Bloom, and Molly. At the end the characters, discombobulated in "Circe," return to their individual identities as if like Kant they had weathered Hume's skepticism. The book revolts against history as made up of hatred and violence, and speaks in its most intense moments of their opposite. It does so with the keenest sense of how love can degenerate into creamy dreaminess or into brutishness, can claim to be all soul or all body, when only in the union of both can it truly exist. Like other comedies, *Ulysses* ends in a vision of reconciliation rather than of sundering. Affection between human beings, however transitory, however qualified, is the closest we can come to paradise. That it loses its force does not invalidate it. Dante says that Adam and Eve's paradise lasted only six hours, and Proust reminds us that the only true paradise is the one we have lost. But the word known to all men has been defined and affirmed, regardless of whether or not it is subject to diminution.

It has been said by Hugh Kenner that Molly Bloom's thoughts may not end. But Joyce has put a full stop to them. The full stop comes just at the moment when her memories culminate in a practical demonstration of the nature of love which bears out what Stephen and Bloom have said more abstractly. It has been asserted by the critic Michael Groden that Joyce never finished *Ulysses*, just abandoned it, the grounds for the statement being that he was revising it up to the last moment. But other writers have stopped writing because of deadlines, and we do not say that their books are unfinished. I should maintain that Joyce finished his book in that sense and in another sense as well. Because Molly Bloom countersigns with the rhythm of finality what Stephen and Bloom have said about the word known to all men, *Ulysses* is one of the most concluded books ever written. (pp. 30-1)

Richard Ellmann, "The Big Word in 'Ulysses'," in The New York Review of Books, Vol. XXXI, No. 16, October 25, 1984, pp. 30-1.

RICHARD ELLMANN

[In the following excerpt from an essay written in 1986, Ellmann questions Gabler's restoration of the passage including the "word known to all men."]

The most important emendation in Gabler's new edition is one in the "Scylla and Charybdis" episode. It comes in the middle of Stephen's explanation of the serenity of Shakespeare's late plays:

> —Marina, Stephen said, a child of storm, Miranda, a wonder, Perdita, that which was lost. What was lost is given back to him, his daughter's child. *My dearest wife,* Pericles says, *was like this maid.* Will any man love the daughter if he has not loved the mother?

Mr. Best acquiesces to Stephen's first question, quoting the title of a book by Victor Hugo: "—The art of being a grandfather, Mr. Best gan murmur. *L'art d'être grandp.* . . ."

In the emendation, Stephen asks a second question of the others and a third of himself:

> —Will he not see reborn in her, with the memory of his own youth added, another image?

> Do you know what you are talking about? Love, yes. Word known to all men. *Amor vero aliquid alicui bonum vult unde et ea quae concupiscimus.*

after which he says to the others, as in the old text:

> —His own image to a man with that queer thing genius is the standard of all experience, material and moral. Such an appeal will touch him. The images of other males of his blood will repel him. He will see in them grotesque attempts of nature to foretell or to repeat himself.

It is extremely helpful to have Joyce confirm that the word known to all men is *love,* and Gabler must be commended for unearthing this passage. But there are reasons for arguing that, however much it may clarify Joyce's outlook, it should not be included in the final text. Stephen's interpretation of Shakespeare is, as he is well aware, specious, but he wants to put as good a face on it as he can. In the quotation from *Pericles,* what is discussed is the resemblance of daughter to mother. Shakespeare's two daughters were born in the 1580's, long before the plays of the late period were written; it is the birth in 1608 of his granddaughter Elizabeth, the child of Susanna Shakespeare and John Hall, that is relevant to Stephen's theme. He is slyly shifting from the resemblance of mother to daughter, to the resemblance of grandmother to granddaughter. Mr. Best reminds him that a granddaughter rather than a daughter is involved.

Stephen then asks the second question: "Will he not see reborn in her, with the memory of his own youth added, another image?" This augments the confusion. For it makes Elizabeth a blend of two of her four grandparents rather than of her parents. Stephen is clumsily making Shakespeare the father of his granddaughter. Joyce, fastidiously scrutinizing these lines, could see that the deliberate confusion of daughter and granddaughter, plausible if got over quickly, was implausible if drawn out.

It might be argued that the word *image* in the second question is necessary because of the passage about "his own image" that follows. But image in the second question means the composite of Shakespeare ("the memory of his own youth added") and his wife, while image in the later passage leaves out Anne Hathaway—in sharp contradiction to Pericles—and makes the granddaughter a reflection only of the artist.

Gabler's emendation continues with the aside by Stephen about love. The passage in Latin has been identified by John T. Noonan, Jr., as from Book I, Chapter 91, of the *Summa Contra Gentiles.* Unfortunately it puts together two passages that are separate in the original and deal with different points. Thomas Aquinas is distinguishing between selfless love and selfless desire. *Amor vero aliquid alicui bonum* means, "love wishes another's good"; *unde et ea quae concupiscimus* means "whence we desire [not love] these things." Joyce must have wanted Stephen to bridge, in silent monologue, from Shakespeare's once genuine love for his wife to his pleasure at seeing in his granddaughter his own image. But in looking at the passage again, he could see that the Latin was without further explanation unintelligible. He could see also that the emphasis on true love was excessive when Stephen was about to dismiss it in favor of artistic narcissism. By striking out the passage, he could avoid drawing undue attention to a weakness in Stephen's argument, and he could save Stephen's celebration of love (of the selfless kind) until later in the book, when in the "Circe" episode Stephen asks his dead mother, "Tell me the word, mother, if you know now. The word known to all men." She will not answer. (pp. 554-55)

Richard Ellmann, "The New 'Ulysses'," in The Georgia Review, *Vol. XL, No. 2, Summer, 1986, pp. 548-56.*

EDITORIAL PRINCIPLES AND PROCEDURES

CHRISTINE FROULA

[In the following excerpt, Froula presents the editorial principles on which Gabler's Ulysses *is based.]*

The highly innovative (and somewhat controversial) editorial principle guiding the construction of Gabler's *Ulysses* is that the "continuous manuscript text"—conceived as the fair copy texts of the chapters together with their extension in autograph notation on later typescripts, serializations, proofs for the first edition, and the first edition itself—is "the highest authority on which to base an edition." This principle modifies W. W. Greg's theory of copytext: whereas for Greg, the copytext is an actual document chosen as the best authority to settle problematic readings, Gabler's copytext is the synoptic text—the synthetic and ideal "document" that his left-hand pages record, gleaned from the many actual documents, extant and inferred, that were produced in the course of *Ulysses*' composition. Gabler's copytext functions not to settle undecidable readings but to array the evidence of Joyce's written, revised, and canceled words through the text's evolution from the chapter fair copies forward; it is for further editorial principles to determine the most authoritative variants for the reading text.

Gabler's conception of his copytext indicates, moveover, the nature of the *Ulysses* his work aims for: not the 1922 text with all errors of transmission corrected but a text that recovers as far as possible the text Joyce left in his own hand in the documents' composite final stage. Gabler's method is to follow the track of Joyce's pen in its journey across manuscript pages and over typed transcriptions and proofs, admitting only those changes whose authority can be proved or inferred from documents with a reasonable degree of certainty. Consequently, what constitutes an "error" for Gabler covers a somewhat wider range of variants that usual: not only does he correct the

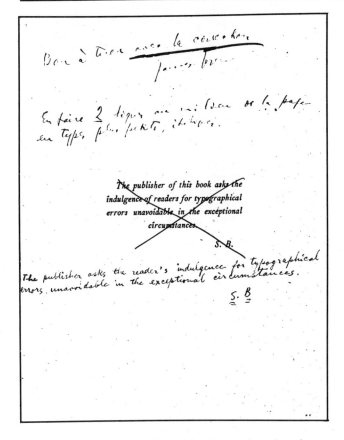

Joyce's corrections of the introductory note from the publisher in the first edition of Ulysses. *The Society of Authors as the literary representatives of the Estate of James Joyce and © 1978 the Trustees of the Estate of James Joyce.*

usual copyist's errors, but many variants from early stages of the text that could be taken as rejected by Joyce the author are construed by Gabler as accidental omissions by Joyce in his capacity as copyist and overseer of his text's transmission. The five thousand variants between Gabler's text and the previous ones, then, are not all "errors" by any usual definition. Gabler's method entails what he terms a "radical conservatism": he returns to the roots of the text to discover what Joyce wrote and to preserve it from change. The text thereby created, although one that Joyce never held in his hands, is in theory a perfect transcription of the text at the point of its latest *autograph* development. Properly speaking, Gabler does not *restore* missing words, *undo* editorial changes, or *correct* existing errors but strives to re-create Joyce's text as it would have stood had such losses, changes, and omissions never occurred. (pp. 456-57)

Only rarely does Gabler depart from his editorial principle of reconstructing and preserving Joyce's text as he wrote it. One striking instance is his decision to correct two errors in "Ithaca," in the elaborate historical dating of Bloom's weight on the chemist's scales. On the third and last proof, Joyce added in script, "Roman indication 2, Julian period 6617, MXMIV," which Gabler corrects in both genetic and reading text to "Roman indiction 2, Julian period 6617, MCMIV," on the ground that Joyce had no further opportunity to catch the errors himself before the book's publication. This argument seems eminently reasonable, and yet the fact that Joyce never noted either error in the errata slips of the early editions nor attempted to correct

them in later ones must give an editor pause. Gabler has considered and rejected Patrick McCarthy's theory that the errors are deliberate ones, intended to exhibit the catechistic narrator's unreliability. I am no more convinced that this was Joyce's design than Gabler is, but I think that the questions raised by his decision to emend the text may be more complicated than he acknowledges. Gabler and McCarthy propose two different ways of reconciling the errors with Joyce's authority, the one by correcting them and the other by rationalizing them. Either way assures the triumph of Joyce's authority over error. But there is a third stance toward Joyce's authorial errors which an editor might plausibly adopt, one that takes into account the fact that the errors, if indeed unintentional, show Joyce himself to be a not entirely reliable narrator—a fact which, although it may not be part of the text's ideal intention, is part of its actual history. *Ulysses*, unlike Pound's *Cantos*, does not contain many such errors; in this respect, its historical text coincides with its ideal text closely enough that it is not necessary to distinguish between them except at such rare and tiny moments as these. But the fact that, when Gabler must choose between them, it is the ideal text and not the historical one that wins the day does constitute a departure from his "radical conservatism" which merits fuller discussion in the apparatus. It would be overstating the matter to say that Gabler here puts himself in the position of those earlier transcribers who enlarged their function for the sake of "improving" Joyce's text—the French printer correcting "Entente cordial," the copyist removing the extra *a*'s in "dearer thaaan them all," the editors who changed "acatalectic" to "catalectic," even the printer of Gabler's own text who, mistaking the period that concludes "Ithaca" for a flyspeck, helpfully whited it out (an error caught in the proofs); for he, unlike them, is very likely right. The fact remains, however, that Joyce wrote what he wrote and did not through many years correct it; and this fact is arguably as integral to the text as the ideal of correctness which Gabler, departing from his own stated principle, here applies.

This question, in any case, is one of critical judgment and does not diminish the definitive value of this edition, which fully documents both Joyce's readings and Gabler's emendations. (pp. 463-64)

Christine Froula, "The Adventures of 'Ulysses'," in The Yale Review, *Vol. 74, No. 3, April, 1985, pp. 454-66.*

MICHAEL GRODEN

[In the following excerpt, Groden discusses in detail the editorial process Gabler followed in reconstructing Ulysses.*]*

The errors in the text of *Ulysses* have never been a secret. Joyce himself complained about them even before the first edition appeared: in a letter to Harriet Weaver in November 1921, he noted that he was "extremely irritated by all those printer's errors" and asked, "Are these to be perpetuated in future editions? I hope not" (*Letters* I 176). In the first edition itself, Joyce and Sylvia Beach alerted readers to the deplorable state of the text by including a note at the front calling attention to the many unavoidable typographical errors in the printing. There are several broad explanations for the corruption of the first edition's text and, therefore, of the text of all the versions published until now, since they all stem from the first edition. Some of the reasons involve the system of composition and transmission that Joyce developed for *Ulysses*. After compiling notes and rough drafts, he brought each episode to a temporary finish in a working draft that he gave to a typist. From that point on in each episode's development, the text was transcribed by a series of other people (the typist and the printers), sometimes as many as eight or nine times. Joyce added new text as he read each transcription. For many pages he himself served as a scribe as he apparently recopied the manuscript he had given to the typist, making some changes and some errors as he went along. As he corrected each transcription, he seems not to have looked back to his original manuscript, so he was relying on his memory. (By 1921, when he was reading, correcting, and augmenting the proofs, he no longer had the manuscript available, since he had sent it to its purchaser, John Quinn.) Other reasons involve the printing process. Joyce complained that he was forced to "write and revise and correct" all at the same time (*Letters* I 168) a necessity due to the startling amount of material he added to the book as he received proofs in mid-1921, while he was writing "Ithaca" and "Penelope." Complicating matters were the state of Joyce's eyes and the condition of the proofs themselves. Only one of the printers knew any English at all, and his limited knowledge was unfortunate, since it inspired him to intervene with what he thought were corrections of some of Joyce's idiosyncracies into standard English. Besides, the printers worked under severe time pressures. They frequently had to reset much type because of Joyce's corrections, and they worked under very short deadlines. All in all, it is less surprising that so many words were misprinted in the first edition than that so many managed to appear correctly.

All subsequent versions of *Ulysses* descend from the first edition. There have been ten previous editions: (1) Shakespeare and Company, 1922; reprinted 1924 (fourth impression), with errata incorporated into the text; (2) Shakespeare and Company, 1926 (eighth printing), set from the first; (3) "Shakespeare and Company, 1927"; actually a pirated edition published by Samuel Roth, 1927, set from the second; (4) Odyssey Press, 1932, set from the second; (5) Random House, 1934, set from the third (yes, the piracy) and corrected from the fourth; (6) Limited Editions Club, 1935, set from the fourth; (7) John Lane, The Bodley Head, 1936, set from the fourth; 1937, reprinted with authorial corrections; (8) Bodley Head, 1960, set from the (uncorrected) seventh; (9) Random House, 1961, set from the eighth; (10) Penguin, 1968, set from the eighth. None of the editions after the first edition—and neither of the errata lists Joyce included in the second and fourth impressions of the first edition—looked back to the manuscript or to other prepublication documents for authorization or corroboration. Rather, they sought primarily to correct mistakes. Due to human error, each new edition introduced as many new mistakes as it eliminated. The textual nadir occurred when Random House inadvertently used Samuel Roth's 1927 piracy as the setting text for its first authorized American edition in 1934; the pirated edition is erroneous probably more often than it is accurate. In the 1960s Jack Dalton worked to produce a corrected edition of the 1961 Random House text, and he used the prepublication documents as the sources for his corrections, but he never completed his project. (pp. 137-39)

Ulysses: A Critical and Synoptic Edition is not a corrected edition, one whose editor looks for places where the printed text is inaccurate and corrects them. Even though the new text does indeed expose some five thousand errors in all the previously published versions of Joyce's text, it corrects them only indirectly. Rather, by establishing and printing the text Joyce wanted—in other words, by producing a "critical edition"—the new edition reveals that the first edition departs

from Joyce's text about five thousand times and that each of the other collated editions departs from Joyce's text about the same number of times, but not always in the same places. To produce a critical edition, Hans Walter Gabler reconstructed Joyce's writing of the book and built the new text up from the beginning as Joyce originally did it. With the help of an editorial team and set of interlocking computer programs, Gabler needed seven years—from March 1, 1977 to February 29, 1984—to reconstruct the text, about as much time as Joyce took to construct it in the first place.

Any editor has to perform a process of reconstruction in order to determine the sequence of original composition and revision of a text and the degree of interference (sometimes authorized, sometimes not) by typists, editors, and printers. Usually one of the editions of the text published during the author's lifetime serves as the critical edition's copytext; the choice is often the first edition even if the text was substantially changed or corrected later. (The first edition can be used as long as the text was not completely recast.) The edition follows the copytext for accidentals (styling, punctuation, spelling) and when necessary emends its substantives (the words themselves and sometimes punctuation as well) on the basis of the editorial reconstruction of the original composition. But even at this basic level of editing theory and practice (a theory and procedure begun by W. W. Greg and extended and developed by Fredson Bowers and his followers), *Ulysses* presents immediate problems because, if all published versions are so error-ridden, none can serve as the copytext for a critical edition. Furthermore, the distinction between substantives and accidentals is blurred beyond recognition in *Ulysses*. Punctuation was extremely important to Joyce, as were spelling and many matters of styling. Thus, preparatory to anything else, especially to a serious plan to edit *Ulysses*, Gabler had to extend and adapt the prevailing editing theory to new circumstances.

The details of these circumstances have gradually become known through textual studies of *Ulysses* during the past forty years, and the new edition builds on several of them. Prominent among these studies are Joseph Prescott's pioneering dissertation on the revisions to the proofs, the series of Columbia University dissertations on individual episodes, A. Walton Litz's *Art of James Joyce*, Phillip Herring's editions of the British Library notesheets and some of the Buffalo notes and drafts, and my own *"Ulysses" in Progress* [see Additional Bibliography], including the stemma of the development of *Ulysses* that I offered there. Most important, the publication in the mid and late 1970s of the Rosenbach Manuscript in facsimile and the other documents in photo-reprints in the *James Joyce Archive* brought the relevant materials together in printed form and made it possible for most of the work to be done in one place, Munich, with periodic visits to the libraries for closer investigation of the original documents. Even with all this scholarship available, however, a critical edition seemed utterly impossible until quite recently. What was missing was a way of merging editorial theory with the unique circumstances of composition that these studies of *Ulysses* brought to light.

Joyce's methods of composition as they are now understood can be briefly summarized. . . . He wrote *Ulysses* episode by episode. For each one he began with notes and rough drafts and eventually consolidated the episode into a final working draft. He sent the final working draft, sometimes amended, to a typist, who prepared an original and from one to three carbon copies. A nearly complete manuscript is extant at the Rosenbach Museum in Philadelphia. Part of this manuscript represents the document the typists used—the final working draft—but almost half is not that document. Joyce made some corrections and additions to the typescript, usually but not always marking all copies identically. For the first fourteen episodes, he sent one copy to Ezra Pound, who sent it (with occasional expurgations) to New York for serial publication in the *Little Review*. When Joyce submitted a typescript he considered that episode finished, at least to the extent that he felt free to move on to the next episode.

When book publication was arranged in 1921, Joyce took another copy of each episode's typescript, wrote new additions onto it, and sent it with its two rounds of revisions to the printer. Each set of proofs—first *placards* (galley proofs in page-proof form) and then page proofs—inspired further additions. For each passage there are at least two and as many as nine sets of proofs. Joyce decided that he wanted his book published on his fortieth birthday, February 2, 1922, so two days before that date he stopped adding to the text and, with a combination of reluctance and relief, considered the book finished.

Neither the Rosenbach Manuscript nor the first (or any other published) edition can serve as the basis for a critical edition. The Rosenbach manuscript is unacceptable because, even if it were in its entirety the document the typists used, it is too far removed from the final text; for some passages Joyce added up to a third of the final text after he inscribed the manuscript. And as I mentioned above, the published texts are too corrupt. It became possible to produce a critical edition only when Hans Walter Gabler realized that a base text does exist in Joyce's handwriting, even if not on any single document. The final working draft (sometimes the existing Rosenbach Manuscript, sometimes the lost document from which the Rosenbach Manuscript was transcribed), plus Joyce's handwritten additions to the typescript and to each successive set of proofs, can constitute the base text for an edition.

Gabler thus saw a real possibility of editing *Ulysses* when he realized that he could arrive at an accurate text by recreating Joyce's writing of the book from beginning to end. This approach is especially applicable to an accretive text like *Ulysses*. From the final working draft onwards, Joyce's revisions are almost all additions; there is some substitution but almost no deletion. Gabler modified the idea of copytext to one of a "continuous manuscript" or, more precisely, a "continuous manuscript text." Almost all of *Ulysses* as Joyce wanted it to appear exists in his own handwriting. The inscriptions are scattered among the many (up to twelve) documents for each passage, but the final working draft plus Joyce's subsequent handwritten additions should add up to the text he wanted. The editorial task, then, was to recover this "continuous manuscript text." In theory, such an approach would bypass all the versions prepared along the way to the first edition (the typescript and each printing on the proofs) and all the published versions of the book as it concentrated exclusively on Joyce's own inscriptions. In reality, several crucial documents (including much of the final working draft) are not extant, so the process was more complicated, and the transmitted versions in the typescripts and proofs served the editor in two ways: they offered evidence of authorial changes from the missing documents, and they provided useful sources of comparison at every stage between the text that Joyce wanted and the text that was produced.

The continuous manuscript text served as the edition's copytext and was emended when necessary, but it had to be editorially

constructed as part of the recreation of Joyce's writing of *Ulysses*. The first step was to establish the earliest beginning-to-end version of each episode, a base onto which subsequent revisions could be grafted. This version represents the state of the text's development at the final-working-draft/typescript/*Little-Review* stage, the provisionally finished state. This "early-version text" is an edited version of each episode of *Ulysses* representing the first (but only temporarily) complete step in its development; and it is an ideal text in that it is free of all the mistakes produced first by Joyce himself as he faircopied his work, then by the typist, and finally by the compositors for the *Little Review* as they transcribed the text.

Establishing the early-version text was relatively simple when the Rosenbach Manuscript (the only extant manuscript) is in the line of transmission, but when it is not, the early-version text had to be editorially constructed from the two documents (the extant manuscript and the typescript) that lie in a collateral relationship to the non-extant final working draft. It used to be assumed that, even though the relationship between the Rosenbach Manuscript and typescript varied among episodes, it was constant within each episode (with the one exception of "Lotus Eaters"); in *"Ulysses" in Progress*, for example, I argued that the manuscript is in the line of transmission for nine episodes, outside it for eight, and partly in and partly out for "Lotus Eaters." There is no question about the claim that the manuscript lies in the line of transmission for nine episodes: the first three ("Telemachus," "Nestor," "Proteus"), the last four ("Circe," "Eumaeus," "Ithaca," "Penelope"), and two in the middle ("Wandering Rocks," "Cyclops"). (Were this not the case the edition might have taken another seven years to complete.) But Gabler discovered that the extant manuscript is not entirely outside the line of transmission for the other nine episodes. Rather, the relationship at times seems to vary from page to page in those nine from the middle of *Ulysses*. By the time Joyce was preparing "Calypso," "Lotus Eaters," and "Hades" for the typist, he was thinking about selling the manuscript, and he apparently decided that the appearance of various pages of the final working draft made them unsuitable for sale. So he probably recopied some pages while preserving others, discarding the pages that he recopied. This theory helps to account for the failure of a single page of the hypothetical final working draft to survive when there is a recopied Rosenbach Manuscript page.

Gabler calls the Rosenbach manuscript a "collective manuscript,". . . since it was assembled from different documents sometime after the typescript was prepared. (Such eclectic assembling was also Joyce's practice with the typescripts, the top copies and carbons of which he mixed indiscriminately.) The relationship between the texts of the extant manuscript and typescript had to be ascertained for each passage individually to determine whether the manuscript is (1) the source of the typed text or identical with the source, (2) an early text subsequently revised on the final working draft before the draft was given to the typist, or (3) a revision to the text of the final working draft that was not recorded in the final working draft itself and so never entered the line of transmission. Through a computer print-out of all variants revealed by a collation of the Rosenbach Manuscript, typescript, and *Little Review* texts, the editor knew which passages required editorial attention to produce the ideal early-version text.

Once the early-version text was established, the editing process was simpler, at least in theory. Joyce's handwritten inscriptions on the typescripts and proofs, representing up to a third of an episode, were added to the early-version text to produce the final text. The editorial team prepared a handwritten list of all the additions and corrections, and at the same time the computer collated all the inscriptions against the first edition text, thus revealing both the corruption in the first edition and any transcription errors on the part of the editorial team. The hand-compiled and computer-complied lists were compared and editorially merged into one set of additions, and the final text resulted from the early-version text plus these subsequent inscriptions. Not surprisingly, this part of the editing procedure was more complicated in practice than in theory, since for many reasons the two lists were not identical. For example, the printers often erred as they set type for a revision. If Joyce corrected the mistake and the printers then set the type as he wanted, Gabler ignored both the error and the correction. (The loss to the inquisitive reader is a record of some funny misprints.) If Joyce missed an error or revised it to a new reading, Gabler had to make an editorial decision regarding Joyce's intentions.

As each word or phrase was entered into the computer, it was coded to indicate the stage in the composition sequence at which it first appears. Only the basic text of the Rosenbach Manuscript received no code. For the rest of the text, "A" stands for the revisions to the final working draft that first appear in the typed text; "R" represents the revisions to the Rosenbach Manuscript that are not in the typescript (Joyce neglected to make these changes on the final working draft, or these revisions postdate the preparation of the typescript); "B"-"D" mean the rounds of revision in the typescript; "1" represents the revisions in the first *placard*, incorporated in the second *placard;* etc. The highest number (8 in some cases) represents the revisions in the final page proofs, incorporated in the first edition.

Because each textual unit was labelled in this way, a different kind of presentation of the edited text became possible. Two versions of the text have been generated; in *Ulysses: A Critical and Synoptic Edition* they are printed on facing pages. On the left is the edition's major innovation, a new type of textual apparatus; Gabler calls it a "synoptic text," since it offers a synopsis of the textual development. . . . Each word or phrase is labelled here with the codes to indicate its first appearance in the text. The identifying letters and numbers appear as superscripts within half-brackets before and after each unit. (A letter or number in parentheses indicates a non-extant document.) Carets indicate changes and additions within a single stage. Full brackets indicate words Joyce eliminated either by revision or, occasionally, by simple deletion. With a little practice, a reader can recreate Joyce's work on *Ulysses*. . . . The codes differ depending upon the number of proofs for each passage; they are identified at the beginning of the textual notes for each episode . . . and in a list of symbols printed at the beginning of each volume. The development of the entire book thus appears in an uninterrupted form, accessible to anyone interested in studying the text's genesis or retracing the editorial process. The synoptic text is accompanied by traditional lists recording changes the editor has made in the continuous manuscript text and variant readings in the different published versions. The editorial changes, the List of Emendations, appear as footnotes to the synoptic text, while the Historical Collation is located after the text of the book along with textual notes and a textual history of each episode.

The right-hand page contains the version most readers want, a clear reading text. This version was produced when the editor instructed the computer to ignore all coding marks and all words within full brackets (deleted or superseded words). The beginnings and ends of the right- and left-hand pages correspond as closely as possible to facilitate cross-checking, and the lines of both pages have been numbered for reference. The synoptic-text lines are numbered for each page, the clear-text lines consecutively from beginning to end of each episode. Because of this beginning-to-end line numbering for the clear text of each episode, compatibility between the scholarly edition and [forthcoming commercial printings] . . . will be possible. The page lengths in the commercial printings may differ from the Garland page lengths (which themselves vary from page to page), but the line numbers will allow a reader to move easily from one printing to another. (pp. 139-46)

Because Joyce's writing of *Ulysses* differs from any of the common models of composition with which editors usually work, *Ulysses: A Critical and Synoptic Edition* opens up several provocative theoretical issues. One of these issues grows out of those passages where the Rosenbach Manuscript is not the final working draft and where its text differs from that on the typescript that was prepared from the final working draft. Here the extant Rosenbach Manuscript and the typescript radiate from the non-extant final working draft. As I noted earlier, if the texts differ, the Rosenbach Manuscript text can be in one of two positions relative to the final-working-draft/typescript text. In the first possibility, the Rosenbach Manuscript text represents the less complete stage of development: Joyce wrote out the final working draft, copied the text onto the Rosenbach Manuscript, then revised the final working draft and sent it to the typist without making the changes in the Rosenbach Manuscript. In this case, and it is the more likely and more common possibility, the revision became part of the transmission process of the text, and Gabler chose the typescript reading over the Rosenbach Manuscript reading. In the second possibility, the Rosenbach Manuscript text represents the more advanced stage of development. Here, once again, Joyce presumably wrote out the final working draft and copied the text onto the Rosenbach Manuscript. But he revised the Rosenbach Manuscript, sometimes as he wrote, sometimes (either then or later) through deletion and substitution of text already written. Joyce did not make these revisions on the corresponding text in the final working draft, or he revised the Rosenbach Manuscript after the text was typed from the final working draft; however and whenever he entered the revisions, they did not enter the transmission process and have never appeared in any published versions. Gabler admitted about one hundred of these readings into the critical edition of *Ulysses*.

A few points can be made to explain Gabler's reasoning and procedures:

—The basic principle is that the text of *Ulysses* developed in a linear fashion with every inscription part of the evolutionary process. Gabler says that Joyce, in inscribing the various documents for *Ulysses*, "carr[ied] forward a continuous manuscript of essentially linear development." A collateral *document* (not in the main line of transmission), as the Rosenbach Manuscript certainly is for many of its pages, does not necessarily mean collateral status for the *text* carried by that document. Gabler considers the Rosenbach Manuscript in these cases to be collateral to the typescript but an extension of the final working draft.

—Because the Rosenbach Manuscript is a collective manuscript, the status of the text it carries can vary from page to page. Thus, every Rosenbach-Manuscript/typescript variant had

Sylvia Beach and James Joyce at Shakespeare and Company. Sylvia Beach Collection, Princeton University Library.

to be considered and decided individually; it is possible that neighboring passages resulted from different circumstances of composition.

—For many of the passages in question, there is no textual evidence to indicate the direction in which Joyce actually revised. Occasionally the Rosenbach Manuscript shows a clear deletion of the typescript reading in favor of a new one, but more often the extant manuscript shows only the variant reading. Here the editor's critical skills came into play as he had to decide which reading probably represents the more advanced of the two inscriptions. Sometimes there seems to be little difference between the two readings. In a passage from "Oxen of the Sun," for example, the typescript, proofs and published versions read, "And he that had erst challenged to be so doughty waxed pale as they might all mark," whereas the text in the Rosenbach Manuscript and the new edition is "waxed wan.". . . The direction of Joyce's revision is not obvious from the documents themselves, and there is no strong critical basis for choosing one reading over the other. (It could be argued, however, that Joyce is more likely to have revised toward an alliterative phrase than away from one.) In other passages the direction of revision is clearer on critical grounds. In "Aeolus," one of Bloom's thoughts in the transmitted versions reads, "It is amusing to view the unpar one ar alleled embarra two ars is it? double ess ment of a harassed pedlar while gauging

au the symmetry of a peeled pear under a cemetery wall," whereas the Rosenbach Manuscript and critical edition read "symmetry with a y.". . . It is unlikely that Joyce deleted "with a y"; either he accidentally omitted it from the final working draft or he added it to the Rosenbach Manuscript while he was transcribing it from the final working draft. The same argument applies to a passage from "Lestrygonians." In the transcribed versions, as Bloom remembers Molly on Howth hill, he thinks, "Mawkish pulp her mouth had mumbled sweet and sour with spittle." The Rosenbach Manuscript and critical edition read "sweetsour of her spittle.". . . It is difficult to imagine Joyce revising from the more complex to the simpler phrasing.

—One kind of textual evidence that helps here is what Gabler calls the rule of the invariant context. If the context (words, phrases, sentences—the length varies from example to example) surrounding an uncertain passage underwent any change in the subsequent development, then the Rosenbach Manuscript reading was rejected in favor of the transmitted reading because the changes in the context imply that Joyce altered the Rosenbach Manuscript text as well. If the context remained invariant, the Rosenbach reading could be accepted. . . .

—A parallel situation exists in a few places where the *Little Review* (also a collateral document) presents a unique reading that was admitted into the critical text. An example is Cyril Sargent's hair in "Nestor," described twice in the Rosenbach Manuscript, proofs (there is no extant typescript), and published versions as "tangled," but in the *Little Review* and critical edition as "thick.". . . Here the *Little Review* reading presumably came about when Joyce entered a revision onto one copy of the typescript but did not make the same revision on the copy he eventually gave to the printer of the book version. In these situations the two typescripts lie in the same relation to each other as do the Rosenbach Manuscript and the typescript.

—For passages like these Gabler rejected the notion of "passive authorization," . . . the argument that the absence of correction implies Joyce's acceptance of the transmitted text. There are several places where Joyce simply missed nonsensical transcriptions, even though he saw the transmitted text between five and ten times on the typescript and proofs. For example, the typist created mathematical nonsense in a passage from "Calypso." In the typescript, proofs, and printed texts Bloom thinks, "You pay eight marks and they plant a dunam of land for you. . . . Can pay ten down and the balance in yearly instalments." In the Rosenbach Manuscript and new edition the total fee is "eighty marks.". . . In another passage, . . . grammatical nonsense resulted when the printer apparently skipped a line of type from the typescript of "Lotus Eaters" and set "His right hand once more more slowly went over again: choice blend, made of the finest Ceylon brands" instead of "went over his brow and hair. Then he put on his hat again, relieved: and read again." . . . It is easy to suggest reasons why Joyce missed these errors; the pressure under which he worked as he revised and corrected the proofs at the same time as he was writing the last two episodes and the state of his eyes are two obvious possibilities. Gabler treated passages like these two as paradigms. "From such cases," he writes, "the edition takes its guidance and classifies the departures from Joyce's autograph notation that were left standing in the documents of transmission as errors and corruptions to be rejected and not as tacit revisions to be followed.". . .

Such a procedure obviously conflicts with a textual theory that is oriented toward the text as published in the first edition, where the broad working principle is to decline to change the text as transmitted unless there is a compelling reason to do so. Gabler would agree that all of Joyce's efforts were directed toward publication, but he argues that it is not the first edition as *document* that represents the culmination of Joyce's work but rather the finished *text*. Following Greg and Bowers, he distinguishes between the documents of composition and the documents of transmission. . . . He calls his procedure "radically conservative" and describes it in this way:

> Going to the roots of the text in the documents where Joyce wrote out each word and sentence and chapter for the novel, it [the edition] traces and records the work's evolution towards publication. In this process of critical recovery it in the main does not follow the departures of typescripts and proofs from the text in autograph. Thus, this critical edition endeavours to conserve intact Joyce's text for *Ulysses*.

In the Afterword [see Additional Bibliography], he succinctly distinguishes between the two types of document:

> In the documents of composition [i.e., the holograph inscriptions], the text is held to possess

full authority, unless it can be shown to be faulty. In the documents of transmission, by contrast [i.e., the typed text on the typescripts and the printed text on the proofs], the text is held to be potentially faulty, unless it can be proved to possess authority.

A second area of theoretical interest involves the role and significance that the editor assigns to the original transmission and publication process. In *A Critique of Modern Textual Criticism,* Jerome J. McGann argues that, for some nineteenth- and twentieth-century authors, the concept of the "author's final intentions" (the usual goal of an editor operating on Greg-Bowers principles) must be modified to include aspects of non-authorial transmission in the process of publication. McGann calls for more attention to "the collaborative or social nature of literary production." Publishers' editors and printers contribute not only to the house style and punctuation of a text but sometimes to the language itself, and this involvement can occur with the knowledge, and maybe even the encouragement, of the author. Gabler paid serious attention to the conditions of printing and publication as they affected the development of *Ulysses,* but he concluded that knowledge of these conditions supports a text based on authorial inscription as it exists in the autograph manuscripts. Nevertheless, Gabler would agree with McGann that recovering the final intentions of an author is not under all conditions the editor's uppermost goal. Gabler aimed to recover and reproduce Joyce's intentions, but these were not necessarily the final chronological ones, the last state of the text Joyce may have seen and approved. Rather, Joyce signalled his intentions through his inscription of a passage's most advanced state of development, and while that state usually appears in the final page proofs, in some cases it is found in the Rosenbach Manuscript that Joyce inscribed before he saw the proofs.

If an awareness of the printing process did not ultimately affect the editorial decisions, it does nonetheless throw important light on other aspects of *Ulysses.* For one thing, Joyce worked toward deadlines, first the regular ones for the *Little Review* serialization and then the arbitrary one of his fortieth birthday for the book publication. Deadlines prodded Joyce to complete individual episodes and the book as a whole, and it can be argued (as I did in *"Ulysses" in Progress*) that "Circe," the longest and most elaborate episode up to that point and the one that most fully reuses material from the earlier parts of the book, grew as it did because Joyce was freed from working toward a deadline for serial publication in the *Little Review.* (By the time he was writing "Circe," a court decision had ended the serialization.) Second, Joyce's rereading of the book for his work on "Oxen of the Sun" and "Circe" may have profoundly affected the form of the book, as it seems likely that this rereading helped to inspire the huge number of revisions that soon followed. The contract for book publication and the subsequent need to read proofs for the early episodes while he was writing "Ithaca" and "Penelope" seem to have prodded Joyce into adding even more new material. . . . Third, even significant aspects of the final ordering of the book appear to be results of the printing conditions. A great deal of background material about Bloom and Molly is included in the last two episodes, and the inclusion of this material here is usually explained on artistic grounds. (Hugh Kenner, for example, refers to Joyce's "aesthetic of delay.") But, as Gabler has shown, by the time Joyce finished "Ithaca" and "Penelope," the printer had distributed type for the first sixteen episodes, and as a result nothing new could be added to them. The only place left to put the new information was the last two episodes. (pp. 152-57)

Finally, I look forward to the ways in which the new edition of *Ulysses* will relate to current literary theory. For example, it seems possible to consider the critical edition not as text (clear text on the right-hand pages) and apparatus (synoptic text on the left), as the 1962 edition of Melville's *Billy Budd*, with its genetic text printed at the back of the book, seems to do, but rather as a parallel text along the lines of editions of Wordsworth's *Prelude*. The clear text on the right represents a privileged state in a series of developing texts, and set alongside the synoptic text, it can be seen in its relationship to the genetic development rather than as an absolute text in relation to which the genetic text is subsidiary. Gabler has spoken of the two texts in Saussurian terms, calling the clear text synchronic and the genetic text diachronic, and the edition attempts to present both texts as fully as is typographically possible. At a time when critics speak of the blurred borders of texts and of the loss of a text's autonomy, this edition shows a "finished" text merging with its own development.

In speculations like these, as in almost every other aspect of criticism and textual study of *Ulysses*, the chance to base our investigations on Joyce's own text has now arrived. "Are these [printer's errors] to be perpetuated in future editions?" Joyce asked in November 1921, even before the book was published, and he added, "I hope not." Sixty-two years later, his hope has finally been realized. (pp. 157-58)

> *Michael Groden, "Foostering over Those Changes: The New 'Ulysses'," in* James Joyce Quarterly, *Vol. 22, No. 2, Winter, 1985, pp. 137-59.*

THEORETICAL ISSUES

IRA B. NADEL

[*Nadel is an American educator and critic whose works include* Jewish Writers of North America *(1981) and* Biography: Fiction, Fact, and Form *(1984). In the following excerpt, he examines the issues of authorial intent, textual authority, and editorial judgment raised by Gabler's* Ulysses.]

In his 1983 study, *A Critique of Modern Textual Criticism* [see excerpt below], Jerome J. McGann declares that "textual criticism is in the process of reconceiving its discipline." He supports this claim by analyzing copy-text, authorial intention, and textual authority. Additionally, McGann argues that the social dynamic between the individual author and the means of literary production always fashions the printed text. He furthermore emphasizes that an author's intentions toward his manuscript may differ from those toward his published text—as in, for example, Joyce's conscious production of a typescript of *Ulysses* with three carbons for prospective sale to the New York lawyer John Quinn, a departure from his usual compositional practice. A textual critic, McGann exlains, is a kind of archaeologist who recreates the past from clues in which a single object or text can be read as containing the entire history of that work as it emerged into the present.

McGann's study poses challenging questions to anyone concerned with the matter of text and the quality of what we read. Joyceans—as Joyce himself demonstrated in his own list of errata to the second and third impressions of *Ulysses*—are

especially conscious of such matters, and the new *Ulysses*, what I shall call the Garland *Ulysses*, is the *summa* of that preoccupation. My interest, however, relates to how the edition responds to the issues McGann outlines and how it might be understood as altering certain procedures of textual criticism. In short, how new is the new *Ulysses?* (pp. 111-12)

In all of the textual studies on *Ulysses* preceding the Garland edition, certain topics remained constant: the impossibility of recovering an uncorrupted text, an analysis of Joyce's compositional method, the divergences between preexistent manuscripts and published sources, and the overall difficulties in editing Joyce. The work in process took precedence over the work as product, with the analysis of textual development rather than the establishment of an authorized text as the focus. The latter was a difficulty more often commented than acted upon until Hans Walter Gabler and his associates undertook . . . the complex task of editing *Ulysses*.

The physical process of producing the text of the Garland *Ulysses* is outlined . . . in various articles by Michael Groden, Gabler, and others. I am more interested, however, in the assumptions that have led to the creation of the Garland *Ulysses* and its implications for future editions of Joyce's work. Two sentences from Gabler's "Afterword" [see Additional Bibliography] concentrate the issues: "The first edition [of *Ulysses*] comes closest to what Joyce aimed for as the public text of *Ulysses*. Yet it does not present the text of the work as he wrote it." This is a radical statement for several reasons. First, Gabler posits a dichotomy between what we have assumed to be the rationale for a work's composition, its appearance in print, and the nature of its critical authority, its reception; he furthermore implicitly argues that the printed, public version of the work substantially differs not only from its actual text but from the author's intention, presumably the public appearance of his work. Gabler's statement also suggests that a phantom text may exist that supersedes the published form of the work. By extension, this implies that the personal or authorial control of the author over his text has become sabotaged by its publication, that the socialization of the production of texts that McGann described is in many ways opposite to the intentions of the author.

Gabler partially recognizes the theoretical and critical implications of his statement by emphasizing that transmission and composition force distinctions between corrections and authorial matters of revisions and expansion. This leads to a critical paragraph summarizing the editorial principles and textual practice of the edition:

> This edition's whole rationale is based on the assumption that the legal act of first publication did not validate the actual text thereby made public to the extent of lending authority to its high incidence of corruption. Instead, the act of publication is conceived of as an ideal act, to which the edition correlates an ideal text freed of the errors with which *Ulysses* was first published. Thus, it is taken to be the main business of the critical edition to uncover and to undo the first edition's textual corruption. Thereby, the edition endeavors to recover the ideal state of development as it was achieved through the traceable processes of composition and revision at the time of the book's publication on 2 February 1922.

The paragraph should give us pause, for in it Gabler comes closest to expressing the theory of his edition and its method, which essentially focuses on prepublication transmission and documents of composition. Again, a dichotomy exists: in documents of composition Gabler holds that the text possesses full authority; in documents of transmission, the text is held to be "potentially faulty" unless proved to possess authority.

Gabler's statement, embedded in the final pages of the three-volume edition, is important theoretically as well as descriptively, for in it he establishes an intersection between textual criticism and literary theory. At the nexus of his dialectic between the printed form and the actual text is the question posed by Roland Barthes, Julia Kristeva, and Stanley Fish: What is a text? Gabler's positing of a text other than the printed version of *Ulysses* is the effort to reconstruct what Barthes calls "that incontrovertible and indelible trace, supposedly of the meaning which the author has intentionally placed in his work." "It is the written in so far as the written participates in the social contract," Barthes continues, and it "marks language with an inestimable attribute which it does not possess in its essence: security." The text for Barthes becomes "the very theatre of a production where the producer and the reader of the text meet." But the text remains what it means etymologically, a

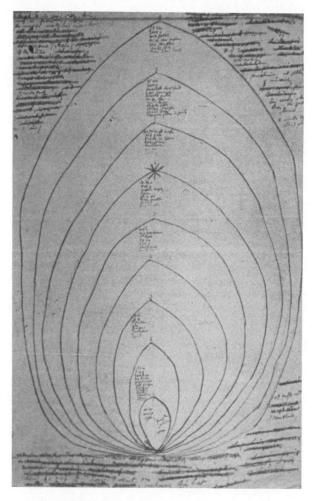

Joyce's notesheet for the "Oxen" section of Ulysses. *The Society of Authors as the literary representatives of the Estate of James Joyce and © 1978 the Trustees of the Estate of James Joyce.*

tissue; the job of the textual critic, which Gabler acknowledges, is then to reconstruct the tissues or interconnections of tissues/texts that comprise *Ulysses*. In Barthes's words, the goal is to secure "the guarantee of the written object," since the text is "a weapon against time" and "authenticates writing."

The effort of Gabler to recover the actual text of *Ulysses* differs little from our own efforts to theorize about texts; his physical quest to reconstitute what he calls the ideal text in its ideal published state freed from error is no different from the goal of critics to obtain an ideal reading of a work. Through the creation of what Gabler will call "the continuous manuscript text," the generation of a manuscript that has never before existed because Joyce never composed a unified, error-free fair copy of the entire novel, he establishes, in Barthes's words, "a methodological field" where a variety of approaches, judgments, decisions, and methods are at work. One might actually argue that the task Gabler sets for himself is literally and theoretically "to expose the grammatological structure of the text," to identify its origin and end, precisely the desire of the deconstructive critic who, in the unmaking of a text, also implies the possibility of its rebuilding. In seeking and recording the vestigial elements of Joyce's text, the ineffable "traces" and erasures Derrida describes, Gabler turns *Ulysses* into a palimpsest pursuing the "ideal act of publication" from "an ideal text . . . freed of errors." By the textual acts of recension and recovery, Gabler hopes to reclaim a work Joyce never totally wrote, in a state of publication the novel never achieved. This parallels the idea of text established by Derrida—"a differential network, a fabric of traces referring endlessly to something other than itself, to other differential traces."

Gabler's procedure is involved. . . . Distinguishing between an "Early-Version Text" and an "Edition Text," Gabler began by inputting a series of holograph, autograph, and compositional documents, including the Rosenbach Ms. (actually fifteen chapters of *Ulysses* in fair copy and three in final working draft), chapter typescripts, and serial publication of the work. The addition of emendations, autograph notations, and revisions to proof soon established a multiple overlay that collectively established the "Early-Version Text," in essence a corrected and emended version of the Rosenbach Ms. This in turn was collated with the "Edition Text," a collation of the 1922 first edition and the 1926 second edition, a corrected eighth printing of the first edition. Computer generated lists of differences between the "Early-Version" and "Edition Text" were then compared. List 1 contained the record of all Joyce did to the "Early-Version Text," and list 2, every discrepancy between that version and the "Edition Text." The two were not identical because of authorial changes the compositors missed and compositors' changes the author never intended. Each discrepancy required judgment and decision, complicated by changes that might have been authorial but, if so, were made on sets of proof no longer extant. Other errors included Joyce's emendations to compositors' changes when he did not remember what he originally intended.

At this juncture in the development of the text, the greatest care is necessary in determining which reading has authority for the text. Knowledge of Joyce's stylistic habits, preferences, and understanding of the compositional process are paramount. Fundamental is the question of authorial intention. Once these decisions had been taken and the corrections made, a continuous manuscript text was created by grafting choices and a coding system on to the "Edition Text," which became the copy-text for the Garland edition. This in turn assumed two forms, the "Synoptic Text," printed on the verso of the new edition and so called because it is a synopsis of the textual development of the novel, and, on the recto page, the "Critical Reading Text," a clean, uncoded, but corrected text eliminating Joyce's deletions.

In its procedure, the edition appears accurate, complete, and, in our custom of computer-generated texts, uncommon. But in methodology, it is innovative if not radical in its approach, beginning with its new idea of copy-text. Gabler demonstrates the compromise position of copy-text enunciated by G. Thomas Tanselle, midway between the hard line of W. W. Greg and Fredson Bowers and the radical view of Philip Gaskell. "[A] copy text," states Tanselle, "is simply the text most likely to provide an authorial reading . . . at points of variation where one cannot otherwise reach a decision." Gabler reconstructs a text that satisfies his goal—the establishment of the novel's corrected text that analyzes the process of its composition. The fragmented state of Joyce's manuscript materials forces Gabler to construct his ideal text which becomes, in a departure from the traditional practice of using either an autograph manuscript or a corrected first edition, his copy-text. The "Continuous Manuscript Text," newly constructed and without precedent, stands as an innovative copy-text based on accumulation rather than single evidence to establish a complete manuscript. This principle is also one of narrative, as though Gabler were reconstructing a story in the process of dismantling a preexistent tale.

But the very establishment of the "Continuous Manuscript Text" causes problems because, although accuracy of text has been achieved based on the formalized collations, the decision-making process of selecting authorized readings remains a discrete activity. Explicit on the procedure, programs, and process for establishing textual variants, Gabler is less clear on why certain readings are chosen over others. Since documents of transmission become those of composition when Joyce begins to revise them, it is difficult to maintain their distinction and integrity despite Gabler's desire to do so. For example, the now well-known restoration of the word "love" in the National Library passage of "Scylla and Charybdis," which appeared in an early fair copy but not in a later typescript or proof. His dislike of proof-reading, poor eyesight, or fallible memory may have caused him not to catch the omission, or he may have decided its absence would not be missed. But Gabler includes it, setting aside the principle of printing the text corrected by the author.

Gabler's "Textual Notes" interestingly confirm the poetics of deconstruction. Questioning the use of a question mark after "it" preceding a comma on p. 1356.23 in "Eumaeus," Gabler writes "R's [Rosenbach's] punctuation would seem an instance of immediate graphic expression of the undecidedness of the episode between spoken and written speech." The theoretical questions of trace, of erasure, and of *différence* in the text appear in an applied manner in the "Textual Notes," and their careful reading would provide a workshop for the application of Derridean grammatology. . . . The critical rather than mechanical establishment of text remains, then, a debatable if not controversial dimension of the Garland *Ulysses;* a variety of passages in the text have readings noted less for their accuracy than for their interpolation. Or, as certain commentators have asked, how much did it really cost Bloom for his cake of "Fry's Plain Chocolate?"

These matters relate to another subject that requires even greater attention if we are to understand the nature of Joyce's texts and their formation. That subject is the phenomenology of error, the first topic Freud addressed in his 1915-17 lectures at the University of Vienna and published in English in 1920 as *A General Introduction to Psychoanalysis.* Errors, Freud argued, have meaning and occur as "mental acts arising from the mutual interferences of two [or more] intentions." What, we may ask, is the nature and significance of Joyce's errors? What do they mean and how do they relate to the analysis of his work? Methodologically, how do we evaluate mistakes Joyce made in manuscript as opposed to errors made by others (and Joyce) in typescript, *placards,* or page proofs—and failed to correct? Why, in fact, did he let some errors stand? Neglect, oversight, forgetfulness? Is it legitimate to propose a philosophy of error for Joyce, accepting the notion of Christopher Ricks, writing of Pater and Arnold, that nothing literary gets into a text by chance? And if misquotation or errors of transcription are always revealing, even if the author was not himself aware of the error, what do these mistakes reveal about Joyce? Or do we have to accept the contention that literary error is so universal that psychological explanation is unnecessary? A possible response appears to be that in making errors we are, in a fashion, taking possession of what passes through our hands, leaving our mark. "What may look like mere sloppiness," the writer Janet Malcolm has noted, "is in (unconscious) fact a studied assertion of personality."

A study of the phenomenology of error in Joyce, based on his own corrections and comments during and after the composition and publication of *Ulysses,* would be revealing. Gabler, providing us with the materials for such a study by including the traces and evolution of errors in Joyce's text, now makes it possible. The culmination of such a study would be, of course, *Finnegans Wake,* because in that work, with its morphological and lexical distortions, "error" is elevated to the status of the correct text. The intentional misspelling of words and their irregular syntax become their proper form in the text. Language renews itself through dislocation, and "error" becomes correction, a new method to establish meaning. As Joyce warns us, "You are deepknee in error, sir, Madame . . . let me then tell you" since "with each word that would not pass away the squidself which he had squirtscreened from the crystalline world waned chagreenold and doriangrayer in its dudhud" (*Wake*). "Erringnesses" are everywhere in the text and a gauge, I would suggest, to its understanding. Freud states that errors are "*compromise*-formations; they express part-success and part-failure for each of the two intentions" that formulate an error (*Gen. Introd.*). *Finnegans Wake,* with its neologisms and private but decipherable language of deviation, embodies this concept. It seems likely, then, that Joyce's errors may be the very "portals of discovery" Stephen refers to in his discussion of mistakes in Shakespeare.

Details on the evolution of *Ulysses* are now available in an unprecedented manner to students of the novel. With the Joyce Archive, Rosenbach facsimile, and now Garland *Ulysses,* readers may witness the process of Joyce's composition. But despite the gathering of an extraordinary amount of data in the new *Ulysses,* despite the scrupulous collation and computer reliability, many of the final editorial readings depend on judgment and not external evidence. Textual decisions are not as indisputable as they may at first appear. These decisions will require continued analysis by scholars, parallel to the reformulation of textual criticism as McGann has outlined, before acceptance of the synoptic and critical text as definitive takes place. The path of the text, traced in detail by Gabler, will now begin a new, Odyssean journey, returning to sources formerly unavailable as readers reassess and judge the quality of the textual changes for themselves.

Bloom, contemplating his "inverted volumes improperly arranged" near the end of the "Ithaca" episode, reflects on "the insecurity of hiding any secret document behind, beneath or between the pages of a book." The Garland *Ulysses* confirms his suspicion, for where a document does not exist, it manages to invent one, and where a text has been lost, it has now been found. (pp. 113-20)

> *Ira B. Nadel, "Textual Criticism, Literary Theory,*
> *and the New 'Ulysses'," in* Contemporary Literature,
> *Vol. 28, No. 1, Spring, 1987, pp. 111-20.*

JEROME J. McGANN

[*An American critic, McGann is the editor of the six-volume* Complete Poetical Works of Byron *and the author of critical studies of Lord Byron and Algernon Swinburne, among other works. In the following excerpt from his* Critique of Modern Textual Criticism (1983), *McGann presents the historical development of textual criticism and the central issues of debate in contemporary textual criticism theory.*]

All current textual critics, whether they work on Homer, Langland, Shakespeare, or a Romantic poet like Byron, agree that to produce a critical edition entails an assessment of the history of the text's transmission with the purpose of exposing and eliminating errors. Ultimately, the object in view is the same in each case: to establish a text which, in the now universally accepted formulation, most nearly represents the author's original (or final) intentions.

This critical commonplace has emerged gradually during the past two hundred years or so. It is a principle which assumes, quite correctly, that all acts of information transmission produce various sorts of corruption from the original material. Classical scholarship, which eventually produced the determinate breakthrough known as the Lachmann Method, established the basic rationale for the general procedures. Lacking the author's original documents, possessing only a more or less extensive set of later manuscripts, the classical editor developed procedures for tracing the internal history of these late manuscripts. The aim was to work out textual errors by revealing the history of their emergence. Ultimately, the method sought to "clear the text" of its corruptions and, thereby, to produce (or approximate)—by subtraction, as it were—the lost original document, the "authoritative text."

These methods were soon applied to national scriptures of various kinds. In England, the New Bibliography centered its work in Shakespeare, where the problems which the Lachmann Method was fashioned to deal with were in certain important respects quite similar. Samuel Johnson's famous lament over the state of the Shakespearean texts contains a neat formulation of the problem.

> The business of him that republished an ancient book is, to correct what is corrupt, and to explain what is obscure. To have a text corrupt in many places, and in many doubtful, is, among the authours that have written since the use of types, almost peculiar to Shakespeare. Most writers, by publishing their own works, prevent all various readings, and preclude all conjectural criticism. Books indeed are sometimes published after the death of him who produced

them, but they are better secured from corruptions than these unfortunate compositions. They subsist in a single copy, written or revised by the authour; and the faults of the printed volume can be only faults of one descent.

> But of the works of Shakespeare the condition has been far different: he sold them, not to be printed, but to be played. They were immediately copied for the actors, and multiplied by transcript after transcript, vitiated by the blunders of the penman, or changed by the affectation of the player; perhaps enlarged to introduce a jest, or mutilated to shorten the representation; and printed at last without the concurrence of the authour, without the consent of the proprietor, from compilations made by chance or by stealth out of the separate parts written for the theatre: and thus thrust into the world surreptitiously and hastily, they suffered another depravation from the ignorance and negligence of the printers, as every man who knows the state of the press in that age will readily conceive.

> It is not easy for invention to bring together so many causes concurring to vitiate a text. No other authour ever gave up his works to fortune and time with so little care: no books could be left in hands so likely to injure them, as plays frequently acted, yet continued in manuscript: no other transcribers were likely to be so little qualified for their task as those who copied for the stage, at a time when the lower ranks of the people were universally illiterate: no other editions were made from fragments so minutely broken, and so fortuitously reunited; and in no other age was the art of printing in such unskilful hands.

The state of the Shakespearean texts corresponded to the state of the classical and biblical texts in this respect: in each case the authorized documents were missing, so that critical editors were faced with the problem of sorting through the mediated texts which developed subsequently, in the scribal process which preserved, disseminated, and reproduced the lost original works. Of course, the Shakespearean problem differed from the classical problem in two important ways. First, the process of reproducing Shakespeare's lost original documents was typographical rather than scribal. Second, unlike the classical texts, the lost Shakespearean documents were not radically separated in time from their subsequent process of preservation and reproduction. Stemmatics is a complex problem in classical scholarship, whereas in Shakespearean studies it is normally a relatively straightforward matter: the textual history in the latter case is, as we now say, monogenous, whereas in the former it is polygenous.

These differentials necessitated some adjustments of the Lachmann Method by Shakespearean scholars. Pollard, McKerrow, and Greg were prominent initiators of these reformulations, and their activities in the field established the direction of the twentieth century's textual criticism of Shakespeare. More than that, however, they exerted a powerful influence upon the textual criticism of all periods of our national scriptures. The influence has been most noticeable in the textual criticism of Restoration and eighteenth-century literature, and, more recently, of various nineteenth-century authors, both English and American. Indeed, these nineteenth-century instances have emerged as the focal point of most current problems with the theory of textual criticism.

In his celebrated essay "Some Principles for Scholarly Editions of Nineteenth-Century American Authors" Fredson Bowers took the case of Hawthorne to lay down some rules for editing novels like *The Blithedale Romance*. This work is typical of the vast majority of works written and published in the modern periods; that is to say, it is a work for which we have the author's original manuscript. Thus, the classical problem which originally established the terms of modern textual criticism— the absence of the authoritative text—no longer pertains. Indeed, that fundamental and complex problem in classical studies—to find and remove textual contaminations—normally subsides in these cases to a secondary, if sometimes complex, operational task. Stemmatics and its related problems of emendation loom over the editors of classical as well as most medieval texts because the processes of textual transmission have been severely ruptured by time and circumstance.

Texts produced and reproduced in the earlier sixteenth and seventeenth centuries—pre-eminently Shakespeare's texts—raise special issues and problems, some of which I shall glance at in the following pages. My chief interest, however, lies with the texts produced and reproduced in the later modern (that is, the post-seventeenth-century) periods, for these texts have served to focus discussion of the theory of final intentions. Specifically, the theoretical interests of textual critics working largely in the modern periods have shifted from the field of stemmatics to the problems of copy-text.

This shift witnesses the profound influence which the earlier work of Fredson Bowers had upon the field of textual criticism. Bowers advanced a theory of final intentions in order to solve certain editorial problems which are typical of works typographically produced in the later modern periods. This theory was based upon a reading and interpretation of W. W. Greg's important essay "The Rationale of Copy-Text," where the main interest lies with Shakespeare and works produced in the early modern periods.

Bowers's altered focus upon the later modern periods, and particularly upon American books, has meant that he typically deals with works for which we have one or more of the author's pre-publication texts. These subjects lead him to the following argument, which I now quote in full.

> When an author's manuscript is preserved, this has paramount authority, of course. Yet the fallacy is still maintained that since the first edition was proofread by the author, it must represent his final intentions and hence should be chosen as copy-text. Practical experience shows the contrary. When one collates the manuscript of *The House of Seven Gables* against the first printed edition, one finds an average of ten to fifteen differences per page between the manuscript and the print, many of them consistent alterations from the manuscript system of punctuation, capitalization, spelling, and word-division. It would be ridiculous to argue that Hawthorne made approximately three to four thousand small changes in proof, and then wrote the manuscript of *The Blithedale Romance* according to the same system as the

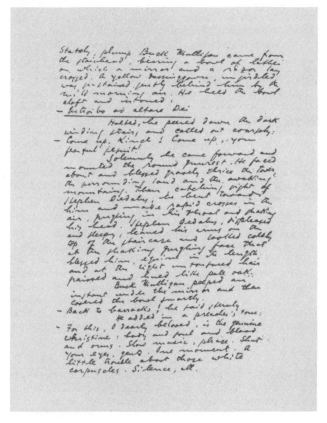

First page of the John Quinn manuscript of Ulysses. *The Society of Authors as the literary representatives of the Estate of James Joyce and © 1978 the Trustees of the Estate of James Joyce.*

manuscript of the *Seven Gables*, a system that he had rejected in proof.

A close study of the several thousand variants in *Seven Gables* demonstrates that almost every one can be attributed to the printer. That Hawthorne passed them in proof is indisputable, but that they differ from what he wrote in the manuscript and manifestly preferred is also indisputable. Thus the editor must choose the manuscript as his major authority, correcting from the first edition only what are positive errors in the accidentals of the manuscript.

Here, though the textual problems are far removed from those faced by Lachmann, the influence of the classical approach is clear. Printing-house punctuation—the editorial intervention by a publisher or his agents between the author's manuscript and the published text—is regarded as a corruption of the authoritative text. It makes no difference, in Bowers's view, that the author oversaw and accepted this editorial intervention. As Bowers says a bit later in the essay.

> One is foolish to prefer a printing-house style. This distinction is not theory, but fact. Hawthorne's punctuation, for example, is much more meaningful in respect to emphasis and to delicate matters of parenthesis and subordination than is the printing-house style in which *Seven Gables* and *The Blithedale Romance* appeared.

In each book, the real flavor of Hawthorne, cumulatively developing in several thousand small distinctions, can be found only in the manuscript.

This "theory of a critical edition is now widely accepted, and it indeed represents a reasonable approach to the choice of copy-text, especially when one reflects upon the historical development of the discipline. Bowers dismisses the chief alternative approach, "that since the first edition was proofread by the author, it must represent his final intentions and hence should be chosen as copy-text." This idea is a "fallacy . . . still maintained" in the teeth of what to Bowers seems manifest: that editorial intervention at the point of initial publication represents a process of deviation from the authoritative original, in fact, a process of corruption.

Bowers's views, then, continue to show the influence of the textual criticism developed in the field of classical studies. Hawthorne's early publisher, his editors, his printers are, for Bowers, entirely comparable to those older scribes who sought to preserve and transmit the classical texts, but who introduced, in the process, various contaminations. The business of the classical critic is to find and remove those corruptions, and the business of the critic of Hawthorne's texts is seen in the same way: to find and remove the corruptions and, by critical subtraction, to restore the sincerity of the authoritative text.

This approach continues to dominate the current theory of textual criticism, though it has of course been challenged from various quarters, particularly by critics who work in the modern periods. The distinguished textual critic G. Thomas Tanselle recently surveyed, and rebutted, the chief lines of attack in an important essay. But the opposition has not been silenced, and Tanselle himself indicated certain key fault lines in the Bowers view.

A vigorous line of dissent from Bowers has been carried by James Thorpe and Philip Gaskell, though Donald Pizer and others have raised some important objections of their own. Tanselle's rebuttal of these dissenting lines is impressive partly because of Tanselle's personal tact, and partly because he is defending a position whose strength lies in its logical coherence and self-consistency. Again and again Tanselle parries the opponents of Bowers by pointing to the irrelevance of the objections for the dominant theory, or to the theoretical and methodological contradictions which appear in the arguments and positions of the dissenting critics. Such contradictions proliferate, it is clear, at least partly because the dissenting positions are not founded upon a carefully articulated theoretical structure. As we shall see later, the contradictions are also the result of the compromised nature of the dissenting views, which have not been able to divorce themselves from certain key aspects of the views they are attacking. This, too, as we shall also see, represents failure of theory.

Up to now I have been discussing this critical dialogue at a rather high level of abstraction, principally in order to expose the general shape of the critical debate, rather than the precise areas of conflict. We will need to keep the larger view in mind, since it is my contention that the dissenting line, though lacking the theoretical rigor of the Bowers position, preserves the latter in a state of crisis by raising over and over again vexing practical problems which the Bowers line cannot easily deal with. In other words, the dissenting line involves alternative theoretical grounds which it has not yet articulated self-consciously in the way that Bowers has done. (pp. 15-22)

Present-day textual criticism . . . is the descendant of the earlier historical critics of biblical and classical texts, among whom Lachmann is by common consent the most notable. Out of this early work in classical philology emerged two of the three principal areas of current interest: the theory of the critical edition, and the theory of the copy-text. The second of these has been a special preoccupation of those inheritors of the Lachmann Method, the New Bibliographers. When the latter began to concern themselves with textual problems of the more modern periods, they opened up the third area in which debate is now frequently joined: the problem (or the theory) of final authorial intentions. We will consider each of these matters in turn. (p. 23)

The attempt by classical philologists to recover, or approximate by historical reconstruction, the lost original works of ancient authors produced a "theory of the critical edition." The chief device for constructing such an edition was then, and still is, the systematic collation of all the relevant texts of the work in question. Out of the collation emerges an analytic picture of the work's historical passage, and, as a natural consequence, the critical opportunity of removing the errors consequent upon such a passage.

The production of this collation entails as well the development of a textual stemma, that is, a summary analysis of the historical relations of the various specific texts of the work in question. The stemma is an especially important tool for an editor when he is choosing his copy-text, which is in a "general sense" an "early text of a work which an editor [selects] as the basis of his own." The copy-text, in fact, permits the critic to sort out and arrange the collations. In a properly critical edition, the editor will produce a critical text which is based upon the copy-text but into which has been introduced a series of emendations and corrections. These changes are designed to bring the critical text into as close an approximation as possible with the author's no longer extant work. A textual apparatus accompanies the critical text, and this contains as complete a record as is possible of the textual variants which have emerged from the collation of the documents. It is this apparatus which displays the "history" of the text.

The above general theory of the critical edition is now accepted, with minor variations and modifications, by all textual critics and critical editors. But the special problems of editing Shakespeare and other English authors of the early-modern periods led Greg to develop a "rationale of copy-text," which is explicitly designed to deal mainly with problems raised by certain national scriptures produced in the early modern typographical periods. As Greg put the matter:

> If I am right in the view that I am about to put forward, the classical theory of the "best" or "most authoritative" manuscript, whether it be held in a reasonable or in an obviously fallacious form, has really nothing to do with the English theory of "copy-text" at all.

The New Bibliography was interested in considering more closely how a critic was to choose, among the possible options, one specific text which would serve him as his base text or copy-text. On what grounds should one make such a choice, what was a coherent theory of copy-text? Greg's interest in this question led him to produce his famous essay ["The Rationale of Copy-Text"; see Additional Bibliography].

According to Greg, in the context of a monogenous textual stemma—that is, in the situation which one frequently encounters in a bibliographical context, but only rarely in a scribal one—textual critics can and should approach the problem of copy-text in a systematic way. Greg followed "the modern editorial practice [of choosing] whatever extant text may be supposed to represent most nearly what the author wrote and to follow it with the least possible alteration." But Greg went on to make his famous distinction between accidentals and substantives in order to set up a rationale for the use of the copy-text:

> Since, then, it is only on grounds of expediency, and in consequence either of philological ignorance or of linguistic circumstances, that we select a particular original as our copy-text, I suggest that it is only in the matter of accidentals that we are bound (within reason) to follow it, and that in respect of substantive readings we have exactly the same liberty (and obligation) of choice as has a classical editor, or as we should have were it a modernized text that we were preparing.

Greg arrives at this formulation because he wants to define a standard of authority between early texts and later revised texts (including those which carry genuine authorial revisions). That standard lies in the so-called accidentals, which will be, in the earliest monogenous textual forms, necessarily closest to "the author's original in so far as the general form of the text is concerned." Because this is the case, the critic's copy-text must be that text in the monogenous series which is historically closest to the author's lost original, for to displace it in favor of a reprint, whether authoritatively revised or not, means receding at least one step further from the general form of the author's original.

> The true theory is, I contend, that the copytext should govern (generally) in the matter of accidentals, but that the choice between substantive readings belongs to the general theory of textual criticism and lies altogether beyond the narrow principle of the copy-text. Thus it may happen that in a critical edition the text rightly chosen as copy may not by any means be the one that supplies most substantive readings in cases of variation. The failure to make this distinction and to apply this principle has naturally led to too close and too general a reliance upon the text chosen as basis for an edition, and there has arisen what may be called the tyranny of the copy-text, a tyranny that has, in my opinion, vitiated much of the best editorial work of the past generation.

This famous passage represents what Greg earlier called the English theory of copy-text," which Greg correctly recognized as the consequence of the developing work of the New Bibliographers. McKerrow supplied Greg with his initial formulation of the theory, but Greg's view was that McKerrow "relapsed into heresy" out of a fear of "conceding too much to eclecticism." The true "English theory" of copy-text means to draw a distinction between a text's substantives and its accidentals, and to argue that whereas the critic should choose "the earliest 'good' print as copy-text" and should follow that in its accidentals, he should be prepared to deviate from the copy-text in the matter of substantive readings.

Greg's argument, we must observe, leaves aside altogether the question of "the choice between substantive readings," nor

does it address directly the question of textual "versions," as they are now called. When "there is more than one substantive text of comparable authority," or as we should say when there is more than one version, Greg owns that the choice between them will be an arbitrary and expedient matter. Greg's purpose here is to free the editor from the tyranny of a copy-text, "to uphold his liberty of judgement" and discretion when decisions have to be made: "In the case of rival substantive editions the choice between substantive variants is . . . generally independent of copy-text."

At this point we should recall that Greg's rationale makes no appeal to any concept of author's intentions (whether original or final). When editing a work, as Tanselle has observed, "It is not necessary to have a copy-text at all in the strict sense of the term which Greg develops." The term can be used in a general sense to refer to the editor's chosen base text or version, of course, but in Greg's determination copy-text is a device for helping an editor choose between "indifferent readings." Tanselle elucidates the theory of copy-text economically.

> Generally speaking, an editor has less to go on when judging variants in punctuation and spelling than when judging variants in wording, and for that reason the text chosen as copy-text often supplies most of the punctuation and spelling for the critical text. But the editor is free, of course, to make rational decisions regarding spelling and punctuation when the evidence permits; conversely, variants in wording can sometimes seem indifferent, and the impasse is resolved by adopting the copy-text reading. . . . [A] copy-text is simply the text most likely to provide an authorial reading . . . at points of variation where one cannot otherwise reach a decision.

This seems to me an accurate translation of Greg's position. As we shall see, however—and as the passages I quoted from Bowers show—whereas Greg never sought to interpret his rationale in terms of authorial intentions, this is precisely what Bowers would later propose. As a consequence, the theory of authorial intentions was formulated not merely as an explanation of the rationale of copy-text, but as a rule which would be asked to govern both the choice of the copy-text and the choice of the textual version as well.

Greg's theory of copy-text was developed to deal primarily with certain problems in Elizabethan bibliography, though it obviously has a general bearing on scribal texts as well. The theory grew from Greg's awareness that when texts were produced in typographical forms in the early modern periods, their orthography—what Greg called "the general form of the text"—was subject to frequent and odd changes (so-called modernizations) as the work passed through the hands of the printers and publishers. In an unpublished essay which takes up this matter, Peter Blayney explains the situation lucidly:

> If the fourth paragraph of "The Rationale" is read with uniform attention it becomes quite clear that there is one overriding reason why the author's (usually lost) manuscript is held up as the final authority for accidentals. Quite simply, before the eighteenth century no other possible "standard" for accidentals exists. Before 1650, while "house style" varied from printing house to printing house and from com-

positor to compositor, rapidly changing "fashions" in orthography can be seen affecting the whole of the London printing trade. . . . Greg never put it in so many words, but was well aware that *all* the compositors of the First Folio (and their contemporaries) scattered punctuation and capitals around in a profusion seldom matched even in the 18th century. In this respect they all differed from *all* the compositors who set Shakespeare's Quartos. . . . The point is that one can legitimately define a hefty percentage of the seemingly arbitrary changes that distinguish (say) a 1605 reprint from its 1595 copy as *modernizations*. And it was modernization that Greg was trying to minimize.

Greg himself refers to these matters only by implication, or obliquely—as in the following passage: "The thesis I am arguing is that the historical circumstances of the English language make it necessary to adopt in formal matters the guidance of some particular early text." The "historical circumstances of the English language" and its processes of transmission led Greg to formulate his rationale for the editing of early modern texts. Subsequent editors and theorists have gone on to apply Greg's rationale to works of later periods when, in Blayney's words, "there *was* such a thing as 'standard' orthography."

Under these new textual circumstances, new problems have emerged, the most pressing of which has come to seem the problem of the author's final intentions. Greg's theory can be made to deal reasonably well with such problems in circumstances where the author's original text is not preserved. But in more recent periods, and especially in those which saw the emergence of modern textual criticism itself, authorial texts abound: draft copies, corrected drafts, fair copies (holograph, or amanuensis copies with or without autograph corrections for the press), proofs (uncorrected or corrected, sometimes by the author, sometimes by his editors). In these circumstances, a theory of final intentions has emerged out of the Lachmann-Greg tradition which has received its most eloquent formulation in the work of Fredson Bowers, whose normative statements on the matter I have already quoted.

I must point out, in passing, that in so far as Greg concerned himself with the problem of author's intentions at all, his position was typically discretionary: "authority is never absolute, but only relative," he observed when he was beginning to attack "the tyranny of the copy-text." Of course, Greg can speak of "the author's original text," and he has in fact endorsed the following editorial principle: "It is . . . the modern editorial practise to choose whatever extant text may be supposed to represent most nearly what the author wrote and to follow it with the least possible alteration. Nevertheless, when he laid aside the problem of textual versions in his theory of copy-text, he was implicitly laying aside the problem of authorial intentions as well. The locus of his concern was a period when such problems did not rise up with the urgency or in the forms which Bowers and others have encountered.

Bowers's appeals to Greg and the previous traditions of textual criticism represent an effort to support Bowers's theory of authorial intentions by an appeal to Greg's rationale for editing early modern texts. But special problems appear when textual critics seek to apply Greg's rationale to texts, especially modern ones, which come down to us in forms that trace back to preserved original manuscripts and other pre-publication documents. Bowers's position—that an editor must choose, other

things being equal, the earliest in the surviving series of completed texts—is based upon the idea that the original in such a series will be closest to the author's final intentions, will be least contaminated by nonauthorial interventions—in particular, by nonauthoritative forms in the so-called accidentals.

Critics have repeatedly attacked this position on the matter of the accidentals, and have argued, in various ways, that the formal features of the authorial manuscripts—even printer's copy manuscripts—do not necessarily lie closest to the author's final intentions. In many cases—Gaskell and Thorpe give a number of typical ones—the first printed edition seems to exert at least as strong a claim to author's final intentions as the author's manuscript; and various particular cases have been raised to show that other textual constitutions—corrected proofs, later revised editions, and so forth—might reasonably claim to represent, in formal as well as in substantive matters, the author's final intentions.

Tanselle has vigorously rebutted these positions—more on that matter in a moment—but what he and most of the parties to the debate have thus far failed to emphasize is that the problems being raised are historically peculiar to circumstances where critics and editors have inherited an unprecedented amount of early textual material and related documentation. Under such conditions the critic is often able to follow the process of literary production through all its principal stages, and from the vantage of all the principal persons engaged in the process. Byron's poetry abounds in illustrative examples, but his case is merely prototypical. Nevertheless, a critic facing the massive textual documentation for a work like *The Giaour*—multiple manuscripts, multiple corrected and uncorrected proofs, a trial edition, a whole series of early editions at least three of which are known to have been proofed and revised by Byron—finds it difficult to accept the idea that one of these texts, and presumably an early manuscript, represents the author's final intentions. The case typifies what Hans Zeller has recently suggested: that texts frequently exist in several versions no one of which can be said to constitute itself the "final" one.

Zeller has in mind famous cases like *The Prelude*, the special problems of which are sometimes handled in special critical formats, such as the facing-page edition. But the example of *The Giaour*—or *Childe Harold*, or *Don Juan*, or any number of Byron's other works—raises the problem of multiple versions beyond the capacity of a facing-page compromise. If, as Tanselle says, "the aim of the editor is to establish the text as the author wished to have it presented to the public, the case of Byron's works can stand as an exemplary one for a host of others: that is, many works exist of which it can be said that their authors demonstrated a number of different wishes and intentions about what text they wanted to be presented to the public, and that these differences reflect accommodations to changed circumstances, and sometimes to changed publics.

Donald Pizer recently brought a similar objection to the Bowers theory of final intentions. Tanselle's answer to Pizer needs to be quoted here because it helps to illuminate the special character of the crisis facing the current theory of final intentions. Pizer argues that a modern critical editor may want to choose as copy-text a first edition rather than some prepublication text in those cases where author, publisher, and house editor worked closely in the production of the work. Tanselle counters Pizer in this way.

> What appears in a prepublication form of a text
> is normally a better representation of the au-

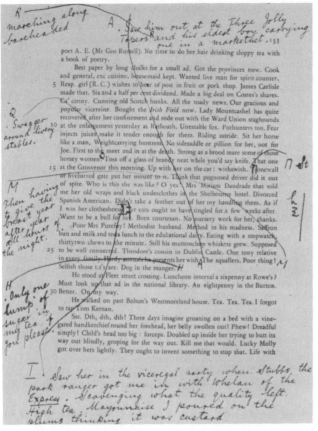

Joyce's corrections of the second page proofs for the first edition of Ulysses. *The Society of Authors as the literary representatives of the Estate of James Joyce and © 1978 the Trustees of the Estate of James Joyce.*

thor's habits than what appears in a first printing, and the text of a fair-copy manuscript or typescript reflects the author's intention, whether or not it turns out to be his final intention in every respect. It is true, as Pizer says, that choosing "an early copy-text encourages a frame of mind which requires later variants to 'prove themselves' as authorial rather than as editorial or printer's variants"; but such would seem to be the safest course in most instances, since the author's responsibility for a later reading—especially in accidentals—is normally less certain than his responsibility for an early one. Of course, such editorial caution may occasionally produce a text reflecting "an author's discarded rather than final intentions," but at least it reflects his, rather than someone else's, intentions. The editor's critical judgment—his literary taste exercised in the light of his intimate knowledge of the author and all known relevant external evidence—must finally determine the case; and there is nothing in Greg's theory to prevent him, on this basis, from deciding that the later variants have indeed "proved themselves." If, however, he starts from the assumption that the author and the publisher's editor are creative collaborators, he will, to be sure, produce an unmodernized text—in the

sense that it reflects the author's period—but it may be far from the text which the author wished (finally, or at any other time).

First, a practical point. It is true that an editor making Pizer's choice may produce a text which is "far from the text which the author wished" to have presented to the public. True—but, by the same token, an editor making Tanselle's or Bowers's choice is equally liable to the danger of producing a text which the author would never have wanted the public to see. The latter is an especially clear and present danger when one chooses to edit some prepublication version of a work, for obvious reasons. In each case a danger exists which must be met by the acuteness and skill of the individual editor, for—in *any* case—the best of imaginable strategies will collapse if the tactics are blundered. Certainly the Bowers *theory* of final intentions will be no protection under the circumstances detailed by Pizer. Such circumstances, needless to say, are common in the more modern periods—indeed, they are the rule.

The second point to be made goes to the issue of "intentions" generally. Following Bowers, Tanselle argues that if their "editorial caution" is open to the danger of choosing less-than-final intentions, "at least" it will capture the author's rather than someone else's intentions. One must note, simply in passing, that the authorial intentions marked in prepublication manuscripts will often represent in only the most tentative way what an author wished to have presented to the public, certainly in the matter of accidentals, and often of substantives as well. But this ambiguity in the concept of author's intention conceals an even more crucial problem in the Bowers's theory of final intentions. Once again it is a historically specific problem and appears in circumstances where the textual critic has in his possession, at the outset of his work, the early authoritative (prepublication) documents.

Tanselle's belief that the theory of copy-text will ensure an edition that "reflects [the author's], rather than someone else's, intentions" assumes that any editorial intervention at the work's point of origin constitutes a contamination of the authoritative text. But Pizer, like Thorpe, Gaskell, and others, has shown what everyone recognizes to be the historical facts: the production of books, in the later modern periods especially, sometimes involves a close working relationship between the author and various editorial and publishing professionals associated with the institutions which serve to transmit literary works to the public. To regard the work done by such institutions as a contamination of authorized material is to equate the editorial work done by an author's original publishing institutions and the (historically belated) editorial work done by the scribes of ancient texts. The original theory of the critical edition was developed to find and remove the contaminations inadvertently produced by those textual transmitters, and Greg's rationale represented a special variation on that theory, one designed to take account of the peculiar typographical conditions which prevailed before the eighteenth century. But the theory of final intentions, though a corollary derivative from the initial theory of the critical text and its special variant, has been asked to perform the same function under conditions which are structurally far different.

The scholarly consequences of this hegemonic use of the theory of final intentions are far reaching, and they extend ultimately to the way we read and comprehend literary works, and not merely to how we edit their texts. More immediately, the consequence has been to retard the development of the theory of textual criticism. Important critics and theorists continue to maintain the dominance of Bowers's theories even when the empirical evidence demonstrates, from many different quarters, that those theories are not adequate under certain circumstances. It is certainly true, as Tanselle has argued, that these theories are the most powerful and coherent that we currently possess; indeed, their continuing power resides in their coherence and methodological consistency, as Tanselle has also argued. Still, the empirical challenges to the theory raised by various learned voices argue that serious problems underlie the theory of final intentions when it is applied to a certain large class of (typically) modern works. But the fact that these challenges have remained largely empirical in character testifies as well to the absence of any substantial theoretic critique. (pp. 23-35)

> *Jerome J. McGann, in his* A Critique of Modern Textual Criticism, *The University of Chicago Press, 1983, 146 p.*

JEROME J. McGANN

[*In the following excerpt, McGann examines several critical issues in modern textual editing raised by the Gabler edition of* Ulysses.]

[In] setting up the general framework for understanding his new edition [of *Ulysses*] Gabler observes:

> The composition of *Ulysses* was directed toward publication. It advanced from notes and drafts via final draft, fair copy, typescript and extensive revisions on the typescripts and multiple proofs to its culmination in the first edition of February 1922. The first edition comes closest to what Joyce aimed for as the public text of *Ulysses*. Yet it does not present the text of the work as he wrote it.

Gabler's intention is not the usual editor's goal: to give what "Joyce aimed for as the public text of *Ulysses*." Rather, he is after "the text of the work as he wrote it." For this reason, "the innovative feature of this edition," according to Gabler, is "the emended continuous manuscript text . . . displayed synoptically by a system of diacritics to analyse its layers of growth." That is to say, Gabler offers a text of *Ulysses* in which we can follow, in a seriatim reading process, the work of *Ulysses* as Joyce actually produced it in a continuous act of writing and rewriting. (pp. 284-85)

Ultimately, what has guided the production of this edition is a certain theory of copytext, on the one hand, and a particular decision about the "compositional development" of *Ulysses* on the other. Since the latter is a simpler matter, I shall take it up first.

Gabler breaks the compositional development of *Ulysses* into two parts. The first part, which includes all the autograph manuscript documents, traces the history of the text from its earliest drafts to its latest autograph copies. Included here are hypothetically reconstructed "lost" documents, and particularly the so-called "final working drafts" for episodes 4-9, 11, and 13-14. For Gabler, the lost final working drafts sometimes represent, in these instances, a later stage of compositional development of the text than the Rosenbach Manuscript, which contains Joyce's fair copies. He arrives at this conclusion by a critical analysis of the relations between the Rosenbach manuscripts and various subsequent (non-autograph) documents.

The latter, taken together, constitute what Gabler sees as the second part of the compositional development. Included at this stage are the typescripts (some lost, and none typed by Joyce), the various proof texts, and finally—the "ultimate stage of compositional development"—the first edition. Other materials are obviously important in establishing the text—the *Little Review* and *Egoist* printings, the errata lists and corrections made subsequent to the book's publication, and so forth. For Gabler, however, these materials fall outside the main line of the work's compositional development and hence only exercise a secondary influence upon the process of critical editing. Of course, numerous readings are incorporated into Gabler's established text from these sources, but this fact does not affect their status in the work's "compositional development."

One further distinction is important for Gabler: that between documents of composition and documents of transmission. In the former, "the text is held to possess full authority, unless it can be shown to be faulty"; in the latter, "the text is held to be potentially faulty, unless it can be proved to possess authority." In making this distinction Gabler argues that Joyce himself must be seen as the producer of both kinds of documents—that not every piece of autograph manuscript should be regarded as part of the line of "compositional development." Joyce is sometimes merely his own scribe, a textual transmitter and not a textual maker.

Gabler seeks, then, to "define a continuous manuscript text for *Ulysses*," to assemble that text in a synoptic act of critical editing, and finally to declare the assembled text to be his "copytext." That is to say, a continuous manuscript text is assembled toward which all editorial decisions gravitate as to their text of presumptive and highest authority. This text represents the ultimate state of the work's composition (not of its transmission). Because Gabler wants to assemble a text of the work's compositional development, therefore, and because he regards the act of composition as an entirely isolated and personal affair, he always sets a privilege on autograph manuscript texts. The typescripts, the proofs, and the first edition involve the intervention of other, purely *transmissive* authorities, and hence they fall outside the process of compositional development. Exceptions are made for certain passages of "compositional overlay" in the typescripts and proofs.

This entire procedure operates with a theory or concept of "copytext" which needs to be clearly understood, since it departs, in certain crucial ways, from the usual understanding of the term. In the post-Greg context, the term signifies what an editor chooses to take as the text of highest presumptive authority in the preparation of an eclectic, or critical, edition. That is to say, after examining the surviving documents in which the text is transmitted forward, the editor chooses one of these—sometimes, a combination of these—as his copytext. The copytext serves as the basis of the critical edition that is to be produced. The theory is that the readings of the copytext will be taken over into the critical edition unless other readings—either readings taken from other documents or original readings produced by the editor through a process of critical inference—are positively shown to carry a higher authority. In this theory of copytext, the latter is practically equivalent to some document or set of documents.

In Gabler's *Ulysses,* what is called the copytext is not a document or set of documents at all; rather, Gabler's copytext is "the ideal state of [the text's] development as it was achieved through the traceable processes of composition and revision at the time of the book's publication." Gabler's copytext is what he calls "the continuous manuscript text." Before this edition its existence was ideal, or perhaps hypothetical. Indeed, it is possible—even probable—that this manuscript text never existed at all in the form that Gabler's edition has hypothesized. The copytext comes into existence with the publication of this edition. It is the basis for the genetic text produced on the verso pages of Gabler's edition as "the continuous manuscript text."

The latter then serves as the basis for the "reading" text on the rectos; as such, it might be called the "copytext" for the reading edition of *Ulysses* produced by Gabler. Gabler does not call it that, and indeed the term is not strictly applicable. Nevertheless, scholars should be aware of these various textual relationships if they are to understand what Gabler has done in his edition. (pp. 286-88)

An edition like Gabler's is inconceivable for any author before the modern period. For pre-19th century authors, the documents that might be assembled for a genetic text of the sort prepared by Gabler simply do not exist. (p. 288)

The theory of copytext was initially deployed in order to deal with editing situations where certain key documents are lacking. As editors began to encounter situations—they are typical of the modern period—where the basic lines of textual transmission are clear and relatively unambiguous, the theory of copytext as rationalized by Greg underwent a slight but important modification. Whereas critical editors of earlier works tried to reconstitute some (now lost) state of the text—ideally, the earliest possible or "original" text—critical editors of modern works are already in possession of the kind of "original" text which those other editors were precisely trying to recover. For modern works, therefore, editorial attention turned to a minute examination of pre-publication documents in an effort to recover what has since been termed "the author's final intentions." Greg's theory of copytext, on the other hand, has nothing to do with authorial intentions as such. For editors of works like *Ulysses,* so much authorial material has been preserved that an editor can imagine the production of a "genetic" text which mirrors the actual process of authorial composition. The "genetic" text for an editor of Lucretius, on the other hand, represents a post-authorial process of transmission rather than a pre-publication process of composition.

Gabler's "continuous manuscript text" is a hypothesized reconstruction of a text which displays Joyce working out what Gabler seems to regard as his final authorial intentions. For Gabler, "the final state of the text's development is considered reached when it is last fully and correctly written out in the author's hand." Since all the pertinent authorial manuscripts are not forthcoming, the editor has to reconstruct critically the missing manuscripts and their readings. Once the synoptic "continuous manuscript text" is assembled and has been critically edited, the reading text can be produced. The latter reconstitutes, in a completed rather than in a genetic form, the text of "the author's final intentions."

In assessing the significance of this achievement we must understand that Gabler did not *have* to proceed in this way. He could have aimed to produce a critically edited corrected edition of the original publication of 1922. In this respect, Hugh Kenner's interesting and otherwise admirable review of the edition [see excerpt above] has misunderstood the situation:

> Given the complex history of transmission, it is pointless to think of starting from an extant text and "correcting" it. Efforts in that direction have been made, with the result that all

available texts contain approximately the same number of errors, the cost of each correction being some novel botch. The technique of the new edition was instead to build up the complex text as it was built up originally, and so arrive at a final version that would have been arrived at in 1922 if no one had made any mistakes. . . .

In the first place, Gabler's edition is not the "final version that would have been arrived at in 1922 if no one had made any mistakes." Gabler's edition alters the text of 1922 in more than five thousand instances, but the 1922 text does not contain more than five thousand mistakes, nor anywhere near that number. The number of errors in the first edition is several hundred at the most, and the vast majority of these are relatively minor.

In the second place, the goal of producing a corrected version of the original publication is quite within the possibility of a critical edition. Far from hindering such a task, the "complex history of transmission" makes it easier, for that history is written in the massive surviving documentation. The fact that the intervening editions between 1922 and Gabler have compounded corrections of the text with new corruptions merely testifies to the unsystematic (and careless) mode of correction. A scrupulous critical editor could—and probably should—produce a fully corrected edition of 1922. It would differ in notable ways from Gabler's edition.

Gabler understands this situation very clearly. "The first edition," he says, "comes closest to what Joyce aimed for as the public text of *Ulysses.*" Were an editor to produce a fully and systematically corrected edition of 1922, then, the result would clearly be the work which Joyce "aimed for as the public text of *Ulysses.*" That text would differ from Gabler's text in many more than four thousand readings, though most of these would be minor. Nevertheless, such an edition would represent a "correct" text of *Ulysses.* Would such a text mean that Gabler's text is "incorrect"?

The answer is no, for the simple and obvious reason that we are dealing with two different conceptions of "the text of *Ulysses.*" Gabler's is an imagination of Joyce's work and not its reconstitution. Gabler invents, by a process of brilliant editorial reconstruction, *Joyce's Ulysses* (as it were), a work that existed, if it ever existed at all in fact, for Joyce the writer rather than Joyce the author. Gabler's edition does not give us the work which Joyce wanted to present to the public; rather, he gives us a text in which we may observe Joyce at work, alone, before he turns to meet his public. Given his purposes, then, Gabler is entirely correct to declare the synoptic text to be the most important feature of his edition. The "reading text" is of secondary importance.

The most important consequence of Gabler's edition, therefore, in my view, is not that it has removed the accumulated corruptions from the text. What Gabler's edition has done is to reveal, in a precise and concrete way, what can be (and therefore what cannot be) entailed in the idea of textual instability. Gabler has shown that another text of *Ulysses* can be imagined and concretely rendered—a text that does not simply offer a large mass of minor textual variations from the previously conceived text, but that completely overhauls *the way we might think about the text as a whole.* By giving priority of importance to the "synoptic" text over the "reading" text Gabler forces us to think of *Ulysses* as something other than a given object of interpretation on the one hand (which is the traditional and

New Critical view), or as an invention of interpretation on the other (which is the common post-structural view).

A number of different *Ulysses* begin to occupy the space of critical possibility. They are finite in number, and although new ones will become possible as time and circumstances change, all must take their orders from pre-established and determinate textual configurations. Some of these *Ulysses* will represent themselves, at the surface, as more stable than others. Gabler's "reading text" seems stable whereas his "synoptic text" seems processive, but the appearance is merely a function of certain conventions of reading which have or have not been mastered. The diacritics in Gabler's edition are a grammar of an artificial language and should present no serious problems for readers of imaginative works, which are always mediated by artificial grammars of various kinds. When we shall have learned to "read" the synoptic text as we read the reading text, we shall have gone a long way toward understanding the nature of texts in general. Such an experience should remove forever that illusion of fixity and permanence we normally take from literary works because they so often come to us wearing their masks of permanence.

The appearances of stability or instability are only formal relativities, as the relations between Gabler's "synoptic" and "reading" texts so clearly show. In fact, all texts are unstable to the extent that they are all processive and (in Gabler's terms) "continuous." At the same time, all are fixed within certain real, determinable limits and they assume certain specific forms. The fact that the texts have always to be re-viewed in terms of a shifting historical perspective does not alter their status as specific things. We should probably think of them—to borrow a metaphor from Modernism—as "vortices."

Gabler's edition helps one to see the formal limits which always constrain the generation of texts. Besides the class of "reading" texts, there is the class of "genetic" texts; and the latter may be conceived either as mirrors of composition or mirrors of production. After Gabler I begin to imagine an entirely different genetic text of *Ulysses*, one which would represent the history of the work's initial *production* rather than its initial composition—the author's rather than the writer's *Ulysses*. This would be the synoptic text that would lie behind, or serve as the basis for, the "reading text" we would then call "the edition of 1922, critically emended."

At the same time, Gabler's work shows that any other imaginations of the text of *Ulysses* must either be versions of the foregoing, or post-productive acts of translation—like Bowdler's or Lamb's Shakespeares. Instability in a text may take many forms, but they can and must take *determinate* forms. In addition, when we are dealing with texts as genetic constructs, we shall have to understand that only two *forms* of text are conceptually possible: either the text that is composed, or the text that is produced. Any number of instances of those forms is hypothetically possible, but that number will always be a small number *in actual fact*.

Gabler's edition also calls one's attention to a peculiar generic quality of modernist writing: that its subject is often the act and process of writing itself. The fluid, not to say unstable, character of poetic and fictional work since the time of Wordsworth and Byron has often been remarked, but almost always in vague and general terms. Gabler's edition calls attention to the necessity of determining precisely what forms of instability we are dealing with. Wordsworth's *The Prelude* is an oft-cited example of an undecidable text because Wordsworth generated,

if only provisionally, several distinct versions, all (and none) of which can make a claim to authority. But Wordsworth never brought this work to its productive phase—that is, he never oversaw its appearance in print. In this respect, the instability of *The Prelude* is quite unlike the instability of Byron's *The Giaour,* or *Don Juan.* In the latter two instances, instability is a problem not of composition but of production.

Further specifications of textual indeterminacy are possible and necessary. I instanced *The Giaour* and *Don Juan* because each epitomizes a different type of productive indeterminacy. In *Don Juan* the text's fluidity is largely a function of Byron's struggle with various censors. Byron agreed to modify his original work in a number of ways, sometimes reluctantly, sometimes willingly, sometimes actively, sometimes passively. He did so in response to various external pressures. Furthermore, deliberate changes were sometimes made in his texts without his knowledge, and these may or may not have gained his subsequent agreement. Finally, the whole phenomenon of pirating *Don Juan* is part of the poem's special type of productive indeterminacy. The pirated texts of the poem differ only in minor verbal ways from the early editions, but they constitute a major—indeed, a radical (in several senses)—shift to a whole new text of Byron's epic.

The situation is different for *The Giaour*. In this case fluidity is a function of Byron's willingness to seize the opportunities offered by the productive medium itself. As the poem moved through successive editions, he revised and augmented it until it grew to four times its original length. The case shows how an author can utilize the media of production to extend the process of composition—something that Tennyson, for example, did repeatedly and in various ways. More significantly, it calls attention to the possibility that several authorized versions of a work may be produced (not simply composed) for different purposes and perhaps readerships. The English and the American editions of *Moby-Dick* are quite distinct affairs; the early cantos of Pound were printed in a number of different versions, as are various poems by Auden; indeed, even the appearance of an author's work in anthologized formats exerts an important change in the status of the text (not merely the document).

All of these are real and realized distinctions which, when kept in mind, enable us to deal more precisely with the so-called "instability" of the text. Gabler's work reminds us that fictive works do not exist in "definitive" forms (or editions); by the same token, it also reminds us that the indeterminacy of texts is a determinate and determinable matter. Like Humpty Dumpty, anyone can make a text to his or her liking, but that act will itself always be of a determinate sort, and will have been carried out within certain structures of possibility that were licensed by specific material conditions which are at once social, institutional, and technological. The significance of any act of textual making (which includes, of course, textual interpretation) is always concrete and specific, and it emerges to critical view when its conditions of existence are made clear. The significance of Gabler's work is clear because he has so fully specified the conditions which made his work possible, and perhaps even—at this point in time—necessary.

When theorists and critics speak of the "undecidable" or "indeterminate" text they mean to indicate that various interpretations can be produced for different passages or whole works, and hence to argue that "meaning" is not something which resides "in" a literary work but is rather something which is "brought to it" or "laid upon it" by the reader, who is now of Queen Victoria ⌐(born 1820, acceded 1837)¬ and the ⌐posticipated¬ opening of the new municipal fish ⌐[market,] market: secondly,¬ apprehension of opposition from extreme circles on the questions of the respective visits of Their Royal Highnesses° the duke and duchess of York (real) and of His Majesty ⌐King¬ Brian Boru ⌐[(imaginary),] (imaginary): thirdly,¬ a conflict between professional etiquette and professional emulation concerning the recent erections of the Grand Lyric Hall on Burgh Quay and the Theatre Royal in Hawkins ⌐[street,°] street:°¬ fourthly,¬ dis-|traction resultant from compassion for ⌐[Fay Arthur's] Nelly Bouverist's¬ non-intellectual, non-political, non-topical expression of countenance and concupiscence caused by ⌐[Fay Arthur's] Nelly Bouverist's¬ re-|velations of white articles of ^non-intellectual, non-political, non-topical^ underclothing while she (⌐[Fay Arthur] Nelly Bouverist¬) was in the ⌐[articles,] articles: fifthly,¬ the ⟨diffi⟩ ⟨rhyming⟩ difficulties ^of >⟨rhyming and⟩ the selection of< appropriate music and ⟨>selection of⟩ humorous° allusions ⟨□⟩ from *Everybody's Book of Jokes* (1000 pages and a laugh in every ⌐[one],] one): sixthly,¬^ ^the rhymes, homophonous and cacophonous,^ associated with the names of the new lord mayor, Daniel Tallon, the new high sheriff, Thomas Pile and the new solicitorgeneral,° Dunbar Plunket Barton.¬

What relation existed between their ages?

16 years before ^in^ 1888 when Bloom was of Stephen's present age Stephen was 6. ⌐[Sixteen] 16¬ years after in 1920 when Stephen would be of Bloom's present age ⟨Blond⟩ Bloom would be 54. ⌐In 1936 when Bloom would be 70 and Stephen 54 their ages initially ^(as) in the ratio of^ 16 to 0 would be as 17 ½ to 13 ½, the proportion ^(diminishing) increasing^ and the disparity diminishing ⌐according¬ as⌐ ⌐arbitrary¬ future> years were added,° for if the proportion existing in 1883 had continued ⌐[immutable] immutable, conceiving that to be possible,¬ till then ^1904^ when Stephen was 22 Bloom would be 374 and in 1920 when Stephen would ^(be,) be 38,^ as Bloom then was, ⟨^38⟩ Bloom would be 646 while in 1952 when Stephen would have attained the ^⌐[postdiluvian maximum] maximum postdiluvian¬^ age of 70 Bloom, ⟨□⟩ being 1190 years alive having been born in the year ⌐[714] 714,¬ would have surpassed by 221 years the

---

4 Highnesses] *STET* aB; Highnesses, a1   8 street] e; Street, aB   8 street:] 1932; Street: a1
16 humorous] a1; humourous aB   20 solicitorgeneral,] e; solicitor-general, aB;

---

and the posticipated opening of the new municipal fish market: secondly,   430 apprehension of opposition from extreme circles on the questions of the respective visits of Their Royal Highnesses the duke and duchess of York (real) and of His Majesty King Brian Boru (imaginary): thirdly, a conflict between professional etiquette and professional emulation concerning the recent erections of the Grand Lyric Hall on Burgh Quay and the Theatre   435 Royal in Hawkins street: fourthly, distraction resultant from compassion for Nelly Bouverist's non-intellectual, non-political, non-topical expression of countenance and concupiscence caused by Nelly Bouverist's revelations of white articles of non-intellectual, non-political, non-topical underclothing while she (Nelly Bouverist) was in the articles: fifthly, the   440 difficulties of the selection of appropriate music and humorous allusions from *Everybody's Book of Jokes* (1000 pages and a laugh in every one): sixthly, the rhymes, homophonous and cacophonous, associated with the names of the new lord mayor, Daniel Tallon, the new high sheriff, Thomas Pile and the new solicitorgeneral, Dunbar Plunket Barton.   445

What relation existed between their ages?

16 years before in 1888 when Bloom was of Stephen's present age Stephen was 6. 16 years after in 1920 when Stephen would be of Bloom's present age Bloom would be 54. In 1936 when Bloom would be 70 and Stephen 54 their ages initially in the ratio of 16 to 0 would be as 17 ½ to 13 ½, the proportion   450 increasing and the disparity diminishing according as arbitrary future years were added, for if the proportion existing in 1883 had continued immutable, conceiving that to be possible, till then 1904 when Stephen was 22 Bloom would be 374 and in 1920 when Stephen would be 38, as Bloom then was, Bloom would be 646 while in 1952 when Stephen would have attained the   455 maximum postdiluvian age of 70 Bloom, being 1190 years alive having been born in the year 714, would have surpassed by 221 years the maximum

---

sollicitor-general, 1; sollicitorgeneral, a1   27 as--future] *STET* a1,a3; *TD:* arbitrary as future 2,3; as future arbitrary a2   28 added,] 1926; added aB

Two pages from "Ithaca" in Gabler's Ulysses. *The Society of Authors as the literary representatives of the Estate of James Joyce and © 1978 the Trustees of the Estate of James Joyce.*

called—by metaphoric license—"the writer." No one has put the case for such a procedure more forcefully than Stanley Fish, particularly, perhaps, in his well-known essay "Interpreting the *Variorum*." I do not wish to address the entire set of arguments put forth in this essay but merely to point out one of its salient features which is characteristic of this kind of approach. Fish's essay centers in the interpretive possibilities which are left open by a series of texts from Milton. Fish is interested in what he calls the "interpretive crux," or those passages where interpreters have carried on (often prolonged) disputes about the meaning of the text.

In his examination, however, Fish acknowledges two types of cruces. The first are purely "interpretive": "what is the two-handed engine in *Lycidas*? what is the meaning of Haemony in *Comus*?" Fish then glances at "Still others" which are, however, "of interest largely to those who make editions: matters of pronoun reference, lexical ambiguities, punctuation." In this case he calls attention to those various matters of textual fact where the issue of what is correct and what is incorrect always impinges, if it often remains insoluble. The texts of antiquity are strewn with passages which we know to be, in their received state, corrupt, wrong, incorrect, but which we also are unable to set right. Modern texts, like *Ulysses*, exhibit similar, though usually less serious, textual problems; less serious only because we are not normally left without any idea about the correct reading, but with alternative possibilities.

In making his case for the indeterminacy of meaning Fish never deals with a textual crux that involves a matter of fact. He avoids this sort of problem because his principal point is that textual indeterminacy is a function of the "reader" rather than of the "text." So far as Fish is concerned, the factive (rather than the fictive) dimension of a text is a documentary matter which is to be set aside when the question of interpretation is raised. Fish wants to take the text as physical object at face value. For him there are, on the one hand, "no fixed texts" because various "interpretive strategies are always being deployed"; on the other hand, there are the stable "documents," or the physical objects which the interpreter simply takes, for the nonce at any rate, as given. This is the structure of Fish's distinctions between the "editor" and the "interpreter" and between the "text" and the "document."

One has to realize, however, that Fish's distinction between a text and a document is not at all the distinction which textual critics intend when they make a similar verbal distinction between the terms. Vinton Dearing is the contemporary scholar most associated with this distinction, which in textual criticism separates two different kinds of physical objects. For Fish, however, a "text" is an *ideal* object from which we can—indeed, from which we must—abstract out its empirical aspects. For modern hermeneutics, meaning is a function of the act of interpretation and not of something antecedently "in" the "text." This view is correct, however, if and only if we make a firm distinction, for interpretive purposes, between "the text" on the one hand and "the document" on the other. Gabler's edition contains, implicitly, an argument that refuses to permit such a distinction. This argument maintains that "texts" and "documents" are always joined together in hypostatic unions. As a result, in this view the interpretive act "constitutes meaning" (as we now say) only in terms that are licensed by the received socio-history of the text. And that socio-history, for *texts,* is constituted at its most elementary level as a set of empirical documents whose meaning is intimately bound up with the socio-history of the documents.

In this context one may begin to understand more clearly the sort of illusions which lie behind the indeterminacy principles of much contemporary theory and criticism. "Rather than restoring and recovering texts," Fish says, "I am in the business of making texts and of teaching others to make them." The main thrust of this deliberately amusing and paradoxical remark is to suggest that texts are "made" not by the originary authors (Milton, Joyce, Byron) or by their editors, but by their "interpreters." But the participial clause ("Rather than restoring and recovering texts") contains a related position which exposes the full significance of what Fish is saying. He draws a distinction between "making" texts and "restoring and recovering" them. But given his non-documentary meaning of the term "text," what he *ought* to have said was: "Rather than restoring and recovering documents, I am in the business of making texts." In fact, however, the word "text" is repeatedly allowed to slip its moorings, as it does here, and carry a documentary meaning. This is a common feature of those interpretive strategies which do not deploy a socio-historical empiric in their discussions of "textual" indeterminacy.

The word "document" is never used by Fish in a similarly ambiguous fashion. "Document" for him means the physical and received object. But whereas Fish and critics like him want "text" to mean the "ideal" and the "made" thing, the "meaning" rather than the "medium" of the message, they cannot preserve the distinction intact. This is because, quite simply, no message is possible outside a concrete medium of some specific kind; indeed, the medium (documentary) is constitutive of the message itself. "Documents" are no more stable—or unstable—than "texts."

What Gabler's edition shows is that unstable "texts," texts that are "in process" or "indeterminate," always appear in material forms that are as determinate as the most "stable" text one might want or imagine. Gabler's edition also shows that these determinate forms of indeterminacy are always limited, and—furthermore—that the limitations are *determined* by certain material, institutional, and historical conditions that can be concretely specified. Criticism—whether in an analytic or a synthetic mode—is not "free play" and endless possibilities; it is structured play and certain particular possibilities. Gabler's own synoptic "continuous manuscript text" is an instance of one of two large and governing models for a process text (the other being what I earlier called the "continuous production text").

I should point out that Gabler's work exemplifies a discernible trend in European theoretical and textual studies. This movement is most directly associated with a series of editions which have been structured as "genetic texts" wherein the process of writing and production is conceived as the editorial object. Rather than aiming to produce a "definitive edition" or an edition which reflects the author's "intended" work, these editions seek to illuminate—in an imitative textual structure—

one or another phase or aspect of the writer's productive activity.

It is highly significant that this theoretical work has been spearheaded by editors and textual critics rather than by hermeneuts and philosophically-oriented "readers." When matters of *textualité* are raised within a hermeneutical or interpretive discourse, a certain abstractness or blurring of focus often occurs. We are all aware of the discontent which so much postmodern and poststructural theoretical work has stirred up in various quarters, even in the academy. In the present instance, however, the idea of textual instability or indeterminacy will always assume a specific and determinate form. The European editions I have alluded to—those of Hölderlin, Kafka, Flaubert, Klopstock, Proust, for example—have already made an important practical and theoretical impact upon the direction which postmodern literary work will have to take. In them we see, with unmistakable clarity, that the study of texts cannot acquire precision unless it is carried out within firmly defined material and technological conditions, and in relation to the particular social and historical structures which are imbedded within those material conditions.

Because Gabler's edition is the first English-language work to illustrate these new European lines, it needs to be carefully pondered by English and American scholars, and especially by theorists and literary interpreters. The edition argues, for example, that textual meaning is not an "idea" or an interpretive function—is not, that is to say, a textual supplement. Rather, textual meaning is always materially constituted *as* some particular text (in the documentary sense). Later glosses or supplementary moves on early texts will not reconstitute the earlier text—they will remain, sometimes literally, "in the margin"—until they constitute themselves, with clear self-consciousness, as a specific material formation.

So we study Gabler's three volumes and are forced to conclude that they represent a postmodern *Ulysses.* The concrete formatting of these books, where the synoptic text is given highest priority, is the most dramatic representation of the work's postmodern textuality. In an earlier edition the "clear text" on the rectos would have been the editor's ultimate object of interest. In Gabler's work, on the contrary, it has to be regarded as a supplementary aid in the reading of the synoptic text, which is this edition's chief goal and ultimate concern. Furthermore, this "text" of Joyce's original work is enmeshed within an editorial network that is extremely self-conscious of itself. That is to say, Gabler seeks actually to specify the material, institutional, and historical conditions which are embodied in his edition. Of course he does this from a certain particular vantage—his chief point of view is that of an internationally mobile scholar, with post-war graduate training in English studies in the United States (U. of Virginia), influenced by the Greg-Bowers line of textual criticism, and with expertise in computer-based word processing and access to the computer facilities at the University of Tübingen. (What does not form a part of that point of view is as pertinent to understanding it as what does.) This set of determinants engages with another large set—those established as the institutional history of Joyce scholarship up to the present time. Gabler's edition takes a concrete form which replicates the conditions of its production. The elementary bibliographical data on Gabler's edition is no less than a coded set of interpretive clues for understanding, and using, the work.

The same is of course true for all literary works, whose meanings are a function of their material, institutional, and social histories. When Fish speaks of "interpretive communities" he has precisely these determinate structures in mind. Unlike Gabler, however, Fish—in this respect he represents the dominant tradition of contemporary hermeneutics, especially in the United States—leaves those structures as undecided as the meanings he deploys in his *explications des textes*. As a consequence, we get no clear presentation of those "interpretive communities" where meanings are founded: neither of Fish's own (empirically concrete) interpretive community, nor of the conceptual category itself. All communities, even interpretive ones, are social structures with specific histories. Fish's "interpretive community," on the other hand, is a purely nominal category, a notional rather than a theoretical structure. In it "meaning" takes the determinate form not of the *in*determinate, but of the *non*determinate.

Gabler's edition of *Ulysses* provides an extremely useful point of contrast. . . . The synoptic continuous manuscript text is an exhibition—a concrete and particular presentation—of a self-deconstructing and unstable text. Unlike a hermeneutical (i.e., critically mediated and narrativized) presentation, however, Gabler's procedures make the structure of fluidity—its finite limits—very clear.

With or without a knowledge of the diacritical marks, a reader of [a passage from Gabler's *Ulysses*] might well take it for a (now so-called) L=A=N=G=U=A=G=E poem out of San Francisco or New York. In fact, Gabler's *Ulysses* is a distinctly postmodern text: the style is impersonal and maintained in a surface mode ("languaged"); the procedure is intertextual and self-referencing; the form of order is stochastic. None of these characteristics dominates the "reading text" offered on the rectos in Gabler's edition. (pp. 289-99)

[A passage] can be "translated" (or "read") if one understands the use of the diacritical marks. . . . [All] the words in full brackets (angled or square) indicate some type of revision or cancellation, and the various superscripts tell the reader at what stage of the composition process the revisions were carried out, and where (in the manuscript material) they are to be found. Carets indicate passages that are added as an "overlay" (e.g., an interlinear insertion) to a particular document, and the superior half-brackets mark off material that has been added to the continuous manuscript text at some "level" of the continuum. The degree sign signals that a textual note at the foot of the page must be consulted in order to understand a relevant but collateral (i.e., non-manuscript) process of revision. Finally, superscripts in parentheses indicate that the initial phase of the reading is being critically reconstructed from an hypothesized, but missing, document.

The reading text provided to the right of the synoptic text is a help in reading the latter because the reading text represents the ultimate stage reached by the continuous manuscript text. It is, however, beside the synoptic text, a pallid, chill, and drear document—disappointingly abstract, simple, and one-dimensional where the other is rich, complex, and many-levelled. Perhaps the most remarkable quality of the synoptic text is its capacity to preserve both the facts and the relationships of many kinds of detail, from the most dominant to the most marginal and tenuous. It is a text which Foucault would have admired, a text which re-presents a socio-history of Joyce's *Ulysses* (not *the* socio-history, of course).

One . . . thing might be noted about [a well-known passage from Episode 8 ("Lestrygonians") in Gabler's rendering]. It contains a textual crux in line 17. The word "gums" does not appear in the first or any of the later standard editions. It appeared in the *Little Review* printing, and Gabler's superscript "(C)" tells us that, in his view, the word must have been added to the (now lost) typescript which served as printer's copy for the *Little Review* printing. The textual note signalled by the degree sign also tells us, however, that the word is not present in the (author-corrected, and extant) typescript which was printer's copy for the first edition. If we turn to Gabler's reading text we find that "gums" is present in the text; as such, it gets numbered among the more than five-thousand "corrections" to the received texts.

But Gabler's own procedures tell us something else, tell us that the text of *Ulysses* is "correct" with or without "gums." Gabler hypothesizes an "error" and a "correction" here when in fact what we have are two different readings, each of which is possible, and neither of which can be shown to be more or less "correct" than the other. This is an "undecidable" matter, and the specific character of its undecidability can be—has already been, by the synoptic text—determined. We understand this if we contrast it with the case of the word "chewchewchew" in line 18. The latter replaced the word "chew" at the stage of the first placard (i.e., the first proof level), which is to say that the word "chew"—authorized through several levels of manuscript and typescript—was superseded at a later, intermediate level of composition. The correction maintained its authority through all the subsequent levels of composition and production—an important point to bear in mind, since this is by no means always the case.

Gabler's synoptic text shows us, in this instance, two types of textual instability. In the case of "chew" v. "chewchewchew" we observe a process by which one reading is marginalized by another. Gabler's *Ulysses* does not erase the marginalized reading, however, but merely places it in its appropriate historical position. The dominant reading, moreover, is also historically located (more or less midway along the complex length of this text's process of composition); as such, its fragility—emphasized nicely by the surrounding diacritics—serves to epitomize the kind of text we are dealing with, where marginality and dominance are distinctly relative terms. In the case of "gums," on the other hand, instability is a function of equivalent authority rather than of dominance and marginality. The effect, in each instance, is very similar, for we are perforce made conscious that this text is to be fundamentally characterized as a thing of many real and concrete details which are, at the same time, extremely fragile, and put together in strange, stochastic orderings.

"Gums" and the lack of "gums": a small matter, in the large scheme of things (of the world, of *Ulysses*), yet not an insignificant matter by any means. The world and the world of *Ulysses* are constituted by myriads of just such matters. Is not this one of the central "meanings" of *Ulysses,* and have we not been told so over and over again for more than sixty years by many literary scholars and ordinary readers as well? We have, but Gabler's *Ulysses* re-explains those meanings for us anew, and more clearly because his explanation has taken a peculiarly appropriate Postmodern form. The appropriate Modernist *Ulysses* is the 1922 first edition—a limited edition and supported by subscriptions of the literati. Its "perfect" form would be a corrected text of this edition. But the Postmodern *Ulysses* is Gabler's edition: a product (a) marketed by Garland Publishing, Inc., a highly specialized house which features academic books, but which locates itself in the world of commercial publishing rather than in the world of the university presses; and (b) electronically typeset by pagina GmbH in Tü-bingen from the processed text generated by the editing program TUSTEP. In Gabler's *Ulysses* the finished and monumental text of Joyce's work is placed in a secondary—might one say marginal?—relation to that fascinating document called the "synoptic continuous manuscript text." Gabler gives us a particular, a *determinate* synoptic text; in so doing, however, he also indicates the limits which his text, and which all texts, necessarily define and incorporate. (pp. 299-301)

> *Jerome J. McGann, "'Ulysses' as a Postmodern Text: The Gabler Edition," in* Criticism, *Vol. XXVII, No. 3 (Summer, 1985), pp. 283-305.*

ADDITIONAL BIBLIOGRAPHY

Dalton, Jack P. "The Text of *Ulysses*." In *New Light on Joyce from the Dublin Symposium*, edited by Fritz Senn, pp. 99-119. Bloomington: Indiana University Press, 1972.

> Examines errors in various editions of *Ulysses*, noting that the 1961 Random House edition was "the kind of book you could use only a few minutes in the chemistry lab before blowing the place up."

Gabler, Hans Walter. "Computer-Aided Critical Edition of *Ulysses*." *Association of Literary and Linguistic Computing* 8, No. 3 (1981): 232-48.

> Utilizes the example of *Ulysses* to demonstrate how the TUSTEP computer "system of text processing and printing programs may be successfully employed in the services of scholarly textual editing."

———. Afterword to *Ulysses: A Critical and Synoptic Edition*, by James Joyce, edited by Hans Walter Gabler, vol. 3, pp. 1859-1911. New York: Garland Publishing, 1984.

> Extensive discussion including: "the composition of *Ulysses*," "Joyce's manner and habits of writing," "the surviving documents and the main patterns of the descent of the text from manuscript to print," and "the editorial procedures" followed by Gabler "for establishing the critical text."

Gaskell, Philip. "Example 11: Joyce, *Ulysses*, 1922." In his *From Writer to Reader: Studies in Editorial Method*, pp. 213-44. Oxford: Clarendon Press, 1978.

> Proposes three approaches to re-editing *Ulysses*. "The first would be to produce a plain, accurate text of the final form of the book, all the available editions being sadly defective. The second would be to edit the first half of *Ulysses*—say up to 'Scylla and Charybdis'—in its first-draft form, before Joyce shifted the emphasis of his work away from narrative and character towards language and symbol. The third would be to illustrate the development of the text by making available the earlier drafts and versions in order both to elucidate it and to illuminate Joyce's mind and art."

Greg, W. W. "The Rationale of Copy-Text." *Studies in Bibliography* 3 (1950-1951): pp. 19-36.

> Presents Greg's seminal theory of copy-text.

Groden, Michael. *"Ulysses" in Progress*. Princeton, N.J.: Princeton University Press, 1977, 235 p.

> Traces the novel's "complicated and bizarre prepublication history," assembling evidence from "letters, notebooks, drafts, the autograph fair copy, typescripts, proofs, and the early version of *Ulysses* that was serialized in the *Little Review*."

———. "Editing Joyce's *Ulysses*: An International Effort." *Scholarly Publishing* 12, No. 1 (October 1980): 37-54.

> Asserts that the Gabler edition of *Ulysses* "will be a major literary event not only because the book is one of the most difficult and notoriously corrupt of modern prose texts, but also because the project involves a revised theory of the editing process and an intimate cooperation between human minds and computer technology."

———. "A Textual and Publishing History." In *A Companion to Joyce Studies*, edited by Zack Bowen and James F. Carens, pp. 71-128. Westport, Conn.: Greenwood Press, 1984.

> Composition and publication history of *Ulysses* and other works by Joyce.

Hettche, Walter, and Melchior, Claus. "A Famous Fighter and Mairy's Drawers: Joyce's Corrections for the 1936 John Lane Edition of *Ulysses*." *James Joyce Quarterly* 21, No. 2 (Winter 1984): 165-69.

> Details corrections made by Joyce in proofreading for the John Lane edition of *Ulysses* in 1936, which, due to their late arrival, were first incorporated into that publisher's 1937 edition of the novel.

Kenner, Hugh. "The Computerized *Ulysses*." *Harper's* 260, No. 1559 (April 1980): 89-95.

> Traces the ever-increasing corruption of the text of *Ulysses* from the time of its first publication and recounts the efforts of scholars to restore Joyce's original intention. Kenner predicts that the Gabler edition will be "a sublimely accurate version."

Pizer, Donald. "On the Editing of Modern American Texts." *Bulletin of the New York Public Library* 75, No. 3 (March 1971): 147-53.

> Debates the applicability of the theory of copy-text, which was formulated in response to problems arising in editing Renaissance texts, to works of modern American literature.

Ryder, John. "Editing *Ulysses* Typographically." *Scholarly Publishing* 18, No. 2 (January 1987): 108-24.

> Typographic history of the various editions of *Ulysses*.

Appendix

The following is a listing of all sources used in Volume 26 of *Twentieth-Century Literary Criticism*. Included in this list are all copyright and reprint rights and acknowledgments for those essays for which permission was obtained. Every effort has been made to trace copyright, but if omissions have been made, please let us know.

THE EXCERPTS IN TCLC, VOLUME 26, WERE REPRINTED FROM THE FOLLOWING PERIODICALS:

American Mercury, v. XV, December, 1928.

American Quarterly, v. XI, Fall, 1959 for "Fiction and the Businessman: Society through All Its Literature" by Van R. Halsey. Copyright 1959, American Studies Association. Reprinted by permission of the publisher and the author.

The Atlantic Economic Review, v. VIII, October, 1958.

The Atlantic Monthly, v. 259, March, 1987 for "The Game's Still Afoot" by Cait Murphy. Copyright 1987 by The Atlantic Monthly Company, Boston, MA. Reprinted by permission of the author.

Black World, v. XXI, June 1972 for "The Fork in the Road: Patterns of the Harlem Renaissance" by George E. Kent. Copyright © 1972 Johnson Publishing Company, Inc. Reprinted by permission of *Black World* and the Literary Estate of George E. Kent.

Books Abroad, v. XXX, Winter, 1956.

California Management Review, v. I, Summer, 1959. © 1959, The Regents of the University of California. All rights reserved. Reprinted by permission of The Regents.

CLA Journal, v. XXIX, September, 1985. Copyright, 1985 by The College Language Association. Used by permission of The College Language Association.

College English, v. 22, January, 1961 for "The Rogue in the Gray Flannel Suit" by Lewis A. Lawson. Copyright © 1961 by the National Council of Teachers of English. Reprinted by permission of the publisher and the author.

Commentary, v. 41, May, 1966. Copyright © 1966 by American Jewish Committee. All rights reserved. Reprinted by permission of the publisher.

Contemporary Literature, v. 28, Spring, 1987. © 1987 by the Board of Regents of the University of Wisconsin System. Reprinted by permission of The University of Wisconsin Press.

The Crisis, v. 36, July, 1929.

Baring-Gould, William S. From " 'I Hear of Sherlock Everywhere since You Became His Chronicler'," in *The Annotated Sherlock Holmes, Vol. I*. By Sir Arthur Conan Doyle, edited by William S. Baring-Gould. Potter, 1967. Copyright © 1967 by Lucile M. Baring-Gould. Used by permission of Clarkson N. Potter, Inc.

Benson, Frederick R. From *Writers in Arms: The Literary Impact of the Spanish Civil War*. New York University Press, 1967. © 1967 by New York University Press. Reprinted by permission of the publisher.

Blake, Patricia. From an introduction to *Half-Way to the Moon: New Writing from Russia*. Edited by Patricia Blake and Max Hayward. Holt, Rinehart and Winston, 1964. Copyright © 1963 by Patricia Blake. All rights reserved. Reprinted by permission of the author.

Bone, Robert A. From *The Negro Novel in America*. Yale University Press, 1958. © 1958 by Yale University Press, Inc. Renewed 1986 by Robert Adamson Bone. All rights reserved. Reprinted by permission of the author.

Brown, Sterling. From *Negro Poetry and Drama*. The Associates in Negro Folk Education, 1937.

Commager, Henry Steele. From *The American Mind: An Interpretation of American Thought and Character since the 1880's*. Yale University Press, 1950. Copyright, 1950, by Yale University Press. Renewed 1978 by Henry Steele Commager. All rights reserved. Reprinted by permission of the publisher.

Cox, Don Richard. From *Arthur Conan Doyle*. Frederick Ungar Publishing Co., 1985. Copyright © 1985 by The Ungar Publishing Company. Reprinted by permission of the publisher.

Cunningham, Valentine. From *Spanish Front: Writers on the Civil War*. Edited by Valentine Cunningham. Oxford University Press, Oxford, 1986. Introduction © Valentine Cunningham 1986. All rights reserved. Reprinted by permission of Oxford University Press.

Czigány, Lóránt. From *The Oxford History of Hungarian Literature: From the Earliest Times to the Present*. Clarendon Press, 1984. © Lóránt Czigány 1984. All rights reserved. Reprinted by permission of Oxford University Press.

Diaz, Janet W. From "Spanish Civil War and Exile in the Novels of Aub, Ayala and Sender," in *Latin America and the Literature of Exile: A Comparative View of the 20th-Century European Refugee Writers in the New World*. Edited by Hans-Bernhard Moeller. Carl Winter Universitätsverlag, 1983. © 1983. Carl Winter Universitätsverlag, gegr. Alle Rechte vorbehalten. Reprinted by permission of the author and the editor.

Eyles, Allen. From *Sherlock Holmes: A Centenary Celebration*. Harper & Row, 1986. Text copyright © 1986 by Allen Eyles. Copyright © 1986 by Justin Knowles Publishing Group. All rights reserved. Excerpted by permission of Harper & Row, Publishers, Inc.

Ford, Hugh D. From *A Poets' War: British Poets and the Spanish Civil War*. University of Pennsylvania Press, 1965. © 1965 by the Trustees of the University of Pennsylvania. Reprinted by permission of the publisher.

Frankel, Edith Rogovin. From *Novy Mir: A Case Study in the Politics of Literature, 1952-1958*. Cambridge University Press, 1981. © Cambridge University Press 1981. Reprinted by permission of the publisher and the author.

Hardwick, Michael. From *The Complete Guide to Sherlock Holmes*. Weidenfeld and Nicolson, 1986, St. Martin's Press, 1987. Copyright © Michael Hardwick 1986. All rights reserved. Reprinted by permission of St. Martin's Press, Inc. In Canada by George Weidenfeld & Nicolson Limited.

Haycraft, Howard. From *Murder for Pleasure: The Life and Times of the Detective Story*. A Hawthorn Book. Appleton-Century, 1941. Copyright 1941 by D. Appleton-Century Co., Inc. Renewed 1968 by Howard Haycraft. All rights reserved. Reprinted by permission of E. P. Dutton, a division of NAL Penguin Inc.

Held, Joseph. From "Young Hungary: The 'Nyugat' Periodical, 1908-14," in *Intellectual and Social Developments in the Habsburg Empire from Maria Theresa to World War I: Essays Dedicated to Robert A. Kann*. Edited by Stanley B. Winters and Joseph Held. East European Quarterly, 1975. Copyright © 1975 by East European Quarterly. Reprinted by permission of the publisher.

Huggins, Nathan Irvin. From *Harlem Renaissance*. Oxford University Press, 1971. Copyright © 1971 by Oxford University Press, Inc. Reprinted by permission of the publisher.

Jenkins, Cecil. From *André Malraux*. Twayne, 1972. Copyright © 1972 by Twayne Publishers. All rights reserved. Reprinted with the permission of Twayne Publishers, a division of G. K. Hall & Co., Boston.

Symons, Julian. From an introduction to _His Last Bow: Some Reminiscences of Sherlock Holmes_. By Sir Arthur Conan Doyle. John Murray and Jonathan Cape, 1974. Introduction © 1974 by Julian Symons. All rights reserved. Reprinted by permission of Jonathan Cape Ltd.

Tezla, Albert. From "Major Developments in the Imaginative Literature of Hungary since 1945," in _Ocean at the Window: Hungarian Prose and Poetry since 1945_. Edited by Albert Tezla. University of Minnesota Press, 1980. Copyright © 1980 by the University of Minnesota. All rights reserved. Reprinted by permission of the publisher.

Turner, Darwin T. From "The Harlem Renaissance: One Facet of an Unturned Kaleidoscope," in _Toward a New American Literary History: Essays in Honor of Arlin Turner_. Louis J. Budd, Edwin H. Cady, and Carl L. Anderson, eds. Duke University Press, 1980. Copyright © 1980 by Duke University Press. Reprinted by permission of the publisher.

Van Nostrand, A. D. From _The Denatured Novel_. The Bobbs-Merrill Company, Inc., 1960. Copyright © 1956, 1959, 1960, by Macmillan Publishing Company. Reprinted by permission of the author.

Vickery, Walter N. From _The Cult of Optimism: Political and Ideological Problems of Recent Soviet Literature_. Indiana University Press, 1963. Copyright 1963 by Indiana University Press. Reprinted by permission of the publisher.

Wall, Cheryl A. From "Poets and Versifiers, Singers and Signifiers: Women of the Harlem Renaissance," in _Women, the Arts, and the 1920s in Paris and New York_. Edited by Kenneth W. Wheeler and Virginia Lee Lussier. Transaction Books, 1982. Copyright © 1982 by Transaction, Inc. All rights reserved. Published by permission of Transaction, Inc.

Watts, Emily Stipes. From _The Businessman in American Literature_. University of Georgia Press, 1982. Copyright © 1982 by the University of Georgia Press. All rights reserved. Reprinted by permission of the publisher.

Whitney, Thomas P. From _The New Writing in Russia_. Edited and translated by Thomas P. Whitney. The University of Michigan Press, 1964. Copyright © by The University of Michigan 1964. All rights reserved. Reprinted by permission of the author.

Yevtushenko, Yevgeny. From _A Precocious Autobiography_. Translated by Andrew R. MacAndrew. Dutton, 1963. English translation copyright © 1963 by E. P. Dutton. All rights reserved. Reprinted by permission of E. P. Dutton, a division of NAL Penguin Inc.

Literary Criticism Series
Cumulative Author Index

This index lists all author entries in the Gale Literary Criticism Series and includes cross-references to other Gale sources. For the convenience of the reader, references to the *Yearbook* in the *Contemporary Literary Criticism* series include the page number (in parentheses) after the volume number. References in the index are identified as follows:

AITN:	*Authors in the News*, Volumes 1-2
CAAS:	*Contemporary Authors Autobiography Series*, Volumes 1-5
CA:	*Contemporary Authors* (original series), Volumes 1-121
CABS:	*Contemporary Authors Bibliographical Series*, Volumes 1-2
CANR:	*Contemporary Authors New Revision Series*, Volumes 1-21
CAP:	*Contemporary Authors Permanent Series*, Volumes 1-2
CA-R:	*Contemporary Authors* (revised editions), Volumes 1-44
CDALB:	*Concise Dictionary of American Literary Biography*
CLC:	*Contemporary Literary Criticism*, Volumes 1-46
CLR:	*Children's Literature Review*, Volumes 1-14
CMLC:	*Classical and Medieval Literature Criticism*, Volume 1
DLB:	*Dictionary of Literary Biography*, Volumes 1-59
DLB-DS:	*Dictionary of Literary Biography Documentary Series*, Volumes 1-4
DLB-Y:	*Dictionary of Literary Biography Yearbook*, Volumes 1980-1986
LC:	*Literature Criticism from 1400 to 1800*, Volumes 1-7
NCLC:	*Nineteenth-Century Literature Criticism*, Volumes 1-17
SAAS:	*Something about the Author Autobiography Series*, Volumes 1-4
SATA:	*Something about the Author*, Volumes 1-48
SSC:	*Short Story Criticism*, Volume 1
TCLC:	*Twentieth-Century Literary Criticism*, Volumes 1-27
YABC:	*Yesterday's Authors of Books for Children*, Volumes 1-2

Author Index

Cabell, James Branch
    1879-1958.................. TCLC 6
    See also CA 105
    See also DLB 9

Cable, George Washington
    1844-1925.................. TCLC 4
    See also CA 104
    See also DLB 12

Cabrera Infante, G(uillermo)
    1929-.................. CLC 5, 25, 45
    See also CA 85-88

Cage, John (Milton, Jr.) 1912-.....CLC 41
    See also CANR 9
    See also CA 13-16R

Cain, G. 1929-
    See Cabrera Infante, G(uillermo)

Cain, James M(allahan)
    1892-1977.............. CLC 3, 11, 28
    See also CANR 8
    See also CA 17-20R
    See also obituary CA 73-76
    See also AITN 1

Caldwell, Erskine 1903-...... CLC 1, 8, 14
    See also CAAS 1
    See also CANR 2
    See also CA 1-4R
    See also DLB 9
    See also AITN 1

Caldwell, (Janet Miriam) Taylor (Holland)
    1900-1985........CLC 2, 28, 39 (301)
    See also CANR 5
    See also CA 5-8R
    See also obituary CA 116

Calhoun, John Caldwell
    1782-1850.................. NCLC 15
    See also DLB 3

Calisher, Hortense
    1911-.................CLC 2, 4, 8, 38
    See also CANR 1
    See also CA 1-4R
    See also DLB 2

Callaghan, Morley (Edward)
    1903-.................. CLC 3, 14, 41
    See also CA 9-12R

Calvino, Italo
    1923-1985........CLC 5, 8, 11, 22, 33,
                      39 (305)
    See also CA 85-88
    See also obituary CA 116

Cameron, Peter 1959-........ CLC 44 (33)

Campana, Dino 1885-1932....... TCLC 20
    See also CA 117

Campbell, John W(ood), Jr.
    1910-1971....................CLC 32
    See also CAP 2
    See also CA 21-22
    See also obituary CA 29-32R
    See also DLB 8

Campbell, (John) Ramsey
    1946-........................CLC 42
    See also CANR 7
    See also CA 57-60

Campbell, (Ignatius) Roy (Dunnachie)
    1901-1957.................. TCLC 5
    See also CA 104
    See also DLB 20

Campbell, (William) Wilfred
    1861-1918.................. TCLC 9
    See also CA 106

Camus, Albert
    1913-1960..... CLC 1, 2, 4, 9, 11, 14,
                          32
    See also CA 89-92

Canby, Vincent 1924-.............CLC 13
    See also CA 81-84

Canetti, Elias 1905-........ CLC 3, 14, 25
    See also CA 21-24R

Cape, Judith 1916-
    See Page, P(atricia) K(athleen)

Čapek, Karel 1890-1938......... TCLC 6
    See also CA 104

Capote, Truman
    1924-1984........CLC 1, 3, 8, 13, 19,
                  34 (320), 38
    See also CANR 18
    See also CA 5-8R
    See also obituary CA 113
    See also DLB 2
    See also DLB-Y 80, 84
    See also CDALB 1941-1968

Capra, Frank 1897-..............CLC 16
    See also CA 61-64

Caputo, Philip 1941-.............CLC 32
    See also CA 73-76

Card, Orson Scott 1951-..... CLC 44 (163)

Cardenal, Ernesto 1925-...........CLC 31
    See also CANR 2
    See also CA 49-52

Carey, Ernestine Gilbreth 1908-
    See Gilbreth, Frank B(unker), Jr. and
      Carey, Ernestine Gilbreth
    See also CA 5-8R
    See also SATA 2

Carey, Peter 1943-.................CLC 40

Carleton, William 1794-1869...... NCLC 3

Carlisle, Henry (Coffin) 1926-......CLC 33
    See also CANR 15
    See also CA 13-16R

Carman, (William) Bliss
    1861-1929.................. TCLC 7
    See also CA 104

Carpenter, Don(ald Richard)
    1931-.......................CLC 41
    See also CANR 1
    See also CA 45-48

Carpentier (y Valmont), Alejo
    1904-1980.............. CLC 8, 11, 38
    See also CANR 11
    See also CA 65-68
    See also obituary CA 97-100

Carr, John Dickson 1906-1977 ......CLC 3
    See also CANR 3
    See also CA 49-52
    See also obituary CA 69-72

Carr, Virginia Spencer
    1929-................. CLC 34 (419)
    See also CA 61-64

Carrier, Roch 1937- ....CLC 13
    See also DLB 53

Carroll, James (P.) 1943-.........CLC 38
    See also CA 81-84

Carroll, Jim 1951-................CLC 35
    See also CA 45-48

Carroll, Lewis 1832-1898......... NCLC 2
    See also Dodgson, Charles Lutwidge
    See also CLR 2
    See also DLB 18

Carroll, Paul Vincent
    1900-1968....................CLC 10
    See also CA 9-12R
    See also obituary CA 25-28R
    See also DLB 10

Carruth, Hayden
    1921-.................CLC 4, 7, 10, 18
    See also CANR 4
    See also CA 9-12R
    See also DLB 5

Carter, Angela (Olive)
    1940-.................. CLC 5, 41
    See also CANR 12
    See also CA 53-56
    See also DLB 14

Carver, Raymond 1938-....... CLC 22, 36
    See also CANR 17
    See also CA 33-36R
    See also DLB-Y 84

Cary, (Arthur) Joyce
    1888-1957.................. TCLC 1
    See also CA 104
    See also DLB 15

Casares, Adolfo Bioy 1914-
    See Bioy Casares, Adolfo

Casely-Hayford, J(oseph) E(phraim)
    1866-1930.................. TCLC 24

Casey, John 1880-1964
    See O'Casey, Sean

Casey, Michael 1947- ....CLC 2
    See also CA 65-68
    See also DLB 5

Casey, Warren 1935-
    See Jacobs, Jim and Casey, Warren
    See also CA 101

Cassavetes, John 1929-............CLC 20
    See also CA 85-88

Cassill, R(onald) V(erlin)
    1919-.................. CLC 4, 23
    See also CAAS 1
    See also CANR 7
    See also CA 9-12R
    See also DLB 6

Cassity, (Allen) Turner
    1929-.................. CLC 6, 42
    See also CANR 11
    See also CA 17-20R

Castaneda, Carlos 1935?-..........CLC 12
    See also CA 25-28R

Castro, Rosalía de 1837-1885 ..... NCLC 3

Cather, Willa (Sibert)
    1873-1947................ TCLC 1, 11
    See also CA 104
    See also SATA 30
    See also DLB 9, 54
    See also DLB-DS 1

Author Index

Deutsch, Babette 1895-1982 . . . .**CLC 18**
See also CANR 4
See also CA 1-4R
See also obituary CA 108
See also DLB 45
See also SATA 1
See also obituary SATA 33

Devkota, Laxmiprasad
1909-1959 . . . . **TCLC 23**

De Vries, Peter
1910- . . . .**CLC 1, 2, 3, 7, 10, 28, 46**
See also CA 17-20R
See also DLB 6
See also DLB-Y 82

Dexter, Pete 1943- . . . . **CLC 34 (43)**

Diamond, Neil (Leslie) 1941- . . . .**CLC 30**
See also CA 108

Dick, Philip K(indred)
1928-1982 . . . . **CLC 10, 30**
See also CANR 2, 16
See also CA 49-52
See also obituary CA 106
See also DLB 8

Dickens, Charles 1812-1870 . . . . . **NCLC 3, 8**
See also SATA 15
See also DLB 21

Dickey, James (Lafayette)
1923- . . . .**CLC 1, 2, 4, 7, 10, 15**
See also CANR 10
See also CA 9-12R
See also CABS 2
See also DLB 5
See also DLB-Y 82
See also AITN 1, 2

Dickey, William 1928- . . . . **CLC 3, 28**
See also CA 9-12R
See also DLB 5

Dickinson, Peter (Malcolm de Brissac)
1927- . . . . **CLC 12, 35**
See also CA 41-44R
See also SATA 5

Didion, Joan 1934- . . . . **CLC 1, 3, 8, 14, 32**
See also CANR 14
See also CA 5-8R
See also DLB 2
See also DLB-Y 81, 86
See also AITN 1

Dillard, Annie 1945- . . . .**CLC 9**
See also CANR 3
See also CA 49-52
See also SATA 10
See also DLB-Y 80

Dillard, R(ichard) H(enry) W(ilde)
1937- . . . .**CLC 5**
See also CANR 10
See also CA 21-24R
See also DLB 5

Dillon, Eilís 1920- . . . .**CLC 17**
See also CAAS 3
See also CANR 4
See also CA 9-12R
See also SATA 2

Dinesen, Isak 1885-1962 . . . . . . **CLC 10, 29**
See also Blixen, Karen (Christentze
Dinesen)

Disch, Thomas M(ichael)
1940- . . . . **CLC 7, 36**
See also CAAS 4
See also CANR 17
See also CA 21-24R
See also DLB 8

Disraeli, Benjamin 1804-1881 . . . . . **NCLC 2**
See also DLB 21

Dixon, Paige 1911-
See Corcoran, Barbara

Döblin, Alfred 1878-1957 . . . . **TCLC 13**
See also Doeblin, Alfred

Dobrolyubov, Nikolai Alexandrovich
1836-1861 . . . . **NCLC 5**

Dobyns, Stephen 1941- . . . .**CLC 37**
See also CANR 2, 18
See also CA 45-48

Doctorow, E(dgar) L(aurence)
1931- . . . .**CLC 6, 11, 15, 18, 37,
44 (166)**
See also CANR 2
See also CA 45-48
See also DLB 2, 28
See also DLB-Y 80
See also AITN 2

Dodgson, Charles Lutwidge 1832-1898
See Carroll, Lewis
See also YABC 2

Doeblin, Alfred 1878-1957 . . . . **TCLC 13**
See also CA 110

Doerr, Harriet 1910- . . . . **CLC 34 (151)**
See also CA 117

Donaldson, Stephen R. 1947- . . . .**CLC 46**
See also CANR 13
See also CA 89-92

Donleavy, J(ames) P(atrick)
1926- . . . .**CLC 1, 4, 6, 10, 45**
See also CA 9-12R
See also DLB 6
See also AITN 2

Donnadieu, Marguerite 1914-
See Duras, Marguerite

Donnell, David 1939?- . . . .**CLC 34 (155)**

Donoso, José 1924- . . . .**CLC 4, 8, 11, 32**
See also CA 81-84

Donovan, John 1928- . . . .**CLC 35**
See also CLR 3
See also CA 97-100
See also SATA 29

Doolittle, Hilda 1886-1961
See H(ilda) D(oolittle)
See also CA 97-100
See also DLB 4, 45

Dorn, Ed(ward Merton)
1929- . . . . **CLC 10, 18**
See also CA 93-96
See also DLB 5

Dos Passos, John (Roderigo)
1896-1970 . . . . . **CLC 1, 4, 8, 11, 15, 25,
34 (419)**
See also CANR 3
See also CA 1-4R
See also obituary CA 29-32R
See also DLB 4, 9
See also DLB-DS 1

Dostoevski, Fedor Mikhailovich
1821-1881 . . . . **NCLC 2, 7**

Doughty, Charles (Montagu)
1843-1926 . . . . **TCLC 27**
See also CA 115
See also DLB 19, 57

Douglass, Frederick
1817-1895 . . . . **NCLC 7**
See also SATA 29
See also DLB 1, 43, 50

Dourado, (Waldomiro Freitas) Autran
1926- . . . .**CLC 23**
See also CA 25-28R

Dowson, Ernest (Christopher)
1867-1900 . . . . **TCLC 4**
See also CA 105
See also DLB 19

Doyle, (Sir) Arthur Conan
1859-1930 . . . . **TCLC 7, 26**
See also CA 104
See also SATA 24
See also DLB 18

Dr. A 1933-
See Silverstein, Alvin and Virginia
B(arbara Opshelor) Silverstein

Drabble, Margaret
1939- . . . .**CLC 2, 3, 5, 8, 10, 22**
See also CANR 18
See also CA 13-16R
See also DLB 14

Dreiser, Theodore (Herman Albert)
1871-1945 . . . . **TCLC 10, 18**
See also SATA 48
See also CA 106
See also DLB 9, 12
See also DLB-DS 1

Drexler, Rosalyn 1926- . . . . **CLC 2, 6**
See also CA 81-84

Dreyer, Carl Theodor
1889-1968 . . . .**CLC 16**
See also obituary CA 116

Drieu La Rochelle, Pierre
1893-1945 . . . . **TCLC 21**
See also CA 117

Droste-Hülshoff, Annette Freiin von
1797-1848 . . . . **NCLC 3**

Drummond, William Henry
1854-1907 . . . . **TCLC 25**

Drummond de Andrade, Carlos 1902-
See Andrade, Carlos Drummond de

Drury, Allen (Stuart) 1918- . . . .**CLC 37**
See also CANR 18
See also CA 57-60

Dryden, John 1631-1700 . . . .**LC 3**

Duberman, Martin 1930- . . . .**CLC 8**
See also CANR 2
See also CA 1-4R

Dubie, Norman (Evans, Jr.)
1945- . . . .**CLC 36**
See also CANR 12
See also CA 69-72

Du Bois, W(illiam) E(dward) B(urghardt)
1868-1963 . . . . **CLC 1, 2, 13**
See also CA 85-88
See also SATA 42
See also DLB 47, 50

Dubus, André 1936- . . . . **CLC 13, 36**
See also CANR 17
See also CA 21-24R

Farrell, James T(homas)
1904-1979............CLC 1, 4, 8, 11
See also CANR 9
See also CA 5-8R
See also obituary CA 89-92
See also DLB 4, 9
See also DLB-DS 2

Farrell, M. J. 1904-
See Keane, Molly

Fassbinder, Rainer Werner
1946-1982....................CLC 20
See also CA 93-96
See also obituary CA 106

Fast, Howard (Melvin) 1914-......CLC 23
See also CANR 1
See also CA 1-4R
See also SATA 7
See also DLB 9

Faulkner, William (Cuthbert)
1897-1962...... CLC 1, 3, 6, 8, 9, 11,
14, 18, 28
See also SSC 1
See also CA 81-84
See also DLB 9, 11, 44
See also DLB-Y 86
See also DLB-DS 2
See also AITN 1

Fauset, Jessie Redmon
1884?-1961...................CLC 19
See also CA 109

Faust, Irvin 1924- ....CLC 8
See also CA 33-36R
See also DLB 2, 28
See also DLB-Y 80

Federman, Raymond 1928- ....CLC 6
See also CANR 10
See also CA 17-20R
See also DLB-Y 80

Federspiel, J(ürg) F. 1931-.........CLC 42

Feiffer, Jules 1929- .... CLC 2, 8
See also CA 17-20R
See also SATA 8
See also DLB 7, 44

Feinstein, Elaine 1930- ....CLC 36
See also CA 69-72
See also CAAS 1
See also DLB 14, 40

Feldman, Irving (Mordecai)
1928-.........................CLC 7
See also CANR 1
See also CA 1-4R

Fellini, Federico 1920- ....CLC 16
See also CA 65-68

Felsen, Gregor 1916-
See Felsen, Henry Gregor

Felsen, Henry Gregor 1916-........CLC 17
See also CANR 1
See also CA 1-4R
See also SAAS 2
See also SATA 1

Fenton, James (Martin) 1949-......CLC 32
See also CA 102
See also DLB 40

Ferber, Edna 1887-1968..........CLC 18
See also CA 5-8R
See also obituary CA 25-28R
See also SATA 7
See also DLB 9, 28
See also AITN 1

Ferlinghetti, Lawrence (Monsanto)
1919?-...............CLC 2, 6, 10, 27
See also CANR 3
See also CA 5-8R
See also DLB 5, 16
See also CDALB 1941-1968

Ferrier, Susan (Edmonstone)
1782-1854...................NCLC 8

Feuchtwanger, Lion
1884-1958...................TCLC 3
See also CA 104

Feydeau, Georges 1862-1921..... TCLC 22
See also CA 113

Fiedler, Leslie A(aron)
1917-..................CLC 4, 13, 24
See also CANR 7
See also CA 9-12R
See also DLB 28

Field, Andrew 1938- .... CLC 44 (463)

Field, Eugene 1850-1895 .... NCLC 3
See also SATA 16
See also DLB 21, 23, 42

Fielding, Henry 1707-1754..........LC 1
See also DLB 39

Fielding, Sarah 1710-1768 ....LC 1
See also DLB 39

Fierstein, Harvey 1954- ....CLC 33

Figes, Eva 1932-...................CLC 31
See also CANR 4
See also CA 53-56
See also DLB 14

Finch, Robert (Duer Claydon)
1900-........................CLC 18
See also CANR 9
See also CA 57-60

Findley, Timothy 1930-............CLC 27
See also CANR 12
See also CA 25-28R
See also DLB 53

Fink, Janis 1951-
See Ian, Janis

Firbank, (Arthur Annesley) Ronald
1886-1926...................TCLC 1
See also CA 104
See also DLB 36

Firbank, Louis 1944-
See Reed, Lou

Fisher, Roy 1930- ....CLC 25
See also CANR 16
See also CA 81-84
See also DLB 40

Fisher, Rudolph 1897-1934 ...... TCLC 11
See also CA 107

Fisher, Vardis (Alvero)
1895-1968....................CLC 7
See also CA 5-8R
See also obituary CA 25-28R
See also DLB 9

FitzGerald, Edward
1809-1883................... NCLC 9
See also DLB 32

Fitzgerald, F(rancis) Scott (Key)
1896-1940..............TCLC 1, 6, 14
See also CA 110
See also DLB 4, 9
See also DLB-Y 81
See also DLB-DS 1
See also AITN 1

Fitzgerald, Penelope 1916-.........CLC 19
See also CA 85-88
See also DLB 14

Fitzgerald, Robert (Stuart)
1910-1985......... CLC 39 (318; 470)
See also CANR 1
See also CA 2R
See also obituary CA 114
See also DLB-Y 80

FitzGerald, Robert D(avid)
1902-........................CLC 19
See also CA 17-20R

Flanagan, Thomas (James Bonner)
1923-........................CLC 25
See also CA 108
See also DLB-Y 80

Flaubert, Gustave
1821-1880................NCLC 2, 10

Fleming, Ian (Lancaster)
1908-1964.................. CLC 3, 30
See also CA 5-8R
See also SATA 9

Fleming, Thomas J(ames)
1927-........................CLC 37
See also CANR 10
See also CA 5-8R
See also SATA 8

Flieg, Hellmuth
See also Heym, Stefan

Flying Officer X 1905-1974
See Bates, H(erbert) E(rnest)

Fo, Dario 1929- ....CLC 32
See also CA 116

Follett, Ken(neth Martin)
1949-........................CLC 18
See also CANR 13
See also CA 81-84
See also DLB-Y 81

Forbes, Esther 1891-1967..........CLC 12
See also CAP 1
See also CA 13-14
See also obituary CA 25-28R
See also DLB 22
See also SATA 2

Forché, Carolyn 1950- ....CLC 25
See also CA 109, 117
See also DLB 5

Ford, Ford Madox
1873-1939................ TCLC 1, 15
See also CA 104
See also DLB 34

Ford, John 1895-1973.............CLC 16
See also obituary CA 45-48

Ford, Richard 1944- ....CLC 46
See also CANR 11
See also CA 69-72

Forester, C(ecil) S(cott)
1899-1966....................CLC 35
See also CA 73-76
See also obituary CA 25-28R
See also SATA 13

Forman, James D(ouglas)
1932-........................CLC 21
See also CANR 4, 19
See also CA 9-12R
See also SATA 8, 21

Author Index

Gallant, Mavis 1922-........**CLC 7, 18, 38**
See also CA 69-72
See also DLB 53

Gallant, Roy A(rthur) 1924-.......**CLC 17**
See also CANR 4
See also CA 5-8R
See also SATA 4

Gallico, Paul (William)
1897-1976....................**CLC 2**
See also CA 5-8R
See also obituary CA 69-72
See also SATA 13
See also DLB 9
See also AITN 1

Galsworthy, John 1867-1933......**TCLC 1**
See also CA 104
See also DLB 10, 34

Galt, John 1779-1839 ....**NCLC 1**

Galvin, James 1951-..............**CLC 38**
See also CA 108

Gann, Ernest K(ellogg) 1910-......**CLC 23**
See also CANR 1
See also CA 1-4R
See also AITN 1

García Lorca, Federico
1899-1936................**TCLC 1, 7**
See also CA 104

García Márquez, Gabriel
1928-....**CLC 2, 3, 8, 10, 15, 27**
See also CANR 10
See also CA 33-36R

Gardam, Jane 1928-..............**CLC 43**
See also CLR 12
See also CANR 2, 18
See also CA 49-52
See also SATA 28, 39
See also DLB 14

Gardner, Herb 1934- ....**CLC 44 (208)**

Gardner, John (Champlin, Jr.)
1933-1982......**CLC 2, 3, 5, 7, 8, 10,**
18, 28, 34 (547)
See also CA 65-68
See also obituary CA 107
See also obituary SATA 31, 40
See also DLB 2
See also DLB-Y 82
See also AITN 1

Gardner, John (Edmund)
1926-.......................**CLC 30**
See also CANR 15
See also CA 103
See also AITN 1

Garfield, Leon 1921-..............**CLC 12**
See also CA 17-20R
See also SATA 1, 32

Garland, (Hannibal) Hamlin
1860-1940..................**TCLC 3**
See also CA 104
See also DLB 12

Garneau, Hector (de) Saint Denys
1912-1943..................**TCLC 13**
See also CA 111

Garner, Alan 1935-..............**CLC 17**
See also CANR 15
See also CA 73-76
See also SATA 18

Garner, Hugh 1913-1979.........**CLC 13**
See also CA 69-72

Garnett, David 1892-1981 ....**CLC 3**
See also CANR 17
See also CA 5-8R
See also obituary CA 103
See also DLB 34

Garrett, George (Palmer)
1929-....................**CLC 3, 11**
See also CAAS 5
See also CANR 1
See also CA 1-4R
See also DLB 2, 5
See also DLB-Y 83

Garrigue, Jean 1914-1972 ....**CLC 2, 8**
See also CA 5-8R
See also obituary CA 37-40R

Gary, Romain 1914-1980.........**CLC 25**
See also Kacew, Romain

Gascoyne, David (Emery)
1916-.......................**CLC 45**
See also CANR 10
See also CA 65-68
See also DLB 20

Gascar, Pierre 1916-..............**CLC 11**
See also Fournier, Pierre

Gaskell, Elizabeth Cleghorn
1810-1865...................**NCLC 5**
See also DLB 21

Gass, William H(oward)
1924-.....**CLC 1, 2, 8, 11, 15, 39 (477)**
See also CA 17-20R
See also DLB 2

Gautier, Théophile 1811-1872.....**NCLC 1**

Gaye, Marvin (Pentz)
1939-1984...................**CLC 26**
See also obituary CA 112

Gébler, Carlo (Ernest)
1954-.................**CLC 39 (60)**
See also CA 119

Gee, Maurice (Gough) 1931-.......**CLC 29**
See also CA 97-100
See also SATA 46

Gelbart, Larry (Simon) 1923-......**CLC 21**
See also CA 73-76

Gelber, Jack 1932- ....**CLC 1, 6, 14**
See also CANR 2
See also CA 1-4R
See also DLB 7

Gellhorn, Martha (Ellis) 1908- .....**CLC 14**
See also CA 77-80
See also DLB-Y 82

Genet, Jean
1910-1986........**CLC 1, 2, 5, 10, 14,**
44 (385), 46
See also CANR 18
See also CA 13-16R
See also DLB-Y 86

Gent, Peter 1942-.................**CLC 29**
See also CA 89-92
See also DLB-Y 82
See also AITN 1

George, Jean Craighead 1919- .....**CLC 35**
See also CLR 1
See also CA 5-8R
See also SATA 2
See also DLB 52

George, Stefan (Anton)
1868-1933................**TCLC 2, 14**
See also CA 104

Gerhardi, William (Alexander) 1895-1977
See Gerhardie, William (Alexander)

Gerhardie, William (Alexander)
1895-1977....................**CLC 5**
See also CANR 18
See also CA 25-28R
See also obituary CA 73-76
See also DLB 36

Gertler, T(rudy) 1946?- ......**CLC 34 (49)**
See also CA 116

Gessner, Friedrike Victoria 1910-1980
See Adamson, Joy(-Friederike Victoria)

Ghelderode, Michel de
1898-1962................**CLC 6, 11**
See also CA 85-88

Ghiselin, Brewster 1903-..........**CLC 23**
See also CANR 13
See also CA 13-16R

Ghose, Zulfikar 1935-.............**CLC 42**
See also CA 65-68

Ghosh, Amitav 1943- ....**CLC 44 (44)**

Giacosa, Giuseppe 1847-1906 .....**TCLC 7**
See also CA 104

Gibbon, Lewis Grassic
1901-1935..................**TCLC 4**
See also Mitchell, James Leslie

Gibran, (Gibran) Kahlil
1883-1931................**TCLC 1, 9**
See also CA 104

Gibson, William 1914-............**CLC 23**
See also CANR 9
See also CA 9-12R
See also DLB 7

Gibson, William 1948- ......**CLC 39 (139)**

Gide, André (Paul Guillaume)
1869-1951................**TCLC 5, 12**
See also CA 104

Gifford, Barry (Colby)
1946-..................**CLC 34 (457)**
See also CANR 9
See also CA 65-68

Gilbert, (Sir) W(illiam) S(chwenck)
1836-1911..................**TCLC 3**
See also CA 104
See also SATA 36

Gilbreth, Ernestine 1908-
See Carey, Ernestine Gilbreth

Gilbreth, Frank B(unker), Jr. 1911-
See Gilbreth, Frank B(unker), Jr. and
Carey, Ernestine Gilbreth
See also CA 9-12R
See also SATA 2

Gilbreth, Frank B(unker), Jr. 1911- and
Carey, Ernestine Gilbreth
1908-.......................**CLC 17**

Gilchrist, Ellen 1935- ....**CLC 34 (164)**
See also CA 113, 116

Giles, Molly 1942-...........**CLC 39 (64)**

Gilliam, Terry (Vance) 1940-
See Monty Python
See also CA 108, 113

Gilliatt, Penelope (Ann Douglass)
        1932- . . . . .CLC 2, 10, 13
    See also CA 13-16R
    See also DLB 14
    See also AITN 2

Gilman, Charlotte (Anna) Perkins (Stetson)
        1860-1935. . . . . TCLC 9
    See also CA 106

Gilmour, David   1944-
    See Pink Floyd

Gilroy, Frank D(aniel)   1925- . . . . .CLC 2
    See also CA 81-84
    See also DLB 7

Ginsberg, Allen
        1926- . . . . .CLC 1, 2, 3, 4, 6, 13, 36
    See also CANR 2
    See also CA 1-4R
    See also DLB 5, 16
    See also CDALB 1941-1968
    See also AITN 1

Ginzburg, Natalia   1916- . . . . CLC 5, 11
    See also CA 85-88

Giono, Jean   1895-1970. . . . . CLC 4, 11
    See also CANR 2
    See also CA 45-48
    See also obituary CA 29-32R

Giovanni, Nikki   1943- . . . . CLC 2, 4, 19
    See also CLR 6
    See also CANR 18
    See also CA 29-32R
    See also SATA 24
    See also DLB 5, 41
    See also AITN 1

Giovene, Andrea   1904- . . . . .CLC 7
    See also CA 85-88

Gippius, Zinaida (Nikolayevna)   1869-1945
    See also Hippius, Zinaida
    See also CA 106

Giraudoux, (Hippolyte) Jean
        1882-1944. . . . . TCLC 2, 7
    See also CA 104

Gironella, José María   1917- . . . . .CLC 11
    See also CA 101

Gissing, George (Robert)
        1857-1903. . . . . TCLC 3, 24
    See also CA 105
    See also DLB 18

Gladkov, Fyodor (Vasilyevich)
        1883-1958. . . . . TCLC 27

Glanville, Brian (Lester)   1931- . . . . . .CLC 6
    See also CANR 3
    See also CA 5-8R
    See also DLB 15
    See also SATA 42

Glasgow, Ellen (Anderson Gholson)
        1873?-1945. . . . . .TCLC 2, 7
    See also CA 104
    See also DLB 9, 12

Glassco, John   1909-1981 . . . . .CLC 9
    See also CANR 15
    See also CA 13-16R
    See also obituary CA 102

Glasser, Ronald J.   1940?- . . . . .CLC 37

Glissant, Édouard   1928- . . . . .CLC 10

Gloag, Julian   1930- . . . . .CLC 40
    See also CANR 10
    See also CA 65-68
    See also AITN 1

Glück, Louise (Elisabeth)
        1943- . . . . .CLC 7, 22, 44 (214)
    See also CA 33-36R
    See also DLB 5

Gobineau, Joseph Arthur (Comte) de
        1816-1882. . . . . NCLC 17

Godard, Jean-Luc   1930- . . . . .CLC 20
    See also CA 93-96

Godwin, Gail   1937- . . . . . . .CLC 5, 8, 22, 31
    See also CANR 15
    See also CA 29-32R
    See also DLB 6

Godwin, William   1756-1836 . . . . . NCLC 14
    See also DLB 39

Goethe, Johann Wolfgang von
        1749-1832. . . . . NCLC 4

Gogarty, Oliver St. John
        1878-1957. . . . . TCLC 15
    See also CA 109
    See also DLB 15, 19

Gogol, Nikolai (Vasilyevich)
        1809-1852. . . . . NCLC 5, 15
    See also CAAS 1, 4

Gökçeli, Yasar Kemal   1923-
    See Kemal, Yashar

Gold, Herbert   1924- . . . . . .CLC 4, 7, 14, 42
    See also CANR 17
    See also CA 9-12R
    See also DLB 2
    See also DLB-Y 81

Goldbarth, Albert   1948- . . . . CLC 5, 38
    See also CANR 6
    See also CA 53-56

Goldberg, Anatol   19??- . . . . . . CLC 34 (433)
    See also obituary CA 117

Golding, William (Gerald)
        1911- . . . . .CLC 1, 2, 3, 8, 10, 17, 27
    See also CANR 13
    See also CA 5-8R
    See also DLB 15

Goldman, Emma   1869-1940 . . . . . TCLC 13
    See also CA 110

Goldman, William (W.)   1931- . . . . . . .CLC 1
    See also CA 9-12R
    See also DLB 44

Goldmann, Lucien   1913-1970 . . . . .CLC 24
    See also CAP 2
    See also CA 25-28

Goldoni, Carlo   1707-1793 . . . . LC 4

Goldsberry, Steven   1949- . . . . . CLC 34 (54)

Goldsmith, Oliver   1728?-1774. . . . . . . LC 2
    See also SATA 26
    See also DLB 39

Gombrowicz, Witold
        1904-1969. . . . . CLC 4, 7, 11
    See also CAP 2
    See also CA 19-20
    See also obituary CA 25-28R

Gómez de la Serna, Ramón
        1888-1963. . . . . .CLC 9
    See also obituary CA 116

Goncharov, Ivan Alexandrovich
        1812-1891. . . . . NCLC 1

Goncourt, Edmond (Louis Antoine Huot) de
        1822-1896
    See Goncourt, Edmond (Louis Antoine
        Huot) de and Goncourt, Jules (Alfred
        Huot) de

Goncourt, Edmond (Louis Antoine Huot) de
        1822-1896   and **Goncourt, Jules (Alfred
        Huot) de**   1830-1870 . . . . NCLC 7

Goncourt, Jules (Alfred Huot) de   1830-1870
    See Goncourt, Edmond (Louis Antoine
        Huot) de and Goncourt, Jules (Alfred
        Huot) de

Goncourt, Jules (Alfred Huot) de   1830-1870
    and **Goncourt, Edmond (Louis Antoine
        Huot) de**   1822-1896
    See Goncourt, Edmond (Louis Antoine
        Huot) de and Goncourt, Jules (Alfred
        Huot) de

Goodman, Paul
        1911-1972. . . . . .CLC 1, 2, 4, 7
    See also CAP 2
    See also CA 19-20
    See also obituary CA 37-40R

Gordimer, Nadine
        1923- . . . . .CLC 3, 5, 7, 10, 18, 33
    See also CANR 3
    See also CA 5-8R

Gordon, Caroline
        1895-1981. . . . . CLC 6, 13, 29
    See also CAP 1
    See also CA 11-12
    See also obituary CA 103
    See also DLB 4, 9
    See also DLB-Y 81

Gordon, Mary (Catherine)
        1949- . . . . CLC 13, 22
    See also CA 102
    See also DLB 6
    See also DLB-Y 81

Gordon, Sol   1923- . . . . .CLC 26
    See also CANR 4
    See also CA 53-56
    See also SATA 11

Gordone, Charles   1925- . . . . CLC 1, 4
    See also CA 93-96
    See also DLB 7

Gorenko, Anna Andreyevna   1889?-1966
    See Akhmatova, Anna

Gorky, Maxim   1868-1936 . . . . TCLC 8
    See also Peshkov, Alexei Maximovich

Goryan, Sirak   1908-1981
    See Saroyan, William

Gotlieb, Phyllis (Fay Bloom)
        1926- . . . . .CLC 18
    See also CANR 7
    See also CA 13-16R

Gould, Lois   1938?- . . . . CLC 4, 10
    See also CA 77-80

Gourmont, Rémy de
        1858-1915. . . . . TCLC 17
    See also CA 109

Goyen, (Charles) William
          1915-1983............CLC 5, 8, 14, 40
     See also CANR 6
     See also CA 5-8R
     See also obituary CA 110
     See also DLB 2
     See also DLB-Y 83
     See also AITN 2

Goytisolo, Juan 1931-.......CLC 5, 10, 23
     See also CA 85-88

Grabbe, Christian Dietrich
          1801-1836.................. NCLC 2

Gracq, Julien 1910-..............CLC 11

Grade, Chaim 1910-1982.........CLC 10
     See also CA 93-96
     See also obituary CA 107

Graham, R(obert) B(ontine) Cunninghame
          1852-1936................. TCLC 19

Graham, W(illiam) S(ydney)
          1918-.......................CLC 29
     See also CA 73-76
     See also DLB 20

Graham, Winston (Mawdsley)
          1910-.......................CLC 23
     See also CANR 2
     See also CA 49-52
     See also obituary CA 118

Granville-Barker, Harley
          1877-1946.................. TCLC 2
     See also CA 104

Grass, Günter (Wilhelm)
          1927-....... CLC 1, 2, 4, 6, 11, 15, 22,
                                              32
     See also CANR 20
     See also CA 13-16R

Grau, Shirley Ann 1929- .... CLC 4, 9
     See also CA 89-92
     See also DLB 2
     See also AITN 2

Graves, Richard Perceval
          19??- .... CLC 44 (474)

Graves, Robert (von Ranke)
          1895-1985............ CLC 1, 2, 6, 11,
                            39 (320), 44 (474), 45
     See also CANR 5
     See also CA 5-8R
     See also obituary CA 117
     See also SATA 45
     See also DLB 20
     See also DLB-Y 85

Gray, Alasdair 1934-..............CLC 41

Gray, Amlin 1946-................CLC 29

Gray, Francine du Plessix
          1930-.......................CLC 22
     See also CAAS 2
     See also CANR 11
     See also CA 61-64

Gray, John (Henry)
          1866-1934................. TCLC 19
     See also CA 119

Gray, Simon (James Holliday)
          1936-................ CLC 9, 14, 36
     See also CAAS 3
     See also CA 21-24R
     See also DLB 13
     See also AITN 1

Gray, Thomas 1716-1771...........LC 4

Grayson, Richard (A.) 1951-.......CLC 38
     See also CANR 14
     See also CA 85-88

Greeley, Andrew M(oran)
          1928-.......................CLC 28
     See also CANR 7
     See also CA 5-8R

Green, Hannah 1932- .... CLC 3, 7, 30
     See also Greenberg, Joanne
     See also CA 73-76

Green, Henry 1905-1974 ...... CLC 2, 13
     See also Yorke, Henry Vincent
     See also DLB 15

Green, Julien (Hartridge)
          1900-.................... CLC 3, 11
     See also CA 21-24R
     See also DLB 4

Green, Paul (Eliot) 1894-1981.....CLC 25
     See also CANR 3
     See also CA 5-8R
     See also obituary CA 103
     See also DLB 7, 9
     See also DLB-Y 81
     See also AITN 1

Greenberg, Ivan 1908-1973
     See Rahv, Philip
     See also CA 85-88

Greenberg, Joanne (Goldenberg)
          1932-.................... CLC 3, 7, 30
     See also Green, Hannah
     See also CANR 14
     See also CA 5-8R
     See also SATA 25

Greene, Bette 1934-..............CLC 30
     See also CLR 2
     See also CANR 4
     See also CA 53-56
     See also SATA 8

Greene, Gael 19??- ....CLC 8
     See also CANR 10
     See also CA 13-16R

Greene, Graham (Henry)
          1904-....... CLC 1, 3, 6, 9, 14, 18, 27,
                                              37
     See also CA 13-16R
     See also SATA 20
     See also DLB 13, 15
     See also DLB-Y 85
     See also AITN 2

Gregor, Arthur 1923-..............CLC 9
     See also CANR 11
     See also CA 25-28R
     See also SATA 36

Gregory, Lady (Isabella Augusta Persse)
          1852-1932.................. TCLC 1
     See also CA 104
     See also DLB 10

Grendon, Stephen 1909-1971
     See Derleth, August (William)

Greve, Felix Paul Berthold Friedrich
          1879-1948

Grey, (Pearl) Zane
          1872?-1939................. TCLC 6
     See also CA 104
     See also DLB 9

Grieg, (Johan) Nordahl (Brun)
          1902-1943.................. TCLC 10
     See also CA 107

Grieve, C(hristopher) M(urray) 1892-1978
     See MacDiarmid, Hugh
     See also CA 5-8R
     See also obituary CA 85-88

Griffin, Gerald 1803-1840 .... NCLC 7

Griffin, Peter 1942-......... CLC 39 (398)

Griffiths, Trevor 1935-...........CLC 13
     See also CA 97-100
     See also DLB 13

Grigson, Geoffrey (Edward Harvey)
          1905-1985............ CLC 7, 39 (330)
     See also CANR 20
     See also CA 25-28R
     See also obituary CA 118
     See also DLB 27

Grillparzer, Franz 1791-1872 ..... NCLC 1

Grimm, Jakob (Ludwig) Karl 1785-1863
     See Grimm, Jakob (Ludwig) Karl and
          Grimm, Wilhelm Karl

Grimm, Jakob (Ludwig) Karl 1785-1863
     and Grimm, Wilhelm Karl
          1786-1859.................. NCLC 3
     See also SATA 22

Grimm, Wilhelm Karl 1786-1859
     See Grimm, Jakob (Ludwig) Karl and
          Grimm, Wilhelm Karl

Grimm, Wilhelm Karl 1786-1859 and
          Grimm, Jakob (Ludwig) Karl
          1785-1863
     See Grimm, Jakob (Ludwig) Karl and
          Grimm, Wilhelm Karl

Grimmelshausen, Johann Jakob Christoffel
     von 1621-1676................. LC 6

Grindel, Eugene 1895-1952
     See also CA 104

Grossman, Vasily (Semënovich)
          1905-1964....................CLC 41

Grove, Frederick Philip
          1879-1948.................. TCLC 4
     See also Greve, Felix Paul Berthold
          Friedrich

Grumbach, Doris (Isaac)
          1918-.................... CLC 13, 22
     See also CAAS 2
     See also CANR 9
     See also CA 5-8R

Grundtvig, Nicolai Frederik Severin
          1783-1872.................. NCLC 1

Grunwald, Lisa 1959-........ CLC 44 (49)

Guare, John 1938-.......... CLC 8, 14, 29
     See also CA 73-76
     See also DLB 7

Gudjonsson, Halldór Kiljan 1902-
     See Laxness, Halldór (Kiljan)
     See also CA 103

Guest, Barbara 1920- .... CLC 34 (441)
     See also CANR 11
     See also CA 25-28R
     See also DLB 5

Guest, Judith (Ann) 1936- ...... CLC 8, 30
     See also CANR 15
     See also CA 77-80

Guild, Nicholas M. 1944-.........CLC 33
     See also CA 93-96

Harris, Mark 1922-..............CLC 19
See also CAAS 3
See also CANR 2
See also CA 5-8R
See also DLB 2
See also DLB-Y 80

Harris, (Theodore) Wilson
1921-.......................CLC 25
See also CANR 11
See also CA 65-68

Harrison, Harry (Max) 1925- ......CLC 42
See also CANR 5
See also CA 1-4R
See also SATA 4
See also DLB 8

Harrison, James (Thomas) 1937-
See Harrison, Jim
See also CANR 8
See also CA 13-16R

Harrison, Jim 1937- .... CLC 6, 14, 33
See also Harrison, James (Thomas)
See also DLB-Y 82

Harrison, Tony 1937-..............CLC 43
See also CA 65-68
See also DLB 40

Harriss, Will(ard Irvin)
1922-................... CLC 34 (192)
See also CA 111

Harte, (Francis) Bret(t)
1836?-1902...............TCLC 1, 25
See also CA 104
See also SATA 26
See also DLB 12

Hartley, L(eslie) P(oles)
1895-1972 .... CLC 2, 22
See also CA 45-48
See also obituary CA 37-40R
See also DLB 15

Hartman, Geoffrey H. 1929-.......CLC 27
See also CA 117

Haruf, Kent 19??- .... CLC 34 (57)

Harwood, Ronald 1934- ....CLC 32
See also CANR 4
See also CA 1-4R
See also DLB 13

Hašek, Jaroslav (Matej Frantisek)
1883-1923................... TCLC 4
See also CA 104

Hass, Robert 1941- ...... CLC 18, 39 (145)
See also CA 111

Hastings, Selina 19??-....... CLC 44 (482)

Hauptmann, Gerhart (Johann Robert)
1862-1946.................. TCLC 4
See also CA 104

Havel, Václav 1936- ....CLC 25
See also CA 104

Haviaras, Stratis 1935-............CLC 33
See also CA 105

Hawkes, John (Clendennin Burne, Jr.)
1925-......CLC 1, 2, 3, 4, 7, 9, 14, 15,
                                        27
See also CANR 2
See also CA 1-4R
See also DLB 2, 7
See also DLB-Y 80

Hawthorne, Julian 1846-1934 .... TCLC 25

Hawthorne, Nathaniel
1804-1864.............NCLC 2, 10, 17
See also YABC 2
See also DLB 1

Hayashi, Fumiko 1904-1951 ..... TCLC 27

Haycraft, Anna 19??-
See Ellis, Alice Thomas

Hayden, Robert (Earl)
1913-1980............CLC 5, 9, 14, 37
See also CA 69-72
See also obituary CA 97-100
See also CABS 2
See also SATA 19
See also obituary SATA 26
See also DLB 5
See also CDALB 1941-1968

Hayman, Ronald 1932-...... CLC 44 (493)

Haywood, Eliza (Fowler)
1693?-1756.....................LC 1
See also DLB 39

Hazzard, Shirley 1931-............CLC 18
See also CANR 4
See also CA 9-12R
See also DLB-Y 82

H(ilda) D(oolittle)
1886-1961..........CLC 3, 8, 14, 31,
                                   34 (441)
See also Doolittle, Hilda

Head, Bessie 1937-................CLC 25
See also CA 29-32R
See also obituary CA 109

Headon, (Nicky) Topper 1956?-
See The Clash

Heaney, Seamus (Justin)
1939-........... CLC 5, 7, 14, 25, 37
See also CA 85-88
See also DLB 40

Hearn, (Patricio) Lafcadio (Tessima Carlos)
1850-1904................... TCLC 9
See also CA 105
See also DLB 12

Heat Moon, William Least
1939-.......................CLC 29

Hébert, Anne 1916-........ CLC 4, 13, 29
See also CA 85-88

Hecht, Anthony (Evan)
1923-................. CLC 8, 13, 19
See also CANR 6
See also CA 9-12R
See also DLB 5

Hecht, Ben 1894-1964..............CLC 8
See also CA 85-88
See also DLB 7, 9, 25, 26, 28

Hedayat, Sadeq 1903-1951....... TCLC 21
See also CA 120

Heidegger, Martin 1889-1976 ......CLC 24
See also CA 81-84
See also obituary CA 65-68

Heidenstam, (Karl Gustaf) Verner von
1859-1940................... TCLC 5
See also CA 104

Heifner, Jack 1946-................CLC 11
See also CA 105

Heijermans, Herman
1864-1924.................. TCLC 24

Heilbrun, Carolyn G(old)
1926-.......................CLC 25
See also CANR 1
See also CA 45-48

Heine, Harry 1797-1856
See Heine, Heinrich

Heine, Heinrich 1797-1856........ NCLC 4

Heiney, Donald (William) 1921-
See Harris, MacDonald
See also CANR 3
See also CA 1-4R

Heinlein, Robert A(nson)
1907-............. CLC 1, 3, 8, 14, 26
See also CANR 1
See also CA 1-4R
See also SATA 9
See also DLB 8

Heller, Joseph
1923-........... CLC 1, 3, 5, 8, 11, 36
See also CANR 8
See also CA 5-8R
See also DLB 2, 28
See also DLB-Y 80
See also AITN 1

Hellman, Lillian (Florence)
1905?-1984........CLC 2, 4, 8, 14, 18,
                              34 (347), 44 (526)
See also CA 13-16R
See also obituary CA 112
See also DLB 7
See also DLB-Y 84
See also AITN 1, 2

Helprin, Mark 1947-.....CLC 7, 10, 22, 32
See also CA 81-84
See also DLB-Y 85

Hemingway, Ernest (Miller)
1899-1961...... CLC 1, 3, 6, 8, 10, 13,
                19, 30, 34 (477), 39 (398; 427), 41,
                                      44 (514)
See also SSC 1
See also CA 77-80
See also DLB 4, 9
See also DLB-Y 81
See also DLB-DS 1
See also AITN 2

Hempel, Amy 1951-.......... CLC 39 (67)
See also CA 118

Henley, Beth 1952- ....CLC 23
See also Henley, Elizabeth Becker
See also DLB-Y 86

Henley, Elizabeth Becker 1952-
See Henley, Beth
See also CA 107

Henley, William Ernest
1849-1903................... TCLC 8
See also CA 105
See also DLB 19

Hennissart, Martha
See Lathen, Emma
See also CA 85-88

Henry, O. 1862-1910 .... TCLC 1, 19
See also Porter, William Sydney

Hentoff, Nat(han Irving) 1925-.....CLC 26
See also CLR 1
See also CANR 5
See also CA 1-4R
See also SATA 27, 42

Author Index

Johnson, Diane 1934- . . . . **CLC 5, 13**
See also CANR 17
See also CA 41-44R
See also DLB-Y 80

Johnson, Eyvind (Olof Verner)
1900-1976 . . . . **CLC 14**
See also CA 73-76
See also obituary CA 69-72

Johnson, James Weldon
1871-1938 . . . . **TCLC 3, 19**
See also Johnson, James William
See also CA 104

Johnson, James William 1871-1938
See Johnson, James Weldon
See also SATA 31

Johnson, Lionel (Pigot)
1867-1902 . . . . **TCLC 19**
See also CA 117
See also DLB 19

Johnson, Marguerita 1928-
See Angelou, Maya

Johnson, Pamela Hansford
1912-1981 . . . . **CLC 1, 7, 27**
See also CANR 2
See also CA 1-4R
See also obituary CA 104
See also DLB 15

Johnson, Uwe
1934-1984 . . . . **CLC 5, 10, 15, 40**
See also CANR 1
See also CA 1-4R
See also obituary CA 112

Johnston, Jennifer 1930- . . . . **CLC 7**
See also CA 85-88
See also DLB 14

Jolley, Elizabeth 1923- . . . . **CLC 46**

Jones, D(ouglas) G(ordon)
1929- . . . . **CLC 10**
See also CANR 13
See also CA 29-32R
See also CA 113
See also DLB 53

Jones, David
1895-1974 . . . . **CLC 2, 4, 7, 13, 42**
See also CA 9-12R
See also obituary CA 53-56
See also DLB 20

Jones, David Robert 1947-
See Bowie, David
See also CA 103

Jones, Diana Wynne 1934- . . . . **CLC 26**
See also CANR 4
See also CA 49-52
See also SATA 9

Jones, Gayl 1949- . . . . **CLC 6, 9**
See also CA 77-80
See also DLB 33

Jones, James
1921-1977 . . . . . . **CLC 1, 3, 10, 39** (404)
See also CANR 6
See also CA 1-4R
See also obituary CA 69-72
See also DLB 2
See also AITN 1, 2

Jones, (Everett) LeRoi
1934- . . . . **CLC 1, 2, 3, 5, 10, 14, 33**
See also Baraka, Amiri
See also Baraka, Imamu Amiri
See also CA 21-24R

Jones, Madison (Percy, Jr.)
1925- . . . . **CLC 4**
See also CANR 7
See also CA 13-16R

Jones, Mervyn 1922- . . . . **CLC 10**
See also CAAS 5
See also CANR 1
See also CA 45-48

Jones, Mick 1956?-
See The Clash

Jones, Nettie 19??- . . . . **CLC 34** (67)

Jones, Preston 1936-1979 . . . . **CLC 10**
See also CA 73-76
See also obituary CA 89-92
See also DLB 7

Jones, Robert F(rancis) 1934- . . . . **CLC 7**
See also CANR 2
See also CA 49-52

Jones, Terry 1942?-
See Monty Python
See also CA 112, 116

Jong, Erica 1942- . . . . **CLC 4, 6, 8, 18**
See also CA 73-76
See also DLB 2, 5, 28
See also AITN 1

Jonson, Ben(jamin) 1572-1637 . . . . **LC 6**

Jordan, June 1936- . . . . **CLC 5, 11, 23**
See also CLR 10
See also CA 33-36R
See also SATA 4
See also DLB 38

Jordan, Pat(rick M.) 1941- . . . . **CLC 37**
See also CA 33-36R

Josipovici, Gabriel (David)
1940- . . . . **CLC 6, 43**
See also CA 37-40R
See also DLB 14

Joubert, Joseph 1754-1824 . . . . **NCLC 9**

Joyce, James (Augustine Aloysius)
1882-1941 . . . . **TCLC 3, 8, 16, 26**
See also CA 104
See also DLB 10, 19, 36

József, Attila 1905-1937 . . . . **TCLC 22**
See also CA 116

Juana Inés de la Cruz
1651?-1695 . . . . **LC 5**

Julian of Norwich 1342?-1416? . . . . . . **LC 6**

Just, Ward S(wift) 1935- . . . . **CLC 4, 27**
See also CA 25-28R

Justice, Donald (Rodney)
1925- . . . . **CLC 6, 19**
See also CA 5-8R
See also DLB-Y 33

Kacew, Romain 1914-1980
See Gary, Romain
See also CA 108
See also obituary CA 102

Kacewgary, Romain 1914-1980
See Gary, Romain

Kafka, Franz
1883-1924 . . . . **TCLC 2, 6, 13**
See also CA 105

Kahn, Roger 1927- . . . . **CLC 30**
See also CA 25-28R
See also SATA 37

Kaiser, (Friedrich Karl) Georg
1878-1945 . . . . **TCLC 9**
See also CA 106

Kaletski, Alexander 1946- . . . . **CLC 39** (72)
See also CA 118

Kallman, Chester (Simon)
1921-1975 . . . . **CLC 2**
See also CANR 3
See also CA 45-48
See also obituary CA 53-56

Kaminsky, Melvin 1926-
See Brooks, Mel
See also CANR 16

Kane, Paul 1941-
See Simon, Paul

Kanin, Garson 1912- . . . . **CLC 22**
See also CANR 7
See also CA 5-8R
See also DLB 7
See also AITN 1

Kaniuk, Yoram 1930- . . . . **CLC 19**

Kantor, MacKinlay 1904-1977 . . . . . . **CLC 7**
See also CA 61-64
See also obituary CA 73-76
See also DLB 9

Karamzin, Nikolai Mikhailovich
1766-1826 . . . . **NCLC 3**

Karapánou, Margaríta 1946- . . . . **CLC 13**
See also CA 101

Karl, Frederick R(obert)
1927- . . . . **CLC 34** (551)
See also CANR 3
See also CA 5-8R

Kassef, Romain 1914-1980
See Gary, Romain

Kauffman, Janet 1945- . . . . **CLC 42**
See also CA 117
See also DLB-Y 86

Kaufman, George S(imon)
1889-1961 . . . . **CLC 38**
See also CA 108
See also obituary CA 93-96
See also DLB 7

Kaufman, Sue 1926-1977 . . . . **CLC 3, 8**
See also Barondess, Sue K(aufman)

Kavan, Anna 1904-1968 . . . . **CLC 5, 13**
See also Edmonds, Helen (Woods)
See also CANR 6

Kavanagh, Patrick (Joseph Gregory)
1905-1967 . . . . **CLC 22**
See also obituary CA 25-28R
See also DLB 15, 20

Kawabata, Yasunari
1899-1972 . . . . **CLC 2, 5, 9, 18**
See also CA 93-96
See also obituary CA 33-36R

Kaye, M(ary) M(argaret)
1909?- . . . . **CLC 28**
See also CA 89-92

Kaye, Mollie 1909?-
See Kaye, M(ary) M(argaret)

Kaye-Smith, Sheila
1887-1956 . . . . **TCLC 20**
See also CA 118
See also DLB 36

Author Index

Kleist, Heinrich von
1777-1811.................. NCLC 2

Klimentev, Andrei Platonovich 1899-1951
See Platonov, Andrei (Platonovich)
See also CA 108

Klinger, Friedrich Maximilian von
1752-1831.................. NCLC 1

Klopstock, Friedrich Gottlieb
1724-1803.................. NCLC 11

Knebel, Fletcher 1911- ....CLC 14
See also CAAS 3
See also CANR 1
See also CA 1-4R
See also SATA 36
See also AITN 1

Knight, Etheridge 1931-...........CLC 40
See also CA 21-24R
See also DLB 41

Knight, Sarah Kemble 1666-1727..... LC 7
See also DLB 24

Knowles, John 1926-......CLC 1, 4, 10, 26
See also CA 17-20R
See also SATA 8
See also DLB 6

Koch, C(hristopher) J(ohn)
1932-......................CLC 42

Koch, Kenneth
1925-.............CLC 5, 8, 44 (239)
See also CANR 6
See also CA 1-4R
See also DLB 5

Kock, Charles Paul de
1794-1871.................. NCLC 16

Koestler, Arthur
1905-1983...... CLC 1, 3, 6, 8, 15, 33
See also CANR 1
See also CA 1-4R
See also obituary CA 109
See also DLB-Y 83

Kohout, Pavel 1928-..............CLC 13
See also CANR 3
See also CA 45-48

Konrád, György 1933- .... CLC 4, 10
See also CA 85-88

Konwicki, Tadeusz 1926-....... CLC 8, 28
See also CA 101

Kopit, Arthur (Lee)
1937-.................. CLC 1, 18, 33
See also CA 81-84
See also DLB 7
See also AITN 1

Kops, Bernard 1926-..............CLC 4
See also CA 5-8R
See also DLB 13

Kornbluth, C(yril) M.
1923-1958.................. TCLC 8
See also CA 105
See also DLB 8

Korolenko, Vladimir (Galaktionovich)
1853-1921............... TCLC 22

Kosinski, Jerzy (Nikodem)
1933-......CLC 1, 2, 3, 6, 10, 15
See also CANR 9
See also CA 17-20R
See also DLB 2
See also DLB-Y 82

Kostelanetz, Richard (Cory)
1940-....................CLC 28
See also CA 13-16R

Kostrowitzki, Wilhelm Apollinaris de
1880-1918
See Apollinaire, Guillaume
See also CA 104

Kotlowitz, Robert 1924-...........CLC 4
See also CA 33-36R

Kotzwinkle, William
1938-.................. CLC 5, 14, 35
See also CLR 6
See also CANR 3
See also CA 45-48
See also SATA 24

Kozol, Jonathan 1936- ....CLC 17
See also CANR 16
See also CA 61-64

Kozoll, Michael 1940?-
See Bochco, Steven and Kozoll, Michael

Kramer, Kathryn 19??- ...... CLC 34 (74)

Kramer, Larry 1935- ....CLC 42

Krasicki, Ignacy 1735-1801 .... NCLC 8

Krasiński, Zygmunt
1812-1859.................. NCLC 4

Kraus, Karl 1874-1936........... TCLC 5
See also CA 104

Krévé, Vincas 1882-1959 .... TCLC 27

Kristofferson, Kris 1936-..........CLC 26
See also CA 104

Krleža, Miroslav 1893-1981........CLC 8
See also CA 97-100
See also obituary CA 105

Kroetsch, Robert 1927-....... CLC 5, 23
See also CANR 8
See also CA 17-20R
See also DLB 53

Kroetz, Franz Xaver 1946- ....CLC 41

Krotkov, Yuri 1917-..............CLC 19
See also CA 102

Krumgold, Joseph (Quincy)
1908-1980...................CLC 12
See also CANR 7
See also CA 9-12R
See also obituary CA 101
See also SATA 1
See also obituary SATA 23
See also SATA 48

Krutch, Joseph Wood
1893-1970...................CLC 24
See also CANR 4
See also CA 1-4R
See also obituary CA 25-28R

Krylov, Ivan Andreevich
1768?-1844.................. NCLC 1

Kubin, Alfred 1877-1959 .... TCLC 23
See also CA 112

Kubrick, Stanley 1928-...........CLC 16
See also CA 81-84
See also DLB 26

Kumin, Maxine (Winokur)
1925-................ CLC 5, 13, 28
See also CANR 1
See also CA 1-4R
See also SATA 12
See also DLB 5
See also AITN 2

Kundera, Milan
1929-.............CLC 4, 9, 19, 32
See also CANR 19
See also CA 85-88

Kunitz, Stanley J(asspon)
1905-............... CLC 6, 11, 14
See also CA 41-44R
See also DLB 48

Kunze, Reiner 1933-..............CLC 10
See also CA 93-96

Kuprin, Aleksandr (Ivanovich)
1870-1938.................. TCLC 5
See also CA 104

Kurosawa, Akira 1910-...........CLC 16
See also CA 101

Kuttner, Henry 1915-1958....... TCLC 10
See also CA 107
See also DLB 8

Kuzma, Greg 1944-................CLC 7
See also CA 33-36R

Labrunie, Gérard 1808-1855
See Nerval, Gérard de

**Laclos, Pierre Ambroise François Choderlos
de** 1741-1803 .... NCLC 4

**La Fayette, Marie (Madelaine Pioche de la
Vergne, Comtesse) de**
1634-1693.................... LC 2

Lafayette, Rene
See also Hubbard, L(afayette) Ron(ald)

Laforgue, Jules 1860-1887....... NCLC 5

Lagerkvist, Pär (Fabian)
1891-1974.............. CLC 7, 10, 13
See also CA 85-88
See also obituary CA 49-52

Lagerlöf, Selma (Ottiliana Lovisa)
1858-1940.................. TCLC 4
See also CLR 7
See also CA 108
See also SATA 15

La Guma, (Justin) Alex(ander)
1925-1985....................CLC 19
See also CA 49-52
See also obituary CA 118

Lamartine, Alphonse (Marie Louis Prat) de
1790-1869.................. NCLC 11

Lamb, Charles 1775-1834 .... NCLC 10
See also SATA 17

Lamming, George (William)
1927-.................... CLC 2, 4
See also CA 85-88

LaMoore, Louis Dearborn 1908?-
See L'Amour, Louis (Dearborn)

L'Amour, Louis (Dearborn)
1908-......................CLC 25
See also CANR 3
See also CA 1-4R
See also DLB-Y 80
See also AITN 2

**Lampedusa, (Prince) Giuseppe (Maria
Fabrizio) Tomasi di**
1896-1957.................. TCLC 13
See also CA 111

Lancaster, Bruce 1896-1963 ....CLC 36
See also CAP-1
See also CA 9-12R
See also SATA 9

L'Engle, Madeleine 1918-.........CLC 12
   See also CLR 1, 14
   See also CANR 3
   See also CA 1-4R
   See also SATA 1, 27
   See also DLB 52
   See also AITN 2

Lengyel, József 1896-1975 ....CLC 7
   See also CA 85-88
   See also obituary CA 57-60

Lennon, John (Ono)
   1940-1980...................CLC 35
   See also Lennon, John (Ono) and
     McCartney, Paul
   See also CA 102

Lennon, John (Ono) 1940-1980 and
   McCartney, Paul 1942-.......CLC 12

Lennon, John Winston 1940-1980
   See Lennon, John (Ono)

Lentricchia, Frank (Jr.)
   1940-.................. CLC 34 (571)
   See also CA 25-28R

Lenz, Siegfried 1926- ....CLC 27
   See also CA 89-92

Leonard, Elmore
   1925-.............. CLC 28, 34 (212)
   See also CANR 12
   See also CA 81-84
   See also AITN 1

Leonard, Hugh 1926- ....CLC 19
   See also Byrne, John Keyes
   See also DLB 13

Lerman, Eleanor 1952-.............CLC 9
   See also CA 85-88

Lermontov, Mikhail Yuryevich
   1814-1841................... NCLC 5

Leroux, Gaston 1868-1927...... TCLC 25
   See also CA 108

Lesage, Alain-René 1668-1747....... LC 2

Lessing, Doris (May)
   1919-....... CLC 1, 2, 3, 6, 10, 15, 22,
                 40
   See also CA 9-12R
   See also DLB 15
   See also DLB-Y 85

Lester, Richard 1932-.............CLC 20

Leverson, Ada 1865-1936....... TCLC 18
   See also CA 117

Levertov, Denise
   1923-.........CLC 1, 2, 3, 5, 8, 15, 28
   See also CANR 3
   See also CA 1-4R
   See also DLB 5

Levi, Peter (Chad Tiger) 1931-.....CLC 41
   See also CA 5-8R
   See also DLB 40

Levi, Primo 1919- ....CLC 37
   See also CANR 12
   See also CA 13-16R

Levin, Ira 1929-............... CLC 3, 6
   See also CANR 17
   See also CA 21-24R

Levin, Meyer 1905-1981............CLC 7
   See also CANR 15
   See also CA 9-12R
   See also obituary CA 104
   See also SATA 21
   See also obituary SATA 27
   See also DLB 9, 28
   See also DLB-Y 81
   See also AITN 1

Levine, Philip
   1928-..........CLC 2, 4, 5, 9, 14, 33
   See also CANR 9
   See also CA 9-12R
   See also DLB 5

Lévi-Strauss, Claude 1908- ....CLC 38
   See also CANR 6
   See also CA 1-4R

Levitin, Sonia 1934- ....CLC 17
   See also CANR 14
   See also CA 29-32R
   See also SAAS 2
   See also SATA 4

Lewis, Alun 1915-1944........... TCLC 3
   See also CA 104
   See also DLB 20

Lewis, C(ecil) Day 1904-1972
   See Day Lewis, C(ecil)

Lewis, C(live) S(taples)
   1898-1963........ CLC 1, 3, 6, 14, 27
   See also CLR 3
   See also CA 81-84
   See also SATA 13
   See also DLB 15

Lewis, (Harry) Sinclair
   1885-1951.............TCLC 4, 13, 23
   See also CA 104
   See also DLB 9
   See also DLB-DS 1

Lewis (Winters), Janet 1899-.......CLC 41
   See also Winters, Janet Lewis

Lewis, Matthew Gregory
   1775-1818.................. NCLC 11
   See also DLB 39

Lewis, (Percy) Wyndham
   1882?-1957................TCLC 2, 9
   See also CA 104
   See also DLB 15

Lewisohn, Ludwig 1883-1955 .... TCLC 19
   See also CA 107
   See also DLB 4, 9, 28

Lezama Lima, José
   1910-1976................ CLC 4, 10
   See also CA 77-80

Li Fei-kan 1904-
   See Pa Chin
   See also CA 105

Lie, Jonas (Lauritz Idemil)
   1833-1908................. TCLC 5
   See also CA 115

Lieber, Joel 1936-1971 ....CLC 6
   See also CA 73-76
   See also obituary CA 29-32R

Lieber, Stanley Martin 1922-
   See Lee, Stan

Lieberman, Laurence (James)
   1935-................... CLC 4, 36
   See also CANR 8
   See also CA 17-20R

Lightfoot, Gordon (Meredith)
   1938-.......................CLC 26
   See also CA 109

Ligotti, Thomas 1953-........ CLC 44 (53)

Liliencron, Detlev von
   1844-1909.................. TCLC 18
   See also CA 117

Lima, José Lezama 1910-1976
   See Lezama Lima, José

Lima Barreto, (Alfonso Henriques de)
   1881-1922.................. TCLC 23
   See also CA 117

Lind, Jakov 1927-.........CLC 1, 2, 4, 27
   See also Landwirth, Heinz
   See also CAAS 4
   See also CA 9-12R

Lindsay, David 1876-1945....... TCLC 15
   See also CA 113

Lindsay, (Nicholas) Vachel
   1879-1931.................. TCLC 17
   See also CA 114
   See also SATA 40
   See also DLB 54

Lipsyte, Robert (Michael)
   1938-.......................CLC 21
   See also CANR 8
   See also CA 17-20R
   See also SATA 5

Lish, Gordon (Jay) 1934-.........CLC 45
   See also CA 113, 117

Lispector, Clarice 1925-1977......CLC 43
   See also obituary CA 116

Littell, Robert 1935?- ....CLC 42
   See also CA 109, 112

Liu E 1857-1909 .... TCLC 15
   See also CA 115

Lively, Penelope 1933- ....CLC 32
   See also CLR 7
   See also CA 41-44R
   See also SATA 7
   See also DLB 14

Livesay, Dorothy 1909-........ CLC 4, 15
   See also CA 25-28R
   See also AITN 2

Llewellyn, Richard 1906-1983.......CLC 7
   See also Llewellyn Lloyd, Richard (Dafydd
     Vyvyan)
   See also DLB 15

Llewellyn Lloyd, Richard (Dafydd Vyvyan)
   1906-1983
   See Llewellyn, Richard
   See also CANR 7
   See also CA 53-56
   See also obituary CA 111
   See also SATA 11, 37

Llosa, Mario Vargas 1936-
   See Vargas Llosa, Mario

Lloyd, Richard Llewellyn 1906-
   See Llewellyn, Richard

Locke, John 1632-1704..............LC 7
   See also DLB 31

Lockhart, John Gibson
   1794-1854.................. NCLC 6

Lodge, David (John) 1935-........CLC 36
   See also CANR 19
   See also CA 17-20R
   See also DLB 14

Author Index

Macpherson, (Jean) Jay 1931-......CLC 14
  See also CA 5-8R
  See also DLB 53

MacShane, Frank 1927-..... CLC 39 (404)
  See also CANR 3
  See also CA 11-12R

Macumber, Mari 1896-1966
  See Sandoz, Mari (Susette)

Madden, (Jerry) David
    1933-.................... CLC 5, 15
  See also CAAS 3
  See also CANR 4
  See also CA 1-4R
  See also DLB 6

Madhubuti, Haki R. 1942-.........CLC 6
  See also Lee, Don L.
  See also DLB 5, 41

Maeterlinck, Maurice
    1862-1949.................. TCLC 3
  See also CA 104

Maginn, William 1794-1842...... NCLC 8

Mahapatra, Jayanta 1928-.........CLC 33
  See also CANR 15
  See also CA 73-76

Mahon, Derek 1941-..............CLC 27
  See also CA 113
  See also DLB 40

Mailer, Norman
    1923-......CLC 1, 2, 3, 4, 5, 8, 11, 14,
                          28, 39 (416)
  See also CA 9-12R
  See also CABS 1
  See also DLB 2, 16, 28
  See also DLB-Y 80, 83
  See also DLB-DS 3
  See also AITN 2

Mais, Roger 1905-1955........... TCLC 8
  See also CA 105

Major, Clarence 1936- .... CLC 3, 19
  See also CANR 13
  See also CA 21-24R
  See also DLB 33

Major, Kevin 1949-..............CLC 26
  See also CLR 11
  See also CA 97-100
  See also SATA 32

Malamud, Bernard
    1914-1986..... CLC 1, 2, 3, 5, 8, 9, 11,
                          18, 27, 44 (411)
  See also CA 5-8R
  See also obituary CA 118
  See also CABS 1
  See also DLB 2, 28
  See also DLB-Y 80, 86
  See also CDALB 1941-1968

Malherbe, François de 1555-1628..... LC 5

Mallarmé, Stéphane
    1842-1898.................. NCLC 4

Mallet-Joris, Françoise 1930-.......CLC 11
  See also CANR 17
  See also CA 65-68

Maloff, Saul 1922-.................CLC 5
  See also CA 33-36R

Malone, Michael (Christopher)
    1942-.......................CLC 43
  See also CANR 14
  See also CA 77-80

Malouf, David 1934-..............CLC 28

Malraux, (Georges-) André
    1901-1976........ CLC 1, 4, 9, 13, 15
  See also CAP 2
  See also CA 21-24R
  See also obituary CA 69-72

Malzberg, Barry N. 1939- ....CLC 7
  See also CAAS 4
  See also CANR 16
  See also CA 61-64
  See also DLB 8

Mamet, David (Alan)
    1947-........ CLC 9, 15, 34 (217), 46
  See also CANR 15
  See also CA 81-84
  See also DLB 7

Mamoulian, Rouben 1898-.........CLC 16
  See also CA 25-28R

Mandelstam, Osip (Emilievich)
    1891?-1938?.............. TCLC 2, 6
  See also CA 104

Mandiargues, André Pieyre de
    1909-.......................CLC 41
  See also CA 103

Manley, (Mary) Delariviere
    1672?-1724................... LC 1
  See also DLB 39

Mann, (Luiz) Heinrich
    1871-1950.................. TCLC 9
  See also CA 106

Mann, Thomas
    1875-1955......... TCLC 2, 8, 14, 21
  See also CA 104

Manning, Frederic
    1882-1935................. TCLC 25

Manning, Olivia 1915-1980 ..... CLC 5, 19
  See also CA 5-8R
  See also obituary CA 101

Mano, D. Keith 1942-......... CLC 2, 10
  See also CA 25-28R
  See also DLB 6

Mansfield, Katherine
    1888-1923................. TCLC 2, 8
  See also CA 104

Manso, Peter 1940-......... CLC 39 (416)
  See also CA 29-32R

Marcel, Gabriel (Honore)
    1889-1973...................CLC 15
  See also CA 102
  See also obituary CA 45-48

Marchbanks, Samuel 1913-
  See Davies, (William) Robertson

Marinetti, F(ilippo) T(ommaso)
    1876-1944................. TCLC 10
  See also CA 107

Marivaux, Pierre Carlet de Chamblain de
    (1688-1763) .... LC 4

Markandaya, Kamala 1924- .... CLC 8, 38
  See also Taylor, Kamala (Purnaiya)

Markfield, Wallace (Arthur)
    1926-.......................CLC 8
  See also CAAS 3
  See also CA 69-72
  See also DLB 2, 28

Markham, Robert 1922-
  See Amis, Kingsley (William)

Marks, J. 1942-
  See Highwater, Jamake

Marley, Bob 1945-1981 ....CLC 17
  See also Marley, Robert Nesta

Marley, Robert Nesta 1945-1981
  See Marley, Bob
  See also CA 107
  See also obituary CA 103

Marmontel, Jean-François
    1723-1799..................... LC 2

Marquand, John P(hillips)
    1893-1960................. CLC 2, 10
  See also CA 85-88
  See also DLB 9

Márquez, Gabriel García 1928-
  See García Márquez, Gabriel

Marquis, Don(ald Robert Perry)
    1878-1937.................. TCLC 7
  See also CA 104
  See also DLB 11, 25

Marryat, Frederick 1792-1848 .... NCLC 3
  See also DLB 21

Marsh, (Edith) Ngaio
    1899-1982....................CLC 7
  See also CANR 6
  See also CA 9-12R

Marshall, Garry 1935?- ....CLC 17
  See also CA 111

Marshall, Paule 1929-..............CLC 27
  See also CA 77-80
  See also DLB 33

Marsten, Richard 1926-
  See Hunter, Evan

Martin, Steve 1945?-..............CLC 30
  See also CA 97-100

Martin du Gard, Roger
    1881-1958................. TCLC 24
  See also CA 118

Martínez Ruiz, José 1874-1967
  See Azorín
  See also CA 93-96

Martínez Sierra, Gregorio 1881-1947
  See Martínez Sierra, Gregorio and Martínez
    Sierra, María (de la O'LeJárraga)
  See also CA 104, 115

Martínez Sierra, Gregorio 1881-1947 and
    Martínez Sierra, María (de la
    O'LeJárraga) 1880?-1974 .... TCLC 6

Martínez Sierra, María (de la O'LeJárraga)
    1880?-1974
  See Martínez Sierra, Gregorio and Martínez
    Sierra, María (de la O'LeJárraga)
  See also obituary CA 115

Martínez Sierra, María (de la O'LeJárraga)
    1880?-1974 and Martínez Sierra,
    Gregorio 1881-1947
  See Martínez Sierra, Gregorio and Martínez
    Sierra, María (de la O'LeJárraga)

Martinson, Harry (Edmund)
    1904-1978...................CLC 14
  See also CA 77-80

Marvell, Andrew 1621-1678 .... LC 4

Marx, Karl (Heinrich)
    1818-1883................. NCLC 17

Masaoka Shiki 1867-1902....... TCLC 18

Mistral, Gabriela 1889-1957 ...... TCLC 2
  See also CA 104

Mitchell, James Leslie 1901-1935
  See Gibbon, Lewis Grassic
  See also CA 104
  See also DLB 15

Mitchell, Joni 1943-..............CLC 12
  See also CA 112

Mitchell (Marsh), Margaret (Munnerlyn)
  1900-1949.................. TCLC 11
  See also CA 109
  See also DLB 9

Mitchell, W(illiam) O(rmond)
  1914-.....................CLC 25
  See also CANR 15
  See also CA 77-80

Mitford, Mary Russell
  1787-1855.................. NCLC 4

Mitford, Nancy
  1904-1973.............. CLC 44 (482)

Mo, Timothy 1950-...............CLC 46
  See also CA 117

Modiano, Patrick (Jean) 1945- .....CLC 18
  See also CANR 17
  See also CA 85-88

Modarressi, Taghi 1931-...... CLC 44 (82)

Mofolo, Thomas (Mokopu)
  1876-1948.................. TCLC 22

Mohr, Nicholasa 1935-............CLC 12 '
  See also CANR 1
  See also CA 49-52
  See also SATA 8

Mojtabai, A(nn) G(race)
  1938-..................CLC 5, 9, 15, 29
  See also CA 85-88

Molnár, Ferenc 1878-1952...... TCLC 20
  See also CA 109

Momaday, N(avarre) Scott
  1934-.................. CLC 2, 19
  See also CANR 14
  See also CA 25-28R
  See also SATA 30, 48

Monroe, Harriet 1860-1936...... TCLC 12
  See also CA 109
  See also DLB 54

Montagu, Elizabeth 1720-1800 .... NCLC 7

Montague, John (Patrick)
  1929-.................... CLC 13, 46
  See also CANR 9
  See also CA 9-12R
  See also DLB 40

Montale, Eugenio
  1896-1981.............. CLC 7, 9, 18
  See also CA 17-20R
  See also obituary CA 104

Montgomery, Marion (H., Jr.)
  1925-.....................CLC 7
  See also CANR 3
  See also CA 1-4R
  See also DLB 6
  See also AITN 1

Montgomery, Robert Bruce 1921-1978
  See Crispin, Edmund
  See also CA 104

Montherlant, Henri (Milon) de
  1896-1972................ CLC 8, 19
  See also CA 85-88
  See also obituary CA 37-40R

Montisquieu, Charles-Louis de Secondat
  1689-1755.................... LC 7

Monty Python....................CLC 21
  See also Cleese, John

Moodie, Susanna (Strickland)
  1803-1885................ NCLC 14

Mooney, Ted 1951- ....CLC 25

Moorcock, Michael (John)
  1939-.................... CLC 5, 27
  See also CAAS 5
  See also CANR 2, 17
  See also CA 45-48
  See also DLB 14

Moore, Brian
  1921-.........CLC 1, 3, 5, 7, 8, 19, 32
  See also CANR 1
  See also CA 1-4R

Moore, George (Augustus)
  1852-1933.................. TCLC 7
  See also CA 104
  See also DLB 10, 18, 57

Moore, Lorrie 1957- ...... CLC 39 (82), 45
  See also Moore, Marie Lorena

Moore, Marianne (Craig)
  1887-1972...... CLC 1, 2, 4, 8, 10, 13, 19
  See also CANR 3
  See also CA 1-4R
  See also obituary CA 33-36R
  See also DLB 45
  See also SATA 20

Moore, Marie Lorena 1957-
  See Moore, Lorrie
  See also CA 116

Moore, Thomas 1779-1852........ NCLC 6

Morand, Paul 1888-1976..........CLC 41
  See also obituary CA 69-72

Morante, Elsa 1918-1985...........CLC 8
  See also CA 85-88
  See also obituary CA 117

Moravia, Alberto
  1907-.........CLC 2, 7, 11, 18, 27, 46
  See also Pincherle, Alberto

Moréas, Jean 1856-1910......... TCLC 18

Morgan, Berry 1919- ....CLC 6
  See also CA 49-52
  See also DLB 6

Morgan, Edwin (George)
  1920-........................CLC 31
  See also CANR 3
  See also CA 7-8R
  See also DLB 27

Morgan, Frederick 1922-..........CLC 23
  See also CA 17-20R

Morgan, Janet 1945-........ CLC 39 (436)
  See also CA 65-68

Morgan, Robin 1941- ....CLC 2
  See also CA 69-72

Morgenstern, Christian (Otto Josef Wolfgang)
  1871-1914.................. TCLC 8
  See also CA 105

Mori Ōgai 1862-1922 .... TCLC 14
  See also Mori Rintaro

Mori Rintaro 1862-1922
  See Mori Ōgai
  See also CA 110

Mörike, Eduard (Friedrich)
  1804-1875.................. NCLC 10

Moritz, Karl Philipp 1756-1793 ...... LC 2

Morris, Julian 1916-
  See West, Morris L.

Morris, Steveland Judkins 1950-
  See Wonder, Stevie
  See also CA 111

Morris, William 1834-1896 ...... NCLC 4
  See also DLB 18, 35, 57

Morris, Wright (Marion)
  1910-............. CLC 1, 3, 7, 18, 37
  See also CA 9-12R
  See also DLB 2
  See also DLB-Y 81

Morrison, James Douglas 1943-1971
  See Morrison, Jim
  See also CA 73-76

Morrison, Jim 1943-1971..........CLC 17
  See also Morrison, James Douglas

Morrison, Toni 1931- .... CLC 4, 10, 22
  See also CA 29-32R
  See also DLB 6, 33
  See also DLB-Y 81

Morrison, Van 1945-..............CLC 21
  See also CA 116

Mortimer, John (Clifford)
  1923-.................... CLC 28, 43
  See also CA 13-16R
  See also DLB 13

Mortimer, Penelope (Ruth)
  1918-........................CLC 5
  See also CA 57-60

Mosley, Nicholas 1923-............CLC 43
  See also CA 69-72
  See also DLB 14

Moss, Howard 1922-........ CLC 7, 14, 45
  See also CANR 1
  See also CA 1-4R
  See also DLB 5

Motley, Willard (Francis)
  1912-1965....................CLC 18
  See also obituary CA 106
  See also CA 117

Mott, Michael (Charles Alston)
  1930-............... CLC 15, 34 (460)
  See also CANR 7
  See also CA 5-8R

Mowat, Farley (McGill) 1921-......CLC 26
  See also CANR 4
  See also CA 1-4R
  See also SATA 3

Mphahlele, Es'kia 1919-
  See Mphahlele, Ezekiel

Mphahlele, Ezekiel 1919-..........CLC 25
  See also CA 81-84

Mqhayi, S(amuel) E(dward) K(rune Loliwe)
  1875-1945.................. TCLC 25

Mrożek, Sławomir 1930- .... CLC 3, 13
  See also CA 13-16R

Mueller, Lisel 1924- ....CLC 13
See also CA 93-96

Muir, Edwin 1887-1959 ....TCLC 2
See also CA 104
See also DLB 20

Mujica Láinez, Manuel
1910-1984....................CLC 31
See also CA 81-84
See also obituary CA 112

Muldoon, Paul 1951-..............CLC 32
See also CA 113
See also DLB 40

Mulisch, Harry (Kurt Victor)
1927-........................CLC 42
See also CANR 6
See also CA 9-12R

Mull, Martin 1943- ....CLC 17
See also CA 105

Munford, Robert 1637?-1784 ....LC 5
See also DLB 31

Munro, Alice 1931-.........CLC 6, 10, 19
See also CA 33-36R
See also SATA 29
See also DLB 53
See also AITN 2

Munro, H(ector) H(ugh) 1870-1916
See Saki
See also CA 104
See also DLB 34

Murasaki, Lady c. tenth
century ....CMLC 1

Murdoch, (Jean) Iris
1919-......CLC 1, 2, 3, 4, 6, 8, 11, 15,
22, 31
See also CANR 8
See also CA 13-16R
See also DLB 14

Murphy, Richard 1927-...........CLC 41
See also CA 29-32R
See also DLB 40

Murphy, Sylvia 19??- .... CLC 34 (91)

Murray, Les(lie) A(llan) 1938-......CLC 40
See also CANR 11
See also CA 21-24R

Murry, John Middleton
1889-1957..................TCLC 16
See also CA 118

Musgrave, Susan 1951-............CLC 13
See also CA 69-72

Musil, Robert (Edler von)
1880-1942..................TCLC 12
See also CA 109

Musset, (Louis Charles) Alfred de
1810-1857..................NCLC 7

Myers, Walter Dean 1937-........CLC 35
See also CLR 4
See also CANR 20
See also CA 33-36R
See also SAAS 2
See also SATA 27, 41
See also DLB 33

Nabokov, Vladimir (Vladimirovich)
1899-1977...... CLC 1, 2, 3, 6, 8, 11,
15, 23, 44 (463), 46
See also CANR 20
See also CA 5-8R
See also obituary CA 69-72
See also DLB 2
See also DLB-Y 80
See also DLB-DS 3
See also CDALB 1941-1968

Nagy, László 1925-1978 ....CLC 7
See also obituary CA 112

Naipaul, Shiva(dhar Srinivasa)
1945-1985.......... CLC 32, 39 (355)
See also CA 110, 112
See also obituary CA 116
See also DLB-Y 85

Naipaul, V(idiadhar) S(urajprasad)
1932-..........CLC 4, 7, 9, 13, 18, 37
See also CANR 1
See also CA 1-4R
See also DLB-Y 85

Nakos, Ioulia 1899?-
See Nakos, Lilika

Nakos, Lilika 1899?-..............CLC 29

Nakou, Lilika 1899?-
See Nakos, Lilika

Narayan, R(asipuram) K(rishnaswami)
1906-........................ CLC 7, 28
See also CA 81-84

Nash, (Frediric) Ogden
1902-1971....................CLC 23
See also CAP 1
See also CA 13-14
See also obituary CA 29-32R
See also SATA 2, 46
See also DLB 11

Nathan, George Jean
1882-1958.................. TCLC 18
See also CA 114

Natsume, Kinnosuke 1867-1916
See Natsume, Sōseki
See also CA 104

Natsume, Sōseki
1867-1916...............TCLC 2, 10
See also Natsume, Kinnosuke

Natti, (Mary) Lee 1919-
See Kingman, (Mary) Lee
See also CANR 2

Naylor, Gloria 1950-..............CLC 28
See also CA 107

Neihardt, John G(neisenau)
1881-1973....................CLC 32
See also CAP 1
See also CA 13-14
See also DLB 9

Nekrasov, Nikolai Alekseevich
1821-1878.................. NCLC 11

Nelligan, Émile 1879-1941 ......TCLC 14
See also CA 114

Nelson, Willie 1933- ....CLC 17
See also CA 107

Nemerov, Howard
1920-....................CLC 2, 6, 9, 36
See also CANR 1
See also CA 1-4R
See also CABS 2
See also DLB 5, 6
See also DLB-Y 83

Neruda, Pablo
1904-1973........CLC 1, 2, 5, 7, 9, 28
See also CAP 2
See also CA 19-20
See also obituary CA 45-48

Nerval, Gérard de 1808-1855 ..... NCLC 1

Nervo, (José) Amado (Ruiz de)
1870-1919.................. TCLC 11
See also CA 109

Neufeld, John (Arthur) 1938- ......CLC 17
See also CANR 11
See also CA 25-28R
See also SAAS 3
See also SATA 6

Neville, Emily Cheney 1919- ......CLC 12
See also CANR 3
See also CA 5-8R
See also SAAS 2
See also SATA 1

Newbound, Bernard Slade 1930-
See Slade, Bernard
See also CA 81-84

Newby, P(ercy) H(oward)
1918-..................... CLC 2, 13
See also CA 5-8R
See also DLB 15

Newlove, Donald 1928-..............CLC 6
See also CA 29-32R

Newlove, John (Herbert) 1938-.....CLC 14
See also CANR 9
See also CA 21-24R

Newman, Charles 1938-......... CLC 2, 8
See also CA 21-24R

Newman, Edwin (Harold)
1919-......................CLC 14
See also CANR 5
See also CA 69-72
See also AITN 1

Newton, Suzanne 1936-............CLC 35
See also CANR 14
See also CA 41-44R
See also SATA 5

Ngugi, James (Thiong'o)
1938-................CLC 3, 7, 13, 36
See also Ngugi wa Thiong'o
See also Wa Thiong'o, Ngugi
See also CA 81-84

Ngugi wa Thiong'o
1938-................CLC 3, 7, 13, 36
See also Ngugi, James (Thiong'o)
See also Wa Thiong'o, Ngugi

Nichol, B(arrie) P(hillip) 1944- .....CLC 18
See also CA 53-56
See also DLB 53

Nichols, John (Treadwell)
1940-........................CLC 38
See also CAAS 2
See also CANR 6
See also CA 9-12R
See also DLB-Y 82

Nichols, Peter (Richard)
1927-...................... CLC 5, 36
See also CA 104
See also DLB 13

Nicolas, F.R.E. 1927-
See Freeling, Nicolas

Olsen, Tillie 1913- . . . . CLC **4, 13**
    See also CANR 1
    See also CA 1-4R
    See also DLB 28
    See also DLB-Y 80

Olson, Charles (John)
        1910-1970. . . . . . CLC **1, 2, 5, 6, 9, 11,**
                                                        29
    See also CAP 1
    See also CA 15-16
    See also obituary CA 25-28R
    See also CABS 2
    See also DLB 5, 16

Olson, Theodore 1937-
    See Olson, Toby

Olson, Toby 1937- . . . . CLC **28**
    See also CANR 9
    See also CA 65-68

Ondaatje, (Philip) Michael
        1943- . . . . CLC **14, 29**
    See also CA 77-80

Oneal, Elizabeth 1934-
    See Oneal, Zibby
    See also CA 106
    See also SATA 30

Oneal, Zibby 1934- . . . . CLC **30**
    See also Oneal, Elizabeth

O'Neill, Eugene (Gladstone)
        1888-1953. . . . . TCLC **1, 6, 27**
    See also CA 110
    See also AITN 1
    See also DLB 7

Onetti, Juan Carlos 1909- . . . . . . CLC **7, 10**
    See also CA 85-88

O'Nolan, Brian 1911-1966
    See O'Brien, Flann

O Nuallain, Brian 1911-1966
    See O'Brien, Flann
    See also CAP 2
    See also CA 21-22
    See also obituary CA 25-28R

Oppen, George
        1908-1984. . . . . CLC **7, 13, 34** (358)
    See also CANR 8
    See also CA 13-16R
    See also obituary CA 113
    See also DLB 5

Orlovitz, Gil 1918-1973 . . . . CLC **22**
    See also CA 77-80
    See also obituary CA 45-48
    See also DLB 2, 5

Ortega y Gasset, José
        1883-1955. . . . . TCLC **9**
    See also CA 106

Ortiz, Simon J. 1941- . . . . CLC **45**

Orton, Joe 1933?-1967 . . . . . . CLC **4, 13, 43**
    See also Orton, John Kingsley
    See also DLB 13

Orton, John Kingsley 1933?-1967
    See Orton, Joe
    See also CA 85-88

Orwell, George
        1903-1950. . . . . TCLC **2, 6, 15**
    See also Blair, Eric Arthur
    See also DLB 15

Osborne, John (James)
        1929- . . . . CLC **1, 2, 5, 11, 45**
    See also CA 13-16R
    See also DLB 13

Osceola 1885-1962
    See Dinesen, Isak
    See also Blixen, Karen (Christentze
    Dinesen)

Oshima, Nagisa 1932- . . . . CLC **20**
    See also CA 116

Ossoli, Sarah Margaret (Fuller marchesa d')
        1810-1850
    See Fuller, (Sarah) Margaret
    See also SATA 25

Otero, Blas de 1916- . . . . CLC **11**
    See also CA 89-92

Owen, Wilfred (Edward Salter)
        1893-1918. . . . . TCLC **5, 27**
    See also CA 104
    See also DLB 20

Owens, Rochelle 1936- . . . . CLC **8**
    See also CAAS 2
    See also CA 17-20R

Owl, Sebastian 1939-
    See Thompson, Hunter S(tockton)

Oz, Amos 1939- . . . . . . CLC **5, 8, 11, 27, 33**
    See also CA 53-56

Ozick, Cynthia 1928- . . . . CLC **3, 7, 28**
    See also CA 17-20R
    See also DLB 28
    See also DLB-Y 82

Ozu, Yasujiro 1903-1963 . . . . CLC **16**
    See also CA 112

Pa Chin 1904-. . . . . CLC **18**
    See also Li Fei-kan

Pack, Robert 1929- . . . . CLC **13**
    See also CANR 3
    See also CA 1-4R
    See also DLB 5

Padgett, Lewis 1915-1958
    See Kuttner, Henry

Padilla, Heberto 1932- . . . . CLC **38**
    See also AITN 1

Page, Jimmy 1944-
    See Page, Jimmy and Plant, Robert

Page, Jimmy 1944- and
        Plant, Robert 1948- . . . . CLC **12**

Page, Louise 1955-. . . . . CLC **40**

Page, P(atricia) K(athleen)
        1916- . . . . CLC **7, 18**
    See also CANR 4
    See also CA 53-56

Paget, Violet 1856-1935
    See Lee, Vernon
    See also CA 104

Palamas, Kostes 1859-1943 . . . . TCLC **5**
    See also CA 105

Palazzeschi, Aldo 1885-1974 . . . . . . .CLC **11**
    See also CA 89-92
    See also obituary CA 53-56

Paley, Grace 1922- . . . . CLC **4, 6, 37**
    See also CANR 13
    See also CA 25-28R
    See also DLB 28
    See also AITN 1

Palin, Michael 1943-
    See Monty Python
    See also CA 107

Pancake, Breece Dexter 1952-1979
    See Pancake, Breece D'J

Pancake, Breece D'J
        1952-1979. . . . . .CLC **29**
    See also obituary CA 109

Papini, Giovanni 1881-1956. . . . . . TCLC **22**

Parker, Dorothy (Rothschild)
        1893-1967. . . . . .CLC **15**
    See also CAP 2
    See also CA 19-20
    See also obituary CA 25-28R
    See also DLB 11, 45

Parker, Robert B(rown) 1932-. . . . . .CLC **27**
    See also CANR 1
    See also CA 49-52

Parkin, Frank 1940- . . . . .CLC **43**

Parkman, Francis 1823-1893. . . . . NCLC **12**
    See also DLB 1, 30

Parks, Gordon (Alexander Buchanan)
        1912-. . . . . CLC **1, 16**
    See also CA 41-44R
    See also SATA 8
    See also DLB 33
    See also AITN 2

Parnell, Thomas 1679-1718 . . . . LC **3**

Parra, Nicanor 1914- . . . . .CLC **2**
    See also CA 85-88

Pasolini, Pier Paolo
        1922-1975. . . . . CLC **20, 37**
    See also CA 93-96
    See also obituary CA 61-64

Pastan, Linda (Olenik) 1932-. . . . . . .CLC **27**
    See also CANR 18
    See also CA 61-64
    See also DLB 5

Pasternak, Boris
        1890-1960. . . . . CLC **7, 10, 18**
    See also obituary CA 116

Patchen, Kenneth
        1911-1972. . . . . CLC **1, 2, 18**
    See also CANR 3
    See also CA 1-4R
    See also obituary CA 33-36R
    See also DLB 16, 48

Pater, Walter (Horatio)
        1839-1894. . . . . NCLC **7**
    See also DLB 57

Paterson, Katherine (Womeldorf)
        1932-. . . . . CLC **12, 30**
    See also CLR 7
    See also CA 21-24R
    See also SATA 13
    See also DLB 52

Patmore, Coventry Kersey Dighton
        1823-1896. . . . . NCLC **9**
    See also DLB 35

Paton, Alan (Stewart)
        1903-. . . . . CLC **4, 10, 25**
    See also CAP 1
    See also CA 15-16
    See also SATA 11

Paulding, James Kirke
        1778-1860. . . . . NCLC **2**
    See also DLB 3

Paulin, Tom 1949-...............CLC 37
See also DLB 40

Paustovsky, Konstantin (Georgievich)
1892-1968....................CLC 40
See also CA 93-96
See also obituary CA 25-28R

Paustowsky, Konstantin (Georgievich)
1892-1968
See Paustovsky, Konstantin (Georgievich)

Pavese, Cesare 1908-1950 .... TCLC 3
See also CA 104

Payne, Alan 1932-
See Jakes, John (William)

Paz, Octavio 1914-..... CLC 3, 4, 6, 10, 19
See also CA 73-76

Peake, Mervyn 1911-1968 ....CLC 7
See also CANR 3
See also CA 5-8R
See also obituary CA 25-28R
See also SATA 23
See also DLB 15

Pearce, (Ann) Philippa 1920-......CLC 21
See also Christie, (Ann) Philippa
See also CA 5-8R
See also SATA 1

Pearl, Eric 1934-
See Elman, Richard

Pearson, T(homas) R(eid)
1956-................... CLC 39 (86)
See also CA 120

Peck, John 1941-..................CLC 3
See also CANR 3
See also CA 49-52

Peck, Richard 1934-..............CLC 21
See also CANR 19
See also CA 85-88
See also SAAS 2
See also SATA 18

Peck, Robert Newton 1928-........CLC 17
See also CA 81-84
See also SAAS 1
See also SATA 21

Peckinpah, (David) Sam(uel)
1925-1984....................CLC 20
See also CA 109
See also obituary CA 114

Pedersen, Knut 1859-1952
See Hamsun, Knut
See also CA 104

Péguy, Charles (Pierre)
1873-1914................. TCLC 10
See also CA 107

Percy, Walker
1916-.......... CLC 2, 3, 6, 8, 14, 18
See also CANR 1
See also CA 1-4R
See also DLB 2
See also DLB-Y 80

Pereda, José María de
1833-1906................. TCLC 16

Perelman, S(idney) J(oseph)
1904-1979........CLC 3, 5, 9, 15, 23,
44 (499)
See also CANR 18
See also CA 73-76
See also obituary CA 89-92
See also DLB 11, 44
See also AITN 1, 2

Péret, Benjamin 1899-1959 ...... TCLC 20
See also CA 117

Peretz, Isaac Leib
1852?-1915................. TCLC 16
See also CA 109

Pérez, Galdós Benito
1853-1920.................. TCLC 27

Perrault, Charles 1628-1703 .... LC 2
See also SATA 25

Perse, St.-John
1887-1975............. CLC 4, 11, 46
See also Léger, (Marie-Rene) Alexis Saint-
Léger

Pesetsky, Bette 1932-..............CLC 28

Peshkov, Alexei Maximovich 1868-1936
See Gorky, Maxim
See also CA 105

Pessoa, Fernando (António Nogueira)
1888-1935 .... TCLC 27

Peterkin, Julia (Mood)
1880-1961....................CLC 31
See also CA 102
See also DLB 9

Peters, Joan K. 1945-........ CLC 39 (91)

Peters, Robert L(ouis) 1924- ....CLC 7
See also CA 13-16R

Petrakis, Harry Mark 1923- ....CLC 3
See also CANR 4
See also CA 9-12R

Petrov, Evgeny 1902-1942 and **Ilf, Ilya**
1897-1937
See Ilf, Ilya 1897-1937 and Petrov, Evgeny
1902-1942

Petry, Ann (Lane) 1908-...... CLC 1, 7, 18
See also CLR 12
See also CANR 4
See also CA 5-8R
See also SATA 5

Phillips, Jayne Anne 1952-..... CLC 15, 33
See also CA 101
See also DLB-Y 80

Phillips, Robert (Schaeffer)
1938-.......................CLC 28
See also CANR 8
See also CA 17-20R

Pica, Peter 1925-
See Aldiss, Brian W(ilson)

Piccolo, Lucio 1901-1969 ....CLC 13
See also CA 97-100

Pickthall, Marjorie (Lowry Christie)
1883-1922.................. TCLC 21
See also CA 107

Piercy, Marge
1936-.......... CLC 3, 6, 14, 18, 27
See also CAAS 1
See also CANR 13
See also CA 21-24R

Pilnyak, Boris 1894-1937? .... TCLC 23

Pincherle, Alberto 1907-
See Moravia, Alberto
See also CA 25-28R

Pineda, Cecile 1942- .... CLC 39 (94)
See also CA 118

Piñero, Miguel (Gomez) 1947?-......CLC 4
See also CA 61-64

Pinget, Robert 1919-........CLC 7, 13, 37
See also CA 85-88

Pink Floyd ....CLC 35

Pinkwater, D(aniel) M(anus)
1941-......................CLC 35
See also Pinkwater, Manus
See also CLR 4
See also CANR 12
See also CA 29-32R
See also SAAS 3
See also SATA 46

Pinkwater, Manus 1941-
See Pinkwater, D(aniel) M(anus)
See also SATA 8

Pinsky, Robert 1940-........CLC 9, 19, 38
See also CAAS 4
See also CA 29-32R
See also DLB-Y 82

Pinter, Harold
1930-........CLC 1, 3, 6, 9, 11, 15, 27
See also CA 5-8R
See also DLB 13

Pirandello, Luigi 1867-1936...... TCLC 4
See also CA 104

Pirsig, Robert M(aynard)
1928-..................... CLC 4, 6
See also CA 53-56
See also SATA 39

Plaidy, Jean 1906-
See Hibbert, Eleanor (Burford)

Plant, Robert 1948-
See Page, Jimmy and Plant, Robert

Plante, David (Robert)
1940-................... CLC 7, 23, 38
See also CANR 12
See also CA 37-40R
See also DLB-Y 83

Plath, Sylvia
1932-1963....... CLC 1, 2, 3, 5, 9, 11,
14, 17
See also CAP 2
See also CA 19-20
See also DLB 5, 6
See also CDALB 1941-1968

Platonov, Andrei (Platonovich)
1899-1951.................. TCLC 14
See also Klimentov, Andrei Platonovich

Platt, Kin 1911-..................CLC 26
See also CANR 11
See also CA 17-20R
See also SATA 21

Plimpton, George (Ames)
1927-.......................CLC 36
See also CA 21-24R
See also SATA 10
See also AITN 1

Plomer, William (Charles Franklin)
1903-1973.................. CLC 4, 8
See also CAP 2
See also CA 21-22
See also SATA 24
See also DLB 20

Plumly, Stanley (Ross) 1939-.......CLC 33
See also CA 108, 110
See also DLB 5

Author Index

Author Index

Author Index

Summers, Hollis (Spurgeon, Jr.)
1916-.........................CLC 10
See also CANR 3
See also CA 5-8R
See also DLB 6

Summers, (Alphonsus Joseph-Mary Augustus)
Montague 1880-1948 .... TCLC 16

Sumner, Gordon Matthew 1951-
See The Police

Surtees, Robert Smith
1805-1864.................. NCLC 14
See also DLB 21

Susann, Jacqueline 1921-1974......CLC 3
See also CA 65-68
See also obituary CA 53-56
See also AITN 1

Süskind, Patrick 1949- ...... CLC 44 (111)

Sutcliff, Rosemary 1920- ....CLC 26
See also CLR 1
See also CA 5-8R
See also SATA 6, 44

Sutro, Alfred 1863-1933.......... TCLC 6
See also CA 105
See also DLB 10

Sutton, Henry 1935-
See Slavitt, David (R.)

Svevo, Italo 1861-1928 .... TCLC 2
See also Schmitz, Ettore

Swados, Elizabeth 1951-...........CLC 12
See also CA 97-100

Swados, Harvey 1920-1972 ....CLC 5
See also CANR 6
See also CA 5-8R
See also obituary CA 37-40R
See also DLB 2

Swarthout, Glendon (Fred)
1918-.........................CLC 35
See also CANR 1
See also CA 1-4R
See also SATA 26

Swenson, May 1919- .... CLC 4, 14
See also CA 5-8R
See also SATA 15
See also DLB 5

Swift, Graham 1949-..............CLC 41
See also CA 117

Swift, Jonathan 1667-1745.......... LC 1
See also SATA 19
See also DLB 39

Swinburne, Algernon Charles
1837-1909.................. TCLC 8
See also CA 105
See also DLB 35, 57

Swinfen, Ann 19??- .... CLC 34 (576)

Swinnerton, Frank (Arthur)
1884-1982....................CLC 31
See also obituary CA 108
See also DLB 34

Symons, Arthur (William)
1865-1945.................. TCLC 11
See also CA 107
See also DLB 19, 57

Symons, Julian (Gustave)
1912-..................... CLC 2, 14, 32
See also CAAS 3
See also CANR 3
See also CA 49-52

Synge, (Edmund) John Millington
1871-1909.................. TCLC 6
See also CA 104
See also DLB 10, 19

Syruc, J. 1911-
See Miłosz, Czesław

Szirtes, George 1948-............CLC 46
See also CA 109

Tabori, George 1914- ....CLC 19
See also CANR 4
See also CA 49-52

Tagore, (Sir) Rabindranath
1861-1941.................. TCLC 3
See also Thakura, Ravindranatha

Taine, Hippolyte Adolphe
1828-1893.................. NCLC 15

Talese, Gaetano 1932-
See Talese, Gay

Talese, Gay 1932-.................CLC 37
See also CANR 9
See also CA 1-4R
See also AITN 1

Tallent, Elizabeth (Ann) 1954- .....CLC 45
See also CA 117

Tally, Ted 1952-..................CLC 42
See also CA 120

Tamayo y Baus, Manuel
1829-1898.................. NCLC 1

Tammsaare, A(nton) H(ansen)
1878-1940.................. TCLC 27

Tanizaki, Jun'ichirō
1886-1965.............. CLC 8, 14, 28
See also CA 93-96
See also obituary CA 25-28R

Tarkington, (Newton) Booth
1869-1946.................. TCLC 9
See also CA 110
See also SATA 17
See also DLB 9

Tasso, Torquato 1544-1595 .... LC 5

Tate, (John Orley) Allen
1899-1979...... CLC 2, 4, 6, 9, 11, 14, 24
See also CA 5-8R
See also obituary CA 85-88
See also DLB 4, 45

Tate, James 1943-................ CLC 2, 6, 25
See also CA 21-24R
See also DLB 5

Tavel, Ronald 1940- ....CLC 6
See also CA 21-24R

Taylor, C(ecil) P(hillip)
1929-1981....................CLC 27
See also CA 25-28R
See also obituary CA 105

Taylor, Eleanor Ross 1920- ....CLC 5
See also CA 81-84

Taylor, Elizabeth
1912-1975.............. CLC 2, 4, 29
See also CANR 9
See also CA 13-16R
See also SATA 13

Taylor, Henry (Splawn)
1917-.................. CLC 44 (300)

Taylor, Kamala (Purnaiya) 1924-
See Markandaya, Kamala
See also CA 77-80

Taylor, Mildred D(elois) 1943- .....CLC 21
See also CLR 9
See also CA 85-88
See also SATA 15
See also DLB 52

Taylor, Peter (Hillsman)
1917-....... CLC 1, 4, 18, 37, 44 (304)
See also CANR 9
See also CA 13-16R
See also DLB-Y 81

Taylor, Robert Lewis 1912-........CLC 14
See also CANR 3
See also CA 1-4R
See also SATA 10

Teasdale, Sara 1884-1933........ TCLC 4
See also CA 104
See also DLB 45
See also SATA 32

Tegnér, Esaias 1782-1846........ NCLC 2

Teilhard de Chardin, (Marie Joseph) Pierre
1881-1955.................. TCLC 9
See also CA 105

Tennant, Emma 1937- ....CLC 13
See also CANR 10
See also CA 65-68
See also DLB 14

Teran, Lisa St. Aubin de 19??-.....CLC 36

Terkel, Louis 1912-
See Terkel, Studs
See also CANR 18
See also CA 57-60

Terkel, Studs 1912-...............CLC 38
See also Terkel, Louis
See also AITN 1

Terry, Megan 1932- ....CLC 19
See also CA 77-80
See also DLB 7

Tesich, Steve 1943?- ....CLC 40
See also CA 105
See also DLB-Y 83

Tesich, Stoyan 1943?-
See Tesich, Steve

Tertz, Abram 1925-
See Sinyavsky, Andrei (Donatevich)

Teternikov, Fyodor Kuzmich 1863-1927
See Sologub, Fyodor
See also CA 104

Tevis, Walter 1928-1984..........CLC 42
See also CA 113

Tey, Josephine 1897-1952 .... TCLC 14
See also Mackintosh, Elizabeth

Thackeray, William Makepeace
1811-1863................NCLC 5, 14
See also SATA 23
See also DLB 21

Thakura, Ravindranatha 1861-1941
See Tagore, (Sir) Rabindranath
See also CA 104

Thelwell, Michael (Miles)
1939-.......................CLC 22
See also CA 101

Webb, Sidney (James) 1859-1947 and
Webb, Beatrice (Potter) 1858-1943
See Webb, Beatrice (Potter) and Webb,
Sidney (James)

Webber, Andrew Lloyd 1948-
See Rice, Tim and Webber, Andrew Lloyd

Weber, Lenora Mattingly
1895-1971...................CLC 12
See also CAP 1
See also CA 19-20
See also obituary CA 29-32R
See also SATA 2
See also obituary SATA 26

Wedekind, (Benjamin) Frank(lin)
1864-1918...................TCLC 7
See also CA 104

Weidman, Jerome 1913-...........CLC 7
See also CANR 1
See also CA 1-4R
See also DLB 28
See also AITN 2

Weil, Simone 1909-1943........TCLC 23
See also CA 117

Weinstein, Nathan Wallenstein 1903?-1940
See West, Nathanael
See also CA 104

Weir, Peter 1944-................CLC 20
See also CA 113

Weiss, Peter (Ulrich)
1916-1982................CLC 3, 15
See also CANR 3
See also CA 45-48
See also obituary CA 106

Weiss, Theodore (Russell)
1916-..................CLC 3, 8, 14
See also CAAS 2
See also CA 9-12R
See also DLB 5

Welch, James 1940-...........CLC 6, 14
See also CA 85-88

Welch, (Maurice) Denton
1915-1948.................TCLC 22

Weldon, Fay
1933-..........CLC 6, 9, 11, 19, 36
See also CANR 16
See also CA 21-24R
See also DLB 14

Wellek, René 1903-...............CLC 28
See also CANR 8
See also CA 5-8R

Weller, Michael 1942-............CLC 10
See also CA 85-88

Weller, Paul 1958-................CLC 26

Wellershoff, Dieter 1925-..........CLC 46
See also CANR 16
See also CA 89-92

Welles, (George) Orson
1915-1985.................CLC 20
See also CA 93-96

Wells, H(erbert) G(eorge)
1866-1946............TCLC 6, 12, 19
See also CA 110
See also SATA 20
See also DLB 34

Wells, Rosemary 19??-............CLC 12
See also CA 85-88
See also SAAS 1
See also SATA 18

Welty, Eudora (Alice)
1909-..........CLC 1, 2, 5, 14, 22, 33
See also SSC 1
See also CA 9-12R
See also CABS 1
See also DLB 2
See also CDALB 1941-1968

Werfel, Franz (V.) 1890-1945.....TCLC 8
See also CA 104

Wergeland, Henrik Arnold
1808-1845..................NCLC 5

Wersba, Barbara 1932-...........CLC 30
See also CLR 3
See also CA 29-32R
See also SAAS 2
See also SATA 1

Wertmüller, Lina 1928-...........CLC 16
See also CA 97-100

Wescott, Glenway 1901-...........CLC 13
See also CA 13-16R
See also DLB 4, 9

Wesker, Arnold 1932-........CLC 3, 5, 42
See also CANR 1
See also CA 1-4R
See also DLB 13

Wesley, Richard (Errol) 1945-.......CLC 7
See also CA 57-60
See also DLB 38

Wessel, Johan Herman
1742-1785.....................LC 7

West, Jessamyn 1907-1984......CLC 7, 17
See also CA 9-12R
See also obituary SATA 37
See also DLB 6
See also DLB-Y 84

West, Morris L(anglo)
1916-......................CLC 6, 33
See also CA 5-8R

West, Nathanael
1903?-1940..............TCLC 1, 14
See Weinstein, Nathan Wallenstein
See also DLB 4, 9, 28

West, Paul 1930-..............CLC 7, 14
See also CA 13-16R
See also DLB 14

West, Rebecca 1892-1983.....CLC 7, 9, 31
See also CA 5-8R
See also obituary CA 109
See also DLB 36
See also DLB-Y 83

Westall, Robert (Atkinson)
1929-......................CLC 17
See also CANR 18
See also CA 69-72
See also SAAS 2
See also SATA 23

Westlake, Donald E(dwin)
1933-......................CLC 7, 33
See also CANR 16
See also CA 17-20R

Whalen, Philip 1923-...........CLC 6, 29
See also CANR 5
See also CA 9-12R
See also DLB 16

Wharton, Edith (Newbold Jones)
1862-1937..............TCLC 3, 9, 27
See also CA 104
See also DLB 4, 9, 12

Wharton, William 1925-...... CLC 18, 37
See also CA 93-96
See also DLB-Y 80

Wheatley (Peters), Phillis
1753?-1784.....................LC 3
See also DLB 31, 50

Wheelock, John Hall
1886-1978...................CLC 14
See also CANR 14
See also CA 13-16R
See also obituary CA 77-80
See also DLB 45

Whelan, John 1900-
See O'Faoláin, Seán

Whitaker, Rodney 1925-
See Trevanian
See also CA 29-32R

White, E(lwyn) B(rooks)
1899-1985.........CLC 10, 34 (425),
39 (369)
See also CLR 1
See also CANR 16
See also CA 13-16R
See also obituary CA 116
See also SATA 2, 29
See also obituary SATA 44
See also DLB 11, 22
See also AITN 2

White, Edmund III 1940-..........CLC 27
See also CANR 3
See also CA 45-48

White, Patrick (Victor Martindale)
1912-...........CLC 3, 4, 5, 7, 9, 18
See also CA 81-84

White, T(erence) H(anbury)
1906-1964...................CLC 30
See also CA 73-76
See also SATA 12

White, Walter (Francis)
1893-1955..................TCLC 15
See also CA 115

White, William Hale 1831-1913
See Rutherford, Mark

Whitehead, E(dward) A(nthony)
1933-......................CLC 5
See also CA 65-68

Whitemore, Hugh 1936-...........CLC 37

Whitman, Walt 1819-1892........NCLC 4
See also SATA 20
See also DLB 3

Whitney, Phyllis A(yame)
1903-......................CLC 42
See also CANR 3
See also CA 1-4R
See also SATA 1, 30
See also AITN 2

Whittemore, (Edward) Reed (Jr.)
1919-......................CLC 4
See also CANR 4
See also CA 9-12R
See also DLB 5

Whittier, John Greenleaf
1807-1892..................NCLC 8
See also DLB 1

Author Index

TCLC Cumulative Nationality Index

Nationality Index